Weight

Metric		Approximate apothecary equivalents		Metric		Approximate apothecary equivalents	
30	g.	1	ounce	30	mg.	$\frac{1}{2}$	grain
15	g.	4	drams	25	mg.	$\frac{3}{8}$	grain
10	g.	$2\frac{1}{2}$	drams	20	mg.	$\frac{1}{3}$	grain
7.5	g.	2	drams	15	mg.	$\frac{1}{4}$	grain
6	g.	90	grains	12	mg.	$\frac{1}{5}$	grain
5	g.	75	grains	10	mg.	$\frac{1}{6}$	grain
4	g.	60	grains (1 dram)	8	mg.	$\frac{1}{8}$	grain
3	g.	45	grains	6	mg.	$\frac{1}{10}$	grain
2	g.	30	grains ($\frac{1}{2}$ dram)	5	mg.	$\frac{1}{12}$	grain
1.5	g.	22	grains	4	mg.	$\frac{1}{15}$	grain
1	g.	15	grains	3	mg.	$\frac{1}{20}$	grain
0.75	g.	12	grains	2	mg.	$\frac{1}{30}$	grain
0.6	g.	10	grains	1.5	mg.	$\frac{1}{40}$	grain
0.5	g.	$7\frac{1}{2}$	grains	1.2	mg.	$\frac{1}{50}$	grain
0.4	g.	6	grains	1	mg.	$\frac{1}{60}$	grain
0.3	g.	5	grains	0.8	mg.	$\frac{1}{80}$	grain
0.25	g.	4	grains	0.6	mg.	$\frac{1}{100}$	grain
0.2	g.	3	grains	0.5	mg.	$\frac{1}{120}$	grain
0.15	g.	$2\frac{1}{2}$	grains	0.4	mg.	$\frac{1}{150}$	grain
0.12	g.	2	grains	0.3	mg.	$\frac{1}{200}$	grain
0.1	g.	$1\frac{1}{2}$	grains	0.25	mg.	$\frac{1}{250}$	grain
75	mg.	$1\frac{1}{4}$	grains	0.2	mg.	$\frac{1}{300}$	grain
60	mg.	1	grain	0.15	mg.	$\frac{1}{400}$	grain
50	mg.	$\frac{3}{4}$	grain	0.12	mg.	$\frac{1}{500}$	grain
40	mg.	$\frac{2}{3}$	grain	0.1	mg.	$\frac{1}{600}$	grain

Pharmacology in nursing

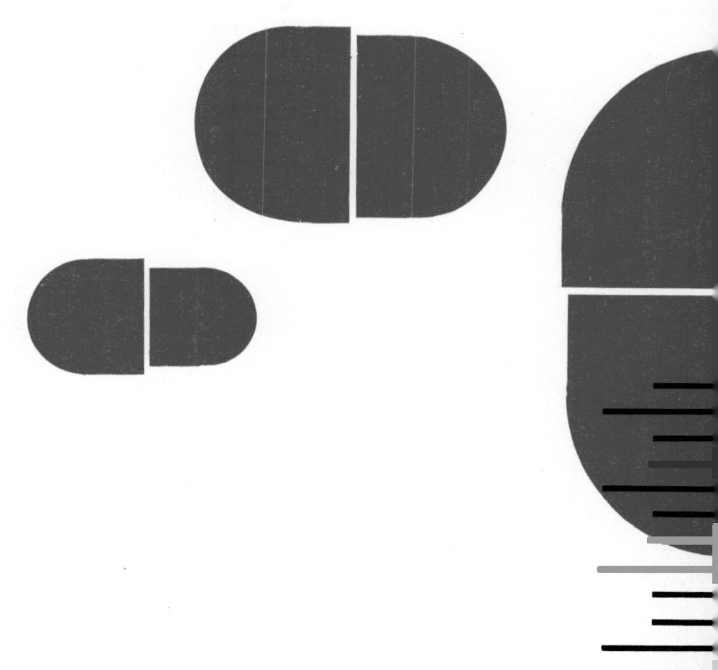

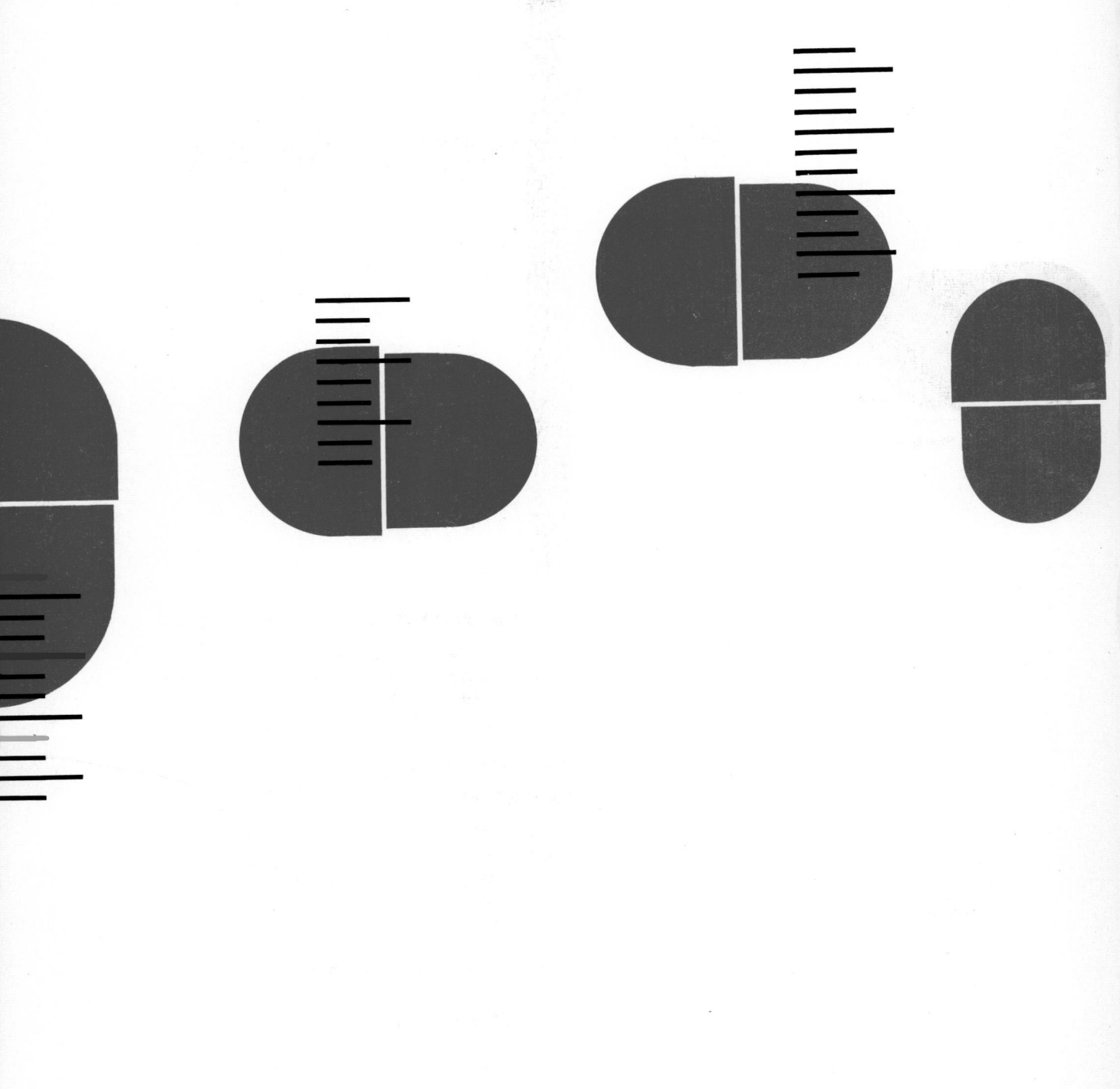

Pharmacology in nursing

BETTY S. BERGERSEN, R.N., M.S., Ed.D.

*Professor of Nursing and Chairman of Graduate
Medical-Surgical Nursing, University of Colorado
School of Nursing, Medical Center,
Denver, Colorado*

In consultation with

ANDRES GOTH, M.D.

*Professor of Pharmacology and Chairman
of the Department,
The University of Texas Southwestern
Medical School,
Dallas, Texas*

With 48 illustrations and 8 color plates

TWELFTH EDITION

The C. V. Mosby Company

Saint Louis 1973

TWELFTH EDITION

Copyright © 1973 by The C. V. Mosby Company

Previous editions copyrighted 1936, 1940, 1942, 1945, 1948, 1951, 1955, 1960, 1963, 1966, 1969

Printed in the United States of America

International Standard Book Number 0-8016-0630-6

Library of Congress Catalog Card Number 66-10935

Distributed in Great Britain by Henry Kimpton, London

Preface

Drugs can be beneficial when used with wisdom but harmful when used with inadequate knowledge. This edition of *Pharmacology in Nursing* outlines current concepts of pharmacology and their relationship to clinical patient care. Included in the text are basic mechanisms of drug action, indications and contraindications for drug therapy, toxicity and side effects, and safe therapeutic dosage range. This information should provide the nurse practitioner or student the means for ensuring rational and optimal drug therapy. Once again the book has been updated and physiologic aspects expanded.

As in the previous edition, each chapter has been critically reviewed by Andres Goth, Professor of Pharmacology and Chairman of the Department, The University of Texas Southwestern Medical School, Dallas, Texas.

Because of the widespread misuse and abuse of drugs it was deemed essential to include a chapter on this subject. The chapter was planned and written by my friend and colleague, Jurate Abromaities Sakalys, Assistant Professor of Nursing, University of Colorado School of Nursing, who also made important contributions to the chapter on drug action.

I also wish to thank Patricia Valoon, Senior Instructor, University of Colorado School of Nursing, for her work on Chapter 31, "Administration of Medicines to Infants and Children." The inclusion of this expanded information is long overdue.

Readers who have used previous editions of this book will note the absence of Elsie Krug's name from this twelfth edition. This was done at her request. Students of nursing and nurse educators owe a debt of gratitude to Elsie Krug for her continued efforts over the past years to provide a pharmacology textbook for nurses that was scholarly, highly informative, up to date, and with minimal error. The fact that this textbook is in its twelfth edition, and used in the Philippine Islands, Canada, and throughout the United States by students of nursing, nurse educators, hospital pharmacists, and other paramedical health workers, attests to her success as an author of a pharmacology textbook.

v

I owe Elsie Krug a debt of gratitude I can never repay for arousing my interest in pharmacology and providing me with the challenge to continue to provide nurses with a highly satisfactory text and reference book. To my very dear friend Elsie Krug I express my heartfelt thanks and affection.

Betty S. Bergersen

Contents

Contents

Color plates

List of tables

x

List of tables

Pharmacology in nursing

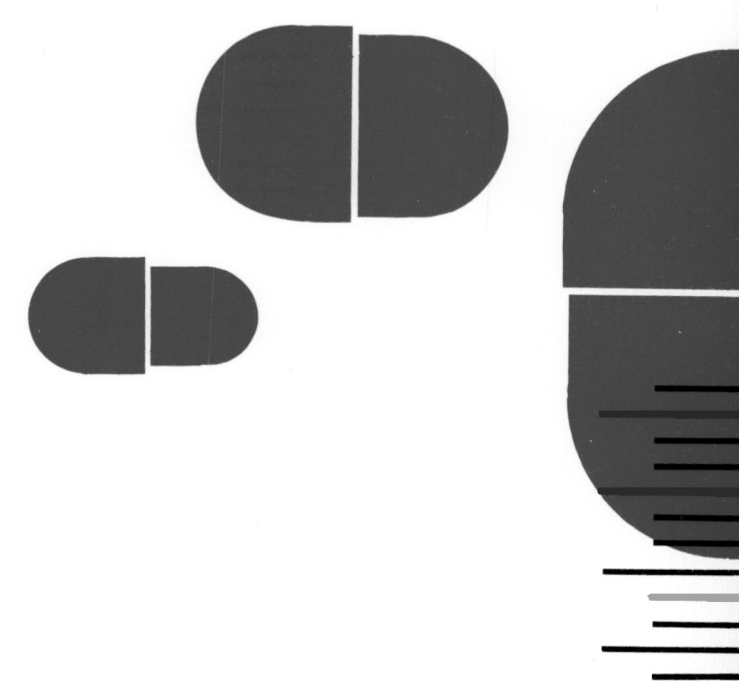

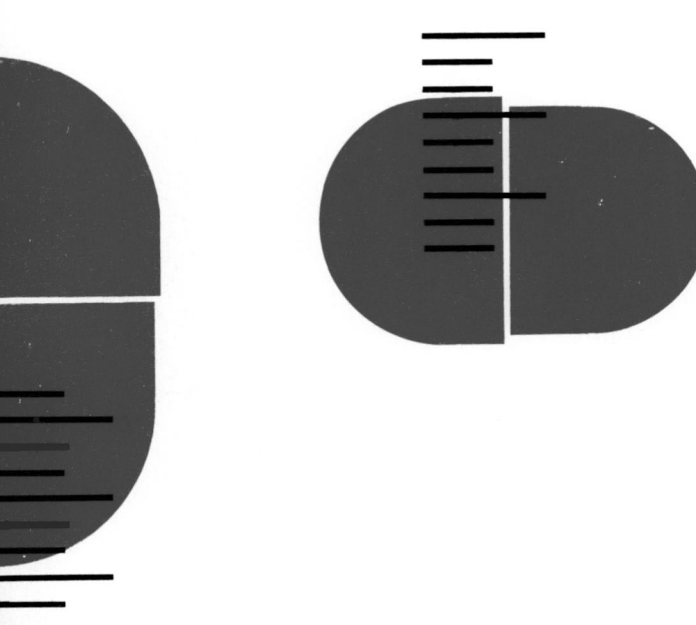

Orientation to pharmacology
Drug information sources

■ Orientation to pharmacology

Medications are an essential part of patient care, and safe administration of drugs requires *sound* and *current* knowledge of their: (1) mode of action, (2) side effects, (3) toxicity, (4) range of dosage, (5) rate and route of excretion, (6) individual differences in response, such as idiosyncratic or allergic reactions, and (7) interactions with other drugs. This knowledge can be obtained from textbooks and periodicals for health professionals, classroom lectures and discussions, and materials available in teaching laboratories. However, actual administration of drugs with careful observation of their effects in individuals and groups of patients will richly supplement and complement a student's knowledge of specific drugs.

Drugs have the power to help or to harm. Nurses, along with physicians and clinical pharmacists, are held legally responsible for safe and therapeutically effective drug administration. A nurse is liable for her actions and omissions and for those duties she delegates to others. She is not exonerated from responsibility when drugs are administered by medication technicians, pharmacy technicians, practical nurses, or even physicians. Indeed, all members of a health team may be held liable for a single injury to a patient. The continued increase in litigation against nurses and physi-

cians indicates that society tolerates only a minimal margin of error in relation to human life. Claims have been brought against health professionals for drug errors that caused loss of life (Norton v. Argonaut Insurance Co., the Somera case) and permanent injury (Honeywell v. Rogers).* When claims against health professionals are supported with evidence that the conduct of one or more health professionals helped to bring about the loss or injury, those parties are held liable. The law, a legal and social norm, requires health professionals to be safe and competent practitioners and permits compensation to those harmed or injured.

However, the law is a protective force for the knowledgeable, competent, and skilled nurse. The nurse who is knowledgeable about the drugs her patients are receiving, who uses proper technique and precautions, who ob-

*Murchison, I. A., and Nichols, T. S.: Legal foundations of nursing practice, New York, 1970, The Macmillan Company, pp. 189, 338, and 116.

serves for and charts explicitly the drug effects, who keeps her knowledge up to date by referring to authoritative sources (pharmacist, pharmacologist, professional literature), who questions a drug order that is unclear or that appears to contain an error, and who even refuses to administer a drug and intervenes to prevent others from administering a drug when she believes harm may come to the patient is safeguarding and protecting her patients from drug-induced harm. The law in turn will protect her from unfair litigation.

Drugs deserve the respect of the nurse, but that respect must be mingled with skepticism. Much remains to be learned about the actual mode of action as well as effects from prolonged use of many commonly prescribed drugs. Furthermore, there is increasing concern about drug-induced disease. Fortunately, drug therapy for most illnesses or for illness prevention is temporary. However, there are those diseases that require life-long use of drugs to sustain life (such as insulin for diabetes mellitus) or prolonged use to maintain relatively normal physiologic or psychologic functioning.

Nurses are entrusted with potent and habit-forming drugs, and they must not abuse or misuse this trust. Used respectfully and intelligently, drugs are comforting and lifesaving. Used unwisely or with undue dependence, they can lead to irreparable tragedy. The nurse who combines diligent and intelligent observation with moral integrity and factual knowledge will be a safe and competent practitioner and a credit to her profession.

Pharmacology is a challenging and interesting subject to study. It requires integrating knowledge from many different disciplines including anatomy and physiology, pathology, microbiology, organic chemistry and biochemistry, psychology, and sociology; thus, clinical drug therapy can be considered to be an applied science. The hundreds of drugs available would make the study of pharmacology formidable if they had to be studied as individual agents. Fortunately, drugs can be classified into a reasonable number of drug groups based on their chemical, pharmacologic, or therapeutic relatedness. Understanding the characteristic effects of a particular group of drugs at the subcellular, tissue, organ, or functional system level permits a student or practitioner to know a variety of facts about many drugs. An individual drug can then be studied according to those characteristics that differentiate it from other drugs within the same classification.

The doses of drugs and indications for use must not be regarded by the student as therapeutic dogma. New knowledge about drugs will be forthcoming from laboratory research and more scientific methods of clinical drug evaluation.

The constant advances in the field of drug therapy, the almost daily appearance of new drugs or new preparations of old drugs on the market and in the hospital, are a challenge to both the student and the graduate nurse to be students always. An examination passed and an R.N. acquired are no lasting guarantees of sufficient knowledge in the field of drugs to make a nurse helpful to the doctor or even safe for the patient. Drugs change and will continue to change. The nurse's pharmacology books become a permanent section of her library, and year by year as new editions or new books appear she must bring her library up to date. In addition, the official current literature on drugs must be followed carefully, since new drugs are slow in making their way into more permanent literature. For the nurse working in a hospital or health service, doctors, instructors, supervisors, and pharmacists will be on hand to help her. In a more isolated practice, greater personal effort will be required to keep her abreast of current practices. In any case, a sustained interest in pharmacology will help to keep the nurse well informed about drugs.

Of primary importance is the understanding that learning is an active process and that learning does not take place without activity. Thus, clinical experience with drugs is invaluable for it enables the student to:

1 Note those drugs most commonly used to treat certain diseases or specific signs and symptoms
2 Note the frequency with which certain drugs are administered

3 Observe the degree of effectiveness between specific drugs for relieving particular signs and symptoms

4 Witness the individual differences in patients' reactions to drug

5 Relate knowledge obtained from authoritative sources with real-life situations

Regardless of what subject matter is to be learned, reasoning and the ability to analyze and synthesize information are prerequisites to understanding. These cognitive skills, along with perceptual skills, permit an individual to see meaningful relationships, make comparisons, and determine significance, all of which are essential for sound decision making. The development of cognitive, perceptual, and manual skills is the foundation for professional competence.

■ Drug information sources

Nurses will find the following sources of drug information very useful in the study of pharmacology and in the practice of nursing involving drug therapy.

The United States Dispensatory and Physicians' Pharmacology

The twenty-sixth edition of the United States Dispensatory and Physicians' Pharmacology was edited by Arthur Osol, Robertson Pratt, and Mark D. Altschule and published by J. B. Lippincott Co. (Philadelphia, 1967).

The Dispensatory is an encyclopedia containing comprehensive monographs on individual drugs and general survey articles on pharmacologic classes of drugs. The monographs contain descriptions, histories, actions, uses, and facts on toxicology and dosage; they are documented by references to medical literature. Official, nonproprietary, trade, and chemical names are given in the monographs. The monographs contain drugs listed in *The Pharmacopeia of the United States of America, The National Formulary,* and the *British Pharmaceutical Codex;* drugs not listed in these official compendia; and drugs used in veterinary practice. Official, nonproprietary, and proprietary names are included in the general alphabetic index.

American Hospital Formulary Service

The *American Hospital Formulary Service* is a drug monograph subscription service for the calendar year published by the American Society of Hospital Pharmacists, Washington, D. C. The monograph of each drug is entered under the nonproprietary name, giving common synonyms and proprietary names. Monographs are full and descriptive and emphasize rational therapeutic procedures. Classification is according to the pharmacologic actions of the individual agents. Each monograph includes a list of the dosage forms most commonly used in hospitals.

Modern Drug Encyclopedia and Therapeutic Index

The *Modern Drug Encyclopedia,* eleventh edition edited by Arthur J. Lewis and published by The Reuben H. Donnelley Corporation (New York, 1970), describes approximately 5000 products of 150 manufacturers of prescription medications. Individual monographs are arranged alphabetically according to trade names. Information for each includes its manufacturer, pharmacologic classification, description and/or nonproprietary name, chemical name with structural formula when possible, action and uses, method of administration and dosage, cautions and contraindications, and forms and sizes supplied. The general alphabetic index includes both nonproprietary and trade names.

Physicians' Desk Reference to Pharmaceutical Specialties and Biologicals (P.D.R.)

P.D.R., twenty-sixth edition published by Medical Economics, Inc. (Oradell, N. J., 1972), contains an annual listing of drugs arranged in five sections. The pink section is a comprehensive alphabetic listing of brand name products and a list of manufacturers with their products. The blue section is a therapeutic index. The yellow section is a drug, chemical, and pharmacologic index to drugs. The white section is a list of the major products of manufacturers, with information on composition, action, uses, administration, dosage, precautions, contraindications, and supply of each drug. A twenty-nine page product identification section shows full-size color photographs of more than 1000 capsules and tablets.

Unlisted Drugs

Unlisted Drugs, published by Special Libraries Association (New York), lists new drugs found in literature or advertising when no entries are located for them in *Modern Drug Encyclopedia*, or other standard sources. Entries are made for experimental compounds under their research numbers as well as for marketed products. Each entry includes a brief statement of composition, manufacturer, action, dosage, and source of information. This is a monthly publication with a cumulative index for volumes.

Remington's Pharmaceutical Sciences

Remington's Pharmaceutical Sciences, thirteenth edition, Eric W. Martin, editor-in-chief, published by Mack Printing Company (Easton, Pa., 1965), classifies drugs according to their therapeutic use as well as to their chemical structure. Almost every drug and chemical used today in medicine and pharmacy is included in the book, along with complete commentary on drugs in *The Pharmacopeia of the United States of America* (the U.S.P.), *The National Formulary, British Pharmacopoeia* (the B.P.), *Pharmacopoeia Internationalis*, and other current reference sources.

Compendium of Pharmaceuticals and Specialties (Canada)

Compendium of Pharmaceuticals and Specialties (Canada), fourth edition edited by F. N. Hughes and published by Canadian Pharmaceutical Association (Toronto, 1968), is the only reference book that contains information on all of the approximately 9000 drugs and drug preparations for human use available to Canadian pharmacists. The book contains monographs (entered under trade names) that provide descriptions, manufacturers' information, indication, instructions for administration, and dosage, as well as forms and sizes in which drugs are available. Veterinary drugs are also included in a separate section. A list of manufacturers

with their products and a therapeutic index are included as well as a cross-reference index for nonproprietary names and chemical names of drugs. This publication consists of three semiannual supplements, which are cumulative.

Package brochures

Before marketing a new drug product, the manufacturer develops a concise description of the product, indications and precautions in clinical use, guidance for dosage, known adverse actions, and other pertinent pharmacologic information. Federal law requires that a brochure accompany each package of the product, and because this is construed as labeling, the brochure must be approved by the Food and Drug Administration.

The Medical Letter

The Medical Letter, a semimonthly periodical published by Drug and Therapeutic Information, Inc. (New York), contains independent brief comments on newly released drug products and related topics by a board of competent authorities who call freely upon specialists in various fields. The letters contain data on drug action and comparative clinical efficacy. They have the advantage of presenting a timely and critical summation of current status in the early phase of promotion of a drug. However, these drug appraisals are tentative.

Clinical Pharmacology and Therapeutics

Clinical Pharmacology and Therapeutics, a bimonthly periodical published by The C. V. Mosby Co. (St. Louis), contains reports of studies of new drugs, reviews of present knowledge of classes of drugs or advances in therapy of various disorders, and abstracts of reports of adverse reactions to drugs appearing in the world literature. It also contains a section on drug-induced diseases.

Drugs of Choice 1972-1973

Drugs of Choice 1972-1973, edited by Walter Modell and published by The C. V. Mosby Co. (St. Louis, 1972), is revised every 2 years and contains contributions from forty-six outstanding specialists who express their opinions of the drugs in current use in their own fields of specialization. The book is designed to provide clear, concise, and practical answers to questions of drugs of choice for actual therapeutic problems. An alphabetically arranged index of drugs in common use is also included.

Journals

Other important sources of drug information are the various nursing, pharmacy, medical, and allied health journals. In addition to the *American Journal of Nursing*, the following prominent periodicals are usually available in medical and health reference libraries:

Pharmacy journals

Journal of the American Pharmaceutical Association
American Journal of Hospital Pharmacy
American Druggist
Pharmacy Times
Drug Topics

Medical journals

Journal of the American Medical Association
New England Journal of Medicine
Postgraduate Medicine
British Medical Journal

2

History of
materia medica

The story of materia medica is as old as the story of man, for sickness has been man's heritage from the beginning of time and the search for ways and means to combat disease has been one of his earliest and most persistent activities. Early man's first experiments in dealing with disease were suggested by the belief common to all primitive people that the world in which they lived teemed with invisible spirits, some of whom were good and some bad. Whatever puzzled man in nature was attributed to these supernatural agencies, and it followed that disease was at first thought to be an evil spirit or the work of such a spirit. If this supposition were true, the logical treatment was to placate the invader by burnt offerings or to frighten it away by resorting to hideous noises or by administering foul-tasting substances. These measures were designed to make the body an uncomfortable habitat for the spirit. The search for obnoxious materials led man to experiment with herbs of the field and the forest, and as the knowledge gained from experience increased, the rudiments of materia medica were assembled. These intuitive efforts of man led to some valuable discoveries. Savages in separate countries knew the properties of the most fatal arrow poisons, such as curare, veratrine, and ouabain, as well as the virtues of drugs like opium. Centuries ago the Indians of Peru discovered the value of cinchona bark for the treatment and prevention of malaria, and the natives of Brazil knew the worth of ipecac for amebic dysentery. The victims of leprosy in the Far East believed that they received relief by rubbing their wounds with chaulmoogra oil, and for some time chaulmoogra oil was used in the treatment of this disease. The Indians of America used arbutus for rheumatism; lobelia for coughs and colds; wild sage tea, goldenseal, and flowering dogwood for fevers; elders, wild cherry, and sumac for colds and quinsies; inhalations of pennyroyal for headache; sassafras leaves for wounds and felons; and the roots of sassafras for cooling and purifying the blood.

As medical lore accumulated, there appeared

individuals who demonstrated a special talent for herb-doctoring, bone-setting, and rude surgery and who employed it as a means of earning a livelihood. They were either the wisewomen who sought by their art to lessen the hardships and dangers of childbirth or certain men of superior intelligence and cunning who, appreciating the credulity of the rank and file, made use of incantations and charms in their therapeutics and established themselves in the community in the role of priest and physician. These nature healers soon perceived not only what substances were good and what were harmful but that a number of poisons were also remedies under certain conditions. This drug and poison lore was the beginning of materia medica and medicine.

■ Ancient period
Egypt

The oldest phase of medicine is the Egyptian. The main sources of data are the medical papyri, the most important of which is the Ebers papyrus, written in the sixteenth century B.C. It is a scroll 22 yards long and about 12 inches wide that contains a collection of prescriptions and formulas covering a wide range of uses. Included among them are many invocations and conjuring forms for driving away disease, as well as specific recipes, calling in many instances for drugs that are in common use today, for example, aloes, castor oil, figs, vinegar, turpentine, opium, wormwood, peppermint, and squill.

Among the mineral and metal substances were iron, copper sulfate, magnesia, niter, sodium carbonate, salt, and precious stones ground into powder.

The animal preparations included such substances as lizards' blood, swine's teeth, putrid meat, stinking fat, milk, goose grease, asses' hoofs, animal fats, flies and excreta of various animals (a soothing syrup for babies was made of the latter), and such ingredients as the thigh bone of a hanged man or the moss grown on a human skull.

The prescriptions were for purges, headache remedies, tonics, hair restorers, and remedies for hookworm, tapeworm, and intestinal worms, to be put up in the form of pills, powders, infusions, decoctions, gargles, salves, plasters, poultices, and confections. Over 700 drugs are mentioned, and one prescription requires thirty-five ingredients.

As the inclusion of invocations and charms in the prescriptions would imply, medicine was closely allied with religion, as it was to remain for many centuries. The doctors were all priests paid out of the royal treasury, but they were allowed to take fees also.

Greece

The pharmaceutical history of Greece begins with legends regarding gods and goddesses. The reputed activities of these mythical characters are so inextricably woven with the authentic doings of real men and women that it is often hard to determine where legend ends and history begins. The story goes, however, that Chiron, the centaur, originated the pharmaceutical art and imparted his valuable knowledge to Aesculapius, son of Apollo. Aesculapius, with the aid of his daughters Hygeia and Panacea, in turn taught mortals the art of healing, but he became so successful in combating disease that he incurred the wrath of Pluto, god of the underworld, because he was diminishing too greatly the number of shades received in Hades. Pluto prevailed upon almighty Zeus to destroy Aesculapius with a thunderbolt, but upon the intercession of Apollo, Zeus deified him as the god of healing. His mortal followers in time made up the organized guild of physicians called Aesclepiades. They built temples in his honor in which they practiced their art and increased their knowledge of healing. These temples were situated in hills or mountains, usually near mineral springs, and were managed by trained priests. Hence they were virtually sanatoriums or hospitals for the sick. The patient was received by the physician priests and, after spiritual purification by prayers and sacrifice, was further cleansed by a bath from the mineral springs, catharsis, massage, and inunction and encouraged with medicated wines and soft music to sleep and to dream. The priest then interpreted the dream as a message from Morpheus and offered medical advice accordingly. If the treatment was a success and the patient recovered, a votive tablet giving the history of the case and the treatment was hung in the temple where anyone who wished might consult it. In this way, a considerable body of empirical knowledge was assembled and these Temples of Health took on some of the characteristics of a medical school. The most celebrated ones were at Cnidus and Cos.

The most famous representative of the Aescleplades was Hippocrates, who was born in the Island of Cos, 460 B.C., of a long line of priest physicians and who was reputed by popular tradition to be the seventeenth in direct descent from Aesculapius. Hippocrates pursued his early studies at Cos and Cnidus but later came under the influence of the great thinkers and philosophers of the period and soon began to give to medicine their scientific and ethical ideas. He denounced the belief in the supernatural origin of disease and the use of charms, incantations, and other superstitious devices of priestcraft. He substituted the doctrine that disease resulted from natural causes and that knowledge of it would be gained only through the study of the natural laws. He taught the use of the senses in collecting data for diagnosis and the use of inductive reasoning in arriving at diagnostic conclusions.

His therapeutic measures were decidedly modern. He believed that the body has great power to recuperate and that the role of the physician should be simply to aid Nature in her work. His treatment consisted usually of fresh air, good food, purgation, bloodletting, massage, and hydrotherapy. Although he mentioned over 400 drugs in his writings, he used only a few of the important ones, among them opium. His preparations included foments, poultices, gargles, suppositories, pills, lozenges, ointments, cerates, and inhalations.

Hippocrates is called the Father of Medicine because his influence has extended through the ages and his teachings have established the sound principles that control the practice of medicine to the present day.

Another early Greek physician was Dioscorides, who was an authority on materia medica. He described 600 plants and plant principles of which no less than seventy-four are in use today. His work was the chief source of pharmaceutical knowledge of antiquity.

Rome

After the Roman conquest of Greece, Greek medicine migrated to Rome. The most famous Greek physician of this period was Galen (A.D. 131-201). He based his teachings and practice largely upon the work of Hippocrates and established a system of medicine and pharmacy that made him the supreme authority for several hundred years. He originated many preparations of vegetable drugs, which even now are spoken of as galenicals, and was the first to prepare rosewater ointment or cold cream.

■ Medieval period (A.D. 400 to 1500)
Early period—the Dark Ages (A.D. 400-1100)

The term *Middle Ages* is given to that period of European history that lies between what are known as ancient and modern times, extending from about the middle of the fifth to the middle of the fifteenth century. The historical event that marked the close of ancient times was the decline and fall of the Roman Empire. This process extended over three or four centuries, during which period successive hordes of Germanic barbarians poured in from the north and east and overran Western Europe. They gradually succeeded in wresting the territory piecemeal from the Romans and in setting up their own tribal organizations. This process of dismemberment of the Roman Empire was completed in the fifth century and was followed by a period of about 600 years known as the Dark Ages, because during this time the old civilization was largely destroyed and there was little progress in learning. The German tribes were slowly learning to combine their primitive institutions with those of Rome and were assimilating the first rudiments of culture through their contact with the Latins. Wars between the tribes were frequent and served to stifle all effort along constructive lines. Their medicine was folklore and tradition, the employment of wonder-cures and temple-sleeps similar to those of the Greeks before the advent of Hippocrates.

Another important movement at the same time was the spread of Christianity. After three centuries of struggle and persecution the Christian church triumphed in 311 through a decree of the emperor, who made it the official church of Rome. Thereupon, religious orders arose whose members scattered throughout Europe preaching the new doctrine and building monasteries, where they could withdraw from the world and devote their lives to the work of the Church. The monasteries, particularly those of the Benedictines, soon became the repositories of all the learning of the period. The Venerable Bede was a Benedictine. The monks collected all available manuscripts and copied and preserved them. Among other things, they preserved the works on pharmacy and medicine. Since it was part of their religious duty to give aid to the sick and needy, they controlled most of the practice of medicine and disseminated much knowledge of healing. Their treatment was usually good food, quiet, rest, and the administration of decoctions of medicinal plants from their gardens. Monastery gardens were an important factor in the development of herbals or books of plant lore, the oldest of which dates 500 years before the invention of printing. Mistletoe was a great panacea. Lycopodium, clover, primrose, henbane, and verbena were common remedies, as were wormwood, belladonna, hellebore, and mandragora.

The first records of the use of some of the remedies now in modern practice are from this period. In the sixth century Alexander of Tralles used colchicum for gout, iron for anemia, cantharides as a blister, and rhubarb for dysentery and liver complaints.

Arabian influence

In the eighth century the Arabs spread over the Holy Land, Egypt, North Africa, and Spain and began a supremacy that lasted over 500 years. They were especially interested in medicine, pharmacy, and chemistry and built hospitals and schools for the pursuit of their study. They carried forward the knowledge obtained from Greece and Rome and preserved the pharmaceutical art from the sixth to the sixteenth centuries. Their medicine was a blend of the practice of the Greeks and Jews and of the astrology and occult lore of Egypt and India. The teachings of Hippocrates and Galen, which had been translated into Arabic in the seventh century, furnished much of their material.

The Arabs contributed many new drugs. Medicine is indebted to them for the use of senna, camphor, musk, myrrh, cassia, tamarind, nutmeg, cloves, cubeb, aconite, ambergris, cannabis, and sandalwood. They were the originators of syrups, juleps, alcohol, and aromatic water. They introduced into Europe the decimal notation, acquired by them from a now forgotten race in India.

The first great Mohammedan author was Geber, who wrote exclusively on chemistry. He is the reputed discoverer of sulfuric acid, nitric acid, nitrohydrochloric acid, corrosive sublimate, and lunar caustic.

Avicenna was an accomplished physician of the tenth century. He wrote the *Canon*, a miscellaneous collection of past medical lore with his interpretations. His works were considered authoritative in universities as late as 1650.

During this period, pharmacy was practiced somewhat as a profession separate from medicine. The first apothecary shops were established and the first pharmaceutical formulary or set of drug standards was produced. This served as a model for the first London pharmacopeia. The Arabian pharmacists were called sandalini. Their stocks were regularly inspected and punishment was meted out to those found guilty of selling spurious or deteriorated drugs.

Rise of universities

The word *university* means an association, and the principal universities of Europe had their origin in the voluntary association of guilds of students banded together for mutual protection and established at some place favorable to the pursuit of their studies. Salerno, which was founded in the eighth century, was the first of the educational institutions of the university type. Others founded later were the University of Paris, 1110; Bologna, 1113; Oxford, 1167; Cambridge, 1209; Padua, 1222; and Naples, 1224. They exerted a great influence upon the development of all science, and especially of medicine and pharmacy. Pharmacy was taught in all as part of the medical course. One of the most eminent pharmaceutical authorities of this period was Nicholas of Salerno, Director of the Medical School. He wrote the *Antidotarium*, which was the standard for pharmaceutical preparations for centuries. It contained the basic units of the present apothecaries' system, the grain, scruple, and dram, just as they are used today. At Salerno, the study of anatomy was resumed under a decree that permitted the dissection of a human body every 5 years. Didactic instruction here was based upon Hippocrates, Galen, Avicenna, and the antidotary of Nicholas Praepositus. A famous woman physician, Trotula of Salerno, first used mercury in the treatment of syphilis.

Late medieval period

In 1095 occurred the first of the Crusades. They extended over a period of nearly 200 years and exerted a profound influence on pharmacy by bringing about a fusion of Arabian science and learning with the primitive practices based upon folklore and tradition in Central and Northwest Europe. Records of the customhouse of the port of Acri in Italy in the early thirteenth century show large traffic in the various spices, opium, and rhubarb. Venetians brought the first sugar to Europe during the time of the Crusades. It was costly and was used exclusively as medicine, as were most of the spices.

Pharmacies as separate places for compounding and dispensing medicines spread through Europe with great rapidity during the thirteenth century. The fourteenth and fifteenth centuries witnessed a great awakening of interest in medicine and pharmacy throughout Europe. The Moors of Spain, who had a great reputation for knowledge and skill in these branches of science and who had been driven out of Granada by Ferdinand in 1492, scattered over Europe, prac-

ticing and teaching. Moreover, during this period, epidemic diseases were very prevalent, especially leprosy, ergotism, and the Black Death. The Black Death (bubonic plague) killed 25% of the human race (60 million people) during this period.

In the fifteenth century alchemy, brought in by the Arabs, swept over Europe like a conflagration. Alchemy was the search for means of transmuting base metals into gold. The mere desire to discover such a substance gave rise to a universal belief that one existed, and the so-called philosopher's stone was as much a reality to the alchemist as the actual substances with which he worked. Gradually belief spread that the philosopher's stone could not only transmute all metals into gold but could also cure all diseases, restore youth, and indefinitely prolong life. It thus also became the elixir of life. While the alchemists were carrying on the search for the stone, they made important inventions and discoveries that laid the foundations of the modern science of chemistry. In 1438 printing was invented and the world was flooded with books. One of the earliest printed works extant contains an illustration of a fifteenth-century pharmacy.

■ Sixteenth century

In the sixteenth century pharmacy came into its own. Drugs were rare and costly, prescriptions were complex, and special art was required in preparing and keeping the drugs. Formularies appeared in such numbers that a need was felt for an authoritative standard. This was furnished by Valerius Cordus, son of a professor of medicine at Marburg. Cordus collected formulas during 12 years of teaching at Wittenberg and compiled these in manuscript form. The physicians of Nuremberg wished a copy for the local druggists and secured the consent of the senate in 1546 to have it printed. This work of Cordus was the first pharmacopeia to be printed and authorized for use in a community for the sake of uniformity. It drew its material from Greek, Roman, and Arabian sources and quoted freely from Galen, Dioscorides, Avicenna, and Nicholas Praepositus. It contained comparatively few types of preparations, namely, aromatics, opiates, confections, conserves, purges, pills, syrups, plasters, cerates, troches, salves, and oils. Editions were published in Paris, Lyons, Venice, and Antwerp. It held its place till 1666 and was revised five times meanwhile.

The outstanding figure of the sixteenth century was Paracelsus, the son of a German physician and chemist. At the age of 16 years he began the study of medicine at the University of Basel, but he soon gave it up to experiment with chemistry and alchemy. He traveled widely, gathering a vast amount of knowledge, especially of folk medicine, from barbers, gypsies, and others with whom he associated. He served some time as a military surgeon in the Low Countries and worked in mines in the Tyrol. Here he investigated processes of preparing metals and made experiments as to their medicinal virtues. His cures gained wide publicity and he was called upon to prescribe for many of the great men of his day. In 1526 he was appointed professor of physics and surgery at Basle. Here he inaugurated his career as a teacher by publicly burning the works of Galen and denouncing the Arabians masters whose doctrines were then generally followed. He also flouted tradition by lecturing in German instead of Latin. His defiance of tradition and his arrogant manner aroused the enmity of the other members of the faculty, and he was compelled to leave the university in 1528 and resume his wanderings. At Salzburg he gave offense to a prominent physician, was thrown from a window by the man's servants, and died from the fall.

In spite of his objectionable methods, Paracelsus exerted a profound influence upon the medical beliefs of his time and of succeeding centuries. He attacked the weak points of the prevailing system of medicine; he destroyed the "humoral pathology" that taught that diseases were caused by an excess or deficiency of the "humors" bile, phlegm, or blood and substituted the doctrine that diseases were actual entities to be combated with specific remedies. He improved pharmacy and therapeutics, introduced some new remedies such as calomel and sulfur,

made some new chemical compounds, and strove to reduce the overdosing then practiced.

■ Seventeenth century

In 1618 the first London pharmacopeia appeared. It was chiefly a compilation of older authorities. It was sponsored by the London College of Physicians, and its use was made obligatory throughout the British realm by a decree of King James. It was very large compared with the modern pharmacopeia, containing 1028 simple drugs and 932 preparations and compounds. The most complex preparation contained 130 ingredients. One substance listed was usnea. This was moss from the skull of a man who had died a violent death. It was not hard to obtain in England in those days, because the bodies of criminals who had been executed were suspended in chains in public places as a warning to other criminals, and the exposure was conducive to growth of moss on the skull.

Great interest was displayed in chemistry and pharmacy in this century, and many preparations that originated then are still in use. Among them are senna or black draught, the alcoholic tincture of opium or laudanum, the compound tincture of benzoin, the balsams of Peru and Tolu, guaiacum, sarsaparilla, and jalap. In 1638 cinchona was imported by the Countess Ana del Chinchon, wife of the Viceroy of Peru, who had been cured of a severe intermittent fever by its use. Coca was likewise introduced from Peru, and ipecac found its way into Europe and was used with such skill by a quack named Helvetius that Louis XIV paid him $4000 for his secret.

■ Eighteenth century

The eighteenth century likewise witnessed great progress in pharmacy. A German practitioner by the name of Hoffmann originated the elixir of orange and Hoffmann's anodyne. A Berlin apothecary identified magnesia, the alums, the potassa, and soda and discovered beet sugar. A French pharmacist published an essay entitled "The Superstitions Concerning the Philosopher's Stone" and thereby helped divert alchemy into more profitable channels. In

11

1775 Louis XVI paid nearly $5000 to a certain Madame Nouffer for a celebrated cure for tapeworm. She inherited the secret from her husband, a Swiss physician. The drug proved to be male fern, commonly known since Galen.

Inoculation against smallpox was introduced in the latter part of the eighteenth century by Edward Jenner, an English physician. For years he had been studying smallpox, swinepox, and cowpox and the development of the two latter diseases when communicated to man. He noticed that milkmaids who were frequently infected with cowpox were immune to smallpox. He made his first public inoculation with vaccine on May 14, 1796, and within a year had won the confidence of the physicians in his theory of immunization.

In 1785 the infusion of digitalis was introduced by William Withering of England for the treatment of heart disease. The foxglove is carved on Withering's monument.

Dover's powder had its origin about this time. Thomas Dover administered the drug in doses of 60 grains and claimed to have given as much as 100 grains. This was equivalent to 10 grains of opium and 10 grains of ipecac. The pharmacists filling his prescriptions usually advised patients first to make their wills.

A great number of important pharmacopeias and works of reference appeared during the century. One of particular interest was the dispensatory of St. Thomas', Guy's, and St. Bartholomew's hospitals in London in 1741. It listed viper's flesh as an ingredient of one preparation and wood lice as an ingredient of several. Dried horses' hoofs were used to check the spitting of blood. The motto of the book was: "Prepare to die, for behold, Death and Judgment is at hand."

■ Nineteenth century

During the nineteenth century, chemistry gradually took its place as a highly specialized science, with pharmaceutical chemistry as an important subdivision. The first great pharmaceutical discovery was that of the alkaloid morphine, obtained from opium by a German apothecary, Serturner, in 1815. This was the first active principle to be isolated and led to enthusiastic research on many vegetable drugs. The result was the discovery of quinine, strychnine, and veratrine by Pelletier and Caventou; of emetine by Pelletier and Magendie; of atropine by Brandes; and of codeine by Robiquet. All of these men were pharmacists. Their discoveries made it possible to administer drugs in an attractive and palatable form. The accurate study of dosage was also possible.

In 1842 Dr. Crawford W. Long of Georgia first used ether as a general anesthetic, and in 1847 Sir J. T. Simpson used chloroform for the same purpose.

About 1856 appeared the first of the numerous coal-tar products. Perkin, in a vain attempt to produce synthetic quinine, discovered instead the first coal-tar dye, called "Perkin's purple" or mauve. This led to the preparation in the laboratory of a great family of remedial agents, some of which, such as salicylic and benzoic acids, duplicated products previously obtained from natural sources, and others of which were new to science, for example, acetanilid and antipyrine.

The discovery of so many new drugs and the invention of new and convenient dosage forms led to the establishment of large-scale manufacturing plants that took over much of the work formerly done by the pharmacist with his mortar and pestle.

This century also witnessed the initial appearance of the important national pharmacopeias. The French *Codex* was first to be produced. It was issued in 1818 and contained one remarkable item, a formula for an extract of opium in which the preparation was to be boiled incessantly for 6 months and the water lost by evaporation to be constantly replaced. The first pharmacopeia for the United States appeared in 1820, the national standard for Great Britain in 1864 to replace those of London, Edinburgh, and Dublin, and that for Germany in 1872, superseding nearly a score of local volumes.

Fewer drugs were prescribed, and the prescriptions given were accompanied with greater knowledge of their expected action. In other words, rational medicine began to replace empiricism. During this period purging and blood-letting became less popular and definite action toward exposing harmful patent medicines and nostrums was taken.

■ Twentieth century

Great progress has been made in pharmacy and medicine since the beginning of the twentieth century. In pharmacy, growth has been chiefly along the lines of strengthening and improving the work of the professional organizations such as the American Pharmaceutical Association and the National Association of Retail Druggists and with the promotion of legislation controlling the manufacture and sale of drugs. The most important acts were the Food and Drug Acts of 1906 and 1938 and the Harrison Narcotic Act of 1914.

It is said that more progress has probably been made during the past 50 years than in all the years prior to that time. As far as therapeutics is concerned this is largely the result of changes in the concept of the cause of disease. When it was believed that evil spirits caused disease, the treatment given was highly varied and used in the hope that one of the measures would be the right one. Since the acceptance of the germ theory there has been rapid advancement in scientific methods of research. Such methods have been greatly aided by animal experimentation, appropriation of money for research work, and efforts of public health organizations to educate the public and to collect valuable vital statistics.

Of interest to both pharmacy and medicine are the many biologic preparations such as the vaccines, antitoxins, and serums now in common use and the valuable group of anesthetics, which is constantly growing through the isolation and duplication in the laboratory of more and more of the potent vegetable substances found in nature. The introduction into medicine by the German physician Ehrlich in 1907 of salvarsan, the great specific for syphilis, and the discovery by Banting in 1922 of insulin for the treatment of diabetes constitute two of the epoch-making events of the century.

With the increased knowledge of drugs has grown an increasing awareness of implications in their misuse and abuse. Among other trends in modern medicine is the use of other therapeutic agencies either to supplement drug therapy or to replace it. Such therapies include vitamin therapy, diet therapy, and various kinds of physical therapy.

To discover chemotherapeutic agents that will be effective in every infectious disease is one of the goals of research workers in medicine. However, for years there were only a few chemicals that acted as specifics. Among the most important were quinine for malaria and the arsenicals for syphilis. In the last few decades several remarkable chemotherapeutic agents have changed chemical therapy tremendously. Infections that a few years ago took a tremendous toll in sickness and deaths are now well controlled by the sulfonamides, penicillin, and other antibiotics. In 1908 sulfanilamide was first prepared by Gelmo, a German organic chemist, who was investigating azo dyes. It was not until 1932, however, that its possible therapeutic value was realized. In 1932 Prontosil was patented in Germany by Klarer and Mietzsch. A German worker, Domagk, is credited with the discovery of the therapeutic value of Prontosil. In 1932 Domagk observed that mice with streptococcal septicemia could be protected by Prontosil. It was later shown that Prontosil breaks down into para-aminobenzenesulfonamide, which is the effective substance. In the next few years more and more interest was aroused in these drugs, and today they have a rightful place as some of the most important drugs. Para-aminobenzenesulfonamide was accepted by the Council on Pharmacy and Chemistry of the American Medical Association for inclusion in N.N.R. in 1937, at which time the name of sulfanilamide was suggested for it. Since then many new sulfonamide derivatives have been tried, and a few of them have become well established in drug therapy.

The story of the development of antibacterial agents of biologic origin, or antibiotics, is one of the most interesting developments in pharmacy. In 1929 Dr. Alexander Fleming at the University of London noted that a mold contaminating a plate of staphylococci produced a zone of inhibition around it in which the staphylococci did not grow. Fleming found that the mold, *Penicillium notatum*, secreted into its medium an antibiotic agent, which he named penicillin. He found it was not toxic to animals, did not hurt white blood cells, and inhibited the growth of certain gram-positive pathogens. He used broth containing penicillin clinically on several cases of skin infections with favorable results. However, little was done clinically about it for the next 10 years.

In 1939 Rene J. Dubos of the Rockefeller Institute for Medical Research published the results of experiments done on certain bacteria found in the soil. Dubos acted on the assumption that all organic matter added to the soil would eventually undergo decomposition by microorganisms. Samples of soil were incubated for a few weeks to bring about decomposition of most of the organic matter present. Then cultures of staphylococci, Group A hemolytic streptococci, and pneumococci were added to the soil at intervals.

After 2 years, a gram-positive, spore-bearing aerobic bacillus capable of lysing the living cells of many gram-positive bacteria was isolated from the soil. The soil bacillus, called *Bacillus brevis*, produced a substance destructive to certain gram-positive bacteria. The destructive substance could be extracted from the bacteria. It was named tyrothricin and was later shown to be composed of two substances, gramicidin and tyrocidine. Gramicidin is much more effective than tyrocidine therapeutically. Unfortunately, gramicidin is hemolytic and can be used only for local infections, never where it can get in contact with the blood.

This story now turns back to penicillin. In 1938 Dr. Howard Florey at Oxford University began to study penicillin and other naturally occurring antibacterial agents. Dr. Florey and his associates are responsible for the isolation of penicillin, its assay and dosage, and proof of its clinical usefulness. The first patient was treated with penicillin early in 1941. Because of World War II it was impossible to start large-scale production in England. Dr. Florey came to the United States in 1941 and asked for the help of the National Research Council in studying penicillin. Production was soon started in the United States, and the first patient in this country was treated with penicillin in March, 1942. Since that time a number of new antibiotics —streptomycin, dihydrostreptomycin, chloramphenicol, chlortetracycline, oxytetracycline, tetracycline, and many others—have been added to the physician's armamentarium.

It should be noted that obtaining antibacterial agents from natural sources is not a new procedure. There are many such substances throughout the plant and animal kingdoms. Quinine, which is produced by a plant, has been used for many years.

In 1935 a series of events occurred that were to have far-reaching significance. Dr. E. C. Kendall and associates of the Mayo Foundation, Dr. Wintersteiner and Dr. Pfiffner of Columbia University, and Professor Reichstein of Switzerland independently isolated a group of crystalline substances from the cortex of the adrenal gland. Continued effort resulted in the discovery of the chemical structure of these compounds. Among these new products was one that proved to be 17-hydroxy-11-dehydrocorticosterone. The name of this compound was shortened to cortisone. It was first used in medicine in 1948. It appears to have opened a new era in medical science. Later (1950) hydrocortisone and (1954) aldosterone were isolated and identified.

In 1955 and later in 1961 the announcement of new poliomyelitis vaccines focused the attention of the world upon another achievement that provided mankind with relief from the dreaded disease of poliomyelitis.

During the 1950's and early 1960's many new drugs were introduced, bringing great benefits but also creating many problems. Since the passage of the 1962 Kefauver-Harris Drug Amendments requiring proof of efficacy as well as safety, the introduction of new medicinal agents has become much less frequent. In addition, the number of preparations available is actually decreasing as many older, ineffective drugs are being removed from the market.

Despite the slowdown in the introduction of new drugs, many valuable agents continue to be made available, such as newer anti-infectives, hormonal agents, and anti-neoplastic agents, to mention a few. Real breakthroughs in therapy continue to occur, such as the discovery of the beneficial effect of allopurinol (Zyloprim) in gout or the dramatic effects of L-dopa in Parkinson's disease. The future of drug therapy continues to be bright.

References

Burger, A.: Approaches to drug discovery, New Eng. J. Med. **270:**1098, 1964.

Fleming, A.: Penicillin: its practical application, London, 1950, Butterworth & Co. Ltd.

Krantz, J. C., Jr.: A portrait of medical history and current medical problems, Baltimore, 1962, The John D. Lucas Company.

Mariott, H. J. L.: Medical milestones, Baltimore, 1952, The Williams & Wilkins Co.

Osler, Sir W.: The evolution of modern medicine, New Haven, Conn., 1921, Yale University Press.

Rose, F. L.: Medicine's debt to the sulphonamide group, Chem. Industr., May 23, 1964, pp. 858-865.

Sonnedecker, G.: Kremers and Urdang's history of pharmacy, ed. 3, Philadelphia, 1963, J. B. Lippincott Co.

Woodham-Smith, C.: Florence Nightingale, New York, 1951, McGraw-Hill Book Company.

3 Drug standards and legislation

Drug standards
Drug legislation

■ Drug standards

Drugs have been known to vary considerably in strength and activity. Drugs obtained from plants, such as opium and digitalis, have been known to vary in strength from plant to plant and from year to year, depending on where the plants are grown, the age at which they are harvested, and how they are preserved. Occasionally, one finds on the market drugs of low concentration or drugs that have been adulterated. Since accurate dosage and reliability of effect of a drug depend on uniformity of strength and purity, it has been necessary to find ways by which drugs can be standardized. The technique by which the strength or potency of a drug is measured is known as *assay*. The two general types of assay method used are chemical and biologic. Chemical assay really means chemical analysis to determine the ingredients present and their amount. A simple example would be the determination of the concentration of hydrochloric acid in a solution to be used medically. Thus the acid content of a solution might be measured by titration and then adjusted, for example, to a standardized tenth-normal solution.

Opium is known to contain certain alkaloids (*active principles* was the older term), and these may vary greatly in different preparations. The United States official standard demands that opium must contain not less than 9.5% and not more than 10.5% of anhydrous morphine. Opium of a higher morphine content may be reduced to the official standard by admixture with opium of a lower percentage or with certain other pharmacologically inactive diluents such as sucrose, lactose, glycyrrhiza, or magnesium carbonate.

In the case of some drugs either the active ingredients are not known or there are no available methods of analyzing and standardizing them. These drugs may be standardized by biologic methods—bioassay. Bioassay is performed by determining the amount of a preparation required to produce a definite effect on a suitable laboratory animal under certain standard conditions. For example, the potency of a certain sample of insulin is measured by its ability to lower the blood sugar of rabbits. The strength of a drug that is assayed biologically is usually expressed in units. For example, insulin injection, U.S.P., possesses a potency of not less than 95% and not more than 105% of the potency stated on the label, expressed in U.S.P. insulin units. Both the unit and the method of assay are defined, so that national and sometimes international standards exist.

Drug standards in the United States

In the United States an official drug is one that is included in *The Pharmacopeia of the United States of America, The National Formulary*, or the *Homeopathic Pharmacopoeia of the United States*. Drugs listed in these publications are official because they are so designated by the *Federal Food, Drug, and Cosmetic Act*.

The Pharmacopeia of the United States of America (usually referred to as the U.S.P. or *The Pharmacopeia*) is a book in which approved medicinal agents used in present-day medical practice are defined as to source, physical and chemical properties, tests for purity and identity, assay, method of storage, category (general type of drug), and dosage (range of dosage as well as the usual therapeutic dosage).

In most instances, preparations included in the U.S.P. are single drugs. They are listed under their official names. The purpose of the U.S.P. is to provide standards for the identification and purity of drugs and to ensure uniformity of strength. When a drug is prescribed by a physician anywhere in the United States, the pharmacist must fill the prescription with a preparation that meets pharmacopeial standards if the drug is listed in the U.S.P. This assures the physician of uniform potency and purity of all official drugs that he prescribes for his patients.

The first pharmacopeia in the United States was published in 1820. The current edition, U.S.P. XVIII, became official in 1970. At one time it was customary to revise the U.S.P. every 10 years, but it is now revised every 5 years. Supplements to the U.S.P. are published between revisions to keep abreast of the rapid changes in this field.

The U.S.P. is revised by a special pharmacopeial committee headed by a full-time director. The committee is made up of outstanding pharmacologists, physicians, and pharmacists who donate their services to this important task. The main committee is assisted by many subcommittees and advisory boards. Drugs included in the U.S.P. are selected on the basis of their therapeutic usefulness and low toxicity. When drugs listed in the U.S.P. have been supplanted in practice by better drugs, the older ones are deleted and the newer or better drugs are added. Sometimes a drug is deleted from the U.S.P. because after extensive use the incidence of toxic reactions is shown to be too high.

Drugs whose content or method of preparation is secret are not admitted to the U.S.P. Trademarked or patented preparations of therapeutic merit may be included; when included they are listed under their official names, not the popular trade names by which they may be commonly known.

The National Formulary (N.F.) serves as a supplement to the U.S.P. It is sponsored by the American Pharmaceutical Association and is usually revised the same year as the U.S.P. The latest edition is the thirteenth, printed in 1970. Originally *The National Formulary* contained only formulas for drug mixtures. It now contains many single drugs as well as formulas for drug mixtures. Standards for those drugs listed in *The National Formulary* but not included in *The Pharmacopeia* are indicated. *The Pharmacopeia* represents a more critical selection of drugs since they are more carefully screened as to their therapeutic value and toxic qualities. Drugs included in *The National Formulary* are selected not only on the basis of their therapeutic value but also on the basis of demand. Preparations deleted from *The Pharmacopeia* are often transferred to *The National Formulary*. It provides standards for many of the older remedies that the pharmacist is still called upon to dispense. As is true of *The Pharmacopeia*, drugs are listed in *The National Formulary* under their official names only.

Drug standards in Great Britain and Canada

British Pharmacopoeia (B.P.) is similar to the U.S.P. in its scope and purpose. Drugs listed in it are considered official and subject to legal control in the United Kingdom and those parts of the British Commonwealth in which the *British Pharmacopoeia* has statutory force. It is published by the British Pharmacopoeia Commission under the direction of the General Medical Council. Dosage is expressed in metric system, although in some cases dosage is indicated in both metric and imperial systems.

The Pharmacopeia of the United States of America is used a great deal in Canada, and some preparations used in Canada conform to the U.S.P. instead of the B.P. because many of the drugs used in Canada are obtained from the United States.

British Pharmaceutical Codex (B.P.C.) is published by the Pharmaceutical Society of Great Britain. In general, it resembles *The National Formulary*.

The *Compendium of Pharmaceuticals and Specialties* is published by the Canadian Pharmaceutical Association. It contains formulas for preparations used extensively in Canada. It also contains standards for new drugs prescribed in Canada but not included in the *British Pharmacopoeia*. This publication has been given official status by the *Canadian Food and Drug Act*.

The Physician's Formulary contains formulas for preparations that are representative of the needs of medical practice in Canada. It is published by the Canadian Medical Association. *New Drugs* is also used in Canada as a source of information about new drugs.

International standards

Various national pharmacopeias have been developed to meet the needs of medical practice in different countries. *The Pharmacopeia of the United States* has been translated into Spanish for the Spanish-speaking parts of the Americas. In addition, an international pharmacopeia has been published.

Pharmacopoea Internationalis (Ph.I.) was first published in 1951. It was published by a committee of the World Health Organization and represents an important contribution to the development of international standards in drugs and unification of national pharmacopeias. The work done on this publication has resulted in better understanding of terms and in uniformity of strengths and composition of drugs throughout the world. It has also demonstrated that members of different nations can sit down together and come to agreement about matters that concern many people of the world.

The *Pharmacopoea Internationalis* is published in English, Spanish, and French. The nomenclature is in Latin, and the system of measurement is metric. It is not intended to convey official status in any country unless it is adopted by the appropriate authority of that country.

■ Drug legislation

Important though pharmacopeias, formularies, and other publications are to the maintenance of standards for drugs, unless provision is made to enforce the standards the public can be defrauded, drugs adulterated, and the market flooded with unreliable and unsafe preparations. Enforcement of standards is partly a responsibility of individual states, but federal legislation is needed to cover interstate commerce in drugs as well as in other items.

The twentieth century ushered in an era of rapidly expanding scientific knowledge. At the beginning of the century federal laws controlling drug distribution were nonexistent. Illness was treated primarily with well-known botanicals or time-honored products of nature, and many preparations of secret composition were sold to the public for all known diseases.

During the first decade of the twentieth century organic chemicals used in medicine increased in number, and it soon became evident that federal legislation was needed to protect the public in a complex area where individuals were unable to protect themselves. The result was enactment of the first federal drug law in 1906.

United States drug legislation

Federal Food, Drug, and Cosmetic Act. In 1906 the Federal Food, Drug, and Cosmetic Act designated *The Pharmacopeia of the United States of America* and *The National Formulary* as official standards and empowered the federal government to enforce these standards. It was "An act for preventing the manufacture of adulterated or misbranded or poisonous or deleterious foods, drugs, medicines, and liquors, and for regulating traffic therein, and for other purposes." This first federal drug law required that drugs comply with the standards of strength and purity professed for them, and it also required that labels on drugs containing morphine or other narcotic ingredients indicate the kind and amount of such substances.

In the second decade of the twentieth century the number of chemicals used in medicine continued to increase, and Congress passed the Sherley Amendment prohibiting use of fraudulent therapeutic claims. Drug research continued to accelerate during the next two decades. Synthetic organic chemicals made their appearance, and the chemotherapeutic age began. The Food and Drug Act of 1906 was updated by the Federal Food, Drug, and Cosmetic Act of 1938. Impetus to revise the 1906 drug act was provided by more than 100 deaths in 1937 resulting from ingestion of a diethylene glycol solution of sulfanilamide. The sulfanilamide preparation had been marketed as an "elixir of sulfanilamide" without benefit of investigation of the toxicity of the solvent. The only charge that could be made against the drug was that it was misbranded since it was labeled an "elixir" and the drug failed to meet the definition of an elixir as an alcoholic solution. The Federal Food, Drug, and Cosmetic Act of 1938 contained a provision to prevent premature marketing of new drugs not properly tested for safety by requiring the manufacturer to submit a new drug application to the government for review of safety studies before the product could be sold.

The Federal Food, Drug, and Cosmetic Act of 1938 conferred status on the drugs listed in the *Homeopathic Pharmacopoeia of the United States* as well as those in *The Pharmacopeia of the United States of America* and *The National Formulary*.

The Durham-Humphrey Law in 1952 further amended the 1938 drug act. The law was aimed at tightening control of barbiturates by restricting the refilling of prescriptions. For the first time Congress enacted legislation specifically dividing drugs into (1) those safe for use without medical supervision, which may therefore be sold over the counter, and (2) those not safe for unsupervised use, which are therefore required to be labeled with the legend: "Caution: Federal law prohibits dispensing without prescription" (provision 10). The law also clarifies the use of written and oral prescriptions (provision 13).

The Kefauver-Harris Drug Amendment in 1962 further changed the Federal Food, Drug, and Cosmetic Act. Impetus for this amendment was provided by the thalidomide tragedy, although for the United States it was more a might-have-been catastrophe than a real one. This amendment authorizes the Food and Drug Administration to insist upon "substantial evidence that the drug will have the effect it purports or is represented to have under the conditions of use prescribed, recommended, or suggested in the proposed labeling thereof." Thus, the drug manufacturer must prove not only that a new drug is safe but also that it is effective. The law provides for greater control and surveillance over the distribution and clinical testing of investigational drugs. The intent of the 1962 drug law is to protect the public and the clinical investigator by ensuring that adequate preclinical studies are done on the drug before the investigator is asked to do human studies.

Provisions of the Federal Food, Drug, and Cosmetic Act. The provisions include many features designed to prevent misbranding and to ensure careful and accurate labeling. Labeling refers not only to the labels on the immediate container but also to circulars, pamphlets, and brochures that may accompany the preparations or in some manner reach the hands of the consumer. The Act prohibits certain statements from appearing on the label and insists upon certain others:

1 Statements on the label must not be false or misleading in any particular.
2 Drugs must not be dangerous to health when used in the dosage or with the frequency prescribed, recommended, or suggested on the label.

19

3 The label must indicate the name and the business address of the manufacturer, packer, or distributor as well as an accurate statement of the contents.

4 The label must indicate quantitatively the presence of all habit-forming drugs, such as narcotics, hypnotics, or other habit-forming drugs or their derivatives. The label must also bear the statement: "Warning—May Be Habit Forming."

5 Labels must designate the presence of official drugs by their official names, and if nonofficial they must bear the usual name of the drug or drugs, whether active or not.

6 The Act requires that official drugs be packaged and labeled as specified by *The Pharmacopeia of the United States*, *The National Formulary*, or the *Homeopathic Pharmacopoeia of the United States*. Deviations in strength, quality, and purity are permitted, provided such deviations are clearly indicated on the label.

7 Labels must indicate the quantity, kind, and proportion of certain specified ingredients, including alcohol, bromides, atropine, hyoscine, digitalis, and a number of other drugs, the presence of which needs to be known for the safety of those for whom it is prescribed.

8 The label must bear adequate directions for use and adequate warnings against unsafe use (a) by children and (b) in pathologic conditions.

9 The label must bear adequate warning against unsafe dosage or methods or duration of administration or application in such manner and form as are necessary for the protection of the users.

10 The label must bear the following statement for all drugs considered unsafe for self-medication: "Caution—Federal Law Prohibits Dispensing Without Prescription." All drugs given by injection (with the exception of insulin) are considered prescription drugs, as well as the following groups of drugs:

A Hypnotic, narcotic, or habit-forming drugs or derivatives thereof as specified in the law.

B Drugs that because of their toxicity or because of the method of their use are not safe unless they are administered under the supervision of a licensed practitioner (physician or dentist).

C New drugs that are limited to investigational use or new drugs that are not considered safe for indiscriminate use by lay persons.

11 New drugs may not be introduced into interstate commerce unless an application has been filed with the Food and Drug Administration and the application has been permitted to become effective. Adequate scientific evidence must be presented to show that the drug is safe for use under the conditions proposed for its use. The applicant does not have to prove the efficacy of the drug in order to obtain an effective application. During the time that the drug is under investigation by experts, the label of the drug must bear the statement: "Caution: New Drug—Limited by Federal Law to Investigational Use."

NOTE: When tests indicate that the requirements of the Food and Drug Administration have been met, the law permits a period of clinical testing by approved clinicians and clinical groups. Pertinent data are collected and submitted to the Food and Drug Administration for further evaluation. If the Administration is satisfied that the drug has therapeutic merit and is not unduly toxic, distribution and sale of the new drug are permitted.

12 Certain drugs must be obtained from a batch that has been certified by the Food and Drug Administration. This applies to insulin and the antibiotics. Samples of each batch of these drugs are examined, and if samples conform to standards set forth by the Food and Drug Administration, the batches are referred to as "Certified Drugs."

13 Provisions of the Act that refer to prescriptions include the following:

A The pharmacist cannot refill from the original prescription unless the physician has authorized him to do so either by designating the number of times or the intervals after which the prescription may be refilled.

B A physician may give a prescription for most drugs orally (over the telephone), but the pharmacist must convert the oral prescription to writing. This provision modifies a previous provision that recognized only written prescriptions. Authorization for refills may also be telephoned to the pharmacist.

NOTE: Nothing in the Federal Food, Drug, and Cosmetic Act, including the Durham-

Humphrey and Kefauver-Harris amendments, modifies the law and regulations regarding prescriptions for narcotics.

The Act also contains provisions pertaining to foods and cosmetics, as indicated in its name. The law is concerned with the prevention of misbranding, adulterating, and incorporating harmful substances into foods and cosmetics.

Fundamentally, there were two objectives advanced by the Kefauver-Harris Amendment: (1) assurance of both the safety and effectiveness of drugs, and (2) improvement of the communication of necessary information concerning these drugs, their side effects and contraindications, as well as their advantages. Specifically, these two related objectives are advanced by provisions that require the following:

1 Substantial evidence of the effectiveness of new drugs before marketing.
2 Manufacture of all drugs under adequate control and good manufacturing practices.
3 Government certification of both the safety and effectiveness of all antibiotics for human use.
4 Prompt reporting by manufacturers to the government of adverse reactions attributed to new drugs and antibiotics.
5 Truthful statements in prescription drug advertisement concerning the effectiveness, side effects, and contraindications of the advertised drugs.
6 Annual registration with the Food and Drug Administration of all persons and firms engaged in the manufacturing, reporting, and labeling of drug products.
7 Inspection of every registered establishment at least once every 2 years.

The law further authorizes the Food and Drug Administration to do the following:

1 Establish official names for drugs in the interest of usefulness and simplicity.
2 Withdraw approval of drugs when substantial doubt arises as to their safety or in the absence of substantial evidence of effectiveness.
3 Have access during inspection of prescription drug manufacturing establishments to all things that have a bearing on violations of the law with respect to such drugs, including records,

files, papers, processes, controls, and facilities.
4 Exercise greater controls over shipments of investigational drugs for testing in humans.

In 1966 the Drug Abuse Control Amendment (D.A.C.A.) became effective. It was designed to curb the illegal use and illegal dispensing of central nervous system depressants and stimulants and other drugs with potential for abuse. This includes the barbiturates, amphetamines, and psychotropic and hallucinogenic drugs.

Under this act, pharmacists are required to keep a record of the receipt and dispensing of all such drugs for a period of at least 3 years and to make the records available to authorized persons. Prescription orders for these drugs cannot be refilled more than five times, nor filled or refilled more than 6 months after the prescription date, nor refilled if refill instructions do not appear on the prescription order.

As of 1968, regulatory and control functions are now under the jurisdiction of the Bureau of Narcotics and Dangerous Drugs within the Department of Justice.

Food and Drug Administration. The Food and Drug Administration is charged with the enforcement of the Federal Food, Drug, and Cosmetic Act. Seizure of offending goods and criminal prosecution of responsible persons or firms in federal courts are among the methods used to enforce the Act.

In addition, the Kefauver-Harris Amendment requires that pharmaceutical firms report at regular intervals to the F.D.A. all adverse effects associated with their new drugs. The F.D.A. also has an adverse-reaction reporting program with approximately 450 cooperating reporting sources. The purpose of this program is to detect reactions not revealed by previous clinical or pharmaceutical studies.

Public Health Service. The Public Health Service is an agency that is also part of the U. S. Department of Health, Education, and Welfare. One of its many functions is the regulation of biologic products. This refers to "any virus, therapeutic serum, antitoxin, or analogous product applicable to the prevention, treatment, or cure of diseases or injuries of man." The control exercised by the Public Health Service over these products is done by inspecting and licensing the establishments that manufacture the products and by examining and licensing the products as well.

Federal Trade Commission. The Federal Trade Commission is an agency of the federal government that is directly responsible to the President. Its principal control with respect to drugs lies in its power to suppress false or misleading advertising to the general public.

Harrison Narcotic Act. The Harrison Narcotic Act was originally passed in 1914. It has been amended several times. The Act regulates the importation, manufacture, sale, and use of opium and cocaine and all their compounds and derivatives. Marihuana and its derivatives are also subject to the Act, as are many synthetic analgesic drugs that have been shown to be addiction-forming or addiction-sustaining.

All persons who manufacture, sell, prescribe, or dispense these drugs must be licensed and registered with the Department of Internal Revenue and pay an annual registration fee. Those who are lawfully entitled to obtain and use narcotics for purposes of instruction, research, or analysis must also register and pay a yearly tax. All persons who handle these drugs must keep accurate records of the drugs that they handle or use and save the records for a period of at least 2 years, during which time they are subject to inspection at any time by a revenue official.

A prescription for preparations listed in the law must bear the physician's name, address, and registry number as well as the name and address of the patient and the date on which the prescription was written. The pharmacist may not refill the prescription.

A prescription for an opiate may not be issued by a physician to satisfy the craving of an addict unless it is done in the course of professional treatment of the addict.

Application of the Harrison law in hospitals. Every hospital must register with the Department of Internal Revenue and conform to many of the same regulations as physicians. Hospital pharmacies order supplies of narcotics, as well as other drugs listed under the Harrison

Narcotic Law, on special order blanks that bear the hospital registry number. A special record is kept on every hospital unit (ward) for every dose of the preparations mentioned. The nurse records the name of the patient receiving the drug, date of administration of the drug, the amount, the name of the physician who ordered the drug, and her own name. In this way nurses can account for the quantities of these drugs that have been dispensed from the pharmacy and help the pharmacists to account for the supplies that have been issued.

Oral prescriptions for narcotics. A pharmacist may dispense certain narcotics on the verbal authority of a physician (via telephone). Narcotics that may be dispensed in this manner are those believed to have little or no addiction liability and include apomorphine, codeine (in limited quantities and when combined with nonnarcotic ingredients or with one of the isoquinoline alkaloids of opium such as papaverine), limited amounts of dihydrocodeinone and ethylmorphine either alone or with other nonnarcotic ingredients, and certain others.

In case of emergency or great necessity, telephone or verbal orders may be given by a physician to a nurse for a patient. The nurse must write the order on the doctor's order sheet, stating that it is a telephone order or an emergency order, give the doctor's name, and sign her own name or initials. This written order must be signed by the doctor with his full name or initials within 24 hours. The Bureau of Narcotics acceded to the latter with some reluctance but permits it because it recognizes that unusual situations arise in hospitals not common to other places. Individual hospitals may choose to adhere to stricter regulations regarding narcotic orders.

Preparations exempt from the Harrison Narcotic Law. Certain preparations (with or without a prescription) in small quantities are exempt from the Harrison Narcotic Law, provided the preparation does not contain more than any one of the following per fluid or solid ounce: gr. 2 of opium, gr. $\frac{1}{4}$ of morphine, gr. 1 of codeine, or any salt or derivative of these drugs, and also contains certain active medicinal drugs (other than narcotics) that provide valuable medicinal qualities other than that possessed by the narcotics alone.

Some state laws, however, cause the sale of such preparations to be restricted just as for any narcotic. For example, camphorated opium tincture (paregoric) may be purchased in some states in small amounts without a prescription, whereas in others the laws are such that the same tight restrictions apply for small amounts as do for larger amounts of any of the narcotics.

The Narcotic Control Act of 1956. The Narcotic Control Act amended the Harrison law by increasing the penalties for violation of the Harrison law and by making it unlawful to have heroin in one's possession. No heroin can be lawfully used or distributed for purposes other than for scientific research. This amendment also makes the acquisition and the transportation of marihuana unlawful. Under the Narcotics Manufacturing Act of 1960, the manufacture of marihuana preparations is not authorized. Special authorization from the Director of the Bureau of Narcotics and Dangerous Drugs is required for licensed physicians or researchers to obtain small quantities of marihuana.

Possession of narcotics. It is important to know that federal and state laws make the possession of narcotics a crime, except in specifically exempted cases. The laws make no distinction between professional and practical nurses in this respect. A nurse may give narcotics only under the direction of a physician or dentist who has been licensed to prescribe or dispense narcotics. She may not have narcotics in her possession unless she is giving them to a patient under a doctor's order, or she is a patient for whom the doctor has prescribed them, or she is the official custodian of a limited supply of narcotics on a ward or department of the hospital.

Narcotics ordered but not used for patients must be returned to the source from which they were obtained (the doctor or the hospital). Violation or failure to comply with the Harrison Narcotic Law is punishable by fine, imprisonment, or both.

Problems in drug legislation. In addition to the federal laws discussed in the preceding pages, it should be mentioned that many states have laws applicable to the sale and manufacture of drugs within the state. This refers to laws other than those applying to the sale of small amounts of narcotics. Outstanding among them are the regulations for the sale of barbiturates.

It is well to remember that the effectiveness of legislation will depend on the appropriation of adequate funds to enforce the laws, the vigor with which enforcement is pushed by proper authorities, and the interest and cooperation of professional and lay groups.

There are still many problems resulting from indiscriminate and unwise use of drugs, misunderstandings about vitamins, glandular preparations, drugs for obesity, and cancer "cures." Although the consumer is often led astray by attractive advertising, clever suggestion, and adroit mishandling of information, there are reliable sources of information concerning drugs, cosmetic preparations, depilatories (hair removers), obesity cures, laxatives, antiseptics, dentifrices, and numerous other things about which the public is often grossly misinformed. Organizations such as the American Medical Association, American Dental Association, American Society for the Control of Cancer, American Heart Association, and local, state, and county health departments will supply accurate information free of charge or for a very small fee, necessary to defray the expense of printing or mailing materials.

Canadian drug legislation

In Canada, the Food and Drug Directorate of the Department of National Health and Welfare is responsible for administration and enforcement of the Food and Drugs Act, as well as the Proprietary or Patent Medicine Act and the Narcotics Control Act. These acts are designed to protect the consumer from health hazards and fraud or deception in the sale and use of foods, drugs, cosmetics, and medical devices. Canadian drug legislation began in 1874 when the Parliament of Canada passed an act to prevent the sale of adulterated food, drink, and drugs. Since that time there has been food and drug control on a national basis.

Canadian Food and Drugs Act. In 1953 the present Canadian Food and Drugs Act was passed by the Senate and House of Commons of Canada. The law states that no food, drug, cosmetic, or device is to be advertised or sold as a treatment, preventative, or cure for certain diseases listed in schedule A of the Act. Among the diseases included in the list are alcoholism, arteriosclerosis, and cancer. In addition, the Act prohibits the sale of drugs that are contaminated, adulterated, or unsafe for use and those whose labels are false, misleading, or deceptive. According to the Act, drugs must comply with prescribed standards as stated in recognized pharmacopeias and formularies listed in schedule B of the Act, or according to the professed standards under which the drug is sold. These include the following:

Pharmacopoea Internationalis
The British Pharmacopoeia
The Pharmacopeia of the United States of America
Codex Français
Compendium of Pharmaceuticals and Specialties (Canada)
The British Pharmaceutical Codex
The National Formulary

Sale of certain drugs is prohibited unless the premises where the drug was manufactured and the process and conditions of manufacture have been approved by the Minister of National Health and Welfare. These drugs are listed in schedules C and D and include injectable liver extracts, all insulin preparations, anterior pituitary extracts, radioactive isotopes, antibiotics, serums, drugs prepared from microorganisms or viruses, and live vaccines. For some drugs the batch from which the drug was taken must meet approval, and these are listed in schedule E. Among the drugs listed are various arsphenamines and sensitivity disks and tablets. Distribution of samples of drugs is also prohibited, with the exception of distribution of samples of drugs to duly licensed individuals such as physicians, dentists, or pharmacists. Schedule F of the Act contains a list of drugs that can be sold only on prescription, and such prescriptions shall not be refilled unless the prescriber has so directed. Drugs listed in schedule F include the antibiotics, sulfonamides, phenothiazine derivatives, and numerous other drugs. These are controlled drugs and can be prescribed and dispensed only by licensed individuals (physicians, pharmacists). They must always be properly and clearly labeled and include directions for use. For more specific information, the nurse can obtain a copy of *The Food and Drugs Act and Regulations*, issued by Department of National Health and Welfare, from the Queen's Printer and Controller of Stationery, Ottawa, Canada.

In 1961 the scope of the Food and Drugs Act was extended to provide greater control over the developing traffic in barbiturates and amphetamines. The Act makes it a legal offense to manufacture, sell, export, import, transport, or deliver the aforementioned drugs without express government authorization. These drugs are also controlled drugs and are listed in schedule G of the Act.

In 1962 the Act was further amended by prohibiting the sale of any drug described in schedule H. The drugs listed in schedule H are thalidomide, lysergic acid diethylamide, diethyltryptamine, dimethyltryptamine, and dimethoxyamphetamine. Thalidomide is known to be a cause of embryopathy while the others are hallucinogenic drugs. The amendments allow the government to withdraw from the market drugs found to be unduly toxic. New drugs introduced to the market must have shown effectiveness and safety in human clinical studies to the satisfaction of the manufacturer and the government.

Canadian Narcotic Control Act. The regulations of the Canadian Narcotic Control Act govern the possession, sale, manufacture, production, and distribution of narcotics. The Canadian Narcotic Control Act was enacted in 1961. This act revoked the Canadian Opium and Narcotic Act of 1952.

Only authorized persons can be in possession of a narcotic. Authorized persons include a licensed dealer, pharmacist, practitioner, or person in charge of a hospital. A licensed dealer is one who has been given permission to manufacture, produce, import, export, or distribute a narcotic. Practitioners include persons registered under the laws of a province to practice the profession of medicine, dentistry, or veterinary medicine. However, persons other than these may be licensed by the Minister of National Health and Welfare to cultivate and produce opium poppy or marihuana or to purchase and possess a narcotic for scientific purposes. Members of the Royal Canadian Mounted Police and members of technical or scientific departments of the government of Canada or of a province or university may possess narcotics for the purpose of, and in connection with, their employment. A person who is undergoing treatment by a medical practitioner and who requires a narcotic may possess a narcotic obtained on prescription. This person may not knowingly obtain a narcotic from any other medical practitioner without notifying that practitioner that he is already undergoing treatment and obtaining a narcotic on prescription.

All persons authorized to be in possession of narcotics must keep a record of the name and quantity of all narcotics received, from whom narcotics were obtained, and to whom narcotics were supplied (including quantity, form, and dates of all transactions). In addition, they must ensure the safekeeping of all narcotics, keep full and complete records on all narcotics for at least 2 years, and report any loss or theft within 10 days of discovery.

The schedule of the Act lists those drugs, their preparations, derivatives, alkaloids, and salts that are subject to the Canadian Narcotic Control Act. Included in the schedule are opium, coca, and marihuana. Before a pharmacist legally may dispense a drug included in the schedule or medication containing such a drug, he must receive a prescription from a physician. A signed and dated prescription issued by a duly authorized physician is essential in the case of all narcotic medication prescribed as such or any preparation containing a narcotic in a form intended for parenteral administration. Oral medication containing a narcotic may be dispensed by a pharmacist on the strength of a verbal prescription received from a physician who is known to the pharmacist or whose identity is established. Prescriptions of any description calling for a narcotic may not be repeated.

There is one exception to the prescription requirement. Certain codeine compounds with a small codeine content may be sold to the public by a pharmacist without a prescription. In such instances the narcotic content cannot exceed $\frac{1}{8}$ grain per unit in tablet, capsule, or other solid form and $\frac{1}{3}$ grain per fluidounce in liquid form. In products of this kind, codeine must be in combination with two or more nonnarcotic substances and in recognized therapeutic doses.

Additionally, items of this nature are required to be labeled in such a fashion as to show the true formula of the medicinal ingredients and a caution to the following effect: "This preparation contains codeine and should not be administered to children except on the advice of a physician." These preparations cannot be advertised or displayed in a pharmacy. It is also unlawful to publish any narcotic advertisement for the general public.

Labels of containers of narcotics must legibly and conspicuously bear the proprietary and proper or common name of the narcotic, name of the manufacturer and distributor, the symbol "N" in the upper left-hand quarter, and net contents of the container and of each tablet, capsule, or ampule.

It should be pointed out that local or provincial laws modify to a certain extent regulations governing the sale and administration of narcotics.

Although the administration of the Canadian Narcotic Control Act is legally the responsibility of the Department of National Health and Welfare, the enforcement of the law has been made largely the responsibility of the Royal Canadian Mounted Police. Prosecution of offenses under the Act is handled through the Department of National Health and Welfare by legal agents specially appointed by the Department of Justice.

Application to nursing. A nurse may be in violation of the Canadian Narcotic Control Act if she is guilty of illegal possession of narcotics. Ignorance of the content of a drug in her possession is not considered a justifiable excuse. Proof of possession is sufficient to constitute an offense. Legal possession of narcotics by a nurse is limited to times when she is administering a drug to a patient on the order of a physician, when she is acting as the official custodian of narcotics in a department of the hospital, or when she is a patient for whom a physician has prescribed narcotics. The nurse may be held liable if she engages in illegal distribution or transportation of narcotic drugs. Heavy penalties are imposed for violation of the Canadian Narcotic Control Act.

Exercises and questions

for study and review

1 State the purpose of the Federal Food, Drug, and Cosmetic Act.
2 Name six specific features of the Federal Food, Drug, and Cosmetic Act that are of interest to medical groups.
3 To what extent do you think present-day legislation ensures adequate control of commerce in drugs? Explain.
4 Preparations of what drugs are included in the federal narcotic laws?
5 How does a nurse account for narcotic drugs that she may have contaminated or lost?
6 How might a nurse be guilty of violating the narcotic laws of her country?
7 What is meant by "prescription drug"? By "nonprescription drug"? Be specific.
8 Prepare a list of sources from which you would expect to secure accurate information about new drugs.
9 Bring to class several examples of drug, cosmetic, or dietary advertisements taken from current magazines. Be prepared to discuss what seems to you to be good or poor advertising from the standpoint of legitimacy of claims made.
10 May any physician who comes to your hospital write an order for a narcotic? Explain.

Objective questions

Circle the correct answer(s).
11 *New Drugs* is issued under the direction and supervision of:
   a. American Pharmaceutical Association
   b. Council on Drugs of American Medical Association
   c. American Association of Hospital Pharmacists
   d. a pharmacopeial committee
12 The letters U.S.P. after the name of a drug provide what information about a drug?
   a. source
   b. therapeutic usefulness
   c. legal status
   d. classification
13 Drugs selected for inclusion in the N.F. are selected largely on the basis of their:
   a. source
   b. low toxicity
   c. therapeutic merit
   d. demand
14 *The Pharmacopeia of the United States of America* and *The National Formulary* are legal standards because they are made so by which of the following?
   a. Council on Drugs
   b. American Pharmaceutical Association
   c. Federal Food, Drug, and Cosmetic Act
   d. National Bureau of Standards

15 The publication in which reports of the Council on Drugs are made periodically is:
   a. *The American Journal of Nursing*
   b. *The Journal of the American Medical Association*
   c. Supplements to the U.S.P.
   d. *American Journal of Medical Science*
16 In the United States an official drug is one listed in the U.S.P., the N.F., or in:
   a. *The Dispensatory of the United States of America*
   b. *New Drugs*
   c. *Homeopathic Pharmacopoeia of the United States*
   d. *Physicians' Desk Reference*
17 A nonprescription drug does *not* need to have which of following included on the label?
   a. adequate warnings about unsafe use
   b. duration of administration of the drug
   c. method of administration
   d. ingredients not classified as drugs

References

General references

Cook, E., and others: Remington's practice of pharmacy, ed. 13, Easton, Pa., 1965, Mack Printing Co.

DiPalma, J. R., editor: Drill's pharmacology in medicine, ed. 3, New York, 1965, McGraw-Hill Book Company.

Goodman, L., and Gilman, A.: The pharmacological basis of therapeutics, New York, 1970, The Macmillan Company.

Ladimer, I., and Newman, R. W., editors: Clinical investigation in medicine: legal, ethical, and moral aspects, Boston, 1962, Boston University Law–Medicine Research Institute.

Lewis, J. R.: Drug evaluation by Council on Drugs, J.A.M.A. **185:**256, 1963.

Shreiner, G. E.: Liability in use of investigational drugs, J.A.M.A. **185:**259, 1963.

Symposium on clinical drug evaluation and human pharmacology, Clin. Pharmacol. Therap. **3:**235, 1962.

The Food and Drug Act and Regulations, Roger Duhamel, F.R.S.C., Ottawa, Ontario, 1970, Queen's Printer and Controller of Stationery.

Official publications

Pharmacopoea Internationalis, ed. 2, Geneva, Switzerland, 1967, The World Health Organization.

British Pharmacopoeia, ed. 10, London, 1963, The Pharmaceutical Press.

Compendium of Pharmaceutical Specialties, ed. 4, Toronto, 1968, Canadian Pharmaceutical Association.

The National Formulary, ed. 13, Easton, Pa., 1970, Mack Printing Company.

The Pharmacopeia of the United States of America, ed. 18, Easton, Pa., 1970, Mack Printing Company.

4 Names, sources, active constituents, and pharmaceutical preparations of drugs

Names of drugs
Sources of drugs
Pharmaceutical preparations

■ Names of drugs

The present-day use of a variety of names for the same drug is cause for confusion for all health professionals. One name under which a drug may appear is its official name, another is the generic name, another is its chemical name, and a fourth by which it may be known is its trade name.

The *official name* is the name under which it is listed in one of the official publications. The official name may also have one or more synonyms by which it is known. Before a new drug becomes official it will have assigned to it a *generic name*. This name is simpler than the chemical name, although it may reflect the chemical family to which the drug belongs. The generic

name is never changed and can be used in all countries. It is not protected by law. It is usually initiated or proposed by the company that develops the drug. When it is selected careful investigation is made to make certain that it does not conflict with already existing names. Then it is usually processed by way of the American Medical Association Council on Drugs and through the World Health Organization, which has a Committee on International Non-Proprietary Names. In that way the name may be adopted on a worldwide basis.

The *chemical name* is meaningful principally to the chemist, who sees in the name a very precise description of the chemical constitution of the drug and the exact placement of atoms or atomic groupings. For example, the chemical name of one of the antibiotics is 4-dimethylamino-1,4,4a,5,5a,6,11,12a-octahydro-3,6,10,12,12a-pentahydroxy-6-methyl-1,11-dioxo-2-naphthacenecarboxamide. Its generic name is tetracycline, and it is known under a number of trade names—Achromycin, Panmycin, Polycycline, Tetracyn, and Tetracyn V.

A *trademark name* or a *brand name* frequently appears in the literature with the sign ® at the upper right of the name to indicate that the name is registered and that its use is restricted to the manufacturer who is the legal owner of the name. The first letter of the trade name is capitalized but the generic name is not capitalized. Many times the generic name is stated and the trade name is given in parentheses.

The name of a drug is not patented but a patent may be issued by the U. S. Patent Office to cover the drug as a chemical entity, the method of manufacture, the method of use, or any combination of these. Patents expire after 17 years; then other manufacturers may make the drug under its generic name but they must select a different trade name. Two or more drug companies may make the same drug under different trade or trademark names. Sometimes a single drug may be sold under ten or twenty different brand names, which results in a great deal of undesirable confusion.

In order to promote sales under the trademark name, extensive advertising is usually necessary. This involves considerable expense, which is borne mainly by the consumer. On the other hand, much of the research in new drugs is done in laboratories of reputable drug firms, and in order to realize a legitimate return for the cost of research, they need to patent their product and have exclusive rights of its manufacture and sale.

There is a real need to give more attention to generic and official names. Some hospital pharmacies in the United States are labeling medications with their official or generic names and placing the trade name or trademark name at the bottom of the label. This would appear to place the emphasis properly.

Further confusion is fostered when mixtures or combinations of otherwise well-known drugs are sold under a name that does not reflect the content. For example, combinations of phenacetin, aspirin, and caffeine are sold under a variety of names such as Empirin compound, APC, and PAC, as well as aspirin compound.

The word *proprietary* is also used in referring to drugs. This means that the drug is protected from competition in some manner. In other words, the drug or its name belongs to someone.

■ Sources of drugs

Drugs are derived from four main sources: (1) plants, examples of which are digitalis,

opium, and belladonna; (2) animals, from which drugs such as epinephrine, insulin, and ACTH are obtained; (3) minerals or mineral products, such as iron, iodine, and Epsom salt; and (4) chemical substances made in the laboratory. The drugs made of chemical substances are pure drugs, and some of them are simple substances, such as sodium bicarbonate and magnesium hydroxide, whereas others are products of complex synthesis, such as the sulfonamides and the adrenocorticosteroids.

Active constituents of plant drugs

The leaves, roots, seeds, and other parts of plants may be dried or otherwise processed for use as medicine and, as such, are known as crude drugs. Their therapeutic effect is caused by chemical substances contained in the crude preparation. When the pharmacologically active constituents are separated from the crude preparation, the resulting substances are more potent and usually produce effects more reliable than those of the crude drug. As might be expected, these active principles are also more poisonous, and the dosage must be smaller. Some of the types of pharmacologically active compounds found in plants, grouped according to their physical and chemical properties, are alkaloids, glycosides, gums, resins and balsams, and oils.

Alkaloids. Alkaloids (alkali-like) are compounds composed of carbon, hydrogen, nitrogen, and oxygen. Alkaloids have a bitter taste; they are often poisonous and hence preparations of them are administered in small doses. They are, for the most part, white crystalline solids. The name of an alkaloid ends in "ine," for example, caffeine, atropine, and morphine. Alkaloids will combine with an acid to form a salt. The salts of alkaloids are used in medicine in preference to pure alkaloids because they are more soluble; for example, morphine sulfate is preferred to morphine since it is much more soluble in water. Increased solubility may make possible administration by injection. A number of alkaloids have been chemically synthesized in the laboratory.

Both alkaloids and their salts are precipitated

by tannic acid and oxidized by potassium permanganate. Hence these substances can be used under certain circumstances as antidotes for poisoning from alkaloids.

Glycosides. Glycosides are active principles that upon hydrolysis yield a carbohydrate (a sugar) and some other chemical grouping such as an aldehyde, acid, or alcohol. The carbohydrate may be glucose, in which case the compound may be called a glucoside, but carbohydrates other than glucose may occur in the molecule, hence the use of the more general term *glycoside*. The carbohydrate molecule is usually not necessary for the action of the glycosides, and in the body it may be removed to liberate the active aglycone or genin. The presence of a sugar in the molecule of the glycoside is thought to modify activity by increasing solubility, absorption, permeability, and cellular distribution. An important glycoside used in medicine is digitoxin.

Gums. Gums are exudates from plants. They are polysaccharides that vary in the degree of their solubility in water. Upon the addition of water some of them will swell and form gelatinous or mucilaginous masses. Some remain unchanged in the gastrointestinal tract, where they act as hydrophilic (water-loving) colloids; that is, they absorb water, form watery bulk, and exert a laxative effect. Agar and psyllium seeds are examples of natural laxative gums. Synthetic hydrophilic colloids such as methylcellulose and sodium carboxymethyl cellulose may eventually replace the natural gums as laxatives. Gums are also used to soothe irritated skin and mucous membranes. Tragacanth gum, upon the addition of water, forms an emulsion used as a basis for a greaseless catheter lubricant or for chapped skin. Acacia (gum arabic), U.S.P., B.P., is used as a suspending agent in making emulsions and mixtures.

Resins. Resins are crude drugs or an extraction from a crude drug. The rosin used by violinists is an example of a solid resin. A few are devoid of color, and some give off an aromatic fragrance as a result of admixture of a volatile oil. Resins form the sap of certain trees. They are insoluble in water but soluble in alcohol,

ether, and various oils. Resins are local irritants and some have been used in medicine as cathartics. Podophyllum resin is a constituent of aloin, belladonna, cascara, and podophyllum pills (Hinkle's Pills) and is a rather irritating cathartic.

Balsams also contain resins in addition to benzoic or cinnamic acids. Benzoin, U.S.P., B.P., Peruvian balsam, N.F., and tolu balsam, U.S.P., B.P., are examples.

Oils. The term *oil* is applied to a large number of liquids characterized by being insoluble in water and highly viscous. Their greasy feel is the result of these properties. Oils are of two kinds, volatile and fixed.

Volatile oils are liquids that impart an aroma to a plant. They evaporate easily and leave no greasy stain. Because of their pleasant odor and taste they are frequently used as flavoring agents. Because of their volatility and consequent power of penetration they may be irritating, mildly stimulating, and antiseptic in effect. Peppermint oil and clove oil are listed in the U.S.P. and the B.P. and are occasionally used in medicine.

Fixed oils are those that feel greasy and do not evaporate readily. They hydrolyze to form fatty acids and glycerin. Some fixed oils are used as food, for example, olive oil. Others are used in medicine, such as castor oil, and some as vehicles in which to dissolve other drugs, such as sesame oil.

■ Pharmaceutical preparations

Pharmaceutical preparations are the preparations that make a drug suited to various methods of administration. They may be made by the pharmacist or by the pharmaceutical company from which they are purchased. A nurse is likely to bring more understanding to the task of administering drugs if she has some knowledge of these preparations.

Solutions and suspensions

Aqueous solutions. Aqueous solutions have one or more substances dissolved in water. *Waters* are saturated (unless otherwise stated) solutions of volatile oils or other aromatic substances in distilled water. Peppermint water and concentrated peppermint water, B.P., are examples. Other aqueous solutions, sometimes referred to as *true solutions*, are made by dissolving a nonvolatile substance in water. Examples are strong iodine solution (Lugol's Solution), U.S.P., epinephrine solution, U.S.P., and aluminum acetate solution, U.S.P.

Syrups are sometimes used for their demulcent* effect on irritated membranes of the throat. Syrup, U.S.P., is an aqueous solution of sucrose (85%). Syrups may be flavored and used as a vehicle in which to disguise unpleasant-tasting medicines and also as a preservative. Examples listed in the U.S.P. are orange, wild cherry, glycyrrhiza, and raspberry syrups. Promethazine hydrochloride syrup, U.S.P., is an example of a syrup that reflects medicinal content, an antihistaminic.

Aqueous suspensions. Aqueous suspensions are defined in U.S.P. XVIII as preparations of finely divided drugs either intended for suspension or already in suspension in some suitable liquid vehicle. Sterile suspensions are prepared by adding sterile, distilled water for injection to the preparation, for example, sterile chloramphenicol for suspension. A sterile suspension ready for use is sterile procaine penicillin G suspension, U.S.P. Sterile suspensions are intended for intramuscular or subcutaneous injection, but they cannot be given intravenously or intrathecally. Oral suspensions may be prepared in much the same way, but they are not sterile and must not be injected. Suspensions for ophthalmic use are sterile and contain a bacteriostatic agent. Hydrocortisone acetate opthalmic suspension, U.S.P., is a good example. Suspensions tend to settle slowly and should be shaken well before use to provide uniform distribution of the drug in the aqueous medium.

Mixtures. Mixtures are any solid material suspended in a liquid. No mixtures are listed in the U.S.P. The B.P. records a mixture of magnesium hydroxide. The term *mixture* is also used to mean any preparation of several drugs, such as a cough mixture. However, the term is usually restricted to mean only preparations for internal use.

Emulsions. Emulsions are suspensions of fats or oils in water with the aid of an emulsifying agent, which lowers the interfacial tension between the two substances, masking its oily feel. These oils are more easily digested than undispersed oils. Emulsions are stabilized by agents such as acacia and gelatin, which coat the tiny droplets of oil and prevent them from coming in direct contact with water. An example is cod liver oil emulsion.

Magmas. Magmas are sometimes called milks because they are white and resemble milk. They are bulky suspensions of insoluble preparations in water. Milk of magnesia, U.S.P., or magnesium hydroxide mixture, B.P., is an example. Magmas tend to settle or separate upon standing and should be shaken well before they are poured.

Gels. Gels are aqueous suspensions of insoluble drugs in hydrated form. The particles suspended are approximately the size seen in colloidal dispersions. Magmas and gels are similar except that the particles suspended in a magma are larger; aluminum hydroxide gel, U.S.P., is an example.

Spirits. Spirits are concentrated alcoholic solutions of volatile substances. They are also known as essences. The dissolved substance may be solid, liquid, or gaseous. Most spirits contain from 5% to 20% of the active drug. The alcohol serves as a preservative as well as a solvent. Peppermint spirit, N.F., is sometimes used as a carminative and also as a flavoring agent.

Elixirs. Elixirs are aromatic, sweetened, alcoholic preparations, frequently used as flavored vehicles, such as aromatic elixir, U.S.P., or as active medicinal agents if they are medicated elixirs, such as phenobarbital elixir, U.S.P., or cascara elixir, B.P.

Tinctures. Tinctures are alcoholic or hydroalcoholic solutions usually prepared from plant drugs or from chemical substances. Tinctures of potent drugs contain 10 Gm. of drug in 100 ml. of tincture. Most other tinctures contain 20 Gm. of drug in 100 ml. of tincture. Tinc-

---

*A demulcent is a substance that exerts a soothing effect.

tures are prepared by extracting the drug from its crude source or by making an alcoholic solution of the drug. Iodine tincture, U.S.P., is made by dissolving iodine in an alcoholic solution of sodium iodide. The alcoholic content of tinctures improves their stability and facilitates solution of drugs that are poorly soluble in water. Tinctures listed in the B.P. are preparations extracted from crude drugs, not simple solutions. The usual dose of a potent tincture is about 1 ml. (0.3 to 1 ml.) or 5 to 15 minims.

Fluidextracts. Fluidextracts are alcoholic liquid extracts of vegetable drugs made so that 1 ml. of the fluidextract contains 1 Gm. of the drug. They are the most concentrated of any of the fluid preparations, being of 100% strength and ten times stronger than potent tinctures. Since many of them precipitate in light, they should be kept in dark bottles and not used if precipitate has formed. Glycyrrhiza fluidextract, U.S.P., is used as a flavoring agent, whereas aromatic cascara sagrada fluidextract, U.S.P., and cascara liquid extract, B.P., are used as cathartics.

NOTE. Spirits, medicated elixirs, tinctures, and fluidextracts are preparations that tend to be potent and therefore the dosage is likely to be small. A nurse would never expect to administer as much as 30 ml. (a fluidounce) of any of them. A fraction of a milliliter (a few minims) up to as much as 2 to 4 ml. (1 to 2 fluidrams) is likely to be the range of dosage. Furthermore, these preparations are never injected, one reason being that they all contain alcohol. Most tinctures contain resins that make them incompatible with water.

Extracts. Extracts are concentrated preparations of vegetable or animal drugs obtained by removing the active ingredients of the drugs with suitable solvents and then evaporating all or part of the solvents. Extracts are made in three forms: semiliquids or liquids of syrupy consistency, plastic masses or pillular extracts, and dry powders known as powdered extracts. Extracts are intended to preserve the useful constituents of a drug in a form suitable for medication or for the making of other dosage forms such as tablets or pills. Liver extract is

a dry extract. Cascara dry extract, B.P., is used to make cascara tablets, B.P.

Dosage forms

Capsules, sustained-release capsules, tablets, pills, and troches are used to divide a drug or mixture of drugs into definite doses and avoid the inconvenience of preparing the dose from dry powders. They are therefore referred to as dosage forms. Capsules and coated tablets are a convenient way of giving drugs that have an unpleasant taste. It has been true in the past and to some extent continues to be true that some patients are more impressed with a vile-tasting medicine than a pleasant-tasting or tasteless preparation. However, most patients appreciate preparations that are not unpleasant to take.

Capsules. Capsules are one of the most popular dosage forms for the oral administration of powders, oils, and liquids. They dissolve readily in the stomach and make the contents available for absorption only slightly less quickly than a liquid medicament. New drugs for oral use are often introduced in capsules in order to avoid problems of disintegration, stability, or taste. When these problems have been solved, tablet forms of the drug are generally used because they are less costly to produce. Capsules are usually made of gelatin and may be hard or soft, depending on the amount of glycerin in the gelatin. Gelatin capsules may be coated with a substance that resists the action of gastric juice and so will not disintegrate until they reach the alkaline secretions of the intestine. Such capsules are said to be *enteric coated.* Sizes of capsules range from 5 to 000 (see Figure 4-1). Capsules are often of a distinctive color or shape to identify the manufacturer.

Dosage forms providing for gradual but continued release of drug are sold under a number of different names, such as Spansules, Gradumets, and Timespans. Sustained-release dosage forms contain small particles of the drug coated with materials that require a varying amount of time to dissolve. This provides for a long continuous period of absorption and effect. Some particles dissolve and are absorbed almost immediately, others require 2 or 3 hours, and some do not dissolve for 10 or 12 hours. An increasing number of drugs is available in one of these forms; prochlorperazine edisylate, U.S.P. (Compazine Edisylate), is available in this dosage form.

Tablets. Tablets are preparations of powdered drug that are compressed or molded into small disks. They may be made with or without a diluent (dextrose, lactose, starch), and they may differ greatly in size, weight, and shape. *Compressed tablets* are made with heavy machinery. The granulated form of the preparation is formed, under great mechanical pressure, into tablets. Compressed tablets usually contain in addition to the drug a diluent, a binder, a disintegrator, and a lubricant. Binders are substances that give adhesiveness to the powdered drug. Diluents are used when the amount of active ingredient is small, and lubricants keep the tablet from sticking to the machines. A disintegrator, such as starch, helps the tablet to dissolve readily when it is placed in water, because the starch expands when it gets wet. Tablets are sometimes scored (marked with an indented line across the surface) so that they can be broken easily if half a tablet is the dose required. Tablets may be coated with sugar or chocolate to enhance their palatability. They may be covered with a colored coating to make them more attractive to patients, easier to swallow, or identifiable by the use of distinctive colors and legible imprinting. Both tablets and capsules may be enteric coated, either to protect the drug from the effect of the gastric secretions or to prevent drug irritation of the gastric mucosa.

Enteric coatings should never render the drug ingredient less available, but this problem may

occur. When enteric-coated medication seems to fail or proves less effective than expected, the patient may be excreting the tablets intact.

Compressed tablets are usually administered orally. *Molded tablets* or *tablet triturates* are made by mixing the moistened powdered drug with dextrose or lactose and powdered sucrose, so as to make a plastic mass suited for manual pressure into small molds. Later the tablets are ejected and dried. They disintegrate readily when placed in water. Molded tablets are administered orally, sublingually, or sometimes by inserting them in the buccal pouch (between the cheek and the teeth), depending on the type of medication they contain and the purpose for which they are given. Hypodermic tablets are compressed or molded tablets that dissolve completely in water, making a solution suitable for injection. They must be prepared under aseptic conditions and dissolved suitably before administration.

Tablets may "case harden" on storage, which would interfere with absorption, or deteriorate when exposed for long periods of time to high humidity, thereby reducing the availability of the drug. Tablets so affected should be discarded.

Numerous sustained-release products are also available as tablets that may (1) disintegrate into discrete particles in the gastrointestinal tract, (2) gradually erode but retain their original shape while getting smaller, and (3) retain their original shape but give up active drug by leaching.

Troches. Troches or lozenges are flat, round, or rectangular preparations that are held in the mouth until they dissolve, liberating the drug or

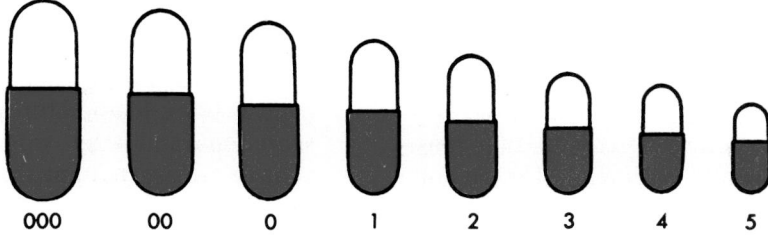

Figure 4-1
Various sizes and numbers of gelatin capsules, actual size.

drugs involved. They usually contain water, sugar, and a mucilage in addition to the drug and are dried in hot air. They temporarily produce a high concentration of the drug in the oral cavity. They are held in the mouth until entirely dissolved. That which is swallowed may produce systemic effects.

Pills. Pills are mixtures of a drug or drugs with some cohesive material. The mass is molded into globular, oval, or flattened bodies convenient for swallowing. Pills are not suitable for injection. They have been replaced to a great extent by capsules and tablets. Although *pill* is a popular, general term for tablets or capsules, this is a misuse of the term. In fact, very few true pills are on the market today.

Powders. Powders are finely divided solid drugs or mixtures of drugs for internal or external use.

Ampules and vials. Ampules and vials contain powdered or liquid drugs usually intended for injection. *Ampules* are sealed glass containers and usually contain one dose of the drug. *Vials* are glass containers with rubber stoppers and usually contain a number of doses of the drug. The powdered drug must be dissolved in sterile distilled water or in isotonic saline solution before administration.

Disposable syringes. Disposable syringes containing doses of drug preparations have become popular. Various antibiotic preparations are commonly given this way. Another dosage form employs the cartridge type of container, which is fitted into a metal framework and a needle attached, such as Tubex. The cartridge contains the drug that is given by injection and the whole resembles a hypodermic (Figure 4-2).

Additional preparations

Liniments. Liniments are liquid suspensions or dispersions intended for external application. They are applied to the skin by rubbing. In addition to one or more active ingredients they may contain oil, soap, water, or alcohol. The oil and the soap of liniments adhere to the skin and serve as lubricants while the preparation is being rubbed on. Liniments usually contain an anodyne (to relieve pain) or a rubefacient (to redden the skin). Liniments may temporarily relieve pain and swelling by counterirritation and by improving circulation of blood to the part.

Lotions. Lotions are liquid suspensions or dispersions intended for external application. Lotions usually should be patted on the skin and not applied by rubbing. This is particularly true if the skin is irritated or inflamed. Lotions can be protective, emollient, cooling, cleansing, astringent, or antipruritic, depending on their content. Calamine lotion, U.S.P., B.P., is an example of a lotion that has a soothing effect. Phenolated calamine lotion, U.S.P., is effective for the relief of itching.

Ointments. Ointments are semisolid preparations of medicinal substances in some type of base such as petrolatum and lanolin that are intended for external application to the skin or mucous membranes. The base helps to keep the medicinal substance in prolonged contact with the skin. Ointments do not wash off readily unless surfactants have been added. A number of other bases can be used in ointments, some of which are miscible with water. Ointments are used for their soothing, astringent, or bacteriostatic effects, depending on the drug or drugs contained in the preparation. Sulfur ointment, U.S.P., B.P., rose water ointment, N.F., and zinc oxide ointment, U.S.P. (zinc ointment, B.P.), are examples.

Ophthalmic ointments are sterile, specially prepared ointments for use in the eye. The ointment base selected must be nonirritating to the eye, must permit free diffusion of the drug throughout the secretions of the eye, and must not alter or destroy the drug that it incorporates. Chloramphenicol ophthalmic ointment, U.S.P., is an example.

Pastes. Pastes are ointment-like preparations suited only for external application. Many of them consist of thick stiff ointments that do not melt at body temperature. They tend to absorb secretions and they soften and penetrate the skin to a lesser extent than do ointments. Zinc oxide paste, U.S.P., and compound zinc paste, B.P., are examples.

Plasters. Plasters are solid preparations that serve as either simple adhesives or counter-

Figure 4-2

How to use Tubex-sterile needle units.

(Courtesy Wyeth Laboratories, Philadelphia, Pa.)

**How to use
Tubex®-sterile needle units**

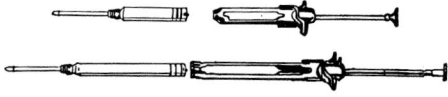

To load the syringe

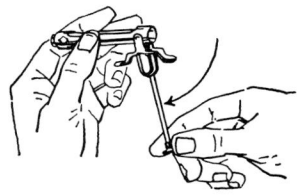

1

Grasp barrel of syringe with one hand. With the other hand, pull back firmly on the plunger and swing the entire handle section downward so that it locks at right angle to the barrel.

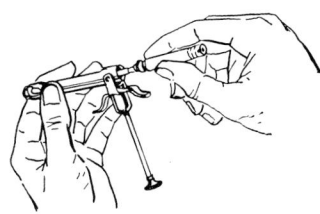

2

Insert Tubex-sterile needle unit, needle end first, into the barrel. Engage needle ferrule by rotating it clockwise in the threads at front end of syringe.

To administer

Method of administration is the same as with conventional syringe. Remove rubber sheath, introduce needle into patient, aspirate, and inject.

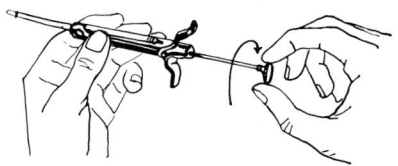

3

Swing plunger back into place and attach end to the threaded shaft of the piston. Hold the syringe barrel with one hand and rotate plunger until both ends of Tubex are fully but lightly engaged. To maintain sterility, leave the rubber sheath in place until just before use. To aspirate before injecting, pull back slightly on the plunger.

To remove the empty Tubex

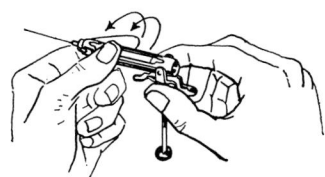

4

Disengage plunger from piston by rotating counterclockwise and open syringe as in step 1. Do not pull plunger back before disengaging or syringe will jam. Rotate Tubex-sterile needle unit counterclockwise to disengage at front end of syringe, remove from syringe, and discard.

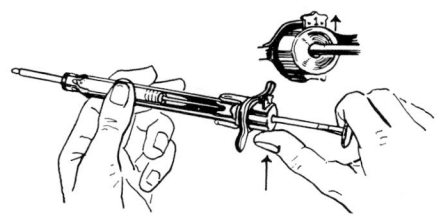

**TO ADAPT 2 CC. SYRINGE
TO 1 CC. TUBEX**

The 2 cc. syringe can be used for a 1 cc. Tubex. Engage both ends of Tubex and push the slide through so the number "1" appears. After use, the syringe automatically resets itself for 2 cc. Tubex.

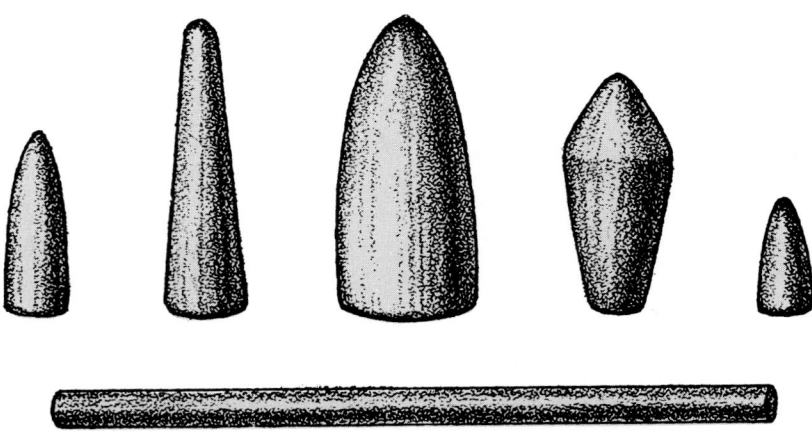

Figure 4-3
Various forms of suppositories: rectal, vaginal, and urethral.

irritants. When applied to the body the heat softens them and makes them adhere. The base is usually a rubber mixture called rubber plaster. Adhesive tape, U.S.P., and salicylic acid plaster, U.S.P., are two examples.

Suppositories. Suppositories are mixtures of drugs with a firm base that can be molded into shapes suitable for insertion into a body cavity or orifice. The base may be glycerinated gelatin, a hard soap, cacao butter (cocoa butter), or carbowax (a polymer of ethylene glycol). These substances melt at body temperature and dissolve in the secretions of mucous membranes to produce local or systemic effects. The shapes and sizes are suitable for insertion into the rectum, vagina, or urethra. Urethral suppositories are called *bougies*. Glycerin suppositories, N.F., B.P., are official preparations. Aminophylline suppositories and aspirin suppositories are listed in the U.S.P.

Poultices. Poultices are soft moist preparations, the purpose of which is to supply moist heat to a skin area. If applied too long they cause maceration of the skin. They tend to be regarded as home remedies. There are no poultices listed in the U.S.P., and the B.P. has only one, kaolin poultice.

Pharmaceutical accessories

Coloring substances. Coloring substances may be added to medicines to make them more acceptable to patients. Red and green colors seem to be favorites. The coloring agent must be either an official agent or one that has been certified under the Federal Food, Drug, and Cosmetic Act. Amaranth solution, U.S.P., imparts a vivid red color to a preparation such as phenobarbital elixir, U.S.P. Compound amaranth solution is listed in the N.F.

Questions

for study and review

1 What is meant by the generic name of a drug? How does it differ from a trade name?
2 What is the advantage of labeling drugs with both their generic and trade names?
3 How can you recognize a trademark name when it is used in medical literature?
4 From what source do most of our new drugs come? What advantages do they have from the standpoint of dosage and reliability of effect?
5 Define an active principle and name several.

6 What is meant by a crude drug? Why were so many of the early drugs used in this country as well as in other countries preparations of crude drugs?

7 What are the main differences between alkaloids and glycosides?

8 What seems to be the main role or function of a carbohydrate in the molecular makeup of a glycoside?

9 Name four medicinal preparations that contain alcohol. How would you expect to administer them to patients and why? What general statement could you make about their dosage?

10 What differences exist between compressed and molded tablets that are of significance to a nurse?

11 What is meant by an enteric-coated tablet? What is the purpose of the enteric coating?

12 What purpose is served by sustained-release dosage forms of drugs?

References

Campbell, J. A., and Morrison, A. B.: Oral prolonged medication, J.A.M.A. **181**:102, 1962.

Claus, E. P., and Tyler, V. E., Jr.: Pharmacognosy, Philadelphia, 1965, Lea & Febiger.

Council on Drugs of the American Medical Association: New drugs, Chicago, 1967, American Medical Association.

Crossland, J.: Lewis's pharmacology, Baltimore, 1970, The Williams & Wilkins Co.

DiPalma, J. R., editor: Drill's pharmacology in medicine, ed. 4, New York, 1971, McGraw-Hill Book Company.

Friend, D. G.: One drug—one name, Clin. Pharmacol. Therap. **6**:689, 1965.

Gaddum, J. H.: Discoveries in therapeutics, J. Pharm. Pharmacol. **6**:497, 1954.

Hallister, L. E.: Studies of delayed action medication, New Eng. J. Med. **266**:281, 1962.

Jerome, J. B.: Selecting generic names for drugs, J. New Drugs **2**:276, 1962.

Jerome, J. B.: Current status of nonproprietary nomenclature for drugs, J.A.M.A. **185**:256, 1963.

Martin, E., editor: Remington's pharmaceutical sciences, ed. 14, Easton, Pa., 1970, Mack Printing Company.

Nelson, E.: Pharmaceutical for prolonged action, Clin. Pharmacol. Therap. **4**:283, 1963.

Official drug compendia

British Pharmacopoeia, ed. 10, London, 1968, The Pharmaceutical Press.

The National Formulary, ed. 13, Easton, Pa., 1970, Mack Printing Company.

The Pharmacopeia of the United States of America, ed. 18, Easton, Pa., 1970, Mack Printing Company.

5 Weights and measures

■ Brief history of weights and measures

The several systems of weights and measures used today have developed over a long period of time and in different cultures. Many measures used by English-speaking nations grew out of Egyptian, Roman, and Greek measures based on the human hand, finger, or foot. The Egyptian cubit was the distance from the elbow to the tip of the middle finger. The Roman mile was 1000 paces, a pace being 5 Roman feet. King Henry I of England is said to have made the yard (cloth yard) the distance from his nose to his outstretched thumb. The drachma (dram) is from the Greek and meant a handful.* The hand meant the breadth of the palm. These were

*This ancient Greek unit of measurement had several values.

early attempts to define a symbol to represent a definite quantity of a substance.

Measures based on common objects or parts of the body were highly variable although useful to meet the simple needs of people at one time. The ruling monarch of a country frequently decided on the amount of a measure in order that some conformity could prevail in his country. The King of England adopted the avoirdupois pound as an outgrowth of trade relations with France where the pound was 16 ounces. This resulted in two weights for pounds in England and later in the United States, the apothecaries' pound (12 ounces) and the avoirdupois pound (16 ounces).

Britons and Americans are not referring to the same measurement when they speak of gallons or quarts. Both the British gallon and the American gallon contain 4 quarts. However, the American quart contains 32 ounces and the British quart contains 40 ounces. Today there are various standards established by state or national authority as a rule for the measure of quantity. Late in the nineteenth century the International Bureau of Weights and Measures was founded and prepared international standards in the metric system.

The metric system is the system prescribed by law in most European countries, and several legislative attempts have been made to render its use obligatory in the United States. It is now used in the sciences, in weighing foreign mail, in weighing at the mints, and in other government departments, particularly the medical departments of the Army and Navy.

There are two systems of weighing and measuring drugs in the United States—the metric system and the apothecaries' system. There is a growing tendency to use the metric system entirely, but until such time that change to the metric system is complete, nurses will need to know something about both. Moreover, since these systems are often used interchangeably, nurses need to be able to change from one system to the other. In the home, patients or nurses may use teaspoons or other common household containers to measure drugs. Therefore, nurses also need to know the approximate equivalents for the household system.

■ Metric system

The metric system of weights and measures was invented by the French in the latter part of the eighteenth century. For this purpose a committee of the Academy of Sciences, consisting of five men, was appointed under authority of the government. They had two preconceived ideas regarding the proposed system: (1) that the standards should be based upon some unalterable object in nature, so that the correctness of the measures accepted as models might be redetermined, if necessary, and (2) that the system should employ the decimal scale. Of the three natural linear bases proposed—namely, the length of a second's pendulum, a fourth of the earth's circumference measured along the equator, and a fourth of the earth's circumference measured across the poles—the committee recommended the last, one ten-millionth of which should be the standard unit of linear measure. They calculated the distance from the equator to the North Pole from surveys made along the meridian that passes through Paris, and this distance, divided by 10 million, was chosen as the unit of length, the meter. The meter is the fundamental unit of the metric system. A bar of platinum of this length was constructed and deposited in the French Archives to serve as a model for the meter measures intended for actual use. There was also construct-

ed and deposited in the Archives a weight of platinum of such size as to counterpoise in vacuo 1 cubic decimeter of water at its greatest density. This weight constituted the fundamental standard of mass and was to serve as the model for the kilogram weights (and indirectly for the other weights) intended for actual use.

The metric standards were adopted in France in 1799. In 1875 the International Metric Convention met in Paris. Seventeen countries including the United States participated. This convention resulted in the foundation of the International Bureau of Weights and Measures, whose first work was the preparation of an international standard meter bar and an international standard kilogram weight with duplicates for each of the countries that had contributed to the support of the bureau. For the international standard meter, a bar of platinum iridium was selected and two lines were drawn on its surface at a distance from each other equal to 1 meter measured when the bar was at the temperature of melting ice (0° C.). The distance between these lines is the official unit of the metric system. The international standards were placed in the custody of the International Bureau of Weights and Measures near Paris. The duplicates were distributed by lot, the United States drawing meters No. 21 and No. 27 and kilograms No. 4 and No. 20. Meter No. 27 and kilogram No. 20 were selected as our national standards and are carefully preserved in the United States Bureau of Standards at Washington, D. C. Meter No. 21 and kilogram No. 4 are used as working standards.

Metric units of measurement

Metric units of measurement are the meter, the liter, and the gram. The *meter* is the unit for linear measurement, the *liter* for capacity or volume, and the *gram* for weight.

The metric system is a decimal system; the basic unit can be divided into 10, 100, or 1000 parts, or the basic unit may be multiplied by 10, 100, or 1000 to form secondary units that differ from each other by 10 or some multiple of 10. The names of the secondary units are formed by joining Greek and Latin prefixes to the

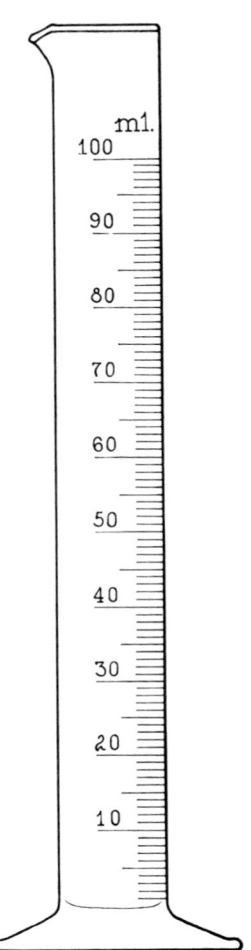

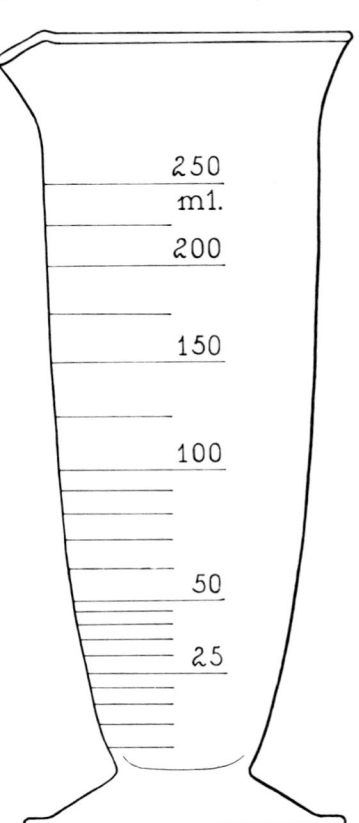

Figure 5-1
Metric measures suited to the measurement of volume. Both containers are marked in milliliters. The cylindrical graduate on the left is marked so that small amounts can be measured more accurately than with the graduate on the right.

Table 5-1 Metric linear measurement

1 meter	=	10 decimeters (dm.)
	=	100 centimeters (cm.)
	=	1000 millimeters (mm.)
10 meters =		1 dekameter (Dm.)
100 meters =		1 hectometer (Hm.)
1000 meters =		1 kilometer (Km.)
		(approx. 5/8 mile)

Table 5-2 Weight

1 gram (Gm.)	=	10 decigrams (dg.)
	=	100 centigrams (cg.)
	=	1000 milligrams (mg.)
	=	1,000,000 micrograms (μg.)
10 grams =		1 dekagram (Dg.)
100 grams =		1 hectogram (Hg.)
1000 grams =		1 kilogram (Kg.)

names of the primary unit. Subdivisions of the basic unit can be made by moving the decimal point to the left, and multiples of the basic unit are indicated by moving the decimal point to the right.

The prefixes used to designate subdivisions of the unit are deci- (0.1), centi- (0.01), and milli- (0.001) and are from the Latin; those used to designate multiples are deka- (10), hecto- (100), and kilo- (1000) and are from the Greek. The subdivisions of a meter are known as decimeters, centimeters, and millimeters; and the multiples of the meter are known as dekameters, hectometers, and kilometers. The following diagram compares the subdivisions or denominations of the metric system with the scheme of the decimal system.

hundred thousands	ten thousands	thousands	hundreds	tens	units	decimal point	tenths	hundredths	thousandths	ten thousandths	hundred thousandths	millionths
0	0	0	0	0	0	•	0	0	0	0	0	0
		kilo	hecto	deka	meter, liter, gram		deci	centi	milli			

Meter. The meter is the unit from which the other metric units were derived (Table 5-1). The meter is comparable to the yard although it is several inches longer (39.37 inches).

The first part of Table 5-1 is most frequently used and is similar to the system of money used in the United States: one dollar = 10 dimes, or 100 cents, or 1000 mills.

Centimeters and millimeters are the chief linear measures used in hospital work. Measurement of the size of body organs is made in centimeters and millimeters, and students will recall that the sphygmomanometer used in measuring blood pressure is calibrated in millimeters. Microns, which are one millionth of a meter, are used in measuring minute distances, such as the length or size of bacteria. There are approximately 2.5 centimeters (25 millimeters) in 1 inch.

Liter. The liter is the unit of capacity. The contents of a cube whose sides measure 1 decimeter (10 centimeters) constitute the unit of capacity. It was originally intended that the liter and the cubic decimeter should be exactly the same. Because of the difficulty of measurement, however, the liter is found to be 1.000028 cubic decimeters.

The liter, therefore, is 28 parts per 1,000,000 larger than intended. The difference is so small that it is of no importance except in determinations of great precision. The weight of a liter of water at 4° C. is 1 kilogram.

If the liter contained exactly 1000 cc., the cubic centimeter and the milliliter would be exactly the same volume and each the one thousandth part of the liter. However, since the liter in common use is 1000.028 cc., the cubic centimeter is less than the milliliter by 0.000028 cc. *In practice the cubic centimeter and the milliliter are considered equal.*

Fractional parts of a liter are usually expressed in milliliters or cubic centimeters. For example, 0.6 L. would be expressed as 600 ml. or 600 cc. Multiples of a liter are similarly expressed: 2.4 L. would be 2400 ml. or cc.

Gram. The gram is the metric unit of weight that is used in weighing drugs and various pharmaceutical preparations. Originally, the unit of measurement of weight was the kilogram, but this proved too large to meet the practical needs of the pharmacist. The gram is the weight of 1 milliliter of distilled water at 4° C. The official abbreviation of gram is Gm.*

In studying Table 5-2 it becomes apparent that 1 decigram is 10 times greater than a centigram and 100 times greater than a milligram. To change decigrams to centigrams one would therefore multiply by 10; to change decigrams to milligrams one would multiply by 100. To change milligrams to centigrams one would divide by 10; to change milligrams to decigrams

---

*The abbreviation for gram has a capital G (Gm.) to avoid confusion with gr. for grain.

one would divide by 100; and to change milligrams to grams one would divide by 1000.

In reading a whole number expressing a metric quantity only one unit is used, however large the number, such as 2750 Gm. is read twenty-seven hundred fifty grams, not two kilograms, seven hectograms, five dekagrams; 7500 ml. is read seven thousand five hundred or seventy-five hundred milliliters.

In expressing a fraction of a gram, the terms *decigram* and *centigram* are seldom used. The quantity is expressed in its equivalent grams or milligrams; for example, 6 decigrams, written 0.6 Gm., is called six-tenths gram; 5 centigrams, written 0.05 Gm., is called preferably fifty milligrams. The thousandth part of a gram and multiples or fractions of it are commonly expressed as milligrams; for example, 0.001 Gm. may be expressed as 1 mg.; 0.003 Gm. as 3 mg.; and 0.0005 Gm. as 0.5 mg.; 0.001 mg. is 1 microgram.

The kilogram is the only multiple of the gram used in medical work. Nurses will observe that this measure is used in weighing patients and in calculation of dosage in terms of kilograms of body weight (1 kilogram = 2.2 pounds avoirdupois weight).

To ensure accuracy in reading, a zero always should be used before the decimal point in writing a fractional part of a metric unit—0.5 Gm., 0.6 ml., or 0.001 L. The misplacement of the period or point may be the cause of serious error. When the abbreviations for gram, milliliter, and cubic centimeter are omitted, it is taken for granted that 1.0 means 1 Gm. when expressing weight or 1 ml. when expressing liquid quantity. When metric abbreviations are used, the numerals are always expressed in Arabic and precede the abbreviation—for example, 20 Gm., 50 ml., 250 mg.

The metric system has many advantages, chief of which are as follows: all the standard units of weight and measure bear a simple relation to the fundamental unit, the meter; the prefixes deci-, centi-, milli-, deka-, hecto-, and kilo- have a numerical significance and have other applications in our language that make them readily understood; the uniform decimal scale of relation between the successive units makes the use of the decimal notation possible; and the system is universal.

The early Greeks had an advantage when they described the quantity of a substance as a handful. The person hearing these words could look at his hand and imagine how much it would hold. To use the metric system to accomplish the same purpose today, it is necessary to obtain a mental picture of the quantity represented by the denominations that are a part of the system. The laboratory suggestions in this chapter are designed to help the student develop these concepts.

Laboratory suggestions

1 Gather the following materials for use: glass measures marked in milliliters, gram scales, salt, water, and colored solution of alcohol.
2 Study the gram scale. Balance it and note how the scale is marked to indicate the subdivisions of the gram.
3 Study the various metric measures that can be used to measure liquids. Note the amount of water contained in 4 ml., 30 ml., 180 ml., and 500 ml. Try to build a mental concept of these quantities.
4 Weigh out 3 Gm. of salt and add it to 30 ml. of water; notice how much constitutes each of these amounts. Is the volume of the liquid noticeably changed? Why? How much salt is there in each milliliter of solution?
5 Normal (physiologic) salt solution is made by adding 9 Gm. of sodium chloride to 1000 ml. of water; weigh out the amount of salt needed for 0.5 liter of normal (physiologic) salt solution.
6 Add 15 ml. of alcohol to 30 ml. of water. Is the volume of the liquid increased? How much? Why? What is the ratio strength of the finished solution? How much alcohol would be needed to make 1 liter of solution of the same strength?
7 Add 10 ml. of alcohol to 60 ml. of water. How much alcohol is there in each milliliter of solution?

Before undertaking any arithmetic operations using the metric system of measure, it is necessary to recall a few basic rules and definitions.

A number such as 2 or 7 taken by itself, without reference to anything concrete, is called an *abstract* or *pure* number. A number that designates a quantity of objects or units of measure, such as 2 grams or 7 milligrams, is called a *concrete* or *denominate* number.

Four basic rules govern the arithmetic operations used here.

1 Numbers of different denominations have no numerical connection with each other and cannot be used together in any arithmetic operation.

2 A denominate number may be added or subtracted from any other number of the same denomination.

> Example: 2 grams + 7 grams = 9 grams

3 A denominate number may be multiplied or divided only by a pure number.

> Example: 2 grams × 7 grams = 14 grams

Note: The result of any of these operations is always a number of the same denomination.

4 When both sides of an equation are multiplied or divided by the same pure number, the resulting products or quotients are equal.

> Example: 1 gram =   1000 milligrams
> 10 × 1 gram =   1000 milligrams × 10
> 10 grams = 10,000 milligrams

Conversion is the process that enables one to describe the same quantity of a substance in different terms. Tables have been developed to show relationships among subdivisions within a system or between systems. Entries from these tables provide the starting point for the conversion process. The arithmetic operation is multiplication or division of both sides of the equation by the same pure or abstract number:

1 To express 4.75 Gm. in terms of milligrams:
1 Gm. = 1000 mg. (Table 5-2, p. 40)
The pure number selected is 4.75; the operation selected is multiplication.

> 4.75 × 1 Gm. = 1000 mg. × 4.75
> 4.75 Gm. = 4750 mg.

2 To express 568 cm. in terms of meters: 1 meter = 100 centimeters (Table 5-1, p. 40)
a. The pure number selected is 100; the operation selected is division.

> 1 M. ÷ 100 = 100 cm. ÷ 100
> .01 M. = 1 cm.

b. The pure number selected is 568; the operation selected is multiplication.

> 568 × .01 M. = 1 cm. × 568
> 5.68 M. = 568 cm.

Exercises

Metric system

1 a. What part of a gram is a decigram?
  b. What part of a gram is a milligram?
  c. What part of a gram is a centigram?
2 a. How many dekagrams are there in a kilogram?
  b. How many centigrams are there in a kilogram?
  c. How many centigrams are there in a hectogram?
3 In the calculation of the following problems, state the process of reasoning:
  a. Convert the following to milligrams: 3 Gm., 7 dg., 4 cg., 0.5 Gm.
  b. Add this series of measurements and express the sum in grams: 200 mg., 40 cg., 15 dg., 2 Gm.
  c. Add this series of measurements and express the sum in centigrams: 250 mg., 1.3 Gm., 12 dg., 0.7 cg.
  d. Add this series of measurements and express the sum in milligrams: 0.02 Gm., 0.13 cg., 0.125 Gm., 0.08 dg.
4 A preparation of medicine is made by dissolving 30 mg. of drug in 200 ml. of water. If 3 mg. is the dose of drug desired, how many milliliters must be given for each dose?
5 If the dose of cascara sagrada is 4 ml., how many doses will there be in 0.2 liter?
6 If 0.2 Gm. of drug is added to 200 ml. of water, how many milligrams of drug is there in each milliliter of solution?
7 If 20 ml. of alcohol is added to 80 ml. of water to make a certain desired strength of solution, how much alcohol would be required to make a liter of solution?

■ Apothecaries' system

The apothecaries' system of weights and measures was a part of the system used in England at the time of colonization in the United States. It has now been superseded by the imperial system, which is official in Great Britain.*

*The imperial system of weights and measures as well as the metric system is used in the *British Pharmacopoeia* and the *Canadian Formulary*. The imperial system is being replaced gradually by the metric system.

1 pound (lb.)	= 16 ounces = 7000 grains
1 ounce (℥)	= 437½ grains
1 dram (ℨ)	= 60 grains (unofficial) — officially 1 grain is 1/7000 part of a pound
1 pint (O)	= 20 fluidounces (f℥)
1 fluidounce (f℥)	= 8 fluidrams (fℨ)
1 fluidram (fℨ)	= 60 minims (min.)

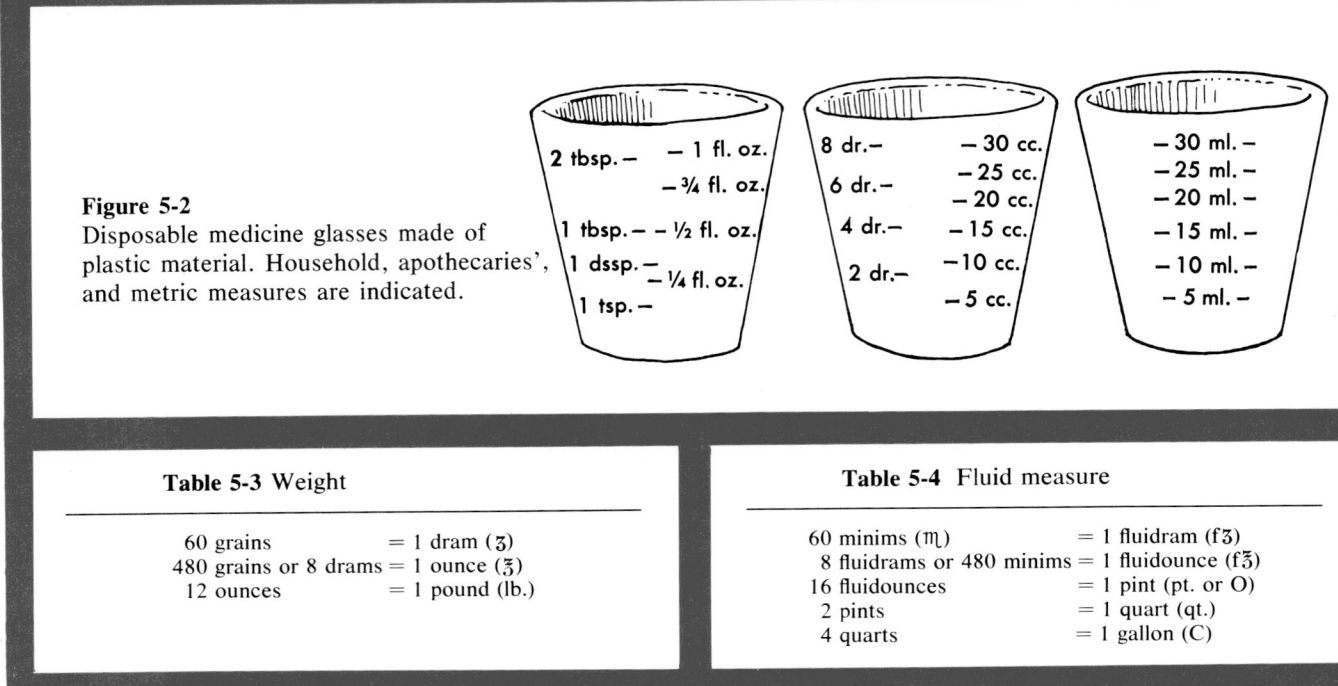

Figure 5-2
Disposable medicine glasses made of plastic material. Household, apothecaries', and metric measures are indicated.

Table 5-3 Weight

60 grains	= 1 dram (ʒ)
480 grains or 8 drams	= 1 ounce (℥)
12 ounces	= 1 pound (lb.)

Table 5-4 Fluid measure

60 minims (♏)	= 1 fluidram (fʒ)
8 fluidrams or 480 minims	= 1 fluidounce (f℥)
16 fluidounces	= 1 pint (pt. or O)
2 pints	= 1 quart (qt.)
4 quarts	= 1 gallon (C)

The basic unit of weight in the apothecaries' system is the grain, which originally meant a grain of wheat. The other units of weight are the scruple, the dram, the ounce, and the pound. The scruple is seldom used and therefore is not included in Table 5-3. Quantities less than 1 dram are usually expressed in grains. The abbreviation lb. is for libra, the Latin word meaning pound.

The unit of fluid measure is a minim (Table 5-4), which is approximately the quantity of water that would weigh a grain. The symbol O is the abbreviation of the Latin word *octarius* meaning an eighth (eighth of a gallon), and the letter C is the abbreviation for the Latin word *congius*, meaning a vessel holding a gallon.

When symbols are used, the quantity is expressed in Roman numerals, which are placed after the symbols: three grains is written gr. iii; five drams, ʒ v; ten ounces, ℥ x. Fractions are expressed in Arabic numerals; gr. $^1/_4$, gr. $^1/_8$, gr. $^1/_2$; the symbol "ss" may be used for $^1/_2$ (ss =

semis, Latin for one-half); thus, two and one-half grains, gr. iiss.*

The minim (♏) is often assumed to be identical with the drop (gtt. from the Latin word *gutta*), but such measurement is inaccurate. A minim of water or of an aqueous solution is approximately equal to a drop; a minim of an alcoholic solution, such as digitalis tincture, equals approximately 2 drops; a minim of ether contains 3 drops; and a minim of chloroform equals approximately 4 drops. A minim of a gummy substance is less than a drop. Minims should always be measured when minims are ordered, and a minim glass or minim pipet should be used to measure accurately. When drops are ordered, they may be measured by means of a medicine dropper.

*When the numeral for "one" is used, a dot is frequently placed over it to avoid confusion with the Roman numeral L, meaning 50, which is sometimes written as a small letter.

Exercises

Apothecaries' system

1 Read the following:
   a. ʒ iiss   **e.** ♏ viii   **h.** ℥ vi
   b. gr. xiii   **f.** gr. xxx   **i.** ♏ xxiv
   c. ℥ ss   **g.** ʒ iv   **j.** O v
   d. ʒ xviii

2 Write the following expressions as they should be written in a prescription: 15 minims, 3 fluidrams, 7 fluidounces, 1 pint, 2½ drams, 20 grains, 12 minims, 5 ounces, ½ ounce.

3 How many grains are there in:
   a. ʒ vi   **d.** ℥ vi   **g.** ʒ iii
   b. ℥ iss   **e.** lb. i   **h.** ʒ ix
   c. ʒ ii   **f.** ℥ ss

4 How many minims are there in:
   a. f℥ ss   **d.** f℥ ii   **g.** f℥ i
   b. fʒ ss   **e.** O ss   **h.** f℥ iiss
   c. fʒ iv   **f.** fʒ viii

5 **a.** What part of a dram is gr. xl, gr. xiii, gr. xv, gr. xx, gr. i?
   b. What part of an ounce is gr. xxx, ʒ ss, ʒ iv, ʒ vi, gr. lx?
   c. What part of a fluidram is ♏ x, ♏ xv, ♏ xlv, ♏ xxx, ♏ i?
   d. What part of a fluidounce is fʒ vi, fʒ iv, fʒ ii, fʒ ss?

6 Add the following amounts and express the sum in fluidounces: O ss, ♏ 160, fʒ x, ♏ 200.

7 A physician's prescription calls for gr. xxiv of a drug. This would be what part of an ounce?

8 One dose contains gr. xv of a drug; how many drams of this drug would be required to make up sixty doses?

9 How much morphine sulfate would be required to make up 2 fluidounces of solution if every 20 minims of the solution is to contain gr. ¼?

10 If a pint of solution contains ʒ ii of drug, how many grains in each fluidounce of solution?

Laboratory suggestions

1 Gather the following materials for use: apothecaries' scales and measures, colored solution of alcohol, and salt.

2 With a minim measure determine the number of minims in:
   a. 1 fluidram
   b. 2 fluidounces
   c. 1 fluidounce
   Why would a minim glass be unsuitable to measure out several fluidounces of a solution?
   d. Observe the various apothecaries' measures set out for your use. Note the amount of their content. Measure out 1 fluidram, 1 fluidounce, 60 minims, 1 pint, and so on. Try to form a mental picture of various quantities and how they compare with each other; for example, compare the amount of water in 15 minims with the amount in 1 fluidram or 1 fluidounce. Compare the weight of 1 grain with 15 grains, with 1 ounce, and with 1 pound.

3 With a fluidram measure determine how many fluidrams there are in 1 fluidounce; in 1 pint. What kind of an apothecaries' measure would you select to measure out ½ pint of a solution if you had the following to choose from: minim glass, fluidram measure, fluidounce measure? Why?

4 Weigh out 60 grains of salt on an apothecaries' scale. This corresponds with how many drams?

5 Dissolve ʒ i of salt in f℥ iv of water. How many grains of salt are there in each fluidounce of solution? In each fluidram?

6 Dissolve gr. xxx of salt in f℥ iiss of water. How many grains of salt would there be in ♏ 40 of the solution?

7 Using the colored solution of alcohol, add 1 fluidram of alcohol to 4 fluidrams of water. What part of the solution will be alcohol? How many minims of alcohol would there be in ♏ 60 of the solution?

8 Add fʒ ii of alcohol to f℥ iv of water. What part of the solution is alcohol? How many minims of alcohol in each fluidram of solution?

■ Conversion from one system to another

The metric system and the apothecaries' system have different size units and subdivisions. The denominations of one system are incompatible with the denominations of the other. Thus, the tables that list the measurement of a denomination of one system in terms of another system are clearly labeled approximate equivalents and should be interpreted in that way.

Since nurses have occasion to use both the apothecaries' and the metric systems in computing dosage of drugs to be given orally or parenterally as well as in preparing solutions for external use, it is essential that they know how to use these systems interchangeably.

Although these systems are used interchangeably, greater emphasis is being placed on the metric system as its convenience is increasingly appreciated. Nevertheless, it is advisable for nurses to learn the tables of weights and measurements and at least some of the approximate equivalents as thoroughly as they learned the multiplication tables. However, the nurse should rely neither on memory alone nor on tables alone. Conversion tables should be available in every medication locker as a means of checking,

Table 5-5 Commonly used approximate
equivalents

Weight		Volume	
1 Gm.	= 15 grains	1 ml.	= 15 minims
0.06 Gm.	= 1 grain	1 cc.	= 15 minims
4 Gm.	= 1 dram	0.06 ml.	= 1 minim
30 Gm.	= 1 ounce	4 ml.	= 1 fluidram
1 Kg.*	= 2.2 pounds (imperial or avoirdupois)	30 ml.	= 1 fluidounce
		500 ml.	= 1 pint
		1000 ml. (1 L.)	= 1 quart

*1 Kg. is equivalent to 2.6 apothecaries' pounds; however, the nurse has little or no occasion to use the apothecaries' pound.

Table 5-6 Additional approximate
equivalents (weight)

gr. xv	= 1.0	Gm. = 1000	mg.
gr. x	= 0.6	Gm. = 600	mg.
gr. viiss	= 0.5	Gm. = 500	mg.
gr. v	= 0.3	Gm. = 300	mg.
gr. iii	= 0.2	Gm. = 200	mg.
gr. 1½	= 0.1	Gm. = 100	mg.
gr. 1	= 0.06	Gm. = 60	mg.
gr. ¾	= 0.05	Gm. = 50	mg.
gr. ½	= 0.03	Gm. = 30	mg.
gr. ¼	= 0.015	Gm. = 15	mg.
gr. ⅙	= 0.010	Gm. = 10	mg.
gr. ⅛	= 0.008	Gm. = 8	mg.
gr. 1/12	= 0.005	Gm. = 5	mg.
gr. 1/15	= 0.004	Gm. = 4	mg.
gr. 1/20	= 0.0032	Gm. = 3	mg.
gr. 1/30	= 0.0022	Gm. = 2	mg.
gr. 1/40	= 0.0015	Gm. = 1.5	mg.
gr. 1/50	= 0.0012	Gm. = 1.2	mg.
gr. 1/60	= 0.001	Gm. = 1	mg.
gr. 1/100	= 0.0006	Gm. = 0.6	mg.
gr. 1/120	= 0.0005	Gm. = 0.5	mg.
gr. 1/150	= 0.0004	Gm. = 0.4	mg.
gr. 1/200	= 0.0003	Gm. = 0.3	mg.
gr. 1/300	= 0.0002	Gm. = 0.2	mg.
gr. 1/600	= 0.0001	Gm. = 0.1	mg.

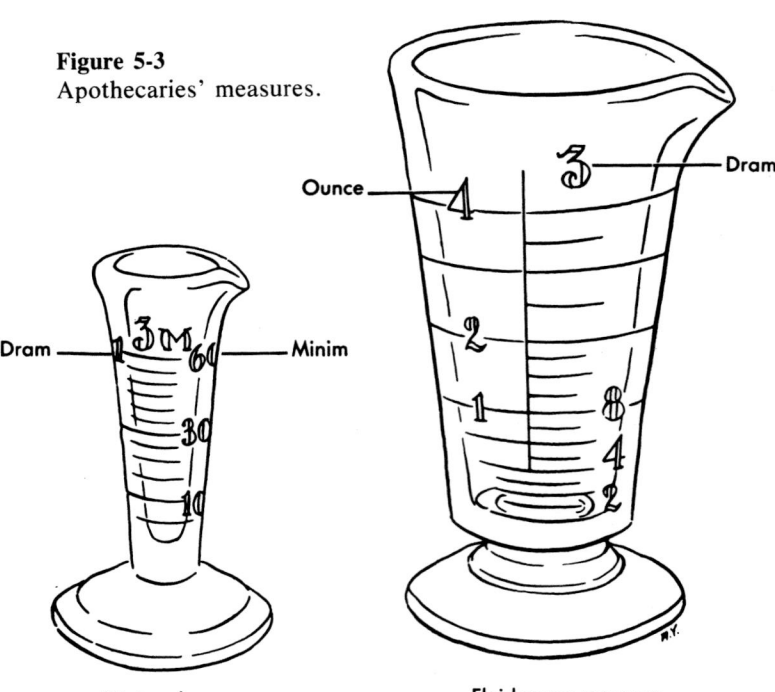

Figure 5-3
Apothecaries' measures.

Minim glass

Fluidounce measure

not as a substitute for the nurse's calculations.

Although it is well to know how to calculate the change from one system to the other, often the accepted equivalent is not the same as the exact amount in the other system, and confusion results. For the most part, exact equivalents are used only by the pharmacist in compounding prescriptions or in converting a pharmaceutical formula from one system to the other. When dosage forms such as tablets and capsules are prescribed in the metric system, the nurse may administer the approximate apothecaries' equivalent and vice versa. If the nurse knows that 1 mg. = gr. $\frac{1}{60}$, she can easily calculate the desired equivalent:

To express 0.2 mg. in terms of grains: gr. $\frac{1}{60}$ = 1 mg. (Table 5-6). The pure or abstract number selected is 0.2; the operation selected is multiplication.

$$0.2 \text{ (or } \frac{2}{10}) \times \text{gr. } \frac{1}{60} = 1 \text{ mg.} \times 0.2$$
$$\text{gr. } \frac{1}{300} = 0.2 \text{ mg.}$$

The approximate equivalents (Table 5-5) are used in *The Pharmacopeia of the United States of America, The National Formulary,* and *New Drugs,* and they have the approval of the F.D.A.

It is important to know how to change from one system to the other in the event that one forgets the corresponding equivalent or that no table with the desired equivalent is available. It must be remembered, of course, that 1 gram is the equivalent of 15 grains and that 1 milliliter is the equivalent of 15 minims. One gram (1 Gm.) divided by 15 is 0.06 Gm., the equivalent of 1 grain, and 0.06 milliliter is the equivalent of 1 minim.

Exercises

Conversion from one system to another

Indicate the process whereby you arrive at an answer.

1 Convert the following to their apothecary equivalents:

a. 30 Gm.	**e.** 45 Gm.	**i.** 0.03 Gm.
b. 4 Gm.	**f.** 0.6 ml.	**j.** 0.010 Gm.
c. 4 ml.	**g.** 0.6 Gm.	**k.** 500 ml.
d. 1 ml.	**h.** 0.1 Gm.	**l.** 1000 ml.
m. 250 ml.	**p.** 15 mg.	**s.** 0.1 mg.
n. 120 ml.	**q.** 10 mg.	**t.** 30 mg.
o. 15 ml.	**r.** 100 mg.	

2 Change to metric equivalents:

a. ℥ i	**h.** gr. iss	**o.** gr. $\frac{1}{8}$
b. ℥ iv	**i.** gr. $\frac{1}{6}$	**p.** gr. v
c. ℥ ii	**j.** gr. $\frac{1}{4}$	**q.** f℥ i
d. O ss	**k.** 6 lb.	**r.** ℥ lx
e. C i	**l.** 3 lb.	**s.** f℥ iv
f. ℥ xv	**m.** 35 lb.	**t.** qt. i
g. gr. viiss	**n.** gr. $\frac{1}{600}$	

3 Without consulting the text, practice giving metric equivalents for:

a. gr. xv	**g.** ℥ x	**m.** gr. $\frac{1}{2}$
b. gr. x	**h.** gr. $\frac{1}{6}$	**n.** qt. ss
c. ℥ v	**i.** qt. i	**o.** O i
d. 11 lb.	**j.** ℥ xv	**p.** gr. viiss
e. gr. iss	**k.** gr. $\frac{1}{60}$	**q.** gr. $\frac{1}{8}$
f. 1 lb.	**l.** ℥ i	**r.** gr. $\frac{1}{150}$

4 In the same way, give apothecaries' equivalents for:

a. 1.0 Gm.	**j.** 0.1 Gm.
b. 0.3 Gm.	**k.** 500.0 ml.
c. 1 Kg.	**l.** 0.0006 Gm.
d. 1.0 ml.	**m.** 30.0 ml.
e. 1½ ml.	**n.** 0.015 Gm.
f. 0.03 Gm.	**o.** 10 Kg.
g. 4.0 ml.	**p.** 0.065 Gm.
h. 1000 ml.	**q.** 0.008 Gm.
i. 0.5 Gm.	**r.** 250.0 Gm.

5 Change:

a. 3 fluidounces to minims	**g.** 1 liter to fluidounces
b. 1 liter to pints	**h.** 36 drams to grams
c. 6.0 ml. to fluidrams	**i.** 5.0 ml. to minims
d. 75 grains to grams	**j.** 3 pints to milliliters
e. 7.0 Gm. to grains	**k.** 75.0 ml. to fluidounces
f. 40 lb. to Kg.	

6 If the dose of milk of magnesia is 15 ml., how many fluidounces would be necessary to give ten doses?

7 If there are 7½ grains of drug in each 5-ml. ampule of the preparation, how many grams of the drug are there in four ampules?

8 If the dose of a certain medication is 0.5 Gm. and the tablets are marked 7½ gr., how many tablets will be given for each dose? How many tablets will be required for ten doses?

9 If the dose of a medication is 4 ml., how many fluidounces would you order from the pharmacy in order to have sixty doses?

10 If a physician orders 15 mg. of a drug and the preparation comes marked "Tablets gr. $\frac{1}{8}$," how many tablets or what part of a tablet will you give?

■ Household measures

When nursing is done in the home, a graduate for accurate measurement may not be available

---

Table 5-7 Approximate equivalents

60 drops (gtt.)	= 1 teaspoonful (t.)	
3 teaspoonfuls	= 1 tablespoonful (T.)	
2 tablespoonfuls	= 1 fluidounce	
6 fluidounces	= 1 teacupful	
8 fluidounces	= 1 glassful	

Household	Apothecaries'	Metric
1 drop	1 minim	0.06 ml.
1 teaspoonful	1 fluidram	5 (4) ml.*
1 tablespoonful	4 fluidrams	15 ml.
2 tablespoonfuls	1 fluidounce	30 ml.
1 teacupful	6 fluidounces	180 ml.
1 glassful	8 fluidounces	240 ml.

*A scant teaspoonful is generally accepted as an equivalent of 4 ml. (cc.) or fʒ i.

and some household article may be used to measure, approximately, the amount required. Household measures include glasses, cups, tablespoons, teaspoons, and drops. Pints and quarts are usually found in the home, but they are defined as apothecaries' measures. Household measures are not accurate and their use should be avoided in the administration of medicines. A teaspoon is said to hold a dram, but the average present-day teaspoon often holds 5 ml. or more.* Drops and minims are also said to be equivalent, but when the physician orders a certain number of minims of a drug, the dose should be measured in minims. If he orders drops, the dose should be measured with a medicine dropper. The volume of a drop varies with the viscosity of the liquid to be dropped, the diameter of the dropper used, the angle at which the dropper is held, and sometimes the temperature of the solution. Approximate equivalents (Table 5-7) are not absolutely accurate, but they are sufficiently accurate for practical purposes.

*An American standard teaspoon has been established by the American Standards Association as containing approximately 5 ml. and is accepted as such in U.S.P. XVII.

Exercises

Approximate equivalents

Choose approximate and appropriate equivalents.
1 Using household measures, how would you measure:
   a. ʒ i   f. ℳ xxx   k. 120 ml.
   b. fʒ i   g. qt. ss   l. C ss
   c. fʒ iii h. 0.3 ml.   m. fʒ iv
   d. 30 ml. i. 4 ml.
   e. 1000 ml. j. ʒ ss
2 Change to the approximate apothecary equivalents:
   a. 1 T.   e. 1 teacupful   i. ½ glassful
   b. 2 t.   f. 1 glassful   j. ½ teacupful
   c. ½ t.   g. 60 drops   k. ½ T.
   d. 2 T.   h. 4 glassfuls   l. 15 drops
3 Give the approximate metric equivalents:
   a. 1 teacupful   g. 2 T.
   b. 1 glassful   h. ¼ t.
   c. 1 T.   i. 20 gtt.
   d. 1 t.   j. ½ T.
   e. 60 gtt.   k. 2 teacupfuls
   f. ½ t.   l. 2 glassfuls

Laboratory suggestions

1 Gather the following materials for use: apothecaries' measures, metric measures, household measures of various sizes and shapes, medicine droppers, water, and oil.
2 Determine the capacity of the household measures provided for you, using apothecaries' and metric measures. Compare the sizes of three or four cups, glasses, teaspoons, and tablespoons. Do you find any discrepancy? What can you say about the reliability of household measures?
3 With a medicine dropper, drop 20 drops of water into a minims glass. How many minims are there? Do the same with a water faucet instead of a medicine dropper. How many minims are there? Under what circumstances would a medicine dropper measure minims accurately?
4 Drop 20 drops of oil into a minim glass. How many minims are there? What factors determine the size of a drop?

■ The preparation of solutions and doses
Methods of making solutions

There are three methods of making solutions. One is on the weight-to-weight basis, commonly designated as W/W. This means that a given part by weight of solute is dissolved in a given number of parts by weight of solvent. This method is used chiefly where a high degree of accuracy is essential, such as in highly technical work.

A second method is the weight-to-volume method, designated W/V, in which a given part by weight of drug (solute) is placed in a graduate and a sufficient amount of solvent is added to make the required amount of solution. This method is commonly used in medicine and pharmacy. Many of the intravenous fluids given to patients, such as the glucose and saline solutions, are prepared on a weight-to-volume basis and are so indicated on the label.

The third method is the volume-to-volume method, in which a liquid solute is added to the liquid solvent and is designated V/V.

The difference in expressing the strength of a solution on a W/V basis or on a V/V basis is very apparent when one considers the difference in weight of two liquids such as alcohol and water. Alcohol weighs considerably less than water so the amount of alcohol in a 50% solution prepared on a weight-to-volume basis would be quite different than if it were prepared on a volume-to-volume basis.

The strength of solutions is frequently spoken of in terms of molarity or normality. A *normal solution* is one that contains 1 Gm. equivalent weight of solute in each 1000 ml. of solution. An equivalent combining weight is the weight of an element in grams that will combine with 1.008 Gm. of hydrogen or 8 Gm. of oxygen. It is obtained by dividing the atomic weight by the valence. Normal solution of sodium chloride contains 58.454 Gm. of sodium chloride per liter of solution. The atomic weight of sodium is 22.997, and the atomic weight of chlorine is 35.457, making a total of 58.454. Since the valence of both sodium and chlorine is 1, the atomic weight and the equivalent weight of each is the same.

Normal solution of sodium chloride should not be confused with physiologic saline solution, particularly since the physiologic saline solution is sometimes referred to as normal saline. Normal solution of sodium chloride is a 5.8% solution of sodium chloride, whereas physiologic or normal saline is approximately 0.9% strength.

Solutions may be designated as normal (1N),

half-normal (0.5N), tenth-normal (0.1N), etc.

A *molar solution* is one that contains a mole (gram molecular weight) of the solute in 1000 ml. of solution. Thus each liter of molar solution of sulfuric acid contains 98.08 Gm. of hydrogen sulfate (H_2SO_4). Since the equivalent weight would be half this amount, a normal solution of sulfuric acid would contain 49.04 Gm. of solute. Solutions containing one tenth of a gram molecular weight of solute in 1 liter of solution are designated as (0.1M) or M/10.

Solutions are made from pure drugs, tablets, or stock solutions. *Pure drugs* are unadulterated substances in solid or liquid form. They are 100% pure unless otherwise stated. Powders and crystalline substances, such as boric acid, magnesium sulfate, sodium chloride, sodium bicarbonate, and a few liquids, such as cresol, alcohol, and glycerin, are pure drugs.

Tablets containing a definite known quantity of drugs may be used in making solutions. They also save the inconvenience of weighing the pure drug. The tablet is essentially a preparation of pure drug.

Stock solutions are relatively strong solutions from which weaker solutions may be made. It is customary to have stock solutions on hand so that dilution of various strengths may be made without the inconvenience and delay of weighing the pure drug. Examples of stock solutions commonly used are bichloride of mercury, phenol, potassium permanganate, and magnesium sulfate.

Solutions from pure drugs. To prepare a solution of a given strength of a pure drug it is necessary to determine the amount of drug to use to make a given quantity of solution. If ratio and proportion is the method of calculation, the proportion may be expressed as follows: The amount of drug is to the finished solution as the strength in percent* (or equivalent ratio expression):

(a)   (b)   (c) (d)

Amount of drug : finished solution :: % : 100

*The term *percent* and its corresponding sign, %, mean "by the hundred" or "in a hundred." Percent is simply a fraction of such frequent use that its numerator is expressed but its denominator is left understood, for example, 4% or $^1/_{100}$.

In this proportion terms *a* and *b* are concrete or denominate numbers; terms *c* and *d* are abstract or pure numbers. To construct a true proportion terms *a* and *b* must be of the same (or equal) denomination.

Right way

(X) Gm. of drug are to ml. of solution
(X) ml. of drug are to ml. of solution
(X) gr. of drug are to ℥ of solution
(X) f℥ of drug are to f℥ of solution

Wrong way

(X) gr. of drug are to ml. of solution
(X) ℥ of drug are to ml. of solution
(X) ml. of drug are to ℥ of solution
(X) f℥ of drug are to f℥ of solution

In a true proportion the product of the means (terms *b* and *c*) equals the product of the extremes (terms *a* and *d*).

Examples (using the above rule):

1   Prepare 500 ml. of a 5% solution of boric acid. Since no strength of solute is indicated, boric acid crystals or powder are considered 100% pure drug.

$$X \text{ (Gm. of drug)} :$$
$$500 \text{ ml. finished solutions} :: 5 : 100$$
$$100 \text{ X} = 2500$$
$$X = 25$$

In any proportion the product of the means equals the product of the extremes.

$$\text{Proof: } 25 \times 100 = 2500$$
$$5 \times 500 = 2500$$

Substitute the number 25 for X in the original proportion and it reads:

$$25 \text{ Gm. of drug} :$$
$$500 \text{ ml. finished solution} :: 5 : 100$$

Another method that can be used to solve this problem or to prove the answer is as follows:

Five percent means that $^5/_{100}$ of the solution is boric acid. 500 ml. weigh 500 Gm. Hence $^5/_{100} \times 500$ (Gm.) = 25 Gm. It is necessary to use 25 Gm. of pure drug. To prepare the solution, place 25 Gm. of boric acid in a graduate,

add enough water to dissolve it, and then add water up to 500 ml.

2   How much drug is needed to make 1 fluidounce of a 1:25 sodium chloride solution?

Amount of drug: finished solution :: specified ratio. Since so small an amount is to be made, it is well to change the fluidounce to minims.

$$X \text{ grains (amount of drug)} :$$
$$480 \text{ minims finished solution} :: 1 : 25$$
$$25 \text{ X} = 480$$
$$X = 19.2$$
$$19.2 \text{ grains of drug} :$$
$$480 \text{ minims finished solution} :: 1 : 25$$

Another method of solving the problem is similar to that mentioned under example 1: the ratio 1:25 means that $^1/_{25}$ of the solution is sodium chloride. One fluidounce weighs 480 grains.

$$^1/_{25} \times 480 = 19.2 \text{ gr.}$$

Dissolve 19.2 grains of sodium chloride in a quantity of water so that the total amount of solution measures 1 fluidounce.

3   Prepare a gallon of 1:1000 bichloride of mercury from tablets of $7^1/_2$ gr.

$$X \text{ (Gm.)} : 4000 \text{ (ml.)} :: 1 : 1000$$
$$1000 \text{ X} = 4000$$
$$X = 4$$
$$4 \text{ Gm.} : 4000 \text{ ml.} :: 1 : 1000$$

Each tablet contains $7^1/_2$ gr. Entry from Table 5-6, p. 46. $7^1/_2$ gr. = 0.5 Gm.

$$1 \text{ tablet} = \text{gr. } 7^1/_2 = 0.5 \text{ Gm.}$$
$$4 \div 0.5 = 8$$
$$8 \times 0.5 \text{ Gm.} = 1 \text{ tablet} \times 8$$
$$4 \text{ Gm.} = 8 \text{ tablets}$$

4   If f℥ 2 of alcohol are added to f℥ 4 of water, what is the percentage strength of the resulting solution? State the strength also as a ratio.

$$\text{Amount of drug : finished solution} :: \% : 100$$
$$2 \text{ (f℥)} : 6 \text{ (f℥)} :: X : 100$$
$$6 \text{ X} = 200$$
$$X = 33^1/_3$$

When a liquid drug is added to a given amount of water, the finished solution is the sum of the two. Addition of a dry drug to the water of a solution will not increase the volume appreciably since it will be soluble.

$$33^1/_3\% \text{ means } 33^1/_3 \text{ parts in 100 parts}$$
$$\text{or } 1 : 3 \text{ ratio}$$

5 How much water would you add to a pint of pure alcohol to make it an 80% solution?

$$500 \text{ ml. drug : X ml.}$$
$$\text{finished solution :: } 80 : 100$$
$$80 \text{ X} = 50,000$$
$$\text{X} = 625$$
$$500 \text{ ml. drug : } 625 \text{ ml.}$$
$$\text{finished solution :: } 80 : 100$$
$$625 \text{ ml.} - 500 \text{ ml.} = 125 \text{ ml. of water}$$

Since the alcohol is a liquid, to determine the amount of water needed the liquid drug must be subtracted from the finished solution.

6 How much potassium permanganate solution 1:100 could you make from fifteen 5-gr. tablets?

Since it is convenient and customary to measure solutions of this type in milliliters, it will be necessary to convert the known available drug to grams.
Entry from Table 5-5, p. 46.

$$1 \text{ Gm.} = 15 \text{ gr.}$$
$$15 \times 5 \text{ gr.} = 75 \text{ gr.}$$
$$5 \times 1 \text{ Gm.} = 15 \text{ gr.} \times 5$$
$$5 \text{ Gm.} = 75 \text{ gr.}$$

Amount of drug : finished solution ::
% : 100 (or ratio of strength)
5 (Gm.) : X (ml.) :: 1 : 100
X = 500; therefore 500 ml.
of finished solution

Exercises

Solutions from pure drugs

1 How much salt would be required to make the following?
  a. 1 gallon of a 0.9% solution
  b. 250 ml. of a 1% solution
  c. O ss of a $\frac{1}{2}$% solution
  d. 1 liter of 1:20 solution
2 How much drug would be required to make up the following?
  a. 4 fluidounces of a 2% Lysol solution
  b. 1000 ml. of a 4% vinegar solution
  c. 2 liters of $\frac{1}{5}$% soda bicarbonate solution
  d. 1 liter of 5% glucose solution
3 Express the strength of the following in percent:
  a. 200 ml. of solution containing gr. xv of mercuric cyanide
  b. 1 pint of solution containing 50 ml. of glycerin
  c. 1000 ml. of solution containing 4 fluidounces of alcohol
  d. 500 ml. of alcohol added to a liter of water

4 Express the strength of the following in ratio:
  a. 500 ml. of solution containing 20 Gm. of boric acid
  b. 4 fluidounces of solution containing 60 gr. of a drug
  c. 120 ml. of solution containing $1\frac{1}{2}$ fluidrams of a drug
  d. O ss containing 1 ounce of a drug
5 How many tablets would you need for each of the following?
  a. 1 liter of 1:1000 mercuric cyanide, using gr. $7\frac{1}{2}$ tablets
  b. 2 quarts of 1:100 potassium permanganate solution using gr. 5 tablets
  c. 1 fluidounce of 2% ammonium chloride solution, using gr. 3 tablets
  d. 1 gallon of bichloride of mercury 1:5000, using 0.5-Gm. tablets
6 How much water would be required:
  a. to prepare a $\frac{1}{2}$% solution from gr. x of soda bicarbonate
  b. to prepare a 40% solution from 200 ml. of pure alcohol
  c. to prepare a 1:10 solution from f3 iii of glycerin
  d. to prepare a 2% solution from 1 level teaspoon of soda bicarbonate

Solutions from stock solutions. Stock solutions are relatively concentrated solutions that are kept on hand and from which weaker solutions can be made. The problem is always how much stock solution of a given strength is needed to make a certain amount of solution of a lesser strength. The rule is much the same as the one used in the previous lesson. *The amount of drug (stock solution) : the finished solution :: the ratio of strength of the two solutions (lesser to the greater)*

The following are some examples:

1 How would you prepare a quart of a 2% solution of formaldehyde from a stock solution labeled 40%?

$$\text{X (ml. of stock sol.) : } 1000 \text{ (ml.) ::}$$
$$2 \text{ (%) : } 40 \text{ (%)}$$
$$40 \text{ X} = 2000$$
$$\text{X} = 50$$

50 ml. of stock solution : 1000 ml. finished
solution :: 2% : 40%

Fifty milliliters of stock solution would be measured in a graduated container and to this amount would be added 950 ml. of water.

2 How would you prepare 2 liters of a 1:2000 potassium permanganate solution from a 1% stock solution?

In this case, the strength of the stock solution is expressed in percent and the strength of the solution to be made is in terms of a ratio. In order to be able to compare the strengths, both must be ratios or both must be in percentage.

$$X \text{ (ml. of stock sol.)} : 2000 \text{ (ml.)} ::$$
$$^1/_{20} \, (\%) : 1 \, (\%)$$
$$X = 100 \text{ ml. of stock solution}$$

The balance of the 2 liters would be water (1900 ml. water).

Exercises

Solutions from stock solutions

1 How much of a 5% solution would be needed to prepare 1 L. of a 2% solution?
2 How much of a 1:5 solution would be needed to prepare 1 pint of a 10% solution?
3 How much water would be needed to prepare 1 gallon of a 3% solution from a 10% solution?
4 How many milliliters of a 20% stock solution would be needed to prepare f℥ ii of a 4% solution?
5 How much water should be added to 50 ml. of a 10% solution to make it a 1:20 solution?
6 How much of a 1:5 stock solution would be needed to prepare 1 gallon of a 1:20 solution?
7 How much of a 25% stock solution would be needed to prepare 10 fluidounces of a 1:25 solution?
8 How much of a $^1/_2$% solution would be needed to make 20 minims of a $^1/_5$% solution?
9 How much stock solution 1:10 would be needed to prepare f℥ ivss of a 1:80 solution?
10 How many milliliters would be needed to prepare 5 fluidrams of a 15% solution from a 1:4 solution?
11 How many fluidounces of a 5% glucose solution could be prepared from 2 fluidrams of a 1:4 solution?
12 How many minims of a 1% solution would be needed to prepare f℥ ss of a $^1/_{10}$% solution?
13 How much of a 1:2000 solution would be needed to prepare 1 gallon of a 1:10,000 solution?
14 How much of a 12% solution could be made from a fluidounce of a 20% solution?
15 How much stock solution 1:3 would be needed to prepare f℥ v of a 1:5 solution?

Doses from stock solutions. In some hospitals, drugs for parenteral use are kept in solutions of various strengths. The strength is expressed either by percentage or as the number of minims that contain a certain dose, as ℳ x = gr. $^1/_8$. The problem for the nurse is to determine how many minims or milliliters of the

stock solution contain the dose she is required to give:

1 How would you give morphine sulfate gr. $^1/_4$ from a stock solution labeled "ℳ 15 contains gr. $^1/_6$"? One half of the proportion describes the relationship between the drug and the solution as it is stated on the label; the other half indicates the relationship between the desired amount of drug and the solution.

$$\text{gr. } ^1/_6 : 15 \text{ minims} :: \text{gr. } ^1/_4 \text{ (desired}$$
$$\text{dosage)} : X \text{ minims}$$
$$^1/_6 \, X = 3^3/_4$$
$$X = 22^1/_2$$
$$\text{gr. } ^1/_6 : 15 \text{ minims} :: \text{gr. } ^1/_4 \text{ (desired}$$
$$\text{dosage)} : 22^1/_2 \text{ minims}$$

If the nurse is expected to determine the amount in milliliters (or cubic centimeters), the equation would read:

$$15 \text{ (mg.)} : X \text{ ml.} :: 10 \text{ (mg.)} : 1 \text{ (ml.)}$$
$$10 \, X = 15$$
$$X = 1.5$$

2 How would you give atropine sulfate gr. $^1/_{300}$ from a solution containing gr. $^1/_{150}$ per ml.?

$$\text{gr. } ^1/_{150} : ℳ \, 15 : \text{gr. } ^1/_{300} : X \, (ℳ)$$
$$^1/_{150} \, X = ^1/_{20}$$
$$X = ℳ \, 7^1/_2$$

Exercises

Doses from stock solutions

1 If the bottle of morphine sulfate is labeled 15 mg. = 1 ml., how would you give the following (how many milliliters or what part of a milliliter would you need to give)?
  a. gr. $^1/_6$ **c.** gr. $^1/_{12}$
  b. gr. $^1/_8$ **d.** gr. $^1/_4$
2 If the solution of Demerol Hydrochloride is labeled 50 mg. = 1 ml., how many milliliters would be required to give the following?
  a. 100 mg.   **c.** gr. ss
  b. gr. i   **d.** 37.5 mg.
3 If the solution of codeine phosphate is labeled gr. i = 1 ml., how many minims would be required to give the following?
  a. 0.03 Gm.   **c.** 60 mg.
  b. 0.015 Gm.   **d.** 8 mg.
4 If a solution of atropine sulfate is labeled gr. $^1/_{150}$ = 1 ml., how many milliliters or what part of a milliliter would be needed to give the following?
  a. gr. $^1/_{200}$ **c.** gr. $^1/_{100}$
  b. gr. $^1/_{300}$ **d.** gr. $^1/_{75}$

5 How would you obtain gr. $^1/_{200}$ of atropine sulfate from bottle of atropine solution marked 0.5 mg. per ml.?

6 How would you obtain 65 mg. of Phenergan from a stock bottle of solution marked 25 mg./cc. Phenergan?

7 How would you obtain gr. $^1/_4$ of morphine sulfate from a solution labeled 1:50?

8 What amount of solution would be necessary if you wished to give gr. $^1/_{150}$ of atropine sulfate and the bottle of atropine solution is marked 0.3 mg./cc.?

Doses from tablets. Potent drugs such as alkaloids and glycosides usually come in tablets containing definite doses. If the dose that the nurse is called upon to give is not the same as that of the tablet, it is necessary for her to calculate how many tablets or what part of a tablet will contain the required dose.

The drug is found in a solid state called a tablet instead of in solution. For these problems the statement of proportion is adjusted to read:

Amount of drug specified on label : one tablet :: desired amount of drug : tablets required

Example:

The physician orders atropine sulfate gr. $^1/_{300}$ (H), the tablets in the medicine cupboard are labeled gr. $^1/_{150}$.

$$\text{gr. } ^1/_{150} \text{ (drug specified on label) : 1}$$
$$\text{tablet :: gr. } ^1/_{300} : X \text{ tablets}$$
$$^1/_{150} X = ^1/_{300}$$
$$X = ^1/_2$$

gr. $^1/_{150}$: 1 tablet :: gr. $^1/_{300}$: $^1/_2$ tablet

It is important to label the answer of this part of the calculation in terms of a tablet or tablets. But in this instance and in most others in which drugs are given hypodermically, the nurse does not cut the tablet. Since the drug is to be given hypodermically, the tablet gr. $^1/_{150}$ will be dissolved in a suitable number of minims of water and half of the solution will be administered to the patient. The volume of solution given hypodermically is usually between 10 and 20 minims. More than this can make the patient uncomfortable, and less than this increases the margin of error should some of the solution be lost. In this example, 30 would be a good choice of minims in which to dissolve the stock tablet, gr. $^1/_{150}$, because half of 30 minims is 15 minims and the patient will get half of gr. $^1/_{150}$ or gr. $^1/_{300}$. The remaining 15 minims would be discarded.

Exercises

Dosage from tablets

1 How would you calculate and prepare the following doses for hypodermic administration?
   a. atropine sulfate gr. $^1/_{200}$ from tablets gr. $^1/_{100}$
   b. atropine sulfate gr. $^1/_{350}$ from tablets gr. $^1/_{150}$
   c. morphine sulfate gr. $^1/_{16}$ from tablets gr. $^1/_6$
   d. codeine sulfate gr. $^1/_4$ from tablets gr. $^1/_2$

2 How would you calculate and prepare the following for hypodermic administration?
   a. dilaudid hydrochloride gr. $^1/_{60}$ from tablets gr. $^1/_{30}$
   b. morphine sulfate 15 mg. from tablets gr. $^1/_6$
   c. codeine sulfate 60 mg. from tablets gr. $^1/_4$
   d. morphine sulfate 0.01 Gm. from tablets gr. $^1/_8$

3 How would you prepare gr. 3 of a drug from a gr. 5 tablet? How would you expect to administer it?

Exercises

Weights and measures

1 Change to appropriate metric equivalents:
a. f℥ iv	**e.** C ii	**i.** gr. 7½
b. ℥ ii	**f.** lb. 2.2	**j.** f℈ ii
c. ℳ xv	**g.** gr. $^1/_8$	
d. ½ cup	**h.** gr. $^1/_{120}$	

2 Change to appropriate apothecaries' equivalents:
a. 30 Gm.	**e.** 0.2 mg.	**i.** 15 gtt.
b. 0.5 Gm.	**f.** 1 cup	**j.** 500 ml.
c. 1 L.	**g.** 1 T.	
d. 30 mg.	**h.** 1 t.	

3 Change to appropriate household equivalents:
a. 4 Gm.	**e.** f℥i	**i.** O ii
b. 30 ml.	**f.** ℳ xxx	**j.** 1 L.
c. quart 1	**g.** ℥ iv	
d. f℈ i	**h.** gr. LX	

For the following problems, state the rule by which you solve the problem, indicate the equation you use, and label all answers. Additional information may be indicated in some instances.

4 The bottle of streptomycin is labeled 1 Gm. = 2.5 ml. How much solution will contain 350 mg.?

5 How many gr. 7½ tablets of salt would you need to make 2 L. of 1:100 solution?

6 A vial of powdered polymyxin B is labeled 50 mg. or 500,000 units. How would you prepare a solution so that you could administer doses of 300,000 units?

7 How would you prepare a gallon of 1:2000 solution from a stock solution labeled $^1/_{10}$%?

8 If sodium pentothal solution is made by adding 400 ml. of distilled water to 10 Gm. of drug, what is the percentage strength of the solution? The ratio of strength?

9 If 4 fluidrams of drug are added to 4 fluidounces of water, what is the strength of the resulting solution? Express the strength also as a ratio.

10 How much water would you add to a pint of 95% alcohol to make a 70% solution?

11 How much salt (sodium chloride) would be required to make a quart of physiologic saline solution (0.9%)?

12 If you have on hand tablets of morphine gr. $^1/_6$ and the doctor orders gr. $^1/_8$, how would you prepare the dose?

13 The vial of kanamycin is labeled 0.25 Gm./ml. You are to give 15 mg. of drug for each kilogram the patient weighs. The patient weighs 11 lb. How large a dose is required?

14 Change to appropriate metric equivalents:

a. f℥ i	**e.** 2 T.	**i.** $^3/_4$ cup
b. 12 lb.	**f.** gr. $^1/_{600}$	**j.** 1 t.
c. C ss	**g.** gr. x	
d. O ii	**h.** 30 lb.	

15 Change to appropriate apothecaries' equivalents:

a. 250 ml.	**e.** 8.4 Kg.	**i.** 54.5 Kg.
b. 1 mg.	**f.** 300 mg.	**j.** 0.3 Gm.
c. 10 mg.	**g.** 10 gtt.	
d. 30 ml.	**h.** 8 mg.	

16 Change to appropriate household equivalents:

a. 80 ml.	**e.** ♏ xb	**i.** 0.5 L.
b. 45 ml.	**f.** 120 ml.	**j.** O i
c. f℥ iv	**g.** 6 ml.	
d. f℥ vi	**h.** 45 Gm.	

For the following problems, state the rule by which you plan to solve each problem, state the equation, and label all answers.

1 How would you prepare a gallon of 1:2000 solution from a stock solution labeled $^1/_5$%?

2 How would you make 2 L. of 1:2000 solution from tablets containing gr. $7^1/_2$ of drug in each tablet?

3 How much water is needed to make a 70% solution from a pint of pure alcohol?

4 How much soda bicarbonate is needed to make $1^1/_2$ L. of 2% solution?

5 If a physician ordered 2 Gm. of drug to be given in four equally divided doses and the drug is available in 250-mg. capsules, how many capsules would you give per dose?

6 How much water would you add to a pint of 95% alcohol to make a 50% solution?

7 If the container of Demerol Hydrochloride solution reads 50 mg. per milliliter (cubic centimeter), how many minims would be required to give gr. iss?

8 If a bottle of codeine sulfate solution is labeled 60 mg. per milliliter (cubic centimeter), how many minims would you need to give gr. $^1/_4$?

9 How would you prepare 2 quarts of a 2% vinegar douche for a patient?

10 If a fluidounce of glycerin is added to 120 ml. of water, what is the strength of the solution?

11 How would you prepare $1^1/_2$ quarts of a physiologic saline solution to be used for a throat irrigation?

12 How much water is needed to make a $^1/_{10}$% solution from gr. 2 of a drug?

Questions

for study and review

1 Explain how you would prepare 1 L. of a 5% solution from a stock solution labeled 12%.

2 Explain how you would prepare 1 L. of 1:1000 solution of Zephiran Chloride using the 17% concentrate solution.

3 How much water would you need to add to 120 ml. of 17% Zephiran Chloride to obtain a 1:5000 solution?

4 How would you give gr. i of sodium phenobarbital from a tablet containing 0.12 Gm.?

5 A 2-ml. ampule of caffeine with sodium benzoate contains gr. $7^1/_2$ of drug; how much would be necessary to give gr. 5?

6 Explain how you would give morphine sulfate gr. $^1/_{64}$ from tablet gr. $^1/_4$.

7 What is the ratio of strength of a solution in which 10 fluidounces contain 2 drams of drug? What is the percentage strength?

8 How much salt is needed to make 2 quarts of physiologic saline solution?

9 If ♏ xx of solution contain gr. $^1/_4$ of a drug, how much of the solution would you use to give gr. $^1/_6$?

10 How would you prepare 1500 ml. of a 7% solution, using gr. 5 tablets?

11 How would you give atropine gr. $^1/_{200}$ from a bottle marked 0.5 mg. per ml.?

12 If 2 fluidounces of alcohol are added to a liter of water, what is the percentage strength of solution? What part of the total solution is alcohol?

13 How would you prepare a dosage of 0.02 mg. of digoxin to be given intramuscularly to a child, if the ampule of digoxin (Lanoxin) is labeled 0.5 mg. in 2 ml.?

14 If a physician orders 10 mg. of morphine sulfate and the bottle is labeled gr. $^1/_4$ ml., how many minims will you give?

15 How would you prepare 750 ml. of half-strength magnesium and sodium citrate solution (Suby-Albright solution) from full-strength stock solution?

16 How much 1:1000 solution could be made from ten gr. $7^1/_2$ tablets of a drug?

Major channels of administration
Orders for medications
Nursing responsibilities relative to medicines
and their administration

■ Major channels of administration

Route of administration of a given drug is determined by its physical and chemical properties, the site of desired action, and the rapidity of response desired. As a rule, drugs are administered for one of two effects: local, in which the effects are confined to the site of application, or systemic, in which the results are realized after the drug is absorbed into the blood and diffuses into one or more tissues of the body. Some drugs given locally may produce both local and systemic effects if they are partly or entirely absorbed. A drug may be injected into a joint cavity and have little or no effect beyond the tissues of that structure.

Administration for local effect

Application to the skin. Medications are applied to the skin primarily for the following effects:

1 *astringent:* resulting in vasoconstriction, tissue contraction, and decreased secretions and sensitivity, thereby counteracting inflammatory effects
2 *antiseptic* or *bacteriostatic:* to inhibit growth and development of microorganisms
3 *emollient:* for a soothing and softening effect to overcome dryness and hardness
4 *cleansing:* for the removal of dirt, debris, secretions, or crusts

These medications may be applied in the form of a lotion, tincture, ointment or cream, wet dressing, baths, or soaks. Effectiveness of medicinals applied to the skin is limited by the fact that the highly specialized layers of skin resist penetration of foreign substances to protect the internal body environment. However, absorption is increased when the skin is thin or macerated, when there is increased drug concentration, or when there is prolonged contact of the drug with the skin.

Application to mucous membranes. Drugs are well absorbed across mucosal surfaces and therapeutic effects are easily obtained. However, mucous membranes are highly selective in their absorptive action and differ in sensitivity. A drug applied to oral mucosa may be twice as strong as that applied to nasal mucosa, while its strength may be reduced one fourth to one half for delicate membranes of the eye or urethra. Aqueous solutions are quickly absorbed from mucous membrane while oily liquids are not. Oily preparations should not be applied to nasal or respiratory mucosa using sprays or nebulae since the droplets of oil may be carried to terminal portions of the respiratory tract and retained there, causing lipoid pneumonia.

Respiratory mucosa may be medicated by means of inhalation or insufflation. The *inhalation* method utilizes *sprays* or *nebulae*, whereby the drug is sprayed into the throat using a nebulizer, or *aerosols*, whereby a flow of air or oxygen under pressure disperses the drug throughout the respiratory tract. In the *insufflation* method a fine powder is blown or sprayed onto nasal mucosa. Drugs so administered tend to have both a respiratory and a systemic effect. The respiratory mucosa offers an enormous surface of absorbing epithelium. If the drug is volatile and capable of being absorbed and if there is more in the inspired air than in the blood, the drug is instantaneously absorbed. This fact is of significance in situations of emergency. Amyl nitrite, ether, oxygen, and carbon dioxide are examples of volatile and gaseous agents that are given by inhalation.

Drugs in suppository form can be used for their local effects on the mucous membranes of the vagina, urethra, or rectum. Packs and tampons may be impregnated with a drug and placed in a body cavity. They are used particularly in the nose, ears, and vagina. Drugs may also be painted or swabbed on a mucosal surface, instilled, or administered by way of a douche or irrigation.

Administration for systemic effects

Drugs that produce a systemic effect must be absorbed and carried to the cells or tissues capable of responding to them. The channel of administration used depends upon the nature and amount of drug to be given, desired rapidity of effect, and general condition of the patient. Channels selected for systemic effect include the following: oral, sublingual, rectal, and parenteral (injection)—intradermal, subcutaneous, intramuscular, intravenous, intraspinal, and sometimes intracardiac, intrapericardial, and intraosseous.

Oral. The oral channel of administration is the safest, most economical, and most convenient way of giving medicines. Therefore, medications should be given orally unless some distinct advantage is to be gained by giving them another way.

Most drugs are absorbed from the small intestine; a few are absorbed from the stomach and colon.

Following oral administration, drug action has a slower onset and *more prolonged* but *less potent effect* than when drugs are given parenterally. This may result from: (1) *variation in absorption* as a result of drug composition, gastric or intestinal pH and motility, food content, and pathology within the gastrointestinal tract; or (2) *alteration of the drug* resulting from its retention, inactivation, or partial destruction by the liver if the drug traverses the hepatic circulation before entering the general circulation.

Disadvantages of oral administration of certain drugs are: (1) they may have an objectionable odor or taste; (2) they may harm or discolor the teeth; (3) they may irritate the gastric mucosa, causing nausea and vomiting; (4) they may be aspirated by a seriously ill or uncooperative patient; and (5) they may be destroyed by digestive enzymes.

Sublingual. Drugs given sublingually are placed under the patient's tongue, where they must be retained until dissolved and absorbed. The thin epithelium and rich network of capillaries on the underside of the tongue permit both rapid absorption and rapid drug action. In addition, there is greater potency since the drug gains access to the general circulation without traversing the liver or being affected by gastric and intestinal enzymes.

The number of drugs that can be given sublingually is limited. The drug must dissolve readily, and the patient must be able to cooperate; the patient must understand that the drug is not to be swallowed and that he must not take a drink until the drug has been absorbed. Tablets of nitroglycerin are usually administered sublingually.

A drug may be applied against the mucosa of the cheek for *buccal absorption*.

Rectal. Rectal administration can be used advantageously when the stomach is nonretentive, when the medicine has an objectionable taste or odor, or when it can be changed by digestive enzymes. It is a reasonably convenient and safe method of giving drugs when the oral method is unsuitable, as when the patient is unconscious.

Use of this route avoids irritation of the upper gastrointestinal tract and may promote higher bloodstream drug titers because venous blood from the lower part of the rectum does not traverse the liver. The suppository vehicle is far superior to the retention enema. Use of suppositories releases drugs at a slow but steady rate to ensure a protracted effect. One disadvantage of the retention enema is unpredictable retention of the drug; another is that much of the fluid passes above the lower rectum and then is absorbed into the portal circulation. An evacuant enema prior to the administration of the medication is usually advisable. The amount of solution that can be given rectally is usually small.

Parenteral. Parenteral administration of drugs includes all forms of drug injection into body tissues or fluids using a syringe and needle or catheter and flask. Drugs given parenterally must be sterile, readily soluble and absorbable, and nonirritating. Since parenteral administration of drugs can be hazardous, precautions are required: (1) sterile aseptic technique must be used to avoid infection, and (2) accurate drug dosage, proper rate of injection, and proper site

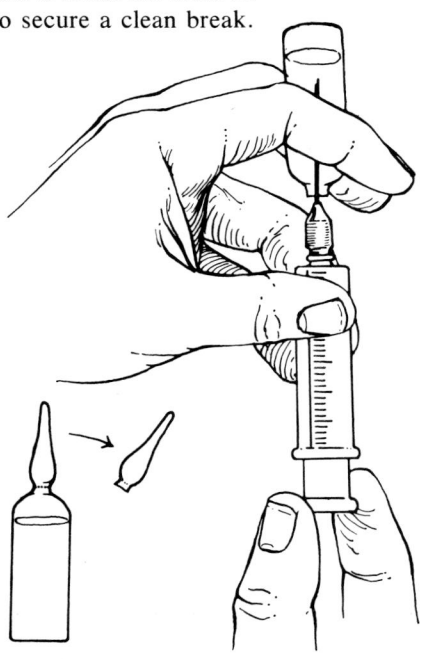

Figure 6-1
Withdrawing medication from an ampule. An ampule may be made like the one in the lower left part of this illustration—it will break easily when pressure is exerted at the constricted portion—or the ampule may be made so that a metal file must be used at the neck to secure a clean break.

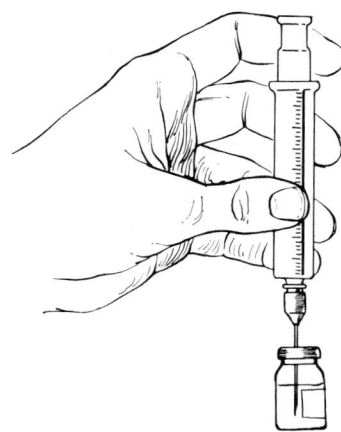

Figure 6-2
Inserting hypodermic needle into a stoppered vial. When a hypodermic needle is inserted into a vial of this type, it is important that air be injected first to facilitate withdrawal of the liquid medication. Note that the plunger has been withdrawn and is supported by the index finger. After the plunger has been pushed down to the end of the barrel, the vial can be turned and held much like the ampule in Figure 6-1. The desired amount is then drawn into the syringe.

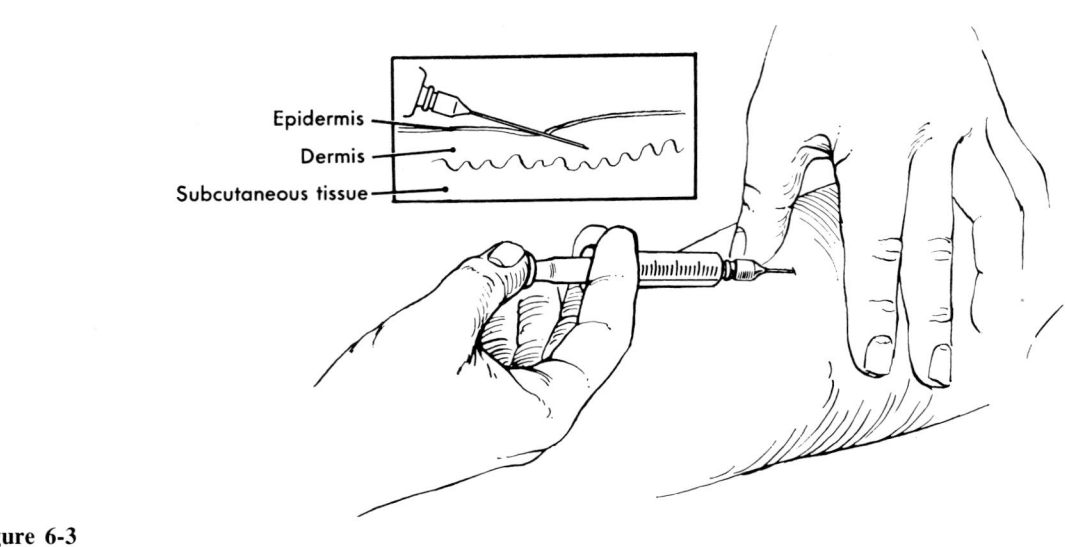

Epidermis
Dermis
Subcutaneous tissue

Figure 6-3
Intradermal injection. Needle penetrates
epidermis into the dermis.

of injection are essential to avoid harm such as
tissue injury and severe or permanent nerve
damage. *An injected drug is irretrievable*, and an
error in dosage or method or site of injection
is not easily corrected.

Given parenterally rather than orally: (1)
onset of drug action is more rapid but of shorter
duration; (2) dosage is often smaller since drug
potency tends not to be altered; and (3) the cost
of drug therapy may be greater. Parenteral administration of drugs requires specialized
knowledge and manual skill to ensure safety and
therapeutic effectiveness. Various methods of
parenteral administration may be performed by
the nurse, but some are done only by a physician.

Intradermal. Intradermal or intracutaneous
injection means that the injection is made into
the upper layers of the skin. The amount of
drug given is small and absorption is slow. This
method is used to advantage when testing for
allergic reactions of the patient. Minute
amounts of the solution to be tested are injected
just under the outer layers of the skin. The me-

dial surface of the forearm and the skin of the
back are the sites frequently used. These injections are best made with a fine, short needle (26
gauge) and a small barrel syringe (such as a tuberculin syringe) (Figure 6-4). A physician is
usually responsible for this procedure.

Subcutaneous. Small amounts of drug in
solution are given subcutaneously (hypodermically) by means of a hypodermic syringe and
needle, usually a fine 25-gauge needle. The needle is inserted through the skin with a quick
movement, but the injection is made slowly and
steadily. The piston of the syringe should be
withdrawn slightly before injecting the drug to
make sure that a blood vessel has not been entered. The angle of insertion should be 45 to 60
degrees and should be made on the outer surface of the upper arm or on the anterior surface
of the thigh. In these locations there are fewer
large blood vessels, and sensation is less keen
than on the medial surfaces of the extremities.
Movement of the part after injection tends to
increase the rate of absorption. Disposable
syringes and needles contribute to accuracy and

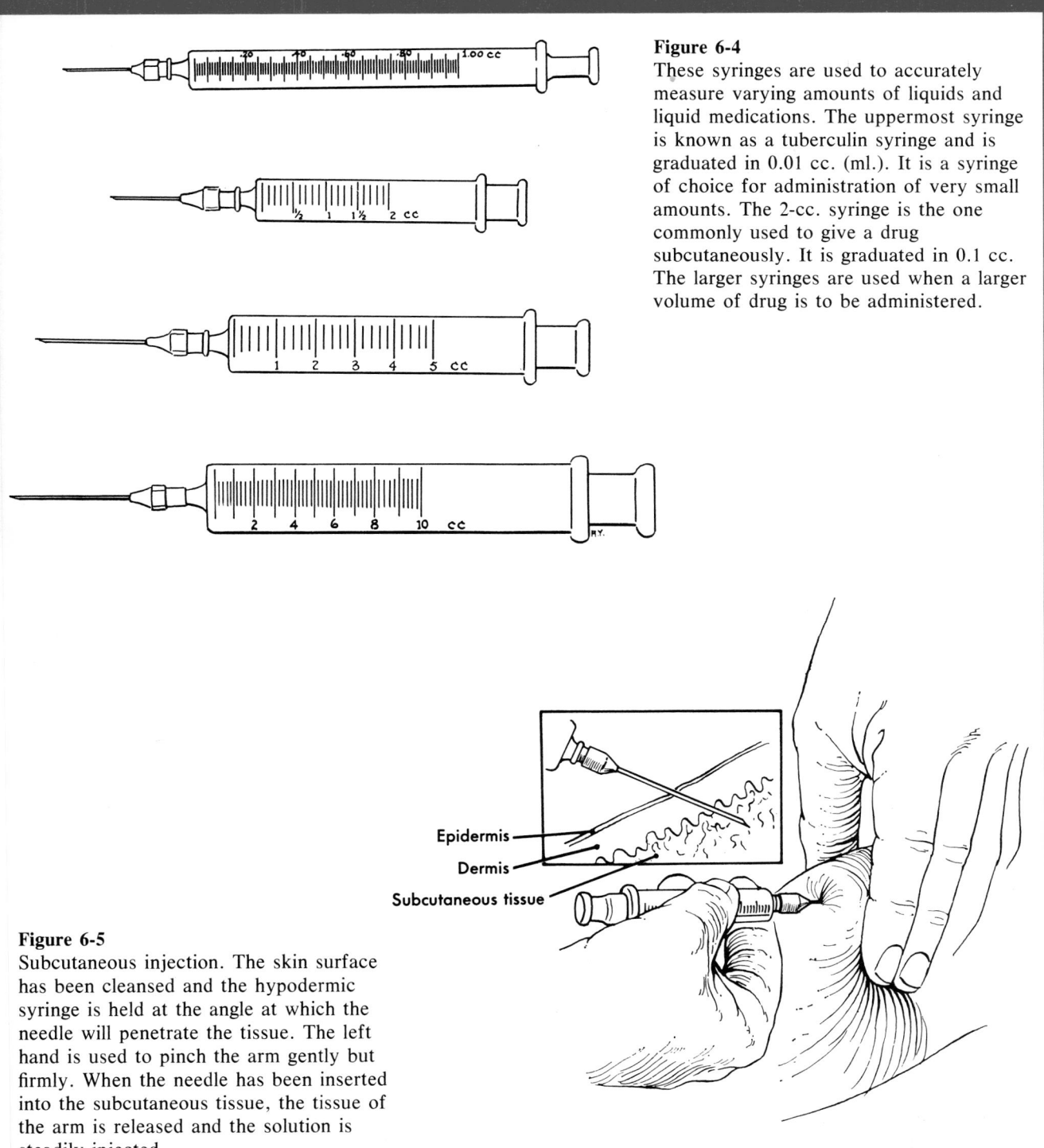

Figure 6-4
These syringes are used to accurately measure varying amounts of liquids and liquid medications. The uppermost syringe is known as a tuberculin syringe and is graduated in 0.01 cc. (ml.). It is a syringe of choice for administration of very small amounts. The 2-cc. syringe is the one commonly used to give a drug subcutaneously. It is graduated in 0.1 cc. The larger syringes are used when a larger volume of drug is to be administered.

Epidermis
Dermis
Subcutaneous tissue

Figure 6-5
Subcutaneous injection. The skin surface has been cleansed and the hypodermic syringe is held at the angle at which the needle will penetrate the tissue. The left hand is used to pinch the arm gently but firmly. When the needle has been inserted into the subcutaneous tissue, the tissue of the arm is released and the solution is steadily injected.

safety of the procedure. Hypodermically inject-ed medicines are limited to the administration of drugs that are highly soluble and nonirritating and to solutions of limited volume (0.5 to 2 ml.).

Irritating drugs given subcutaneously can re-sult in the formation of sterile abscesses and necrotic tissue. Infection can also occur more easily after subcutaneous administration than when drugs are given intravenously. Care should be exercised to avoid contamination. Subcutaneous injections are not satisfactory in individuals with sluggish peripheral circulation.

The introduction of large amounts of solution (500 to 1000 ml. in adults) into subcutaneous tis-sues is known as *hypodermoclysis.* Isotonic solutions of sodium chloride or glucose are ad-ministered this way. The needle is longer than that used for a hypodermic injection and it is inserted into areas of loose connective tissue such as that under the breasts, in the upper sur-faces of the thighs, and into the subscapular re-gion of the back. Fluids must be given slowly to avoid overdistention of the tissues. Hyal-uronidase is sometimes added to the solution to facilitate the spread and absorption of the fluid by decreasing the viscosity of the ground sub-stance in connective tissues. Some physicians prefer intravenous infusion of fluids to hypoder-moclysis because the amount of absorption is more readily determined.

Intramuscular. Injections are made through the skin and subcutaneous tissue into muscular tissue when prompt absorption is desirable and the drug is too irritating to be given subcuta-neously. Larger doses can be given intramuscu-larly than can be given subcutaneously (1 to 10 ml.). Muscles into which injection can usually be made conveniently are those of the buttock, the lateral side of the thigh, and the deltoid re-gion of the arm. The gluteal muscles are usually thick and well suited to the injection of the larger intramuscular doses. The drug spreads along the muscle fibers and along the fasciae. This affords a large absorbing surface and rela-tively few sensory nerves.

A drug may be given intramuscularly in an aqueous solution, an aqueous suspension, or a solution or suspension of oil. Suspensions form

a depot of drug in the tissue, and slow gradual absorption usually results. Two disadvantages are sometimes encountered when preparations in oil are used: the patient may be sensitive to the oil or the oil may not be absorbed. In the latter case, incision and drainage of the oil may be necessary.

The type of needle used for intramuscular in-jection depends upon the site of the injection, the condition of the tissues, and the nature of the drug to be injected. Needles from 1 to 3 inches in length may be used. The usual gauge is 19 to 22 (the larger the number, the finer the needle). Fine needles can be used for thin solu-tions and heavier needles for suspensions and oils. Needles for injection into the deltoid area should be 1 to 1$^1/_2$ inches in length, the gauge again depending on the material to be injected. The deltoid can readily absorb up to 2 ml. of drug. For many intramuscular injections the preferable site of injection is the buttock. The needle must be long enough to avoid depositing the solution of drug into the subcutaneous or fatty tissue. The depth of insertion depends upon the amount of subcutaneous tissue and will vary with the weight of the patients. The buttock should be divided into four parts and the injection made into the upper outer quad-rant. The crest of the ileum serves as a good landmark and should be palpated to confirm the location of the upper outer quadrant, and then the needle should be inserted straight in, with a firm bold pressure, about 2 to 3 inches below the iliac crest. In this region the muscle is thick and the nerve supply is less profuse than in an area near the middle of the buttock or in the region closer to the rectum. Nurses sometimes make the mistake of giving intramuscular injec-tions too near the rectum or too near the middle of the buttock, where it is possible to cause the patient unnecessary discomfort or actually to in-jure the sciatic nerve and cause paralysis of the lower extremity. To avoid this injury, von Hochstetter has described the V method of lo-cating the ventral gluteal muscle. Using the left hand, the index finger is placed on the right iliac spine of the patient and the middle finger stretched back to form a V with the index

Figure 6-6
Intramuscular injection.

A
Posterior gluteal site. In determining the location of the upper outer quadrant it is important to locate the crest of the ilium above and the inferior gluteal fold below before marking the buttocks into fourths. The **x**'s indicate two of a number of sites that may be used in the upper outer quadrant, although it is well to keep about 2 inches below the iliac crest. An injection near the middle of the buttocks may result in an injury to the sciatic nerve. It is, of course, important to vary the sites of injection, preferably using alternate buttocks. The needle is inserted in with a quick firm movement. After aspirating to make certain the needle is not in a blood vessel, the solution is injected slowly and steadily.

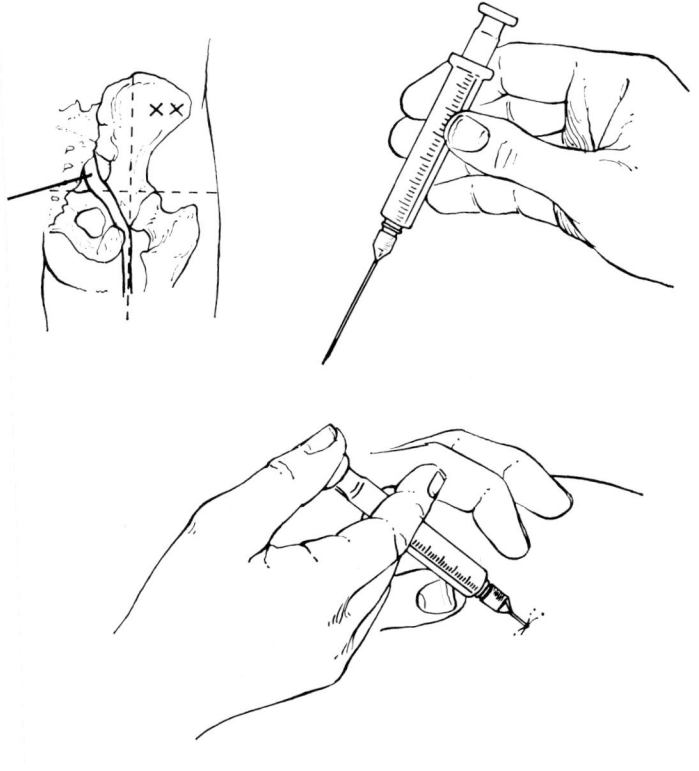

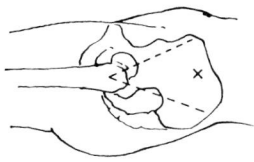

B
Ventrogluteal intramuscular injection site. The **V** fans out from the greater trochanter. The injection site (**x**) is centered at the bottom of the triangle.

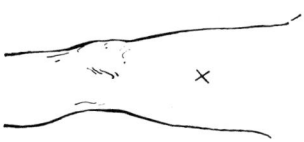

C
Midlateral thigh intramuscular injection site a handsbreadth below the greater trochanter and a handsbreadth above the knee.

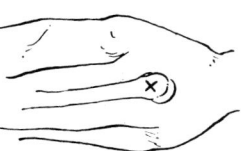

D
Mid-deltoid intramuscular injection site—below the acromion and lateral to the axilla.

finger. The middle finger is slipped to a point just below the crest of the ilium. The palm of the hand rests on the patient's hip. The triangle between the index and middle fingers is the injection site. The positions of the middle and index fingers are reversed in finding the site on the patient's left side. In case the needle is inserted all the way to the hub, it should be withdrawn just enough to have something to grasp should the needle break.

After the needle is inserted the plunger should be slightly withdrawn to make certain that the needle is not in a blood vessel. Although this problem seldom occurs when the injection is made in the sites mentioned, it is not justifiable to take a chance of injecting a drug into a blood vessel when this is not the route of administration selected for the drug. In certain instances injection of oily or particulate medicines or killed bacteria by inadvertent intravenous administration could result in a serious emergency.

When giving an intramuscular injection, it is usually preferable to have the patient in a prone position, with his head turned to one side and with a pillow under the legs just below the knees. He should be instructed to toe inward; this will help to promote relaxation of the gluteal muscles. If this is not a convenient position for the patient to take, he may be placed on his side with the leg flexed at the knee.

To prevent excessive scar formation or tissue irritation, no two injections should be made in the same spot during a course of treatment. When injection is made into the buttocks, it should be given first on one side and then on the other. The technique in which the tissue is pinched between the fingers, rather than spread, may be desirable for patients with very little subcutaneous tissue but is contraindicated for patients who are bruised as a result of repeated injections.

Intravenous. When an immediate effect is desired, or when for any reason the drug cannot be injected into other tissues, or when absorption may be inhibited by poor circulation, it may be given directly into a vein as an *injection* or *infusion*. The technique of this method requires skill and sterile asepsis, and the drug must be highly soluble and capable of withstanding sterilization. This method is of great value in emergencies. The dose and amount of absorption can be determined with accuracy, although the rapidity of absorption and the fact that there is no recall once the drug has been given constitute dangers worthy of consideration. From this standpoint it is one of the least safe methods of administration. Precautions must be taken to prevent extravasation of drug or fluids into surrounding tissue.

Injection. In intravenous injection a comparatively small amount of solution (also referred to as a *bolus*) is given by means of a syringe. The drug is dissolved in a suitable amount of normal (physiologic) saline solution or some other isotonic solution. The injection is usually made into the median basilic or median cephalic vein at the bend of the elbow (Figure 6-7). However, any accessible vein may be used. Factors that determine the choice of a vein are related to the thickness of the skin over the vein, the closeness of the vein to the surface, and the presence of a firm support (bone) under the vein. The veins in the antecubital fossa, though readily accessible, are uncomfortable sites for the patient requiring long-term intravenous therapy. For this reason they are frequently reserved for obtaining samples of blood. A vein that is normally distended with blood is much easier to enter than a partially collapsed vein. If a vein of the arm has been chosen, a tourniquet is drawn tightly around the middle of the arm to distend the vein, the air is expelled from the syringe, and the needle should be introduced quickly and forcefully pointing upward toward the heart. A few drops of blood aspirated into the syringe indicates the needle is in the vein; the tourniquet is then removed; and the solution is injected very slowly. The needle, syringe, and solution must be sterile, and the hands of the doctor and nurse and the skin of the patient at the point of insertion of the needle must be clean.

Infusion. In intravenous infusion a larger amount of fluid is usually given, varying from 1 to 5 pints, and the method differs somewhat.

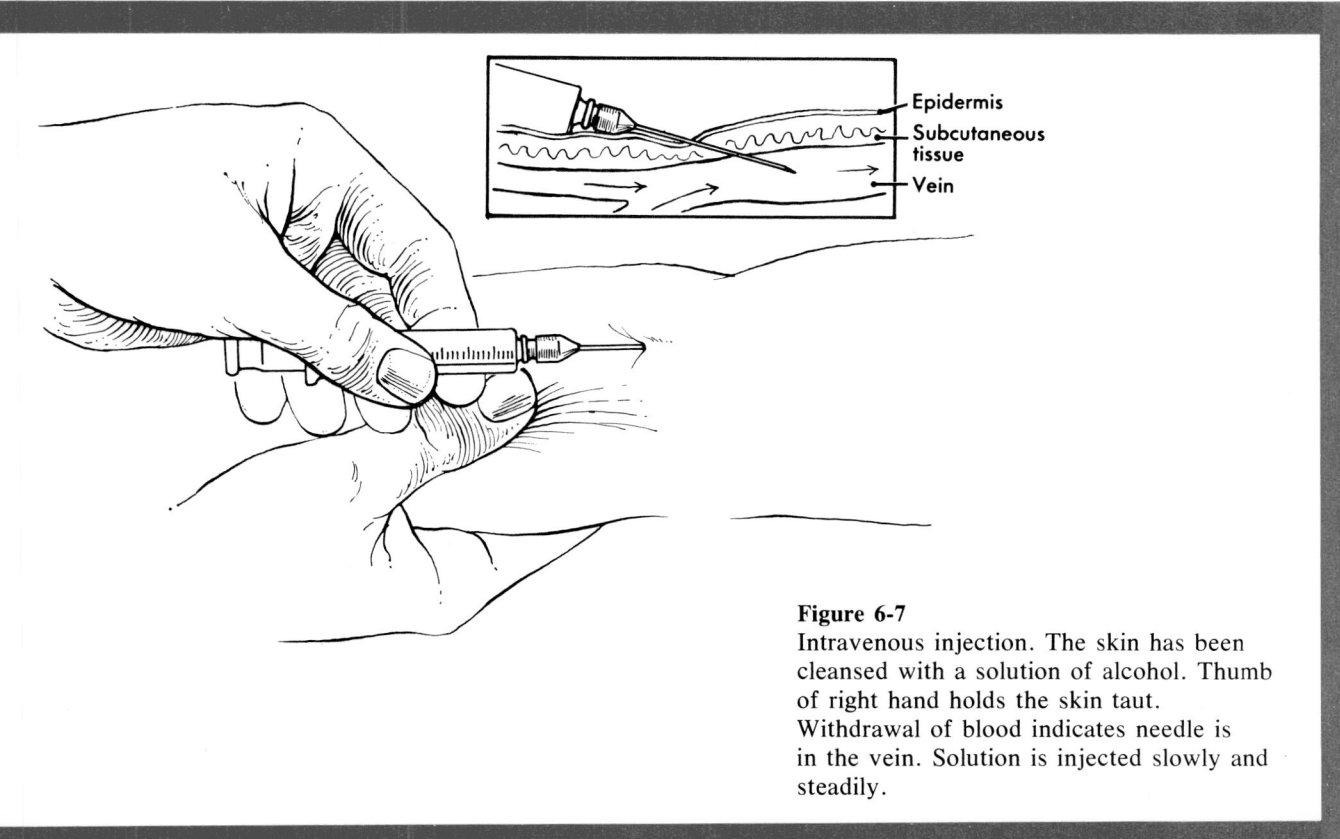

Figure 6-7
Intravenous injection. The skin has been
cleansed with a solution of alcohol. Thumb
of right hand holds the skin taut.
Withdrawal of blood indicates needle is
in the vein. Solution is injected slowly and
steadily.

The solution flows by gravity from a graduated glass flask through tubing, connecting tip, and needle or catheter into a vein.

Infusions are most commonly given to relieve tissue dehydration, to restore depleted blood volume, to dilute toxic substances in the blood and tissue fluids, and to supply electrolytes, drugs, and foods.

During the administration of the intravenous infusion, the patient must remain quiet to prevent the displacement of the needle. The fluid is usually given slowly to prevent reaction or fluid overload, which may impair cardiac and pulmonary function. Ordinarily 3 to 4 hours are required for every 1000 ml. of fluid, depending on the condition of the patient, the nature of the solution, and the reasons for giving it. For children the rate will be slower and is determined by age; weight, and urinary output.

Sodium chloride (0.9%) solution, commonly known as physiologic or isotonic salt solution, is the fluid of choice for intravenous infusion to relieve dehydration not complicated by acidosis.

Five percent dextrose solution is frequently administered and is of value because it provides a means of administering water and a sugar, which is a food. A concentration of 5.5% is approximately isotonic with normal body fluids. Dextrose in physiologic saline solution is sometimes given.

A special gelatin solution may be given intravenously as an infusion colloid to support blood volume in the management of various types of shock.

A number of commercial solutions are used in intravenous replacement therapy. Some contain not only salts of sodium and potassium but also salts of calcium and magnesium. Vitamins

63

are also added to intravenous fluids when their need is indicated.

Whole blood and blood plasma are likewise given intravenously to restore depleted blood volume as well as constituents of the blood.

Intraspinal. Intraspinal injection is also known as intrathecal (into a sheath), subdural, subarachnoid, or lumbar injection. The technique is the same as that required for a lumbar puncture. Nurses do not administer drugs intraspinally.

In addition, drugs are occasionally administered by intracardiac, intrapericardial, and intraosseous injections; however, nurses do not administer drugs by these routes.

■ Orders for medications

The procedure used for ordering medicines for a patient depends on whether the patient is in the hospital, in his home, in the doctor's office, or in some institution other than a hospital. On the ward of the hospital there is usually a book or file in which the physician writes his orders. Sometimes orders are written on the patient's chart. In an emergency there may be no time to write an order and it is given verbally. Sometimes the physician gives an order over the telephone. It is customary for the nurse to write the order that she has been given verbally. She indicates the name of the physician who gave the order and how it was given (in person or by telephone), and the physician later confirms the order by signing his name or initials.

Written orders are a form of protection to everyone concerned with medicines—the patient, physician, pharmacist, and the nurse. They constitute permanent legal records that can be referred to as often as necessary or submitted as evidence in case of litigation. No nurse may modify or in any way alter a physician's order. If she has reason to think that an error has been made, she should ask the physician about it. If inquiry is made courteously, the physician is usually pleased that the nurse is alert and conscientious. If the head nurse is available, she will appreciate being asked regarding an order about which there is question. She may be able to explain something about the order that will clarify matters. *The nurse should not go ahead and give a medicine if she believes there is an error involved.* On the other hand, she may not disregard the order; she is obligated to seek clarification.

Prescriptions

Outside the hospital the physician will write a prescription when he wishes to order a drug. Only persons legally licensed to prescribe—physicians, dentists, and veterinarians—may write prescriptions. Medicines should be labeled by a pharmacist.

A number of medicinal agents may be purchased over the counter without a prescription, but an amendment to the Federal Food, Drug, and Cosmetic Act (as mentioned in Chapter 3) requires that all drugs that can be used safely and effectively only under the supervision of a physician must have a prescription. Such prescriptions can be refilled only if authorization is granted by the prescriber. Authorization may be made in writing by indicating on the written prescription the number of times or the frequency with which the prescription may be refilled, or the physician may authorize the pharmacist by telephone. Sometimes the pharmacist telephones the physician if a patient requests that a prescription be refilled and no previous authorization has been given. Prescriptions for narcotics cannot be refilled; they must be rewritten.

A typical prescription is a written formula given by a physician to a pharmacist for dispensing medicine to a patient. It consists of four parts:

1. The *superscription*, which includes the patient's name, address, the date and the symbol ℞, an abbreviation for "Recipe" meaning "Take thou." The age of an infant or young child should be included to permit the pharmacist to check the correctness of the dose.

2. The *inscription*, which states the name of the drug, dose form, and amount per dose.

3. The *subscription*, which contains the directions to the pharmacist, which are now usually limited to the number of doses to be dispensed.

Superscription	Mr. James Wiley	Age:	Date	7/1/72
	210 Elmwood Pl., Minneapolis, Minn.			
Inscription				
	Ammonium Chloride	15 Gm.		
	Syrup Citric Acid	48 ml.		
	Syrup Glycyrrhiza to make	120 ml.		
Subscription	Mix			
Signature	Sig.: one teaspoonful every 3-4 hours			
		J. B. Tanner, M.D.		
		(address)		

4. The *signature*, which is abbreviated "S." or "Sig." and means "Write on the label." This indicates the directions for the patient who is to take the medicine and should include that the name of the drug be placed on the label. This permits identification of the drug if toxicity occurs or patient changes physicians. Instructions for refilling the prescription should also be included.

The physician's name is also indicated. His name, address, and telephone number are frequently printed on his prescription blanks. If the prescription is for a narcotic or any other drug listed in the Harrison Narcotic Law, the physician's registry number as well as his address must appear on the prescription form. Quantities are expressed in either the apothecaries' or metric system. An example of a prescription is shown above.

The abbreviations in Table 6-1 are used in written orders, prescriptions, and labels on medicines, and it is necessary for the nurse to know what they mean. A difference exists between the abbreviations s.o.s. and p.r.n. The former, when used in connection with medicines, means if necessary and refers to one dose only. The latter means when required, as often as necessary, or according to circumstances. The nurse is expected to use her judgment about repeating the dose. For example, a physician may leave an order for a patient that reads:

For Mrs. Smith, Room 210, elixir terpin hydrate dram i q. 3 h. p.r.n. for cough.
John Doe, M.D.

The order means that the patient may have a dose of cough medicine every 3 hours. However, if the patient is not coughing and has no need for the medicine, the nurse may allow longer intervals to elapse between doses.

"Morphine sulfate 10 mg. q. 4 h. p.r.n." means that the dose of morphine sulfate may be given every 4 hours if the patient has need of it. If the nurse thinks that the patient has no need for it—the patient seems to have no pain, is resting comfortably, is asleep most of the time —she will allow a longer interval than 4 hours to elapse before repeating the dose. If, however, the order reads "Morphine sulfate 10 mg. s.o.s.," the nurse would give one dose of the drug if the patient seemed to need it and then would give no more. If a dose of the drug is to be given immediately, it would read "Morphine sulfate 10 mg. stat."

■ Nursing responsibilities relative to medicines and their administration
Care of medicines

Regulations vary in different hospitals, but, regardless of the place, certain principles of organization should be observed in the care of drugs and associated equipment.

1 All medicines should be kept in a special place, which may be a cupboard, closet, or room. It should not be freely accessible to the public.
2 Narcotic drugs and those dispensed under special legal regulations must be kept in a locked box or compartment.

Table 6-1 Abbreviations for orders, prescriptions, and labels

Abbreviation	Derivation	Meaning	Abbreviation	Derivation	Meaning
a̅a̅	ana	of each	o.h.	omni hora	every hour
a.c.	ante cibum	before meals	o.m.	omni mane	every morning
ad	ad	to, up to	o.n.	omni nocte	every night
ad lib.	ad libitum	freely as desired	os	os	mouth
aq.	aqua	water	oz.	uncia	ounce
aq. dest.	aqua destillata	distilled water	p.c.	post cibum	after meals
b.i.d.	bis in die	two times a day	per	per	through or by
b.i.n.	bis in noctis	two times a night	pil.	pilula	pill
c.	cum	with	p.r.n.	pro re nata	when required
caps.	capsula	capsule	q.h.	quaque hora	every hour
comp.	compositus	compound	q. 2 hr.		every two hours
dil.	dilutus	dilute	q. 3 h.		every three hours
elix.	elixir	elixir	q. 4 h.		every four hours
ext.	extractum	extract	q.i.d.	quater in die	four times a day
fld.	fluidus	fluid	q.s.	quantum sufficit	as much as is required
Ft.	fiat	make	Ŗ	recipe	take thou
Gm.	gramme	gram	s	sine	without
gr.	granum	grain	Sig. or S.	signa	write on label
gtt.	gutta	a drop	s.o.s.	si opus sit	if necessary
h.	hora	hour	sp.	spiritus	spirits
h.s.	hora somni	hour of sleep (bedtime)	ss	semis	a half
M.	misce	mix	stat.	statim	immediately
m.	minimum	a minim	syr.	syrupus	syrup
mist.	mistura	mixture	t.i.d.	ter in die	three times a day
non rep.	non repetatur	not to be repeated	t.i.n.	ter in nocte	three times a night
noct.	nocte	in the night	tr. or tinct.	tinctura	tincture
O	octarius	pint	ung.	unguentum	ointment
ol.	oleum	oil	vin.	vini	wine
o.d.	omni die	every day			

3 In some hospitals each patient's medicines are kept in a designated place on a shelf or compartment of the medicine cupboard or room. Such an arrangement means that the nurse must be careful to keep the patient's medicines in the right area and to make certain that when he leaves the hospital his medicines are returned to the pharmacy, unless he is taking them with him. Many hospitals require that medicines be returned to the pharmacy for relabeling if they are to be taken home at the time of dismissal. It is imperative that the medicines have the patient's full name on the label of the container. In some hospitals the medicines are dispensed wholly or in part from a stock supply kept on the ward. Misplaced medicines and equipment can contribute to errors in administration.

4 If stock supplies are maintained they should be arranged in an orderly manner. Preparations for internal use should be kept separate from those used externally.

5 Some preparations, such as serums, vaccines, certain suppositories, certain antibiotics, and insulin, need to be kept in a refrigerator.

6 Labels of all medicines should be clean and legible. If they are not, they should be sent to the pharmacist for relabeling. *Nurses should not label or relabel medicines.*

7 Bottles of medicines should always be stoppered.

The administration of medicines

Experience has demonstrated that it is wise to abide by established policies and regulations pertaining to the administration of medicines. Such regulations vary from hospital to hospital, but principles of safety do not vary appreciably. They have been established to protect patients and to save nurses from the traumatizing effects of errors that other nurses have had the misfortune to experience. This does not mean that deviation from the rule or regulation under special circumstances is always bad judgment. The nurse must consider the situation carefully before departing from established policy. If possible she should consult with a more experienced person, such as her instructor or the nurse in charge. Policies and regulations are protective guides to live by, not to be followed so blindly that thinking and good sense do not enter into the making of decisions. Safety regulations are effective only when they are understood and readily interpreted by the nursing staff as being necessary for the patient's protection. The following are policies or regulations that have been found to be sound relative to the administration of medicines. They are not listed in order of importance.

1 When preparing or giving medicines, concentrate your whole attention on what you are doing. Do not permit yourself to be distracted while working with medicines.
2 Make certain that you have a written order for every medication for which you assume the responsibility of administration. (Verbal orders should be written out as soon as possible.)
3 Develop the habit of reading the label of the medicine carefully before removing the dose from the container.
4 Make certain that the data on the medicine card corresponds exactly with the doctor's written order and with the label on the patient's medicine. A medicine card should accompany each medicine (Figure 6-9). Sometimes skipping a dose of medicine may be as dangerous as an overdose. It is important that for every drug listed in the Kardex there be a corresponding medicine card.
5 Never give a medicine from an unlabeled container or from one on which the label is not legible.
6 Do not administer medicines that have been prepared by some other person unless that person is a clinical pharmacist.

Figure 6-8
Read the label carefully.

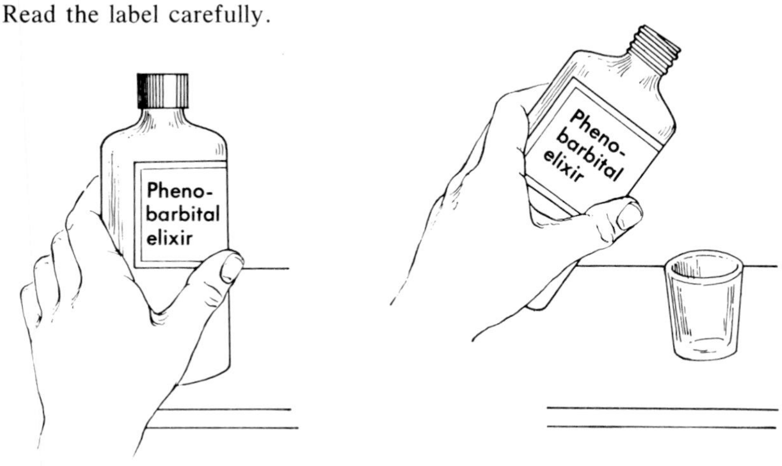

1
As the medicine is taken from the shelf

2
Before pouring the medicine

3
As the medicine is replaced on the shelf

Mrs. Melvin Nigon
(Name)
2 - 190
(Room no.)

Digitoxin

0.2 mg. bi d.

(orally)

8 ⁻

4 ⁻

.

Count Pulse

Michael Morris
(Name)
3-160
(Room no.)

Compazine

Syrup

ʒ ī   T.i.d.

8 ⁻

1 ⁻

5 ⁻

Figure 6-9
Samples of medicine cards used to
accompany medications. Cards should bear
the following information: name and room
of patient; name of medicine; dosage; time
of administration; route of administration if
there is any question about how it might
be given; and special precautions.

Figure 6-10
Two medicine trays with cards.
The small tray at the left may
be used for a number of
patients, as in a double room
or a small ward. Souffle cups
instead of medicine glasses
may be used for capsules or
tablets. The large tray is
arranged for the administration
of medications to a group of
patients.

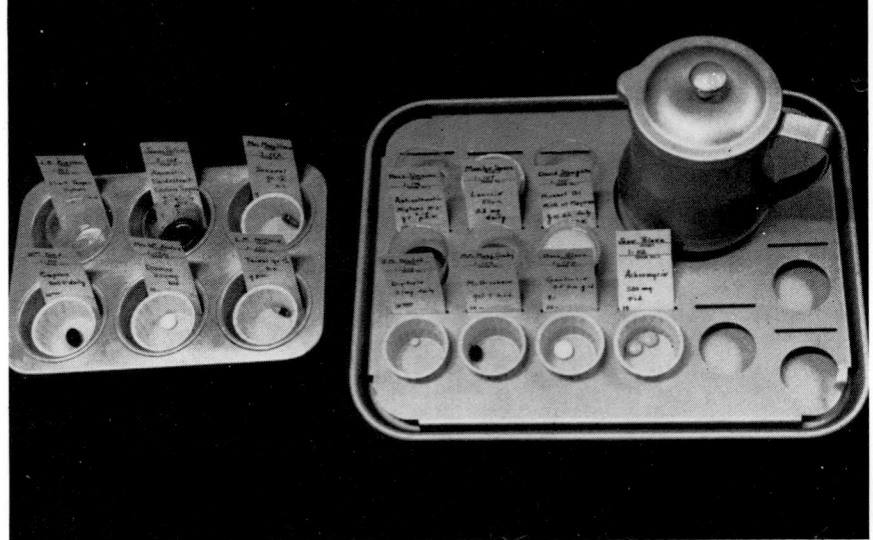

7 If you must in some way calculate the dosage for a patient from the preparation on hand and you are uncertain of your calculation, verify your work by checking with some responsible person—an instructor, nurse in charge, or pharmacist.

8 Measure quantities as ordered, using the proper apparatus, graduated containers for milliliters, fluidounces, or fluidrams, minim glasses, or calibrated pipets for minims and droppers for drops. When measuring liquids, hold the container so that the line indicating the desired quantity is on a level with the eye. The quantity is read when the lowest part of the concave surface of the fluid is on this line (Figure 6-11).

9 Even though you have cared for a particular patient all morning or for several days, you should have developed the habit of checking his identification each time you give him a medication. If the patient wears an identification band, the name on it must correspond with the name on the medicine card. The problem of identification presents an even greater haz-

ard to the nurse who is responsible for the administration of medications to a group of patients, perhaps an entire unit. For this nurse a 10:00 A.M. injection may be her initial or only contact with the patient. It is important that each patient be called by name. If there is the least doubt of his identity, ask him to state his name. Patients have been known to answer to names other than their own, but they are not likely to give the wrong name when asked to speak it.

10 Remain with the patient until the medicine has been taken. Most patients are very cooperative about taking medicines at the time that the nurse brings them. However, sometimes patients are more ill than they appear and have been known to hoard medicines until they had accumulated a lethal amount and then have taken the entire amount, with fatal results.

11 Never return an unused dose of medicine to a stock bottle.

12 Never chart a medicine as having been given until it has been administered. Sometimes it may be necessary to check the chart before

Figure 6-11
When pouring liquid medicine, the thumbnail is placed at the mark on the medicine glass and the medicine is poured on a level with the eye. The bottle should be held so that the medication is not poured over the label.

giving the medication. All medications are recorded, but the manner of recording may vary from hospital to hospital. The name of the drug, the dosage, the time of administration, and the channel of administration as well as the patient's reaction to the medication should be recorded.

Additional suggestions relative to the giving of medicines. The following suggestions constitute habits of thought and behavior developed by experienced professional nurses that the nursing student will also be expected to develop.

1 Dosage forms such as tablets, capsules, and pills should be handled in such a way that the fingers will not come in contact with the medicine. Use the cap of the container or a clean medicine card to guide or lift the medicine into the medicine glass or container you will be taking to the bedside of the patient.

2 When pouring liquid medicines, hold the bottle so that the liquid does not run over the side and obscure the label. Wipe the rim of the bottle with a clean piece of paper tissue before replacing the stopper or cover.

3 Assist weak or helpless patients in taking their medications.

4 Most liquid medicines should be diluted with water or other liquid. This is especially desirable when medicines have a bad taste. Exceptions to this rule include oils and cough medicines that are given for a local effect in the throat. The patient should be supplied with an ample amount of fresh water after swallowing solid dosage forms, such as tablets or capsules, unless for some reason the patient is allowed only limited amounts of fluid.

5 Medicine glasses should be thoroughly washed with hot soapy water and scalded with hot water. Glasses used for oils should be washed separately. Disposable medicine containers provide a more sanitary means of dispensing medicines.

6 The nurse should avoid waste of medicines. Medicines tend to be expensive; in some instances a single capsule may cost the patient several dollars. Dropping medicine on the floor is one way of wasting it.

7 If a patient expresses doubt or concern about a medication or the dosage of a medication, the nurse should do everything possible to make certain that no mistake has occurred. Occa-sionally, the patient may be right. The nurse should reassure the patient as well as herself by rechecking to make certain that there is no error. She may need to recheck the order, the label on the medicine container, or the patient's chart.

8 Do not leave a tray of medicines unattended. If you are in a patient's room and must leave, take the tray of medicines with you.

9 As a rule nurses should not prepare mixtures of drugs. They should be prepared by the pharmacist.

Nurse's approach. The reaction of a patient to medicine may be an expression of fear, frustration, or hostility. The nurse who has been caring for a patient can appreciate the many incidents that may disturb him. A physician calls upon a patient to discuss the possibility of serious surgery that will benefit the patient. The proposition leaves the patient rather shaken. He also knows that sometime during the day he must make financial arrangements for continued hospitalization. The nurse who understands this patient is not content to simply chart on her notes that the patient refused his 10:00 A.M. medication. She may encourage him to talk about the things that are concerning him so deeply and thus make him feel that she is able to accept his reaction, whatever it may be. The nurse who realizes that a particular medication is an essential part of the patient's care will provide him with other opportunities to refuse less essential care. Recognition of the patient's right to express feelings can lead to greater security for the patient and deeper insight for the nurse.

The medicine containers from which the patient is served his medicine should be scrupulously clean, and the water supplied immediately after the medicine should be fresh and cold. Carelessly prepared medicines and lack of consideration in the way a medicine is handed to a patient can disgust him in the same way that poor food, cracked dishes, and inefficient service affect him in a restaurant.

When giving a medicine with an unpleasant taste it is better to admit that it is unpleasant and thereby agree with the patient than to make him feel that his reaction is grossly exaggerated or silly. The nurse can attempt to improve the taste by diluting the medicine (if possible) or by offering chewing gum or a Life Saver immediately after the medicine.

Administration of medicines on the psychiatric ward

The giving of medicines on a psychiatric unit automatically assumes symbolic meanings present in lesser degree on any hospital ward. All individuals need and seek meaningful interpersonal relationships; most individuals find such relationships outside medical situations. Psychiatric patients, however, are often starved for affection and yearn for some person to whom they may look for security and interest. Frequently, their emotional deprivation is concealed by an appearance of hostility or disdain.

In addition, the immediate personal needs of the patient and the current symptoms against which the patient is fighting must be considered. Overwhelming anxiety, depression to the point of suicide, pain of an uncanny nature, or distortions of thought that constantly separate the patient from his fellow men demand of the nurse much care in any contact, particularly that of medication. To the patient in a state of psychologic disequilibrium, that which is taken by mouth or given by injection may hold threats and symbolic meanings rarely felt by the medical or surgical patient. The fear of poisons or supernatural effects of capsules or the suggestions of witchcraft inherent in a needle often reaches the degree of catastrophe unless the nurse is able to interrelate her action and the thought processes of the patient. The psychiatric patient's tendency toward impulsiveness and his high titer of emotional sensitivity must constantly be kept in mind.

No practical suggestions can ever take the place of the techniques practiced by the psychiatrically oriented nurse, but the following factors should be considered in the general handling of medications for the psychiatric patient:

1 Drugs used in emergencies must be anticipated and such drugs must be made available.
2 Medicines should be given in paper, not glass, containers. The psychiatric patient is often so impulsive that all possible precautions must be taken to avoid accidents, and glass is always a potential weapon for suicide.
3 Precautions should be used whenever drugs are administered.
4 *The nurse must remain with the patient until oral medications have been swallowed.* This principle is basic in the giving of all medications but one of particular importance to the depressed and suicidal patient; such patients may conceal capsules in the mouth for long periods, only to hoard them until a lethal supply has been accumulated. Frequently, measures such as the piercing of the capsule case and staying with the patient until the drug is dissolved or the practice of using liquid preparations will enforce the actual ingestion of the drug.
5 It is often necessary not only to urge the psychiatric patient to take medication but also to insist upon its acceptance. The psychiatric patient is frequently an indecisive, emotionally confused individual who tends to doubt everything. He often presses the nurse for detailed information about the drug prescribed and frequently rebels because of minor discrepancies in information. Paradoxically, however, he complies quickly if a positive yet interested attitude is presented without undue explanation.
6 It is of utmost importance to report all drug refusals to the physician in charge. But in the meantime it is frequently also of importance to persuade the patient to take the medicine. Omission of doses may cause the blood level of psychotropic drugs to be lowered so that larger doses than usual may eventually be needed. Intramuscular administration of psychotropic drugs assists in calming the patient within a relatively short period of time, so that oral preparations may then be given. The oral route of administration is preferred and should be instituted as soon as possible.

Changes in drug administration

One of the major changes that will undoubtedly occur (which will affect all hospitals, patients, hospital pharmacists, and nurses) will be safer and more expedient methods of drug distribution to hospitalized patients. While numerous improvements in patient care have taken place (such as monitoring equipment, electric beds, piped-in oxygen, and specialized units) little progress has been made in improving the methods by which drugs are distributed to hospitalized patients. In most hospitals nurses still transcribe drug orders, make out medicine cards, keep a Kardex containing the patient's medicine orders, and count, pour, and request medicines from the pharmacy. In one study it was found that in more than 300 hospitals located throughout the United States, 89% of all drug orders were still being written on the patients' charts in the nurses' station and that 60% of the time nurses assumed major responsibility for transcribing all drug orders and requisitioning medicines from the pharmacy. There is no doubt that most methods of drug ordering and drug distribution in the hospital now in use are serious usurpers of the nurses' valuable time.

Unit dose package. A number of hospitals are slowly converting to unit dose packages, and it is safe to predict that in the future the use of unit dose packages will be commonplace in all hospitals. A unit dose package contains the ordered amount of a drug for a single administration in the proper form for administration by the prescribed route. All unit dose packages are labeled with the drug's generic name, trade name, strength of dose, warning terms or precautions, expiration date (if this is appropriate), and recommendations for storing (such as the need to store in a cool place or away from direct light). Tablets, capsules, and liquids can be prepared in single unit packages.

Disadvantages of using unit dose packages are primarily those of space for storage and increased cost. In addition, it is practical at this time for pharmaceutical companies to manufacture unit dose packages or single unit packages for only the most widely and commonly used drugs. It has been estimated that 30% to 50% of all drugs commonly used are available in single unit packages. However, small and inexpensive single unit package machines are available for purchase that permit hospital pharmacists to make up unit dose packages from their own stock supplies for medications ordered for patients in their hospital.

The advantages of using unit dose packages far outweigh their disadvantages. The most important advantage is medication safety and a decrease in error, since drug computations are eliminated. The drug is already properly labeled and the nurse does not have to pour the drug. All she needs to do is deliver the package to the patient where it is opened at the bedside and administered. This permits the patient to check on his own drug and be assured of proper medication and dosage, particularly when the drugs are distributed by nonprofessional personnel. Packaging also decreases chance of deterioration and permits giving financial credit to the patient for drugs not used. Often because of fear of contamination, bottles of unused drugs must be discarded and not relabeled for any other patient. Because of this the patient for whom the drug was originally ordered does not get financial credit for drugs he did not receive.

Strip packages permit ease of narcotic counting since all packages in the strip are numbered and only the number needs to be checked. This also prevents contamination caused by pouring narcotic tablets into the hands for ease of counting.

Prefilled disposable syringes. Prefilled disposable syringes for all medications to be given subcutaneously, intramuscularly, and even intravenously will be commonplace in all hospitals. Advantages of prefilled and disposable syringes are the following:

1 Accuracy of dosage
2 Sterile product
3 Sharp needle
4 Elimination of suspected source of serum hepatitis
5 Less danger of allergic sensitization of personnel handling the drugs
6 Immediate availability of drug for use
7 Charge only for medicine used
8 Reduced likelihood of pilferage of narcotics
9 Less waste by breakage or incomplete use
10 Safer use of practical nurses permitted to administer subcutaneous or intramuscular drugs

Clinical pharmacists. In the future there will also be more extensive use of the newly emerging clinical pharmacist and around-the-clock pharmacy service with professional pharmacists. Clinical pharmacists will be stationed in nursing areas to work closely with physicians, nurses, and dietitians. They will be drug clinicians and will hold pharmacology conferences to discuss not only drug action but whether or not a particular drug is compatible with other drugs and foods the patient is receiving. In addition these clinical pharmacists will:

1 Obtain a drug history on all patients, including what medicines (prescription or nonprescription) the patient took prior to hospitalization
2 Interpret the physician's medication orders to the nurse and to the patient
3 Recommend drug therapy for particular patients to the physician
4 Work with the nurse in observing patients for drug reactions and keep logs or records of suspected reactions to particular drugs
5 Advise patients about the medications they are to take home with them

Since pharmacists are well educated in the compounding, dispensing, and control of drugs, it is only natural they become more involved in drug therapy for the hospitalized patient. They should not be isolated from the clinical areas where much of the actual compounding and dispensing of drugs in the hospital really takes place.

In the future there will also be hospital pharmacies with special "clean rooms" that the pharmacist will enter after donning scrub gown, mask and cap, and sterile gloves. The air in this room will be specially filtered. This sterile atmosphere will be used for compounding various parenteral solutions. The pharmacist will be responsible for putting all additives into intravenous solutions and checking all such solutions for compatibility reactions.

The emergence of clinical pharmacists is long overdue, and nurses will find them to be valuable and irreplaceable members of the health team. In some hospitals clinical pharmacists or clinical pharmacy technicians may actually distribute and administer drugs to patients. It goes almost without saying that whoever is responsible for drug administration is also responsible for being highly knowledgeable about each and every drug administered.

Role of the nurse. What does all this mean for the nurse? Will her role change where drug therapy is concerned? Regardless of the changes that may come about in the ordering, distribution, or administration of drugs, the nurse is still responsible for her patients and their care 24 hours a day. Automation, clinical pharmacists, and unit package doses do not simplify the task of the nurse but serve to increase the complexity of patient care and responsibility of the nurse. As a result of these changes nurses will be better informed about drugs and their reactions. Nurses will still need to make their observations of patients, determine whether p.r.n. orders are to be given, and consult with physicians about withholding, discontinuing, or changing the drug dosage. They will continue to assist the physician and pharmacist in teaching patients about drugs and their effects and help patients plan their drug therapy upon returning home. The nurse will become more involved in taking drug histories and in working more closely with the pharmacist.

Questions

for study and review

1 What are some of the habits that you think would help you to develop safety and accuracy in the administration of drugs?
2 Make a list of precautions that should be observed in a home to prevent accidents in the care and handling of medicines.
3 Write out a plan of instruction for one of your patients who expects to go home and will continue to take several of the medicines that he has been taking while in the hospital. What explanation does the patient need to help him understand what to do, how to do it, and when to do it?
4 How would you interpret the following orders?
Sherry wine ℥ ii t.i.d. a.c.
Nitroglycerin gr. $1/100$ stat. and p.r.n.
Mineral oil and milk of magnesia ℥ ss a̅a̅ b.i.d. and p.r.n.
Phenobarbital gr. ss q.i.d.
5 What advantages does oral administration of drugs have over parenteral administration (subcutaneous, intramuscular, or intravenous)?

6 What is meant by buccal administration of a drug? When is this form of administration used?

7 When are drugs most likely to be administered intravenously?

8 What would you do if one of your patients refuses to take the oral medications prescribed for him by his physicians?

9 What precautions should be taken and what are the responsibilities of the nurse for narcotics stored in the clinical area?

10 What length and gauge of needle are usually recommended for the administration of drugs to adults by the following routes?
  a. intramuscular
  b. subcutaneous
  c. intravenous
  d. intradermal

11 What is meant by the following?
  a. Store in a tight container.
  b. Keep in a cool place.
  c. Do not expose to direct light.
  d. Do not use if solution is cloudy.

12 Write a paper on the predictions for the future in relation to drug administration in hospitals. Information can be obtained from nursing and pharmacy journals.

Objective questions

Select the answer that in your opinion is the one best answer.

13 If a drug is injected into the cavity of a joint where its effect is limited to the tissue of the joint, its action is said to be:
  a. general   **c.** systemic
  b. local   **d.** selective

14 Which of the following channels of administration is likely to afford least dependable absorption?
  a. oral   **c.** intravenous
  b. intraspinal   **d.** rectal

15 Which of the following must be characteristic of a drug if it is to be administered by inhalation?
  a. volatile   **c.** nontoxic
  b. sterile   **d.** water soluble

16 Which of the following routes of administration will afford the most rapid rate of absorption and action?
  a. intramuscular   **c.** rectal suppository
  b. sublingual   **d.** subcutaneous

17 Which of the following routes of administration is least likely to cause a systemic reaction?
  a. rectal suppository
  b. application of ointment to the skin
  c. inhalation
  d. spraying of a drug onto mucous membrane

References

Campbell, E.: A nurse analyzes unit dose dispensing, Amer. Prof. Pharmacist **33**:43, 1967.

Capps, R. B.: A syringe-transmitted epidemic of infectious hepatitis, J.A.M.A. **136**:819, 1948.

Hanson, D. J.: Intramuscular injection injuries and complications, GP **27**:109, 1963.

Hingson, R. A., Danis, H. S., and Rosen, M.: Jet injection in medicine, Milit. Med. **128**:516, 1963.

Krantz, J. C., and Carr, C. J.: The pharmacologic principles of medical practice, Baltimore, 1969, The Williams & Wilkins Co.

Lovejoy, F. J., Constantine, H., and Dautrebande, L.: Importance of particle size in aerosol therapy, Proc. Soc. Exp. Biol. Med. **103**:836, 1960.

Lowe, C. A.: Principles of parenteral fluid therapy, Amer. J. Nurs. **53**:963, 1953.

O'Brien, G.: How the nurse views the pharmacist's role in nursing homes, Amer. Prof. Pharmacist **33**:50, 1967.

Pike, M.: Nurse-℞ man teamwork cuts medication errors, Amer. Prof. Pharmacist **33**:65, 1967.

Price, E.: Five activities of nurses that ℞ men can handle, Amer. Prof. Pharmacist **33**:29, 1967.

Safar, P., editor: Respiratory therapy, Philadelphia, 1965, F. A. Davis Company.

Shallowhorn, G.: Intramuscular injections, Amer. J. Nurs. **54**:438, 1954.

Skipper, J. K., Tagliacozzo, D. L., and Mauksch, H. O.: What communication means to patients, Amer. J. Nurs. **64**:101, 1964.

Travell, J.: Factors affecting pain of injection, J.A.M.A. **158**:368, 1955.

Pharmacodynamics 7

Because of the constantly increasing number of drugs utilized in medical therapeutics and the nurse's expanded responsibility in this area, it is essential that the nurse have a coherent, rational, and scientifically accurate understanding of the principles underlying pharmacology. The time is long past when anyone can expect to acquire complete knowledge about all drugs. Thousands of drugs exist, requiring that health professionals have some fundamental theoretical framework through which to approach their study and understanding of drug therapy.

Historically, the administration of drugs has been a prominent nursing task. This task, however, is changing in nature and prominence. A shift in responsibility is occurring away from the actual administration of drugs to greater responsibility in relation to other aspects of drug therapy. The nurse's expanded role currently includes a variety of functions, all of which are predicated upon a sound understanding of drug action. In many health care delivery settings, for example, the nurse is no longer the primary administrator and dispenser of drugs. In such settings, her responsibility has shifted to assuring safe administration of drugs by a variety of specially educated health workers and to observing and interpreting the patient's response to drug therapy. The moral, ethical, and legal responsibility of drug administration remains the nurse's. In addition, other nursing roles in relation to drug therapy have been developed and expanded. Today, more than before, the nurse has the responsibility of *teaching* patients about the drugs they are receiving. She has a *data-gathering role* in relation to the patient's previous drug therapy and present and past responses to drug therapy, as exemplified in the function of obtaining a drug history from the patient. She is a *decision-maker* regarding p.r.n. medications. By virtue of her interpersonal skills, she may also function as a *potentiator* of drug effects. And last, but certainly not least, she is a *communicator* of her knowledge and observations to other health care professionals, notably the physician who prescribes drug therapy.

These responsibilities require more than memorization of specific drugs, their actions, and their dosages. Rather, their effective implementation is predicated upon a sound comprehension of the theory of drug action, which the nurse can transfer to the individual patient with a specific diagnosis and definable, individualistic needs. Such a background necessitates knowledge of theories of drug action, physiologic processes mediating drug action, variables affecting drug action, and unusual and adverse responses to drug therapy.

The field of pharmacodynamics encompasses such theoretical knowledge. It is defined as the study of biochemical and physiologic effects of drugs and their mechanisms of action. As such, it is concerned with the response of tissues to a chemical agent being used and with the absorption, distribution, biotransformation, and excretion of the chemical agent in the body.

■ Empiric versus scientific medicine

Early medicines could be described frequently as empiric remedies—that is, experience with them revealed that they were sometimes useful in certain conditions, but very little was actually known about the basis of their therapeutic effects. This type of remedy has been replaced by drugs whose effects are often highly predictable and whose action in the body has, to a great extent, been substantiated through scientific research.

Once a chemical agent is found to be biologically active, pharmacologists perform a variety of tests. The major studies performed include: (1) investigation of the drug's site and mechanism of action; (2) determinations of the drug's metabolic fate in the body; (3) determination of dose-response relationships—that is, how much of the agent is required to produce various effects; and (4) investigation of structure-activity relationships—that is, exploration of the extent to which the agent's effects resemble those of other compounds that have similar chemical structures. A principal method of this scientific research in pharmacology is *biologic assay*, or *bioassay*, the study of the effect of a certain kind and certain amount of a drug upon living organisms.

In utilizing the method of bioassay, it is assumed that a definite quantity of a drug will always produce a certain response in the same animal or in animals of the same species. Methods of bioassay require rigorous statistical control in order to account for biologic variations (such as sex, age, and genetic background) that can exert a major influence on sensitivity to drugs and also in order to account for inevitable variations in laboratory conditions. In order to overcome such variables, reference standards and international standards have been established, as mentioned in Chapter 3. Consequently, contemporary knowledge about drug effects is predicated upon knowledge of chemical structures of drugs, which enable the scientists to predict to some extent what effects a drug will have in the body and what those effects will be. It has been found, for example, that drugs containing a certain molecular structure have a tendency to produce allergic responses in patients, hence, any new drug with this general type of molecular structure may have a tendency to produce hypersensitivity in some patients.

It must be said that scientists still do not have a definite theoretical scheme that allows them to predict accurately which chemical groupings will have specific desired physiologic effects. The advances made in knowledge regarding the chemistry of proteins, the nature and behavior of enzymes, and the metabolism of microbes have contributed greatly to understanding the responses that living systems make to drugs.

■ Theories of drug action

When a drug enters a living system, one can think of its molecules immediately beginning to react with the molecules of the cells and tissues with which they come in contact. The effects a drug produces must be regarded as ultimate consequences of complex physical and chemical interactions between the drug and molecules in the living organism. Therefore, in order to understand drug action, drug and tissue interactions at the molecular level must be studied.

Most drugs are believed to produce their effects by combining with cell membranes, enzymes, or other specialized components of cells. The interaction between the drug and the cell is presumed to change the function of the cell, thereby initiating biochemical and physiologic changes. According to some authorities, pharmacologically active compounds can be conceptually divided into two groups: those that are structurally specific and those that are not. Structural specificity refers to the ability of a drug to produce its effects by combining with a specific receptor. Structurally nonspecific drugs, on the other hand, do not combine with specific receptors and may instead penetrate into cells or accumulate in cell membranes.

Structurally specific drugs

Receptor theory of drug action. Structural specificity is an essential postulate of the receptor theory of drug action. Receptor theory hypothesizes that drugs are selectively active substances that have a special affinity for certain chemical groups or parts of cells and not for others. Therefore, receptor theory states, drugs exert their action by becoming attached to specialized regions of a cell. This relationship of a drug to its receptor has often been likened to the fit of a key into a lock. That is, some sort of reciprocal, or complementary, relationship exists between the chemical structure of the drug molecule and the drug receptor. The "fit" implies a mutual adaptation between the drug and the receptor in regard to respective physical shapes and electric charge distributions. Why the "fit" occurs is not entirely clear. It is believed that drug receptor binding may result from the formation of hydrogen, covalent, or ionic bonds or from weak binding forces that operate when any atoms are brought together. When this "fit" occurs, the drug is then able to initiate a chain of biochemical reactions.

The term *affinity* is used to describe the propensity of a drug to be found at a given receptor site and the term *efficacy* is used to describe the drug's ability to initiate biologic activity as a result of such binding. A drug that combines with receptors and initiates a sequence of biochemical and physiologic changes is said to possess both properties and is termed an *agonist*. A drug that combines with the same receptor site but does not initiate drug action is considered to lack efficacy and is termed a *competi-*

tive antagonist. Drug antagonism refers to the selective activity of many compounds that may be specifically blocked by other compounds. Not infrequently, antagonists share some structural common denominators with their agonists. It is hypothesized that they react with receptors by virtue of the affinity characteristics they share with their agonists, but, as previously indicated, they are not efficacious. Their major purpose, then, is to prevent the access of agonist molecules to the receptor site.

Because of some basic similarities between the receptor theory and theories of enzymatic action, many drugs are thought to produce their effects by combining with enzymes. Those drugs that are believed to combine with enzymes are thought to do so by virtue of their structural resemblance to an enzyme's substrate molecule (the substance acted upon by an enzyme). A drug may resemble an enzyme's substrate so closely that it may combine with the enzyme instead of with the normal substrate. Drugs resembling enzyme substrates are termed *antimetabolites* and can either block normal enzymatic action or result in the production of other substances with unique biochemical properties. The enzyme, then, becomes the receptor for the drug. However, while enzymes may be receptors, not all receptors are enzymes.

Rate theory of drug action. The rate theory assumes that the most important factor determining drug action is the rate at which drug-receptor combinations take place. It postulates that if a drug-receptor complex dissociates rapidly, it has high efficacy. Conversely, if there is slow dissociation, there is firm binding, prolonged occupancy, and low efficacy. Therefore, drug antagonism is associated with slow kinetics and drug agonism with fast kinetics.

The validity of rate theory is controversial at this time, although it does explain drug phenomena in quantitative as well as qualitative terms.

Structurally nonspecific drugs

It is not to be concluded from the previous discussion that all drugs operate through receptor mechanisms. Some drugs demonstrate no structural specificity and presumably act by more general effects on cell membranes and cellular processes. These drugs may penetrate into cells or accumulate in cellular membranes where they interfere, by physical or chemical means, with some cell function or some fundamental metabolic processes. Structurally nonspecific drugs are exemplified by the general anesthetics, which are lipid-soluble compounds of unrelated chemical structure but having similar properties. It is hypothesized that some structurally nonspecific drugs such as the general anesthetics exert their effects on cell membranes. These membranes are complex lipoprotein structures that regulate the flow of ions and metabolites in a highly selective manner, thereby maintaining an electrochemical gradient between the interior and exterior surfaces of the cell. General anesthetics, for example, are thought to act on the cells of the central nervous system by dissolving in the lipids of nerve cell membranes. It is presently believed that many drugs having rapid and potent effects cause selective changes in the permeability of certain cell membranes. Acetylcholine, histamine, and the catecholamines, all important naturally occurring regulators of body functions, are believed to act by such a mechanism.

Other structurally nonspecific drugs are believed to act by biophysical means that do not affect cellular or enzymatic functions. Drugs acting as a result of their obvious physical properties include the ointments and emollients. Hydrophilic indigestible substances exert a cathartic action because of their physical action on the bowel.

■ Physiologic processes mediating drug action

As previously mentioned, pharmacodynamics deals not only with mechanisms of drug action but also with the study of a drug's process through the body. The fate of drugs in the body includes everything that happens to a drug from the time the foreign chemical enters the biologic system until it and all of its products have been eliminated from the body.

In order to produce its effects, a drug must reach appropriate concentrations at its sites of action. That is, the molecules of the chemical must proceed from their point of entry into the body to the vicinity of the tissues with which they react. Therefore, it is evident that a drug must have the ability to affect a specific receptor site and the physicochemical characteristics to allow it to reach its site of action. The concentration the drug attains at its site of action is influenced by a number of factors, the primary ones being: (1) the rate and extent to which the drug is *absorbed* into body fluids; (2) the rate and extent to which the drug is transported or *distributed* to sites of action or storage in the body; (3) the rate and extent to which the drug is *biologically transformed* in the body to breakdown products; and (4) the rate and extent to which the drug is *excreted* from the body via various routes.

An ideal drug should be able to reach its site of action within a given time and in sufficient concentration, but it should not be too concentrated at the site as to be toxic. (Exceptions to this rule are the antineoplastic agents, which are often administered for their selective toxicity to malignant cells.) Moreover, the ideal drug should not be metabolized and/or excreted too rapidly to be effective.

In order to accomplish these processes necessary for drug action, however, the drug must traverse a number of cell membranes. In brief review, a drug may cross cell membranes by either passive transport processes or by specialized transport processes. In *passive transport*, the motion of substances is largely the result of the process of diffusion in proportion to a concentration gradient. After diffusion reaches a steady state, the concentration of the drug is equal on both sides of the cell membrane. Many drugs, however, are absorbed against a concentration gradient and require specialized active transport processes. *Active transport* processes influence the movement of substances by the production of energy and are generally more rapid than simple diffusion. All of the physiologic processes mediating drug action—absorption, distribution, biotransformation, and excretion—are predicated upon these transfer processes.

Absorption

Absorption refers to the process by which a drug is transferred from its site of entry into the body to the circulating fluids of the body. With the exception of locally acting drugs, all drugs must reach the bloodstream in order to be carried to their receptors. Absorption of the drug from its site of administration is largely influenced by the following factors.

Routes of drug administration. A drug may enter the circulatory system either by being injected there directly—for example, intravenously—or by absorption from depots in which it has been placed. The routes of drug entry into the body can be classified into three categories: the enteral (drugs administered via any portion of the gastrointestinal tract); the parenteral (drugs administered by routes that bypass the gastrointestinal tract and that are generally given by injection, thereby avoiding the necessity for absorption across a mucosal barrier); and the percutaneous (drugs absorbed from mucous membranes, either through sublingual administration or by inhalation). Of these three routes of administration, the enteral route generally results in slowest absorption. Drugs injected parenterally are usually speedily and completely absorbed, with a few exceptions. Some parenteral drugs, such as protamine zinc insulin, are deliberately prepared in a depot form so that absorption is delayed. Drugs that are applied sublingually are very rapidly absorbed by the highly vascular sublingual mucosa. Inhalation drugs, such as gaseous drugs or those administered in aerosol form, are also extremely rapidly absorbed from the respiratory tract or alveolar surfaces. A more detailed discussion of routes of administration is contained in Chapter 6.

Drug solubility. The more soluble the drug, the more rapidly it will be absorbed. Therefore, oral drugs given in solution form are generally absorbed more quickly than drugs administered in capsule or tablet form. Moreover, because cell membranes contain a fatty acid layer, lipid solubility is a valuable attribute of a drug that is to be absorbed from the alimentary tract. Chemicals and minerals that form insoluble precipitates in the gastrointestinal tract, such as barium salts, or drugs that are not soluble in water or lipids cannot be absorbed. Parenterally administered drugs prepared in oily vehicles, such as streptomycin, will be absorbed more slowly than drugs dissolved in water or isotonic sodium chloride.

Local conditions at the site of administration. These local conditions include circulation to the site and the area of the absorbing surface. Generally, the more extensive the absorbing surface, the greater the absorption of the drug and the more rapid its effects. For example, anesthetics are very rapidly absorbed from the pulmonary epithelium because of its vast surface area and its vascularity. Circulation to the site of administration is also a significant factor in the absorption of parenteral drugs. A patient in shock, for example, may not respond to intramuscularly administered drugs because of poor peripheral circulation. Drugs injected intravenously, on the other hand, are directly placed into the circulatory system and are totally absorbed. This route of administration is desirable when speedy drug effects are necessary, but it carries the potential danger of achieving temporarily toxic effects in vital organs such as the heart or the brain.

Circulation to the site of administration can also be externally manipulated in order to hasten or retard the rate of drug absorption. Local cooling of the site will hinder absorption, as will the application of a tourniquet proximally to the injection site. On the other hand, applying heat or friction to the site of administration will hasten absorption.

Drug concentration or dosage. Drugs administered in high concentrations or dosages are more rapidly absorbed than drugs administered in low concentrations. In certain situations, a drug may be initially administered in large doses that temporarily exceed the body's capacity for excretion of the drug. In this way, active drug levels are rapidly reached at the receptor site. Once an active drug level is established by such cumulation of effects, smaller daily doses of the drug can be administered in amounts designed to replace only the amount of the drug excreted since the previous dose. The initial and temporary overloading doses of the drug are *"priming doses,"* while the smaller daily doses are *"maintenance doses."* Such manipulation of drug dosage is frequently used, for example, with digitalis and steroid preparations in acute situations.

Another way in which drug concentration can be manipulated is by pharmaceutical processing. It is possible to combine an active drug with a resin or another substance from which it is only slowly released or to prepare a drug in a vehicle that offers relative resistance to the digestive action of stomach contents (enteric coating). Repository dosage forms are produced by suspension of a drug in a substance from which it is slowly released, producing uniform drug absorption for at least 8 hours or longer. For example, protamine zinc insulin is suspended in protamine for slow, sustained release so that its duration of action is 24 to 36 hours. Drug "Spansules" are gelatin capsules containing drug pellets having different coatings designed for timed release of the drug contained within. Advantages of this dosage form include decreased frequency of administration and prolonged maintenance of therapeutic effects. Disadvantages are related to possible failure of the sustained release mechanism, which could result in release of unexpectedly high and toxic levels of the drug or in therapeutically inadequate levels.

Distribution

After a drug is absorbed or injected into the bloodstream, it is distributed throughout the body by means of the circulation. Drug distribution is the transport of a drug across cell membranes, resulting in accumulations of the drug in certain tissues. The rate of entry of a drug into the various tissues of the body depends upon the relative rate of perfusion and the permeability of the capillaries for the particular drug molecules. The distribution may be general or restricted. Some drugs cannot pass particular cell membranes and are restricted in their distribution, while other drugs, such as ethyl alcohol, can eventually be found in solution in all body fluids.

Differential distribution of drugs may result from the binding of a drug to plasma proteins and from the unequal passage of a drug across biologic membranes, most notably into the central nervous system and the placenta. The binding of drugs to plasma proteins, particularly albumin, which reacts with a wide variety of drugs, creates higher concentrations of the drug in the blood than in the extracellular fluid and prolongs the action of the drug. In relation to the passage of drugs into the central nervous system, it has long been noted that many drugs fail to penetrate into those tissues as readily as into other tissues. This phenomenon has led to the conceptualization of a "blood-brain barrier." Currently, this concept is undergoing scrutiny, and recent research indicates that what has been termed the "blood-brain barrier" is not an absolute barrier. It has been postulated that it is a quantitative rather than a qualitative difference in capillary permeability as compared with other tissues. Still, the fact remains that the distribution of some drugs will be more readily achieved into other parts of the body than into the central nervous system. There is a very slow rate of entry of water-soluble and ionized drugs, such as penicillin, into the brain and spinal cord. Lipid-soluble compounds, on the other hand, enter the brain easily and rapidly. Moreover, some drugs that have no effects on the central nervous system when administered systemically have striking effects when injected directly into the cerebrospinal fluid.

Passage of drugs across the placenta to the fetus is a well-established fact. Again, lipid-soluble substances diffuse across the placenta readily and other substances are assisted by energy-coupled specific transport systems. Some drugs that are easily transported across the placenta include steroids, narcotics, anesthetics, various teratogenic agents, and some antibiotics.

In addition to differential distribution affected by plasma protein binding, the blood-brain barrier, and placental transfer, drugs are differentially distributed as a result of preferential accumulation. Accumulation of a drug after its distribution may be at the receptor site or in some other location. Some drugs have preferential sites of accumulation in certain tissues. For example, body fat has a high affinity for some drugs such as thiopentone. Other common sites of drug accumulation are muscle and plasma protein, which may be considered as storage depots for a drug. The stored drug is in equilibrium with the amount of drug contained in plasma and is released as plasma levels are reduced. Consequently, plasma levels of the drug are maintained for longer periods and, therefore, pharmacologic effects are also prolonged. Such drug effects, however, are predicated upon the administration of initially adequate priming doses in order to saturate the storage depots or binding sites.

Biotransformation

As soon as a drug is absorbed and distributed to either receptor sites or selective areas of accumulation, the effective concentration of the drug is depleted. The bodies of animals and human beings possess mechanisms for converting foreign molecules into harmless substances, and most drugs undergo metabolic transformation in the body. Biotransformation is the metabolic transformation of a foreign substance into one that is either harmless or more rapidly excreted. Metabolic and excretory processes, therefore, work together to keep the body free of foreign compounds.

The term *detoxication* has often been used to describe the metabolism of drugs, but it is not an optimally accurate conceptualization of the process. Although most types of biotransformation result in inactivation of a drug, occasionally the result of this metabolic process is a more active compound that requires further biotransformation before being excreted. For example, the active ingredient of chloral hydrate is its metabolite, which must then undergo a second reaction to facilitate its excretion. The term *detoxication*, however, implies that all drugs are toxic to the body and that all are metabolized to less toxic products. As indicated, this is not always the case. In addition to biotransformation sometimes resulting in active metabolites, drugs may be changed to other chemical forms or inactivated before excretion. In other instances, drugs may be excreted from the body unchanged, as

is the case with ether, for example. In short, the chemical reactions of biotransformation result in the formation of new chemicals that are ultimately less active than the parent compound and/or more readily eliminated.

The chemical alterations of biotransformation are produced by enzyme systems in the blood and in all body cells, but particularly those of the liver. The hepatic enzyme systems responsible for the biotransformation of many drugs seem to be located in the hepatic endoplasmic reticulum and are generally called microsomes, because they are located into the microsomal fraction of the liver. These hepatic microsomal enzymes effect the process of biotransformation through two general classes of chemical reactions: the synthetic and the nonsynthetic. The synthetic chemical reactions, also called "*coupling*" or "*conjugation*," involve the union of the drug (or its metabolite) with another substance. This chemical reaction generally produces a soluble, inactive product that is readily excreted. Nonsynthetic chemical reactions of drug metabolism include oxidation, hydrolysis, or reduction, which can result in activation, a change in activity, or inactivation of a drug.

Research indicates that drug metabolism can be depressed or stimulated. Depression of the microsomal drug-metabolizing system can be produced by conditions that have a deleterious effect on hepatic function, such as starvation and obstructive jaundice. Individuals with any type of hepatic disease, severe cardiovascular disease, or renal disease may be expected to have prolonged drug metabolism. Immaturity of drug-metabolizing enzymes in infants and degeneration of these enzymes in the aged also produce depression of biotransformation. In addition, some drugs are known to inhibit the metabolism of other drugs when they are administered simultaneously. If metabolism of drugs is delayed, cumulative drug effects may be expected and may be manifested as excessive or prolonged responses to ordinary doses of drugs. Stimulation of drug metabolism, on the other hand, may produce a state of apparent drug tolerance. A number of drugs are also known to cause an increase in the activity of hepatic microsomal drug-metabolizing enzymes. It is possible that repeated administration of some drugs stimulates the formation of new microsomal enzymes. This is thought to be the case with some hypnotic drugs, whose effect diminishes with prolonged administration.

Biotransformation of drugs does not occur exclusively in the liver. The plasma, the kidneys, and the intestinal mucosa also function to metabolize drugs, although to a lesser degree.

Excretion

Drug molecules, intact, changed, or inactivated, are ultimately removed from their sites of action by the physiologic channels and mechanisms of excretion. Excretion through the kidneys, biliary system, intestines, and lungs accounts for most drug elimination, renal excretion being by far the most important of these routes. Some drug metabolites are excreted via the bile into the intestinal tract, but the majority are then reabsorbed into the blood and excreted in the urine. Other routes of drug elimination include the nursing mother's milk, perspiration, tears, and saliva, although the latter three constitute relatively unimportant routes.

Drugs may also be eliminated through the use of extracorporeal dialysis, which was originally designed to substitute for renal function in cases of severe but temporary renal shutdown. Overdosage of drugs may lead to just such a situation. By an artificial process resembling glomerular filtration, dialysis can achieve rapid reduction of high plasma levels of the drugs.

Prerequisite to successful excretion is the maintenance of effective physiologic mechanisms of transport (the circulatory system) and of excretion (kidney and bowel function, respiratory function, and sweating). It can be seen, therefore, that metabolism, storage, and excretion are the three mechanisms by which drugs are ultimately removed from their sites of action.

Excretion via the kidneys remains by far the most important route of drug elimination. It accomplishes this process through passive glomerular filtration, active tubular secretion, and reabsorption. The kidney receives a large blood supply, the afferent arterioles bringing blood to the glomeruli for filtration and the efferent arterioles carrying the majority of the same blood to the tubules and then to the venous collecting system. The availability of a drug for glomerular filtration, however, is dependent upon its concentration in unbound form in plasma. Some drugs are cleared by tubular secretion and all of the drug, bound and free, becomes available for active secretion. When free drug is eliminated by tubular cells, the bound drug dissociates its bond rapidly in order to maintain a level of equilibrium with plasma water. The renal excretory mechanisms, then, have the net effect of removing the amount of free drug that is brought to the kidneys by the renal arterial blood.

In newborn infants, whose renal tubular secretory mechanisms are incompletely developed, and in individuals with renal dysfunction, drug elimination is severely hampered and drug toxicity may result.

Variables predictably influencing drug action

There are some factors that will alter an individual's response to drug therapy. Deviant drug reactions can frequently be traced to the predictable influence of such variables. It is important for the nurse to be cognizant of factors that modify cell conditions and, therefore, modify the activity of a drug. Some of these factors include the following.

Age. It is generally recognized that children and elderly persons are highly responsive to drugs. Infants often have immature hepatic and renal systems and, therefore, incomplete excretory and metabolic mechanisms. Aged individuals will often demonstrate different responses to drug therapy because of deterioration of hepatic and renal function, which is often accompanied by concurrent disease processes, such as cardiovascular disease. The usual adult dose of a drug is considered to be a dose suitable for an adult 20 to 60 years of age. Modifications of dosage for children may be calculated as a fraction of the adult dose on the basis of body weight or surface area.

Body mass. The relationship between body mass and amount of drug administered influences the distribution and concentration of a drug. In order to maintain a desired drug concentration in individuals of various sizes, drug dosage must be adjusted in proportion to body mass. Therefore, particularly for children and for very lean and for very obese individuals, drug dosage is frequently determined on the basis of amount of drug per kilogram of body weight or body surface area.

Sex. Differential drug effects related to the variable of sex result, in part, from size differences between men and women. Women are usually smaller than men, which will lead to high drug concentrations if dosage is prescribed indifferently. There are also demonstrable differences in relative proportions of fat and water in the bodies of men and women, and some drugs may be more soluble in one or the other. Some authorities also indicate that subjective factors regarding drug effects may vary with sexual differences, stating that women are more suggestible to drug effects than men. This, however, is a controversial hypothesis. Differential drug reactivity by sex is most pronounced during pregnancy, since drugs taken by the pregnant woman might affect the uterus and/or the fetus as a result of placental transfer. As a precaution, the use of drugs is best avoided during pregnancy unless an absolute necessity exists.

Environmental milieu. Drugs affecting mood and behavior are particularly susceptible to the influence of the patient's environment. With such drugs one has to consider effects in light of four factors: (1) the drug itself; (2) the personality of the user; (3) the environment of the user; and (4) the interaction of these three components. Sensory deprivation and sensory overload may also affect responses to drugs. Physical environment may also modify drug effects, for example, temperature affects drug activity. Heat relaxes peripheral vessels and so intensifies the actions of vasodilators and diaphoretics, while cold has the opposite effect. The relative oxygen deprivation at high altitudes may also increase sensitivity to some drugs.

Time of administration. It is well known that drugs are absorbed more rapidly if the gastrointestinal tract is free of food, while irritating drugs are more readily tolerated if there is food in the stomach. Circadian rhythms also affect drug action in that body resistance to drugs is generally greater in the early morning when the body is at its lowest point of physiologic functioning. Conversely, the body is more sensitive to drug effects during times of maximal activity and optimal physiologic functioning.

Pathologic state. The presence of pathology and the severity of symptoms may call for careful consideration of the type of drug administered and for adjustment in dosage. For example, the presence of severe pain tends to increase a patient's resistance to opiates, and an extremely anxious patient can prove resistant to very large doses of tranquilizing and sedating drugs. When acetylsalicylic acid is administered to a patient with a fever, he will respond with a decrease in temperature, whereas a patient taking the drug for its analgesic effects will show no temperature change at all. Larger doses of insulin may be required for the diabetic patient whose condition is complicated by fever or infection. In addition, it bears repeating that the presence of circulatory, hepatic, and/or renal dysfunctions will interfere with the physiologic processes of drug action.

Genetic factors. Although the influence of genetic factors on drug action has not been specifically identified, it appears that genetic differences contribute to quantitative as well as qualitative differences in drug effects.

■ Adverse responses to drugs

There are many ways in which drugs may react in the patient to produce unpredictable, harmful, and sometimes unexplainable responses. No drug is totally safe and absolutely free of toxic effects. Sometimes these effects are immediately apparent. At other times, they may take weeks or months to develop. Some drugs result in aberrant pharmacologic actions when administered individually; other aberrant actions are precipitated by the concurrent administration of certain chemicals. Some adverse reactions to drugs are relatively mild; others can be fatal. With the increasing numbers of drugs being utilized, the incidence of adverse reactions has increased and is presently a significant problem in medical therapeutics.

Untoward effects of drugs can be classified as iatrogenic diseases or as adverse reactions. Generally, iatrogenic diseases refer to groups of adverse effects produced unintentionally by the physician in treating his patient. Iatrogenic diseases induced by drugs manifest themselves in five major syndromes: (1) blood dyscrasias, such as agranulocytosis, thrombocytopenia, aplastic anemia, and bone marrow depression; (2) hepatic toxicity, which is common and may take the form of biliary obstruction, hepatitis-like syndromes, and hepatic necrosis; (3) renal damage, particularly glomerular damage, which is a significant toxic effect of a number of drugs, including some antibiotics; (4) teratogenic effects, or drug effects causing malformations in the fetus as a result of placental transfer of drugs taken by a pregnant woman; and (5) dermatologic effects, such as acne, psoriasis, eczema, maculopapular rashes, and, rarely, erythema multiforme.

In addition to these common and well-known drug-induced diseases, there are numerous other iatrogenic syndromes specific to certain drugs. Ulceration of the gastrointestinal tract, for example, is a common result of long-term therapy with drugs such as acetylsalicylic acid, steroids, and potassium chloride. The current relationship being investigated between oral contraceptive agents and cerebrovascular occlusion is another phenomenon that may eventually be defined as an iatrogenic drug-induced disease, although present studies are inconclusive.

Adverse drug reactions, on the other hand, refer to one way of characterizing unpredictable and sometimes unexplainable drug responses that have not been optimally, clearly, and distinctly defined. Among the most common and best defined adverse drug reactions are the following.

Drug allergy is an altered state of reaction to a drug resulting from previous sensitizing exposure and the development of an immunologic mechanism. Substances foreign to the body act as antigens to stimulate the production of antibodies. Later, when a previously sensitized individual is again exposed to the foreign substance, the antigen reacts with the antibodies in ways that are damaging to body tissues. Allergic reactions can be either immediate or delayed.

Immediate reactions occur within minutes of exposure to the chemical to which the person has been previously sensitized. The antigen-antibody reaction is believed to release histamine from the tissues, which then exerts a pharmacologic action on the smooth muscles of small blood vessels and other organs. Immediate and severe reactions are called anaphylactic reactions and are frequently fatal if not recognized and treated quickly. Signs and symptoms are severe, occur suddenly, and produce shock. The most dramatic form of anaphylaxis is sudden, severe bronchospasm, vasospasm, severe hypotension, and rapid death. Signs are largely caused by contraction of smooth muscles and may begin with irritability, extreme weakness, nausea, and vomiting and may proceed to dyspnea, cyanosis, convulsions, and cardiac arrest. Antihistamine drugs, epinephrine, and bronchodilators are indispensable in the treatment of anaphylactic shock.

Mild allergic reactions may be characterized by the development of a rash, angioedema, rhinitis, fever, asthma, and pruritus. Some allergic reactions are delayed and may appear anywhere from 7 to 14 days after initial administration of the drug. Delayed reactions are frequently analogous to "serum sickness" and are characterized by angioedema, arthralgia, fever, lymphadenopathy, and splenomegaly. Contact dermatitis, which results from direct skin contact with the eliciting drug, is also a delayed allergic response.

An individual who has had a mild allergic response to a particular drug should avoid reexposure to that drug and, optimally, should have skin tests performed in order to more definitely diagnose his response. Reinstitution of therapy with the same drug is always dangerous to patients who manifest allergic reactions since an anaphylactoid reaction may occur.

The term *hypersensitivity* is frequently used synonymously with allergy, but it is inappropriate because it is frequently confused with other kinds of adverse drug reactions. Since there is a lack of precision to defining hypersensitivity, it may be wisest to avoid usage of the term.

Idiosyncrasy is any abnormal or peculiar response to a drug that may manifest itself by: (1) overresponse or abnormal susceptibility to a drug; (2) underresponse, demonstrating abnormal tolerance; (3) a qualitatively different effect from the one expected, such as excitation after the administration of a sedative; or (4) unpredictable and unexplainable symptoms. Idiosyncratic reactions are generally thought to result from genetic enzymatic deficiencies that lead to abnormal mechanism of metabolizing drugs. This term has been used rather vaguely to cover drug reactions that are qualitatively different from the usual effects obtained in the majority of patients and that cannot be attributed to drug allergy.

Tolerance is said to exist when there is a decreased physiologic response to the repeated administration of a drug. It is a reaction that necessitates an excessive increase in dosage to maintain a given therapeutic effect. Drugs well known for their propensity to produce tolerance are tobacco, opium alkaloids, nitrites, barbiturates, and ethyl alcohol. The actual mechanism of tolerance is unknown. Recent research indicates that prolonged administration of some drugs somehow induces the synthesis of extra drug-metabolizing enzymes in the liver, which may account for the patient's increased ability to tolerate drug doses that previously affected him. Cross tolerance between related chemicals (such as between alcohol and some anesthetics) is a well-documented phenomenon.

Cumulation occurs when the body cannot metabolize one dose of a drug before another dose is administered. In other words, when drugs are excreted more slowly than they are absorbed, each new dose adds more to the total quantity in the blood and organs than is lost in the same amount of time by excretion. Unless drug administration is adjusted, sufficiently high concentrations can be reached to produce toxic effects. Cumulative toxicity can occur rapidly, as dramatically illustrated in ethyl alcohol intoxication, or it can occur insidiously, as is the case in poisoning with heavy metals, such as lead. The latter is stored in many body tissues and deposited in bones, therefore having prolonged effects on the body while accumulation continues.

Tachyphylaxis refers to a rapidly developing tolerance to a drug after only a few doses of the drug. It is quick in onset and the patient's initial response to the drug cannot be reproduced with even larger doses of the drug.

Drug dependence is the term preferred over the previous terminology of habituation and addiction. The World Health Organization has suggested the usage of the term *dependence* in conjunction with the drug being described (for example, barbiturate dependence or opiate dependence). Dependence can be physical or psychic. Physical dependence refers to an adaptive physiologic state to a drug that manifests itself by intense physical disturbance when the drug is withdrawn. Psychic dependence is a state of emotional reliance upon a drug in order to maintain a state of well-being. Its manifestations may range from a mild desire for a drug, to craving, and to compulsive use of the drug. Drug dependence will be explored in greater breadth and depth in Chapter 17.

Drug interaction results from concurrent administration of a number of drugs and is caused by the interaction of two different drugs on the same receptor site. Serious and sometimes fatal consequences may result from the interaction of drugs with other drugs, with certain foods, or with some chemicals utilized in diagnostic procedures.

Drug interaction may take the form of drug antagonism, which has been previously discussed, or it may take the form of synergism or potentiation—that is, one drug enhancing the action of another by interfering with its biotransformation. In such a situation, the combined effects of both drugs would be greater than the effects of each drug administered individually. For example, phenergan potentiates the depressant effect of narcotics. More frequently, the term *drug interaction* has come to have the connotation of an adverse reaction, and, indeed, in the great majority of cases, drug interactions do manifest themselves generally as adverse reactions. Drug interactions may arise from either alteration of the absorption, distribution, biotransformation, or excretion of one drug by another or from combination of their actions or effects. They may generally manifest themselves as enhanced or diminished effects. For example, the effects of hypotensive agents may be antagonized by the effects of nasal decongestants, which contain catecholamines; the effect of digitalis preparations may be undesirably potentiated by the concomitant administration of thiazide diuretics. Every mechanism of physiologic processing of drugs may potentially yield an adverse drug interaction. The potential combinations of drugs that may interact in an adverse manner are astronomical in number. It is possible that many drug interactions go undetected. To keep herself informed, the nurse should be cognizant of hospital pharmacy and drug manufacturers' releases regarding drug incompatibilities. Handbooks of undesirable drug interactions and interferences are also available for reference. When in doubt, the nurse should consult one of these resources in the pharmacy department of her health care delivery agency.

Questions

for study and review

1 Define pharmacodynamics.
2 Differentiate between structurally specific and structurally nonspecific drugs.
3 Briefly explain the receptor theory of drug action.
4 Define the terms *affinity* and *efficacy* as they relate to drug action.
5 Briefly explain the rate theory of drug action.
6 Identify and describe the four physiologic processes mediating drug action.
7 Describe how the following factors may influence drug absorption: route of drug administration, drug solubility, local conditions at the site of administration, and drug concentration.
8 Define and explain the rationale underlying the administration of drugs in "priming" and "maintenance" doses.

9 Define repository dosage forms of drugs. Identify their advantages and disadvantages.
10 Explain why drug distribution in the body is unequal.
11 Explain why the term *detoxification* is not an optimally accurate conceptualization of the process of biotransformation.
12 Identify the system primarily responsible for the biotransformation of drugs.
13 Explain how drug metabolism can be depressed or stimulated.
14 Describe how the following variables influence drug action: age, body mass, sex, environmental milieu, time of drug administration, and pathologic state.
15 Define iatrogenic disease and identify the five major syndromes by which drug-induced iatrogenic disease may be manifested.
16 Define adverse drug reactions and list some of these reactions.
17 Explain how drug allergy occurs. Describe the manifestations of immediate and delayed allergic reactions.
18 Explain why drug interaction has become a vital issue in contemporary medical therapeutics.

References

Brodie, B. B.: Physiochemical and biochemical aspects of pharmacology, J.A.M.A. **202**:600, 1967.

Burns, J. J.: Implications of enzyme induction for drug therapy, Amer. J. Med. **37**:327, 1964.

Bush, M. T., and Sanders, E.: Metabolic fate of drugs: barbiturates and closely related drugs, Ann. Rev. Pharmacol. **7**:57, 1967.

Crossland, J.: Lewis's pharmacology, Baltimore, 1970, The Williams & Wilkins Co.

DiPalma, J. R., editor: Drill's pharmacology in medicine, ed. 3, New York, 1971, McGraw-Hill Book Company.

Evaluation and mechanisms of drug toxicity, Ann. N. Y. Acad. Sci. **123**:1, 1965.

Evans, D. A. P.: Pharmacogenetics, Amer. J. Med. **34**:639, 1963.

Fouts, J. R.: Drug interactions: effects of drugs and chemicals on drug metabolism, Gastroenterology **46**:486, 1964.

Gaddum, J. H., and others: Symposium on drug antagonism, Pharmacol. Rev. **9**:211, 1957.

Goldstein, A., Aronow, L., and Kalman, S.: Principles of drug action: the basis of pharmacology, New York, 1969, Harper and Row, Publishers.

Goodman, L., and Gilman, A.: The pharmacological basis of therapeutics, New York, 1970, The Macmillan Co.

Goth, A.: Medical pharmacology: principles and concepts, ed. 6, St. Louis, 1972, The C. V. Mosby Co.

Grollman, A., and Grollman, E.: Pharmacology and therapeutics, Philadelphia, 1970, Lea & Febiger.

Kern, R. A.: Anaphylactic drug reactions, J.A.M.A. **179:**20, 1962.

Krantz, J. C., Jr., and Carr, C. J.: The pharmacological principles of medical practice, Baltimore, 1969, The Williams & Wilkins Co.

Meyers, F., Jawetz, E., and Goldfein, A.: Review of medical pharmacology, Los Altos, Calif., 1970, Lange Medical Publications.

Motulsky, A. G.: Drug reactions, enzymes and biochemical genetics, J.A.M.A. **165:**835, 1957.

O'Reilly, R. A., and others: Hereditary transmission of exceptional resistance to coumarin anti-coagulant drugs, New Eng. J. Med. **271:**809, 1964.

Parker, C. W., and others: Hypersensitivity to penicillenic acid derivatives in human beings with penicillin allergy, J. Exp. Med. **115:**821, 1962.

Paton, W. D. M.: The principles of drug action, Proc. Royal Soc. Med. **53:**29, 1961.

Paton, W. D. M., and Payne, J. P.: Pharmacological principles and practice, Boston, 1968, Little, Brown and Company.

Penn, R. G.: Pharmacology, London, 1970, Baillière, Tindall & Cassell Ltd.

Sluester, L.: Metabolism of drugs and toxic substances, Ann. Rev. Biochem. **33:**571, 1964.

Wadell, W. J., and Butler, T. C.: The distribution and excretion of phenobarbital, J. Clin. Invest. **36:**1217, 1957.

Williams, R. T.: Detoxication mechanisms in man, Clin. Pharmacol. Ther. **4:**234, 1963.

Weiner, I. M.: Mechanisms of drug absorption and excretion, Ann. Rev. Pharmacol. **7:**39, 1967.

8 Psychologic aspects of drug therapy and self-medication

Psychologic aspects of drug therapy
Aspects of self-medication

■ Psychologic aspects of drug therapy

Every drug administered to the patient has a symbolic meaning and a potential psychologic effect in addition to its pharmacodynamic action. A drug not only alters in a useful way the function or structure of some part of the body, but it may also influence the behavior, sense of well-being, and mental state of the patient. Psychologic responses of patients to the symbol of medication may mimic pharmacologic reactions, adverse effects, or even allergic reactions to drugs. The most profound psychologic reactions may be observed in patients receiving placebos.

A patient's reaction to the symbolic meaning and pharmacologic action of drugs is extremely complex. Only an introduction to this aspect of drug therapy can be included here. For more detailed information, the student should consult the references listed at the end of this chapter.

Symbolic meaning of drugs

Medications may be a symbol of help to the patient. This meaning is strengthened and drug effectiveness enhanced when doctors or nurses inform a patient that a particular drug will benefit or help him. Repeated suggestions to the patient that the drug is beneficial further reinforce the therapeutic value of the drug. This is similar to the relief a mother's kiss gives to the pain of her child; the assurance it gives makes the child feel better. Investigation of the effects of drugs on the mind has resulted in the conclusion that some drugs are effective only in the presence of an appropriate mental state. The patient's faith and belief are able to confer positive benefits.

Another important symbolic meaning of a drug is related to the power inherent in the drug. This symbolic power is united with the patient physically and emotionally. Although the emotional unity is most often unconscious, it provides the patient with strength and even a temporary sense of security. However, it is also this symbolic power that may propel an insecure and dependent individual into a state of addiction. When an individual's needs cannot be met independently, his incapacity can be overcome with the help of an external factor such as a narcotic, drug, or alcohol. One of these might be the crutch that makes the patient feel he can more successfully meet the stresses with which he is confronted.

Drugs may also be viewed as symbols of

danger. The patient may interpret the prospect of cure as a serious threat to his emotional security if he uses illness to meet a need such as dependence. The result may be the occurrence of adverse symptoms from medications. The patient may complain of dry mouth, nausea, vomiting, palpitation, fatigue, and other vague feelings of discomfort. He may resist taking the medication, refuse to have the prescription refilled, or even throw the drug away. If he does take the medication to please his family, doctor, or nurse, or because he can no longer withstand their pleading, he may immediately feel worse.

A patient may have ambivalent feelings about medications; he may wish to regain his health and may recognize the importance of drug therapy in achieving this goal, but he may also feel that his illness is essential for the gratification of his needs. Drug therapy may then result in some of his symptoms being relieved while others are intensified.

Drug fantasies. Patients may also harbor fantasies or irrational notions about medications. A patient may think a medication is too strong and therefore refuse to take the drug, decrease the amount of drug taken at any one time, or decrease the number of times the drug is taken. This type of fantasy may be suspected when a drug known to be effective for a specific condition is ineffective in a particular patient with that condition.

If a patient believes the drug is too weak, he may take the drug too often or request the drug more often than prescribed; he may increase the amount of drug he takes or continue drug therapy for a longer period of time than prescribed. A patient with this type of fantasy is quite likely to develop symptoms of overdosage.

Some fantasies may revolve around fear. Patients tend to fear radioactive drugs such as ^{32}P or ^{131}I and dependence on drugs that have an antidepressant, analgesic, or sedative effect. Although few people today believe in the claims of a cure-all remedy, there are some who believe that a certain medicament or combination of medicaments is essential to general good health and should, therefore, be taken habitually.

An honest presentation to the patient of the action of drugs and of his own responsibility in drug therapy will help alleviate the problem of drug fantasies. In addition, what the patient thinks and believes about drugs should be learned prior to instituting drug therapy; this information may be used as a basis for the teaching of positive aspects of drug therapy.

Other reactions to drugs. Not only does a patient react to the symbol of medication but also to the pharmacodynamic properties of the drug and, if they occur, to the toxic, allergic, or other adverse reactions to the drug. A patient's reaction to the side effects of a particular drug may be somewhat reduced if the patient has been prepared in advance of their occurrence. Medical personnel may be reluctant to warn patients of ill effects from drugs, not wanting to cause unnecessary worry and anxiety. On the whole, patients prefer knowing the potential risks of drug therapy. Failure to prepare the patient for side effects may result in anxiety, panic, or rejection of therapy when these effects occur.

Patients who believe they are allergic to a certain drug, for real or imagined reasons, are likely to react with fear or panic when administration of that drug is contemplated. A detailed personal history and (if possible) tests for hypersensitivity should be used to corroborate or refute the patient's belief. Rejection of a patient's claim of hypersensitivity without evidence could result in dire consequences.

The route of administration of a drug and the financial cost of treatment as well as a patient's conscious and unconscious attitudes toward his drugs, doctor, nurse, illness, and so on determine the extent, duration, and intensity of the patient's response to medication. Studies indicate that when a patient is angry, resentful, or hostile, certain medications used in normal doses may not be effective.

A patient's illness may affect his emotional response to a drug. When a patient's illness is short, his recovery is complete, and medical and drug expense is not too great, he tends to have a positive reaction to drugs, hospitals, and medical and nursing personnel. Strong negative reactions toward drugs or medical personnel result when a patient has been led to believe that he will make a quick and complete recovery, and then drugs are both ineffective and expensive or symptoms of allergy, side or toxic effects, or overdosage occur. Preparing patients for limited beneficial effects of drugs, for side and toxic effects, and for drug expense tends to reduce or prevent negative reactions.

In any chronic illness a patient may suddenly rebel against ill health and may irrationally resist therapy with life-sustaining medications. When this occurs, the patient may be testing himself to see if he is really dependent on the drugs, or he may be attempting a real or symbolic act of self-destruction. Usually, the ill effects experienced from drug omission bring about reinstitution of drug therapy from which the patient does not deviate for a long time. The patient's denial of need for drug therapy is directly related to denial of illness. Rejection of medications is often associated with increase in stress. Such a patient usually needs supportive and reconstructive psychotherapy.

Effects of drugs on the mind

Many drugs used in the treatment of nonpsychotic patients have an effect on the patient's mind. Drugs may interfere with judgment, mood, sense of values, motor ability, and coordination. Certain antihistaminics used to treat allergies may decrease the individual's alertness and cause him to be drowsy, depressed, or even accident prone. Rauwolfia compounds used to treat hypertension may cause depression. The barbiturates and ataractic agents may induce inattentiveness and confusion and reduce initiative and the ability to think creatively. Drug-induced depression calls for discontinuance of the offending drug. These patients should be watched for self-destructive tendencies, since pharmacologic literature is abundant with examples of those with drug-induced depressions who have attempted suicide.

Medications tend to be more effective when the patient believes in his capacity to get well, when he has a strong desire to get well, and when he believes that the health personnel caring for him are sincerely interested in his health.

The patient's past and present conditioning to drugs, illness, hospitals, nurses, and other health personnel as well as his health goal are determinants in his reaction to drugs. Nurses must keep in mind that one of the most important deterrents to successful drug therapy occurs when the patient and the health personnel have divergent goals. An accurate determination of the patient's goal in seeking medical advice and therapy is important to planning and implementing an effective plan of care.

■ Aspects of self-medication

Development of the science of public health has led to the realization that the state of a nation's health is not exclusively dependent upon the interplay between professional medical practice on the one hand and bacteria, malignancy, and other causes of disease on the other. The influence on community health of the individual's personal attempts to relieve his ailments has frequently been ignored or underestimated. Here are a few of many varied aspects that affect self-medication either positively or negatively.

In the United States nearly $2 billion is spent annually for medicines that require no prescription or physician's advice. The amount spent on drugs for self-medication has been increasing yearly in Canada, the United States, and other nations. However, in the United States, sales of nonprescription drugs have not risen as much as have sales of prescription drugs. Nonprescription drugs accounted for 80% of all pharmaceutical products sold in the United States during the 1920's; in 1962 this figure had fallen to 28%.*

Drugs sold without prescription can induce sleep or wakefulness, relieve pain or tension, or supply the body with vitamins and minerals. Remedies can be purchased for any part of the body from head to toe. Widespread use of self-medication (autotherapy) is primarily the result of advertising via mass communication media. Concern over the use of home remedies and

*Backman, J.: Economics of proprietary medicines, speech given at The New York Academy of Sciences, November, 1964.

self-medication is not new. Self-medication continues to be a controversial subject with adherents for and against it. A critical assessment of the problem should include the investigation of the realistic and practical aspects of self-medication, so that the lay person's rights and obligations become apparent to the student and the practicing nurse.

Autotherapy is based on the tradition of folk remedies. Among the many reasons given for the continuing popularity of autotherapy are convenience, fear or embarrassment with regard to medical consultation, disappointment with professional medical methods or results, and the fact that home remedies are more economical than medical consultation.

Advantages of self-medication

Historical records and present-day surveys indicate that man has a desire and a need to practice self-medication. Man insists that self-medication is an inherent right, and he has guarded this right from time immemorial. Throughout history man has searched for medicines to relieve his ailments, and he has tried almost every natural material known to him in his battle against pain, discomfort, and disease.

The public is health conscious; otherwise there would be no across-the-counter sales or use of nonprescribed drugs. Many of man's ailments are trivial and temporary, and he seeks to alleviate these discomforts in the most expedient way possible. Minor ailments do not require the time or energy of a busy physician. The success with which minor complaints are treated by members of the public attests to this fact. Indeed, if individuals sought medical advice for every minor ailment (colds, headaches, slight wounds, temporary gastrointestinal upsets, or minor burns), physicians would be unable to give attention to patients with illnesses requiring professional medical care. Although self-medication if misused or abused may harm an individual, available data indicate that there is a greater amount of harm caused by prescription drugs than by nonprescription drugs. Hazards of autotherapy can be minimized by educating the public about drugs.

Disadvantages of self-medication

Although man has jealously guarded his inherent right to self-medication for hundreds of years, most preparations available to him before the twentieth century were harmless vegetable concoctions. The advent of modern chemistry and pharmacology produced literally thousands of preparations for self-medication, some of which are capable of causing harm.

Today, many drugs can be bought in supermarkets, restaurants, and vending machines. The desire for self-medication can be easily gratified. Sales promotion via radio and television encourages self-medication for real or fancied ills. Since the hazards of medications are insufficiently outlined, persistent abuse of drugs may occur and toxic effects may result. Many drugs considered harmless by the general public, such as aspirin and vitamin tablets, can actually cause untoward reactions. Aspirin may depress bone marrow function, while multiple-vitamin preparations containing iron, minerals, and salts may disturb gastrointestinal function. Calcium preparations and excessive amounts of vitamin D may cause kidney damage. Persistent use of bromides may result in bromism, and habitual use of antihistaminics can cause cardiac irregularities. Habitual self-medication may also mask a serious condition, endanger the individual's life, and create a need for prolonged and expensive medical therapy. The public's lack of knowledge of drugs and illness requires restriction of availability of potentially harmful drugs.

Proper limits of self-medication

The limits of self-medication must be made clear to the public through health education programs. The layman must be taught to recognize the boundaries of his own therapeutic competence and the dangers involved in exceeding them. This will offer some protection from his own lack of knowledge as well as from the bad advice of others. Through education, society can be guided rather than limited in freedom of action.

Many ailments cannot be alleviated by self-treatment, and such attempts at autotherapy may be dangerous. These conditions include, **91** among others, neoplastic diseases, tuberculosis, cardiovascular diseases, peptic ulcers, diseases of the genitourinary system, and diseases of the sense organs.

Most often the layman engages in autotherapy to relieve symptoms rather than a particular disease. His level of knowledge does not often permit him to associate certain symptoms with disease or to recognize that the coexistence of symptoms may indicate a serious underlying pathologic process. Thus, the layman should be taught that it is permissible to treat diarrhea with a nonprescription drug, but it is unwise to do so if diarrhea alternates with constipation or if it is accompanied by indigestion, recurring fever, tiredness, and rectal bleeding.

Any chronic, persistent, unresponsive, or frequently recurring condition or symptom should not be subject to autotherapy. Medical advice should be sought to determine the cause for recurrent complaints. A good rule for the layman to follow is—any ailment that he cannot clearly diagnose should be presented to a physician for medical advice.

Many individuals are induced to purchase dietary aids, particularly "slimming" products. It has been estimated that in the United States approximately $50 million is spent annually on worthless antiobesity products. Laymen should seek medical advice in order to rule out a pathologic cause for obesity. They should be aware that for nonpathologic obesity a reduction in caloric intake according to a well-planned diet that avoids nutritional risks plus a sound program of physical activity are the best methods available to achieve and maintain normal weight.

The public is able to classify drugs. They recognize certain products as being antacids, tonics, nasal decongestants, or analgesics even though they may not use these terms.

Table 8-1 contains a list of medications that can be considered permissible for home treatment. Every home medicine cabinet probably contains a number of these medications. The layman should be advised to seek the help of his local pharmacist in stocking his medicine cabinet.

Safety precautions should be observed to prevent unnecessary accidents. These precautions include the following:

1 Properly label all medications; labels should be legible.
2 Check all medications periodically for deterioration by heat, light, or dampness and discard accordingly.
3 Discard any unused portion of a prescription medicine.
4 Keep medicines out of the reach of children.

Control of proprietary drugs

An important factor in determining the limits of autotherapy is governmental control of nonprescription drugs. Control of over-the-counter drugs has increased in Canada, the United States, and most European countries in the past few decades. Home remedies have existed from time immemorial, but their legislative history is of recent vintage. Drug laws in Canada and the United States were not intended to restrict the availability of drugs for self-medication but were intended to make self-medication safer and more effective. As a result of these laws, the use of secret formulas and deceptive advertising at its worst have disappeared.

Many nonprescription drugs available to the layman have limitations of effectiveness. Thus, analgesics such as aspirin are available for the relief of minor aches and pains, but agents such as morphine that relieve visceral pain are unavailable without a prescription. A nonprescription drug, like a prescription drug, must be proved safe and effective for the conditions for which it is recommended. It is this rule that has resulted in the withdrawal of many harmful and ineffective agents from the market. Nonprescription medicines must be safe and effective within a wide range of dosage. This provides protection against misuse. Most drugs capable of causing dependence or addiction such as amphetamines and barbiturates are no longer available across the counter. Nonprescription drugs are of low toxicity and pose no threat to the average consumer when directions are followed.

Not many medications can be released to the public without a warning of some sort to the user. These warnings include statements regard-

Table 8-1 Medications for home treatment

Medication	Use
Analgesic balm or ointment	Muscular aches
Analgesic tablets (aspirin and aspirin combinations for adults and children)	Headaches, minor aches, pains, fever
Antacids	Indigestion or upset stomach
Antidiarrheal compounds	Mild or noncomplicated diarrhea
Antiseptics	
liquid, cream, spray	Minor cuts and scrapes
mouthwash	Mild sore throat
throat lozenges	Mild sore throat
Calamine cream or lotion	Insect bites, minor itching, poison ivy
Cough syrup	Coughing caused by colds
Laxatives, mild	Constipation
Motion or travel sickness remedies	Dizziness, nausea, vomiting from travel
Nasal decongestants	Nasal stuffiness resulting from colds or allergies
Skin creams or lotions	Chapped skin, diaper rash
Sunburn and other burn treatments	Sunburn, other minor burns
Universal antidote	Accidental poisoning emergency
Vitamin preparations	Dietary supplement

ing avoidance of use by children, avoidance of chronic use of the drug, and avoidance of use during pregnancy and in the presence of various pathologic conditions, for example, high blood pressure. Typical warnings include the following:

1 How to use a medication safely.
  "Do not apply to broken skin."
  "Do not exceed recommended dosage."
2 When not to use the drug.
  "Do not drive or operate machinery while taking this medication."
3 When to stop taking the drug.
  "Discontinue use if rapid pulse, dizziness, or blurring of vision occurs."
4 When to see a doctor.
  "If pain persists for more than 3 days or redness is present or in conditions affecting children under 12 years of age, consult a physician immediately."

According to law, all nonprescription drugs must bear these seven points on their labels:

1 Name of the product
2 Name and address of the manufacturer, packer, or distributor
3 Net contents of the package
4 Active ingredients and the quantity of certain ingredients
5 Name of any habit-forming drug contained in the prescription
6 Cautions and warnings needed for the protection of the user
7 Adequate directions for safe and effective use

Labeling and warnings that accompany nonprescription drugs help protect the layman against misuse and potential harmful effects.

Retail sale of home remedies can also be important to proper use of autotherapy. Allowing drugs to be purchased in grocery stores or supermarkets, from mail-order houses or vending machines promotes the use of medications without benefit of the professional advice that can be given by the pharmacist. Restricting the sale of drugs to pharmacies or stores where a registered pharmacist is employed provides an opportunity for advice on the purchase of drugs and enables the pharmacist to observe which customers repeatedly buy the same medications to treat the same ailment; he can advise these customers to see a physician.

References

Beecher, H. K.: The powerful placebo, J.A.M.A. **159:**1602, 1955.

Dukes, M. N. G.: Patent medicines and autotherapy in society, Den Haag, Holland, 1963, Drukkerij Pasmans, v.d. Vennestraat 76.

Fischer, H. K.: Psychiatric progress and problems of drug therapy, GP **16:**92, 1957.

Fischer, H. K., and Olin, B.: The dynamics of placebo therapy, Amer. J. Med. Sci. **232:**504, 1956.

Hollender, M. H.: The psychology of medical practice, Philadelphia, 1958, W. B. Saunders Co.

Hundley, J. M.: Change and challenge, J. Amer. Pharm. Ass. **3:**515, 1963.

Jaco, E. G., editor: Patients, physicians, and illness, New York, 1970, The Free Press of Glencoe, Inc.

Kaufman, W.: Some psychological aspects of therapy with drugs, Parts I to IV, Conn. Med. **25:**300-304; 368-371; 438-441; 506-509, 1961.

Lasagna, L.: Placebos, Sci. Amer. **193:**68, 1955.

Pennes, H. H., editor: Psychopharmacology, New York, 1958, Harper & Row, Publishers.

Rome, H. P.: Doctors: drugs: patients, Med. Clin. N. Amer. **34:**973, 1950.

Rosenheim, M. L., and Moulton, R., editors: Sensitivity reactions to drugs, Springfield, Ill., 1950, Charles C Thomas, Publisher.

St. Whitelock, O. V., editor: Techniques for the study of behavioral effects of drugs, Ann. N. Y. Acad. Sci. **65:**247, 1956.

Wikler, A.: The relation of psychiatry to pharmacology, Baltimore, 1957, The Williams & Wilkins Co.

Wolf, S.: Effects of suggestion and conditioning on the action of chemical agents in human subjects—the pharmacology of placebos, J. Clin. Invest. **29:**110, 1950.

Autonomic drugs 9

■ Autonomic nervous system

Autonomic (from the Greek words *auto*, self; *nomos*, law) means a law unto itself, or self-governing. The autonomic nervous system has been known by other names. Winslow (1732) called it sympathetic because he thought it controlled the sympathies of the body; Bichat (1800) called it vegetative to designate its control over nutrition, as opposed to voluntary processes. Gaskell called it the involuntary nervous system, to contrast it with the voluntary system, which controls skeletal movement.

The autonomic nervous system ramifies, primarily, outside the substance of the brain and spinal cord. It has been said that to describe the anatomy of the autonomic nervous system is like "setting down the anatomy of a fisherman's net; there is neither head nor tail to start on." While there are chains of ganglia located on either side of the vertebral column with tenuous connections with outgoing spinal nerves, at either end the autonomic nerves dissolve into a tassel of fibers like a length of rope frayed at both ends.

The autonomic nervous system automatically regulates a multitude of physiologic tasks necessary for the preservation of a constant internal environment (homeostasis), emergency mechanisms, and repair. Digestion of a meal, heart rate, pressure of circulating blood, and many other processes are quietly supervised by a system of control whose measure of efficiency is the silence of its working.

There are a number of centers that lie in the central nervous system that are concerned with integration of all autonomic nervous system activities. There is evidence that the hypothalamus, in particular, is concerned with such integrating activities. It contains centers that function in the regulation of body temperature, water balance, carbohydrate and fat metabolism, and blood pressure. It also integrates mechanisms concerned with emotional behavior, the waking state, and sleep. The medulla oblongata integrates the control of blood pressure and respiration. Other centers of integration may be located in higher levels of the brain.

The autonomic nervous system is composed of two systems of nerves, the parasympathetic and the sympathetic, whose actions are opposed in a balanced antagonism. The parasympathetic system is the stabilizing force; its functions are conservative, constructive, reparative, and creative. The sympathetic system is an emergency protective system that uses runaway patterns; it is geared for mass response and the expenditure of large amounts of energy.

Differences between the sympathetic and parasympathetic divisions

Although anatomic and physiologic differences do exist between the sympathetic and parasympathetic divisions, these differences are not always clear-cut and absolute. The anatomic

concept of the autonomic or visceral nervous system comprises all the nerves, peripheral ganglia, and motor centers of the internal organs or viscera (see Table 9-1).

Efferent nerves conduct messages from the central portions of the nervous system to the periphery. However, the efferent system is closely controlled by information received from the periphery via the afferent system. The efferent connections of the autonomic nervous system are built upon the principle of the two-

Table 9-1 Differentiating characteristics between the sympathetic and parasympathetic nervous systems

Characteristics	Sympathetic nervous system	Parasympathetic nervous system
Origin	Thoracolumbar	Craniosacral
Structure innervation	Cardiac muscle Smooth muscle Glands Viscera	Cardiac muscle Smooth muscle Glands Viscera
Position of cell body	Central nervous system + periphery	Always central nervous system (brain and spinal cord)
Denervation response	Continued function Denervation hypersensitivity to particular chemical mediator	Paralysis
Ganglia	Near central nervous system	Near the effector (vagus, atria of heart)
Length of fibers	Preganglionics (short) Postganglionics (long)	Preganglionics (long) Postganglionics (short)
Ratio of pre- to postganglionics	High degree of divergence (1:11, 1:17)	Divergence is minimal (1:2), very discrete, fine responses
Response	Diffuse	Discrete
Ganglion transmitter	Acetylcholine (ACh)	Acetylcholine
Transmitter substance	Norepinephrine (most cases) Acetylcholine for sweat glands and blood vessels of skeletal muscles	Acetylcholine

Blocking drugs	Adrenergic blocking agents
	Alpha-phenoxybenzamine
	    (Dibenzyline)
	Beta-propranolol
	    (Inderal)
		Cholinergic blocking agents
		(atropine)

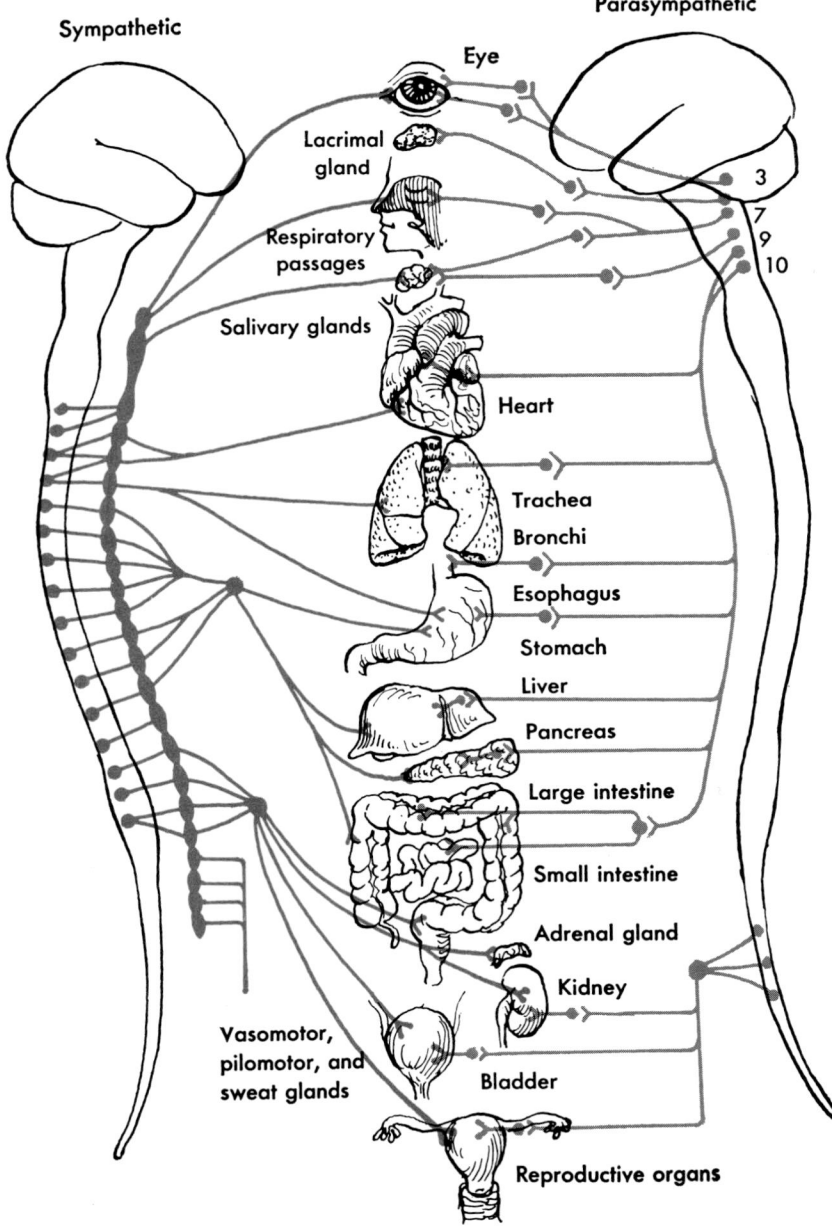

Plate 1
Diagram of autonomic nervous system. Craniosacral (parasympathetic) division is shown in gray. Thoracolumbar (sympathetic) division is shown in red.

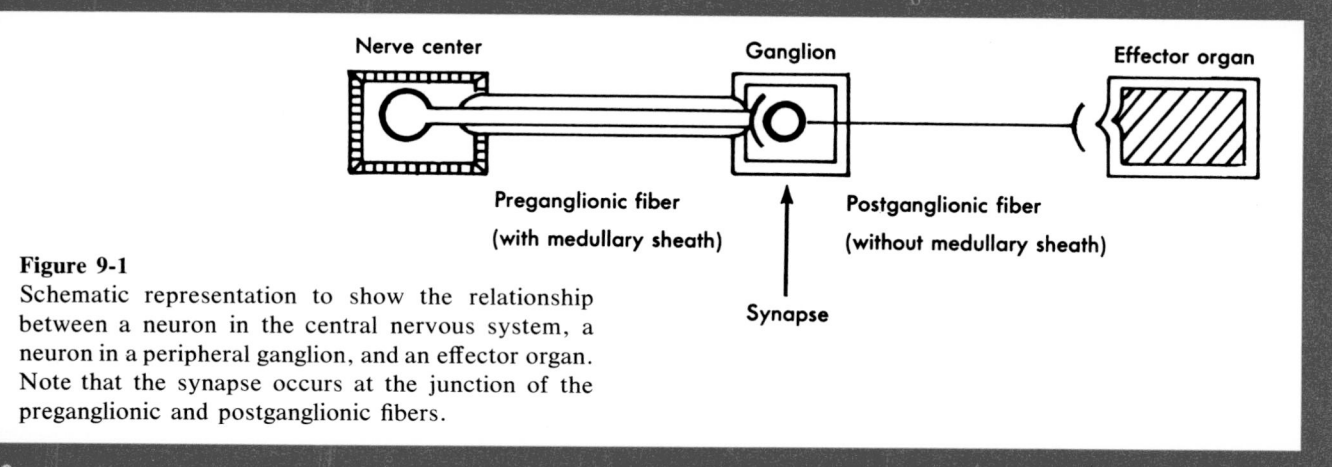

Figure 9-1
Schematic representation to show the relationship between a neuron in the central nervous system, a neuron in a peripheral ganglion, and an effector organ. Note that the synapse occurs at the junction of the preganglionic and postganglionic fibers.

neuron system, the two neurons being in series (see Figure 9-1).

Transmission of the impulse from one neuron to another takes place at the junction or synapse. The peripheral synapses of the autonomic nervous system are generally to be found in the ganglia (in groups of nerve cells situated at the periphery). The neuron that conducts the impulse from the central nervous system to the peripheral ganglion is termed *preganglionic;* the neuron that transmits the impulse from the ganglion to the effector organ is termed *postganglionic.* A preganglionic fiber may pass through several ganglia, but it forms only a single synapse.

The effect of the sympathetic and parasympathetic systems on individual organs and functions can be seen in Table 9-2. The functions stimulated by the parasympathetic system are mainly those concerned with digestion, excretion, acute vision, cardiac deceleration, and anabolism. Functions stimulated by the sympathetic system are primarily those concerned with the expenditure of energy; they are called into play by physical or emotional stress (pain, hemorrhage, extremes of temperature, intense emotion).

Understanding the anatomy and physiology of the autonomic nervous system facilitates understanding the pharmacology of autonomic drugs.

Nerve impulse transmission

There is now general agreement that transmission of nerve impulses at synaptic connections and at myoneural junctions is brought about by the activity of chemical substances called mediators. These mediators are acetylcholine and the catecholamines. The classification of autonomic nerves presently in widespread use is not an anatomic one but one based on the type of chemical mediator responsible for nerve impulse transmission. Those nerve fibers that synthesize and liberate acetylcholine are known as *cholinergic* fibers; those that synthesize and secrete norepinephrine (noradrenalin) are called *adrenergic* fibers.

Drugs that bring about effects in the body similar to those produced by acetylcholine are called cholinergic drugs. An older term used to designate this group of drugs is parasympathomimetic, because they appear to mimic the action produced by stimulation of the parasympathetic nervous system. Drugs that produce effects like those produced by the adrenergic mediator are called adrenergic drugs; the older term for these drugs is sympathomimetic.

$$CH_3-\overset{\overset{\displaystyle CH_3}{|+}}{\underset{\underset{\displaystyle CH_3}{|}}{N}}-CH_2-CH_2-O-\overset{\overset{\displaystyle O}{\|}}{C}-CH_3$$

Acetylcholine

Table 9-2 Effects produced by divisions of the autonomic nervous system

Organ or function	Sympathetic effect	Parasympathetic effect
Metabolism:		
Basal metabolic rate	Increase	Decrease
Blood sugar	Increase	Decrease
Liver glycogen	Decrease	—
Body temperature	Increase	Decrease
Heart	Acceleration	Inhibition
Blood pressure (mean)	Increase	Decrease
Blood vessels:		
Skin	Constriction	—
Muscle	Dilatation and constriction	—
Coronary vessels	Dilatation	Constriction
Salivary glands	Constriction	Dilatation
Lungs	Constriction and dilatation	Dilatation and constriction
Brain	Constriction	Dilatation
Abdominal and pelvic organs	Constriction	Dilatation
External genitalia	Constriction and dilatation	Dilatation
Smooth musculature:		
Ciliary muscle	—	Contraction
Constrictor muscle of iris	—	Contraction
Dilator muscle of iris	Contraction	—
Skin (piloerector)	Contraction	—
Bronchi	Inhibition	Constriction
Esophagus	Inhibition	Contraction
Cardia	Contraction	Relaxation
Stomach	Inhibition (or contraction)	Contraction (or inhibition)
Pylorus	Inhibition (or contraction)*	Contraction (or inhibition)
Intestine	Decrease in tone and motility	Increase in tone and motility
Sphincter ani	Contraction	—
Detrusor	Inhibition	Contraction
Vesical sphincter	Contraction	Inhibition
Uterus (human)	Mainly inhibition*	—
Glands:		
Sweat	Increase in secretion	—
Salivary	Increase in secretion†	Increase in secretion
Gastric	Decrease in secretion*	Increase in secretion
Pancreatic	Increase in secretion*	Increase in secretion
Adrenal medulla	Increase in secretion	—
Islets of Langerhans	—	Increase in secretion*
Striated muscle	Inhibition of fatigue	—

*Questionable response—uncertain about origin of response.
†Occurs at times in some glands.

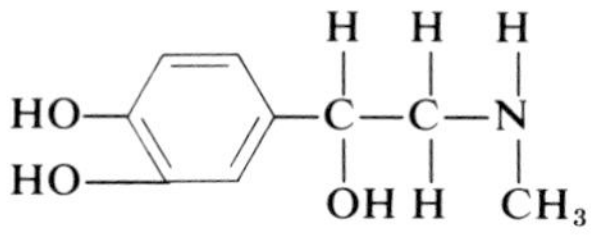

**Epinephrine
(Adrenalin)**

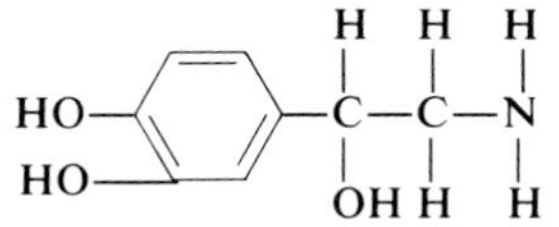

**Norepinephrine
(Noradrenalin; levarterenol)**

All preganglionic fibers of the autonomic nervous system, whether parasympathetic or sympathetic, release acetylcholine at the ganglion where synapse occurs. Also, parasympathetic postganglionic fibers release acetylcholine at the effector cell. Recent evidence indicates that acetylcholine (ACh) and norepinephrine are liberated from postganglionic sympathetic fibers. It is now hypothesized by some researchers that norepinephrine release is triggered by ACh. If further research supports this hypothesis, this will confer upon ACh the role of universal transmitter substance.

■ The catecholamines

During the past two decades great interest was evoked by confusing and conflicting reports that the effects of sympathetic nerve stimulation and the effects of epinephrine injection did not always correspond. In the mid-1940's it was shown that epinephrine had a twin, norepinephrine. With the recognition that these were separate substances that occurred naturally in the body, the confusion began to resolve. With further research two more catecholamines have been positively identified—dopamine and isoproterenol (isoprenaline). Dopamine is a precursor of norepinephrine and epinephrine (see Figure 9-2). Epinephrine acts mainly as a hormone, while norepinephrine acts as a hormone, a transmitter of nerve impulses, and an intermediary in epinephrine formation.

In 1948 Ahlquist helped to clarify the varied actions of the catecholamines by showing that in the sympathetic nervous system the adrenergic effector cells contained two distinct receptors, the alpha (α) and beta (β) receptors. Norepinephrine acts mainly on alpha receptors, isoproterenol acts mainly on beta receptors, and epinephrine acts on both, although the alpha effect is usually stronger. The most important alpha adrenergic activities in man are: (1) vasoconstriction of arterioles in the skin and splanchnic area, resulting in a rise in blood pressure; (2) pupil dilation; and (3) relaxation of the gut. Beta adrenergic activity includes: (1) cardiac acceleration and increased contractility; (2) vasodilation of arterioles supplying skeletal muscles; (3) bronchial relaxation; and (4) uterine relaxation. The effects of both alpha and beta stimulation will result from a summation of action where they are interrelated. That is, a change in blood pressure will depend on the degree of vasoconstriction in the skin and splanchnic area *and* the extent of vasodilation in skele-

Figure 9-2
Synthesis of norepinephrine and epinephrine.

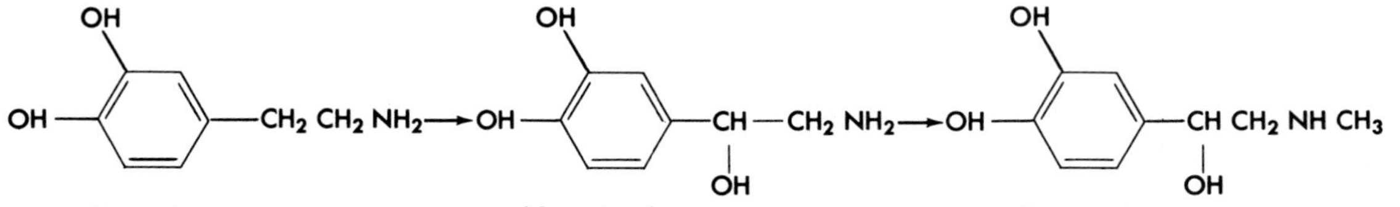

Table 9-3 Adrenergic receptor stimulation

Organ	Alpha receptor	Beta receptor
Heart 　Cardiac muscle 　Sinoatrial node 　Atrioventricular node 　Conductive tissue	–	Increase contractility of atria 　and ventricles Increase heart rate Increase conduction velocity; 　shorten refractory period
Arteries	Constriction	Relaxation
Veins	Constriction	Relaxation
Bronchial smooth muscle		Relaxation

tal muscles. Large arteries and veins contain both alpha and beta receptors; the heart contains only beta receptors (see Table 9-3).

While there are specific drugs that stimulate the alpha or beta receptors, there are also drugs that selectively block alpha or beta receptors. Most adrenergic blocking agents are alpha blockers; these drugs include ergot derivatives, phenoxybenzamine, and dibenamine. Only recently has a beta receptor blocking agent, propranolol, become available for clinical use. These agents effect blockade at peripheral autonomic sites, which distinguishes them from ganglionic blocking agents that act at the ganglia. It should be noted that no drugs presently available are *pure* alpha or beta blockers (agonists) or stimulators.

The catecholamines norepinephrine and epinephrine are neurohormones, and they serve important functions in neural and endocrine integration. They are synthesized in the brain, in the sympathetic ganglia and nerve endings, and in the adrenal medulla. Norepinephrine and epinephrine are secreted into the circulation from the adrenal medulla. Norepinephrine is also released locally as a neurotransmitter by sympathetic nerve endings. Norepinephrine and epinephrine influence a number of physiologic target organs, which include vascular smooth muscle, the heart and liver, adipose tissue, and uterine muscle. Nervous impulses from the cen-

tral nervous system control the synthesis of norepinephrine; hormones such as glucocorticoids regulate epinephrine synthesis.

The catecholamines are stored in specialized subcellular particles called granules, storage granules, or granulated vesicles. These storage granules (1) take up dopamine from cytoplasm, (2) oxidize it to norepinephrine, (3) bind and store the norepinephrine to prevent its diffusion out of the cell and destruction by enzymes, and (4) release norepinephrine after appropriate physiologic stimuli. Storage of catecholamines appears to require ATP and magnesium. This uptake process serves to terminate the actions of released or administered catecholamines and to conserve norepinephrine. Metabolism of norepinephrine and epinephrine is primarily dependent on two enzymes, monamine oxidase (MAO) and catechol-o-methyltransferase (COMT). Metabolism by MAO occurs within the neuron, while COMT catabolizes circulating catecholamines, primarily in the liver and kidney. Drugs inhibiting these enzymes prolong the actions of catecholamines.

Norepinephrine and epinephrine are continuously present in arterial blood, although the amount varies widely during any one day. Certain physiologic stimuli such as stress and exercise significantly increase catecholamine blood levels. Most of the catecholamine secreted by the human adrenal medulla is norepinephrine.

Only a small amount is epinephrine, although most epinephrine in the blood comes from the adrenal glands. Recent evidence indicates that the release of catecholamines from the adrenal gland occurs in spurts in response to proper stimuli.

Studies indicate that the major source of circulating norepinephrine comes from stimulated sympathetic nerve endings. Organs that receive a large fraction of blood and contain large numbers of sympathetic nerve endings contain the greatest amount of catecholamines. (Examples of such organs are the heart and blood vessels.) Thus the number of sympathetic nerve endings or adrenergic nerves to various organs determines the magnitude of response of these organs to increased levels or injections of catecholamines.

Epinephrine (Adrenalin)

General characteristics. Epinephrine can be prepared synthetically or obtained from the adrenal glands of domestic animals. Most of the epinephrine used in medicine at the present time is a pure synthetic preparation. Chemically, epinephrine is an amine and reacts with acids to form salts. Epinephrine hydrochloride solutions are unstable, react to light, and should be kept in the refrigerator.

Epinephrine's adrenergic effects are both excitatory and inhibitory since it acts on both alpha and beta receptors. It is a more potent alpha receptor stimulator than norepinephrine. Beta receptors are also more sensitive to epinephrine than to norepinephrine. Small doses of epinephrine will not act on alpha receptors but will act on beta receptors. Large doses of epi-

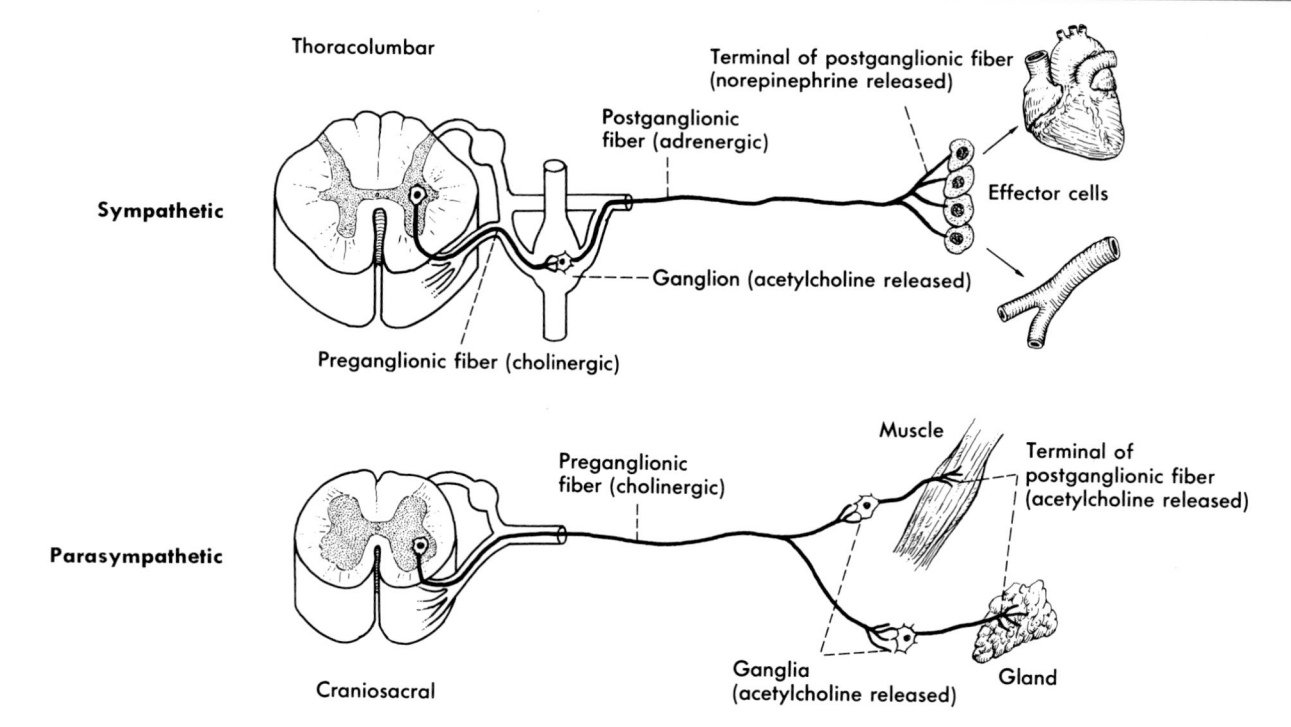

Figure 9-3
Pre- and postautonomic ganglionic fibers and neurohormone transmitters.

nephrine activate both alpha and beta receptors.

Local action and use. The ability of epinephrine to constrict blood vessels makes it useful for topical application in stopping capillary bleeding from the nose, mouth, mucosal surfaces, and skin abrasions. It is often added to local anesthetic solutions to delay their absorption from the site of injection by promoting local vasoconstriction, which in turn restricts the action of the anesthetic to that given area, prolongs the anesthetic action, and checks bleeding.

This same vasoconstrictor ability accounts for the use of epinephrine to relieve congestion and swelling of particular tissues—thus its use in treating urticaria and angioneurotic edema. When applied to the eye in a 2% solution, it dilates the pupil, decreases the blood flow, and reduces intraocular tension. This last effect makes it useful in treating chronic simple glaucoma.

Epinephrine may also be given by inhalation (in a 1:100 solution) to asthmatics to relieve bronchial spasm and swelling and to promote a patent airway. However, the time-honored treatment of an acute asthmatic attack is the subcutaneous injection of epinephrine, 0.2 to 0.5 ml. of a 1:1000 solution. Dosage may be repeated every 10 to 15 minutes or hourly if necessary. However, the patient may develop tolerance to epinephrine. Therefore, its use should be restricted to *acute* asthmatic attacks.

Epinephrine has not proved to be an effective drug in the relief of nasal congestion because of its rebound or secondary vasodilator effect, which brings about a greater swelling of the nasal mucosa than was present initially.

Systemic uses. While epinephrine mimics the actions of adrenergic stimulation, its inherent beta adrenergic properties result in responses different from that of norepinephrine with alpha adrenergic properties.

Cardiac. Epinephrine is a potent cardiac stimulant. It increases myocardial contraction (positive inotropic effect) and cardiac rate (positive chronotropic effect). (See Chapter 10 for a more detailed discussion of inotropic and chronotropic effects.) It has been shown experimentally and clinically that 0.5 mg. injected into arterial or venous blood and circulated by cardiac compression or massage may stimulate spontaneous and vigorous cardiac contractions. Even though the heart is in ventricular fibrillation, epinephrine increases fibrillation vigor and frequently promotes successful electric defibrillation of the patient. In these situations the drug may be repeatedly injected. Use of other drugs, such as sodium bicarbonate, to overcome acidosis is also necessary in these cases.

The strong myocardial contractions result in more complete emptying of the ventricles, which increases cardiac output and promotes a rise in blood pressure. It was these effects that provided the rationale for its use in cardiac arrest and the injection of epinephrine directly into heart muscle. It should be noted, however, that a reflex bradycardia may occur with a resultant fall in cardiac output.

Since epinephrine shortens the refractory period of atrial and ventricular muscle and since it speeds atrioventricular conduction, cardiac arrhythmias may develop. It also increases oxygen consumption by cardiac muscle but decreases the conversion of oxidative energy into mechanical work. It is not, therefore, a drug that can be used repeatedly to improve the function of a failing heart (congestive heart failure). It is known to cause anginal pain in patients with angina pectoris. Therefore, although it increases coronary blood flow, its use is contraindicated for patients with angina. Increased blood flow through the heart and brain results from increased systolic pressure produced by epinephrine. It is used by some cardiologists for treatment of heart block.

Blood vessels. Epinephrine is a skeletal muscle vasodilator. This is an unwanted action when it is important to increase or maintain blood flow to vital organs. When large amounts of epinephrine are given, a lethal form of shock can occur; visceral vessels become congested, stasis of blood flow occurs, hypotension ensues, and death results if these effects cannot be reversed. Therefore, epinephrine is not the drug of choice in most cases of shock or hypotension.

Blood vessels to the skin, mucosa, and kidney are constricted by epinephrine; this is an alpha receptor effect. The increased renal vascular resistance may reduce renal blood flow as much as 40%.

Smooth muscle. Vascular smooth muscle effects of epinephrine have been described. Other important effects on smooth muscle include the following.

Epinephrine is a potent dilator of bronchial smooth muscle. Its ability to inhibit bronchial secretions and constrict pulmonary blood vessels makes it a valuable drug in the treatment of acute asthmatic attacks. It is used for treatment of various allergies and is the drug of choice for anaphylactic shock.

The smooth muscle of the stomach and intestine is relaxed by large doses of epinephrine, and the sphincters are usually contracted, although sphincter action depends on the state of tonus. Intestinal tone is decreased and peristalsis is diminished. This retards the propulsion of food and gastrointestinal emptying. However, therapeutic doses rarely produce these effects.

Epinephrine stimulates the musculature of the splenic capsule, thereby increasing contractions of that organ. This action results in increasing the number of circulating red cells and blood viscosity. However, this effect is not of great significance in man.

In the urinary bladder, epinephrine causes relaxation of the bladder wall, trigone and sphincter contraction, and a delay in desire to void. Epinephrine's effect on the pregnant uterus is one of relaxation.

Metabolic effects. Epinephrine produces a significant rise in blood sugar by mobilizing liver and skeletal muscle glycogen, thus providing for increased energy. Glycosuria may be present after an injection of epinephrine. Fat metabolism is also affected, as shown by an increase in free fatty acids.

Other effects. Liberated or injected epinephrine may evoke sensations of fear and anxiety with weakness and tremor of the limbs. Sweating and salivation are stimulated by epinephrine; other gland secretions are inhibited.

Absorption and excretion. Although epinephrine is readily absorbed from mucous mem-

branes, it is destroyed by digestive enzymes and is therefore useless if given by mouth. Rapid effects may be noted when the drug is given hypodermically or intramuscularly, and almost immediate effects occur when it is given intravenously. The drug is rapidly inactivated in the body by enzymatic alteration.

Preparation, dosage, and administration. The following are available preparations of epinephrine.

Epinephrine solution, **U.S.P.** The 1:1000 aqueous solution is for topical application only. This solution is not sterile.

Epinephrine injection, **U.S.P.;** *adrenaline injection,* **B.P.** This 1:1000 solution is available in ampules and 30-ml. vials. Dosage is 0.1 to 1 ml. (gr. $1/300$ to $1/60$) given subcutaneously or intramuscularly. This preparation is sterile and contains 1 mg. of drug in each milliliter of solution. Subcutaneous administration is most often used. When the intravenous route is used, the drug must be given very slowly and in a very low concentration.

Epinephrine inhalation, **U.S.P.** This is 1:100 epinephrine solution. It should be administered with a special nebulizer to provide a fine mist for oral inhalation. Epinephrine is well absorbed from mucous membranes. The effectiveness of this preparation for the asthmatic patient is explained on the basis of achieving a relatively high concentration of the drug in the throat and respiratory passages rather than from a systemic action. Special precautions should be observed to avoid confusing the 1:100 solution with the 1:1000 solution.

Sterile epinephrine suspension, **U.S.P.** (epinephrine in oil injection). Dosage for adults is 0.2 to 0.5 ml. intramuscularly. It is available in 1-ml. ampules (1:500). The duration of action is prolonged.

Epinephrine bitartrate, **U.S.P.** This preparation is available as a 2% ophthalmic solution.

Adrenaline solution, **B.P.** This is a 1:1000 solution of epinephrine tartrate for topical application. It is not a sterile solution.

Unofficial preparations of epinephrine are also available, such as epinephrine suppositories (1:1000 with cocoa butter).

Solutions of epinephrine do not keep well; deterioration is evidenced by formation of sediment and brownish discoloration.

For children the recommended subcutaneous injection dose for asthma is 0.01 ml. of 1:1000 aqueous solution per kilogram of body weight, with a maximum dose of 0.5 ml. This dosage may be repeated every 4 hours. When the intramuscular injection of epinephrine in oil (1:500) is used, the dose is 0.01 to 0.02 ml. per kilogram of body weight every 12 to 24 hours p.r.n.

Because epinephrine is such a potent drug, the nurse must be particularly careful to give the right dose. If the preparation at hand is an ampule containing 1 ml. of the drug, it does not follow that 1 ml. is the usual dose. Very often, the dose is only a few minims. The minimum fatal dose of epinephrine subcutaneously seems to be about 10 ml. of a 1:1000 solution.

Toxic effects. Toxic effects and death from epinephrine may result from overdosage caused by errors in preparation of solutions or the intravenous administration of a subcutaneous dose. Symptoms of toxicity include tachycardia, palpitations, dyspnea, pulmonary edema, severe headache, pallor, pupillary dilation, anxiety, high blood pressure, and rapid collapse. Toxic effects may be counteracted by rapid-acting vasodilators or alpha blocking agents.

A nurse is expected to recognize an obvious error. She should carefully check the strength of solution, dosage ordered, and route of administration.

Contraindications. Epinephrine should not be used for patients on a regimen of digitalis, since together these drugs have a synergistic action and predispose the heart to premature beats or arrhythmias. Epinephrine should be avoided in patients with hyperthyroidism, hypertension, cerebral arteriosclerosis, and nervous instability. The drug should not be used in elderly or debilitated patients.

Norepinephrine

Norepinephrine is predominantly an activator of alpha receptors of smooth muscle. Norepinephrine, like epinephrine, has positive inotropic and chronotropic effects; it increases myocardial contraction and heart rate. However, norepinephrine is less likely to produce severe tachycardia, arrhythmias, and fibrillation. Norepinephrine can actually cause a reflex bradycardia. Its ability to cause vasoconstriction, an increase in total peripheral resistance to blood flow, and a rise in blood pressure activates the baroreceptors (pressure receptors). The baroreceptors then stimulate the cardioinhibitory center and slow the heart through increased vagal nerve activity. This is an example of the homeostatic mechanism in man counteracting the changes produced from an administered drug.

In addition to these actions, when the effects of norepinephrine and epinephrine are compared it is noted that:

1 They have many similar effects.
2 Toxicity from norepinephrine is less than that from epinephrine.
3 Norepinephrine is less effective than epinephrine in relieving bronchospasm, inhibiting intestinal activity, and causing hyperglycemia.
4 Norepinephrine is a more potent pressor agent than epinephrine. It has a systemic vasoconstricting effect while epinephrine causes more profound cutaneous vasoconstriction; its vasoconstricting effects are not as easily reversed with adrenergic blocking agents as are those of epinephrine.
5 Oxygen consumption by the heart is increased to a lesser extent with norepinephrine than when epinephrine is used.

The drug preparation of norepinephrine is known as levarterenol.

Levarterenol bitartrate, U.S.P.
(Levophed Bitartrate, norepinephrine);
noradrenaline acid tartrate, B.P.

$$HO \underset{OH}{\underbrace{\bigcirc}} \overset{H}{\underset{OH}{C}} \overset{H}{\underset{H}{C}} \overset{H}{\underset{H}{N}} \cdot COOH - (CHOH)_2 - COOH \cdot H_2O$$

Levarterenol bitartrate is a grayish white, crystalline powder, freely soluble in water. It darkens on exposure to light and air. It has been synthesized, but, like epinephrine, levarterenol is obtained chiefly from the medullary portion of the adrenal glands of animals.

Uses. Levarterenol bitartrate is used to maintain blood pressure in acute hypotensive conditions caused by vasomotor depression, trauma, and shock. It does not take the place of intravascular fluids if the fall in blood pressure is caused by diminished blood volume.

Levarterenol may be life saving in cardiogenic shock because of its direct stimulating effect on the myocardium and its vasoconstricting action. These effects restore the cardiac output and blood pressure to a more normal level.

Preparation, dosage, and administration. Levarterenol bitartrate is available in 4-ml. ampules containing 0.2% solutions of the drug (8 mg.). Four milliliters is usually added to 1000 ml. of 5% glucose in distilled water or to 5% glucose in physiologic saline solution. It is administered slowly by intravenous infusion with a control drip bulb, 2 to 3 ml. per minute at first. The amount may be decreased to 0.5 to 1 ml. per minute, depending on the response of the patient. Since the drug is quickly metabolized, its pressor effects disappear within 1 to 2 minutes after the infusion is stopped. The drug is also available in 2-ml. ampules of 0.02% solution for immediate intravenous or intracardiac administration in patients with cardiac arrest. The drug is ineffective when given orally.

During administration the blood pressure of the patient must be taken frequently (every 2 to 5 minutes), since the rate of infusion is determined by changes in the patient's heart rate and blood pressure. Direct arterial measurement with an intra-arterial catheter is the preferred method of taking the blood pressure. However, the indirect measurement of blood pressure using the sphygmomanometer may be used. It should be kept in mind that blood pressure measurement obtained indirectly is significantly lower than that obtained by direct measurement; the difference may be as much as 15 mm. Hg.

Cautions. Overdosage can produce marked hypertension, severe headache, photophobia, chest pain, pallor, and vomiting. Great care must be taken that the drug does not leak into subcutaneous tissue, since its marked local vasoconstricting effect may cause the tissues to slough.

Isoproterenol

Isoproterenol has predominant beta adrenergic action. It is a synthetic catecholamine with potent cardiovascular properties. Its chemical structure resembles that of epinephrine and norepinephrine.

Its positive inotropic and chronotropic actions are greater than those of epinephrine. These effects result in increased stroke volume, cardiac output and cardiac work, and coronary flow. Therefore, it is a useful drug for patients with heart failure.

Uses. Isoproterenol's chronotropic effects improve atrioventricular conduction and enhance the rhythmicity of the sinoatrial and ventricular pacemakers. This makes isoproterenol an important drug—and for many authorities the drug of choice—for the treatment of atrioventricular heart block, ventricular tachycardia, and asystole. By accelerating the action of the basic pacemakers of the heart, ectopic pacemaker activity and arrhythmias are suppressed. However, its effect on cardiac automaticity can enhance ventricular irritability. Thus, some cardiologists recommend its use in atrioventricular block only for patients with slow ventricular responses who do not respond to atropine. Pacemaker implantation may be preferred.

In addition isoproterenol relaxes arterial and bronchial smooth muscles. Isoproterenol produces both pulmonary and systemic arterial dilation, which decreases vascular resistance. It can be used to reverse pulmonary hypertension caused by pressor agents, pulmonary embolism, and incompatible blood transfusion.

Isoproterenol is a more potent bronchodilator than epinephrine. Following inhalation it facilitates liquefaction of tenacious mucus. It shrinks **107**

Table 9-4 Direct adrenergic drug effects —
catecholamine type

	Epinephrine	*Norepinephrine*	*Isoproterenol*
Trade names	Adrenalin	Noradrenalin Levarterenol	Isuprel
Mode of action Alpha receptors Beta receptors	Stimulates Inhibits	Stimulates — *	N.S.† Stimulates
Effects Cardiovascular Myocardium	Increases rate and strength of contractions Increases output	Slows rate reflexly	Like epinephrine
Pacemaker cells	Stimulates Increases irritability May cause arrhythmias	Stimulates — like epinephrine	Like epinephrine
Coronary vessels	Dilates — increases blood flow	Dilates	Like epinephrine
Blood pressure	Increases	Increases	Decreases diastolic Slightly increases systolic
Bronchi	Relaxes Improves airway	Relaxes less than epinephrine	Potent bronchodilator — more effective than epinephrine
Blood vessels Skeletal muscle	Dilates — increases blood flow	—	Dilates — increases blood flow
Kidney	Constricts — decreases blood flow	Constricts — decreases blood flow	N.S.
Gastrointestinal tract	Relaxes smooth muscle Inhibits peristalsis	Like epinephrine	N.S.
Metabolic	Increases oxygen consumption Mobilizes glycogen Causes hyperglycemia	Increases metabolic rate but less than epinephrine	N.S.
Remarks	Tolerance does not develop	Infiltration into tissues may cause necrosis and sloughing	
Uses	Widely used for allergic states, cardiac arrest; with local anesthetics Given by injection or inhalation	To elevate blood pressure, give by slow intravenous infusion	Heart failure Asthma

* —, Effect is slight, none, or unknown in man.
†N.S., Not significant.

swollen mucous membrane and reduces mucous secretion. This makes it a useful drug in the treatment of bronchial asthma and pulmonary emphysema and for the prevention and treatment of bronchospasm and laryngospasm during anesthesia. It is also used for the patient who is no longer benefited by the use of epinephrine or the patient in status asthmaticus.

Isoproterenol is also used during cardiac catheterization to simulate exercise to help determine its effects on cardiovascular activity, particularly in evaluating congenital cardiac defects and acquired valvular disease. The use of isoproterenol for patients in shock is still experimental.

Preparation, dosage, and administration. The following are the preparations available of isoproterenol.

Isoproterenol hydrochloride, **U.S.P. (Isuprel Hydrochloride, Aludrine Hydrochloride).** Isoproterenol hydrochloride is available in 10- and 15-mg. sublingual tablets. However, their absorption is variable, unreliable, and at times associated with pronounced side effects such as nausea, tachycardia, and palpitations. Isoproterenol is used as a solution for inhalation in concentrations of 1:100, 1:200, and 1:400 and as a solution for injection in 1:5000 concentration.

Isoproterenol sulfate, **N.F. (Norisodrine Sulfate, Isonorin Sulfate);** *isoprenaline sulfate,* **B.P.** This is available in the form of a powder for inhalation (10% and 25%), as a solution for inhalation (1:100), and in tablets (10 mg.) for sublingual administration.

Isoproterenol may be given intravenously. From 1 to 4 mg. per minute may be given in a continuous drip. From 5 to 40 mg. per minute have been used to arouse a pacemaker. It has been shown that isoproterenol is an effective drug in the treatment of Stokes-Adams syndrome when 1.0 mg. is administered in 200 ml. of 5% dextrose in water starting at 20 drops per minute. Thereafter, flow is regulated to maintain ventricular rate at 35 to 50 beats per minute.

Side effects and toxic effects. Untoward effects include precordial pain, heart palpitation, anginal pain (pain down one or both arms), headache, nausea, tremor, and flushing of the skin. There may be a fall in arterial blood pressure. It is contraindicated for patients who have insufficient coronary blood flow.

Precautions. Isoproterenol must be used cautiously in patients with valvular stenosis since cardiac output may be seriously compromised. Caution should also be exercised when the patient has digitalis-induced heart block.

Ephedrine

$$\text{C}_6\text{H}_5-\underset{\underset{\text{OH}}{|}}{\overset{\overset{\text{H}}{|}}{\text{C}}}-\underset{\underset{\text{CH}_3}{|}}{\overset{\overset{\text{H}}{|}}{\text{C}}}-\underset{\underset{\text{CH}_3}{|}}{\overset{\overset{\text{H}}{|}}{\text{N}}}$$

Ephedrine is the name given to an active principle isolated from an Asiatic drug, ma huang (*Ephedra vulgaris,* var. *helvetica*), which has been used in the practice of medicine in China for more than 5000 years. In chemical composition it is an amine, closely allied to epinephrine, and it is an alkaloid. At the present time, most of the ephedrine used is produced synthetically. The ephedrine alkaloid is levorotatory.

Action and result. Ephedrine has both a direct and an indirect sympathomimetic action. Its indirect action is caused by its release of norepinephrine or the impairment of norepinephrine uptake by storage granules. Ephedrine has been found to be both an alpha and beta adrenergic stimulant. Like epinephrine and norepinephrine, ephedrine has positive inotropic (myocardial stimulation) and chronotropic (increased heart rate) activity, but it is a less effective vasoconstrictor. However, it does raise the blood pressure and is used for this purpose during spinal anesthesia and some types of hypotension. It is beneficial for the treatment of hypotension caused by shock from any cause.

Ephedrine resembles epinephrine but differs from it in a number of ways. Ephedrine is more stable than epinephrine, it is well absorbed from the gastrointestinal tract, and it is effective when given orally. Its action is slower, more prolonged, but less intense than that produced by epinephrine. In addition, ephedrine stimulates the central nervous system by acting on the cerebral cortex and medulla. This accounts for its use in the treatment of narcolepsy, a state in which the patient persistently falls asleep. However, this use for ephedrine has been largely replaced by the amphetamines.

Its ability to stimulate the respiratory center in the medulla makes ephedrine a useful drug for the treatment of narcotic, barbiturate, and alcohol poisoning.

Ephedrine relaxes hypertonic muscle in the bronchioles and in the gastrointestinal tract. Emptying time of the stomach and intestine is delayed. Sphincter muscles in the urinary as well as in the gastrointestinal tracts are stimulated. The effect on metabolism is similar to that of epinephrine.

In the treatment of bronchial asthma, ephedrine is useful in preventing acute attacks. Epinephrine is preferable when attacks are acute because of its more rapid effect.

As a constituent of nasal drops, jellies, and sprays, ephedrine relieves acute congestion of hay fever, sinusitis, head colds, and vasomotor rhinitis. Shrinkage of mucous membranes begins immediately and lasts for several hours. Vasodilation does not ordinarily follow vasoconstriction, as may occur after epinephrine.

Ephedrine exhibits a tendency to increase the tone of skeletal muscle. It is used in the treatment of muscle weakness associated with myasthenia gravis. It is most effective, however, when combined with prostigmine.

Ephedrine may be used in solution as a mydriatic when a cycloplegic action is not necessarily desired. It is not useful if inflammation is present. It acts as a mydriatic in the eye by acting on the radial muscles of the iris. This occurs with local application to the eye and with systemic administration of the drug.

A 3% to 4% solution is used for eyedrops, and the oral range of dosage is 20 to 50 mg. (gr. $^1/_3$ to $^3/_4$) every 3 or 4 hours. The oral dose for children is 3 mg. per kilogram of body weight daily, divided into four or six portions.

Preparation, dosage, and administration. The following are the preparations and dosages of ephedrine.

Ephedrine sulfate capsules, **U.S.P.;** *ephedrine sulfate tablets,* **N.F.** These are available in 25 and 50 mg. for oral administration. The usual dose is 25 mg. (gr. $^3/_8$) taken three or four times daily.

Ephedrine sulfate injection, **U.S.P.** This is available in 1-ml. ampules containing 25 or 50 mg. (gr. $^3/_8$ to $^3/_4$) of drug in solution for injection. The usual dose is 25 mg. (gr. $^3/_8$).

Ephedrine hydrochloride, **N.F., B.P.** This is available in capsule and tablet form and the usual dose is 25 mg. (gr. $^3/_8$).

Ephedrine sulfate solution, **U.S.P.** This is available in 1% and 3% solutions of the drug in 0.36% sodium chloride solution, to be further diluted with an equal amount of isotonic saline before use.

Ephedrine sulfate syrup, **U.S.P.** The usual dose is 5 ml. (20 mg. ephedrine sulfate).

Ephedrine sulfate and phenobarbital capsules, **N.F.** Each capsule contains 25 and 50 mg. of ephedrine sulfate and 30 and 60 mg. of phenobarbital.

(The main difference between the hydrochloride and the sulfate salts of ephedrine is that the latter are more freely soluble in water.)

Side effects and toxic effects. Older men may experience difficulty with voiding because of ephedrine's ability to relax bladder musculature. Anxiety, irritability, headache, tremor, palpitation, and insomnia are common side effects. Nausea and vomiting may also occur. Occasionally a patient will exhibit symptoms of hypersensitivity. The same precautions are recommended for the use of ephedrine as for epinephrine. Barbiturates or some type of sedative is sometimes prescribed for the patient who is receiving the drug over a period of time. This is to counteract the central stimulating effect of ephedrine. Diminished response to the drug occurs with repeated administration. Although tolerance develops, it has not been known to cause addiction.

Phenylephrine hydrochloride, U.S.P., B.P. (Neo-Synephrine Hydrochloride)

Phenylephrine hydrochloride is a synthetic adrenergic drug chemically related to epinephrine, norepinephrine, and ephedrine.

Action and uses. Phenylephrine hydrochloride is relatively nontoxic, exhibits fewer side effects than epinephrine, and has longer lasting therapeutic effects. It has no effect on the central nervous system.

Phenylephrine hydrochloride is a powerful stimulator of alpha receptors and is therefore a potent vasoconstrictor. It elevates both the systolic and diastolic blood pressures. Its vasoconstricting action is more prolonged than that of epinephrine—it lasts 20 minutes after intravenous administration and 50 minutes after subcutaneous injection. For these reasons it is often used to treat hypotension caused by myocardial infarction, orthostatic hypotension, and hypotension resulting from loss of vasomotor tone from spinal anesthesia. It is not effective in shock caused by loss of blood volume.

Phenylephrine has very little inotropic or chronotropic effect. It does cause a reflex bradycardia as a result of its ability to elevate the blood pressure, which stimulates the baroreceptors and vagal activity. It is therefore an effective drug in converting paroxysmal tachycardia to a normal rate.

When applied topically to mucous membranes, it reduces swelling and congestion by constricting the small blood vessels.

It is useful in the treatment of sinusitis, vasomotor rhinitis, and hay fever. It is sometimes combined with local anesthetics to retard their systemic absorption and to prolong their action.

Phenylephrine hydrochloride is used as a mydriatic for certain conditions in which dilation of the pupil is desired without cycloplegia (paralysis of the ciliary muscle).

It is occasionally used for patients who have allergic symptoms and used alone or with other drugs for the relief of bronchial asthma.

Preparation, dosage, and administration. Phenylephrine hydrochloride is marketed in 10- and 25-mg. capsules for oral administration, as a 0.2% and a 1% solution for injection, and in a number of forms for topical application—solutions, an ophthalmic solution, a jelly, and an emulsion. Phenylephrine hydrochloride, U.S.P. (2 and 10 mg. per milliliter) and phenylephrine hydrochloride solution, U.S.P. (0.25%, 0.5%, and 1%) are official preparations.

For topical application to the nasal mucous membrane, 0.25% solution is ordinarily used. For parenteral injection, 0.1 to 1 ml. of a 1% solution is used. The intravenous dose should be about one tenth the subcutaneous or intramuscular dose. As a mydriatic, 1 or 2 drops of the 1% solution or emulsion or the 2.5% ophthalmic solution are used. The oral dose needs to be about fifty times the subcutaneous dose—30 to 75 mg. (in divided doses) daily for allergic conditions.

Mephentermine sulfate, U.S.P., B.P. (Wyamine Sulfate)

$$\text{CH}_2\!-\!\underset{\underset{\text{CH}_3}{|}}{\overset{\overset{\text{CH}_3}{|}}{\text{C}}}\!-\!\text{NH}\!-\!\text{CH}_3 \cdot {}^{1}\!/_{2}\,\text{H}_2\text{SO}_4 \cdot \text{H}_2\text{O}$$

Mephentermine sulfate is a white crystalline powder that is freely soluble in water.

Action. Its effects are similar to those of the amphetamines and ephedrine, but it brings about far less cerebral stimulation. Local application in the eye produces dilation of the pupil.

Mephentermine is an indirectly acting sympathomimetic. It releases catecholamines from storage sites in the heart and other tissues. Therefore, it tends to bring about both alpha and beta stimulating effects and inotropic and chronotropic effects on the heart.

Its vasoconstrictor effect is used to treat hypotensive states not associated with hemorrhage. In these cases the drug is given intramuscularly or intravenously. Onset of action occurs within 5 to 15 minutes and lasts 1 to 2 hours. Since it improves cardiac contraction and mobilizes blood from venous pools, thereby increasing cardiac output, it is also used in heart failure following a myocardial infarction. Mephentermine also increases cardiac conduction and shortens the refractory period of the heart. This makes it useful in treating certain cardiac arrhythmias.

Like ephedrine, mephentermine constricts the small blood vessels of the nasal mucosa and can be used topically or by inhalation to relieve nasal congestion. It does not cause rebound congestion.

It should be noted that if catecholamine storage sites have been depleted, there may be no pressor response from mephentermine. In this case, administration of norepinephrine resupplies these depots or storage sites, which restores the action of mephentermine.

Preparation, dosage, and administration. Mephentermine sulfate is administered topically for nasal congestion and orally, intramuscularly, and intravenously for systemic effects. It is available in 1- and 2-ml. ampules containing 15 and 30 mg. per milliliter for injection; as an elixir, 5 mg. per milliliter; in tablets (12.5 and 25 mg.) for oral administration; and as a solution (0.5%) for topical administration to nasal membranes (2 or 3 drops every 4 hours as needed). Dosage for systemic effect varies from 10 to 30 mg. Inhalers are also marketed that contain 250 mg. of the drug.

When given by continuous intravenous drip, 600 to 1000 mg. may be added to 1 L. of 5% glucose in water. Continuous blood pressure monitoring is required, since adverse blood pressure responses may be obtained.

Metaraminol bitartrate, U.S.P., B.P. (Aramine Bitartrate, Pressonex Bitartrate)

Metaraminol is a vasopressor agent with both direct and indirect effects on the sympathetic system. It acts indirectly by releasing norepinephrine from tissues and storage sites and directly as a neurohormone. Metaraminol also has positive inotropic effects. Since it constricts blood vessels, increases peripheral resistance, elevates both systolic and diastolic blood pressure, and improves cardiac contractility and cerebral, coronary, and renal blood flow, it is a valuable drug for the treatment of shock. It is used to overcome hypotension associated with myocardial infarction, surgical procedures, barbiturate poisoning, and trauma.

Since it exhibits beta as well as alpha adrenergic activity, it is often effective in raising blood pressure when alpha adrenergic agents are ineffective. This may be because of its ability to bring about a more effective venous flow. It does not appear to cause arrhythmias.

While the action of metaraminol is similar to that of norepinephrine, it is a less potent drug. Its onset of action is more gradual than that obtained from norepinephrine, but it is longer acting. It exerts a smoother blood pressure response than some of the other vasopressor agents, which makes it easier to determine rate of flow when given intravenously.

Preparation, dosage, and administration. Metaraminol is available in 1- and 10-ml. units containing 10 mg. per milliliter. It may be given subcutaneously or intramuscularly in a 2- to 10-mg. dose, or by intravenous drip, 15 to 100 mg. in 500 ml. of 5% dextrose in physiologic saline. Effects appear in 5 to 20 minutes after subcutaneous injection, 10 minutes after intramuscular injection, and within 1 or 2 minutes following intravenous administration. In emergency situations, 500 μg. to 5 mg. of metaraminol may be injected intravenously.

The same precautions should be employed when giving metaraminol as when giving other powerful vasoconstrictors.

Methoxamine hydrochloride, U.S.P. (Vasoxyl)

Methoxamine is an alpha adrenergic stimulator and appears to be devoid of beta receptor activity. Therefore, it is almost exclusively a vasoconstrictor. It is used in treating nasal congestion and hypotension. Since it has no stimulating effect on the heart, the rise in blood pres-

Table 9-5 Adrenergic drug effects —
noncatecholamine type

	Ephedrine	*Phenylephrine*	*Mephentermine*	*Metaraminol*	*Methoxamine*
Trade names		Neo-Synephrine	Wyamine	Aramine Pressonex	Vasoxyl
Mode of action Alpha receptors Beta receptors	Stimulates Stimulates More prolonged but less intense action than epinephrine	Stimulates N.S.	Stimulates	Stimulates	Stimulates —
Effects Cardiovascular Myocardium	Variable	N.S. Bradycardia may occur reflexly	Increases contractility and rate May cause bradycardia	Some increase in contractility Bradycardia may occur	— Reflex bradycardia may occur
Pacemaker cells	N.S.*	N.S.	N.S.		
Coronary vessels	Dilates — increases blood flow	Dilates — increases blood flow	Dilates — increases blood flow	—	—
Blood pressure	Increases	Increases	Increases	Increases	Increases
Bronchi	Dilates	Dilates but less than epinephrine	Dilates but less than epinephrine	N.S.	
Cerebral effects	Stimulating action	N.S.	N.S.	—	—
Blood vessels Skeletal muscle	N.S.	—†	N.S.	N.S.	—
Kidney	Constricts	Constricts	Constricts but less than ephedrine	Constricts — decreases blood flow	Decreases blood flow
Gastrointestinal tract	Decreases peristalsis	Decreases mobility	Relaxes smooth muscle — inhibits	Some inhibition	Inhibits
Metabolic	Increases metabolic rate	Some increase in metabolic rate	N.S.	N.S.	N.S.
Remarks	Serious arrhythmias may occur if used with digitalis Can be given orally			Prolonged duration of action, cumulative effects may occur — give drug slowly May cause tissue sloughing — do not give subcutaneously	
Uses	Vasopressor Allergic states Nasal decongestant Enuresis Myasthenia gravis	Nasal decongestant Vasopressor Paroxysmal atrial tachycardia Mydriatic	Vasopressor Nasal decongestant	Vasopressor Nasal decongestant	Vasopressor Paroxysmal atrial tachycardia Nasal decongestant

*N.S., Not significant.
†—, Effect is slight, none, or unknown in man.

Table 9-6 Principal uses of adrenergic drugs

Vasoconstrictor (pressor) action (treatment of hypotensive states)

Epinephrine	Mephentermine
Isoproterenol	Norepinephrine
Levarterenol (norepinephrine)	Phenylephrine
Metaraminol	Phenylpropanolamine
Methoxamine	

Local vasoconstrictor action (hemostasis; prolong local anesthetic action)

Epinephrine	Methoxamine

Nasal decongestant action (in treatment of allergic rhinitis, common cold, hay fever)

Ephedrine	Phenylephrine
Mephentermine	Phenylpropanolamine
Methoxamine	Propylhexedrine

Bronchodilator action (in treatment of asthma)

Ephedrine	Levarterenol (norepinephrine)
Epinephrine	Phenylpropanolamine
Isoproterenol	Protokylol
Methoxyphenamine	

Vasodilator action (in treatment of peripheral vascular disease)

Nylidrine

Mydriatic action (for ophthalmologic examination)

Ephedrine	Phenylephrine

sure causes a reflex bradycardia. It is this effect that makes it useful in treating paroxysmal tachycardia.

Preparation, dosage, and administration. Methoxamine hydrochloride is supplied in solution form for intramuscular or intravenous injection. It is available in 1-ml. ampules containing 20 mg., in 10-ml. vials containing 10 mg. per milliliter, and in 1-ml. ampules containing 15 mg. of methoxamine and 10 mg. procaine hydrochloride. It is also available in a 0.5% nasal solution.

When it is given intravenously its effects occur almost immediately and last for 1 hour; intramuscularly, effects occur within 15 minutes and persist for about 90 minutes. Slow intravenous infusions of the drug may also be used—60 to 70 mg. methoxamine in 500 ml. of 5% dextrose.

Side effects. Side effects include severe headache, urinary urgency, and vomiting.

■ Alpha blocking agents

Most alpha adrenergic blocking agents are competitive blockers; that is, they compete with the catecholamines at receptor sites and inhibit adrenergic sympathetic stimulation. They are more effective against action of circulating catecholamines than against catecholamines released from storage sites. These drugs may be obtained from natural sources, such as ergot and its derivatives, or they may be synthesized.

Alpha blocking agents are used in the treatment of peripheral vascular disease and migraine headache. Phentolamine is used in the diagnosis and surgical management of pheochromocytoma (tumors of the medullary portion of the adrenal gland that secrete large amounts of epinephrine and norepinephrine). Most of the adrenergic blocking agents are not drugs of choice in the treatment of essential hypertension, because their action is too unpredictable and side effects too troublesome.

Phenoxybenzamine hydrochloride, B.P. (Dibenzyline)

Phenoxybenzamine abolishes or decreases the receptiveness of alpha receptors to adrenergic stimuli. Its effects are predominantly those of vasodilation and inhibition of vasospasm. This drug lowers peripheral resistance and increases the size of the vascular space. For these reasons it is a useful drug in the treatment of peripheral vascular diseases, such as Raynaud's disease.

Since this agent competes with the catecholamines, it is also useful in decreasing the blood pressure of patients with pheochromocytoma. It does not block sympathetic impulses on the heart and therefore does not impair cardiac output. It has mild antihistaminic activity and may cause nasal drying.

Phenoxybenzamine may be used as an antishock agent because of its ability to increase the vascular space and permit adequate flow of blood to tissues. However, it should not be used in hypovolemic shock without the use of volume expanders or blood replacement. In hypovolemia, an increase in vascular space will cause the blood pressure to fall even further. Phenoxybenzamine causes little change in supine blood pressure, but it is known to cause orthostatic hypotension and reflex tachycardia. It is also used to prevent epinephrine-induced cardiac arrhythmias.

Preparation, dosage, and administration. Phenoxybenzamine is available in 10-mg. capsules for oral use. The initial dose is usually 10 mg. daily. Dosage may be increased by increments of 10 mg. at 4-day intervals. Maintenance dosage is usually 20 to 60 mg. daily. Onset of action occurs in about 2 hours, and duration of action is 24 to 36 hours. Daily administration causes cumulative effects, intensifies side effects, and predisposes to toxic effects.

Phentolamine hydrochloride, N.F. (Regitine Hydrochloride); phentolamine mesylate, U.S.P., B.P. (Regitine Mesylate)

Phentolamine is a direct vasodilator and inhibitor of hypertension because of excessive levels of epinephrine and norepinephrine. Its direct effect is more potent than its adrenergic blocking action.

Phentolamine is used in the diagnosis of pheochromocytoma. Since this tumor secretes large amounts of catecholamines, which produce elevated blood pressure, a marked fall in blood pressure following administration of phentolamine suggests the presence of pheochromocytoma. However, this test lacks precision.

This drug is also used to reverse the vasoconstrictive action of an overdose or excessive response to injected norepinephrine (levarterenol). The subcutaneous injection of phentolamine following extravasation of intravenous norepinephrine will prevent tissue necrosis. Phentolamine also has a stimulant action on cardiac muscle and the gastrointestinal tract.

Preparation, dosage, and administration. Phentolamine hydrochloride is available in 50-mg. tablets for oral use. The usual adult dose is 50 mg. four to six times daily; for children the dose is 5 mg. per kilogram of body weight daily divided into four or six doses.

Phentolamine mesylate is administered intramuscularly or intravenously. It is prepared in 5-mg. vials to which 1 ml. of diluent is added for injection. The amount used in the test for pheochromocytoma is 5 mg. The preoperative dose for removal of the adrenal tumor is 2 to 5 mg. For children the dose is usually 1 mg.

Side effects. Side effects include tachycardia, orthostatic hypotension, nausea and vomiting, diarrhea, weakness, dizziness, and flushing. Phentolamine should be used with caution in patients with gastritis, peptic ulcer, or coronary artery disease.

Ergot alkaloids

Alkaloids found in extracts of a fungous disease of rye called *ergot* are derivatives of lysergic acid; some of these alkaloids cause alpha receptor blockade. At the present time, it is not clear to what extent their vasoconstrictor action results from alpha blockade of direct vasoconstriction.

Ergotamine tartrate

Ergotamine has marked vasoconstrictor activity. All ergot alkaloids stimulate uterine smooth muscle; both tone and amplitude of uterine contractions are increased. However, ergotamine is no longer used as an oxytocic. It is now used chiefly to treat migraine headache and is considered almost a specific for this condition. Its efficacy in migraine is thought to result from cerebral vasoconstriction, which decreases the amplitude of the pulsations of cranial arteries. The earlier the drug is taken, the smaller the dose needed and the more rapid the effect. Administration of the drug should be followed by bed rest for an hour or two.

This drug also has been used to relieve intense itching and hives associated with jaundice, cirrhosis of the liver, or Hodgkin's disease.

Since this drug has a cumulative action, it must be used with caution. It is capable of producing all the symptoms of ergotism: numbness and tingling of the fingers and toes, muscle pains and muscle weakness, as well as gangrene and blindness. Its use is contraindicated in patients with diabetes mellitus or hepatic disease.

Preparation, dosage, and administration. The following are the ergotamine preparations available.

***Ergotamine tartrate*, U.S.P., B.P. (Gynergen).** The usual oral dose is 2 mg., and the usual intramuscular dose is 0.25 mg. Ergotamine tartrate is available in tablets for oral administration (1 mg.), in ampules of solution for parenteral administration (0.25 mg. in 0.5 ml. and 0.5 mg. in 1 ml.), and as suppositories for rectal administration.

***Ergotamine with caffeine*, N.F. (Cafergot).** Each tablet contains 1 mg. ergotamine tartrate and 100 mg. caffeine. Usual dose is one to two tablets for headache. Dosage may be repeated if necessary. The caffeine presumably increases the effectiveness of ergotamine because of its own vasoconstrictor action.

***Dihydroergotamine* (D.H.E. 45).** This compound is prepared by hydrogenating ergotamine and is used in the treatment of migraine headache. It is available in 1-ml. ampules that contain 1 mg. of the drug. Administration is intramuscular, subcutaneous, or intravenous. It is said to produce fewer side effects than ergotamine tartrate.

Methysergide maleate, N.F. (Sansert)

Methysergide maleate, a drug related structurally to the ergot alkaloids, has been introduced into therapeutics for the prophylactic treatment of vascular headaches, such as migraine, cluster headaches, and others. Each tablet contains 2 mg. of methysergide maleate. The drug is a serotonin antagonist.

Retroperitoneal fibrosis has been noted in a small number of patients on methysergide therapy. Its signs and symptoms usually present themselves as urinary tract obstruction. Because of this serious complication and numerous side effects, the approved package insert should be consulted before the drug is used. The usual dose is two to four tablets, preferably one tablet with each meal. Because of the potential dangers of prolonged therapy, treatment with methysergide should not exceed 6 months without a rest period of 3 to 4 weeks. In addition, patients should be instructed to report promptly any dysuria or back pain.

■ Beta blocking agents

Drugs that block the beta adrenergic receptors have been developed only within the past few years and have been released for clinical use only recently. In the United States, the only agent presently in clinical use is propranolol (Inderal). This drug is chemically related to isoproterenol. Other drugs are undergoing experimental clinical trials.

Beta blockers inhibit the sympathetic actions of beta receptors by competing with the catecholamines at the effector site. The exact mode of action is not known. These agents *block* vasodilation, cardiac acceleration, increased cardiac output, bronchial dilation, and hyperglycemia.

Propranolol, B.P. (Inderal)

Propranolol inhibits the inotropic and chronotropic actions caused by beta adrenergic stimulation and has a quinidine-like effect. Propranolol inhibits pacemaker activity and atrioventricular conduction and prolongs cardiac diastole. These actions account for its clinical effectiveness in controlling various ventricular arrhythmias including digitalis-induced arrhythmia when hypokalemia is not present. It may be used in the preparation of patients for cardioversion when digitalis must be withheld prior to cardioversion.

Propranolol has been found effective in the treatment of some cases of angina. It probably acts by preventing an increase in cardiac activity in response to exercise. There is evidence that patients treated with propranolol can undertake a greater amount of exercise before experiencing anginal pain.

Dosage and administration. Propranolol may be administered orally or intravenously. When given orally, it is most readily absorbed in the fasting state and therefore should be given before meals. It is effective within 1 to 4 hours, and the effect lasts about 6 hours. The usual oral dose is from 30 to 120 mg. daily.

When propranolol is administered intravenously, maximal effect occurs within 10 minutes. The range of dose for intravenous administration is usually 1 to 5 mg. This drug *must* be given slowly with careful monitoring of vital signs and electrocardiographic control. Administration should be discontinued when a change in heart rate or rhythm is noted.

Side effects. Side effects include nausea and vomiting, lightheadedness, and mild paresthesia.

Toxic effects. These include hypotension, bradycardia, heart block, congestive heart failure in patients with limited cardiac reserve, and intensified hypoglycemia in diabetic patients receiving insulin or oral hypoglycemic drugs. The latter effect occurs because beta-receptor activity is necessary for a rise in blood sugar and free fatty acids and for manifestations of insulin overdosage. Special precautions should be taken when propranolol is used along with other adrenergic blocking agents, since the effects are additive, or when used with MAO inhibitors, since the enhanced alpha effect may lead to hypertension.

Contraindications. Propranolol is contraindicated in patients with congestive heart failure, hypotension, asthma, and atrioventricular heart block.

Acetylcholine

Bethanechol
(carbamyl-β-methylcholine)

Methacholine

■ Cholinergic drugs

Acetylcholine plays an important role in transmission of nerve impulses in both the sympathetic and parasympathetic divisions of the autonomic nervous system.

Acetylcholine has two major actions on the autonomic nervous system: (1) it has stimulant effects on the ganglia, adrenal medulla, and skeletal muscle, and (2) it has stimulant effects at postganglionic nerve endings in cardiac muscle, smooth muscle, and glands. The first action resembles the effects of nicotine and therefore is referred to as the "nicotinic action" of acetylcholine. The effects of acetylcholine at the effector cell is like that of muscarine (an alkaloid obtained from the toadstool *Amanita muscaria*), and it is referred to as the "muscarinic action" of acetylcholine. These terms are used in describing acetylcholine effects because both nicotine and muscarine and their effects on nerve impulses were studied long before acetylcholine was identified or synthesized. See Table 9-7 for these actions.

It is hypothesized by some prominent present-day researchers that acetylcholine is released by all postganglionic fibers and that a function of acetylcholine is to liberate norepinephrine for adrenergic stimulation. This hypothesis that acetylcholine is involved at adrenergic nerve endings as an intermediary

Table 9-7 Nicotinic and muscarinic actions of acetylcholine

	Nicotinic action	*Muscarinic action*
Cardiovascular		
Blood vessels	Constriction	Dilation
Heart rate	Increased	Slowed
Blood pressure	Increased	Decreased
Gastrointestinal		
Tone	Increased	Increased
Motility	Increased	Increased
Sphincters	−	Relaxed
Glandular secretions	Initial stimulation then inhibition of salivary and bronchial secretions	Increased salivary, lacrimal, intestinal, and sweat secretion
Central nervous system	Stimulation—tremors, convulsions with large doses	Cortical arousal
Skeletal muscle	Stimulated	−
Autonomic ganglia	Stimulated	−
Eye	−	Pupil constriction Decreased accommodation
Blocking agent	Tubocurarine	Atropine
Remarks	Increased dosage inhibits effects and causes receptor blockade	Effects increase as dosage increases

transmitter for the release of norepinephrine is, at the present time, controversial. It is also theorized that acetylcholine acts by making the fiber membrane permeable to calcium; the rise in calcium concentration within the fiber causes a release of norepinephrine. These theories are based on evidence from electron microscopy.

Those drugs chemically related to acetylcholine that produce similar effects are cholinergic drugs. These drugs may be obtained from plant sources or synthesized. The synthetic drugs are more stable and have a more selective action on particular organs.

Cholinergic fibers are widespread; they are present in heart, spleen, uterus, vas deferens, and colon and in the vessels of the skin and muscles. It is quite likely that cholinergic fibers are present in many more tissues of the body. In the gastrointestinal tract parasympathetic innervation predominates; it inhibits both motor and secretory action.

Acetylcholine (ACh) is synthesized in motor nerve terminals under the control of the enzyme choline-acetylase. ACh is stored in vesicles within the nerve terminals and released by (1) spontaneous rupture of small numbers of vesicles or (2) rupture of large numbers of vesicles simultaneously with nerve impulse stimulation. The former action releases amounts of ACh too small to generate a propagated muscle contraction; the latter action releases ACh in amounts sufficient to initiate muscle fiber contraction. Influx of calcium ions into the nerve apparently increases the fragility of the vesicles, promoting their rupture. When the depolarizing action occurs, the ACh is hydrolyzed within milliseconds by cholinesterase located on the surface of the end plate to allow for rapid transmission of the next impulse. Hence, the effect of acetylcholine is brief. When the enzyme is made ineffective, as it is by certain drugs (anticholinesterase drugs), the effect of acetylcholine is intensified and prolonged.

Cholinergic drugs are used:

1 To stimulate the intestines and bladder postoperatively
2 To lower intraocular pressure in glaucoma
3 To promote salivation and sweating
4 To dilate peripheral blood vessels in conditions of vasospasm
5 To terminate curarization
6 To symptomatically treat myasthenia gravis

The use of cholinergic agents to treat cardiac arrhythmias has been almost abandoned, since new and more effective antiarrhythmic agents have been developed. Therapeutic effectiveness of cholinergic drugs depends primarily upon their muscarinic action; however, some of them also possess nicotinic action. This latter action usually requires doses much larger than those used therapeutically. However, some drugs may exhibit more nicotinic than muscarinic effects.

The ideal cholinergic or anticholinesterase drug would:

1 Mimic or inhibit the effect of acetylcholine on a particular structure or organ
2 Be effective when administered orally
3 Be more stable and less easily inactivated than the drugs now available
4 Produce a therapeutic effect with minimal side effects

While these ideal drugs are not yet available, progress has been and is being made in this direction.

Cholinergic drugs used primarily to lower intraocular pressure will be discussed in Chapter 22; these include pilocarpine and carbachol.

Bethanechol chloride, U.S.P. (Urecholine Chloride)

Bethanechol is a cholinergic agent that has rather selective effects on the smooth muscle of the gastrointestinal and urinary tracts, where it promotes motility of the intestines and contraction of the bladder. Its action is primarily muscarinic. It does not exhibit any ganglion-stimulating effect. Bethanechol is not destroyed by cholinesterase; therefore, its action is of comparatively long duration. It is less potent than some of the other choline derivatives but is also less toxic. Cardiovascular effects are minimal.

Uses. This compound is useful in conditions in which stimulation of the parasympathetic nervous system is indicated. It is used to treat gastric retention after vagotomy or gastric surgery, for postoperative abdominal distention, and for urinary retention. It is sometimes used to prevent paralytic ileus and urinary retention in patients receiving certain drugs for hypertension (ganglion-blocking agents).

Preparation, dosage, and administration. Bethanechol chloride is available in 1-ml. ampules containing 5 mg. of the drug and also in 5-, 10-, and 25-mg. tablets. Bethanechol chloride is administered orally, sublingually, or subcutaneously. It must not be given intramuscularly or intravenously.

Oral and sublingual doses of 10 to 30 mg. three or four times daily will usually control symptoms. The effect of the drug can usually be observed in about 30 minutes. The usual subcutaneous dose is 2.5 to 5 mg. When given orally it should be administered with meals since it increases volume and acidity of gastric secretions.

When used in children and infants the dose is 0.6 mg. per kilogram of body weight divided into three oral doses. For subcutaneous use the dose is one third to one fourth the oral dose.

Side effects and toxic effects. Side effects are sometimes seen after subcutaneous administration and include headache, flushing, abdominal cramps, sweating, asthmatic attacks, and sometimes a drop in blood pressure. Parenteral administration of atropine promptly abolishes side effects. The major advantage of bethanechol over other choline derivatives is its greater margin of safety and low incidence of severe toxic effects.

Contraindications. Bethanechol should not be used after gastrointestinal anastomosis until healing has occurred; it should not be used when peritonitis is present or when there is vesical neck obstruction. Its use is also contraindicated during pregnancy or in patients with coronary disease, hyperthyroidism, or asthma.

Methacholine chloride, N.F. (Mecholyl Chloride)

At the present time methacholine is not a popular drug. It has been used for many different conditions—to improve muscle tone of various organs, increase secretions, treat paroxysmal atrial tachycardia—and in the diagnosis of pheochromocytoma. For the latter, a positive test results when the patient responds to a subcutaneous injection of methacholine with a

Table 9-8 Prominent cholinergic agents*

Generic name	Trade name	Single adult dose	Usual route of administration
Ambenonium	Mytelase	5-25 mg.	Oral
Benzpyrinium	Stigmonene	2 mg.	Intramuscular
Bethanechol	Urecholine	10-30 mg.	Oral
			Sublingual
		2.5-5 mg.	Subcutaneous
Isoflurophate	Floropryl	1-3 gtt. 0.1% solution	Topical (eye)
Neostigmine	Prostigmin		
Bromide	Bromide	15 mg.	Oral
Methylsulfate	Methylsulfate	0.5 mg. (1-2 mg.)	Intramuscular
Physostigmine	Eserine	0.02%-1% solution	Topical (eye)
Pilocarpine		0.5%-4% solution (1 gtt.)	Topical (eye)
Pyridostigmine	Mestinon	Highly variable	Oral

*Effects to be expected are similar to those that can be expected from stimulation of the parasympathetic nervous system (see Table 9-2). Drugs are listed in alphabetical order. The majority of drugs mentioned are administered in the form of their salts.

rise in blood pressure. It has primarily muscarinic action and little nicotinic action.

Futrethonium iodide (Furmethide)

Futrethonium is used to stimulate the bladder and cause contractions to combat urinary retention. It is administered subcutaneously in 3-mg. doses.

■ Anticholinergic agents (belladonna group)

Anticholinergics are those agents that selectively act on postganglionic effector sites and block or inhibit the muscarinic effect of acetylcholine by competing with it. These drugs are also known as antimuscarinics. Anticholinergics relax smooth muscle, inhibit secretions of duct glands, and dilate the pupils. In the toxic doses these agents will produce skeletal muscle paralysis. Anticholinergic agents may be obtained from natural sources or they may be synthesized. The synthetic drugs tend to have fewer side effects.

A number of plants belonging to the potato family (Solanaceae) contain similar alkaloids. Included are *Atropa belladonna* (deadly nightshade), *Hyoscyamus niger* (henbane),* *Datura stramonium* (Jimson weed or thorn apple),† and several species of scopola. The principal alkaloids of these plants are atropine, scopolamine (hyoscine), and hyoscyamine.

Atropa belladonna was the name conferred on one of these plants by Linnaeus in 1753. The first part of the name was selected because of the poisonous qualities of the plant and is called Atropa after Atropos, the eldest of the Greek Fates who supposedly cut the thread of life. The second part of the name, belladonna, means beautiful lady and was chosen because of the custom practiced by certain Roman women who

---

*Henbane is thought to be a corruption of hennebell, which suggests a musical instrument. In medieval Latin, henbane was referred to as *Symphoniaca herba,* symphoniaca being a rod with many bells on it. (Wootton.) Henbane is the bane of domestic fowl.

†Jimson weed is a corruption of Jamestown weed, so called because it was early observed as a weed in Jamestown, Virginia. It is given its other name, thorn apple, because of its spiny capsule.

placed belladonna preparations in their eyes to make them appear larger and more lustrous.

Atropine and scopolamine resemble each other closely, both in effects and in chemical structure, as can be seen in the accompanying formulas.

$$H_2C-CH-CH_2$$
$$|\quad\quad N-CH_3\quad CH-O-CO-C(CH_2OH)(C_6H_5)H$$
$$H_2C-CH-CH_2$$

Atropine

$$HC-CH-CH_2$$
$$O<\quad N-CH_3\quad CH-O-CO-C(CH_2OH)(C_6H_5)H$$
$$HC-CH-CH_2$$

Scopolamine

Atropine

Atropine is the chief alkaloid of the plant *Atropa belladonna*, which is grown for commercial purposes in Germany, England, Austria, and North America. It is also synthesized.

Atropine is the prototype of the anticholinergic drugs. It has been in use for over half a century and continues to be a popular drug because of its therapeutic effectiveness.

Action and result. There may be a local, central, or peripheral action.

Local. There is a slight amount of absorption when atropine or belladonna is applied to the skin, especially if it is an oily or alcoholic preparation or in the form of a plaster. Belladonna ointment or suppositories were sometimes used on mucous surfaces. The local effect for the relief of pain is slight, however, and these preparations are seldom used.

When an aqueous solution of atropine is dropped into the conjunctival sac of the eye, it quickly produces dilatation of the pupil, diminished secretion of tears, and impaired ability to focus objects close to the eye. If the eye is normal there is little change in intraocular tension, but it may increase in patients who have glaucoma.

121

Central. Cholinergic receptors are widely distributed in the central nervous system and are found in both excitatory and inhibitory systems. Thus atropine can cause excitatory or inhibitory central effects. However, its central effects are primarily inhibitory. The electroencephalogram usually shows slow, high amplitude waves characteristic of depression.

Cerebrum. Small or moderate doses of atropine have little or no effect. Large or toxic doses cause the patient to become restless, wakeful, and talkative. This condition may develop into delirium and finally stupor and coma. The exalted, excited stage has sometimes been called a "belladonna jag." A rise in temperature is sometimes seen, especially in infants and young children. This is probably the result of suppression of sweating rather than action on the heat-regulating center.

Atropine has been used to diminish tremor in Parkinson's disease. It causes a fall in the ACh content of the brain; this probably reduces cholinergic synaptic transmission.

Medulla. Therapeutic doses of atropine stimulate the respiratory center and make breathing faster and sometimes deeper. When respiration is seriously depressed, atropine is not always reliable as a stimulant; in fact, it may deepen the depression. Large doses stimulate respiration but they can also cause respiratory failure and death.

Small doses stimulate the vagus center in the medulla, causing primary slowing of the heart. The vasoconstrictor center is stimulated briefly and then depressed. Because depression follows rather soon after stimulation, atropine has been called a borderline stimulant of the central nervous system.

Peripheral. The main therapeutic uses of atropine are the result of its peripheral action rather than its central action. The more important effect is on the smooth muscle, cardiac muscle, and gland cells, which are supplied by postganglionic cholinergic nerves. These cells are so affected by atropine that they become insensitive to acetylcholine. The drug apparently does not interfere with the formation of acetylcholine nor does it combine with acetylcho-line. To some extent, atropine brings about effects similar to those produced by stimulation of postganglionic fibers in the sympathetic nervous system. The following results of peripheral action are seen.

Eye. The pupil is dilated (mydriasis) and the muscle of accommodation is paralyzed (cycloplegia). The sphincter muscle of the iris and the ciliary muscle are both innervated by cholinergic nerve fibers and therefore are affected by atropine. Since the sphincter muscle is unable to contract normally, the radial muscle of the iris causes the pupil to dilate. Pupil dilation may reduce outflow of aqueous humor, causing a rise in intraocular pressure, a hazardous situation for patients with glaucoma. These effects in the eye are brought about by both local and systemic administration of atropine, although the usual single therapeutic dose of atropine given orally or parenterally has little effect on the eye. After the pupil is dilated photophobia occurs, and when the drug has reached its full effect the usual reflexes to light and accommodation disappear.

Respiratory tract. Secretions of the nose, pharynx, and bronchial tubes are decreased. The muscles of the bronchial tubes relax and the airway widens to ease breathing. Atropine and scopolamine are less effective than epinephrine as bronchodilators and are seldom used for asthma.

Heart and blood vessels. When the usual clinical doses are given, the cardiac rate is temporarily and slightly slowed because of the central action of the drug on the cardiac center in the medulla. Moderate-to-large doses accelerate the heart by interfering with the response of the heart muscle to vagal nerve impulses. The latter is a peripheral action. The ability of atropine to interfere with vagal stimuli explains its use in the treatment of sinus bradycardia and atrioventricular heart block. In therapeutic doses atropine has little or no effect on blood pressure, although large and sometimes ordinary doses cause vasodilatation of vessels in the skin of the face and neck. This may result from a direct dilator action or from histamine release. Reddening of the face and neck is seen, especially after large or toxic doses.

Glands. Since the sweat glands of the skin are supplied by cholinergic nerves, atropine decreases or abolishes their activity. This causes the skin to become hot and dry. The flow of saline and mucus from glands lining the respiratory tract is reduced, and drying of the mucous membranes of the mouth, nose, pharynx, and bronchi occurs. Patients who have been given atropine, particularly for preoperative preparation, often complain of a dry mouth and thirst. Some of this discomfort may be relieved by frequent rinsing of the mouth.

Although some difference of opinion exists among authorities as to the effect of atropine on the activity of gastric glands, it appears that the amount and character of the gastric secretion are little affected by atropine when given in ordinary therapeutic doses. The secretion of acid in the stomach is presumably less under vagal control than under hormonal or chemical control. The effect of atropine on the secretion of the pancreas and intestinal glands is not therapeutically significant.

Smooth muscle. Atropine and other belladonna alkaloids decrease tone as well as peristalsis in the stomach and small and large intestine. Atropine does not affect the secretion of bile, but it exerts a mildly antispasmodic effect in the gallbladder and bile ducts. It exerts a relaxing effect on the ureter, especially when it has been in a state of spasm. Therapeutic doses decrease the tone of the fundus of the urinary bladder. When the detrusor muscle is hypertonic, it is relaxed by atropine.

The power of atropine to decrease the activity of uterine muscle is thought to be negligible. It is at best only mildly antispasmodic. However, atropine is said to have a relaxing effect on the circular muscle of a hypertonic uterus, which probably explains its use for dysmenorrhea.

Uses. Atropine is especially useful as a preliminary medication prior to surgical anesthesia. It decreases secretions of the mouth and respiratory passages and is effective in the prevention of laryngospasm.

Atropine may be used as a mydriatic and cycloplegic in examinations of the eye and in the treatment of certain eye conditions. It is used especially for the refractions of the eyes of children who need a potent drug to paralyze the muscle of accommodation. (Homatropine, a shorter-acting cycloplegic and mydriatic, is usually satisfactory for adults.)

Atropine is sometimes given with morphine to relieve biliary and renal colic. Atropine tends to relieve the muscular spasm induced by morphine.

Preparations of belladonna or its alkaloids are administered for their antispasmodic effects in conditions characterized by hypermotility of the stomach and bowel—pylorospasm, spastic colon, biliary and renal colic, and hypertonicity of the urinary bladder and ureters. These drugs are also found in certain cough remedies (antiasthmatic mixtures), in which case they are given to relieve mild conditions of bronchial spasm and excessive secretions. Atropine has a mild antihistaminic effect.

Belladonna derivatives are sometimes useful for the relief of painful menstruation.

Symptoms in selected cases of Parkinson's disease are also relieved—the tremor, muscular rigidity, and cramps. However, other drugs are superior to atropine for this use.

Preparation, dosage, and administration. The following are the preparations available of atropine.

Atropine sulfate, **U.S.P., B.P.** Tablets containing 0.3, 0.4, and 0.6 mg. of drug are available. These correspond to gr. $^1/_{200}$, $^1/_{150}$, and $^1/_{100}$, respectively. The drug is also available in multiple-dose vials (gr. $^1/_{150}$ per milliliter) for injection and in the form of atropine sulfate ophthalmic ointment. Atropine sulfate is usually administered subcutaneously, orally, or topically (in the eye). The usual subcutaneous or oral dose is 0.5 mg. (gr. $^1/_{120}$), although 0.4 mg. (gr. $^1/_{150}$) is frequently ordered. The ophthalmic solution and the ointment are usually used in a 0.5% or 1% concentration.

Belladonna extract, **N.F., B.P.** The extract is prepared from belladonna leaf and contains alkaloids of the leaf. It is given orally, usually in doses of 15 mg. (gr. $^1/_4$).

Belladonna tincture, **U.S.P., B.P.** The usual dose is 0.6 ml. (10 minims), although the range of dosage may be from 0.3 to 2.4 ml. It is given orally.

Absorption, distribution, and excretion. Atropine (and also scopolamine) is readily absorbed after oral and parenteral administration. It is also absorbed from mucous membranes, as is noted when ophthalmic solutions escape through the lacrimal ducts to the mucous membrane of the nose. To a lesser extent, atropine is also absorbed from the skin. The drug is widely distributed in the fluids of the body and easily passes the placental barrier to the blood of the fetus. It is excreted chiefly by way of the kidney. Some is excreted through the bile. The remainder is apparently metabolized in the liver. Traces are found in other secretions, such as the milk.

Side effects and toxic effects. Atropine is a potent alkaloid, but it has a wide margin of safety. Poisoning occurs but is rarely fatal. The fatal dose is said to be about 100 mg. for adults and 10 mg. for children. Survival has occurred after much larger doses.

Symptoms develop rapidly after overdosage and consist of dry mouth, great thirst, and difficulty in swallowing and talking. Vision becomes blurred, pupils are dilated, and photophobia is present. A rash may develop, which is seen chiefly over the face, neck, and upper trunk. Rash is seen particularly in children, although it may be seen in adults. The body temperature is elevated, and in young children and infants it may reach 107° F. and more. The skin of the face and neck is flushed; the pulse becomes rapid and may be weak. Urinary urgency and difficulty in emptying the bladder may be noted. The patient becomes restless, excited, talkative, and confused. This may progress to delirium and mania and may be mistaken for an acute psychosis. The patient may also experience giddiness, staggering, stupor, coma, and respiratory and circulatory failure.

Young children who are given atropine or scopolamine as a preanesthetic medication often have a pronounced cutaneous flush after administration of the drug. Parents may be much disturbed about this and think that the child is ill with an acute disease. This is a side effect and is not seen as often in adults as in children.

Contraindications. Atropine and related alkaloids are usually contraindicated for patients with glaucoma because of the tendency of mydriatics to increase intraocular tension.

Treatment of overdosage. If the drug has been taken by mouth, the stomach should be lavaged promptly with tannic acid solution. Administration of the universal antidote or activated charcoal will help to inhibit further absorption of the drug. Neostigmine or pilocarpine is sometimes ordered to be given subcutaneously in doses of 10 mg. until the mouth is moist. Physostigmine has also been recently recommended. Artificial respiration, oxygen, or oxygen and carbon dioxide may be indicated. Short-acting barbiturates, chloral hydrate, or paraldehyde may be given to relieve excitement. Cautious use of central nervous system stimulants is recommended should the patient become stuporous. Ice bags and alcohol sponge baths aid in reducing the fever.

Scopolamine (Hyoscine)

Action. Scopolamine resembles atropine in its peripheral effects but differs in its central action, since doses of the drug given parenterally depress the central nervous system, producing drowsiness, euphoria, relief of fear, relaxation, sleep, and amnesia. Some "over-the-counter" sleeping pills (for example, Sleep-Eze) contain small amounts of scopolamine.

Uses. Scopolamine is used as a preanesthetic medication, usually along with morphine or one of the barbiturates, to check secretions and to prevent laryngospasm, as well as for its sedative (twilight sleep) and its amnesic effects.

It is used for motion sickness because of its depressant action on vestibular function, but this use has largely been supplanted by newer drugs. It is employed as a sedative for certain maniacal and delirious patients and also for postencephalitic parkinsonism and paralysis agitans.

It is also used as a mydriatic and cycloplegic. Its effects appear more promptly and disappear more rapidly than those of atropine. Scopolamine is less likely to cause irritation in the eyes than atropine.

Preparation, dosage, and administration. The following are the available preparations of scopolamine.

Scopolamine hydrobromide, **U.S.P.;** *hyoscine hydrobromide,* **B.P.** This drug is available in 0.6-mg. (gr. $^1/_{100}$) tablets, which can be given orally or parenterally. The usual dose is 0.6 mg. or gr. $^1/_{100}$. Ophthalmic solutions are applied topically to the eye in 0.2% concentration.

Hyoscine eye ointment, **B.P.** The ointment contains 0.25% hyoscine hydrobromide.

Scopolamine hydrobromide injection, **U.S.P.;** *hyoscine injection,* **B.P.** The injection is available in ampules containing 0.3, 0.4, and 0.6 mg. in 1 ml. and 0.4 mg. in 0.5 ml. Dosage is 0.3 to 0.8 mg. subcutaneously.

Synthetic substitutes for atropine (antispasmodics)

The usefulness of atropine is limited by the fact that it is a complex drug and produces effects in a number of organs or tissues simultaneously. When it is administered for its antispasmodic effects it will also produce prolonged effects in the eye, causing dilated pupils and blurred vision, as well as dry mouth and possibly rapid heart rate. When the antispasmodic effect is the one desired, other effects become side effects, which may be distinctly undesirable.

A large number of drugs have been synthesized in an effort to capture the antispasmodic effect of atropine without its other effects. Drugs of this type are frequently used to relieve hypertonicity and hypersecretion in the stomach and to treat patients with gastric and duodenal ulcers.

The ideal drug for the management of peptic ulcer should block the mechanism of gastric secretion without producing blockage in the autonomic ganglia and without causing curariform effects (muscular weakness). It should be relatively nontoxic and palatable and should reduce both the volume and the acidity of the gastric secretion over long periods of time. It should be effective when given orally. It should not produce troublesome or adverse side effects. The ideal drug has not been found, which prob-ably explains why so many different preparations are available. Seemingly no single preparation excels all others.

Continued synthesis of new anticholinergic drugs takes place, and if the claims for longer action and greater effectiveness are substantiated after long trial, more useful therapeutic agents may become available.

Like most of the cholinergic blocking agents, they are contraindicated for patients with glaucoma, pyloric obstruction, and prostatic hypertrophy.

Methscopolamine bromide (Pamine Bromide)

Action. Methscopolamine bromide is an anticholinergic drug that produces antispasmodic and antisecretory effects. It can suppress both volume and acidity of gastric secretion if large enough doses are given. It slows the emptying of the stomach and reduces peristalsis in the bowel. It decreases secretion of saliva and sweat. Tolerance to the medication does not seem to develop.

Uses. Methscopolamine bromide is used as an antispasmodic in the treatment of patients with peptic ulcer and forms of gastritis associated with hypermotility and hyperacidity. It is also occasionally used to relieve excessive salivation and sweating.

Preparation, dosage, and administration. Methscopolamine bromide is available in 2.5-mg. tablets and in solution for injection (1 mg. per milliliter). The usual dosage for adults is 2.5 mg. administered before meals and at bedtime. The usual parenteral dose is 0.5 mg. intramuscularly or subcutaneously every 6 to 8 hours as needed to control symptoms. It is also available as a syrup and as an elixir containing phenobarbital.

Side effects and toxic effects. The side effects most frequently encountered include dry mouth, constipation, and blurred vision. Other effects encountered less frequently may include dizziness, palpitation, flushed dry skin, difficult urination, headache, and nausea.

Overdosage may bring about a ganglionic blocking action and a curare-like effect on skeletal muscle.

Methantheline bromide, N.F.
(Banthine Bromide)

Action. Methantheline bromide has an anticholinergic action similar to that of atropine. It has a ganglionic blocking action in the autonomic nervous system, as well as a curare-like effect on skeletal muscle. It inhibits motility of the stomach and delays emptying time, inhibits motility of the small intestine and genitourinary tract, and diminishes secretions.

It is used as an antispasmodic in the treatment of patients with pylorospasm, hypermotility of the intestine, spastic colon, and spasm of the ureter and urinary bladder. Some degree of pupillary dilatation accompanies the antispasmodic effect.

Preparation, dosage, and administration. Methantheline bromide is available in 50-mg. tablets for oral administration and in ampules, each containing 50 mg. The content of the ampule is dissolved in physiologic saline solution for the purpose of injection (intramuscularly or intravenously). Parenteral administration is not recommended if the patient can take the drug orally. The tablets should not be chewed because they have an unpleasant taste.

The usual initial dose for adults is 50 mg., although the usual effective dose is 100 mg. four times a day, before meals and at bedtime. Some patients require more, some less, than this amount. The recommended dosage is the smallest amount that will effectively relieve the symptoms. Onset of action occurs within 30 to 45 minutes and persists for 4 to 6 hours.

Side effects and toxic effects. Patients may experience side effects in the form of dryness of the mouth, dilated pupils, and inability to read fine print. Some may develop constipation and require a laxative. Varying degrees of urinary retention have been observed in patients with prostatic hypertrophy. A small percentage of patients complains of general malaise and weakness and does not tolerate the drug well.

Propantheline bromide, U.S.P., B.P.
(Pro-Banthine Bromide)

Action. Propantheline bromide is an analogue of methantheline bromide and is said to be more effective than the latter drug to reduce the volume and acidity of gastric secretions. It is also said to produce less severe effects. It has come to replace the older drug to a great extent.

Preparation, dosage, and administration. Propantheline is available in 7.5- and 15-mg. tablets, 30-mg. prolonged action tablets, and 30-mg. vials as a powder for injection. The content of the vial is dissolved in not less than 10 ml. of water for injection prior to intravenous administration. Parenteral administration is reserved for patients who cannot take the drug orally. Propantheline bromide is also available in tablets that contain phenobarbital.

The dosage of propantheline must be carefully adjusted to the needs of individual patients. The initial recommended dose is one tablet (15 mg.) with meals and two tablets at bedtime, with subsequent adjustment depending on the patient's reaction and tolerance to the medication. The bitter taste of methantheline bromide has been controlled by sugar-coating the Pro-Banthine tablet.

Side effects. Propantheline is thought to show less severe but not less frequent side effects than methantheline bromide.

Homatropine methylbromide, N.F.
(Novatrin, Mesopin)

Action. Homatropine methylbromide is one of the older cholinergic blocking agents used in the United States. Its effects are similar to those of atropine, but it is without the latter drug's effect on the central nervous system. Its an-

Table 9-9 Side effects characteristic of cholinergic blocking agents

Dryness of mouth	Mental confusion
Dilatation of pupils (mydriasis)*	Excitement
Blurred vision	Dizziness; headache
Heart palpitation	Constipation
Flushing and dryness of skin	Urinary retention

*It must be understood that a symptom such as mydriasis is not a side effect when this is the purpose for which a drug is given.

Table 9-10 Summary of some of the anticholinergic agents*

Generic name	Trade name	Usual single adult dose	Usual route of administration
Atropine		0.5 mg. 0.5%-1% ophthalmic solution	Oral or subcutaneous Topical
Scopolamine		0.6 mg.	Oral or subcutaneous
Hyoscine		0.2% ophthalmic solution	Topical
Synthetic mydriatics and cycloplegics Homatropine hydrobromide		1%-2% ophthalmic solution	Topical
Synthetic antispasmodics Homatropine methylbromide	Novatrin, Mesopin	5-10 mg.	Oral
Methscopolamine bromide	Pamine, Lescapine	2.5-5 mg. 0.25-1 mg.	Oral Subcutaneous or intramuscular
Methantheline bromide	Banthine	50 mg.	Oral
Propantheline	Pro-Banthine	15 mg.	Oral
Pipenzolate	Piptal	5 mg.	Oral

*Drugs listed are usually administered in the form of their salts.

ticholinergic potency is said to be considerably less than that of atropine, but it is also less toxic. Its effect on gastric secretion, hypermotility, and the duration of action are said to be much the same as that for atropine.

Uses. Homatropine methylbromide is used for the treatment of gastrointestinal spasm and as an adjunct in the treatment of patients with peptic ulcer.

Preparation, dosage, and administration. Homatropine methylbromide is available in 2.5-, 5-, and 10-mg. tablets and as an elixir (2.5 mg. per 4 ml.). The usual oral dose is 5 mg. three or four times daily. Solutions are also available for injection and for oral administration.

Side effects. Side effects include dryness of the mouth and blurring of vision.

Pipenzolate bromide (Piptal)

Action and result. Pipenzolate bromide is a synthetic anticholinergic drug with effects comparable to atropine. It diminishes gastric acidity and gastric motility and relieves spasms. It is used to treat peptic ulcers. The ability of pipenzolate to relax spasms of the lower gastrointestinal tract and of the sphincter of Oddi makes it useful in the treatment of ileitis, irritable colon, and biliary colic.

Side effects and toxic effects. Pipenzolate has a minimum of side effects and those are chiefly atropine-like in nature. No serious toxic reactions have been reported to date.

Preparation, dosage, and administration. Pipenzolate bromide is available in 5-mg. tablets for oral administration. The average adult dose is 5 mg. three times daily before meals and 5 to 10 mg. at bedtime. Onset of action is about 1 hour; duration of effect is 4 hours.

■ Anticholinesterase drugs

Some drugs act as cholinergic agents, not by directly affecting the cells innervated by postganglionic cholinergic nerves but by inactivating or inhibiting the enzyme that normally degrades acetylcholine. In this way the activity of acetylcholine is prolonged and its concentration at the myoneural junction increased.

Drugs used for treatment of myasthenia gravis

Myasthenia gravis is a rare chronic disease manifested by extreme fatigability of the skeletal muscles. Although any skeletal muscle may be involved, those concerned with movement of the eyeballs, eyelids, and face and those used in chewing, swallowing, and speech are most likely to show involvement. Ptosis of the eyelids is an almost constant symptom. Diplopia is also likely to be present. The cause of this disease is not known, although recent studies suggest that the synaptic vesicles of motor nerves have a lower than normal acetylcholine content. The disease is usually subject to remissions and exacerbations (periods of improvement followed by periods of decline). Judicious use of neostigmine or other anticholinesterase drugs may produce dramatic results, but overdosage tends to aggravate the muscular fatigue and cause side effects such as nausea and vomiting, abdominal cramps, diarrhea, and muscle twitching. It is important that the patient have sufficient therapy to maintain function of the chewing and swallowing muscles to avoid malnutrition.

Neostigmine (Prostigmin)

Neostigmine is a synthetic drug available only in the form of its salts, which are freely soluble in water and stable in aqueous solutions. Neostigmine has become the standard drug for therapy of myasthenia gravis. It has both muscarinic and nicotinic actions. Neostigmine preserves endogenous ACh and has a direct cholinomimetic action. This results in increased

muscle power and relief from characteristic signs and symptoms of myasthenia gravis (ptosis, dyspnea, difficulty in swallowing, and so on).

Uses. Neostigmine is used to relieve abdominal distention caused by accumulation of gas and insufficient peristaltic activity after surgical operations. It is also used for the prevention and treatment of atonic conditions of the urinary bladder. It will enable the patient to empty the bladder completely.

Neostigmine is also used as a test for pregnancy. It is given intramuscularly for 3 days, and if the patient is not pregnant bleeding will occur usually within 72 hours.

Neostigmine (ophthalmic solution) is sometimes used as a miotic for patients with glaucoma.

Preparation, dosage, and administration. The following are the preparations available of neostigmine.

Neostigmine bromide, **U.S.P., B.P. (Prostigmin Bromide).** This drug is available in 15-mg. tablets and also in the form of a slow-release tablet for oral administration. The usual dosage is 15 mg. three times a day. This preparation is also available as a 5% ophthalmic solution. The slow-release dosage form decreases the need for administration of the drug at night.

Neostigmine methylsulfate injection, **U.S.P., B.P.** This is available in 1-ml. ampules containing 0.25-mg. (1:4000), 0.5-mg. (1:2000), and 1-mg. (1:1000) solution. The total daily dosage must be determined in accordance with the severity of the symptoms and the response of the patient. A dose of 0.5 mg. of neostigmine intramuscularly is said to be equivalent to 15 mg. given orally. In the treatment of myasthenia gravis 1 to 2 mg. given intramuscularly every 3 hours is generally satisfactory when the patient is unable to swallow. Sometimes neostigmine bromide is given orally and neostigmine methylsulfate is given intramuscularly to reinforce the oral dosage when symptoms are severe. Some patients will require only one 15-mg. tablet two or three times a day and other patients may require twenty or more tablets a day. Increased physical activity and/or emotional strain usually causes the patient to require more medication.

Side effects and toxic effects. Side effects include nausea and vomiting, diarrhea, abdominal cramps, muscle twitching, excessive secretion, urinary urgency, rapid weak pulse, and low blood pressure. In addition the patient feels faint and apprehensive. With acute toxicity pulmonary edema and respiratory failure may occur. Excessive doses of any of the anticholinesterase compounds may cause severe weakness accompanied by parasympathetic side effects and various degrees of muscular tightness and twitching. Atropine is the physiologic antidote and should be given intravenously or subcutaneously.

Pyridostigmine bromide, U.S.P., B.P. (Mestinon Bromide); ambenonium chloride (Mytelase)

Pyridostigmine and ambenonium are two anticholinesterase compounds that are being used for myasthenia gravis. They differ from neostigmine mainly in their longer action and decreased severity of side effects. The longer duration of their action often makes it possible for the patient to sleep undisturbed without the administration of the drug during the night.

Both drugs are available in tablet form for oral administration. Mestinon Bromide is available in a slow-release dosage form.

Edrophonium chloride, U.S.P., B.P. (Tensilon Chloride)

Edrophonium is a cholinergic drug that is discussed further in Chapter 15. It is mentioned here because its action resembles that of neostigmine and because it is used in the emergency treatment of patients with myasthenia gravis and as a diagnostic agent. When it is given to a patient suspected of having myasthenia gravis, he will show prompt improvement in muscular strength should the disease be present. The duration of the action of the drug is too brief to be of value for maintenance therapy.

As a diagnostic agent, 10 mg. of the drug is administered intravenously. In myasthenia crisis, the drug is given by continuous intrave-

nous drip. Edrophonium chloride is available in 10-ml. vials that contain 10 mg. per milliliter.

Nicotine

Nicotine is a liquid alkaloid, freely soluble in water. It turns brown on exposure to air. It is the chief alkaloid found in tobacco.

It has no therapeutic use but is of great pharmacologic interest and toxicologic importance. Its use in experiments performed on animals has helped to increase understanding of the autonomic nervous system.

Absorption. Nicotine is readily absorbed from the gastrointestinal tract, respiratory mucous membrane, and skin.

Action and result. Nicotine produces a temporary stimulation of all sympathetic and parasympathetic ganglia. This is followed by depression, which tends to last longer than the period of stimulation. It affects skeletal muscle in a way similar to the way it affects the ganglia; that is, a depressant phase follows stimulation. During the depressant phase nicotine exerts a curare-like action on skeletal muscle.

In addition, nicotine stimulates the central nervous system, especially the medullary centers (respiratory, emetic, and vasomotor). Large doses may cause tremor and convulsions. Stimulation is followed by depression. Death is caused by respiratory failure, although it may be caused more by the curariform action of nicotine on nerve endings in the diaphragm, which prevents respiratory muscles from responding, than by action on the respiratory center.

The actions and effects of nicotine on the blood-vascular system are complex. The rate of the heart is frequently slowed at first, but later it may beat faster than usual. Various disturbances in rhythm have been observed. The small blood vessels in peripheral parts of the body constrict but may later dilate, and the blood pressure will fall. The latter condition is observed in nicotine poisoning. Nicotine also has an antidiuretic action.

Repeated administration of nicotine causes tolerance to develop.

Toxic effects. Acute or chronic poisoning can result.

Acute poisoning. Nicotine is a rapid-acting, extremely toxic drug. Cases have been reported of gardeners who were poisoned while handling the drug as an insecticide. Death occurred in a few minutes. Black Leaf 40 is a commercial preparation that contains nicotine and is used as a spray to kill various types of insects.

Symptoms of poisoning include increased flow of saliva, nausea, vomiting, abdominal cramps, diarrhea, cold sweat, confusion, fainting, drop in blood pressure, rapid pulse, prostration, and collapse. Convulsions sometimes occur. Death results from respiratory failure.

Treatment is directed toward keeping the patient breathing. Artificial respiration with oxygen is said to be more effective than central respiratory stimulants. If life can be prolonged to give the tissues an opportunity to detoxify the drug, the patient may recover.

If the poison has been swallowed, gastric lavage with solution of potassium permanganate (1:10,000) is recommended. Other forms of treatment indicated depend upon the symptoms presented.

Tobacco smoking and nicotine. The effect of tobacco in the individual who smokes is a subject about which there is considerable difference of opinion. The effects of excessive smoking seem to afford more agreement than the effects of mild or moderate use of tobacco. Excessive smoking is known to cause irritation of the respiratory tract, and there is a real possibility that tobacco smoke exerts carcinogenic effects in the lungs of man. Chronic dyspepsia may develop in heavy smokers, and patients with gastric ulcer are usually advised to avoid overindulgence. Of considerable importance is the fact that sufficient nicotine is absorbed by smokers to exert a variety of effects on the autonomic nervous system.

In patients with peripheral vascular disease such as thromboangiitis obliterans (Buerger's disease), nicotine is generally believed to be a contributing factor in the disease and may precipitate spasms of the peripheral blood vessels and thus reduce the blood flow through the affected vessels. Vasospasm in the retinal blood vessels of the eye, associated with smoking of tobacco, is thought to be the cause of a serious disturbance of vision.

Grace Roth found that nicotine in cigarettes must be reduced more than 60% before vascular effects of smoking fail to appear or are only slight.

Some physicians recommend that patients with hypertension and peripheral vascular disease sharply limit their smoking habits or discontinue smoking entirely. The adverse effects of cigarette smoking on the cardiovascular system are increasingly emphasized.

Questions

for study and review

1 Explain what is meant by the muscarinic action of a drug; by the nicotinic action of a drug.
2 What is the difference between cholinergic fibers and adrenergic fibers? Between cholinergic drugs and adrenergic drugs?
3 Explain why epinephrine should not be administered to patients receiving digitalis.
4 Explain the important nursing care aspects for patients receiving intravenous infusion of powerful vasoconstrictors such as levarterenol, metaraminol, or methoxamine.
5 Explain why after prolonged use of a pressor drug the drug may no longer have a vasoconstrictor effect.

Multiple choice

6 Choose the correct answer(s).
Acetylcholine:
  a. promotes sympathetic stimulation by releasing norepinephrine at postganglionic fibers
  b. promotes a rise in calcium concentration within nerve fibers to enhance muscle activation
  c. is the transmitter substance for both the sympathetic and the parasympathetic nervous systems
  d. is inactivated by cholinesterase
7 Which of the following are correct statements about anticholinergic drugs?
  a. They are also known as antimuscarinics.
  b. Natural sources of these drugs have fewer side effects than the synthetic drugs.
  c. The most widely used anticholinergic is atropine.
  d. They block the action of norepinephrine.

Plate 2
Atropa belladonna (deadly nightshade).

8 Choose the *incorrect* answer(s).
The use of epinephrine in local anesthetic solutions is for the purpose of:
a. prolonging the anesthetic action by vasoconstriction
b. delaying absorption from the site of injection
c. promoting distribution of the drug
d. inhibiting bleeding

9 Choose the correct answer(s).
Epinephrine:
a. stimulates vascular beta receptors
b. is a catecholamine secreted from the adrenal medulla
c. has a direct cardioaccelerator action
d. is therapeutically effective in the treatment of heart failure because it increases myocardial oxygen uptake

10 Which of the following are toxic effects of high doses of epinephrine?
a. reflex bradycardia
b. anxiety
c. palpitation
d. cardiac arrhythmias
e. hypotension

11 Choose the *incorrect* answer(s).
Epinephrine:
a. has both excitatory and inhibitory effects on the autonomic nervous system
b. is used in treating simple glaucoma by reducing intraocular pressure via pupil and blood vessel dilation
c. is an effective drug for relieving nasal congestion since it does not produce a rebound vasodilator or mucosal swelling effect
d. is effective in treatment of acute asthmatic attacks by its dilating effect on bronchial smooth muscle, which promotes a resistant airway

12 Which of the following effects does epinephrine have on the heart?
a. It brings about more complete emptying of the ventricles by increasing myocardial contraction.
b. It increases the heart's refractory period.
c. It inhibits stimulation of the vagus nerve causing cardiac acceleration.
d. It inhibits atrioventricular conduction.

13 In comparing the effects of ephedrine and epinephrine it will be noted that:
a. both are adrenergic drugs; ephedrine also stimulates the central nervous system
b. ephedrine is effective orally; epinephrine is not
c. the actions of ephedrine are slower and weaker but more prolonged than those of epinephrine
d. both drugs cause rebound vasodilation after their vasoconstricting effect

14 Choose the *incorrect* answer(s).
When the effects of norepinephrine and epinephrine are compared it is noted that:
a. epinephrine brings about a greater increase in oxygen consumption by the heart
b. norepinephrine is a more potent systemic vasoconstrictor
c. epinephrine is a less toxic substance than norepinephrine

d. the effects of norepinephrine are more easily reversed than those of epinephrine

15 Choose the correct answer(s).
Norepinephrine
a. has little or no effect on beta receptors of the heart
b. will cause tissue sloughing if infiltration occurs with an intravenous infusion
c. is predominantly an activator of alpha receptors of smooth muscle, which accounts for its vasoconstrictor effect
d. has a positive inotropic effect

16 Which of the following statements about the alpha and beta adrenergic receptors of the sympathetic nervous system are *incorrect?*
a. Drugs affecting the alpha receptors cause an inhibitory action.
b. Large arteries and veins contain both alpha and beta receptors.
c. The heart contains only beta receptors.
d. Norepinephrine acts mainly on alpha receptors.

17 Atropine:
a. produces dilatation of the pupil and diminished secretion of tears when instilled into the eye
b. decreases gastric secretion
c. has an antispasmodic effect on the gastrointestinal tract
d. decreases muscle tremor in Parkinson's disease

18 Atropine is frequently given as a preanesthetic drug not only to inhibit oral and bronchial secretions but also to prevent:
a. cardiac arrest
b. respiratory failure
c. laryngospasm
d. hypotension

19 If the stock supply of atropine sulfate is in solution and the vial is labeled 0.4 mg. per milliliter, how many minims (approximately) would be required to give gr. $^1/_{200}$?
a. 11
b. 15
c. 20
d. $7^1/_2$

20 Anticholinesterase drugs are used therapeutically for:
a. glaucoma
b. increasing intestinal peristalsis
c. urinary retention
d. atropine poisoning

21 Anticholinergic drugs are frequently given to patients with peptic ulcer for which of the following reasons?
a. to control the gastric acidity
b. for their direct analgesic effect
c. to soothe and coat the ulcer
d. to diminish hypermotility and hypersecretion of the stomach

22 Patients with hypertension and cardiovascular disease are often encouraged to stop smoking for which of the following reasons?
a. Nicotine stimulates the central nervous system.
b. Nicotine has a tendency to cause vasospasm.
c. Tobacco smoke contains substances thought to be carcinogenic.
d. Tobacco smoke is irritating to the respiratory mucous membrane.

References

Abboud, F. M.: Clinical importance of adrenergic receptors, Arch. Intern. Med. 118:418, 1966.

Acheson, G. H.: Second symposium on catecholamines, Baltimore, 1966, The Williams & Wilkins Co.

Almquist, R. F.: Development of the concept of alpha and beta adrenotropic receptors, Ann. N. Y. Acad. Sci. 139:549-553, 1967.

Bachrach, W. H.: Anticholinergic drugs: survey of the literature and some experimental observations, Amer. J. Digest. Dis. 3:743, 1958.

Boura, A. L. A., and Green, A. F.: Adrenergic neuron blocking agents, Ann. Rev. Pharmacol. 5:183, 1965.

Bowsler, D.: Introduction to the anatomy and physiology of the nervous system, Oxford, 1967, Blackwell Scientific Publications.

Burn, J. H.: The autonomic nervous system, Oxford, 1965, Blackwell Scientific Publications.

Burn, J. H., and Rand, M. J.: Acetylcholine in adrenergic transmission, Ann. Rev. Pharmacol. 5:163, 1965.

DiPalma, J. R.: Drill's pharmacology in medicine, New York, 1971, McGraw-Hill Book Company.

Eckstein, J. W., and Abboud, F. M.: Circulatory effects of sympathomimetic anemia, Amer. Heart J. 63:119, 1962.

Epstein, S., and Braunwald, E.: Clinical and hemodynamic appraisal of beta adrenergic blocking drugs, Ann. N. Y. Acad. Sci. 139:952-968, 1967.

Fleming, A. R.: The use of urecholine in the prevention of postpartum urinary retention, Amer. J. Obstet. Gynec. 74:569, 1957.

Friend, D.: Gastrointestinal anticholinergic drugs, Clin. Pharmacol. Therap. 4:559, 1963.

Furchgott, R. F.: The pharmacological differentiation of adrenergic receptors, Ann. N. Y. Acad. Sci. 139:553-571, 1967.

Gershon, S., Neubauer, H., and Sundland, D. M.: Interaction between some anticholinergic agents and phenothiazines, Clin. Pharmacol. Therap. 6:749, 1965.

Goodman, L., and Gilman, A., editors: The pharmacological basis of therapeutics, ed. 4, New York, 1970, The Macmillan Company.

Haggerty, R. J.: Levarterenol for shock, Amer. J. Nurs. 58:1243, 1958.

Hunter, A. R., and Miller, R. A., editors: Symposium on adrenergic drugs and their antagonists, Brit. J. Anaesth. 38:666, 1966.

Ingelfinger, F. J.: Anticholinergic therapy of gastrointestinal disorders, New Eng. J. Med. 268:1454, 1963.

Jones, A.: Ganglionic actions of muscarinic substances, J. Pharmacol. 141:195, 1963.

Kirsner, J. B., Ford, H., and Kassriel, R. S.: Anticholinergic drugs in peptic ulcer, Med. Clin. N. Amer. 41(2):495-521, 1957.

Lawrence, D. R.: Clinical pharmacology, London, 1966, J. & A. Churchill, Ltd.

Levy, P., and Ahlquist, R. P.: A study of sympathetic ganglionic stimulants, J. Pharmacol. Exp. Therap. 137:219, 1962.

Lucchesi, B.: Antiarrhythmic effects of beta adrenergic blocking agents, Ann. N. Y. Acad. Sci. 139:940-952, 1967.

Richins, C. A., and Young, P. A.: The autonomic nervous system, Progr. Neurol. Psychiat. 15:209, 1960.

Roberts, T. D.: Basic ideas in neurophysiology, New York, 1966, Appleton-Century-Crofts.

Roth, G.: The effects of smoking tobacco on the cardiovascular system of normal persons and patients with hypertension, Collected Papers of the Mayo Clinic 45:435, 1953.

Roth, G., McDonald, J. B., and Sheard, C.: The effect of smoking cigarettes, J.A.M.A. 125:761, 1944.

Ruffin, J. M., and Doyer, D.: Role of anticholinergic drugs in the treatment of peptic ulcer disease, Ann. N. Y. Acad. Sci. 99:179, 1962.

Second symposium on catecholamines, Pharmacol. Rev. 18:1, 1966.

Smith, V. M.: Newer anticholinergic drugs, Med. Clin. N. Amer. 48:399, 1964.

Swan, H. J. C.: Noradrenaline, adrenaline and the human circulation, Brit. Med. J. 1:1003, 1952.

Udenfriend, S., Levenberg, W., and Shoerdsma, A.: Physiologically active amines in common fruits and vegetables, Arch. Biochem. Biophys. 85:487, 1959.

Varagic, V., and Belesin, D.: Comparison of adrenergic activation by anticholinesterases and by hypoxia, Circ. Res. 11:916, 1962.

VonEuler, V. S.: Epinephrine and norepinephrine: action and uses in man, Clin. Pharmacol. Therap. 1:65, 1960.

VonEuler, V. S.: Noradrenalin: chemistry, physiology, pharmacology and clinical aspects, Springfield, Ill., 1956, Charles C Thomas, Publisher.

Wurtman, R. J.: Catecholamines, New Eng. J. Med. 273:637, 1965.

Cardiovascular drugs

The development of microelectrode techniques and recordings in the past two decades has resulted in new knowledge and greater understanding of cardiovascular activity. The resulting new anatomic, electrophysiologic, and pharmacologic information has permitted greater precision in diagnosing and treating cardiac disease, particularly the arrhythmias. Concomitant with these advances has been the increasing use of electrocardiographic monitoring of acutely ill patients and of those with known or suspected cardiovascular disorders. In addition, the nurse's clinical role has continued to expand and now includes responsibility for the care of patients on monitoring equipment. This in turn requires the nurse to be able to recognize and understand abnormal electrocardiographic patterns and in some cases to institute therapy, including pharmacologic therapy, to prevent serious complications and unnecessary deaths. Therefore, it is necessary for the nurse to understand electrophysiology of the heart and drug effects on cardiac activity if she is to keep her knowledge current and her nursing care therapeutically effective.

■ Cell metabolism and the circulatory system

Vital processes in living cells involve the use of oxygen and metabolic fuels and simultaneous elimination of metabolic waste products. In uni-cellular organisms such as the ameba, exchange of these substances occurs primarily by the process of diffusion (the movement of particles from regions of high concentration to regions of low concentration). For example, as a single cell uses oxygen, the oxygen concentration in the protoplasm decreases, and oxygen from regions of higher concentration outside the cell diffuses into the cell. The exchange of gases and metabolic products can occur rapidly since the distance of diffusion from the surface to the center of the cell or simple organism is not great.

In complex organisms, cells are grouped together, which increases the distance of diffusion to the center of the cell mass. To maintain rapid diffusion, a circulatory system is necessary—thus, the need in man for billions of thin-walled capillaries. If capillary flow is not interrupted, diffusion distances are small and diffusion gradients are steep. When the need for oxygen and nutrients by cells is increased, faster capillary flow is required. The heart, through its pumping action, distributes blood to the capillaries by means of the numerous ramifications of the arterial system. Blood leaving the capillaries returns to the heart via numerous venous channels.

Fundamental requirements of the cardiovascular system are circulation of blood flow without interruption and regulation of blood flow in response to varying tissue demands. The heart must continuously adapt its output to balance blood flow through the billions of capillaries in the body. To meet these requirements there must be an adequate pump, effective peripheral vascular resistance, and an effective circulating blood volume.

■ The heart muscle

Heart muscle resembles other muscles in the possession of three qualities: (1) tone or maintained mild contraction, (2) excitability or readiness to respond to stimulation, and (3) contractility. The contractility of heart muscles differs from that of other muscles in that it is rhythmic and depends upon certain intrinsic properties of the muscle itself and not only upon neural impulses. Moreover, the atria and ventricles of the heart can contract independently of one another; the atria are capable of beating three times as fast as the ventricles.

Normally, atrial contraction is followed in about a fifth of a second by ventricular contraction. The whole contraction forms the systole, which occurs about seventy-two times each minute in the adult. Each systole is followed immediately by a period of relaxation called diastole. Heart muscle differs from skeletal muscle in that its refractory period is relatively long, which helps to preserve the cardiac rhythm.

Electrophysiology of the heart

Current information on cardiac electrophysiology is organized around the major concepts of excitation, conduction, contraction, and automaticity, which are major physiologic properties of the heart. Understanding these concepts requires an understanding of numerous other concepts, principles, and laws, such as the refractory period and Ohm's law.

Ohm's law states that when there are two regions in conductive media with different electromotive force, there is an electric current running between them.

The "law of excitation" states that the larger the stimulus required to bring about a response, the lower the excitability. Therefore, when membrane potential is increased in magnitude, the cell is less excitable. (For greater detail on this subject, the student should refer to the references listed at the end of the chapter.)

Excitation and conduction. The efficiency of the heart depends upon a sequential pattern of excitation and subsequent contraction proceeding in an orderly and coordinated manner from atria to ventricles. *Excitation* is a property of specialized cell membranes that maintain and alter their permeability to ions in a special manner. It should be remembered that the cell membrane serves as a semipermeable barrier between extracellular and intracellular fluid, both of which contain ions such as sodium (Na^+) and potassium (K^+). Outside the cell, the sodium concentration is high and the potassium level is low. Within the resting cell, potassium is predominant and the sodium concentration is small. Since substances tend to move from areas of greater to areas of lesser concentration, active transfer of sodium (via the sodium pump) is required to maintain the low sodium concentration within the cell. This transfer requires energy, and a potential difference develops across the cell membrane. In addition, any environmental change (which may result from a local electric current or chemical agent) results in a sudden, transient increase in the ionic permeability of the cell membrane. This also causes a change in the electric potential difference across the membrane. The permeability of the membrane to sodium and potassium increases and permits these ions to pass through the membrane. When the electric potential of the membrane reaches

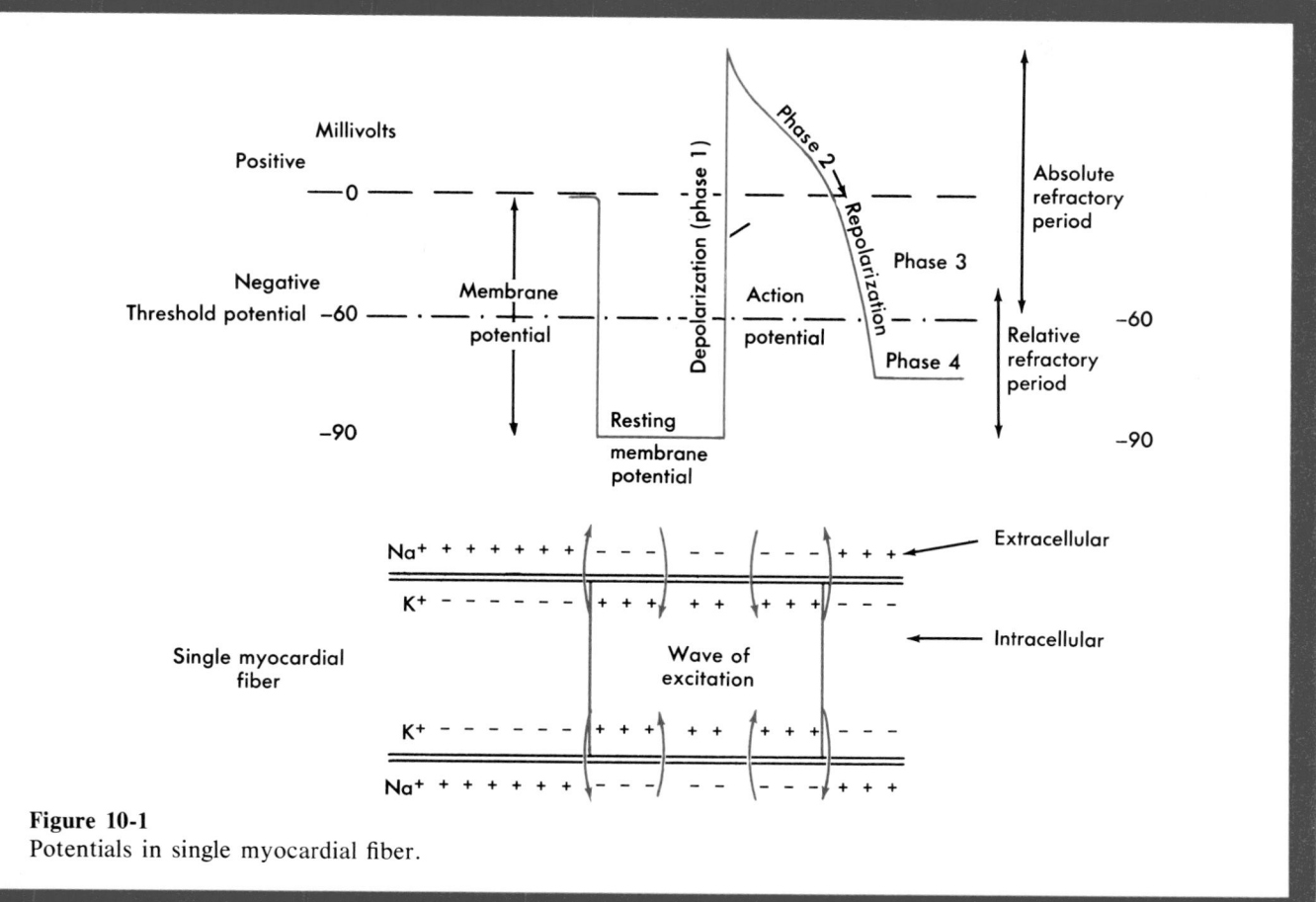

Figure 10-1
Potentials in single myocardial fiber.

a critical level, the cell is excited or stimulated. The result is an action potential, or a propagated impulse (see Figure 10-1).

Conduction occurs when there is a progressive spread of excitation from one fiber to neighboring fibers to more remote fibers.

Action potential is the conducted impulse, the result of interaction between excitation and electroionic conduction.

Resting membrane potential (RMP) is the potential difference between the inside and outside of a single fiber after complete repolarization or recovery from a prior action potential. The resting state exists when there is unequal *but normal* ion distribution between the inside and outside of the cell (a higher potassium concentra-

tion inside the cell and a higher sodium concentration outside the cell). The resting membrane potential varies for different cells. In cardiac cells it ranges from 50 to 95 millivolts (mv.). It is a period of electric quiescence and is designated phase 4.

Threshold potential is the critical level of membrane potential at which the fiber develops a self-sustaining depolarization. It is the point at which the membrane becomes excited and capable of starting a conducted impulse. Threshold potential varies for different cardiac cells.

Depolarization is the result of sodium ions diffusing into the cell attracted by the negative charge within and driven by the concentration **135** gradient. During the initial depolarization phase the increase of ionized sodium inside the cell decreases the negativity within until a zero potential exists between the inside and outside of the cell (the inside of the cell is no longer negative). A reversal of polarity now occurs within the cell and it becomes positive. This is referred to as the "overshoot"—the height of the upstroke of the action potential in terms of positive millivolts. Depolarization is also referred to as phase 1 of the action potential. The velocity of depolarization determines the rate of firing of pacemaker fibers.

Repolarization is the period during which the membrane potential is restored to the resting level. Phase 2 is the first repolarization phase; it is also known as the plateau or slow recovery stage. Phase 3 is the more rapid recovery phase that proceeds to phase 4, the resting potential. During repolarization the excess sodium within the cell is actively transported, via the sodium pump, out of the cell and potassium is again taken up by the cell to restore the negativity within the cell.

Absolute refractory period is the interval during which the fiber does not respond to any stimulus. This period occurs from the onset of depolarization to the time when repolarization reaches the threshold potential. Another action potential, or propagated response, cannot occur until the threshold potential is reached.

Relative refractory period is that phase of repolarization that occurs between the threshold potential and reestablishment of the resting potential. A stimulus can elicit a response during this period, but the stimulus must be stronger or larger than a stimulus eliciting a response during the fully recovered or resting phase (phase 4). In addition the response occurs at a slower velocity.

Excitation-contraction coupling. Excitation-contraction coupling is initiated by depolarization of the cell membrane and involves the movement of calcium ions into the cell or the release of ionized calcium from intracellular binding sites. Increased concentration of free or active calcium in the vicinity of the contractile proteins (myosin and actin), which are contained in the myofibrils, apparently initiates contraction. Relaxation is associated with rebinding of ionized calcium to intracellular sites and outward displacement of calcium ions across the cell membrane.

It is theorized that in resting muscle, actin and myosin are separate and repel each other. Actin is bound by ADP (adenosine diphosphate) and myosin is bound by ATP (adenosine triphosphate). With activation of muscle, calcium is liberated and forms strong links between the actin and myosin, producing muscle shortening or tension. Since the repulsion charge has been obliterated, contraction can occur. With con-

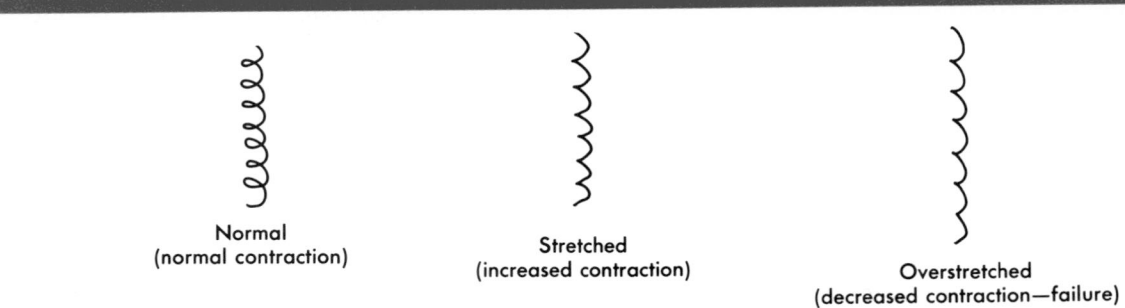

Normal
(normal contraction)

Stretched
(increased contraction)

Overstretched
(decreased contraction—failure)

Figure 10-2
Length of single myofibril and contractile force.

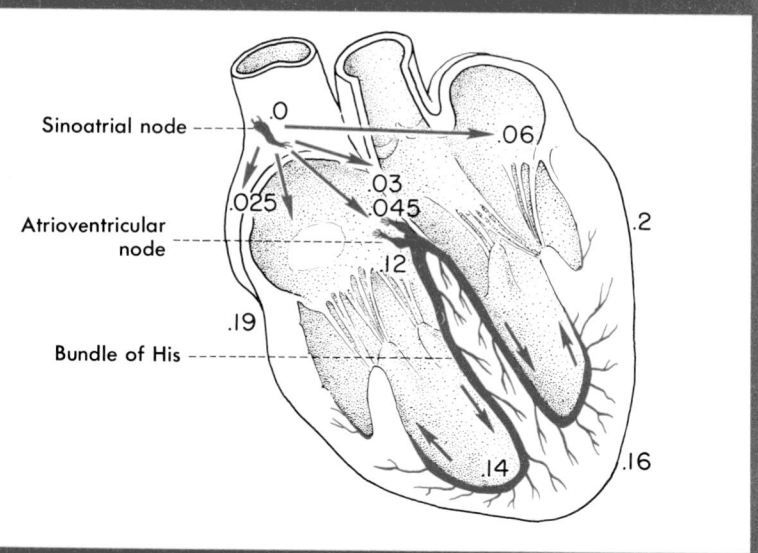

Figure 10-3
General ramification of conductive tissue in the heart and normal time sequence of depolarization (or electric conduction) from the sinoatrial node through the atria, to the atrioventricular node down the bundle of His (including right and left branches), to the terminal Purkinje fibers. Ventricular contraction then occurs.

traction there is a splitting of ATP by ATPase, and the link between actin and myosin is broken. One fundamental characteristic of cardiac muscle is that it will contract more forcefully if its precontraction, or resting, phase is increased.

Up to a certain point, increasing or lengthening the myofibrils increases the force of contraction. Beyond this point stretching no longer brings about forceful contractions but decreases contractile effectiveness. This explains why an enlarged heart is often a less efficient pump than a normal size heart. When cardiac cells are excited and a wave of excitation is conducted throughout muscle causing the muscle fibers to shorten or contract, excitation-contraction coupling has occurred. This fundamental physiologic phenomenon helps to explain the sequential and coordinated pump action of the heart.

Automaticity. Automaticity refers to the capacity for spontaneous, repetitive self-excitation. Cells with automaticity have an unstable resting potential; as soon as the cells repolarize they spontaneously depolarize. A large number of specialized cardiac cells possess normal automaticity and can initiate a propagated impulse that excites all or some part of the nonautomatic fibers of the heart. These automatic or *pace-*

maker cells are clustered in (1) the sinoatrial node and adjacent tissue, (2) the other automatic atrial cells, and (3) the His-Purkinje system (see Figure 10-3). The nonautomatic fibers of the heart include atrial and ventricular muscle fibers. The speed at which spontaneous depolarization proceeds in pacemaker cells is a primary factor in determining which cells will initiate the cardiac impulse. The fastest rate occurs in automatic cells of the sinoatrial node and adjacent tissue, and these are the primary pacemakers of the heart. The rate of depolarization is slower for the automatic cells of the His-Purkinje system; this system ordinarily functions as a reserve pacemaker. Any factor that significantly changes the firing rate of the automatic cells can cause arrhythmia. If the automaticity of normal pacemaker tissue is decreased, other tissue with *latent* or *potential* pacemaker ability will function as the pacemaker.

Blood supply

The entire blood supply to the myocardium is provided by the right and left coronary arteries, which arise from the base of the aorta (Figure 10-4). The right ventricle and atrium are supplied with blood from the right coronary ar-

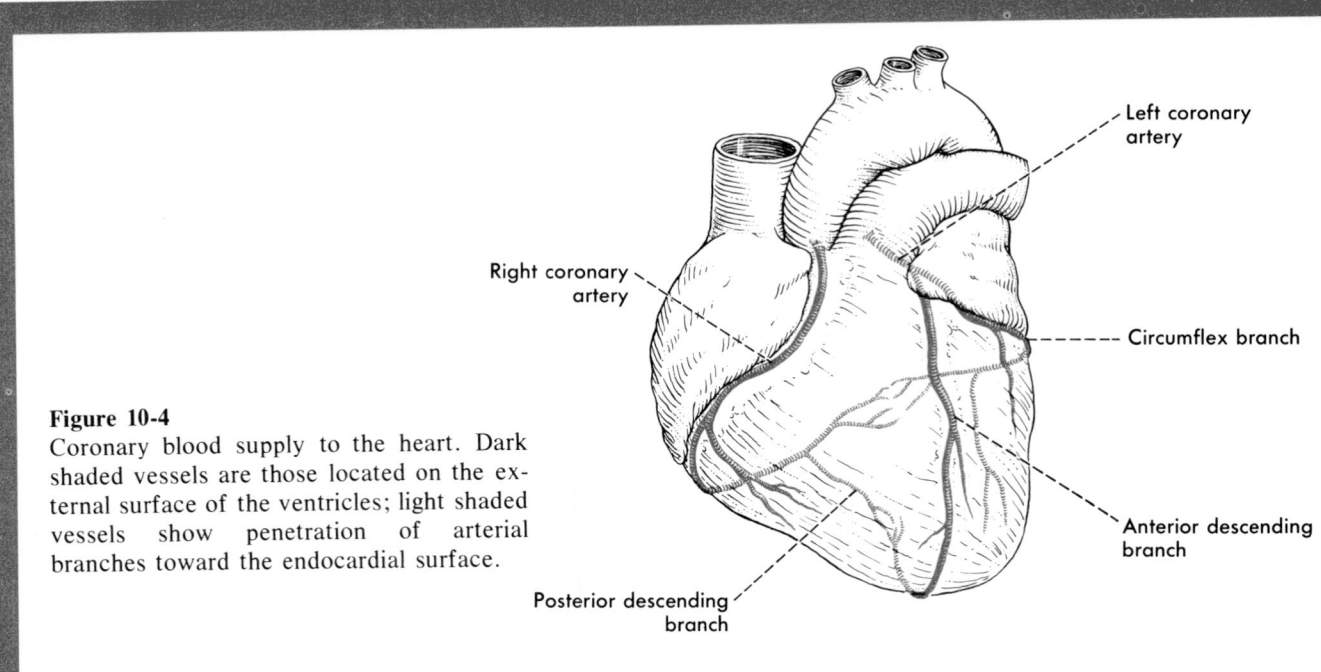

Figure 10-4
Coronary blood supply to the heart. Dark shaded vessels are those located on the external surface of the ventricles; light shaded vessels show penetration of arterial branches toward the endocardial surface.

tery. The left coronary artery divides into the anterior descending branch and the circumflex branch and supplies blood to the left ventricle and atrium. These main coronary vessels continue to divide, forming numerous branches. The result is a profuse network of coronary vessels. The major arterial vessels are located on the external surface of the ventricles. Arterial branches penetrate the myocardium toward the endocardial surface.

Increased oxygen delivery to the myocardium is supported almost exclusively by increased coronary blood flow. When there is increased demand for oxygen and nutrients by body tissues, the heart must increase its output. At the same time, the heart itself must be supplied with enough oxygen and nutrients to replace the energy expended. In other words, a balance must be maintained between energy expenditure and energy restoration.

During systole the myocardial contraction compresses the coronary vascular bed. This restricts coronary inflow but increases coronary outflow. Coronary inflow occurs primarily during diastole when the ventricles have relaxed and the coronary vessels are no longer compressed. Blood is driven through the coronaries by aortic pressure, perfusing the myocardium.

A change in heart rate is accomplished by shortening or lengthening diastole. With tachycardia the increased amount of time required for the increased number of systolic contractions per minute reduces the time available for diastole and coronary inflow. There is also an increase in the metabolic needs of the rapidly beating heart. Coronary dilation occurs in an attempt to overcome restricted blood inflow. With bradycardia, the decreased number of systolic contractions per minute prolongs the diastolic period. There is a decrease in resistance to coronary flow and a decrease in the metabolic requirements of the myocardium.

Whenever the delivery of oxygen to the myocardium is inadequate to meet the heart's oxygen consumption needs, myocardial ischemia occurs. One of the major causes of ischemia is coronary artery disease.

Nerve supply

Normally, the heart rate is primarily controlled by the parasympathetic and sympathetic divisions of the autonomic nervous system. Cardiac parasympathetic fibers (vagal fibers) originate in the medulla and synapse with ganglionic cells located near the sinoatrial node and atrioventricular conduction tissue. The right vagus nerve has its greatest effect on the sinoatrial node, and right vagal stimulation inhibits sinoatrial nodal activity, which causes a slowing of the heart rate. The left vagus nerve primarily influences atrioventricular conduction tissue, and stimulation of this nerve produces various degrees of atrioventricular block. Parasympathetic control is usually more dominant than sympathetic control.

Sympathetic fibers originate in the upper fourth, fifth, or sixth thoracic segments of the spinal cord. Some fibers synapse with corresponding spinal sympathetic ganglia; others ascend to the cervical ganglia. Postganglionic fibers from the superior, middle, and inferior cervical ganglia travel to the heart as the superior, middle, and inferior cardiac accelerator nerves. Accelerator fibers to the heart are also supplied by the thoracic ganglia. Stimulation of sympathetic fibers to the right side of the heart (accelerator fibers) elicits greater cardiac acceleration than does stimulation of the left sympathetic fibers, while stimulation of the left sympathetic fibers (augmentor fibers) has a more profound effect on myocardial contractility than upon heart rate.

Neurohormones

Neurohumoral agents are chemical substances released from nerve endings to transmit information to adjacent cells. In man, neurohormonal transmission involves autonomic innervation (the vagus and sympathetic nerves) and two chemical agents (acetylcholine and the catecholamines, epinephrine and norepinephrine). The vagus nerves are inhibitory and the sympathetic nerves are accelerator nerves. Norepinephrine is the primary catecholamine involved in the transmission of neural impulses.

Acetylcholine is released from the vagal nerve endings in the heart at the sinoatrial and atrioventricular nodes and the bundle of His. It slows the heart rate by inhibiting impulse formation and atrioventricular conduction, decreasing the rate of depolarization, increasing the refractory period and resting potential, and hyperpolarizing the cell membrane. Acetylcholine is also a vasodilator; it is rapidly destroyed in the blood. The antagonist for acetylcholine is atropine.

Norepinephrine exists in inactive bound form in sympathetic nerve endings of the heart and with appropriate stimuli it can be released as free active norepinephrine. The catecholamines have a potent positive inotropic effect on myocardial contractility. They speed impulse formation, increase atrioventricular conduction velocity, decrease the refractory period of the atrioventricular node, and induce spontaneous depolarization in Purkinje fibers. Catecholamines increase the work load on the heart and cause a shorter systole with more complete systolic ejection of blood. Norepinephrine is a powerful vasoconstrictor, and this effect tends to impede coronary flow.

Electrocardiogram

Electrocardiograms are graphic representations of the sequence of cardiac excitation. Nurses caring for patients on monitor equipment should be able to detect and interpret changes in the cardiac rate or rhythm or in the conduction of the wave of electric activity or excitation. The electrocardiogram is a useful tool in determining the therapeutic effectiveness of certain drugs. Drugs used in the treatment of cardiovascular disease may alter the electric activity of the heart. The electrocardiogram may provide the earliest objective evidence of a drug's effectiveness or its toxic manifestations. A knowledgeable and observant nurse can use the information she obtains from the electrocardiogram for assessing the effectiveness of drug therapy in the treatment of various cardiac arrhythmias.

Electric activity always precedes mechanical contraction. Immediately after a wave of electric activity moves through atrial muscle, the

139

Figure 10-5
Graphic representation of the normal electrocardiogram. Vertical lines represent time, each square represents 0.04 second, and every five squares (set off by heavy black lines) represents 0.20 second. The normal P-R interval is less than 0.20 second; the average is 0.16 second. The average duration of the P wave is 0.08 second; the QRS interval is 0.08 second; the S-T segment is 0.12 second; the T wave is 0.16 second; and the Q-T interval is 1.36 seconds. Each horizontal line represents voltage; every five squares equals 0.5 millivolt.

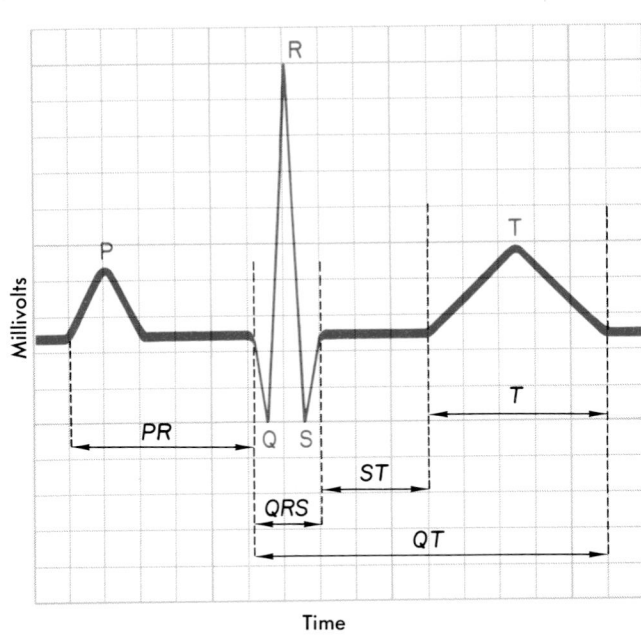

muscle contracts and blood flows from the atria into the ventricles. (See Figure 10-5 for the graphic illustration of the normal electrocardiogram.) The P wave is produced by a wave of excitation through the atria (atrial depolarization). The onset of the P wave follows the firing of the sinoatrial node. After the P wave, a short pause or interval (P-R interval) occurs while the electric activity is transmitted to the atrioventricular node and conduction tissue and the ventricles. The electrocardiogram now records the QRS complex, or ventricular depolarization. This leads to contraction of the ventricles. Repolarization, or recovery, of the ventricles is indicated by the T wave. Atrial recovery or repolarization does not show on the EKG because of being hidden in the QRS complex. The EKG records receding activity as a negative potential, downward deflection; activity approaching an exploring electrode is recorded as a positive potential, an upward stroke on the graph paper or oscilloscope.

Drugs that affect the heart

Drugs may change the rate, force, and rhythm of the heart. Pharmacologic terms that have specific meaning for the actions of drugs on the cardiovascular system include the terms *inotropic, chronotropic, dromotropic,* and *pressor effects.*

Drugs with an *inotropic* (Gr. *inos,* fiber; *tropikos,* a turning or influence) effect influence myocardial contractility. If the drug has a positive inotropic effect it strengthens or increases the force of cardiac contraction. A drug with a negative inotropic effect weakens or decreases the force of muscular contraction.

Drugs with *chronotropic* (Gr. *chronos,* time) action affect the rate of the heart. If the drug increases the heart rate by increasing the rate of impulse formation in the sinoatrial node, it has a positive chronotropic effect. A negative chronotropic drug has the opposite effect and slows the heart rate by decreasing impulse formation.

When drugs have a *dromotropic* (Gr. *dromos*, a course) effect, they affect conduction through the specialized conducting tissues. A drug having a positive dromotropic action speeds conduction. A drug with negative dromotropic action delays conduction.

Drugs with *pressor* effect increase blood pressure by increasing peripheral arteriolar resistance through vasoconstriction.

■ Cardiac glycosides
Digitalis and digitalis-like drugs

Drugs in the digitalis group are among the oldest and most effective therapeutic agents available to the physician for treatment of congestive heart failure. Cardiac glycosides act with specificity and rapidity and have unrivaled value in the treatment of congestive heart failure. Their use in medicine dates from the thirteenth century. However, it was not until 1785, when the English physician and botanist William Withering published his rigorous and systematic observations on the treatment of various ailments with digitalis, that cardiac glycosides became indispensable to a physician's drug armamentarium.

Chemically, all cardiac glycosides are closely related; each is composed of a sugar (glycoside), a steroid, and a lactone. This is illustrated in the structural formula of digitoxin, below, one of the therapeutically important glycosides present in purple foxglove *(Digitalis purpurea)*.

The sugar portion of the molecule will vary in different glycosides. These sugars increase the substance's water solubility and cell penetrability, alter absorption, and modify toxicity. Removal of the sugar portion from the glycoside leaves a molecule known as an aglycone or genin. An aglycone retains its glycosidal activity but to a lessened degree. However, the lactone portion is essential to the characteristic cardiotonic properties of the molecule. The basic digitalis nucleus, the steroid portion, is similar to that of the sex hormones and corticosterones. The difference in this portion from other steroids is responsible for the inability, to date, to synthesize digitalis. The primary therapeutic use of digitalis glycosides is in treatment of congestive heart failure.

Many substances, of which digitalis is the most important, are characterized by their action on the heart. These substances belong to many different botanical families. For ages they have been used empirically in therapeutics. The action of each is fundamentally the same, so that the description for digitalis, with minor differences, will apply to all.

The most important plants that contain digitaloid substances are as follows:

Digitalis purpurea—purple foxglove
Digitalis lanata—white foxglove
Strophanthus hispidus, S. kombé—an African arrow poison
Scilla maritima—squill or sea onion

Digitalis

Digitalis is the dried leaves of *Digitalis purpurea,* or purple foxglove. This plant is cultivat-

| (Digitoxose)₃ | Steroid portion | Lactone portion |
| Sugar portion | | |

Digitoxin

ed for the drug market in England, North America, and Germany and grows wild in Europe, the United States, and Australia. Early investigators gave the plant the name *Digitalis purpurea* because the flower is purple and resembles a finger. Digitalis leaves contain a number of glycosides; the most important are digitoxin, gitoxin, and gitalin.

While all cardiac glycosides have similar pharmacologic properties, they differ in absorption and rate of elimination, time of onset of action, and duration of action. Selection of which cardiac glycoside to use is based on the needs of a particular individual and his reactions to the drug.

The primary circulatory actions of digitalis have been established only within the past two decades. However, the underlying cellular mechanisms remain uncertain.

Digitalis affects cardiac function through two important mechanisms:

1 Digitalis has positive inotropic action. It influences the mechanical performance of the heart by increasing the strength of myocardial contraction.
2 Digitalis alters the electric behavior of heart muscle through its actions on myocardial automaticity, conduction velocity, and refractory period.

Inotropic action. The inotropic action of digitalis results from direct action on the myocardium independent of extracardiac factors. Digitalis does not alter the amount of energy available for myocardial contraction; the increased contractility is associated with more efficient use of available energy. The exact mechanism by which digitalis affects the complex phenomenon of myocardial contraction remains to be established. However, present evidence suggests that digitalis increases myocardial contractility by potentiating excitation-contraction coupling. There is evidence that digitalis brings this about by:

1 Increasing the influx of calcium ions across the membrane
2 Releasing intracellular bound ionized calcium during depolarization

3 Decreasing outward movement or binding of intracellular calcium ions during and after depolarization

The increased strength of myocardial contraction produced by optimal digitalis dosage will be lessened if there is (1) increased extracellular concentration of ionized calcium, (2) frequent contractions, or (3) decreased extracellular sodium concentration.

Electrophysiologic action. It has long been known that digitalis affects the movement of monovalent ions (Na^+, K^+) across the cell membrane. This permits digitalis to alter the electric properties of myocardium. (See Figure 10-6 for typical changes in the electrocardiographic pattern resulting from digitalization.) Both the outward movement of sodium and the inward movement of potassium across the cell membrane are decreased by digitalis. Digitalis inhibits the sodium- and potassium-activated membrane ATPase. It is believed that this action is responsible for its influence on ion movements.

Automaticity of cardiac tissue is not directly affected by therapeutic concentrations of digitalis. The slower heart rate or abolishment of a sinus tachycardia in heart failure results from an increased cardiac output. However, toxic concentrations of digitalis can directly increase automaticity in all cardiac tissues capable of self-excitation. The result is an increased rate of both action potentials and spontaneous depolarization. This is one of the mechanisms responsible for digitalis-induced ectopic arrhythmias. Toxic doses of digitalis may significantly increase impulse formation in latent or potential pacemaker tissue. In some cases the vagus-accelerating and adrenergic-inhibiting action of digitalis may predominate and decrease automaticity of the normal sinoatrial node pacemaker, with a resultant sinus bradycardia. This depression of normal pacemaker function further enhances the occurrence of ectopic arrhythmias.

Conduction velocity is decreased with all concentrations of digitalis. The atrioventricular conduction system is particularly affected. This slowing of conduction is partly caused by the direct action of digitalis but mostly by an in-

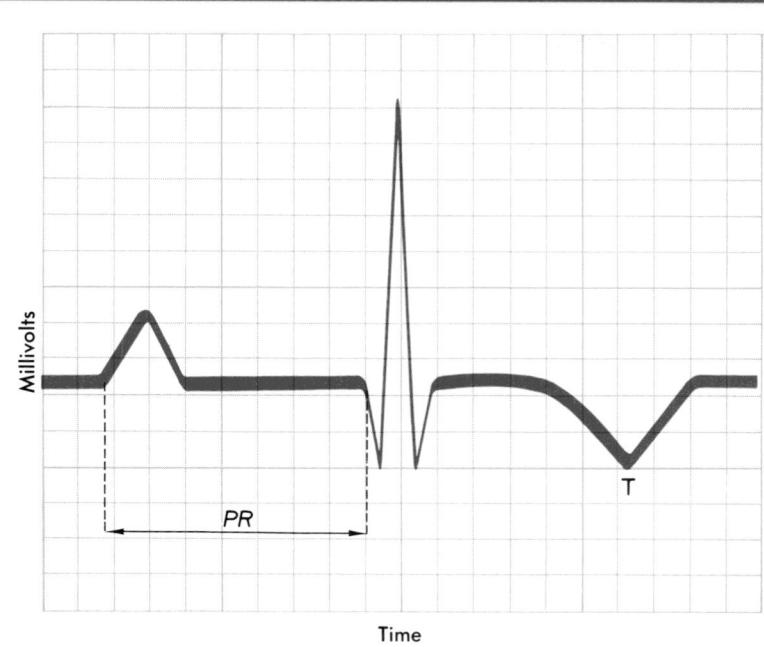

Figure 10-6
Representation of typical effects of digitalization on the electric activity of the heart as shown on the electrocardiogram. Note the prolonged P-R interval, the shortened Q-T interval, and the T wave inversion. (Compare with Figure 10-5.)

crease in vagal action and a decrease in adrenergic action. This is shown on the electrocardiogram by a prolonged P-R interval.

The refractory period in most parts of the heart is lessened by digitalis. Reduction of the refractory period in the ventricles requires nearly toxic amounts of digitalis. A prolonged refractory period occurs in the atrioventricular conduction system, which is very sensitive to digitalis action. This action is partly direct and partly caused by increased vagal and decreased sympathetic (adrenergic) tone. Toxic doses of digitalis may prolong the refractory period and depress conduction in the atrioventricular conduction system to the point where a partial or complete block occurs.

Clinical or therapeutic use of digitalis. As stated previously, the primary therapeutic use of digitalis is to treat congestive heart failure. However, digitalis is also a valuable drug in the treatment of atrial fibrillation and in the management of atrial flutter and paroxysmal tachycardia.

Congestive heart failure. Congestive heart failure is also referred to as cardiac insufficiency, heart or pump failure, and cardiac decompensation. Heart failure most often occurs as a late event of various congenital or acquired disorders of the heart or blood vessels, which place the heart under constant stress. A heart in failure is no longer capable of supplying body tissue with adequate oxygen and nutrients or of removing metabolic waste products. When pump failure occurs, there is usually failure of both sides of the heart, although failure of one side may have preceded and precipitated failure of the other side. Most of the signs and symptoms are caused by pulmonary and systemic congestion, the result of inadequate systolic outflow, and delayed venous return. The mortality for congestive heart failure is high.

The positive inotropic effect of digitalis that results in increased myocardial contractility has many important benefits for the patient with a failing heart. The increased force of systolic contraction causes the ventricles to empty more

143

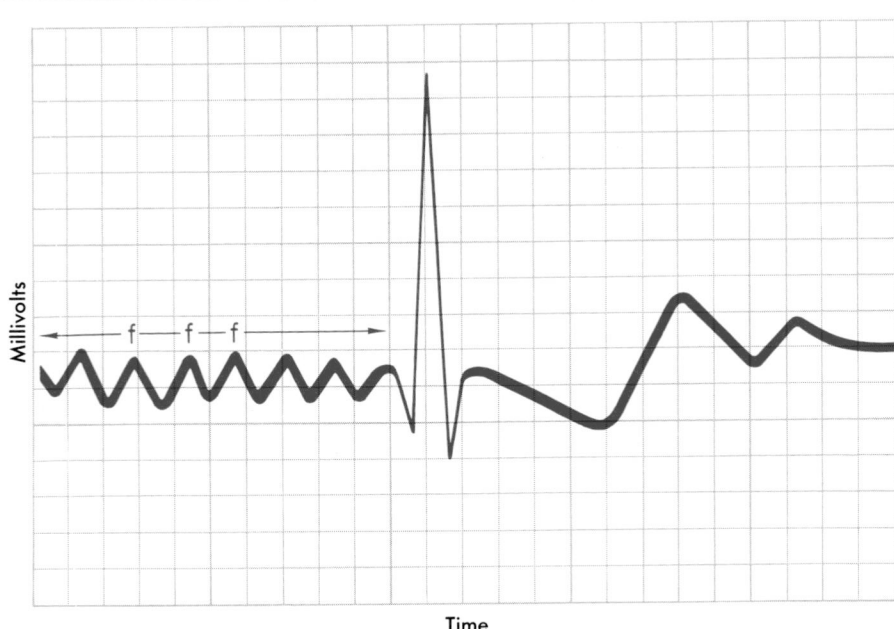

Millivolts

f — f — f

Time

Figure 10-7
Graphic representation of atrial fibrillation as seen on the electrocardiographic monitor or tracing paper. No true P waves are noted; but f (fibrillation) waves consisting of rapid, small, and irregular waves are noted. The QRS complex is normal in configuration and duration but occurs irregularly.

completely. This permits a slower heart rate and more complete filling, which result in the following:

1 Venous pressure falls, and the pulmonary and systemic congestion and their accompanying signs and symptoms are either diminished or completely abolished.
2 Coronary circulation is enhanced, myocardial oxygen demand is reduced, and the supply of oxygen and nutrients to the myocardium is improved.
3 Heart size is often decreased toward normal.

It has been demonstrated that some of the cardiac glycosides have a true but mild diuretic effect. However, marked diuresis in the edematous patient is primarily the result of improved heart action, improved circulation to all body tissue, and improved tissue and organ function including renal function. When digitalis is effec-

tive, the patient is noticeably improved and has an increased sense of well-being.

Atrial fibrillation. The dromotropic action (conduction delay) of digitalis is ideal for control of atrial fibrillation. (See Figure 10-7 for electrocardiographic pattern of atrial fibrillation.) Impairment of conduction reduces the number of impulses reaching the ventricle, the number of ineffective beats is reduced or eliminated, and a more normal rate is established. Controlling atrial fibrillation may prevent or eliminate cardiac failure.

Protective and prophylactic use. There is no general agreement concerning the value of prophylactic digitalization in the absence of congestive heart failure. Some authorities believe the cardiac glycosides may exert a protective effect on myocardial function in the absence of cardiac failure when: (1) an unusual work load is to be placed on the heart or (2) when a patient is to be subjected to the risk of having his myocardial function depressed. Patients who may be digitalized in the absence of cardiac failure by the proponents of prophylaxis include prepartum cardiac patients and elderly or cardiac patients who are to undergo the acute stress of anesthesia and major surgery. More extensive studies are needed before the therapeutic effectiveness of prophylactic digitalization can be established.

Absorption and excretion. The absorption of various cardiac glycosides varies from a minimal amount to almost 100% after oral administration. Digitoxin is almost completely absorbed, digoxin is 80% to 90% absorbed, less than 50% of lanatoside C is absorbed, while ouabain is even less completely absorbed. Oral preparations are readily absorbed from the intestinal tract. Distribution is widespread throughout body tissues. The liver is the major organ for detoxifying cardiac glycosides. Since the drugs are eliminated gradually, repeated doses produce accumulation. This accounts for the persistence of digitalis' cardiac effects for several days or weeks after discontinuance of the drug.

Only a small percentage of a cardiac glycoside is excreted unchanged. Most of the drug is excreted in the urine; some is excreted in the feces. Since digitalis excretion is primarily by the kidneys, patients with renal insufficiency retain the drug longer and show greater sensitivity to the drug.

Administration. The preferred route of administration of digitalis and the cardiac glycosides for congestive heart failure is oral. Because of variation in rapidity of onset of action, duration of action, and individual response, the oral route is safest to use. It is also least expensive. Local gastric mucosal irritation is decreased by giving the drug with or just after meals.

Digitalis preparations should not be given subcutaneously or intramuscularly because of the local irritating effect of the drugs (producing pain and abscess formation) and uncertain absorption. The intravenous route is usually re-served for cases of emergency (such as patients with pulmonary edema or acute ventricular failure) or when the patient has a condition preventing the use of oral medications (such as vomiting or coma). Rectal administration has been used for patients who have difficulty tolerating the drug orally. However, this is an uncommon route of administration.

Standardization of digitalis preparations. Preparations of digitalis are assayed biologically. The U. S. Digitalis Reference Standard contains 1 unit of activity in 0.1 Gm. This is equal to the International Digitalis Standard. While many digitalis preparations must be assayed by the official U.S.P. method in pigeons, the pure glycosides such as digitoxin, digoxin, or deslanoside, U.S.P., are assayed colorimetrically.

Digitalization and choice of preparations. In the treatment of heart failure, the aim is to give digitalis until optimum cardiac effects are achieved and most of the signs and symptoms of heart failure have disappeared. When the patient has reached that state in which he has profited all that he can from the drug, he is said to be digitalized. The amount of drug required for digitalization may vary with each patient.

Usually digitalization is accomplished by giving the patient, over a period of hours or days, a total amount necessary to produce the desired cardiac effect—the digitalizing dose—and then keeping him on a smaller daily dose—the maintenance dose—designed to replace the daily loss of the drug from his body by destruction or excretion to maintain the desired effect. For example, a common schedule for an average adult, using whole-leaf digitalis, would include a digitalizing dose of 1 to 1.5 Gm., given in divided doses over 1 to 2 days, followed by a maintenance dose of 0.1 Gm. daily. Naturally, both the digitalizing and the maintenance doses must be adjusted to the particular patient in terms of toxic reactions and clinical signs of adequate digitalization. If digitoxin were administered orally, 1 to 1.5 mg. would constitute an average digitalizing dose of the drug and 0.1 to 0.2 mg. the maintenance dose. The rate of drug destruction following adequate digitalization is about **145** one tenth the digitalizing dose per 24 hours. This is the rationale usually used for determining the maintenance dose. Many patients who receive digitalis must continue to take the drug the rest of their lives. In children, the dose of digitalis and the rapidity of administration depend on weight and age, body surface, severity of cardiac impairment, and response of the patient.

Differences among the preparations available occur chiefly in absorption from the gastrointestinal tract, local emetic action, and speed of excretion. The glycosides of digitalis are poorly absorbed when the whole drug is administered, which accounts for the fact that only one fifth as much of the intravenous preparation is required as the oral preparation. The digitalis glycosides are irritating to mucous membranes and subcutaneous tissues. Large oral doses of whole drug may produce nausea and vomiting shortly after administration. Smaller doses are less likely to produce emesis from local irritation. The nausea and vomiting occasioned by small doses result from a central effect on the vomiting center. All preparations capable of exerting cardiac effects are capable of emetic action, and this untoward effect cannot be avoided by changing to other members of the digitalis group or by changing the method of administration. All preparations of digitalis or digitalis-like drugs have a cumulative action, although some are more cumulative than others. Digitoxin and digitalis leaf have an especially pronounced cumulative action.

In spite of differences of opinion, the use of the whole drug in the form of digitalis tincture or powdered digitalis has to a certain extent been replaced by the use of refined preparations or by the use of the crystalline glycosides. These are frequently preferred because they are more stable and can be injected and because dosage can be determined more accurately. They are absorbed much more readily when given by mouth and cause less gastrointestinal irritation. Several glycosides are available in a high degree of purity, such as digitoxin, digoxin, and lanatoside C. These make rapid digitalization by oral administration possible with a mini-

mum of local irritant action caused by nonabsorbable glycosides.

It should be emphasized that some of the purified digitalis glycosides are extremely potent compounds, and if looked upon as poisons they are among the most powerful poisons known. Some of the glycosides have a lethal dose for man of about 0.1 mg. per kilogram of body weight. The nurse should therefore handle these compounds with great care and respect.

Purple foxglove—preparation, dosage, and administration

Powdered digitalis, **U.S.P.;** *prepared digitalis,* **B.P.** This preparation is available in tablets and capsules.

Digitalis tincture, **N.F.** This is the only acceptable form of liquid preparation for oral use; 1 ml. is equal to 1 U.S.P. digitalis unit. Calibrated medicine droppers or medicine glasses should be used to ensure accuracy.

Gitalin (amorphous), **N.F. (Gitaligin).** This is a mixture of glycosides obtained from *Digitalis purpurea.* Its action and uses are the same as those of digitalis, and the same precautions should be taken with its administration. The rate of elimination or destruction is slower than that of digoxin but faster than that of digitoxin. Gitalin is administered orally or intravenously. It is marketed in tablets (0.5 mg.), as a solution for injection (2.5 mg. in 5 ml.), and as a solution (drops) for oral administration.

Digitoxin, **U.S.P., B.P.** Digitoxin is the chief active glycoside of *Digitalis purpurea.* It is available in crystalline form and is readily absorbed from the intestinal tract. One milligram of digitoxin has the same effect as 1 Gm. of U.S.P. digitalis when given by mouth. It is available in tablet form as well as in ampules for intravenous therapy. It is extremely poisonous. Digitoxin is sold under a number of trade names: Crystodigin, Unidigin, Purodigin, and Digitaline Nativelle. *Digitoxin tablets,* U.S.P., are available in amounts of 0.1 and 0.2 mg.

White foxglove—preparation, dosage, and administration

Digilanid. This is a mixture of the crystallized cardioactive glycosides, lanatoside A, lanatoside B, and lanatoside C, obtained from the leaves of white foxglove, *Digitalis lanata*. The three components are present in this preparation in the same proportion as found in the crude drug. When these glycosides are hydrolyzed, they yield, respectively, digitoxin, gitoxin, and digoxin. The actions and uses of digilanid are similar to those of digitalis, U.S.P. It can be administered orally, intramuscularly, intravenously, and rectally. Dosage is 0.67 to 1.33 mg. (two to four tablets). It is usually given daily in tablet form until desired effects are obtained and then one to two tablets are given daily as maintenance dosage. Precautions to be observed are the same as those for any digitalis preparation. It is marketed in solution for injection (0.4 mg. in 2 ml.) and in tablets (0.33 mg.).

Acetyldigitoxin (Acylanid). This is a cardiac glycoside derived from lanatoside A. It resembles digitoxin in many ways but has a more rapid onset and a shorter duration of action than digitoxin. It is available in 0.1- and 0.2-mg. tablets for oral administration.

Lanatoside C, N.F. (Cedilanid). This glycoside of *Digitalis lanata* is thought to be more active, therapeutically, than the other two glycosides of the white foxglove. Lanatoside C is a white powder that is practically insoluble in water. Absorption after oral administration is said to be irregular. It is marketed in tablets for oral administration. Lanatoside C tablets usually contain 0.5 mg. of the drug, and 0.5 mg. (gr. $^1/_{120}$) is the usual dose.

Deslanoside (deacetyllanatoside C), U.S.P. *(Cedilanid-D).* This preparation is derived from lanatoside C and has the advantage of being more soluble and more stable than the parent substance. For practical purposes it constitutes the injectable form of lanatoside C. *Deslanoside injection,* U.S.P., is marketed in 2- and 4-ml. ampules containing 0.4 mg. and 0.8 mg. of the drug, respectively.

Digoxin, U.S.P., B.P. *(Lanoxin).* This is a hydrolytic product formed from lanatoside C. It has an advantage over digitalis for the patient who must be rapidly digitalized. Some patients seem to tolerate digoxin better than digitalis. The drug may be given intravenously, in which case saturation of the tissues may be accomplished much more rapidly than with digitalis. Digoxin may also be given orally. It should be administered with caution because it is extremely poisonous. It may bring about digitalization within a few hours when it is administered by mouth and within a few minutes when given intravenously. Official (U.S.P.) preparations of digoxin are available in tablets (0.25 and 0.5 mg.) and as an injectable solution (0.5 mg. in 2 ml.). The proprietary name Lanoxin has an advantage in that it helps to differentiate digoxin and digitoxin, which are sometimes mistaken one for the other by the student. Digoxin (Lanoxin) is widely used in pediatrics and is available as an elixir (0.05 mg. per millimeter) for oral administration to children.

Contraindications. Digitalis is contraindicated in severe myocarditis and heart block and usually when ventricular tachycardia is present. Valvular disease, pneumonia, diphtheria, and thyrotoxicosis are not in themselves considered indications for digitalis therapy.

Side effects and toxic effects. Not all undesired effects of digitalis are toxic effects. While anorexia, nausea, and vomiting can occur with digitalis toxicity, these symptoms can also be caused by gastric irritation from oral digitalis preparations and stimulation of the vomiting center. These effects are often self-limiting and disappear as the patient adjusts to the drug.

Additional signs and symptoms of digitalis toxicity include diarrhea, headache, visual disturbances, weakness, restlessness, and nervous irritability. These are *extracardiac* manifestations of digitalis excess. These toxic effects, while troublesome to the patient, are rarely serious and are often eliminated by omission of the drug for several days. Once the toxic signs or symptoms are gone, drug therapy can again be reinstituted at a lower dosage.

Almost every type of arrhythmia can be produced by digitalis toxicity. The type of arrhythmia produced varies with the age of the patient. Premature ventricular contractions and bigeminal rhythm (two beats and a pause) are common signs of digitalis toxicity in adults, while children tend to develop ectopic nodal or atrial beats. Digitalis-induced arrhythmias are caused

Table 10-1 Dosage of digitalis and cardiac glycosides (adults)

Preparation (generic name and trade name)	Administration	Usual digitalizing quantity (given in divided doses)	Usual daily maintenance dose
Purple foxglove			
Powdered digitalis (leaf)	Oral	1.5 Gm. (1 to 2 Gm.)	0.1 Gm. (100 to 200 mg.)
Digitalis tincture	Oral	10 to 15 ml.	1 ml.
Cardiac glycosides			
Acetyldigitoxin (Acylanid)	Oral	1.8 mg. (0.6 to 2 mg.) over 24 hr.	0.15 mg. (0.1 to 0.2 mg.)
Digitoxin (Crystodigin, Digitalline Nativelle,	Oral	1.0 to 1.5 mg. over 24 to 48 hr.	0.1 to 0.2 mg.
Purodigin)	Intravenous	0.5 mg. (0.5 to 1.2 mg.)	0.1 mg. (0.1 to 0.2 mg.)
Digoxin (Lanoxin)	Oral	1.5 mg. (0.5 to 2 mg.)	0.5 mg. (0.25 to 0.75 mg.)
	Intravenous	1 mg. (0.5 to 1.5 mg.)	0.5 mg. (0.25 to 0.75 mg.)
Lanatoside C (Cedilanid)	Oral	8 mg.	1.0 mg.
Gitalin (Gitaligin)	Oral	6.5 mg. (2.5 mg. initially and then 0.75 mg. every 6 hr.)	0.5 mg.
	Intravenous	2.5 to 3.0 mg. in two injections at 24-hr. intervals	2.5 mg. two times per week
Ouabain	Intravenous only (slowly)	0.5 mg. (0.12 to 0.25 mg.)	
Deslanoside (deacetyl-lanatoside C, Cedilanid-D)	Intravenous only (slowly)	1.6 mg. (1.2 to 1.6 mg.)	0.4 mg. (0.2 to 0.6 mg.)

by depression of the sinoatrial and atrioventricular nodes. The sinoatrial node depression is often greater than that for the atrioventricular node. This results in various conduction disturbances (first, second, or complete heart block). Digitalis may also cause increased myocardial irritability, producing extra systoles or tachycardias.

Predisposing factors to digitalis toxicity. Nurses need to be aware of the predisposing factors to digitalis toxicity. Presence of any of these factors in patients indicates need for close observation of these patients for signs and symptoms of digitalis intoxication.

Potassium loss. Hypopotassemia is a common cause of digitalis cardiotoxicity. Since potassium inhibits the excitability of the heart, a depletion of body or myocardial potassium increases cardiac excitability. Low extracellular potassium is synergistic with digitalis and enhances ectopic pacemaker activity (arrhythmias). The following are causes of potassium loss:

1 Hypopotassemia occurs if large amounts of body fluids are lost as a result of vomiting, diarrhea, or diuresis from administration of diuretics. The use of various diuretic agents (mercurials, carbonic-anhydrase inhibitors, ammonium chloride, and thiazide preparations) induce potassium diuresis along with sodium and water diuresis.
2 Poor dietary intake or severe dietary restrictions decreasing electrolyte intake can cause loss of potassium.
3 Adrenal steroids cause potassium loss and sodium retention.

4 Surgical procedures associated with severe electrolyte disturbances such as abdominal-perineal resection, colostomy, ileostomy, colectomy, and ureterosigmoidostomy can cause loss of potassium.
5 Use of potassium-free intravenous fluids can cause hypopotassemia.

Pathologic conditions. Kidney, liver, and severe heart disease are major factors in digitalis toxicity. From 60% to 80% of the digitalis glycosides are excreted by the kidneys. Therefore, renal disease promotes digitalis cumulation and intoxication. Since the liver is the primary organ for inactivating digitalis, any impairment of liver function decreases an individual's tolerance to digitalis. Severe cardiac disease impedes the function of all body organs and increases myocardial sensitivity to digitalis.

Administration of purified glycosides. Because purified glycosides produce fewer side effects than the whole leaf, there may be continued administration of digitalis without awareness that toxicity is occurring.

Slower body function. Elderly persons have a slowing of body functions and decreased tolerance to drug therapy. Older patients often show signs of toxicity with small doses of digitalis.

Intravenous administration of digitalis and rapid digitalization. The risk of digitalis overdosage is increased by intravenous administration and rapid digitalization.

Treatment of digitalis intoxication. The treatment of digitalis toxicity may consist entirely of omitting administration of digitalis until toxic signs and symptoms have disappeared, or it may include the administration of other drugs such as potassium chloride or EDTA. Administration of potassium chloride will tend to decrease myocardial excitability and abolish arrhythmias. Disodium ethylenediamine tetra-acetic acid (EDTA) is a calcium chelating agent. Digitalis is known to increase the influx of calcium to myocardial cells. Since increased intracellular calcium increases myocardial excitability, inactivating cellular calcium can reduce arrhythmias. Successful treatment of digitalis toxicity has also been reported with the use of diphen-ylhydantoin and propranolol. There is no specific antidote for digitalis intoxication.

Ouabain; G-Strophanthin, U.S.P.

This preparation is obtained from *Strophanthus gratus.* For many years it was the standard against which all digitalis preparations were measured. It is not absorbed well from the gastrointestinal tract and hence must be given parenterally (usually intravenously). Its action is relatively rapid. Effects appear within about 30 minutes after intravenous injection, and the peak of effect is secured in about 90 minutes. Most of its effects have disappeared within 24 hours. It is one of the preparations of choice for rapid digitalization. It is relatively soluble and not likely to cause venous thrombosis when given intravenously. It is available in 1- and 2-ml. ampules containing 0.25 mg. per milliliter of solution.

Nursing measures for care of patients receiving digitalis preparations

Of great importance is the careful observation by the nurse of patients receiving digitalis preparations who have one or more of the predisposing factors to digitalis intoxication. If the patient is being monitored, careful observation should be made of his electrocardiogram before and after the institution, reduction, or increase in digitalis dosage. The pulse should be checked prior to giving each dose to determine any marked change in rate or rhythm. It is still a safe precaution to report and record a pulse below sixty in the adult or ninety to one hundred and ten beats per minute in the child. A decision may be made to withhold the drug.

Understanding on the part of the nurse of the relationship between dosage and potency is fundamental to intelligent cooperation with the physician in the care of the patient who is receiving digitalis or related drugs. When medication is ordered in terms of a small fraction or a decimal fraction, the inference is not only that the drug is potent but also that a mistake in dosage can be especially dangerous even if the amount is small in terms of milligrams. Considerable difference exists among dosages of 1 mg., **149**

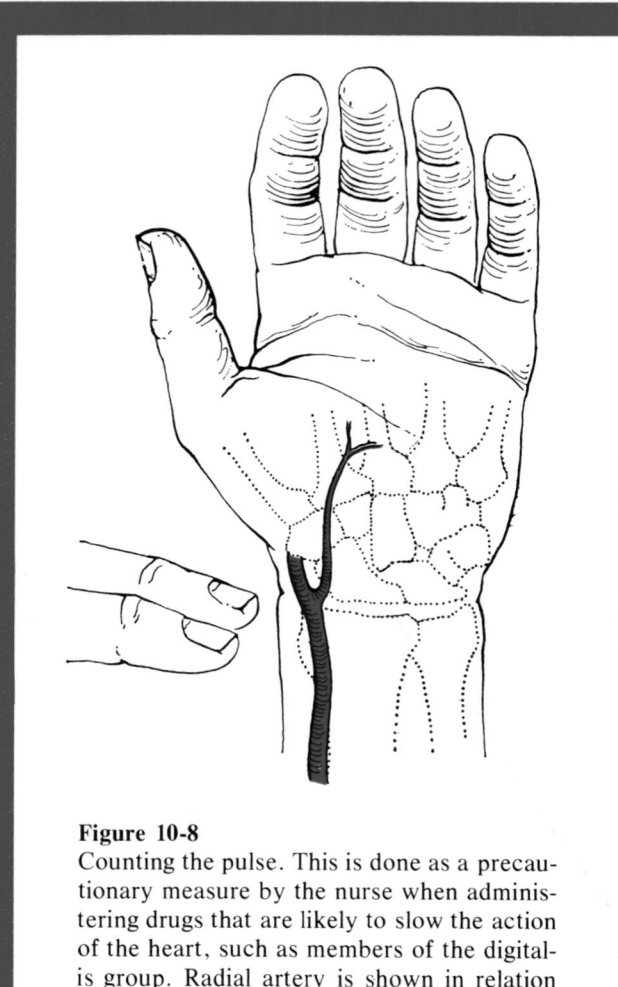

Figure 10-8
Counting the pulse. This is done as a precautionary measure by the nurse when administering drugs that are likely to slow the action of the heart, such as members of the digitalis group. Radial artery is shown in relation to the bones of the hand and radius and ulna.

0.1 mg., 0.15 mg., and 0.2 mg. Differences of a fraction of a milligram can make a great deal of difference when dealing with a potent preparation. The nurse must exert particular care to see that the correct dosage is given.

■ Antiarrhythmic drugs

Antiarrhythmic agents, also known as cardiac depressants, are used to treat various departures from the regular rhythm of the heart. Arrhythmias may cause abnormally slow or rapid heart rates or irregular rhythms such as heart block, series of premature beats, or independent atrial and ventricular rhythms. Arrhythmias can seriously affect cardiac performance and may even be fatal. The ideal antiarrhythmic drug should reestablish and maintain normal cardiac rhythmicity and excitability with minimal toxic or side reactions.

Quinidine

Quinidine is considered to be the prototype of antiarrhythmic drugs. Like quinine, quinidine is contained in cinchona bark and was used by Peruvian Indians for the treatment of malaria. It was introduced as an antiarrhythmic drug early in the twentieth century following a demonstration by a patient of Wenckebach's that he could control his atrial fibrillation by self-administration of quinine. It was not until 1962 that the electrophysiologic mechanisms of quinidine were identified. Of the antiarrhythmic agents now available, quinidine is the one most widely used.

Action. Quinidine has a chronotropic, dromotropic, and inotropic action. In addition, quinidine is known to have a vasodepressor, a vagolytic, and an antiadrenergic effect.

Quinidine has a negative *chronotropic* effect; that is, it inhibits the rate of electric impulse formation from the pacemakers and thereby decreases heart rate. Abnormal or ectopic pacemaker tissue appears to be more sensitive to quinidine than normal pacemaker tissue (sinoatrial node). The blocking of abnormal electric impulses permits the sinoatrial node to reestablish control over cardiac impulse formation, which abolishes ectopic arrhythmias. The best available evidence to date indicates that quinidine inhibits the movement of sodium and potassium ions across the membrane. This in turn inhibits impulse formation by slowing depo-

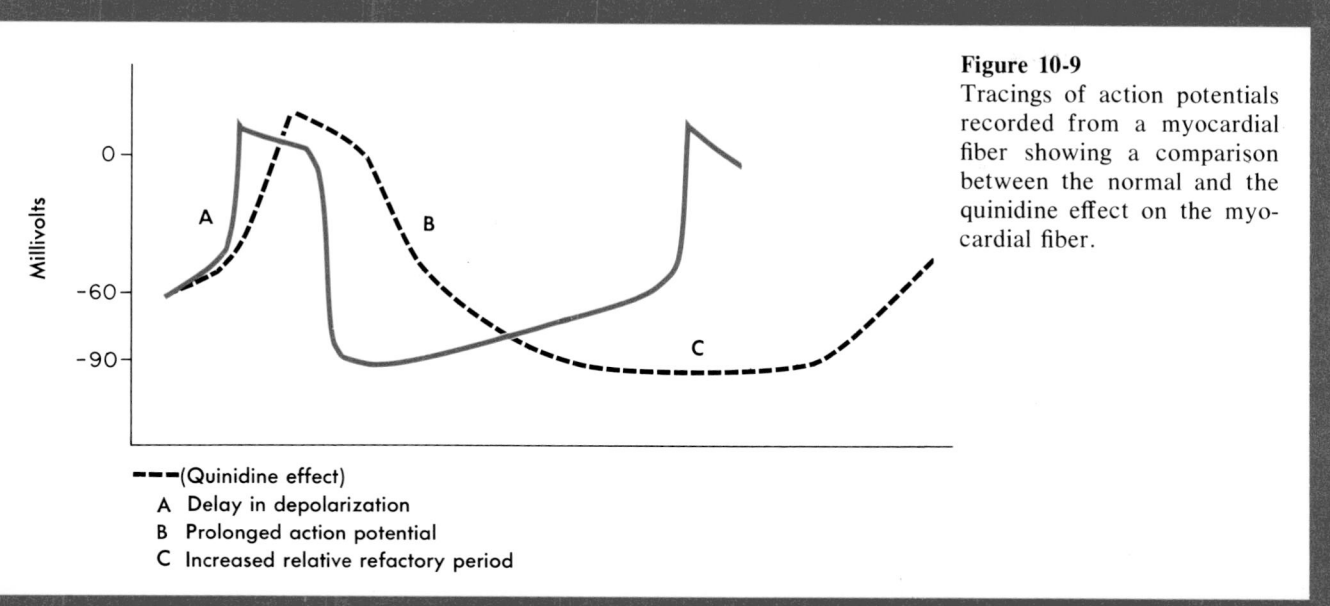

Figure 10-9
Tracings of action potentials recorded from a myocardial fiber showing a comparison between the normal and the quinidine effect on the myocardial fiber.

- - -(Quinidine effect)
A Delay in depolarization
B Prolonged action potential
C Increased relative refractory period

larization, prolonging the action potential, and increasing the relative refractory period (see Figure 10-9). Quinidine increases the interval between the application of a stimulus to myocardial fibers and their response to the stimulus (latent period of the heart). This provides protection from rapidly repeated stimuli.

Quinidine's *dromotropic* action is a negative one since it delays or depresses atrioventricular and intraventricular conduction. This is reflected in the electrocardiogram by prolongation of the P-R interval and QRS duration. With increased drug effect more advanced degrees of heart block can occur.

A negative *inotropic* action is exhibited by quinidine; that is, it depresses myocardial contractility. This is not a serious hazard when therapeutic doses of quinidine are used. However, marked depression of myocardial contractility may be associated with a reduction of cardiac output.

Quinidine has an effect on smooth muscle that accounts for its *vasodepressor* action resulting in vasodilation. This peripheral vasodilating effect is caused by quinidine's ability to interfere with catecholamine (epinephrine and norep-

inephrine) action on vascular smooth muscle. This is referred to as quinidine's antiadrenergic effects. The resultant decrease in peripheral vascular resistance may cause hypotension and/ or decreased cardiac output. This is more likely to occur with intravenous administration of quinidine.

The *vagolytic* effect of quinidine inhibits vagal action on the sinoatrial node. This accounts for the tachycardia seen in some patients. It should be noted that potassium concentrations enhance the depressive effects of quinidine—hypopotassemia counteracts the antiarrhythmic effect of quinidine.

Uses. Quinidine is effective against many arrhythmias—atrial tachycardia, atrial flutter and fibrillation, ventricular tachycardia, and premature systoles. Quinidine has proved to be a valuable drug in the treatment of recurrent paroxysmal atrial tachycardia. With improved techniques, electric cardioversion may be the agent of choice to convert an arrhythmia to a normal sinus rhythm. However, quinidine continues to have an important role in the management of chronic and paroxysmal arrhythmias.

Absorption and excretion. Quinidine is readily absorbed from the gastrointestinal tract. Therefore, effective concentrations of the drug can be achieved by the oral as well as parenteral route. It is rapidly taken up by body tissue (with the exception of brain tissue). It is excreted from the body via the urine. From 10% to 50% of a given dose is excreted within 24 hours after administration. Degradation of quinidine takes place in the liver.

Preparation, dosage, and administration. The maximal effect of an oral dose of quinidine occurs within 1 to 3 hours after administration and the effect persists for 6 to 8 hours. Quinidine sulfate is used for oral administration and the hydrochloride, lactate, gluconate, or sulfate preparations are used for intramuscular administration. Intravenous administration should be used for emergency situations only because of the potentially dangerous effects of the drug. Quinidine should not be given rectally because it has a severe irritating effect on rectal mucosa.

Quinidine sulfate, **U.S.P., B.P.** This drug is available in 100-, 200-, and 300-mg. tablets. Quinidine sulfate is given orally in doses of 0.2 to 0.4 Gm. (gr. 3 to 6) and repeated every 2, 4, or 6 hours. When given every 2 hours, peak blood levels are usually achieved after the fifth dose; when given orally every 4 hours peak blood levels are achieved within 48 to 72 hours; when given every 6 hours or four times a day, peak blood levels may not be reached until the fifth day of administration. The oral maintenance dose is usually from 200 to 600 mg. daily.

Quinidine gluconate, **U.S.P.** This drug is sometimes administered intramuscularly. The initial dose is from 300 to 500 mg. The drug begins to act within 15 to 30 minutes; maximum effect is reached within 1 to 3 hours. Quinidine gluconate is also given orally.

Toxic effects. Quinidine is a potentially hazardous drug. A number of sudden deaths have been reported in patients on quinidine therapy.

The toxic effects of quinidine in approximate order of frequency of occurrence include cinchonism (nausea, vomiting, diarrhea, tinnitus, vertigo, and visual disturbances), thrombocytopenic purpura, rashes and urticaria, hypotension, and ventricular fibrillation.

Some of these effects, such as thrombocytopenic purpura, are thought to be a true allergic hypersensitivity to the drug. Therefore, some clinicians give a test dose of the drug before instituting intensive therapy.

Quinidine can cause cardiac arrest since it is a depressant of myocardial excitability. In patients with conduction defects, a complete block may occur. Since quinidine depresses atrioventricular and intraventricular conduction and ventricular impulse formation, an intrinsic ventricular rhythm may fail to develop and the patient may die of cardiac arrest. Reducing or stopping the dosage of quinidine may be sufficient to overcome toxic or side effects. A true hypersensitivity to the drug necessitates absolute withdrawal of the drug.

The most effective treatment of quinidine toxicity at the present time appears to be intravenous angiotensin alone or in combination with disodium calcium versenate. These drugs significantly increase peripheral vascular resistance and enhance myocardial contractility.

Contraindications. Quinidine is contraindicated in patients who are hypersensitive to the drug. Its use is also contraindicated in patients with second-degree or complete heart block, since it can further enhance conduction delay and lead to asystole.

Nursing measures. Patients with liver disease, congestive heart failure, or renal insufficiency should be closely observed for toxic reactions, since interference with metabolism of quinidine or its excretion from the body can greatly increase the body's response to any given dose of the drug.

Since the drug can cause thrombocytopenic purpura, patients on quinidine therapy should be closely observed for bleeding tendencies, petechiae, or ecchymotic or purpuric areas. Patients with decreased platelets require protection from injury that could result in hemorrhage.

Early evidence of quinidine toxicity is best detected by having the patient monitored electrocardiographically and observing for changes in the patient's cardiac electric activity pattern. Abnormal prolongation of the QRS complex, evidence of second-degree or complete heart block, or appearance of premature ventricular contractions precludes continued quinidine administration.

It is recommended that the patient's blood pressure be checked before administration of quinidine. If hypotension is noted, the physician should be notified.

Procainamide hydrochloride, U.S.P., B.P. (Pronestyl Hydrochloride)

$$H_2N - \bigcirc - CONH - CH_2CH_2 - N \begin{array}{c} C_2H_5 \\ \\ C_2H_5 \end{array} \cdot HCl$$

Procainamide is a synthetic drug that is an effective antiarrhythmic agent with fewer toxic effects than quinidine. Procainamide is the result of investigations to produce a drug similar to the local anesthetic procaine, but with fewer central nervous system effects. It had been demonstrated that topical application of procaine to the myocardium during thoracic surgery reduced the occurrence of premature cardiac contractions during surgery.

Action. The cardiac effects of procainamide are similar to those of quinidine. Procainamide has a negative chronotropic effect since it depresses the rate of pacemaker discharge. It has negative dromotropic action since it slows down conduction in the atria, across the atrioventricular node, through the atrioventricular conducting tissue, and within the ventricles. It has a negative inotropic action since it depresses myocardial contractility. Procainamide has the same effect on ion transfer as does quinidine. Its ability to prolong the refractory period helps to terminate circus movement.* Also, like quinidine, procainamide can cause hypotension.

Electrocardiographic changes that may be noted are prolonged P-R, QRS, and QT intervals.

---

*Circus movement or rhythm refers to a widely held reentry theory that states that flutter and fibrillation occur when initial impulses meet a local block during transmission and the impulses return to the original pacemaker when the latter is no longer refractory; thus constant firing of the pacemaker occurs.

Uses. Procainamide is used to treat a wide variety of ventricular and supraventricular arrhythmias. It is inferior to quinidine in the treatment of atrial fibrillation and flutter.

Absorption and excretion. When given orally procainamide is readily absorbed from the gastrointestinal tract and is rapidly excreted in the urine. Intravenously its action is almost immediate; orally, it acts within 30 to 60 minutes, with peak action occurring in 1 to 2 hours.

Preparation, dosage, and administration. The following is the available preparation of procainamide.

Procainamide hydrochloride, U.S.P., B.P. (**Pronestyl Hydrochloride**). This preparation is available in 250-mg. capsules and in solution for injection (100 mg. per milliliter). It is usually administered orally or intravenously, although it can be administered intramuscularly. A continuous intravenous drip of procainamide in 5% glucose in water may be used to control acute arrhythmias.

Side effects and toxic effects. Side effects of procainamide include gastrointestinal and central nervous system disturbances and hypotension. Bone marrow depression has been reported as well as allergic reactions. Tachycardia or other arrhythmias may result from use of procainamide. More than forty cases have been reported of patients developing a systemic lupus erythematosus type syndrome while on prolonged oral maintenance doses of procainamide. If the drug is discontinued at onset of symptoms, they disappear in a few days or few weeks. It is not known what the outcome would be if procainamide administration were continued.

Vasopressor drugs or molar sodium lactate may be required to overcome the hypotensive effect of procainamide. Frequent blood examinations should be done to determine the drug's effect on the leukocytes and agranulocytes.

Contraindications. Procainamide is usually contraindicated in patients with severe heart damage and shock, since increasing the hypotension may result in fatality. It is also contraindicated in patients with complete heart block and in patients manifesting allergic reactions. Increased widening of the QRS complex caused by procainamide contraindicates further administration of the drug.

Nursing measures. When the drug is given intravenously, electrocardiographic and blood pressure monitoring is required. Further administration of the drug should be questioned when hypotension, progressive widening of the QRS complex, or undesirable changes in the EKG pattern occur. Vasopressors, such as norepinephrine, should be readily available if hypotension occurs. Patients should be observed for and told to report symptoms of arthralgia and fever (lupus syndrome).

Lidocaine, U.S.P. (Xylocaine)

Lidocaine is better known and extensively used as a local and topical anesthetic agent. However, in recent years it has become one of the most frequently used drugs and in some institutions it is the drug of choice in the treatment of ventricular arrhythmias. It has gained considerable acclaim as an effective antiarrhythmic agent.

Action. The action of lidocaine is similar to that of procainamide. Lidocaine has greater antiarrhythmic potency at a lower dosage.

Uses. Lidocaine is used to treat ventricular arrhythmias that occur during surgery or cardiac diagnostic procedures or that are caused by acute myocardial infarction or cardioversion. It may be used preoperatively in patients with a history of ventricular arrhythmia for prophylaxis. Lidocaine is effective in decreasing the frequency of premature beats.

Administration. Lidocaine is administered intravenously, 1 mg. per kilogram of body weight, and by slow intravenous injection or continuous intravenous drip. The onset of action of lidocaine occurs within 2 minutes. Duration of action of a single dose is 10 to 20 min-

utes; 20 minutes after discontinuing intravenous administration, none of lidocaine's effects persists. Lidocaine is metabolized by the liver and rapidly excreted by the kidneys.

Side effects and toxic effects. Drowsiness is a very common side effect but this is often desirable, particularly in patients with acute myocardial infarction.

Toxic effects of lidocaine are not well documented at the present time and are conflicting. Some investigators report central nervous system disturbances (agitation, disorientation, muscle twitching, and convulsions), heart block, and hypotension, particularly with high dosage or rapid rate of administration. Toxic effects rapidly disappear upon discontinuance of drug administration. More extensive clinical investigation is necessary to better establish the toxic and side effects of lidocaine.

Infusions of lidocaine should be carefully monitored for cardiac depressant effects. The blood pressure should be checked for hypotensive effect, and the patient should be carefully observed for other undesirable effects.

Diphenylhydantoin, U.S.P.
(DPH, Dilantin); phenytoin sodium, B.P.

Diphenylhydantoin was introduced 30 years ago for control of epilepsy. In 1950 diphenylhydantoin was found effective in controlling arrhythmias in experiments on dogs, and during the past decade there has been evidence of the drug's ability to control arrhythmias in man.

The structure of diphenylhydantoin is related to that of the barbiturates.

Action. Diphenylhydantoin apparently decreases the excitability of myocardial tissue by increasing the rate of transport of sodium ions across the cell membrane. Diphenylhydantoin increases the ratio of extracellular to intracellular ionized sodium concentration. This decrease in intracellular sodium increases the membrane threshold or potential, decreases the cells' excitability, and inhibits the cells' response to stimuli. Therefore DPH has a stabilizing effect on excitable cells.

The electrophysiologic mechanisms of DPH are similar to those for quinidine. DPH decreases

154

Plate 3
Digitalis purpurea (foxglove).

conduction velocity between myocardial fibers (negative dromotropic effect), it reduces myocardial contractility (negative inotropic effect), and it has a direct vasodilating effect. This same mechanism of action to inhibit arrhythmias is believed to be similar to its action in controlling epilepsy.

Uses. DPH is equally effective in supraventricular and ventricular arrhythmias and in digitalis-induced arrhythmias. It is used in patients unable to tolerate quinidine or procainamide.

Absorption and excretion. Diphenylhydantoin is readily absorbed from the gastrointestinal tract. Only a small amount of the drug is excreted in the urine; most is excreted from the body via the gastrointestinal tract. The liver is the major site for detoxification of DPH.

Preparation, dosage, and administration. When given for prevention of recurrent tachycardia or suppression of premature beats, the oral maintenance dose of DPH is usually from 200 to 400 mg. daily.

Given intravenously constant EKG monitoring is required. Clinical doses may range from 5 to 10 mg. per kilogram of body weight. The average dose is 250 mg. The drug should *not* be administered in less than 10 minutes. It may be given by intravenous drip over a period of several hours.

When given intravenously, diphenylhydantoin is effective within 5 minutes. When given orally, peak action is not reached for 8 hours.

Toxic effects. DPH's ability to depress conduction may result in heart block; its ability to reduce the sinus rate and to cause vasodilation may result in bradycardia and hypotension. Rapid intravenous administration of DPH may result in cardiac or respiratory arrest. DPH may cause extracardiac toxic effects including nervousness, confusion, drowsiness, ataxia, tremors, visual disturbances, cutaneous eruptions, and hyperplasia of the gums.

Heart block or bradycardia caused by DPH may be reversed with intravenous administration of atropine.

Contraindications. DPH is contraindicated in patients with bradycardia or second-degree or complete heart block.

Drugs that affect blood vessels

Some drugs that affect the circulatory system have effects primarily on blood vessels. Drugs producing vasoconstriction tend to increase the blood pressure, whereas those producing vasodilation tend to lower blood pressure. Increased blood flow to the extremities—often desirable in case of arteriosclerosis or of abnormal contraction of blood vessels—can also be promoted by the use of drugs that increase the lumen of arterioles.

Drugs acting on the peripheral circulation can do so either directly or indirectly. (The mechanism by which drugs affect the alpha and beta receptors in blood vessels, thereby effecting vasodilation or vasoconstriction, is discussed in Chapter 9.) Other drugs affect vascular tone by action at still higher centers; reserpine produces vasodilation and lowers blood pressure by acting at centers in the hypothalamus. Still other compounds, of which the nitrites are examples, do not appear to act on blood vessels through their nervous control but relax the muscle cells by direct action. As with many classes of other drugs, it should therefore be kept in mind that the same physiologic effect, such as vasodilation with a resultant drop in blood pressure, may result from the action of a drug at one of several different sites—brain, autonomic ganglia, or the muscle cell itself.

Drugs are also used to sclerose and obliterate the lumen of blood vessels (veins) and in this way alter the course of the circulating blood in veins that have developed varicosities.

■ Vasodilators

Drugs that bring about vasodilation have a number of uses. They play a part in the treatment of coronary disease, peripheral vascular disease, and hypertension. A number of drugs act either on the smooth muscle of the blood vessels or on the vasomotor center in the medulla. Some agents exhibit other actions or combinations of actions. These are indicated under the discussion on the individual drug.

Coronary vasodilators

The term *angina pectoris* implies transient myocardial ischemia (temporary interference with the flow of blood, oxygen, and nutrients to heart muscle). Angina pectoris occurs when the work load on the heart is too great and oxygen delivery is inadequate. Since coronary flow is very responsive to oxygen requirements of the heart, inadequate myocardial oxygenation implies inadequate coronary flow in relation to need. This inadequate oxygenation may be caused by coronary atherosclerosis or various disorders of the coronary vessels, such as vasomotor spasm. Angina pectoris is characterized by chest pain of short duration and its relationship to stress.

Drug therapy of angina pectoris is based on the belief that relaxation of coronary smooth muscle will bring about coronary vasodilation, which in turn will improve blood flow to the myocardium. There are three therapeutic objectives for the use of antianginal drugs:

1. To decrease the duration and intensity of pain during an attack
2. To prophylactically decrease frequency of attacks and improve work capacity even though angina may occur
3. To prevent or delay the onset of myocardial infarction

While evidence exists that the first objective may be achieved, less evidence exists that the second objective can be attained, and no real proof exists that the third objective is attainable. The ideal antianginal drug would:

1. Establish a balance between coronary blood flow and the metabolic demands of the myocardium
2. Have a local rather than a systemic effect—it would act directly on coronary vessels to promote coronary vasodilation with absence of effects on other organ systems
3. Promote myocardial oxygen extraction from arterial flow
4. Have oral effectiveness with sustained action
5. Have absence of tolerance

No drug at the present time meets these criteria. Drugs presently available provide only temporary relief.

Nitrites

Certain members of the nitrite group of drugs have been used clinically for more than 100 years. Organic and inorganic nitrites and organic nitrates possess the pharmacologic effect of vasodilation. However, the exact mechanism of action of the organic nitrates remains obscure.

Since the nitrites and organic nitrates exert similar qualitative effects on the blood and circulatory system, the term *nitrite* as used in the following discussion will include both nitrates and nitrites.

Action and use. The nitrites have a direct cellular action that causes relaxation of most smooth muscles in the body including bronchial, biliary, ureteral, uterine, and gastrointestinal smooth muscle. The most important pharmacologic effects are on vascular smooth muscle. The nitrites dilate all large arteries (temporal, radial, and coronary arteries) as well as arterioles (retinal, skin, meningeal, and splanchnic), capillaries, and venules. For this reason they can be called universal vasodilators. The nitrites are used extensively for patients with angina pectoris.

Because of the vasodilating effect, there is a reduction in vascular resistance and blood pressure, resulting in decreased work load on the heart. In patients with advanced coronary arteriosclerosis there may be an absence of response to the nitrites; no change in coronary resistance is noted, since blood vessel elasticity has been severely diminished.

The rapid-acting nitrites (nitroglycerin) remain the drug of choice for treatment of angina pectoris.

Side effects. The side effects of the nitrites result from their vasodilator action. Severe headache, flushing of the skin, nausea and vomiting, hypotension, and vertigo may occur. Nitrites should be used with caution in patients with glaucoma since dilated retinal vessels may increase intraocular pressure.

Tolerance. Tolerance to the nitrites is easily developed and necessitates the employment of the smallest dose of the drug that will give satisfactory results so that dosage may be increased as tolerance develops. Tolerance begins to appear within a few days and is well established within a few weeks. On the other hand, tolerance is rather easily broken by stopping administration, and the patient is again susceptible to the effects of the drug.

Preparation, dosage, and administration. The following are available preparations of nitrates.

Nitroglycerin tablets, **U.S.P.;** *glyceryl trinitrate tablets,* **U.S.P., B.P.** These tablets are available in 0.3, 0.4, and 0.6 mg. The usual sublingual dose is 0.4 mg. (gr. $^1/_{150}$) and may be repeated several times during the day. Hypodermic tablets of this preparation are used when it is desirable to give the drug subcutaneously.

$$CH_2-O-NO_2$$
$$CH-O-NO_2$$
$$CH_2-O-NO_2$$

Nitroglycerin

When taken sublingually the drug appears in the blood in about 2 minutes; peak blood level is reached in 4 minutes; the effect begins to disappear in 10 minutes and is virtually dissipated within 30 minutes. Fall in blood pressure occurs in 1 to 5 minutes after administration and maximum fall occurs in 5 to 10 minutes. There is a return to initial blood pressure readings within 15 to 40 minutes.

During an acute anginal attack, if pain is not relieved within 5 to 10 minutes, the dose may be repeated. If pain persists after two or more tablets have been taken the physician should be notified. However, some patients take as many as thirty tablets per day without harm.

For prophylactic use the patient should be instructed to insert a nitroglycerin tablet sublingually prior to undertaking any effort that may cause him to have an anginal attack.

EKG patterns are unchanged by nitroglycerin.

Nitroglycerin readily deteriorates, for it is inactivated by time, light, heat, air, and moisture. Patients should be instructed as follows:

1 A *fresh* supply of drug should be kept on hand. A fresh supply should be obtained at least every 3 months.

2 The drug should always be kept in a dark, airtight container.
3 All but a few days' supply of drug should be kept refrigerated.
4 The drug should not be kept close to the body to protect it from body heat.

Ineffectiveness of nitroglycerin may be caused by failure to adhere to these few simple rules. The drug is rapidly destroyed when taken orally. It is ineffective except when taken sublingually.

Mannitolhexanitrate (Nitranitol). This drug is one of the longer-acting nitrites. It is given orally, and the usual dose is 30 mg. It is available in 15- and 30-mg. tablets.

Pentaerythritol tetranitrate, **N.F., B.P.** (Peritrate, Pentritol, Quintrate, Vasodiatol, Pentafin). This preparation is available in 10- and 20-mg. tablets, sustained-release preparations of 80 mg., and a sublingual preparation consisting of 10 mg. pentaerythritol and 0.3 mg. of nitroglycerin. The usual oral dose is 10 to 20 mg. four times a day, or one sustained-release tablet on arising and another 12 hours later. Onset of action of the tablets occurs within 30 to 60 minutes and disappears in 4 to 5 hours. Sustained-release preparations persist for about 12 hours. Tolerance rapidly develops with continuous administration.

Amyl nitrite, **N.F.** This preparation is available in glass ampules (pearls) that are fitted into a loosely woven material so that the pearl can be crushed and the drug inhaled. Each pearl contains about 0.3 ml. (5 minims). It has a strong unpleasant odor, and the patient should not inhale more than two or three times to prevent overdosage. The drug is effective within 30 to 60 seconds. Amyl nitrite is very flammable. It is likely to cause a throbbing headache, facial flushing, nausea, and vomiting.

Erythrityl tetranitrate, **N.F.** (Cardilate, Erythrol Tetranitrate, Tetranitrol). This drug is available in 5-, 10-, and 15-mg. tablets for oral or sublingual use. Initial dose is usually 5 to 10 mg. three times a day. Dosage may be increased to 30 mg. three times a day. When taken sublingually onset of action occurs within 5 to 10 minutes, orally within 30 minutes. Duration of action for either route is 2 to 4 hours.

Table 10-2 Coronary vasodilators

Generic name	Trade name or synonym	Route of administration	Dose*	Onset of action	Duration
Amyl nitrite	—	Inhalation	0.3 ml.	10 to 20 sec.	—
Nitroglycerin	Glyceryl trinitrate	Sublingual	gr. $1/150$	2 min.	15 to 30 min.
Pentaerythritol tetranitrate	Peritrate	Sublingual	10 mg.	10 min.	30 min.
	Pentritol	—	—	—	—
	Pentafin	Oral	10 to 20 mg.	30 to 60 min.	4 to 5 hr.
	Quintrate	Oral	—	—	—
	Vasodiatol	Sustained-release	80 mg.	30 to 60 min.	12 hr.
Erythrityl tetranitrate	Cardilate	Sublingual	5 to 30 mg.	5 to 10 min.	2 to 4 hr.
	Tetranitrol	—	—	—	—
	Erythrol tetranitrate	Oral	5 to 30 mg.	30 min.	2 to 4 hr.
Isosorbide dinitrate	Isordil	Sublingual, oral	5 to 10 mg. 5 to 30 mg.	2 min. 15 to 30 min.	1½ to 2 hr. 4 hr.
Trolnitrate phosphate	Metamine	Oral	2 to 10 mg.	10 min.	Up to 1 week
	Nitretamine	—	—	—	—
Dipyrimadole	Persantin	Oral	25 to 50 mg.	2 to 5 min.	20 to 30 min.

*Single dose only; dose may be repeated three or four times a day or as necessary.

Isosorbide dinitrate (Isordil). This preparation is available in 5- and 10-mg. tablets for oral and sublingual use four times a day. Onset of action sublingually is 2 minutes; orally it is 15 to 30 minutes and lasts about 4 hours. Sustained-release tablets of 40 mg. are also available (Isordil Tembids). These provide onset of action in 30 minutes with the effect lasting for 12 hours.

Trolnitrate phosphate (Metamine, Nitretamin, Triethanolamine Trinitrate Biphosphate). This drug is marketed as 2- or 10-mg. tablets for oral use only, one to two tablets four times a day. Sublingual administration produces stomatitis. Sustained-release tablets are also available.

Monamine oxidase inhibitors

In 1957 it was noted that monamine oxidase (MAO) inhibitors seemed to decrease symptoms of angina pectoris in patients given these drugs for mental depression. The role of these drugs in relieving angina is not known. However, some investigators claim that the antianginal effectiveness of monamine oxidase inhibitors results from their psychic energizing action; mood elevation makes angina more tolerable. There is an association between anxiety and the pain of angina. The use of these drugs in angina pectoris has been virtually abandoned.

Papaverine hydrochloride, N.F., B.P.

Action. Although papaverine is one of the alkaloids of opium, it is free of analgesic and sedative action and has a low level of toxicity. Neither tolerance nor habituation to its use has been reported. The main action of papaverine is seen in cardiac and smooth muscle, especially the smooth muscle of blood vessels.

Papaverine acts directly on cardiac muscle, depresses conduction, and increases the refractory period. It is capable of causing arrhythmias when given intravenously in large doses. Relaxation of muscle in blood vessels occurs especially if spasm has been present. Its effects are seen particularly in the coronary, peripheral, and pulmonary arteries.

Uses. Good results have been obtained by the use of papaverine for peripheral or pulmonary embolism. It acts by increasing the collateral circulation in vascular beds that have been reflexly constricted. When given intravenously in doses of 20 to 100 mg., disturbance of sensation or pain may be relieved. However, papaverine is not considered to be as reliable as nitroglycerin for angina pectoris.

Preparation, dosage, and administration. Papaverine hydrochloride is available in 1-, 2-, and 10-ml. ampules containing 30 mg. per milliliter and in 30-, 60-, 100-, and 200-mg. tablets. It is given orally and parenterally (usually intravenously or intramuscularly). The usual range of dosage is 30 to 60 mg. intramuscularly and 60 to 200 mg. orally.

Ethyl alcohol

It has been common practice to permit and even recommend the use of alcoholic drinks for patients with angina. The beneficial action of alcohol probably results from its sedative action; there is no evidence that alcohol dilates the coronary arteries.

Xanthines

The xanthine derivatives (caffeine, theobromine, theophylline, and aminophylline) have been widely used for many years for treatment of angina. However, their use in angina has been steadily decreasing.

Beta adrenergic blockers

In clinical studies, propranolol has shown some effectiveness in improving exercise tolerance in patients with angina. However, its use in angina is experimental at this time. There is some evidence of adverse myocardial effects.

Peripheral vasodilators

The use of vasodilating drugs in chronic occlusive arterial disease or peripheral vascular disease has to date been very discouraging. Adrenergic blocking agents are frequently used to treat peripheral vascular diseases.

However, several drugs that are not adrenergic blocking agents have been used with some success in the treatment of these diseases.

Nicotinyl tartrate (Roniacol Tartrate)

Nicotinyl tartrate is the tartrate salt of nicotinyl alcohol. By its conversion to nicotinic acid in the body, nicotinyl tartrate produces direct peripheral vasodilation and increases blood flow to the extremities. Since it is oxidized slowly, it has a more prolonged effect than nicotinic acid.

Nicotinyl tartrate is used in the treatment of peripheral vascular diseases. It has been reported to be beneficial in relieving intermittent claudication of peripheral arteriosclerosis and thromboangiitis obliterans.

It is available in 50-mg. tablets and as an elixir, 50 mg. per 5 ml. It is given in doses of 50 to 150 mg. three times a day after meals.

Cyclandelate (Cyclospasmol)

Cyclandelate has a direct relaxation effect on the smooth muscles of peripheral arterial walls. It increases peripheral circulation of the extremities and digits and elevates skin temperature of the extremities.

The drug is available in 100-mg. tablets and 200-mg. capsules for oral use. The usual dose is 100 mg. four times a day.

Side effects include tingling, flushing, sweating, dizziness, and headache.

Isoxsuprine hydrochloride, N.F. (Vasodilan)

Isoxsuprine hydrochloride has potent inhibitory effects on vascular and uterine smooth muscle. It is used in the treatment of peripheral vascular spasm, Raynaud's and Buerger's disease, and arteriosclerotic vascular disease. Isoxsuprine produces a slight to moderate increase in the blood flow of resting muscle. Reports indicate that isoxsuprine produces significant uterine relaxation, and it is used by some clinicians in the treatment of dysmenorrhea, threatened abortion, and premature labor.

Side effects are relatively mild and include lightheadedness, dizziness, nausea, and vomiting. These effects usually subside with a reduction in dosage. Transient hypotension and tachycardia have also been reported.

It is available in 10-mg. tablets. Oral dosage is 10 to 20 mg. three or four times daily. Action occurs within 1 hour and persists for 3 hours after oral administration. An intramuscular preparation of 5 mg. per milliliter in 2-ml. containers is also available for acute and severe symptoms of arterial insufficiency. However, for prolonged use oral therapy is preferred.

■ Antihypertensives

Arterial hypertension is characterized by increased peripheral vascular resistance resulting in a consistent elevation of the diastolic pressure above the accepted range of normal (above 90 mm. Hg) and pathologic changes in the retinal arterioles. Hypertension is associated with a variety of cardiac, cerebrovascular, and renal complications and decreased life expectancy. When there is no known cause for the elevated blood pressure (such as no preexisting kidney disease or atherosclerosis) the condition is termed essential or primary hypertension. For this form of hypertension, the only possible means for adequate control is drug therapy. Research indicates that two factors may be responsible for essential hypertension: (1) a defect in catecholamine metabolism and (2) a concentration of sodium in vascular smooth muscle.

Evidence indicates that successful therapy in essential hypertension results in a decrease in free norepinephrine available for vasoconstriction. Drugs may decrease free norepinephrine by:

1   Inhibiting release of norepinephrine
2   Depleting stores of norepinephrine
3   Competing with norepinephrine effector sites

The belief that norepinephrine is a causative agent in essential hypertension is based on the following findings:

1   The hypertensive patient's blood pressure is lowered by blocking sympathetic nerve transmission surgically (via lumbar sympathectomy) or medically (via drug therapy).
2   All tissues innervated by the sympathetic nervous system contain norepinephrine.
3   Transmission of impulses from postganglionic fibers to arteriolar muscles requires the release of norepinephrine at the neuromuscular junction.
4   Maintenance of a constant level of stored norepinephrine is dependent upon its extraction from blood and its synthesis in nerve tissue.
5   Hypertensives are more reactive than normotensives to norepinephrine and other vasoactive substances.

Clinical and experimental literature indicates that sodium and potassium ions are undoubtedly involved in regulating vascular smooth muscle tension. It has been shown that acute vasoconstriction and vasodilation by vasoactive drugs are associated with cellular and extracellular sodium and potassium exchange.

The exact role of sodium as a causative factor in human essential hypertension is not known. However, there is available evidence that a relationship does exist between excess salt ingestion and human essential hypertension; susceptibility is undoubtedly on a genetic basis. It is claimed that high blood pressure is more prevalent in cultures with a high salt intake. It has been demonstrated that children fed large amounts of salt developed hypertension, and it is well known that drastic salt restriction or use of a salt-depleting diuretic like chlorothiazide reduces the blood pressure of some hypertensive individuals. A high salt intake, or retention of sodium and fluids, may cause ionic disturbances in peripheral arterioles, which may in turn increase vascular tone and vascular reactivity (particularly to adrenergic agents).

The judicious use of antihypertensive drugs can effectively control the blood pressure in a majority of hypertensive individuals with less risk of serious complications and intolerable side reactions than was true for older methods of treatment (especially sympathectomy). However, antihypertensive drug therapy remains empirical since essential hypertension is a disease of unknown etiology and the mechanism of action of many antihypertensive drugs also remains unknown.

The ideal antihypertensive drug would:

1   Maintain blood pressure within normal limits for various body positions

2 Maintain or improve blood flow, not compromise tissue perfusion or blood flow to brain
3 Reduce the work load on the heart
4 Have no undesirable effects
5 Permit long-term administration without development of tolerance

The use of sedatives, diets low in sodium chloride, and weight reduction continue to be advocated for hypertensive patients, although these measures alone are insufficient for many patients. Some patients, such as those with severe renal insufficiency or severe psychiatric disturbance, do not respond well to treatment of hypertension with drugs. On the other hand, many patients benefit from therapy and are spared damage to the heart, kidneys, and brain. The severity of hypertensive disease is often estimated in terms of the level of the diastolic blood pressure and the degree of change in the retinal vessels of the eye.

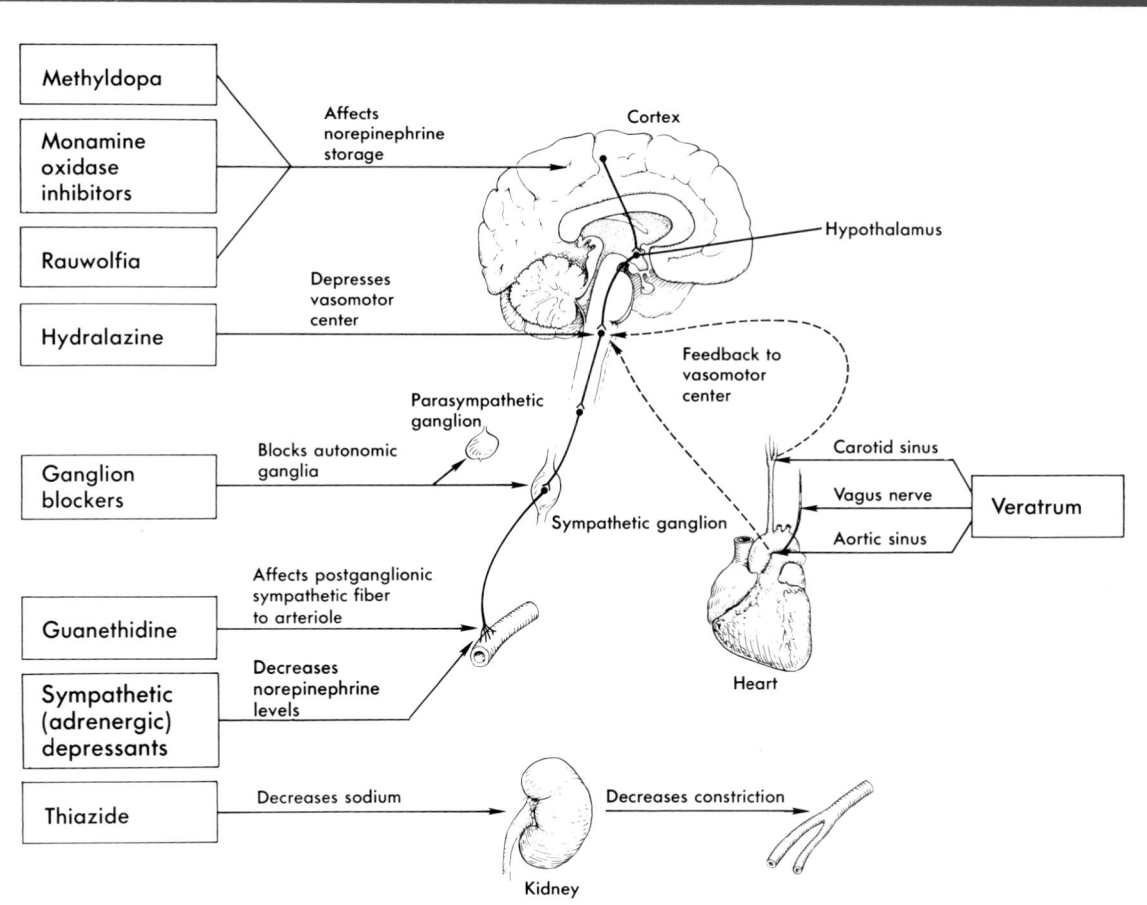

Figure 10-10
Site and method of action of various antihypertensive drugs based on reported clinical and experimental evidence.

Among the drugs presently used in antihypertensive therapy are:

1 Sympathetic nervous system depressants
2 Drugs with selective or obscure sympathetic action
3 Veratrum alkaloids
4 Ganglionic blocking agents
5 Monamine oxidase inhibitors

Figure 10-10 shows the action sites of various antihypertensive drugs discussed in the following sections.

Antihypertensives

■ Sympathetic nervous system depressants

Drugs that most effectively reduce blood pressure are those inhibiting sympathetic nervous system function. The distinction between sympathetic depressants and ganglion blocking agents is that the former agents do not interfere with parasympathetic innervation. It is this characteristic that accounts for clinicians preferring sympathetic depressants to ganglion blockers for lowering blood pressure. The following discussion on the action of rauwolfia compounds is typical of the pharmacologic effects of a number of sympathetic depressants.

Alkaloids of Rauwolfia

Rauwolfia serpentina is a large climbing or twining shrub that grows in India and various tropical regions of the world. The botanical name given to a whole group of these plants was *Rauwolfia,* after an early German physician and botanist, Leonard Rauwolf. The root of the shrub from which the drug is obtained resembles a snake, hence the term *serpentina.* Extracts of the root of the plant have been used for a long time (in countries where the plant is indigenous) for a variety of ills, including snake bites, hypertension, and emotional disturbances. A report of its effectiveness in treating hypertension and mental disorders first appeared in an Indian medical journal in 1931. In 1952, the alkaloid reserpine was isolated. In 1953, western investigators began using the drug and publishing their findings on the sedative and antihypertensive effects of the drug. The rauwolfia compounds are still widely used, particularly for their antihypertensive effect. Their use as sedatives for emotional disorders has declined as other more effective psychotropic drugs have become available.

Individual rauwolfia alkaloids differ in chemical structure and pharmacologic action but in general have similar actions, uses, and cautions. These agents have a cumulative action; maximum response takes several days to 2 weeks after treatment is initiated. Upon discontinuance of drug administration effects from the drug may last 4 weeks. No tolerance or habituation has been reported.

These drugs are not recommended for patients with peptic ulcer, colitis, or mental depression. Parkinsonian rigidity may occur when large doses are administered. This symptom disappears when administration of the drug is discontinued.

Reserpine, U.S.P., B.P. (Serpasil, Sandril, Serfin, Reserpoid, Rau-Sed)

Reserpine is an ester-containing alkaloid obtained from the root of a certain species of *Rauwolfia.* It is a complex heterocyclic compound that was first synthesized in 1956, although the principal source continues to be the plant. It is a whitish crystalline powder, slightly soluble in water and alcohol but very soluble in organic acids such as acetic acid. It is considered the most potent of the alkaloids of *Rauwolfia.*

Reserpine

Action. Reserpine greatly reduces norepinephrine levels in sympathetic postganglionic nerves (peripheral nerve endings). The reason for this action is unknown. It is thought not to be caused by interference with norepinephrine synthesis but by an increased release of norepinephrine resulting in storage depletion. Released norepinephrine is rapidly destroyed by amine oxidases and related enzymes. Studies indicate that reserpine alters the ability of storage granules in nerve cells to take up and bind norepinephrine. Without adequate norepinephrine available for release, discharges of impulses from the sympathetic nervous system produce little or no effect on the effector organ (blood vessels). Since stimulation of vascular smooth muscle is inhibited, vasomotor tone is lowered, vascular relaxation occurs, and blood pressure is decreased. Reserpine is used in the treatment of moderate forms of hypertension.

Reserpine also depletes norepinephrine from various organs. Depletion of brain norepinephrine and serotonin may account for the sedative action of reserpine. It does not alter the brain waves (EEG); it produces calm and quietude without undue drowsiness and without mental confusion or difficulty in movement. It also increases the sense of well-being. When given it, hostile and vicious animals become gentle, calm, and manageable, without loss of alertness and muscle coordination. The animal may go to sleep if undisturbed, but it is easily aroused. The drug seems to reduce attention and responsiveness to outside stimuli, but it does not produce general centralized depression. It potentiates the central nervous system depressant actions of drugs such as barbiturates and alcohol. Depletion of cardiac norepinephrine results in bradycardia. In addition there are constriction of the pupil and increased secretion and motility of the gastrointestinal organs. These effects are believed to be the result of suppression of sympathetic centers that allow the activity of the parasympathetic centers to be more prominent and noticeable. Reserpine is not an analgesic, and it does not potentiate the effects of analgesics.

Preparation, dosage, and administration. Reserpine is available in tablets, in sustained-release spansules, as an elixir, and in liquid forms for oral use. It is available in solutions for injection and in preparations containing a thiazide diuretic, potassium chloride, and other antihypertensive agents.

Reserpine is administered orally or by intramuscular or intravenous injection. The usual dose for adults for mild hypertension is 0.1 to 0.5 mg. daily, in two or three divided doses. It is a preparation of choice for most hypertensive emergencies, in which case doses of 2.5 to 5 mg. may be given parenterally every 6 to 12 hours. Blood pressure should be determined before each injection of reserpine to avoid marked hypotension.

Side effects. Reserpine is considered to have a low level of toxicity, but undesirable effects may occur as dosage levels rise. Nasal stuffiness, gain in weight, and diarrhea are common side effects. Other effects include dryness of mouth, nosebleeds, insomnia, itching, and skin eruptions. The drug sometimes causes gastric irritation, and occasionally it brings about reactivation of old gastric ulcers or causes a new one to form. Postural hypotension may occur after parenteral administration.

Rauwolfia serpentina, N.F. (Raudixin, Rautina, Rautotal, Rauwoldin)

This drug is the powdered whole root of *Rauwolfia serpentina*, N.F. It is administered orally. The daily oral dose for adults is 100 to 150 mg. It is usually divided into two doses. If larger doses are required, a more potent antihypertensive drug is indicated. It is available in 50- and 100-mg. tablets. It is also available in preparations containing a thiazide diuretic and potassium chloride.

Alseroxylon (Rauwiloid, Rautensin)

This preparation is the fat-soluble alkaloidal fraction extracted from the root of *Rauwolfia serpentina*. It is administered orally. The average adult dose is 2 to 4 mg. daily. It is available in 2-mg. tablets.

Syrosingopine, N.F. (Singoserp)

Syrosingopine is a derivative of reserpine. It is the least potent of the rauwolfia derivatives and has minimal central action.

Deserpidine (Harmonyl)

Deserpidine's pharmacologic action is like that of reserpine. It is administered orally and is available in 0.1- and 0.25-mg. tablets and in combination with a thiazide diuretic. Average daily dose is 0.25 to 1.0 mg.

Rescinnamine, N.F. (Moderil)

The pharmacologic actions of rescinnamine are indistinguishable from those of reserpine, with the exception that sedation and bradycardia are less common. It is available for oral administration in 0.25- and 0.5-mg. tablets. Average initial adult dose is 0.5 mg. once or twice daily for 2 weeks. Maintenance dose is usually 0.25 mg. daily.

Antihypertensives

■ Selective sympathetic nervous system inhibitors

Certain antihypertensive drugs have the distinctive property of blocking the postganglionic nerves to arterial smooth muscle, but because they are highly ionized they do not cross the blood-brain barrier and therefore do not act on the central nervous system.

Guanethidine sulfate, U.S.P., B.P. (Ismelin)

Guanethidine depletes norepinephrine from the heart and other peripheral organs. It causes a release and subsequent depletion of norepinephrine from adrenergic nerve endings. Unlike the rauwolfia compounds it does not have additional central action, and unlike the ganglionic blocking agents it does not inhibit the parasympathetic system. Therefore, it does not produce a definite sedative effect or the serious side effects of parasympathetic blockade (urinary retention, paralytic ileus).

Guanethidine's blocking actions are very selective. It is a potent antihypertensive agent with fewer side effects than the older ganglionic blocking agents (pentolinium tartrate and hexamethonium chloride). Its prolonged therapeutic effect and the need for only one dose daily make it a clinically advantageous drug in the treatment of severe and malignant hypertension. The drug is only partially absorbed from the gastrointestinal tract and is primarily excreted by the kidney.

Venodilation occurs in addition to arteriolar dilation, which causes blood to pool in the splanchnic and peripheral areas. This results in some reduction in cardiac, renal, cerebral, and coronary flow. It must be kept in mind that these effects are increased in the standing position, and the drug may cause serious side effects in patients with cerebrovascular, coronary, or renal disease.

Preparation, dosage, and administration. Guanethidine is available in 10- and 25-mg. tablets for oral administration. Initial dose is often 10 to 25 mg. daily, which is increased by 10 mg. weekly until a desirable antihypertensive response is attained. No increased dosage should be given until the patient's blood pressure has been taken in the standing position. Average daily dose may range from 10 to 75 mg. Maintenance dose must always be individualized.

The onset of action of guanethidine is slow, and the antihypertensive effect may not be noted for 48 to 72 hours after treatment has been started. The action of the drug is prolonged and the hypotensive effect may persist for 7 to 10 days after drug discontinuation.

Side effects. The most frequently noted side effects from guanethidine are lightheadedness and weakness, especially when the patient first gets out of bed in the morning. This is caused by orthostatic hypotension, the arteriolar and venodilation permitting pooling of the blood in the lower extremities with a reduction in cerebral flow. These symptoms will disappear as the day progresses. (See section on nursing care measures and instructions for patients with orthostatic hypotension, p. 171.) Some patients receiving guanethidine show marked variation in blood pressure during the day, going from orthostatic hypotension in the morning to severe hypertension by late afternoon or evening. This effect may be alleviated by rest periods during the after noon or early evening.

The orthostatic hypotension actually reflects the therapeutic potency of the drug and is not a true side reaction. This effect may be lessened or eliminated by reduced drug dosage.

Other common side effects are diarrhea occurring after meals and at night and ejaculation failure. Impotence has been reported in a few cases. These effects result from the unopposed action of the parasympathetic nervous system.

Bradycardia occurs with guanethidine since the drug blocks the sympathetically innervated cardioaccelerator nerves and leaves the vagal influence unopposed. Other side effects include abdominal distress, fatigue, nausea, nasal stuffiness, and weight gain. These symptoms may be relieved by reducing drug dosage.

Precautions. Guanethidine should be used cautiously in patients with coronary insufficiency, recent myocardial infarction, cerebrovascular disease, renal disease with nitrogen retention, or history of peptic ulcer. The increased parasympathetic tone resulting from guanethidine therapy may aggravate these conditions.

Prior to surgery, guanethidine should be discontinued or reduced, anesthetics should be given with caution, and atropine and vasopressor drugs should be immediately available. These are essential precautions since the stress of surgery in the presence of depleted norepinephrine levels may result in cardiac arrest.

In addition, guanethidine should not be used in conjunction with monamine oxidase inhibitors.

Methyldopa, U.S.P. (Aldomet)

$$HO \quad \text{---} \quad CH_2\text{---}\overset{\overset{\displaystyle NH_2}{|}}{\underset{\underset{\displaystyle CH_3}{|}}{C}}\text{---}COOH$$

Methyldopa is another drug with selective sympathetic inhibition. Methyldopa lowers brain and heart norepinephrine. Some investigators claim that in the body, methyldopa is converted to methyldopamine and then to methylnorepinephrine. This biosynthesis is competitive with the conversion of dopa to dopamine to norepinephrine.

Methylnorepinephrine is stored in the norepinephrine storage sites and, therefore, it is methylnorepinephrine that is released when sympathetic nerve stimulation occurs. This false neurotransmitter is a less potent pressor substance than norepinephrine, and the result is reduced sympathetic activity. The precise antihypertensive mechanism of methyldopa remains unidentified.

Methyldopa reduces blood pressure by lowering peripheral vascular resistance. Since it also reduces renal vascular resistance it is often used in patients with renal hypertension and in hypertensive patients with impaired renal function. The drug has little or no effect on cardiac output. Lowered blood pressure occurs in both the lying and standing positions. Although the standing response is greater, the difference between the standing and lying blood pressures is not as great as that obtained with guanethidine or ganglionic blocking agents.

Sedation does occur with methyldopa since it readily penetrates brain tissue and lowers norepinephrine levels. Methyldopa is absorbed from the gastrointestinal tract and excreted by the kidney.

Preparation, dosage, and administration. Methyldopa is available in 250-mg. tablets for oral use. The usual starting dose is 500 mg. daily with increments of 250 mg. weekly or biweekly until an optimum blood pressure response is obtained. Daily dosage may range from 500 to 3000 mg. (0.5 to 310 Gm.). Effect occurs within 4 to 6 hours; duration of action is 8 to 12 hours. Upon discontinuance of the drug, pretreatment blood pressure levels return within 24 to 48 hours.

Methyldopa is also available in 5-ml. ampules containing 50 mg. per milliliter for intravenous use in hypertensive crises. From 250 to 500 mg. of the drug is given at 6-hour intervals. The drug may also be given by intravenous infusion in 100 to 200 ml. of 5% dextrose in water over a

165

period of 30 to 60 minutes. Frequent blood pressure monitoring is highly recommended.

Side effects. Side effects from the use of methyldopa are sedation, depression, dry mouth, nasal congestion, fluid retention (edema), fever, altered liver function tests (although no liver toxicity has been reported), and decreased white and platelet cell counts. Liver function tests and blood cell determinations should be done at regular intervals. Numerous other side effects may occur, and their elimination may be brought about by a reduction of dosage.

Precautions. Methyldopa is contraindicated in patients with liver disease, eclampsia, or a history of mental depression.

Hydralazine hydrochloride, N.F. (Apresoline Hydrochloride)

Hydralazine hydrochloride is an effective antihypertensive agent, particularly when used in combination with other drugs for treating the patient with moderately severe hypertension. The exact mechanism by which hydralazine lowers blood pressure is unknown. However, hydralazine is thought to produce its effects by depressing the vasomotor center and inhibiting sympathetic stimulation and by direct action on blood vessels. These actions reduce vascular resistance by producing arteriolar vasodilation. Hydralazine also has the ability to partially block the pressor effects of norepinephrine and angiotensin and to interfere with enzymes such as histaminase necessary for vasoconstriction. In combination with a rauwolfia preparation or a thiazide, it often lowers diastolic blood pressure in both the recumbent and upright positions, and toxic effects from hydralazine are decreased. Its use is now limited because of the availability of more effective and less toxic drugs.

Preparation, dosage, and administration. Hydralazine hydrochloride is usually administered orally, although it may be given intravenously or intramuscularly when the patient is unable to take the drug orally. It is available in 10-, 25-, 50-, and 100-mg. tablets and as a sterile solution for injection of 20 mg. per milliliter. As with other antihypertensive drugs, medication is started with small doses and the dosage increased gradually until desired effects are obtained or symptoms of toxicity appear. The initial oral dose for patients with moderate to severe hypertension is 10 mg. given after meals and at bedtime. Patients may receive larger doses, depending on the severity of the hypertension and their response to the drug. Repeated blood pressure readings must be taken not only to determine the effect of the drug but also to avoid serious side effects.

Side effects and toxic effects. Side effects associated with hydralazine hydrochloride vary all the way from merely unpleasant effects to those that are serious and require cessation of administration. Headache, heart palpitation, anxiety, mild depression, dry mouth, unpleasant taste in the mouth, and nausea and vomiting are symptoms that are unpleasant but may not necessitate discontinuance of administration. More serious symptoms include symptoms of coronary insufficiency, edema, chills, fever, and severe depression. Toxic symptoms that may result from prolonged administration of hydralazine hydrochloride in large doses resemble those of early rheumatoid arthritis or acute systemic lupus erythematosus.

Antihistaminic drugs, salicylates, or barbiturates are useful to control headache, palpitation, anxiety, and nausea and vomiting. The more severe symptoms require cessation of therapy with this drug. Fortunately, most symptoms subside when the drug is withdrawn. However, the lupoid state may persist for an indefinite period.

Antihypertensives

■ Veratrum preparations

Veratrum viride and *Veratrum album* (green and white hellebore) are two species of plants that contain alkaloids with the capacity to slow the heart and lower blood pressure. Protoveratrines A and B (Veralba) constitute a mixture of two alkaloids that have been isolated from *Veratrum album.* Alkavevir (Veriloid) is a preparation of the ester alkaloids of *Veratrum viride.*

The hypotensive effect of veratrum alkaloids results from their rather unique ability to reflexly depress the vasomotor center and sympathetic activity, which inhibits vasoconstriction and promotes vasodilation. This results from their stimulating effect on receptors in the carotid sinus and aortic arch. These receptors (baroreceptors) and the vasomotor center are an example of a feedback control loop. They have opposing effects for the purpose of moderation and control of body function. The veratrum compounds also stimulate the vagus, which slows the heart and dilates peripheral blood vessels with a fall in blood pressure.

The veratrum alkaloids all have a central emetic effect and the resulting nausea and vomiting is a serious disadvantage. In addition, the range between toxic and therapeutic dose is narrow. These disadvantages have limited their usefulness.

Veratrum preparations such as alkavervir (Veriloid), protoveratrine (Protalba, Beralba), or cryptenamine (Unitensin) have been used effectively for hypertensive emergencies. They reduce blood pressure almost immediately upon intravenous use. Constant expert supervision and blood pressure monitoring are required to regulate the dose according to blood pressure response and to avoid serious side effects such as respiratory depression and collapse.

Side effects. Side effects of the veratrum preparations include epigastric distress, increased flow of saliva, nausea, vomiting, hiccoughing, and slow pulse. These effects may be stopped with atropine. Overdosage causes bradycardia, hypotension, respiratory depression, and collapse. Ephedrine is useful in overcoming the hypotension.

Contraindications. Veratrum products are contraindicated in patients with high intracranial pressure (which is not secondary to hypertension), in cases of digitalis intoxication, and in patients with uremia or with cerebrovascular disease.

Antihypertensives

■ Ganglionic blocking agents

Among the earliest effective agents for treatment of hypertension (and still the most potent of the antihypertensive drugs) are the ganglionic blocking agents. These drugs block transmission of both sympathetic and parasympathetic nerve impulses at the ganglia. The parent compound of this group of drugs is a quaternary ammonium compound, tetraethylammonium chloride. It is not well suited for the treatment of hypertension because of its short duration of action, its ineffectiveness when given orally, and its distressing side effects.

In 1950 the methonium derivatives were introduced and hexamethonium chloride became the drug of choice in managing severe and malignant hypertension. Despite the difficulties in managing patients receiving hexamethonium because of its erratic absorption and action and severe side effects, its use demonstrated that severe hypertension could be controlled with an improvement in morbidity and mortality. Since 1961, however, the ganglionic blocking agents have been seldom used. Newer antihypertensive drugs that have more selective action and less severe side effects are preferred.

Ganglionic blocking agents block the action of acetylcholine (ACh) upon the ganglion cells by competing with acetylcholine at the synapse of autonomic ganglia. This results in reduced transmission of impulses from preganglionic to postganglionic fibers in both sympathetic and parasympathetic nerves (see Figure 9-3, p. 103). Blocking transmission of impulses through the sympathetic ganglia abolishes vasoconstrictor tone; the blood vessels dilate and arterial pressure falls. This is the desired clinical effect. The greatest antihypertensive effect occurs when the patient stands, since compensatory vasoconstrictor reflexes regulating blood pressure with position change are suppressed. The result is that blood pools in the leg veins, venous return

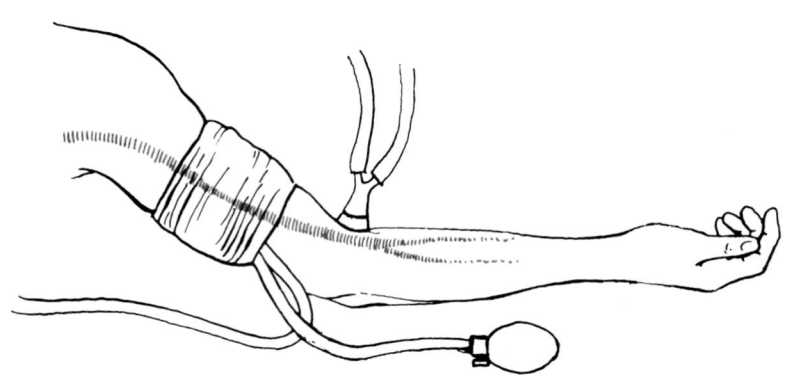

Figure 10-11
Determining the blood pressure prior to the administration of antihypertensive drugs such as thexamethonium chloride or pentolinium tartrate (Ansolysen) in order that adjustments in dosage may be made according to the patient's response to the drug. Dosage may need to be increased, decreased, or omitted. The blood pressure may need to be taken with the patient in standing, sitting, and lying positions.

to the heart is decreased, and cardiac output falls. If blood supply to the brain is inefficient, fainting occurs. These are of course undesired effects but a natural result of the drugs' pharmacologic action. Sympathetic block also causes loss of body heat and lowered body temperature as a result of vasodilation in the skin. Sweating is also inhibited.

Major disadvantages in the use of ganglion blockers result from parasympathetic blockade. This causes dry mouth, reduced gastric secretion, paralytic ileus, constipation, urinary retention, blurred vision, and loss of visual accommodation.

Impotence may also occur, owing to the combined sympathetic and parasympathetic block. Erection is prevented by the latter, while the former prevents ejaculation.

These drugs do not penetrate the blood-brain barrier and therefore do not exert central nervous system actions.

Ganglion blockers still have a place in modern medicine in the treatment of hypertensive emergencies when it is necessary to lower the blood pressure rapidly, in management of the patient resistant to other antihypertensive therapy, and in combination with other less potent drugs. Withdrawal of these drugs must be gradual to avoid a rebound in pressure and the possibility of a vascular accident. Tolerance may develop with prolonged administration of any of the ganglionic blocking agents.

Hexamethonium chloride (Methium Chloride); hexamethonium tartrate

Hexamethonium is rarely used today except in emergencies. Many of its previous dosage forms are no longer available. It is not given orally since it is poorly and irregularly absorbed from the gastrointestinal tract. When it is given parenterally its effects are achieved rather promptly and last 4 to 6 hours.

Pentolinium tartrate, B.P. (Ansolysen Tartrate)

Pentolinium is administered orally, subcutaneously, and intramuscularly. It is available in 20-, 40-, 100-, and 200-mg. tablets and as a sterile solution, 100 mg. in 10 ml. The total daily oral dosage may vary from 60 to 600 mg. The initial oral dose is usually 20 mg. The initial dose is made as small as possible and increased gradually while the patient is under careful medical supervision. The initial parenteral dose recommended is 2.5 to 3.5 mg.

Pentolinium is about five times more potent than hexamethonium and has a longer duration of action (8 to 12 hours).

Chlorisondamine chloride (Ecolid Chloride)

Chlorisondamine is more potent than hexamethonium or pentolinium but less potent than mecamylamine. It is available in 25-mg. tablets for oral administration. The initial dose is 12.5 mg.; daily increments are determined by the patient's response. The average daily dose is 50 to 100 mg. twice daily. Duration of action is 8 to 12 hours.

Mecamylamine hydrochloride, U.S.P., B.P. (Inversine Hydrochloride)

Mecamylamine is marketed in 2.5- and 10-mg. tablets for oral administration. The dosage recommended is that which will reduce the blood pressure and maintain it without the appearance of severe side effects. Treatment is usually started with a dosage of 2.5 mg. twice daily and is gradually increased. The average total daily maintenance dose is about 25 mg. (divided into three portions). Dosage must be determined in relation to blood pressure readings.

Mecamylamine is well absorbed from the intestinal tract. It lowers the blood pressure of both normal persons and hypertensive patients. Its duration of action is 6 to 12 hours. Mecamylamine is absorbed by the central nervous system; confusion, tremors, and psychologic difficulties have been observed in some patients being treated with mecamylamine.

Trimethaphan camsylate, U.S.P. (Arfonad Camsylate); trimethaphan camphorsulphonate, B.P.

Trimethaphan camsylate is a rapid-acting ganglionic blocking agent that lowers blood pressure in both normotensive and hypertensive persons. The duration of its action is brief, which makes it unsuited to the treatment of hypertension.

This drug is used for the production of controlled hypotension during certain types of surgical procedures in which the production of some degree of hemostasis in capillary beds, arterioles, and venules helps to prevent excessive bleeding and increases visualization and exposure of the surgical field. It is used especially in neurosurgery and peripheral vascular surgery.

Preparation, dosage, and administration. Trimethaphan camsylate is administered by continuous intravenous infusion as a 0.1% solution in 5% dextrose in water or in isotonic salt solution. It is available in 10-ml. ampules containing 500 mg. Blood pressure returns to normal levels about 5 minutes after administration is stopped.

The use of this drug is recommended for administration only by experienced anesthetists. Respiratory depression is a complication, particularly when a muscle relaxant has been used. Tachycardia is a potential complication.

Antihypertensives
■ Amine oxidase inhibitors

The monamine oxidase inhibitors have the ability to lower blood pressure. Monamine oxidase is an enzyme active in the metabolic breakdown of catecholamines. Agents that inhibit this enzyme and its actions, resulting in increased concentrations of norepinephrine, cause reduction in blood pressure. Studies also indicate that the monamine oxidase inhibitors suppress release of norepinephrine from peripheral sympathetic neurons. The precise mechanism by which monamine oxidase inhibitors reduce blood pressure remains undetermined.

Pargyline hydrochloride, N.F. (Eutonyl)

$$\text{C}_6\text{H}_5-\text{CH}_2-\underset{\underset{\text{CH}_3}{|}}{\text{N}}-\text{CH}_2-\text{C}\equiv\text{CH} \cdot \text{HCl}$$

Pargyline is used for moderate to severe hypertension. It is a potent amine oxidase inhibitor that, like guanethidine and ganglionic blocking agents, exerts a predominant orthostatic antihypertensive effect. Onset of action is slow, about 3 to 4 days. It takes 7 days for the cumulative effect to be sufficient to bring about a decrease in blood pressure. Maximum response to the drug may take as long as 3 weeks.

Upon discontinuance of the drug, blood pressure returns to pretreatment levels in 10 to 14 days.

Preparation, dosage, and administration. The drug is available in 10-, 25-, and 50-mg. tablets. **169**

The usual initial dose is 10 to 25 mg. daily. Because of the cumulative effect, drug dosage should be increased slowly by increments of 10 mg. at weekly or biweekly intervals until the desired blood pressure response is obtained. The usual maintenance dose is 25 to 75 mg. per day.

Pargyline is usually used along with an oral diuretic since this reduces the amount of pargyline required, reduces side effects, and promotes more effective lowering of blood pressure in the supine position.

Side effects. The most common side effects are dry mouth, insomnia, daytime drowsiness, nervousness, weight gain, and impotence or inability to ejaculate. Reducing drug dosage may eliminate these side effects. For some patients a different antihypertensive drug may be needed.

Pargyline has been known to exert a euphoric action in some patients; this is particularly helpful for the depressed hypertensive patient.

Cautions. Since pargyline is an amine oxidase inhibitor, the patient must be cautioned against ingesting foods or liquids that contain large amounts of tyramine. Since monamine oxidase inhibitors increase the concentration of norepinephrine and tyramine is a precursor of norepinephrine, a "flooding" of the body with norepinephrine may result. Severe vasoconstriction can occur with marked blood pressure elevation. Several deaths reported in the literature have been attributed to this effect. Foods known to contain high tyramine content are cheese products, particularly cheddar cheese; excluded are cream and cottage cheese. The more aged and the less acid the cheese, the greater its tyramine content. Some alcoholic beverages, beer and wine (especially chianti), and some meats, fruits, and vegetables have sufficient concentrations of tyramine and tyrosine to cause the patient on monamine oxidase inhibitors to have extreme headaches, serious blood pressure elevation, and tachycardia. Since these reactions can occur with use of pargyline and amphetamines, amphetamines and antidepressants should not be taken concomitantly. Fortunately these reactions disappear in 1 to 2 hours in most cases, but these reactions

may be serious and caution must be exercised.

Since pargyline may potentiate action of drugs affecting the central nervous system, it should not be given with imipramine, amitriptyline, ganglionic blocking agents, or sympathomimetic amines. If barbiturates are used, they must be given in reduced dosage.

Antihypertensives

■ The thiazides

Chlorothiazide, N.F., B.P. (Diuril); hydrochlorothiazide, U.S.P., B.P. (HydroDiuril, Esidrix, Oretic)

The effectiveness of chlorothiazide and certain related compounds, when given alone or in conjunction with other antihypertensive agents in the treatment of hypertension, has now been established.

Action. Although introduced and primarily useful as a diuretic agent, chlorothiazide has also been found to have significant blood pressure lowering action in hypertensive subjects, perhaps because of its effect in reducing the amount of water, sodium, and chloride in the body and possibly because of certain inherent properties of the drug. It also augments the effects of other drugs used in treatment of hypertension.

Uses. Chlorothiazide is used either alone, in cases of mild hypertension, or in combination with other antihypertensive drugs. This permits lower drug dosage, reduction of unpleasant side effects, and enhanced hypotensive effects.

Preparation, dosage, and administration. Chlorothiazide is available in tablets of 250 and 500 mg. for oral administration. When given alone, doses of 500 mg. may be prescribed to be given from one to three times daily. When combined with other antihypertensive drugs, the dosage is lower, usually 250 mg. twice daily.

Hydrochlorothiazide is available in tablets of 25 and 50 mg. for oral administration. There are also tablets containing hydrochlorothiazide and potassium. Some pharmaceutical companies market a combination of this drug and another antihypertensive in the same tablet. The usual antihypertensive dose is 25 to 50 mg. one or two times a day, but doses as high as 200 mg. a day may be used.

Side effects. Unlike many antihypertensive drugs, chlorothiazide produces few unpleasant side effects. Patients occasionally experience weakness, fatigue, nausea, abdominal pain, distention, and diarrhea. A fairly high percentage of patients has been known to show some disturbance of blood electrolytes. The blood uric acid may be elevated and the level of serum potassium lowered. Chlorothiazide is administered cautiously to patients with renal insufficiency. Some physicians recommend that the patient on prolonged therapy with this drug be given supplemental amounts of potassium chloride. Skin rash has been observed occasionally. Leukopenia, thrombocytopenia, and agranulocytosis have occurred but are rare.

Other thiazide compounds

A number of preparations chemically related to chlorothiazide have been marketed, such as hydrochlorothiazide, U.S.P. (HydroDiuril), polythiazide, N.F. (Renese), and bendroflumethiazide, N.F. (Naturetin). These drugs have helped to eliminate need for parenteral injection of mercurial diuretics and have permitted liberalization of sodium chloride intake. (See Table 11-2 for comparison of the various thiazides and Chapter 11 for more detailed information on the thiazides.)

Nursing measures for care of patients on antihypertensive therapy

Instructions to patients to avoid or decrease orthostatic hypotensive effect. The nurse should give the patient on antihypertensive therapy the following instructions:

1 The patient should rise slowly from a lying to a sitting position and from a sitting to a standing position. This allows for physiologic adjustment of the vascular system. It also allows vasoconstriction of lower extremity vessels to occur, which prevents pooling of blood and syncope.
2 The patient should never stand perfectly still in one place for any length of time, especially within 2 hours after taking drug. Standing still causes relaxation of leg vessels with pooling of

blood and may result in syncope or weakness. This is particularly true in the early morning since this is the time when postural hypotension is often most severe. The patient should avoid standing still in church, waiting in line, standing on buses and subway trains, and in telephone booths. He should use caution while shaving or showering.

3 If weakness and dizziness occur it can be relieved by muscular activity or recumbency.
   a. If standing or sitting, the patient should flex his calf muscles, wiggle his toes, rise up on his toes, and allow his feet to return to flat position. This results in alternate vasoconstriction and vasodilation and prevents blood from pooling in lower extremities.
   b. If possible, the patient should lie flat with his legs slightly higher than his head to promote cerebral flow and decrease pooling of blood in legs.
4 The patient should be instructed to be careful within 2 hours after taking drugs. He should avoid driving a car if blurred vision or hypotension occurs. He should be cautious when working with or around heavy and dangerous machinery.
5 The patient should not take hot baths or steambaths since this promotes peripheral vasodilation and may cause a hypotensive reaction.

Other instructions to patient

1 The patient should take precautions in the heat or when in the sun, or at the beach, since heat increases peripheral blood flow through vascular relaxation from heat dissipation, and since some antihypertensive drugs cause decreased sweating, hypotension, heat stroke, and other serious side effects from vasodilation can occur.
2 If impotency occurs he should consult his doctor. Omission of an occasional dose or a decrease in dosage may overcome this effect.
3 The patient should *not suddenly omit drug therapy.* If the drug is suddenly discontinued blood pressure tends to rise higher because of increased sensitivity to pressor substances. Gradual withdrawal of the drug is therefore necessary.
4 The patient should carry an identification card with the name of the drug, dosage, and the times the drug is taken.
5 If chest pain occurs after taking the drug, the patient should discontinue taking the drug and

consult his doctor. This is especially important in patients with history of angina pectoris.

6 Alcohol in moderation is acceptable.

7 If headache occurs at night or early in the morning, the patient should sleep with his head elevated or in a sitting position.

8 When the patient is on a monamine oxidase inhibitor he should be cautioned to avoid foods or beverages high in tyramine or tyrosine (see p. 170). In addition, he should not take any medicine not prescribed for him by his physician, since drug incompatibilities may occur.

9 Another important aspect is moderation with salt intake or the ingestion of foods high in sodium content. Such foods include bacon, ham, sausage, tuna, crabmeat, various cheeses, and crackers.

Nursing care of patients with orthostatic hypotension. An Ace bandage or an elastic stocking should be used to overcome vascular relaxation in lower extremities. It should be applied with the legs slightly elevated or horizontal. Bandages should be snug but not excessively constricting. The bandages need be applied only when the patient is up and about; they should be removed when he returns to bed. A snug abdominal binder or girdle may help overcome orthostatic hypotension.

The patient's blood pressure should be checked in lying, sitting, and standing positions. The readings should be charted and reported. Dosage is often regulated according to blood pressure obtained in standing or upright position. With some drugs blood pressure is lowest in standing position and highest in lying position. Blood pressure in the sitting position may be lower than that obtained in the lying position but higher than that recorded for the standing position. The patient should stand for at least 3 minutes before reading is taken. For patients on bedrest, the patient should be in a semireclining position with the head of the bed elevated.

Nursing care of patients with side effects. Visual disturbances may occur with the use of some drugs such as ganglion blockers. There may be interference with pupillary response and sensitivity to light because of poor accommodation. The patient may need to wear sunglasses and avoid bright lights.

Constipation is a common effect with some antihypertensive drugs such as ganglion blockers. Daily elimination is very important when antihypertensive drugs are given orally or if the drug is primarily eliminated via the intestinal tract. Constipation may cause either irregular or constant absorption of the drug, and cumulative effects may occur. Adequate diet, liquids, and exercise are important to avoid this effect. Cathartics (such as 30 to 45 ml. daily of milk of magnesia) or enemas may be necessary during early stages of treatment. The antihypertensive agent may need to be changed if regular and unassisted elimination cannot be established.

Other side effects include diarrhea, urinary retention, and dry mouth and nasal mucosa. Diarrhea is likely to occur with guanethidine therapy. This may require changing the drug or use of antidiarrheic agents. Urinary retention is likely to occur in the older male with prostatic hypertrophy. These patients should be placed on recorded intake and output. Dry mouth is likely to occur with any drug that inhibits sympathetic activity, since the salivary glands are innervated by the sympathetic nerves. Dry mouth interferes with carbohydrate digestion. In addition, the patient is more prone to oral infections. Good oral hygiene is essential for these patients. Dry nasal mucosa is not a serious side effect, but it is an annoying one. Nonirritating lubricants, such as lanolin or glycerine, may be used to relieve this effect.

Teaching the patient to take his own blood pressure. Some authorities believe that the patient should be taught to take, record, and graph his own blood pressure at home. This often lessens nonadherence to the therapeutic program and serious side effects from overdosage.

■ Vasoconstrictors

Vasoconstrictor drugs usually exert their effects by bringing about contraction of the muscle fibers in the walls of the blood vessels or by stimulation of the vasomotor center in the medulla. They may be used to stop superficial hemorrhage, relieve nasal congestion, raise and sustain the blood pressure, and sometimes increase the force of the heart action.

Angiotensin amide, N.F. (Hypertensin)

Since 1898 it has been known that a relationship exists between the kidneys and elevated blood pressure. Research revealed that a substance released from the kidneys was converted in the bloodstream to a vasoconstrictor. In 1940 reports appeared in the United States and Argentina describing this vasopressor substance. In the United States it was named angiotonin and in South America, hypertensin. In 1957 this agent was synthesized and renamed angiotensin.

It has been shown experimentally that ischemic kidneys release an enzyme-like substance known as renin, which acts on a globulin in plasma in the blood to form angiotensin I, which is vasoinactive. Angiotensin I is then converted by a plasma enzyme to angiotensin II, the most powerful vasoconstrictor known. A simplified schematic representation of this action is shown below.

Renin   +   Angiotensinogen ⟶ Angiotensin I
(enzyme liberated   (globulin of hepatic
by renal cortex)   origin and angio-
               tensin precursor)
Angiotensin I + Converter enzyme ⟶ Angiotensin II

Angiotensin II is destroyed by an enzyme called hypertensinase (an antipressor substance) produced by both the normal kidney and gut and found in red blood cells and pancreas and in small amounts in the liver.

The renin-angiotensin system appears to be a homeostatic mechanism for regulating blood pressure. A drop in blood pressure results in release of renin and the eventual formation of angiotensin II. Angiotensin amide is the synthetic preparation of angiotensin II with identical pharmacologic properties.

Angiotensin amide acts directly on the smooth muscle of arterioles, causing vasoconstriction. It has no effect on venules. Its ability to elevate blood pressure is probably the result of (1) its arteriolar vasoconstricting effect, and (2) its ability to stimulate aldosterone release, which causes renal tubular absorption of sodium and an increase in body sodium and water, with a resultant rise in blood volume.

Angiotensin has no direct stimulating effect on the heart, and a rise in blood pressure may cause a reflex bradycardia and decreased cardiac output.

Angiotensin amide is a controversial substance and its therapeutic role is not yet clearly delineated. It is used by some clinicians to treat hypotension, particularly refractory hypotension when the use of other vasopressor agents have been ineffective.

Preparation, dosage, and administration. Angiotensin amide is supplied in powdered form in vials containing 2.5 mg. of the compound to which 5 ml. of sterile distilled water is added before use. The mixture is then added to saline or glucose for slow intravenous administration. It is a stable substance and may be stored for months without loss of pressor activity. Angiotensin is destroyed by enzymes in tissues, in whole blood, and in plasma and therefore it cannot be mixed with blood or plasma for infusion. If extravasation into subcutaneous tissue occurs, no sloughing results. Angiotensin acts immediately; *continuous monitoring of the blood pressure is required.*

Drugs that act on the blood and blood-forming tissue

The following information includes only those drugs used to treat certain anemias, to replace blood volume, or to influence blood clotting.

■ Antianemic or hemopoietic drugs

The formation of both red cells and hemoglobin is a complex process, and deficiency in any one of a number of constituents may result in failure to produce the needed number of red cells or an adequate amount of hemoglobin. The hemoglobin molecule is composed of globin (a protein) and hematin (an iron-containing pigment). A related protein (myoglobin) is found in the muscle cells of mammals.

Some of the factors that promote formation of red blood cells are:

1 A diet adequate in essentials for production of mature red blood cells; namely, iron, vitamin C, vitamin B complex, the antianemic factor (vitamin B_{12}), and animal protein

173

2 Normal gastrointestinal tract activity to assure adequate digestion and absorption of needed essentials

3 A liver able to store iron as well as the antianemic factor. It has been observed that chronic disease of the liver leads to anemia. Much of the iron needed for synthesis of hemoglobin is salvaged from erythrocytes. The antianemic factor is vital for the maturation and formation of normal red blood cells.

4 Normal activity of blood-forming tissues, particularly the red bone marrow of the adult

Although an adequate diet is the preferable way to acquire the essential constituents for blood formation, various disease conditions require treatment that brings about more rapid results than can be obtained from diet alone.

Antianemic drug therapy is aimed at eliminating the cause of the anemia or at symptomatic relief. Vitamin or hormonal deficiency may lead to anemia; specific examples are deficiency of ascorbic acid or of thyroid or adrenocortical hormones. Replacement of any of these missing substances can be considered specific therapy for the corresponding anemia. The major antianemic substances under this heading are iron, vitamin B_{12}, and folic acid.

Iron

Iron is a metallic element that is rather widely distributed in the body. It is found not only in hemoglobin but also in the cytochrome pigments of cells and as a reserve supply in the blood-forming organs. Iron is essential to the normal transport of oxygen and to normal tissue respiration.

Iron deficiency results in a form of anemia in which the red blood cells are hypochromic and microcytic—the red blood cells contain less hemoglobin (and therefore have a low color index) and are smaller than normal. Iron-deficiency anemia is associated with symptoms of low vitality, pallor of the skin and mucous membrane, fatigue, and poor appetite.

Absorption, metabolism, and excretion of iron compounds. Absorption of iron is influenced by a number of factors: (1) the presence of acid in the gastric content (the acid is thought to favor

dissociation of iron compounds and the reduction of ferric to ferrous iron, although some doubt has been expressed about this); (2) the presence of reducing substances in the alimentary canal, such as ascorbic acid, which helps to keep iron in a soluble form; and (3) the dietary intake of iron.

Iron is absorbed primarily from the upper part of the duodenum where the acidity prevents formation of insoluble iron compounds. Iron is stored in the form of ferritin or hemosiderin in bone marrow, liver, spleen, and other reticuloendothelial tissue. Both forms can be mobilized and used for hemoglobin synthesis. Iron transport is carried on by transferrin, a specific iron-binding protein in plasma. The transfer of iron to maturing erythrocytes occurs by release of iron from transferrin to specific receptor sites on the membranes of immature red blood cells.

Most iron used for new erythrocyte formation comes from disintegrated red blood cells, whose life span is about 120 days. Approximately 25 mg. of iron daily comes from this source. At best the amount of iron actually absorbed from the gastrointestinal tract is small, about 1 to 2 mg. daily. This is usually adequate since the body is extremely protective of its iron supply.

Iron is not readily eliminated from the body; that which is eliminated was probably not absorbed. It is primarily excreted via the intestinal tract. Only minute traces of iron are excreted via the urinary tract.

Uses. Iron therapy is indicated by hypochromic (iron-deficiency) anemia that occurs following hemorrhage or in persons with an inadequate supply of iron. The major and only significant way of losing iron from the body to such an extent that anemia develops is by blood loss resulting from a sudden acute large hemorrhage or a slow insidious loss from menorrhagia, hemorrhoids, or a silent ulcer or tumor of the gastrointestinal tract.

Iron is used prophylactically in pregnancy, for premature infants, and for those whose diet contains an inadequate amount of iron (such as a diet for peptic ulcer).

Iron requirements in man. Since much of the iron salvaged from worn-out red cells is reused in the body, only a small amount (1 to 2 mg.) needs to be absorbed from the diet to maintain a positive iron balance. During periods of rapid growth and development the body's need for iron is correspondingly increased. Pregnancy, early childhood, early adolescence (especially in girls), and menopause constitute periods when the iron content should probably be increased either by increased dietary intake or medicinal iron or both. Women up through the age of menopause require two to four times as much iron as the adult male because of pregnancy and loss of menstrual blood. The body requirements are ordinarily met by a diet adequate in red meats, green vegetables, eggs, whole wheat, and other foods rich in iron.

Action and result. The local action of iron salts constitutes a side action.

Local. When inorganic iron compounds are administered orally, iron acts as an irritant and astringent. It reacts with tissue proteins and forms an insoluble iron compound. Irritation and astringent effects along the gastrointestinal tract may cause nausea and vomiting, constipation or diarrhea, and abdominal distress. Solutions of ferric iron are sometimes used for their strong astringent properties. They are applied externally as styptics. Ferric solutions are also occasionally used as gargles for their astringent effects. Organic forms do not cause the same irritation because of the fact that they dissociate with difficulty.

Systemic. The action for which iron is most often administered is its hematopoietic one. If iron reserves of the body are depleted, they are restored when ample amounts are administered. It is believed that the action of iron in conditions of deficiency is largely to supply that which is needed for the hemoglobin molecule. The exact mechanism by which iron is utilized by the bone marrow is unknown. Iron is of value only in hypochromic anemias or those in which the color index is low. Iron therapy in this condition can be expected to result in increased vigor on the part of the patient, increased resistance to fatigue, inproved condi-

tion of the skin and nails, improved appetite, and general feeling of well-being. In other words, it brings about a tonic effect. When administered to individuals with normal blood values it does not bring about an increase in the hemoglobin but only increases the reserve supply of iron in the body.

Maximum response may be expected in the case of hypochromic anemias between the second and the fourth week. Favorable response may, however, be inhibited by vitamin deficiency, infection, achlorhydria, hepatic disorder, or disorders of absorption in the intestine. If the iron deficiency is a severe one, other forms of therapy may be needed to supplement the iron therapy. Blood transfusion will restore the blood more rapidly than anything else that can be done. The physician is likely to maintain that the major medical indication, apart from replacing iron, however, is to find the source of blood loss. To treat iron-deficiency anemia without investigating the possible cause has been vigorously criticized by leading hematologists.

Chlorosis, an iron-deficiency condition in its classic form, has largely disappeared, but a similar although mild grade of anemia in girls of adolescent years (ages 14 to 20) is still a common finding. It responds well to iron therapy.

Preparation, dosage, and administration. It is widely accepted that ferrous salts are better absorbed than ferric salts, and that oral administration is preferable to parenteral. Large doses of iron are usually given, since only 15% of an oral dose is absorbed. Administration after meals tends to reduce gastrointestinal irritation. The concomitant administration of orange juice or ascorbic acid is sometimes used since either acts as a reducing agent to aid absorption.

Oral iron preparations. Ferrous sulfate, U.S.P., is the most widely used form of iron and is very economical. It is always given orally as a tablet, extended release capsule, or elixir. The tablets are often enteric coated, since ferrous sulfate rapidly oxidizes in air to form ferric sulfate. The average dose of ferrous sulfate for adults is 300 mg. daily. Dosage range for infants and children is usually 300 to 600 mg. daily. **175**

Dosage must be individually determined according to the severity of anemia.

Ferrous gluconate, N.F., B.P. (Fergon). This preparation of iron is available in tablet, capsule, and liquid forms. Dosage is usually the same as that for ferrous sulfate. It is said to have less tendency to cause gastric distress and is better tolerated by some patients than is ferrous sulfate.

Ferrous fumarate, U.S.P., B.P. (Ircon). It is claimed that this oral preparation of iron is better tolerated than either the sulfate or gluconate preparations. It is available as tablets, chewable tablets, and sustained-release forms. Usual adult dose is 200 mg. three or four times daily.

Ferrocholinate (Chel-Iron, Ferrolip). This preparation is a chelated (bound) form of iron, which is believed to be less toxic and better tolerated than some of the older preparations such as ferrous sulfate and ferrous gluconate. At the same time it is said to be clinically effective in the treatment of iron-deficiency anemia. It is administered orally and can be given between meals. It is available in tablets, as a syrup, and as a solution. The proposed dose is 330 mg. three times daily for adults and children.

Side effects and toxic effects. Long-continued administration of iron may cause headache, loss of appetite, gastric pain, nausea, vomiting, and constipation or diarrhea. Patients should be forewarned of the possibility of experiencing abdominal cramps and diarrhea when taking certain preparations of iron. If only the latter symptoms develop, the drug can be stopped for a day or two and then resumed. They should also be told that oral preparations will usually cause the stool to be dark red or black. If many untoward symptoms develop, it may be necessary to take a longer rest period before resuming administration. Tolerance to iron is apparently not developed. Serious acute poisoning can result from ingestion of large doses of iron compounds. This is particularly true when it occurs in infants or young children. Preparations of iron should be kept out of the reach of children. The signs and symptoms of poisoning are those of gastrointestinal irritation, destruction of tissue, and shock.

Most cases of severe poisoning have occurred in young children who have swallowed many tablets of ferrous sulfate. Some deaths have been reported.

Precautions. To avoid injury or staining of the teeth, solutions should be well diluted with water or fruit juice and taken through a glass tube or straw. Because of the astringent property of these preparations, they may be combined with or be accompanied by a cathartic to ensure regular bowel evacuation.

Iron stains silver; a silver spoon should never be used in giving iron. Such stains may be removed with strong ammonia water. Iron stains on linen and clothing may be removed with oxalic acid.

Parenteral iron preparations. The preferable route of administration of iron is usually the oral one. However, the following conditions are indications for parenteral administration: (1) for patients with hypochromic anemia who do not tolerate oral iron preparations, (2) for those who do not absorb iron well from the gastrointestinal tract or have gastrointestinal complications such as ulceration or severe diarrhea, (3) for those who for one reason or another cannot be relied upon to take the iron orally, such as the aged or the mentally disturbed, and (4) for those in whom a maximal rate of hemoglobin regeneration is needed, such as patients with severe iron deficiency (patients prior to surgery for which there is immediate need or for patients in the last trimester of pregnancy).

Intramuscular administration is preferable to intravenous injections.

Iron-dextran injection, U.S.P., B.P. (Imferon). This is a colloidal suspension of ferric hydroxide in complex with partially hydrolyzed low molecular weight dextran. The preparation is stable, has a pH of 6, and contains 50 mg. of elemental iron per milliliter. It is available in 2- and 5-ml. ampules and in 10-ml. vials. Total dosage is calculated by determining the approximate extent of the hemoglobin deficit and adjusting the daily dose accordingly. The initial dose is usually 50 mg. on the first day, and amounts up to 250 mg. may be given every day or every other day thereafter until the amount needed has been given. This preparation is given by deep intramuscular injection into the gluteal muscle. The subcutaneous tissue should be pushed aside before insertion of the needle to prevent leakage along the tract of the needle. It is not administered intravenously.

Dextriferron injection, N.F. (Astrafer). This preparation is an iron-carbohydrate complex that is administered intravenously. It is recommended that the initial dose not exceed 1.5 ml. of a 2% solution (30 mg. of iron).

Iron sorbitex, U.S.P. (Jectofer). This is an intramuscular preparation of iron in combination with sorbitol and citric acid. It is available in 2-ml. ampules that contain 50 mg. of iron per milliliter. Iron sorbitex is rapidly absorbed (50% to 70% within 3 hours and up to 95% within 24 hours after injection). It is primarily excreted in the urine, and the urine of patients receiving this drug may turn dark. Dosage must be determined individually for each patient.

Side effects. Side effects from parenteral administration of iron include headache, nausea, vomiting, muscle ache, fever, and mild urticaria. Severe anaphylactic reactions can occur with parenteral administration of iron.

Pain is sometimes experienced at the site of intramuscular injection, and there may be permanent brownish discoloration of the skin at the injection site. Injection of an iron preparation outside a vein may cause a severe local reaction. When iron is administered orally there is a limit to which it will be absorbed, but when it is injected into the bloodstream an overdose may be serious, partly because there is no satisfactory way for the body to excrete the amount taken in, over and above what the body can use or can store as a normal reserve. It is deposited in organs such as the liver or pancreas, causing hemochromatosis.

Iron-chelating agents
Deferoxamine
(Desferrioxamine B, Desferal)

Deferoxamine is a polyhydroxamic acid found in combination with iron in certain microorganisms. Deferoxamine is an iron-chelating agent; that is, it has great affinity for iron, re-

moves iron from its tissue storage form (ferritin), binds the iron, and blocks its absorption.

Deferoxamine is used to treat iron poisoning, iron overloading that may result from ingestion of large quantities of iron over a long period of time or from a metabolic abnormality that permits absorption of large amounts of iron from the diet, thereby increasing iron storage. This condition is termed hemosiderosis if no tissue damage occurs and hematochromatosis if tissue damage results. Deferoxamine is also used to treat iron poisoning.

Deferoxamine may be given orally, intramuscularly, or intravenously and by direct instillation into the stomach via gastric tube. Rapid urinary excretion of iron occurs after parenteral administration.

Vitamin B$_{12}$ (cyanocobalamin)

One of the major developments in nutrition in the past 40 years began with the recognition by Minot and Murphy in 1926 that a substance in liver could cure the hitherto fatal disease pernicious anemia. Their discovery led to the eventual isolation by other scientists of the pure compound, at first called "antianemic factor" in 1948, and in 1956 the elucidation of the structure of this molecule—vitamin B$_{12}$. Vitamin B$_{12}$ is an extremely complex and large organic molecule containing the metal cobalt. It has a structure similar to heme, the iron-bearing porphyrin in the hemoglobin molecule.

Today it is believed that persons with pernicious anemia (now a misnomer since the disease can be arrested) lack the ability to absorb vitamin B$_{12}$ from dietary sources, at least at the normal rate. They must therefore be supplied with enormous doses of the vitamin by mouth (so that a sufficient amount can be absorbed) or else be given rather small doses parenterally (since by this route all is made available to the tissues). The exact role of the vitamin in body chemistry is not well understood, but it is clearly required for some chemical step in the formation and normal development of the mature red cell.

Vitamin B$_{12}$ is believed to act as a coenzyme in certain biologic reactions necessary for the normal synthesis of methionine, deoxynucleic acids, and other essential constituents of all cells.

The exact nature of the disease process in pernicious anemia that prevents the absorption of vitamin B_{12} is not well understood. There is good evidence, however, that these patients fail to manufacture in their gastric mucous membrane a specific substance required for the normal absorption of vitamin B_{12}. The absorption factor has been called the intrinsic factor to distinguish it from vitamin B_{12}, which, before its chemical nature was understood, used to be somewhat mysteriously identified as extrinsic factor.

There is no lack of vitamin B_{12} in a normal diet. Even without a dietary supply, evidence shows that there is sufficient formation of the vitamin by bacteria normally present in the intestine of man and other mammals. The patient with pernicious anemia therefore, in a sense, starves in the midst of plenty since he lacks the substance necessary for absorption of vitamin B_{12}.

For this reason, it is also possible to supply the vitamin indirectly by giving the patient a preparation of dried gastric mucosa containing the intrinsic factor and thereby enabling him to absorb his own vitamin B_{12} from the diet. The surest way of remedying a deficiency, however, is to give the vitamin directly by injection, and this is the most common way of treating pernicious anemia.

When the body is deficient in vitamin B_{12} over a period of time, a series of characteristic symptoms and pathologic changes develop. The onset is gradual, and the early symptoms are usually fatigue, sore tongue, and achlorhydria. The patient develops a peculiar yellowish pallor and complains of increasing weakness, breathlessness, itching, dyspepsia, and diarrhea. Degenerative changes in the nervous system also occur, giving rise to incoordination of movement, loss of vibratory sense (as a result of changes in the dorsal columns of the spinal cord), peripheral neuritis, optic atrophy, and, sometimes, psychosis. Death may result from the changes associated with pernicious anemia unless the changes are arrested. This is accom-

plished effectively with the administration of vitamin B_{12}.

Uses. Pernicious anemia is one of the macrocytic hyperchromic anemias for which the administration of vitamin B_{12} is effective either as the pure vitamin or in a preparation of liver. It constitutes a form of replacement therapy, and administration must be continued indefinitely. It corrects the abnormalities of the red blood cells, relieves the sore mouth and tongue, restores normal function of the peripheral nerves, and arrests the progression of changes in the central nervous system. In some cases the changes in the nervous system are reversed if the irreversible stage of degeneration has not been reached. Vitamin B_{12} is also used in certain nutritional macrocytic anemias and for tropical and nontropical sprue. Beneficial effects have been reported in a number of neurologic disorders, such as trifacial neuralgia. These effects have been secured only after very large doses.

Preparation, dosage, and administration. Cyanocobalamin is a red crystalline substance that contains cobalt; it is obtained from cultures of *Streptomyces griseus* as a by-product in the manufacture of antibiotics. Because there is a group of closely related B_{12} factors, the activity of any preparation coming from natural sources may result from several members of this group. Prior to the availability of pure vitamin B_{12}, liver was administered extensively since it contains B_{12}, but it is now considered scientifically obsolete since liver preparations have no advantage over the pure vitamin but have several distinct disadvantages—liver is more expensive, may be painful to give, and is allergenic in some persons.

Cyanocobalamin (vitamin B_{12}), **U.S.P., B.P.** This is available in a variety of preparations for oral administration and in powder or solution for injection. The minimum effective dose is thought to be 1 *mg.* per day or multiples of this amount at appropriate intervals, such as 15 *mg.* twice a month. The dosage may need to be larger or be given more frequently if the patient is very ill or has neurologic complications. Vitamin B_{12} is usually given intramuscularly. If it is administered orally, much larger dosage is required, and the body response is slower.

Vitamin B₁₂ with intrinsic factor concentrate. This is a mixture of vitamin B_{12} with preparations of gastric mucosa obtained from the stomachs of domestic animals used for food. It is available in capsule and tablet form. It may be desirable for an occasional patient for whom parenteral therapy is difficult or undesirable. However, the administration of vitamin B_{12} by injection is considered more dependable. It is no longer an official preparation.

Side effects and toxic effects. No undesirable side effects or toxic effects have been reported following administration of vitamin B_{12}, even after large parenteral doses.

Use of hydrochloric acid. Since nearly all patients with pernicious anemia have a lack of hydrochloric acid in the stomach, full doses of the official dilute hydrochloric acid may be prescribed for the patient, to be given with meals not only to aid digestion but also to act as a gastric antiseptic. The usual dose is $^1/_2$ to 1 fluidram, which is well diluted with water (one-third to one-half glass).

Folic acid

The chemical name for folic acid is pteroylglutamic acid. It is a member of the vitamin B complex and can be prepared synthetically. It is found only in small amounts in the free state in a number of foods.

Folic acid is an important growth factor for a large number of cells. It participates in the synthesis of amino acids and deoxyribonucleic acid (DNA). DNA deficiency interferes with cell mitosis, and this may result in the development of large cells (megaloblasts) that are characteristic of megaloblastic anemias.

Folic acid has been used as a supplement to liver therapy in the treatment of pernicious anemia. It produces a response in blood similar to that produced by liver extract. The hemoglobin and red cells increase to normal, and bone marrow returns to its normal state. The appetite improves, and the patient feels better in general. In most patients the blood response is apparently maintained indefinitely with folic acid. It does not, however, prevent the development or the progression of neurologic changes that are often a part of the disease, and it may in fact make them worse. Because of this, it cannot be recognized as adequate therapy for pernicious anemia and cannot replace vitamin B_{12}. Its use is therefore dangerous when used alone for this condition, and the presence of folic acid in many multivitamin preparations adds to the hazard of this type of irrational therapy when it is used in the treatment of an undiagnosed anemia.

Uses. Although folic acid should not be employed in the treatment of pernicious anemia except possibly as a supplement to adequate therapy with vitamin B_{12}, it is used for the treatment of selected cases of macrocytic anemias and of nutritional and metabolic disorders associated with such anemia. It frequently is useful in the treatment of an anemia of pregnancy. It is sometimes used in the treatment of anemia associated with tropical sprue and celiac disease, although there is some question as to whether it constitutes complete therapy.

Preparation, dosage, and administration

Folic acid, U.S.P., B.P. (Folvite). This preparation is marketed in 5-mg. tablets and as an elixir, 1 mg. per milliliter, for oral administration, and as a solution for injection, 15 mg. per milliliter. The usual oral dose is 5 to 15 mg. daily, in divided doses. The usual parenteral dose is 10 mg. once daily, intramuscularly. Folic acid injection, U.S.P., is the same as sodium folate. It is the preparation preferred for parenteral therapy.

■ Whole blood and its constituents

Transfusions of whole blood are of value not only to replace red cells but also to restore blood volume and blood pressure. The latter value is seen particularly in the treatment of shock. Whole blood, since it contains all of the necessary fluid-holding constituents, does not pass out of the vascular system as rapidly as most parenteral fluids.

Blood transfusion plays an important although passive role in the treatment of anemic conditions. Transfusions do not apparently stimulate the bone marrow to greater activity but in times of crises they may save the patient's life when the patient cannot wait for iron or liver to become effective.

For blood transfusions to be used satisfactorily, it is important that the blood be readily available and of the suitable type. It is also essential that a careful technique be developed and strictly adhered to in order to help prevent reactions. The blood should be administered slowly, particularly if the patient's anemia is severe. Sometimes one transfusion of whole blood will suffice, but under other conditions a series of small transfusions may accomplish better results.

Treatment of hypovolemic shock

Adequate blood volume is absolutely essential to maintain viability of cells, normal tissue function, and life itself. Extensive trauma and hemorrhage that seriously lower blood volume usually require blood replacement. Whenever 30% of the blood volume is lost, prompt treatment is essential. Fresh whole blood replaces not only blood volume but vital clotting factors (platelets) and essential cellular elements (red and white blood cells). Stored blood rapidly loses its platelets and clotting factors. In cases of severe and continued blood loss, blood may need to be administered under pressure and even through more than one infusion route. Need for blood volume replacement may be determined not only by estimating blood loss when hemorrhage is visible and blood loss is measurable, but also by severity of shock, serial measurement of arterial blood pressure and blood volume, central venous pressure, hematocrit, pulse, and hourly urine output. Blood pressure alone, without the use of other physiologic parameters, is a very unreliable criterion for the presence or severity of shock. Prompt control of bleeding as well as blood replacement is essential.

It is important, of course, that blood used for replacement match the patient's specific type of blood. While blood may not always be the fluid of choice for volume replacement, it is usually the most dependable. If the loss of blood volume is the result of hemorrhage, whole blood replacement is the therapy of choice, along with control of hemorrhage. Whole blood contains all

the necessary fluid-holding constituents and does not pass out of the vascular system as rapidly as most parenteral fluids. The use of plasma expanders and noncolloid fluids, such as isotonic saline, offers only temporary support. Blood should not be used for transfusion if more than 21 days have passed since it was obtained from the donor. With massive transfusions, hypocalcemia may occur from the citrate used to prevent the blood from clotting. Citrate binds and inactivates calcium. Calcium gluconate is given to replace the calcium content.

If lost blood volume is replaced promptly with adequate amounts of blood, there is no problem. However, if treatment is delayed, more and more blood is required to maintain blood pressure and other vital signs. Actually more blood will be required than has been lost from hemorrhage. The reason for this is that some of the blood remaining in the circulatory system becomes trapped in the capillaries and small blood vessels, particularly in the liver and splanchnic area. The trapped cells may form microclots or small thrombi. Trapping is probably caused by increased resistance to blood flow from compensatory vasoconstriction. In addition, with decreased velocity of flow, there is increased viscosity. As blood viscosity increases, the plasma cannot keep red cells in suspension, and they settle out of the plasma causing sludging or aggregation of cells in the microcirculation. As blood flow slows and red blood cells bump into one another in the small vessels, a sticky substance forms on the outside of the red blood cell, and this further promotes sludging or red cell aggregation.

The use of high molecular weight dextran (see p. 182) may further increase viscosity as well as red blood cell aggregation. Clinical studies have shown that low viscosity dextran infusions help to mobilize noncirculating red cells, thus its use along with whole blood for treatment of shock caused by hemorrhage.

Avoidance of sludging. The following are methods used to avoid aggregation of red blood cells:

1 Adequate mechanical respiratory movements should be maintained by encouraging the pa-

tient to breathe deeply and regularly or by using mechanical assistance. These respiratory movements help to bring blood into the thorax and assist blood flow. (From 30% to 50% of the patients who die following shock show signs of pulmonary insufficiency and pulmonary emboli.)

2 Muscle movement is promoted by having the patient contract and relax the muscles in his extremities, shoulders, and buttocks. Circulation can be assisted by massaging and moving the patient's muscles and by position movement of the patient (if this is not contraindicated by his condition).

Use of vasoconstrictors and vasodilators in shock therapy. The use of vasoconstrictors (such as norepinephrine) is considered by researchers to be *contraindicated* in this form of shock. These drugs will further reduce capillary blood flow and hasten cell death.

In some cases where significant vasoconstriction is present, vasodilators such as phenoxybenzamine or phentolamine have been used to reduce peripheral resistance to blood flow and to increase capillary perfusion. The use of vasodilators plus volume replacement has resulted in a decrease in mortality from hypovolemic shock.

Since hypovolemic shock can be more successfully treated than other forms of shock, its prompt recognition and safe management are of great importance.

Packed human blood cells, U.S.P.

Packed human blood cells are citrated whole blood from which plasma has been removed. Its use is indicated when blood cell replacement is necessary but an increase of plasma volume is unnecessary or undesirable. It is used for treating certain cases of anemia. Expiration date should be noted.

Blood plasma

Blood plasma is the fluid part of the blood that may be procured by separating the blood cells from the whole citrated blood. Plasma may be given irrespective of the donor's group. Many authorities believe that blood plasma, since it contains the protein fibrinogen, albumin, gamma globulins, hemagglutinins, prothrombin, sugar, and salts, is an ideal transfusion medium to restore effective blood volume in the treatment of peripheral circulatory failure associated with severe burns, traumatic shock, or hemorrhage. It is also used to maintain colloid osmotic pressure and to supplement blood proteins. Blood plasma can be used as it is for transfusions or it can be concentrated, dehydrated, and stored for long periods of time without deterioration. The addition of sterile distilled water is all that is needed to make it ready for immediate use. Plasma in the dried form is particularly stable and useful when transportation, storage, and contamination are problems that must be considered.

Normal human plasma. Normal human plasma is obtained by pooling equal parts of citrated whole blood from eight or more adult human beings who qualify as donors by virtue of their having passed physical examinations and various clinical tests. Procedures are carried out under definite aseptic conditions, and the cell-free plasma is obtained by centrifugation or by sedimentation. It is dispensed in liquid, dried, or frozen form. The usual amount given whole or restored is 500 ml. It is administered to combat surgical and traumatic shock, in the treatment of burned persons when much plasma has been lost, and in cases in which whole blood is not immediately available for the treatment of hemorrhage.

A serious problem with the use of pooled human plasma is the transmission of viral hepatitis. Since plasma from one infected donor may appear in many bottles of plasma, the incidence of transmitting viral hepatitis is far greater than when whole blood is used.

Blood proteins

Blood plasma can be further broken down to many useful parts. Albumin is just as effective as plasma in shock treatment, and effective treatment requires less of the albumin than of the plasma.

Thrombin and fibrinogen also can be separated from plasma and then purified and concentrated into fine white powders. When put into solution they coagulate to form fibrin. The solution is sometimes applied locally to stimulate blood clotting and to provide a sort of glue in skin grafting.

Fibrinogen, U.S.P., B.P., is available as a powder for injection along with a suitable amount of diluent.

Normal human serum albumin, U.S.P., is a brownish, viscous, clear, relatively odorless liquid obtained from the blood of healthy human donors. It is made free of the hazard of the virus of serum jaundice by heating at 60° C. for 10 hours. It is available in a solution (25 Gm. in 100 ml.) or as a dried preparation. The normal unit is composed of 25 Gm. of human albumin to which sterile water or physiologic saline solution can be added before use. This is then equivalent to about 500 ml. of whole human plasma, in terms of protein osmotic pressure. It is used in the treatment of shock and in situations in which it is important to raise the serum protein of the blood. It is administered intravenously.

Antihemophilic human plasma, U.S.P., is normal human plasma that has been processed promptly to preserve the antihemophilic globulin component. Hemophilia is the result of a congenital deficiency in a particular globulin, and this reduces the ability of the blood to clot. Antihemophilic human plasma is administered to bring about temporary relief of the dysfunction of the clotting mechanism in the patient with hemophilia. It is dispensed in the frozen or the dried form.

Plasma substitutes
Dextran (Expandex, Gentran); dextran injection, B.P.

Dextran is a glucose polymer made by the action of special bacteria *(Leuconostoc mesenteroides)* on sucrose. The resulting polysaccharide does not easily pass through capillary walls. The molecules are like those of serum albumin and have a molecular weight of about 75,000.

Uses. Dextran is used to expand plasma volume and maintain blood pressure in emergency conditions resulting from shock and hemorrhage. It is not a substitute for whole blood or its derivatives when the latter are needed for the treatment of anemia secondary to hemorrhage or when it is essential to restore blood proteins after traumatic injuries, burns, and so forth. It has no oxygen-carrying property. The effect of an injection of 500 to 1000 ml. of dextran (6%) usually persists for a period of 24 hours. From 30% to 50% is excreted in the urine and the remainder is metabolized in the body.

Preparation, dosage, and administration. Dextran is administered intravenously in isotonic solution of sodium chloride. The usual dose is 500 ml. of 6% solution infused at the rate of 20 to 40 ml. per minute. Repeated infusions can be given when necessary, if blood or its derivatives are not at hand or if their use is not indicated. Solutions of dextran do not require refrigeration and are easily stored. The 6% solution of dextran is osmotically equivalent to serum albumin.

Although high molecular weight dextran is effective in replacing lost blood volume, it has been shown clinically and experimentally that this form of dextran has an adverse effect on flow in minute vessels and capillaries because it increases blood viscosity. Another disadvantage of this form of dextran is that it interferes with normal clotting by coating platelets.

Side effects and toxic effects. Untoward effects are rare with the exception of an antigen-antibody type of reaction in certain persons. It has been established that bleeding time of recipients may be increased. This seems to be a temporary effect. Patients with cardiovascular disease who receive dextran infusions should be watched for congestive heart failure and pulmonary edema. Temporary depression of renal tubule functioning has been reported.

Dextran 40
(LMD, Rheomacrodex)

Low molecular weight dextran with a molecular weight of 40,000 is a less effective expander of plasma volume than high molecular dextran. However, it has been used effectively to restore flow in the microcirculation and to improve tissue perfusion by reducing blood viscosity and sludging and preventing intravascular coagulation.

Dextran 40 is also used as a priming agent for pump oxygenators or bypass machines used for open-heart surgery.

Action. Dextran 40 may reduce blood viscosity by drawing fluid from the tissues into the vascular system, and therefore patients should be watched for signs of dehydration (warm dry skin and mouth, thirst, rise in body temperature). Prevention of intravascular clotting is theorized by some researchers to result from the ability of Dextran 40 to maintain the electronegativity of red blood cells, which causes the cells to repel one another. In addition, red blood cell rigidity may be decreased, which promotes flow of red cells through the small blood vessels.

Absorption and excretion. Dextran 40 is rather rapidly excreted by the kidneys in patients with normal renal function. The viscosity and specific gravity of the urine may be increased during the administration of dextran 40 and throughout the duration of its effects, particularly in patients with decreased urine flow. A low specific gravity of urine with dextran 40 may indicate inability of the kidneys to remove dextran and is an indication for discontinuance of therapy. This drug should not be used in patients with renal disease. Its use is not contraindicated in patients with reduced urine output caused by shock. However, its use should be discontinued if no improvement in urine flow occurs. Unexcreted dextran is slowly degraded to glucose, which is then metabolized to respiratory carbon dioxide and water.

Preparation, dosage, and administration. Dextran 40 is available for intravenous injection as a 10% solution in 500- and 1000-ml. bottles in combination with dextrose 5% or sodium chloride 0.9%. When used in shock therapy total dosage in the first 24 hours should not exceed 2 Gm. per kilogram of body weight (10 ml. of a 10% solution equals 1 Gm. of dextran). Thereafter, total dosage should not exceed 1 Gm. per kilogram of body weight per 24 hours. It is not recommended that therapy be continued for longer than 5 days.

Side effects and toxic effects. Side effects to dextran 40 include urticarial reactions, nausea,

vomiting, wheezing, a tight feeling in the chest, and hypotension. However, these are not common reactions.

■ Drugs that affect blood coagulation

Drugs affecting the clotting of blood are used both to hasten clotting (hemostatics) and to retard clotting (anticoagulants). In some instances normal components necessary for blood clotting must be supplied.

Drugs that affect blood coagulation

■ Hemostatics
Absorbable gelatin sponge, U.S.P., B.P. (Gelfoam)

Absorbable gelatin sponge is an especially prepared form of gelatin having a porous nature. It is used to control capillary bleeding and may be left in place in a surgical wound. It is completely absorbed in 4 to 6 weeks. It should be well moistened with isotonic saline solution or thrombin solution before it is applied to a bleeding surface. Its presence does not induce excessive scar formation.

The hemostatic action is the result of its action as a tampon and liberation of thromboplastin from damaged platelets traumatized by contact with the sponge.

Fibrin foam, B.P.

This is a sterile dry preparation of human fibrin that, when applied to a bleeding surface, acts as a mechanical coagulant. In combination with thrombin it gives a chemical as well as a mechanical matrix for coagulation. It is used in surgery of organs such as the brain, liver, or kidneys where ordinary methods for the control of bleeding are ineffective or inadvisable.

It is absorbed within a short period of time and need not be removed after bleeding has stopped.

Oxidized cellulose, U.S.P., B.P. (Oxycel, Hemo-Pak)

This is a specially treated form of surgical gauze or cotton that exerts a hemostatic effect but is absorbable when buried in the tissues. **183**

The hemostatic action is caused by the formation of an artificial clot by cellulosic acid. Absorption of oxidized cellulose occurs between the second and the seventh day following implantation, although absorption of large amounts of blood-soaked material may take 6 weeks or longer. Oxidized cellulose is of value in the control of bleeding in surgery of such organs as the liver, pancreas, spleen, kidney, thyroid, and prostate. Its hemostatic action is not increased by the addition of other hemostatic agents. It should not be used as a surface dressing except for the control of bleeding, because cellulosic acid inhibits the growth of epithelial tissue. Since it interferes with bone regeneration it should not be implanted in fractures.

Thrombin, N.F., B.P.

This is a preparation of thrombin isolated from bovine plasma. It is intended as a hemostatic agent for *topical application* to control capillary bleeding. It may be applied as a dry powder or dissolved in sterile isotonic saline solution. It is not injected.

Vitamin K

Vitamin K was discovered by Dam of Copenhagen in 1935 as a result of a study of newly hatched chicks that had a fatal hemorrhagic disease. This condition, he found, could be prevented and cured by the administration of a substance found in hog liver and in alfalfa. It was later discovered that the delayed clotting time of the blood was caused by deficiency of prothrombin content. Vitamin K occurs naturally in two forms known as K_1 and K_2. Both have a naphthoquinone nucleus and exhibit similar physiologic properties.

Vitamin K–like compounds

In natural vitamin K (K_1 or K_2), R is a long alkyl chain of twenty or thirty carbons. In synthetic vitamin K (Menadione), R is only hydrogen, but this is as potent as the natural compound. These compounds are called naphthoquinones from the parent nucleus. The synthetic analogues greatly resemble the natural vitamin and have even greater physiologic activity. Certain of the analogues are water soluble, whereas the natural vitamin is fat soluble. The fat-soluble vitamin requires the presence of bile in the intestine to ensure adequate absorption after oral administration. This is not essential for the water-soluble preparations.

Vitamin K is widely found in foods; deficiency is rarely caused by lack of it in the diet. It is also synthesized by intestinal bacteria.

Action and result. Vitamin K is essential to the synthesis of prothrombin by the liver. The exact mechanism of its action is not known, although it is thought to contribute to the activation of an enzyme necessary to the formation of prothrombin.

Prothrombin deficiency may occur because of inadequate absorption of vitamin K from the intestine (usually because of biliary disease in which bile fails to enter the intestine) or because of destruction of intestinal organisms, which may occur with antibiotic therapy. It is also encountered in the newborn, in which case it is probably caused by the fact that the intestinal organisms have not yet become established. It may result from therapy with certain anticoagulants.

Uses. Vitamin K is useful only in conditions in which the prolonged bleeding time is the result of low concentration of prothrombin in the blood, which is not in turn the result of damaged liver cells. Vitamin K has been recommended for hemorrhagic conditions in the newborn for which prophylactic doses are administered during the last stages of pregnancy and first few weeks after birth.

It is also indicated in the preoperative preparation of patients with deficient prothrombin, particularly those with obstructive jaundice. In addition, it is given as an antidote for overdosage of systemic anticoagulants such as bishydroxycoumarin, as well as for hemorrhagic disorders and hypoprothrombinemia secondary to large doses, or overdosages, of drugs such as salicylates, quinine, sulfonamides, arsenicals, and barbiturates. Hemorrhagic conditions not caused by deficiency of prothrombin are not successfully treated with vitamin K.

The natural concentrates have, to a great extent, been replaced by the synthetic preparations. It is important that the prothrombin activity of the blood be measured frequently when the patient is receiving a preparation of vitamin K. Parenteral preparations should be administered if for some reason the intestinal absorption is impaired.

Preparation, dosage, and administration. The following are the preparations of vitamin K available.

Menadione, **N.F.** This drug is a synthetic substitute for natural vitamin K. The presence of bile is essential for adequate absorption after oral administration. Menadione tablets, N.F., and menadione injection, N.F., are official preparations. The usual dose is 1 to 2 mg. daily.

Menadione sodium bisulfite, **N.F. (Hykinone).** This form is similar to menadione but it is water soluble, and oral doses need not be accompanied by bile salts. It is available in tablet form for oral administration as well as in solution for subcutaneous, intramuscular, and intravenous injection. Menadione sodium bisulfite injection, N.F., and menaphthone sodium bisulfite injection, B.P., are official preparations for injection. Average daily dose is 0.5 to 2 mg. daily. Dosage is determined in relation to the prothrombin level of the blood.

Various other commercial water-soluble vitamin K analogues are also available. Synkamin is marketed in 1-ml. ampules containing 1 mg. of the drug and in capsules containing 4 mg. of the drug.

Menadiol sodium diphosphate, **U.S.P. (Synkayvite).** This is a derivative of menadione and has the same action and uses as other analogues of vitamin K. It is water soluble and is adequately absorbed after oral administration without bile salts. It is administered orally, subcutaneously, intramuscularly, and intravenously.

The dosage is approximately three times that of menadione. It is available in 5-mg. tablets for oral administration and in solution for injection. The usual dose is 4 to 75 mg.

Phytonadione, **U.S.P. (vitamin K$_1$, Mephyton, Konakion);** *phytomenadione,* **B.P.** This preparation acts more promptly and over a longer period of time than the vitamin K analogues. It is a fat-soluble vitamin, and the presence of bile salts in the intestine is essential to adequate absorption. It will stop bleeding 3 to 4 hours after intravenous administration and produces a normal prothrombin level in 12 to 14 hours. It is useful to reverse the effects of anticoagulant therapy that have produced a serious deficiency of prothrombin in the blood. Phytonadione is available in 5-mg. tablets and as an emulsion for intravenous injection. The emulsion is diluted with isotonic salt solution or sterile water before it is injected. Phytonadione is administered orally or parenterally, depending upon the severity of the condition being treated. The dosage varies greatly; 2 to 20 mg. may be given daily, although much larger doses have been given in emergency situations. However, small doses of vitamin K$_1$ orally administered will effectively correct the reduced prothrombin activity induced by certain anticoagulants (coumarin drugs). Effects are said to be less predictable when severe liver damage is present. The dosage must be determined according to the level of prothrombin activity, the length of time during which the patient has received anticoagulant therapy, and the hazard of restoring the risk of thrombosis. Large doses of vitamin K$_1$ are said to make subsequent regulation of anticoagulant therapy with coumarin drugs more difficult.

Phytonadione solution **(Aqua Mephyton, Konakion).** This preparation is a water-soluble form of vitamin K$_1$ that has recently been made available. It may be given subcutaneously or intramuscularly.

Drugs that affect blood coagulation

■ Anticoagulants

Diseases associated with abnormal clotting within vessels take a great toll of lives. It is esti-

Table 10-3 Blood coagulation factors

Name	Factor
Fibrinogen	I
Prothrombin	II
Tissue thromboplastin	III
Calcium	IV
Proaccelerin (labile factor, accelerator globulin)	V
(Accelerin)*	VI
Proconvertin (stable factor, serum prothrombin conversion accelerator, SPCA)	VII
Antihemophilic factor	VIII
Plasma thromboplastin component, Christmas factor	IX
Stuart-Prower factor	X
Plasma thromboplastin antecedent (PTA)	XI
Hageman factor	XII

*Existence of factor VI is disputed. It was previously called accelerin, but it is no longer believed to be involved in hemostasis. There is no name or function now assigned to "factor VI."

mated that over a million persons suffer from thrombosis or embolism in the United States each year. Diseases caused by intravascular clotting include some of the major causes of death from cardiovascular sources—coronary occlusion and cerebral accidents. Drugs that inhibit clotting are therefore important.

Anticoagulation therapy is directed toward preventing intravascular thrombosis by decreasing blood coagulability. This therapy has no direct effect on a blood clot that has already formed or on an ischemic tissue injured by an inadequate blood supply because of the clot.

Anticoagulants are indicated in:

1 Occlusive vascular disease, such as thromboangiitis obliterans
2 Sudden arterial occlusion
3 Venous thrombosis
4 Pulmonary embolism
5 Cerebrovascular thrombosis
6 Coronary artery occlusion or myocardial infarction

Anticoagulants are used prophylactically in:

1 Major surgery where there is previous history of thrombosis or when prolonged immobilization will be necessary
2 Pelvic surgery in the male or female, since pelvic surgery is notorious for its high incidence of postoperative thrombophlebitis
3 Patients on bedrest for more than 2 or 3 days, since this predisposes them to vascular stasis
4 Rheumatic heart disease

Anticoagulants are also used to prevent clotting of blood to be used for transfusion, laboratory, or experimental work. The mechanism of blood coagulation is very complex. During the past two decades many new coagulation factors have been discovered and new terminology has come into existence. Three stages of blood coagulation are recognized:

Stage I—formation of thromboplastin
Stage II—conversion of prothrombin to thrombin
Stage III—conversion of fibrinogen to fibrin

It is stage I that is most complex, and at least eight of the twelve blood coagulation factors (IV, V, VIII, IX, X, XI, XII, and phospholipid) are essential for formation of intravascular thromboplastin (see Table 10-3). Formation of extravascular or tissue thromboplastin requires only factors IV and VII. Tissue or extrinsic thromboplastin is released from injured tissue; intravascular or intrinsic thromboplastin is released from platelets.

The following is a summary of the last stages of the coagulatory process:

$$\text{Prothrombin} \xrightarrow{\text{Thromboplastin + Calcium}} \text{Thrombin}$$

$$\text{Fibrinogen} \xrightarrow{\text{Thrombin}} \text{Fibrin}$$

Local trauma, vascular stasis, and systemic alterations in coagulability of blood are still considered the principal etiologic factors in the initiation of thrombosis.

Arterial thrombosis is most frequently associated with atherosclerotic plaques, high blood pressure, and turbulent blood flow that damages the inner lining of the blood vessel and causes platelets to stick and aggregate and release thromboplastin. Arterial thrombi are platelet or white thrombi.

Venous thrombosis occurs most often in areas where blood flow is reduced or static. This appears to initiate clotting and produce a red thrombus. Current anticoagulants are more effective in preventing venous than arterial thrombosis. To prevent arterial thrombosis will require a drug that will control platelet aggregation, and such a drug is not yet available.

Anticoagulant therapy is primarily prophylactic. These agents act (1) by preventing fibrin deposits, (2) by preventing extension of a thrombus, and (3) by preventing thromboembolic complications. Anticoagulation therapy is still empirical and is based largely on clinical experience. Long-term anticoagulant therapy remains controversial. Nevertheless there is evidence that anticoagulant therapy reduces the incidence of thrombosis and therefore prolongs life.

Bleeding tendencies constitute the most important side effect of the anticoagulants. Hematuria, epistaxis, ecchymosis, and bleeding gums may occur as well as other signs of bleeding.

Contraindications to the use of anticoagulants include blood dyscrasias, liver or kidney disease, peptic ulcer, chronic ulcerative colitis, and active bleeding. Patients undergoing spinal cord or brain surgery should not use anticoagulants since even minor bleeding may cause serious consequences. Certain drugs such as salicylates, cincophen, phenylbutazone, and reserpine increase the risk of bleeding and should not be given with anticoagulants. Use of barbiturates and anticoagulants is also somewhat hazardous; discontinuance of the barbiturate with continued administration of the anticoagulant may result in active bleeding. In the presence of barbiturates, higher doses of the anticoagulants are required for optimum effect. Unless the anticoagulant dosage is reduced when barbiturates are discontinued, excessive loading of the anticoagulant may occur, resulting in toxic or bleeding effects. The combination of anticoagulant and adrenocorticosteroid therapy has proved to be lethal and therefore should not be used.

Sodium citrate

Sodium citrate is used as an anticoagulant in blood that is to be used for a transfusion or that is to be stored for a time. Anticoagulant sodium citrate solution, N.F., is an approximately 4% sterile solution of sodium citrate in water. It is used as an anticoagulant for blood plasma and for blood for fractionation. Anticoagulant citrate dextrose solution, U.S.P., is used as an anticoagulant for storage of whole blood. Sodium citrate acts by binding plasma calcium and preventing the formation of thrombin.

Sodium heparin injection, U.S.P.; heparin injection, B.P.

Heparin is a mucopolysaccharide that is strongly acidic because of the presence of sulfate groups in the molecule. Heparin, as the name implies, was first found in the liver and subsequently in the lungs and intestinal mucosa. It is present in the mast cells of these tissues; it has also been found in the tunica intima of blood vessels.

Action and uses. Heparin prevents coagulation by (1) interfering with the formation of thrombin from prothrombin, (2) preventing thrombin from acting as a catalyst in converting fibrinogen into fibrin, and (3) preventing agglutination and disintegration of platelets and release their thromboplastin. Therefore heparin increases the clotting time of blood. The effects of heparin are thought to be caused by its strong electronegative charge by which it blocks enzymatic reactions. The action of heparin can be inhibited or reversed by protamine sulfate, which has a strong positive charge. Heparin is also known to be antilipemic; that is, it reduces blood lipids or fats. It has been shown to dissolve clots in the sludge stage.

Heparin is the drug of choice for sudden arterial occlusion since its action is immediate and readily reversible if surgery becomes necessary for clot removal. In thrombophlebitis there is evidence that heparin is superior to the coumarin drugs in preventing pulmonary complications. It is also preferred for treating thrombophlebitis occurring during pregnancy since it does not cross the placental barrier and is not excreted in the mother's milk. Since coumarin drugs can go through these channels their use can cause complications to the fetus and hemorrhage in the newborn.

Heparin is usually used when rapid anticoagulant action is desired. It is used prior to the use of oral anticoagulants (coumarin derivatives). Heparin approaches the ideal anticoagulant—it is rapidly absorbed, readily excreted, and almost nontoxic. Its main disadvantages are its short action, high cost, need for parenteral injection, and local reactions at injection sites. Hypersensitivity to heparin is rare but allergic reactions have been reported. Alopecia may occur, but it is reversible after withdrawal of the drug. Osteoporosis has been reported in patients on large doses of heparin for long periods of time (6 months or more).

Preparation, dosage, and administration. Heparin is inactive orally and must be administered parenterally. It is obtained commercially from domestic animals slaughtered for food. It may be given by a single injection or continuous intravenous drip. The response to heparin

occurs almost immediately and lasts for a relatively short time (3 to 4 hours) unless the dose is repeated. When administration is discontinued, the clotting time returns to normal rather quickly, and there is danger of massive clot formation should the drug be discontinued too soon. Dosage needs to be determined for each individual patient and maintained at a level that keeps the clotting time well above normal (15 to 20 minutes). The potency of heparin sodium is expressed in units. When it is given intravenously at spaced intervals, 50 mg. (5000 units) may be given at a time. For continuous drip, 100 to 200 mg. (10,000 to 20,000 units) are added to 1000 ml. of 5% sterile glucose solution or to isotonic saline solution and the flow started at about 20 to 25 drops per minute. Dosage for the repository form is 20,000 to 40,000 units.

Subcutaneous injections of 10,000 to 12,000 units every 8 hours or 14,000 to 20,000 units every 12 hours are also acceptable.

Intramuscular injection of heparin in a slowly absorbed medium repository form has been recommended, and this does reduce the frequency

Table 10-4 Comparison of various anticoagulants

Generic name	Trade name	Peak effect	Recovery	Average initial dose	Average maintenance dose	Route of administration
Acenocoumarol	Sintrom	24 to 48 hr.	48 hr.	16 to 28 mg.	2 to 10 mg.	Oral
Anisindione	Miradon	36 to 72 hr.	24 to 72 hr.	300 mg.	50 to 100 mg.	Oral
Bishydroxycoumarin	Dicumarol	24 to 72 hr.	7 to 9 days	200 to 300 mg.	25 to 100 mg.	Oral
Diphenadione	Dipaxin	48 hr.	20 days	20 to 30 mg.	2.5 to 5 mg.	Oral
Ethyl biscoumacetate	Tromexan	18 to 24 hr.	48 hr.	1.5 to 1.8 Gm.	0.6 to 0.9 Gm.	Oral
Phenindione	Danilone Hedulin Eridone	18 to 24 hr.	24 to 48 hr.	200 to 300 mg.	50 to 100 mg.	Oral
Phenprocoumon	Liquamar	36 to 48 hr.	7 to 14 days	20 to 30 mg.	0.75 to 6 mg.	Oral
Sodium warfarin	Coumadin Sodium Prothromadin	12 to 18 hr.	5 to 7 days	10 to 50 mg.	2.5 to 10 mg.	Oral Intramuscular Intravenous

of the injections to one every 48 hours. There are accompanying disadvantages, however. The injections may be painful and the absorption may not be even, so that sometimes there is inadequate heparinization and at other times an excessive effect may be obtained. Nurses need to watch the patient's skin carefully because of the possibility that a local hematoma will develop.

Heparin antagonist—protamine sulfate injection, U.S.P., B.P.

Protamine sulfate is a protein-like substance derived from the sperm and mature testes of the salmon and other fish. Protamine by itself is an anticoagulant and will cause prolongation of clotting time; it is an antithromboplastin but is not as active as heparin. When protamine is given in the presence of heparin, they are attracted to each other instead of to the blood elements, and each neutralizes the anticoagulant activity of the other. Because it is a basic protein (many free amino groups), it is able to combine with the sulfuric acids of heparin and inactivate them.

Uses. Protamine is used as a heparin antagonist to combat the bleeding tendency from an overdosage of heparin.

When given intravenously to treat the bleeding tendency resulting from an overdose of heparin, protamine acts almost instantaneously, and its effects persist for about 2 hours. Its availability is therefore essential for safe management of a patient having anticoagulant therapy with heparin. It has been used experimentally to treat certain bleeding states believed to be characterized by increased amounts of heparin or heparin-like substances in the circulation.

Preparation, dosage, and administration. Protamine sulfate is administered intravenously and, occasionally, intramuscularly. In the treatment of overdosage of heparin, the extent of the overdosage can be determined from the amount of heparin given over the previous 3 or 4 hours; the amount of protamine needed is approximately equal to the amount of heparin overdosage. The commercial preparation of prota-

mine sulfate consists of a solution containing 10 mg. in 1 ml.

Coumarin derivatives

When cattle are allowed to eat improperly cured sweet clover, they may develop a hemorrhagic disorder believed to be caused by a deficiency of prothrombin. In 1941 Link and his associates were able to show that the substance responsible for the prothrombin deficiency was a coumarin derivative. These workers later synthesized bishydroxycoumarin (Dicumarol), and since that time other coumarin derivatives have been synthesized. These compounds differ mainly in their speed and duration of action. (See Table 10-4, p. 188, for comparison of various anticoagulants.)

Action and result. Although the coumarin drugs are referred to as anticoagulants, they do not appreciably affect coagulation time or bleeding time when they are administered in therapeutic amounts. Dosage is computed on the basis of the plasma prothrombin time. Decreased prothrombin activity seems to act as a deterrent to intravascular clotting. Adequate and safe therapy therefore depends in part on accurate determinations of the patient's plasma prothrombin time.

Coumarin derivatives are prothrombin depressants and depress hepatic synthesis of factors II, VII, IX, and X. These agents probably compete with vitamin K, which functions enzymatically in the clotting process.

Vitamin K and a coumarin compound like bishydroxycoumarin show similarity of structure, as indicated in the accompanying formulas. This has led to the supposition that the coumarin compounds act as competitors to prevent the utilization of vitamin K by the liver. Thus, the antagonist to the anticoagulant effect of coumarin agents is vitamin K.

Bishydroxycoumarin (Dicumarol)

Menadione (vitamin K)

Uses. Coumarin derivatives are the drugs of choice for long-term anticoagulant therapy to protect against sudden acute arterial occlusion or thromboembolic phenomena from any predisposing factor that may cause loss of limb or life. They are the drugs of choice for recurrent phlebitis, chronic occlusive arterial disease, and myocardial infarction.

Major advantages of these drugs are: (1) they are effective with oral administration, (2) they are inexpensive, and (3) they need be given only once a day when the maintenance dose has been established.

However, coumarin drugs depress factors other than prothrombin, and this may account for unexplained bleeding at "safe" levels of prothrombin. Since it is impractical to measure each factor separately, and since it is not known which factor when excessively depressed results in bleeding, Quick's prothrombin test remains the standard test in most clinical laboratories. Prothrombin time is usually maintained at a "safe" level of 35 to 60 seconds or 15% to 30% of normal.

**Bishydroxycoumarin, U.S.P.
(Dicumarol)**

Official preparations of bishydroxycoumarin are available in 25-, 50-, and 100-mg. tablets and also in capsules. It is administered orally. The usual initial dose is 200 to 300 mg. daily. Subsequent dosage for a day or two depends on the prothrombin time of the patient and may vary from 50 to 200 mg. Some authorities attempt to keep prothrombin activity between 10% and 30% of normal and others between 15% and 25% of normal. In most patients, 25 to 50 mg. daily are required as maintenance doses. Dosage is determined not only by the prothrombin time but also by the direction in which it is changing. Bishydroxycoumarin requires 24 to 72

hours for its action to develop, and its action persists 24 to 72 hours after its administration is discontinued.

**Ethyl biscoumacetate, N.F.
(Tromexan)**

This synthetic derivative of bishydroxycoumarin produces a similar anticoagulant action. It is available in 150- and 300-mg. tablets for oral administration. Its action and uses are similar to those of Dicumarol, but it is more rapidly absorbed, acts over a shorter period of time, is detoxified and excreted faster, and has less cumulative effect than Dicumarol. Average initial dose for a 24-hour period is 1.5 Gm. given at one time or in divided dosage. Subsequent doses of 600 to 900 mg. per day are usual, but maintenance dosage is regulated by determinations of prothrombin activity. This compound is more expensive than bishydroxycoumarin.

**Sodium warfarin, U.S.P.
(Coumadin Sodium, Prothromadin)**

Sodium warfarin is available in 5-, 10-, and 25-mg. tablets for oral administration and as a powder from which a solution is made for injection (intravenous and intramuscular). Its action is more rapid than that of bishydroxycoumarin and it more prolonged. The initial oral and intravenous dose is 25 to 50 mg., then 5 to 10 mg. daily, depending on prothrombin activity.

Acenocoumarol (Sintrom)

Acenocoumarol is a synthetic coumarin type of anticoagulant. Its action is faster than that of

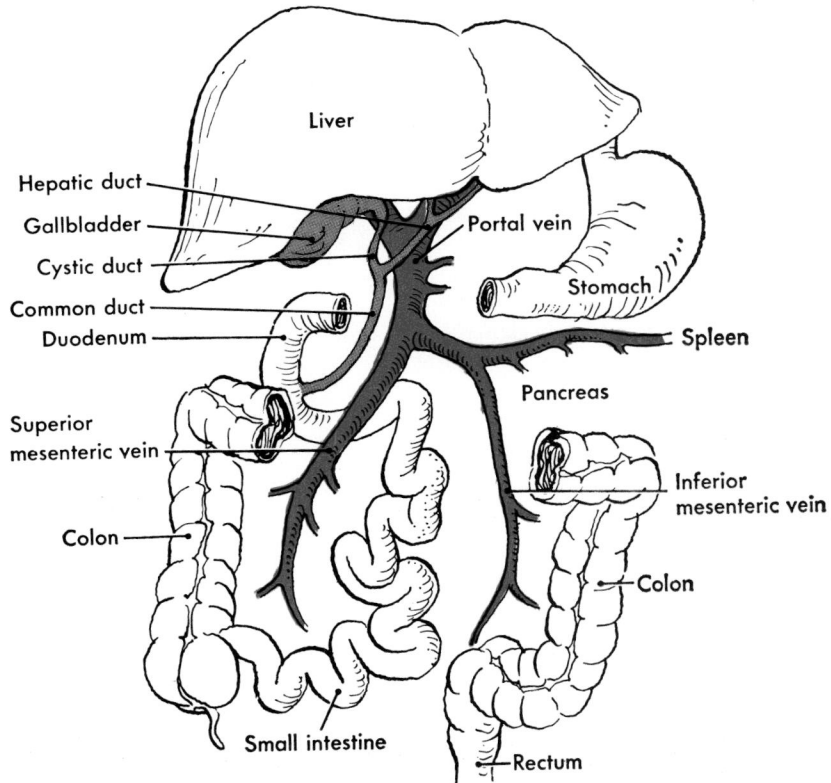

Liver

Hepatic duct

Gallbladder

Cystic duct

Common duct

Duodenum

Portal vein

Stomach

Spleen

Pancreas

Superior
mesenteric vein

Inferior
mesenteric vein

Colon

Colon

Small intestine

Rectum

Plate 4

Diagram of portal-biliary circulation showing related structures. Bile containing bile
salts is discharged into duodenum after eating to assist in process of digestion. Bile
salts are absorbed into capillaries of the gastrointestinal tract, transported via mesenteric veins into the portal vein and then to
the liver, where they are again secreted.
Portal-biliary circulation is directly related
to absorption of fats and fat-soluble vitamins.

bishydroxycoumarin but less rapid than that of ethyl biscoumacetate. It is available in 4-mg. tablets for oral administration. The initial dose is 16 to 28 mg. on the first day of therapy followed by 8 to 16 mg. on the second day. The average maintenance dose is 2 to 10 mg. daily, depending on the response of the patient as measured by frequent determinations of the prothrombin time.

Phenindione derivatives
Phenindione, B.P. (Danilone, Hedulin, Eridone)

Phenindione is a synthetic anticoagulant similar in action to bishydroxycoumarin but unrelated chemically. It acts more promptly than bishydroxycoumarin and in smaller doses. Therapeutic levels are obtained within 18 to 24 hours usually, and prothrombin time usually returns to normal 24 to 48 hours after administration of the drug has been discontinued.

This drug may produce an orange or reddish discoloration of the urine that patients may mistake for hematuria. Phenindione is administered orally in initial doses of 200 to 300 mg.; one half is given in the morning and one half at bedtime. Continued dosage is adjusted as determinations of prothrombin activity indicate.

Periodic examinations of the blood, liver, and kidneys have been recommended because this drug has been known to cause agranulocytosis and hepatic and renal damage.

Diphenadione, N.F. (Dipaxin)
Diphenadione is closely related to phenindione and is one of the most potent and long-acting depressants of prothrombin activity. It is therefore effective in smaller doses than most oral anticoagulants. The initial dose is 20 to 30 mg. orally, followed by 10 to 15 mg. on the second day. Subsequent dosage is determined in accordance with the prothrombin time. The precautions to be observed for these drugs are much the same as those for the coumarin derivatives.

Effective anticoagulant therapy

Both heparin and coumarin derivatives are important anticoagulants. They can be used to complement each other. In some instances the administration of both heparin and one of the synthetic anticoagulants such as bishydroxycoumarin is started simultaneously. The heparin is discontinued as soon as the prothrombin activity has been sufficiently reduced and the coumarin compound is producing a full therapeutic effect. Heparin is needed when rapid anticoagulant effect is required or when adequate facilities for determining the prothrombin time are not available (this prevents the use of one of the synthetic anticoagulants).

In certain conditions when a rapid but not immediate anticoagulant effect is desired, bishydroxycoumarin and ethyl biscoumacetate are given together on the first day of therapy and only the former drug is given on successive days.

Nursing measure for patients on anticoagulant drug therapy

The following are aspects of care for patients taking anticoagulant drugs.

1 Patients should be observed for bleeding
   a. Nosebleeds or bleeding gums
   b. Petechiae, purpura, or ecchymotic areas
   c. Blood in urine or stools
2 Patients on anticoagulant therapy should be instructed to carry an identification card that lists the patient's and physician's names and phone numbers and the name and dosage of drug.
3 Because there is some evidence that dietary factors, especially the ingestion of fat, are associated with increased tendency of thrombosis, it may be of benefit to advise the patient of a diet with moderate to low fat content. The relationship between high fat content and thrombosis has not been proved, however.
4 Patients should be advised to protect themselves from injury.
5 When heparin is used, blood should be drawn for clotting time when heparin activity is least,

193

just before another injection of heparin is to be given.

6 Vitamin K should be readily accessible if bleeding occurs. Outpatients should carry vitamin K with them, and 5 to 20 mg. should be taken at once if bleeding occurs. Statistics show that bleeding occurs in approximately 10% of all patients on long-term anticoagulant therapy. However, fatalities are rare.

7 Patients on long-term therapy must be instructed to take their medication *as prescribed* and to report without fail for their blood tests. Cooperation of the patient is important for safe and effective anticoagulation therapy. Some physicians do not advocate long-term anticoagulant therapy for unreliable patients— those patients who do not eat properly, go on alcoholic binges, do not take their medicine as directed, and do not report for the test of their prothrombin activity (prothrombin time) as they have been directed to do.

▪ Antilipemic agents

From both clinical and experimental studies there is evidence that an important relationship exists between atherosclerosis and high levels of circulating blood lipids or fats (glycerides, phospholipids, and cholesterol). Atherosclerosis is a causative factor in coronary artery disease and myocardial infarction, in cerebral arterial disease that results in senility or cerebral vascular accidents, in peripheral arterial occlusive disease (which may cause gangrene and loss of limb), and in renal arterial insufficiency. It is also a factor in hypertension. Therefore there is intensive research to develop antilipemic drugs. If serum lipid levels could be controlled within normal limits, the development and progression of atherosclerosis might be inhibited or prevented.

That a positive relationship exists between high serum lipid levels and atherosclerosis is controversial; some individuals with high serum lipid levels have no objective evidence of atherosclerosis, while others with marked atherosclerotic signs and symptoms have normal serum lipid levels. However, more persons with high blood lipid levels have atherosclerosis than those with so-called normal blood lipid levels. Consequently, some researchers and clinicians believe that if lipid levels can be controlled, so can the atherosclerotic process. At the present time the available antilipemic drugs are also controversial, and their place in drug therapy requires more long-term critical studies. None of the antilipemic drugs is thought to have any effect on reversing the atherosclerotic process once it has begun. Means of preventing atherosclerosis remain obscure. Multicausative factors are undoubtedly involved and include dietary saturated fats, faulty fat metabolism, genetic influence, and other factors as yet unknown.

Clofibrate, N.F. (Atromid)

Clofibrate is a new antilipemic drug that is a preparation of p-chlorophenoxyisobutyric acid. It is particularly effective in lowering serum triglycerides, serum cholesterol, and phospholipids. The exact mode of action of clofibrate is unknown, but the drug appears to block the synthesis of blood lipids. It is administered orally in doses of 500 mg. three or four times daily. Several weeks or even 2 or more months of therapy are required before the serum lipid level is reduced to the desirable level. Clofibrate has also been shown to enhance the action of anticoagulants. Side effects reported include nausea, abdominal discomfort, urticaria, abnormal liver function tests, and alopecia. Further clinical trials are necessary before the role of clofibrate in the control of atherosclerosis can be determined.

Cholestyramine resin, U.S.P. (Cuemid, Questran)

Cholestyramine is a chloride salt of a quaternary ammonium anion exchange resin. In the intestinal lumen it exchanges chloride ions for bile acids. Since the resin and the bile acids bound to the resin are nonabsorbable, there is increased fecal excretion of bile acids. To compensate for this loss of bile acids, the body increases the rate of oxidation of cholesterol to

194

convert the sterol to bile acids. This in turn lowers serum cholesterol.

Cholestyramine was originally introduced for the treatment of pruritis associated with biliary stasis. It is now under clinical investigation as an antilipemic drug.

Preparation, dosage, and administration. Cholestyramine is available as a powder for oral administration. The powder should be mixed with fruit juice, soup, milk, water, or pureed fruit prior to administration and given with the patient's meal. Adult dosage is 3.33 to 4 Gm. given three or four times daily. It should not be given simultaneously with other drugs, particularly acid drugs such as aspirin, because of its ability to bind acids. A period of 1 to 4 hours should intervene between the administration of cholestyramine and other oral medications.

Side effects. Side effects from cholestyramine include nausea, vomiting, constipation, diarrhea, and skin reactions. Bleeding tendencies have been noted during prolonged treatment with cholestyramine. This effect is thought to be caused by hypoprothrombinemia associated with vitamin K deficiency. It is recommended that fat-soluble vitamins be given intramuscularly to patients receiving cholestyramine.

Niacin (nicotinic acid, nicotinamide), U.S.P.

Nicotinic acid decreases serum lipids. Its exact mode of action is unknown. Niacin is the generic name now used for both nicotinic acid and nicotinamide.

Reductions in serum lipids have been sustained for 2 to 5 years with nicotinic acid therapy. However, with discontinuance of therapy, serum lipid levels return to pretreatment levels within 2 to 6 weeks. Resistance to nicotinic acid therapy occurs in about 25% of patients.

Preparation, dosage, and administration. Nicotinic acid is available in tablets of varying strengths for oral administration. The usual adult dose is 1 to 2 Gm. three times daily with meals.

Side effects. Numerous and often disagreeable side effects may occur from nicotinic acid. Common side effects include severe gastrointestinal upset, flushing pruritis, nervousness, and urticaria. The drug should be used cautiously in patients with allergies and peptic ulcers since nicotinic acid causes a release of histamine and stimulates hydrochloric acid secretion. Giving the drug with meals or with antacids may reduce the incidence and severity of side effects.

Dextrothyroxine sodium (Choloxin, D-thyroxine Sodium)

It has long been known that a definite relationship exists between thyroid function and serum cholesterol levels. Hypothyroidism is associated with high serum cholesterol levels, and administration of thyroid hormones lowers serum cholesterol. Dextrothyroxine apparently increases the rate of oxidation of cholesterol, increases biliary excretion of cholesterol, and promotes intestinal excretion of cholesterol and other lipids.

Preparation, dosage, and administration. Dextrothyroxine sodium is available in 2- and 4-mg. tablets for oral administration. The initial dose is usually 1 to 2 mg. daily, with increments of 1 to 2 mg. every 4 weeks until the desired response is obtained. Maintenance dosage usually ranges from 4 to 8 mg. daily for adults.

Side effects. Numerous side effects from dextrothyroxine have been reported. The most frequent side effects are caused by the metabolic effects of the drug and include insomnia, palpitation, tremor, loss of weight, diuresis, and menstrual irregularities. Other less common side effects include headache, dizziness, tinnitus, malaise, muscle pain, and other subjective complaints.

Precautions. Since dextrothyroxine may potentiate anticoagulant therapy, dosage of anticoagulant drugs should be decreased, prothrombin times should be determined weekly, and patients should be observed for bleeding tendencies.

Dextrothyroxine also tends to elevate blood sugar levels in diabetic persons, which necessitates increased dosage of insulin or hypoglycemic agents.

The increases in metabolism from dextrothyroxine must be used cautiously for patients with angina pectoris because the drug may precipitate attacks. An increase in incidence or severity of anginal attacks indicates need to discontinue the use of dextrothyroxine.

This drug is contraindicated for patients with advanced liver or kidney disease, hypertension, or organic heart disease and in pregnant women and nursing mothers.

Estrogens and androgens

It has been repeatedly demonstrated that gonadal hormones influence serum lipid levels. The incidence of atherosclerosis increases with age while secretion of gonadal hormones decreases with age. Estrogen therapy to reduce serum lipids has received more study than the effect of androgens on serum lipids. Studies show that estrogens are able to sustain lowered serum lipid levels. However, even the estrogen studies have not been sufficiently extensive to obtain definitive answers on survival and mortality associated with estrogen therapy and lowered serum lipids.

Feminizing effects in males treated with estrogens create a serious disadvantage and often result in rejection of estrogen therapy. At the present time, there is intensive research on androgens to establish whether or not they have clinical usefulness in the treatment of elevated blood lipids.

Questions

for study and review

1 What do you think you need to understand about digitalis and its preparations in order to give intelligent nursing care to the patient getting the drug?

2 What special precautions would you observe and what observations would you be expected to make when caring for a patient getting digitalis for congestive heart failure?

3 What should a patient who is to be on long-term anticoagulant therapy with Dicumarol have in the way of instruction before treatment is begun?

4 Explain how quinidine can cause cardiac arrest.

5 For what condition are anticoagulants used prophylactically?

6 Why are the coumarin or phenindione drugs the drugs of choice for long-term anticoagulant therapy?

7 What electrocardiographic changes would contraindicate further administration of quinidine? of procainamide? of Dilantin?

8 What instructions would you provide a patient on nitrate therapy?

9 Explain how the monamine oxidase inhibitors effect a lowering of the blood pressure.

10 What instructions should be given to the patient who experiences orthostatic hypotension from his antihypertensive therapy?

11 Under what circumstances would vasoconstrictors be used to treat hypotension accompanying shock? When would vasodilators be used?

12 Explain why, in treatment of patients with hypochromic anemia, different drugs are used than are used for treatment of patients with pernicious anemia.

13 What it thought to be the role of vitamin B_{12} in the treatment of anemia? When is its use indicated rather than a preparation of iron? of folic acid?

14 Why would you encourage a patient to continue taking vitamin B_{12} when he says that he feels perfectly well and sees no reason for spending his money this way, in spite of the fact that the doctor says he should continue taking it?

15 What is the rationale for the use of antilipemic agents? What precautions must be taken when certain antilipemic agents are used?

Multiple choice

16 Of the following, choose the *incorrect* answer:
   a. Digitalis toxicity may be caused by the drug's ability to lower potassium levels.
   b. A decrease in body sodium is responsible for digitalis toxicity.
   c. Nausea and vomiting from digitialis may result from digitalis' stimulating effect on the vomiting center in the medulla.
   d. All cardiac glycosides have the same type of effects on the heart.

17 Which of the following are the most common effects seen on the EKG tracing or monitor with therapeutic doses of digitalis?
   a. S-T segment depression
   b. P-R interval lengthening
   c. peaked P wave
   d. T wave inversion

18 Select the desired effects of digitalis on the heart.
   a. decreased vagal stimulation
   b. increased amount of energy available for myocardial contraction
   c. prolonged refractory period of the heart
   d. increased impulse formation in potential pacemakers

19 Digitalis intoxication is most likely to occur:
   a. with intravenous rather than oral administration of digitalis
   b. in patients with severely impaired heart function
   c. with rapid digitalization
   d. when diuretic agents are not used

20 The action of digitalis is enhanced by:
   a. potassium   c. sodium
   b. chloride   d. calcium

21 Longest duration of drug action occurs with:
   a. lanoxin   **c.** gitalin
   b. digitoxin   **d.** lanatoside C

22 Which one of the following does not occur in digitalis intoxication?
   a. heart block   **c.** decreased urinary output
   b. bradycardia   **d.** visual disturbances

23 Desirable effects of digitalis in treatment of heart failure include:
   a. increased venous pressure
   b. decreased heart size
   c. slowed conduction
   d. increased urinary output

24 Digitalization of the patient refers to:
   a. the development of early symptoms of digitalis poisoning
   b. a state in which the patient is free of symptoms of heart failure
   c. a state in which the failing heart is receiving maximum benefits from the digitalis preparation
   d. a condition in which the heart has been slowed to normal

25 Symptoms that may indicate cumulative effects of digitoxin are:
   a. marked increase in urine output
   b. pulse rate below 60
   c. nausea and vomiting
   d. diarrhea

26 Which of the following statements about quinidine are *incorrect?*
   a. Quinidine often causes ventricular arrhythmias because of its ability to depress conduction and the sinoatrial node.
   b. Quinidine depresses the excitability of the heart.
   c. Quinidine increases the refractory period of the heart.
   d. Administration of potassium counteracts the antiarrhythmic effect of quinidine.

27 Desirable effects from quinidine include:
   a. increased heart rate
   b. delayed conduction of impulses
   c. blocking impulses from latent pacemaker tissue
   d. increasing depolarization time

28 Which of the following do not occur with the use of quinidine?
   a. thrombocytopenic purpura
   b. heart block
   c. premature ventricular contractions
   d. a lupus erythematoid reaction

29 Procainamide has which of the following actions?
   a. slows conduction
   b. depresses cardiac excitability
   c. depresses myocardial contractility
   d. has a hypertensive effect

30 Nitrites have which of the following desirable actions?
   a. dilation of retinal vessels and increase of intraocular pressure
   b. reduction in blood pressure from the vasodilating effect

   c. decreased coronary vascular resistance
   d. overcoming of decreased vascular elasticity

31 Which of the following statements about nitrites is *incorrect?*
   a. Nitroglycerine is ineffective when taken orally.
   b. Amyl nitrite is the most rapidly acting of the nitrites.
   c. Nitroglycerine increases blood flow through the skin capillaries.

32 Which of the following statements are true?
   a. Hydralazine used in combination with other antihypertensive drugs helps reduce the high incidence of toxic effects from hydralazine.
   b. Hydralazine interferes with the vasoconstricting effects of norepinephrine.
   c. Peripheral resistance refers to resistance of blood flow through the systemic circulation.
   d. Hydralazine has a marked effect on the parasympathetic nervous system.

33 Antihypertensive drugs that lower blood pressure by depleting the body of stored norepinephrine include:
   a. reserpine   **c.** guanethidine
   b. veratrum preparations   **d.** methyldopa

34 Choose the *incorrect* answer.
   Veratrum preparations:
   a. may cause bradycardia as a result of their vagalstimulating ability
   b. have a central emetic effect that causes nausea and vomiting
   c. have a wide margin of safety
   d. reduce blood pressure by reflex inhibition of vasomotor activity

35 Select the correct statement:
   a. Suppressing the sympathetic nervous system also decreases the activity of the parasympathetic nervous system.
   b. Dosage for antihypertensive drugs is based on the blood pressure obtained in the sitting rather than standing or lying positions.
   c. Ganglionic blocking agents are the most potent antihypertensive drugs.
   d. Withdrawal of antihypertensive drugs is not likely to cause a pressure rebound.

36 Repeated prothrombin time determinations are required with administration of:
   a. Dicumarol   **c.** vitamin K
   b. heparin   **d.** protamine

37 Which of the following is used to counteract the effects of Dicumarol?
   a. thrombin   **c.** vitamin K
   b. whole blood   **d.** protamine sulfate

38 Heparin therapy is regulated by determining the patient's:
   a. prothrombin time   **c.** platelet count
   b. clotting time   **d.** bleeding time

39 Which of the following statements are *not* true?
   a. Heparin inhibits the conversion of prothrombin to thrombin.
   b. Normal blood clotting requires calcium for conversion of prothrombin to thrombin.

   c. Heparin prevents agglutination of platelets.
   d. Heparin is not effective in preventing clot extension.
40 The use of heparin is based on:
   a. its inability to cross the placental blood barrier
   b. its low toxicity
   c. the ease with which vitamin K reverses its anticoagulant effects
   d. the need for rapid anticoagulant action
41 Which of the following laboratory findings would indicate a favorable response of a patient to treatment with vitamin B_{12}?
   a. increased hemoglobin
   b. increased reticulocyte count
   c. increased color index
   d. increased white blood cell count
42 Which of the following preparations may produce a favorable hematopoietic response in a patient with pernicious anemia but will not arrest degenerative changes in nervous system?
   a. vitamin B_{12} c. liver extract
   b. folic acid   d. defatted hog stomach
43 Iron is best absorbed from the duodenum for which of the following reasons?
   a. The duodenum has a better absorbing surface than the rest of the bowel.
   b. The duodenal secretions are alkaline in reaction.
   c. Iron is best absorbed from an acid medium.
   d. The jejunum and ileum excrete the salts of heavy metals rather than absorb them.
44 If a patient has developed a thrombosis, which of the following drugs would you expect the physician to order first?
   a. menadione sodium bisulfite
   b. bishydroxycoumarin (Dicumarol)
   c. heparin
   d. ethyl biscoumacetate (Tromexan)

References

Allen, E. V., Barker, N. W., and Waugh, J. M.: The preparation from spoiled sweet clover, J.A.M.A. **120**:1009, 1942.

Berne, R. M., and Levy, M. N.: Cardiovascular physiology, ed. 2, St. Louis, 1972, The C. V. Mosby Co.

Blinds, J. R.: Evaluation of the cardiac effects of several beta adrenergic blocking agents, Ann. N. Y. Acad. Sci. **139**:673, 1967.

Braunwald, E., and Klocke, F. J.: Digitalis, Ann. Rev. Med. **16**:371, 1965.

Brest, A. N., editor: Arrhythmias, Philadelphia, 1970, F. A. Davis Co.

Brest, A. N., editor: International cardiology, Philadelphia, 1971, F. A. Davis Co.

Brest, A. N., and Moyer, J. H., editors: Cardiovascular drug therapy, New York, 1965, Grune & Stratton.

Briller, S. A., and Conn, H. L., Jr., editors: The myocardial cell: structure, function and modification by cardiac drugs, Philadelphia, 1966, University of Pennsylvania Press.

Brunings, K. J., and Lindgren, P., editors: Proceedings of the First International Pharmacological Meeting: Vol. 7. Modern concepts in the relation between structure and pharmacological activity, New York, 1963, The Macmillan Company.

Castle, W. B.: Treatment of pernicious anemia: historical aspects, Clin. Pharmacol. Therap. **7**:147, 1966.

Conn, H. L., Jr.: Quinidine as an antiarrhythmic agent, Med. Clin. N. Amer. **48**:286, 1964.

Conn, H. L., Jr., and Luchi, R.: Some cellular and metabolic considerations relating to the action of quinidine as a prototype antiarrhythmic agent, Amer. J. Med. **37**:685, 1964.

Conn, R.: Newer drugs in the treatment of cardiac arrhythmia, Med. Clin. N. Amer. **51**:1223, 1967.

Dreifus, L. S., and Likoff, W., editors: Mechanisms and therapy of cardiac arrhythmias, New York, 1966, Grune & Stratton.

Evarts, C. M.: Low molecular weight dextran, Med. Clin. N. Amer. **51**:1285, 1967.

Finnerty, F. A., Jr.: Newer antihypertensive drugs, Med. Clin. N. Amer. **48**:329, 1964.

Fisch, S.: Antianginal drugs: I. The therapeutic role of coronary vasodilators, Amer. Heart J. **71**:281, 1966.

Fisch, S.: Antianginal drugs: II. Human pharmacology of nitroglycerin, Amer. Heart J. **71**:417, 1966.

Fisch, S.: Antianginal drugs: III. Clinical use of nitroglycerin, Amer. Heart J. **71**:564, 1966.

Fisch, S.: Antianginal drugs: IV. The long-acting nitrates, Amer. Heart J. **71**:712, 1966.

Fisch, S.: Antianginal drugs: V. Monoamine oxidase (MAO) inhibitors, Amer. Heart J. **71**:837, 1966.

Fisch, S.: Antianginal drugs: VI. Beta-adrenergic blocking drugs, Amer. Heart J. **71**:131, 1966.

Fisch, S., and DeGraff, A. C.: Coronary vasodilators, Dis. Chest **44**:533, 1963.

Friedberg, C., editor: Current status of drugs in cardiovascular disease, New York, 1969, Grune & Stratton, Inc.

Frieden, J.: Lidocaine as an antiarrhythmic agent, Amer. Heart J. **70**:713, 1965.

Friend, D. G.: Iron therapy, Clin. Pharmacol. Therap. **4**:419, 1963.

Glass, G. B. J.: Gastric intrinsic factor and its function in the metabolism of vitamin B_{12}, Physiol. Rev. **43**:529, 1963.

Goldreng, W., and Chasis, H.: Antihypertensive drug therapy—an appraisal, Arch. Intern. Med. **115**:523, 1965.

Goodman, L., and Gilman, A.: The pharmacological basis of therapeutics, New York, 1970, The Macmillan Company.

Gorlin, R.: Drugs and angina pectoris, Amer. J. Cardiol. **9**:419, 1962.

Goth, A.: Medical pharmacology, ed. 6, St. Louis, 1972, The C. V. Mosby Co.

Hoffman, B. F., and Cranefield, P. F.: Electrophysiology of the heart, New York, 1960, McGraw-Hill Book Company.

Horowitz, D., and Sjoerdsma, A.: A basis for the use of MAO inhibitors in angina pectoris, Ann. N. Y. Acad. Sci. **107** (part 3):1033, 1963.

Jandl, J. H., editor: Symposium on the mechanisms of disorders of erythropoiesis, Medicine **43**:615, 1964.

Kayden, H.: Pharmacology of procaine amide, Amer. Heart J. **70**:423, 1965.

Kayden, H., Brodie, B., and Steele, J.: Procaine amide, a review, Circulation **15**:118, 1957.

Kayden, H.: Clinical use of procaine amide, Amer. Heart J. **70**:567, 1965.

Koch-Weser, J.: Mechanism of digitalis action on the heart, New Eng. J. Med. **277**:417, 1967.

Lewis, J. H., and Bayer, W. L.: Therapy in coagulation defects, Med. Clin. N. Amer. **51**:1241, 1967.

Luchi, R. J., Helwig, J., and Conn, H. L., Jr.: Quinidine toxicity and its treatment, Amer. Heart J. **65**:340, 1963.

Lyon, A.: Antiarrhythmic drugs: II. Clinical use of quinidine, Amer. Heart J. **69**:834, 1965.

Lyon, A.: Quinidine toxicity, Amer. Heart J. **70**:139, 1965.

Lyon, A., and DeGraff, A.: Antiarrhythmic drugs: I. Mechanism of quinidine action, Amer. Heart J. **69**:713, 1965.

Mariott, H. J. L.: Rational approach to quinidine therapy, Mod. Conc. Cardiov. Dis. **31**:745, 1962.

McKenna, P. J., and Erslev, A. J.: Treatment of anemias, Med. Clin. N. Amer. **49**:13715, 1965.

McPherson, R. C., and Halles, J. A.: The comparative effects of blood, saline, and low molecular dextran on irreversible hemorrhagic shock, J. Trauma **4**:415, 1964.

Miller, R., Harvey, W. P., and Finch, C. A.: Antagonism of Dicumarol by vitamin K preparation, New Eng. J. Med. **242**:211, 1950.

Moe, K., and Mendey, C.: Bases of pharmacotherapy of cardiac arrhythmias, Mod. Conc. Cardiov. Dis. **31**:739, 1962.

Moser, M.: Use and abuse of antihypertensive drugs, GP **35**:87, 1967.

Nash, H. L., and others: Cardiorenal hemodynamic effects of ethacrynic acid, Amer. Heart J. **71**:153, 1966.

Page, I. H.: A story of hypertension, Fed. Proc. **23**:693, 1964.

Page, I. H.: The drug treatment of arterial hypertension, Clin. Pharmacol. Therap. **7**:567, 1966.

Page, I. H., editor: Symposium on hypertension and its treatment, Med. Clin. N. Amer. **45**:233, 1961.

Pritchard, J. A., and Mason, R. A.: Iron stores of normal adults and replenishment with oral iron therapy, J.A.M.A. **190**:897, 1964.

Riseman, J. E. F.: Nitroglycerin and other nitrites in the treatment of angina pectoris, comparison of six preparations and four routes of administration, Circulation **17**:22, 1958.

Ross, J. D.: Current concepts in therapy: treatment and prevention of iron deficiency anemia of infancy, New Eng. J. Med. **266**:1372, 1962.

Ruthen, G. C.: Diphenylhydantoin in cardiac arrhythmias, Amer. Heart J. **70**:275, 1965.

Sherrod, T. R.: The cardiac glycosides, Hosp. Pract. **56**:59, 1967.

Shoemaker, W., and others: Hemodynamic and microcirculatory effects of high and low viscosity dextrans, Surgery **58**:518, 1965.

Shoemaker, W.: Principles of therapy in shock from hemorrhage, trauma and sepsis, Mod. Treatm. **4**:256, 1967.

Sise, H. S., and others: The risk of interrupting long-term anticoagulation therapy: a rebound hypercoagulable state following hemorrhage, Circulation **24**:1137, 1961.

Sokolow, M., and Perloff, Z. B.: The clinical pharmacology and the use of quinidine in heart disease, Prog. Cardiov. Dis. **3**:316, 1960.

Thomson, G. W.: Quinidine as a cause of sudden death, Circulation **14**:757, 1965.

Weatherall, M.: Ions and the action of digitalis, Brit. Heart J. **28**:497, 1966.

11

Diuretics and other urinary tract agents

■ The kidneys

The kidneys are the chief organs that excrete nonvolatile, water-soluble substances from the body. These substances include products of metabolism such as urea, uric acid, and creatinine, as well as electrolytes such as sodium chloride and potassium salts. Foreign substances that may have gained entrance into the blood are also excreted by the kidneys.

The normal kidney does not excrete colloids, such as plasma proteins, or large molecular weight colloids introduced into the bloodstream, such as gelatin or gum acacia. The kidney plays an important part in maintaining the osmotic pressure of the blood. It also acts to maintain optimum concentrations of the individual constituents of the plasma. This is accomplished by the excretion of water and specific solutes in carefully regulated amounts. It is largely the re-sponsibility of the renal tubules to effect this precise regulation of the substances excreted into the urine. The tubules accomplish this function in a number of ways. Some substances such as glucose and amino acids are completely reabsorbed from the tubular urine and are returned to the blood quantitatively. Others, such as sodium and chloride, are partially reabsorbed. Substances such as inulin and creatinine are not reabsorbed at all and are excreted quantitatively. The renal tubules also add some substances to the urine by a process of secretion. Potassium and hydrogen ions are secreted by the cells of the renal tubule.

Histology of the kidneys

The kidneys are composed of many functional units called nephrons (Figure 11-1), each of which begins as a dilated ovoid-shaped structure known as Bowman's capsule. Into Bowman's capsule is invaginated a tuft of capillary vessels, the glomerulus, through which flows blood that originally came from the renal arteries.

The glomerulus is connected to a long tortuous tubule that is divided into several segments. The first part is called the proximal convoluted tubule. This is followed by a narrowed hairpin-shaped structure called Henle's loop. The initial part of Henle's loop descends toward the pelvis of the kidney and is called the descending limb. This is lined with flattened squamous cells. This descending limb is followed by

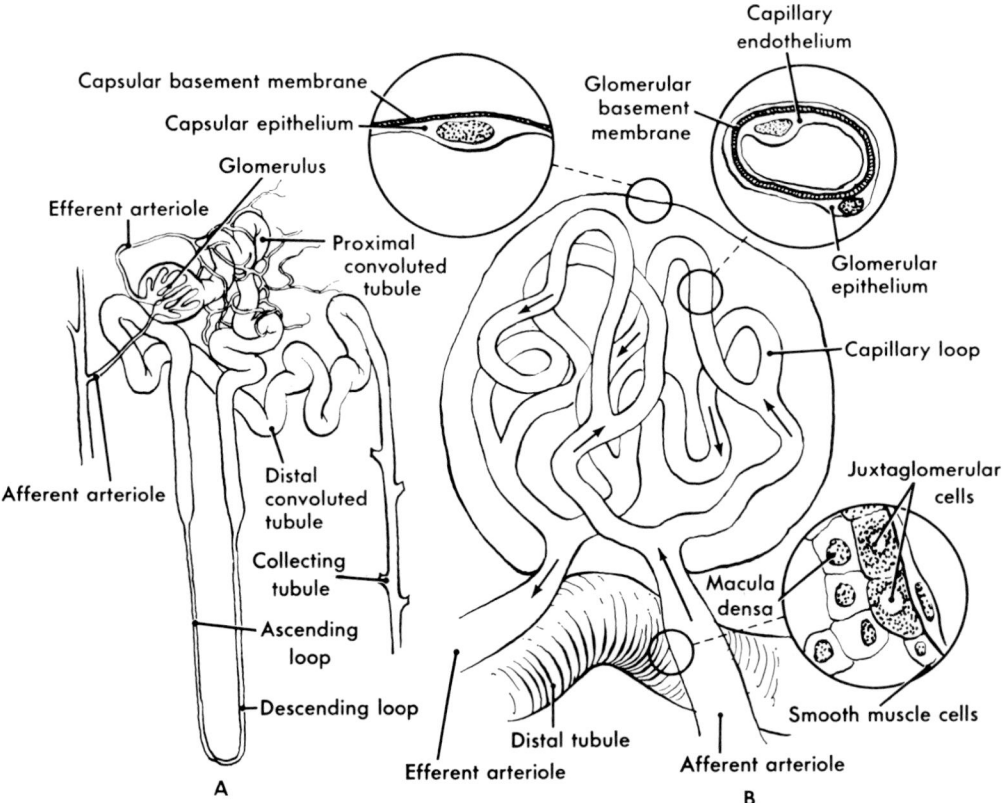

Figure 11-1
A, Diagram of a nephron. The nephron consists of the glomerulus, the ball of capillaries at upper left; the tubule, which twists from the glomerulus to the urine-collecting duct at right; and the bed of capillaries around the tubule. The water of the blood containing small molecules such as urea and sodium chloride is filtered out of the glomerulus into the tubule where virtually all of the water and other useful substances are reabsorbed. Blood enters the glomerulus via the afferent arteriole and leaves it via the efferent arteriole. **B,** Diagram of a glomerulus showing cross sections of its various component parts.

the ascending limb, which is lined with cuboidal epithelium. The next part of the tubule is the distal convoluted tubule, which is also lined with cuboidal epithelium. The distal part of the tubule empties into the collecting tubule, which eventually terminates in the renal pyramid and pelvis of the kidney. The collecting tubule is also lined with cuboidal epithelium. The number of glomeruli in the kidney of man is estimated to be 1 million in each kidney. The total tubule length of both kidneys is estimated to be approximately 75 miles.

In general, the excretion of urine is attuned to the needs of the body. For most substances the kidney serves to maintain constant amounts and concentrations in the body fluids. This is accomplished by excreting the same amounts of solutes and water as are acquired each day (minus the amounts lost through sweat, feces, and other extrarenal routes). In physiologic terms, the kidney acts to preserve balance of most major constituents of body fluids.

Volume and composition of urine

Factors that most affect the formation of urine include glomerular filtration, tubular reabsorption, and tubular secretion.

Glomerular filtration. The force needed for filtration through the glomerular capillaries and into the glomerular capsule is derived from the force of the blood (blood pressure). It is sometimes referred to as hydrostatic pressure. The osmotic pressure of the plasma proteins represents an opposing force to hold fluid in the blood. Various constituents dissolved in the plasma filter through the glomerulus and are found in the filtrate in about the same concentration as they are found in the blood. Blood cells, plasma proteins, and lipids do not diffuse through the capillary walls and are not found in the glomerular filtrate if the kidney is functioning normally. Increased glomerular filtration caused by dilution of the plasma or by increased intraglomerular pressure usually achieves a moderately increased formation of urine.

Tubular reabsorption. The cells lining the renal tubules exhibit a high level of metabolic activity and expend considerable energy in recovering and transporting electrolytes and water back into the extracellular fluid (blood, lymph, and interstitial fluid) of the body. Because they tend to be active cells they are also the cells that are most easily injured when renal damage occurs. For every 100 ml. of fluid filtered through the glomerulus, approximately 99 ml. are reabsorbed in the tubule. Most diuretics used clinically act by interference with tubular reabsorption (water and electrolyte reabsorption). The activity of the tubule cells is greatly affected by the pituitary hormone, antidiuretic hormone (ADH), and certain adrenal hormones. Reabsorption of water is also affected by the amount of nonreabsorbable substances in the blood, which in turn enter the tubule and obligate the excretion of water.

Tubular secretion. It has been found that the tubule cells actively secrete certain substances into the urine as well as absorb certain other substances from the urine. Penicillin is an example of a drug that is excreted this way.

The secretion of hydrogen ions by the tubule cells is an effective way whereby the kidney helps to maintain acid-base equilibrium. The hydrogen ions in the tubular cells are exchanged for the sodium ions in the urine. The rate of this exchange can be greatly affected by drugs and this constitutes a basis of diuresis.

Diuretics

Diuretics are drugs that increase the flow of urine. The purpose of a diuretic is to increase the net loss of water, and to achieve this there must also be a loss of sodium. Diuretics are not all equally effective in removing fluid of edema.

Diuretics act in one of the following ways. (1) Some inhibit reabsorption of sodium by a direct action on the kidney tubules. These agents include the xanthines, mercurials, pyrimidines, carbonic anhydrase inhibitors, benzothiazides, furosemide, and ethacrynic acid. (2) Some inhibit tubular reabsorption of sodium by an indirect mechanism. Included in this group are the osmotic diuretics (such as potassium salts, urea, glucose, and sucrose) and inhibi-

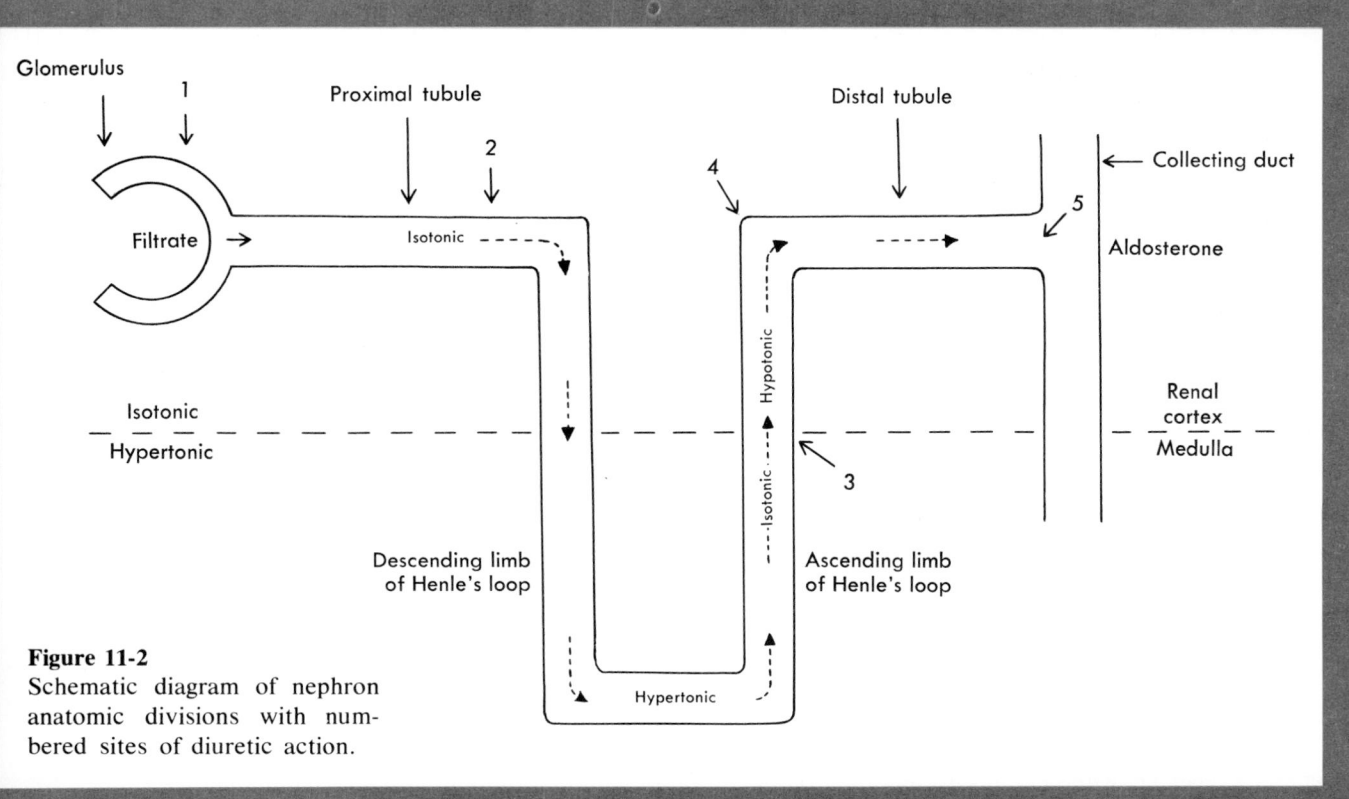

Figure 11-2
Schematic diagram of nephron anatomic divisions with numbered sites of diuretic action.

tors of aldosterone secretion. (3) Others increase glomerular filtration of sodium. Examples of these drugs are the acidifying salts and plasma expanders. Only the acid-forming salts will be discussed in this chapter. Inhibiting the secretion of antidiuretic hormone from the posterior pituitary will also increase urine output. Water and ethyl alcohol produce this effect. However, they do not increase the excretion of electrolytes and therefore do not relieve edema. The cause of a patient's edema is an important factor in determining which diuretic should be used. See Figure 11-2 for a schematic representation of diuretic action sites.

Sites of diuretic action of various agents

Site 1—renal vasculature. Agents effecting renal vasodilation will increase renal blood flow, promoting diuresis. Isoproterenol and papaverine are examples of drugs that exert this

effect. While the diuretic effect is often desirable, such drugs are not administered solely for this renal effect.

Site 2—proximal tubule. Mercurial diuretics, the thiazides, and acetazolamide appear to exert their primary diuretic effect on the proximal tubule, although they probably also act at other sites. Agents acting at this site inhibit sodium and chloride ion reabsorption. A large volume of isosmotic filtrate is thus presented to the distal tubule, where some sodium is reabsorbed and a large volume of free water is generated. The urine becomes more alkaline and contains increased amounts of sodium, potassium, bicarbonate, and chloride.

Site 3—ascending limb of Henle's loop. Furosemide and ethacrynic acid appear to exert their major effect at this site. These agents block the exchange mechanisms, diminish the amount of medullary and cortical sodium, alter

203

osmotic concentration gradients, and impair urinary concentration ability. These drugs probably act at other sites also.

Site 4—renal cortical diluting site. Triamterene apparently blocks sodium reabsorption in the distal tubule. The result is increased sodium excretion accompanied primarily by chloride. There may be no or only slight increase in potassium excretion and at times only slight alkalinization of urine.

Site 5—distal convoluted tubule and collecting duct site. Spironolactone, the aldosterone antagonist, probably exerts its major effect at this site. In the distal portions of the tubule sodium is reabsorbed from tubular fluid in exchange for potassium and hydrogen ions. Blocking the action of aldosterone results in increased sodium and chloride excretion and decreased potassium and ammonium excretion.

An inadequate or poor response to diuretic therapy, particularly when treatment consists of a single drug, may result from:

1 Unrestricted or liberal salt or sodium intake
2 Low glomerular filtration rate, which occurs in patients with renal insufficiency
3 Increased tubular reabsorption of sodium and water, which may be caused by:
   a. Hyperaldosteronism, nephrosis, or cirrhosis
   b. Heart failure, which results in low cardiac output and reduced renal blood flow
   c. Impaired venous or lymphatic drainage, which traps fluid in various tissues

The most frequent side effects of diuretic therapy include:

1 Hypokalemia
2 Hyperuricemia
3 Impaired glucose tolerance
4 Hyperkalemia
5 Hyponatremia
6 Reduced glomerular filtration rate
7 A transient decrease in plasma volume, cardiac output, blood pressure, and renal function

■ Diuretics that act directly on kidney tubules
Xanthines

Xanthine diuretics include caffeine, theobromine, and theophylline, all of which exert similar actions in the body but differ in degree of effect upon various tissues and organs. Caffeine exerts a marked action on the central nervous system but is relatively weak in its action on the kidney. Theobromine and theophylline are weak in their action on the nervous system but have a somewhat greater effect on the kidney and cardiovascular system.

Xanthines produce their diuretic effect by: (1) inhibiting tubular reabsorption of sodium and chloride (most pronounced with theophylline), (2) improving glomerular function by increasing renal blood flow (caffeine and theobromine have this effect), and (3) improving renal blood flow as a result of their ability to stimulate heart action and improve cardiac output; this also enhances their direct action on the kidneys.

Theophylline

Theophylline is the more effective diuretic, but its action is of short duration. Theobromine is somewhat less active, but its effects last longer.

The effects of the xanthine diuretics are inferior to those that can be obtained from the organic mercurials. For the patient with cardiac edema, especially the patient who has become refractory to other forms of treatment, theophylline compounds are sometimes used to supplement therapy with digitalis and the mercurials. The oral forms of the xanthines are little used as diuretics since more effective oral drugs are available.

The xanthines are primarily used in combination with other diuretics, such as the mercurials. Tolerance to these drugs develops with repeated dosages. Xanthines are contraindicated in patients with renal insufficiency.

Aminophylline, U.S.P., B.P.

Aminophylline, a preparation of theophylline and ethylenediamine, is the most commonly used form of theophylline.

204

Preparation, dosage, and administration. Aminophylline is available for oral administration in plain or enteric-coated tablets of 100 to 200 mg. and in combination with aluminum hydroxide to decrease gastrointestinal irritation. Solution forms for intramuscular or intravenous injection are also available (2-, 10-, and 20-ml. ampules containing 250 or 500 mg. of aminophylline).

Caution is recommended when the drug is given intravenously. It should be injected slowly and this method of administration should be reserved for emergencies. Aminophylline is also marketed in suppositories of 125, 250, and 500 mg. All these preparations are official in both the U.S.P. and the B.P. The dose is 100 to 500 mg. several times daily.

Side effects and toxic effects. Although the xanthines have a low level of toxicity, when given orally they are likely to cause gastric discomfort, nausea, and vomiting. Stimulation of the central nervous system often occurs after large doses or when idiosyncrasy is present. This may produce symptoms such as headache, restlessness, dizziness, anxiety, delirium, and convulsions. Aminophylline, when given intravenously, can cause cardiac arrest or ventricular fibrillation. This is why it must be administered slowly. Repeated administration results in the development of tolerance. Xanthines could therefore be expected to be less effective in persons who habitually drink tea and coffee.

Mercurial diuretics

Mersalyl

The organic mercurial diuretics are considered to be among the more potent drugs for increasing the output of urine. Development of newer and orally effective diuretics has limited their use. While the mercurials, under optimal conditions, are four times as effective as thiazides in increasing sodium excretion, they have the disadvantages of requiring repeated parenteral administration and causing nephrotoxicity. Table 11-1 lists some of the mercurial diuretics.

Action. Mercurials do not alter filtration rate and do not affect renal blood flow. Their diuretic effect appears to be that of affecting proximal tubular reabsorption, impairing active reabsorption of sodium. The loss of sodium decreases the body's capacity to retain water, which relieves edema. Loss of chloride and water is a passive action. Mercurials also increase calcium and magnesium excretion with prolonged use; potassium excretion may also increase but not to the same extent as with thiazides.

Uses. The organic mercurial diuretics are used chiefly to relieve cardiac edema or the edema associated with nephroses, cirrhotic conditions of the liver, or portal obstruction and for patients resistant to less potent diuretics.

Preparation, dosage, and administration. The preferred route of administration is intramuscular. Although the subcutaneous route can be used, it can cause local irritation. Oral administration may cause gastric distress. In addition, absorption after oral administration is highly variable, and loss of edema is less dramatic than that obtained from parenteral administration. Chlormerodrin is the only mercurial diuretic that is not injectable.

Certain preparations may be administered intravenously, but they should be given slowly and only under the most carefully controlled conditions. Injections, as a rule, are not repeated more often than every 3 or 4 days. The drug is preferably given in the morning so that the major effects occur during the day.

After parenteral administration of an average dose, the diuretic effect of the organic mercurials can be expected to begin within 1 to 3 hours and to reach a peak effect in 6 to 9 hours. The diuretic effect can be expected to end within 12 to 24 hours. As much as 8 or 9 liters of urine may be excreted the first day by an edematous patient.

The addition of theophylline to the mercurial preparations increases their diuretic effects by improving absorption, and it also decreases irritation at the site of injection. At present, most

205

Table 11-1 Some mercurial diuretics

Name Generic	Name Trade	Route of administration	Range and frequency of dosage	Remarks
Mersalyl	Salyrgan	Intramuscular	0.5 to 2 ml. (40 mg. per ml.)	Most widely used of all mercurials
Meralluride	Mercuhydrin	Intramuscular, intravenous	1 to 2 ml. (40 mg. per ml.) one or two times per week	Each milliliter may also contain 48 mg. of theophylline
Mercaptomerin	Thiomerin	Intramuscular or subcutaneous Rectal suppositories	0.5 to 2 ml. of 13% solution 500 mg. suppository daily	Requires refrigeration, destroyed by heat May cause local irritation
Chlormerodrin	Neohydrin	Intramuscular Oral	10 to 40 mg. daily 10-mg. tablets	
Mercumatilin	Cumertilin	Intramuscular, intravenous	0.5 to 2 ml. (39 mg. per ml.)	

mercurial preparations are available in combination with theophylline. Mercaptomerin is the only mercurial diuretic that is not combined with theophylline to promote absorption when given intramuscularly. Administration may be preceded by large doses of an acidifying salt such as ammonium chloride to enhance the diuretic effect.

Side effects and toxic effects. The signs of toxic reactions of mercurial diuretics include stomatitis, gingivitis, increased salivation, diarrhea, albuminuria, hematuria, circulatory collapse, flushing, febrile reactions, and skin eruptions. Severe reactions are characterized by sudden fall in blood pressure, cardiac irregularity, cyanosis, and severe dyspnea. Renal damage may result from prolonged usage.

Contraindications and precautions. Mercurials are contraindicated in acute nephritis and in advanced chronic kidney disease. Patients who are sensitive to one mercurial may, however, tolerate another satisfactorily. Caution needs to be exercised when mercurials are given intravenously because sudden fatalities,

thought to be caused by ventricular arrhythmia, have occurred. Patients who have frequent ventricular beats or myocardial infarction or who have been heavily digitalized may react to mercurials unfavorably. Patients who receive mercurials are carefully selected and initial tests for sensitivity are given. When it is necessary to give these drugs repeatedly, the urine is examined periodically for blood cells, albumin, and casts.

Intense chloride diuresis after the administration of these drugs may produce hypochloremic alkalosis, which may be treated by the administration of ammonium chloride.

Pyrimidines (aminouracils)

Among the orally effective diuretics are a number of pyrimidine derivatives. The best known are aminometradine and amisometradine. These are synthesized nitrogenous compounds derived from aminouracil and are more effective than the xanthines but less potent than the mercurial diuretics. They are not popular drugs.

Carbonic anhydrase inhibitors

Agents that inhibit carbonic anhydrase, such as certain sulfonamides that cause sodium diuresis, are no longer used clinically as diuretics. They are used, however, for other clinical conditions such as glaucoma.

■ The thiazides
Benzothiadiazines

All thiazides are carbonic anhydrase inhibitors, but this is not the main mechanism for their diuretic action. Thiazides appear to act directly on the proximal tubule with some action occurring in the distal tubule. Thiazide diuretics have the following characteristic effects:

1 They decrease reabsorption of sodium, potassium, chloride, bicarbonate, and water.
2 They decrease urinary diluting capacity. This property accounts for thiazide effectiveness in the treatment of diabetes insipidus.
3 Thiazides have an antihypertensive effect. This effect remains obscure but may result from decreased body sodium and a reduction of potassium from vascular walls. There is also indication that thiazides decrease pressor effects of catecholamines (epinephrine and norepinephrine).
4 They have no marked effect on acid-base balance, and their diuretic effectiveness is not influenced by changes in acid-base balance. They remain effective in both acidosis and alkalosis.
5 They cause less elimination of bicarbonate than acetazolamide and related carbonic anhydrase inhibitors.
6 They potentiate mercurial diuretics and antihypertensive drugs.
7 Resistance to their effects is slow to develop.
8 They have no serious effects on diseased kidneys.

The thiazides are synthetic drugs chemically related to the sulfonamides. They are the result of studies that began with the observation that sulfonamides inhibit carbonic anhydrase. The development of the thiazides marked a major breakthrough in the search for potent nonmercurial diuretics. Chlorothiazide is considered the prototype of this class of drugs. All thiazides are equally effective as diuretics and antihypertensive agents. Although dosage and duration of

action vary, as well as their differing ability to cause chlorine loss, their mode of action and precautions for use are similar.

Chlorothiazide

Hydrochlorothiazide

Thiazides are potent drugs capable of seriously disturbing the fluid and electrolyte balance. Hypokalemia (less than normal amount of potassium in the blood) may precipitate digitalis toxicity. This is of significance in the patient who is receiving digitalis as well as chlorothiazide or a related compound. Chlorothiazide and related drugs have been known to promote the retention of urea, and particularly uric acid, which in turn has been known to cause an attack of gouty arthritis. This effect, however, is considered an unusual response. The drugs may also aggravate diabetes mellitus.

Chlorothiazide was the first of the benzothiadiazine group of drugs, and since then a number of compounds have been made available. They all resemble chlorothiazide, both as diuretics and as antihypertensive agents. Some of these compounds are indicated in Table 11-2. These drugs offer certain advantages over older diuretics.

1 They are convenient to use since they can be taken orally and are relatively inexpensive.
2 They are effective over long periods of time.
3 On the whole, they are regarded as drugs of low toxicity and seem to have a low incidence of side effects (although these do occur).
4 Their effectiveness is comparable to the organic mercurial diuretics, and in some instances they have the advantage of being more effective than the oral forms of the mercurial diuretics.

Table 11-2 Comparison of various thiazide compounds

Generic name	Trade name	Average daily dose (mg.)	Peak action (hours)	Duration of action*(hours)
Chlorothiazide	Diuril	1000	4	6 to 12
Chlorothiazide sodium†	Lyovac Diuril	1000	4	6 to 12
Hydrochlorothiazide	HydroDiuril Esidrix Oretic	100	3 to 4	12
Hydroflumethiazide	Saluron	100	2 to 4	12
Benzthiazide	NaClex	100	4 to 6	12 to 18
Methychlothiazide	Enduron	5 to 10	6	24
Bendroflumethiazide	Naturetin	5 to 10	4 to 6	10 to 18
Trichlormethiazide	Naqua	2 to 8	6	24
Polythiazide	Renese	2 to 8	6	24 to 48
Chlorothalidone‡	Hygroton	100 to 200	6 to 18	48 to 60
Quinethazone‡	Hydromox	50 to 100	6	18 to 24

*Onset of action of all thiazides is approximately 2 hours.
†Suitable for parenteral administration.
‡Not a thiazide but resembles one.

5 Although they produce electrolyte imbalance, this can be kept to a minimum when proper precautions are taken.

Their main pharmacologic effect as diuretics seems to be the excretion of sodium and chloride and secondarily of water. They are useful for the relief of practically all kinds of fluid retention in the body. Thiazides do not depress reabsorption of sodium in the distal tubule where exchange of sodium for potassium takes place. The increased load of sodium ions causes increased secretions of potassium ions. This plus inhibition of carbonic anhydrase and decreased hydrogen ion secretion accounts for the hypokalemic effect of the thiazides.

Thiazides are used for management of edema resulting from congestive heart failure, certain forms of renal disease, portal cirrhosis, pregnancy, and the use of certain drugs such as cortisone. These drugs may also be used to relieve fluid retention during premenstrual tension. Their use as antihypertensive agents is discussed in Chapter 10.

Thiazides do not penetrate the blood-brain barrier or the blood-ocular barrier and therefore have no effect in glaucoma. Side effects produced by these preparations are similar to those of chlorothiazide.

The introduction of new derivatives is based on the hope of obtaining a compound that is (1) more potent, (2) less likely to produce loss of potassium, and (3) less likely to cause other side effects. The search for a compound of greater potency has been successful, since some of the thiazides now available are many times more potent than the parent substance, chlorothiazide. Potency alone, however, is not a meaningful advantage. If a smaller dose produces the same amount of diuresis with decreased incidence and severity of side effects, then a real advantage has been achieved. The loss of potassium can be prevented to a great extent by the oral administration of potassium. Furthermore, some pharmaceutical houses sell their products in fixed combination with a potassium salt, such as bendroflumethiazide with potassium chloride.

Chlorothiazide (Diuril)

Chlorothiazide is a synthetic drug chemically related to the sulfonamides. It first became available for clinical use in 1958.

Action and result. Chlorothiazide was the first member of the thiazide group to be synthesized. Diuretic doses of chlorothiazide bring about diminished reabsorption of sodium and chloride ions, which result in an increased urine output. Potassium is also excreted after diuretic doses of the drug. This may necessitate the administration of potassium chloride or a food rich in potassium such as orange juice (8 oz.) to avoid serious depletion of potassium (hypokalemia). At higher dose levels, inhibition of carbonic anhydrase causes excretion of bicarbonate. Chlorothiazide potentiates a number of antihypertensive agents.

Uses. Chlorothiazide is effective in relieving edema associated with congestive heart failure and cirrhosis of the liver. It is said to be much less effective when there is a reduction of glomerular filtration in the kidney. It is also used to diminish fluid retention in toxemia of pregnancy, in the management of hypertension, and for the relief of premenstrual tension and dysmenorrhea associated with the retention of fluid. Its diuretic effectiveness is said to be only slightly less that that of the parenterally administered mercurials.

Preparation, dosage, and administration

Chlorothiazide, **N.F., B.P.** (**Diuril**). This drug is available in 250- and 500-mg. tablets for oral administration. The usual diuretic dose for adults is from 500 mg. to 1 Gm. daily or twice daily. Diuretic effects occur within 2 hours after oral administration and last over a period of 6 to 12 hours. To avoid disturbing the patient at night, it is better to give the drug early in the day.

It is also available as a syrup, 250 mg. per 5 ml. Oral dosage range for children is from 20 to 40 mg. per kilogram of body weight per day in two divided doses. Infants under 6 months may require 30 mg. per kilogram of body weight in two divided doses.

Chlorothiazide sodium (**Lyovac Diuril**). This is the sodium salt of chlorothiazide; it is more soluble than chlorothiazide and is therefore better suited to parenteral administration. It is available in vials that contain 500 mg. of the drug in the form of a powder.

Side effects and toxic effects. Side effects include allergic reactions, skin eruptions, nausea, epigastric discomfort, weakness, dizziness, paresthesias, and muscle cramps. A lowering of the number of leukocytes and thrombocytes, as well as agranulocytosis, has occurred, but the incidence is said to be low. Bicarbonate is excreted when large doses are administered, and this can cause acidosis.

Chlorothiazide may be contraindicated for patients with severe hepatic or renal dysfunction.

Thiazides may cause hyperglycemia and glycosuria in patients with latent diabetes. These drugs should be used with caution in diabetic patients.

Hydrochlorothiazide, U.S.P., B.P. (HydroDiuril, Oretic, Esidrix)

Hydrochlorothiazide is ten times more effective than chlorothiazide; thus its dosage is about one tenth that for chlorothiazide. It is available for oral administration in tablets, capsules, and extended-release forms and in combination with other drugs such as hydralazine, reserpine, and potassium chloride. The usual adult diuretic dose is 25 to 100 mg. once or twice daily. The recommended daily dosage for children is 2 mg. per kilogram of body weight, and for infants under 6 months, the dosage is 3 mg. per kilogram of body weight daily in divided doses. Infants apparently are more resistant to the effects of the drug.

Furosemide, U.S.P. (Lasix); frusemide, B.P.

Furosemide is a powerful diuretic that has been introduced recently. While its use is likely to be more limited than those of the previously discussed thiazides, it may be very important in selected cases.

Furosemide is rapidly absorbed. Its maximum effect occurs 2 to 4 hours after oral ingestion, and its action lasts for 6 to 8 hours. The ascending limb of Henle's loop appears to be the principal site for the action of furosemide, although it probably also acts on the proximal tubule. In maximum effective doses it is probably eight to ten times as powerful as the thiazides. Its potency is unaltered by the acid-base balance. Since it causes a high rate of chloride excretion, hypochloremic alkalosis may occur.

Uses. Furosemide finds its greatest application in congestive heart failure, cirrhosis of the liver, and nephrosis whenever a diuretic of very great potency is required.

Preparation, dosage, and administration. Furosemide is supplied in tablets of 40 mg. The usual dose is one to two tablets, preferably given as a single dose in the morning. In some cases additional doses may be required, but no more than 200 mg. should be administered in 24 hours.

Side effects and toxic effects. The great potency of furosemide makes careful medical supervision mandatory. Dehydration and reduction of blood volume can lead to vascular collapse, thrombosis, and embolism. Hepatic coma may occur in cirrhotic patients who receive the drug. Potassium supplementation may be necessary when furosemide is used, and the possibility of small bowel lesions from coated tablets of potassium salts should be kept in mind.

Ethacrynic acid, U.S.P. (Edecrin)

$$CH_3-CH_2-\underset{\underset{CH_2}{\parallel}}{\overset{\overset{O}{\parallel}}{C}}-C \left\langle \begin{array}{c} Cl \quad Cl \\ \end{array} \right\rangle -OCH_2COOH$$

Ethacrynic acid is also a new powerful diuretic. Like furosemide, it is more powerful than the thiazides, but its usefulness will probably be more limited. The action of ethacrynic acid is of short duration. However, it is so powerful that excessive diuresis with marked loss of water and salt can result from its use.

Uses. Patients with congestive heart failure who are unresponsive to other diuretics may respond to ethacrynic acid. Acute pulmonary edema caused by heart failure may also respond to the intravenous administration of the drug. The drug has also been used successfully in renal edema in patients with nephrotic syndrome and for the removal of ascites in hepatic cirrhosis.

Preparation, dosage, and administration. Ethacrynic acid is supplied in capsule-shaped tablets of 25 and 50 mg. Injectable Lyovac Sodium Edecrin is available in vials containing sodium ethacrynate equivalent to 50 mg. of ethacrynic acid for intravenous use.

Dosage must be regulated carefully to prevent an excessive loss of water and electrolytes. The smallest effective dose is determined by administering 50 mg. after a meal the first day, 50 mg. twice daily the second day, and 100 mg. in the morning and 50 to 100 mg. in the evening the third day. Onset of diuresis usually occurs at 50 to 100 mg. for adults.

When intravenous use is indicated, Lyovac Sodium Edecrin is injected in the average adult dose of 50 mg. The drug should not be given subcutaneously or intramuscularly because of local pain and irritation.

Side effects and toxic effects. Ethacrynic acid is contraindicated in anuria or increasing oliguria and azotemia. Severe diarrhea may be produced in some patients, in which case the administration of the drug should be stopped. Severe loss of water and electrolytes, hepatic coma in cirrhotic patients, weakness, loss of appetite, tetany, hyperuricemia, dizziness, skin rash, and hypokalemia constitute some of the additional reasons why ethacrynic acid should be used only under very close medical supervision. A few deaths have occurred following its use. These were probably caused by acute hypokalemia in cardiac patients who had been taking digitalis at the same time or in cirrhotic patients who developed hepatic coma.

■ Diuretics that act indirectly

Drugs that cause diuresis by decreasing sodium reabsorption through indirect mechanisms include the osmotic diuretics and inhibitors of aldosterone secretion. The antialdosterone drugs are still in the experimental stage.

Antialdosterone compounds
Spironolactone, U.S.P., B.P. (Aldactone A)

Spironolactone is a diuretic that acts by blocking certain effects of the adrenocortical hormone, aldosterone. This hormone is known to promote the retention of sodium and the excretion of potassium. Spironolactone, by blocking the effects of aldosterone, brings about the excretion of sodium and chloride and the retention of potassium. Excretion of water, of course, accompanies the excretion of sodium and chloride. Thus, this agent promotes diuresis and also helps to counteract the loss of potassium when administered with other diuretics such as chlorothiazide or one of the mercurials. The latter drugs block reabsorption in the proximal part of the renal tubule, whereas spironolactone inhibits reabsorption in the distal tubule; a type of synergism is produced.

Spironolactone is said to be particularly effective in promoting diuresis in patients who are more or less resistant to the usual diuretics. It is employed in the management of edema associated with cirrhosis of the liver (ascites), congestive heart failure, and the nephrotic syndrome. Edematous conditions that do not respond to the administration of spironolactone or to a combination of this drug and another diuretic sometimes respond favorably when one of the glucocorticoids is added to the therapeutic regimen. This is because certain glucocorticoids are capable of diuretic effects in certain patients. Their action is believed to be either a direct one on the kidney or an indirect action

on the pituitary gland, where they inhibit the secretion of antidiuretic hormone. In treatment of patients with nephrotic syndrome the physician may try one of the glucocorticoids first, and if the response is not satisfactory, he will prescribe spironolactone alone or in combination with another diuretic.

Spironolactone is said to have an antihypertensive effect similar to that produced by chlorothiazide, but its value in the treatment of hypertension has not been well established.

One of the disadvantages of spironolactone is that it is poorly absorbed from the gastrointestinal tract; furthermore, it is expensive.

Preparation, dosage, and administration. Spironolactone is administered orally. It is marketed in 25-mg. tablets, and the initial dose is usually 100 mg. in four divided doses daily. Its full effect cannot be evaluated for several days because of its slow onset of action.

Side effects and toxic effects. Although spironolactone is not considered a toxic drug, serious electrolyte imbalance has been known to occur. Skin rash, drowsiness, and ataxia have been reported. The drug is not thought to be toxic to the normal liver and kidney, but stupor and coma have been known to develop in persons with severe disease of the liver. It is not recommended for patients with severe renal disorder.

Triamterene, U.S.P. (Dyrenium)

Although triamterene is not a very powerful diuretic and not a specific aldosterone antagonist, it is occasionally used for purposes similar to the spironolactones. The drug potentiates other diuretics and causes the increased elimination of sodium but does not cause a loss of potassium. For that reason triamterene is used sometimes in combination with the thiazides. The usual dose is 150 to 200 mg. by mouth daily.

211

Table 11-3 Action and effects of urinary
excretion of various diuretics

Diuretic agent	Onset of diuresis (hours)	Peak action (hours)	Duration of action (hours)	Effects on excretion*			
				Na^+	K^+	Cl^-	HCO_3^-
Mercurials	1 to 3	6 to 9	12 to 24	↑	↓	↑	—
Thiazides	2	4 to 6	12 to 24	↑	↑	↑	↑
Ethacrynic acid	½ to 1	2 to 4	6 to 8	↑	↑	↑	—
Furosemide	½ to 1	2 to 4	6 to 8	↑	↑	↑	↑
Acetazolamine	½	2	12	↑	↑	—	↑
Spironolactone	Gradual	72	48 to 72	↑	↓	—	↑
Triamterene	2	4 to 6	12 to 24	↑	↓	—	↑

* ↑, Increased; ↓, decreased; —, no change.

Osmotic diuretics

Substances exerting an osmotic pressure that is additive to that of the solutes already present in tubular fluid cause a reduction in sodium chloride and water reabsorption and increased water excretion. When the amount of any solute delivered to the tubules exceeds tubular reabsorptive capacity, diuresis will occur. The body attempts to compensate for high concentrations of solute through dilution so that equal concentrations of solute will exist on both sides of the cell membrane. It is a physiologic principle that fluids flow from areas of less concentration to areas of higher concentrations. Potassium, urea, glucose, and sucrose may be used for osmotic diuresis.

Osmotic diuretics are rarely used today. They are not very effective agents for increasing sodium excretion and must often be given in very large amounts.

Potassium salts

The diuretic action of potassium salts is the result of competition in the distal tubule to exchange potassium ions for sodium ions, resulting in increased excretion of sodium and water. Potassium salts also appear to dilate renal blood vessels, which increases renal blood flow.

They should be administered only when renal function is normal. Potassium salts can produce toxic effects if the function of the kidney is impaired and the daily urinary volume is low (less than 500 ml.).

Potassium chloride, U.S.P., B.P.; *potassium nitrate,* B.P. These are the preparations used, although the bicarbonate, citrate, and acetate salts of potassium are also used. The usual dosage is 1 Gm. several times a day, given orally during or just after meals. Enteric-coated tablets or capsules decrease the incidence of gastric irritation. These preparations, however, have fallen into disuse with the advent of newer and better diuretics.

Small bowel lesions leading to obstruction, hemorrhage, and perforation have occurred in patients who have been taking enteric-coated potassium chloride tablets and capsules. Although some of these patients have been receiving thiazide diuretics also, it is believed that the bowel lesions are caused by the irritant effect of the highly concentrated potassium salt.

Urea, U.S.P., B.P. (Carbamide)

Urea, though normally present in body fluids, serves as an osmotic diuretic when given in sufficiently large amounts. In a person with normal kidneys it is rapidly eliminated and is not toxic. It should not be administered when there is renal disease characterized by retention of nitrogen. Since a large amount of it is not reabsorbed by the tubular cells it prevents the reabsorption of a proportional amount of water.

At present, urea is not widely used because of the large dosage, bitter taste, and its ineffectiveness in terms of net sodium removal.

Sterile preparations are available, from which solutions can be prepared for intravenous administration. The dosage is 0.1 to 1 Gm. per kilogram of body weight.

Glucose and sucrose

Glucose, when given in quantity sufficient to exceed the renal threshold for this substance, is excreted into the urine and results in increased excretion of water and, to a lesser degree, sodium and chloride. To bring about this effect the glucose in the blood must be increased significantly and, in general, the route of administration must be intravenous. The usual dose is 50 ml. of a 50% solution.

Sucrose solution also acts as an osmotic diuretic, and in some ways it is more efficient than glucose. It is little used, however, because it can cause severe renal damage (sucrose nephrosis). When given directly into the bloodstream its form is too complex to be utilized by the tissues and the kidney excretes it as a foreign substance with little or no reabsorption in the tubule. It exerts osmotic effects similar to those produced by glucose. Since so little is reabsorbed in the tubule, its effects are greater than those of glucose.

Mannitol, U.S.P., B.P. (Osmitrol)

Mannitol is a sugar alcohol that occurs naturally in a number of plants and fungi. It is also synthesized. Since mannitol is not reabsorbed by the tubules, it is excreted along with the water that is bound to it. It is considered to be the most effective osmotic diuretic. Mannitol is also used to test kidney function.

Mannitol is used for its diuretic action to relieve cerebral and other forms of edema, for treatment of oliguria resulting from transfusion reactions and accidents, and to promote excretion of toxic substances resulting from overdosage of sedatives.

Preparation, dosage, and administration. Mannitol is available in 5%, 10%, and 20% solutions in bottles of 250, 500, and 1000 ml. for intravenous injection. The adult dosage is 50 to 200 Gm. infused over 24 hours. Dosage must be regulated according to the patient's fluid and electrolyte balance, urinary output, and clinical signs.

Side effects. Side effects include headache, nausea, chills, mild chest pain, and low sodium and chloride blood levels. Fatal convulsions have also been reported.

Precautions. Mannitol should not be given to patients with severe congestive heart failure or to patients with edema associated with capillary fragility or membrane permeability. Its use in patients with impaired renal function should be preceded by administration of a test dose of 200 mg. per kilogram of body weight over a period of 3 to 5 minutes. Mannitol may be given if the patient produces 40 ml. or more of urine within 1 hour.

■ Diuretics that increase glomerular filtration of sodium

Agents that increase glomerular filtration of sodium include the acid-forming salts and the plasma expanders. The latter act by increasing plasma colloid osmotic pressure, which mobilizes edema fluid and promotes diuresis. Only the acid-forming salts will be discussed here.

Acid-forming salts

Diuretics that produce acidosis exert only transient action. The acidifying diuretics are chiefly ammonium chloride, ammonium nitrate, and calcium chloride. Of these, only ammonium chloride continues to be used with any regularity.

Ammonium chloride, U.S.P., B.P.

Action. After absorption, the ammonium portion of the compound is converted in the liver to urea with the liberation of hydrogen ions and chloride ions. Neutralization of the hydrogen ions is accomplished by a shift in the buffer system $\dfrac{H_2CO_3}{BHCO_3}$, with a compensatory loss of carbon dioxide via the lungs and a loss of available base to the excess of chloride ions. A state of acidosis results.

The number of chloride ions reaching the renal tubules is greatly increased, causing an increase in the urinary loss of chloride with an equivalent amount of cation (chiefly sodium) and water. By achieving a net loss of water and electrolytes (sodium chloride), ammonium chloride promotes the movement and excretion of edema fluid.

The action of ammonium chloride would soon deplete the body of sodium were it not for several compensatory mechanisms that effect a return to a state of equilibrium. The diuretic effect of this compound is therefore greatest during the first day or two of administration. The principal compensatory mechanisms include increased renal excretion of cations (hydrogen and potassium) and the formation of ammonia by the renal cells with the recovery of corresponding amounts of sodium ions.

Preparation, dosage, and administration. Ammonium chloride is available in 0.5-Gm. enteric-coated tablets or capsules for oral administration. The dose varies, although 8 to 12 Gm. is sometimes given daily in divided doses. It may cause gastric irritation, nausea, and vomiting. It should not be used if renal function is seriously impaired because of the danger of causing uncompensated acidosis. The chief value of ammonium chloride as a diuretic is observed when it is used in combination with the mercurial diuretics.

Nondiuretic agents that affect diuresis

Cation exchange resins

Cation exchange resins are occasionally used in the management of sodium retention associated with chronic heart failure, cirrhosis of the liver, and nephrosis. They are used to remove sodium from food, and they cause sodium to be eliminated from the gastrointestinal tract, which prevents its absorption. Use of these exchange resins appeals to patients whose diet must be low in salt or salt free. Prevention of absorption of sodium can result in considerable loss of edema fluid. Unfortunately, potassium and calcium ions may be removed as well as sodium.

This can result in potassium and calcium deficiencies unless suitable precautions are taken. The patients who receive these drugs should be watched for constipation. Some will object to the disagreeable texture of these substances or to the gastric distress that may follow the taking of large doses. These resins may supplement the action of mercurial diuretics in the treatment of recurring edema, but they are not intended to supplant the use of them.

Water

Water is a physiologic diuretic. Fluid intake is frequently forced to increase urine output. The barrier to water reabsorption presented by the tubule cells appears to be related to the concentration of the posterior pituitary secretions in the blood. When fluid intake is increased, posterior pituitary activity is decreased, less water is removed from the urine, and diuresis results. Water is not a diuretic in the sense that it causes the excretion of edema fluid from the tissues. It frequently is considered unnecessary to restrict fluids for edematous patients, provided there is a restriction placed on intake of sodium.

Drugs that act on the bladder

Disturbance of bladder function as seen in hospitalized patients frequently results from one of two causes. Either the patient's bladder has too much muscle tone or too little. If the bladder is hypertonic and irritable, the emptying reflex is stimulated very easily and the bladder feels full although it really has not filled to anywhere near its normal capacity. The patient then has symptoms of frequency of urination, and voiding may be accompanied by painful contractions. In such instances derivatives of belladonna are more effective than the opiates. Hyoscyamus tincture is sometimes the preparation of choice. It acts like other belladonna derivatives to relax the hypertonic muscle of the bladder. When the bladder is lacking in muscle tone, the patient is often unable to empty the organ completely, and this condition may predispose the patient to the development of infection, particularly when he is catheterized. Neostigmine and bethanechol chloride have been used to improve the atonic condition, encourage micturition, and eliminate the need for catheterization.

Urinary antiseptics

Urinary antiseptics are substances that, when given by mouth or other suitable channel, exert antibacterial activity in the urine or urinary tract with little or no systemic antibacterial effect. Present-day urinary antiseptics of choice include some of the older drugs such as methenamine and mandelic acid, either alone or in combination, as well as a number of sulfonamides and antibiotics. The selection of one of these preparations in preference to another is made on the basis of identification of the pathogens by Gram's stain or by urine culture in the severe, recurrent, or chronic infections. The relative cost of antibacterial agents, too, is worthy of consideration, especially when the infection is mild. The cost of a sulfonamide is much less for the patient than the cost of tetracycline, penicillin, or nitrofurantoin. Many physicians advocate the treatment of a urinary infection for at least a week after symptoms have subsided or the results of cultures have become negative. No available drug will inhibit or destroy all the organisms that cause urinary infections. Each of the agents used has its own bacterial spectrum against which it is effective. Some infections subside without specific therapy. General measures of importance are rest and a fluid intake that will result in at least 2000 ml. of urinary output daily.

Specific organisms that may be found in the urinary tract

The most common organisms found in the urinary tract are gram-negative bacilli and of this group *Escherichia coli* is found to be responsible for many of the infections. *Aerobacter aerogenes* is also frequently found, as well as the organisms of the genera *Proteus* and *Pseudomonas*. Since these are often regarded as contaminants, strict aseptic technique assumes a role of major importance in the examination or treatment of disorders of the urinary tract. The most commonly found coccus in urinary tract infections is *Streptococcus faecalis,* which is an enterococcus commonly found in the large bowel. *Staphylococcus aureus* is the next most commonly found coccus. Hemolytic streptococci are found only occasionally.

There appears to have been a decided change in the bacterial flora of urinary tract infections since the introduction of some of the newer antiseptics. *Aerobacter aerogenes* and *Pseudomonas aeruginosa* seem to be isolated with greater frequency. As the surviving strains, they may be responsible for a higher percentage of infections as the more susceptible strains are destroyed.

Sulfonamides

Sulfonamides are often effective against gram-negative bacilli that infect the urinary tract, although the incidence of resistant strains has increased in recent years. Sulfonamides may also be effective against gram-positive cocci such as *Staphylococcus aureus* but are usually ineffective against *Streptococcus faecalis.* Sulfonamides are easily administered since they can be given orally. In a small percentage of patients this route of administration may not be possible, in which case the sodium salt of a sulfonamide may be given intravenously. The sulfonamides are discussed in greater detail in Chapter 28.

Sulfisoxazole, U.S.P. (Gantrisin). This is an effective chemotherapeutic agent that, because of its high solubility in body fluids (including acid urine), is less likely to cause crystalluria and renal blocking than some of the less-soluble sulfonamides employed singly. In other respects it is potentially as toxic as other drugs of this group. When used as a urinary antiseptic, forcing of fluids or alkalinization of the urine is not thought to be essential, although the output of fluid should be within the normal range. The initial dose may be as high as 4 Gm. followed by 0.5 to 1 Gm. every 4 to 6 hours.

Sulfamethoxypyridazine, B.P. (Kynex, Midicel). This agent is readily absorbed after oral administration, but it is eliminated slowly. It is available in 500-mg. tablets. The usual adult dose is 0.5 Gm. daily.

Sulfacetamide, N.F. (Sulamyd). This compound has the advantage of a high degree of solubility in urine, even when it is acid in reaction. The likelihood of crystalluria is therefore reduced to a minimum. Sulfacetamide is excreted rapidly, exhibits good antibacterial activity, and is, in general, of a low level of toxicity. The dosage is the same as that for sulfisoxazole. This dosage rarely produces toxic symptoms.

Sulfadimethoxine, N.F. (Madribon). This drug has properties and uses very similar to those of sulfamethoxypyridazine.

Acetyl sulfamethoxypyridazine (Kynex Acetyl); acetyl sulfisoxazole (Gantrisin Acetyl, Lipo-Gantrisin Acetyl). These are similar to the parent sulfonamides except that they are tasteless and therefore are more suitable for pediatric preparations.

Nalidixic acid, N.F. (NegGram)

Nalidixic acid is a urinary antiseptic chemically unrelated to other antimicrobial agents. Since it is rapidly excreted in the urine, the drug is effective when administered orally.

It is bacteriostatic or bactericidal against many gram-negative bacteria, especially those caused by strains of *Proteus*. It is not effective against most strains of *Pseudomonas* or enterococci. Its effectiveness is the result of its inhibition of DNA synthesis.

Preparation, dosage, and administration. Nalidixic acid is available in 250- and 500-mg. tablets for oral administration. The usual adult range of dose is 0.5 to 1 Gm. four times daily. Maximal doses are usually given during initiation of therapy to minimize development of bacterial resistance, which may develop within 48 hours. Dosage for children is about 50 mg. per kilogram of body weight in divided doses.

Adverse effects. Among adverse effects are gastrointestinal disturbances and pruritus. Rashes and neurologic disturbances (confusion or convulsions) are infrequent. The drug should not be given to epileptics.

Antibiotics

A number of systemic antibiotics may be used to treat urinary tract infections. These are discussed in Chapter 29.

Methenamine mandelate, U.S.P. (Mandelamine)

Methenamine mandelate combines the action of methenamine and mandelic acid and is used for treatment of infections of the urinary tract caused by most of the common urinary tract pathogens. Methenamine owes its antiseptic action to the formaldehyde that it yields in the presence of free acid. It is effective only in acid urine; therefore, the administration of an acid-forming agent such as ammonium chloride may be necessary to produce the proper urinary pH. Methenamine mandelate is sometimes effective against organisms that have developed resistance to other agents. Microorganisms do not acquire resistance to this antiseptic.

Uses. It is useful in the treatment of pyelitis, pyelonephritis, and cystitis.

Preparation, dosage, and administration. Methenamine mandelate is available in 250- and 500-mg. tablets and as a suspension, 50 mg. per milliliter, for oral administration. The average initial dose is 1 to 1.5 Gm. four times a day. Dosage thereafter is usually 0.5 to 1.0 Gm. three times a day.

Side effects and toxic effects. When the drug is given in therapeutic amounts, gastric disturbance and other toxic effects rarely occur.

Contraindications. It is contraindicated for patients with renal insufficiency.

Nitrofurantoin, U.S.P., B.P. (Furadantin)

Nitrofurantoin is a nitrofuran derivative and is chemically related to nitrofurazone. It is a yellow bitter-tasting powder.

Action and result. Nitrofurantoin exhibits antibacterial activity against a wide range of both gram-negative and gram-positive microorganisms. It is both bacteriostatic and bactericidal to many strains of *Staphylococcus (albus* and *aureus), Streptococcus pyogenes, Escherichia coli, Aerobacter aerogenes,* and *Paracolobactrum* species. It is less effective against *Proteus vulgaris, Alcaligenes faecalis, Pseudomonas aeruginosa,* and *Corynebacterium* species. It has no effect on viruses and fungi.

Uses. Nitrofurantoin is used in the treatment of bacterial infections of the urinary tract caused by microorganisms sensitive to the drug. It is rapidly and completely absorbed from the intestinal tract and hence has little effect on the intestinal flora. About 40% to 50% of the drug is excreted unchanged in the urine and with sufficient rapidity to require administration at intervals of 4 to 6 hours. Much of the remainder of the drug is changed in the body tissues to inactive compounds that have a brownish color. These compounds may cause the urine to be tinted.

Preparation, dosage, and administration. Nitrofurantoin is available in 50- and 100-mg. tablets and as a suspension, 5 mg. per milliliter, for oral administration. This drug is also available for intravenous injection. The average total daily dose is 5 to 8 mg. per kilogram of body weight. The total daily dose should be divided into four equal doses and given after meals and at bedtime with some food to minimize the possibility of nausea. Some physicians prescribe this drug in doses of 100 mg. four times a day for adults. Administration of the drug should be continued at least 3 days after the urine has become sterile. Large doses may be required for refractory infections.

Side effects and toxic effects. Nitrofurantoin has a low level of toxicity. It occasionally causes nausea and vomiting, and an occasional case of sensitization has been observed. The low dosage required for an effective urinary concentration is not associated with a noticeable amount of the drug in the blood. The two advantages of the drug as a urinary antiseptic are (1) its high solubility in urine even when the urine is acid and (2) the small dosage required. Both of these factors operate to minimize the likelihood that the drug will precipitate out of solution and cause crystalluria in the kidney.

Contraindications. It is not recommended for patients with anuria, oliguria, or severe renal damage.

Phenazopyridine hydrochloride (Pyridium)

Phenazopyridine is an azo dye that occurs as a fine crystalline red powder. It is slowly soluble in cold water but is readily soluble in hot water, in alcohol, and in glycerin. It was used at one time as a urinary antiseptic, but now it is used more for the analgesic effect it produces on the urinary mucosa. It is used to bring about relief of symptoms such as urgency and frequency of micturition. It is also used to achieve preoperative and postoperative surface analgesia in urologic surgical procedures and after diagnostic tests in which instrumentation has been necessary. It is sometimes given to patients who experience discomfort from a retention catheter.

It causes the urine to be orange or red in color, and patients should be informed of this so they do not become alarmed.

Preparation, dosage, and administration. Phenazopyridine hydrochloride is available in 100-mg. tablets for oral administration. The usual adult dose is one to two tablets three times a day before meals.

Side effects and toxic effects. Patients occasionally exhibit symptoms of sensitivity.

Contraindications. Its use for patients with diminished renal function or severe hepatitis is not recommended.

■ Nursing measures for patients receiving diuretic therapy

It is important that patients receiving diuretic therapy be placed on recorded intake and output. If the patient is ambulatory or has bathroom privileges, he can be instructed in maintaining daily records of his intake and output.

A weight record should also be maintained on these patients if at all possible. Weight should be recorded prior to and during therapy. Daily weight may be required during the first few days of therapy. Thereafter it may be sufficient to record the weight only once or twice weekly.

When giving care to patients who tend to develop edema, the nurse should examine those areas most susceptible to edema formation because of gravitational forces and dependency (sacral, ankle, and pedal tissue) for increase in tissue fluid (swelling or pitting). Signs of increased tissue fluid and gain in weight may indicate the development of refractoriness or tolerance to therapy. Diuretics should be administered early in the day to avoid nocturnal diuresis and disturbance of sleep patterns.

Nurses should remember that the most common toxic response to diuretic therapy is systemic acidosis, which results from excessive elimination of sodium and potassium. To avoid undue potassium loss, patients on diuretic therapy may be instructed to increase dietary intake of potassium. Foods high in potassium include oranges, tomatoes, grapefruit juice, and whole milk. Many other foods are high in potassium and are listed in most hospital or clinic diet manuals.

Questions

for study and review

1 Explain the important nursing care aspects for patients on diuretic therapy.
2 How do plasma expanders mobilize edema fluid and promote diuresis?
3 What aspects of nursing intervention can be used by the nurse to prevent or inhibit urinary tract infections?
4 Explain how antialdosterone compounds promote diuresis.
5 Explain the need for caution when diuretics are administered to patients receiving digitalis preparations.

Multiple choice

6 As much as 90% of the glomerular filtrate is reabsorbed in the:
   a. loop of Henle
   b. proximal convoluted tubule
   c. distal convoluted tubule
   d. collecting tubule
7 Which of the following statements about diuretics are *incorrect?*
   a. Mercurial diuretics are more potent than the thiazides in increasing sodium excretion.
   b. Tolerance to xanthine diuretics develops with repeated dosages.
   c. The combined use of diuretics and digitalis may precipitate digitalis toxicity.
   d. Mannitol exerts its diuretic effects by being reabsorbed by the kidney tubules and attracting fluid from the tissues.
8 Which of the following statements about mercurial diuretics are correct?
   a. Their diuretic effect is the result of inhibiting proximal tubular reabsorption.
   b. During mercurial diuresis the urine contains more chloride than sodium, which may cause alkalosis.
   c. They increase the flow of urine by increasing filtration pressure.
   d. Most mercurials are combined with theophylline to promote absorption of injectable mercurials.
9 Toxic reactions to mercurials do not include which of the following?
   a. renal damage   c. stomatitis
   b. hypertension   d. ventricular arrhythmias
10 After parenteral administration of an organic mercurial diuretic to an edematous patient, peak effects can be expected in:
   a. 1 to 2 hours   c. 6 to 8 hours
   b. 3 to 4 hours   d. 12 to 18 hours
11 Xanthine diuretics:
   a. increase renal blood flow
   b. improve urine output by a stimulating effect on the heart, which improves cardiac output
   c. cause diuresis by inhibiting tubular reabsorption
   d. are more effective than mercurial diuretics
12 The diuretic action of the thiazides:
   a. is not influenced by changes in the acid-base balance
   b. is not primarily the result of carbonic anhydrase inhibition
   c. does not account for their antihypertensive effects
   d. promotes the excretion of equal amounts of sodium and chloride
13 The antidiuretic hormone exerts its action on the:
   a. bladder   c. glomerulus
   b. proximal tubule d. distal tubule
14 Which of the following factors is likely to receive priority in selecting a drug for a severe urinary infection?
   a. cost of the urinary antiseptic
   b. sensitivity of infecting organism to the drug
   c. ease of administration
   d. side effects

References

Baer, J. E., and Beyer, K. H.: Renal pharmacology, Ann. Rev. Pharmacol. **6**:261, 1966.

Beyer, K. H.: The mechanism of action of chlorothiazide, Ann. N. Y. Acad. Sci. **71**:363, 1958.

Beyer, K. H., and Baer, J. E.: Physiological basis for the action of newer diuretics, Pharmacol. Rev. **13**:517, 1961.

Earley, L. E.: Diuretics, New Eng. J. Med. **276**:966, 1967.

Earley, L. E., and Friedler, R. M.: Renal tubular effects of ethacrynic acid, J. Clin. Invest. **43**:1495, 1968.

Earley, L. E., and Orloff, J.: Thiazide diuretics, Ann. Rev. Med. **15**:149, 1964.

Friedberg, C. K., editor: Heart, kidney and electrolytes, Progr. Cardiov. Dis. **3**:395; **4**:1, 1961.

Garrod, L. P., and O'Grady, F. O.: Antibiotic and chemotherapy, ed. 3, Baltimore, 1971, The Williams & Wilkins Co.

Goodman, L., and Gilman, A., editors: The pharmacological basis of therapeutics, ed. 4, New York, 1970, The Macmillan Company.

Hagedorn, C. W., Kaplan, A. A., and Hulet, W. H.: Prolonged administration of ethacrynic acid in patients with renal disease, New Eng. J. Med. **272**:1152, 1965.

Laragh, J. H., and others: Physiologic and clinical observations in furosemide and ethacrynic acid, Ann. N. Y. Acad. Sci. **139**:453, 1966.

Levitt, M. F., and Goldstein, M. H.: Mercurial diuretics, Bull. N. Y. Acad. Med. **38**:249, 1962.

Liddle, G. W.: Aldosterone antagonists and triamterene, Ann. N. Y. Acad. Sci. **139**:466, 1966.

Milne, M. D.: Renal pharmacology, Ann. Rev. Pharmacol. **5**:119, 1965.

Mudge, G. H.: Renal pharmacology, Ann. Rev. Pharmacol. **7**:163, 1967.

Nash, H. L., and others: Cardiorenal hemodynamic effects of ethacrynic acid, Amer. Heart J. **71**:153, 1966.

Pitts, R. F.: The physiological basis of diuretic therapy, Springfield, Ill., 1959, Charles C Thomas, Publisher.

Ramos, B., Rivera, A., and Pena, J. C.: Mechanism of the antidiuretic effect of saluretic drugs, Clin. Pharmacol. Therap. **8**:557, 1967.

Saxena, K. M., and Crawford, J. D.: Current concepts: the treatment of nephrosis, New Eng. J. Med. **272**:522, 1965.

Seneca, H., and Peer, P.: Drug susceptibility of pathogens of the urinary tract system: changing patterns, Surgery **60**:652, 1966.

Smith, L. H., and Martin, W. J.: Infections of the urinary tract, Med. Clin. N. Amer. **50**:1127, 1966.

Stahl, W. M.: Effect of mannitol on the kidney: changes in intrarenal hemodynamics, New Eng. J. Med. **272**:381, 1965.

Walker, W. G.: The clinical use of furosemide and ethacrynic acid, Med. Clin. N. Amer. **51**:1277, 1967.

Walker, W. G.: Indications and contraindications for diuretic therapy, Ann. N. Y. Acad. Sci. **139**:481-496, 1966.

12

Histamine and antihistaminics

Histamine

Histamine-antagonizing drugs

■Histamine

Histamine is the enigma of pharmacology. Although it is widely distributed throughout the body with high concentrations in the lungs, skin, and stomach, its role in normal physiology remains a mystery. Histamine means "tissue amine." It was isolated from extracts of ergot in 1910 and firmly established as a natural body substance in 1927. When liberated from binding sites it causes untoward reactions that range in intensity from mild itching to angioneurotic edema, shock, and death. There is some evidence that histamine has some function in anaphylaxis, allergies, drug reactions, and inflammatory processes. It is possible that histamine is important to anabolic events such as growth and repair, for it is found wherever there is protein breakdown or putrefaction.

Histamine release

Histamine release can provoke allergic responses and troublesome side effects, and health professionals should know which substances are most commonly implicated in this phenomenon. Histamine-releasing agents can be classified into seven groups.

1 Antigens and substances that combine with proteins to form antigens and provoke formation of antibodies. The antigen-antibody reaction releases histamine (and other substances) from sensitized tissue, giving rise to an "altered response" or allergic reaction—asthma, hay fever, urticaria. Antigens are also known as allergens and include pollens and food, particularly dietary protein such as eggs, milk, shellfish, and fresh berries.
2 Proteolytic enzymes such as trypsin and penicillinase
3 Surface-active agents such as detergents and bile salts
4 Monamines
5 High molecular weight compounds such as the plasma expanders and dextrans
6 Mechanical and chemical trauma to the skin: abrasion, laceration, wasp and bee stings, snake venom, plant poisons (poison ivy, poison oak), or toxins
7 Drugs that are histamine liberators—that "explosively" release histamine

Histamine phosphate, U.S.P., B.P.

$$H-C{=\!=\!=}C-CH_2-CH-COOH \longrightarrow H-C{=\!=\!=}C-CH_2-CH_2 + CO_2$$

Histidine   Histamine

Histamine, like epinephrine, norepinephrine, and 5-hydroxytryptamine, is a compound of pharmacologic and physiologic interest, since, in contrast to most drugs, it occurs naturally in the body. Like the other natural-body constituents just named it is an amine possessing the basic group NH_2. Histamine is derived from the amino acid histadine by the removal of the carboxyl group as carbon dioxide—a reaction that takes place in body cells and intestinal contents.

Histamine's interest to medicine is multiple; the compound itself can be used to produce certain pharmacologic effects employed chiefly for diagnostic tests. Much more important than this use, however, is the fact that certain compounds that prevent the pharmacologic action of histamine (histamine antagonists, antihistaminics) have very useful effects, including the prevention or relief of allergic symptoms and motion sickness.

Action and result. The principal actions of histamine are: (1) contraction of smooth muscle, (2) dilation of capillaries, and (3) promotion of gastric acid secretion. In man a noticeable dilation of the arterioles also occurs.

An intradermal injection of histamine causes a series of reactions called the "triple response." Blood vessels (capillaries) immediately affected by the histamine dilate and produce a *flush* or redness. Surrounding blood vessels then dilate to produce a *flare* or diffuse redness. This reaction is probably the result of a neural mechanism—axon reflexes stimulate sensory nerves and their branches to produce dilatation of blood vessels. Widely dilated blood vessels have increased permeability. There is an increase in tissue fluid or local edema, which is termed a *wheal*. Any chemical or mechanical injury to the skin can cause this triple response of flush, flare, and wheal. Therefore, it is believed that histamine is released from injured skin. The triple response is believed to be one of the body's protective mechanisms, since increased permeability of blood vessels permits the passage of plasma proteins and white cells into the tissues.

The marked dilation of the arterioles and capillaries by histamine produces a definite flushing of the skin, a rise in skin temperature, an itching or burning sensation, and a fall in blood pressure. Vasodilation in the meningeal vessels is accompanied by an increase in intracranial pressure, which may cause headache. The fall in blood pressure after small doses of histamine is followed by rather quick recovery, caused by the release of epinephrine and the activity of cardiovascular reflexes.

A marked fall in blood pressure may follow a large dose of histamine, and the same vascular changes that take place in surgical shock may occur. The permeability of capillary beds increases, and sufficient blood proteins are lost to the tissues so that blood volume cannot be maintained and circulation is slowed. While an increase in cardiac rate and output occur after injection of histamine, this is mainly reflexly induced by the fall in blood pressure.

Uterine and intestinal muscle is stimulated, as well as the smooth muscle of the bronchial tubes. Bronchospasm may be induced in man after large doses of the drug, especially if the patient suffers from chronic conditions of the respiratory tract, such as asthma and bronchitis.

Histamine stimulates the gastric, salivary, pancreatic, and lacrimal glands. The chief effect in man, however, is seen in the gastric glands. The resulting secretion in the normal stomach is high in acid because of the selective action on the acid-forming cells.

Some investigators maintain that histamine is liberated in the body in large amounts as a result of extensive tissue damage or of antigen-antibody reactions. Attempts to demonstrate that histamine tolerance can be achieved by desensitization of the patient have been inconclusive.

Because the symptoms of acute histamine poisoning and those of anaphylactic shock are quite similar, it was suggested long ago that acute allergic reactions (resulting from the exposure of a sensitive individual to an antigen) resulted in the release of histamine. Since then it has been found that when allergic shock is produced either in the whole animal or in an isolated organ (such as the guinea pig uterus), histamine is released. The thesis is now well accepted that abnormal release of histamine from

221

storage sites accompanies acute allergic reactions, both mild and severe, and accounts for at least some of the changes observed in the patient. A further convincing finding has been that antihistaminics can modify and significantly lessen the picture of an acute allergic reaction.

Wasp, bee, and snake venom, gnats, and plant poisons contain histamine that can cause the triple response in man. Other agents known to release histamine are detergents and surface-active agents, trypsin and proteolytic enzymes, and basic protein substances such as amines. Many drugs are histamine liberators that may be responsible for side effects; examples are morphine and codeine. Certain foods are potent histamine releasers, for example, fresh berries, shellfish, and eggs.

Ordinarily, histamine is altered in the body partly by methylation and by the enzyme diamine oxidase, which converts histamine to imidazole-acetic acid. Diamine oxidase is present in greatest amounts in the intestinal mucosa and kidney. It acts slowly to inactivate histamine.

Uses. Histamine is rarely used therapeutically but has occasionally been used for diagnostic purposes.

One diagnostic use is concerned with gastric acid production. Histamine is a potent stimulus to the secretion of gastric hydrochloric acid, and there is some evidence suggesting that it may be the natural trigger that starts the secretion of hydrochloric acid. Accordingly, it can be used to reveal the absence of gastric acid (achlorhydria), a diagnostic aid for certain anemias. If a patient does not respond with a significant secretion of gastric acid to the challenge of a small dose of histamine, it is likely that he cannot make gastric acid. This is believed to be caused by a degenerative change in the gastric mucosa.

Another use is in the diagnosis of pheochromocytoma. Tumors of the medullary portion of the adrenal gland that secrete epinephrine and norepinephrine are uncommon, but their discovery is important since they represent one type of hypertension that can be permanently cured by surgery. Small doses of histamine stimulate the secretion of the adrenal medulla; in the normal individual the pressor amines secreted by the adrenal gland are insufficient to produce a marked rise in blood pressure, but in the patient with pheochromocytoma histamine may lead to a very prominent secretion of medullary amines with a resultant striking rise in blood pressure. The histamine test is one of several "pharmacologic" provocative tests for pheochromocytoma.

Histamine may also be used to test the capacity of capillaries to dilate in certain peripheral vascular diseases.

Preparation, dosage, and administration. Prior to the test for gastric acid production the patient should have fasted and rested for 12 hours. A gastric tube is inserted and the gastric contents are aspirated. The patient may then be given 300 ml. of water. The histamine is injected subcutaneously; the dose is usually 0.25 to 0.5 mg. of histamine in the form of a 1:1000 solution. Pulse and blood pressure should be taken immediately after injection; the usual response is increased pulse rate and slightly decreased blood pressure. Observations for side effects should be continued during the test. Epinephrine hydrochloride 1:1000 (0.5 to 1.0 ml.) should be readily available to treat severe reactions if they occur. After injection of histamine, gastric contents are aspirated every 10 to 15 minutes for 1 hour and tested for volume, total acidity, blood, bile, and mucus. Maximum secretory response to histamine usually occurs in 30 minutes. Gastric achlorhydria after histamine injection is an essential finding in the diagnosis of pernicious anemia.

In the test for pheochromocytoma, 25 to 50 μg. of histamine is injected intravenously. The patient should be at rest and his basal blood pressure level should have been determined. Following a decrease in blood pressure within 30 seconds, if a marked rise in blood pressure occurs (60 mm. Hg systolic, 30 mm. Hg diastolic) in 1 to 4 minutes associated with symptoms of pallor, fear, sweating, and so on, the test is positive for the presence of the tumor. Blood pressure usually returns to preinjection levels within 5 to 15 minutes. Pulse rate and blood pressure must be frequently determined both during and following the test. This test is contraindicated for elderly persons or for those

Table 12-1 Histamine effects

Blood vessels	
Capillaries	Dilation, increased permeability
Arterioles	Dilation
Arteries	Dilation
Cerebral vessels	Dilation (headache)
Heart	Increased rate, indirect effect
Blood pressure	Decrease
Secretions	
Bronchial	Increase
Gastric	Definite increase
Intestinal	Slight increase
Salivary	Slight increase
Uterus	Mild contraction
Gastrointestinal tract	Contraction
Adrenal medulla	Stimulated epinephrine and norepinephrine release
Skin	Flush, flare, wheal

with marked hypertension (blood pressure in excess of 150 mm. Hg systolic and 100 mm. Hg diastolic).

Side effects and toxic effects. Symptoms of overdosage include rapid drop in blood pressure, intense headache, dyspnea, flushing of the skin, vomiting, diarrhea, shock, and collapse. The toxic symptoms are rarely dangerous, although they may be alarming. If the patient goes into shock, the blood volume may need to be restored. Epinephrine is a specific physiologic antagonist and will prevent or counteract symptoms if administered promptly.

■ Histamine-antagonizing drugs

Histamine can be antagonized by the use of drugs that: (1) produce pharmacologic effects opposed to those of histamine, of which the best example is epinephrine, and (2) in some way prevent histamine from showing its typical actions. The latter drugs are the group generally called antihistaminics.

Epinephrine

Epinephrine is a lifesaving drug in anaphylactic shock. The most serious effects of anaphylaxis (or severe acute allergic reactions) in man

are the extensive arteriolar dilatation with hypotensive shock and collapse and the marked constriction of bronchial tubes that can lead to extreme respiratory difficulty and even suffocation. By promoting vasoconstriction and by dilating the bronchial tubes epinephrine can antagonize the physiologic effects of anaphylaxis or of histamine poisoning.

Antihistaminics

Antihistaminics are believed to act not by opposing but by preventing the physiologic action of histamine. It is postulated that the antihistaminics act by preventing histamine from reaching its site of action, that is, by competition for the receptors. The first antihistaminic was found in 1933 as a result of a conscious attempt to discover a compound with this activity. Although the initial compounds were quite toxic and therefore not very useful, hundreds of antihistaminics have been synthesized and tested. Many of these compounds have similar chemical features, represented by three typical compounds:

Diphenhydramine (Benadryl)

Tripelennamine (Pyribenzamine)

Chlorpheniramine (Chlor-Trimeton)

It can be seen that a common structural feature is the short straight chain terminating in a tertiary amine, $-C-C-N\begin{smallmatrix}R'\\ \\R''\end{smallmatrix}$, and it has been suggested that this portion of the antihistaminics is an analogue of the $-C-C-NH_2$ chain of histamine.

Pharmacologically, it is known that antihistaminics block histamine action somewhat selectively. They tend to prevent the muscular (circulatory and bronchiolar) action of histamine but are not as effective against the secretory actions of histamine. For example, antihistaminics do not prevent the normal gastric acid secretory response to histamine.

During the past few years histamine antagonists of various types have been tried for histamine shock, anaphylactic reactions, and allergy. The antihistaminics have the greatest therapeutic effect on nasal allergies, particularly on seasonal hay fever. They relieve symptoms better at the beginning of the hay fever season than during its height but fail to relieve the asthma that frequently accompanies hay fever. These preparations are palliative and do not immunize the patient or protect him over a period of time against allergic reactions. Their benefits are therefore comparatively short lived and provide only symptomatic relief. They must be regarded only as adjuncts to more specific methods of treatment. They do not begin to replace such remedies as epinephrine, ephedrine, and aminophylline. In acute asthmatic reactions, the antihistaminic drugs serve only as supplements to these older remedies. Furthermore, relief of various symptoms of allergy is obtained only while the drug is being taken. It does not appear to have a cumulative action and can therefore be taken over a period of time.

One peculiar and unanticipated action of many of the antihistaminics is their ability to relieve or abolish the symptoms of motion sickness, both in animals and in man. Thus a number of anti-motion sickness agents are also potent antihistaminics. The commonly used compound dimenhydrinate, for example, is simply diphenhydramine with a different acid neutralizing the basic nitrogens of the antihistaminic itself.

The most common untoward effect of these preparations is drowsiness, which may become so marked that deep sleep may result. Other untoward symptoms include dizziness, dryness of the mouth and throat, nausea, disturbed coordination, lassitude, muscular weakness, and gastrointestinal disturbances. Sedation may disappear after 2 or 3 days of treatment. However, in some patients symptoms of excitation occur, such as insomnia, nervousness, and even convulsions.

Patients receiving these preparations for continuous treatment should have the benefit of periodic medical examinations.

Antazoline hydrochloride, B.P. (Antistine)

Antazoline hydrochloride is one of the milder antihistaminics and is less irritating to tissues than other drugs of this group. Nausea and drowsiness are the side effects most commonly encountered. The usual range of oral dosage is 50 to 100 mg. three or four times daily for adults. A 0.5% solution made with isotonic saline can be instilled in the nose or given with a nebulizer every 3 or 4 hours. Antazoline phosphate, N.F. (Antistine Phosphate) is used for ophthalmic solutions (0.5%).

Chlorcyclizine hydrochloride, N.F., B.P. (Di-Paralene Hydrochloride, Perazil)

Advantages claimed for chlorcyclizine hydrochloride are a prolonged action and low incidence of side effects. A dose of 50 mg. or more is given orally up to four times a day. Chlorcyclizine hydrochloride tablets, U.S.P., are available in 25 and 50 mg. each. It is contraindicated in pregnancy because of potential harm to the fetus.

Chlorpheniramine maleate, U.S.P., B.P. (Chlor-Trimeton Maleate, Teldrin)

This preparation produces a low incidence of side effects but compares favorably with other antihistaminics in therapeutic usefulness and does so after comparatively low dosage. The effect of the drug is prolonged by the use of a special tablet form that contains twice the average single dose, half of which is contained in an enteric-coated core that delays absorption. The drug is available in dosage forms suited for parenteral as well as oral administration. Its action tends to be slow. The usual adult oral dose is 2 to 8 mg. Tablets of 4 mg. are available. The repeat-action tablet is available in 8 and 12 mg. The usual parenteral dose is 5 to 10 mg.

Diphenhydramine hydrochloride, U.S.P., B.P.
(Benadryl Hydrochloride)

Diphenhydramine is similar to other members of the group. In addition to its antihistaminic activity it has a moderate antispasmodic action. This is sometimes significant in cases of bronchial asthma. When given in full therapeutic doses, it causes a high incidence of sedation, which makes it more suitable for use at night than during the day. The average oral dose for adults is 25 mg. given three or four times daily. It is available in a number of dosage forms suited for topical, oral, and parenteral administration. The usual intravenous dose is 10 to 50 mg.

Promethazine hydrochloride, U.S.P., B.P.
(Phenergan Hydrochloride)

Promethazine hydrochloride exhibits a number of pharmacologic effects and therefore has a number of clinical uses. It is a potent antihistaminic, it can be used for the relief of motion sickness, and it relieves apprehension. It potentiates the action of drugs that depress the central nervous system, making possible a reduction of their dosage. It has a relatively prolonged action, lasting up to 18 to 24 hours. Its sedative action is utilized clinically for surgical and obstetric patients. Promethazine hydrochloride is administered orally, parenterally, and rectally. The usual oral dose is 25 mg., although the range of dosage may be 6 to 75 mg. Parenterally, the dosage is up to 1 mg. per kilogram of body weight. It is available in 12.5- and 25-mg. tablets, as a syrup, and as a sterile solution for injection (25 mg. per milliliter). Promethazine suppositories are available (25 mg.).

Pyrilamine maleate, N.F. (Neo-Antergan Maleate); mepyramine maleate, B.P. (Anthisan)

This compound is available in 25- and 50-mg. tablets and as a syrup, 2.5 mg. per milliliter, for oral administration, after which effects last 4 to 6 hours. The usual adult dose is 25 to 50 mg. three or four times daily. The incidence of sedation is low, but it may cause gastrointestinal irritation.

Tripelennamine hydrochloride, U.S.P., B.P.
(Pyribenzamine Hydrochloride)

This drug is therapeutically effective, and the incidence of untoward reactions is low. Stimulation of the nervous system does occur as well as gastrointestinal irritation, but the latter is not severe. Sedation is moderate. This agent is available in a number of dosage forms for topical, oral, and parenteral (subcutaneous, intramuscular, and intravenous) administration. The usual adult dose is 25 to 75 mg. up to three times a day when given orally, although doses of 100 to 150 mg. are tolerated by most patients.

Tripelennamine citrate, U.S.P. (Pyribenzamine Citrate)

This preparation is more palatable than the hydrochloride when administered in a liquid form. It provides the same therapeutic action as does the hydrochloride. The dosage is greater for the citrate than for the hydrochloride preparation of the drug because of the difference in the molecular weights of the compounds. The usual adult dose is 50 mg. three times a day.

Other antihistaminics. There are a number of additional antihistaminic agents listed in the N.F. These include brompheniramine maleate (Dimetane), carbinoxamine maleate (Clistin), chlorothen citrate (Tagathen), methapyrilene hydrochloride (Dozar, Histadyl), pheniramine maleate (Trimeton Maleate), pyrathiazine hydrochloride (Pyrrolazote), pyrrobutamine phosphate (Pyronil), and thonzylamine hydrochloride (Anahist).

Drugs used for motion sickness

Motion sickness is a reaction to certain kinds of movement, sometimes any kind if it is sufficiently severe. Most persons are well adjusted to horizontal movements, but some are unable to tolerate continuous vertical movements. Such persons are likely to become ill when traveling in cars, trains, airplanes, or ships. Disturbance of the cells in the labyrinth of the ear is believed to be the cause of motion sickness. As a result of this disturbance contact is made with parts of the brain, including the vomiting center in the medulla. The person usually becomes pale, perspires, feels chilly or warm, and salivates freely. If he continues to be subjected to the motion, symptoms usually progress to nausea and vomiting.

A number of drugs have been used for motion sickness, including sedatives such as barbiturates, autonomic drugs such as scopolamine, as well as a number of the tranquilizing agents. Promethazine, mentioned previously, has been widely tested and found effective. The following agents have also been found useful for prevention of motion sickness and vestibular dysfunction (disturbance of functions of the inner ear). The exact mechanism of their action is unclear, but most of them appear to depress the central nervous system and decrease sensitivity of the labyrinth of the ear. Like other antihistaminics they should be used with caution by persons who are responsible for the operation of power machines.

Cyclizine hydrochloride, U.S.P. (Marezine Hydrochloride)

Cyclizine is an antihistaminic drug that has been found effective in a high percentage of cases in the prevention of nausea and vomiting associated with motion sickness.

Although dry mouth, drowsiness, and blurred vision can be observed after large doses, these symptoms seldom appear after ordinary therapeutic doses. Cyclizine is teratogenic in the rat. This fact should be taken into consideration before its use in pregnancy is contemplated.

Cyclizine hydrochloride is administered orally and rectally. The usual adult dose is 50 mg. 30 minutes before departure and 50 mg. three times daily before meals. Reduction of dosage may be indicated after the initial dose, depending on the duration of the trip, type of travel, and reaction of the individual person. For the relief of dizziness and associated symptoms of vestibular disorder (in conditions other than motion sickness) the usual dose is 50 mg. three times a day.

Cyclizine hydrochloride is available in 50-mg. tablets and 50- and 100-mg. suppositories. Cyclizine lactate has the same effects as cyclizine hydrochloride but is suited for intramuscular injection. The dosage is the same as that for hydrochloride.

Dimenhydrinate, U.S.P., B.P. (Dramamine)

As mentioned previously (p. 224), dimenhydrinate is chemically related to diphenhydramine (Benadryl). It produces mild sedation. It is effective for a high percentage of persons who suffer from motion sickness. It is also used to control nausea, vomiting, and dizziness associated with a number of conditions such as stapedectomy operations, radiation sickness, and Meniere's disease. It has also been employed for the relief of postoperative nausea and vomiting. Its status as an antiemetic for this purpose is not well established because of the variety of factors that contribute to the illness.

Dimenhydrinate is available in a number of dosage forms for oral, rectal, or intramuscular administration. The usual oral dose is 50 mg. 30 minutes before departure to prevent motion sickness. Dosage up to 100 mg. every 4 hours may be prescribed not only for motion sickness but also for the control of nausea and vomiting associated with other conditions. The usual intramuscular dose is 50 mg.

Meclizine hydrochloride, U.S.P. (Bonine Hydrochloride*)

Meclizine hydrochloride exerts a mild but prolonged antihistaminic action and is effective in the prevention of motion sickness. The duration of its effects may be as long as 24 hours.

---

*Formerly known as Bonamine Hydrochloride.

Like other members of this group of drugs, it appears to affect the central nervous system and the inner ear.

The incidence of its side effects seems to be low, although like most other antihistaminic drugs it can cause drowsiness, blurred vision, dryness of the mouth, and fatigue. Meclizine is teratogenic in the rat and thus should not be taken during pregnancy.

It is administered orally. The usual adult dose is 25 to 50 mg. once a day for the prevention of motion sickness (1 hour before departure). For the relief of nausea and vomiting from other reasons the dosage is similar or the same. The drug is available in tablets of 25 mg., as well as an elixir containing 12.5 mg. in 5 ml.

Trimethobenzamide hydrochloride, N.F. (Tigan Hydrochloride)

Trimethobenzamide hydrochloride exhibits an antiemetic action similar to the phenothiazine derivatives but has a weak antihistaminic action. It is believed to depress the chemoreceptor trigger zone in the medulla rather than the vomiting center directly. It has the advantage of long duration of action and little or no sedative effect. It is recommended for the prevention or relief of nausea and vomiting caused by radiation sickness, infection, motion sickness, and the action of other drugs. It has also been used to relieve nausea and vomiting caused by a number of other conditions.

Trimethobenzamide hydrochloride is marketed in 100- and 250-mg. capsules for oral administration, in vials and ampules for intramuscular injection containing 100 mg. per ml., and in 200-mg. rectal suppositories. The usual adult oral dose is 100 to 250 mg. The usual adult parenteral dose is 200 mg. After oral or parenteral administration the drug is effective in 20 to 40 minutes, and action persists 3 to 4 hours or more.

No indications of toxicity in vital organs have been reported for this drug. However, further study is needed to establish its safety for prolonged use. Dizziness, diarrhea, irritation after rectal administration, and pain at the site of injection have been noted. Occasionally, the patient's nausea is intensified.

Questions

for study and review

1 Explain the rationale for linking histamine with allergic reactions.
2 What are the advantages and disadvantages of the various antihistaminics?
3 Explain what is meant by the "triple response."
4 Explain how histamine may be used for diagnosing achlorhydria; for diagnosing pheochromocytoma.

References

Brand, J. J.: The pharmacologic basis for the control of motion sickness by drugs, Pharmacol. Physicians 2(3):1, 1968.

Brand, J. J., and Perry, W. L. M.: Drugs used in motion sickness, Pharmacol. Rev. 18:895, 1966.

Chinn, H. I., and Smith, P. K.: Motion sickness, Pharmacol. Rev. 7:33, 1955.

DiPalma, J. R., editor: Drill's pharmacology in medicine, New York, 1970, McGraw-Hill Book Company.

Friend, D. G.: The antihistamines, Clin. Pharmacol. Ther. 1:5, 1960.

Goodman, L. S., and Gilman, A.: The pharmacological basis of therapeutics, New York, 1970, The Macmillan Co.

Goth, A.: Medical pharmacology, ed. 6, St. Louis, 1972, The C. V. Mosby Co.

Greenberg, H. R., and Lustig, N.: Misuse of Dristan inhaler, N. Y. J. Med. 66:613, 1966.

Harris, M. C., Shure, N., and Unger, L.: Asthmalytic and antihistamine compounds, Dis. Chest 48:106, 1965.

Hildreth, E. A.: Some common allergic emergencies, Med. Clin. N. Amer. 50:1313, 1966.

Hughes, F. W., and Forney, R. B.: Comparative effects of three antihistaminics and ethanol on mental and motor performance, Clin. Pharmacol. Ther. 5:414, 1964.

Isaac, L., and Goth, A.: The mechanism of the potentiation of norepinephrine by antihistaminics, J. Pharmacol. Exp. Therap. 156:463, 1967.

Jillson, O. F.: Treatment of urticaria and contact dermatitis, Mod. Treat. 2:895, 1965.

Michelson, A. L., and Lowell, F. C.: Antihistaminic drugs, New Eng. J. Med. 258:994, 1958.

West, G. B.: Studies on the mechanism of anaphylaxis: a possible basis for a pharmacologic approach to allergy, Clin. Pharmacol. Ther. 4:749, 1963.

Wilhelm, R. E.: The newer anti-allergic agents, Med. Clin. N. Amer. 45:887, 1961.

Wood, C. D., Kennedy, R. S., and Gaybriel, A.: Review of anti-motion sickness drugs from 1954-64, Aerospace Med. 36:1, 1965.

13 Central nervous system drugs

■ The central nervous system

Drugs act to increase or decrease the activity of nerve centers and conducting pathways. Stimulants and depressants of the brain, the spinal cord, or specific centers of each have been developed, and their effects, on the whole, are highly predictable.

Physiologically man is constituted of numerous cells that have been organized into tissues, the tissues into organs, and the organs into systems; and all of these taken as a whole provide man with his structure and vital functions. All of man's functions, from the most basic (respiration and elimination) to the most complex and highly developed (abstract reasoning and creative thought), require coordination if he is to function as a whole. The main coordinator of man's body functions is his nervous system.

The central nervous system is composed of the brain, spinal cord, and numerous nerve cells called neurons. It is often referred to as the somatic or cerebrospinal nervous system. Striated muscle (skeletal or voluntary muscle) control and the unique functions of the brain (reasoning and memory) are primary concerns of the central nervous system.

The central nervous system of man functions much like a computer. Information from the external world (such as that related to sight, sound, touch, smell, and taste) and from the internal world (such as that related to oxygen or carbon dioxide blood levels, muscle tension, and body temperature) is sent to the appropriate part of the central nervous system. The information is integrated and instructions relayed to appropriate cells or tissues to produce the necessary actions and environmental adjustments. Information concerning these actions and adjustments is again fed back into the central nervous system. The constant feeding of information into the central nervous system permits continuous adjustment to be made in the instructions sent to various tissues to ensure effective control of body functions.

The central nervous system and drug action

The *cerebral cortex* constitutes the outer layer of gray matter covering each of the two hemispheres of the brain and the four lobes into which each hemisphere is divided. These lobes are named for the bones of the skull under which they lie—frontal, parietal, occipital, and temporal. The frontal lobe contains the motor and speech areas and centers that coordinate autonomic and muscle activity. The sensory cortex is located in the parietal lobe, the visual cortex in the occipital lobe, and the auditory cortex in the temporal lobe. Association areas lie near these areas and act in conjunction with them. In addition, large parts of the cortex are concerned with higher mental activity—reasoning, creative thought, judgment, memory—those attributes that are unique to man and separate him from other animals.

Drugs that depress cortical activity may decrease acuity of sensation and perception, inhibit motor activity, decrease alertness and concentration, and even promote drowsiness and sleep. Drugs that stimulate the cortical areas may cause more vivid impulses to be received and greater awareness of the surrounding environment. In addition increased muscle activity and restlessness may occur. The specific response brought forth by a drug depends to a large extent on the personality of the individual, his emotional and physiologic state, the specific attributes of the drug, and a host of other factors.

The *thalamus* is composed of sensory nuclei and serves as a relay center for impulses to and from the cerebral cortex. It also serves as a center of unlocalized sensations. It enables the individual to have impressions of agreeableness or disagreeableness about a sensation. Drugs that depress cells in the various portions of the thalamus may interrupt the free flow of impulses to the cerebral cortex. This is one way pain is relieved.

The *hypothalamus* lies below the thalamus and contains centers that regulate body temperature, carbohydrate and fat metabolism, and water balance. There is evidence that there is also a center for sleep and wakefulness here. Some of the sleep-producing drugs are thought to depress centers in the hypothalamus; others, such as aspirin, are known to affect the heat-regulating center. The thalamus and hypothalamus constitute important regions of the brain known as the diencephalon.

The *medulla oblongata* contains the so-called vital centers, the respiratory, vasomotor, and cardiac centers. If the respiratory center is stimulated, it will discharge an increased number of nerve impulses over nerve pathways to the muscles of respiration. If it is depressed, it will discharge fewer impulses, and respiration will be correspondingly affected. Other centers in the medulla that respond to certain drugs are the cough center and the vomiting center. The medulla, pons, and midbrain constitute the brainstem and contain many important correlation centers (gray matter) as well as ascending and descending pathways (white matter).

The *reticular formation* is a part of the central nervous system that has been studied increasingly in recent years. Its importance is only beginning to be appreciated. It is made up of cells and fine bundles of nerve fibers that extend in many directions. The formation extends from the upper part of the spinal cord forward through the brainstem to the diencephalon. It exhibits both inhibitory as well as excitatory functions in relation to other parts of the nervous system. It receives afferent impulses from all parts of the body and relays impulses to the cortex to promote wakefulness and alertness, which affects many cerebral functions, such as consciousness and learning. It also inhibits or excites activity in motor neurons, promoting both reflex and voluntary movements. Its overall function is thought to be that of an integrating system that influences activities of other parts of the nervous system. Depression of the reticular formation produces sedation and loss of consciousness. Many drugs are believed to exert an effect on the reticular formation. It is particularly sensitive to certain depressant drugs, such as barbiturates.

The *cerebellum* contains centers for muscle

coordination, equilibrium, and muscle tone. It receives afferent impulses from the vestibular nuclei as well as the cerebrum and plays an important role in the maintenance of posture. Drugs that disturb the cerebellum or vestibular branch of the eighth cranial nerve cause loss of equilibrium and dizziness.

The *spinal cord,* a center for reflex activity, also functions in the transmission of impulses to and from the higher centers in the brain and may be affected by the action of drugs. Large doses of spinal stimulants may cause convulsions; smaller doses may increase reflex excitability.

When a drug is described as having a central action, it means that it has an action on the brain or the spinal cord.

Synaptic transmission in the central nervous system

There is evidence that transmission of impulses at synapses in the central nervous system is humoral. For example, it is known that some parts of the central nervous system contain acetylcholine (ACh) and acetylcholinesterase. Since acetylcholine is a known chemical transmitter of nerve impulses, it can be assumed that its presence in the central nervous system is for the purpose of transmission of nerve impulses. Not all parts of the central nervous system contain acetylcholine. Those areas that contain high concentrations are the motor cortex, thalamus, hypothalamus, geniculate bodies, and anterior spinal roots; very low concentrations are found in the cerebellum, optic nerves, and dorsal roots of the spine. The former areas are considered to be cholinergic and are known to be very responsive to acetylcholine levels. Increased acetylcholine levels can cause nausea, vomiting, muscle tremors, and convulsions. Atropine blocks the action of acetylcholine and is used in treating some of the symptoms of Parkinson's disease, which is characterized by rigidity, tremors, and disturbance of voluntary and involuntary movements.

Central nervous system areas with low concentration of acetylcholine are considered to be predominantly noncholinergic. It is believed that neurons in these areas transmit impulses by a chemical transmitter not yet identified.

The extent and strength of muscle contractions depend on the number of motor neurons involved and the frequency with which they discharge impulses. Inhibition of motor neuron activity may be presynaptic or postsynaptic.

Studies indicate that presynaptic inhibition occurs in the brain and is widespread at the spinal level affecting transmission in afferent fibers from skin and muscle. The function of presynaptic inhibition is probably to suppress weak inputs that would otherwise cause unnecessary responses. It has also been demonstrated that impulses in some nerves can depolarize the presynaptic terminals of other nerves. When a fiber is somewhat depolarized, the nerve impulse traveling along that fiber is smaller than normal, and this decreased impulse causes less than the normal amount of transmitter to be liberated with decreased stimulation to the postsynaptic nerve fibers and terminals. The convulsant drug picrotoxin is known to reduce presynaptic inhibition.

Postsynaptic inhibition may be the result of changes in the membrane permeability of the postsynaptic cells caused by release of chemical transmitters from presynaptic nerve endings.

Lower motor neurons release acetylcholine at the neuromuscular junction, causing contraction in striated (voluntary) muscle. The concentration of acetylcholine must be high since a large number of muscle fibers must respond synchronously for striated muscle contraction to occur, and also because acetylcholine is very rapidly destroyed by the enzyme cholinesterase. In all likelihood this constitutes a protective mechanism for the body and prevents man from being a constantly quivering organism.

Renshaw cells are special interneurons. Nerve fibers that innervate skeletal muscle give off side branches that synapse with the Renshaw cells. These cells in turn synapse with the large anterior horn cells in the spinal cord. They are inhibitory cells and cause muscle contraction to be less vigorous and to terminate sooner than would otherwise be possible. When a motor neuron is stimulated, the Renshaw cell is also excited, thereby dampening any excessive activity in the motor neurons.

Upper motor neurons are scattered throughout the cerebral cortex; a number of them are located in the motor cortex. About three fourths of the nerve fibers from these motor neurons cross to the opposite side at the level of the medulla, descend to the spinal cord, and synapse with interneurons, which in turn synapse with the lower motor neurons. Almost all motor neurons of one side are controlled by the motor cortex of the other side. Therefore, injury to the motor cortex of the right side causes paralysis on the left side of the body (hemiplegia). Systems other than the upper and lower motor neuron systems are concerned with voluntary movement, but lower motor neurons form the common final pathway for stimuli for voluntary movement.

Catecholamines (dopamine, norepinephrine, and epinephrine) and serotonin are synthesized, stored, and metabolized in the brain. These substances do not easily penetrate the blood-brain barrier, but their precursors do. The effect of injected catecholamines on the central nervous system is slight in comparison to the effect on the autonomic nervous system. However, an increase in catecholamines and serotonin causes cerebral stimulation. Drugs, such as reserpine, that release catecholamines and reduce amine concentration in the brain have a depressing or sedative action. Methyldopa lowers the serotonin level and this, too, has a cerebral depressing effect.

Special staining techniques indicate that there are adrenergic and serotoninergic tracts within the central nervous system. Dopamine, a catecholamine, is especially concentrated in the basal ganglia. The study of dopamine at this site in individuals suffering from Parkinson's disease led to the new therapeutic approach of utilizing its precursor L-dopa with good results in many cases.

The blood-brain barrier prevents drug penetration to the brain and spinal cord. This has impeded both physiologic and pharmacologic research on the central nervous system. Therefore, less is known about the central nervous system than about the autonomic nervous system.

Stimulants

Drugs included under the heading of stimulants will be limited, for the most part, to those whose major effect is on the central nervous system. There are drugs, such as atropine, cocaine, and ephedrine, that are central nervous system stimulants but, medically, they have more important actions on other systems of the body.

The central nervous system stimulants may produce dramatic effects, but their therapeutic usefulness is limited because of the multiplicity of their actions and side effects. Also, repeated administration and large doses are prone to precipitate convulsive seizures, coma, and exhaustion. The number of drugs that stimulate the central nervous system is large, but the number actually employed for this purpose is limited. Those having particular therapeutic value are the respiratory stimulants and the analeptics. Central nervous system stimulants used to antagonize depressant drugs are referred to as analeptics. They restore consciousness and mental alertness.

Stimulants are classified on the basis of where in the nervous system they exert their major effects—on the cerebrum, on the medulla and brainstem, or on the spinal cord. Amphetamine is mainly a stimulant of the cerebral cortex; nikethamide acts mainly on the centers in the medulla and the brainstem; and strychnine is a spinal stimulant. These drugs may also affect other parts of the nervous system. The drugs that act primarily on the medullary centers are said to be the best analeptics.

Xanthines

Caffeine, theobromine, and theophylline are known as methylated xanthines. Their actions are similar, although their effect on specific structures varies in intensity.

Caffeine is a trimethylxanthine (three methyl groups) and theobromine and theophylline are

Xanthine Theobromine Caffeine Theophylline

dimethylxanthines (two methyl groups). Caffeine, theophylline, and theobromine are alkaloids that all act on the central nervous system, the kidney, the heart, the skeletal muscle, and the smooth muscle, but the degree of their action on these structures varies considerably. Of the three xanthines, caffeine is the most effective stimulant of the central nervous system, theophylline is less effective, and theobromine has little effect. On the kidney, theophylline ranks first in effectiveness, theobromine second, and caffeine third. Aminophylline (a theophylline compound) is the xanthine preparation of choice to produce relaxation of the bronchial tubes and to produce diuresis. Theobromine and theophylline will be discussed further in later chapters (see Index).

Caffeine

Caffeine is a white crystalline powder commercially obtained from tea leaves. It is the active alkaloid occurring in a number of plants used as beverages—coffee, the seed of *Coffea arabica;* tea, the leaves of *Thea sinensis;* the kola nut of Central America; and guarana, derived from the seeds of a Brazilian plant and from yerba maté or Paraguay tea. Tea contains from 1% to 5% caffeine*; coffee, from 1% to 2%. Tea contains 10% to 24% tannin. Coffee contains a variable amount of caffetannic acid (average, about 12%), which is not very astringent.

*Although tea contains more total methylated xanthines than coffee, less tea is usually used in preparing the beverage (at least in the United States), and it therefore usually contains less caffeine.

Action and result

Cortical and medullary. Caffeine stimulates the central nervous system, especially the cerebral cortex (Plate 5). Its action is a descending one; small doses (100 to 150 mg.) stimulate the cerebrum, and larger doses stimulate the medullary centers and the spinal cord. Doses large enough to stimulate the spinal cord are never ordered. As a result of the cortical stimulation the individual is more alert, thinks faster, has a better memory, forms judgments more quickly, learns faster (temporarily), and has a decreased reaction time. Drowsiness and fatigue disappear. The sense of touch may be more discriminating and the sense of pain more keen. Stimulation is not necessarily followed by depression, except as it brings about exhaustion of natural reserves.

Caffeine, when taken orally in ordinary therapeutic doses, has little or no effect on medullary centers. Large doses given parenterally will stimulate the respiratory center, especially if it is moderately depressed. There is some stimulation of the vagus and vasoconstrictor centers of the medulla, although this is partially masked by the peripheral action on the heart and blood vessels.

Decreased susceptibility to fatigue has also been observed, but whether the action is a direct one on the striated muscle cells or whether the effect is produced by masking the sense of fatigue through cerebral stimulation is not fully understood.

Large doses of caffeine stimulate the entire central nervous system, including the spinal cord. There is first an increased reflex excitability that may, with increasing dosage, result

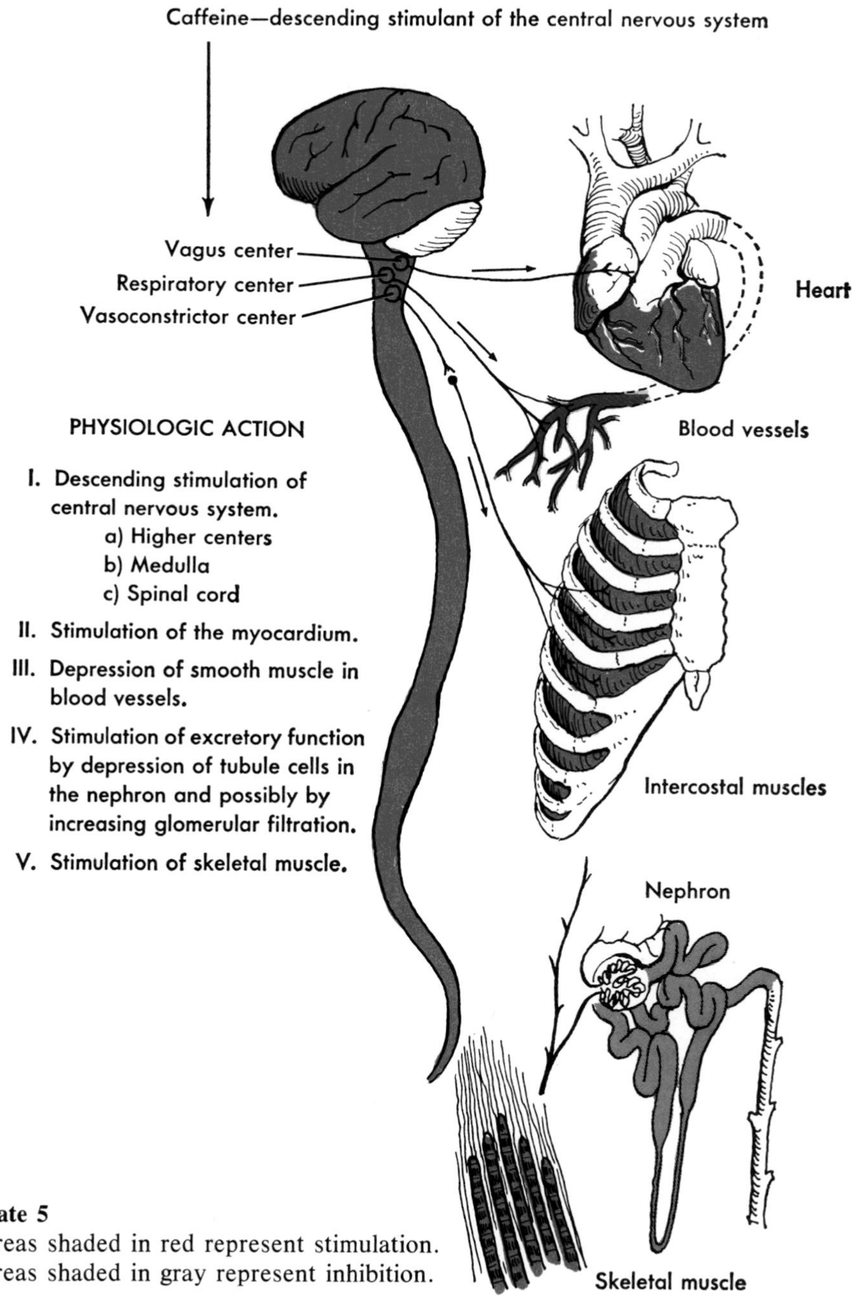

Caffeine—descending stimulant of the central nervous system

Vagus center
Respiratory center
Vasoconstrictor center

Heart

Blood vessels

PHYSIOLOGIC ACTION

I. Descending stimulation of central nervous system.
   a) Higher centers
   b) Medulla
   c) Spinal cord

II. Stimulation of the myocardium.

III. Depression of smooth muscle in blood vessels.

IV. Stimulation of excretory function by depression of tubule cells in the nephron and possibly by increasing glomerular filtration.

V. Stimulation of skeletal muscle.

Intercostal muscles

Nephron

Plate 5
Areas shaded in red represent stimulation.
Areas shaded in gray represent inhibition.

Skeletal muscle

in muscle twitching, especially in the limbs and face.

Cardiovascular. Caffeine stimulates the myocardium, bringing about both an increased cardiac rate and an increased cardiac output. This effect is antagonistic to that produced on the vagus center; consequently, a slight slowing of the heart may be observed in some individuals and an increased rate in others. The latter effect usually predominates after large doses. Overstimulation may cause a harmful tachycardia and cardiac irregularities.

A slight and somewhat transitory elevation of blood pressure is sometimes noted. Some investigators are of the opinion that caffeine constricts the intracranial blood vessels and brings about some lowering of intracranial pressure.

Renal. Like the other xanthines, caffeine increases the flow of urine, but its action is relatively weak. The mode of action seems to be that of depressing the tubule cells and preventing reabsorption of fluid.

Metabolic. The metabolic rate is slightly increased by caffeine. An appreciable tolerance to certain effects of caffeine is readily established, although apparently not to the cerebral effects. Caffeine is also used to relieve fatigue, depression, and headache.

Gastric. Caffeine stimulates the output of pepsin as well as hydrochloric acid in the gastric juice. Thus coffee is usually omitted from the diet of patients with gastric or duodenal ulcer.

Uses. Caffeine is used as a mild cerebral stimulant. It is used also occasionally as a respiratory stimulant, provided the depression of the medullary center is not severe. In cases of severe respiratory depression there are better respiratory stimulants. Caffeine is no longer used for the relief of narcotic depression unless more effective drugs are not available.

Caffeine is used with one or more analgesic drugs or with ergotamine tartrate for the relief of headache. Its effect in such cases is thought to be caused by its effect on the cerebral blood vessels.

Preparation, dosage, and administration. The following are the preparations and dosages of caffeine.

Caffeine, U.S.P., B.P. The usual dose is 0.2 Gm. (gr. 3).

Caffeine and sodium benzoate injection, U.S.P. It is available in 2-ml. ampules and 10-ml. vials, 250 mg. per milliliter. The usual dose is 0.5 Gm. (500 mg.) to 1 Gm.

Citrated caffeine, N.F. This is available in 60- and 120-mg. tablets. The average dose is 60 to 120 mg. orally.

Ergotamine tartrate with caffeine, N.F. (Cafergot). Each tablet contains 1 mg. of ergotamine tartrate and 100 mg. of caffeine. The drug is given orally for migraine headache (one to two tablets).

Caffeine is usually prescribed as citrated caffeine or caffeine and sodium benzoate because they are more soluble than caffeine itself. Caffeine and sodium benzoate is usually given intramuscularly, whereas the citrated form is given orally. Caffeine may also be given in the form of a liquid, either orally or by rectum. The caffeine content of an average cup of coffee as made in the United States is between 100 and 150 mg. Twelve ounces of a cola drink contains 35 to 55 mg. of caffeine, while a cup of cocoa may contain as much as 50 mg. of caffeine. Caffeine sometimes exhibits a local irritant action on the gastric mucosa, resulting in nausea and vomiting or gastric distress. Sick persons often do not tolerate coffee well as a beverage especially if they are slightly nauseated. Weak tea is often better tolerated.

Side effects and toxic effects. Fatal poisoning by caffeine is rare, partly because it is readily excreted. The fatal dose is presumably about 10 Gm. Toxic doses produce excessive irritability, restlessness, insomnia, nervousness, profuse flow of urine, nausea, vomiting, headache, and heart palpitation, particularly in susceptible individuals. The more chronic symptoms of poisoning include insomnia, anxiety, and functional cardiac symptoms. The signs of chronic caffeine poisoning are more commonly seen among workers such as night nurses, who use coffee to keep awake and continue to work when physically tired. The symptoms of nervousness disappear when the overuse of coffee is remedied. Stopping the intake of caffeine and providing rest and quiet is sufficient treatment. In certain individuals a short-acting sedative may be indicated. The use of coffee to combat fatigue is like a whip to a tired horse, and it would be better to get needed rest than to continue using coffee to keep going.

The question is sometimes raised as to whether or not caffeine causes habituation and addiction. Many persons note that if they do not have their usual cup or two of coffee in the morning, they feel irritable and nervous and develop a headache. This probably indicates habituation.

Amphetamines

Amphetamines are synthetic sympathomimetic amines. Amphetamines are weak inhibitors of monamine oxidase (MAO). However, their central nervous system stimulation is not thought to be a result of monamine oxidase inhibition. The exact mechanism by which amphetamines act is unknown. However, they do exert a stimulating effect on the cerebral cortex and probably on the reticular activating system. This effect produces feelings of wakefulness, alertness, and euphoria or elation.

Amphetamines can produce emotional dependence but physical dependence does not occur. Prolonged use of amphetamines leads to tolerance. Amphetamines may be used to treat nonpsychotic, mild depressive states, but they are of little or no value in psychotic depressive states. They are widely used for their ability to depress appetite and reduce obesity.

Amphetamine

Amphetamine is prepared synthetically from ephedrine. The following formulas indicate points of similarity and difference.

Ephedrine

Amphetamine

Action and result. Amphetamine stimulates the central nervous system, particularly the cerebral cortex. The effects depend upon the personality of the individual, the mental state, and the amount of drug administered. The results of action seen after oral administration usually include an elevation of mood that may become a true euphoric exhilaration, decreased feeling of fatigue, increased willingness to work, increased confidence, alertness, power of concentration, and sometimes talkativeness. Continued use may cause irritability, sleeplessness, dizziness, and anorexia. Large doses tend to be followed by fatigue and mental depression. Amphetamine may fortify a person for prolonged physical and mental exertion, but the end result in terms of fatigue is correspondingly greater and requires a longer period for rest than usual. When the respiratory center is depressed, amphetamine exerts a stimulating effect upon it; this is significant in treatment of poisoning from depressant drugs.

Uses. Amphetamine is used to bring about symptomatic treatment of narcolepsy and relieves many patients of overpowering attacks of sleep.

For various manifestations of postencephalitic parkinsonism the drug is given to bring about improvement in muscle strength, decreased rigidity, and a sense of increased energy. Subjective improvement may be more marked, however, than objective decrease in tremor and rigidity. This drug is useful in the treatment of mild psychogenic states, particularly those attending childbirth, menopause, old age, and chronic fatigue.

Amphetamine may be useful to depress the appetite of the patient who is dieting to overcome obesity. Many physicians, however, do not recommend its use for this purpose because as soon as the drug is withdrawn the former appetite returns, and unless the patient has established a new food pattern he usually returns to the old habit of overeating. Furthermore, obese persons may have disturbances of the cardiovascular system, such as hypertension, that contraindicate the use of the amphetamines.

A number of derivatives of amphetamine are marketed as anorexigenic drugs (drugs to decrease the appetite). Generally, they have a lower potency than amphetamine. The sustained-dosage forms afford more economy and in many instances produce fewer side effects.

Amphetamine may be used as an analeptic in certain cases of poisoning from depressant drugs.

Preparation, dosage, and administration. The drug is available with the hydrochloride, sulfate, or phosphate salt and in combination with analgesics or barbiturates to depress excessive irritability and tension.

Amphetamine sulfate, N.F., B.P. (Benzedrine Sulfate). This drug is marketed in tablets of 5, 10, and 15 mg., in solution for injection (20 mg. per milliliter), and in 10- and 15-mg. sustained-release capsules. It is marketed under the trade name of Benzedrine. Amphetamine sulfate is usually administered orally and given in divided doses—the total daily dose is divided into several smaller doses and distributed through the day. To prevent interference with sleep the final dose of the day should not be given after 4:00 P.M. When injected, it is given intramuscularly or by slow intravenous drip.

Amphetamine phosphate (Raphetamine Phosphate). This form is available in 2- and 5-mg. tablets for oral administration and in solution for injection (100 mg. per 10 ml.). Small initial doses, 5 mg. or less, are recommended, to be followed with gradually increased amounts if necessary. Amphetamine phosphate has the same effects and uses as amphetamine sulfate, but its physical property of increased solubility in water makes it better suited for parenteral administration.

Side effects and contraindications. There is danger in the promiscuous use of amphetamine to overcome sleepiness and lack of alertness, because the natural warning signs associated with fatigue may be eliminated. Furthermore, amphetamine has high drug abuse potential. It is to be avoided by persons with hypertension and cardiovascular disease and by persons who are unduly restless, anxious, agitated, and excited. Side effects include dryness of the mouth,

headache, insomnia, irritability, a sense of intoxication, and anxiety.

Elevated blood pressure, tachycardia, and gastrointestinal disorders may occur. Abrupt withdrawal after prolonged use may cause depression and lethargy. Some clinicians advocate gradual withdrawal of the drug to avoid these effects. Despite the numerous side effects caused by these drugs, there is a wide margin of safety between therapeutic and toxic doses.

**Dextroamphetamine sulfate, U.S.P.
(Dexedrine Sulfate); dexamphetamine, B.P.**

Action and uses. Dextroamphetamine sulfate, for the most part, has the same action and uses as amphetamine sulfate, although it exhibits a greater stimulating effect on the central nervous system. It is considered to be less toxic than amphetamine sulfate because of its diminished sympathomimetic activity. It seldom causes rapid pulse, changes in blood pressure, or tremor. However, the same dangers attend its indiscriminate use as is true of the other amphetamines.

Preparation, dosage, and administration. Dextroamphetamine sulfate is available in 5- and 10-mg. tablets, as an elixir (5 mg. per 5 ml.), and in sustained-release capsules (Spansules) containing 5, 10, or 15 mg. of drug. It is also marketed in combination with analgesics, such as aspirin or phenacetin, or with one of the barbiturates, such as amobarbital. The latter combination is sometimes used when elevation of blood pressure and insomnia constitute problems. The usual dose of dextroamphetamine is 2.5 to 15 mg. daily given orally.

It may be taken three times a day 30 minutes to 1 hour before meals. The last dose should be taken at least 6 hours before retiring to avoid insomnia. Sustained-release forms are taken once daily in the morning.

In the treatment of barbiturate intoxication, 10 to 20 mg. of dextroamphetamine is administered intramuscularly or intravenously. This dosage may be repeated at 30-minute intervals until the desired response has been obtained. It is available for injection as dextroamphetamine sulfate in 10- and 30-ml. vials containing 20 mg. of dextroamphetamine per milliliter.

Methamphetamine hydrochloride, U.S.P. (Desoxyephedrine Hydrochloride); methylamphetamine hydrochloride, B.P.

Methamphetamine hydrochloride greatly resembles amphetamine sulfate; the two drugs differ in their action only in degree. The central stimulant action of this drug is slightly greater, and the cardiovascular action is slightly less than that of amphetamine. Like amphetamine, it is used in the treatment of narcolepsy, to relieve symptoms of postencephalitic parkinsonism, as part of the treatment of alcoholism, and in various types of depressed states. Because it allays hunger and depresses motility in the gastrointestinal tract, it has been used in the treatment of obesity. It has the same disadvantages as a form of treatment for obesity as was mentioned under amphetamine sulfate.

It is contraindicated for patients with hypertension, cardiovascular disease, hyperthyroidism, anxiety states, or undue restlessness. Severe toxic psychoses have occurred in individuals who abuse methamphetamine, commonly referred to as "speed."

Preparation, dosage, and administration. Methamphetamine hydrochloride is marketed in 5- and 10-mg. capsules, 2.5-, 5-, 7.5-, and 10-mg. tablets, as an elixir (0.667 and 1 mg. per milliliter), and in solution for injection (20 mg. per milliliter). Methamphetamine is given parenterally as well as orally. The beginning oral dose is 2.5 mg. daily; this is increased to 2.5 to 5 mg. two or three times a day until the desired response is obtained. In case of emergency, 10 to 15 mg. may be given slowly by intravenous injection. In emergency, the usual dose is 15 to 30 mg. when the drug is given intramuscularly.

Phenmetrazine hydrochloride, N.F., B.P. (Preludin)

Phenmetrazine hydrochloride resembles amphetamine pharmacologically, especially in its ability to depress appetite. It is a mild stimulant of the central nervous system, and it rarely causes changes in pulse rate and blood pressure.

It is administered orally in 25-mg. doses two or three times a day, an hour before meals, or in an oral extended-release form containing 75 mg. of the drug, which is taken once daily.

Other central nervous system stimulants used primarily as appetite suppressants are diethylpropion hydrochloride (Tenuate, Tepanil), phendimetrazine tartrate (Plegine), phentermine (Ionamin, Wilpo), and chlorphentermine (Pre-Sate).

Medullary or convulsant stimulant
Picrotoxin injection, N.F.

Picrotoxin is a drug obtained from a climbing shrub, *Anamirta cocculus,* indigenous to the regions of Malabar and the East Indies. The drug is present in the berries of the shrub, commonly called fishberries because of a native custom of throwing the berries onto the water to catch fish. The fish are stupefied by the berries and float on the surface of the water.

The stimulant action of picrotoxin is thought to be the result of altering the electric properties of the cell membranes of excitable cells (neurons or nerve cells).

Action and result. Picrotoxin is a powerful central nervous system stimulant and convulsant. Its most prominent action is apparently on the midbrain and medulla. It stimulates the respiratory, vasomotor, vomiting, and vagus centers in the medulla, producing increased respiration, elevation of blood pressure, emesis, and slowing of the heart. These effects are seen particularly in the anesthetized or narcotized individual. It is a dangerous stimulant because the range of safety between the therapeutic dose and the toxic dose is a narrow one. Large doses produce convulsions.

Uses. Although highly toxic to normal persons, this drug is less toxic to individuals who have taken an overdose of barbiturates. It has, in fact, a special analeptic action against the narcosis produced by a large dose of barbiturates. It is also useful in combating depression caused by paraldehyde and tribromoethanol, but it is not useful in overcoming depression of the nervous system caused by alcohol or morphine. The drug is rapidly destroyed in the body.

Preparation, dosage, and administration. Picrotoxin injection is available as a 3% solution in isotonic saline (3 mg. per milliliter). Total dosage is determined on an individual basis according to the needs of the patient. Picrotoxin is administered intravenously. In cases of barbiturate poisoning it is recommended by some that 6 mg. of picrotoxin be given initially and an additional 3 mg. at 15-minute intervals until 15 mg. has been injected or until the desired response has been obtained. Other restorative measures should accompany the administration of picrotoxin—oxygen administration, intravenous fluids, and artificial respiration. It is worth noting here, however, that there is considerable difference of opinion among physicians about the optimal treatment for barbiturate poisoning, and many hospitals avoid the use of analeptics entirely on the basis that their hazards do not justify their beneficial effects.

Depressants

Mild drug-induced depression of the central nervous system is frequently characterized by lack of interest in surroundings, inability to focus attention on a subject, and lack of inclination to move or talk. The pulse and respiration may become slower than usual, and as the depression deepens, acuity of all sensations such as touch, vision, hearing, heat, cold, and pain diminish progressively. Psychic and motor activities decrease; reflexes become sluggish and finally are abolished. If the depression is not checked, it progresses to unconsciousness, stupor, coma, respiratory failure, and death. Some depressant drugs, such as the general anesthetics, act upon the entire central nervous system; others, such as the anticonvulsant drugs, are more selective in their action. The nonselective depressants include the following: (1) analgesics, which are drugs that relieve pain; (2) hypnotics and sedatives, which produce sleep and rest; and (3) general anesthetics, which produce loss of sensation and loss of consciousness.

■ Analgesics

Analgesics are drugs that relieve pain without producing loss of consciousness and reflex activity. Pain may be defined as a feeling or sensation of unpleasantness. It is believed that any neutral sensation (a sensation not recognized by the individual as being either pleasant or unpleasant) can become converted into pain when the stimulus causing the sensation becomes sufficiently intense. Physical pain is a part of a larger experience called "pain experience," which includes, in addition to the sensation of pain, all the associated emotional sensations for a particular person under particular circumstances. This accounts for the wide variation in individual response to the sensation of pain. It is known that the stimuli that cause pain must be more intense than those evoking other sensations. There is a strong link between pain and tissue damage.

Pain perception and response are influenced by such psychologic factors as past experience, attention, and emotion. In addition, the intensity, duration, and location of harmful stimuli also influence pain perception and response. Pain that increases rapidly in intensity (such as that accompanying acute myocardial infarction or extensive partial thickness burns) does not usually permit the individual to achieve any control over the pain. Pain that is less severe with a slow rise in intensity permits the individual to exert some control over the pain. The latter may be achieved by the person thinking about something else or engaging in activity that diverts his attention.

There appears to be a relatively constant pain threshold for each individual. Although the pain threshold varies from individual to individual, tolerance to pain appears to be far more variable than pain threshold. For example, certain stimuli, such as heat applied to the skin at an intensity of 45° to 48° C., will initiate the sensation of pain in almost all individuals. Pain threshold is the minimum intensity of a harmful stimulus that produces the sensation of pain, while tolerance to pain refers to the point beyond which the pain can no longer be endured. There is evidence that some sensitization or adaptation to pain occurs, that is, there is a diminution of response with constant stimulation.

Action. Analgesics act in several ways: (1) by inhibiting conduction of noxious impulses or abnormal motor responses; (2) by altering the attitude or mood of the patient from one of concern to one of detachment, promoting a sense of well-being or mild euphoria; and (3) by producing sedative and soporific effects.

Opium and its derivatives, related synthetic compounds, and the analgesic antipyretics, such as aspirin and phenacetin, belong to the analgesic group of drugs.

The search for an ideal analgesic continues, but it is difficult to find one that does all desired of it. It should (1) be potent, so that it will afford maximum relief of pain; (2) be nonaddicting; (3) exhibit a minimum of side effects, such as constipation, respiratory depression, nausea, and vomiting; (4) not cause tolerance to develop; (5) act promptly and over a long period of time with a minimum amount of sedation, so that the patient is able to remain awake and be responsive; and (6) be relatively inexpensive. Needless to say, no present-day analgesic has all of these qualifications, and so the search continues.

Nonsynthetic narcotic analgesics—opiates

Opium is one of the oldest analgesics about which there is any record. Opium is described in Chinese literature written long before the time of Christ. The name comes from the Greek *opos*, meaning "juice of plants."

Opium is the hardened dried juice of the unripe seed capsules of *Papaver somniferum,* a species of poppy grown largely in China, India, Iran, and Asia Minor. The poppy plant is indigenous to Asia Minor, and from there knowledge of opium spread to Greece and Arabia, where physicians became well versed in its use. Arabian traders were responsible for its introduction into the Orient, where it was known as "smoking dirt." The Chinese used it chiefly to control some of the symptoms of dysentery until its cultivation was exploited for commercial reasons by European powers, and the opium habit spread through many parts of the Orient.

Paracelsus is credited with compounding the preparation "laudanum." Paregoric was first used as an elixir for asthma and was prepared by a chemistry professor at Leyden. Thomas Dover, an English physician, used the powder as a sweating agent for gout in 1732.

Opium in the crude form was used until well into the nineteenth century, before the chief alkaloid, morphine, was isolated. The discovery of other alkaloids soon followed, and their use came to be preferred to that of the crude preparations.

Composition. The active principles of opium are alkaloids, of which there are some twenty in number, although only three are used widely in the practice of medicine—morphine, codeine, and papaverine.

Morphine

Codeine
(methylmorphine)

Papaverine

diet that should be given to a patient who has had morphine. It is obvious that the patient is not likely to have either the inclination or ability to enjoy or digest a full meal. Tolerance to the effects of morphine on the gastrointestinal muscle develop slowly if at all.

Genitourinary tract. The tone of the muscle in the ureters and the detrusor muscle of the urinary bladder is said to be affected much the same as the tone of the muscle in the gastrointestinal organs. Increased tone in the sphincter muscle of the bladder may contribute to difficulty in urination. In addition there is decreased perception of the stimulus to void. This sometimes explains a patient's inability to void and the need for catheterization. Morphine also releases the antidiuretic hormone and therefore has an antidiuretic effect. This is an important factor to keep in mind when checking the patient's urinary output.

Other smooth muscle. Morphine promotes contraction of the bronchial musculature, but this effect is significant only in persons subject to allergic reactions and asthma. Allergic reactions to morphine and related alkaloids are said to be rather common.

Although there seems to be no direct action of morphine on uterine muscle, normal labor may be delayed because of central depression, and the respiration of both the mother and the child will be depressed.

Therapeutic uses and the natural alkaloids. Morphine, especially, is used primarily as an analgesic for control of severe pain. It should not be used if other analgesics will suffice, but when pain is severe, the narcotic analgesics have no rival. When morphine is given to a patient who is already in severe pain, the chief effect seems to be that the patient's emotional reaction to the pain is altered. He is no longer afraid of the pain or thrown into a panic because of it. If the nurse asks such a patient about his condition half an hour or so after she has given him a hypodermic of morphine, he is likely to say: "I still have pain, but I can stand it."

If morphine is given before the patient begins to experience pain, its effect seems to be somewhat different; a better blocking of the pain impulses occurs and the patient may experience no pain. This explains why, on the first or possibly the second postoperative day, a patient should not be allowed to wait until he is in full pain if the greatest analgesic effect of morphine is to be achieved.

In surgical conditions in which the alleviation of severe pain may make diagnosis more difficult and lead to undue delay in operating, morphine should not be used or it should be employed only in very small doses and with great caution. It should not be used in chronic conditions in which there is pain, since prolonged administration is almost certain to result in dependence. Exceptions to this rule are to be found in cases of inoperable cancer in which the patient cannot recover and may be spared much unnecessary suffering by its use. The administration of a drug such as chlorpromazine or promethazine can be used to potentiate the action of morphine and reduce the amount of morphine needed. Morphine is not recommended for the relief of pain in persons of neurotic or hysteric temperaments unless its use is absolutely necessary.

Ordinarily, morphine or related alkaloids are not given to produce sleep unless sleeplessness is caused by pain or dyspnea. There are conditions in which the relief of restlessness and apprehension is essential, such as the patient suffering from a myocardial infarction.

Morphine is used to check peristalsis in conditions such as hemorrhage and severe diarrhea and after surgery on the stomach and bowel. Preparations of opium are prescribed more often than morphine to check diarrhea because of opium's slow absorption and effect on smooth muscle.

Morphine is frequently used as premedication prior to the administration of a general anesthetic to relieve apprehension and decrease resistance to the anesthetic.

Codeine is the opiate of choice in relieving a cough because it effectively depresses the cough center and is less likely to produce dependence than morphine.

Papaverine is sometimes used to relieve the reflexly constricted blood vessels associated with pulmonary embolism, peripheral arterial embolism, and coronary occlusion. These are instances in which the antispasmodic effects of papaverine may be beneficial.

Tolerance. Different individuals require varying periods of time before the repeated administration of opium derivatives fails to have the effect that it originally produced. This condition is known as tolerance. A patient who suffers considerable pain may be relieved at first by gr. $\frac{1}{4}$ of morphine, but if the painful condition persists, the time will come when he requires an ever-increasing dose to experience the same relief. The person who has developed tolerance may eventually take doses that would have caused death if given as an initial dose. Tolerance does not develop uniformly—tolerance is developed to the hypnotic, analgesic, and respiratory depressant effects of opiates but not to their effects on the pupil of the eye and on the gastrointestinal muscle. Tolerance develops faster when the dosage is administered regularly and is large and may occur after 2 weeks of repeated administration. The exact mechanism of action whereby tolerance develops is not known.

Side effects. Side effects may include one or more of the following.

Nausea and vomiting may be caused by pronounced stimulating effects on the vomiting center. These effects may be counteracted by some phenothiazine derivatives, but these drugs should not be given in the presence of hypotension, since they will augment it.

Constipation may outlast the analgesic effect. Cathartics and enemas are frequently required. *Urinary retention* may require catheterization.

Postural hypotension with dizziness and faintness may occur. These patients should be instructed to arise or change positions slowly to allow compensatory mechanisms to become effective. These symptoms may not occur if the patient remains recumbent.

Depression of respiration and coughing tends to result in retained secretions and predisposition to atelectasis. Coughing and deep breathing should be encouraged in these patients. Mechanical assistance with intermittent positive

pressure breathing (IPPB) may be necessary to promote adequate respiratory excursions.

Behavioral changes, such as increased restlessness and excitement, tremors, delirium, and insomnia, may occur. These usually require use of a different analgesic.

Allergic reactions, which include urticaria, skin rash, itching (itching of the nose is a common occurrence), or activation of other allergic phenomena such as asthma, may occur in the allergic individual. In these cases the drug should be discontinued and another analgesic substituted.

Contraindications. Because of its depressant effect on respiration, its tendency to increase intracranial pressure, and its tendency to make the patient less responsive, morphine is contraindicated or used cautiously for patients with head injuries and for patients who have had a craniotomy performed. Other persons for whom it may not be indicated are those with bronchial asthma, hypertrophy of the prostate gland, or stricture of the urethra (because of the effect on smooth muscle). Morphine is also contraindicated in acute alcoholism and in convulsive disorders, and it must be used with caution for patients with inadequate oxygen–carbon dioxide exchange.

Acute poisoning. Poisoning with opium or morphine occurs from overdoses taken as a medicine or with suicidal intent. As a rule, the toxic dose of morphine for the adult who is not in pain is about 60 mg. (gr. 1), and the lethal dose is approximately 250 mg. (gr. 4). Death may come within the hour after ingestion of a fatal dose, or the patient may linger for 6 to 12 hours. The longer the patient lives, the better his chances for recovery since the drug is being destroyed and excreted and restorative measures can be instituted. The nurse is often in a position to detect the early symptoms of poisoning, and if she is knowledgeable and alert to her responsibilities, she will not allow the poisoning to reach an advanced stage.

Symptoms begin with depression, which progresses into a deep sleep from which the patient at first is easily aroused; then it becomes increasingly difficult to arouse him (stupor); and

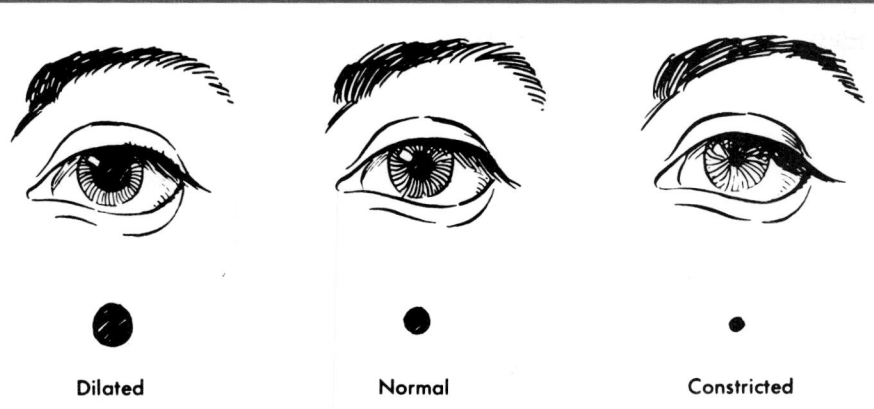

Dilated   Normal   Constricted

Figure 13-1
Salts of morphine produce constriction of the pupil. Pinpoint pupils occur only in advanced states of poisoning.

finally he cannot be aroused at all (coma). A significant early symptom of overdosage is slow respirations (10 to 12 per minute). In advanced poisoning the respirations may be 2 to 4 per minute, and Cheyne-Stokes breathing may be observed. Death usually results from asphyxia brought on by a developing respiratory failure; hence, this condition becomes a focal point toward which therapy must be directed. The pupils of the eyes are at first constricted, later they become pinpoint sized, and as the asphyxia deepens, the pupils dilate. The patient, as a rule, perspires freely and increasingly as poisoning advances. In early stages the skin is warm as well as moist, and the color is fairly normal, but later the body temperature falls and the skin feels cold and clammy and appears cyanotic or gray. The heart action is not much affected at first, but later the pulse becomes weak and irregular. The blood pressure is usually maintained near normal until the lack of oxygen becomes pronounced and shock develops.

The symptoms of poisoning that the nurse should regard as particularly significant are slow respirations (less than 12 per minute), deep sleep, and constricted pupils. Further doses of morphine should be withheld when these symptoms appear and the patient carefully watched

to prevent the development of more serious symptoms. If a toxic dose has already been taken, however, prompt treatment is necessary to save the patient's life. Attention must be focused on respiration. The older respiratory stimulants have been replaced by the morphine antagonists, which give very good results. (See the discussions on nalorphine hydrochloride and levallorphan tartrate later in this chapter.) Artificial respiration should be given without delay if breathing has become dangerously slow.

Treatment is directed toward elimination of the poison from the body. If the drug has been taken orally, the stomach should be emptied. Repeated lavage, however, is not recommended. Tannic acid or dilute potassium permanganate solution (1:2000) may be used to wash out the stomach, since these agents attack alkaloids chemically and thereby inactivate them. Strong black coffee, as hot as may be given with safety, may be administered by tube, by mouth, and also by rectum. Additional measures consist largely of keeping the patient awake, as warm and dry as possible, and by changing the patient's position frequently to prevent the development of hypostatic pneumonia. Prolonged stupor also requires that attention be given to food intake, fluids, and disten-

245

tion of the bladder. Measures that uselessly exhaust the patient should be avoided.

Opium

The following are the preparations of whole opium drugs.

Opium tincture, **B.P.** *(Laudanum).* The usual dose is 0.6 ml. (10 minims) and the range of dosage 0.3 to 1 ml. It is used to check intestinal peristalsis. It contains approximately 10 mg. of morphine per milliliter.

Paregoric, **U.S.P.;** *camphorated opium tincture,* **B.P.** The usual dose is 5 ml. and range of dosage 5 to 10 ml. This is a 1:250 solution of opium together with benzoic acid, camphor, oil of anise, glycerin, and diluted alcohol. Paregoric is given to check intestinal peristalsis. It contains approximately 0.4 mg. of morphine per milliliter.

The foregoing preparations of whole opium must be given by mouth and are not suited to parenteral injection. This is partly because the two tinctures contain alcohol and because preparations of whole opium contain resins and other substances that are not readily soluble in water and tissue fluids.

Opium and belladonna suppositories. These are no longer official preparations, but they continue to be prescribed for the analgesic action of opium and the antispasmodic effect of belladonna. Some physicians prescribe them for relief of painful hemorrhoids and for patients who have had a transurethral resection. The usual dose is one suppository inserted rectally every 3 to 4 hours. Each suppository contains 65 mg. (gr. 1) of opium and 8 mg. (gr. $\frac{1}{8}$) of belladonna in a suitable base.

Morphine

Morphine sulfate, **U.S.P., B.P.** Morphine sulfate is available as tablets, capsules, and a solution for injection in vials or ampules. The injection form may also contain atropine or scopolamine. The usual dose is 10 mg. (gr. $\frac{1}{6}$); the range of dosage is 5 to 15 mg. (gr. $\frac{1}{12}$ to $\frac{1}{4}$).

Morphine hydrochloride, **B.P.** The usual dose is 15 mg. (gr. $\frac{1}{4}$); the range of dosage is 8 to 20 mg. (gr. $\frac{1}{8}$ to $\frac{1}{3}$).

Although the dosage (15 mg.) for both mor-

phine sulfate and morphine hydrochloride is sometimes ordered, investigators are of the opinion that 10 mg. (gr. $\frac{1}{6}$) per 70 kilograms of body weight comes closer to being an optimal dose than 15 mg. Larger doses may be needed sometimes, but they are associated with a higher incidence of untoward effects. The action and uses of these two salts are the same.

Morphine is readily absorbed after subcutaneous or intramuscular injection; more than half the drug is absorbed within 30 minutes after injection. Onset of action occurs within 5 to 10 minutes, a euphoric action (pleasant drowsiness, freedom from anxiety and fear) occurs within 30 minutes, and peak action (rise in pain threshold) or maximum analgesic action occurs in 60 to 90 minutes. Actual increase in the pain threshold may last only a few hours, but the decreased emotional reaction to pain may permit the patient to endure the pain for 4 to 6 hours or more. This, of course, depends upon the patient's reaction to the drug, dosage given, and severity of pain. About 90% of the drug is excreted in the urine within 24 hours. The drug is inactivated by the liver.

Morphine may be given orally, and onset of action then occurs in 10 to 15 minutes. However, since absorption from the gastrointestinal tract is highly variable, this route is less dependable for therapeutic effectiveness and is seldom used.

Morphine may be given intravenously; peak action occurs in 5 minutes. The drug must be administered slowly to avoid severe reactions in patients with hypersensitivity to morphine.

Dosage for children is 0.1 to 0.2 mg. per kilogram of body weight given subcutaneously.

Morphine injection, **U.S.P., B.P.** This is a sterile solution of a suitable salt of morphine in water for injection.

Codeine

Codeine phosphate, **U.S.P., B.P.;** *codeine phosphate tablets,* **U.S.P., B.P.** The usual dose is 30 mg. (gr. $\frac{1}{2}$); the range of dosage, 15 to 60 mg. (gr. $\frac{1}{4}$ to 1). After subcutaneous injection peak effect is reached in 30 to 60 minutes; duration of effect is 3 to 4 hours. Codeine is a natural alkaloid of opium, but it is made from morphine.

Codeine sulfate, N.F., is like the phosphate, except that it is less soluble in water. Codeine is about one sixth as analgesic as morphine. It is also less constipating (although it does cause constipation) and less depressing to respiration. Codeine is less habit-forming than morphine, although drug dependence does occur. It is a preparation of choice in cough mixtures for the treatment of a dry, unproductive cough. Doses beyond 60 mg. are thought to be inadvisable because if effect is not secured with 60 mg. it will not be accomplished with a higher dosage. Large doses of codeine tend to stimulate the brainstem. Codeine has a greater tendency to excite nerve centers than morphine.

Dosage for children for pain is 3 mg. per kilogram of body weight for a 24-hour period in divided doses; for cough the dose is one third to one half that for pain.

Codeine is available in a variety of forms as tablets or capsules, in solution for injection in vials and ampules, and in elixir and syrup form for coughs. Codeine is also prepared in combination with other drugs such as aspirin.

Terpin hydrate and codeine elixir, **N.F.** Usual dose is 5 ml., which contains 10 mg. of codeine (gr. $^1/_6$).

Dihydrocodeinone bitartrate **(Dicodid, Hycodan, Tussionex).** This is similar in action to codeine sulfate (or phosphate) but more active and more likely to cause drug dependence. It is used to relieve cough. The dose is 5 to 15 mg. (gr. $^1/_{12}$ to $^1/_4$). It is marketed in oral tablets and a syrup.

Pantopon

Pantopon is an artificial mixture composed of the purified alkaloids of opium in the same proportion as they are found in opium but in about five times the concentration. It is free from gums, resins, and the like. Some think it is more valuable than opium itself; however, this is questionable. Pantopon has an advantage in that it can be injected and opium cannot. Patients who are hypersensitive to morphine can sometimes tolerate pantopon satisfactorily. The dosage is twice that of morphine. It may be administered orally or subcutaneously. The usual therapeutic dose is 20 mg. (gr. $^1/_3$).

Papaverine hydrochloride, N.F., B.P.; papaverine hydrochloride injection, N.F.

The usual intramuscular dose is 30 mg. (gr. $^1/_2$); the range of dosage is 30 to 60 mg. (gr. $^1/_2$ to 1), although larger doses are sometimes given. The usual oral dose is 100 mg. (gr. $1^1/_2$). It can be administered orally, intramuscularly, or intravenously. In emergencies it is usually given slowly by intravenous injection; however, this route may cause cardiac arrhythmias. The depressant effects on the brain are much less than those of morphine. Papaverine has an antispasmodic action on smooth muscle of the body. It has a relaxing effect on the coronary arteries and on the smooth muscles of the bronchi, the gastrointestinal tract, the ureters, and the biliary system. Since papaverine is one of the alkaloids of opium, it formerly came under the federal narcotics law, although it is practically devoid of narcotic action. *Copavin* contains 15 mg. each of codeine sulfate and papaverine hydrochloride. It is a cough depressant.

Dihydromorphinone hydrochloride (Dilaudid Hydrochloride)

This is prepared from morphine. The usual dose of dihydromorphinone is 2 mg., which is about five times as analgesic as morphine. It may be given orally, subcutaneously, or by suppository. The last preparation allows for slower absorption and more prolonged effect, which is an advantage because the duration of analgesic effect is shorter than that of morphine. Its analgesic effect is accompanied by minimal hypnotic effect, which is desirable when the drug is given to patients in whom it is important to relieve pain without producing a stupefying effect. It depresses respiration, but side actions such as euphoria, nausea, vomiting, and constipation seem to be less marked than with morphine. Both drug dependence and tolerance can occur. Federal narcotics regulations apply to this drug.

Synthetic narcotic analgesics

Mention has been made that morphine falls short of being an ideal analgesic, not because it is not sufficiently potent but because it depresses respiration, produces constipation, and may produce drug dependence. Consequently,

Table 13-1 Selected effects of opiates

	Morphine	*Codeine*	*Dilaudid*	*Papaverine*
Potency of analgesic action	Potent	One-sixth to one-tenth that of morphine	Ten times more potent than morphine	None
Potency of narcotic action	Potent	Mild	Ten times more potent than morphine	None
Effects Respiration	Markedly depressed Carbon dioxide retention	Depression one-fourth that of morphine	Like morphine	None or slight bronchial relaxation
Gastrointestinal	Decreased activity, spasm, and constipation	Like morphine but less prominent	Like morphine but less constipating	Relaxes
Biliary	Increased intrabiliary pressure Possibility of spasm	Less intense spasms than from morphine	Like codeine	Relaxes
Genitourinary Ureters	Possibility of spasms Increased tone, decreased motility	Increased tone, decreased motility	Like morphine	Relaxes
Bladder	Increased sphincter tone Retention of urine	Increased tone, decreased motility	Like morphine	Relaxes
Uterus	Tone increased Contractions decreased	N.S.*	Like morphine	None
Eyes	Pupil constriction	Less than morphine	Like morphine	None
Cerebral	Stimulation of vomiting center—nausea and vomiting Depressed cough center Cortical sedation Rise in pain threshold Euphoria	Less than morphine Large doses required to produce euphoria	Less than morphine	None

*N.S. = not significant.

Table 13-2 Comparison of narcotic analgesics for subcutaneous or intramuscular administration

Generic name	Trade name	Average adult dose	Usual range of single dose	Onset of action	Peak action	Duration of action
Nonsynthetic narcotic analgesics						
Morphine	—	10 mg. (gr. 1/6)	5 to 15 mg. (gr. 1/12 to 1/4)	5 to 10 min.	1 hr.	4 to 6 hr.
Codeine	—	30 mg. (gr. 1/2)	15 to 60 mg. (gr. 1/4 to 1)	5 to 10 min.	30 to 60 min.	3 to 4 hr.
Dihydromorphinone	Dilaudid	2 mg.	1 to 4 mg.	5 to 10 min.	1 hr.	3 to 4 hr.
Pantopium	Pantopon	20 mg. (gr. 1/3)	5 to 20 mg. (gr. 1/12 to 1/3)	5 to 10 min.	1 hr.	3 to 4 hr.
Synthetic narcotic analgesics						
Meperidine	Demerol Pethidine	50 to 100 mg.	50 to 150 mg.	15 min.	1 hr.	2 to 4 hr.
Anileridine	Leritine	25 to 50 mg.	25 to 100 mg.	15 min.	1 hr.	2 to 4 hr.
Methadone	Adanon Amidone Dolophine	7.5 mg.	2.5 to 10 mg.	10 min.	1 to 2 hr.	4 to 6 hr.
Phenazocine	Prinadol	2 mg.	1 to 3 mg.	5 to 20 min.	1 hr.	2 to 6 hr.
Alphaprodine	Nisentil	40 to 60 mg.	40 to 60 mg.	5 min.	30 min.	2 hr.
Levorphanol	Levo-Dromoran	2 to 3 mg.	1 to 3 mg.	15 min.	1 to 1 1/2 hr.	4 to 8 hr.

there has been an almost continuous search for an analgesic with fewer of the disadvantages of morphine. Some of the newer agents have been found to exhibit some advantages over morphine. For a comparison of dosage and action time of various nonsynthetic and synthetic narcotic analgesics administered subcutaneously or intramuscularly, see Table 13-2.

Meperidine hydrochloride, U.S.P. (Demerol Hydrochloride)

Meperidine hydrochloride is a synthetic substitute for morphine discovered by two German scientists who were searching for a substitute for atropine. It is a stable, white crystalline powder that is soluble in alcohol and very soluble in water.

Action and result. Meperidine depresses the central nervous system, probably at both the cortical and subcortical levels. The exact mechanism of action is unknown. Its most outstanding effect is to produce analgesia. It is especially effective for visceral pain, although it also relieves pain in structures of the body wall. Its analgesic potency is said to be slightly greater than codeine and lasts 2 to 4 hours, depending on the dosage. The onset of action occurs in 15 minutes, and peak action occurs in 1 hour. It

249

is about one tenth as analgesic as morphine; hence, severe pain is not well controlled by meperidine. Euphoria is produced in some patients and lasts for an hour or so. Compared to morphine it is less likely to cause sleep and sedation unless large doses are given. There is little depression of the respiratory center with the usual therapeutic doses; however, toxic doses can produce marked depression. Compared to morphine, it is less likely to cause nausea and vomiting and it does not produce pupillary constriction or depress the cough center.

Meperidine in therapeutic doses has little or no effect on the cardiovascular system, particularly if the patient is in a recumbent position. When given to patients who are up and about or when given by rapid intravenous injection, postural hypotension and fainting may result. Like morphine it is prone to cause an elevation of intracranial pressure and must be used cautiously in patients with head injuries or conditions in which there is an elevation of cerebrospinal pressure.

Meperidine was formerly thought to be a useful agent to relieve the spasm of smooth muscle, but it has been found that it resembles morphine in some of its effects on smooth muscle; it has been found to promote spasm of muscle in the biliary tract. It exerts a rather weak antispasmodic effect on the bronchial musculature and can more safely be used than morphine for the asthmatic patient who has need for an analgesic. The tendency to produce spasm in the smooth muscle of the gastrointestinal tract is said to be somewhere between that of morphine and codeine. It is rather mildly spasmogenic and does not produce constipation; therefore, it is of no value in the therapy of severe diarrhea. It has more effect on the small intestine than on the colon. The emptying of the stomach is somewhat retarded.

Uses. Meperidine is used primarily as a substitute for morphine to produce analgesia. When so used it has the advantage of producing much less sedation and constipation. However, it does not take the place of morphine for the relief of severe pain. It is quick acting and short

acting. It is suited to the management of intermittent pain such as renal colic.

Meperidine is widely used as a preanesthetic agent.

In obstetrics it is frequently combined with scopolamine, promethazine, or one of the short-acting barbiturates to produce obstetric amnesia.

Preparation, dosage, and administration. Meperidine hydrochloride is available for oral use in 50- and 100-mg. tablets and in ampules, vials, and disposable injection units for parenteral administration. The single oral or parenteral dose usually varies from 50 to 100 mg. For severe pain doses up to 150 mg. may be given. The usual dosage for children is 6 mg. per kilogram of body weight for 24 hours, given in divided doses. It is also available as a syrup. Although meperidine can be given orally, it is more effective when given intramuscularly. Occasionally it is given rectally, and it is rarely administered intravenously. It may be given orally for relief of chronic pain. It is irritating to subcutaneous tissue.

Side effects and toxic effects. Side effects include dizziness, nausea and vomiting, dry mouth, sweating, headache, fainting, and drop in blood pressure. Toxic effects include dilated pupils, mental confusion, tremor, incoordination, convulsions, and respiratory depression. Death may result. Toxic effects are said to produce more physical impairment than any of the narcotic drugs.

Meperidine has a distinct capacity to produce drug dependence. Some physicians are of the opinion that dependence develops more rapidly than with morphine. Withdrawal symptoms develop more rapidly but are thought to be less severe. At one time tolerance was thought to develop more slowly than with morphine, but if pain is to be controlled, the drug must be given more often because of the short duration of action, and therefore tolerance develops more quickly. It is subject to provisions of the Harrison Narcotic Law.

Treatment of acute intoxication depends upon the severity of the symptoms. If respiratory depression becomes severe it can be antagonized by the administration of nalorphine.

Plate 6
Papaver somniferum (opium poppy).

Contraindications. Meperidine is contraindicated in severe dysfunction of the liver (since the drug is inactivated in the liver), in certain conditions involving the gallbladder and the bile ducts (since meperidine causes contraction of these structures), and in cases in which there is increased intracranial pressure.

Anileridine hydrochloride, N.F.
(Leritine Dihydrochloride)

Anileridine is a synthetic analgesic closely related to meperidine. It is available as a dihydrochloride for oral use. Anileridine is also available as a phosphate for parenteral administration.

Action and result. The action of anileridine is like that of meperidine. Its analgesic activity is three to six times greater than that of meperidine but less than that of morphine. Duration of action is slightly less than that of meperidine and considerably less than that of morphine.

Uses. Anileridine is used to relieve moderate to severe pain and many medical, surgical, obstetric, and dental situations.

Preparation, dosage, and administration. Anileridine hydrochloride is available in 25-mg. tablets for oral use. Anileridine phosphate is available as a solution in which 25 mg. is contained in each milliliter for parenteral administration. The usual adult dose is 25 to 50 mg. subcutaneously or intramuscularly every 4 to 6 hours. Peak action occurs in 1 hour and duration of action may last up to 4 hours.

Side effects and toxic effects. Side effects are similar to those of meperidine. Nervousness and restlessness caused by cerebral excitement have been reported. Toxic effects include respiratory and circulatory depression. Its addiction liability

is equivalent to that of morphine. Anileridine is antagonized by nalorphine.

Methadone hydrochloride, U.S.P., B.P.

Methadone was synthesized during World War II by German chemists. It occurs as a white crystalline substance that has a bitter taste and that is soluble in both alcohol and water.

Action and result. Methadone resembles morphine in a number of respects. It also depresses the central nervous system and acts as a potent analgesic, although it has a weaker sedative effect than morphine. Only in minimal doses does it cause less respiratory depression than morphine. Euphoria is less intense than that produced by morphine. The effects of methadone on smooth muscle are somewhat more variable than morphine, but, on the whole, the results are similar.

Uses. Methadone is used primarily as an analgesic. The duration of its effect is about the same as for morphine. It is somewhat more satisfactory for the relief of chronic pain than morphine, but it is not as useful as a preanesthetic medication.

It is given to relieve cough because of its depressant effect on the cough center. This type of drug is called an antitussive.

Methadone is sometimes substituted for morphine in the treatment of morphine addiction. This can be done because addiction develops more slowly and the withdrawal symptoms are less severe than those associated with morphine.

Preparation, dosage, and administration. Methadone hydrochloride is available in 2.5-, 7.5-, and 10-mg. tablets and in solutions dispensed in ampules or multiple-dose vials containing 10 mg. per milliliter. It is also available as an elixir (1 mg. per milliliter) and as a syrup (0.34 mg. per milliliter). The usual oral or parenteral dose is 7.5 mg. every 4 hours as necessary; the range of dosage is 2.5 to 10 mg. To relieve cough 1.5 to 2 mg. is given. Methadone is sometimes administered orally but more often parenterally. It is more effective than morphine when given orally. Subcutaneous injections sometimes cause local irritation, in which case intramuscular injection is preferred. If it is given intravenously the patient should be in recumbent position.

Side effects and toxic effects. Methadone exhibits some of the same disadvantages as morphine. It causes nausea and vomiting, itching of the skin, constipation, light-headedness, and respiratory depression. Death results from respiratory failure.

Both tolerance and addiction occur following repeated doses of methadone. The same precautions need to be observed in the administration of methadone as for morphine. Nalorphine acts as an antagonist to methadone as it does for morphine and meperidine. The use and administration of methadone is subject to restrictions of the federal narcotics laws.

Phenazocine hydrobromide (Prinadol)

Phenazocine is a potent synthetic narcotic analgesic similar to morphine, although it is effective in smaller doses and is said to be more rapid in producing analgesia. It seems to produce less sedation than morphine, but its capacity to produce respiratory depression and addiction is very similar to the older drug. It is said to have no effect on uterine contractions.

It is employed as a preanesthetic narcotic, in obstetrics, and in the control of severe pain. It is reported to be useful as an analgesic for patients who are to have angiograms under local anesthesia.

Preparation, dosage, and administration. Phenazocine hydrobromide is available in 10-ml. vials and 1-ml. ampules (2 mg. per milliliter) for intramuscular and intravenous administration. The usual intramuscular dose is 1 to 3 mg. every 4 to 6 hours. It is incompatible with a number of drugs; therefore, it should not be administered in the same syringe with another medication.

Side effects and toxic effects. Side effects other

than those mentioned previously include nausea and vomiting, headache, hypotension, and mild constipation. Severe respiratory depression is relieved by the administration of levallorphan or nalorphine.

Alphaprodine hydrochloride, N.F. (Nisentil Hydrochloride)

Alphaprodine hydrochloride is a white crystalline powder with a bitter taste and a fishy odor. It is a synthetic narcotic analgesic that is chemically related to meperidine.

Action and result. Its analgesic potency is said to be between that of meperidine and morphine. It resembles morphine in that it produces euphoria, mild sedation, slight dizziness, itching, and sweating. It is less likely to cause depression of respiration, nausea, and vomiting than morphine. Its analgesic and general depressant actions are less intense than those of morphine, but it acts more quickly and over a shorter time (about 2 hours). It passes the placental barrier easily, especially if given in conjunction with a barbiturate, and can depress respiration in the fetus unless it is given long enough before the time of delivery. Its effect on smooth muscle is similar to that of morphine. It has little or no cumulative action.

Uses. Alphaprodine is said to be suited for use as an analgesic for obstetric patients and patients undergoing urologic examination. It is also useful as a preanesthetic narcotic prior to minor surgery involving the musculoskeletal system and the eyes, nose, and throat.

Preparation, dosage, and administration. Alphaprodine hydrochloride is available in 1-ml. ampules containing 40 or 60 mg. and 10-ml. vials of solution containing 60 mg. per milliliter. The usual dose is 40 to 60 mg., depending on the size of the patient. The dose may be repeated after 2-hour intervals. Alphaprodine hydrochloride is usually administered subcutaneously. When very rapid and brief analgesia is desired, it is given intravenously; action occurs in 1 to 2 minutes and persists for 30 to 60 minutes.

Side effects and toxic effects. The undesirable effects are similar to those of morphine. Death can result from respiratory failure. Nalorphine

Table 13-3 Selected effects of some
synthetic narcotic analgesics

	Meperidine (Demerol)	*Methadone*	*Levorphanol (Levo-Dromoran)*
Analgesic potency	Between that of codeine (60 mg.) and morphine (15 mg.)	Like morphine	Five times that of morphine Hypnotic effect similar to morphine
Action Onset Duration	15 min. 2 to 4 hr. (intramuscular)	20 to 30 min. 4 to 6 hr.	60 to 90 min. (intramuscular) 4 to 8 hr.
Effects Respiratory	Mild depression Bronchodilation Sometimes bronchospasm	Depression—similar to morphine Bronchial constriction	Depression—like morphine Apnea caused by overdose
Gastrointestinal	Decreased motility Spasm No constipation effect	Increased tone Decreased motility Spasms—like morphine	Decreased motility Spasms Moderate constipation
Genitourinary Ureters	Decreased motility and tone	Spasms—like morphine	—
Bladder	Increased tone Retention uncommon	—	—
Kidney	Not significant Some decrease in urinary output	Antidiuretic action Reduced urinary output	Reduced urinary output
Uterus	Decreased tone and contractions	No relief of pain of labor or uterine contractions	Reduced motility
Eyes	No pupil change with therapeutic dose Blurred vision	Miosis with large dose	Miosis
Salivary glands	Moderate decrease in secretions Dryness of mouth	Stimulation Slight increase in secretions	—
Cerebral	Euphoria Mild depression Drowsiness Dizziness Giddiness	Not significant with therapeutic dose Cortical depression with large doses	—

is an effective antidote. Drug dependence may develop, although this is considered unlikely under conditions in which this drug is used.

Levorphanol tartrate, N.F., B.P. (Levo-Dromoran Tartrate)

Levorphanol tartrate is a white, odorless crystalline powder. It has a bitter taste and is slightly soluble in water. It is a synthetic analgesic pharmacologically and chemically related to morphine.

Action and result. Its analgesic potency is comparable to that of morphine but in smaller dosage. The analgesic effect is said to last somewhat longer than in the case of morphine (4 to 8 hours). Maximum analgesic effects are obtained in 60 to 90 minutes after subcutaneous injection. In man, 2 to 3 mg. of levorphanol tartrate is said to relieve pain as effectively as 10 to 15 mg. of morphine. It has less effect than morphine on the smooth muscle of the gastrointestinal tract. Tolerance develops slowly. (See Table 13-3.)

Uses. This drug is useful to relieve severe visceral pain, such as that associated with terminal carcinoma, renal and biliary colic, myocardial infarction, and gangrene. It is also used as a preanesthetic narcotic as well as for the relief of postoperative pain. It can be used for practically all the same conditions for which morphine is employed.

Preparation, dosage, and administration. Levorphanol tartrate is available in solution, dispensed in 1-ml. ampules and 10-ml. vials of solution containing 2 mg. per milliliter. It is also available in scored 2-mg. tablets for oral administration. Recommended average dose for adults is 2 to 3 mg. The initial dose should be as small as possible to delay the development of tolerance. This drug is usually given subcutaneously, but, unlike morphine, it is almost as effective after oral administration as when given subcutaneously. This constitutes a possible advantage over morphine.

Side effects and toxic effects. The side effects are the same as those for morphine except for a lower incidence of constipation. As is true of most narcotics, dizziness and vomiting are ob-

Table 13-4 Comparison of analgesic dose of certain narcotic compounds

Generic name	Trade name	Equivalent analgesic dose (mg.)
Morphine		10
Codeine		60
Dihydromorphinone	Dilaudid	2
Meperidine	Demerol	100
Methadone	Dolophine (and others)	10
Alphaprodine	Nisentil	40
Levorphanol	Levo-Dromoran	2
Phenazocine	Prinadol	2

served more in ambulatory patients than in those who must remain in bed. The drug is capable of causing drug dependence and must be used with the same precautions that are observed in the use of other such drugs. It is subject to the restrictions of the federal narcotics law.

Oxycodone hydrochloride (Eucodal, Percodan)

Oxycodone is a derivative of morphine and related to codeine. It is five to six times more potent than codeine and also more addicting than codeine, but it is less potent and addicting than morphine. It is used as an analgesic for the treatment of moderate pain and as a cough suppressant. Oxycodone has therapeutic side and toxic effects similar to the other narcotic analgesics. The usual oral dose is 3 to 20 mg.; subcutaneous dose is 5 mg. The same precautions should be used when administering oxycodone as when giving other narcotics. Onset of action occurs in 10 to 15 minutes and peak action in 30 to 60 minutes, with duration of action lasting 3 to 6 hours after oral administration.

Oxymorphone hydrochloride, N.F. (Numorphan)

Oxymorphone is a semisynthetic narcotic with a pharmacologic action resembling that of morphine. It is a potent drug and is useful for treating severe pain. Although the dose of oxymorphone is about one tenth that of morphine, its duration of effect is no greater. Oxymorphone is said to cause fewer untoward effects (constipation, nausea, and vomiting) than morphine. It has high drug abuse potential. Precautions are necessary to prevent respiratory depression and other toxic effects. It may be administered orally in 5- or 10-mg. doses or parenterally in 0.75- to 1.5-mg. doses. Rectal suppositories are also available containing 2 and 5 mg. of the drug. When given subcutaneously the drug acts in 5 to 10 minutes, peak action occurs in 10 to 20 minutes, and duration of action is 3 to 6 hours.

Narcotic antagonists

The antinarcotic drugs nalorphine and levallorphan are weak narcotics rather than stimulating agents. They exert an antagonistic action only when there is an overdosage of narcotics. They are said to act by competitive inhibition; that is, they displace the offending depressant from the receptors of cells where the depressant usually exerts its effect. It is a case of weak depressants replacing a strong one. They cause depression when given alone.

Nalorphine hydrochloride, U.S.P. (Nalline Hydrochloride); nalorphine hydrobromide, B.P.

Nalorphine, a synthetic congener of morphine, acts as an antagonist of morphine, meperidine, and methadone in the event of narcotic poisoning. There is evidence that it also reverses the respiratory depression caused by overdoses of dihydromorphinone, levorphanol, and alphaprodine. It does not reverse the respiratory depression caused by barbiturates or some general anesthetics.

Uses. Nalorphine is of value in the treatment of acute poisoning from morphine and related analgesics, but its use should not exclude the use of other supportive measures for the patient. It is not recommended for the treatment of drug abuse. It can be used to prevent respiratory depression in the newborn when given to mothers shortly before delivery, provided they

have been given morphine or one of the related analgesics.

Large doses of nalorphine hydrochloride cause drowsiness, lethargy, sweating, and dysphoria (misery). In morphine abusers it produces rapid onset of withdrawal symptoms and can therefore be used in diagnosing cases of addiction. Doses beyond 40 mg. are not recommended.

Preparation, dosage, and administration. Nalorphine hydrochloride is a white powder, and nalorphine injection, U.S.P., B.P., is a solution suited for parenteral administration. It is available in 1- and 2-ml. ampules and in 10-ml. vials. The concentration of the solutions varies from 0.2 to 5 mg. per milliliter. It can be given subcutaneously, intramuscularly, or intravenously. The usual adult dose is 5 to 10 mg., which can be repeated if the respirations are not adequate. Since it is a derivative of morphine, it had been subject to the restrictions of the federal narcotics law, but it has now been reclassified and is no longer under such restrictions.

Levallorphan tartrate, U.S.P., B.P. (Lorfan)

Levallorphan is a narcotic antagonist chemically related to levorphanol. It relieves the respiratory depression caused by the action of narcotics but not the depression that may result from the action of anesthetics, barbiturates, or pathologic conditions. It is said to abolish the respiratory depression without affecting the state of analgesia. When given alone, however, it acts as a respiratory depressant and produces slight analgesia.

Uses. The action and uses of levallorphan are much the same as those of nalorphine. When given after or together with narcotics it relieves or prevents respiratory depression. It is fully as effective as nalorphine to antagonize the respiratory depression of morphine, and some physicians consider it more effective. It is less expensive than nalorphine.

Preparation, dosage, and administration. Levallorphan tartrate is available for adults as a solution in which 1 mg. is contained in each milliliter; for children, it is available in concentration of 0.05 mg. per milliliter. Total dosage varies with the patient and the degree of depression. One or more doses of 0.4 to 0.6 mg. may be given as necessary. In acute poisoning with morphine, 1 mg. may be the initial dose. Levallorphan is administered intravenously, as a rule, although it may be given subcutaneously and intramuscularly.

Synthetic nonnarcotic analgesics
Pentazocine, N.F. (Talwin)

Pentazocine is a potent nonnarcotic analgesic for parenteral use. It is a new synthetic compound that may be used in place of morphine and other narcotic analgesics. It is not classified as a narcotic. With repeated and frequent use some tolerance develops. Drug dependence potential appears to be less than that of codeine.

Uses. Pentazocine has been used for the relief of pain in connection with surgical procedures, during labor, in urologic procedures, and in many medical disorders.

Preparation, dosage, and administration. Pentazocine is supplied in ampules of 1 ml. containing 30 mg. of the base. It is also available in disposable syringes and multiple-dose vials and in 50-mg. tablets for oral use. Pentazocine should not be mixed in the same syringe with soluble barbiturates because precipitation will occur.

The average single parenteral dose is 30 mg. by intramuscular, subcutaneous, or intravenous injection. The dose may be repeated every 3 to 4 hours. Following subcutaneous or intramuscular administration, pentazocine acts in 10 to 30 minutes with a duration of effect of 2 to 3 hours. For patients in labor a single intramuscular 30-mg. dose has been found useful. An intravenous 20-mg. dose may give adequate pain relief to some patients in labor when contractions become regular. This dose may be given two or three times at 2- to 3-hour intervals, as needed. Because of limited clinical experience, the use of pentazocine in children is not recommended.

Side effects and toxic effects. Nausea, vertigo, dizziness, lightheadedness, vomiting, and euphoria may occur following the use of pentazocine. Respiratory depression was reported in about 1% of the patients. The usual narcotic antagonists are not effective in the treatment of respiratory depression produced by pentazocine. Artificial respiration and respiratory stimulants such as methylphenidate should be useful.

Propoxyphene hydrochloride, U.S.P. (Darvon)

Propoxyphene hydrochloride is a synthetic analgesic compound with about half the potency of codeine. Like codeine, it does not depress respiration when given in ordinary therapeutic amounts, but unlike codeine, it produces little or no relief of cough. It relieves mild to moderate pain better than severe pain. The onset of its action and the duration of its effects are similar to codeine. It does not act as an antipyretic.

Uses. It is used alone or along with certain other analgesics, such as aspirin, for the relief of pain associated with chronic or recurring diseases like rheumatoid arthritis and migraine headache.

Preparation and dosage. Propoxyphene hydrochloride is available in 32- and 65-mg. capsules. The usual dose for adults is 65 mg. four times a day with or without other medication for the relief of pain.

Darvon compound contains the following: propoxyphene hydrochloride, 32 mg. (65 mg. in Darvon Compound-65); phenacetin, 162 mg.; aspirin, 227 mg.; and caffeine, 32.4 mg. Dosage is one to two capsules three or four times a day.

Darvon and Darvon Compound are given orally. Propoxyphene hydrochloride is not suited to parenteral administration because of a local irritating action.

Side effects and toxic effects. Therapeutic doses do not produce euphoria, tolerance, or physical dependence. Sudden cessation of administration has not been known to produce withdrawal symptoms. It appears to have a low level of toxicity. Side effects of nausea, vomiting, and constipation are considered minimal. Large doses may cause drowsiness and dizziness. Patients are occasionally hypersensitive to this drug. There are no known contraindications except hypersensitivity. It is not subject to the restrictions of the federal narcotics law.

Ethoheptazine citrate, N.F. (Zactane Citrate)

Ethoheptazine is a synthetic nonnarcotic analgesic structurally similar to meperidine. It is without antipyretic and sedative effects and seemingly has no effect on cough and respiration. It is said to be more effective than aspirin when given alone. It is used for its analgesic effects for mild to moderate pain rather than for severe pain. Its greatest use seems to be for the control of pain associated with musculoskeletal disorders, for postpartum and postoperative patients, and for patients in the early stages of neoplastic disease. It is not particularly effective for headaches. It has been combined with aspirin to enhance its effectiveness. This combination is marketed under the name of Zactirin.

Preparation, dosage, and administration. Ethoheptazine citrate is marketed in 75-mg. tablets for oral administration. The dosage may be from 75 to 150 mg. three or four times daily.

Ethoheptazine citrate with aspirin contains 75 mg. of ethoheptazine citrate and 325 mg. (gr. 5) of aspirin in each tablet. Dosage is one to two tablets three or four times a day.

Side effects and toxic effects. Side effects are not often seen. Epigastric distress, dizziness, and pruritus are effects that are observed occasionally. It does not cause addiction.

Nonnarcotic analgesics that are also antipyretics

During the latter part of the nineteenth century, when chemists were trying to find a cheaper source of quinine than the natural source, they discovered a number of compounds that differed in some respects from quinine but resembled it in their ability to reduce fever and relieve pain. Several of these compounds have survived chiefly because of their analgesic properties.

Salicylates

The natural source of salicylic acid is willow bark, although it is now made synthetically from phenol. The cheaper synthetic product is identical with, and therefore as effective as, the natural product. Salicylic acid itself is irritating and can be used only externally, necessitating the synthesis of derivatives for systemic uses. All of these compounds will be referred to as "salicylates" and will be discussed as a group. Usefulness of the various members of the group depends upon their solubility, their salicylic acid content, and their tendency to cause local irritation. Aspirin is by far the most widely used of all the salicylates; 113 million tablets per day were manufactured in the United States in 1967. A chemical relationship among several members of the group can be seen in the following formulas.

Salicylic acid

Aspirin

Sodium salicylate

Methyl salicylate

257

Action and result. Both local and systemic effects may occur.

Local. Salicylic acid is irritating to both skin and mucous membrane. It softens epidermis without producing inflammation. The salts of salicylic acid have no effect on skin, but when salicylic acid is released, after their oral ingestion, it is likely to cause gastric irritation, nausea, and vomiting. Methyl salicylate produces irritation of both skin and mucous membranes and at one time was used for its counterirritant effects. It was rubbed on sore and painful joints and muscles to produce some degree of redness and improved circulation. It now is rarely prescribed for this purpose. In solution the salicylates are weakly bacteriostatic and are capable of inhibiting certain fermentative and putrefactive processes.

Systemic. The systemic action may, in turn, be either analgesic or antipyretic.

Analgesic. The salicylates demonstrate a selective type of depression of the central nervous system. Since all sensory impulses from the surface of the body (with the exception of smell) are conveyed to the thalamus, and most of these sensations are then relayed to the cerebral cortex, the site of action of the salicylates is probably in or near the thalamus and/or cortex. The thalamus appears to be responsible for the conscious appreciation of pain while the cortex is concerned with the sensation and perception of pain. Analgesic doses of the salicylates do not produce dulling of consciousness, mental sluggishness, or disturbances of memory. Unlike the opiates, analgesia produced by the salicylates is not accompanied by euphoria or sedation. They do not cause drug dependence.

There is evidence that salicylates have a selective peripheral action that protects pain receptors against bradykinin, which may be a mediator of the inflammatory process. Salicylates are therefore effective in treating peripheral pain (musculoskeletal pain or muscle and joint pain) and in relieving headache. Salicylates are not effective in relieving visceral pain or severe traumatic pain. Their analgesic potency is less than that of codeine.

The salicylates seem to exert other important actions in the relief of symptoms associated with rheumatic conditions, which are often referred to as anti-inflammatory effects. Exactly how these are brought about is not clear. It is likely, however, that the anti-inflammatory actions of the salicylates play an important part in their analgesic effect.

Antipyretic. Little or no effect is observed in persons with a normal body temperature, but in the febrile patient, a marked fall in temperature may be brought about. The salicylates seem to reduce fever by increasing the elimination of heat. It is believed that they act upon the heat-regulating center in the hypothalamus. As a result of this action, peripheral blood vessels dilate, and heat is lost from the body by radiation and by evaporation of increased perspiration. There is evidently no effect on heat production.

Respiratory. Therapeutic doses of aspirin and sodium salicylate do not affect respiration. Large or toxic doses stimulate the respiratory center, producing increased depth and rate of respiration and can cause *respiratory alkalosis*. Later, toxic doses can cause respiratory acidosis.

Cardiovascular. In patients receiving large doses of salicylates, the plasma volume of the blood increases as much as 20%, hematocrit falls, and cardiac output and work are increased. If the patient has cardiac insufficiency, these effects may lead to cardiac failure and pulmonary edema.

Gastrointestinal. Salicylates in large doses are prone to produce gastrointestinal irritation (gastric distress, nausea, and vomiting). This effect is attributed to both a local and a central action—the gastric mucosa may be affected and also the vomiting center in the brain. The administration of sodium bicarbonate with the oral doses of salicylates helps to prevent irritation, but it also promotes excretion via the kidney. This is not an advantage when the maintenance of a definite blood level is desirable. It is claimed that gastric irritation is decreased appreciably when aspirin is buffered with aluminum glycinate and magnesium carbonate and that it is also absorbed more rapidly. A recent study fails to support this claim. Unlike sodium bicarbonate, these substances do not increase the sodium intake, which is an advantage in certain instances.

Liver damage from salicylates seldom occurs, although massive doses may lower the prothrombin content of the blood. Salicylates should not be taken when anticoagulants (coumadin derivatives) are being administered since this may result in gastrointestinal bleeding.

Absorption and excretion. Salicylates are rapidly absorbed from the stomach and duodenum and are rapidly excreted from the kidney. Rapid excretion explains the need for large and frequent dosage. Salicylic acid, as well as methyl salicylate, to some extent, is absorbed from the skin.

Uses based on local effects. *Salicylic acid* is a constituent of some corn and callus removers, and it is used to remove warts and upper layers of the skin in the treatment of certain skin diseases. It is also used for the treatment of fungal infections. Whitfield's ointment contains benzoic acid and salicylic acid; it loosens the outer horny layers of the skin and is known as a *keratolytic.*

Sodium salicylate is sometimes used as a sclerosing agent in the treatment of varicose veins.

Uses based on systemic effects. The major use of salicylates (aspirin and sodium salicylate) is for the relief of pain (analgesia). When compared on the basis of weight, the former compound is said to be the more potent analgesic. These preparations are especially effective for headache, neuralgia, dysmenorrhea, myalgia, fibrositis, neuritis, rheumatoid arthritis, and rheumatic fever. Aspirin is probably more widely used than any other single therapeutic agent. Feldman, in quoting from a report of the U. S. Tariff Commission, states that 13,481,000 pounds were produced in 1951. A more recent figure of the estimated amount used yearly in the United States is approximately 10,500 tons.

Salicylates are also used to produce antipyresis when reduction of fever is beneficial to the patient. Care must be exercised to avoid giving any of these preparations if the patient is bene-

fiting from the fever or if the cause of the illness is obscured by the reduction of the temperature.

The preparations are helpful in the symptomatic treatment of gout. They are less valuable for this purpose than certain other agents, but they are also less toxic. They decrease the renal threshold of uric acid and promote its excretion.

Unpleasant symptoms associated with a cold or attack of influenza may be relieved by one or more of the salicylates since they relieve muscular aching, headache, and fever, but their use should be accompanied by rest in bed. They exert no effect on the progress of the infection. In other words, it is impossible to "break up" a cold with aspirin as is commonly believed.

Preparation, dosage, and administration. The following are the preparations and dosages of salicylates.

Aspirin, **U.S.P., B.P.** This is a white, crystalline, odorless powder. It has a bitter taste and is poorly soluble in water. In the presence of moisture it hydrolyzes slowly to acetic acid and salicylic acid. It is available in capsule and tablet form. Enteric-coated tablets are available for patients with gastric or duodenal ulcers who would not tolerate the plain tablets well. The usual dose is 0.6 Gm. (gr. 10) every 3 to 4 hours as necessary. It is available in 150-, 300-, and 600-mg. tablets (gr. $2^1/_2$, 5, and 10) for adults and 65-mg. (gr. 1) tablets for children. The latter are coated with a sweet-tasting material that may lead the child to think of aspirin as candy. Aspirin Suppositories, U.S.P., are also available.

Sodium salicylate, **U.S.P., B.P.** This preparation is a white or pinkish powder with a sweetish saline taste. The usual dose is 0.6 Gm. (gr. 10) every 2 to 4 hours as needed. It is relatively soluble in water and is absorbed more rapidly than aspirin. It is available in 300- and 600-mg. tablets (gr. 5 and 10) plain or enteric coated. It is also available in ampules of sterile solution for injection.

Both aspirin and sodium salicylate may be given in large doses to patients with acute rheumatic conditions, as much as 1 Gm. every hour until untoward symptoms appear, such as ringing in the ears. The route of administration is usually oral, and both preparations should be accompanied by ample amounts of water. Sodium salicylate is occasionally given intravenously when high concentrations in the blood are desired and it is difficult to attain them with oral administration.

Salicylic acid, U.S.P., B.P. This form is too irritating for oral administration, but it is a component of many ointments and preparations for external use.

Methyl salicylate, U.S.P., B.P. (Wintergreen Oil). This preparation is too irritating to be used internally except in low concentrations as a flavoring agent.

Salicylamide, N.F. (Salamide). Salicylamide, the amide of salicylic acid, shares the actions and uses of aspirin. It has no advantage over aspirin with the exception that it can be used effectively for patients who are allergic to aspirin. Administration and dosage are essentially the same as for aspirin.

Side effects and toxic effects. The safety range of the salicylates is wide, and most cases of poisoning are mild. However, the indiscriminate use of these drugs by lay persons for every kind of ache or pain has resulted in numerous instances of toxic reactions. Mild poisoning is called salicylism and consists of ringing in the ears, dizziness, disturbances of hearing and vision, sweating, nausea, vomiting, and diarrhea. The so-called salicylic jag results from stimulation of the central nervous system and may progress to a state of delirium. Skin eruption and other allergic manifestations as well as deaths from salicylate poisoning have been reported. Intensive therapy with salicylates and massive doses can produce a decreased prothrombin level in the blood and hemorrhagic manifestations. This appears to accompany a deficiency or diminished intake of vitamin K. There is little likelihood of hemorrhage if the dosage is kept at 1 Gm. or less a day. Methyl salicylate in doses as small as 6 ml. has caused death in children. Other dangerous symptoms of salicylate poisoning include depression, coma, inconstant pulse, first a rise and then a fall in blood pressure, and deep labored respirations

that become slower and slower until respiratory failure results. Poisoning and untoward reactions to the salicylates are frequently a matter of personal idiosyncrasy.

There is no specific antidote for salicylate poisoning; hence, treatment is largely symptomatic. All that is usually necessary in mild cases of poisoning is to stop the administration of the drug and give plenty of fluids. If massive doses have been taken, it may be necessary and desirable to empty the stomach, preferably with gastric lavage, and then instill a saline evacuant. If the symptoms are those of depression, stimulants may be ordered; if the symptoms are those of overstimulation, mild sedatives may be prescribed. The artificial kidney may be useful in eliminating some of the salicylate from the body.

Overdosage in children. Although aspirin and aspirin compounds are among the safest analgesics known, the ease with which they can be purchased has contributed to carelessness in their use. The so-called baby aspirin, which is available in 1-gr. flavored tablets or dulcets, has been responsible for a high incidence of poisoning in young children. Children eat it thinking it is candy. This has produced severe and sometimes fatal poisoning. The younger the child, the more dangerous overdosage is likely to be. Methyl salicylate should not be left where children can obtain it. The fact that it is used as a flavoring agent suggests to the child that it is good to eat.

All salicylates should be kept out of the hands of children, and mothers should be helped to understand that indiscriminate administration of these drugs to children, and particularly to young children, can be dangerous.

Drugs that may be combined with salicylates. Codeine and aspirin are frequently given together, and aspirin is also combined with other analgesics and sedatives. Such combinations are believed to bring more effective relief of pain than any one of the drugs given alone. Carefully controlled studies may in time cause a reversal of this opinion.

Para-aminobenzoic acid (PABA), when administered with sodium salicylate, was found to raise the level of salicylate in the blood plasma. It acts by inhibiting the metabolism of the salicylates as well as their excretion from the kidney. Para-aminobenzoic acid can be given orally for this purpose.

Phenacetin; acetaminophen

$$H_5C_2-O-\underset{}{\bigcirc}-\overset{H}{\underset{|}{N}}-\overset{O}{\underset{\|}{C}}-CH_3$$

Phenacetin

$$HO-\underset{}{\bigcirc}-\overset{H}{\underset{|}{N}}-\overset{O}{\underset{\|}{C}}-CH_3$$

Acetaminophen

These drugs are often referred to as coal-tar analgesics and antipyretics. They are phenol derivatives.

Action and result. The two chief effects of these drugs are to produce analgesia and to reduce fever. Their effects are the same as those described for aspirin. However, they do not cause gastric irritation or uricosuria nor do they affect carbohydrate metabolism or respiration.

Uses. These drugs have been used as analgesics especially for the relief of headache, and have been the active ingredient of many headache remedies. They also have been used to relieve muscular aches and pains of various kinds.

Antipyretics were more in demand when effort was made to cure fevers by antipyresis. Today many physicians look upon fever as a reaction of the body that helps the individual combat infection, and therefore reduction of the fever is not always desirable. Antipyretic drugs are still used for the relief of high fever, especially in children. Aspirin is probably used more than any other single agent for this purpose.

Preparation, dosage, and administration

Phenacetin, **U.S.P., B.P.** Phenacetin is available in powder, capsule, and tablet form. The usual dose is 0.3 Gm. (gr. 5).

Acetaminophen, **N.F. (Apamide);** *paracetamol,* **B.P.** These are available in drops, tablets, and syrup. The usual dose is 0.3 Gm. (gr. 5). The B.P. preparation is available in 0.5-Gm. tablets.

Aspirin, phenacetin, **and** *caffeine capsules,* **N.F.** Each capsule contains 200 to 250 mg. aspirin, 120 to 150 mg. phenacetin, and 15 to 30 mg. caffeine. These same drugs are found in combination and marketed as Empirin Compound, Aspirin Compound, APC Capsules, and a number of others. These three drugs are also combined with codeine or with one of the barbiturates. These preparations are preferably given orally.

Side effects and toxic effects. Side effects are negligible, but the toxic effects are serious and have caused a number of deaths. Poisoning may occur from a single dose or overdose, but it is usually the result of the prolonged use of some proprietary headache remedy. The symptoms include profuse sweating, nausea, and vomiting, skin eruption, weakness, cyanosis caused by the formation of methemoglobin, slow weak pulse, and slow respirations. Most severe cases of poisoning show subnormal temperature, leukopenia, and collapse. Large doses of phenacetin administered over a long period may cause renal papillary necrosis.

Acetanilid may cause hemolytic anemia and has caused neutropenia, pancytopenia, and leukopenia. Phenacetin produces allergic reactions. Considerable individual susceptibility to these drugs seems to exist; some persons are unharmed by them, whereas others develop severe reactions.

These drugs can damage the blood, bone marrow, kidneys, and liver if the patient is adversely susceptible to the drug. This constitutes a strong point against prolonged self-medication. There is some evidence that phenacetin may be carcinogenic.

In cases of mild poisoning it is usually sufficient simply to discontinue the drug and wait for its elimination from the body. In more severe cases gastric lavage may be indicated if the drug has been recently ingested. Blood transfusions and shock therapy may be necessary. Oxygen is sometimes indicated if the patient is cyanotic.

Phenylbutazone, U.S.P., B.P. (Butazolidin)

Phenylbutazone is a white or light yellow powder with a slightly bitter taste and a slight aromatic odor. It is a synthetic preparation that is chemically related to aminopyrine and antipyrine and exhibits similar analgesic and antipyretic actions. It is absorbed rapidly and completely from the digestive tract and more slowly from intramuscular sites of injection. It is likely to cause some irritation regardless of the channel of administration. Renal excretion of sodium and chloride is reduced, causing retention of fluid. In patients with gout the drug brings about a reduction of uric acid in the blood.

Uses. Phenylbutazone is regarded as a potent analgesic to relieve the pain of rheumatoid arthritis and associated conditions (bursitis, peritendinitis, painful shoulder). It is said to suppress inflammation, to relieve stiffness and swelling, and to shorten the period of disability. However, because of the high incidence of toxic effects, its use is recommended only for those patients who do not respond to less toxic drugs. It is used particularly to relieve symptoms of gout when the patient has an acute episode of this disease and does not respond well to conservative measures.

Preparation, dosage, and administration. Phenylbutazone is available in 100-mg. enteric-coated tablets. The initial daily dose for adults is 300 to 600 mg., given in divided portions. The minimal effective dose is then determined and may be as low as 100 to 200 mg. Phenylbutazone is usually administered orally. To avoid gastric irritation it should be given at mealtime, just after a meal or with a glass of milk. Nonsodium antacids also help to minimize irritation without increasing the ingestion of sodium. A diet restricted in sodium chloride is recommended while the patient is receiving this drug.

Side effects and toxic effects. The administration of phenylbutazone is accompanied by a rather high incidence of side effects (approximately 40% of the patients). Side effects include edema, nausea, gastric distress, stomatitis, rash, and dizziness. Toxic effects include hepatitis, hypertension, temporary psychosis, leukopenia, thrombocytopenia, and agranulocytosis. Chronic ingestion of the drug may be associated with acute leukemia and renal and liver necrosis. Some patients experience a reactivation of peptic ulcers with bleeding, and others complain of nervousness, confusion, visual disturbances, and fever and may develop cardiac arrhythmias.

Contraindications. Phenylbutazone is contraindicated for patients with edema, cardiac insufficiency, a history of peptic ulcer or blood dyscrasia, or hepatic or renal dysfunction. Patients receiving this drug should be under close medical supervision, and periodic examination of their blood is recommended to detect early indications of toxic effects.

Oxyphenbutazone, N.F., B.P. (Tandearil)

Oxyphenbutazone is a metabolic product of phenylbutazone. Its uses and toxic effects are similar to those of the parent drug. It is available in tablets containing 100 mg. The average daily dose for adults is 300 to 400 mg. given in three to four equal portions. The administration of the drug after meals is preferable to minimize gastric irritation. Like phenylbutazone, oxyphenbutazone can cause liver damage and depression of the bone marrow. Its use should also be restricted.

Indomethacin, N.F. (Indocin)

Indomethacin is a new antirheumatic drug that is chemically unrelated to the previously discussed analgesic agents or corticosteroids. It has potent anti-inflammatory, analgesic, and antipyretic activity, but it may cause some serious adverse effects.

Uses. The drug has been found effective in the treatment of rheumatoid arthritis, degenerative joint disease of the hip, and gout.

Preparation, dosage, and administration. Indomethacin is supplied in capsules of 25 and 50 mg. each. The average dose for adults is 25 to 50 mg. two or three times daily by mouth.

Side effects and toxic effects. Indomethacin is a potent drug that can cause serious side effects and toxic effects. It may cause peptic ulceration and gastric irritation and is contraindicated in patients who have peptic ulcer, gastritis, or ulcerative colitis. The safety of the drug in pregnant women and the pediatric age group has not been established. Adverse effects also include headache, dizziness, skin rashes, and bone marrow depression.

Drugs used in the treatment of gout

Gout is a metabolic disease of unknown origin. Heredity is thought to have a bearing on the incidence of the disease since it occurs more often in relatives of persons with gout than in the general population. It is seen mostly in males. It is characterized by defective purine metabolism and manifests itself by attacks of acute pain, swelling, and tenderness of joints such as those of the great toe, ankle, instep, knee, and elbow. The amount of uric acid in the blood becomes elevated, and tophi, which are deposits of uric acid or urates, form in the cartilage of various parts of the body. These deposits tend to increase in size. They are seen most often along the edge of the ear. Chronic arthritis, nephritis, and premature sclerosis of blood vessels may develop if the disease is uncontrolled.

Drugs given to relieve gout are those given to relieve pain and increase elimination of uric acid. The latter are called *uricosuric agents*. Salicylates, probenecid, and colchicine are drugs of choice at the present time. Colchicine, how-

ever, is not uricosuric. Other drugs that are used are phenylbutazone and indomethacin. They are effective in relieving attacks of acute gouty arthritis and may be used when the administration of colchicine is not feasible.

The salicylates increase urinary output of uric acid and, in milder cases of gout, may afford considerable relief. The dosage must be large to accomplish this effect. The recommended dose is 5 or 6 Gm. a day in divided portions for 3 to 5 consecutive days of the week with omission of the drug for the remainder of the week. Dosage must be determined according to the needs of the patient. The effect and dosage of aspirin and sodium salicylate in the treatment of gout are the same. The former preparation is preferable for patients who must have a diet restricted in sodium. The salicylates should not be administered with probenecid, since each is said to counteract the uricosuric effect of the other.

Since uric acid is not very soluble in acid urine but is readily soluble in alkaline urine, the use of an alkalinizing agent is indicated in conjunction with uricosuric agents. The maintenance of an alkaline medium in the kidney prevents the deposit of uric acid and the formation of renal stones and gravel. The amount needed differs with individual patients.

Colchicine, U.S.P., B.P.

Colchicine is an alkaloid obtained from the seeds and corm (bulbous root) of the *Colchicum autumnale* (meadow saffron), which belongs to the lily family of plants. Extracts of this plant have been used for hundreds of years in the treatment of gout.

Action and result. Locally, colchicine is an irritant. The mechanism of its systemic action remains unknown. It does not affect the amount of uric acid in the blood or in the urine (thus it is not uricosuric) and it has no effect on the size of tophi. It does not effectively relieve pain other than that of acute gouty arthritis. It is an interesting drug not only because of its potent analgesic effect in gout but also because of its ability to arrest mitotic division of cells when they are in metaphase. During this phase it prevents the development of the spindle. This occurs in both normal and cancer cells. It has been suggested that colchicine may relieve gout by arresting the formation of lactic acids. Inflammation of synovial tissues is associated with lactic acid production, and this favors a local decrease in pH, which promotes uric acid deposition. Colchicine decreases lactic acid production and the inflammatory response. These effects are apparently caused by colchicine-inhibiting leukocyte mobility and phagocytoses.

Uses. Colchicine is used to prevent or relieve acute attacks of gout. The response is often dramatic, and pain may be relieved within a few hours, the fever and swelling diminishing sometimes after the relief of pain. It frequently must be used in doses large enough to cause some gastrointestinal irritation. Tolerance does not seem to develop. It is sometimes given every night or every other night to prevent the development of an acute attack.

Preparation, dosage, and administration. Colchicine is available in 0.5- and 0.6-mg. tablets. The initial dose of 1 mg. is usually followed by 0.5 mg. every hour or every 2 hours until the pain is relieved or the patient begins to have diarrhea, nausea and vomiting, or abdominal pain. Camphorated opium tincture or bismuth subcarbonate may be required to control the diarrhea. A preparation of colchicine has been prepared for intravenous injection. An ampule contains 1 mg. in 2 ml. of solution. Colchicine is usually administered orally. Inflammatory symptoms usually subside in 12 hours and are completely gone in 48 to 72 hours. The drug should not be administered for the next 3 days to avoid toxic effects from accumulation. Occasionally, it is given by intravenous injection when rapid relief is important or when oral ad-

ministration is not feasible. It is very irritating if injected outside a vein and therefore cannot be given subcutaneously or intramuscularly.

To be effective, colchicine must be given promptly at the first indication of an oncoming attack, and dosage must be adequate. Once the dose that will cause diarrhea has been determined, it is often possible to reduce subsequent doses to prevent diarrhea and still achieve satisfactory relief of pain. Caution should be used when this drug is given to elderly or feeble persons and those with cardiac, renal, or gastrointestinal disease.

Side effects and toxic effects. Prolonged use can cause agranulocytosis, peripheral neuritis, and aplastic anemia. In acute poisoning the patient complains of abdominal pain, nausea, vomiting, and diarrhea, which may become bloody as poisoning advances. Excessive loss of fluid and electrolytes and the dilatation of capillaries result in shock. Scanty urine and blood in the urine indicate damage to the kidney. The pulse becomes rapid and weak, and the patient becomes exhausted.

The main measures used in the treatment of poisoning depend upon the patient and the symptoms that are presented. Treatment is directed toward removal of the poison if possible (gastric lavage) and the prevention of shock. Atropine and morphine will relieve abdominal pain. Artificial respiration and the administration of oxygen are indicated should there be symptoms of respiratory involvement.

Probenecid, U.S.P., B.P. (Benemid)

$$CH_3CH_2CH_2 \diagdown N SO_2 - \bigcirc - COOH \diagup CH_3CH_2CH_2$$

Probenecid is a white crystalline powder that is soluble in alcohol but relatively insoluble in water. Chemically, it is related to the sulfonamides and was first introduced as an agent to inhibit the excretion of penicillin by the kidney.

Action and result. It has been found to inhibit renal excretion of a number of other substances including para-aminosalicylic acid (which is used in the treatment of tuberculosis) and uric acid. It inhibits the reabsorption of urate in the kidney tubules, and this results in reduction of uric acid in the blood. This uricosuric action helps to prevent or retard tophi and joint changes in chronic gouty arthritis. Probenecid is not an analgesic.

Uses. Probenecid is especially useful for the treatment of chronic gout and gouty arthritis. It is not effective in acute attacks of gout. Precipitation of urates in the kidney can be prevented by keeping the urine alkaline. It is also used in penicillin therapy when it is desirable to maintain high levels of the antibiotic in the blood plasma.

Preparation, dosage, and administration. Probenecid is available in 500-mg. tablets. The usual dose is 0.5 to 2 Gm. daily in divided portions. The daily dose must be increased for some patients.

From 2 to 5 Gm. of probenecid is administered orally (frequently with sodium bicarbonate) to maintain alkalinity of the urine. In gout, probenecid should not be given with salicylates because their effects are said to be antagonistic. A high fluid intake to produce copious volumes of urine is recommended to minimize formation of uric acid stones and occurrence of renal colic and hematuria.

Side effects and toxic effects. Probenecid is well tolerated by most patients. A few persons may experience nausea, constipation, or skin rash. Blood dyscrasias, liver necrosis, and serious hypersensitive reactions have been reported, but these are rare. Precautions should be taken against formation of renal calculi.

Sulfinpyrazone, U.S.P., B.P. (Anturane)

Sulfinpyrazone, a drug related to phenylbutazone, is useful in the prevention of attacks of gout because of its potent uricosuric action. The drug is available in 100-mg. tablets and 200-mg. capsules. The drug is administered in doses of 200 to 400 mg. daily in two divided doses, preferably with meals. Uricosuric effects may last for 10 hours after oral administration. The dose may be gradually increased. If acute attacks

occur, it may be necessary to add colchicine, phenylbutazone, or other medications.

Side effects. Sulfinpyrazone may provoke renal colic because of the precipitation of uric acid. It may increase incidence of acute attacks of gout in the early weeks of treatment. The drug may activate peptic ulcers and may cause some blood dyscrasias.

Allopurinol, U.S.P. (Zyloprim)

Allopurinol represents an entirely new approach to the treatment of gout. It blocks the terminal steps in uric acid formation by inhibiting xanthine oxidase.

Uses. Allopurinol is intended for the treatment of either primary or secondary gout.

Preparation, dosage, and administration. Allopurinol is supplied in 100-mg. scored tablets. The dosage varies with the severity of the disease, but the average dose for adults is 200 to 300 mg. per day divided into two or three doses. Larger doses have been used for severe cases of gout. Fluid intake should be sufficient to maintain urinary output of 2 liters.

Side effects and toxic effects. Allopurinol should not be used in pregnant women and in children except in those children whose hyperuricemia is caused by a malignant disease. Allopurinol should not be used in nursing mothers. Toxic effects include liver damage, skin rash, fever, and leukopenia. Allopurinol is not an innocuous drug, and strict attention should be given to the approved package insert before it is used.

■ Hypnotics and sedatives

A hypnotic is a drug that produces sleep, and as a group these drugs have been widely used both for hospitalized patients and by the public at large. Sedatives are drugs that soothe and relieve anxiety.

Hospitalized patients often find it difficult to obtain rest and sleep for a variety of reasons. The surroundings are unfamiliar; they may be subjected to sensory overload or sensory deprivation, and their anxiety level is usually increased. In addition, pain or discomfort may prevent them from sleeping. Equally important

265

as a deterrent to sleep are minor discomforts, such as cold feet, an aching back, a wrinkled bed, lack of sufficient ventilation, too few or too many blankets, a full bladder, or a distended rectum. Occasionally, a patient cannot sleep because he is hungry. It would be a poor nurse who would rely entirely on the effects of a hypnotic or sedative to remedy such discomforts.

The only difference between a hypnotic and a sedative action is one of degree. When a drug is given at the hour of retirement and in full dosage, producing sleep soon after administration, it is known as a hypnotic. When it is given in reduced dosage several times during the day and perhaps again at bedtime, it is called a sedative. Sedation is a calming, quieting effect, and the patient who is calm and relaxed during the day usually sleeps better at night. The terms *soporific* and *somnifacient* are synonymous with *hypnotic*. Many of the drugs known as tranquilizers are used for some of the same effects as the sedatives. Hypnotics act much like general anesthetics if large enough doses are given. They characteristically spare the medullary centers until large doses have been given.

Sleep and various aspects of nursing care

Sleep can be defined as a recurrent, normal condition of inertia and unresponsiveness during which an individual's overt and covert responses to stimuli are markedly reduced.

During sleep man is no longer in sensory contact with his immediate environment, and stimuli that have bombarded him during his waking hours through his senses of sight, hearing, touch, smell, and taste will no longer attract his attention or exert a controlling influence over his voluntary and involuntary movements or functions. It certainly is not difficult to understand that man needs to escape from constant stimuli.

Present-day knowledge about man's sleep has been obtained from research on normal man using the electroencephalogram (EEG) and electro-oculogram (EOG). The electroencephalogram provides graphic illustrations of brain waves, and this permits comparisons to be made

between brain wave patterns of sleep and wakefulness. Brain waves are, of course, an indication of the electric activity occurring in the brain. The electric activity is greater during wakefulness than during sleep; during sleep the greatest electric activity occurs during dreaming sleep, with the least activity occurring in deep sleep. The electro-oculogram provides graphic illustrations of eye movements. Electrodes placed near the outer canthus of each eye monitor the amount, rate, and size of eye movements. These are also recorded as wave patterns. Rapid eye movements during sleep are associated with dreaming sleep.

Sleep research has shown that sleep is not one level of unconsciousness; it actually consists of four main sleep stages that occur in regular cyclic patterns characterized by variations in depth of sleep and variations in brain waves and eye movements (see Figure 13-2).

Onset of sleep is a drowsy period, and brain wave activity is similar to that seen in normal awake individuals, that is, the brain waves are relatively fast and frequent. As sleep gradually deepens to Stage II sleep, a change in brain waves is seen, with the waves becoming slower in frequency. Stages III and IV are deep sleep stages—the brain waves are slow and have great height and depth. In other words, large brain wave deflections are seen.

After the first deep sleep, sleep decreases in depth and the sleep stages reverse themselves. About 1 to $1\frac{1}{2}$ hours after sleep onset, Stage I sleep reoccurs accompanied by rapid eye movement. It is during these rapid eye movement periods, the period of light sleep, that dreaming occurs. This period usually lasts 20

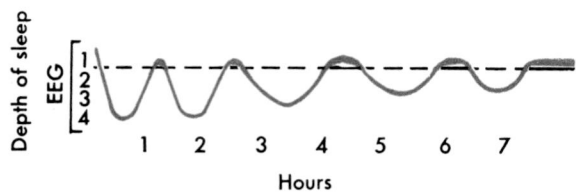

Figure 13-2
Cyclic variation of a night of sleep.

minutes. Following this period of dreaming sleep, there is a gradual deepening of sleep back to Stage IV or deep sleep.

Cycles from light to deep sleep back again to light sleep occur about every 90 minutes. Therefore, in a night's sleep of about 8 hours there are about four to six dreaming periods. Deep sleep occurs primarily in the first half of a night's sleep, with the second half of the night's sleep devoted primarily to dreaming sleep. It is now believed by researchers that everyone dreams every night, even though an individual may not recall having dreamed.

Sleep research indicates that there is both a psychologic and physiologic need for the body to maintain an equilibrium between the various stages of sleep. Physiologic functions of the body tend to be depressed during nondreaming sleep. For example it is known that:

1 There is a fall in blood pressure (10 to 30 mm. Hg)
2 Pulse rate is slowed
3 Metabolic rate is decreased
4 Activity of the gastrointestinal tract is slowed
5 Urine formation slows
6 Oxygen consumption and carbon dioxide production are lowered
7 Body temperature decreases slightly
8 Respirations are slower and more shallow
9 Body movement is minimal

Dreaming sleep, in contrast to deep sleep, tends to increase most of these parameters, and body movements are more noticeable—turning, jerking, arm and leg movements, talking, crying, or laughing—and of course, eye movements can be seen under the closed lids. The dynamic physiologic equilibrium of the body continues to be maintained even during sleep. Depression of physiologic functions occurs during deep sleep and an increase in functions occurs during dreaming. Repeated studies have shown that when individuals are deprived of deep sleep, they become physically uncomfortable, tend to withdraw from society and their friends, are less aggressive and outgoing, and manifest concern over vague physical complaints and changes in bodily feelings. The overall impression made by persons deprived of deep sleep is

that of a depressive and hypochondriac reaction.

However, dreaming sleep is also important. From studies during which individuals were deprived of dreaming sleep (every time the subjects attempted to dream, as evidenced by rapid eye movements, they were awakened and not permitted to dream) the following results were observed. The individuals during their waking hours became less well integrated and less effective. They showed signs of confusion, suspicion, and withdrawal. They appeared anxious, insecure, and irritable, they had greater difficulty concentrating, they had a marked increase in appetite with a definite weight gain, and they were introspective and unable to derive support from other people.

It is the belief of many psychologists and psychiatrists that wish fulfillment finds expression in dreams, and potentially harmful thoughts, feelings, and impulses are released through the dream so as not to interfere in the functioning of the personality during waking hours.

It is also known that in dream deprivation studies, the longer dream deprivation continues, the greater the increase in attempts to dream, until the individual begins to dream almost upon falling sleep. When subjects are finally permitted to dream, a marked increase of dreaming is noted for the entire night, and as much as 75% of the night may be spent in dreaming. This amount diminishes for each succeeding recovery night until the individual has once again established his normal sleep pattern.

Research has shown that deep sleep takes priority over dreaming sleep when there has been prolonged sleep deprivation. In other words, deep sleep needs will be met first, after which dreaming sleep needs will be met. The body attempts to reestablish the normal equilibrium between the sleep stages.

Each individual establishes his own normal sleep pattern, which will vary somewhat from night to night and which is influenced by the individual's emotional and physical state. For most individuals, any alteration in sleeping habits will cause problems in falling asleep, staying asleep, or both. Since drugs affect an individual's physical or emotional state, they also influence his sleep pattern.

Sleep research has also provided important knowledge about drugs and their effects on sleep and dreaming. Drugs commonly used in the hospital and in the home to promote rest and muscle relaxation and to ensure a good night's sleep actually alter the occurrence and length of sleep stages. The stage particularly affected is Stage I in which rapid eye movement occurs.

The drugs known to definitely affect the sleep pattern of man are:

1 Sleeping medications—hypnotics or sedatives (such as glutethimide or pentobarbital)
2 Tranquilizers (such as chlorpromazine)
3 Amphetamines
4 Ethyl alcohol (such as that contained in whiskey or cocktails)

In no study reported in the literature up to the present time has any sleep medication failed to alter the individual's pattern of sleep, and these patterns continue to be disrupted long after the sleeping medication has been discontinued. Sleep research studies also show that it may take as long as 3 to 5 weeks after sleeping medications have been discontinued before the individual's sleep pattern returns to its predrug or normal pattern.

Since both the amphetamines and barbiturates reduce dreaming time, when both these drugs are administered to the same individual the effect on dreaming is an additive one; that is, dreaming sleep is more greatly reduced than when either drug is used alone. Some drugs, such as reserpine, increase dreaming time, which may account for the bizarre dreams reported by patients receiving this drug. Other drugs, such as tranylcypromine parnate (an antidepressant), when withdrawn have been known to cause nightmares, suggesting they may markedly decrease dreaming sleep, which is made up upon withdrawal of the drug. It is theorized by some researchers that the chronic alcoholic has hallucinations upon withdrawal because whiskey reduces total dreaming sleep and he is making up for lost dream time.

Side effects from alteration in sleep pattern include irritability, tremors, tenseness, agitation, confusion, decreased attentiveness, sluggishness or lethargy, and many other symptoms. A new hypnotic, Dalmane, appears to correct abnormal sleep patterns; it reduces sleep induction time and increases sleep-duration time. It does not decrease dream time. However it does decrease Stage IV sleep (deep sleep). The significance of this is yet to be determined.

It is therefore important for nurses to remember:

1 Sleeping medications (hypnotics or sedatives) cause dreaming sleep to be less than normal.
2 When sleeping medications or hypnotics are discontinued, a rebound occurs, and dreaming sleep increases markedly until the loss has been overcome.
3 Sleeping medications cause a prolonged alteration in the individual's normal sleep pattern, which may still be present 3 to 5 weeks after the sleeping medication has been discontinued.
4 Altering the sleep pattern affects the individual physically and emotionally.

Since nurses are in a strategic position to influence the sleep their patients receive, it cannot be stressed enough that nurses must exercise caution when making decisions about giving or repeating an h.s. or p.r.n. order for a sleeping medication, hypnotic, or sedative. Nurses who immediately resort to administering a sleeping medication when a patient complains of being unable to sleep may be doing the patient more harm than good. It is so very important for nurses to keep informed about the drugs they administer, since there continues to be new knowledge about drugs, and this includes the so-called old drugs.

Nurses must also teach their patients and families ways to promote good sleep without resorting to drugs—including those that can be bought across the drug store counter.

Nurses should find out from their patients what their sleep habits are and what they do to ensure good sleep at home. For example:

1 What do they do about environmental control, which includes ventilation, lighting, and noise?

2 What do they do about physical care? Do they shower before retiring or go for a walk?

3 What do they do about food? Do they ingest a snack before retiring?

4 What do they do about quiet recreation before sleep such as reading?

The patient's sleep history and drug history can be valuable aids to help plan the nursing care for the patient that will best promote good sleep.

Another very important factor is that every effort should be made not to disrupt the patient while he is sleeping, if at all possible. Numerous interruptions for various aspects of care can do nothing but alter the patient's sleep pattern.

Characteristics of a satisfactory hypnotic

Since rest and sleep are so important to relieve the effects of fatigue, stress, and strain in everyday life, it is equally if not more important that the sick person have adequate help in securing the benefits of sleep and relaxation. A hypnotic should produce sleep that is refreshing and as much like natural sleep as possible. In addition, the hypnotic should act within a reasonable length of time after administration and allow the patient to awaken somewhere near his usual time of awakening with no hangover effects. The hypnotic should not be habit-forming and should produce no adverse effects on body organs. Some investigators would add as a desirable characteristic a lack of influence on rapid eye-movement (REM) sleep, but this may be premature.

Barbiturates

The barbiturates were among the first drugs to be synthesized. The first one was introduced into medicine by Emil Fischer and Joseph von Mehring in 1903 under the name of Veronal. Phenobarbital, known also as Luminal, is the second oldest of the barbiturates. Since the time of their introduction, hundreds of similar compounds have been synthesized, but only a limited number have proved clinically useful. New compounds have resulted from slight changes in the basic barbiturate molecule, and these changes have resulted in compounds that vary from the earlier compounds mostly in speed and duration of action. The formulas on the following page show the relationship of certain present-day compounds with the basic structure of barbituric acid and barbital. Various members of this family of drugs are made by substituting other substances for hydrogen atoms at position 5.

Some of the barbiturates have stood the test of time very well. Large amounts of these drugs are prescribed and used, as is evident from the fact that thousands of pounds are produced annually.

The barbiturates are all colorless, white crystalline powders that have a more or less bitter taste. They are sparingly soluble in water but freely soluble in alcohol. The sodium salts of these compounds are freely soluble in water.

Action and result. Important actions of the barbiturates are those of sedation and hypnotic effect. Barbiturates have been shown to depress the neurons and synapses of the ascending reticular formation of the brainstem, and this effect may be responsible for the reduction in electric activity of the cortex. Since the ascending reticular formation receives stimuli from all parts of the body and relays impulses to the cortex (thus promoting wakefulness and alertness), depression of the ascending reticular formation decreases cortical stimuli, reducing the need for wakefulness and alertness.

Barbiturates have also been shown to depress the excitability of pre- and postsynaptic membranes; this may be caused by barbiturates inhibiting the release of transmitter substance. However, there is evidence that the barbiturates act at all levels of the central nervous system. The extent of effect varies from mild sedation to deep anesthesia, depending upon the drug selected, the method of administration, the dosage, and also the reaction of the individual's nervous system. The barbiturates are not usually regarded as analgesics and cannot be depended upon to produce restful sleep when insomnia is caused by pain. However, when combined with an analgesic the sedative action seems to reinforce the action of the analgesic and to alter

269

the patient's emotional reaction to pain. Therapeutic doses of the longer-acting barbiturates may result in depression and lowered vitality on the following day ("hangover effect").

All of the barbiturates used clinically depress the motor cortex of the brain in large doses, but phenobarbital, mephobarbital, and metharbital exert a selective action on the motor cortex, even in small doses. This explains their use as anticonvulsants.

Ordinary therapeutic doses have little or no effect on medullary centers, but large doses, especially when administered intravenously,

depress the respiratory and vasomotor centers. Death from overdosage is caused, as a rule, by respiratory failure accompanied by hypotension.

Smooth muscles of blood vessels and of the gastrointestinal organs are depressed after large amounts of barbiturates, but clinical doses do not usually produce untoward effects. The motility of the gastrointestinal organs may be reduced and the emptying of the stomach delayed slightly, but there is apparently little interference with the ability to respond to normal stimuli. Uterine muscle is affected little by hypnotic

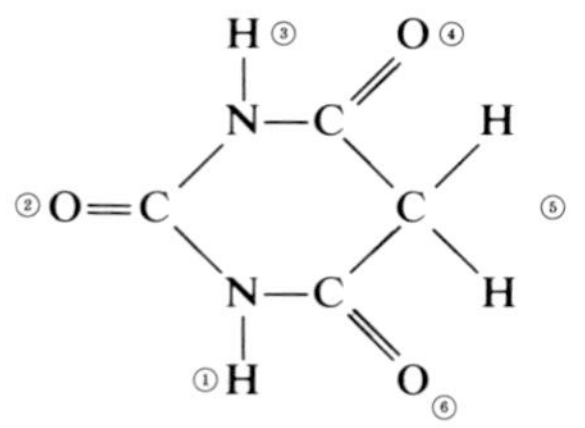

Barbituric acid (contains no carboxyl group but is capable of forming a salt)

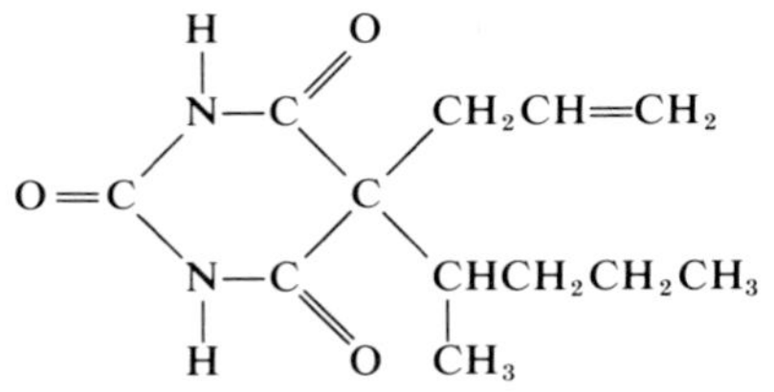

Secobarbital (Seconal)

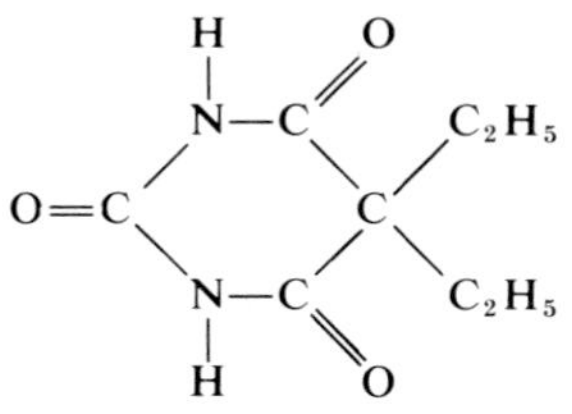

Barbital (diethyl barbituric acid)

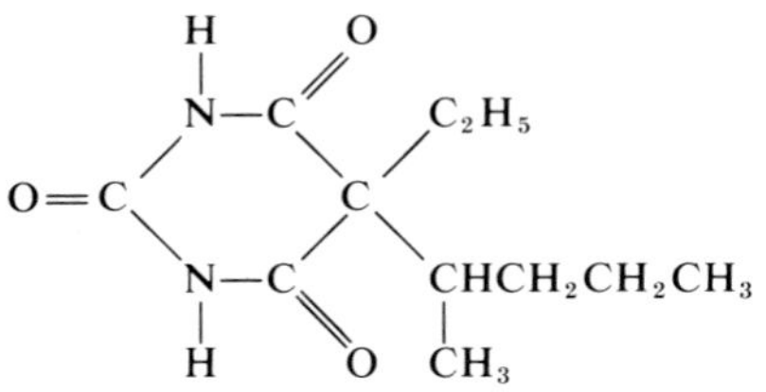

Pentobarbital (Nembutal)

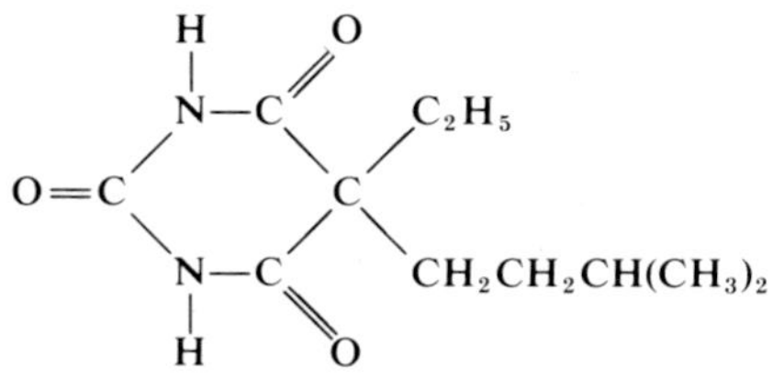

Amobarbital (Amytal)

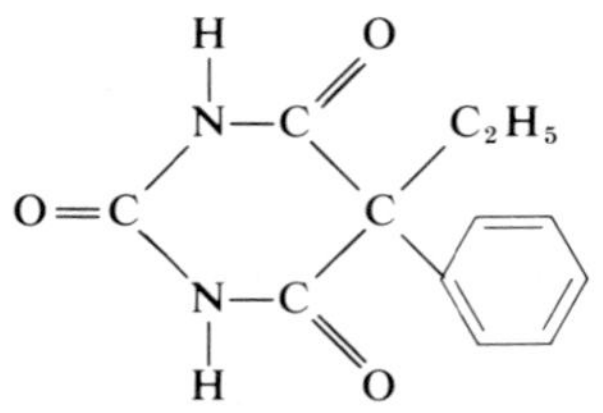

Phenobarbital (Luminal)

doses of barbiturates, and the force of uterine contractions at the time of childbirth is not diminished unless anesthesia has been produced by one of these drugs.

Uses. The barbiturates have many uses and are very popular drugs.

Hypnotics. For best effects the barbiturates should be administered at such times as will coincide with the usual hour of retirement. Long-, short-, or intermediate-acting barbiturates are chosen to meet the needs of individual patients.

Sedatives. The barbiturates have, for purposes of sedation, a wide range of therapeutic uses. Although the tranquilizing drugs have come into a position of great prominence, the barbiturates are still used to calm and sedate the nervous patient and for patients who have physical illness in which there is usually an emotional factor, as in the case of hypertension, chronic ulcerative colitis, and gastric ulcer.

Anticonvulsants. Barbiturates are used to prevent or control convulsive seizures associated with tetanus, strychnine poisoning, cerebral pathology, and epilepsy. Phenobarbital has been especially valuable in the prevention and control of grand mal epilepsy. It may be prescribed alone or in conjunction with other anticonvulsant drugs. Mephobarbital and metharbital are also effective in the symptomatic treatment of certain types of epilepsy.

Anesthetics. For selected forms of surgical procedures, and especially for surgery of short duration, the rapid-acting barbiturates are employed. Thiopental sodium is the preparation most widely used in the United States. These barbiturates are further discussed under "Basal anesthetics" (see p. 309).

Preanesthetic medications. The short-acting barbiturates, such as pentobarbital sodium, are selected for this effect. They are often ordered to be given the night before surgery to enable the patient to sleep and may also be ordered to be given the morning of the operation. They are frequently supplemented by other medications just before the patient is taken to the operating room.

Obstetric sedation and amnesia. For obstetric sedation and amnesia the barbiturates are used either alone or in combination with other drugs, such as scopolamine or meperidine. However, drugs that cause respiratory depression of the mother are likely to cause respiratory depression in the infant as well.

Psychiatry. Barbiturates are sometimes used in psychiatry to temporarily release a patient from strong inhibitions and enable him to cooperate more effectively with his therapist. Amobarbital, pentobarbital, and thiopental are the barbiturates likely to be chosen for this purpose.

Absorption and excretion. Barbiturates are readily absorbed after both oral and parenteral administration. The more soluble sodium salts are more rapidly absorbed than the free acids. Most of the barbiturates, with the exception of barbital, undergo change in the liver before they are excreted by the kidney. Some are excreted partly in an altered form and partly unchanged, and others are excreted in a completely altered form. The longer-acting barbiturates are said to be metabolized or chemically altered more slowly than the rapidly acting members. The more slowly a barbituate is altered or excreted, the more prolonged is its action. If excretion is slow and administration prolonged, cumulative effects will result.

Classification. The barbiturates are classified according to the duration of their action as long-, intermediate-, short-, and ultrashort-acting. This means that the short-acting drugs produce an effect in a relatively short time (10 to 15 minutes) and also act over a relatively short period (3 hours or less). Short-acting barbiturates are used in the treatment of insomnia, for preanesthetic sedation, and in combination with other drugs for psychosomatic disorders. Long-acting barbiturates require 30 to 60 minutes to become effective and act over a period of 6 hours or more. Long-acting barbiturates are used for treating epilepsy and other chronic neurologic disorders and for sedation in patients with high anxiety. Ultrashort-acting barbiturates are used as intravenous anesthetics. Thiopental sodium, which belongs to the ultrashort-acting group of barbiturates, acts rapidly and can produce a state of anesthesia in a few seconds. See

271

Table 13-5 Dosage, administration, and
length of action of barbiturates

Preparation	Usual adult dose	Usual method of administration	Length of action
*Barbital (Veronal); barbitone sodium, B.P.	300 mg. (gr. 5)	Oral	Long
*Phenobarbital, U.S.P. (Luminal); pheno-barbitone, B.P.	30 to 100 mg. (gr. ½ to 1½)	Oral	Long
Mephobarbital, N.F. (Mebaral)	400 to 600 mg. (gr. 6 to 10)	Oral	Long
Metharbital, N.F. (Gemonil)	100 mg. (gr. 1½)	Oral	Long
*Amobarbital, U.S.P. (Amytal)	100 mg. (gr. 1½)	Oral	Intermediate
Aprobarbital, N.F. (Alurate)	60 to 120 mg. (gr. 1 to 2)	Oral	Intermediate
Probarbital sodium (Ipral Sodium)	120 to 250 mg. (gr. 2 to 4)	Oral	Intermediate
Butethal (Neonal)	100 mg. (gr. 1½)	Oral	Intermediate
Sodium butabarbital, N.F. (Butisol Sodium)	8 to 60 mg. (gr. ⅛ to 1)	Oral	Intermediate
Pentobarbital sodium, U.S.P. (Nembutal Sodium); pentobarbitone sodium, B.P.	100 mg. (gr. 1½)	Oral, rectal	Short
Secobarbital sodium, U.S.P. (Seconal Sodium); quinalbarbitone sodium, B.P.	100 to 200 mg. (gr. 1½ to 3)	Oral, rectal	Short
Calcium cyclobarbital, N.F. (Phanodorn); cyclobarbitone, B.P.	200 mg. (gr. 3)	Oral	Short
Butallylonal (Pernoston)	200 mg. (gr. 3)	Oral	Short
Sodium hexobarbital, N.F. (Evipal Sodium)	2 to 4 ml. 10%	Intravenous	Ultrashort
Thiopental sodium, U.S.P. (Pentothal Sodium); thiopentone sodium, B.P.	2 to 3 ml. 2.5% in 10 to 15 sec.; repeated in 30 sec. as required	Intravenous	Ultrashort

*Sodium salts are available.

Table 13-5 for dosage, methods of administration, and length of action.

Administration. The oral channel of administration is preferred and should be used whenever possible. Certain preparations may be given subcutaneously, intramuscularly, intravenously, or rectally, depending on the purpose to be achieved and the general condition of the patient. The intravenous route is the most dangerous and used only for production of anesthesia or in emergencies. Parenteral administration is also used when a patient is too ill to take the drug orally or has nausea and vomiting or when it is important to have a rapid depressant action.

Contraindications. Barbiturates should be avoided for patients who manifest hypersensitivity toward them or who have been previously addicted to them. If a patient tells the nurse that he is hypersensitive to this group of drugs, she should record the statement and make the infomation known to the physician. Seriously impaired hepatic or renal function may also constitute a contraindication for the use of these drugs, although only the physician can decide whether the degree of damage warrants the use of a different type of drug.

Side effects and toxic effects. Unusual effects or reactions may be exhibited as one or more of the following: (1) marked symptoms of hangover—listlessness, prolonged depression, nausea, and emotional disturbances; (2) skin rash, urticaria, swelling of the face, and asthmatic attack; and (3) bad dreams, restlessness, and delirium.

This last category of symptoms may be experienced especially by elderly or debilitated patients. Night nurses find that they need to watch older patients carefully when they have been given a hypnotic dose of a barbiturate. Such patients tend to go to the bathroom more frequently than younger adults and under the influence of a barbiturate may become confused and have difficulty orienting themselves. Barbital, amobarbital, and pentobarbital are said to exert this effect more often than phenobarbital.

Restlessness is also produced when barbiturates are administered to patients in severe pain. The drug, in this instance, does not relieve pain but depresses the higher centers that normally serve as control centers. Mental confusion and delirium may result. An analgesic is usually prescribed to be given with a barbiturate if the patient has pain.

Acute poisoning. Because barbiturates are widely known and obtained with comparative ease, they have been one of the agents of choice for suicide. Poisoning also occurs accidentally and can occur when these drugs are given intravenously by persons insufficiently experienced in giving anesthetics. The fatal dose varies, but when fifteen to twenty times the usual therapeutic dose is absorbed, severe poisoning and possibly death will result. The lethal dose is said to be 1 to 1.5 Gm. or more. When seen in the

earlier stages of poisoning, the patient is usually in a deep sleep or stupor. Occasionally, confusion and excitement precede heavy sleep. When poisoning is fully advanced, the patient is comatose and many of his reflexes are sluggish or absent. Respiration is either slow or rapid and shallow. Lack of oxygen affects the cardiovascular system and results in shock. The blood pressure drops; the pupils may become pinpoint in size; and the pulse is rapid and weak. Death is usually the result of respiratory failure, especially if a rapidly acting barbiturate has been taken. If death is delayed, it is more likely to be caused by hypostatic pneumonia or pulmonary edema.

Treatment. The treatment for acute poisoning will vary with the condition and needs of the patient. Sometimes little more than general supportive measures are required (keeping the patient warm and turned periodically, providing for adequate fluids and nutrition, and so on). If the patient is deeply comatose and unresponsive and having serious difficulty with respiration, great effort may be required to save his life.

If the drug has been swallowed and there is reason to think that part or most of it remains in the stomach, prompt gastric lavage may be done. A saline cathartic is sometimes instilled, after lavage, to hasten elimination of the drug. The danger of aspiration of gastric content at the time of lavage is always a calculated risk. The nurse should have some of the gastric washings saved in the event that a toxicologic examination becomes necessary. At all times the maintenance of an open airway is of primary importance. In severe depression the physician may plan to use an endotracheal tube or a respirator and administer oxygen or oxygen and carbon dioxide. The nurse will be expected to keep a careful check and to make repeated observations of the respirations, pulse, blood pressure, and degree of responsiveness.

Extensive use of analeptic drugs is looked upon with disfavor by some clinicians because many of these drugs are themselves capable of producing toxic symptoms. Picrotoxin and pentylenetetrazol are analeptics that may be prescribed for certain patients to overcome severe general depression as well as respiratory depression. Amphetamines, ephedrine, and nikethamide are examples of central nervous system stimulants that are advocated for the less severe types of depression associated with poisoning from barbiturate drugs. Levarterenol, amphetamines, and phenylephrine may be used to combat circulatory collapse. Hemodialysis is an effective procedure for removing the drug from the patient's system; this procedure may be resorted to only if renal failure occurs. Shock from barbiturates causes a decrease in intravascular volume, and reversal of this phenomenon requires intravenous infusion of volume expanders such as dextran or concentrated albumin.

Chronic poisoning. Drug dependence to the barbiturates can develop. Tolerance is said to develop slowly and to a lesser degree than it does to morphine and related drugs. Occasional doses of barbiturates in quantities of 0.1 Gm. (gr. $1\frac{1}{2}$) do not cause drug dependence. In fact, it takes an appreciably larger daily dose of 0.4 to 0.8 Gm. or more over a period of time to establish drug dependence.

In recent years the abuse of barbiturates has become a problem of increasing concern. The seriousness of the situation is reflected in the large number of state laws passed to regulate the sale of barbiturates and in the continued effort for federal control.

Symptoms of chronic intoxication include slowness of thought, mental depression, incoherent speech, failing memory, skin rash, weight loss, gastrointestinal upsets, and anemia. There is frequently an ataxic gait; coarse tremor of the lips, fingers, and tongue; increased emotional instability; and mental confusion. The clinical manifestations are similar to those of chronic alcoholism. Because of the poor motor coordination, patients may fall and be injured. They are likely to fall asleep while smoking and set the bed or room furnishings on fire. They are unable to work, and they constitute a real hazard if they attempt to drive power machinery. Their judgment may be so impaired that they take additional doses of their drug when they are already seriously intoxicated; this may

account for some cases of reported suicide with barbiturates. Long-continued use of the short-acting barbiturates in large doses results in withdrawal symptoms characterized by great weakness, tremor, anxiety, nausea and vomiting, and a series of grand mal convulsions or psychosis or both. Withdrawal symptoms are precipitated when the drug is appreciably reduced or stopped altogether.

Many opium users are also barbiturate users. They resort to barbiturates when they have difficulty getting their supply of opiates. The barbiturates most commonly selected seem to be pentobarbital, secobarbital, and amobarbital or the sodium salts of these compounds. Some authorities feel that the dependence resulting from the overuse of the barbiturates is, in some respects, more dangerous and undesirable than the dependence resulting from the misuse of opiates.

Treatment. The best treatment results are obtained in an institution with well-prepared personnel, and even then there is a rather high percentage of discouraging results. Abrupt withdrawal of the drug is not recommended.

Advantages and disadvantages encountered in the use of barbiturates. Barbiturates lend themselves to a variety of uses. They are anticonvulsants, anesthetics, hypnotics, and sedatives, although no one of them excels in all of these types of action. They are easily administered in tablets or capsules, and may be given rectally or parenterally. They have a reasonably wide margin of safety.

The main disadvantages are that in large doses they all depress the respiratory center and they are often used for suicide. In addition, they are habit-forming. These are drugs that should never be left at the bedside for the patient to take at will. Patients have been known to hoard barbiturates until they had enough to commit suicide.

In the past these drugs had wide use and were easily obtained, which resulted in indiscriminate use and use for suicidal purposes. State laws patterned after the Harrison Narcotic Act, restrict the sale of hypnotic drugs and prohibit the sale or possession of barbiturates except under proper licensure. Barbiturates may not be purchased or dispensed without a physician's prescription, and the prescription may not be refilled without the physician's personal sanction.

Choice of barbiturate. In choosing barbiturate preparations, consideration is given primarily to the duration of effect produced by the drug and to individual needs of patients. Phenobarbital is an outstanding member of the group of barbiturates because of its anticonvulsant action. Secobarbital and pentobarbital are good examples of short-acting barbiturates, and the ultrashort-acting ones are described under anesthetics.

Barbiturates may be combined in the same capsule so that a long-acting and a short-acting or moderately long-acting preparation can be used to advantage for the patient who has difficulty both in getting to sleep and remaining asleep for the desired number of hours. Tuinal is an official combination of secobarbital sodium and amobarbital sodium, U.S.P. It is available in capsules containing gr. $^3/_4$ (0.05 Gm.) of each barbiturate (total 0.1 Gm., gr. $1^1/_2$) or gr. $1^1/_2$ of each (total 0.2 Gm., gr. 3).

Phenobarbital (Luminal)

Phenobarbital not only requires a relatively long time to take effect but also exerts an effect over a long period (6 or more hours) and is used when prolonged sedation is required. It is used as a hypnotic as well as a sedative for a variety of nervous conditions, such as chorea, gastrointestinal neuroses, disturbances of menopause, and preoperative and postoperative states of tension. It is also proposed as a sedative in certain circulatory and cardiac disorders. Because its action is rather slow, it is not the best drug for certain kinds of insomnia or for use as a preanesthetic medication.

Phenobarbital has a selective depressant action on the motor cortex of the brain when given in sedative doses to epileptic patients. When effective anticonvulsant doses are given, unfortunately some degree of central depression also results. (The patient feels tired, relaxed, and perhaps dull and sleepy.) In this respect phenobarbital is inferior to the anticonvulsant drug diphenylhydantoin (Dilantin). On the other hand, phenobarbital is regarded as one of the least, if not the least, toxic of the antiepileptic drugs. The adult dose varies between 0.1 and 0.13 Gm. (gr. $1^1/_2$ and 2). This may be given in one dose at the time the patient retires, or it may be given in divided doses and spread throughout the day. Should it be necessary to discontinue the drug for an epileptic patient, it should be done gradually and never stopped suddenly or severe epileptic seizures may be precipitated. Phenobarbital is often given to patients after surgical operation on the brain to minimize the irritating effect of the procedure. Patients may continue to take the drug for a year or more under medical supervision.

The action and uses of phenobarbital sodium are the same as those of phenobarbital except that it can be injected when phenobarbital either cannot be given by mouth or the desired effects are not being secured following oral administration.

Caution: Errors sometimes occur if the nurse forgets, or does not understand, that phenobarbital (Luminal) and phenobarbital sodium (Sodium Luminal) are not one and the same drug. The latter, the sodium salt, can be given parenterally but the former cannot.

Preparation, dosage, and administration. The following are the preparations and dosages of phenobarbital and sodium phenobarbital.

Phenobarbital tablets, **U.S.P.;** *phenobarbitone tablets,* **B.P.** The usual dose is 30 mg. (gr. $^1/_2$) orally.

Phenobarbital elixir, **U.S.P.** The usual dose is 4 ml. (1 fluidram) orally.

Sodium phenobarbital, **U.S.P.;** *phenobarbitone sodium,* **B.P.** The usual dose is 100 mg. (gr. $1^1/_2$). This is a powder dispensed in ampules for parenteral or oral administration.

Sodium phenobarbital injection, **U.S.P.** The usual parenteral dose is 100 mg. (gr. $1^1/_2$). A sterile solution of phenobarbital sodium in a suitable solvent is used intramuscularly or subcutaneously. Aqueous solutions of phenobarbital sodium decompose upon standing.

275

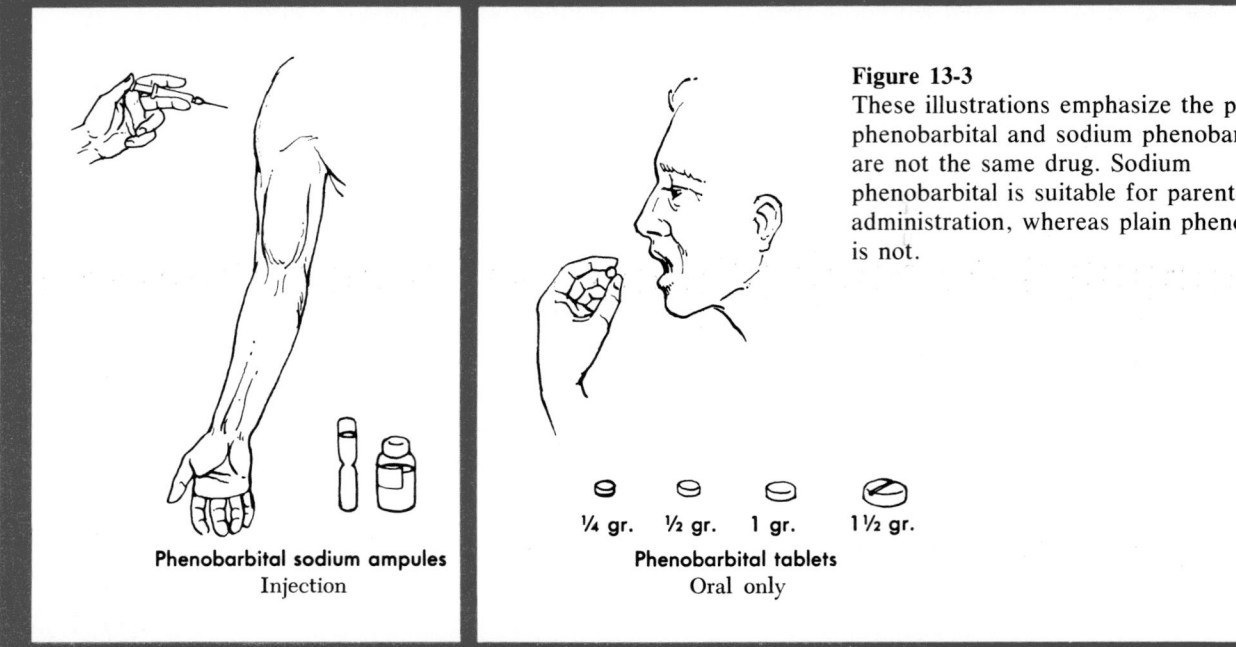

Figure 13-3
These illustrations emphasize the point that phenobarbital and sodium phenobarbital are not the same drug. Sodium phenobarbital is suitable for parenteral administration, whereas plain phenobarbital is not.

Phenobarbital sodium ampules
Injection

¼ gr.   ½ gr.   1 gr.   1½ gr.
Phenobarbital tablets
Oral only

Sodium phenobarbital tablets; phenobarbitone sodium tablets, **B.P.** The usual dose is 30 mg. (gr. $^1/_2$) orally.

Phenobarbital is also available in 50-, 65-, and 100-mg. sustained-release dosage forms.

Sodium secobarbital, U.S.P. (Seconal Sodium); quinalbarbitone sodium, B.P.

Sodium secobarbital is a short-acting barbiturate, more active than barbital, and given in correspondingly smaller doses. Small doses produce a sedative effect and larger doses, a hypnotic effect.

Preparation, dosage, and administration. Dosage of sodium secobarbital is 0.1 to 0.2 Gm. (gr. $1^1/_2$ to 3) for adults. As a preanesthetic agent, 0.2 to 0.3 Gm. is given 30 minutes to 1 hour before the patient goes to the operating room. It is available in 30-, 50-, and 100-mg. capsules and in 30-, 65-, 130-, and 200-mg. rectal suppositories. Sodium secobarbital may also be given by intramuscular or intravenous injection.

Sodium pentobarbital (Nembutal Sodium); pentobarbital calcium (Nembutal Calcium)

Sodium pentobarbital acts over a rather brief period of time (3 to 6 hours), which is sometimes an advantage, particularly if large doses have been given. It is used as a hypnotic and as a sedative prior to anesthesia.

Pentobarbital is one of the short-acting derivatives of barbituric acid, and both pentobarbital and pentobarbital calcium are similar in action and use to pentobarbital sodium. Pentobarbital calcium has no advantage except that it is better suited for making compressed tablets than sodium pentobarbital.

Preparation, dosage, and administration

Sodium pentobarbital elixir, **U.S.P.** (Nembutal Sodium Elixir). The usual dose is 4 ml. (1 fluidram). It is marketed in the form of an elixir for preoperative sedation of children or for elderly patients.

Sodium pentobarbital, **U.S.P.** (Nembutal Sodium); *pentobarbitone sodium,* **B.P.** The usual dose is 0.1 Gm. (gr. 1$^1/_2$) and the range of dosage may vary from 0.1 to 0.5 Gm. for oral hypnotic or sedative use. The preparation is available in capsules, ampules containing the drug in powder form or in solution for injection, suppositories for rectal administration, and sustained-release dosage forms for slow, continuous absorption. Sodium pentobarbital injection, U.S.P., may be given intravenously if prompt action is essential to control convulsive seizures associated with some types of drug poisoning, rabies, tetanus, chorea, and eclampsia. Aqueous solutions of pentobarbital are not stable and decompose on standing or after boiling.

Pentobarbital calcium (**Nembutal Calcium**). Dosage is 0.1 Gm. (gr. 1$^1/_2$). It is available in tablet form rather than capsules for oral administration. It is usually administered orally or rectally.

Nonbarbiturate sedatives and hypnotics
Ethchlorvynol, N.F., B.P. (Placidyl)

$$CH\equiv C-\underset{\underset{CH_2CH_3}{|}}{\overset{\overset{OH}{|}}{C}}-CH=CHCl$$

Ethchlorvynol is a colorless-to-yellow liquid with a pungent odor. It is a mild hypnotic somewhat less predictable than the barbiturates. It acts within 15 to 30 minutes after administration, and the duration of its effects is about 5 hours.

Uses. Ethchlorvynol is said to be useful in the treatment of insomnia if pain and anxiety are not complicating factors. It is also useful for patients who are unable to take barbiturates. It may be used as a daytime sedative. In addition it has anticonvulsant and muscle-relaxing actions.

Preparation, dosage, and administration. Ethchlorvynol is available in 100-, 200-, and 500-mg. capsules. The usual adult hypnotic dose is 500 mg.; sedative doses are correspondingly smaller. It is administered orally.

Side effects. This drug seems to have a wide margin of safety. Side effects include headache, fatigue, ataxia, dizziness, mental confusion, nightmares, and nausea and vomiting.

Ethinamate, N.F. (Valmid)

Ethinamate exerts a mild sedative effect upon the central nervous system. The duration of its effect is shorter than that produced by the barbiturates. It is effective within 15 to 25 minutes, and the duration of its effect is about 4 hours. It has not been known to cause habituation or addiction, and tolerance does not seem to develop. It is readily absorbed from the gastrointestinal tract and rapidly destroyed or excreted from the body.

Uses. It is used chiefly as a rapid-acting hypnotic for the treatment of simple insomnia. It can be used for patients with impaired function of the liver and kidney. It is not a hypnotic of choice for patients requiring heavy or continuous sedation.

Preparation, dosage, and administration. Ethinamate is available in 500-mg. tablets. The minimal effective hypnotic dose for adults is 500 mg. Larger and repeated doses may be required to produce a full night's sleep. It is administered orally.

Side effects. Toxic effects have not been reported, but careful observation of patients who receive the drug over long periods of time is recommended.

Glutethimide, N.F., B.P. (Doriden)

Glutethimide is a hypnotic and sedative that depresses the central nervous system and produces effects similar to those produced by the short-acting barbiturates. The main advantage claimed for it is that it can be used for patients who do not tolerate the barbiturates. It is effective in 15 to 30 minutes and its effects last 4 to 8 hours. Hangover effects do not seem to be noticeable unless the drug is administered late at night or unless the dose is repeated in the course of the night. It is not considered an addicting agent in the same sense as morphine, but some patients have become addicted to the drug.

Uses. At present, the greatest use for glutethimide seems to be for relief of simple or nervous insomnia, provided it is uncomplicated by pain or severe agitation. It can be used both as a preoperative and as a daytime sedative.

Preparation, dosage, and administration. Glutethimide is marketed in 125-, 250-, and 500-mg. tablets. The usual hypnotic dose for adults is 500 mg. given orally at bedtime. For daytime sedation, 250 mg. may be given orally three times daily after meals.

Side effects. The principal side effects seem to be nausea and, occasionally, rash on the skin. Toxic effects and treatment are much the same as those for poisoning with barbiturates. Treatment of poisoning may be quite difficult.

Methyprylon, N.F., B.P. (Noludar)

Methyprylon depresses the central nervous system in a manner similar to the barbiturates except that it has less tendency to depress the respiratory center. The onset of action is about 30 minutes and duration of action is about 7 hours. Its capacity to cause addiction is thought to be less than that of the barbiturates, although further study may prove otherwise.

Uses. Methyprylon is used in the treatment of simple and nervous insomnia.

Preparation, dosage, and administration. Methyprylon is marketed in 50- and 200-mg. tablets and as an elixir containing 10 mg. per milliliter. Doses of 50 to 100 mg. three or four times daily are prescribed to produce sedation, and 200 to 400 mg. is the usual adult hypnotic dose given at bedtime.

Side effects. The incidence of side effects is thought to be low, although the following have been observed: nausea, vomiting, constipation, diarrhea, headache, itching, and rash on the skin. No serious toxic effects on the kidney, liver, or bone marrow have been reported.

Flurazepam (Dalmane)

Flurazepam is a new hypnotic related to the benzodiazepine compounds, which are widely used as minor tranquilizers. It is claimed that flurazepam is useful in the therapy of all sleep disorders and that it does not suppress dream or REM sleep. More extensive investigation is needed to validate this claim. It is available in 15- and 30-mg. capsules.

Older hypnotics

There are a number of hypnotics that were almost abandoned when the barbiturates became popular. They seem to be gradually regaining some of their lost popularity. They include chloral hydrate and paraldehyde as well as a number of others.

Chloral hydrate, U.S.P., B.P. (Noctec)

$$Cl_3-CHOH$$
$$|$$
$$OH$$

Chloral hydrate was first synthesized in 1862. It is the oldest of the hypnotics and is still used. It is a chlorinated derivative of acetaldehyde, or a hydrate of trichloracetaldehyde. It is a crystalline substance that has a bitter taste and a penetrating odor. It is readily soluble in water, alcohols, and oils such as olive oil.

Action and result. Locally, chloral hydrate is an irritant. Systemically, it depresses the central nervous system and decreases awareness of external stimuli. It acts promptly (10 to 15 minutes) and produces sleep that lasts 5 hours or more. The sleep greatly resembles natural sleep; the patient can be awakened without difficulty. It produces little or no analgesic effect, and it is neither an anesthetic nor an anticonvulsant.

In therapeutic doses there is little or no effect on the heart and respiratory center. The pulse and blood pressure are not lowered more than can be observed in ordinary sleep. In large doses chloral hydrate depresses the respiratory and vasomotor centers, resulting in slowed respiration and dilatation of cutaneous blood vessels. Effect on the heart is said to be like that of chloroform. Overdoses will cause cardiac depression, especially in patients with heart disease.

Uses. Chloral hydrate is used as a sedative. It produces sedation similar to paraldehyde and the barbiturates. It is sometimes used to relieve symptoms during the withdrawal phase of drug addiction (alcoholism, opiate, or barbiturate).

Chloral hydrate is used as a hypnotic when

insomnia is not the result of pain. It is one of the cheapest hypnotics. Its chief disadvantage is that it can produce gastric irritation. It also has an unpleasant taste, but this problem is remedied by administering the drug in capsule form.

Preparation, dosage, and administration. The usual adult dose of chloral hydrate is 500 mg. given up to three times a day. Larger doses may also be prescribed (250 mg. to 1 Gm.). It is marketed in soft gelatin capsules containing 250 and 500 mg. and in suppository form. It can be prepared as an aqueous solution or a syrup.

If the liquid solution is administered it should be well diluted with water or given in a syrup or milk to disguise the taste. It is sometimes given to children in the form of a retention enema (dissolved in oil). It is too irritating to be given parenterally. It should not be given with alcohol to avoid the additive effects of two depressant drugs. Such a combination is sometimes referred to as a "Mickey Finn" or knockout drops.

Side effects and toxic effects. Symptoms of both acute and chronic toxicity are sometimes observed.

Although chloral hydrate has a wide safety range, acute poisoning can occur. Symptoms are similar to those of any central depressant and include deep sleep, stupor, coma, lowered blood pressure, slow weak pulse, slow respiration, and cyanosis. The local effects of the drug may cause nausea and vomiting when it is taken orally. Death is usually caused by respiratory depression or it may result from sudden heart failure in patients who have cardiac damage. If the patient survives, there is a possibility that damage may have been done to the liver and kidneys.

Treatment is essentially the same as that for acute poisoning with barbiturates.

Chloral hydrate habitués develop some tolerance to the drug, but habit formation is not common. It sometimes results in chronic poisoning, manifested by degenerative changes in the liver and kidneys, nervous disturbances, weakness, skin manifestations, and gastrointestinal disturbances. Treatment consists in gradual withdrawal of the drug and rehabilitative measures similar to those used in the treatment of the chronic alcoholic.

Contraindications. Chloral hydrate is contraindicated for patients with serious heart disease or impaired function of the liver and kidney and sometimes for patients with gastric or duodenal ulcer.

Petrichloral (Periclor)

Petrichloral is a derivative of chloral that exhibits a hypnotic and sedative action similar to chloral hydrate. It is better tolerated than the latter drug because it has no odor or aftertaste, and it does not produce gastric irritation. It has a wide margin of safety.

Preparation, dosage, and administration. Petrichloral is available in 300-mg. gelatin capsules. The usual hypnotic dose is 600 mg., and the sedative dose for daytime effect is 300 mg. every 6 hours.

Chloral betaine, N.F. (Beta-Chlor) tablets

This is a formulation providing chloral betaine in tablet form. Each tablet contains 870 mg. of chloral betaine, equivalent to 500 mg. of chloral hydrate. It is administered by mouth in a dose of one to two tablets as a hypnotic 15 to 30 minutes before bedtime. The effects, uses, toxic actions, and contraindications are the same as for chloral hydrate.

Paraldehyde, U.S.P., B.P.

Paraldehyde has been used as a hypnotic since 1882, when it was introduced into medicine. It is a colorless, transparent liquid with a strong odor and a disagreeable taste. It is only slightly soluble in water but freely soluble in oils and in alcohol.

Action and result. Paraldehyde depresses the central nervous system, producing drowsiness and sleep in 10 to 15 minutes after a hypnotic dose. The sleep closely resembles a natural sleep and lasts for 4 to 8 hours. Therapeutic doses do not depress the medullary centers and do not affect the heart and respiration. It is less potent than chloral hydrate but also less toxic. It is not an analgesic, but it may compel sleep in spite of pain.

Paraldehyde is rapidly absorbed from the mucosa of the gastrointestinal tract and also from intramuscular sites of injection, although it may cause some irritation when given parenterally. The fate of paraldehyde in the body is not known, but a large part of it is thought to be destroyed in the liver. It is therefore contraindicated for patients who have serious impairment of liver function. It is not contraindicated for patients with renal disease. A part of the drug is excreted by the lungs, where it tends to increase bronchial secretions, and for this reason it is avoided for patients with bronchitis and pneumonia.

Uses. Paraldehyde is employed for its hypnotic and sedative effects in treatment of conditions in which there is a threat of convulsive seizures or nervous hyperexcitability. It is used therefore in delirium tremens, tetanus, strychnine poisoning, and mania. It is sometimes used as a basal anesthetic, particularly for children; when so used it is given rectally.

Preparation, dosage, and administration. Paraldehyde is available as a plain liquid for oral administration or as a sterile solution dispensed in ampules (2 and 10 ml.) for parenteral use. The usual adult oral dose is 8 ml. (2 fluidrams) but may be increased to 10 or 15 ml. in some instances. When paraldehyde is given orally it should be disguised in a suitable medium such as a flavored syrup, fruit juice, wine, or milk, and it should be very cold to minimize the odor and taste. It can also be given as a retention enema (mixed with a thin oil). When given intramuscularly a pure sterile preparation should be used. The usual intramuscular dose is 5 ml. It is rarely given intravenously.

Side effects and toxic effects. The chief disadvantages of paraldehyde are its obnoxious odor, disagreeable taste, and irritating effect on the throat and stomach if the drug is not well diluted in a suitable medium. Because of the odor it is not suitable for patients who are up and about, for they will reek with the odor of the drug. Fortunately, if the patient is capable of noticing the odor, his sense of smell becomes dulled after a time. Paraldehyde is not as safe a drug as was once thought; it is now known that the margin between an anesthetic and a lethal dose is very narrow. Symptoms of overdosage resemble those of alcohol in that mild poisoning can usually be "slept off." The incidence of acute toxicity is low, although deaths from paraldehyde depression have been reported. The symptoms of poisoning and treatment are essentially the same as those for chloral hydrate. In spite of the taste and odor, some patients do become addicted to paraldehyde.

Bromides

The term *bromides* frequently refers to sodium bromide, although a number of bromide salts have been popular. They have been used for their sedative, hypnotic, and anticonvulsant effects, but their range of usefulness has been narrowed because of the appearance of better drugs. They are slow-acting depressants of the nervous system. Bromide intoxication, however, is still encountered. A number of headache remedies contain bromides and are easily procured.

■ Alcohols

Although there are many alcohols that vary physically from liquids to solids, the alcohol usually meant, unless otherwise specified, is ethyl alcohol. Methyl alcohol, propyl alcohol, butyl alcohol, and amyl alcohol are examples of other alcohols. Chemically speaking, they are hydroxy derivatives of aliphatic hydrocarbons.

Ethyl alcohol

$$H-\overset{\overset{\displaystyle H}{|}}{\underset{\underset{\displaystyle H}{|}}{C}}-\overset{\overset{\displaystyle H}{|}}{\underset{\underset{\displaystyle H}{|}}{C}}-OH$$

Ethyl alcohol has been known in an impure form since earliest times, and it is the only alcohol used extensively in medicine. It was formerly thought to be a remedy for almost any disease or disorder. It is a colorless liquid and lighter than water with which it mixes readily. It lowers surface tension and acts as a good solvent for a number of substances. In concentrations above 40% it is flammable. Ethyl alcohol, also referred to as grain alcohol, is the product of the fermentation of a sugar by yeast. If the carbohydrate used for fermentation to alcohol is a starch, the starch must first be broken down to a sugar before the molecules can be fermented.

Action and result. Ethyl alcohol may have either a local or systemic action.

Local. Ethyl alcohol denatures proteins by precipitation and dehydration. This is said to be the basis for its germicidal, irritant, and astringent effects. It irritates denuded skin, mucous membranes, and subcutaneous tissue. Considerable pain may be experienced from a subcutaneous injection of alcohol, and slough of the tissue may result. When it is injected into or near a nerve it may produce degeneration of the nerve and anesthesia. Alcohol evaporates readily from the skin, produces a cooling effect, and reduces the temperature of the skin. When rubbed on the surface of the body it acts as a mild counter-irritant. It dries and hardens the epithelial layer of the skin and helps to prevent bed sores when used externally. However, its use on skin that is already dry and irritated is usually contraindicated. Solutions of ethyl alcohol that measure 70% by weight seem to exert the best bactericidal effects. High concentrations have a. marked dehydrating effect but do not necessarily kill bacteria. Ethyl alcohol in proper concentration is considered an effective germicide for a number of uses, but it does not kill spores.

Systemic. According to modern scientific authorities alcohol is not considered a stimulant (popular ideas to the contrary). It is thought to interfere with the transmission of nerve impulses at synaptic connections, but how this is accomplished is not known. It exerts a progressive and continuous depression on the central nervous system (cerebrum, cerebellum, cord, and medulla). Its action is comparable to that of the

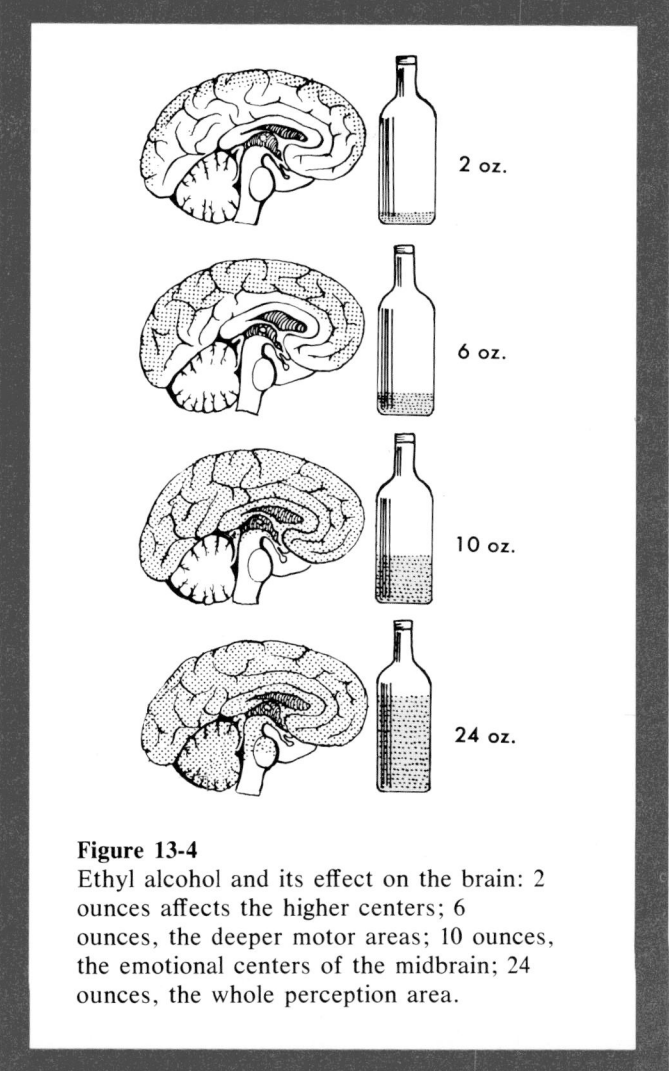

Figure 13-4
Ethyl alcohol and its effect on the brain: 2 ounces affects the higher centers; 6 ounces, the deeper motor areas; 10 ounces, the emotional centers of the midbrain; 24 ounces, the whole perception area.

general anesthetics (see Figure 13-4). The excitement stage, however, is longer, and when the anesthetic stage is reached, definite toxic symptoms are present. Also, when alcohol is taken socially, attempts are usually made to stay in an early stage rather than to pass rapidly to unconsciousness. The margin between the anesthetic and fatal dose is a narrow one. What sometimes appears to be stimulation results from the depression of the higher faculties of man's brain and represents the loss of learned inhibitions

281

acquired by civilization. The results of the action of alcohol vary with the individual, his tolerance, the presence or absence of extraneous stimuli, and the rate of ingestion. Small or moderate quantities produce a feeling of well-being, talkativeness, greater vivacity, and increased confidence in one's mental and physical power. The personality becomes expansive, and there is a general loss of inhibitions. The finer powers of discrimination, concentration, insight, judgment, and memory are gradually dulled and lost. Large quantities of the drug may cause excitement, impulsive speech and behavior, laughter, hilarity, and in some cases, pugnaciousness. Others may become melancholy or unduly sentimental. The individual usually becomes ataxic, mutters incoherently, has disturbance of the special senses, is often nauseated, may vomit, and eventually lapses into stupor or coma.

The respiratory center is not depressed except by large doses.

Cardiovascular. Alcohol depresses the vasomotor center in the medulla and in this way brings about dilatation of the peripheral blood vessels, especially those of the skin. This causes a feeling of warmth. Because of the dilatation of the capillaries, heat is lost from the surface of the body and more must be brought from the interior. This accounts for the fact that an intoxicated person may freeze to death more quickly than a normal person. Alcohol also depresses the heat-regulating mechanism in a manner similar to the antipyretics, and before the advent of the modern antipyretics it was used to reduce fever.

Small doses (10 to 25 ml.) in man produce an insignificant increase in the pulse rate, caused mainly by the excitement and the reflex effect on the gastrointestinal tract. Larger doses produce the same effect but may be followed by lowered blood pressure caused by the effect on the vasoconstrictor center. Only high concentrations of alcohol depress the heart.

Gastrointestinal. The effect of alcohol upon the function of the digestive organs depends upon the presence or absence of gastrointestinal disease, the degree of alcoholic tolerance, and the concentration of the beverage used as well as the type and amount of food present. Small doses in the patient who likes alcohol will stimulate the secretion of gastric juice rich in acid. Salivary secretion is also reflexly stimulated. Large and concentrated doses of alcohol tend to inhibit secretion and enzyme activity in the stomach, although the effect in the intestine seems to be negligible. However, when large quantities of alcohol are taken over a period of time, gastritis, nutritional deficiencies, and other untoward results have been observed.

Absorption and excretion. Since alcohol does not require digestion in the stomach or intestine it is readily absorbed from both organs. Ninety percent or more of the alcohol that is absorbed is metabolized, chiefly in the liver. It is oxidized first to acetaldehyde and eventually to carbon dioxide and water. It is oxidized at the rate of about 10 grams per hour, which amounts to about 70 calories. Alcohol does not form glycogen and hence it cannot be stored, so that it is a food only in the sense that it contributes calories. It supplies no minerals or vitamins.

Alcohol that escapes oxidation is excreted by way of the lungs and kidneys, and some is found in a number of excretions such as sweat.

Alcohol produces an increased flow of urine because of increased fluid intake, which ordinarily accompanies the drinking of alcoholic beverages. Recently it has been suggested that alcohol may also act as a diuretic through central nervous system depression and inhibition of the ADH (antidiuretic hormone) release. If the patient has preexisting renal disease, there may be further damage to the kidney. Large and concentrated doses of alcohol are thought to injure the renal epithelium.

Since alcohol, after absorption, is distributed in the tissues of the body in approximately the same ratio as their water content, a rough estimate of the quantity taken may be obtained from an analysis of the blood and urine. Muehlberger gives his analysis as shown in Table 13-6.

The National Safety Council regards concentration of alcohol in the blood up to 0.05% as evidence of unquestioned sobriety. Concentrations between 0.051% and 0.149% are regarded as grounds for suspicion and for use of

Table 13-6 Relation between clinical indications of alcoholic intoxication and concentration of alcohol of the blood and urine

Stage	Blood alcohol (%)	Urine alcohol (%)	Clinical observations
Subclinical	0 to 0.11	0 to 0.15	Normal by ordinary observations, slight changes detectable by special tests
Emotional instability	0.09 to 0.21	0.13 to 0.29	Decreased inhibitions; emotional instability; slight muscular incoordination; slowing of responses to stimuli
Confusion	0.18 to 0.33	0.26 to 0.45	Disturbance of sensation; decreased pain sense; staggering gait; slurred speech
Stupor	0.27 to 0.43	0.36 to 0.58	Marked decrease in response to stimuli; muscular incoordination approaching paralysis
Coma	0.36 to 0.56	0.48 to 0.72	Complete unconsciousness; depressed reflexes; subnormal temperature; anesthesia; impairment of circulation; possible death
Death (uncomplicated)	Over 0.44	Over 0.60	

performance tests, and anything more than 0.15% is evidence of unquestionable intoxication. The states differ as to what is accepted as a legal limit.

Effects of alcohol that may not be discernible to the casual observer become apparent when the individual who has had a number of doses of alcohol attempts to operate a piece of power machinery such as an automobile. Visual acuity (especially peripheral vision) is diminished, reaction time is slowed, judgment and self-control are impaired, and the individual tends to be complacent and pleased with himself. Many drivers will take chances when under the influence of alcohol that they would never take ordinarily. This leads to disaster, as statistics reveal.

Uses. Ethyl alcohol is used topically as an astringent and antiseptic. It is rubbed on the backs and buttocks of patients to prevent decubiti. It is used to cleanse the skin, and it is poured on dressings over wounds. It is a popular disinfectant for the skin.

It is an excellent solvent and preservative for many medicines and medicinal mixtures (spirits, elixirs, fluidextracts).

Alcohol sponges are given to lower the temperature of the patient with a high fever since it increases heat dissipation. Caution must be exercised when alcohol sponges are given, particularly to children, since alcohol intoxication can occur.

At times alcohol is injected into a nerve to destroy sensory nerve fibers and relieve pain associated with a severe and protracted neuralgia, such as trifacial neuralgia (tic douloureux) or inoperable cancer. An injection of 80% ethyl alcohol is used. Effects may persist for 1 to 3 years or until regeneration of the peripheral nerve fibers takes place.

Alcohol is used to produce vasodilation in peripheral vascular disease. Concentrated solutions often produce greater peripheral vasodilation than any other drug. The pain associated with Buerger's disease may be relieved with the use of ethyl alcohol administered orally. It may be prescribed to decrease the frequency of anginal attacks but effects are said to be unreliable. Benefits to the cardiac patient, if they occur, are believed to result from the rest and relaxation that the alcohol produces.

Alcohol is also used as an appetizer for patients with poor appetite during periods of convalescence and debility. From 5% to 10% solutions of alcohol have also been given in intravenous fluids (5% dextrose and isotonic saline solution) to supplement the caloric intake.

The use of some form of alcohol has long been advocated to thwart the development of a head cold, perhaps because it makes the patient more comfortable, drowsy, and sleepy, thereby promoting sleep and rest. Increased circulation of blood through the skin will relieve feelings of chilliness. It seems to have no effect on the course of the cold itself.

It may be used as a hypnotic for older persons who do not tolerate other hypnotics. It is used as a home remedy or for a hospitalized patient who requests it. It is occasionally given in intravenous fluids for its sedative effects—to reduce the amount of opiate or barbiturate needed to keep a patient comfortable.

Preparations. The following are various preparations of ethyl alcohol.

Alcohol (ethyl alcohol, ethanol), U.S.P., B.P. Alcohol contains not less than 92.3% by weight corresponding to approximately 94.9% by volume of C_2H_5OH.

Diluted alcohol, U.S.P. The diluted form contains not less than 41% and not more than 42% by weight of ethyl alcohol. The B.P. lists a number of dilute alcohols.

Whiskey (Spiritus Frumenti). Whiskey is an alcoholic liquid that is obtained by the distillation of the fermented mash of wholly or partly malted cereal grain and contains approximately 50% by volume of ethyl alcohol. It usually is stored in charred wood containers for a period of not less than 2 years.

Brandy (Spiritus Vini Vitis). Brandy is an alcoholic liquid obtained by the distillation of the fermented juice of sound, ripe grapes. It contains approximately 50% by volume of ethyl alcohol. It is stored in wood containers, frequently as long as 2 years.

Other spirits are solutions of volatile substances in alcohol. In most cases the dissolved substance has a more important action than the alcohol, which is used merely as a solvent.

Wines. Wines are fermented liquors made from grapes or other fruit juices. Besides alcohol, wines may contain various acids, such as tartaric, tannic, or malic.

Dry wines are those that contain no added sugar. They contain about 10% alcohol.

Sweet wines are those to which sugar has been added. They contain about 15% alcohol.

Sparkling wines contain carbon dioxide, which makes them effervescent. Examples are champagne and sparkling burgundy.

Dosage varies with the purpose for which the alcohol is administered. When whiskey is prescribed as a vasodilator, 30 ml. may be ordered to be given two or three times a day. When an alcoholic beverage is given for its effects as an appetizer, it should be given before meals. From 30 to 60 ml. are usually given.

Acute alcoholism. In states of acute intoxication the patient is stuporous or comatose, the skin is cold and clammy, respirations are noisy and slow, and pupils are dilated or normal. The breath is usually heavy with alcoholic fumes. Death may result if the coma is prolonged or if injury, hypostatic pneumonia, or infection complicates the picture.

Ordinary intoxication treats itself with time and sleep. In severe intoxication the stomach should be emptied. Emetics in cases of deep narcosis are inactive and worse than useless because they add to the depression. The stomach, therefore, should be emptied with a stomach tube. Difference of opinion exists as to the use of analeptic drugs, but if the depression is deep and the patient cannot be aroused, drugs such as amphetamine phosphate, pentylenetetrazol, methylphenidate hydrochloride, and others have been recommended. In case of threatened respiratory failure, artificial respiration and the inhalation of oxygen and carbon dioxide may be beneficial. The patient's position should be changed frequently to combat development of hypostatic pneumonia. As the patient emerges from a comatose state he may become acutely active and require the administration of a sedative. (Chlorpromazine should *not* be given; it potentiates the effects of alcohol.) Recovery is comparable to recovery from an anesthetic.

The headache, nervousness, and gastric irritability that frequently follow acute alcoholism are best relieved by antacids and demulcents, such as sodium bicarbonate and bismuth subcarbonate. The combined use of glucose and insulin therapy has been advocated by some because it promotes slightly the detoxication of alcohol. The administration of isotonic saline solution intravenously will help the dehydrated patient by reestablishing the electrolyte pattern of the blood.

Chronic alcoholism. The more common manifestations of chronic alcoholism are redness of the face, nose, and conjunctivae caused by the injection of the blood vessels, gastroenteritis, cirrhotic changes in the liver, nephritis, arteriosclerosis and chronic myocardial changes, amblyopia caused by orbital optic neuritis, dulling of the mental faculties, tremors caused by degeneration, and muscular weakness. Not infrequently, the prolonged use of alcohol leads to mental change, which may manifest itself in the gradual weakening of the mental powers, with hallucinations and delusions or other forms of psychosis. To be successfully treated the chronic alcoholic must want to be treated and must want to get well. Early establishment of rapport between the patient and his physician as well as with his nurse is very important. Treatment must include rehabilitation and help in making better adjustments to the patient's living conditions. The best results are probably obtained in a hospital or sanitarium.

Careful attention should be given to the patient's physical needs, such as his diet, fluid balance, and general hygiene, since optimal physical fitness makes the patient feel better and increases his ability to deal with the problems that have contributed to his illness or have caused it to continue. Particular attention is given to supplying adequate amounts of vitamin B complex and ascorbic acid.

Sedatives and tranquilizing agents make the patient more comfortable, help him to sleep better, and relieve anxiety. The patient is also likely to eat better.

There is need for adequate medical supervision at all times as well as for good nursing care if good results are to be attained. Relapses are frequent but are said to be fewer than those seen after the treatment for morphine addiction.

In the treatment of chronic alcoholism, two additional aspects of treatment are deserving of mention because of the success that has been attained. The first is the psychologic approach to the problem or problems of the chronic alcoholic as made by Alcoholics Anonymous. This is an organization composed entirely of rehabilitated alcoholics who are, therefore, in a unique position to understand the problems of other alcoholics. The organization has its headquarters in New York and has many local groups in cities and towns throughout the United States. Frequent meetings, mutual assistance and understanding, and a definite program of constructive rehabilitation have resulted in the fact that approximately 50% of those who enter the organization with a sincere desire to stop drinking do so. Another 25% are reclaimed after one or more failures, and most of the remaining 25% are for one reason or another never successfully reclaimed. Another technique has involved the administration of a drug that the subject knows will produce unpleasant symptoms if he then takes alcohol. Such a drug, called disulfiram (Antabuse), has been reported favorably by some Danish physicians. Disulfiram is said to interfere with the metabolism of alcohol by retarding the oxidation of acetaldehyde. Increased amounts of acetaldehyde in the blood account for the unpleasant effects. The drug must be used cautiously because it has been known to cause personality changes as well as death. Psychotherapy aimed at mental and social rehabilitation should accompany the use of such drugs if permanent effects are likely to be obtained.

Delirium tremens is a form of psychosis that sometimes develops in the chronic alcoholic. It usually occurs after prolonged excessive drinking followed by abstinence and can be viewed as a type of withdrawal syndrome comparable to that seen after withdrawal of barbiturates in persons addicted to them. In the alcoholic who has been drinking for some time it may be precipitated by exposure, surgical operation, or serious illness, especially pneumonia. There may

285

be warning symptoms such as restlessness, insomnia, anorexia, anxiety, fear, and tremor. Chronic alcoholics refer to the first stage of delirium tremens as the "shakes." During the attack the patient continues to have tremor, insomnia, delirium, and terrifying hallucinations of such things as snakes and small animals creeping over him. The patient may have a temperature of 102° to 103° F. Death may result from collapse, traumatism, or infection.

Many methods of treatment have been tried. Sedatives such as paraldehyde, amobarbital sodium, mephobarbital, and some of the tranquilizing agents are tried when the patient is maniacal. Symptomatic treatment of the patient includes attention to fluids, nutrition, and vitamins. Some physicians have found ACTH and cortisone beneficial in promoting recovery.

Contraindications. Ethyl alcohol is contraindicated for certain persons and should be avoided by others. This includes the following:

1. Patients who have ulceration of the gastrointestinal tract, especially patients with hyperacidity and gastric or duodenal ulcers
2. Patients with acute infections of the genitourinary organs
3. Pregnant women
4. Epileptic persons
5. Patients with liver or kidney disease
6. Persons with personality problems, maladjusted persons, or those who have at one time been alcohol or drug dependent

Alcohol and lifespan. The effect of alcohol on resistance to infection and on the life span has been a subject of controversy for many years. It is believed that evidence is lacking to prove that moderate amounts of alcohol have much effect one way or the other. Statistics show, however, that chronic alcoholics and heavy drinkers have a shorter life span than those who abstain from alcohol. Some of the ill effects that have been attributed to alcohol have been found to be caused by general impairment of health, which in turn is caused by malnutrition and poor hygiene. Apparently, it often is not so much the direct effect of alcohol that injures the person as the inability of the alcoholic to take care of himself and others.

Methyl alcohol (wood alcohol)

Methyl alcohol is prepared on a large scale by the destructive distillation of wood. It has also been prepared synthetically. It is important in medicine chiefly because of the cases of poisoning that have resulted from its ingestion. The main effects are on the central nervous system. However, intoxication does not occur as readily as with ethyl alcohol unless large amounts are consumed. Methyl alcohol is oxidized in the tissues to formic acid, which is poorly metabolized. This is the basis for the development of a severe acidosis. Symptoms of poisoning include nausea and vomiting, abdominal pain, headache, dyspnea, blurred vision, and cold clammy skin. Symptoms may progress to delirium, convulsions, coma, and death. In nonfatal cases the patient may become blind or suffer from impaired vision. Treatment is directed toward the relief of acidosis since this seems to be related to the severity of the visual symptoms. Large amounts of sodium bicarbonate may be needed to treat acidosis successfully. Obviously, methyl alcohol is much more toxic than ethyl alcohol. One dose of 60 ml. has been known to cause permanent blindness. Fluids containing methyl alcohol usually bear a "Poison" label, although this may be disregarded or overlooked.

Isopropyl alcohol, N.F.

Isopropyl alcohol is a clear, colorless, liquid with a characteristic odor and a bitter taste. It is miscible with water, chloroform, and ether but insoluble in salt solutions. It is a good solvent for creosote and compares favorably with ethyl alcohol in its antiseptic action. It has been recommended for disinfection of the skin and for rubbing compounds and lotions to be used on the skin. Its bactericidal effects are said to increase as its concentration approaches 100%. It differs in this respect from ethyl alcohol.

It is occasionally misused as a beverage. It can cause severe poisoning and death. The first symptoms are similar to intoxication from ethyl alcohol, but the symptoms progress to coma from which the patient may not recover.

Butyl and amyl alcohols

Butyl and amyl alcohols are said to be several times as toxic as ethyl alcohol.

■ Selective depressants
Anticonvulsant drugs

In this part of the chapter dealing with depressants of the central nervous system a number of drugs used for the symptomatic treatment of various kinds of convulsive seizures will be described.

Epilepsy is regarded as a symptom of disease or disorder of the brain rather than a disease in itself. It is associated with marked changes in the electric activity of the cerebral cortex, and these alterations are often detected in the electroencephalogram. Therefore, the EEG is often a valuable aid to the physician in making a diagnosis. Sometimes the convulsive seizure is associated with a brain tumor, growth of scar tissue, or the presence of a toxin or a poison, but at other times no specific cause can be found. Epileptic seizures vary and are often grouped according to grand mal seizures, petit mal seizures, jacksonian epilepsy, and psychomotor attacks. There are about 1 million epileptic persons in the United States.

Grand mal epilepsy is the type most frequently seen. Such attacks are characterized by sudden loss of consciousness. The patient falls forcefully and experiences a series of tonic and clonic muscular contractions. The eyes roll upward, the arms are flexed, and the legs are extended. The force of the muscular contractions causes air to be forced out of the lungs, which accounts for the cry which the patient may make as he falls. Respiration is suspended temporarily, the skin becomes cyanotic, perspiration and saliva flow, and the patient may froth at the mouth and bite his tongue if it gets caught

between his teeth. When the seizure subsides the patient regains partial consciousness and may complain of aching. He then tends to fall into a deep sleep.

Petit mal seizures are most often seen in childhood and consist of temporary lapses of consciousness that last for a few seconds. Patients appear to be staring into space and may exhibit a few rhythmic movements of the eyes or head. They do not convulse. They may experience many attacks in a single day. Sometimes an attack of petit mal is followed by one of grand mal.

Jacksonian epilepsy is described by some authorities as a type of focal seizure; it is associated with irritation of a specific part of the brain. A single part, such as a finger or an extremity, may jerk and such movements may end spontaneously or spread over the whole musculature. Consciousness may not be lost unless the seizure develops into a generalized convulsion.

Psychomotor attacks are characterized by brief alterations in consciousness, unusual stereotyped movements (such as chewing or swallowing movements) repeated over and over, temperamental changes, confusion, and feelings of unreality. It is often associated with grand mal seizures and is likely to be resistant to therapy with drugs.

Some patients have more than one type of seizure or have mixed seizures. This is significant because different types of seizures respond rather specifically to certain anticonvulsant drugs. The aim of therapy is to find the drug or drugs that will effectively control the seizures and will at the same time cause a minimum of undesirable side effects.

Mechanism of action of the anticonvulsant drugs. The effectiveness of anticonvulsant drugs is often measured by the amount of increased voltage necessary to provoke an electroconvulsion in an animal who has previously received the anticonvulsant to be tested or by the degree of their antagonism to chemical substances capable of producing convulsions. Pentylenetetrazol is a drug against which anticonvulsants are measured for effectiveness.

The mode and site of action of these drugs are still regarded as uncertain. The convulsive seizure may be effectively suppressed, but the abnormal brain waves may or may not be altered. All clinically useful drugs for epilepsy inhibit the seizure.

Although there is no ideal anticonvulsant drug, if one could be synthesized to order, a number of characteristics would be considered highly desirable:

1 The drug should be highly effective but exhibit a low incidence of toxicity.
2 It should be effective against more than one type of seizure and for mixed seizures.
3 It should be long acting and nonsedative so that the patient is not incapacitated with sleep or excessive drowsiness.
4 It should be well tolerated by the patient and inexpensive, since the patient may have to take it for years or for the rest of his life.
5 Tolerance to the therapeutic effects of the drug should not develop.

The present-day drugs that are considered especially satisfactory and safe are phenobarbital, diphenylhydantoin sodium, and trimethadione. The bromides are among the oldest anticonvulsants known, but because they tend to cause states of chronic toxicity, they seldom are used. The barbiturates have been discussed but their use as anticonvulsants will be emphasized again. They are an important group of drugs for this purpose, especially the longer-acting members. Phenobarbital is effective against all types of epileptic seizures except certain petit mal types. It is considered one of the safest of the anticonvulsants. Its chief disadvantage is that it must often be given in doses that produce apathy and sleepiness. Amphetamines or methylphenidate may be ordered to counteract the drowsiness. Mephobarbital is similar to phenobarbital, especially when given in comparable doses. The same can be said for metharbital.

Diphenylhydantoin, U.S.P. (Dilantin); phenytoin sodium, B.P.

$$
\begin{array}{c}
C_6H_5 \\
| \\
C_6H_5 - C - NH \\
| \\
| C - O - Na \\
O = C - N
\end{array}
$$

Diphenylhydantoin is a synthetic agent chemically related to the barbiturates. It is an odorless white or cream-colored powder with a bitter taste.

Action and result. Diphenylhydantoin exerts a selective action on the cerebral cortex of the brain without appreciably affecting the sensory areas. It is an anticonvulsant but not a hypnotic. It is somewhat more effective in controlling grand mal seizures than phenobarbital, although patients vary in their response to these drugs. It is strongly alkaline in solution and may produce gastric irritation.

Uses. In the treatment of epilepsy it is more effective for grand mal than petit mal seizures. It may for a time increase the attacks of petit mal. Psychomotor seizures are sometimes controlled. It does not cure the mental deterioration sometimes found in the epileptic. On the other hand, it does not cause mental deterioration. It is frequently prescribed in combination with phenobarbital. It may be prescribed for patients following surgical operations upon the brain to prevent convulsive seizures.

Preparation, dosage, and administration. Diphenylhydantoin is marketed in 30- and 100-mg. capsules (delayed action), in 50-mg. scored tablets, and in an oral suspension (100 mg. per 4 ml.). It is also available for parenteral administration in "Steri-Vials," each containing 250 mg. of the drug. When used alone, the beginning daily dose for adults is 100 mg. orally with one-half glass of water three times a day. The dosage may be gradually increased until optimum effects are obtained. Most adults seem to tolerate 300 to 400 mg. daily without toxic effects. Children over 6 years of age may be given the adult dose. Dosage for children under 6 years should be less. Increase in dosage is made slowly and with careful observation of the patient. When the drug is combined with one or more other anticonvulsants, the dosage of individual drugs is often reduced. The transition from phenobarbital, bromides, and other hypnotics to diphenylhydantoin is made gradually, with some overlapping of drugs to prevent the precipitation of convulsive seizures.

There are a number of preparations available

that are mixtures of barbiturates and one of the hydantoins. Phelantin contains diphenylhydantoin, phenobarbital, and methamphetamine hydrochloride. Hydantal contains methyl-phenylethyl hydantoin and phenobarbital. Mebroin contains diphenylhydantoin and methobarbital. These preparations have the advantages of convenience (two or more drugs in one tablet) and slightly lower cost, but there is the disadvantage of always having a fixed amount of each drug. It is advantageous for the physician to be able to make adjustments of dosage when several drugs are taken together.

Side effects and toxic effects. The incidence of toxic reactions with diphenylhydantoin is greater than with phenobarbital. The less serious side effects include apathy, nervousness, dizziness, ataxia, blurred vision, hyperplasia of the gums (excessive formation of gum tissues), and hirsutism (excessive growth of hair, especially on the face). Other reactions that sometimes occur are tremor, excitement, hallucinations, psychosis, nausea, and vomiting. If the patient is particularly sensitive to the drug he may develop skin rash, exfoliative dermatitis, fever, and difficult breathing. Hepatitis and lupus erythematosus from diphenylhydantoin have been reported.

Mephenytoin (Mesantoin); methoin, B.P.

$$CH_3CH_2-\underset{\substack{|\\O=C-N-CH_3}}{\overset{\substack{C_6H_5\\|}}{C}}-NH,\ C=O$$

Mephenytoin is an anticonvulsant drug similar in chemical structure and activity to diphenylhydantoin. It is less potent as an anticonvulsant than the latter preparation. It produces more sedation than Dilantin but less than phenobarbital.

Uses. Mephenytoin seems to be more effective for grand mal and psychomotor seizures than for petit mal seizures since it may provoke attacks of petit mal. Certain patients who do not respond favorably to diphenylhydantoin or to phenobarbital may benefit from this drug.

Preparation, dosage, and administration. Mephenytoin is available in 100-mg. tablets for oral administration. The average daily dose for adults is 400 to 600 mg.; for children, 100 to 400 mg. As for all anticonvulsants, the optimum daily dosage must be calculated to meet the needs of each patient.

Side effects and toxic effects. This is a drug that can produce serious toxic effects and therefore caution in its use is recommended. In cases of hypersensitivity to the drug, destruction of blood cells can occur, which may vary from leukopenia to agranulocytosis and aplastic anemia. Some patients become jaundiced, indicating damage to the liver. Other symptoms of toxicity include fever and dermatitis.

Ethotoin, B.P. (Peganone)

Ethotoin belongs to the hydantoin group of anticonvulsants.

Uses. It is said to be less effective than diphenylhydantoin, but it is also less toxic. It is effective in grand mal epilepsy but does not always bring about complete relief of seizures. To be satisfactory it may need to be used with other anticonvulsants. It is of limited usefulness in petit mal and psychomotor seizures. However, in certain patients, seizures that cannot be controlled by other drugs may be controlled.

Preparation, dosage, and administration. The average daily dose of ethotoin is 2 to 3 Gm. given orally after meals in four to six divided portions. It is available in 250- and 500-mg. tablets.

Trimethadione, U.S.P. (Tridione); troxidone, B.P.

289

Trimethadione belongs to a group of compounds known as the oxazolidine diones.

Action. Its primary action is on the central nervous system, although it is not restricted to the motor cortex. It exerts an analgesic effect in some instances as well as an anticonvulsant action. It is said to surpass all other anticonvulsants in raising the threshold to pentylenetetrazol-induced seizures. The precise mechanism of action, however, is unknown.

Uses. Trimethadione is used chiefly in the treatment of petit mal epilepsy and is considered to be the drug of choice for this condition. It appears to be more effective for petit mal in children than in adults. It is not effective for grand mal seizures. It is frequently given with diphenylhydantoin or phenobarbital if the patient has attacks of both petit mal and grand mal. It rarely seems to be adequate to control psychomotor seizures.

Preparation, dosage, and administration. Trimethadione is available in 150-mg. tablets, 300-mg. capsules, and solution (37.5 mg. per milliliter) for oral administration. The dose for children is 300 to 900 mg. daily and for adults, 900 to 1200 mg. daily, in divided portions. Dosage may need to be increased.

Side effects and toxic effects. Symptoms of toxicity appear infrequently, but they may be serious. Nausea and vomiting, skin eruption, blurring of vision, and sensitivity to light are considered indications for reduction of dosage or temporary withdrawal of the drug. Careful medical supervision of the patient receiving the medication is essential. Rare instances of aplastic anemia explain why it is thought advisable for the patient to have periodic examinations of the blood to detect early signs of toxic effects.

The drug is not recommended for patients with hepatic or renal disease, with disease of the optic nerve, allergic reactions to drugs, or blood dyscrasias.

Action and uses. The action and uses of paramethadione are similar to those of trimethadione. It belongs to the same chemical group, and no significant pharmacologic difference between them is known. Some patients not benefited by trimethadione are benefited by paramethadione and vice versa.

Preparation, dosage, and administration. The initial dose of paramethadione for adults is 900 mg. given orally in divided doses. Thereafter, dosage is adjusted to the minimum effective dose. Initial dosage for children varies from 300 to 600 mg., depending on age.

Side effects. Side effects are similar to those of trimethadione, except the incidence of skin rash and photophobia is said to be less with paramethadione.

Phenacemide (Phenurone)

Phenacemide bears a close chemical relationship to the hydantoin compounds, as can be seen in the accompanying formulas.

Phenacemide

Diphenylhydantoin

Uses and toxic effects. Phenacemide is a synthetic anticonvulsant that has the advantage of being effective in the treatment of grand mal, petit mal, psychomotor epilepsy, and mixed seizures. It is often effective when other anticonvulsants are not, but it is one of the more toxic

Paramethadione, U.S.P., B.P. (Paradione)

agents and may cause personality changes, liver damage, and depression of bone marrow. Some physicians regard it as being too toxic for routine use.

Preparation, dosage, and administration. Phenacemide is available in 300- and 500-mg. tablets for oral administration. It may be prescribed alone or with other anticonvulsants. The dosage recommended is as small as will permit control of seizures.

Other anticonvulsants. There are a number of other anticonvulsants that are in current use. These include phensuximide (Milontin), methsuximide (Celontin), and ethosuximide (Zarontin), which are effective for petit mal seizures. However, recent evidence of serious blood cell depression makes these drugs controversial. Primidone (Mysoline) is chemically similar to phenobarbital. It is about as effective as phenobarbital for the management of grand mal seizures and is quite effective in psychomotor epilepsy. Acetazolamide, U.S.P. (Diamox), is sometimes used as a supplement to routine medication with anticonvulsants. It is primarily a diuretic and a carbonic anhydrase inhibitor.

Role of the nurse

The nurse sometimes plays an important role in helping the patient with epilepsy to learn how to live with his handicap. The patient often needs encouragement and help to enable him to understand why strict adherence to the routine the physician has worked out for him is so important. The patient may never be cured, but with care he may experience minimal symptoms and be able to lead a full and useful life. The patient or a family member should be instructed to keep a record of the frequency, duration, and symptoms of attacks and to report signs and symptoms of undesirable drug effects. Urinalyses and blood counts should be performed every 1 to 3 months.

Questions

for study and review

1 Differentiate between the "short-acting," "ultrashort-acting," and "long-acting" barbiturates. Give five examples of each.
2 How should narcotics be stored in hospital clinical units?
3 Explain what is meant by the term *narcotic*.
4 Define alcoholism. What, if any, are the therapeutic uses of alcohol?
5 Explain the Harrison Narcotic Act.
6 Explain the following statement: "Drugs that decrease or release catecholamine concentration in the brain have a depressing or sedative action."
7 What rationale is used by some clinicians for not using analeptics for treatment of barbiturate poisoning?
8 Explain how a drug may be used as a sedative, a hypnotic, or an anesthetic.
9 What are the signs of salicylate poisoning?
10 Discuss the pros and cons of administration of sleeping medications.

Multiple choice questions

11 Which of the following statements about central nervous system stimulants are *not* correct?
 a. Since caffeine stimulates the output of pepsin and hydrochloric acid, coffee is often restricted for patients with peptic ulcers.
 b. Theophylline has a greater stimulant effect on the central nervous system than caffeine.
 c. Caffeine's ability to increase mental alertness is a result of cerebral cortical stimulation.
 d. Caffeine is a drug of choice for respiratory depression.
12 A cup of coffee before writing an examination may be considered a good use of caffeine because:
 a. caffeine depresses the higher centers and thus relieves worry and tension
 b. caffeine stimulates the cerebral cortex
 c. caffeine stimulates the myocardium and thus improves circulation
 d. caffeine stimulates fatigued muscle
13 Choose the *incorrect* answer.
 The amphetamines:
 a. are contraindicated in patients with cardiovascular disease or hypertension
 b. may be used to overcome respiratory depression from depressant drugs
 c. are anorexigenic agents
 d. are not known to cause depression upon withdrawal
14 The nausea and vomiting that may accompany the administration of morphine are caused by:
 a. stimulation of cerebral cortex
 b. irritation of gastrointestinal tract

c. stimulation of chemoreceptor emetic trigger zone in the medulla

d. stimulation of stomach contractions

15 Choose the *incorrect* answer.

Morphine poisoning is indicated by the following signs:

a. hypotension

b. abnormally slow respiratory rate

c. tachycardia

d. pin-point pupils

16 Important factors for the nurse to know about morphine include:

a. Morphine has an antidiuretic effect.

b. Morphine may cause intestinal spasms or "gas pains."

c. Constipation is likely to be a postoperative complication when morphine is given pre- and postoperatively.

d. Morphine is the most valuable analgesic available.

17 The greatest use of morphine lies in its ability to act as a(n):

a. antispasmodic

b. analgesic

c. cough remedy

d. antidiarrheic

18 The habit-forming quality of opium is explained by its effect on:

a. higher centers of the cerebral cortex

b. respiratory center

c. vasomotor center

d. smooth muscle of the bowel

19 Select the correct statements about meperidine.

a. With therapeutic doses, meperidine depresses respirations to the same degree as morphine.

b. Severe pain is not well controlled with meperidine.

c. Syncope may occur when meperidine is given to an ambulatory patient.

d. Meperidine is an effective antispasmodic.

20 Which of the following statements about salicylates are true?

a. Aspirin can cause erosion of the gastric mucosa resulting in gastric bleeding because of its poor solubility in gastric juice.

b. Salicylates are better tolerated when given with an alkaline substance such as sodium bicarbonate because salicylate excretion is increased.

c. Since salicylates lower the prothrombin level, patients receiving both salicylates and anticoagulants should be on reduced anticoagulant therapy.

d. For more rapid absorption, buffered salicylates should be administered.

21 Select the correct statements.

a. Salicylate poisoning is more likely to occur from accidental ingestion than from administration of salicylates for therapeutic effect.

b. Therapeutic doses of aspirin will not lower the temperature of nonfebrile individuals.

c. Salicylates do not cause euphoria, sedation, or addiction.

d. Salicylates will effectively relieve visceral as well as peripheral pain.

22 Choose the *incorrect* answer.

Barbiturates:

a. have a depressant effect on the entire central nervous system

b. primarily depress the motor areas of the cerebral cortex

c. are not effective analgesic agents when used alone

d. do not enhance the analgesic action of salicylates

23 Phenobarbital is one of the best of the barbiturates to prevent convulsive seizures because it:

a. depresses the motor centers in the brainstem

b. depresses the entire cerebral cortex

c. exerts a highly selective depressant action on the motor cortex

d. acts as an anticonvulsant in ordinary doses

24 Indicate which of the following channels of administration you would expect to use to give phenobarbital sodium.

a. oral

b. rectal

c. sublingual

d. intramuscular

25 Indicate which of the following statements are correct.

a. The effects of alcohol can be reduced by caffeine.

b. Nutritional complications are commonly found in the alcoholic.

c. Episodic use of alcohol is not characteristic of the chronic alcoholic.

d. An alcoholic has psychologic dependence on alcohol but not physical dependence.

26 Which of the following statements about alcohol are *incorrect?*

a. When applied locally alcohol may denature proteins.

b. A 70% by weight solution of ethyl alcohol is bactericidal.

c. Alcohol is a stimulant.

d. Toxic amounts of alcohol will impair respiration.

e. Alcohol injected into a nerve only temporarily destroys the sensory nerve endings.

27 The method by which alcohol exerts a vasodilator effect is by:

a. depression of muscle in the blood vessels

b. depression of vasomotor center

c. general cerebral depression

d. depression of motor cortex

28 Which of the following statements about anticonvulsant therapy are *incorrect?*

a. Sudden withdrawal of antiepileptic drugs may precipitate epileptic seizures.

b. Preferred antiepileptics decrease muscle tone without loss of voluntary control.

c. Phenacemide is the least toxic of the clinically available antiepileptics.

d. Diphenylhydantoin suppresses grand mal seizures.

References

Danforth, D. N., and Baldwin, C. A.: Pain relief in the parturient, Med. Clin. N. Amer. **52**:137, 1968.

Gildea, J.: The relief of postoperative pain, Med. Clin. N. Amer. **52**:81, 1968.

Prescott, F.: The control of pain, London, 1964, The English Universities Press, Ltd.

Swafford, L. I.: Pain relief in the pediatric patient, Med. Clin. N. Amer. **52**:81, 1968.

Central nervous system stimulants

Adriani, J.: The use of respiratory stimulants, Postgrad. Med. **27**:723, 1960.

French, J. D.: The reticular formation, Sci. Amer. **196**:54, May, 1957.

Stuart, D. M.: To depress the craving for food, Amer. J. Nurs. **62**:88, 1962.

Sedatives, hypnotics

Adams, E.: Barbiturates, Sci. Amer. **198**:60, 1958.

Bush, M. T., Berry, G., and Hume, A.: Ultra-short acting barbiturates as oral hypnotic agents in man, Clin. Pharmacol. Therap. **7**:373, 1966.

Essig, C. F.: Addiction to nonbarbiturates sedative and tranquilizing drugs, Clin. Pharmacol. Therap. **5**:334, 1964.

Friend, D. G.: Sedative hypnotics, Clin. Pharmacol. Therap. **1**:5, 1960.

Isbell, H., and others: Chronic barbiturate intoxication, Arch. Neurol. Psychiat. **64**:1, 1950.

Lasagna, L.: Efficacy of new drugs: the newer hypnotics, Med. Clin. N. Amer. **41**(2):359-367, 1957.

Lasagna, L.: Across-the-counter hypnotics; boon, hazard or fraud? J. Chron. Dis. **4**:552, 1956.

Lasagna, L.: The pharmacological basis for the effective use of hypnotics, Pharmacol. Physicians **1**(2):1, 1967.

Mark, L. C., and Papper, E. M.: Changing therapeutic goals in barbiturate poisoning, Pharmacol. Physicians **1**(2):1, 1967.

Sadove, M. S., and Albrecht, R. F.: Sedatives and tranquilizers in the treatment of pain, Med. Clin. N. Amer. **52**:47, 1968.

Shideman, F. E.: Clinical pharmacology of hypnotics and sedatives, Clin. Pharmacol. Therap. **2**:313, 1961.

Narcotic analgesics

Eckenhoff, J. E., and Oech, S. R.: The effects of narcotics and antagonists upon respiration and circulation in man, Clin. Pharmacol. Therap. **1**:483, 1960.

Faucett, R. L.: Drug addiction and other considerations in the management of pain with narcotic drugs, Proc. Staff Meet. Mayo Clin. **32**:45, 1957.

Foldes, F. F.: The human pharmacology and clinical use of narcotic antagonists, Med. Clin. N. Amer. **48**:421, 1964.

Foldes, F. F., Swerdlow, H. M., and Siker, E. S.: Narcotics and narcotic antagonists, Springfield, Ill., 1964, Charles C Thomas, Publisher.

Fraser, H. F.: Human pharmacology and clinical uses of nalorphine, Med. Clin. N. Amer. **41**:393-402, 1957.

Jaffe, J. H.: Narcotics in the treatment of pain, Med. Clin. N. Amer. **52**:33, 1968.

Kaufman, M. A., and Brown, D. E.: Pain wears many faces, Amer. J. Nurs. **61**:48, 1961.

Lasagna, L.: The clinical evaluation of morphine and its substitutes as analgesics, Pharmacol. Rev. **16**:47, 1964.

Lasagna, L., and Beecher, H. K.: The optimal dose of morphine, J.A.M.A. **156**:230, 1954.

Modell, W.: The search for a morphine substitute, Amer. J. Nurs. **57**:1565, 1957.

Murphree, H. B.: Clinical pharmacology of potent analgesics, Clin. Pharmacol. Therap. **3**:473, 1962.

Sadove, M. S., and Schiffrin, M. J.: Analgesic agents for the relief of acute pain, Postgrad. Med. **29**:346, 1961.

Seevers, M. H.: Medical perspectives on habituation and addiction, J.A.M.A. **181**:93, 1962.

Shearer, N. M.: The evolution of premedication, Brit. J. Anaesth. **32**:554, 1960; **33**:119, 1961.

Vandam, L. D.: Clinical pharmacology of the narcotic analgesics, Clin. Pharmacol. Therap. **3**:827, 1962.

Way, E. L., and Adler, T. K.: The pharmacologic implications of the fate of morphine and its surrogates, Pharmacol. Rev. **12**:383, 1960.

Nonnarcotic analgesics

DeKornfeld, T. S.: Aspirin, Amer. J. Nurs. **64**:60, 1964.

Done, A. K.: The nature of the antirheumatic action of salicylates, Clin. Pharmacol. Therap. **1**:141, 1960.

Done, A. K.: Salicylate poisoning, Amer. J. Med. **36**:167, 1964.

Friend, D. G.: Current concepts in therapy, analgesic drugs: II. Non-narcotics. I. The salicylates, New Eng. J. Med. **256**:1149, 1957.

Friend, D. G.: Current concepts in therapy, analgesic drugs. Sedative-hypnotic drugs: IV. The barbiturates. II. New Eng. J. Med. **256**:77, 1957.

Guzman, F., and Lim, R. K. S.: The mechanism of action of the non-narcotic analgesics, Med. Clin. N. Amer. **52**:3, 1968.

Nordenfelt, O., and Ringertz, N.: Phenacetin takers dead with renal failure: 17 men and 3 women, Acta Med. Scand. **170**:385, 1961.

Alcohol

Chafitz, M. E.: Drugs in the treatment of alcoholism, Med. Clin. N. Amer. **51**:1249, 1967.

Golbert, T. M., Sanz, C. J., Rose, H. D., and Leitschuk, H.: Comparative evaluation of treatments of alcohol withdrawal syndromes, J.A.M.A. **201**:99, 1967.

Isselbacher, K. J., and Greenberger, N. J.: Metabolic effects of alcohol on the liver, New Eng. J. Med. **170**:351, 1964.

Jacobsen, E.: Metabolism of ethyl alcohol, Pharmacol. Rev. **4**:107, 1952.

McCarthy, R. G.: Alcoholism, Amer. J. Nurs. **59**:203, 1959.

Webb, W. R., and Degerlis, I. U.: Ethyl alcohol and the cardiovascular system, J.A.M.A. **191**:1055, 1965.

14 Anesthetic agents

General anesthetics
Local anesthetics

Anesthetic drugs are central nervous system depressants that possess three characteristics: (1) they depress all types of cells; (2) they have an affinity for nervous tissue; and (3) their action is reversible, with cells returning to normal upon elimination of the drug from the cells. There are two major classifications for these drugs. *Local anesthetic agents* block nerve conduction when applied locally to any type of nerve tissue in any part of the nervous system and thereby abolish sensation in that region; they do not produce unconsciousness. *General anesthetic agents* are capable of producing *narcosis,* that is, stupor or loss of consciousness, and thereby general loss of sensation. Loss of consciousness is preceded by analgesia and accompanied by varying degrees of muscular relaxation.

■ General anesthetics
Discovery

It is more than 100 years since the first volatile anesthetics were used to produce relief of pain and unconsciousness during a surgical operation. Prior to that, agents to relieve pain were limited to alcoholic beverages, belladonna preparations, and opium. The psychic as well as physical trauma associated with surgery without a good anesthetic definitely limited what the surgeon could do for a patient. Surgical skill was equated with speed. An English physician, Sir Clifford Allbutt, is quoted as follows: "When I was a boy, surgeons operating upon the quick were pitted one against the other like runners on time. He was the best surgeon both for the patient and the onlooker, who broke the three minute record in an amputation or a lithotomy."*

Nitrous oxide was discovered in 1772 by Joseph Priestley, who did not realize that the gas had anesthetic properties. Sir Humphrey Davy in 1799 suggested that because of its pain-relieving property, it might be tried in connection with surgery, but his suggestion passed unheed-

*Beckman, H.: Pharmacology; the nature, action, and use of drugs, Philadelphia, 1961, W. B. Saunders Co., p. 272.

ed for many years. Three hundred years elapsed from the time of the discovery of ether until it began to be used for the relief of pain during surgery. Dr. Crawford Long of Georgia in 1842 had a patient inhale ether while he removed a tumor from the neck. Dr. Long failed to publish a report of this administration in the medical literature and therefore failed to receive full credit for being the first to discover the value of ether as an anesthetic agent.

Horace Wells, a dentist, observed some of the properties of nitrous oxide and began to use it in connection with his dental practice. In 1845 he attempted to demonstrate its capacity to relieve pain during a surgical operation. The demonstration failed and his efforts were ridiculed, with the result that this useful agent received little attention for some time thereafter. It was not recognized in that day how difficult it is to produce a good level of anesthesia with nitrous oxide alone for the period of time required for a surgical operation.

In 1846 William Morton, another dentist, who later studied medicine, successfully anesthetized a patient with ether at the Massachusetts General Hospital in Boston. The success of this undertaking launched a new era in surgery.

Chloroform was discovered in 1831, and in 1847 James Simpson of England successfully demonstrated its usefulness. Queen Victoria knighted him for his contribution to the relief of pain.

More than 80 years elapsed before any other general anesthetic gained a permanent place in anesthesia. Since 1935 many new anesthetic agents have been introduced.

Action of general anesthetics

General anesthetics affect all excitable tissues of the body. They vary widely in chemical structure, and there is also great variation in the concentrations required of different anesthetics to produce a given state of anesthesia. There are a number of interesting theories to explain the mechanism whereby anesthetics act.

Theories of action

Although many theories of narcosis have been proposed, none satisfactorily explains the basic mechanisms of action. Indeed, it is possible that different anesthetics have different modes of action and that no one theory will suffice.

The Iverton-Meyer theory stresses the relationship between the lipid solubility of an anesthetic agent and its potency; the greater the solubility in fat, the greater the narcotic power. Since the nervous system has a high lipid content, this theory explains why anesthetics are preferentially taken up by the brain. However, not all lipid-soluble substances possess anesthetic activity, and some narcotics are not fat soluble.

In 1939 Ferguson proposed that anesthetic potency is related to its thermodynamic potential; that is, in addition to the concentration or percentage saturation of a drug in tissue, it is the proportion of molecules that are free to react with enzyme systems, nerve membranes, and other biologic sites that determines drug potency. Molecules not free to react this way react with one another or with other molecules that are present.

In 1961 Miller and Pauling put forth the theory that anesthetic action is essentially a physical event whereby an anesthetic reacts with the water in brain tissue to form microcrystals of ice, which then form an *ice cover* at nerve cell membranes. This blocks the passage of ions across the membranes, reducing their excitability and interfering with synaptic transmission. This event results in narcosis. The ice cover could also interfere with enzyme activity or other fundamental processes. The ice crystals are stabilized by electrically charged side chains of proteins. It is also hypothesized that an ice cover is always present, even in the absence of an anesthetic, and that the ice cover increases as the body temperature falls. This provides an explanation for anesthesia caused solely by hypothermia and the need for less anesthetic drug with hypothermia.

Biochemical theories of anesthesia have also been proposed. These theories claim that various biochemical processes are interfered with, such as oxidation, phosphate uptake, and synthesis of adenosine triphosphate (ATP) and acetylcholine (ACh), causing impaired synaptic transmission in the brain. Although there is some experimental support for these theories, there is also evidence against them.

Recent investigations show that some anesthetics inhibit sodium-stimulated ATPase activity in the brain, which could disturb the processes maintaining ion transport across nerve cell membranes, presumably at synapse sites. Theories that propose that anesthesia results from interference with energy utilization rather than energy expenditure tend to be more acceptable to physiologists.

When anesthesia is first induced, the concentration gradient from alveolar air to blood is steep and therefore absorption of the gas into the blood is rapid. With time, the concentration of gas in alveolar air, blood, and tissues approaches equilibrium and absorption of the gas slows. When the anesthetic is stopped, the reverse process occurs. Elimination is very rapid at first and then slower. Concentration of anesthetics in the fat depots of the body is more slowly reached than in other tissues and is more slowly eliminated. This is probably caused by the relatively small blood supply to fat depots. Alveolar walls are highly permeable to anesthetics, and free diffusion occurs between the alveolae and capillary membranes. A great deal of investigational work is being done, but regardless of the ultimate explanation, anesthesia is produced by progressively increasing the amount of the anesthetic agent, first in the blood and subsequently in the nervous system.

Unlike many other drugs, the anesthetics that can be given by inhalation are absorbed, transported, and excreted by the body without undergoing chemical change. For the most part, they are exhaled and excreted by way of the lungs, except for small amounts lost by way of the kidneys and skin. They are therefore relatively safe agents, since their anesthetic effect can be rapidly reversed by elimination from the lungs, provided respiration is maintained satisfactorily. This possibility of rapid removal of the drug by breathing permits the safe use of drugs that show surprisingly small difference between an anesthetic dose and a fatal dose.

The pattern of depression is similar for all anesthetics—*irregular descending depression.* The cerebral cortex is depressed first, then structures of the diencephalon, midbrain, spinal cord, and finally the medullary centers. It is fortunate that the medulla is spared temporarily, since it contains the vital centers concerned with heart action, blood pressure, and respiration.

Balanced anesthesia

Balanced anesthesia consists of the following:

1 Premedication with a basal anesthetic (barbiturate), a narcotic analgesic (meperidine), and a vagal inhibitor (atropine)
2 Induction using a basal or short-acting anesthetic (thiopental)
3 Maintenance of anesthesia using an anesthetic gas (nitrous oxide), possibly in conjunction with an intravenous narcotic or barbiturate
4 Maintenance of muscle relaxation using a curare type drug or neuromuscular blocking agent (succinylcholine)

The advantages of this procedure are:

1 Rapid induction
2 Reduction in amount of drug required to maintain a desired state of anesthesia
3 Minimal adverse effects
4 Minimal disturbance of physiologic functions and of organs of detoxification and excretion
5 No need for deep state of anesthesia for optimal muscle relaxation

Factors influencing drug choice are the patient's physical condition and previous drug therapy, the operative procedure to be performed, and the estimated length of the operation.

Preanesthetic medications

Satisfactory anesthesia is partly dependent on the preparation of the patient. Preanesthetic medications are administered for: (1) sedative and amnesic effects (barbiturates and narcotic analgesics); (2) inhibition of salivary and mucous secretions (atropine and scopolamine); (3) inhibition of anticipated undesirable side effects such as vagal stimulation (abolished by

Table 14-1 Preanesthetic agents

Drug classification	Agent most frequently used		Desired effect
	Generic name	*Trade name*	*Desired effect*
Narcotic analgesics	Morphine Meperidine	Demerol	Sedation to decrease tension and anxiety
Barbiturates	Pentobarbital Secobarbital	Nembutal Seconal	Rapid induction Rapid induction
Phenothiazines	Promethazine Triflupromazine	Phenergan Vesprin	Rapid induction Antihistaminic Antiemetic Decreased motor activity
Anticholinergics	Atropine Scopolamine	– –	Inhibition of secretions, vomiting, and laryngospasms Sedation
Skeletal muscle relaxants	Succinylcholine *d*-Tubocurarine	Anectine	Promotion of relaxation
Basal anesthetic	Thiopental	Pentothal	Rapid induction

atropine) and spasms (relieved by succinylcholine); and (4) a decrease in the metabolic rate. (See Table 14-1.)

Barbiturates may be administered the night before the operation to ensure a sound and restful sleep. Narcotics, barbiturates, or tranquilizers administered prior to the patient being taken to the operating room promote serenity, amnesia, and smooth induction. It is important that the nurse administer the medications at the time they are ordered to be given, since a narcotic given too close to the time of administration of the general anesthetic may achieve its full effect during anesthesia and cause severe respiratory depression.

Patients have been known to faint after receiving phenergan along with morphine or meperidine. Ambulatory patients receiving these drugs should be carefully watched.

Preparation of the patient for general anesthesia. Preparation of the patient for general anesthesia is very important. Vital signs should be carefully checked before the patient is taken to the operating room, and any alteration from normal should be recorded and immediately reported. The mental state of the patient should be noted and any undue anxiety or expressions of fear or death should be reported immediately. Severe anxiety or fear, unless allayed, affects both the autonomic and central nervous systems and may cause reactions that are deleterious physiologically and psychologically. These patients may resist relaxation and fight the anesthetic. A greater amount of anesthetic is therefore required, and toxic levels of drug may be administered inadvertently. Preparation for surgical procedures should be carefully explained to patients. It may be helpful to highlight the safety factors incorporated in today's modern operative procedures.

Food is usually withheld after the evening meal, and standard procedure is to give the patient nothing to eat or drink after midnight. This helps prevent aspiration if nausea and vomiting occur.

Patients may complain of dry mouth caused by the use of atropine or scopolamine to minimize secretions of saliva and mucus. Frequent rinsing of the mouth may be helpful. The necessity for coughing, deep breathing, and frequent turning during the postoperative period should be taught to the patient preoperatively. This promotes patient cooperation postoperatively when he is asked to perform procedures that often induce pain.

Requirements of an ideal general anesthetic

The following are the requirements of an ideal general anesthetic:

1   It is highly desirable that the anesthetic agent have a sufficiently wide safety range; considerable difference should exist between the therapeutic and the toxic dose.
2   It should produce anesthesia rapidly and not be unpleasant to take.
3   Recovery should be rapid and free from discomfort.
4   It should be readily excreted from the body without damage to body tissues.
5   It should produce maximum muscular relaxation and should not increase capillary bleeding.
6   It should be of such potency that the levels of anesthesia are easily controlled and that oxygen may be administered freely with it.
7   It should be a stable substance and not explosive.
8   It should be a nonirritant and free from side effects.

There is no known anesthetic that fulfills all of the foregoing requirements, but these criteria may be used to evaluate the properties of the various anesthetic agents.

Stages of general anesthesia

Anesthetists have learned to observe a patient's reactions while under anesthesia and have come to know when conditions are satisfactory for surgical procedure and when a reaction constitutes a danger signal.

The stages of anesthesia vary with the choice of anesthetic, speed of induction, and skill of the anesthetist. Present-day practice of inducing anesthesia with an intravenously administered anesthetic prior to inhalation anesthesia promotes rapid transition from consciousness to surgical anesthesia, and the early stages of anesthesia are not seen. However, if the drug is given slowly enough, usually all stages can be observed. They are most easily seen when ether is used as the only anesthetic. (See Table 14-2.)

Stage 1: analgesia. This stage begins with onset of anesthetic administration and lasts until loss of consciousness. Smell and pain are abolished before consciousness is lost. Vivid dreams and auditory or visual hallucinations may be experienced. Speech becomes difficult and indistinct. Numbness spreads gradually over the body. The body feels stiff and unmanageable. When ether is used alone its irritating effects may cause choking, coughing, a feeling of asphyxia, and increased secretions.

Stage 2: excitement. This stage varies greatly with individuals but begins with loss of consciousness. Reflexes are still present and may be exaggerated, particularly with sensory stimulation such as noise. The patient may struggle, shout, laugh, swear, or sing. There is an increase in autonomic activity, muscle tone, eye movement, and rapid and irregular breathing. Irregular respiration may be the cause of uneven absorption of anesthetic; a period of apnea followed by a few deep breaths may produce a toxic concentration of anesthetic in the blood. Most anesthetic deaths have occurred in this stage.

The variability in this stage results from: (1) amount and type of premedication; (2) the anesthetic agent used; and (3) the degree of external sensory stimuli. Since the advent of balanced anesthesia, excitement during induction is rare. However, this stage is important for classifying and analyzing drug effects in investigational studies.

Stages 1 and 2 constitute the *stage of induction.*

Stage 3: surgical anesthesia. The third stage is divided into four planes of increasing depth of anesthesia. Whether a patient is in one or the other of these four planes is determined by the character of the respirations, eyeball movement, pupil size, and degree to which reflexes are present or absent. Most operations are done

Table 14-2 Stages and planes of anesthesia and selected central nervous system effects

Central nervous system effects	*Stage 1*	*Stage 2*	*Stage 3 planes*				*Stage 4*
			1	*2*	*3*	*4*	
Consciousness	Maintained Analgesia Euphoria Some distortion of perceptions Variable amnesia	Lost	Absent	Absent	Absent	Absent	Absent
Respiration	No alteration or increased rate with some irregularity	Rapid, irregular	Regular	Regular but expirations longer than inspirations	Diaphragmatic	Thoracic ceases Diaphragmatic depressed	No respiratory movement Respiratory paralysis
Skeletal muscles	Normal tone	Tone increased	Small muscles relaxed	Large muscles relaxed	Complete relaxation	Complete relaxation	Diaphragm paralyzed
Eye Pupils Movements Tear secretion	Reaction to light Unchanged	Dilated Increased	Constriction Increased	Mid-dilatation None Decreased	None Decreased	Dilated None Absent	Dilated None
Reflexes Lid Corneal Pharyngeal "or gag" Laryngeal Cough	Present Present	Present Present	Absent Present Absent	Absent Absent Absent	Absent Absent Absent in large bronchi	Absent Absent Absent in small bronchi	Absent Absent
Heart rate		Increased	Decreased				
Blood pressure	Unchanged	Increased	Normal	Normal	Decreased	Decreased	Decreased
Venous pressure	Unchanged	Increased	Unchanged				Increased

in plane 2 or in the upper part of plane 3. As the patient moves into plane 1 the respiratory irregularities of the second stage have usually disappeared and respiration becomes full and regular. As anesthesia deepens, respiration becomes more shallow and also more rapid. Paralysis of the intercostal muscles is followed by increased abdominal breathing; finally, only the diaphragm is active. The eyeballs, which exhibit a rolling type of movement at first, gradually move less and then cease to move at all. Normally, if the pupils were reflexly dilated in the second stage, they now constrict to about the size they are in natural sleep. The reaction to light becomes sluggish. The pupils dilate as plane 4 is approached.

The face is calm and expressionless and may be flushed or even cyanotic. The musculature becomes increasingly relaxed as reflexes are progressively abolished. Most abdominal operations cannot be performed until the abdominal reflexes are absent and the abdominal wall is soft. The body temperature is lowered as the anesthetic state continues. The pulse remains full and strong. Blood pressure may be slightly elevated, but in plane 4 the blood pressure drops and the pulse becomes weak. The skin, which was warm, now becomes cold, wet, and pale.

With an anesthetic such as ether the third stage (upper planes) may be maintained for hours with little change by the repeated administration of small amounts of the drug.

Stage 4: medullary paralysis (toxic stage). The fourth stage is characterized by respiratory arrest and vasomotor collapse. Respiration ceases before the heart action, so that artificial respiration may lighten the anesthetic state (if a gaseous agent has been used) and save the patient's life.

Administration of anesthetics by inhalation

Open-drop method. Liquid anesthetics, such as ether, are frequently given by dropping the anesthetic on gauze placed on a wire mask that fits over the patient's nose and mouth. The anesthetic vaporizes, mixes with air, and is inhaled. There is free access to air. No attempt

is made to confine the vapor, and there is no rebreathing of the anesthetic mixture. Its major advantage is its simplicity; it can be used when no other equipment is available. This method is used only for operations of short duration or for obstetric delivery. Major disadvantages include inability to control rate of vaporization resulting in uneven anesthesia; waste of drug; fire hazard if drug is flammable; and irritation to mucous membranes or skin, causing increased secretions and burns. Another form of the open method is seen when a gaseous agent such as nitrous oxide merely flows over the patient's face.

Semiclosed method. This refers to the use of some means to decrease the escape of the anesthetic vapor. A mixture containing gases or vapors mixed with air or oxygen is inhaled from a closed mask that communicates with a reservoir or breathing bag. Recirculation of expired gases is prevented by valves. Exhalations pass through a valve on the top of the mask. There is greater retention of carbon dioxide than with the open method, but a higher concentration of anesthetic vapor is provided. This method sacrifices simplicity, and the exhaled gases may be a fire hazard.

Closed method. This method can be used for both gases and volatile liquids. An anesthetic machine is used and an apparatus fits over the nose and face of the patient, or an endotracheal tube connects the respiratory tract of the patient with the anesthetic machine, thus forming a closed system. Provision is made for removal of carbon dioxide, absorption of moisture, and regulation of the intake of the anesthetic agent or agents, as well as oxygen. Regulation of respiration by the anesthetist is made possible by the periodic and rhythmic compression of the breathing bag. The closed method affords better control of the anesthetic state, as well as greater economy of the anesthetic, since rebreathing of the mixture occurs. Minimal waste of drug makes it more economical and the fire hazard is decreased.

Volatile and nonvolatile anesthetics

Volatile anesthetics are gases or liquids that can be administered by inhalation when mixed with oxygen and can effect a concentration in the blood and brain to depress the central nervous system and cause anesthesia or narcosis. (See Table 14-3.) They have the following characteristics:

1 They are complete anesthetics and thus can abolish superficial and deep reflexes.
2 They provide for controllable anesthesia since depth of anesthesia is easily varied by changing the inhaled concentration.
3 Allergic reactions to these agents are uncommon.
4 Rapid recovery can occur as soon as administration ceases since the anesthetic is excreted in expired air.

Nonvolatile anesthetics include organic solids or liquids that are water soluble and lend themselves to intravenous or intramuscular injection or rectal instillation. Although they can produce loss of consciousness, cortical activity is not completely interrupted, a number of reflexes remain active, and patients respond to painful stimuli. These are not controllable anesthetics because of variation in individual tolerance, which differs with time and metabolic status. Nonvolatile anesthetics are suitable only for basal narcosis.

Volatile or general anesthetics
Ether, U.S.P., B.P. (Diethyl Ether)

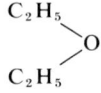

Ether is a clear, colorless liquid with a pungent odor and a bitter, burning taste. It is formed by the action of sulfuric acid on ethyl alcohol. It is highly volatile and very flammable. Mixtures of ether and air or ether and oxygen are explosive. It is decomposed by light, air, and moisture and should therefore be kept in sealed metal containers. Ether is a good solvent for fats, oils, resins, and adhesive plaster.

Action and result. Ether may have either a local or systemic action.

Local. When applied to the skin and allowed to evaporate, ether cools the skin. If it is not allowed to evaporate, it reddens the skin and acts as a rubefacient. Ether irritates mucous membranes and causes increased secretion of mucus, saliva, and tears. When moderately dilute, it acts as a carminative in the digestive tract. Nausea and vomiting may result from gastric irritation or from central stimulation of the vomiting center.

Systemic. The systemic action of ether has been described in the presentation of the stages of anesthesia. Ether has an action similar to that of curare at the myoneural junctions (see p. 392). It is said to be the only anesthetic to possess this action. When ether and a member of the curariform drugs are used together, the dose of the latter must be reduced. The induction period is comparatively slow, and the period of recovery is longer than for a number of the other general anesthetics. Nausea and vomiting are common in the recovery phase.

For a time, ether makes the heart beat faster and stronger; then, as the vagus nerve is blocked, the heart is reflexly accelerated for a time. In the deeper planes of surgical anesthesia the myocardium is directly depressed. Ether produces peripheral vasodilatation by depressing the vasomotor center and also by directly depressing the smooth muscle of blood vessels, particularly the peripheral blood vessels in the skin. As a result there may be oozing of blood from the cut edges of skin during and after surgery. Blood pressure is lowered as anesthesia deepens. The skin feels warm, and the face is frequently flushed. The temperature of the body may be reduced several degrees during a long operation. Sudden marked pupil dilatation is regarded as a danger signal, since it may mean the beginning of respiratory failure. Of course, the size of the pupil may be modified by the action of the preanesthetic drugs such as morphine and atropine.

Some degree of irritation in the kidney is indicated by the presence of albumin in the urine and scanty urine formation for several hours after anesthesia. Postoperative urinary retention may result from poor tone in the bladder. There is no evidence that ether causes any damage to the liver.

Contractions of the uterus are not much affected by moderate degrees of anesthesia, but they are slowed and decreased by deep anesthe-

Table 14-3 Properties of major volatile liquid anesthetics

Properties	*Ether (diethyl)*	*Chloroform*	*Halothane*
Inflammable and explosive	Yes	No	No
Induction	Slow – unpleasant	Rapid – pleasant	More rapid than ether – pleasant
Recovery	Slow	Rapid	More rapid than ether
Mucous membrane irritant	Yes – coughing, laryngeal spasms, profuse mucous secretions	Less than ether	Nonirritant
Sympathetic stimulant	Yes	No	No
Results in increased capillary bleeding	Yes	No	No
Cardiovascular effects: Sensitization of myocardium to epinephrine	No	Yes – may cause arrhythmia	Yes
Heart rate	Decreased in plane 3	Decreased	Bradycardia
Blood pressure	Decreased in plane 3	Decreased	Hypotension
Skeletal muscle relaxation	Excellent	Good	Not adequate when used alone
Postoperative effects	Nausea, vomiting	Nausea, vomiting, possibly permanent liver and kidney damage	Rare (a few cases of severe liver damage have been reported)
Use	Major and prolonged operations Obstetric labor	Not common	Widely used, often used with nitrous oxide

sia. Ether is not an entirely satisfactory anesthetic to relieve the pain of childbirth, because its analgesic effect cannot be obtained fast enough. There are better analgesics for this purpose.

In the early stages of anesthesia there may be sufficient stimulation of smooth muscle of the gastrointestinal tract to cause nausea and vomiting. During moderate or deep surgical anesthesia ether produces diminished peristalsis and tone of smooth muscle of the gastrointestinal organs. This is sometimes responsible for the development of distention. Early ambulation is helpful in preventing local accumulations of gas.

Recovery from ether anesthesia proceeds in reverse order; the patient goes from the stage of surgical anesthesia through the stage of excitement and on through the stage of analgesia before becoming fully conscious. The nurse must make sure that the patient's face is turned to the side to prevent aspiration of mucus or vomitus. No patient should ever be left alone until he is fully conscious.

The sense of hearing returns comparatively early. This is a fact worth noting by attendants, who might discuss the patient's medical status, assuming that he is still unconscious. Postanesthetic doses of morphine or similar narcotics should be withheld until the gagging, swallowing, and coughing reflexes have returned fully. Return of function of these reflexes coincides with the return of consciousness.

Uses. Ether continues to be used widely as a general anesthetic especially in a combination of nitrous oxide gas, oxygen, and ether (G-O-E). Nitrous oxide may be used for induction to avoid the unpleasant suffocating effects of ether and the excitement of the second stage. Ether can be used to check convulsive seizures associated with tetanus and strychnine poisoning. It is used as a fat solvent to cleanse the skin prior to surgical procedures.

Preparation, dosage, and administration. The dose of ether depends upon the patient, the length of operation, and the depth of anesthesia to be maintained.

Ether is administered in any of the ways mentioned under administration of anesthetics in this chapter. It is often given by the open-drop method, although the closed system is also employed, especially if ether is combined with other agents.

Side effects and toxic effects. Acute toxicity caused by overdosage may occur during administration. If induction occurs too rapidly there may be a temporary respiratory arrest. Removal of the mask or facepiece is usually all that needs to be done. Respiration is usually resumed at the normal rate. Prolonged administration of ether may result in respiratory depression and respiratory failure. The pulse becomes feeble and irregular, and the blood pressure drops. The skin becomes cold, clammy, and gray. The pupils dilate widely and do not react to light. Other dangers associated with ether anesthesia are those that arise from aspiration of mucus or vomitus or from some other form of airway obstruction.

Treatment of overdosage is prevented by keeping the patient in the lighter planes of surgical anesthesia. Oxygen and artificial respiration will hasten elimination of the ether and lighten the anesthesia.

Advantages. Ether is considered to be a relatively safe anesthetic. There is a wide margin of safety between the anesthetic and the toxic dose. It brings about excellent muscular relaxation. It is said that if anesthetists could have but one anesthetic agent they would probably choose ether.

Disadvantages. Ether is flammable and potentially explosive. It is irritating to mucous membranes and unpleasant to inhale. The recovery period from ether anesthesia may be unpleasant because of nausea and vomiting.

Contraindications. Although ether has long been thought to be contraindicated in pulmonary disease, this opinion has, to some extent, been reversed. Ether depresses activity of the vagus nerve, which is desirable in thoracic surgery. When ether is administered in a closed system with adequate amounts of oxygen and continual removal of carbon dioxide and when steps are taken to prevent accumulation of secretions in the the bronchial tubes and trachea, this anesthetic seems to serve satisfactorily for thoracic surgery even when pulmonary disease is present. Its use is not recommended for patients in acidosis or for those who have advanced renal disease. Unless special precautions are taken it should not be administered when an open flame or cautery must be used.

Chloroform, N.F., B.P.

$$H-\underset{\underset{Cl}{|}}{\overset{\overset{Cl}{|}}{C}}-Cl$$

Chloroform is a heavy, clear, colorless liquid. It has a characteristic odor and a sweet taste. It is prepared by the action of chlorine on alcohol or by the direct chlorination of methane. It should be protected from bright light when stored. It is not flammable, and when mixed with oxygen it does not form an explosive mixture.

Action and result. Chloroform, like ether, progressively depresses the central nervous system. It resembles ether in that all degrees of surgical anesthesia may be obtained along with adequate oxygenation of the patient. Chloroform is more pleasant to inhale than ether. It provides a faster induction and is not as irritating to mucous membranes, since a lower concentration can be used. It provides excellent muscular relaxation. It is excreted mainly from the lungs much the same as ether.

Uses. Chloroform is little used in the United States. It is used more often in tropical countries as an emergency anesthetic and for surgical or obstetric patients, where it is difficult to give ether by the open-drop method because of its high volatility. In the United States it has been replaced by safer anesthetics.

Preparation and dosage. Chloroform is marketed in brown bottles to retard decomposition. The solution is sweet-smelling and colorless and contains 99% to 99.5% chloroform. The remainder consists of alcohol. Dosage is determined on an individual basis.

Side effects and toxic effects. Chloroform is said to have caused five times as many deaths as ether. It may disturb the rhythm of the heart and cause it to slow or to stop beating. This is thought to be preventable by the proper use of atropine. Chloroform has also been blamed for damage of the liver and the kidney. Some authorities are of the opinion that the dangers of chloroform have been exaggerated and believe that, because of its advantages, its status should be reevaluated. They maintain that with present-day facilities for supplying adequate oxygen and removing carbon dioxide, chloroform is not necessarily more toxic than a number of other anesthetics.

Halothane, U.S.P., B.P. (Fluothane)

$$\begin{array}{cc} F & Cl \\ | & | \\ F-C-C-H \\ | & | \\ F & Br \end{array}$$

Halothane is a volatile, nonflammable, nonirritating general anesthetic whose potency is said to be about twice that of chloroform and four times that of ether. Induction with this agent is made rapidly and smoothly, and during recovery the return of consciousness is also rapid. Pharyngeal and laryngeal reflexes are easily suppressed. This means that there is little likelihood of complications such as laryngospasm, coughing, or bronchospasm. Since the agent is nonirritating, and because it depresses salivary and mucous secretions, there is little or no increase in bronchial and salivary secretions. Muscular relaxation is moderately satisfactory; muscle relaxants are sometimes needed to promote adequate relaxation. There is a low incidence of postoperative nausea and vomiting.

Preparation, dosage, and administration. Halothane is administered by closed inhalation. The drug is usually vaporized with oxygen or an oxygen–nitrous oxide mixture; 1% to 2% halothane concentration will maintain surgical anesthesia.

Side effects and toxic effects. Some degree of hypotension has been noted with most patients. Severe hypotension may result from a suddenly increased concentration of the anesthetic or when deep planes of anesthesia are attempted. Alterations in the cardiac rate and rhythm are frequently produced by halothane, the most common of which is a slow pulse. This can usually be prevented by the administration of atropine or a related type of drug. Halothane sensitizes the cardiac muscle to epinephrine and levarterenol; therefore, the administration of these drugs during anesthesia with halothane is avoided. Anesthetists are using ephedrine or Neo-Synephrine to combat hypotension.

Respiration is frequently depressed, and the depression progresses with increasing depth of anesthesia. Uterine contractions during labor cease. Halothane apparently does not harm the kidneys. Severe, even fatal liver damage has occurred in a few individuals following halothane anesthesia. It is difficult to avoid the impression of a causal role of the anesthetic in some of these cases. Halothane is such a potent anesthetic that the margin of safety between the toxic dose and the therapeutic dose is not great.

Uses. Halothane is widely used. It can be used alone or with nitrous oxide and muscle relaxants for a wide variety of operations.

Advantages. Halothane is nonexplosive, does not burn, provides rapid induction and rapid recovery, is nonirritating, has a relatively pleasant odor, and depresses salivary and bronchial secretions. It is potent and can be given with adequate amounts of oxygen. Patients may need respiratory assistance, but completely controlled respiration is easily achieved.

Disadvantages. Halothane is a strong respiratory and circulatory depressant. It causes vasodilatation, hypotension, and tachypnea (rapid shallow respirations) in the upper planes of anesthesia. In addition the drug is expensive. It is destructive to steel, rubber, and plastic materials if the liquid drug is permitted to come in contact with them.

Nitrous oxide, U.S.P., B.P. (Nitrogen Monoxide)

Nitrous oxide, one of the oldest and safest anesthetics, is a colorless gas somewhat heavier than air, with a slight odor and a sweetish taste. It long has been known as "laughing gas." It is unique among volatile anesthetics in that it is an inorganic compound (contains no carbon atoms) and is made from ammonium nitrate. It is nonflammable and nonexplosive, but at sufficiently high temperatures it will dissociate, release oxygen, and support combustion. It will therefore increase explosiveness of certain other anesthetics, such as ethylene and ether.

Action and result. The central nervous system is the only part of the body that seems to react to nitrous oxide. When the gas is mixed with air and inhaled it produces an effect similar to that of a mild intoxicant. The patient feels merry, laughs, and talks, but he does not go to sleep.

When the pure gas is inhaled, the patient first feels warm, numb, dizzy, and confused. Vivid dreams and hallucinations may be experienced.

After a few deep inspirations the patient becomes pale and soon loses consciousness. If administration is continued the patient becomes cyanosed and death results from asphyxia. The upper planes of surgical anesthesia are reached in 1 or 2 minutes, but by this time the patient is already becoming seriously depleted of oxygen. Respirations are deep and rapid, later becoming irregular and shallow. If administration is stopped before cyanosis is marked, consciousness is regained rapidly. Because many untoward effects are associated with anoxia, administration of undiluted nitrous oxide is not recommended. Anesthesia can be safely prolonged when a mixture of 20% oxygen and 80% nitrous oxide is used, but this combination is insufficiently potent to produce satisfactory surgical anesthesia without premedication. Nitrous oxide has no untoward effects on circulation, respiration, and the liver or kidneys unless oxygen deficiency is allowed to develop and persist. Nitrous oxide does not irritate the respiratory mucous membrane. Muscular relaxation is not as complete as it is with ether or cyclopropane.

Uses. If nitrous oxide were more potent it would probably be regarded as an ideal anesthetic. It is an excellent analgesic and can be given with oxygen to produce this effect in dental procedures, surgical procedures that are brief and do not require muscular relaxation, and obstetrics. It is also used as an agent for induction prior to the use of other anesthetics. G-O-E refers to the use of gas (nitrous oxide), oxygen, and ether in that sequence. Its greatest use is as a component of balanced anesthesia for prolonged or complicated surgical procedures.

Preparation and administration. Nitrous oxide is available in the compressed state in steel cylinders for closed system administration. It is also available for self-administration during childbirth.

Side effects and toxic effects. Nitrous oxide itself is a very innocuous substance and has remarkably low side and toxic effects. It can cause bone marrow depression with prolonged administration. If anoxia occurs it is probably the result of poor technique and not the gas itself. The disadvantages of nitrous oxide is its low anesthetic potency, although this can be remedied by proper use of supplemental agents. Satisfactory administration requires an experienced anesthetist.

Ethylene, N.F.

$$H_2C = CH_2$$

Ethylene is a colorless, highly volatile gas with a slightly sweet taste and an unpleasant but not intolerable odor. When mixed with a certain amount of oxygen it is highly explosive and flammable. However, it is believed to be no more explosive than ether-oxygen or ether-oxygen–nitrous oxide mixtures when comparable precautions are taken. Ethylene was first used for clinical surgery in 1923.

Action and result. Induction is smooth and rapid. Ethylene is less powerful as an anesthetic than either ether or cyclopropane but slightly more potent than nitrous oxide. It is difficult to reach more than plane 1 or possibly plane 2 of surgical anesthesia with ethylene.

Ethylene does not irritate the respiratory mucosa, and it does not increase salivary secretion. The patient awakens readily when administration of ethylene is stopped. Respiratory depression and vasomotor depression are uncommon, and postoperative complications are rare.

Uses. Because of its explosiveness, the availability of more potent anesthetics, and its slight increase in potency over nitrous oxide, the use of ethylene has been almost abandoned.

Preparation and administration. Ethylene is available in steel tanks in which the gas is kept under pressure. It is administered with oxygen in a closed system technique with a gas machine. It is important for the patient to receive a preliminary medication so that adequate amounts of oxygen may be given during anesthesia to prevent hypoxia.

Disadvantages. The chief disadvantage associated with the use of ethylene is the hazard of fire and explosion. As is true of certain other anesthetics, the time of greatest danger is at the end of the operation, when the mask is lifted from the patient's face. For this reason no one should touch the anesthetist or the anesthetic machine other than those constantly working with the patient or with the machine. A small spark of static electricity may set off an explosion. This precaution applies to all explosive mixtures.

Cyclopropane, U.S.P., B.P.

$$\begin{array}{c} CH_2 \\ \diagup \quad \diagdown \\ H_2-C \underline{\hspace{1.2cm}} C-H_2 \end{array}$$

Cyclopropane is a colorless gas, heavier than air, flammable, and explosive in most anesthetic concentrations when mixed with air or oxygen. It has a mildly pungent but not unpleasant odor. It is stable and is stored in metal cylinders where, under pressure, it liquefies easily.

Action and result. Cyclopropane is a potent anesthetic. Adequate amounts of oxygen can be given with it, to the extent of 20% or more, and it will still produce satisfactory anesthesia. A wide margin of safety exists between the anesthetic and the toxic dose. Induction is pleasant and rapid. It does not irritate the respiratory mucous membrane. There is little change in respiration until deep depression is produced. Laryngospasm occasionally develops; therefore, atropine or scopolamine is likely to be prescribed as a preliminary medication. Cyclopropane produces a fair amount of muscle relaxation, although the supplemental effect of a muscle relaxant may be required. Uterine and intestinal muscles are not affected unless the patient is in the lower planes of surgical anesthesia.

Uses. Cyclopropane has been used successfully as a general anesthetic for a wide variety of operations. It has been approved as an anesthetic for chest surgery in which quiet respirations and absence of bronchial irritation are important. It is also used in obstetrics, since it can be administered in amounts that do not affect uterine activity or the respirations of the child. Its explosiveness has limited its use in favor of newer, nonflammable agents. However, it is still often selected for patients in shock or impending shock.

Preparation and administration. Stored in steel cylinders, cyclopropane is administered by in-

Table 14-4 Properties of gaseous anesthetics

Properties	Cyclopropane	Ethylene	Nitrous oxide
Inflammable and explosive	Yes	Yes	No—but supports combustion
Induction	Rapid	Rapid	Rapid
Recovery	Rapid	Rapid	Rapid
Results in increased capillary bleeding	Yes	No	No
Sensitization of myocardium to epinephrine	Yes—may cause arrhythmia	No	No
Skeletal muscle relaxation	Adequate at deep levels of anesthesia	Incomplete except at deep levels of anesthesia	Poor when used alone
Postoperative effects	Nausea and vomiting Excitement and laryngospasm may occur	Nausea and vomiting	Anoxia if oxygen supply inadequate
Use	Widely used	Not common	To induce anesthesia For brief anesthesia (dental extraction) Principal agent in balanced anesthesia

halation preferably with the use of the closed system because it is both expensive and explosive.

Side effects and toxic effects. As anesthesia with cyclopropane deepens, disturbance of cardiac rhythm may occur. Sudden death has been known to result. This effect seems to be related to the development of hypoxia and the retention of carbon dioxide. It can be prevented by maintaining adequate ventilation. The incidence of nausea, vomiting, and postoperative distention is said to be less than after ether anesthesia but more than that seen after anesthesia with nitrous oxide or ethylene.

Vinyl ether, N.F., B.P.
(Divinyl Ether, Vinethene)

$$H—C=C—O—C=C—H$$
$$\quad\ |\quad\ |\qquad\ |\quad\ |$$
$$\quad\ H\quad H\qquad H\quad H$$

Vinyl ether is a clear, colorless fluid that greatly resembles ether. It is more volatile but about as flammable and explosive as diethyl ether. Partial decomposition may occur when it is exposed to light and air.

Action and result. Vinyl ether rapidly depresses the central nervous system, which means that the toxic stage is also reached rapidly. To prevent overdosage the patient must be watched with more than the usual care. Induction is rapid and smooth, and surgical anesthesia is produced two or three times more quickly than with ordinary ether. Continuous administration is necessary to maintain anesthesia; otherwise, the patient promptly recovers consciousness. The effects on respiration and circulation are similar to those produced by diethyl ether. It produces

307

satisfactory muscular relaxation with minimal respiratory irritation.

Uses. Vinyl ether is used especially for minor operations or surgical procedures of short duration. It is sometimes used as an induction agent prior to the administration of another anesthetic. It is a useful anesthetic in dentistry, for postpartum repair work, and in surgery of the ear, eye, nose, and throat.

Preparation and administration. Vinyl ether is available in 10-, 25-, 50-, and 75-ml. bottles with droppers. It can be administered by the open-drop, semiclosed, and closed methods.

Side effects and toxic effects. This drug has a narrow safety range and can cause liver and kidney damage. It may cause increased flow of saliva, even after the administration of atropine. It is contraindicated in the aged and for patients with hepatic and renal insufficiency. It is particularly important to prevent hypoxia during its administration, since lack of oxygen is believed to be the cause of the hepatic damage. Repeated administration of vinyl ether after short intervals or prolonged administration at any time is not recommended. Nausea and vomiting seldom occur.

Methoxyflurane, N.F., B.P. (Penthrane)

$$H-\overset{\overset{\displaystyle Cl}{|}}{\underset{\underset{\displaystyle Cl}{|}}{C}}-\overset{\overset{\displaystyle F}{|}}{\underset{\underset{\displaystyle F}{|}}{C}}-O-CH_3$$

Methoxyflurane is an inhalation anesthetic suitable for both induction and maintenance of anesthesia. It is not flammable or explosive in any concentration mixed with air or oxygen at operating room temperatures. It is a colorless liquid with a boiling point of 104.65° C. and it has a fruity odor. It is stable in light and in the presence of oxygen, moisture, and carbon dioxide absorbers. Methoxyflurane can be administered by any of the usual techniques—closed, semiclosed, and open-drop. Induction is slow and recovery prolonged. It produces as good muscle relaxation as does diethyl ether. When muscle relaxants are used with it, they should

be administered in less than the usual dose. Since it is a halogenated compound, there is the possibility it may cause acute or delayed liver damage; its administration in the presence of liver disease is contraindicated.

Fluroxene, **N.F. (Fluoromar).** This is a derivative of vinyl ether with an odor similar to vinyl ether. Fluroxene is a volatile liquid. It is explosive and flammable but its flammability is thirty times less than that of ethyl ether. It provides a more rapid and pleasant induction than ethyl ether. Potency and depressant effects are less than that of halothane. It can be used alone or with nitrous oxide; it is used primarily for minor surgery not requiring profound muscle relaxation. This is not a widely used anesthetic.

Trichloroethylene **(Trilene).** This is a nonflammable, nonirritating, volatile liquid with an odor similar to chloroform. Induction with trichloroethylene is pleasant and rapid, and recovery is also rapid. It is a potent analgesic and used primarily for this purpose in obstetrics and minor surgical procedures and as an analgesic for ambulatory patients (such as for relief of trigeminal neuralgia). It can be self-administered. Trichloroethylene is not suitable for major surgery since it is cardiotoxic and causes arrhythmias, is a poor muscle relaxant and is slowly eliminated after long use, causing prolonged recovery.

Common postoperative complications. A wide variety of signs and symptoms may be observable in the postoperative patient. The nurse should be aware of the more common postoperative complications and the possible causative factors to enable her to determine effective modes of intervention.

Hypotension may result from an excess of nonvolatile drugs that depress the vasomotor center. Avoid use of narcotics; these may increase the hypotension.

Nausea and vomiting may be caused by stimulation of the vomiting center as a result of anoxia during anesthesia.

Hypoventilation may result from excess or cumulative effects of drugs administered during anesthesia. It may be a lingering effect of neuromuscular blocking agents.

Oliguria caused by anesthesia is very common, as are *atony and urinary retention* after perineal and genital operations.

Nerve injury may follow spinal anesthesia or malpositioning during general anesthesia. Brachial, radial, ulnar, and perineal nerves are most likely to be injured.

Intestinal distention and at times paralytic ileus may occur from the anesthetic agent, postoperative sedation, or a combination of both. *Thrombosis* may also be observed.

Ethyl chloride, N.F., B.P.

$$C_2H_5Cl$$

Ethyl chloride is a colorless, highly volatile liquid with an agreeable odor and a sweetish, burning taste. It is flammable and explosive and should be kept from any contact with fire.

Ethyl chloride is a powerful, rapid-acting general anesthetic. It closely resembles chloroform in its effects, but it acts more rapidly. It does not provide complete muscular relaxation. Because of the ease with which the anesthesia progresses beyond the surgical stage and because of the danger of cardiac arrest associated with its administration, it is rarely used except for short and minor procedures, It is occasionally used as an agent for induction prior to the administration of ether. For this purpose it is given by the open-drop method, although the closed technique can also be used.

Ethyl chloride also acts as a local anesthetic. After it is sprayed on the area to be anesthetized, it evaporates so rapidly that it freezes the underlying tissues and produces insensibility to pain. It thus permits incision and drainage of boils, carbuncles, and the like. The edema and erythema that result from the thawing of the tissues can be rather painful.

Preparation. Ethyl chloride is marketed in sealed glass tubes or small metal cylinders.

Basal anesthetics

Basal anesthesia means the induction of unconsciousness by a nonvolatile anesthetic or soporific before the production of surgical anesthesia. Basal anesthetics are usually given intravenously. They are valuable to allay emotional distress, since many patients dread having a tight mask placed over the face while they are fully conscious. Basal anesthetics reduce the amount of general anesthetic required. The principal drug used for this purpose is thiopental sodium.

The intravenous anesthetics most commonly used are the ultrashort-acting barbiturates. These drugs are rapidly taken up by brain tissue because of their high oil-water solubility. For example, equilibrium between brain and blood occurs within 1 minute after injection of thiopental. Shortness of action results from the drug being quickly redistributed into the fat depots of the body. Amount of body fat affects drug action. The greater the amount of body fat, the briefer the effect of a single intravenous dose. However, with prolonged administration or large doses, there is prolonged drug action resulting in delayed recovery; this is caused by saturation of fat depots and the slow rate of drug release (10% to 15% per hour).

Advantages for using intravenous anesthetics include the rapidity with which unconsciousness is induced, amnesic effects, prompt recovery with minimal doses, and simplicity of administration. They are nonirritating to mucous membranes and use is not accompanied by the hazard of fire or explosion.

Disadvantages of using this type of anesthetic include tissue sloughing and necrosis of drug infiltrates into tissue; thrombosis if arterial injection occurs; and hypotension, laryngospasm, and respiratory failure from overdosage or prolonged administration.

Sodium thiopental, U.S.P. (Pentothal Sodium); thiopentone, B.P.

Barbiturates are used both as general anesthetics and as basal anesthetics. Sodium thiopental is an ultrashort-acting barbiturate and seems to be the most popular. Its use has steadily increased since it was first introduced by Dr. John S. Lundy in 1934.

Action and result. Sodium thiopental produces rapid loss of consciousness. Induction is smooth, easy, and pleasant for the patient. Recovery is uneventful and rapid, and complications are rare. Opinion has been expressed that the experienced, skillful anesthetist finds the control of anesthesia with this agent as easy or easier than with many of the anesthetics given by inhalation. Abdominal relaxation is likely to be inadequate even with deep anesthesia, and if used as a general anesthetic its effects are frequently supplemented with those of one of the curariform drugs. Due attention must be given to the possible dangers of hypoxia, obstruction of the air passages, and respiratory depression.

Uses. Sodium thiopental is used as a basal anesthetic to carry the patient through the period of induction prior to the use of an anesthetic given by inhalation or injection. It is also used in combination with a number of other drugs for many kinds of minor and major types of surgery. It may be given by intermittent intravenous injection along with a muscle relaxant and nitrous oxide and oxygen.

Preparation, dosage, and administration. Sodium thiopental is marketed in glass ampules containing 0.5, 1, 5, and 10 Gm. of the powder with anhydrous sodium carbonate, which acts as a buffer and makes the resulting solution less irritating to tissues. Sodium thiopental is unstable when in solution and must be freshly made. The usual dose is 2 to 3 ml. of a 2.5% solution; it is given intravenously in about 10 or 15 seconds and is repeated in 30 seconds as required. A 10% solution is sometimes given rectally as a basal anesthetic for children (0.2 ml. per pound of body weight).

Side effects and toxic effects. The rapid onset of action of this barbiturate is both a desirable effect and a potential danger. Medullary paralysis may develop rapidly when an overdose is given. It also has a tendency to produce laryngospasm. This can be prevented or handled successfully with the use of atropine or succinylcholine or by the use of endotracheal intuba-

tion. Although some difference of opinion seems to exist as to how thiopental is metabolized, there seems to be agreement that it is detoxified chiefly in the liver and the metabolic products are excreted by the kidney. This accounts for the prolonged emergence phase associated with this drug. Its use is not recommended for patients with severe heart disease, hepatic disease, anemia, or respiratory difficulties.

Tribromoethanol, N.F. (Avertin)

$$Br—\underset{\underset{Br}{|}}{\overset{\overset{Br}{|}}{C}}—\underset{\underset{H}{|}}{\overset{\overset{H}{|}}{C}}—OH$$

Tribromoethanol is a white, crystalline powder with a slightly aromatic taste and odor. Chemically, it is related to ethyl alcohol and chloral. It is unstable in light and air; it is sparingly soluble in water but very soluble in amylene hydrate. Amylene hydrate is flammable. In basal anesthetic amounts it produces drowsiness, amnesia, and sleep in about 15 minutes, reaching its maximal effect in about 30 minutes.

This was once a very popular basal anesthetic but it is now rarely used because of (1) its ability to markedly depress the respiratory and circulatory systems; (2) the difficulty in estimating dosage as a result of variations in susceptibility and absorption from the rectum; (3) its ability to cause liver damage; (4) the fact that it does not lend itself to controllable anesthesia; (5) and the availability of better and safer basal anesthetics. Tribromoethanol is now used primarily to control convulsive states.

Preparation, dosage, and administration. Tribromoethanol solution (Avertin with amylene hydrate) contains 1 Gm. of tribromoethanol and 0.5 Gm. of amylene hydrate in each milliliter. Dosage is usually calculated on the basis of body weight, but dosage should not exceed 8 ml. for women and 10 ml. for men. It is administered rectally in 2.5% solution in warm distilled water at a temperature not to exceed 40° C. or 104° F.

Propanidid

Propanidid is a new drug recently introduced by clinical investigation as an intravenous anesthetic. It is a phenoxy–acetic acid derivative. Propanidid is a water-insoluble yellow oil available in a 0.5% solution. It has a rapid action. Onset of action usually occurs in 20 to 25 seconds. Following a single injection, consciousness is regained in about 4 minutes.

Sodium hexobarbital, sodium thiamylal, N.F.; sodium methohexital, N.F.

Sodium hexobarbital (Evipal Sodium), sodium thiamylal (Surital Sodium), and sodium methohexital (Brevital Sodium) are ultrashort-acting barbiturates with properties similar to those of sodium thiopental.

■ Local anesthetics

Local anesthetics are drugs used to abolish pain sensation in a particular part of the body. Basic mechanism of action of these drugs is unknown, but most of these drugs act by stabilizing or elevating the threshold of excitation of the nerve cell membrane without affecting resting potential. This is a result of reduction of membrane permeability to all ions. Thus depolarization and transmission of nerve impulses are prevented. Local anesthetics are capable of abolishing all sensation, but pain fibers are affected first, probably since they are thinner, unmyelinated, and more easily penetrated by these drugs. Loss of pain is followed in sequence by loss of response to cold, warmth, touch, and pressure. Most motor fibers can also be anesthetized when there is sufficient concentration of the drug over a long enough period of time.

The quantity of local anesthetic needed to block conduction of nerve impulses is much less than the quantity of a general anesthetic used in surgical anesthesia. A similar amount of local anesthetic in the blood would cause death, and even relatively small doses of local anesthetics reaching the heart or brain may cause serious reactions. For this reason, effort is made to confine the local anesthetic to a limited region or small area near a nerve or among nerve endings. The action of the local anesthetic is reversible; it is followed by complete recovery and, as a rule, produces no damage to the nerve cells.

Reactions to local anesthetics

Local anesthetics produce vasodilation by direct action on blood vessels and by anesthetizing sympathetic vasoconstrictor fibers. This can cause rapid absorption of the drug; when rate of absorption exceeds rate of elimination, toxic effects can occur. To decrease rate of absorption and incidence of toxic effects by allowing more time for metabolic degradation and to prolong local anesthetic effects, epinephrine or other vasoconstrictor drugs are used. Dosage of the latter drugs must be carefully determined to prevent ischemic necrosis at the injection site. Since local anesthetics are potentially toxic drugs, a patient's age, weight, physical condition, and liver function must be taken into account in determining drug dosage.

Most reactions to local anesthetics result from overdosage, rapid absorption into systemic circulation, and individual hypersensitivity or allergic response.

Central nervous system. At first the central nervous system may be stimulated and cause anxiety, restlessness, confusion, dizziness, tremors, and even convulsions. Then depression may occur and unconsciousness and death may ensue.

Cardiovascular system. Myocardial depression, bradycardia, and hypotension can occur because of smooth muscle relaxation and inhibition of neuromuscular conduction. The patient suddenly becomes pale, feels faint, and has a drop in blood pressure. Cardiac arrest can be the end result of a cardiovascular reaction.

Allergic reaction. True allergic reactions are said to be uncommon. Sometimes a reaction is thought to be allergic when it is really caused by overdosage. However, allergic reactions can occur. They may be relatively mild (hives, itching, skin rash) or they may be of an acute anaphylactic nature. Small test doses are frequently given by the physician to gauge the extent of the patient's sensitivity to the anesthetic agent. The anesthetic agent chosen, its concentration, the rate of injection, and physical and emotional factors in the patient all influence reactions to local anesthetics.

Preparation of the patient

Preliminary medication is frequently prescribed prior to the use of a local anesthetic, much the same as before a general anesthetic. The use of a barbiturate is believed to prevent or decrease toxic reactions. Some anesthesiologists recommend the administration of a systemic analgesic and a tranquilizing agent, such as levorphan tartrate and promethazine hydrochloride, prior to the administration of a local anesthetic.

Methods of administration of local anesthetics

Some local anesthetics are suited only for surface anesthesia, some must be injected, and some are suitable for both topical administration and injection. See Table 14-5.

Surface or topical anesthesia. Surface or topical anesthesia is restricted to mucous membranes, damaged skin surfaces, wounds, or burns. The local anesthetic is applied in the form of a solution, ointment, cream, or powder to produce loss of sensation by paralyzing afferent nerve endings. Local anesthetics do not penetrate unbroken skin. Topical anesthesia is used to relieve pain and itching and to anesthetize mucous membranes of the eye, nose, throat, or urethra for minor surgical procedures. Cocaine in a 4% to 10% solution continues to be one of the most widely used agents for topical anesthesia. To minimize toxicity from local anesthetics, the smallest amount of the lowest effective concentration should be used.

Anesthesia by injection. Anesthesia by injection is accomplished by infiltration, conduction, spinal, caudal, and saddle block.

Infiltration anesthesia is produced by injecting dilute solutions (0.1%) of the agent into the skin and then subcutaneously into the region to be anesthetized. Epinephrine is often added to the solution to intensify the anesthesia in a limited region and to prevent excessive bleeding and systemic effects. Repeated injection will prolong the anesthesia as long as it may be

Table 14-5 Local anesthetics — administration and use

Method	Tissue affected	Preparation used	Examples of drugs used	Therapeutic use
Topical	Sensory nerve of mucous membranes and dermis	Solution Ointment Cream Powder	Cocaine Benzocaine Butacaine	Relieve pain or itching Examination of conjunctiva
Infiltration	Sensory nerve endings in subcutaneous tissues or dermis	Injection	Procaine Lidocaine	Minor operations
Block	Nerve trunk	Injection	Procaine Lidocaine	Dental and limb operations Muscle relaxation
Spinal	Spinal roots	Injection	Pontocaine Dibucaine	Abdominal operations Muscle relaxation

needed. The sensory nerve endings are anesthetized. This is used for minor operations such as incision and drainage or excision of a cyst.

Conduction or block anesthesia means that the anesthetic is injected into the vicinity of a nerve trunk that supplies the region of the operative site. The injection may be made at some distance from the site of surgical procedure. A single nerve may be blocked or the anesthetic may be injected in a location where several nerve trunks emerge from the spinal cord (paravertebral block). A more concentrated solution (2%) is required because of the thickness of nerve trunk fibers. This method of anesthesia is often used for operations on the foot and hand.

Spinal anesthesia is a type of extensive nerve block, sometimes called a subarachnoid block. The anesthetic solution is injected into the subarachnoid space and affects the lower part of the spinal cord and nerve roots.

Spinal anesthesia. For *low spinal anesthesia* the patient is placed in a flat or Fowler's position. A solution with a specific gravity greater than that of spinal fluid is used, since it tends to diffuse downward. For high spinal anesthesia the Trendelenburg position with the head sharply flexed is used in conjunction with an anesthetic solution of lower specific gravity than that of spinal fluid (which tends to diffuse upward) or a solution with the same specific gravity as spinal fluid (may diffuse upward or downward, depending upon position used). Solutions with the same specific gravity as spinal fluid act primarily at the site of injection.

Onset of anesthesia usually occurs within 1 to 2 minutes after injection. Duration of anesthesia is 60 to 180 minutes, depending upon the anesthetic used. Spinal anesthesia is used for surgical procedures on the lower abdomen, inguinal area, or lower extremities; it may be the method of choice for patients with severe respiratory problems or with liver, kidney, or metabolic disease. Marked hypotension, decreased cardiac output, and respiratory inadequacy tend to occur during anesthesia and are considered to be disadvantages of this method of anesthesia.

Postoperatively, headache is the most common complaint; this may be accompanied by difficulty in hearing or seeing. Headache may be postural and occur only in the head-up or sitting or standing position. This is the result of the opening in the dura made by the large spinal needle, which may persist for days or weeks, permitting loss of cerebrospinal fluid. Headache and auditory and visual problems following lumbar puncture result from decreased intracranial pressure. These symptoms are usually alleviated when spinal fluid pressure returns to normal. Paresthesias, such as numbness and tingling, may occur after spinal anesthesia; these are usually located in the lumbar or sacral areas and disappear within a relatively short period of time. The success and safety of spinal anesthesia depends primarily upon the anesthetist's skill and knowledge.

Caudal anesthesia is produced by injecting an anesthetic solution into the caudal canal, the sacral part of the vertebral canal containing the caudal equina or bundle of spinal nerves that innervates the pelvic viscera. It is used in obstetrics and for operations on pelvic or genital organs. Its advantage over spinal anesthesia is that the anesthetic does not have direct access to the spinal cord and medullary centers. Thus the respiratory muscles and blood pressure are not directly affected, and undesirable effects are less likely to occur.

Saddle block is sometimes used in obstetrics and for surgery involving the perineum, rectum, genitalia, and upper parts of the thighs. The patient sits upright while the anesthetic is injected, after a lumbar puncture has been done. The patient remains upright for a short time until the anesthetic has had a chance to be effective. The parts that would have been in contact with a saddle when riding become anesthetized, hence the name.

Drugs used as local anesthetics
Cocaine, N.F., B.P.; cocaine hydrochloride, U.S.P.

Cocaine is one of the oldest local anesthetics and the prototype of all local anesthetics. It is an alkaloid derived from the leaves of the coca shrub, which grows in Peru, other parts of

South America, and the Far East. The native people have been known to chew the leaves to give them added energy and ability to endure fatigue. In medicine, cocaine is used chiefly in the form of cocaine hydrochloride, which occurs as a white crystalline powder that is freely soluble in water and alcohol.

Action and result

Local action. Cocaine is unrivaled in its power to penetrate mucous membranes to produce surface anesthesia of the eye, nose, and throat. It is two to three times more potent than procaine. Onset of action is immediate, occurring within 60 seconds; duration of action is about 1 hour. It also causes local vasoconstrictor actions. Applied to the eye it causes pupil dilation; applied to the tongue it removes the taste of bitter substances; applied to nasal mucosa the sense of smell is paralyzed.

Systemic action. Today it is not recommended that cocaine be injected for anesthetic effects because of its toxicity. However, its systemic effects are of interest since it is one of the drugs of addiction. Cocaine potentiates the effects of norepinephrine by inhibiting its uptake into the sympathetic nerve terminals from which it is liberated. This causes a higher concentration of norepinephrine and increased sympathetic stimulation. Cocaine may also inhibit monamine oxidase, the enzyme that inactivates catecholamines. In addition, cocaine has a direct stimulant action on the central nervous system and autonomic centers in the brain.

As a result of its stimulant action, there is a feeling of euphoria, increased mental and muscular power, and increased resistance to fatigue. The individual is more talkative and active. The pulse is stronger and faster, blood pressure is elevated, respirations are faster and deeper, and vomiting may occur.

Toxic effects. Toxic doses of cocaine cause hyperexcitability and convulsions. Depression of the central and autonomic nervous systems follows stimulation.

Body temperature may increase 3° to 5° C. as a result of increased muscular activity, decreased heat loss as a result of vasoconstriction, and direct action of cocaine on the temperature-regulating center. Death is usually caused by respiratory failure but circulatory failure may also occur.

Treatment includes the control of convulsions by the administration of a muscle relaxant such as succinylcholine, evacuation of the stomach if the drug has been taken orally, and artificial respiration.

Uses. Cocaine is used chiefly for surface anesthesia of the nose and throat. Since cocaine causes opacity of the cornea and retards corneal epithelial regeneration, its use in ophthalmology has been virtually abandoned.

It is also injected in low concentrations for the removal of tonsils and similar procedures, although some authorities do not recommend its administration by injection.

Preparation and dosage. Concentrations of 1% to 4% are used for surface anesthesia of the eye and 2% to 5% for mucous membranes of the nose and throat. Epinephrine hydrochloride is frequently added to the cocaine solutions. Cocaine crystals may be moistened in epinephrine hydrochloride solution (1:1000) for placement on the nasal mucosa prior to surgical operation in the nose. A 0.2% concentration is the strength usually used for injection.

Cocaine habit. Habituation to cocaine evidently occurs as a result of its ability to produce euphoria and an illusion of power and superiority that enables an individual to forget the inadequacies and drabness of his life.

A difference exists betweeen habituation to cocaine and habituation to morphine or opium derivatives. Cocaine users tend to be gregarious and euphoric; drug taking tends to be intermittent; there is minimal or no abstinence syndrome, since tolerance or physical dependence does not occur with the use of cocaine. However, the cocaine habit leads to more rapid mental, moral, and physical deterioration than the morphine habit. The cocaine habit can produce a strong paranoid psychosis along with heightened excitement and energy that cause the cocaine user to not only see enemies everywhere but also to physically attack them. Traditionally, cocaine has been taken in the form of snuff ("snow") which may cause ulceration, gangrene, or perforation of the nasal septum because of prolonged vasoconstriction. It is now more common for users to inject the drug intravenously and to mix it with heroin. Cocaine has decreased in popularity among drug users. Continued use of the drug results in chronic poisoning. The earliest effects may be digestive disturbances and loss of appetite and weight, but the nervous system suffers most, and gradual degeneration of mind and morals usually results. Sleeplessness, tremors, spasm, delirium, and insanity are some of the consequences of long-continued use. To help combat the danger of habituation and addiction, cocaine and all its derivatives are under the regulations of the Harrison Narcotic Law.

Procaine hydrochloride (Novocain)

Procaine is a synthetic local anesthetic. Many synthetic local anesthetics have points of similarity in their chemical structure; they are amino esters of aromatic acids. Procaine is a white powder that is readily soluble in water. In solution it withstands sterilization with heat, although a precipitate may form when the solution stands for a long time.

Procaine is less potent than cocaine but also less toxic. It is rapidly destroyed by enzymes in the blood and other tissues. It does not constrict blood vessels and does not dilate the pupil of the eye. It produces no particular central action like cocaine, and it is not habit-forming.

Uses. Procaine is the best known of the local anesthetics and it is said to be the safest for both nerve block and infiltration. It is probably used more than any other single local anesthetic. Reactions occur comparatively seldom and tend to be mild; elimination is rapid and tissue damage is seldom produced. Procaine is not well absorbed from mucous membranes; hence, it is not suited for topical administration. It is

useful for many types of local anesthesia when given by injection. Procaine hydrochloride has been used to overcome cardiac arrhythmias, although procainamide is used more often for this purpose.

Preparation and dosage. The following are the procaine preparations available.

Procaine hydrochloride, **U.S.P., B.P.** This is available as a white crystalline powder intended for parenteral solutions.

Procaine hydrochloride injection, **U.S.P.;** *procaine and adrenaline injection,* **B.P.** The U.S.P. preparation is available in concentrations of 1% and 2% procaine hydrochloride. It may or may not contain epinephrine.

The dosage of procaine used for anesthesia varies with the technique of administration employed. Concentrations of 1% or 2% are adequate for most purposes, although concentrations of 0.25% to 0.5% may be used for infiltration. The duration of anesthesia for a nerve block is about 45 minutes and for spinal anesthesia about 1 hour.

Lidocaine hydrochloride, U.S.P. (Xylocaine Hydrochloride); lignocaine hydrochloride, B.P.

Lidocaine hydrochloride is another synthetic local anesthetic. It is said to produce effects more promptly and with greater intensity than those produced by an equal amount of procaine. Lidocaine is suited for surface anesthesia as well as for infiltration and block anesthesia.

Preparation and dosage. Solutions are available in 0.5% to 2% concentration, with or without epinephrine hydrochloride. A 2% jelly is used for mucous membranes of the urethra, and a 5% ointment is available for application to burns and skin lesions.

Toxic effects. In low concentrations its toxicity is thought to be about the same as that of procaine. It has an advantage of being effective in small amounts of low concentrations. Overdosage may result in many of the toxic symptoms associated with local anesthetics, such as drop in blood pressure, nausea, vomiting, pallor, apprehension, muscular twitching, and convulsions.

315

Table 14-6 Properties of commonly used local anesthetics

	Cocaine	*Procaine*	*Ethyl aminobenzoate*
Trade names	–	Novocain	Benzocaine Anesthesin
Potency	Two to three times more potent than procaine		Very low
Onset of action	1 min.	2 to 5 min.	Immediate
Duration of action	1 hr.	1 hr.	During contact only
Dose	2% to 4% topically	0.5% to 2%, depending upon method of administration	5% to 10% ointment topically
Toxicity	Four times more toxic than procaine when injected subcutaneously	Least toxic of all local anesthetics	Relatively nontoxic
Precautions	Not recommended for infiltration, nerve block, or spinal anesthesia Repeated use causes psychic dependence	Overdose or rapid injection may cause stimulation	Suitable for topical use only

Chloroprocaine hydrochloride, N.F. (Nesacaine Hydrochloride)

Chloroprocaine is more potent and acts more quickly than procaine.

Preparation and administration. Solutions of chloroprocaine for injection in 1%, 2%, and 3% concentrations are available.

The drug is not a potent surface anesthetic. It apparently can be given in all the ways that procaine can be given by injection, although its use for spinal anesthesia has not been fully evaluated.

Toxic effects. Its toxic effects are said to be similar to those produced by procaine. Since it does not produce vasoconstriction, its toxicity can be decreased by giving it with epinephrine to delay absorption.

Cyclomethycaine sulfate, B.P. (Surfacaine)

Cyclomethycaine sulfate is used as a topical anesthetic for certain types of skin lesions and abrasions in which discomfort is caused by pain and itching. It is also used on vaginal and rectal mucous membranes to reduce pain from fissures and ulcerations.

Preparation and administration. Cyclomethycaine sulfate is available in preparations that in-

Lidocaine	Tetracaine	Mepivacaine	Dibucaine
Xylocaine Lignocaine	Pontocaine	Carbocaine	Nupercaine
Two times more potent than procaine	Ten times that of procaine	Two times that of procaine	Ten to twenty times that of procaine
Immediate 1 to 2 hr.	5 to 10 min. 1½ to 2 hr.	Similar to procaine Similar to lidocaine	10 min. 2½ to 3 hr.
0.5% to 2% for injection 4% topically	1% to 2% topically 0.15% to 0.25% for injection	1% to 2% solution	0.05% to 0.1% solution
	More toxic than procaine, but toxic effects rare because of low dosage used	Two times that of procaine—less than lidocaine	Ten to twenty times that of procaine
When administered rapidly or in large doses may cause convulsions and hypotension	May cause vasodepressor effects	Has vasoconstrictor action	Tissue sloughs when injected subcutaneously

clude a topical cream and ointment, a urethral jelly, topical solutions, and suppositories. The concentration of the drug in various preparations varies from 0.25% to 1%. Suppositories contain 10 mg. of the drug.

Tetracaine hydrochloride, U.S.P.
(Pontocaine Hydrochloride);
amethocaine hydrochloride, B.P.

Tetracaine hydrochloride is a synthetic local anesthetic, the effects of which are said to be more potent and more prolonged than those of procaine. It is also more toxic. It can be employed in dilute concentrations and serves as a useful anesthetic for a number of purposes. It can be used to produce surface anesthesia of the eye, nose, and throat, as well as for infiltration and spinal and caudal anesthesia. Effects are believed to be more prolonged than those with procaine.

Preparation and dosage. Tetracaine hydrochloride is available in solutions of various concentrations and also in tablets. An official ophthalmic ointment, 0.5% in white petrolatum, is also available. The concentration used varies with the part to be anesthetized; a 0.5% solution is commonly employed for the eye, a 2% solution for mucous membranes of the nose and

317

throat, 0.5% is used for spinal anesthesia, and 0.15% to 0.25% is used for caudal anesthesia. It can be given with epinephrine.

Butacaine sulfate (Butyn Sulfate)

Butacaine sulfate acts rapidly and produces a prolonged effect. It does not produce constriction of blood vessels. Butacaine is used for surface anesthesia particularly of the eye, nose, and throat and has, to some extent, replaced cocaine. This drug is usually used in a 2% solution.

Toxic effects. Its toxicity is similar to that of cocaine, and its administration by injection is not recommended.

Dibucaine hydrochloride, N.F. (Nupercaine Hydrochloride); cinchocaine hydrochloride, B.P.

Dibucaine hydrochloride is not only one of the more potent local anesthetics but also one of the most toxic. Onset of action is slow and may be delayed for 15 minutes, but its effects may last $2^1/_2$ to 3 hours.

It is used to produce surface anesthesia but can be used for all types of local anesthesia. It can be given with epinephrine.

Preparation and dosage. Dibucaine hydrochloride is marketed in ampules and vials containing various amounts of the drug. The drug is used in concentrations of 0.05% to 0.1% solution for injection and topical application. It is a constituent of certain ointments used to relieve the discomfort of burns and hemorrhoids.

Toxic effects. Caution in its use is recommended because of its potential toxicity.

Hexylcaine hydrochloride, N.F. (Cyclaine Hydrochloride)

Hexylcaine hydrochloride is used in concentrations up to 5% for surface anesthesia, 1% for infiltration and nerve block, and 2% to 2.5% for spinal anesthesia. For surface anesthesia it is said to be as effective as cocaine, and for infiltration and nerve block it is thought to be faster and longer acting than equal amounts of procaine.

Toxic effects. It exhibits toxic effects similar to other local anesthetics and must be employed with the same precautions.

Piperocaine hydrochloride (Metycaine Hydrochloride)

Piperocaine hydrochloride is chemically related to cocaine but produces effects similar to procaine. It differs from procaine in that it is suited to topical application for surface anesthesia as well as for injection. It is slightly more potent and more toxic than procaine and lasts for about the same length of time. It is compatible with epinephrine and is used for anything for which procaine can be used unless the patient is hypersensitive to the agent.

Preparation, dosage, and administration. Solutions of various concentrations are available for injection, as well as 150-mg. tablets and a 4% or 5% ointment. The drug is used in concentrations that vary from 0.25% to 5%, depending on the route of administration.

Butethamine hydrochloride, N.F. (Monocaine Hydrochloride)

Butethamine hydrochloride is a local anesthetic similar to procaine. It has about one third more anesthetic and toxic potency than procaine but is inferior to cocaine or butacaine. It is used for surface anesthesia and for nerve block anesthesia in dentistry. It is a stable compound. It must be used with the same precautions as with other local anesthetics.

Mepivacaine hydrochloride, N.F. (Carbocaine Hydrochloride)

Mepivacaine is a relatively nontoxic, nonirritating, potent local anesthetic similar in action to lidocaine. Its action is more rapid and more prolonged than that of lidocaine. It can be used for infiltration, regional nerve block, caudal, and peridural anesthesia. It exerts its effect without the use of a vasoconstrictor, thereby eliminating the necessity to use agents such as epinephrine. Thus, mepivacaine has a definite advantage over other local anesthetics for use with elderly patients or patients with cardiovascular disease, diabetes mellitus, or thyrotoxicosis. Mepivacaine may cause adverse reactions similar to those noted for lidocaine. It is available in solutions of 1%, 1.5%, and 2%.

Ethyl aminobenzoate (Benzocaine)

Ethyl aminobenzoate is very insoluble in water, slowly absorbed, nonirritating, and almost nontoxic. It can be applied as a powder or ointment to relieve the pain of wounds or inflammation and to alleviate itching. Suppositories containing this drug are used to relieve pain from hemorrhoids.

Butacaine (Butyn)

Butacaine has a rapid action and prolonged effect. It is used for surface anesthesia of the nose and throat but particularly of the eye. Anesthesia is produced in 1 minute with a single application; repeated instillation permits ocular surgery. Since it does not cause vasoconstriction, pupil dilation, or drying, it has largely replaced cocaine in ophthalmic surgery. It is more powerful than cocaine and, when injected, is more toxic than cocaine. Thus, Butacaine is unsuitable for injection. It is used principally in the form of a 2% solution.

Eugenol, U.S.P., B.P.

Eugenol is a pale yellow liquid obtained from clove oil. It is applied topically to the skin and mucous membrane and is used especially by dentists for the relief of pain caused by dental caries.

Phenolated calamine lotion, U.S.P.

Phenolated calamine lotion contains 1% phenol, which is included because the phenol anesthetizes the sensory nerve endings of the skin. It is used for the relief of itching caused by mild allergic reactions.

Local anesthesia by freezing

Low temperatures in living tissues produce diminished sensation. This form of anesthesia is sometimes employed for minor operative procedures. Packing an extremity in ice may be used for the major operative procedure of amputation of part of an extremity, particularly in elderly and debilitated persons or in patients con-sidered to be "high risk" patients if given a general anesthetic. Tissues that are frozen too intensely and over too long a period of time may be destroyed.

Ethyl chloride is a local anesthetic that can be used to produce this effect, although it is not employed extensively (see p. 309).

Slightly soluble local anesthetics

A number of local anesthetic agents are only slightly soluble and therefore cannot be injected. Because they are absorbed slowly they can be used safely on open wounds, ulcers, and mucous surfaces. They occasionally cause dermatitis, which necessitates discontinuation of their use.

Benzocaine, N.F., B.P. (Anesthesin). This agent acts as a local anesthetic when applied to painful wounds and ulcers of the skin and mucous membranes. It may be applied as a dusting powder or as an ointment to denuded areas of the skin and to mucous membranes. It is used to relieve itching and discomfort associated with hemorrhoids and rectal fissures. It is also available in the form of rectal and vaginal suppositories.

Benzocaine ointment, N.F. This is a 5% preparation of the drug in white ointment.

Butyl aminobenzoate, N.F. This preparation is used with or without a diluent as an anesthetic dusting powder. It is also marketed in the form of troches, suppositories, and ointments.

Drug-induced reactions to anesthetics

Treatment of disease with a variety of drugs having varying degrees of potency and diverse effects on body systems establishes a propensity for drug-induced reactions to anesthetics. Interactions between drugs and anesthetics may be responsible for anesthetic morbidity and mortality. Certain drugs and anesthetic agents are hepatotoxic, and their administration to the same patient can result in severe and even fatal liver damage. Drugs that have depressant effects on cardiac function in conjunction with the depressant action of anesthetics can cause decreased cardiac output and hypotension, which may result in ventricular fibrillation or

Table 14-7 Drug-induced reactions to anesthetics

Type of drug	Example of drug		Reaction	Prevention
	Generic name	*Trade name*		
Antihypertensives	Bretylium Reserpine Guanethidine	Darenthin Ismelin	Circulatory depression Reduced cardiac output Hypotension Bradycardia	Use of vasopressors during anesthesia
Antidepressants	Pargyline Tranylcypromine Phenelzine	Eutonyl Parnate Nardil	Hypertension Potentiation of action of narcotics, hypnotics	Avoid use of narcotics and barbiturates with these drugs
Adrenergics	Epinephrine Norepinephrine		Cardiac arrhythmias Tissue slough when used with local anesthetics	Avoid use with anesthetics that sensitize myocardium to catecholamines, (halothane, cyclopropane)
Antibiotics (parenteral)	Neomycin Kanamycin Streptomycin		Enhancement of neuromuscular blockade Muscle paralysis, apnea, bradycardia, hypotension	
Adrenal steroids	Cortisone Cortisol		Adrenal insufficiency and hypotension during stress of surgery after prolonged use Circulatory collapse	Administer steroids preoperatively and if necessary during surgery and postoperatively
Tranquilizers (phenothiazines)	Chlorpromazine Promazine	Thorazine Sparine	Potentiation of action of narcotics, hypnotics Central nervous system depression Hypotension Respiratory depression	Use minor tranquilizers with no adrenergic blocking effect Reduce dosages of drugs and anesthetics
Pituitary hormones	Oxytocin Vasopressin	Pitocin Syntocinon Pitressin	Coronary vasoconstriction Myocardial ischemia Hypotension	
Ergot alkaloids	Ergonovine Methylergonovine	Ergotrate Methergine	Potentiation of effects of vasopressors used to overcome hypotension caused by spinal anesthesia Severe hypertension during third stage of labor	Use pressor drugs sparingly in obstetric patient

cardiac arrest. Drug-induced reactions to anesthesia are not uncommon and not decreasing; indeed, this problem appears to be rapidly increasing. Not all drug interactions occur during anesthesia; some reactions are delayed or latent. The nurse needs to closely observe postoperative patients for undesirable signs and symptoms. Early detection and treatment of drug interactions may be vital.

Questions

for study and review

1 Explain the role of preliminary medications in the production of a satisfactory anesthetic state.
2 What is the difference between a basal anesthetic and a general anesthetic?
3 Discuss the difference between the various stages of anesthesia.
   a. between analgesia and excitement
   b. between the various planes of surgical anesthesia
4 Explain the use of a vasoconstrictor with a local anesthetic.
5 What are some important nursing care aspects for the postanesthetic patient?

Multiple choice questions

6 Which of the following statements about preanesthetic medications are correct?
   a. Preanesthesia is used to reduce apprehension.
   b. Preanesthesia decreases the amount of anesthetic required.
   c. Preanesthesia promotes smoother induction and emergence from general anesthesia.
   d. Preanesthesia may have the undesirable action of prolonging awakening from anesthesia.
7 Which of the following are *incorrect* statements?
   a. Cyclopropane is the most potent of the anesthetic gases.
   b. Vinyl ether is preferable for surgical procedures of short duration since it requires continuous administration to maintain anesthesia.
   c. Although ether (diethyl ether) is volatile and highly flammable, it continues to be widely used because of its nonirritating effects.
   d. Nitrous oxide is a highly desirable anesthetic because of its nonexplosiveness and its ability to promote optimum muscular relaxation without the use of other drugs or gases.

8 Choose the *incorrect* answer.
   Ethylene:
   a. is a more potent anesthetic than ether
   b. has a rapid induction
   c. does not irritate the respiratory mucosa
   d. is not noted as a good muscle relaxant
9 Choose the *incorrect* answer.
   Halothane:
   a. tends to cause hypotension
   b. has a low incidence of postoperative nausea and vomiting
   c. is not as potent as ether
   d. depresses salivary and mucous secretions
10 Ether has continued to be one of the widely used anesthetics because:
   a. muscular relaxation can be secured
   b. induction is easy and safe
   c. it has a wide safety range
   d. it is readily transported and used in a variety of circumstances
11 Indicate which of the following constitutes the chief disadvantage in the use of cyclopropane.
   a. cost   c. explosiveness
   b. availability   d. narrow safety range
12 Choose the correct statements about open-drop anesthesia.
   a. It does not permit controlled concentration of anesthetic.
   b. It is inexpensive and does not require elaborate equipment.
   c. It is used with liquid anesthetics.
   d. It can be safely administered without anesthesia education.
13 Select the *incorrect* answer.
   a. Ethyl chloride produces local anesthesia by freezing.
   b. Procaine is an effective topical anesthetic.
   c. Local anesthetics are potentially hazardous drugs and should be used in low concentrations.
   d. Sodium thiopental is a basal anesthetic.

References

General anesthetics

Adriani, J.: Some newer anesthetic agents, Amer. J. Nurs. **61:**60, 1961.

Adriani, J., and Zepernick, R.: Anesthesia for infants and children, Amer. J. Nurs. **64:**107, 1964.

Artusio, J. R., Jr., editor: Halogenated anesthetics, Clinical anesthesia series, Philadelphia, 1963, F. A. Davis Co.

Beecher, H. K.: Anesthesia, Sci. Amer. **196:**70, 1957.

Bendixen, H. H., and Laver, M. B.: Hypoxia in anesthesia: a review, Clin. Pharmacol. Therap. **6:**510, 1965.

Block, M.: Some systemic effects of nitrous oxide, Brit. J. Anaesth. **35:**631, 1963.

Bromage, P. R.: Physiology and pharmacology of epidural analgesia, Anesthesiology **28:**592, 1967.

Dingle, H. R.: Antihypertensive drugs and anesthesia, Anesthesia **21:**151, 1966.

Dobkin, A. B., and Po-Giok Su, J.: Newer anesthetics and their uses, Clin. Pharmacol. Therap. **7:**648, 1966.

Dripps, R. D., Eckenhoff, J. E., and Vandam, L. D.: Introduction to anesthesia, Philadelphia, 1967, W. B. Saunders Co.

Dundee, J. W.: Clinical pharmacology of general anesthetics, Clin. Pharmacol. Therap. **8:**91, 1967.

Eckenhoff, J. E.: Science and practice in anesthesia, Philadelphia, 1965, J. B. Lippincott Co.

Eger, E. I., II: Atropine, scopolamine and related compounds, Anesthesiology **23:**365, 1962.

Elliott, H. W.: Influence of previous therapy on anesthesia, Clin. Pharmacol. Therap. **3:**41, 1962.

Faulcomer, A., and Keys, T. E.: Foundations of anesthesiology, Springfield, Ill., 1965, Charles C Thomas, Publisher.

Gillespie, N. A.: The signs and reflex reactions of the stages of anesthesia, Anesth. Analg. **22:**275, 1943.

Katz, R. L., Weintraub, H. D., and Papper, E. M.: Anesthesia, surgery and rauwolfia, Anesthesiology **25:**142, 1964.

Little, D. M., and Stephan, C. R.: Modern balanced anesthesia; a concept, Anesthesiology **15:**246, 1954.

Lundy, J. S.: Contributions of modern anesthesia to improvement in surgical technic, collected papers of Mayo Clinic and Mayo Foundation, Philadelphia, 1956, W. B. Saunders Co.

Lundy, J. S.: New drugs and an era of analgesia and amnesia, J.A.M.A. **162:**97, 1956.

Miller, S.: A theory of gaseous anesthetics, Proc. Nat. Acad. Sci. **47:**1515, 1961.

Ngai, S. H., and Papper, E. M.: Anesthesiology, New Eng. J. Med. **269:**28, 1963.

Ngai, S. H., and Papper, E. M.: Metabolic effects of anesthesia, Springfield, Ill., 1962, Charles C Thomas, Publisher.

Patton, W. D. M., and Speden, R. M.: The uptake of anesthetics and their action on the central nervous system, Brit. Med. Bull. **21:**44, 1965.

Price, H. L.: General anesthesia and circulatory homeostasis, Physiol. Rev. **40:**187, 1960.

Rapper, E. M.: The pharmacologic basis of anesthesiology, Clin. Pharmacol. Therap. **2:**141, 1961.

Ridley, R. W.: Safety in anesthesia, collected papers of the Mayo Clinic and Mayo Foundation, Philadelphia, 1953, W. B. Saunders Co.

Schnider, S. M.: A review: fetal and neonatal effects of drugs in obstetrics, Cur. Res. Anesth. Analg. **45:**373, 1966.

Symposium: post-anesthetic complications, Anesthesiology **22:**657, 1961.

Symposium on muscle relaxants, Brit. J. Anaesth. **35:**510, 1963.

Vandam, L. D.: Anesthesia, Ann. Rev. Pharmacol. **6:**379, 1966.

Vandam, L. D.: The unfavourable effects of prolonged anesthesia, Canad. Anaesth. Soc. J. **12:**107, 1965.

Wise, R. P.: Muscle disorders and the relaxants, Brit. J. Anaesth. **35:**558, 1963.

Woolbridge, P. D.: The components of general anesthesia, J.A.M.A. **186:**641, 1963.

Local anesthetics

Adriani, J.: Local anesthetics, Amer. J. Nurs. **59:**86, 1959.

Adriani, J.: Reactions to local anesthetics, J.A.M.A. **196:**405, 1966.

Adriani, J., and Campbell, D.: Fatalities following topical application of local anesthetics to mucous membranes, J.A.M.A. **162:**1527, 1956.

Adriani, J., and others: The comparative potency and effectiveness of topical anesthetics in man, Clin. Pharmacol. Therap. **5:**49, 1964.

Adriani, J., and Zepernick, R.: Clinical effectiveness of drugs used for topical anesthesia, J.A.M.A. **188:**511, 1964.

Campbell, D., and Adriani, J.: Absorption of local anesthetics, J.A.M.A. **168:**873, 1958.

Moore, D. C.: Regional block, Springfield, Ill., 1965, Charles C Thomas, Publisher.

Sinclair, J. C.: Intoxication of the fetus by a local anesthetic: a newly recognized complication of maternal caudal anesthesia, New Eng. J. Med. **273:**1173, 1965.

Respiratory system drugs

Respiration is essentially the utilization of oxygen and the elimination of carbon dioxide. It provides for rapid adjustment to meet metabolic needs and is one of the regulating systems to help maintain physiologic dynamic equilibrium. The respiratory system in man includes the nasal cavity, larynx, trachea, bronchi, lungs, bronchioles and alveolar sacs, striped and unstriped muscles of the larynx, intercostal muscles and diaphragm, respiratory center in the medulla, and the blood.

■ Regulation of respiration

Breathing is controlled and coordinated involuntarily by the respiratory center located in the lateral reticular formation of the medulla. However, breathing can also be voluntarily influenced. Two groups of neurons comprise this center; one group is concerned with inspiration, the other with expiration. Each of these groups is antagonistic to the other, is self-reexciting, and discharges or fires impulses alternately. When inspiratory neurons are stimulated, they discharge impulses to motor neurons innervating inspiratory muscles and at the same time send inhibitory impulses to the expiratory neurons. As inspiration occurs, inhibition of expiratory neurons decreases and they discharge impulses to stimulate expiratory muscles and in-hibit impulses in the inspiratory neurons. This brings about rhythmic breathing movements.

The respiratory center is also influenced by various forms of sensory stimuli, the vasomotor center, reflex mechanisms (such as the Hering-Breuer reflex), the chemoreceptors in the carotid and aortic bodies, and the baroreceptors in the carotid sinus and aortic arch. Pain, blood pressure, stretch fibers in the lungs, and the blood levels of oxygen and carbon dioxide affect respiratory rate and force.

Carbon dioxide is the chief respiratory stimulant. An increase in the carbon dioxide tension of the blood directly stimulates the inspiratory and expiratory centers, which increases both the rate and depth of breathing. This results in a blowing off of carbon dioxide to keep the carbon dioxide tension of the blood constant. The pH of the blood is determined by the ratio of bicarbonate ion (HCO_3) to carbon dioxide. Elevated carbon dioxide levels result in acidosis, while abnormally low levels result in alkalosis. Therefore, respiration is important for regulating the pH of the blood by controlling the carbon dioxide tension of the blood.

Air passages. The air passages serve the dual purpose of permitting air to flow from the external environment to pulmonary blood and of modifying the air taken in by warming and moistening it and removing noxious substances. Man's airway efficiency is determined by the following factors:

1. Shape and size of each portion of the respiratory tract (nasal cavity, pharynx, larynx, trachea, bronchi, bronchioles, alveolar sacs)
2. Presence of a ciliated, mucus-secreting, epithelial lining throughout most of the respiratory tract
3. Character and thickness of respiratory tract secretions
4. Compliance of the cartilaginous and bony supports
5. Pressure gradients
6. Traction on airway walls
7. Absence of foreign substances in the lumen of the respiratory tract

An alteration from normal of any of these factors will affect the ease with which air flows through the air passages. Congenital anomalies, injuries, allergies, or disease will cause air flow resistance if the preceding factors are abnormally affected. Resistance occurs, for example, if there is stenosis or narrowing of any portion of the respiratory tract, loss of cilia that ordinarily sweep out foreign substances, presence of thick or tenacious secretions, loss of elasticity, or presence of foreign objects.

Lungs. The lungs are elastic, membranous sacs. Air flowing to the lungs passes through the trachea, bronchi, bronchioles, and alveolar sacs. The bronchiolar musculature is regulated by bronchoconstrictor fibers in the vagi and bronchodilator fibers in the sympathetic nervous system. The wall of each alveolus is composed of a single layer of respiratory epithelium. Across this layer and the endothelium of the capillaries, gaseous exchange occurs between the inhaled air and the blood by free diffusion. The total number of alveoli in the lungs of man has been estimated at about 725 million and their total surface at about 200 square meters, or 100 to 130 times the surface area of the body. The surface area of the capillaries of the lungs is estimated to be about 90 square meters.

Alveoli are lined with an insoluble film of lipoprotein called *surfactant*, which lowers surface tension to prevent alveolar collapse, particularly during exhalation. Atelectasis can occur from lack of surfactant in cases of hypoventilation or respiratory distress. This can be counteracted to some extent by intermittent positive pressure breathing.

The efficacy of detergents (such as Tergemist and Alevaire) to liquefy and loosen thick pulmonary secretions has been questioned by the Food and Drug Administration. These agents may coat alveolar walls and interfere with the stabilizing properties of pulmonary surfactant.

Gaseous exchange in the lungs. The interchange of gases between the outside air and the blood depends on (1) the difference in tension of the gases, (2) the rate of blood flow through the lungs, (3) the area of the lungs, and (4) the resistance offered by the alveolar walls to the diffusion of gases. The tension of the gases depends on the composition of the air inspired and upon the rate and volume of inspiration. A man at rest may inspire 6 to 8 liters of air per minute, breathing fourteen times per minute, whereas an athlete in maximal effort may inspire thirty times that volume and breathe four to five times as rapidly. This is evidence of the great adaptive power of the respiratory mechanism.

Drugs that act on the respiratory center

Oxygen and carbon dioxide are the two respiratory gases commonly administered for the treatment of hypoventilation and hypoxia. Oxygen is given to increase oxygen tension in the blood and promote adequate oxygenation of cells and thereby protect cell viability. Carbon dioxide is used for its direct stimulating effect on the respiratory center to increase rate and depth of breathing.

Oxygen, U.S.P., B.P.

Oxygen is a gas that constitutes 20% of ordinary air and is necessary to maintain life. Oxygen, U.S.P., is oxygen in a compressed state. It is a colorless, odorless, and tasteless gas. It is not flammable, but it supports combustion much more vigorously than does air.

Oxygen is compressed and marketed in steel cylinders that are fitted with reducing valves for the delivery of the gas. Because it is under considerable pressure, the tanks must be handled carefully to prevent their falling or bumping into each other or into anything that may cause undue jarring.

Oxygen must be continuously supplied to tissue cells, for no fiber or cell can remain hypoxic for very long and survive. Oxygen consumption by the brain is very high, about 20% of the total body basal oxygen consumption. It has been estimated that cerebral oxygen consumption is about 3.5 ml. per 100 Gm. per minute or about 49 ml. per minute for the entire brain. Cerebral oxygen consumption proceeds without respite, and the replenishment of oxygen by the blood must be maintained continuously. Whenever any circulatory stress exists, cerebral blood flow tends to be preserved at the expense of other less vital organs. A fall in oxygen tension dilates cerebral vessels and increases cerebral blood flow. Increased blood oxygen levels have the opposite effect. The respiratory center is particularly sensitive to a lack of oxygen and fails before the circulatory or vasomotor center.

The kidneys constitute other vital organs in which there must be considerable constancy of blood flow and oxygen supply. Oxygen consumption is greater in the renal cortex; renal medullary tissue has an oxygen consumption that is 15% less than that of the renal cortex. This difference is related to the variation in pressure gradient and the fact that cortical flow is rapid while the medullary flow is slower. The renal cortex is highly dependent on oxygen, while the medulla can function relatively independently of the oxygen supply.

The kidneys' oxygen consumption is approximately 0.06 ml. per gram per minute. They consume more oxygen than most other tissues. For each 100 ml. of blood entering the kidney, 1.4 ml. of oxygen is consumed. Renal hypoxia is under intensive study at the present time. The high oxygen consumption by the kidneys is primarily used for sodium reabsorption.

In skeletal muscle, oxygen consumption is related to blood flow. Oxygen consumption and blood flow are decreased when muscle is at rest, and both are significantly increased during exercise.

Reduction of oxygen supply to the intestinal tract is regarded by some investigators as a key factor for inadequate splanchnic vascular compensation (splanchnic vasoconstriction) during hypotension.

Inadequate oxygen supply will impair myocardial metabolism and function. Arterial blood pressure determinations, when used alone, are unreliable indicators of the adequacy of tissue oxygenation. Oxygen deprivation is known to be a factor in the production of ectopic beats and arrhythmias.

Purposes for giving oxygen. Oxygen is used in medicine chiefly to treat hypoxia and hypoxemia (oxygen lack and diminished oxygen tension in the blood). It is indicated therefore in the following:

1 Conditions associated with inadequate oxygenation in the lungs such as pneumonia (both lobar and bronchopneumonia), pulmonary edema, and poisoning from gases such as carbon monoxide
2 Severe asthma
3 Cardiac failure or decompensation and coronary occlusion
4 Anesthesia to increase the safety of general anesthetics
5 Treatment of abdominal distention caused by intestinal ileus
6 Treatment of certain types of headache

325

7 Certain conditions involving injury to the nervous system and threatened respiratory failure

The gas causing gastrointestinal distention is mostly nitrogen. When the patient inhales pure oxygen or a high concentration of oxygen, the nitrogen that is dissolved in the blood gradually leaves by way of the lungs. The blood is then able to absorb the nitrogen from body cavities, such as the intestine, discharge it into the expired air, and thus relieve distention and gas pain.

Administration of oxygen. Oxygen is administered in a number of ways, including oxygen tent, nasal catheter or cannula, face mask, hood, and oxygen chamber. Each of these methods of administering oxygen has advantages and disadvantages.

When a *nasal catheter* is used it should be lubricated with a water-soluble jelly and passed through the nose until the tip is just above the epiglottis. This distance is usually the same as the distance from the patient's external nares to the tragus of the ear, minus 1 cm. The catheter should not be inserted so far that the patient swallows oxygen, for this will cause stomach distention and abdominal discomfort. The catheter is fastened with tape to the forehead and/or nose. Flow rate varies according to patient need, but 3 to 6 L. of oxygen per minute is commonly used. Since this form of therapy is very drying to the mucous membrane the oxygen should be humidified. In addition, nasal and oral hygiene is important to maintain cleanliness, maintain intact mucous membrane, and prevent infection and discomfort. Most patients receiving oxygen therapy are mouth breathers, and frequent mouth care is required to prevent sordes. Nasal catheters become obstructed with encrusted secretions and must be removed and cleaned or replaced several times a day.

Nasal cannulae are much more comfortable for patients than catheters. They are less likely to become obstructed with secretions. Nasal and oral mucosa still require frequent attention. A flow of 3 L. of oxygen is adequate for many patients.

Oxygen masks are the most effective means of delivering needed oxygen. Oxygen concentrations of 90% to 100% can be administered by mask. To be effective the mask must fit well over nose and mouth; high flow rates can compensate to some extent for a poor fit. Masks are better tolerated when used intermittently or when disposable plastic masks are used. Only absolutely clean and uncontaminated rubber masks should be used, since they can be a source of hospital-acquired infection.

Oxygen tents and hoods have the advantage of temperature and humidity regulation. Disadvantages include oxygen loss, carbon dioxide accumulation, and claustrophobic effect. Oxygen concentration in a tent rarely reaches 50%; in a hood the concentration may reach 90% to 100%. The tent and hood should be periodically tested with an oxygen analyzer for oxygen concentration. Oxygen should be flowing into the tent *before* it is secured over the patient. The usual rate of flow is 15 L. per minute for the first 15 to 30 minutes after the patient is in the tent, and 10 to 12 L. per minute thereafter. Tent leakage should be prevented by careful planning of care so that the tent is removed or opened as little as possible. The tent should also be securely tucked under the mattress and around the patient. The mattress should be covered with plastic or a rubber sheet to prevent oxygen saturation of the mattress and undue loss of oxygen. Oxygen tents and hoods are less popular today than formerly since the advent of plastic face masks and face tents.

For a child with a respiratory infection adequate oxygen concentration can be maintained in a croup tent with an open top. When indicated, the top may be covered to increase the mist.

Face tents are the most convenient, comfortable way to administer high concentrations of oxygen. A flow of 15 L. per minute can provide an oxygen concentration of 70%.

Since oxygen supports combustion and combustible material burns with greater ease and intensity, and since the patient is surrounded with combustible materials (linens, wooden furniture), smoking and the use of matches or electric equipment that may cause sparks are strictly forbidden in rooms where oxygen is being administered.

The effectiveness of oxygen administration will depend on the carbon dioxide content of the blood. Patients with emphysema have difficulty with carbon dioxide and oxygen exchange and are subject to hypercapnia (high carbon dioxide concentration), which decreases the patient's sensitivity to carbon dioxide and its respiratory stimulating effect. These patients become dependent upon oxygen lack for respiratory stimulation. Administration of oxygen removes this stimulating effect and carbon dioxide may accumulate to narcotic and toxic levels, further depressing the central nervous system and respiration. As a result, hypoventilation and acidosis may occur. Neurologic symptoms may be observed, including paresthesias, confusion, and visual disturbances. This problem may be overcome by gradually increasing the concentration of administered oxygen or by using intermittent positive pressure breathing. When there is no accumulation of carbon dioxide, the respiratory center retains its sensitivity and high concentrations of oxygen can be administered.

Nursing care of the premature baby. Nurses who care for premature babies in incubators must constantly be aware of the potential damage that can occur to the retina of the premature baby when exposed to high concentrations of oxygen. When the orders for the infant include oxygen p.r.n., the nurse must make certain that it is administered only as needed and at low concentrations, rather than continuously. Frequently, the removal of a very small plug of mucus can clear the baby's airway, thus enabling him to inhale oxygen without assistance. The hazard of oxygen poisoning, with resulting blindness, can be reduced if nurses are alert to detect and prevent the oxygen concentration from rising above 40% inside the incubator. Some models are equipped with a safety valve that automatically releases the excess oxygen outside the chamber.

Helium-oxygen mixtures. Helium-oxygen mixtures have been used for some time to treat obstructive types of dyspnea. Helium is an inert gas and so light that a mixture of 80% helium and 20% oxygen is only one third as heavy as air. Helium is only slightly soluble in body fluids and has a high rate of diffusion. Its low specific gravity makes it possible for mixtures of this gas with oxygen to be breathed with less effort than either oxygen or air alone when there is obstruction in the air passages.

It is recommended for status asthmaticus, bronchiectasis, and emphysema, and for anesthesia when dealing with a respiratory tract in which there is obstruction.

Carbon dioxide, U.S.P., B.P.

Carbon dioxide is a colorless odorless gas that is heavier than air. It functions in the physiologic control of the respiratory center and can be used as a valuable respiratory stimulant. Whether it affects the respiratory center directly or by increasing the hydrogen ion concentration is not entirely agreed upon. The fact remains that inhalation of carbon dioxide for a short period of time increases both the rate and depth of respiration unless the respiratory center is depressed by narcotics or disease.

Carbon dioxide has two opposing effects in the human body:

1 It stimulates cells of the sympathetic nervous system, the respiratory center, and the peripheral chemoreceptors.
2 It depresses the cerebral cortex, myocardium, and smooth muscle of the peripheral blood vessels.

Carbon dioxide may also interfere with nerve conduction and transmission. When carbon dioxide increases the rate and force of respiration, venous return to the heart is usually enhanced as a result of decreased peripheral resistance; there is improved rate and force of myocardial contraction and less likelihood of myocardial irritability and arrhythmias.

Too much carbon dioxide has a depressant effect and results in acidosis as well as unresponsiveness of the respiratory center to carbon dioxide. It is therefore important that carbon dioxide be administered with caution.

Uses. When administered in 2% to 5% concentration, carbon dioxide exerts a definite effect on the respiratory center. Inhalation of a

3% concentration doubles the pulmonary ventilation and may be used to relieve Cheyne-Stokes breathing. In 5% to 7% concentration mixed with oxygen, it may be used before, during, or after anesthesia.

Most general anesthetics cause a reduction in response to carbon dioxide, which reflects central nervous system depression. The degree of depression is directly related to depth of anesthesia. The more deeply the patient is anesthetized, the greater the depression of the central nervous system. In the beginning carbon dioxide speeds up anesthesia by increasing pulmonary ventilation. By lessening the sense of asphyxiation, it reduces struggling. After anesthesia it hastens the elimination of many anesthetics. Inhalation of 5% to 7% carbon dioxide increases cerebral blood flow by approximately 75%, primarily by dilation of cerebral vessels.

Carbon dioxide is used as a respiratory stimulant in the treatment of specific types of asphyxia, such as asphyxia neonatorum and carbon monoxide poisoning. Inhalation of carbon dioxide and oxygen mixtures has been used in the treatment of postoperative singultus (hiccough). Relief of singultus is apparently accomplished by stimulating the respiratory center, causing large excursions of the diaphragm that submerges spasmodic contractions of that muscle, thereby promoting regular contractions.

Deep breathing, coughing, and frequent turning of the postoperative patient may be just as effective as administration of carbon dioxide to prevent pulmonary complications. However, when carbon dioxide is used, these nursing care measures should also be used. Postoperative pneumonia and pulmonary atelectasis may be prevented by increasing depth of breathing and preventing lung congestion.

Administration. Carbon dioxide is kept in a storage tank and may be administered by means of a close-fitting mask. The patient should inhale the mixture until the depth of respirations is definitely increased, which is usually within 3 minutes. For the postoperative patient the procedure should be repeated, for short periods every hour or two for the first 48 hours, and then several times a day for several days.

Another way of administering carbon dioxide is to allow the patient to hyperventilate with a paper bag held over his face. He reinhales his expired air in which the carbon dioxide content is continually increased.

Signs of carbon dioxide overdosage are dyspnea, breath-holding, markedly increased chest and abdominal movements, nausea, and increased systolic blood pressure. The administration of the gas should be discontinued when these symptoms appear. The administration should, in fact, be stopped as soon as the desired effects on respiration have been obtained.

■ Nebulization therapy

Nebulization therapy is used to deposit medication in the respiratory tract in the form of droplets that have been suspended in air. The medication is inhaled as a fine mist. Nebulization therapy is used to promote:

1 Bronchodilation and pulmonary decongestion
2 Loosening of secretions
3 Topical application of antibiotics, steroids, and antifoaming agents
4 Moistening, cooling, or heating of inspired air

The effectiveness of nebulization therapy is dependent upon the number of droplets that can be suspended in an inhaled aerosol. The number of droplets that can be suspended is directly related to the size of the droplets. Small droplets can be suspended in greater numbers than large droplets. Smaller droplets (about 2 microns in diameter) are more likely to reach the periphery of the lungs—the alveolar ducts and sacs. Larger droplets (8 to 15 microns in size) will be deposited primarily in the bronchioles and bronchi. Droplets of more than 40 microns will be deposited primarily in the upper airway (mouth, pharynx, trachea, and main bronchi).

Rate and depth of breathing are other important factors. Rapid or shallow breathing decreases the number of droplets reaching the periphery of the lungs as well as their retention. Rapid breathing permits the escape of significant amounts of fine droplets during expirations. Few droplets will escape if the breath is held long enough after deep inspiration to permit droplet deposit in the lung periphery. Small droplets are considered more effective for maximum absorption of antibiotics and bronchodilators.

Almost all large droplets will be retained somewhere in the air passage. Large droplets are used for keeping large airways moist (nose, trachea) and for loosening secretions. Slow and deep breathing is required for proper lung aeration and penetration of the mist into peripheral lung areas. The breath should be held for a few seconds after a full inspiration. Nebulizers commonly used in hospitals all produce similar mists. Droplet size can be controlled by the amount of pressure used to force oxygen or room air through the solution to produce a mist. The tubing used, its length, and number of bends affect turbulent flow and mist temperature. More precise studies are required to settle controversies and to determine how to provide more effective nebulization therapy for various respiratory disorders. With most nebulizers maximum density of the inhaled mist is achieved by making the flow of mist as smooth and direct as possible.

Drugs used for nebulization therapy include bronchodilators, mucolytic agents, antibiotics, steroids, and antifoaming agents.

Bronchodilators

Drugs that cause bronchodilation are used for their ability to relax the smooth muscle of the tracheobronchial tree. This permits an increase in lumen size of the bronchioles and alveolar ducts and decreases resistance to air flow. These drugs also decrease congestion in the respiratory tract through vasoconstriction and a decrease in mucous membrane swelling. Bronchodilators are adrenergic agents (sympathomimetic drugs). A more detailed discussion of these agents is given in Chapter 9. Aerosol therapy varies in length of time. Range in minutes may be from 3 to 15 minutes. Epinephrine and isoproterenol are the major aerosol bronchodilators. Epinephrine is usually given in a 1:100 concentration (1% solution); isoproterenol in concentrations of 1:100 or 1:200.

Mucolytic agents

Mucolytic agents reduce the thickness and stickiness of purulent and nonpurulent pulmonary secretions. This facilitates removal of the secretions by coughing, postural drainage, or suction, permitting more adequate pulmonary ventilation. These drugs are quite effective in removing mucous plugs obstructing the tracheobronchial airway. They are used in the treatment of patients with acute and chronic pulmonary disorders, following chest surgery, pre- and postbronchoscopy, and as an adjunct for tracheostomy care.

Acetylcysteine (Mucomyst, Respaire)

Acetylcysteine is an amino acid derivative that is administered by nebulization as a 10% or 20% solution. The 20% solution may be converted to a 10% solution by dilution with isotonic sodium chloride or sterile water. Range of dosage is from 3 to 5 ml. of the 20% solution, or 6 to 10 ml. of the 10% solution for about 15 minutes, three or four times daily. It may also be administered for a single continuous treatment by means of a closed tent or croupette. This may require up to 300 ml. of a 20% solution.

Acetylcysteine may cause stomatitis, nausea, and rhinorrhea. Bronchospasm may occur in patients with bronchial asthma. This drug has a wide margin of safety.

Solutions of acetylcysteine will harden rubber and become discolored on contact with certain metals. It should be used with equipment made out of glass, plastic, or stainless steel. If the vacuum seal has been broken on the bottle, it should be refrigerated to retard oxidation and be used within 48 hours.

Deoxyribonuclease (Dornavac)

Deoxyribonuclease is an enzyme that degrades DNA. It is obtained from beef pancreas. It reduces the tenacity or thickness of pulmonary secretions. Deoxyribonuclease is available in powder form, 100,000 units per vial. The powder is dissolved in 1 to 2 ml. of sterile saline. The average dose is 50,000 to 100,000 units three times a day by aerosol inhalation for 2 to 6 days. It is an expensive drug.

Other agents used for nebulization therapy

Other drugs administered by aerosol inhalation include antibiotics, steroids, and antifoaming agents.

Systemic antibiotics are often the drugs of choice to combat pulmonary infection. Certain antibiotics that can be given in limited doses only when administered systemically because of their toxicity can often be given in large doses by nebulization. These antibiotics include polymyxin, colistin, neomycin, and bacitracin. Since these antibiotics are irritating and may cause bronchospasm, bronchodilators are usually given prior to, or along with, the antibiotic.

Nebulized steroids are given for their effect on respiratory mucosa. The true effectiveness of nebulized steroids has not been established.

Antifoaming agents (ethyl alcohol or octyl alcohol) have been used to supplement therapy to reverse severe fulminating pulmonary edema. Alcohol reduces the surface tension of pulmonary edema bubbles and causes them to break. In addition, alcohol produces some bronchodilation. The result is better ventilation. This form of aerosol therapy must not be administered rapidly since it will cause irritation and coughing. This therapy should be used in conjunction with intermittent positive pressure breathing (IPPB) for effective oxygenation. Aerosol alcohol should be discontinued as soon as the lungs are dry to prevent ciliary damage.

■ Direct respiratory stimulation

While drugs are available for stimulating depth of respiration and concomitantly, but to a lesser degree, rate of respiration, the importance of mechanical or physiologic stimulation of respiration must never be ignored. Indeed the latter is often superior to the use of drugs. However, in cases of respiratory depression caused by drug intoxication, both mechanical and pharmacologic therapies are frequently used.

Ethamivan, N.F. (Emivan)

Ethamivan is a centrally acting respiratory stimulant used for treating respiratory depression resulting from barbiturate poisoning, tranquilizers, and chronic lung disease.

Ethamivan is available for intravenous injection in a solution containing 50 mg. per milliliter in 2- and 10-ml. ampules. Onset of action occurs in 1 minute; duration of action is about 10 minutes. Dosage depends on the degree of respiratory depression. In barbiturate poisoning or carbon dioxide narcosis where there is severe respiratory depression, 0.5 to 5 mg. per kilogram of body weight may be administered slowly over a period of several minutes, or 1.0 Gm. of ethamivan may be given in 250 ml. of dextrose or saline by intravenous infusion. Rate of infusion or amount of drug administered is determined by respiratory response. The drug may be given until eyelid reflex is obtained. Administration should be reduced or stopped if signs of central nervous system irritation occur (sneezing, coughing, restlessness, muscular twitching).

Ethamivan is also available in 20- and 60-mg. tablets for oral use as a mild respiratory stimulant for patients with chronic lung disease. Dosage ranges from 20 to 60 mg. two to four times daily. The effectiveness of this form of therapy requires further study. This drug is contraindicated for epileptics or in association with other drugs that may cause convulsions.

Doxapram hydrochloride, N.F. (Dopram)

Doxapram is a centrally acting respiratory stimulant. It is particularly useful for treatment of postanesthetic respiratory depression and to hasten return of protective pharyngeal and laryngeal reflexes after anesthesia. Depth of respiration is significantly increased by doxapram, and the rate of respiration may also increase. The action of doxapram is thought to be primarily caused by stimulation of the respiratory center. It may also have some effect on the chemoreceptors. Mild vasopressor activity is noted with the use of doxapram, resulting in elevation of blood pressure and heart rate. In addition, doxapram produces an increase in salivation, body temperature, gastric secretions, and tone and motility of the gastrointestinal tract and urinary bladder.

Preparation, dosage, and administration. Doxapram is available in solution form for intravenous injection, 20 mg. per ml. in 20-ml. vials. When it is administered postoperatively, a single dose of 0.5 to 1.5 mg. per kilogram of body weight may be given over a period of 30 to 90 seconds. Repeated doses may be necessary, but maximum dosage, even when multiple injections are used, should not exceed 2 mg. per kilogram of body weight. Intravenous infusion may also be used. With this method of administration dosage of doxapram is usually 5 mg. per minute initially; this is reduced to 1 to 3 mg. per minute when the desired response has been obtained. During administration the patient's blood pressure, heart rate, and other vital signs should be carefully monitored to prevent overdosage and toxic reactions.

Side effects. Doxapram can cause a wide variety of side effects as a result of its central stimulating effect. Nausea, vomiting, sneezing, coughing, tachycardia, elevated blood pressure, spontaneous urination, headache, fever, confusion, and other symptoms may occur.

Precautions. Doxapram is contraindicated for patients with hypertension, convulsive disorders, cardiac arrhythmias, cerebral edema, or hyperthyroidism. It is not recommended for use in patients with chronic pulmonary disease.

Bemegride, B.P. (Megimide)

Bemegride is used to treat respiratory depression resulting from drugs and anesthesia. Side effects are those of central nervous system stimulation. It is available in solution form for intravenous injection, 5 mg. per milliliter in 10-ml. ampules and 30-ml. vials. Dosage depends upon degree of respiratory depression, but 50 mg. may be injected every 3 to 5 minutes until signs of improvement or toxicity occur.

Nikethamide, B.P., N.F. (Coramine)

Nikethamide is a synthetic compound chemically related to nicotinamide, the vitamin that prevents pellagra. Apparently nikethamide has its most pronounced effect upon the respiratory center when the center is in a state of depression. When used on experimental animals, the medullary centers give evidence of stimulation, resulting in increased rate and depth of respiration and peripheral vasoconstriction.

Nikethamide may be used to treat acute respiratory depression caused by hypnotics, anesthetics, or alcohol. It has low toxicity and is considered to be a relatively safe stimulant since it is less likely to cause convulsions than other centrally acting stimulants.

Nikethamide is available in solution form for parenteral injection. It is usually given intravenously. Dose varies according to degree of respiratory depression and may range from 1.0 to 10.0 ml. of a 25% solution (250 mg. to 2.5 Gm.). Anxiety, nausea, and vomiting may occur, but side effects are usually mild.

Caffeine sodium benzoate, U.S.P.

Caffeine, when given in large doses or when given parenterally, definitely stimulates the respiratory center. Tolerance to caffeine, which is established in many persons, is a disadvantage in the use of the drug as a respiratory stimulant. Some authorities believe that better respiratory stimulants are available.

Caffeine sodium benzoate is available for parenteral injection in solution form, 250 mg. per milliliter in 2-ml. ampules and 10-ml. vials. It is usually used to counteract depressant effects of an overdose of drugs (barbiturates). It is occasionally used in cardiac arrest.

Atropine sulfate, U.S.P., B.P.

Atropine has some action as a respiratory stimulant because it produces stimulation of the medullary centers. Ordinary therapeutic doses, however, seem to affect only the vagal center and the respiratory center; the latter is affected to a mild degree. The rate and, occasionally, the depth of breathing are increased. When respiration is markedly depressed, atropine cannot be depended upon to produce stimulation, since large or continued doses of atropine may actually further depress the respiratory center.

Atropine is commonly given with morphine in hypodermic injections to lessen the effect of the latter drug on respiration, to check the secretion of mucus, and to prevent laryngospasm.

331

■ Reflex stimulation

Camphor, ammonia, and carminatives act as mild respiratory stimulants when taken by mouth. Ammonia, however, is the only drug given by mouth or inhalation for its action as a reflex respiratory stimulant. Ammonia is used as a heart and respiratory stimulant in the form of aromatic ammonia spirit, 2 ml. in half a glass of water. It is the type of stimulant that could be safely kept in the home medicine chest. It is also administered by vapor inhalation in cases of fainting.

■ Respiratory depressants or sedatives

The most important respiratory depressants are the central depressants of the opium group and those of the barbiturate group of drugs. These drugs depress the respiratory center, thereby making breathing slower and more shallow and lessening the irritability of the respiratory center. Respiratory depression, however, is seldom desirable or necessary, although it is sometimes unavoidable. It is sometimes a side effect in otherwise very useful drugs. Occasionally, a cough is so painful or harmful that an opiate, such as codeine, is administered to inhibit the rate and depth of respiration. A greater value, however, lies in its action to depress the cough reflex. Too-high concentrations of carbon dioxide in inhalation mixtures may paradoxically act to depress respiration.

Drugs that affect the cough center and the respiratory mucosa

Coughing is a protective reflex for clearing the respiratory tract of environmental irritants, foreign bodies, or accumulated secretions and thus should not be depressed indiscriminately. A cough is *productive* when irritants or secretions are removed from the respiratory tract; it is *nonproductive* when it is dry and irritating. The severity of frequent and prolonged coughing should be diminished since it can be exhausting,

painful, and taxing to the circulatory system and the elastic tissue of the respiratory system, particularly in the elderly and in young children. Most coughs can be suppressed without danger to the patient and thereby foster comfort and rest. Some coughs occur primarily at night or when the patient is recumbent because of the accumulation of secretions, and some coughs occur in the morning upon arising as a result of gravitational movement of secretions. Coughing is to some extent under voluntary control; an individual can cough at will and at times can suppress coughing. However, coughing is usually initiated by respiratory tract reflexes responding to irritations by sending impulses to the cough center. The value of adequate hydration of the patient, by oral intake of fluids as well as by inhalation of fully water-saturated vapors (steam), should be stressed as one of the most important means of producing increased amounts of mucus as well as thinning such sputum.

Treatment of the cough is secondary to treatment of the underlying disorder. Antitussives should not be given in situations in which retention of respiratory secretions or exudates may be harmful. Medications that may be used to relieve the cough include narcotic and nonnarcotic antitussives, demulcents, antiseptics, expectorants, and others.

Narcotic antitussives

Narcotics such as morphine, dihydromorphinone, and levorphanol are potent suppressants of the cough reflex, but their clinical usefulness is limited by their side effects. They inhibit the ciliary activity of the respiratory mucous membrane, depress respiration, and may cause bronchial constriction in allergic or asthmatic patients. In addition, they can cause drug dependence.

Codeine and dihydrocodeinone exhibit less pronounced antitussive effects but they also have fewer side effects. They have been widely used. Dihydrocodeinone is more active than codeine, but its drug dependence liability is also greater. The usual dose is 5 to 10 mg. three to four times a day.

Methadone is not an opiate, but it resembles morphine in a number of respects. Its ability to suppress the cough reflex is similar to that of morphine. A dose of 1.5 to 2 mg. will effectively relieve a cough. Its main disadvantage as an antitussive agent lies in its drug dependence qualities.

Nonnarcotic antitussive agents

The instillation of a local anesthetic agent prior to procedures such as bronchoscopy is effective in suppressing the cough reflex. This has led to the investigation of other agents that exert a similar action. Benzonatate and carbetapentane are two such preparations.

Benzonatate, N.F. (Tessalon)

Benzonatate is chemically related to the local anesthetic tetracaine. It relieves cough without depressing respirations. It selectively anesthetizes stretch receptors in the lungs, thus depressing cough by a peripheral action. Direct suppression of the cough center may also occur. After oral administration its effects are noticed within 15 to 20 minutes, and they last for several hours. Side effects do not seem to be serious but may include drowsiness, nausea, tightness in the chest, dizziness, and nasal congestion. Side effects like those associated with the narcotic antitussives have not been reported. This preparation is administered orally. It is marketed in 50- and 100-mg. capsules, and the dosage is 100 mg. several times daily.

Carbetapentane citrate, N.F. (Toclase)

This is a synthetic preparation said to exhibit properties similar to atropine and certain local anesthetics. Its antitussive potency seems to be similar to that of codeine phosphate. It is marketed in 25-mg. tablets and as a syrup (1.45 mg. per milliliter) for oral administration. The proposed dosage for adults is 15 to 30 mg. three to four times a day.

Noscapine, N.F., B.P. (Nectadon)

Noscapine is one of the isoquinoline alkaloids of opium, formerly known as narcotine. It resembles papaverine in its effects on smooth muscle, but its present use is based on its ability to depress the cough reflex. It resembles codeine in potency but does not produce opiate effects such as constipation, respiratory depression, constriction of the pupils, analgesia, or sedation. Side effects after therapeutic dosage are minimal. Nausea occurs occasionally. It does not cause addiction. The usual dosage is 15 to 30 mg. administered orally three or four times daily.

Dextromethorphan hydrobromide, B.P., N.F. (Romilar Hydrobromide)

This drug is a synthetic derivative of morphine but is employed only as an agent to relieve cough. However, it possesses no significant analgesic properties, does not depress respiration, and does not cause addiction. Its toxicity is low and side effects appear to be negligible. Its antitussive effects appear to be well established by extensive experimental and clinical studies. It is administered orally. The usual adult dose is 10 to 20 mg. once to several times daily. It is available in 15-mg. tablets and as a syrup (3 mg. per milliliter).

Demulcents

Respiratory demulcents are sticky substances that protect the lining of the respiratory tract from the irritation of contact with air and in this way they check coughing. They are used as gargles, lozenges, and syrups and as vehicles for other drugs. The most common are syrups (tolu, citric acid, acacia, or glycyrrhiza).

Cough syrups are soothing partly because of their local effect in the throat; hence, they should not be diluted and the patient should not drink water immediately after their administration.

Home remedies include simple syrup, honey, or hard candy. The soothing effect of steam inhalations upon irritated mucous membranes has a well-known demulcent effect. Plain or medicated steam may be administered with a special apparatus or by placing a basin of hot water over a hot plate to increase room humidity. There is little value, however, in administering steam when the doors or windows are open. Therefore, if the patient is to have the benefit of moisture-laden air to soothe the irritated respiratory tract, it is important to keep the patient's room warm and the doors and windows closed. The addition of some aromatic substance such as menthol or oil of pine may make the inhalation more pleasant or soothing.

Expectorants

Expectorants are drugs that increase or modify the secretion of mucus in the bronchi and reduce the viscosity of the mucus, thereby facilitating the expulsion of secretions. They are therefore used in the treatment of coughs, bronchitis, and pneumonia.

Experimentally, little is known of their mode of action, but clinical experience attests to their value. They are used empirically to modify respiratory tract physiology. The respiratory tract is lined with ciliated epithelium that normally carries secretions of the tract toward the exterior. Mucus that becomes thick and tenacious probably interferes with these ciliated movements and coughing results. It is not known whether or not expectorants modify these movements.

Ammonium chloride, U.S.P., B.P.; ammonium carbonate, N.F.

Ammonium chloride is frequently administered in some vehicle such as wild cherry syrup, citric acid syrup, or orange syrup. It apparently exerts its action by causing gastric irritation. Ammonium chloride is given in doses of 0.3 Gm. (gr. 5) four times a day in some suitable medium. It should be accompanied by a full glass of water because the increased fluid intake plays a part in the formation of increased mucus.

Ammonium carbonate acts like ammonium chloride except that it causes gastric distress more easily. It is given in much the same manner and dosage as ammonium chloride. It is an alkaline salt and cannot be given in acid syrups. The usual dose is 0.3 Gm. (gr. 5).

Sodium iodide, U.S.P., B.P.; potassium iodide, U.S.P., B.P.

Iodides increase bronchial secretions reflexly by causing gastric irritation. These preparations are too irritating to be used in acute inflammatory conditions of the respiratory tract. When sputum becomes particularly tenacious, they are given to fluidify the secretion or loosen the cough. The average expectorant dose is 0.3 Gm. (gr. 5) three times a day, but quantities up to 2 Gm. (gr. 30) may be given. The salts may be administered in a saturated solution or in a cough mixture. If use is long continued, these drugs frequently produce symptoms of iodism. These are caused by irritation of the nasal passage, bronchi, and skin and include coryza and pain in the region of the frontal sinus and various skin eruptions, generally of a papular character. When such toxic symptoms occur, the drug should be discontinued, but it may be resumed in smaller doses after the disappearance of the symptoms.

Ipecac syrup, U.S.P.; ipecacuanha liquid extract, B.P.

Ipecac syrup is prescribed in doses of 1 to 8 ml. for adults and 5 minims for infants 1 year of age. A small increase of dosage is made for each additional year. In children, it is used to increase secretions and relieve bronchitis associated with croup. Ipecac syrup is also used as an emetic, particularly in children.

Terpin hydrate, N.F.

Terpin hydrate occurs as colorless, lustrous crystals, nearly odorless, having a slightly aromatic odor and somewhat bitter taste. Terpin hydrate is antiseptic, diaphoretic, and diuretic in action, but it is used chiefly to lessen secretion in bronchitis accompanied by free secretion. Usual dose of terpin hydrate elixir, N.F., and terpin hydrate and codeine elixir, N.F., is 4 ml. (1 fluidram). The recommended dosage is usually too small to exert a significant effect and therefore it acts only as a vehicle.

Atropine

Atropine, although not classed as an expectorant, may be given cautiously to check secretion and excessive expectoration in certain forms of bronchitis.

Many remedies used to treat colds contain atropine. Morphine, codeine, and papaverine not only act as sedatives but also tend to dry the mucous membranes. In many cases the best treatment of a cold or inflammation of the respiratory mucous membranes consists of prescribing extra rest, forcing fluids, and simple but nutritious food.

■ Preparations to relieve nasal congestion and cold symptoms
Nasal decongestants

Perhaps the attribute for which vasoconstricting drugs are most commonly used is their capacity to shrink the engorged nasal mucous membranes in mild upper respiratory infections. Many drugs are used exclusively as nasal vasoconstrictors. Because of their wide popular use and lack of serious hazard (when used topically), a confusingly large number of preparations have been provided by the pharmaceutical industry, as well as many patent preparations, for direct sale to the public. Some of the more widely used agents in this group are phenylephrine hydrochloride (Neo-Synephrine), ephedrine sulfate, mephentermine sulfate (Wyamine Sulfate), propylhexadrine (Benzedrex), tuaminoheptane (Tuamine), xylometazoline hydrochloride (Otrivin Hydrochloride), phenylpropylmethylamine hydrochloride (Vonedrine), and naphazoline hydrochloride (Privine). Students will recognize these drugs as adrenergic agents. They are used to shrink engorged mucous membranes of the nose and to relieve nasal stuffiness. However, there is a tendency on the part of patients to misuse them by using them in too large an amount and too frequently. This may result in "rebound" engorgement or swelling of the mucous membranes. Preservatives, antihistaminics, detergents, and antibiotics are sometimes added to the preparation of the decongestant. In some cases untoward reactions are believed to be caused by the additive rather than by the decongestant. Too-frequent interference with the vasomotor mechanism in the nose may do more harm than good, and there is always the possibility of spreading the infection deeper into the sinuses or to the middle ear. Sprays and nose drops are of benefit when used judiciously under the advice of a physician.

Antihistaminic agents for colds

Considerable difference of opinion exists at the present time as to the usefulness of the antihistaminic drugs for the prevention or treatment of the common cold. These drugs include diphenhydramine hydrochloride (Benadryl) and tripelennamine hydrochloride (Pyribenzamine) as well as a number of others. They are discussed in Chapter 12. Some investigators are of the opinion that if these drugs are taken early during the onset of a cold, the allergic manifestations of the disease are relieved. The patient experiences relief from the tickling sensation in the nose, sneezing, and the continuous irritating discharge from the nasal mucous membrane. The Council on Drugs warns that their indiscriminate use is not without harmful effects —people may become excessively drowsy and fall asleep while driving a car or operating machinery. It is also possible that profound effects may occur in the central nervous system and the blood-forming tissues after prolonged use of these drugs.

Questions

for study and review

1 Explain the therapeutic uses of carbon dioxide and state what precautions should be taken when carbon dioxide is administered.
2 What precautions must be taken when oxygen is administered to patients with severe respiratory disease?
3 Discuss the beneficial and harmful effects of coughing.
4 Discuss the advantages and disadvantages of "across-the-counter" preparations for coughs and nasal congestion.
5 What are the advantages of nebulization therapy?
6 Discuss the effects of the following, and give an example of each:
    a. detergent   **c.** antifoaming agent
    b. mucolytic agent   **d.** bronchodilator
7 What nursing care measures are important for the patient receiving oxygen via:
    a. nasal catheter
    b. mask
    c. tent
8 When is it advantageous to use large droplets for nebulization therapy? To use small droplets?

9 Under what conditions is it preferable to stimulate expectoration?

10 Why does increased humidity of atmosphere in itself help to relieve coughing?

11 Discuss the therapy and nursing care for a patient with an acute asthmatic attack.

12 How do drugs act to produce relief from a cough?

References

A. M. A. Council on Drugs: New drugs, Chicago, 1967, American Medical Association.

Bickerman, H. A.: Antitussive drugs. In Modell, W., editor: Drugs of choice 1972-1973, St. Louis, 1972, The C. V. Mosby Co.

Bickerman, H. A.: Clinical pharmacology of antitussive agents, Clin. Pharmacol. Therap. 3:353, 1962.

Bickerman, H. A., and Irkin, S. W.: Aerosol steroid therapy and chronic bronchial asthma, J.A.M.A. 184:533, 1963.

Burch, G. E., DePasquale, N., and Hyman, A. L.: Influence of temperature and oxygen concentrations in oxygen tents, J.A.M.A. 176:1017, 1961.

Campbell, E. J. M.: A method of controlled oxygen administration which reduces the risk of carbon dioxide retention, Lancet 2:10, 1960.

Chernick, R. M., and Hakimpour, K.: The rational use of oxygen in respiratory insufficiency, J.A.M.A. 199:146, 1967.

Chodosh, S.: Newer drugs in the treatment of chronic bronchitis, Med. Clin. N. Amer. 51:1169, 1967.

Cohen, B. M., and Crandall, C.: Physiologic benefits of "thermofog" as brochodilator, Amer. J. Med. Sci. 247:57, 1964.

DuBois, A. B.: Oxygen toxicity, Anesthesiology 23:473, 1962.

Eggers, G. W. N., and others: Hemodynamic responses to oxygen breathing in man, J. Appl. Physiol. 17:75, 1962.

Flatter, P.: Hazards of oxygen therapy, Amer. J. Nurs. 68:80, 1968.

Geddes, A. K.: Premature babies: their nursing care and management, Philadelphia, 1960, W. B. Saunders Co.

Goodman, L., and Gilman, A.: The pharmacological basis of therapeutics, ed. 3, New York, 1965, The Macmillan Company.

Graham, J. D. P.: Cough suppressants, Practitioner 183:344, 1959.

Hatch, T. F., and Gross, P.: Pulmonary deposition and retention of inhaled aerosols, New York, 1964, Academic Press, Inc.

Kanig, J. L.: Pharmaceutical aerosols, J. Pharm. Sci. 52:513, 1963.

Kirby, W. M. M., guest editor: Modern managements of respiratory diseases, Med. Clin. N. Amer. 51(2):269, 1967.

Levine, E. R.: Inhalation therapy—aerosols and intermittent positive pressure breathing, Med. Clin. N. Amer. 51:307, 1967.

Lovejoy, F. W., and Morrow, P. E.: Aerosols, bronchodilators, and mucolytic agents, Anesthesiology 23:460, 1962.

Nett, L. M., and Petty, T. L.: Acute respiratory failure, Amer. J. Nurs. 67:1947, 1967.

Safar, P.: Respiratory therapy, Philadelphia, 1965, F. A. Davis Co.

Segal, M. S., and Weiss, E. B.: Current concepts in the management of the patient with status asthmaticus, Med. Clin. N. Amer. 51:373, 1967.

Symposium on carbon dioxide and man, Anesthesiology 21:585, 1960.

Symposium on inhalation therapy, Anesthesiology 23:407, 1962.

Psychotropic drugs

■ Role of drug therapy in psychiatry

Drugs play an important role in contemporary approaches to psychiatric care. The development of the tranquilizing drugs opened many avenues of treatment that were not available before. Although emphasis in therapy is placed on milieu factors by many workers in the field, drug therapy is a valuable adjunct to providing comprehensive psychiatric care. The effect of drug therapy in psychiatric illness can be neither ignored nor overestimated. Because the use of the psychotropic drugs is not presently thought of as a "cure," consideration is given to the patient's total life situation as an important determinant of his health status. The use of drugs alleviates symptoms and allows the patient an opportunity to participate more easily in other forms of treatment. Drugs temporarily modify behavior while other therapies, such as psychotherapy, can shape behavior and produce a permanent change. Some drugs disrupt patterns of behavior or modify the electric patterns or fields within the brain that produce changes. However, any enduring effects on behavior are more likely to result from the individual's concurrent interaction with the environment. Since incoming information must be translated into biochemical changes before it can affect the nervous system function, environmental transactions, like drugs, may affect similar pathways before influencing behavior. Their effects can be additive, potentiating, or antagonistic, depending on their nature and direction. The milieu may potentiate the effectiveness of the drug or detract from it.

Drugs affect behavior indirectly as the chemical composition of a drug interacts with other chemicals, enzymes, or enzyme substrates. The alteration of the biochemical cell environment produces a change in cellular, tissue, and organ function. A modification of the behavior state of the patient results and determines the nature of his interaction with the environment. Drugs affect various levels of integration, from simple to complex—from cellular activity to psychosocial interaction.

Anatomy and physiology of emotions

In order to understand the action of drugs in alleviating the symptomatology of mental illness, the nurse must have knowledge of the functioning of the nervous system. The trend in nursing toward a holistic view of man and his phenomenologic experience no longer allows the practitioner to separate out the functions of the mind from the body. Neurophysiologists have traditionally identified each part of the nervous system by a specific function or made tentative architectonic maps of the cerebral cortex, allocating specific functions to various areas of the brain. Recent research has indicated a change in this perspective. The brain is considered to be a single organ composed of various structures that produce a final unified effect when they react on each other in a normal fashion. The interrelationship of various structures is extremely intricate, and it is difficult to allocate special functions to each structure. Papez in 1937 was one of the first to suggest the function of a reverberating circuit in the brain as an explanation of emotional experience. Research has revealed methods for measuring certain types of brain activity, and such information has made it possible to speculate in some detail on the physiologic substrates of emotional activity. For purposes of clarity in discussing the neuroanatomic and neurophysiologic bases of emotions, the various parts of the nervous system will be discussed under the following headings:

1. Central nervous system
2. Autonomic regulation
3. Biochemical mechanisms

Central nervous system

The central nervous system functions in the coordination and direction of activities in the tissues and organs of the body. The various parts and levels of the central nervous system form a closely related and integrated series of mechanisms and systems through which the human being achieves adjustment and adaptation to his environment. The central nervous system is responsible for consciousness, behavior, memory, recognition, learning, and the more highly developed attributes of man such as imagination, abstract reasoning, and creative thought. In addition, it serves to coordinate such vital regulatory functions as blood pressure, heart rate, respiration, salivary and gastric secretions, muscular activity, and body temperature. Discussion will be limited to consideration of the functions of the central nervous system that are believed to affect the emotions and behavior.

The cerebrum is the largest part of the brain and is divided into two hemispheres. The outer surface of the cerebral hemispheres is composed of gray matter known as the cerebral cortex. It is thought to be the site of consciousness and is divided into sensory, motor, and association areas. These areas receive sensations from organs of special sense (sight, hearing, smell, and taste) as well as from the skin, muscles, joints, and tendons (touch, pain, and temperature). Large parts of the cortex now appear to function as a whole in providing the anatomic basis for such mental attributes as recognition, memory, intelligence, imagination, and creative thought.

Beneath the cortex are tracts of fibers comprising the white matter, which connect the lower centers of the brain, spinal cord, and associated areas of the cortex with each other. The nuclei located in this area control the extrapyramidal system that regulates muscular movement. The basal ganglia (corpus striatum, claustrum, and amygdaloid nucleus) are located in the lateral ventricle of the cerebrum. The hippocampus, a mass of gray matter lying close to the lateral ventricle, is connected by a tract of fibers (the fornix) to the mamillary bodies in the hypothalamus. The hippocampus, the fornix, the amygdaloid nucleus, the hippocampal gyrus, and the uncus are collectively referred to as the limbic system. This system is believed to be concerned with the conscious experience of emotion.

The midbrain, pons, and medulla form the part of the brain below the cerebrum. The midbrain is the seat of the cranial nerves. The pons is mainly a pathway for ascending and descend-

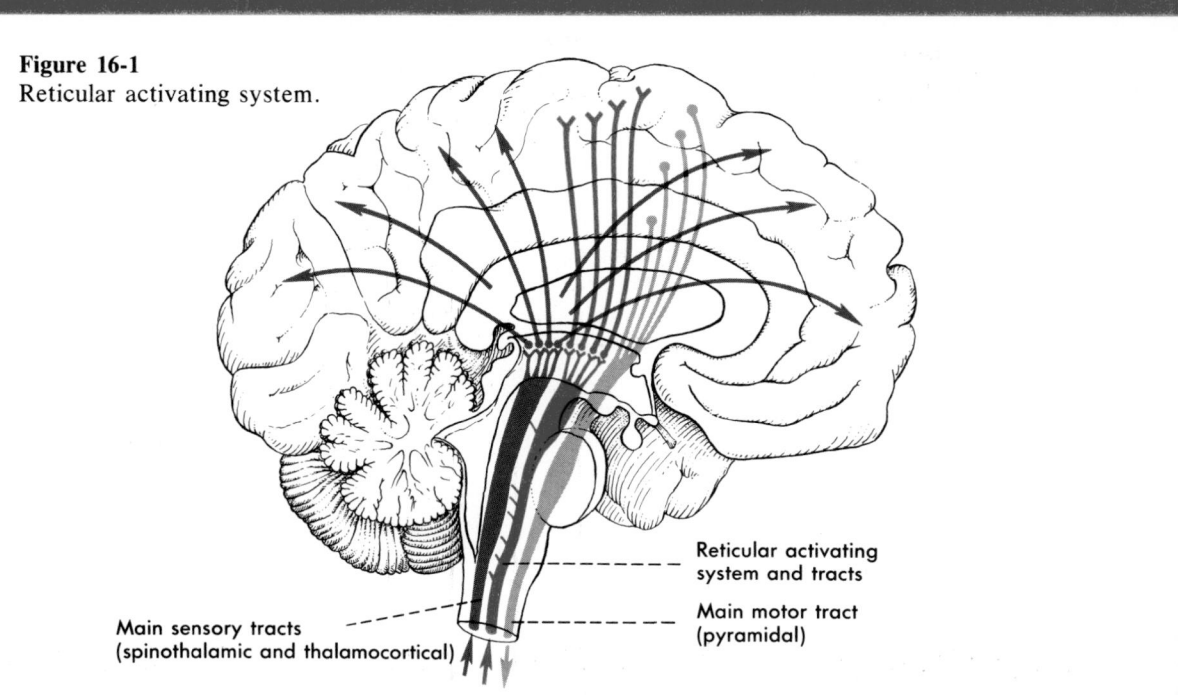

Figure 16-1
Reticular activating system.

Reticular activating
system and tracts

Main motor tract
(pyramidal)

Main sensory tracts
(spinothalamic and thalamocortical)

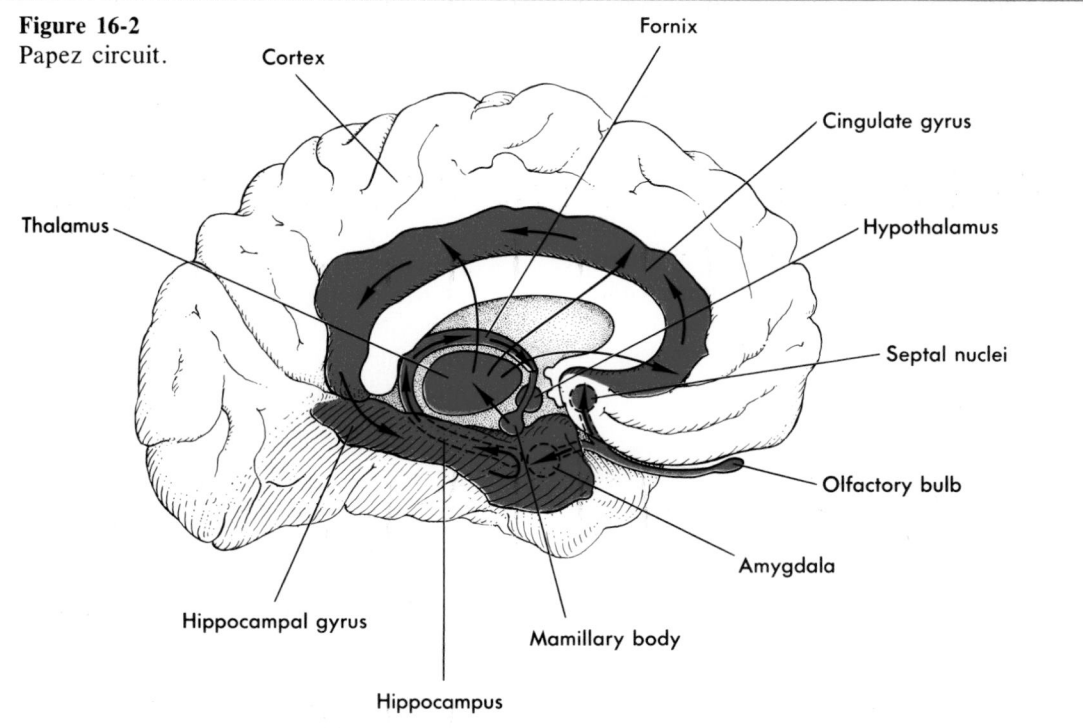

Figure 16-2
Papez circuit.

Cortex

Fornix

Cingulate gyrus

Hypothalamus

Thalamus

Septal nuclei

Olfactory bulb

Amygdala

Hippocampal gyrus

Mamillary body

Hippocampus

ing tracts of the fibers. The reticular formation of the brainstem is located in the gray matter of the pons. The medulla oblongata is continuous with the spinal cord. It contains vital groups of synapses that are concerned with the reflex control of blood pressure (vasomotor center), heart rate and force (cardiac center), respiration (respiratory center), vomiting (vomiting center), and temperature. The gray matter of the medulla consists of a complex network of cell bodies and interlacing fibers that comprise the brainstem reticular formation (reticular activating system). The reticular activating system is thought to function in alerting the cortex to sensory stimuli and in originating the emotional reactions associated with somatic sensory experiences (pain, touch, hearing, sight). Experimental stimulation of this system produces alertness in behavior, whereas decrease in its activity leads to relaxation and drowsiness. The reticular activating system has its upper end in the posterior hypothalamus and lower thalamus.

The cerebellum lies on the dorsal side of the hindbrain and is attached to the brainstem. It functions as part of the feedback mechanisms concerned with subconscious control of equilibrium, posture, and movement.

The thalamus and hypothalamus are located in the region of the brain that is called the diencephalon (the between brain). Most sensations are relayed through the thalamus to the cerebral cortex. The conscious appreciation of pain is said to be located in the thalamus along with another complex network of nerve cells and fibers known as the thalamic reticular formation. In recent years there has been a gradual increase of knowledge relative to the functions of the hypothalamus. In spite of extensive research and experimentation there still seems to be some question of its specific mode of function. It has been conjectured that the hypothalamus contains integrative mechanisms that, in addition to their effect on behavior patterns, also aid in regulating the basic life functions of man (control of water excretion, appetite, sleepwake mechanisms, temperature, and blood pressure). The hypothalamus seems to function through its relationships with other parts of the

nervous system and endocrine system. It is part of a system of complex circuits within the brain so strategically placed that its derangement may have profound effects. These interrelationships between cerebral cortex, thalamus, hypothalamus, and various other circuits in the brain produce patterns of behavior that are modifiable by situations and autonomic adjustments to adapt the individual to changes in both external and internal environments.

Papez proposed that "the hypothalamus, the anterior thalamic nuclei, the gyrus cingulum, the hippocampus, and their interconnections constitute a harmonious mechanism which may elaborate the functions of central emotion as well as participate in emotional expression."* The Papez circuit functions in the following sequence:

On stimulation of the hippocampus this structure relays impulses via the fornix to the mammillary bodies of the hypothalamus. From that area they continue to the anterior thalamic nuclei and to the cingulate gyrus of the cerebral cortex. The functional circuit is completed by fibers leaving the cingulate gyrus by way of the cingulum and returning to the hippocampus via the hippocampal gyrus.*

This proposed circuit provides an understanding of the anatomic basis for the expression of emotion and behavior. The intricate balance of positive and negative controls leads to a better conceptualization of the function of the central nervous system in the regulation of emotions and behavioral patterns in human beings. In recent years increasing evidence implicates these areas of the central nervous system with control of behavior and emotions; however, at best, these data have been superficial, inconclusive, and merely theoretical.

Autonomic regulations

The functions of the sympathetic and parasympathetic visceral nervous system are discussed in Chapter 9. The importance of the reactions of these systems in the production of behavior is paramount in gaining an understanding of drug action and/or the behavioral manifestations of side effects from the use of drugs.

*Marks, J.: Scientific basis of drug therapy, New York, 1965, Pergamon Press, Inc., p. 5.

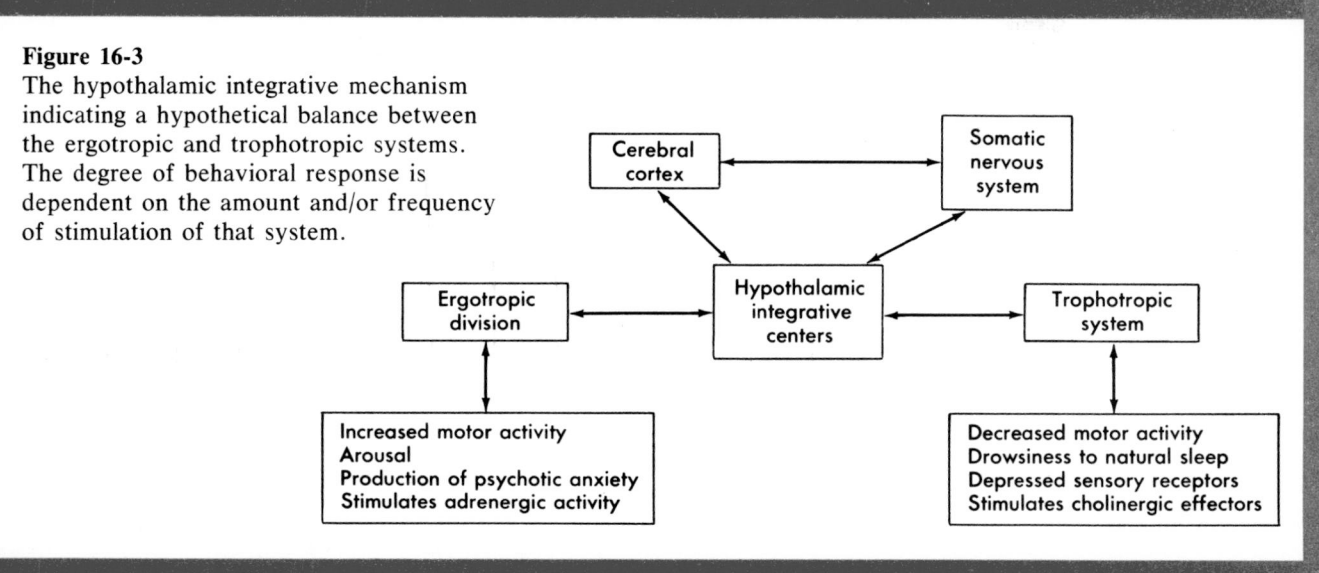

Figure 16-3
The hypothalamic integrative mechanism indicating a hypothetical balance between the ergotropic and trophotropic systems. The degree of behavioral response is dependent on the amount and/or frequency of stimulation of that system.

Since the central nervous system functions in the regulation of integrated behavior, considerable effort has been extended toward locating and defining the integrative centers. Scientific evidence is accumulating for grouping the functions of the subcortical systems into two separate and antagonistic divisions. Two such systems have been identified by Hess in the hypothalamus and have been labeled the "ergotropic division" and the "trophotropic system." Much of the work in defining and locating these divisions is based on the behavioral and physiologic responses elicited by their stimulation.

It is hypothesized that the ergotropic division integrates the sympathetic and reticular activity systems with the somatosensory motor system. This activity produces an activated psychic state, such as seen in severe anxiety, and an increase in physiologic responses of the sympathetic nervous system. These combined responses ready the body for positive action.

It is postulated that the trophotropic system integrates the parasympathetic system, the somatosensory motor system, and probably a part of the limbic system. Stimulation of this system produces such behavioral patterns as relaxation, subdued psychic state, or diminished response to external stimuli (increased parasympathetic activity).

The degree of behavioral response elicited by stimulation of either of these divisions is probably on a continuum. Stimulation of the trophotropic system may produce relaxation and reduced response to external stimuli on one end of the continuum or drowsiness and sleep on the other. The degree of behavioral response is dependent on the amount and/or frequency of stimulation of that system.

Biochemical mechanisms

The functions of the central nervous system are dependent upon the action of certain neurohormonal agents located in the brain and peripheral tissues. These neurohormones are stored in inactive forms, and at the right moment nerve impulses release their free forms, which then stimulate transmission of appropriate reactions (see pp. 101 to 106). It is postulated that norepinephrine (noradrenalin) and serotonin (5-hydroxytryptamine) may qualify as respective agents for the ergotropic and trophotropic divi-

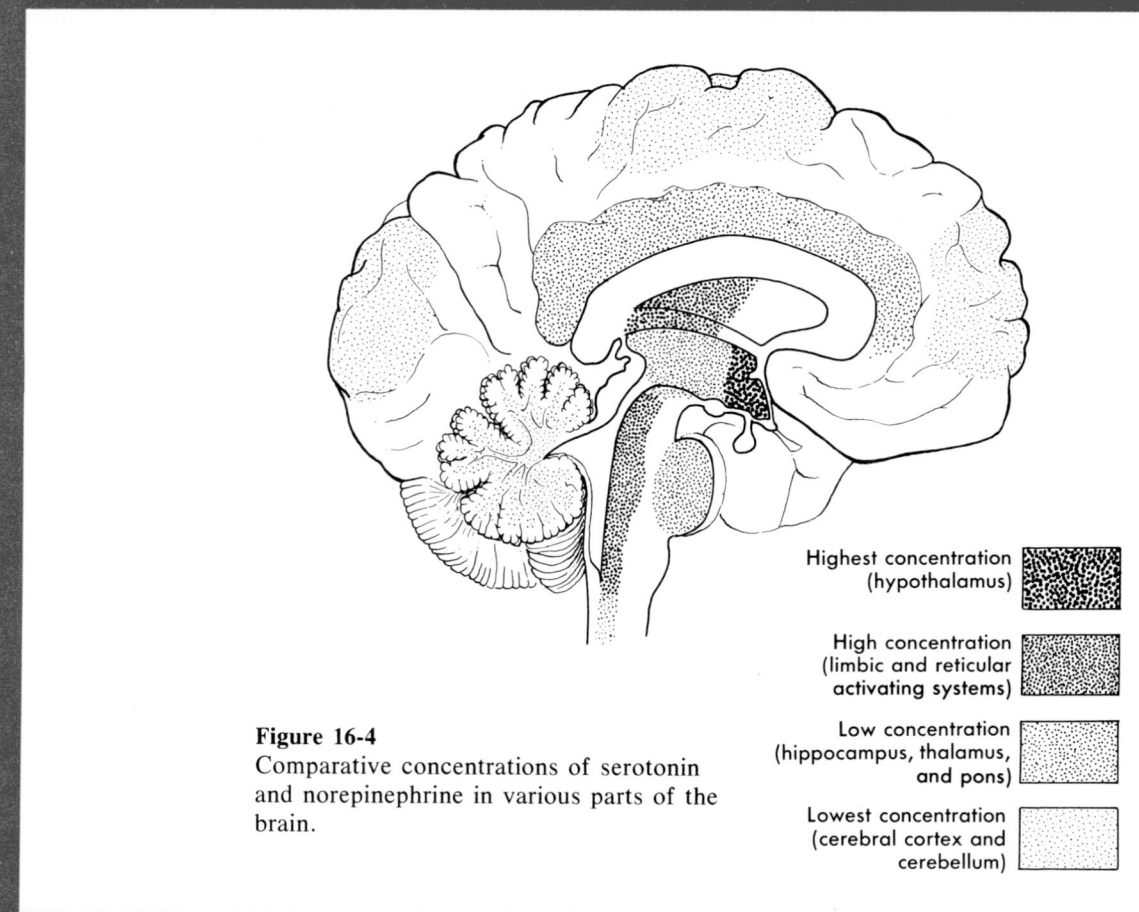

Figure 16-4
Comparative concentrations of serotonin and norepinephrine in various parts of the brain.

Highest concentration (hypothalamus)

High concentration (limbic and reticular activating systems)

Low concentration (hippocampus, thalamus, and pons)

Lowest concentration (cerebral cortex and cerebellum)

sions of the nervous system. Acetylcholine has been identified as a neurotransmitter at central synapses (see pp. 118 and 119); however, this does not imply that other substances are not neurotransmitters.

The highest concentrations of norepinephrine in the central nervous system are located in the hypothalamus and medulla. Sensory impulses from the viscera are transmitted to the sensitive areas in the brain where deposits of norepinephrine are stored. This causes a subsequent release of free norepinephrine, which activates the ergotropic division and produces increased initiative and emotional responses, increased reaction to sensory stimuli, arousal and excitement, increase in muscular tone, motor excitement, and an increase in the predominant sympathetic activity of elevation of blood pressure, tachycardia, hyperthermia, and mydriasis (see Figure 16-4).

Serotonin occurs in the central nervous system in about the same distribution as norepinephrine, but is also found in the hippocampus, cerebellum, and pineal gland. Serotonin is synthesized in the brain and stored in the subcellular particles and does not penetrate the blood-brain barrier. Alteration of the level of serotonin in the nervous system is associated with changes in behavior. Many drugs mimic or block the action of serotonin on peripheral tissues and produce changes in mood and behavior, which suggests that they interfere with the action of serotonin in the brain. It is hypothesized that serotonin serves as the central neurohormone for the trophotropic division.

Sensory impulses from the somatic structures and the viscera are transmitted to deposits of serotonin in the brain, which causes a release of free serotonin and activates the trophotropic division. This produces lack of volition and verve, decreased reaction to sensory stimuli, drowsiness and sleep, decreased muscular tone, and a general decrease in psychomotor activity. It is a predominantly parasympathetic activity; it causes a lowering of blood pressure, decreased salivation, miosis, and hypothermia.

There is enough evidence available to suggest that the degree of psychomotor activity of the cortex is in some way dependent on the balance of serotonin and norepinephrine in the hypothalamus. Further research and investigation in this has led to the identification of another enzyme, monamine oxidase, which is present in brain tissue. This enzyme acts in the breakdown of the neurohormones serotonin and norepinephrine. When monamine oxidase is inhibited, brain levels of various amines rise and cause a subsequent change in behavior.

Psychotropic drugs

The two major drug groups that comprise the classification of psychotropic drugs are the *tranquilizers* and the *antidepressants*. The term *tranquilizer* reflects the action of this group of drugs in effecting a change toward tranquility in the affective and behavioral state of the individual. Tranquilizers have a direct effect on the levels of anxiety that create a pathologic adjustment to intrapersonal and interpersonal experiences. Anxiety is reduced without subsequent impairment of consciousness, and hyperactivity is controlled. The delusions, hallucinations, and confusion associated with psychopathology are decreased to a tolerable level. The tranquilizers are commonly classified as *major* and *minor* tranquilizers. The major tranquilizers are some-

times referred to as "neuroleptics" or "ataractics" (from the Greek word *ataraktos* meaning "undisturbed" or "peace of mind"). The major tranquilizers are those substances that affect psychotic symptoms and extrapyramidal and autonomic manifestations, as well as lower the convulsive threshold. Minor tranquilizers are those substances that are characterized by their action in the relief of mild or moderate anxiety and that are not usually known to be effective as antipsychotic agents. The main therapeutic action of the minor tranquilizers seems to be in treatment of anxiety that accompanies neurotic symptomatology. The minor tranquilizers do not evoke extrapyramidal symptoms such as tremor, rigidity, or dystonic reactions; they produce few autonomic symptoms and tend to raise the convulsive theshold.

The antidepressant drug group has recently attracted a great deal of attention and has led to an effective psychopharmacologic treatment of depression states. The newly developed antidepressants, called "psychostimulants" or "psychic energizers" because of their stimulating and energy-producing action, have replaced some of the older drugs (amphetamine, caffeine) in the treatment of depressive states. The older drugs were found to cause rise in blood pressure, increase in heart rate, and loss of appetite. Drugs such as the amphetamines are high-risk drugs for causing psychic dependency, which reduces their effectiveness for long-term treatment.

Another group of drugs, the psychomimetics, are included in the psychotropic drug classification. This group of drugs will not be given consideration in this discussion of the psychotropic drugs since their mechanism of action is unknown and their usefulness in the treatment of mental illness is still in the experimental stages. The action of these drugs has been known to mimic or produce psychotic states and therefore they are sometimes called *hallucinogenic drugs*. The most publicized and best known of these drugs is lysergic acid diethylamide (LSD). These drugs cause initial autonomic disturbances (tachycardia, dilation of the pupil, tightness in the chest and abdomen, and nausea) **343** followed by vivid visual hallucinations, severe anxiety, and delusions. Use of these drugs should be restricted to controlled experimental research because of the grave danger of irreversible sequelae.

Selection and use of psychotropic drugs

In the past physicians have selected psychotropic agents on the basis of the diagnostic category that the patient's psychopathology fit into—schizophrenia, manic-depressive syndrome, or psychoneurosis. More recent proposals have indicated a radical change in the physician's approach to selecting drugs for the mentally ill person. The pharmacologic treatment of psychiatric disorders would appear to be similar to that of somatic disorders—modification of the most disabling components of the patient's behavior so that the patient may more effectively cope with his environment and take advantage of the therapeutic milieu available. It would seem more rational to deemphasize the diagnostic classifications of psychiatric disorders as a basis for drug selectivity and to consider instead the most disabling behavioral manifestations that can be observed. This implies a thorough assessment of the patient prior to the administration of drugs. This assessment should include the specific disabling features of the patient's behavior, a decision as to the goals of therapy, the dynamics involved, and the specific directional changes sought. Other factors helpful in making an accurate assessment of the patient's need for drug therapy are:

1 The degree of agitation or behavioral arousal
2 The degree of over- or underactivity
3 Patterns of affective response to stress (avoidance or escape, aggression, fear, inhibited withdrawal)
4 The degree of social withdrawal
5 The nature and dynamics of depressive elements present
6 Sleep problems
7 Need for environmental control
8 Medical complaints
9 Possible drug dependence
10 Past drug history—effectiveness of response to drugs

When the physician establishes the need for drug therapy, he must then decide on the agent or combination of agents best suited for the behavioral and medical needs of the patient. Since there are many drugs available, it is judicious for the physician to familiarize himself with a few drugs rather than make a haphazard selection of several agents. This requires an intimate knowledge of the behavioral actions, the pharmacologic effects, and the potential adverse reactions of the agents used, as well as an awareness of the many individual and environment-related factors present. Upon selection of the agent or agents to be used, the dosage is then increased until the desired and expected effects are produced. Continuous reevaluation based on observation of the effects of the drug selected is needed. Increase or reduction of dosage may be indicated in order to gain the desired effects. The nurse plays an important role in the evaluation and reassessment of a patient's response to drug therapy. It is important for her to be aware of the criteria the physician uses in selecting psychotropic drugs and the expected effects so that she may observe and report the patient's progress. Knowledge of the action of drugs also assists the nurse in understanding the interpersonal responses that take place in the therapeutic nurse-patient relationship.

■ Major tranquilizers—antipsychotic agents
Rauwolfia alkaloids

The first of the drugs to play an important part in the pharmacologic treatment of mental illness were the rauwolfia alkaloids. These drugs came into prominence around 1953, although they have been used in India for many years for the treatment of mental disorders. The most widely used of these compounds is reserpine. The principal use of the rauwolfia alkaloid compounds today is in the treatment of hypertension. Their use in this respect is described in Chapter 20. The rauwolfia alkaloids are still considered as antipsychotic agents; however, they are not widely used because of the toxic side effects present with large single doses. It is necessary to administer these compounds in small daily dosages that prolong the effects of their action and delay their therapeutic effectiveness. As a tranquilizer, reserpine produces many of the same effects as the phenothiazine drug groups; however, its use is now restricted to those patients who do not respond to phenothiazine treatment. Since the phenothiazine drugs achieve the same tranquilizing effects, can be administered in larger doses, and produce a therapeutic effect sooner, the rauwolfia compounds have been replaced by these drugs.

Phenothiazine derivatives

Discovery of the phenothiazine derivatives arose out of research in the area of the antihistamines. Chlorpromazine hydrochloride was introduced in 1951 and has found wide acceptance in the treatment of mental illness. Additional investigation of the action of chlorpromazine in producing undesirable side effects led to the development of numerous derivatives, which now comprise the largest group of psychotropic agents.

Most of the antipsychotic drugs are phenothiazine derivatives. They are commonly divided chemically into the following three subgroups: (1) the dimethylaminopropyl compounds (chlorpromazine, promazine, and triflupromazine); (2) the piperidyl compounds (thioridazine and mepazine); and (3) the piperazine compounds (acetophenazine, fluphenazine, perphenazine, prochlorperazine, thiopropazate, and trifluoperazine). The chemical structure of these compounds and specific information regarding their action, effects, and adverse reactions will be presented separately following the general discussion of commonalities that have been identified. The type of action is essentially similar with all phenothiazine derivatives; individual compounds vary chiefly in their potency and in the nature and severity of their side effects.

Site and mechanism of action of phenothiazine derivatives. It has been pointed out earlier (p. 341) that at the hypothalamic level the homeostatic control of the emotional reaction to the environment is determined by two opposing systems—the ergotropic system, which pro-duces arousal activity and increased sympathetic tone, and the trophotropic system, which has the opposite effects and causes reduced activity and increased parasympathetic tone. At the higher level of the limbic system the hippocampus and the amygdala appear to exert opposing influences—stimulation of the hippocampus produces calmness and tranquility, while inhibition of the amygdala will also produce similar effects. Reverse procedures are known to evoke rage reactions.

Impulses activated by sensory input from the external environment as well as the viscera travel via the reticular formation to the thalamus, hypothalamus, and limbic system. It has been postulated that there is a two-way neuronal connection between all these regions and systems and that the experience and expression of emotion follows the integration of sensory input by this complex system. Evidence supports the supposition that tranquilizers act within this system, but the precise sites are difficult to determine because of the synergistic action of the system. Attempts have been made to link the effects of the antipsychotic agents to interaction with substances normally found in the brain— norepinephrine, serotonin, and acetylcholine.

Brodie has postulated that norepinephrine is the transmitter in the neurons of the ergotropic system and that serotonin is the transmitter for the trophotropic system. The phenothiazines are thought to act centrally as an antiepinephrine drug, blocking the adrenergic synapses of the ergotropic system. By inactivating the ergotropic system, the trophotropic system is allowed to predominate (Figure 16-5). This raises the threshold for sympathetic excitation at the hypothalamic level and prevents norepinephrine from exciting those nerve cells that generate widespread sympathetic effects.

The administration of phenothiazines to the human being seems to support this theory in that a widespread reduction of sympathetic tone in the body can be observed. There is vasodilatation and hypotension with compensatory tachycardia, relaxation of smooth muscle, alteration of pupillary size, and salivary and gastric secretions. Because the phenothiazines act to **345**

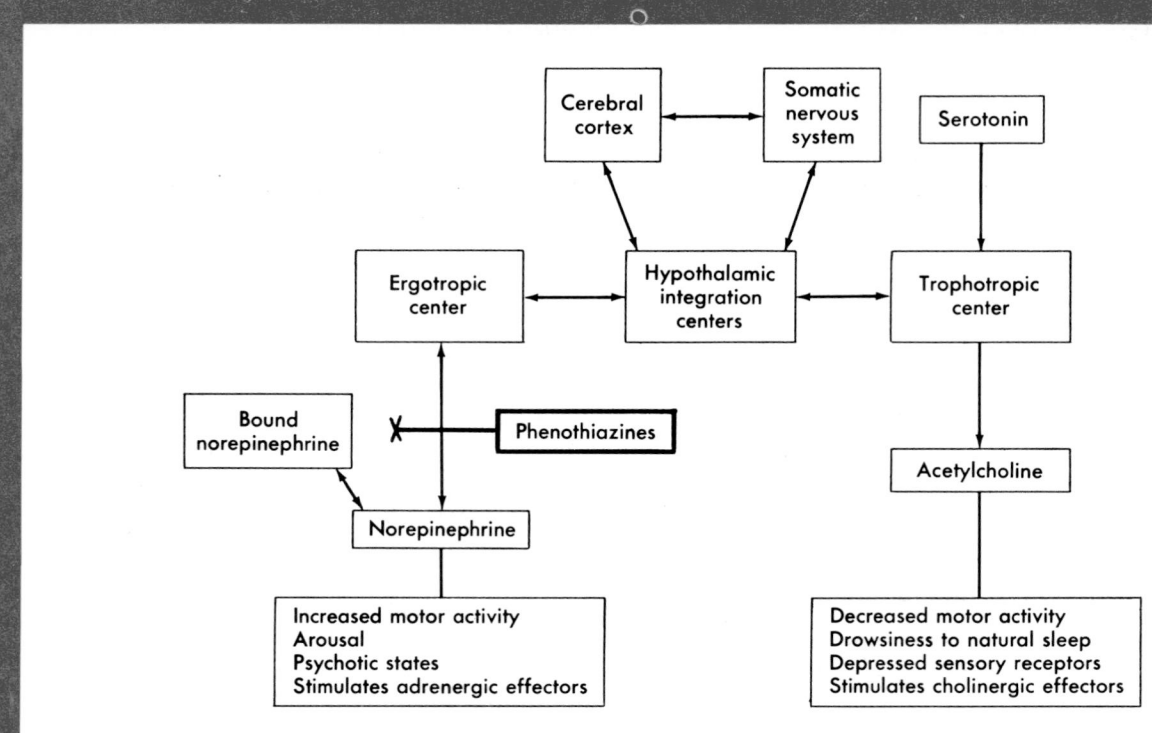

Figure 16-5
Effect of phenothiazine derivatives on the hypothalamic integration of the ergotropic and trophotropic centers. Normal physiologic and psychologic behavior depends on maintaining a balance in the concentrations of norepinephrine and acetylcholine. Anxiety or psychosis may result with too much epinephrine or too little acetylcholine. Too much acetylcholine or too little epinephrine produces tranquility. Phenothiazine derivatives shift the balance to predominant concentrations of acetylcholine in the trophotropic system.

suppress central sympathetic activity without significantly depressing the reticular activating system, their use is favored in the control of psychomotor agitation, since this effect is produced without significant loss of cortical functioning or consciousness. The hallucinations and delusions associated with psychosis are mitigated or eliminated by the action of the phenothiazines.

This seems to point to the direct effect of the phenothiazine drug group on the neocortical functions that control interpretation of sensory data and thought processes. The phenothiazines indirectly affect the neocortex via the Papez circuit and similar feedback systems that involve both neocortical and limbic areas. It would appear then that the phenothiazines reduce the intensity of emotional reactions with a resulting decrease of anxiety and subsequent abandonment of defenses such as hallucinations or delusions.

Pharmacologic characteristics and uses. The most important pharmacologic characteristics of these substances are: (1) antipsychotic activity (an ability to calm aggressive, overactive, disturbed patients); (2) failure of large doses to produce deep coma and anesthesia (patients show both behavioral and electroencephalographic arousal when stimulated); (3) production of reversible and irreversible effects on the extrapyramidal system, leading to the development of related signs and symptoms; and (4) lack of any notable tendency to cause psychogenic or physical dependence.

The phenothiazine derivatives are used to reduce psychotic symptoms and therefore are useful in the treatment of acute and chronic psychoses. Control of deeply disturbed patients is achieved without causing depression of vital centers. Psychotic conditions marked by excessive psychomotor activity, panic, fear, and hostility respond well to the administration of the phenothiazines. Relief of emotional tension, excitement, and agitation lessens the patient's response to hallucinations and delusions. Destructive and combative behavior is notably reduced. On the other hand, some of the piperazine compounds are useful in stimulating the withdrawn apathetic patient so that he becomes more alert, sociable, and communicative. The phenothiazines may make some depressive reactions worse and do not seem to be of value in treating hysteria or obsessive-compulsive reactions. However, phenothiazines seem to be helpful in allaying the agitation and anxiety that occurs prior to electroconvulsive treatments.

Small doses of the antipsychotic agents are sometimes used to control the anxiety, tension, and emotional disturbance in the psychoneurotic patient. Anxiety that often accompanies diseases with psychogenic components is easily controlled with small doses of the phenothiazine derivatives. However, the risk involved from the side effects does not seem to warrant their use in these instances. The minor tranquilizers appear to be more useful in these conditions.

Some of the phenothiazine derivatives have been used in nonpsychiatric settings because of their secondary actions (antiemesis; potentiation of hypnotic, analgesic, and anesthetic agents).

Side effects and precautions. The phenothiazine derivatives produce a wide variety of un-toward effects. Individuals vary in their ability to tolerate these compounds, and difficulty with side effects may determine the effectiveness of the compound. The pattern of adverse reactions is one of the important factors that the physician considers in choosing among the compounds. Some of these side effects result from the secondary action of the drugs on the central and autonomic nervous systems, while others are idiosyncratic or allergic in nature.

Common side effects that may occur with any of the phenothiazines are dry mouth, blurred vision, constipation, excessive weight gain, edema, and vivid dreams. Nursing care should be directed toward conscientious and consistent attention to the hygienic needs of the patient.

Patients should be cautioned against driving an automobile, operating dangerous machinery, or performing tasks that require absolute precision, motor coordination, and mental alertness.

Decreased libido may be a troublesome side effect for patients on a maintenance dosage of these drugs. Careful explanation of the cause of this side effect may alleviate the patient's anxiety. Some patients refuse medications before home visits for this reason.

Liver. Cholestatic hepatitis with obstructive jaundice is the most frequent form of liver disorder observed. It usually develops within the first 5 weeks of treatment. If bilirubinuria and icterus are detected in liver function tests, the drug should be withdrawn immediately. Since the subsequent changes in the liver persist for a much longer time, it is not advisable to change treatment to another phenothiazine compound. Fatality is rare, and recovery from phenothiazine jaundice usually occurs within a few weeks. It is undesirable to use these drugs in patients who have known liver disease. Such patients are probably no more susceptible to such reactions than other patients, but the consequences might be more serious should they occur.

Hematologic complications. Leukopenia, granulocytopenia, agranulocytosis, purpura, and pancytopenia are hematologic complications that occur. The incidence of their occurrence is low; however, the mortality rate is high. Physicians and nurses should be alert to the appearance of such signs as sore throat, fever, or weakness in patients taking these drugs. With the appearance of these symptoms the drug is usually discontinued and a white blood cell and differential count are made to determine the cause of the disturbance. Some physicians order routine monthly or bimonthly laboratory tests to avoid such complications. However, most physicians believe that this is of little value, since blood dyscrasias occur so rapidly that it is impractical to do blood counts frequently enough to protect the patient.

Postural hypotension. Postural hypotension is usually mild and occurs with initial dosage of the phenothiazines. Compensatory adjustment usually takes place in a few days. It can be especially serious, though, with patients in whom a sudden drop in blood pressure would be undesirable (elderly patients with evidence of arteriosclerosis or patients with cardiovascular disease). If this side effect is causing an unusual amount of difficulty or serious hazards, the following remedial measures may be instituted: (1) a change of medication to one of the phenothiazine derivatives that is not known to produce this side effect with such frequency, (2) reduction of dosage, or (3) discontinuation of medication for a 24-hour period with a gradual buildup of dosage as tolerated. The patient who complains of dizziness, lightheadedness, or palpitation may be experiencing orthostatic (postural) hypotension. This can easily be confirmed by comparing the patient's blood pressure in the prone and standing positions. The nurse may instruct the patient to rise slowly from the recumbent position and to sit on the edge of the bed for a few minutes before attempting to stand. Support and reassurance may be necessary to allay the patient's anxiety. Explanation of this phenomenon may also aid in the patient's understanding of this experience and reduce his anxiety. Patients should be encouraged to remain in a recumbent position for 1 hour after initial doses, parenterally administered doses, or large oral doses of the phenothiazines.

Dermatoses. Dermatoses are usually mild and can be controlled by discontinuing the drug.

It is often possible to resume treatment later with another compound, or even the same one, without recurrence of the allergic skin reaction. If photosensitivity develops, the patient should stay out of the sunlight or wear protective clothing to prevent solar erythema. Nurses should instruct patients regarding this side effect and/or assist them in providing the necessary protective measures to avoid exposure. A dark purplish-brown skin pigmentation, induced by light, has been reported in hospitalized psychiatric patients who were given large dosages of phenothiazines for 3 to 10 years.

Endocrine imbalance. Endocrine imbalance is caused by depression of hypothalamic functions. These symptoms have been reported infrequently and include delayed ovulation and menstruation, amenorrhea with false positive results from pregnancy tests, lactogenic response in female patients, and weight gain. These symptoms may cause unwarranted anxiety and compound the patient's problems. After ordinary steps are initiated to determine other possible causative factors for these symptoms without positive results, the patient should be reassured that the medication she is receiving is the causative factor. Depending on the patient's current symptomatology, reinforcement of these facts may be necessary.

In pregnancy the risk of administration of this drug should be weighed against the expected therapeutic outcome.

Extrapyramidal symptoms. Extrapyramidal symptoms may appear after the administration of a single dose of phenothiazines or after prolonged usage. Extrapyramidal symptoms are considered to be a rather normal consequence of drug action and usually indicate that the phenothiazines are affecting the deeper brain centers where much of the antipsychotic activity presumably takes place. Extrapyramidal reactions are of four general types: pseudoparkinsonism, akinesia, akathisia, and dyskinesia. Pseudoparkinsonism resembles true parkinsonism and manifests symptoms such as tremor, mask-like facial expression, rigidity, drooling, loss of associated movements of the arms, and some restlessness. Akinesia is usually less dis-

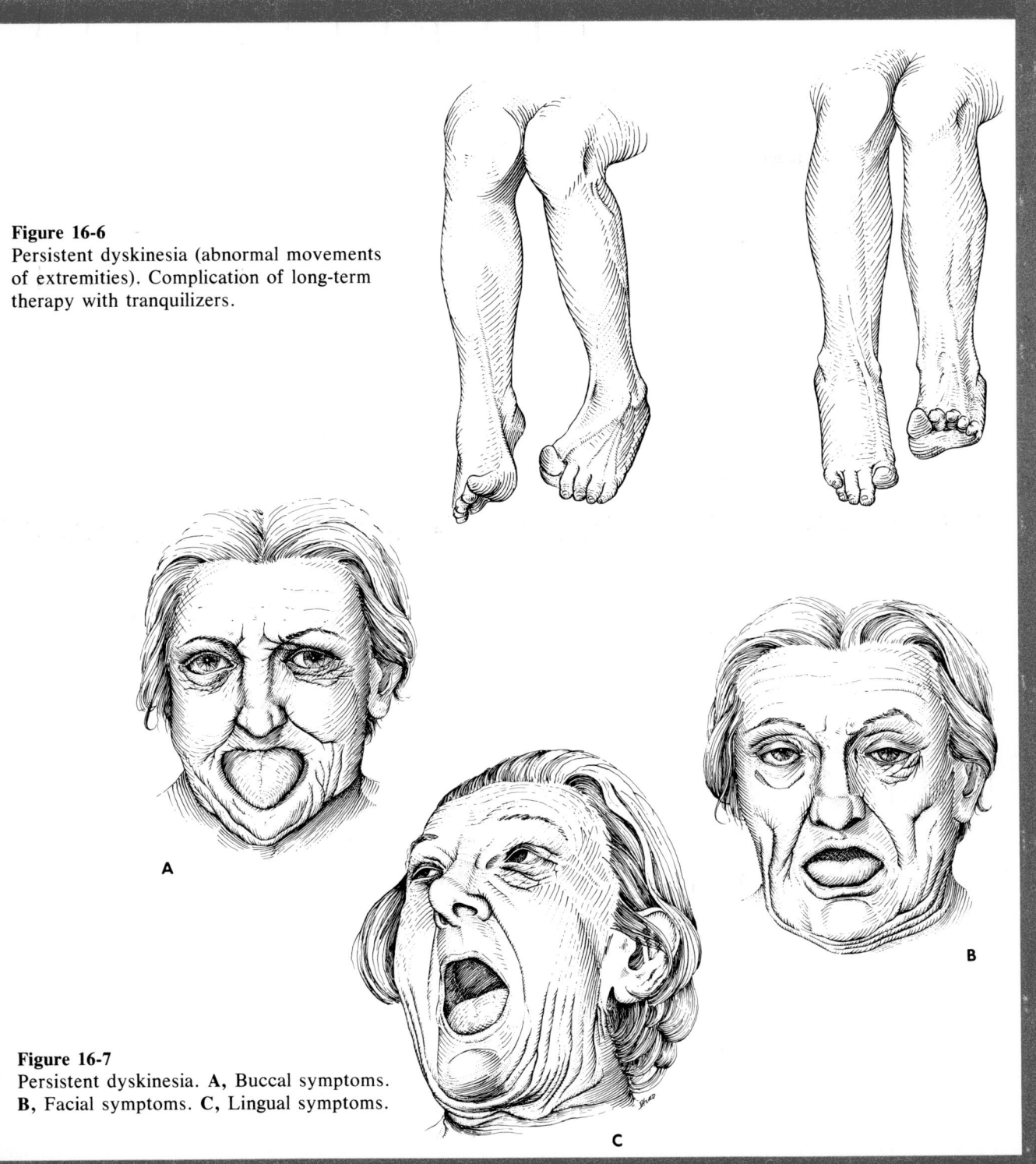

Figure 16-6
Persistent dyskinesia (abnormal movements
of extremities). Complication of long-term
therapy with tranquilizers.

Figure 16-7
Persistent dyskinesia. **A,** Buccal symptoms.
B, Facial symptoms. **C,** Lingual symptoms.

tressing to the patient and becomes evident to medical personnel when the patient complains of fatigue and weakness of the arms and legs. Akathisia (the inability to sit still) becomes apparent when the patient is observed to be extremely restless, continually moving his hands, mouth, and body. Dyskinesia is a less common disturbance that takes many forms such as torsion spasm, opisthotonos, oculogyric crises, drooping of the head, protrusion of tongue, and other facial disturbances (Figure 16-7). Patients complain of stiff neck and inability to swallow and usually become very frightened with the onset of these symptoms. The dramatic suddenness of onset is often frightening to nursing personnel as well. Recognition of the cause of this symptomatology is helpful in allaying the anxiety of both nurse and patient. Immediate action should be instituted to reverse this extrapyramidal reaction. The administration of an antiparkinsonian agent orally (when possible) or parenterally will produce a reversal of symptoms in as dramatic a fashion as the onset of the symptoms. The nurse should stay with the patient and reassure him that the symptoms will subside, which also gives her an opportunity to observe the patient closely. Pseudoparkinsonism, akathisia, and akinesia may have a more gradual onset than dyskinesia; however, they may be just as troublesome to patients. Generally these extrapyramidal symptoms are easily controlled by lowering the dosage or discontinuing the medication, using a compound that has a low incidence of these reactions (see Table 16-1), or controlling these reactions with use of antiparkinsonian drugs. Antiparkinsonian agents most commonly used are Benztropine Methanesulfonate, biperiden, and procyclidine.

Precautions. There are several precautions that should be observed in the use of phenothiazine compounds.

Autonomic blockade may occur as one of the most serious effects resulting from the adrenergic blocking action of the phenothiazines. If circulatory collapse occurs, a vasopressor agent such as levarterenol or angiotensin amide should be given. *Epinephrine* should *never* be used since its administration to a patient with

Table 16-1 Frequency of incidence of extrapyramidal symptoms from antipsychotic agents

	Generic name	Trade name
Highest incidence	Fluphenazine	Permitil; Prolixin
	Trifluoperazine	Stelazine
	Perphenazine	Trilafon
	Prochlorperazine	Compazine
	Thiopropazate	Dartal
	Acetophenazine	Tindal
	Triflupromazine	Vesprin
	Chlorpromazine	Thorazine
Lowest incidence	Mepazine	Pacatal
	Thioridazine	Mellaril

partial adrenergic blockade may result in further fall of blood pressure.

Potentiation of other drugs is a common effect produced by the phenothiazine derivatives. They should be used cautiously in patients who are under the influence of alcohol or barbiturates or of morphine-like analgesics. Dosage of anesthetics should be reduced. These drugs should also be used with care in patients who are taking antihypertensive drugs.

Antiemetic effects of these agents may obscure the cause of nausea and vomiting in various organic disorders.

Other adverse reactions that have been observed are melanosis of internal organs such as the heart, liver, and kidneys after the administration of chlorpromazine in large doses. Electrocardiographic alterations resembling those caused by quinidine or by hypokalemia and pigmentary retinopathy have been noted, especially when large doses of thioridazine have been administered. These drugs should be administered cautiously to patients with suspected heart disease. Because of the pronounced anticholinergic action of these agents, they should not be administered to patients with a history of glaucoma or prostatic hypertrophy. During

Table 16-2 Major tranquilizers
(phenothiazine derivatives)

Generic name	Trade name	Side effects*	Dosage range† per 24 hour period (mg.)
Dimethylamine subgroup			
Chlorpromazine hydrochloride	Thorazine	1-9, 11, 13-16, 32	30 to 1200
Triflupromazine	Vesprin	1-11, 13	60 to 150
Piperidyl subgroup			
Thioridazine	Mellaril	1-3, 6, 7, 13, 14, 19-21	30 to 800
Mepazine	Pacatal	1-11, 13, 14	50 to 400
Piperazine subgroup			
Acetophenazine	Tindal	1, 6	40 to 80
Fluphenazine	Permital; Prolixin	1-9, 11, 13, 16, 20	1 to 20
Perphenazine	Trilafon	1-9, 11, 13	6 to 64
Prochlorperazine	Compazine	1-7, 9, 11, 13, 16, 22	15 to 150
Thiopropazate	Dartal	1, 3-7, 11, 13, 15, 16	15 to 100
Trifluoperazine	Stelazine	1, 2, 4-9, 11, 13, 16, 20	2 to 20

Key to table
1. Sedation or sleep
2. Ataxia
3. Dry mouth
4. Constipation
5. Dermatitis
6. Extrapyramidal symptoms
7. Hypotension
8. Blood dyscrasia (usually agranulocytosis)
9. Jaundice
10. Convulsions
11. Antiemetic
12. Thrombophlebitis
13. Blurred vision
14. Hypothermia
15. Tachycardia
16. Nasal congestion
17. Mental depression
18. Menstrual irregularities
19. Nausea and vomiting
20. Edema
21. Impotence
22. Increased appetite
23. Bradycardia
24. Cutaneous flushing
25. Salivation
26. Increased intestinal motility or diarrhea
27. Activation of peptic ulcer
28. Decreased libido
29. Increased gastric secretions
30. Insomnia
31. Diaphoresis
32. Photosensitivity

*Side effects here are not intended to be a complete account of possible adverse reactions.
†Since drug dosage varies with the patient's response and the severity of the disease, consult drug digest for dosage schedules.

the summer months, instances of hyperthermia and heat prostration have been reported. The phenothiazines should be used cautiously and in small doses in patients with a history of convulsive disorders because of their action in reducing the convulsive threshold. These drugs are contraindicated in comatose patients because of their central nervous system depressive effect.

Cardiac findings in sudden death after pro- longed use of the phenothiazines have been inconclusive. Patients have been known to die suddenly and unexpectedly. Postmortem examinations of these patients have revealed the presence of a brown glandular pigment in the heart and other viscera. It has been hypothesized that death is caused by ventricular arrhythmia or asphyxia during a convulsive seizure. Some researchers conjecture that the drugs act in the alteration of cell membrane. They may act on the substrate or enzyme-forming system in the mitochondria, or they may act upon the metallic balance of sodium, potassium, and manganese.

Dimethylamine subgroup
Chlorpromazine hydrochloride, U.S.P., B.P. (Thorazine Hydrochloride)

The structural formulas of phenothiazine and chlorpromazine are represented as follows.

Phenothiazine

Chlorpromazine

Chlorpromazine was introduced for clinical trial in 1951. It is a grayish white, crystalline powder that is soluble in water. It is chemically related to the antihistaminic promethazine (Phenergan) but in comparison chlorpromazine has little antihistaminic activity. It was introduced in Europe under the name of Largactil.

Preparation, dosage, and administration. Chlorpromazine hydrochloride is marketed in sustained-release capsules (30, 75, 150, 200, and 300 mg.); in solution, in ampules, and in multiple-dose vials (25 mg. per milliliter); in syrup (2 mg. per milliliter); in tablets (10, 25, 50, 100, and 200 mg.); and as a concentrate (30 mg. per milliliter). Chlorpromazine is available also in suppository form (25 and 100 mg.).

The smallest effective dose is the one recommended. Oral dosage varies from 10 mg. to 1 Gm. or more per day. Total daily amounts are usually given in three evenly spaced doses.

Chlorpromazine hydrochloride is administered orally, intramuscularly, and intravenously. It is usually given orally unless for some reason

the patient is unable to take the dose by mouth. Often patients will conceal tablets in the back of their mouth or around the teeth and lip area. The concentrate may be used effectively in this case. If chlorpromazine concentrate is used for long periods of time, close attention must be given to proper oral hygiene. The taste of chlorpromazine hydrochloride concentrate can become more palatable when given in fruit juice; however, the patient should be told there is medication in the juice. Chlorpromazine concentrate is a highly irritating substance on contact with skin and eyes. Care should be taken to wash areas of the body that come into contact with this substance immediately. Nurses have been known to contract very uncomfortable dermatologic conditions as a result of their contact with this substance. Chlorpromazine hydrochloride is considered too irritating to be given subcutaneously. When given intramuscularly it should be injected deeply and slowly in divided doses of not more than 1 ml. per injection site. Massage of the site of injection helps to reduce local irritation. Some patients have been known to develop abscesses at the injection site, which are thought to result from large doses of this substance in one area. Use of the intramuscular route of administration of chlorpromazine is usually indicated when the patient refuses the tablet or concentrate form or when the most immediate effect of the drug is desired. If the patient is severely agitated, combative, or struggling, care should be taken to follow safe administration technique. This usually requires enough well-trained personnel to adequately restrain the patient while the medication is being given.

Triflupromazine hydrochloride, N.F. (Vesprin)

Action and uses. This compound is at least twice as active as chlorpromazine but otherwise is similar to chlorpromazine in its spectrum. It has been found to be useful in the management of the pernicious vomiting of pregnancy, postoperative emesis, and the nausea and vomiting following encephalograms or ventriculograms.

Preparation, dosage, and administration. Triflupromazine Hydrochloride can be administered orally in tablets of 10, 25, and 50 mg., in a suspension of 50 mg. per 5 ml., and intramuscularly in solutions of 10 and 20 mg. per milliter. Oral therapy should be substituted for parenteral administration as soon as possible. The usual dose for hospitalized psychotic adults is 100 to 150 mg. daily. The initial daily dosage for elderly patients with psychoses is 10 mg. three times a day. For prevention and treatment of nausea and vomiting in adults, the oral dose is 20 to 30 mg. daily.

Piperidyl subgroup
Mepazine hydrochloride and mepazine acetate (Pacatal)

Mepazine base

Action and uses. Mepazine is a phenothiazine compound that has not appeared to be too effective in treating psychotic disorders. It has been noted to have a slight euphorigenic effect. Its administration is associated with rather severe atropine-like effects, and bladder dysfunction commonly occurs. Because of these side effects and its apparent inability to control psychotic symptoms, its use has been limited.

Preparation, dosage, and administration. Mepazine hydrochloride is administered orally. The initial dose for psychiatric patients varies from 25 to 100 mg. per day, depending upon the nature and severity of the symptoms. Antiemetic doses range from 50 to 100 mg. daily. The

drug is marketed in 25-, 50-, and 100-mg. tablets.

Mepazine acetate is like mepazine hydrochloride except that it is suited for parenteral administration (intramuscular or intravenous). Dosage varies from 50 to 200 mg.

Thioridazine hydrochloride, U.S.P., B.P. (Mellaril)

This phenothiazine derivative is chemically similar to mepazine. It is not a highly potent tranquilizer. It does not exert an antiemetic effect, and it seems to have no effect on temperature regulation. It has a broad spectrum of useful antipsychotic activity and is considered by many to be a good all-round tranquilizer. It is believed to have the advantage of producing minimal extrapyramidal effects. However, patients taking large doses have been known to develop pigmentary retinopathy. Sudden death has been reported in some patients after prolonged usage of this drug.

Preparation, dosage, and administration. Thioridazine hydrochloride is available in 10-, 25-, 50-, 100-, and 200-mg. tablets and as a concentrate (30 mg. per milliliter) for oral administration. Dosage varies from 20 to 800 mg. daily. Dosage for this preparation as well as for other tranquilizers is adjusted to meet the needs of the individual.

Side effects and toxic effects. Drowsiness is a frequent side effect, especially after large doses. Many other side effects associated with therapy with the phenothiazine compounds have been seen after the administration of this drug, but on the whole, toxic effects are said to occur less often than after the administration of chlorpromazine. (For other side effects see discussion of phenothiazine derivatives, p. 347.)

353

Piperazine subgroup
Acetophenazine maleate, N.F. (Tindal)

Action and uses. Acetophenazine maleate is a member of the piperazine group of phenothiazine derivatives and may be effective in the management of patients with chronic brain syndrome. Large doses have been effective in the treatment of psychotic patients. It has limited usefulness in the treatment of patients whose anxiety is associated with psychosomatic conditions (peptic ulcer, hypertension). It is much less potent than other derivatives. It is more sedative and produces fewer extrapyramidal phenomena.

Preparation, dosage, and administration. Acetophenazine maleate is available for administration in tablets of 20 mg. only. It is not available for parenteral administration. The usual oral dosage is 40 to 80 mg. a day. In patients who have difficulty sleeping, the last tablet should be taken 1 hour before retiring.

Fluphenazine hydrochloride, N.F. (Permitil, Prolixin)

In terms of potency fluphenazine hydrochloride is one of the most active compounds and is considered more than twenty times as potent as chlorpromazine. It offers the advantage of sustained and prolonged action as an antipsychotic agent.

Preparation, dosage, and administration. Fluphenazine hydrochloride can be administered either orally or intramuscularly. An initial daily dose of 2.5 to 10 mg. is suggested for adults with psychotic conditions. The dosage may be gradually increased to 20 mg. a day; however, the usual maintenance dose is 1.5 to 5 mg. Elderly patients may require much less than the average amounts. Children should rarely receive more than 2 mg. per day. Oral preparations include a concentrate of 5 mg. per milliliter (Permitil); an elixir of 2.5 mg. per 5 ml. (Prolixin); 0.25-, 1-, 2.5-, 5-, and 10-mg. tablets (Permitil or Prolixin); and repeat-action tablets of 1 mg. (Permitil Chronotab). The intramuscular preparation is in a solution of 2.5 mg. per milliliter in 10-ml. containers.

Fluphenazine enanthate, N.F. (Prolixin Enanthate)

Fluphenazine enanthate is an esterified derivative of fluphenazine hydrochloride. It maintains all the properties and actions of the phenothiazines; however, it has gained increasing popularity because of its prolonged action. One injection of 25 mg. per milliliter solution maintains its action and effects for 1 to 3 weeks. This seems to facilitate its use with outpatients or individuals who might not otherwise be disposed to taking medication on a daily basis. Because of its potency and the high incidence of extrapyramidal symptoms, some physicians feel a concomitant treatment with antiparkinsonian agents is necessary. The risk of irreversible extrapyramidal symptoms seems to be the greatest in elderly female patients with organic brain disease or damage who have received fairly high dosages of phenothiazines for prolonged periods.

Perphenazine, N.F. (Trilafon)

Perphenazine is similar to chlorpromazine in action and clinical uses. Milligram for milligram it is said to be six times more potent than chlorpromazine. It has an antiemetic effect.

Preparation, dosage, and administration. Administration of perphenazine may be oral, rectal, intramuscular, and, occasionally, intravenous. The oral dosage for psychotic adults varies from 16 to 64 mg. daily given in two to four divided doses. It is marketed in solution for injection, 5 mg. per milliliter in 1- and 10-ml. containers; as a syrup of 2 mg. per 5 ml.; as a solution, 16 mg. per 5 ml.; and in tablets of 2, 4, 8, and 16 mg. Rectal suppositories are available in 2, 4, and 8 mg. Perphenazine should not be administered intravenously except during surgery to counteract retching, hiccoughs, and vomiting; this route is not recommended for psychiatric conditions.

Prochlorperazine, N.F. (Compazine)

Prochlorperazine is approximately four times as potent as chlorpromazine. It has a rapid and stimulating effect, which makes it useful in the treatment of psychomotor retardation, apathy, and withdrawal. It shares all the additional effects of the phenothiazines in antipsychotic activity. In small doses it has been effective in controlling nausea and vomiting associated with some somatic conditions.

Preparation, dosage, and administration. Prochlorperazine is administered rectally. The suggested dose for adults is one 25-mg. suppository twice daily. Suppositories are available in 2.5, 5, and 25 mg.

Prochlorperazine edisylate, **U.S.P. (Compazine Edisylate).** Administration may be oral in doses similar to those given for the maleate salt. Intramuscular injection is given of 10 to 20 mg., repeated at intervals of 1 to 6 hours, for control of psychotic symptoms. Intramuscular dose for adults with nonpsychiatric conditions is 5 to 10 mg., repeated once if necessary. It is available in solution for injection, 5 mg. per milliliter in 2- and 10-ml. containers; the solution concen-

trate contains 10 mg. per milliliter and the syrup contains 5 mg. per 5 ml.

Prochlorperazine maleate, **U.S.P. (Compazine Maleate).** This preparation is administered orally to psychotic adults. It is given initially in divided doses that range from 30 to 40 mg. daily. Dosage is gradually increased to 75 to 150 mg. a day. Tablets come in 5-, 10-, and 25-mg. strengths and sustained-release capsules of 10, 15, 30, and 75 mg.

Thiopropazate hydrochloride, N.F. (Dartal)

Thiopropazate hydrochloride shares its therapeutic effectiveness with prochlorperazine. It is useful in the management of psychotic symptoms marked by agitation and aggression.

Preparation, dosage, and administration. Thiopropazate hydrochloride is administered only through the oral route. The usual dose for adults with psychotic conditions is 10 mg. three times a day. The dosage may be increased to 100 mg. as a maximal dose to produce the desired effects. Increments or decreases in dosage are recommended at 3- or 4-day intervals at 10 mg. per day. Tablets of 5- and 10-mg. strengths are available.

Trifluoperazine hydrochloride, N.F., B.P. (Stelazine)

Trifluoperazine is fast acting and approximately ten times as active as chlorpromazine. It has been successful in stimulating patients with symptoms of psychomotor retardation, apathy, and withdrawal. Its use in psychoneurotic and psychosomatic conditions has not been established. It has been proved to be an effective antipsychotic agent.

Preparation, dosage, and administration. Trifluoperazine hydrochloride is available in concentrate solution of 10 mg. per milliliter and in 1-, 2-, 5-, and 10-mg. tablets for oral administration. A solution is also available for intramuscular injection, 2 mg. per milliliter in 10-ml. containers.

Dosage varies considerably, depending upon the severity of symptoms to be controlled. For mild anxiety reactions, oral dosage may range from 1 to 4 mg. daily. The dosage for patients with major psychosis may start at 2 to 5 mg. daily, but the optimum dosage may become 15 to 20 mg. daily. Some patients require as much as 40 mg. daily.

Other antipsychotic agents
Chlorprothixene, N.F. (Taractan)

Action and uses. Although chlorprothixene is not a phenothiazine, its action and effects are very similar to the phenothiazine compounds. It is used in similar conditions, and adverse reactions associated with phenothiazine therapy should be borne in mind when this agent is used. This compound is thought to be less likely to produce troublesome side effects such as extrapyramidal symptoms, agranulocytosis, and cholestatic hepatitis. However, a few incidences of these effects have been reported. This agent has also been reported to be useful as an antiemetic agent.

Preparation, dosage, and administration. Chlorprothixene is administered orally and intramuscularly. Oral dosages range from 30 to 600 mg. per day. The drug is administered orally in tablets of 10, 25, 50, and 100 mg. Intramuscular dosage for the acutely agitated patient with

a psychotic condition is 75 to 200 mg. per day; for treatment of nausea and vomiting 12.5 to 25 mg. seems to be adequate. Preparations for injection come in a solution of 12.5 mg. per milliliter in 2-ml. containers.

Haloperidol, N.F. (Haldol)

Action and uses. Haloperidol has recently been introduced in the United States as an antipsychotic agent. Research conducted in Europe in the area of anesthesia brought this compound into view as a possible antipsychotic agent. Subsequent use indicated its effectiveness in the control of hyperactivity associated with the manic phase. Extrapyramidal symptoms occur frequently and, as the manic phase becomes controlled, severe depressive elements may be seen in some patients, precipitating a suicide risk. Adverse reactions discussed earlier in regard to the phenothiazines also apply to this compound.

Preparation, dosage, and administration. Haloperidol is administered orally in tablets of 0.5, 1, and 2 mg. and as haloperidol concentrate of 2 mg. per milliliter. Initial dosages should be gradually increased in increments of 0.5 to 1 mg. every 3 days until the desired effects are attained. Daily doses greater than 15 mg. are not recommended.

■ Minor tranquilizers

Minor tranquilizers have been recommended for the treatment of symptoms associated with psychoneurotic and psychosomatic conditions. The advantage of their use in these conditions is their effect in allaying moderate anxiety states and the muscle tension associated with psychomotor agitation. Psychoneurotic conditions with severe disabling symptoms are treated more effectively with the stronger phenothiazine derivatives. In milder forms of psychoneuroses, the minor tranquilizers act as a valuable adjunct to psychotherapy by diminishing anxiety and tension associated with the treatment process.

The antianxiety agents are not recommended for the long-term treatment of psychotic conditions; however, large doses have been effective in controlling the psychomotor hyperexcitability of acute psychotic episodes. Chlordiazepoxide has been especially effective in treating hyperactive alcoholic patients with withdrawal reactions or delirium tremens. Most of the compounds in this group can be given alone or in conjunction with antispasmodics, analgesics, vasodilators, adrenal corticosteroids, and estrogens. They have been effective in relieving the symptoms of certain gastrointestinal, musculoskeletal, and cardiovascular disorders as well as menopausal discomforts. They differ in their sedative effects from barbiturates in that they

Table 16-3 Minor tranquilizers (antianxiety agents)

Generic name	Trade name	Side effects*	Average daily dosage range (mg.)
Phenothiazine group			
Promazine	Sparine	1-4, 6-12, 14	50 to 1500
Diphenylmethane group			
Hydroxyzine hydrochloride	Atarax	2-5, 9, 14, 15, 24, 27	50 to 400
Hydroxyzine pamoate	Vistaril	2-5, 9, 14, 15, 24, 27	50 to 400
Benactyzine	Suavitil	1-7, 9, 23, 33, 37, 38	3 to 10
Benzodiazepine group			
Chlordiazepoxide	Librium, Libritabs	1-3, 6, 7, 10-12, 15, 23, 29, 33, 34, 36	15 to 300
Diazepam	Valium	1-3, 5, 7, 10-12, 23, 34, 38	4 to 10
Oxazepam	Serax	2, 3, 9-11, 23, 32	30 to 200
Propanedol group			
Meprobamate	Equanil, Miltown	1-4, 7, 9, 10, 12, 14, 17, 23, 27, 28, 33-35	200 to 1200

Key to table
1. Anxiety or agitation
2. Sedation and sleep
3. Ataxia
4. Dry mouth
5. Blurred vision
6. Constipation
7. Dermatitis
8. Extrapyramidal symptoms
9. Hypotension
10. Blood dyscrasias
11. Jaundice
12. Convulsive seizures
13. Hypothermia
14. Antiemetic
15. Increased appetite
16. Tachycardia
17. Edema
18. Retinitis
19. Impotence
20. Nasal congestion
21. Anorexia
22. Polyuria
23. Nausea and/or vomiting
24. Bradycardia
25. Cutaneous flushing
26. Salivation
27. Increased gastric motility or diarrhea
28. Activation of peptic ulcer
29. Decreased libido
30. Increased gastric secretions
31. Miosis
32. Depressive symptoms
33. Mental confusion
34. Habituation
35. Hyperthermia
36. Menstrual irregularities
37. Mydriasis
38. Hallucinations

*Side effects here are not intended to be a complete account of possible adverse reactions.

do not produce a significant loss of mental acuity.

Chemical structure, site, and mechanism of action. The antianxiety agents share similar central depressant action, but their secondary central and peripheral effects vary. Chemically they can be divided according to the following subgroups: (1) phenothiazine derivatives, (2) diphenylmethanes, (3) benzodiazepines, and (4) propanedol. One action of these drugs that accounts for their antianxiety response is their depressive effect on the polysynaptic reflexes of the spinal cord. This effect suggests that their main mode of action is that of reducing skeletal muscle tension, which indirectly reduces the number of afferent proprioceptive impulses aggravating existing anxiety.

These drugs are thought to exert very little effect, if any, on the neocortex and neurotransmitter centers. However, their antianxiety action seems to parallel their depressant action on the limbic structures (septum, amygdala, and hippocampus). Since it has been postulated that the amygdala and the hippocampus influence behavior, the action of these drugs may inhibit their stimulation and thus inhibit the subsequent behavioral responses that they regulate. A similar reduction of sensitivity brought about by their depressant effect reduces reactions to stressful influences and stimuli. They have the ability to produce mild sedation without adversely affecting the level of consciousness or the quality of psychomotor performance.

Side effects and precautions. The minor tranquilizers are relatively safe when used in small dosages. They have fewer disabling side effects than the phenothiazine derivatives; however, numerous reports of untoward effects have appeared. Drowsiness, ataxia, dizziness, and headache occur occasionally after initial doses. Patients should be cautioned against driving an automobile, operating dangerous machinery, or performing tasks that require absolute precision, motor coordination, and mental alertness. Drowsiness, ataxia, and confusion are more commonly seen in the elderly. This can be avoided by gradually increasing the dosage until the desired effects are produced. Some patients have been known to exhibit mild forms of inappropriate behavior that were not related to their current condition after initial doses. Other signs of drug hypersensitivity have been noted such as rash, fever, chills, nausea, vomiting, and dry mouth. Blood dyscrasias and jaundice have been reported occasionally. Some of these drugs are habit-forming, and withdrawal of the drug may cause mild to severe withdrawal reactions including delirium and convulsions. Caution should be taken to avoid habituation of these drugs. Physicians should maintain close supervision of individuals who are taking these drugs for prolonged periods, especially individuals who have a history of alcoholism, drug addiction, or severe dependency problems. Overdosage with massive amounts of these drugs produces coma, shock, and death. Patients with a history of blood dyscrasias, impaired renal function, hepatic disease, or allergies should be evaluated carefully before the administration of these drugs is initiated, even though there have been relatively few reports of adverse effects in these conditions. Use of any drug in pregnancy or lactation requires that the potential benefit of the drug be weighed against its possible hazards to mother and child.

Phenothiazine compounds and antidepressant drugs that potentiate the action of other drugs should not be used concomitantly with the antianxiety agents.

Paradoxic reactions of rage, excitement, stimulation, hostility, confusion, and depersonalization have occurred when these agents have been administered to severely disturbed or psychotic patients.

Phenothiazine subgroup

Promazine hydrochloride, N.F., B.P. (Sparine Hydrochloride)

Promazine hydrochloride is perhaps the weakest of the phenothiazine derivatives. It has very little tendency to induce pseudoparkinsonism; however, it has the potential to manifest all the side effects common to the phenothiazine derivatives.

Preparation, dosage, and administration. Promazine hydrochloride is administered orally, intramuscularly, and intravenously. Oral administration is used whenever possible. The drug is marketed in solution for injection (25 mg. per milliliter for intramuscular or intravenous use; 50 mg. per milliliter for intramuscular use only); in tablets (10, 25, 50, 100, and 200 mg.); in syrup (10 mg. per 5 ml.); and in concentrates of 30 and 100 mg. per milliliter. When this drug is used intravenously it should be given in concentrations no greater than 25 mg. per milliliter. It should be administered slowly and should always be diluted. The dosage ranges from 10 to 1000 mg. per day. Initial dosages no larger than 50 mg. are recommended for inebriated patients because of this drug's potentiating effects.

Diphenylmethanes

Hydroxyzine hydrochloride, N.F. (Atarax); hydroxyzine pamoate, N.F. (Vistaril)

Hydroxyzine is an antianxiety agent that has been useful in the management of acute and chronic urticaria and other manifestations of allergic dermatoses. It has also been used as an antiemetic for the nausea and vomiting associated with pregnancy and motion sickness. It produces sedation preoperatively and postoperatively; however, it usually potentiates the action of opiates and barbiturates used during these periods, which necessitates reduction of their dosage.

Preparation, dosage, and administration. Both drugs may be administered orally, intravenously, and intramuscularly. The usual dosage for adults is 25 to 100 mg. given three or four times daily. Parenteral administration should be reserved for emergency situations only and oral dosages should be substituted as soon as possible.

Hydroxyzine hydrochloride comes in 10-, 25-, 50-, and 100-mg. tablets and in syrup, 10 mg. per 5 ml. It is also prepared in solution for injection, 25 and 50 mg. per milliliter.

Hydroxyzine pamoate is available in capsules of 25, 50, and 100 mg.; as a suspension of 25 mg. per 5 ml.; and in solutions for injection of 25 and 50 mg. per milliliter.

Benactyzine hydrochloride (Suavitil)

Benactyzine hydrochloride has been used in the treatment of mild psychoneurotic conditions. This drug has no apparent sedative or hypnotic action and tends to cause blocking of thought processes (apathy, indifference, and retarded mental activity). These actions differentiate it from other antianxiety agents.

Action and uses. This agent is an autonomic suppressant and is capable of blocking certain conditioned reflexes. Its use in the treatment of psychoneurotic conditions has not been widely accepted. Some patients experience a sense of unreality and an inability to concentrate, while others who manifest a frankly hostile attitude have been known to deteriorate considerably after the administration of this drug.

Precautions. This drug is contraindicated before electroshock therapy and in patients with glaucoma or benign prostatic hypertrophy.

Preparation, dosage, and administration. The oral route is used in the administration of this drug. Tablets are available in 1 and 5 mg. The

359

suggested initial dose is 1 mg. given three times daily for 2 or 3 days, with a gradual increment to 3 mg. three times a day until the desired effect is attained. Dosages over 10 mg. per day are undesirable.

Benzodiazepine group

Chlordiazepoxide hydrochloride, N.F. (Librium, Libritabs)

Action and uses. The actions and uses are similar to all antianxiety agents. Chlordiazepoxide has been effective in controlling the acute withdrawal symptoms of chronic alcoholic conditions (delirium tremens and agitation). However, since alcoholics in general are addiction-prone, caution should be exerted in its use for these patients over prolonged periods. It is known to have a muscle relaxant effect and has been beneficial in treating musculoskeletal conditions in which anxiety and tension intensify the symptoms. Its direct action in these instances is unknown and may well be the result of its sedative effect. It has found a wide range of uses as an antianxiety agent in nonpsychiatric settings, mainly for the control of mild to moderate anxiety associated with psychosomatic conditions. This drug should be limited to small dosages in elderly patients.

Preparation, dosage, and administration. This drug can be administered orally, intramuscularly, or intravenously. It is prepared as capsules of 5, 10, and 25 mg.; as tablets of 5, 10, and 25 mg.; and as a powder for injection of 100 mg. per ampule. The average daily dosage should not exceed 300 mg. The usual daily adult dosage for relief of mild to moderate anxiety is 15 to 40 mg. and 10 to 20 mg. for elderly or debilitated patients. This compound is excreted slowly and has a cumulative effect that should be ex-

pected after the first few days. In the patient with alcoholic agitation or delirium tremens, intramuscular injections initially may be as high as 50 to 100 mg.

Adverse reactions. Paradoxic reactions of rage, excitement, stimulation, hostility, confusion, and depersonalization have resulted from the administration of this drug to severely disturbed psychotic patients.

Diazepam, N.F. (Valium)

Diazepam is effective in the treatment of anxiety and tension related to organic or functional conditions. It has been found to be useful in treating mild to moderate depression occurring alone or with anxiety and tension. Because of its muscle relaxant properties, it is a useful adjunct in the treatment of muscle spasms (conditions such as cerebral palsy and athetosis).

Preparation, dosage, and administration. This drug is available in tablets of 2, 5, and 10 mg. and in 2-ml. capsules, 5 mg. per milliliter, for injection. Daily doses for adults range from 4 to 10 mg. Since this drug is excreted slowly, a cumulative effect can be expected after a few days of therapy.

Oxazepam, N.F. (Serax)

Oxazepam is closely related in its effects to chlordiazepoxide. It has been effective in the treatment of patients with anxiety, tension, and irritability associated with psychoneurotic conditions. It is said to be particularly valuable in the management of anxiety in elderly patients; however, scientific data have not validated this belief as yet.

Preparation, dosage, and administration. This drug is administered orally in capsules of 10, 15, and 30 mg. Daily doses range from 30 to 120 mg. for adults.

Propanedol compounds

Meprobamate, U.S.P., B.P. (Equanil, Miltown)

$$H_2N-\overset{\overset{\displaystyle O}{\|}}{C}-O-CH_2-\overset{\overset{\displaystyle C_3H_7}{|}}{\underset{\underset{\displaystyle CH_3}{|}}{C}}-CH_2O-\overset{\overset{\displaystyle O}{\|}}{C}-NH_2$$

Meprobamate is a synthetic drug that is chemically related to mephenesin, a skeletal muscle relaxant. As can be observed from the formula, the chemical structure differs markedly from that of reserpine or the phenothiazine derivatives. Meprobamate is a straight-chain aliphatic compound. It is a crystalline white powder with a bitter taste.

Action and result. The effects of meprobamate depend on the dosage employed. When used in large doses, as in animal experiments, the drug is not only an antianxiety agent but also a muscle relaxant and anticonvulsant. It acts as an interneuronal blocking agent and causes relaxation of skeletal muscle. It is also referred to as a centrally acting muscle relaxant. It is believed by some investigators, however, that meprobamate as employed in ordinary doses acts mainly as a sedative. Some even believe that its action under these circumstances does not differ significantly from that of phenobarbital.

Uses. Meprobamate has been effective in bringing about relief of anxiety and tension, abnormal fears, psychosomatic disorders, behavior disorders, and insomnia. It is not a potent hypnotic, but the relief of tension that it produces is conducive to sleep. Improvement after administration of this drug is usually characterized by decreased irritability, improved sense of well-being, and greater relaxation.

Preparation, dosage, and administration. Meprobamate is marketed in sustained-release capsules of 200 mg., in an oral suspension of 40 mg. per milliliter, and in tablets of 200 and 400 mg. It is administered orally. The usual adult dose is 400 mg. three or four times daily.

Side effects and toxic effects. Although meprobamate is not considered a toxic drug, it has been known to cause a number of side effects and untoward reactions. The more common reactions are allergic manifestations, such as skin rash, itching, and urticaria. This reaction is sometimes sufficiently severe to require the administration of a corticosteroid and cessation of administration, but the symptoms usually respond well to administration of one of the antihistaminic drugs. Evidence exists that both habituation and physical dependence can develop. Some patients seem to develop tolerance as well. Withdrawal symptoms, including convulsions, have been observed. Such symptoms are seen only after prolonged administration and abrupt discontinuance of administration.

Gradual withdrawal of meprobamate therapy is essential in the event that physical or psychic dependence develops.

◼ Antidepressants

The recent interest in psychotherapeutic agents useful for alleviating depressions has brought about a significant change in the treatment of these conditions. Depressive states appear to be unique to the human being and have been classified by psychiatrists as endogenous psychotic depressions and reactive depressions. Endogenous psychotic depressions are characterized by the absence of external causes for depression (death of a loved one, loss of employment, or debilitating illness), and the apparent grief and depression are of psychopathologic origin. Reactive depressions usually are abnormal depressive responses to environmental factors and are associated with emotional tension and instability. Psychomotor hyperexcitability (agitation) often occurs. Other behavioral manifestations characterizing depression are the expression of feelings of worthlessness, inadequacy, hopelessness, ambivalence, dependence,

361

guilt, and suicidal tendencies. Delusions are common, the content of which express self-accusatory and guilt feelings. Initiative is lost and the patient is apathetic. The eyes are often directed downward, the corners of the mouth sag, lower eyelids droop, and the skin on the forehead may be furrowed. Depression is usually accompanied by poor appetite, loss of weight, coated tongue, foul breath, and constipation. About 30 years ago depressed patients were treated with analeptic drugs, such as leptazol, to induce convulsions, which seemed to improve their condition. Later insulin was used to produce convulsions resulting from hypoglycemia. Electroconvulsive therapy (ECT) was developed and found to be much safer than the aforementioned treatments. Electroconvulsive therapy is still used today, specifically for the depressed patient with manifestations of agitation.

Short-acting neuromuscular blocking agents and barbiturates are used prior to these treatments to prevent damage to the patient's limbs during the convulsions. These convulsions are induced by passing an AC current, for a fraction of a second, through electrodes fixed to the scalp. It is thought that the cycle of events leading to the depressive symptoms is broken by the electric change that allows neuronal activity to return to normal. Electroconvulsive therapy has also been known to increase the free amines in the brain. The psychoactive drugs used in the treatment of depression have not replaced electroconvulsive treatment; however, they have occasionally been a valuable adjunct to this form of treatment. Other measures such as psychotherapy, reduction of environmental stresses, and milieu therapy should also accompany electroconvulsive therapy. The psychoactive drugs commonly used in the treatment of depression are the tricyclic compounds and the monamine oxidase inhibitors. All of these drugs appear to be most therapeutic in the treatment of endogenous depression. The monamine oxidase inhibitors have produced favorable results in both endogenous and reactive depressions. Favorable responses to these drugs include elevation of mood, increased physical activity and mental alertness, and improved appetite and sleep patterns, accompanied by a reduction of premorbid preoccupation and delusions.

The tricyclic compounds, the monamine oxidase inhibitors, and the amphetamines provide relief for some of the symptomatology related to depression. However, they do not treat the underlying causes of depression. They may relieve the depressive effects of temporary situational stress, but caution should be exerted to avoid using these drugs without a thorough evaluation of causative factors. The amphetamines act to stimulate the nervous system directly with little or no monamine oxidase inhibition. Their action is brief (3 to 4 hours) and is frequently followed by a letdown. Hypertensive effect and reduced appetite are additional effects. Dependency can result from prolonged use of amphetamines. The difficulties involved with the use of these drugs should be weighed against the expected therapeutic results.

Since the amphetamines are not widely used for the treatment of depression, further discussion of antidepressant drugs will be confined to the tricyclic compounds and monamine oxidase inhibitors.

Monamine oxidase inhibitors (psychic energizers)

Site and mechanism of action. One of the most significant discoveries in psychopharmacology was the accidental discovery of isoniazid, an antitubercular drug that produced euphoria, appetite stimulation, nervousness, insomnia, and orthostatic hypotension. It was abandoned in the treatment of tuberculosis because of these side effects. In the mid-1950's it became known for its monamine oxidase inhibitory function. At about the same time the function of serotonin was defined in its relationship to central neuronal activity.

Serotonin is thought to be in high concentrations in certain areas of the brain. It functions in the stimulation of the ganglion cells and releases epinephrine (adrenaline) from the adrenal medulla.

Monamine oxidase is an enzyme found in the brain, blood platelets, liver, spleen, and kidneys and is responsible for destroying body chemicals such as the neurohormones epinephrine, norepinephrine, and serotonin. Monamine oxidase inhibitors produce their central stimulation indirectly by inhibiting the monamine oxidase enzyme. By decreasing or modifying the rate of destruction of the neurohormones, these inhibitors increase their longevity. This activates the ergotropic (adrenergic) centers and results in an increase in the sympathetic tone within the hypothalamus, which initiates an arousal behavior pattern. Increased levels of the serotonin metabolite in the cerebrospinal fluid of depressed patients have been reported. There is much evidence to suggest that the degree of psychomotor activity of the cortex is dependent upon the balance of serotonin, epinephrine, and norepinephrine. Monamine oxidase inhibitors act to increase psychomotor activity, increase appetite, and potentiate other drugs. They also act to prevent the release of epinephrine from storage sites in the adrenergic neurons with subsequent inhibition of uptake of the amines into these sites. This accounts for the delayed action of monamine oxidase inhibitors (1 to 2 weeks), since it takes time to increase the amine levels to effect behavior change.

Side effects and precautions. The occurrence of a wide variety of side effects after the administration of the monamine oxidase inhibitors has been cause for concern among most authorities. These side effects have often resulted in fatalities and/or severe medical conditions (see Table 16-4). The existence of hypertension is a contraindication for the use of monamine oxidase inhibitors.

The suicidal tendencies present in the patient's condition may compound his nursing care problem because of the delayed effect of these drugs in relieving suicidal tendencies. This presents an additional risk to the patient during initial phases of drug therapy. The nurse should be alert to the possibility of any impulsive ingestion of these substances.

Since the risk of suicide is frequently near the end of the depressive cycle, attention should be given to the possibility of suicidal attempts during this period. Overt patient behavior may

Table 16-4 Frequent side effects from monamine oxidase inhibitors*

Postural hypertension	Nausea	Tachycardia
Dizziness	Vomiting	Edema
Restlessness	Diarrhea	Palpitation
Insomnia	Abdominal pain	Impotence
Weakness	Constipation	Headaches (not
Drowsiness	Anorexia	from rise
Anxiety	Dryness of mouth	in blood
Agitation	Blurred vision	pressure)
Manic episodes	Chills	

*These side effects can usually be relieved with reduction of dosage. Most of the side effects reported are related to failure to recognize the cumulative action of these drugs with subsequent incorrect dosage. It is important to reduce dosage as soon as improvement of symptoms is observed to avoid precipitating side effects caused by the cumulative action of the drug.

indicate a remission of depressive symptomatology; however, this may be caused by drug action and not by alleviation of pathologic processes. Antidepressants should generally be continued for several months after the remission of symptoms and should never be discontinued abruptly, since a relapse may occur. Most authorities feel that these drugs should only be used in a psychiatric hospital setting for patients who are severely depressed and have serious suicidal tendencies.

Paradoxic hypertension. Paradoxic hypertension has been reported during the use of the monamine oxidase inhibitors. Hypertensive crises have occurred after the ingestion of certain foods or beverages that are rich in amines (such as tyramine) or in amino acids (such as tyrosine) that may be decarboxylated in the body to form pressor amines normally inactivated by monamine oxidase (see Chapter 9). Foods and beverages known to contain these amines are cheese (especially strong or aged varieties), bananas, avocados, beer, and Chianti wine. Drugs containing pressor agents (certain cold remedies, hay fever preparations, or anorexiants) should be avoided. The physician may instruct the patient initially in these precautions; however, nurses must provide the continued reassurance, support, and reinforcement of these restrictions.

During hospitalization, the depressed patient's anorexia may prompt well-meaning family members or friends to bring supplementary foods to the patient or a little wine to stimulate his appetite. Careful nursing observation during visiting hours and instruction of the family regarding these restrictions can avoid serious consequences. Communication with the hospital dietitian may also prevent these foods from appearing on the patient's hospital menu. As the patient's depression lifts or if electroconvulsive therapy is used concomitantly with drug therapy, reinstruction of the patient may be necessary. These foods and beverages should not be ingested for at least 2 to 3 weeks after discontinuance of drug therapy.

Intracranial bleeding associated with paradoxic hypertension and severe occipital headache that may radiate frontally has been known to occur. Symptoms that accompany this condition are stiffness or soreness of the neck, nausea, vomiting, sweating (with fever or with cold clammy skin), dilated pupils, photophobia, constricting chest pain, tachycardia, and bradycardia or other arrhythmias. Discontinuation of the drug immediately is recommended when any of these signs and symptoms occur. Fever is managed by external cooling and either phentolamine mesylate (5 mg. intravenously) or pentolinium tartrate (3 mg. intravenously) is used to control hypertension.

Hepatic toxicity. Jaundice and leukopenia are known side effects of the monamine oxidase inhibitor compounds. It is recommended that patients receiving these drugs have periodic blood cell counts and tests of hepatic function.

The monamine oxidase inhibitor compounds should be used with caution in patients who have a history of impaired kidney function or epilepsy. Overactive, overstimulated, or agitated patients usually do not respond well to these drugs. These drugs are also contraindicated in many other conditions (see Table 16-5).

Table 16-5 Contraindicated conditions for administration of monamine oxidase inhibitors

Cardiovascular disease
Cardiac decompensation
Congestive heart failure
Cerebrovascular disorders
Pheochromocytoma
Hepatic disease
Blood dyscrasias—anemia, hepatitis
Pregnancy
Angina pectoris*
Epilepsy
Kidney dysfunction
Depressions accompanying:
  Chronic brain syndromes
  Schizophrenia
  Alcoholism
  Drug addiction
Conditions manifesting:
  Overactivity
  Overstimulation
  Agitation

*May suppress the warning signal of pain. Should be used with caution.

The effects of alcohol, barbiturates, and morphine-like analgesics are potentiated by the monamine oxidase inhibitors thiazide and phenothiazine. Compounds that lower blood pressure should be administered carefully in conjunction with monamine oxidase inhibitors. Reduction of dosage of both agents may be necessary.

The monamine oxidase inhibitors should not be given with amitriptyline, desipramine, imipramine, or nortriptyline. These combinations may produce severe atropine-like reactions, tremors, hyperpyrexia, generalized clonic convulsions, delirium, and even death. Other monamine oxidase inhibitors should not be administered concomitantly or soon after the administration of another agent in this group. Such combinations also produce hypertensive crises or convulsive seizures. A 2- to 3-week interval

It is recommended that the lowest effective dosage be used.

Nialamide, N.F., B.P. (Niamid)

Nialamide is an effective antidepressant used primarily in the management of endogenous depressions. It is also known to be effective in some reactive depressions.

Preparation, dosage, and administration. The only route of administration of nialamide is oral. It is marketed in tablets of 25 and 100 mg. strength. The usual dosage is 75 to 200 mg. a day in single or divided dosage with maintenance dosages as low as 12.5 mg. every other day.

Isocarboxazid, N.F. (Marplan)

Isocarboxazid is administered to patients with symptoms of depression and withdrawal, and seems to be an effective antidepressant in selected psychiatric conditions. It is useful in treating the depressed phases of anxiety or the depression of manic-depressive syndromes, as well as certain involutional, obsessive, and disassociative reactions. It does not appear to be as effective as electroconvulsive therapy in the treatment of severe psychiatric disorders. Its effects are cumulative and require 3 to 4 weeks of therapy before improvement is noted.

Preparation, dosage, and administration. Isocarboxazid is administered orally in 10-mg. tablets. The proposed initial dosage is 30 mg. daily given in single or divided doses. The average daily dosage should not exceed 30 mg., and the suggested maintenance dose is 10 to 20 mg. a day or less.

Table 16-6 Drug incompatibility with administration of monamine oxidase inhibitors

Monamine oxidase inhibitors

Generic name	Trade name	Incompatible drugs
Isocarboxazid	Marplan	Combination of any monamine oxidase inhibitor
		Other antidepressants
Nialamide	Niamid	Amphetamines
		Alcohol
		Barbiturates
		Morphine-like analgesics
		Cocaine, procaine, ether
Phenelzine	Nardil	Phenothiazine compounds
		Methyldopa, dopamine
		Tryptophan
		Antihypertensives
		Antiparkinsonian drugs
		Insulin
Tranylcypromine	Parnate	Thiazide diuretics
		Sympathomimetic amines —phenylephrine

should follow the discontinuance of any of these drugs before another is started (Table 16-6).

Tranylcypromine sulfate, N.F., B.P. (Parnate)

Tranylcypromine sulfate should be reserved for use in patients with severe depressive conditions who have not responded to electroconvulsive treatment, or in whom such therapy is contraindicated, and for patients who do not respond to other antidepressant therapy.

Preparation, dosage, and administration. Tranylcypromine sulfate is administered orally in 10-mg. tablets. Initial dosage per day is 20 mg. with gradual increments not to exceed 60 mg.

Phenelzine sulfate, U.S.P., B.P. (Nardil)

$$\text{C}_6\text{H}_5-\text{CH}_2-\text{CH}_2-\text{NH}-\text{NH}_2$$

Phenelzine sulfate is useful in the treatment of both endogenous and reactive depressions. There is a latent period before onset of action, and the maximal effect occurs within 1 or 2 weeks.

Preparation, dosage, and administration. Phenelzine sulfate is administered orally in 15-mg. tablets. The initial daily dosage is 15 mg. three times a day. The average daily dosage should not exceed 75 mg. and maintenance dosages as low as 15 mg. every other day have been reported.

Anticholinergic antidepressants (psychostimulants, cholinergic depressants)

Anticholinergic drugs bear close structural resemblance to the phenothiazine compounds. They produce potent antidepressant and mild tranquilizing effects. Investigations were conducted to develop an antidepressant drug that did not affect monamine oxidase and therefore produced fewer side effects than the monamine oxidase inhibitors. The anticholinergic antidepressants have advantages that prompt many physicians to favor these drugs over monamine oxidase inhibitors. There is very little risk of excessive stimulation (hypertensive crises and so on). There have been no reports of irreversible retinal or liver damage, and there is a higher incidence of successful therapy. Imipramine is still the most widely used antidepressant drug for endogenous psychotic depression.

Site and mechanism of action. This group of antidepressant drugs does not inhibit monamine oxidase or change the concentration of serotonin or other amines in the brain. Their mechanism of action is not known. However, it is hypothesized that the action of the drugs may be to affect brain amine levels by interfering with their uptake into the binding sites. The drugs have atropine-like, antihistamine, antiadrenaline, and antiserotonin actions. Autonomic

Table 16-7 Common reversible side effects from anticholinergic antidepressants*

Muscular hypertension	Excessive perspiration
Drowsiness	Dizziness
Dry mouth	Excitement
Tremor	Headache
Fatigue	Numbness and tingling
Weakness	of extremities
Blurring of vision	Epigastric distress
Constipation	Nausea, vomiting
Urinary retention	Insomnia
Tachycardia	Headache
Orthostatic hypotension	Flushing
Anorexia	Impotence
Generalized convulsions	Mild extrapyramidal
	stimulation

*These reactions can be relieved or controlled by reducing drug dosage.

Table 16-8 Drug incompatibility with administration of anticholinergic antidepressants

Tricyclic compounds

Generic name	Trade name	Incompatible drugs
Imipramine	Tofranil	Monamine oxidase inhibitors
		Alcohol
		Barbiturates
Desipramine	Norpramin	Control nervous system
		depressants
		Thiazide diuretics
Nortriptyline	Aventyl	Vasodilators
		Anticholinergic agents
Amitriptyline	Elavil	Thyroid

Table 16-9 Conditions that contraindicate administration of anticholinergic antidepressants

Glaucoma	Angina pectoris
Kidney disease	Congestive heart failure
Pyloric stenosis	Paroxysmal tachycardia
Epilepsy	Benign prostatic hypertrophy
Overactivity, overstimulation, or agitation	Before surgery

side effects associated with these actions occur but are not serious and usually subside as treatment continues. They have only a slight depressant effect on the central nervous system.

Side effects and precautions. This group of drugs has been known to produce a wide variety of side effects. The most common side effects (Table 16-7) can be controlled by reduction of dosage. Skin rash has occurred and usually requires discontinuance of medication for relief.

First-degree atrioventricular block is one of the most serious side effects produced by these tricyclic compounds. The action of these drugs tends to prolong atrioventricular conduction time and, therefore, is contraindicated in patients with congestive heart failure, angina pectoris, or paroxysmal tachycardia.

Although there have been few reports of blood dyscrasias or liver damage, it is recommended that frequent liver function and blood counts be done when these drugs are administered in large doses over long periods of time.

Other agents may potentiate the action of these drugs (Table 16-8), and their use in selected conditions is contraindicated (Table 16-9).

The risk of suicide is the same with anticholinergic drugs as it is with monamine oxidase inhibitors. The precautions regarding continued administration and abrupt discontinuance of the drug are also the same as for monamine oxidase inhibitors.

The anticholinergic antidepressants should not be administered concomitantly with the monamine oxidase inhibitors. They should not be given less than 2 or 3 weeks after the discontinuance of the monamine oxidase inhibitors.

These drugs should not be given in the late afternoon or evening because their stimulating effect can cause insomnia.

Imipramine hydrochloride, U.S.P. (Tofranil)

Imipramine hydrochloride is an effective antidepressant drug that has found wide acceptance in the treatment of endogenous and reactive depressions. Initial improvement in depressive symptomatology may be noted within the first few days; however, maximal benefit is usually achieved in 1 to 2 weeks.

Preparation, dosage, and administration. Imipramine hydrochloride is administered orally in tablets of 10 and 25 mg. and intramuscularly in solution for injection of 12.5 mg. per milliliter. Initial dosage for hospitalized patients is 100 to 150 mg. daily in divided dosages. Gradual increment of dosage is suggested until the desired effects are observed; however, these dosages should not exceed 300 mg. per day. Outpatients may receive 75 mg. initial daily dosages in divided amounts and with gradual increments not exceeding 200 mg. per day. Reduction of dosage to a maintenance level of 50 to 150 mg. per day may be indicated as soon as desirable effects are noted. High dosages are not recommended for the elderly or adolescent patient.

Amitriptyline hydrochloride, U.S.P., B.P. (Elavil Hydrochloride)

Amitriptyline hydrochloride produces antidepressant and mild tranquilizing effects. Its uses and actions are as effective as imipramine in the treatment of endogenous depression. Reports indicate that this drug is effective in neurotic patients with excessive ruminative tendencies related to their depression; however, it has not been successful with other neurotic depressive conditions.

Preparation, dosage, and administration. Amitriptyline hydrochloride is marketed for oral administration in 10-, 25- and 50-mg. tablets and for intramuscular uses in solution for injection, 10 mg. per milliliter. The usual initial dosage is 75 mg. a day in divided doses with gradual increments to 150 mg. per day. Additional doses

367

may be added to the bedtime dosage in 25-mg. increments if this is necessary. Elderly and adolescent patients may find 10 mg. three times a day with 20 mg. at bedtime a satisfactory regimen.

Desipramine hydrochloride, N.F. (Norpramin, Pertofrane)

$$CH_2CH_2CH_2NHCH_3$$

Desipramine hydrochloride is thought to be as useful as imipramine in the treatment of endogenous and reactive depressions. Desipramine hydrochloride has been identified as the primary active metabolite of imipramine and, therefore, is thought to influence the action of imipramine. The effectiveness of this drug may be reduced after a few weeks in some patients.

Preparation, dosage, and administration. Desipramine hydrochloride is only administered orally in 25-mg. capsules (Pertofrane) and in 25-mg. tablets (Norpramin). The average initial dosage per day is 75 to 150 mg. given in divided doses. When the desired results are achieved the average daily maintenance dose is 50 to 100 mg. in divided doses. Daily doses should not exceed 200 mg.

Nortriptyline hydrochloride, N.F., B.P. (Aventyl Hydrochloride)

$$CHCH_2CH_2NHCH_3$$

Nortriptyline hydrochloride is as effective as amitriptyline in the treatment of endogenous and reactive depressions and produces similar results. Patients who respond to this drug ordinarily indicate a change in behavior within the first week of therapy. The effectiveness of nortriptyline as an adjunct to electroconvulsive treatment is unpredictable. It is used as an antidepressant and has some tranquilizing action.

Preparation, dosage, and administration. Nortriptyline hydrochloride is administered orally in 10- and 25-mg. capsules and as a liquid of 10 mg. per 5 ml. The average initial daily dosage is 20 to 40 mg. given in divided dosages. This dosage may be continued for 5 to 7 days or until the desired results are attained. Reduction of dosage may then be necessary for maintenance therapy. Usual maintenance doses are from 30 to 75 mg. per day. Daily dosages should not exceed 100 mg. per day as adverse side effects may occur.

Questions

for study and review

1 Traditionally neurophysiologists have identified each part of the nervous system by allocating specific functions to certain areas of the brain. Recent research has indicated the following change in this perspective:
   a. The brain functions as a result of the independent action of specific areas contributing to total body functioning.
   b. The brain is now considered to be an intricate system of specific structures to which unique functions can easily be allocated.
   c. The brain acts as a unit.
   d. The interrelationship of various structures of the brain are extremely intricate; however, recent research has identified specific functions for each structure.
2 The highest mental activities—recognition, memory, intelligence, imagination, and creative thought—are attributed to:
   a. the cerebral cortex only
   b. interaction of the thalamus, epithalamus, and hypothalamus
   c. interaction among the cerebral cortex, thalamus, epithalamus, and hypothalamus
   d. interraction of the cerebral cortex and hypothalamus
3 The reticular activating system appears to function by:
   a. alerting the cerebral cortex to emotion
   b. alerting the cerebral cortex to emotional stimuli from the environment
   c. alerting the hypothalamus and cerebral cortex to somatic sensory experience
   d. alerting the cerebral cortex to sensory experience and originating emotional reactions associated with somatic sensory experience
4 The term *psychotropic drugs* encompasses which of the following drug groups?

a. major and minor tranquilizers, antidepressants

b. major tranquilizers and antidepressants

c. major tranquilizers and rauwolfia drugs

d. antidepressants, amphetamines, and minor tranquilizers

5 Nurses should be aware of the physician's criteria for selection of psychotropic drugs:

a. so she can look up the side effects of the drugs

b. so she can evaluate the patient's response to drug therapy in light of the physician's goals for selecting the drug

c. so she can interpret these criteria to the patient

d. so she can observe and report any side effects that may occur

6 Rauwolfia alkaloids are considered antipsychotic agents but are not widely used as a tranquilizer because:

a. large single doses cause severe side effects

b. large single doses are expensive

c. their therapeutic action is delayed for several weeks

d. prolonged administration causes hypertension

7 Most of the antipsychotic drugs are phenothiazine derivatives. Commonalities can be identified because:

a. the type of action is essentially similar with all phenothiazine derivatives

b. individual compounds vary chiefly in their potency

c. individual compounds vary slightly in the nature and severity of their side effects

d. individual compounds vary only in number and kind of adverse reactions reported

8 The phenothiazines are thought to have which of the following modes of action on the central nervous system?

a. blocking of adrenergic synapses of the ergotrophic system

b. depression of the reticular activating system

c. stimulation of central sympathetic activity

d. acetylcholine blockage

9 The most important pharmacologic characteristics of the phenothiazines are:

a. antipsychotic activity

b. failure of large doses to produce coma or anesthesia

c. extrapyramidal symptoms

d. causes physical and psychogenic dependence with large doses

10 The phenothiazine derivatives are used to reduce psychotic symptoms and, therefore, are useful in the treatment of acute and chronic psychoses. The nurse may notice which of the following behavior changes after the administration of the phenothiazine drugs?

a. drooling, ataxia, akinesia

b. weight gain, dry mouth, blurred vision

c. increased motor activity, less frequent hallucinatory experiences

d. reduction of agitation, destructive or combative behavior, delusions

11 Measures known to be effective in the management of the most common side effects resulting from phenothiazine administration are:

a. reduction of dosage or discontinuance of drug

b. administration of antiparkinsonian drugs

c. intravenous administration of levarterenol (Levophed)

d. administration of milk of magnesia, Cepacol mouthwash, and reduction diet

12 A common side effect known to occur with the administration of large dosages of phenothiazine derivatives is photosensitivity. The nurse's responsibility in avoiding unnecessary complications is:

a. instructing the family and patient in the appropriate preventive measures

b. reporting the occurrence of dark purplish brown skin pigmentations to the doctor

c. providing protective clothing and/or keeping the patient out of the sun

d. restricting or limiting the patient's outdoor activities during times of the day when solar exposure would be maximal

13 Extrapyramidal symptoms may appear after the administration of phenothiazine drugs. The most severe and distressing extrapyramidal symptom experienced by the patient is:

a. ataxia   c. akinesia

b. dyskinesia   d. akathisia

14 Antiparkinsonian agents most commonly used are:

a. Cogentin, Kemadrin, Artane, and Akineton

b. Benadryl

c. Coramine, Dexedrine, Ritalin

d. Lorfan, Nalline, Megimide

15 Phenothiazine drugs are known to potentiate the action of other drugs. Phenothiazine drugs should be given cautiously to persons who are known to have ingested which of the following substances?

a. alcoholic beverages

b. barbiturates

c. morphine-like analgesics

d. monamine oxidase inhibiting drugs

16 Which of the following precautions should be observed when administering chlorpromazine hydrochloride intramuscularly?

a. Slowly rotate the vial from left to right in order to diffuse the white crystalline powder before drawing the medication up for injection.

b. Avoid getting solution for injection into contact with skin or eyes.

c. Inject the medication slowly, taking care to administer only 1 ml. per injection site.

d. Massage the injection site to avoid local irritation.

17 Indicate the generic name for each of the following antipsychotic agents and number according to approximate incidence of extrapyramidal symptoms:

Tindal _____ _____

Stelazine _____ _____

Compazine _____ _____

Thorazine _____ _____

Mellaril _____ _____

Prolixin _____ _____

Vesprin _____ _____

18 Minor tranquilizers are thought to be effective for which of the following conditions?
   a. some gastrointestinal, musculoskeletal, and cardio-vascular conditions
   b. acute psychotic episodes marked by agitation
   c. psychosomatic or psychoneurotic conditions
   d. withdrawal reactions or delirium tremens

19 Minor tranquilizers differ from barbiturates in their sedative effects because:
   a. minor tranquilizers have longer duration of action
   b. minor tranquilizers have fewer side effects
   c. minor tranquilizers have little effect on levels of awareness
   d. minor tranquilizers tend to cause disorganization of thought processes in high dosages

20 The mechanism of action that best explains the effect minor tranquilizers have in controlling the anxiety related to psychoneurotic conditions is:
   a. their central depressant action on the neocortex
   b. their stimulation of the different proprioceptive impulses
   c. their depressive effects on the polysynaptic reflexes of the spinal cord
   d. their stimulation of adrenergic binding sites

21 Patients taking any of the minor tranquilizers are cautioned against activities such as driving an automobile, operating dangerous machinery, or performing tasks requiring precision because of the common occurrence of which of the following side effects?
   a. drowsiness, ataxia, dizziness, headache
   b. rash, fever, dry mouth, chills
   c. nausea, vomiting, confusion
   d. jaundice, increased white blood counts, diarrhea

22 Occasionally patients taking chlordiazepoxide hydrochloride (Librium) experience a paradoxic reaction, which means:
   a. anxiety increases instead of decreasing
   b. rage, hostility, confusion, and depersonalization result
   c. shock and respiratory embarrassment occurs
   d. nothing happens at all

23 Meprobamate (Equanil, Miltown) is no longer considered an effective antianxiety agent because:
   a. it is too expensive for use in a long-term treatment program
   b. it is habit-forming
   c. it precipitates exaggerated behavior patterns
   d. its usefulness is restricted to middle-aged persons with psychoneurotic behavior patterns

24 Antidepressant drug therapy is used in the treatment of endogenous or reactive depressions. Its effectiveness is thought to be most helpful in:
   a. relief of the symptomatology of depression
   b. treating depressive effects resulting from temporary situational stress
   c. treating the underlying causes of reactive depression
   d. relief of the underlying causes of endogenous depressions

25 Monamine oxidase is an enzyme found in the brain, blood platelets, liver, spleen, and kidneys and is responsible for:
   a. stimulation of ganglion cells releasing adrenaline from the adrenal medulla
   b. destroying body chemicals such as the neurohormones epinephrine and norepinephrine
   c. increasing the sympathetic tone within the hypothalamus
   d. restoring the balance of serotonin, epinephrine, and norepinephrine in cortex

26 Monamine oxidase inhibiting drugs act:
   a. to decrease high concentrations of serotonin in the brain
   b. to stimulate sympathetic tone in the hypothalamus
   c. to increase the activity of the trophotropic centers

27 Check the following side effects most commonly seen with the administration of monamine oxidase inhibitors.
   a. chest pain   g. drowsiness
   b. severe occipital   h. dilated pupils
      headache   i. vomiting
   c. dizziness   j. diarrhea
   d. drowsiness   k. agitation
   e. seizures   l. dry mouth
   f. postural hypotension

28 Which of the following drugs should not be given in conjunction with monamine oxidase inhibitors?
   a. Tofranil   e. Elavil
   b. Norpramin   f. Darvon compound
   c. chloral hydrate   g. Aventyl
   d. Enovid   h. elixir terpin hydrate

29 Anticholinergic antidepressant drugs are more widely used in the treatment of depression for the following reasons:
   a. There is very little risk of hypertension crises.
   b. There is a higher incidence of successful therapy.
   c. They have fewer side effects than monamine oxidase inhibitors.
   d. They are less expensive.

30 Monamine oxidase inhibitors and anticholinergic antidepressants should only be administered in the hospital setting because:
   a. the hospital diet controls the incidence of ingestion of contraband food or beverages
   b. their side effects are serious
   c. patients taking these medications should not be operating dangerous machinery
   d. the risk of suicide is high

References

Benson, W. M., Schiele, B. C., and Thomas, C.: Tranquilizing and antidepressive drugs, Springfield, Ill., 1962, Charles C Thomas, Publisher.

Bowman, W. C., Rand, M. J., and West, G. B.: Textbook of pharmacology, Oxford, England, 1968, Blackwell Scientific Publications.

Brill, H., and others, editors: Neuropsychopharmacology, International Congress Series No. 129, Excerpta Medica Foundation, New York, 1967.

Cole, J. O., and Wittenborn, J. R.: Psychotherapy of depression, Springfield, Ill., 1966, Charles C Thomas, Publisher.

Freed, H.: The chemistry and therapy of behavior disorders in children, Springfield, Ill., 1962, Charles C Thomas, Publisher.

Goodman, L. A., and Gilman, A.: The pharmacological basis of therapeutics, ed. 4, New York, 1970, The Macmillan Company.

Gordon, M., editor: Psychopharmacological agents, vol. II, New York, 1967, Academic Press, Inc.

Hess, W. R.: The biology of the mind, Chicago, 1964, The University of Chicago Press.

Hess, W. R.: Diencephalon, London, 1954, William Heinemann Medical Books Ltd.

Hoch, P. H.: Drug therapy. In Arieti, S., editor: The American handbook of psychiatry, New York, 1959, Basic Books.

Hollister, L. E.: Overdose of psychotherapeutic drugs, Clin. Pharmacol. Ther. 7:142, 1966.

Klotz, M.: The role of drugs in community psychiatry, Brit. J. Soc. Psych. 2(1):12-21, 1967-1968.

Krantz, J. C., Jr., and Carr, C. J.: The pharmacologic principles of medical practice, ed. 7, Baltimore, 1969, The Williams & Wilkins Co.

Mark, J.: Scientific basis of drug therapy, New York, 1965, Pergamon Press, Inc.

Morris, R. W.: Pharm. Index, Vol. 6, May 1964.

Morris, R. W.: Pharm. Index, Vol. 7, March 1965.

Morris, R. W.: Pharm. Index, Vol. 8, May 1966.

Morris, R. W.: Pharm. Index, Vol. 9, June 1967.

Morris, R. W.: Pharm. Index, Vol. 10, May 1968.

Netter, F. H.: CIBA collection of medical illustrations: vol. I. A compilation of paintings on the normal and pathologic anatomy of the nervous system, New York, 1962, CIBA Pharmaceutical Co.

Ranson, S. W., and Clark, S. L.: The anatomy of the nervous system, ed. 10, Philadelphia, 1959, W. B. Saunders Co.

17 Drug abuse

Although most drugs are prescribed and administered with a high degree of discrimination, all drugs can potentially be misused or abused. The prescription of drugs without adequate exploration of the patient's presenting complaint, for example, is representative of drug misuse by a physician. Prolonged and unsupervised administration of drugs for symptomatic relief is another such example. In general, drug misuse refers to nonspecific or indiscriminate use of drugs. Drug abuse, on the other hand, refers to self-medication or self-administration of a drug in chronically excessive quantities, resulting in psychic and/or physical dependence, functional impairment, and deviation from approved social norms.

Drug abuse is neither a new nor a recent phenomenon. Rather, it has been known throughout history as one expression of man's search for relief of his physical and psychosocial problems. Indeed, one recent study suggests that epidemics of drug abuse such as we are now experiencing have occurred throughout man's history. Contemporary drug abuse has attained prominence as an issue with moral, legal, social, intrapsychic, and medical aspects and as an issue that is difficult to examine objectively. In order to fulfill her professional responsibility to society in relation to this pressing social issue, the nurse needs current knowledge about drugs most frequently abused, reasons for drug abuse, crisis intervention in relation to drug abuse, and knowledge of regional treatment facilities to which she can refer patients either for emergency care or for long-term treatment.

It is beyond the scope of this chapter to explore all aspects of drug abuse in depth. Instead this chapter will focus upon the psychopharmacologic aspects of drug abuse. However, the nurse is urged to explore other aspects of this complex phenomenon independently in order to achieve a more holistic frame of reference.

■ Drug dependence

In the past, drug abuse was defined in terms of *habituation* and *addiction*. These terms, however, have been used in so many ways that no longer is there any consensus regarding their definitions. Moreover, the terms *habituation* and *addiction* are nonspecific in that they do not describe the nature of the problem. Characteristics of drug abuse will vary according to the particular agent abused, and different drugs will have entirely different patterns of dependence and different characteristics of withdrawal. In an attempt to reduce the conceptual ambiguity of "habituation" and "addiction," the World Health Organization in 1964 suggested that the use of these terms be replaced by the concepts of *physical* and *psychic dependence*. Its statement regarding this issue reads as follows:

Drug dependence is a state of psychic or physical dependence or both on a drug arising in a person following administration of that drug on a periodic or continuous basis. The characteristics of such a state will vary with the agent involved and these characteristics must always be made clear by designating the particular type of drug dependence in each specific case—e.g., drug dependence of the barbiturate type, of the morphine type...*

Physical dependence to a drug refers to an adaptive physiologic state that occurs after prolonged administration of that drug and that manifests itself by intense physical disturbances (withdrawal symptoms) when the drug's administration is discontinued. That is, physical dependence on a drug can be demonstrated only by a production of a withdrawal syndrome. This syndrome can be relieved by readministering the drug or by administering a pharmacologically related drug. (Drugs are cross-dependent when they are mutually capable of relieving withdrawal symptoms that result from the withdrawal of either drug.) Closely related to physical dependence is the production of drug tolerance with a tendency to increase the drug dose.

Psychic dependence, by contrast, is a state of emotional reliance upon a drug in order to maintain a drug-induced state that, to the involved individual, is preferable to a drug-free state of being. The manifestations of psychic dependence can range from a mild desire for a drug, to "craving," and to compulsive use. Either type of dependence can exist independently of one another or simultaneously. Both types of dependence can potentially lead to a compulsive pattern of drug use that, Goodman and Gilman state,* is characterized by a narrow, almost exclusive, and highly invested involvement in procuring and using the drug.

■ Etiologic factors in drug abuse

A characteristic common to most drugs that cause dependence is that they are initially taken because the individual believes that a desirable pharmacologic effect will result. In order to cause dependence, then, a drug must produce favorable, pleasant, unusual, or desirable effects. The person who is dependent on a drug has found something that will give him relief from his problems, and the drug is generally used as an adjustive mechanism. Since very few drugs without central nervous system effects are abused, one of the predominant factors contributing to drug abuse appears to be intrapsychic and motivated by a desire to alter one's state of mind. This desire may derive from a number of conditions. Pleasure-seeking behavior often seems to be an etiologic factor in drug abuse and may represent escape from inner tensions, a search for euphoria, an attempt to explore unknown aspects of cognitive function, or an attempt to discover one's self, among other goals. More specifically, some psychologic hypotheses have been advanced in relation to persons prone to use drugs as escape mechanisms. Descriptions of potentially drug-dependent personalities have included characteristics of strong psychologic dependence, low threshold of frustration, fear of failure, and feelings of inadequacy. Other authorities dispute the "addiction-prone" personality hypothesis, maintaining that everyone has the potential to become dependent on something.

Other factors related to the development of drug abuse may derive from social conditions.

---

*Wilder Smith, A. E.: The drug users: the psychopharmacology of turning on, Wheaton, Ill., 1969, Harold Shaw Publishers, p. 109.

*Goodman, L. S., and Gilman, A.: The pharmacological basis of therapeutics, ed. 4, New York, 1970, The Macmillan Company.

In today's society, anxiety, tension, insomnia, and other manifestations of stress are common. Many people seek relief by self-medication with either over-the-counter agents or prescription drugs. According to Fort,* dependence upon chemically active substances to treat some problems of living has spread to almost all areas of life. Indeed, Fort cites, our society has in many ways accepted the slogan of "better living through chemistry." Drugs are available for almost every purpose—to help us to relax, to help us to awake, to promote concentration, and to prevent conception, for example—and their use is generally socially acceptable.

Other authorities have cited social factors such as peer-group pressure, the permissiveness of our present generation, and the rapid cultural-technologic changes occurring in our society as other factors influencing drug abuse. Drug abuse may also symbolize alienation from society and rejection of society's mores.

■ Types of drugs abused

All drugs have some abuse potential, and some sources indicate that drug abuse may be more related to the personality of the user than to the drug itself. Perhaps among the most frequently abused chemically active substances are the xanthines and theobromines, which are contained in beverages such as coffee, tea, chocolate, and colas. Although these substances are rarely perceived as drugs by the lay public, they do produce mild stimulant and euphoriant effects and their use may lead to psychic dependence. Nicotine and ethyl alcohol are also frequently abused, with consequent physical and psychic dependence. Atropine, epinephrine, steroids, belladonna alkaloids, and cardiac glycosides are examples of other drugs that may induce altered states of perception, thought, and feeling as a result of their prolonged and concentrated therapeutic use.

However, as previously indicated, few drugs without central nervous system effects are abused. Therefore, the four major categories of commonly abused drugs are narcotics, general

*Fort, J.: The pleasure seekers, Indianapolis, 1969, The Bobbs-Merrill Company.

central nervous system depressants, central nervous system stimulants, and other mind-altering drugs that have been variably classified as hallucinogenic, psychotomimetic, and psychedelic. When used for prolonged periods of time, depressant drugs like the opiates, barbiturates, and alcohol generally produce both physical and psychic dependence. Stimulant drugs like the amphetamines and cocaine tend to produce psychic but not physical dependence. The other mind-altering drugs have variable and, at this time, questionable dependence-producing qualities, but it seems generally agreed that they all produce psychic dependence.

Before proceeding, it is necessary to differentiate among the terms *hallucinogenic, psychotomimetic,* and *psychedelic.* Although all three terms have been utilized interchangeably, they have some distinct differences. *Hallucinogenic* refers to the tendency of a drug to produce auditory and/or visual hallucinations. Hallucinogenic effects, however, are neither a uniform nor a primary property of all consciousness-altering drugs, and the term should be used with discrimination. The term *psychotomimetic* refers to the ability of a drug to chemically induce a psychotic state that mimics a "natural" psychosis. Again, this term must be used with discrimination when referring to mind-altering drugs, since not all induce psychosis. The term *psychedelic* was originally intended to be a nonjudgmental adjective referring to the "mind-manifesting" properties of a drug, that is, to a drug's ability to effect states of consciousness an individual would not usually experience. It has, however, become more ambiguous in definition and has acquired some valuational connotations. It may be used to refer to self-administered mind-altering drugs for their subjective effects of inducing states of altered perception, thought, and feeling. Because of such imprecision of terms, the broad term *mind-altering* will be used throughout this chapter.

■ Pharmacologic basis of physical drug dependence

Several hypotheses exist that attempt to explain the pharmacologic basis of the physiologic adaptation that occurs in tolerance and physical drug dependence.

According to Martin's pharmacologic redundancy theory,* there are two or more pathways mediating the physiologic functions influenced by the opiates. Martin assumes that morphine sulfate interrupts one of the redundant pathways but does not interrupt the other. This results in hypertrophy of the uninterrupted pathway (pathway A), which then assumes the functions mediated by the interrupted pathway (pathway B). Therefore, tolerance to morphine is the result of hypertrophy of pathway A. When the drug is withdrawn, pathway B resumes its normal level of excitability but, because pathway A is still overfunctioning, the total system then functions at a level that is higher than the predrug state of function. This exaggerated function, Martin states, is the hyperexcitability that is characteristic of the abstinence syndrome.

Collier, on the other hand, hypothesizes that tissue may contain two types of receptors for particular drugs. One of these types, the "pharmacologic receptors," produces a pharmacologic response when contact is made with the drug. The other receptors are "silent receptors" that elicit no response. The development of drug tolerance results from a change in the number and production of these receptor types, the pharmacologic receptors decreasing in number and the silent receptors increasing in number.

From a third frame of reference, Crossland† states that physical adaptation to depressant drugs simply involves an increase in the amount of excitatory transmitter that is adequate to overcome the drug-depressed condition of the nerve cells. When the drug is withdrawn, hyperexcitability (abstinence symptoms) occurs if the nerve cells return to normal condition more rapidly than the transmitter supply.

Although all of these and other theories of

physical drug dependence are in hypothetical stages and are still being researched, they generally seem to agree that, in a state of dependence, a condition of latent hyperexcitability develops in the cells of the central nervous system following frequent and prolonged administration of depressant drugs.

■ Altered states of consciousness produced by abused drugs

The effects of various mind-altering drugs are unpredictable and highly variable. The same drug in the same dose may produce quite disparate effects in two different individuals. The primary factors influencing the effects of any drug are generally defined as: (1) the pharmacologic properties of the drug itself; (2) the personality of the user; (3) the environment of the user; and (4) the interaction of these three components. The effects of mind-altering drugs, specifically, are also thought to be related to the purity of the drug used (drugs transferred illegally are frequently adulterated, or "cut," with other substances), the underlying psychopathology in the user, and the age of the user. Many drug users, for example, are adolescents who are dealing with the intrapsychic problems accompanying this stage of maturation. The tenuous emotional equilibrium of this stage may particularly predispose to negative reactions to mind-altering drugs. The effects of mind-altering drugs also appear to be particularly subject to the user's mood, expectations, and social environment. Most adverse reactions to marihuana, for example, are said to occur in novice users, since they may enter the experience with a mental set of fear.

Adequate preparation for the drug experience, therefore, is a significant factor influencing the nature of that experience. In addition, the presence or lack of a supportive environment (particularly the presence and guidance of a trusted and knowledgeable person) and the presence or lack of an opportunity to understand and to reintegrate the experience following recovery from the drug are variables that may influence a drug experience either positively or negatively.

---

*Phillipson, R. V., editor: Modern trends in drug dependence and alcoholism, London, 1970, Butterworth & Co. (Publishers) Ltd.

†Crossland, J.: Lewis's pharmacology, ed. 4, Baltimore, 1970, The William & Wilkins Co.

In describing the phenomenon of the "psychedelic" experience, Houston* identifies some general effects that are commonly observed and experienced after the administration of mind-altering drugs. Among the most common and repeated effects she identifies the following: changes in auditory, visual, olfactory, tactile, gustatory, and kinesthetic perception; changes in body image; changes in experiencing time and space; changes in rate and content of thought; abrupt and frequent changes in mood and affect; heightened suggestibility; possible occurrence of depersonalization and ego dissolution; possible activation of repressed materials; awareness of internal organs and body processes; multiple and fragmentized consciousness; concern with philosophic, cosmologic, and religious questions; perception of a world released from its normal ordering; a sense of capacity to communicate better through nonverbal means; and feelings of empathy.

Houston states that these are not the only effects of psychedelic drugs but that this description should serve to convey some idea of their mind-altering effects. She goes on to categorize the effects of these drugs into four major levels of consciousness as follows:

1 Sensory level. The drug user may experience a great variety of sensory awareness, including heightened awareness of visual phenomena, such as colors, lines, textures, and spatial relationships. This sensory awareness may also be focused upon internal processes of the body. It may be pleasant heightened awareness or a frightening one. Often, Houston states, it is the only alteration in consciousness the drug user experiences.
2 Recollective-analytic level. In this level of altered consciousness, the drug user is described as experiencing psychologic involution and introspection and engaging in self-analysis of personal problems, values, and potentialities. Emergence of unconscious material may occur and the drug user may experience regression.

In an unsupportive context or in a context of latent psychosis, this experience may result in an acute panic psychosis. With an appropriate, predetermined mental set and knowledgeable guidance, Houston states, the experience may be therapeutic.

3 Symbolic level. At this level of consciousness, the drug user is described as experiencing rich symbolism in which his life expands beyond the particular-personal orientation to a personal-universal orientation, and the individual may see his life in terms of a guiding pattern or goal.
4 Integral level. The experience of this level of consciousness is described as extremely rare and is characterized as being similar to religious and mystic experiences in which profound and fundamental value and behavior changes occur or in which "self-actualization" occurs.

Houston's categorization provides a conceptual tool for comprehending experiences with mind-altering drugs, although it is by no means the only frame of reference to apply to the drug experience. Again, it must be emphasized that (1) expanding and continuing research is necessary to validate information regarding drug abuse and (2) at this time the illicit drug experience appears to have as much (if not more) potential for being frightening and negative as it has for being pleasant and constructive.

Central nervous system depressants

Cannabis drugs

The cannabis drugs are derived from the leaves, stem, fruiting tops, and resin of the female hemp plant *Cannabis sativa*. The potency of the active ingredient, tetrahydrocannabinol ($\triangle^9$-THC), is greatest in the resin of the plant and seems to vary according to the climatic conditions under which the plant is grown. In the United States, the plant generally grows wild rather than being cultivated and thus is generally low in potency.

---

* Houston, J.: Phenomenology of the psychedelic experience. In Hicks, R. E., and Fink, P. J.: Psychedelic drugs, Hahnemann symposium, New York, 1969, Grune and Stratton, Inc., pp. 1-7.

Tetrahydrocannabinol (Δ^9-THC)

Preparations. Marihuana and hashish are the most common forms of cannabis drugs used in the United States. Hashish refers to the powdered form of the plant's resin, which is five to eight times as potent as marihuana. Other forms of cannabis drugs used in different parts of the world include "bhang," "ganja," and "charas," which are commonly used in India and which correspond, respectively, to American marihuana, hashish, and unadulterated resin. In Morocco, "kif" is used, while in South America, a cannabis drug often used is called "dagga."

Mode of administration. Cannabis drugs may be absorbed when administered by oral, subcutaneous, or pulmonary routes but are most potent when inhaled. Either the pure resin or the dried leaves of the cannabis plant may be smoked in pipes or cigarettes. Because the smoke is acrid and irritating, some users prefer to smoke marihuana through a water pipe. The smoke is deeply inhaled and retained in the lungs as long as possible in order to achieve maximum saturation of the absorbing surface. Powdered hashish and marihuana may also be mixed with foods, a mode of administration that delays the drug's absorption. The effects of smoking are rapid and generally last 2 to 3 hours, while the effects of the orally ingested drug may not begin for several hours.

Mechanism of action. All of the cannabis drugs seem to act as central nervous system depressants, their "high" resulting from depression of higher brain centers and consequent release of lower centers from inhibitory influence. While there is some controversy regarding their classification, the cannabis drugs are not narcotics and are more frequently classified as sedative-hypnotic-anesthetics or psychedelic drugs.

Like the sedative-hypnotics, they appear to depress the ascending reticular activating system and, as their dosage increases, their effects will proceed from relief of anxiety, disinhibition, and excitement to anesthesia. If dosage is high enough, respiratory and vasomotor depression and collapse may occur.

Little is known about the metabolism of the active principle found in cannabis extracts. Research has yielded some marihuana homologs and analogs (such as synhexyl), which should permit standardization of dosage and yield more information regarding structure-activity relationships of the cannabis drugs.

Effects. The drugs have mind-altering properties and induce an anxiety-free state of relaxation characterized by a feeling of extreme well-being. Perceptions of time and space are distorted; ideas flow freely and disconnectedly; there may be interruptions in thought that are blanks or gaps similar to "epileptic absence"; and there may be states of inwardness and/or occasional excitement in the form of hilarity. Hallucinations can occur with high doses of the drug but are generally reported to be pleasant. There is little controlled research with these drugs, but some experiments suggest some impaired decision-making and psychometric performance is related to the use of these drugs. The drug experience is highly subjective and the presence of an altered state of consciousness may not be perceived by the novice until he is sensitized to it by his colleagues.

The incidence of adverse reactions to marihuana appears to be low. Minor side effects include immediate tachycardia and delayed bradycardia, delayed hypotension, conjunctival vascular congestion, dryness of the mouth and throat, hyperphagia, delayed gastrointestinal disturbances, and possible vasovagal syncope. More serious side effects that may occur are psychologic and include fear, panic, feelings of paranoia, disorientation, memory loss, confusional states, and a variety of perceptual alterations. Moreover, marihuana has been known to precipitate acute psychotic reactions in poorly organized personalities. The incidence of adverse effects appears to be highest in novice users of the drug. However these adverse effects generally appear to be short-lived and self-limiting.

Apparently psychic dependence and tolerance to marihuana develop but not physiologic dependence.

The effects of prolonged abuse of marihuana have not yet been scientifically proved. However, there seems to be some indication that amotivational states, apathy, memory problems, and some loss of mental acuity may occur. Physiologically, the possibility of chronic, long-term use of marihuana cigarettes leading to chronic bronchitis and emphysema cannot be discounted.

There has also been some question regarding the use of marihuana leading to the use of opiates, a progression termed the "stepping-stone" theory. This theory, however, appears somewhat controversial and some authorities state that any progression in drug use stems from personality and environmental factors rather than from the pharmacologic properties of marihuana. The multiple drug use theory lends support to this hypothesis, stating that a person predisposed to abuse one drug is also likely to abuse other, and perhaps stronger, drugs.

Withdrawal symptoms. Since marihuana is not known to produce physical dependence, there appear to be no physiologic withdrawal symptoms associated with discontinuation of its use. Some restlessness, anxiety, irritability, and insomnia may be associated with withdrawal of the drug, but these symptoms are generally mild and of short duration.

Opiates

The opium derivatives comprise the most abused narcotics, although some other narcotics are also abused. The pharmacologic types of drugs that cause dependence similar to that produced by the opiates include the morphine group (heroin, Dilaudid, codeine), the morphinon group (racemorphan, levorphanol), the meperidine group (Demerol, Nisentil), and the methadone group. Of the opiates, heroin, codeine, and morphine are most often abused, heroin (diacetylmorphine) being the most potent of the three.

Mode of administration. The opium derivatives generally appear as a white powder and can be administered through the percutaneous route (absorption through the mucous membranes) by sniffing, in the form of subcutaneous injections (known in street language as "skin popping"), or directly intravenously ("mainlining"). The rate of absorption is correspondingly increased, with "mainlining" producing almost immediate drug effects.

Mechanism of action and effects. The opium derivatives, being narcotics, act as central nervous system depressants, probably acting on the sensory cortex, psychic or higher centers, and thalami. Because these drugs elevate mood, relieve fear and anxiety, and produce feelings of peace and tranquility, they are particularly likely to lead to physical and psychic dependence. Rapid intravenous injection of these drugs produces warm, flushing sensations described as being similar to sexual orgasm. This is followed by a soothing state that seems to be best characterized as a state of complete drive satiation. The individual "high" on opiates feels no need to satisfy drives for basic biologic needs and is often described as being "on the nod" — drowsy, content, and euphoric. The drugs do not produce hallucinogenic or psychotomimetic effects.

Physical dependence upon heroin is evident in the withdrawal syndrome that develops if the drug is withheld and in the marked tolerance that develops with continued use of the drug. Also, because persons dependent upon heroin so frequently feel satiated, physical, emotional, and social deterioration often occurs. The individuals may feel little need for food and become grossly malnourished and weak. Preoccupation with obtaining the drug makes participation in the usual social and vocational aspects of life difficult, if not impossible. While the drug craving grows, tolerance to the drug is also marked and, eventually, the motivation for using the drug becomes oriented more to the avoidance of withdrawal symptoms and less to the achievement of euphoria.

Withdrawal symptoms. Symptoms of withdrawal from heroin are autonomic in origin and appear within 8 hours after the last dose in individuals who are physically dependent. They may originally be manifest as restlessness, chills and hot flashes, pilomotor erection on the skin (which gave rise to the term *cold turkey*), nasal secretions, drowsiness, lacrimation, sneezing, yawning, cramping of the abdomen, the back, and the lower extremities (the latter probably resulted in the phrase "kick the habit"), vomiting and diarrhea, perspiration, muscular twitching, and a craving for the drug. Such symptoms are usually followed by a restless sleep known as "yen" from which the patient may awaken irritable, weak, and depressed.

Occasionally, withdrawal symptoms are severe enough to result in cardiovascular collapse. If withdrawal is untreated, it may continue for up to 7 to 10 days, after which the physical dependence of the body upon the presence of opiates is eventually lost. Psychic dependence continues for a longer period; some authorities claim it continues forever.

Treatment of opiate dependence

Withdrawal programs. Generally, opiate withdrawal is a difficult task, with repeated relapses to drug abuse expected. Abrupt and complete withdrawal ("cold turkey") can be accomplished but is generally avoided as a dangerous and inhumane approach. Therapeutic withdrawal from an opiate may be somewhat more comfortably achieved by successively tapering the drug's dosage over a period of several days. A currently preferred method is immediate withdrawal with concurrent substitution of methadone hydrochloride, a program pioneered by Drs. Vincent Dale and Marie Nyswander. Methadone hydrochloride is a synthetic opiate analgesic that, by virtue of cross-tolerance, permits effective substitution of methadone dependence for heroin dependence. Its effectiveness against heroin dependence results from its ability to block the euphoriant effects of heroin and the craving for the drug without producing heroin's deleterious physical and mental effects. As long as methadone is administered, the individual will not experience the "kick" from a dose of heroin. When properly administered, methadone allows the individual to function with vigilance and without intellectual or emotional impairment. Methadone is taken orally, generally in daily doses of 100 to 180 mg. in a "carrier" of cherry syrup, orange juice, or the like. In its eighteenth report, the W.H.O. Expert Committee on Drug Dependence defined methadone maintenance as follows: "Methadone maintenance is the continuing daily oral administration of methadone under adequate medical supervision, the dose being adjusted to (a) prevent the occurrence of abstinence phenomena (b) suppress partially or completely any continuous preoccupation with the taking of drugs of the morphine-type and (c) establish a sufficient degree of tolerance and cross tolerance to blunt or suppress the acute effects of such agents."* Because the injection procedure of administering heroin ("fixing") itself may be one factor in producing dependence, the oral administration of methadone discourages dependence upon injections. Methadone is also available in pill form and this form is known as dolophine.

Methadone dependence does occur, but it is less serious than heroin dependence and withdrawal symptoms are less severe. Methadone withdrawal programs generally include supplemental rehabilitation techniques such as vocational and social rehabilitation. After the individual has functioned free of heroin for a sufficient period of time, secured steady employment, and readjusted his life style, he theoretically can be withdrawn from methadone maintenance. Some treatment centers report having accomplished withdrawal from methadone through the use of chlorpromazine, while others maintain that the drug may need to be taken indefinitely. Whether the latter can be avoided is still being researched.

Opiate antagonists. Some drugs, such as nalorphine (Nalline), levallorphan (Lorfan), and cyclazocine, are opiate antagonists and block or diminish the effects of concurrently adminis-

*Council on Mental Health: Narcotics and medical practice, J.A.M.A. **218**(4):578-583, 1971.

tered opiates, thereby facilitating withdrawal. These drugs are also useful in counteracting the respiratory depression found in narcotic overdose.

Therapeutic community programs. Therapeutic community programs include programs such as group psychotherapy, self-help approaches such as Synanon, and halfway houses. Because persons withdrawing from drugs frequently cannot make the transition easily, groups of persons who have decided to abstain from drug use can meet or live together in an attempt to support and guide one another through this transition. Ultimately, an individual should emerge from such a program with sufficient personal growth and appropriate support systems so that he will be able to manage his life satisfactorily without resorting to drug abuse.

Narcotic maintenance. In a number of countries, notably Great Britain, physicians have been permitted to prescribe opiates to persons who have a history of intractable dependence, thereby maintaining them and preventing withdrawal symptoms. Prescriptions are presently issued only through designated hospitals and only through the National Health Service. When such a system is implemented appropriately, it appears that the drug user can feel normal, function normally, and will seldom seek supplemental or illicit sources of drugs. There are, however, several reasons why such programs sometimes do not operate effectively and may be abused. Allowing the patient to determine his own dose of the drug or supplying the drug in such form and quantity that it can be easily resold or misused are examples of the ways in which such systems can be abused.

The choice of withdrawal program is partly influenced by the following factors: the patient's physical condition; the duration of drug dependence; the type of drug being taken and its daily dose; motivation for drug abuse; motivation for withdrawal; and whether the patient is also dependent on other drugs. In some instances, depending on these factors, opiate withdrawal may need to be accomplished within a hospital and with close medical supervision.

In identifying criteria for evaluating opiate withdrawal, the Council on Mental Health emphasizes that recovery from dependence of the morphine type is not to be equated with cure. Regardless of repeated relapses to drug abuse, therapeutic programs should continue. Progress in withdrawal may be indicated by progressively longer periods of abstinence from opiates without resort to the use of other psychoactive drugs and by the patient's growing confidence in his ability to function effectively without drugs.

Ethyl alcohol

Ethyl alcohol is one of the most abused drugs in the world and, contrary to popular opinion, is not a stimulant. Rather, it is a primary and continuous depressant of the central nervous system.

Mode of administration and pharmacodynamics. Ethyl alcohol is ingested orally and is well absorbed from the stomach and intestines. Distribution to all tissues including the brain is rapid. The drug is metabolized in the liver to acetaldehyde at the rate of 10 to 20 ml. per hour. Ninety percent is metabolized; 5% is excreted through the lungs and 5% through the kidneys.

Mechanism of action. Ethyl alcohol acts by depressing the reticular activating system, which is thought to be largely responsible for integration of central nervous system activity.

Effects. The drug can foster a pseudostimulant effect that is a consequence of hyperactivity of various parts of the brain that have been suddenly released from the inhibitory control of the cortex. Some of the first mental processes affected are those that depend on this control. Further effects of alcohol on the central nervous system are proportionately related to blood concentrations of alcohol. Memory, concentration, and finer discrimination abilities are successively lost with higher drug concentrations. Emotional lability may result with sensory-motor disturbances following. Incoordination may be accompanied by slurred speech and followed by stupor as the drug continues to cause irregular descending depression of the central nervous system. Large doses of alcohol will produce anesthesia, which may be followed by medullary paralysis.

Physiologically, ethyl alcohol causes diuresis because of depressed secretion of antidiuretic hormone and vasodilatation as a result of depression of the vasomotor center.

Repeated and prolonged use of large doses of ethyl alcohol results in the development of marked tolerance and physical and psychic dependence. Malnutrition may result, because while alcohol contains calories, it contains no vitamins. Cirrhosis of the liver, gastritis, peripheral polyneuropathy, portal hypertension, and lowered resistance to disease are also common adverse effects of dependence of the ethyl alcohol type.

Another significant and potentially adverse effect of alcohol lies in the fact that it potentiates the actions of many drugs and may, therefore, be instrumental in many drug fatalities.

Withdrawal symptoms. The intensity of the ethyl alcohol withdrawal syndrome depends upon the duration of dependence on the drug and the degree of intoxication. Generally, within a few hours after the last dose of alcohol, the physically dependent person begins to experience weakness, tremulousness, anxiety, gastrointestinal disturbances, and hyperreflexia. Within 24 hours, acute alcoholic hallucinosis results, followed by disorientation, confusion, and delusional thinking. Convulsive seizures may occur and death from cardiovascular collapse may occur at the height of the withdrawal syndrome. If the person lives, recovery from the syndrome is complete by the fifth or seventh day of abstinence.

Treatment of the abrupt withdrawal syndrome may include the administration of longer-acting depressant drugs, such as pentobarbitone or paraldehyde, if the patient is seen in early stages of delirium tremens, when withdrawal is severe. Once the withdrawal symptoms are controlled, the drug dosage can be safely and progressively reduced at a rate that prevents the development of further symptoms.

Long-term treatment of alcohol dependence includes methods similar to treatment of dependence of the opiate type, such as halfway houses and other therapeutic communities like Alcoholics Anonymous.

Aversion therapy is also utilized in treatment of alcohol dependence and involves the administration of drugs to prevent complete metabolism of alcohol, thereby causing unpleasant physical symptoms. Drugs such as emetine, apomorphine, and disulfiram are used as adjuncts in the treatment of chronic alcoholism. If ethyl alcohol is administered after treatment with any of these drugs, the "aldehyde syndrome" is produced, with resulting bodily vasodilatation, hypotension, pulsating headache, nausea, vomiting, diaphoresis, thirst, chest pain, vertigo, weakness, and blurred vision. If the patient wishes to avoid the experience of this symptom, he must not ingest alcohol.

Barbiturates

Although it is not generally known by the lay public, the barbiturates and some nonbarbiturate sedative-hypnotics can cause physical as well as psychic dependence. It appears that short-acting barbiturates, in addition to drugs like glutethimide (Doriden), chloral hydrate, paraldehyde, and methyprylon (Noludar), are most likely to produce physical dependence, possibly because they produce more sudden and more forceful desired effects.

Because these drugs have been more extensively described in previous chapters, mechanism of action and effects will not be explored. Rather, the focus of this section will relate to acute intoxication and withdrawal syndromes resulting from dependence on these drugs.

Both the acute and chronic effects of barbiturate intoxication resemble those of alcoholic intoxication. Manifestations may include emotional lability, muscular incoordination, difficulty in cognitive processes, and sedation. Toxic doses lead to stupor and respiratory depression. The reasons for barbiturate abuse are similar to those of ethyl alcohol abuse—both drugs produce disinhibition and mild euphoria.

The withdrawal syndrome accompanying cessation of barbiturate and previously identified nonbarbiturate hypnotic administration has been termed one of the most dangerous in the field of drug abuse. It may begin with weakness, tremulousness, restlessness, anxiety, insomnia, gastrointestinal disturbances, and orthostatic hypotension. Within the first 24 hours, the patient may be too weak to get out of bed. Symptoms may progress to confusion, delirium, and hallucinations. In addition, major convulsive seizures are more common in barbiturate withdrawal than in alcohol withdrawal. Agitation and hyperthermia may lead to exhaustion, cardiovascular collapse, and death. If the withdrawal syndrome is untreated, it generally ends by the eighth day of drug abstinence and its end is generally preceded by prolonged sleep. It is recommended that patients experiencing barbiturate withdrawal be hospitalized because, even when the syndrome appears mild, it may herald impending convulsions and cardiovascular collapse.

Treatment of barbiturate withdrawal generally consists of substitution of the drug with a longer-acting barbiturate such as pentobarbitone, which is then slowly tapered over a period of several weeks until it is completely withdrawn.

Minor tranquilizers

The fact that the use of tranquilizers can lead to psychic dependence is well known. Less well known is the fact that the use of these drugs can also produce physical dependence similar to dependence of the barbiturate type.

Phenothiazine type tranquilizers, while not known to produce physical dependence, will result in anxiety, insomnia, and gastrointestinal disturbances if abruptly withdrawn. Drugs such as meprobamate, diazepam (Valium), and chlordiazepoxide (Librium), however, will frequently manifest withdrawal syndromes marked by the occurrence of major convulsions.

Central nervous system stimulants

Amphetamines

It is of interest to note that persons who are amphetamine abusers often begin the cycle of abuse inadvertently. Amphetamine dependence often begins as infrequent use of the drug to stay awake (such as by college students studying for exams, night shift workers, or overambitious achievement-oriented persons) or use of the drug for appetite control purposes. Although the use of the drug often begins for legitimate purposes and with legitimate prescription, its exhilarating effects may become so attractive as to lead to high rates of dependence.

Mechanism of action. The amphetamines are synthetic sympathomimetic amines that are chemically and pharmacologically related to epinephrine and norepinephrine. The exact mechanism by which amphetamines act is unknown, but they result in central nervous system stimulation, probably by stimulating the reticular activating system.

Preparations. Chemically, there are three types of amphetamines: salts of racemic amphetamines, dextroamphetamines, and methamphetamines, all of which vary in degree of potency and peripheral effects. Dextroamphetamine is said to have fewest peripheral effects, such as hypertension and tachycardia.

Other agents that have been called "psychotomimetic amphetamines" include dimethyltryptamine (DMT), dimethoxymethyl amphetamine (DOM), and diethyltryptamine (DET). These drugs seem to span the line between the amphetamines and lysergic acid diethylamide in producing their effects. DMT and DET produce short (1 to 2 hours) psychotomimetic reactions that are characterized by more pronounced autonomic nervous system effects than those produced by LSD. DOM (also called STP for Dr. Timothy Leary's slogan "serenity, tranquility, and peace" and for the brand name of a motor oil additive that promises added power) appears to produce longer psychotomimetic reactions (16 to 72 hours) with much more intense physiologic effects than the other two drugs.

Effects. The amphetamines are most commonly abused because they produce an elevation of mood, a reduction of fatigue, a sense of increased alertness, and "invigorating aggressiveness." It must be noted that amphetamines do not create extra physical or mental energy—

rather, they promote expenditure of present resources, sometimes to the hazardous point of fatigue that is often unrecognized. Intravenous injection results in marked euphoria, an orgasmic feeling known as the "flash" or "rush," a sense of great physical strength and capacity, and a sense of "crystal-clear" thinking. The user feels little or no need for rest, sleep, or food and may continually engage in vigorous activity that he may perceive as exhilarating and creative. To an objective observer, inefficient, stereotyped, and repetitious behavior is common during an amphetamine "high," and the drug user may engage in perseverating behavior such as repeatedly reconstructing mechanical devices. Depending on the dosage of the drug taken (as much as 1500 mg. is known to have been injected in one dose by long-term users), the individual may experience a "run" of variable length, perhaps for several days. Some amphetamine users will force themselves to lie down and to close their eyes for a few hours during such a "run" and will also "force-feed" themselves in an attempt to prolong the "run." Termination of the drug's use may result from a variety of factors, such as exhaustion, fright, or inability to obtain more of the drug. Withdrawal of the drug is followed by long periods of sleep. Upon awaking, the individual often feels hungry, extremely lethargic, and profoundly depressed, a phenomenon known as "crashing." This phenomenon may be very severe, and the risk of suicide must be considered.

The stimulant properties of the amphetamines can cause dramatic cardiorespiratory effects, such as tachycardia, dyspnea, and chest pain. Users of amphetamines may panic because of association of these signs and symptoms with those of a myocardial infarction. To deal with these disturbing symptoms, amphetamine users often utilize depressants or "downers." Some drugs, such as Dexamyl (dextroamphetamine sulfate and amobarbital) combine a central nervous system stimulant with a central nervous system depressant in an attempt to minimize the overstimulation produced by the amphetamine ingredient.

Amphetamines are also said to be psychotomimetic drugs. Although there is some conflicting evidence regarding the etiology of amphetamine psychosis, it is claimed that heavy users may develop psychosis characterized by delusions of persecution, paranoia, and fully formed visual and auditory hallucinations. Some authorities suggest that these phenomena may be related to the insomnia produced by prolonged amphetamine abuse because sleep deprivation, in and of itself, leads to psychologic disturbance such as deterioration in performance, misperceptions, and hallucinations.

In addition marked tolerance to amphetamines occurs.

Withdrawal symptoms. Although amphetamines do not appear to lead to physical dependence, as identified by the criterion of a characteristic and reproducible withdrawal syndrome, some authorities maintain that the signs and symptoms characteristic of "crashing" may constitute just such a syndrome.

Cocaine

A potent central nervous system stimulant, cocaine is therapeutically used largely as a local anesthetic, since it is likely to cause toxic side effects when administered by other routes. When it is used for its stimulant effects, it produces euphoria and increased expenditure of energy similar to that produced by the amphetamines and may even lead to a similar psychotic state with strong elements of paranoia.

Cocaine may be administered by sniffing the white, fluffy crystalline powder (that resembles snow, hence the name) or by direct intravenous injection. Sometimes it is mixed with heroin for heightened effects, this combination being known as a "speedball."

Adverse effects. Chronic use of cocaine results in nausea, weight loss, insomnia, gastrointestinal disturbances, hyperexcitability of the nervous system with twitching or spasm of muscles, or convulsions. Prolonged sniffing of cocaine may result in perforation of the nasal septum, which results from ischemic necrosis produced by cocaine's vasoconstrictor properties.

Physical dependence does not seem to be

characteristic of cocaine abuse, but strong psychologic dependence is evident.

Hallucinogenic agents

Classification of the most common hallucinogenic agents included: (1) those drugs containing the indole nucleus, such as lysergic acid diethylamide and its variants, dimethyltryptamine (DMT) and its analogs, and psilocybin and (2) those drugs containing the phenyl ring, such as mescaline, STP, and the anticholinergic hallucinogens.

Lysergic acid diethylamide

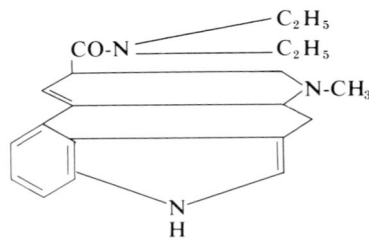

Lysergic acid diethylamide is a colorless, odorless, and tasteless substance that is a synthetic derivative of lysergic acid, a compound that naturally occurs in ergot and some varieties of morning glory seeds.

Therapeutic uses. A number of potentially therapeutic uses of LSD have been proposed, all of which merit more investigation. These include the drug's use in the treatment of chronic alcoholism and in the reduction of intractable pain as found in malignant disease and in phantom limb sensations. For a time, some psychiatrists also used the drug to induce psychosis, thereby helping the patient to revive repressed memories, the influence of which could then be dealt with by the patient and his therapist. The psychotomimetic effects of the drug have also generated the theory that some chemical imbalance may be involved in the etiology of schizophrenia. However, such preliminary data regarding the therapeutic uses of LSD merit much more research.

Mode of administration. LSD is usually distributed as a soluble powder and can be ingested in capsule, liquid, or tablet form. A frequent, but now obsolete, mode of ingestion was from an aqueous solution on sugar, although the drug can be licked off any object impregnated with it, such as a cookie, a stamp, or blotting paper. The drug may also be administered subcutaneously, intramuscularly, or intravenously. It is readily absorbed from the intestinal tract and mucous membranes as well as from body fluids.

Dosage. Pharmacologically, on a weight-for-weight basis, LSD is more active than almost any other drug and can be detected in the body at concentrations of 1 part per billion. The human body reacts to relatively minute doses of the drug, and 100 to 250 μg. administered orally can produce a potent experience up to 12 hours long in the majority of subjects.

Mechanism of action. LSD acts pharmacologically as a sympathomimetic agent. These effects, however, are secondary to the profound psychologic changes that it also produces. The drug is believed to be a serotonin antagonist and inactivates monamine oxidase and acetylcholinesterase. Cross-tolerance to mescaline and psilocybin has been demonstrated. The biochemical mechanism of action, however, is more complex than is currently known.

Effects. The effects of LSD usually begin within 20 to 50 minutes after administration and, like effects of other mind-altering drugs, cannot be reliably predicted. Autonomic nervous system changes are relatively mild and may include tachycardia, hypertension, nausea, vertigo, and perspiration. Effects vary widely among individuals and are in part related to the dosage, the mental set of the individual, and the environment of the individual. The drug experience may also vary for the same individual from time to time; while he may have a pleasant experience or a "good trip" one time, while the next may be an unpleasant or "bad trip."

The initial reaction to the drug may be one of vague anxiety and sometimes nausea. Later, there are general changes of perception involving sound, sight, touch, body image, and time. The brightness of colors may be intensified, for example, and there is generally heightened awareness of the environment, creating a flood of sensations and impressions. There may be synesthesia, that is, the translation of one type of sensory experience into another sensory modality, such as "hearing a color." Every perception assumes an increased sense of significance and meaning. Changes in cognitive functioning and value judgment formation may occur (good and bad may become equal). There may be blurring of boundaries between the self and the environment, and an ineffable state of transcendence may be achieved.

However, unpleasant experiences with LSD are also rather frequent. Clinically, evidence of impaired judgment in the toxic state is frequent and examples of such behavior are well known, as demonstrated, for example, by LSD users attempting to stop traffic with their bodies. Some authorities state that if the previously described altered state of consciousness develops in the context of fear and disorganization, psychosis may occur. Moreover, one of the chief dangers of the drug is that it will precipitate a latent psychosis into activity. With the release of repressed material with which the individual cannot cope, an acute panic psychosis may result. Feelings of acute panic and paranoia during a toxic LSD psychosis can result in homicidal thoughts and actions. Toxic delirium, with altering and alternating levels of consciousness, follows toxic psychosis, and the experience generally resolves in a stage of exhaustion in which the user feels empty, unable to coordinate his thoughts, and depressed. During this time, suicide is a decided risk.

The chemical effects of LSD might be antidoted by administration of a tranquilizer, a barbiturate, or nicotinic acid. It is specifically recommended that the administration of chlorpromazine be avoided in LSD toxicity because it may accentuate anticholinergic-like drug effects and may, in high doses, lead to severe hypotension or confusion, further compounding the situation. However, the administration of medication is recommended only as an adjunct to psychotherapy of a crisis intervention nature. The latter is directed primarily to the restoration of a positive mental set under the guidance of a stable and consistent human point of reference whom the patient trusts. A "talk-down" approach in a quiet environment is often utilized and consists of directing the patient's attention away from perceptions producing panic, reassuring him that the experience will dissipate, and reassuring him that he has not permanently harmed himself. Hospital practices of administering massive doses of tranquilizers, applying restraints, and isolating such patients are to be avoided. The patient's dramatically heightened awareness of his environmment and distorted perceptions may render these measures traumatic rather than therapeutic.

Markedly unfavorable reactions induced by LSD include prolonged, delayed, and recurrent reactions. The last have been described as "flashback phenomena," referring to the repetition of a previous LSD-induced experience that is unrelated to renewed administration of the drug. Moreover, a "bad trip" on LSD is likely to be a paranoid experience, and tendencies to violence can be characteristic of LSD intoxication. Research reports of chromosomal damage related to LSD ingestion are increasing, although there appears to be some variation in susceptibility to chromosomal breaks that is of unknown etiology. The drug does not seem to cause physical dependence, but tolerance to the drug occurs rapidly and psychic dependence is frequent.

Pregnant women should be especially cautioned against taking LSD. Because lysergic acid is the base of all ergot alkaloids, it has uterine stimulant properties that can adversely affect a pregnancy.

Withdrawal symptoms. Insofar as is known, LSD does not produce physical dependence, and there are no withdrawal symptoms following discontinuation of long-term use.

Mescaline

Mescaline is the chief alkaloid extracted from the peyote cactus, and it produces hallucinogenic effects similar to those produced by LSD. Like the amphetamines, mescaline belongs to the amine group and its chemical structure distantly resembles that of norepinephrine. It is usually ingested in the form of a soluble crystalline

Table 17-1 Signs and symptoms of acute drug intoxication

Drug abused	Signs and symptoms
Cannabis drugs	Tachycardia and postural hypotension; conjunctival vascular congestion; clear sensorium; distortions of perception; dryness of mouth and throat; possible panic
Opiates	Depressed blood pressure and respirations; fixed, pinpoint pupils; depressed sensorium; coma; pulmonary edema
Barbiturates and other general central nervous system depressants	Depressed blood pressure and respirations; ataxia; slurred speech, confusion; depressed tendon reflexes; coma; shock
Amphetamines	Elevated blood pressure; tachycardia; other cardia arrhythmias; hyperactive tendon reflexes; pupils dilated and reactive to light; hyperpyrexia; perspiration; shallow respirations; circulatory collapse; clear or confused sensorium; possible hallucinations; paranoid feelings
Hallucinogenic agents	Elevated blood pressure; hyperactive tendon reflexes; piloerection; perspiration; pupils dilated and reactive to light; anxiety; distortion of body image and perception; delusions; hallucinations

powder that is either dissolved or capsulated. The usual dose of mescaline is about 500 mg.

The effects of mescaline appear within 2 or 3 hours and may last 4 to 12 hours or longer. They are characterized by prodromal abdominal pain, nausea, vomiting, and diarrhea, which are followed by vivid and colorful visual hallucinations.

Psilocybin

Psilocybin is a drug derived from Mexican mushrooms (*Psilocybe mexicana*) that produce hallucinogenic effects similar to those produced by mescaline but of shorter duration.

■ Pathophysiologic complications resulting from drug abuse

Physical and psychic dependence on drugs is frequently associated with debilitated physical states caused by the exclusive degree of the user's involvement in procuring and using the drug. Malnutrition, dehydration, and avitaminosis are often evident. Respiratory complications such as pneumonia, pulmonary emboli, and abscesses are frequently associated with neglect, debilitation, and the respiratory depression produced by central nervous system depressants. The intravenous administration of illicit drugs often leads to a high incidence of sepsis and hepatitis as a result of the use of contaminated equipment. In addition, cellulitis, sclerosis of the veins, phlebitis, and skin abscesses may occur. Last but not least, death from accidental overdose is not uncommon. The latter complication is a particularly significant potential danger because illegal drugs are notoriously unreliable in regard to the potency of their active ingredient. The drugs are frequently well adulterated, or "cut," by the time they reach the user. If an individual who has unknowingly been using "cut" drugs receives pure or stronger drugs, he runs the risk of toxicity and even death. Overdosage may also occur when an individual who has been withdrawn from drugs for some time, thereby having lost his accumulated tolerance, injects his previous usual dose, which now is in excess of his tolerance level.

Parenthetically, it must be said that the dose unreliability of most mind-altering drugs also affects research findings. Because dosage is difficult to control and because most drug abuse research is ex post facto, research results frequently may be skewed.

As a consequence of all of these factors, the life expectancy of persons who are physically dependent upon drugs is generally lower than that of nondependent individuals.

■ Legal aspects of drug abuse

Four principal statutes—the Narcotic Drugs Import and Export Act, the Harrison Narcotic Act, the Narcotics Manufacturing Act of 1960, and the Marihuana Tax Act—govern the use of opiate derivative drugs and marihuana in the United States. Presently, there is particular and considerable controversy in relation to the laws governing the use of marihuana. The chief argument revolves about the classification of marihuana as a narcotic in the same category as the opiates and cocaine. The outcome of this deliberation is uncertain, but it is probable that marihuana traffic will continue to be illegal but that its possession will be reduced to the misdemeanor class of offenses. Presently, in most states the possession, traffic and utilization of marihuana is a felony. Several states, however, have already passed statutes making the possession and use of marihuana a misdemeanor rather than a felony. Sale of marihuana, however, remains a felony.

■ Nursing interventions related to drug abuse

The nurse may be called upon to function in any aspect of health care related to drug abuse: in prevention, in case-finding, in treatment of acute intoxication, and in long-term rehabilitation. To function with optimal effectiveness, the nurse not only needs current knowledge of drugs most frequently abused but must also add

other aspects of nursing process, such as patient teaching, crisis intervention, administration of acute emergency care, and support of therapeutic and rehabilitative regimens. Because drug abuse is such a complex, multifaceted behavioral phenomenon, the nurse must relate to and treat the whole patient in all of her functions. Therefore, she must take into account the patient's reality and his environment, and she must evolve an understanding of what mind-altering drugs realistically can and cannot do.

In her preventive role, the nurse may function either inside or outside the hospital environment. Within the hospital, she will be required to make decisions regarding a patient's need for a narcotic or any other drug that may produce dependence. Many nurses are reluctant to administer narcotics to a patient in pain, for example, for fear of producing dependence. The tendency to avoid the use of narcotics should not be carried to such extremes, but it behooves the nurse to exercise her repertoire of skills in a therapeutic attempt before administering a narcotic. A large component of pain is one's subjective response to pain. Many patients experiencing pain are also anxious and/or depressed. It has been found that if these conditions are relieved, the physical pain will also be alleviated. When medication is indicated, if a nonnarcotic analgesic will relieve the pain, it should be administered in place of a narcotic analgesic. Or, when narcotic analgesics are indicated, return to nondependent drugs should be accomplished as soon as possible. It must be emphasized that, when other nursing interventions fail, prescribed drugs should never be withheld from patients who are experiencing physical or psychologic pain.

Preventive nursing roles both inside and outside the hospital environment also include education regarding drugs of all types, but particularly regarding drugs prone to producing dependence. The promotion of the use of functional coping mechanisms rather than the use of drugs is another crucial aspect of the nurse's preventive role in drug abuse. Persons who abuse drugs because of psychologic problems frequently have lost sight of their strength to deal with their problems in other ways. In such situations, the nurse can apply her knowledge of crisis intervention and of supportive psychotherapy.

Because she is a health professional, the nurse also has a responsibility in identifying persons who are dependent on drugs in order to refer them to appropriate resources. The diagnosis of drug dependence is usually not difficult, and often the individual will admit to his need for drugs. Observation for physical signs of drug abuse will frequently yield substantial evidence. Needle marks and scars of abscesses along intravenous routes and pupillary dilatation are some overt signs that are often indicative of chronic drug abuse. Signs of acute toxication differ according to the drug abused and may manifest themselves variably, as indicated in Table 17-1. Striking changes in personality, interest patterns, and social relationships may also be indicative of drug abuse. A medical history of hepatitis, abscesses, or bacterial endocarditis may further substantiate an assumption, and diagnostic tests are available to detect the presence of some drugs in the bloodstream and in urine. Conclusive evidence of chronic drug dependence is the appearance of a withdrawal syndrome.

The nurse's role in acute drug intoxication, or in treatment of overdoses, can be twofold: support of medical therapy and/or interviewing the patient or his companions in an attempt to discover the specific agent that precipitated intoxication. With drugs increasingly being mixed, it is often difficult to identify the drug used and to provide an antidote. In such cases, persistent, patient, nonjudgmental, and painstaking probing of the patient's history may be necessary.

The nurse may also be called upon to care for a patient undergoing withdrawal, a most difficult physiologic phenomenon that requires astute observation of the patient's physical condition as well as a firm but supportive and reassuring interpersonal approach.

When withdrawal of the drug is completed, however, the role of the nurse does not terminate. Indeed, physiologic withdrawal may be defined as the starting point for meeting the problem of the patient's drug dependence. Continuing help and contact are necessary and must be maintained for a long period of time. If such help is not available, relapse to the abuse of drugs is almost inevitable.

Questions

for study and review

1 Differentiate between drug misuse and drug abuse.
2 Define physical and psychic drug dependence.
3 Identify the four major categories of drugs that are abused.
4 Identify four factors that are significant in influencing the nature of an individual's experience after administration of a mind-altering drug.
5 Describe some factors that are believed to be etiologic in the development of drug abuse.
6 Differentiate among the following terms: hallucinogenic, psychotomimetic, and psychedelic.
7 Compare and contrast the primary forms of the cannabis drugs utilized in the United States.
8 Identify the active ingredient of the cannabis drugs.
9 Describe the effects and adverse effects produced by the cannabis drugs.
10 Describe the pharmacologic effects of the opium derivatives. Explain why these drugs can lead to dependence.
11 If heroin is withheld from an individual dependent upon the drug, what physiologic effects might the nurse expect the patient to experience?
12 Explain the rationale for the use of methadone hydrochloride, itself a dependency-producing drug, for accomplishing heroin withdrawal.
13 List three narcotic antagonists that may be used in the treatment of dependence of the opiate type.
14 Identify the effects for which the amphetamines are most frequently abused, and describe the experience of an amphetamine "high."
15 Identify the three most commonly used amphetamines.
16 Explain why high doses of amphetamines may be dangerous to persons with cardiac problems.
17 Explain why individuals who abuse amphetamines often use depressants in conjunction with these drugs.
18 Describe the psychologic effects produced by LSD.
19 Identify the currently known major adverse effects of LSD.
20 Explain why pregnant women should be especially cautioned against taking LSD.
21 Identify some therapeutic goals for which the use of LSD has been proposed.
22 Describe how LSD intoxication or a "bad trip" might be antidoted.
23 List the most common pathophysiologic complications that result from physical drug dependence and explain why they occur.

24 Explain the significance of dosage control in relation to frequently abused drugs.

References

A.M.A. Committee on Alcoholism and Addiction and Council on Mental Health: Dependence on barbiturates and other sedative drugs, J.A.M.A. **193**(8):107-111, 1965.

Council on Mental Health: Narcotics and medical practice, J.A.M.A. **218**(4):578-583, 1971.

Crossland, J.: Lewis's pharmacology, Baltimore, 1970, The Williams & Wilkins Co.

Dole, V. P., and Nyswander, M. E.: A medical treatment for diacetylmorphine (heroine) addiction, J.A.M.A. **193**(8):80-84, 1965.

Dole, V. P., Nyswander, M. E., and Kreek, M. J.: Narcotic blockade, Arch. Intern. Med. **193**(8):80-84, 1965.

Fort, J.: The pleasure seekers, New York, 1969, The Bobbs-Merrill Company.

Goodman, L. S., and Gilman, A.: The pharmacological basis of therapeutics, ed. 4, New York, 1970, The Macmillan Company.

Hicks, R. E., and Fink, P. J.: Psychedelic drugs, a Hahnemann symposium, New York, 1969, Grune and Stratton, Inc.

Hollister, L. E.: Marijuana in man: three years later, Science **172**(3978):21-28, 1971.

Journal of Psychedelic Drugs

Kramer, J. C.: New directions in the management of opiate dependence, New Physician **18**:203-211, 1969.

Louria, D. B.: Current concepts—lysergic acid diethylamide, New Eng. J. Med. **278**(8): February 2, 1968.

Louria, D. B.: The drug scene, New York, 1968, McGraw-Hill Book Company.

Methadone in the management of opiate addiction, Med. Letter Drugs Therap. **11**(24):97-99, 1969.

Phillipson, R. V., editor: Modern trends in drug dependence and alcoholism, London, 1970, Butterworth & Co. (Publishers) Ltd.

Russo, J. R.: Amphetamine abuse, Springfield, Ill., 1968, Charles C Thomas, Publisher.

Smith, D. E., editor: The new social drug: cultural, medical and legal perspectives on marijuana, Englewood Cliffs, N. J., 1970, Prentice-Hall, Inc.

Ungerleider, J. T.: The problems and prospects of LSD, Springfield, Ill., 1968, Charles C Thomas, Publisher.

Wilder Smith, A. E.: The drug users: The psychopharmacology of turning on, Wheaton, Ill., 1969, Harold Shaw Publishers.

Wittenborn, J. R., and others: Drugs and youth: proceedings of the Rutgers symposium on drug abuse, Springfield, Ill., 1969, Charles C Thomas, Publisher.

18

Skeletal muscle relaxants and their antagonists

Skeletal muscle relaxants
Antagonists of curariform drugs
Antiparkinsonism drugs

Skeletal muscles are striated or striped muscles attached to the skeleton that are usually under voluntary control. These muscles function to produce body movements, maintain body position against the force of gravity, and counteract environmental stresses such as wind. An anatomic muscle is composed of numerous muscle cells or muscle fibers. Each muscle cell is connected to only one motor nerve fiber, but each of the nerve fibers is connected to several muscle cells. Therefore, stimulation of one nerve fiber will cause stimulation and activation of a group of muscle cells. Muscle cells and motor nerve cells have action potentials and rest periods similar to that described in Chapters 10 and 13; contraction is followed by relaxation.

The region where a motor nerve fiber makes functional connection with a skeletal muscle fiber (synaptic contact) is known as the motor end plate or neuromuscular junction. The transmitter substance is acetylcholine (ACh). Since ACh is rapidly destroyed by cholinesterase, end-plate depolarization and muscle contractions occur in rapid succession when the motor nerve is repetitively stimulated. Neuromuscular transmission is very susceptible to interference by drugs. Preventing transmission of a message from motor nerve to skeletal muscle fiber results in paralysis or a flaccid muscle.

■ Skeletal muscle relaxants

Muscle relaxants exert their therapeutic effect as: (1) *depolarizing blocking agents,* which prolong depolarization of the end plate during which time the end plate is incapable of responding to motor nerve stimulation; (2) *nondepolarizing, antidepolarizing,* or *competitive blocking agents* (synonymous terms), which do not cause depolarization but which compete with ACh for end-plate receptors and thus reduce or prevent muscle contraction in response to motor nerve stimulation (these drugs may also be referred to as *stabilizing agents*).

Depolarizing agents resemble ACh in structure (see structural formulas, p. 391) and, like ACh, first excite and then paralyze the motor end plate. These drugs are used primarily for muscular relaxation during surgery and permit the use of lower levels of anesthesia. Depolarizing agents antagonize the neuromuscular block-

Decamethonium

Acetylcholine

Succinylcholine

ade of the nondepolarizing drugs. Succinylcholine is an example of a depolarizing agent.

Tubocurarine is an example of a nondepolarizing agent. Neuromuscular blockade of nondepolarizing drugs are: (1) antagonized by depolarizing agents, potassium, and epinephrine; (2) reversed by anticholinesterases (physostigmine, neostigmine, edrophonium), which increase ACh concentration at the end plate; and (3) intensified or prolonged by ether anesthesia. These drugs are also referred to as curariform-blocking agents.

In addition, there are muscle relaxants that exert their effects by action on the central nervous system, thereby decreasing voluntary muscle hyperactivity. These drugs exert a selective action on internuncial neurons of the spinal cord and reduce multisynaptic but not monosynaptic spinal reflexes. Actually, these drugs can be classified as sedatives. In large doses these drugs cause depression similar to that of the sedative-hypnotics.

Muscle spasm is a symptom associated with many conditions and is the result of several processes. These processes include injury to the muscle itself, presence of an inflammatory process of the tissues around the muscle that precipitates muscular contraction, and damage to the nerve fibers of the central nervous system responsible for the control of motor activity of muscles. Skeletal muscle relaxants are advocated for the management of almost every musculoskeletal and neuromuscular condition associated with muscle pain or spasticity. There appear to be as many skeletal muscle relaxants available as there are conditions for which they are prescribed.

Some of the more potent skeletal muscle relaxants may cause undesirable side effects, such as respiratory paralysis, circulatory collapse, and untoward effects in the central nervous system. The patient receiving a drug of this type requires constant, close attention for signs of respiratory embarrassment.

Since these are potent drugs, not without danger, it is recommended that they be used only by persons thoroughly familiar with their effects and under conditions where adequate equipment, antidotes, and measures for prompt treatment of overdosage are readily available.

Neuromuscular blocking agents

Neuromuscular blocking agents are used primarily to produce adequate muscle relaxation during anesthesia in order to reduce excessive use of general anesthetics. They are sometimes used for facilitating endotracheal intubation, for management of tetanus, and to decrease muscular activity in convulsant therapy for certain mental diseases.

391

Curariform or nondepolarizing neuromuscular blocking agents
Curare

d-**Tubocurarine chloride**

Curare is a generic name for a number of arrow poisons obtained from tropical vines used by South American Indians. A number of separate alkaloids are extracted from the plant genus *Strychnos* and certain species of *Chondodendron. Chondodendron tomentosum* is a source of *d*-tubocurarine. The latter alkaloid was isolated by King in 1935 and is available as a pure crystalline compound of known chemical structure.

Action and result. In therapeutic doses curare blocks transmission at the myoneural junctions of skeletal muscle. Curare interrupts the functional connection between peripheral nerve endings and striated muscle in much the same way as atropine affects the response of certain smooth muscle to parasympathetic nerves. The muscle can be made to respond to direct electric stimulation or certain chemical agents but not to nerve stimulation. When large doses are given, one muscle after another becomes weak and flaccid, until complete paralysis occurs.

After therapeutic doses of curare the patient notices the first effects in the short muscles such as those found in the eyes, eyelids, fingers, and toes. Within 2 to 3 minutes after an intravenous injection of an ordinary clinical dose the patient experiences haziness of vision, difficulty in talking and swallowing, ptosis of the eyelids, and weakness of the muscles of the jaw, neck, and legs; then follows relaxation, and finally paralysis of the muscles of the neck, spine, legs, arms, and abdomen. With larger doses the last muscles to be affected are the intercostals and the diaphragm. In recovery after the ordinary clinical dose the paralysis disappears in reverse order and may require 15 to 20 minutes.

A secondary undesirable action of curare is that of blockage of transmission in the autonomic ganglia. This may have the result of lowering the blood pressure. (See Chapter 10 for discussion of ganglionic blocking agents as antihypertensive drugs.)

Absorption and excretion. Because of its poor absorption, curare may be swallowed (ordinary doses) without ill effect, provided there are no wounds or abrasions along the digestive tract. It is rapidly excreted by the kidney and also rapidly destroyed by the liver. For this reason the patient who has paralysis of the muscles of respiration can be kept alive with artificial respiration, particularly if an airway is used.

Uses. Curare can be used to enhance muscular relaxation during anesthesia, particularly when certain lighter anesthetic agents are used, or to permit adequate relaxation without subjecting patients to deep planes of anesthesia that border on medullary paralysis. The margin of safety between the dose that produces good relaxation of voluntary muscle and the one producing paralysis of respiratory muscles, however, is small. Curare is less popular today because better drugs are available.

It was formerly used to prevent trauma and excessive muscular contraction in electroshock therapy and to provide muscular relaxation during endoscopy and the reduction of fractures and dislocations. It has been replaced to a great extent by succinylcholine.

With curare it is possible to relieve spasticity of muscles in certain convulsive states and neuromuscular conditions. It is also used as a diagnostic agent for myasthenia gravis. An injection of one-fifteenth to one-fifth the average adult dose will produce profound exaggeration of symptoms if the patient has myasthenia gravis. Peak action occurs 2 minutes after administration. This test should be terminated in 2 to 3 minutes by an intravenous injection of 1.5 mg. neostigmine and 0.6 mg. atropine.

Table 18-1 Curare type muscle relaxants

	Tubocurarine	d-*Tubocurarine* (*Mecostrin*)	*Benzoquinonium* (*Mytolon*)
Onset of action			
Intravenous	3 min.	1 to 2 min.	3 min.
Intramuscular	15 min.	5 to 10 min.	10 to 15 min.
Oral	No effect	No effect	Effective
Peak of action	—	5 to 7 min. (intravenous)	6 to 10 min.
Duration of action	Variable: 20 to 30 min.; with anesthesia, 40 to 60 min.	25 to 30 min.	12 to 15 min.
Mode of action	Competitive blocker of acetylcholine	Competitive blocker of acetylcholine	Competitive blocker of acetylcholine
Effects			
Central	None	None	None
Cardiovascular	N.S.*	N.S.*	Possibly bradycardia and decreased blood pressure
Respiratory	Hypoventilation, apnea from cumulative effects	Hypoventilation, apnea	Minimal depression
Antagonists	Neostigmine Edrophonium	Neostigmine Edrophonium	Atropine Difficult to reverse effects

*Not significant when administered slowly. Rapid induction may cause a precipitous fall in blood pressure.

A recent finding indicates that 75% to 80% of the drug is eliminated from the body in the urine, with some of the drug being eliminated through the intestinal tract via the bile. Thus its action is prolonged in patients with renal disease, hypotension, and liver dysfunction.

Preparation, dosage, and administration. The following are the preparations of curare.

Tubocurarine chloride, U.S.P., B.P. (*d*-tubocurarine). This drug is available in vials of solution for intravenous injection. It is also available in vials, in which it is contained in a slow-release menstruum and sold under the name of Tubadil Injection.

Dimethyl tubocurarine chloride (Mecostrin, Tubarine). This form is administered by slow in-travenous injection. It is available as a solution (10 mg. in 10 ml.).

Dimethyl tubocurarine iodide injection, N.F. (Metubine Iodide). This form is administered intravenously in physiologic saline solution. The dimethyl derivatives of *d*-tubocurarine are comparable to the parent compound, *d*-tubocurarine, in general characteristics.

Dosage must be determined individually for each patient. It varies with the preparation used as well as with the anesthetic to be administered. With ether anesthesia the total dose must be reduced because ether itself has a curare-like effect on skeletal muscle. A test dose prior to a curarizing dose is recommended. Tubocurarine is poorly absorbed by mouth and therefore must be given either intravenously or intramuscularly. Onset of action occurs in about 1 to 3 minutes; duration of action is 15 to 20 minutes. Its main use is in major abdominal and intrathoracic operations. The usual range of dosage is 40 to 60 units (3 to 6 mg.). After 3 to 5 minutes an additional dose may be given, and small supplemental doses are injected as needed.

Side effects and toxic effects. If large doses are injected rapidly, histamine is apparently released from muscle tissue, resulting in hypotension, circulatory collapse, and occasionally bronchospasm. Depression of the muscles of respiration causes hypoxia and possibly death. Treatment includes early establishment of an open airway (endotracheal tube) and the use of positive pressure artificial respiration with oxygen. The use of antihistamines may prevent bronchospasm and hypotension when these two are caused by the release of histamine from the tissues.

Neostigmine methylsulfate (Prostigmin Methylsulfate) and edrophonium chloride (Tensilon Chloride) are used as antidotes under certain conditions but only as supplements to artificial respiration with oxygen. These antidotes inactivate cholinesterase and permit acetylcholine to be built up, and unless large overdoses of curare have been given, this increased level of acetylcholine tends to overcome the paralysis. However, overdosage with the antidote can also produce untoward effects. Effective doses of neostigmine are likely to produce increased flow of saliva, slowing of the heart, hypotension, and increased motility of the intestine. Atropine is sometimes given to counteract the latter effects. The anticurare drugs are said to be most safely used when employed in small and, if necessary, repeated doses.

Contraindications. Patients with myasthenia gravis are very sensitive to curare and show a pronounced response to small doses of the drug. It is therefore contraindicated for such patients except as a diagnostic agent. It is also contraindicated for patients with respiratory depression, pulmonary disorder, liver depression, and renal disease.

Gallamine triethiodide, U.S.P. (Flaxedil Triethiodide)

Gallamine triethiodide is a synthetic compound whose action, uses, and contraindications are similar to those of the curare drugs. It is about one-fifth as potent as tubocurarine. Advantages claimed for this preparation include the following: (1) it has no effect on autonomic ganglia, (2) it does not cause bronchospasm from histamine release, and (3) it affords a high degree of flexibility because of rapid onset and short duration of action.

Preparation, dosage, and administration. Gallamine triethiodide is administered intravenously in an aqueous solution. It may be mixed with a 2.5% thiopental sodium solution. The average dose of 50 to 60 mg. or 1 mg. per kilogram of body weight reaches its peak action in 3 to 5 minutes and is effective for approximately $1/_2$ to 1 hour. Dosage must be individually adjusted for each patient.

Side effects and toxic effects. This drug may produce an allergic reaction in patients sensitive to iodine and a marked tachycardia because of its acetylcholine blocking action in the myocardium. It must be used with the same precautions as with other potent skeletal muscle relaxants. It is not the relaxant of choice for patients with cardiovascular disease.

Depolarizing neuromuscular blocking agents
Decamethonium bromide (Syncurine)

Action. Decamethonium bromide is a very potent relaxant of skeletal muscle with a rapid onset of action but rather short duration of effect.

Decamethonium bromide is more potent than

tubocurarine, but the duration of its effect is said to be intermediate between that of tubocurarine and succinylcholine. It does not produce a ganglionic blocking action and it does not cause bronchospasm from a liberation of histamine. It has no cumulative effect even after repeated dosage.

Uses. Decamethonium bromide is useful in producing marked but short-term relaxation, and it can be used in connection with procedures such as endoscopy, endotracheal intubation, and closure of the peritoneum during surgical procedure.

Preparation, dosage, and administration. The usual dose varies from 0.5 to 3 mg., depending on the response of the patient and the degree of relaxation desired. It is administered by a single intravenous injection that may be repeated as necessary. Muscle relaxation occurs in 3 to 4 minutes; muscle activity begins to return in about 10 minutes and is back to normal in about 30 minutes.

Side effects. Despite its relatively short duration of action this drug may cause respiratory depression. Neostigmine and edrophonium chloride are of no value as antagonists; therefore, facilities for controlled artificial respiration with oxygen are essential.

Succinylcholine chloride, U.S.P.
(Anectine Chloride);
suxamethonium chloride, B.P.

Action and result. Succinylcholine chloride is an ultrashort-acting myoneural blocking agent. Although the end result of its action is similar to that of curare, its action is the same as that of decamethonium—it intensifies the depolarizing effect of acetylcholine to such an extent that repolarization of the end plate, which is necessary for muscle contraction, does not occur.

Its action is of shorter duration than that of tubocurarine chloride. This is explained by the fact that is easily hydrolyzed by cholinesterase to form choline and succinic acid. Alkaline solutions of the drug undergo rapid hydrolysis; therefore, succinylcholine chloride is not mixed with alkaline solutions of anesthetics such as thiopental sodium. The intensity of its effect can be modified readily by varying the rate of administration.

Clinical doses do not seem to produce significant effects on the circulatory system and autonomic ganglia and they cause no significant liberation of histamine.

Uses. Some authorities are of the opinion that succinylcholine approaches the ideal muscle relaxant. It is the relaxant of choice whenever it is important to have rapid skeletal muscle relaxation.

It is used to produce muscular relaxation during anesthesia and in conjunction with electroshock therapy. Because of its short action, it is particularly well suited to procedures of short duration such as endotracheal intubation and endoscopy.

Preparation, dosage, and administration. Succinylcholine chloride is available as succinylcholine chloride injection, U.S.P., and is administered intravenously, either in separately repeated injections or as a continuous drip infusion. The range of dose is 10 to 40 mg. for an adult when used for short procedures. Relaxation occurs in about 1 minute with peak action in 2 minutes, after which there is rapid recovery in about 5 minutes. Sustained relaxation for prolonged procedures is obtained by continuous drip infusion in which approximately 2.5 mg. is given per minute. Succinylcholine is said to require closer attention during its administration than other muscle relaxants, but it also affords greater ease of control.

Side effects and toxic effects. Succinylcholine exhibits a low level of toxicity and is characterized by a lack of undesirable side effects on vital organs of the body. On the other hand, large doses produce respiratory depression, and facilities to combat respiratory paralysis must be at hand. There is no effective antagonist. Neostigmine and edrophonium chloride prolong the effect of succinylcholine and are therefore contraindicated as antidotes in case of overdosage. However, because it loses its potency rapidly when administration is discontinued, it is a relatively safe drug. The patient must be observed closely to prevent undue respiratory depression. The drug is not well tolerated by patients with severe disease of the liver, severe anemia, or malnutrition. It is of interest that a small percentage of human beings lack an enzyme that destroys succinylcholine. Such otherwise normal persons may be extremely sensitive to small doses of succinylcholine.

Skeletal muscle relaxants that act centrally

Action and uses. The most beneficial results from the administration of these drugs seem to be associated with their ability to relieve acute muscle spasm of local origin. They are used as adjuncts to physiotherapy in the treatment of sprains, strains, or trauma to ligaments. They often accompany the administration of other drugs (salicylates, adrenal corticosteroids) in the treatment of myositis, fibrositis, spondylitis, bursitis, and arthritis. These agents have been used effectively to lessen motor activity in certain neurologic disorders (cerebral palsy and so on) and in other dyskinesias characterized by abnormal reflex activity, increased muscle tonus, involuntary movements, and incoordination. Many physicians feel that benefits from their administration come from the sedative effects produced, rather than from actual muscle relaxation.

The exact mechanism of action of the central skeletal muscle relaxants is not known at present. They do not seem to affect muscle, myoneural junctions, monosynaptic pathways, or motor nerves. However they do affect the central pathways and neuronal systems that control tone and movement of muscles. These drugs are known to produce relaxation of striated muscle spasm by depression of the central nervous system (brainstem, thalamus, and basal ganglia). Skeletal muscle relaxants exert a selective action on internuncial neurons of the spinal cord, thereby reducing multisynaptic spinal reflexes.

Central skeletal muscle relaxants most commonly used are mephenesin, carisoprodol, chlorphenesin carbamate, chlorzoxazone, metaxalone, methocarbamol, and styramate.

Side effects and precautions. Usually the side effects associated with the centrally acting skeletal muscle relaxants have been mild and transient. Mild symptoms such as drowsiness, dizziness, blurred vision, lightheadedness, headache, feelings of weakness, lassitude, and lethargy occur during initial phases of drug therapy. Physicians and nursing personnel should caution patients taking these agents to avoid undertaking activities that require mental alertness, judgment, and physical coordination—such as operating dangerous machinery or driving an automobile. After a sufficient period of time these activities are possible when it is known that the drug no longer causes drowsiness or vertigo. Large oral dosages have caused nausea, vomiting, heartburn, abdominal distress, constipation, or diarrhea. With the occurrence of other signs or symptoms of drug incompatibility, administration of these agents should be discontinued. Some of the centrally acting skeletal muscle relaxants (chlorzoxazone and metaxalone) have been reported to cause jaundice. Periodic liver function tests and blood counts are recommended to avoid complications. This group of muscle relaxants is contraindicated in patients with myasthenia gravis or muscular dystrophy, since their effects may reduce the strength of remaining active muscle fibers and produce further impairment and/or debilitation. Patients with a history of liver disease should not be given these drugs, and the therapeutic effect should be weighed against the possible side effects in their administration during pregnancy.

Mephenesin

$$CH_3$$

$$-OCH_2CH(OH)CH_2OH$$

Action. Mephenesin exhibits a selective depressant action on the basal ganglia, brainstem, and synaptic connections in the spinal cord. Large doses produce a temporary paralysis of skeletal muscle, although the drug does not directly influence muscle as is true of curare. It also has a local anesthetic action, although it is too irritating to be used for this effect. Mephenesin also has a weak sedative action.

Uses. The transient action of mephenesin seriously limits its usefulness. It has been of value as an experimental tool and has also prompted an active search for drugs more effective for motor disturbances. It has been used to relieve spasticity of muscle associated with back injuries, bursitis, cerebral palsy, tetanus, and various neurologic disorders, but its beneficial effects are brief. It has not been found effective as an adjunct to anesthesia or to be useful in the treatment of Parkinson's disease.

Preparation, dosage, and administration. Mephenesin is marketed under a number of trade names* and in a number of dosage forms for oral administration and in a solution for intravenous injection. Mephenesin is marketed in capsules containing 250 and 500 mg., in elixir containing 100 mg. per milliliter, and for injection containing 2.0 Gm. in 10 ml. The usual adult daily dosage is 1 to 3 Gm. given three to five times a day. Its duration of action is about 3 hours regardless of the mode of administration. The average dosage for intravenous injection of this drug is 30 to 150 ml. of a 2% solution injected at the rate of 6 or 7 ml. per minute. Slow injection of the solution avoids possible intravascular hemolysis and hematuria. Hemoglobinuria and fatalities caused by renal impairment and anuria have been reported after injection with mephenesin.

Side effects. Side effects are said to be infrequent after oral administration of mephenesin. However, lassitude, anorexia, nausea, and vomiting may occur.

Carisoprodol (Rela, Soma)

$$H_2N-\overset{\overset{\displaystyle O}{\|}}{C}-O-CH_2-\overset{\overset{\displaystyle C_3H_7}{|}}{\underset{\underset{\displaystyle CH_3}{|}}{C}}-CH_2-O-\overset{\overset{\displaystyle O}{\|}}{C}-NH-\overset{\overset{\displaystyle CH_3}{|}}{CH}-CH_3$$

Carisoprodol is related to meprobamate and has approximately the same actions and limited degree of effectiveness as other mephenesin-like compounds.

*Some are Tolserol, Tolansin, Myoten, Spasmolyn, Dioloxol, and Daserol.

Preparation, dosage, and administration. Carisoprodol is administered orally in capsules of 250 mg. and tablets of 350 mg. The average daily adult dose is 350 mg. given four times a day. Onset of action occurs in 30 minutes, and the duration of action is about 6 hours.

Chlorphenesin carbamate (Maolate)

$$Cl-\underset{}{\bigcirc}-OCH_2CHCH_2O\overset{\overset{\displaystyle O}{\|}}{C}HN_2$$
$$\underset{\displaystyle OH}{|}$$

Chlorphenesin carbamate is chemically and pharmacologically related to mephenesin and produces similar actions and side effects.

Preparation, dosage, and administration. Chlorphenesin carbamate is administered orally in 400-mg. tablets. The average daily dosage ranges from 1.6 to 2.4 Gm. for adults.

Chlorzoxazone (Paraflex)

The actions and effects of chlorzoxazone are similar to those of the other centrally acting skeletal muscle relaxants.

Preparation, dosage, and administration. Chlorzoxazone is administered orally in tablets of 250 mg. The average adult daily dosage is 250 to 750 mg. three to four times a day. Peak action occurs within 2 to 3 hours; duration of action is about 6 hours.

Methocarbamol, N.F. (Robaxin)

$$\underset{\displaystyle OCH_3}{\bigcirc}-OCH_2CH-CH_2O\overset{\overset{\displaystyle O}{\|}}{C}NH_2$$
$$\underset{\displaystyle OH}{|}$$

Methocarbamol is chemically related to mephenesin carbamate and has similar actions and effectiveness.

Preparation, dosage, and administration. Routes of administration of methocarbamol are oral, intramuscular, and intravenous. Initial daily dosage for adults is 1.5 to 2 Gm. given four times a day for 2 or 3 days. Dosages of 1 Gm. given four times a day may be given as a maintenance dosage. When given intramuscularly the dosage should not exceed 500 mg. Intramuscular injection should be given in divided dosages in each buttock at 8-hour intervals. Oral administration should be initiated as soon as possible. Intravenous solutions are highly irritating and should be injected slowly at no more than 3 ml. per minute. Average dosage per injection is 1 to 3 Gm. and should not exceed 3 Gm. daily. Solutions are available for injection in 100 mg. per milliliter with polyethylene glycol in 10-ml. containers. Tablets are available in 500- and 750-mg. strengths.

■ Antagonists of curariform drugs
Edrophonium chloride, U.S.P. B.P.
(Tensilon Chloride)

Edrophonium chloride is an antagonist of skeletal muscle relaxants, such as tubocurarine and similar preparations that act by competing with acetylcholine for end-plate receptors at the myoneural junction. Edrophonium chloride probably displaces the curariform drugs from their sites of attachment to the muscle cell and thus allows the normal transmission of nerve impulses to be restored.

Uses. Edrophonium chloride can be used to terminate the effects of curariform agents when muscular relaxation is no longer desired or to reverse respiratory muscle paralysis produced by overdosage. It is used as a diagnostic agent for myasthenia gravis. This is based on its ability to increase muscle strength in myasthenia gravis; improvement in muscle strength occurs in 30 seconds to 5 minutes. It is also used for emergency treatment of myasthenic crises. Since its action is brief it cannot be used for maintenance therapy.

It is not used as an antidote for succinylcholine chloride or decamethonium.

Preparation, dosage, and administration. Edrophonium chloride is administered intravenously. The dosage employed for antagonism of appropriate curariform drugs varies from 5 to 10 mg. or more. It is not recommended if apnea is present. To counteract overdosage of appropriate muscle relaxants, therefore, it is used along with artificial respiration and oxygen therapy and only when some definite sign of voluntary respiration can be observed.

Side effects and toxic effects. Side effects of edrophonium chloride include increased flow of saliva (salivation), bronchiolar spasm (especially in asthmatic patients), slow pulse, and disturbance of cardiac rhythm (especially in elderly patients). When edrophonium chloride is used in large doses, it intensifies the peripheral effects of the curariform drugs instead of antagonizing them. Furthermore, it does not combat circulatory collapse that is associated with respiratory depression.

Other agents. Neostigmine and other cholinesterase inhibitors are also useful in combating effects of the compounds of curare. Like edrophonium chloride they promote the accumulation of acetylcholine by competing with acetycholine for the enzyme cholinesterase.

■ Antiparkinsonism drugs
Levodopa (L-dopa, Dopar, Laradopa)

Levodopa is the precursor to dopamine, which in turn is the precursor to norepinephrine. Autopsy findings on patients with parkinsonism indicated low dopamine content in the caudate nucleus, which suggested that restoring dopamine levels to normal might overcome the signs and symptoms of parkinsonism.

Levodopa in a majority of patients relieves bradykinesia, rigidity, tremors, and mental depression, symptoms of Parkinson's disease.

Following oral administration, levodopa is well absorbed from the gastrointestinal tract; it is metabolized in the gastrointestinal tract and liver.

Preparation, dosage, and administration. Levodopa is available in 100- and 500-mg. capsules and in 250- and 500-mg. tablets. Dosage must be individualized, and optimal dosage may not be achieved until 6 to 8 weeks of therapy. Average daily dosage appears to be 4 to 6 Gm. daily in three or more divided doses. Constant observation along with constant dosage adjustment is a necessity.

Side effects and toxic effects. Numerous side effects occur in almost all patients receiving levodopa. *Gastrointestinal* side effects range from nausea, vomiting, and anorexia to bleeding, constipation, diarrhea, and abdominal distress.

Cardiovascular side effects include a variety of arrhythmias, orthostatic hypotension, palpitation, hypertension, and phlebitis.

Musculoskeletal side effects are numerous and include various involuntary muscular movements such as grimacing, jerky movements of the shoulders or pelvis, and rhythmic movements of the neck, hands, feet, mouth, and head. Opisthotonos may also occur.

A host of *psychologic* and *neurologic* side effects can occur. These include anxiety, confusion, depression, hallucinations, insomnia, paranoia, and suicidal tendencies. Ataxia, convulsions, headaches, tremors, weakness, and numbness also occur.

Respiratory, urinary, ocular, and *hematologic* disorders have also been reported.

While many of the side effects are dose related and disappear after reduction of dosage, neurologic and psychologic side effects may persist for several months after reduction or discontinuance of the drug.

Precautions. Levadopa should be administered only with great caution to patients with almost any physiologic disorder with an organic basis. Periodic evaluations of most body system functions (hepatic, cardiovascular, and so on) should be performed periodically. Levodopa is *not* recommended for children under 12 years of age, pregnant women, or nursing mothers.

Questions

for study and review

1 Explain the differences in action and uses between the centrally acting skeletal muscle relaxants and the neuromuscular blocking agents.
2 Explain the difference in the use of edrophonium and tubocurarine as diagnostic agents for myasthenia gravis.
3 Which of the following is an untrue statement?
   a. Neostigmine antagonizes the action of curare or tubocurarine.
   b. Anticurare drugs inactivate or inhibit cholinesterase, thereby permitting acetylcholine to accumulate and effect its action.
   c. Acetylcholine is important for skeletal muscle contraction.
   d. Centrally acting skeletal muscle relaxants block the liberation of acetylcholine at nerve endings.
4 Choose the *incorrect* answers.
   Mephenesin:
   a. has a strong neuromuscular blocking action
   b. has a depressant effect on the central nervous system
   c. exerts its primary effect on the autonomic nervous system
   d. causes skeletal muscle relaxation without loss of consciousness
5 Tubocurarine may cause a fall in blood pressure as a result of:
   a. adrenergic blockade
   b. ganglionic blockade
   c. histamine release
   d. catecholamine release
6 Choose the *incorrect* statements.
   Decamethonium:
   a. prolongs depolarization, which inhibits repolarization
   b. causes a flaccid muscle paralysis
   c. is easily antagonized by anticurare drugs
   d. does not cause respiratory depression because of its short duration of action
7 Of the following choose the *incorrect* statement.
   a. Skeletal muscle relaxants cause spinal cord depression.
   b. Succinylcholine is an ultrashort-acting myoneural blocking agent because it is chemically altered by cholinesterase.
   c. An overdose of tubocurarine paralyzes respirator muscles.
   d. Skeletal muscle relaxants are not known to depress the medullary respiratory center.

References

Bowman, W. C.: Mechanisms of neuromuscular blockade, Prog. Med. Chem. **2:**88, 1962.

Cohen, E. N., Brewer, H. W., and Smith, D.: The metabolism and elimination of *d*-tubocurarine, J. Pharmacol. Exp. Therap. **147:**120, 1965.

Friend, D. G.: Pharmacology of muscle relaxants, Clin. Pharmacol. Therap. **5:**871, 1964.

Foldes, F. F.: The pharmacology of neuromuscular blocking agents in man, Clin. Pharmacol. Therap. **1:**345, 1960.

Karczman, A. G.: Neuromuscular pharmacology, Ann. Rev. Pharmacol. **7:**241, 1967.

Katz, F. L., Wolf, C. E., and Papper, E. M.: The nondepolarizing neuro-muscular blocking action of succinylcholine in man, Anesthesiology **24:**784, 1963.

Levine, J. M.: Muscle relaxants in neurospastic diseases, Med. Clin. N. Amer. **45:**1017, 1961.

Riker, W. F.: Pharmacologic considerations in a reevaluation of the neuromuscular synapse, Arch. Neurol. **3:**488, 1960.

Symposium on muscle relaxants, Brit. J. Anaesth. **35:**510, 1963.

Thesleff, S., and Quastel, D. M. J.: Neuromuscular pharmacology, Ann. Rev. Pharmacol. **5:**263, 1965.

■ Anatomy and physiology of the eye

The eye is the receptor organ for one of the most delicate and valuable senses, vision; as such, it demands only the most thoughtful and expert care. The eyeball itself has three layers or coats: the protective external (corneoscleral) coat, the nutritive middle vascular (uveal) coat, and the light-sensitive inner neural receptor (retinal) layer.

The anterior segment of the eye serves as an optic system to focus images upon the retina (Figure 19-1). This system is composed of the cornea, the iris, and the lens. The lens is capable of changing its shape in response to contraction or relaxation of the ciliary muscle and can bring objects various distances from the eye into sharp focus. Strong contraction of the ciliary muscle is necessary to allow the lens to bring nearby objects into focus (accommodation), and relaxation is necessary to focus objects at a distance. Drug-induced paralysis of the ciliary body so that it is incapable of contraction is called cycloplegia. The iris forms the pupillary opening, and in response to strong light or accommodation it contracts to make this opening smaller (miosis), whereas in dim light or in cases in which the eye is focusing an object at a distance the iris relaxes and allows the pupil to become larger (mydriasis).

The eyeball is protected in a deep depression of the skull, the orbit, and is moved in the orbit by six small extraocular muscles. The retina is connected to the brain by the optic nerve, which leaves the orbit through a bony canal in the posterior wall. The anterior surface of the eye is kept moist by the tears, which then drain away into the nose through two small ducts (the lacrimal canaliculi) at the inner corners of the eyelids.

There are numerous drugs used in ophthalmology, many of which have made their appearance within the past two decades. Drugs used in the treatment of eye disorders or for eye examinations include cholinergics, anticholinesterases, adrenergics, antiadrenergics, chemotherapeutics, anesthetics, antiseptics, and others.

Autonomic drugs

The muscles of the ciliary body and the iris receive both parasympathetic and sympathetic innervation and respond to drugs that affect these systems.

401

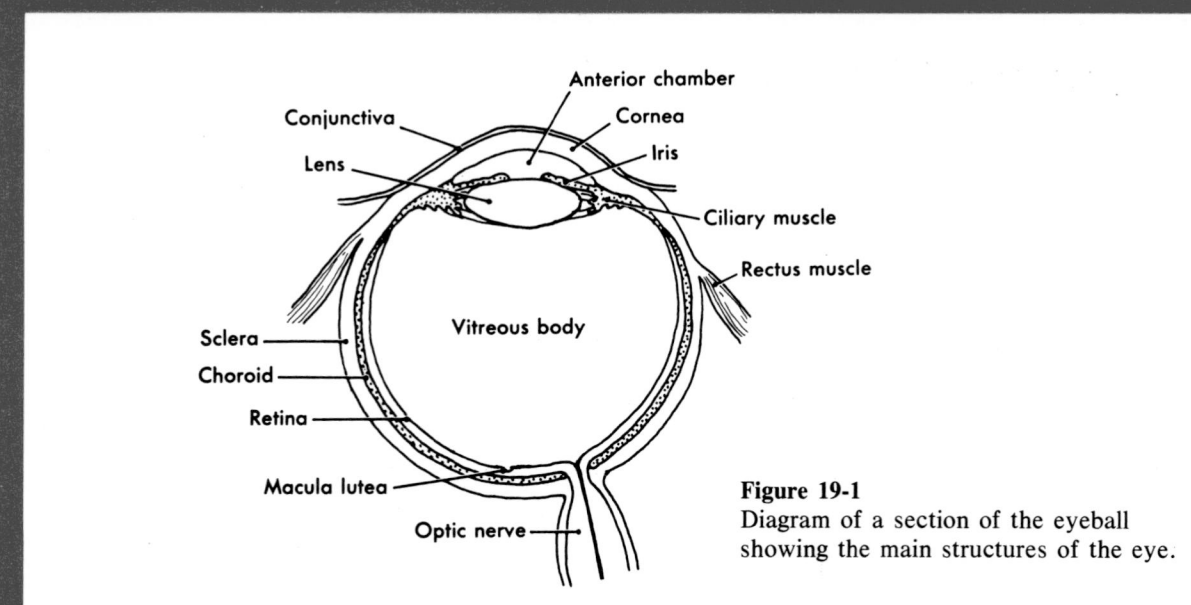

Figure 19-1
Diagram of a section of the eyeball showing the main structures of the eye.

Autonomic drugs are among the most commonly used drugs in ophthalmology. These drugs are used to produce miosis, mydriasis, and cycloplegia. The mechanisms by which autonomic drugs act are discussed in Chapter 9.

Cholinergic drugs

Cholinergic drugs produce strong contractions of the iris (miosis) and ciliary body musculature (accommodation). These drugs have been found to lower the intraocular pressure in patients with glaucoma and to treat patients with certain types of strabismus (crossed eyes).

Glaucoma refers to an abnormally elevated intraocular pressure that may result from excessive production of aqueous humor or from diminished absorption. When the pupil is dilated and the ciliary muscle is relaxed, the filtration angle is reduced and access of aqueous humor to the canal of Schlemm is hindered. Contraction of the ciliary muscles and constriction of the pupil may widen the filtration angle and permit outflow of aqueous humor. This effect may also result from dilation of collector channels and veins peripheral to Schlemm's canal. The cholinergic and anticholinergic drugs are used to bring about these latter effects in the treatment of glaucoma. Unless this elevated pressure is lowered, the result is an impaired blood supply to the optic nerve with eventual atrophy of the nerve and visual field loss.

Clinical toxicity from overdosage or unusual sensitivity to these drugs is manifested by headache, salivation, sweating, abdominal discomfort, diarrhea, asthmatic attacks, and a fall in blood pressure.

Acetylcholine chloride (Miochol)

A 1% solution of acetylcholine chloride is instilled into the anterior chamber or upon the iris for rapid and intense miosis during surgery on the anterior chamber of the eye or for cataract removal, keratoplasty, peripheral iridectomy, or cyclodialysis. Acetylcholine is promptly destroyed by cholinesterase; thus, miosis may last for only 10 minutes. This fact plus its poor corneal penetration makes it of no value in the treatment of glaucoma.

Carbachol, U.S.P. (Carcholin)

The only dosage form of carbachol that is official in the United States is the solution for ophthalmic use. The ophthalmic preparation is applied topically to the conjunctiva as 0.75%, 1.5%, or 3.0% solution two to six times daily.

Carbachol must be combined with a wetting agent, such as benzalkonium chloride, for increased corneal penetration. Carbachol produces intense and prolonged miosis since it is resistant to destruction by cholinesterase. Its miotic action lasts 4 to 8 hours, and it is usually prescribed for use two or three times daily.

Pilocarpine nitrate, U.S.P., B.P.; pilocarpine hydrochloride, U.S.P.

Pilocarpine is used in 0.5% to 6% solution. One drop in the eye will cause miosis and spasm of accommodation in 15 minutes. The pupillary effect lasts for as long as 24 hours, but the fixation of the lens for near vision disappears in about 2 hours.

Dosage of pilocarpine is usually 1 to 2 drops of a 1% or 2% solution several times a day or every 2 hours. Miosis occurs within 1 hour and may persist for 2 or 3 hours. For acute glaucoma, pilocarpine in a 4% solution may be instilled every 10 minutes, three or more times. Excess solution must be wiped away promptly to prevent its flow into the lacrimal system and the production of systemic symptoms. Pilocarpine is also used to neutralize mydriatics used during eye examinations. It is the safest and most widely used miotic.

Anticholinesterase drugs
Isofluorophate, U.S.P. (diisopropyl fluorophosphate, DFP, Floropryl)

The effects of this drug are similar to those of physostigmine, but it is more powerful. It is used in a 0.01% to 0.1% concentration in peanut oil since it is rapidly hydrolyzed in water. One drop is instilled into the eye every 12 to 72 hours. Isofluorophate produces miosis within 20 minutes and the effect may last 2 or more weeks. Care must be taken to prevent tears or other moisture from contaminating the solution.

Physostigmine salicylate, U.S.P., B.P. (Eserine Salicylate)

Physostigmine is used in solutions as strong as 0.5% and 1% every 4 to 6 hours. The aqueous solutions of this compound tend to oxidize on exposure to light and air and turn pink or brown. Such colored solutions should never be used. Maximum effect of topical application is reached in 30 minutes and may last as long as 2 days.

Physostigmine ointment may be prescribed for bedtime use to prevent nocturnal rise in ocular tension.

Demecarium bromide, U.S.P. (Humorsol)

Demecarium bromide is prepared as a 0.125% and 0.25% ophthalmic solution. It is an extremely powerful agent, and 1 drop will produce miosis within 1 hour and ciliary muscle contraction for as long as 5 to 12 days. Care must be taken to prevent general systemic absorption. One drop is instilled every 12 to 48 hours.

Echothiophate iodide, U.S.P. (Phospholine Iodide)

Echothiophate is used as a 0.06% to 0.125% solution and is another very potent agent with prolonged effects similar to those of demecarium bromide. It is extremely effective in the control of chronic wide-angle glaucoma, aphakic glaucoma, and congenital glaucoma.

When used for treatment of convergent strabismus, 0.05 ml. (1 drop) of a 0.125% solution is instilled in each eye at bedtime once daily or every other night for 2 to 3 weeks. Dosage or concentration is then reduced. The drug should be gradually withdrawn.

Miosis occurs within 10 to 45 minutes and may persist from several days to 4 weeks. Solutions of echothiophate are relatively unstable and gradually lose their potency at room temperature; refrigeration prolongs potency.

Disadvantages and advantages of cholinergic and anticholinesterase drugs. There are disadvantages to the instillation of cholinergic and anticholinesterase drugs into the eye. Among these are the following:

1 Visual blurring and headache result from stimulation of accommodation.
2 Constriction of the pupil (miosis) makes it difficult to adjust quickly to changes in illumination. This may be serious in elderly persons, since their light adaptation and visual acuity are often reduced. Night time is particularly hazardous for these patients.
3 They may cause irritation, conjunctivitis, blepharitis, dermatitis, and so on.
4 Cysts of the iris, synechiae, retinal detachments, obstruction of tear drainage, and even cataracts may develop.
5 Tolerance and resistance may develop; this can occur with any of the miotics.
6 Instillation must be frequent.
7 Systemic side effects include precipitation of an asthmatic attack, nausea, fall in blood pressure, and other symptoms of parasympathetic stimulation (refer to Chapter 9).
8 Anticholinesterase drugs may cause spasm of the wink reflex, which is annoying to the patient.

The cholinergic agents are very effective in many cases of chronic glaucoma. Their side effects are less severe and less frequent than those caused by anticholinesterase agents.

These drugs are often effective in treating chronic glaucoma when other agents have been ineffective. Instillations are less frequent with these drugs because of their prolonged action. Another advantage is better control over the intraocular pressure and less fluctuation in pressure.

Antidotes to cholinergic drugs. Two antidotes are available for overcoming effects caused by cholinergic stimulation—atropine and pralidoxime. Pralidoxime chloride (Protopam) reacts chemically with the cholinesterase inhibitor and reactivates the cholinesterase.

Anticholinergic drugs

Parasympatholytic drugs cause the smooth muscle of the ciliary body and iris to relax, which produces mydriasis and cycloplegia. Ophthalmologists take advantage of these effects to examine the interior of the eye, measure the proper strength of lenses for eyeglasses (refraction), and also put the eye at rest in inflammatory conditions. Systemic absorption of these drugs can result in serious side effects, such as dryness of the mouth, inhibition of sweating, flushing, tachycardia, fever, delirium, and coma. Pupillary dilatation from either local or systemic administration can precipitate acute glaucoma in predisposed persons, which, if unrecognized or untreated, can result in blindness.

Atropine sulfate, U.S.P., B.P.

Atropine is used in 0.5%, 1%, and 3% aqueous solutions. Mydriasis produced by the local application of atropine occurs within 30 to 40 minutes; cycloplegia occurs within a few hours. Both of these effects may persist for 12 days or longer. Atropine in a 1% solution is used to treat inflammation of the ciliary body and iris. In severe cases drops may be instilled three times a day; in more mild cases administration is usually once daily. Atropine may be used for refraction in children with squint.

A drop of a 1% solution of atropine contains about 0.5 mg. of drug. Since atropine is highly toxic, bottles of atropine are potentially hazardous. They should be stored in a safe place and kept out of the reach of children.

Patients should be instructed that if side effects occur and are present when drops are to be instilled (dryness of mouth, tachycardia) the instillation should be omitted. Atropine is contraindicated in patients with glaucoma. The patient must be aware that during therapy he may be unable to focus on nearby objects and will be unusually sensitive to light.

Scopolamine hydrobromide, U.S.P.; hyoscine hydrobromide, B.P.

Scopolamine in aqueous solutions of 0.25% to 0.5% has actions and side effects similar to those of atropine. The instillation of a 0.5% scopolamine solution causes cycloplegia within 40 minutes; its effect may persist for more than a week.

Homatropine hydrobromide, U.S.P., B.P.; homatropine hydrochloride

These preparations are available in 2% to 5% solutions. The effects are similar to those of atropine, but the duration of action is only 24 hours. Its maximum effect occurs in 1 to 2 hours. It is used primarily for cycloplegic refraction.

Cyclopentolate hydrochloride, U.S.P. (Cyclogyl Hydrochloride)

This drug in 0.5% to 1% solution produces rapid and brief mydriasis and cycloplegia. It finds its greatest use as an aid to eye examination and refraction. One drop of a 1% solution, or 2 drops of 0.5% solution 5 minutes apart, will produce cycloplegia within 45 minutes. In children, 3 drops 10 minutes apart may be used. The cycloplegic effect lasts about 24 hours; the mydriatic effect may last several days.

Negro patients are particularly resistant to the effects of cyclopentolate and to other cycloplegics. A stronger solution and repeated instillations may be necessary.

Tropicamide, U.S.P. (Mydriacyl)

Tropicamide is a rapid-acting cycloplegic and mydriatic agent with a short duration of action. Two drops of a 1% solution of tropicamide 5 minutes apart are effective within 20 to 35 minutes; there is complete recovery from the cycloplegic effect in 2 to 6 hours.

Oxyphenonium (Antrenyl)

Oxyphenonium is a potent long-acting anticholinergic agent with effects similar to those of atropine. It may be used interchangeably with atropine as a 1% solution in 1:5000 concentration of benzalkonium chloride.

Eucatropine hydrochloride, U.S.P. (Euphthalmine Hydrochloride)

This agent is administered locally as a 2% to 5% solution and produces pupillary dilatation that persists for only a few hours. It has little effect on the power of accommodation.

Adrenergic drugs

It is theorized by some researchers that alpha adrenergic receptors are present in the outflow mechanism of the eye and that stimulation of these receptors increases outflow of aqueous humor with a resultant drop in intraocular pressure. It has long been known that stimulation of the cervical sympathetic nerve causes a decrease in eye pressure. It has been shown experimentally and in studies of human beings that vasoconstriction decreases the rate of aqueous humor formation. However, more study with electron microscopy is required before the controversies regarding the action of adrenergic drugs in relieving eye disorders are resolved.

Adrenergic drugs produce mydriasis. This effect absolutely contraindicates the use of adrenergics in the treatment of narrow-angle glaucomas, since dilation of the pupil causes closure of the anterior chamber and may cause a marked increase in ocular pressure. They are used to treat other types of glaucoma, to relieve congestion and hyperemia, and to produce mydriasis for ocular examination. Serious systemic side effects with these drugs are unusual, but care must be taken in patients with cardiovascular disease. The cautionary comments concerning mydriasis and glaucoma apply here just as well as with the parasympatholytic drugs.

Epinephrine hydrochloride, U.S.P.; adrenaline, B.P.

Epinephrine has several uses in ophthalmology. Dilute solutions are employed at times in treating local allergies and superficial hyperemia. It is mixed with other agents for injection because its vasoconstrictive effects prevent too rapid absorption of the other drugs. Concentrated preparations such as 2% Epitrate are used in lowering intraocular pressure in certain types of glaucoma in which pupillary dilatation is not harmful.

Instillation of 1 drop of a 2% solution of epinephrine causes immediate vasoconstriction that lasts for 2 to 3 hours; mydriasis occurs within a few minutes and lasts for several hours; fall in intraocular pressure occurs in 2 or 3 hours and persists for several days. Systemic effects such as tachycardia, elevated blood pressure, and hemorrhage can occur with these agents.

405

Phenylephrine hydrochloride, U.S.P. B.P. (Neo-Synephrine)

This preparation is commonly used in 0.125% to 10% solutions to produce mydriasis for ocular examination. Care must be taken to prevent systemic absorption since 1 drop of a 10% solution contains about 5 mg. of drug. This is equal to the usual subcutaneous dose and can produce a considerable rise in blood pressure. Phenylephrine's effects are produced within 30 minutes.

■ Chemotherapy of ocular infection

The basic principles guiding the use of chemotherapy are the same in all branches of medicine. The drug of choice and the dose required must be established by adequate laboratory isolation of the offending organism; the initial culture from the infected area must be obtained before any chemotherapeutic agent is applied. Prophylactic use of antibiotic agents in general is useless as well as wasteful and potentially dangerous. A large proportion of the inflammatory diseases seen in ophthalmology are caused by viruses or other agents that are not susceptible to any currently available antibiotic; obviously the use of antibiotics in such situations is unwarranted.

Antibiotics

All known systemically administered antibiotics are available and used at indicated times to treat ocular infections. In addition, frequent use is made of topical ointments and solutions to treat superficial infections. Care must be taken to use an antibiotic that will not cause local or general sensitivity and to use drugs that are unlikely to ever be used systemically. Solutions are preferred, since ointment bases often tend to interfere with healing.

Penicillin

Topical application of penicillin is not recommended. Local hypersensitivity reactions are very common, and unfortunately the patient may develop a generalized hypersensitivity that will forever prohibit the use of penicillin in any form.

Tetracyclines; chloramphenicol; erythromycin; streptomycin

These drugs are all used topically as ointments, suspensions, or solutions in 0.5% to 1% preparations. They are commonly used systemically and therefore are not employed topically without positive indication.

Amphotericin B, U.S.P. (Fungizone)

Amphotericin B is an effective fungistatic drug against yeast-like fungi. Unfortunately its toxicity is high. It is well tolerated by the eye when applied as a 0.5% ointment. It is used for fungal infections of the cornea.

Bacitracin, U.S.P., B.P.

Bacitracin is rarely used systemically because of its nephrotoxic effects. Ophthalmic bacitracin ointments contain 500 to 1000 units per gram of suitable base and are particularly useful in treating superficial infections caused by gram-positive bacteria. Bacitracin does not penetrate the cornea in therapeutic amounts, it is nonirritating to the eye, and it causes no systemic effects. Since bacitracin solutions are unstable they should be refrigerated. Solutions remain potent for about 3 weeks. Ointment preparations are stable for about 1 year at room temperature. Bacitracin is preferable to penicillin for topical use, since fewer organisms are resistant to it, allergy is less frequent, and sensitization to penicillin is avoided.

Chloramphenicol, U.S.P., B.P. (Chloromycetin)

Chloramphenicol's effectiveness against a wide variety of gram-positive and gram-negative organisms makes it an extremely useful drug for intraocular infections. It penetrates the eye much more readily than many other antibiotics. Chloramphenicol is applied topically as a 1% ointment or a 0.25% to 0.5% solution. Drops may be instilled three times a day or every 3 hours, and the ointment may be applied at bedtime.

Isoniazid, U.S.P., B.P.

Isoniazid is used for tuberculous infection of the eye as a topical 10% solution or ointment;

it may be given as a subconjunctival injection containing 10 to 20 mg. of the drug. Corneal penetration occurs with isoniazid. The drug is well tolerated by the eye. Resistance develops rapidly.

Neomycin sulfate, U.S.P., B.P.

Neomycin is available as an ointment containing 3.5 mg. per gram of base or as a 0.5% solution. It has a broad antibacterial spectrum and a low index of allergenicity. Because of auditory and renal toxicity it is generally not used parenterally.

Polymyxin B sulfate, U.S.P., B.P.

Polymyxin is used largely for its activity against gram-negative bacteria. Hypersensitivity reaction to the 0.25% topical solution is practically unknown. It is also available as a 0.2% ointment. An intact corneal epithelium prevents penetration of polymyxin B into the eye, but epithelial damage from abrasion or ulceration permits effective penetration.

Sulfonamides
Sulfacetamide sodium, U.S.P., B.P.
(Sodium Sulamyd)

Used in a 10% ointment or a 30% solution, sulfacetamide provides high local concentrations that are relatively nonirritating. The presence of purulent drainage or exudate interferes with the action of the sulfonamides, since the purulent matter contains para-aminobenzoic acid. Sulfacetamide is used for minor ocular infections.

Sulfisoxazole diethanolamine
(Gantrisin Diethanolamine)

Sulfisoxazole is available in a 4% ophthalmic solution and a 4% ophthalmic ointment. It is applied topically to the conjunctiva three or more times per day.

Other antiinfectives
Nitrofurazone, N.F. (Furacin)

Nitrofurazone is a highly bacteriostatic agent that has a fairly broad spectrum. Unfortunately the rate of patient sensitization is high. Nitrofurazone is available for topical application in the eye as a 1% ointment and a 0.02% solution. The drug is well tolerated by the eye. Since its ocular penetration is insignificant, it is useful only for surface infections of the eye.

Idoxuridine, U.S.P. (Herplex, Dendrid, Stoxil)

Idoxuridine inhibits the replication of certain viruses when applied directly to the eye. The drug is too toxic for systemic use. When applied locally in the eye in a 0.1% solution, the drug is effective in the treatment of keratitis caused by the herpes simplex virus and the vaccinia virus. One drop of the drug may be applied to the conjunctiva every 1 to 2 hours (day and night) for several days. The solution should be kept refrigerated and the expiration date observed.

Idoxuridine is also available as a 0.5% ointment; it is usually applied five times a day. Its effectiveness is reported to be equal to that of the drops.

Antiseptics

Many of the antiseptics that were used to treat surface infections of the eye prior to the advent of antibiotics are now obsolete. Not only were many of these drugs relatively ineffective, they also delayed healing and in some cases caused permanent damage to the eye. Antiseptic solutions are employed in ophthalmology for irrigation, dissolution of secretions, and precipitation of mucus and in certain instances in which specific antimicrobial agents cannot be used. A 2.2% boric acid solution is used as an irrigant; this concentration is thought to be isotonic with tear fluid.

Silver nitrate, U.S.P., B.P.

A solution of 1% or 2% silver nitrate is routinely employed as a prophylaxis against ophthalmia neonatorum in newborn infants. The gonococci are particularly susceptible to silver salts. Silver nitrate is preferred to effective antibiotic agents, since these may sensitize the patient. Silver nitrate ophthalmic solution, U.S.P., is available in collapsible capsules containing about 5 drops of a 1% solution.

Mercury compounds

Inorganic mercuric salts such as yellow mercuric oxide ophthalmic ointment, N.F., and ammoniated mercury, U.S.P., B.P., formerly served as bacteriostatic agents. Today they are seldom used.

Benzalkonium chloride, U.S.P.

This is a cationic surface-active wetting agent that has several applications in ophthalmology. Its antiseptic properties make it useful in the preservation of other solutions and the sterilization of small instruments. It is also used in balanced salt solutions to aid in the cleansing and application of contact lenses. For topical application to the conjunctiva a 1:10,000 solution is used (1 ml. of a 0.01% solution).

Zinc sulfate, U.S.P., B.P.

An aqueous solution of 0.1% to 1% zinc sulfate is used as an astringent and mildly antiseptic eyewash in conjunctivitis caused by the Morax-Axenfeld bacillus.

Iodine tincture, U.S.P.

Iodine tincture contains 2% iodine and 2% sodium iodide in dilute alcohol. Its only ophthalmologic use is for the chemical cautery of corneal lesions produced by the herpes simplex virus.

Steroids

Corticosteroid therapy is indicated for all allergic reactions of the eye, nonpyogenic inflammations, and severe injury. Allergic reactions of the eye may be caused by drugs applied to the eye or by contact with substances such as weed pollen to which the individual is hypersensitive.

Ophthalmic corticosteroid therapy is not used for pyogenic (pus-producing) inflammations of the eye, since corticosteroids decrease defense mechanisms and reduce resistance to pathogenic organisms.

Eye structures are relatively delicate, and inflammation can cause functional damage, scarring, and impaired vision. Inflammation increases capillary permeability. In the eye, this results in the escape of proteins and cells from the blood vessels into the aqueous humor; this, in turn, may cause a rise in intraocular pressure.

The glucocorticoids used in ophthalmology may be applied topically, injected into the conjunctiva, or given systemically.

Corticosteroid therapy is not recommended for minor corneal abrasions. Steroids may actually increase ocular susceptibility to fungous infection. When steroids are used for various eye conditions, they should be used for a limited period of time only and the eye should be checked for increase in ocular pressure. Clinical evidence indicates that prolonged ocular steroid therapy can cause glaucoma and cataracts.

The following corticosteroids are available for topical use as solutions, suspensions, or ointments. They are available in varying strengths and in combinations with various antibiotics.

Cortisone acetate, U.S.P.
Dexamethasone, U.S.P.
Fludrocortisone acetate
Hydrocortisone, U.S.P.
Methylprednisolone, N.F.
Prednisolone, U.S.P.
Triamcinolone acetonide, U.S.P.

Topical anesthesia

Local anesthetics are used to prevent pain during surgical procedures and examinations. Unfortunately, all of the topical anesthetic drugs interfere with healing of epithelial tissue, particularly of the cornea. The practice of repeatedly applying such an anesthetic to an eye after removal of a foreign body is to be condemned.

Cocaine hydrochloride, U.S.P., B.P.

Cocaine was the first drug to be used for anesthesia of the eye (1884). One drop of cocaine produces anesthesia of the cornea in 5 to 10 minutes. Complete anesthesia lasts for approximately 10 minutes; less anesthetic effect persists for 1 or 2 hours. In addition to its anesthetic effects cocaine produces mydriasis and constriction of conjunctival vessels. Since the surface of the eye becomes dry, this may cause damage to the corneal surface. For this reason, cocaine has largely been replaced by newer anesthetics.

Solutions of 1% to 4% are used for deep topical anesthesia of the eye. The drug has both anesthetizing and adrenergic effects. Local administration may produce acute cocaine poisoning with sudden severe confusion, delirium, and convulsions. Short-acting barbiturates must be given at once to prevent a fatal termination.

Benoxinate hydrochloride
(Dorsacaine Hydrochloride)

Benoxinate is similar to proparacaine. Anesthesia occurs within 1 minute after instillation of 1 drop of a 0.4% solution and lasts about 10 to 15 minutes. A series of three instillations may extend the anesthesia to 20 minutes.

Tetracaine hydrochloride, U.S.P.
(Pontocaine Hydrochloride)

Tetracaine is used topically in a 0.5% to 2% solution for rapid, brief, superficial anesthesia. At present it is one of the most widely used local ocular anesthetics. One drop of a 0.5% solution of tetracaine will produce anesthesia within 30 seconds, during which time a burning sensation may be felt by the patient. The anesthetic effect lasts for 10 to 25 minutes. Tetracaine can cause epithelial damage; therefore, it is not recommended for prolonged home use by patients.

Proparacaine hydrochloride, U.S.P.
(Ophthaine, Ophthetic)

This drug is similar to tetracaine. A 0.5% solution is administered by topical instillation. Anesthesia is produced within 20 seconds and lasts for 15 minutes. It is relatively free from the burning and discomfort of other anesthetics and is often the drug of choice.

Instillation of topical preparations. The patient's head is placed on a suitable rest so that his face is directed upward. He is then instructed to fix his gaze on a point above his head. Gentle traction with clean fingertips is applied to the lid bases at the bony rim of the orbit; care is taken not to apply any pressure to the eyeball itself. The dropper or ointment tube approaches the eye from below, outside the patient's field of vision, with due care to avoid contact with

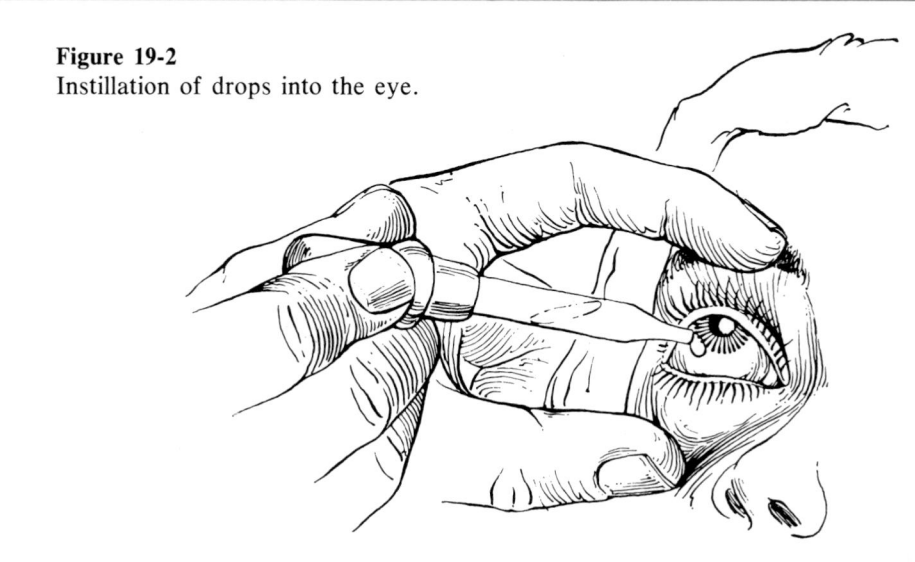

Figure 19-2
Instillation of drops into the eye.

the eye. The drop is applied gently and is not allowed to fall more than 1 inch before it strikes the eye (Figure 19-2). Following the instillation of common ophthalmic drugs, ocular massage is not necessary since these drugs have solubility characteristics that permit adequate corneal penetration.

Many of the solutions employed in opthalmology are extremely potent and care must be taken to prevent their systemic absorption. Gentle pressure is applied for 2 minutes to the lacrimal canaliculi at the inner corner of the eyelids and is directed inward and downward against the bones of the nose. This will prevent the solution from entering the nasal cavity and being absorbed through the highly vascular nasal mucosa.

Injection agents for local anesthesia
Procaine hydrochloride, U.S.P., B.P. (Novocain)

Injections of 1% to 2% solutions are used for local nerve block or regional anesthesia. Its poor penetration makes it unsatisfactory for topical application.

Lidocaine hydrochloride injections, U.S.P. (Xylocaine Hydrochloride)

Lidocaine is similar to procaine in its anesthetic effect, but it produces a wider area of anesthesia for a longer period of time and is more toxic than procaine. About 10 to 15 ml. of a 1% solution is usually used. Systemic absorption results in drowsiness.

Carbonic anhydrase inhibitors

The intraocular pressure is maintained by the production of an aqueous humor inside the eye. It has been found that one of the substances necessary for the production of this fluid is the enzyme carbonic anhydrase. In glaucoma, where the intraocular pressure is abnormally high, it is desirable to slow the production of this fluid and thus decrease the pressure. The specific drugs used to inhibit carbonic anhydrase are quite effective when taken orally. Side reactions are usually not severe and consist of lethargy, anorexia, numbness, and tingling of the face and extremities. Diuresis is produced and potassium depletion can occur. The duration of action of a single oral therapeutic dose is 6 to 8 hours.

The commonly used preparations are as follows:

Acetazolamide, U.S.P., B.P. (Diamox)—available in 250-mg. tablets

Ethoxzolamide (Cardrase)—available in 125-mg. tablets

Methazolamide (Neptazane)—available in 50-mg. tablets

Dichlorphenamide, U.S.P., B.P. (Daranide)—available in 50-mg. tablets

Enzymatic preparations
Hyaluronidase for injection, N.F.; hyaluronidase, B.P.

This enzyme is available in ampules containing 150 turbidity-reducing units. It is employed in local nerve block anesthesia to increase the dispersal of the local anesthetic. Seven and one-half turbidity units are mixed with each milliliter of the anesthetic.

Alpha-chymotrypsin

This enzyme is used in selected cases to facilitate cataract extraction. It is irrigated into the open eye and loosens the attachment of the lens. It is available in ampules containing 750 units of lyophilized enzyme dissolved in 10 ml. of diluent.

Miscellaneous agents
Sodium chloride ointment

This 5% ointment is used to reduce the corneal edema that occurs in certain corneal dystrophies.

Methylcellulose, U.S.P.

A preparation of methylcellulose is used as a 0.5% to 2% solution to provide moisture and lubrication in diseases in which tear production is deficient. It is sometimes referred to as "artificial tears." Methylcellulose is also used as a vehicle in ophthalmic solutions to prolong contact time of topically applied drugs.

Silicone

Silicone fluids are being used for patients with artificial eyes to lubricate the socket, reduce irritation, and increase comfort. They prevent crusting in the lids and impart a more lifelike glistening effect to the artificial eye.

Fluorescein sodium, U.S.P., B.P.

This is a dye that is used as a diagnostic aid. When applied to the cornea, only areas denuded of epithelium are stained a bright green color. Solutions of this dye are easily contaminated by *Pseudomonas aeruginosa,* which cause intense corneal ulceration. For this reason prepared solutions are never used, but strips of filter paper impregnated with the dry dye are moistened just before use. Staining of the eye disappears in one-half hour.

Questions

for study and review

1 Define the following and give an example of a drug used to bring about this effect.
   a. accommodation   **c.** miosis
   b. cycloplegia   **d.** mydriasis
2 What are the major disadvantages to the use of cholinergic and anticholinesterase drugs instilled into the eye?
3 Explain why ophthalmic corticosteroid therapy is not used for pus-producing inflammations of the eye or for minor corneal abrasions.
4 Define glaucoma. Explain why adrenergic drugs should not be used in the treatment of narrow-angle glaucoma.
5 What precautions should be taken by the nurse concerning the following?
   a. storage of eye drops and eye ointments
   b. instillation of eye medication

References

Benedict, W. L., and Birge, H. L.: Survey of recent contributions: 1. Vascular problems as they relate to blindness; 2. The increasing commentary on drugs as visual hazards, Amer. J. Med. Sci. **247:**223, 1964.

Crews, S. J.: Anti-inflammatory drugs in ophthalmology, Practitioner **197:**36, 1966.

Ellis, P. P.: Pharmacology and toxicology, Arch. Ophthal. (Chicago) **76:**117, 1966.

Goldfarb, H. J., and Turtz, A. I.: A detergent-lubricant solution for artificial eyes, Amer. J. Ophthal. **61:**1502, 1966.

Haddad, H.: Drugs for ophthalmologic use, Amer. J. Nurs. **68:**324, 1968.

Havener, W.: Ocular pharmacology, ed. 2, St. Louis, 1970, The C. V. Mosby Co.

Leopold, I. H.: Cholinesterase and the efforts and side-effects of drugs affecting cholinergic systems, Amer. J. Ophthal. **62:**771, 1966.

Leopold, I. H.: New dimensions in ocular pharmacology, Amer. J. Ophthal. **62:**396, 1966.

Leopold, I. H., and Keates, E.: Drugs used in the treatment of glaucoma, Clin. Pharmacol. Ther. **6:**130, 1965.

Magoon, R. C., and Sexton, R.: Wet or dry contact lens storage, Arch. Ophthal. (Chicago) **77:**197, 1967.

Smith, C. L.: Corticosteroid glaucoma: a summary and review of the literature, Amer. J. Med. Sci. **252:**239, 1966.

20 Drugs acting on gastrointestinal organs

Drugs that affect the mouth
Flavoring agents
Mouthwashes and gargles
Dentifrices

Drugs that affect the stomach
Antacids
Digestants
Emetics
Antiemetics
Diagnostic aids

Drugs that affect the intestine
Cathartics
Antidiarrheics
Carminatives

Drugs affecting the digestive tract exert their action mainly on muscular and glandular tissues. The action may be directly on the smooth muscle and gland cells or indirectly on the autonomic nervous system. Both divisions of the autonomic system innervate the tissues of the digestive tract and discharge nerve impulses into these structures almost continuously. Under normal conditions they maintain a delicate balance of control of functions.

Drugs may bring about increased or decreased function, tone, emptying time, or peristaltic action of the stomach or bowel. In addition, drugs may be used as to relieve enzyme deficiency, to counteract excess acidity or gas formation, to produce or prevent vomiting, or as diagnostic aids.

Drugs that affect the mouth

On the whole, drugs have little effect upon the mouth. Good oral hygiene that includes adequate measures for mechanically cleansing the mouth and teeth has more influence than most medicines.

■ Flavoring agents

Oral medications that have an unpleasant taste are usually encapsulated, but occasionally it is necessary to give a drug in a liquid or powder form. Licorice syrup is particularly effective to disguise the taste of a saline substance because of its colloidal properties and because the taste lingers in the mouth. Other popular syrup flavors are raspberry and cherry.

Unpleasant-tasting drugs that are disguised in a suitable flavoring agent are further improved (psychologically, at least) by the addition of a coloring agent. A chocolate-colored medicine is often thought to have the taste of chocolate even when the flavoring agent added is something entirely different. Since the oral route of drug administration is most acceptable, consultation with the pharmacist is useful when taste problems arise.

◼ Mouthwashes and gargles

The efficacy of a mouthwash or gargle depends largely on the length of time it is allowed to remain in contact with the tissues of the mouth and throat. Ordinarily, these preparations cannot be used in sufficient concentration or over a period of time sufficient to ensure germicidal effects.

A 1% solution of sodium bicarbonate ($^{1}/_{2}$ teaspoonful in a glass of water) is useful to remove mucus from the mouth and throat. A 0.9% sodium chloride solution is probably as good a gargle as most mixtures used.

Chloraseptic mouthwash and *Cepacol mouthwash* are used in some institutions. Chloraseptic mouthwash provides surface anesthesia when this is indicated for oropharyngeal discomfort, as well as maintaining oral hygiene. It is to be diluted with equal parts water or sprayed full strength.

Cepacol is also available commercially. It is to be used full-strength and is also produced in lozenge form.

Sodium perborate is a white, odorless, salty-tasting powder that contains not less than 9% available oxygen. It is used in 2% solution as a mouthwash and local disinfectant. Its action results from the liberation of oxygen. It may be obtained in flavored preparations that disguise the salty taste. It is a popular ingredient of tooth powder and is said to be particularly effective against Vincent's infection and pyorrhea. *Potassium permanganate* (0.1%), *potassium chlorate* (1%), or *hydrogen peroxide* (25%) may also be used; they are also oxidizing agents.

Other substances used in the treatment of stomatitis include boric acid, formalin, gentian violet, and zinc chloride.

Many hospital pharmacies prepare the mouthwash used in that particular institution. Nurses should inquire regarding the content of the preparation and should know whether or not the mouthwash should be diluted prior to use.

◼ Dentifrices

The ordinary dentifrice contains one or more mild abrasives, a foaming agent, and flavoring materials made into a powder or paste to be used as an aid to the toothbrush in the mechanical cleansing of accessible parts of the teeth.

The following ingredients, alone or mixed, are found in a number of dentifrices:

Glycerin	Pumice (flour)
Alcohol	Stannous fluoride
Sweetening agents	Soap
Propylene glycol	Sodium borate
Precipitated calcium carbonate	Milk of magnesia

The essential requirement of a tooth powder or cleaner is that it must not injure the teeth or surrounding tissues. In the absence of a tooth paste the nurse may feel justified in having the patient use only a toothbrush since thorough mechanical cleansing of bacterial plaques and food debris is the primary objective.

Therapeutic dentifrices. Intensive research over a period of 25 years seems to show that drinking water containing a proper amount of fluoride reduces dental decay by about 65%.* The American Dental Association and the American Medical Association have recommended the fluoridation of public water supplies. The cost is only a few cents per person per year. Sodium fluoride is effective when added to water supplies in a concentration of one part of fluoride to a million parts of water. Research has shown that this amount is perfectly safe and causes no bodily harm. A 2% solution may be applied directly to the teeth of children.

Dentifrices containing stannous fluoride are presently on the market, and initial research has indicated their efficacy in reducing the incidence of dental caries.

In those parts of the country where fluoridation of water supplies is not technically feasible

---

*Flemming, A. S.: Fluoridation, Pub. Health. Rep. **74:**511, 1959.

or has been legally blocked, various vehicles have been proposed for the systemic administration of fluoride. The most important of these seem to be milk, table salt, and fluoride tablets; the feasibility of all of these is undergoing investigation.

Drugs that affect the stomach

Conditions of the stomach requiring drug therapy include hyperchlorhydria, hypochlorhydria, peptic ulcer, nausea and emesis, and hypermotility. Drugs are also used for diagnostic test purposes. Some of the drugs utilized for these conditions are not unique in their treatment of gastric dysfunction but are members of other major groups of drugs, such as anticholinergic preparations and sedatives.

■ Antacids

Antacids are chemical substances utilized in treatment of hyperchlorhydria and peptic ulcer. Although peptic ulcer is thought to be the result of several pathogenic processes, the control of hyperacidity complements other therapeutic measures.

The major digestive substances secreted by the stomach are hydrochloric acid and pepsin. Hydrochloric acid activates the secretion of pepsin. Pepsin, in turn, begins protein digestion. Oversecretion of hydrochloric acid, however, may result in erosion, ulceration, and possible perforation of the gastric walls. Antacids are used to lower the acidity of gastric secretions by direct neutralization, buffering the hydrochloric acid (normally pH 1 or 2) to a lower hydrogen ion concentration, or by combined absorption of the hydrogen ions of hydrochloric acid, buffering, and partial neutralization of the acid.

Buffering hydrochloric acid to a pH of 3 or 4 is most desirable, since then the proteolytic action of pepsin is reduced and the gastric juice loses its corrosive effect. As pH approaches 7 or 8, as it does with some antacids, pepsin be-

comes completely inactive, the stomach empties rapidly, and a rebound of gastric secretion occurs. It is, therefore, thought to be preferable to lower gastric acidity rather than to raise pH to a state of neutral or above.

Antacids constitute one of the largest groups of drugs used in medicine and by the laity and are frequently abused drugs. Excess alkalinity can cause an uncompensated alkalosis. The nurse frequently hears requests from patients for "just a little something to settle my stomach" and must constantly be aware of her responsibility to explore the basis of that request and to instruct the patient when indicated.

When antacids are appropriately prescribed, they may be given every 1 or 2 hours throughout the 24 hours because of the continuous and often rapid gastric emptying. Many patients will prove receptive to instruction regarding this regime and will be pleased to assume some responsibility in taking the drugs.

The following are the properties of an ideal antacid:

1 Efficiency, so that small amounts of the drug will control a relatively large amount of gastric acid
2 Absence of interference with electrolyte balance when administered in therapeutic amounts
3 Exertion of prolonged effect without secondary increase of gastric secretion
4 Palatability
5 Inexpensiveness, since administration may be prolonged
6 Will not cause constipation or diarrhea
7 Absence of release of carbon dioxide after reaction with hydrochloric acid; this may increase distention and discomfort and may lead to perforation

Antacids may be classified as systemic or nonsystemic. Systemic antacids are soluble in gastric and intestinal secretions and are readily absorbed. Therefore they are capable of altering electrolyte balance and of producing systemic alkalosis. The kidney must then bear the burden of electrolyte readjustment and failure of the renal mechanisms would result in a more enduring metabolic alkalosis. Renal insufficiency and calcinosis have been described in patients on prolonged systemic antacid administration. Another disadvantage of systemic antacids is acid rebound, caused by increased hydrochloric acid secretion as a result of neutralization.

Nonsystemic antacids form relatively insoluble compounds that are not readily absorbed. Because they have no direct effect on the acid-base balance of the blood, they are unlikely to produce alkalosis.

Systemic antacids

Systemic antacids are found in many widely advertised proprietary preparations but are, because of aforementioned reasons, prescribed by the physician much less often than they were at one time. Their use is particularly avoided for patients who have pyloric obstruction or renal disease. However, patients sometimes experience greater relief from systemic antacids, and physicians may prescribe them in conjunction with one or more of the nonsystemic preparations. Systemic antacids are sometimes freely available on nursing units, and it is frequently a temptation to the nurse to give a patient the baking soda he requests without first obtaining a physician's order. The implications of such action should be apparent.

Sodium bicarbonate, U.S.P., B.P. (baking soda); sodium citrate, U.S.P., B.P.

Sodium bicarbonate is the most common systemic antacid used medically and by the laity. Administered as a tablet or a powder, it is readily soluble and easily absorbed. It produces high pH levels (8.5) that inactivate pepsin and predispose to overneutralization and rebound secretion. Furthermore, its reaction with hydrochloric acid liberates carbon dioxide, which may produce gastric distention, an undesirable phenomenon for patients with ulcers.

$$NaHCO_3 + HCl \rightarrow NaCl + H_2CO_3(H_2O \text{ and } CO_2)$$

Preparation, dosage, and administration. Sodium bicarbonate is a white crystalline powder that may be compressed into tablets. The usual dose is 1 to 2 Gm. (gr. 15 to 30) taken up to four times daily.

Sodium citrate is an absorbable systemic antacid similar to sodium bicarbonate. It differs from the latter in action in that it does not release carbon dioxide. It is seldom prescribed as an antacid in the treatment of peptic ulcer, but it is commonly found in proprietary preparations recommended to relieve gastric distress. Sodium citrate is subject to oxidation, which results in the formation of sodium bicarbonate and is therefore capable of causing alkalosis when given in large amounts.

Nonsystemic antacids
Aluminum hydroxide gel, U.S.P., B.P. (Amphojel, Creomolin, Al-U-Creme, Alkagel)

Aluminum hydroxide gel is one of the more popular of the nonsystemic antacids. It is an insoluble drug that reacts with gastric acid to form aluminum chloride that, in turn, reacts with intestinal secretion to form insoluble salts.

$$Al(OH_3) + 3\ HCl \longrightarrow AlCl_3 + 3\ H_2O$$

The formation of aluminum chloride is responsible for both the astringent and constipating effects of the drug. The use of a mixture of aluminum hydroxide with either magnesium trisilicate or magnesium hydroxide helps to prevent constipation.

The chief action is believed to be chemical neutralization of hydrochloric acid; aluminum hydroxide has been found to buffer the gastric secretion to a pH of about 4. It is also thought to possess some adsorptive properties, but evidence regarding this is inconclusive.

Aluminum hydroxide interferes with absorption of phosphates from the intestine and, in the presence of a low phosphorus diet, may cause a deficiency.

Preparation, dosage, and administration. Aluminum hydroxide gel is available in the form of a liquid suspension and as tablets of 300 and 600 mg. The tablets should be chewed slowly. The patient may prefer the tablet form, but the liquid preparation affords a better antacid effect. Flavoring agents are available. Aluminum hydroxide gel is given orally in doses of 4 to 8 ml. every 2 to 4 hours, although as much as 15 to 30 ml. may be given hourly. Some physicians like

415

to have their patients take the aluminum hydroxide gel diluted in a small amount of water or milk or to drink a small amount of liquid after swallowing the antacid. Unless some fluid is taken with a small amount of the antacid it may only coat the esophagus and little or none of it may reach the stomach. It may also be administered by continuous drip through a stomach tube, in which case it is diluted and given 1 part to 2 or 3 parts of water at the rate of 15 to 20 drops per minute (1500 ml. in 24 hours).

Aluminum phosphate gel, N.F. (Phosphaljel)

The properties of this preparation are similar to those of aluminum hydroxide gel, but it does not interfere with absorption of phosphate. Larger doses of this preparation are necessary because its acid-combining power is less than half that of aluminum hydroxide gel of the same concentration.

Uses. Aluminum phosphate gel is a preparation of choice for patients with an ulcer who are unable to be maintained on a high phosphate diet or who suffer an accompanying diarrhea.

Preparation, dosage, and administration. Aluminum phosphate gel is available as a 4% suspension for oral administration. During the active phase of the ulcer 15 to 30 ml. may be given alone or with milk every 2 hours. Later, the dose may be reduced and given after each meal, at bedtime, and between meals if necessary.

Other compounds. There are a number of other aluminum compounds used as antacids, such as dihydroxyaluminum aminoacetate, N.F. (Alglyn is one of many names under which it is sold) and basic aluminum carbonate (Basaljel). They are not believed to have any marked advantage over aluminum hydroxide.

Magnesium trisilicate, U.S.P., B.P.

Magnesium trisilicate is a compound of silicon dioxide and magnesium oxide with water.

$$MgO \cdot 3\,SiO_2 \cdot n\,H_2O$$

It occurs as a white, odorless, tasteless powder, insoluble in water but partially soluble in acids. It is said to compare favorably with other nonsystemic antacids and acts effectively as an adsorbent as well as providing chemical neutralization. In the stomach it has a gelatinous consistency, which explains its ability to coat and protect the crater of the ulcer. In therapeutic amounts it apparently does not affect the motility of the gastrointestinal tract.

$$2\,MgO \cdot 3\,SiO_2 \cdot n\,H_2O + 4\,HCl \rightarrow$$
$$2\,MgCl_2 + 3\,SiO_2 + (n+2)H_2O$$

In the intestine the magnesium chloride reacts with the bicarbonate in the intestinal secretions to form magnesium carbonate (which is excreted) and sodium chloride (which is subject to absorption). This follows a pattern similar to that of the neutralization of the bicarbonate by the hydrochloric acid of the stomach under normal circumstances and helps to explain why electrolyte balance is not disturbed. The magnesium chloride formed after neutralization of the hydrochloride acid is also responsible for a cathartic action in the bowel. Large doses may produce diarrhea, although therapeutic doses do not seem to disturb normal motility of the gastrointestinal tract.

Uses. Magnesium trisilicate is an effective antacid for the relief of gastric hyperacidity and for pain associated with peptic ulcer. A judicious combination of magnesium trisilicate and aluminum hydroxide has resulted in an antacid preparation that is efficient, safe when given in large amounts over prolonged periods, and relatively free from constipating effects.

Preparation, dosage, and administration. Magnesium trisilicate is available in 500-mg. tablets and in powder form. The usual dose is 1 Gm. four times a day, but as much as 2 to 4 Gm. may be given hourly during the treatment of the acute phase of an ulcer. The tablets should be chewed before they are swallowed.

A combination of magnesium trisilicate and aluminum hydroxide gel is available under the trade name Gelusil (tablet and liquid form). The dosage of this preparation varies with the severity of the symptoms to be controlled; 4 to 8 ml. is an average dose, although more may be prescribed.

Mucin, aluminum hydroxide, and magnesium

trisilicate (Mucotin) is an antacid mixture that provides an additional protective coating to the ulcer and the gastric mucosa because of the mucin content. The preparation is available in tablets that should be well chewed before they are swallowed. The dose recommended is two tablets every 2 hours.

Precipitated calcium carbonate, U.S.P., B.P.

Calcium carbonate (chalk) is a fine white powder that is practically insoluble in water but is somewhat soluble in water containing carbon dioxide. It is decomposed by acids, forming a salt of calcium and carbonic acid that in turn yields water and carbon dioxide.

$$CaCO_3 + 2\ HCl \rightarrow CaCl_2 + H_2CO_3\ (CO_2 + H_2O)$$

The calcium chloride will react with the sodium bicarbonate in the intestinal secretions to form calcium carbonate and sodium chloride. The sodium chloride is absorbable, but the calcium carbonate is excreted.

Uses. Calcium carbonate is used chiefly as an antacid and as a protective for patients with hyperacidity, gastritis, and peptic ulcer. Its effects are rapid and prolonged with a high neutralizing capacity.

Preparation, dosage, and administration. Precipitated calcium carbonate is administered orally in doses of 1 to 2 Gm. hourly when acute symptoms are to be controlled. Thereafter, the dosage may be lowered. The official dose is 1 Gm. four or more times a day.

Side effects. Calcium carbonate has a tendency to cause constipation, a disadvantage that may be avoided by alternating the administration of calcium carbonate with the use of magnesium oxide. The release of carbon dioxide may be dangerous if an ulcer is close to perforation. Large doses and prolonged administration may cause an accumulation of chalky formations in the bowel. Difference of opinion has been expressed concerning whether calcium carbonate causes a gastric rebound of acid secretion.

Some cases of hypercalcemia have occurred during chronic usage, especially in conjunction with milk and cream therapy. When large quantities are prescribed, physicians frequently measure serum calcium periodically. The nurse should be aware of symptoms of hypercalcemia, such as depression and bradycardia.

Magnesium oxide, U.S.P., B.P. (light magnesia); magnesium oxide, U.S.P. (heavy magnesium)

Magnesium oxide is a widely used nonsystemic antacid. It is a bulky white powder that is relatively insoluble in water. It reacts with hydrochloric acid to form magnesium chloride and water.

$$MgO + 2\ HCl \rightarrow MgCl_2 + H_2O$$

In the intestine magnesium chloride acts as a saline cathartic and eventually reacts with sodium to form magnesium carbonate, which is excreted, and sodium chloride, which may be absorbed. The neutralizing capacity of magnesium oxide is outstanding among the various antacids. It does not act rapidly, but its effect is prolonged since any excess remains in the stomach and serves to neutralize subsequently secreted acid. Its chief disadvantage is that it may cause diarrhea. Therefore, a frequent practice has been utilization of the laxative effect of magnesium oxide to counteract the constipating effect of certain other antacids.

Magnesium oxide is unlikely to cause alkalosis since little is absorbed, but the little that is absorbed is rapidly excreted by the kidneys and alkaline urine may result.

Preparation, dosage, and administration. The two compounds of magnesium oxide are identical in chemical composition but differ in physical properties. The former is lighter and five times more bulky than the latter. The light magnesia is more difficult to administer but affords a greater surface for reaction with the gastric content because of its greater capacity for dispersion. Recommended (U.S.P.) antacid dose is 250 mg. (250 to 500 mg., B.P.).

Magnesium carbonate, N.F., B.P.

This preparation has antacid properties almost identical with those of magnesium oxide, except that it liberates carbon dioxide upon the neutralization of hydrochloric acid. It is a bulky white powder. The official dose as an antacid is 0.6 Gm. (600 mg.) (300 to 600 mg., B.P.).

Milk of magnesia, U.S.P.; magnesium hydroxide mixture, B.P.

These preparations exhibit the characteristic antacid effect of the basic salts of magnesium. The usual antacid dose is 5 ml. In larger doses, its effect is predominantly cathartic. Maalox is a trade name for a mixture of aluminum hydroxide gel and magnesium hydroxide. It is comparable to Gelusil (aluminum hydroxide and magnesium trisilicate). The usual dosage of Maalox is 8 ml. It should be given with a little water, or a small quantity of water or milk should be swallowed after the dose.

■ Digestants

Digestants are drugs that promote the process of digestion in the gastrointestinal tract and constitute a type of replacement therapy in deficiency states. The most common drugs employed for this purpose are hydrochloric acid, bile salts, and gastric and pancreatic enzymes.

Hydrochloric acid

Hypochlorhydria is a term that denotes decreased secretion of hydrochloric acid in the stomach. *Achlorhydria* means an absence of hydrochloric acid, and when both acid and enzymes are absent in the gastric secretion, the condition is known as *achylia gastrica*. A deficiency of acid is said to occur in approximately 10% to 15% of the population. It is more commonly found in elderly persons. Achlorhydria is associated with gastric carcinoma, pernicious anemia, some types of gastritis, and a number of other conditions, although it is occasionally found in apparently normal individuals. Symptoms of achlorhydria are poorly defined but may consist of vague epigastric distress after meals, eructation, abdominal distention, coated tongue, nausea, and vomiting.

The hydrochloric acid of the stomach has several important functions. It is essential for the conversion of pepsinogen to active pepsin, which is important for the digestion of protein;

it has a germicidal effect on numerous bacteria; it stimulates secretion of secretin in the duodenum; it neutralizes bicarbonate of the intestinal secretions and thus helps to maintain electrolyte balance; and it activates pancreatic and hepatic secretions.

Uses. Hydrochloric acid is administered to relieve symptoms that result from gastric achlorhydria.

Preparation, dosage, and administration. The following are available preparations of hydrochloric acid.

Hydrochloric acid diluted, N.F.; dilute hydrochloric acid, B.P. This preparation contains 10% hydrochloric acid, which should be further diluted in at least one-half glass of water and should be administered through a tube to avoid injury to the enamel of the teeth. The usual dose is 5 ml., although some physicians recommend doses up to 10 ml. The acid may be sipped with the meal or taken just after the meal. Even though the acid is diluted well, the taste is very sour. Food should be eaten after the last swallow of the acid or the mouth rinsed with an alkaline mouthwash.

Glutamic acid hydrochloride, N.F. (Acidulin). This preparation is a combination of glutamic acid and hydrochloric acid and is available in capsules, which avoids exposure of dental enamel to the acid. The hydrochloric acid is released when the preparation comes in contact with water. The dose is 0.3 Gm., which is equivalent to 0.6 ml. of dilute hydrochloric acid. The preparation is usually administered before meals.

Gastric and pancreatic enzymes
Pepsin

Pepsin is an enzyme secreted by the stomach that initiates the hydrolysis of protein. Proteolytic enzymes in the intestinal and pancreatic secretions are capable of digesting proteins completely, so that gastric pepsin is not an indispensable enzyme. Its absence occurs only as an accompaniment to achlorhydria. The absence of both pepsin and hydrochloric acid is known as gastric achylia and is most frequently observed in patients with pernicious anemia or gastric carcinoma. Pepsin is seldom used at the

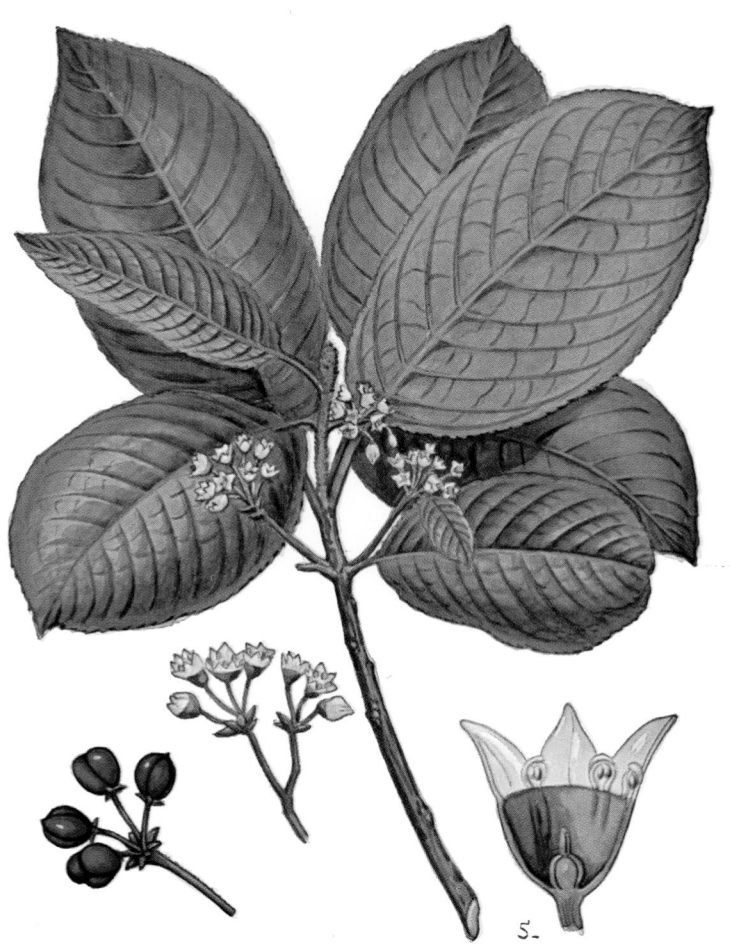

Plate 7
Rhamnus purshiana.

present time, but when it is given, the dose is 0.5 to 1 Gm. taken after meals. Pepsin contains the proteolytic enzyme obtained from fresh hog's stomach.

Pancreatin, N.F., B.P.

Pancreatin is a powdered substance obtained from the pancreas of the hog or ox. It principally contains pancreatic amylase, trypsin, and pancreatic lipase. Acid chyme entering the duodenum and vagal stimulation regulate pancreatic secretion, so replacement therapy may be necessary for patients who have had vagal fibers surgically severed, who have had surgical procedures that cause food to bypass the duodenum, who have had surgery of the jejunum, or with pancreatitis. Some doubt has been expressed concerning the usefulness of pancreatin. The drug is available in enteric-coated capsules to avoid destruction in the stomach and is administered in 500-mg. doses. Viokase and Cotazym are also utilized for patients with pancreatic deficiencies.

Choleretics and hydrocholeretics
Bile and bile salts

Drugs that stimulate the liver to increase bile production are known as choleretics, the most important of which are bile salts and bile acids. Hydrocholeretics are drugs stimulating the production of bile of a low specific gravity, which is desirable in disorders of the biliary tract unassociated with liver disease.

Bile is secreted by the liver into the bile duct, which drains into the duodenum. It is not an enzyme and is composed of water, bile salts, bile pigments, cholesterol, lecithin, and inorganic salts. Of these, bile salts are most important in the digestion of fats because of their hydrotropic effect. They lower surface tension of fats and are partially responsible for the emulsification of fats before digestion and absorption in the small intestine. Bile acids stimulate the production of bile salts. Both of these substances are normally absorbed from the intestine, pass through the portal blood to the liver, are reexcreted by the liver, then pass through the bile ducts and again enter the intestine.

Bile and bile salts are used for patients with various hepatic disorders to aid digestion and absorption and to increase biliary drainage. They are sometimes used for patients with prolonged drainage of the common bile duct.

Outstanding effects of parenterally administered bile salts are manifested in the circulatory and neuromuscular systems, causing hypotension, bradycardia, and skeletal muscular hyperactivity.

Dehydrocholic acid, N.F. (Decholin)

Dehydrocholic acid is a hydrocholeretic; it increases bile volume without increasing total bile acid quantity. In addition to its function in improving lipid absorption, it is frequently used to flush the biliary ducts to remove mucus, debris, and small obstructions and to prevent ascent of infections. It is also used to determine arm-to-tongue circulation time, in which case the drug is administered intravenously and the patient normally experiences a bitter taste within 8 to 16 seconds. Prolonged circulation times are frequently indicative of cardiac decompensation. Although dehydrocholic acid is the least toxic of the hydrocholeretic drugs, caution regarding its use in determining circulation time has been recommended. Dehydrocholic acid is not recommended for patients with complete mechanical obstruction of the biliary tract or in cases of severe hepatitis. The usual dose is 250 to 500 mg. two or three times daily.

Florantyrone (Zanchol)

Florantyrone is a hydrocholeretic of a synthetic nature that is closely related to dehydrocholic acid in action. It is available in 250-mg. tablets and is usually administered in doses of 750 mg. to 1 Gm. daily.

■ Emetics

Emetics are agents given to produce vomiting, the use of which has been largely supplanted by gastric lavage. They are occasionally used as a first-aid measure when prompt evacuation of the stomach is essential.

Vomiting is a complex reflex mechanism, and drugs given to induce vomiting may act at one

419

or more locations in the reflex arc. Vomiting can sometimes be brought about simply by tickling the back of the throat with a finger. A number of household substances can also be used to produce emesis. They include mustard water (1 level teaspoonful of mustard to a glass of tepid water), mild soapsuds solution, warm salt water, or plain starch in warm water. Copious amounts of warm or tepid water will usually induce vomiting. Other emetics include copper sulfate, zinc sulfate, and ipecac fluidextract.

Apomorphine hydrochloride, N.F., B.P.

This drug acts by direct stimulation of the vomiting center in the medulla. The dose is 5 mg. (2 to 8 mg.), and it is administered subcutaneously or intramuscularly. Vomiting is usually produced in a few minutes. Large does produce central depression, so that the drug should be avoided for patients who are already depressed. Since the drug is prepared from morphine, conformity with regulations of the Harrison Narcotic Law is essential.

■ Antiemetics

Antiemetics are drugs given to produce symptomatic relief of nausea and vomiting. Control of vomiting is important and often difficult. Numerous preparations have been used, but effective treatment usually depends upon the removal of the cause. Vomiting may result from diverse phenomena, such as strong emotion, severe pain, increased intracranial pressure, and labyrinthine disturbances. Other factors include motion sickness, endocrine disturbances, the action of certain drugs, gastrointestinal pathology, reaction to roentgen treatments, heart disease, and severe pain.

When there is reason to believe that the nausea and vomiting are associated with a mild disturbance of some kind, a cup of plain hot tea will often relieve a nauseated patient. Carbonated drinks are popular remedies when medication is unavailable and seem to be more effective when administered at room temperature. In patients who cannot eructate, however, they will only increase gastric distention and discomfort. Gastric lavage may be indicated at other times

to empty the stomach of irritating material. A glass of warm solution of sodium bicarbonate may provoke emesis and empty the stomach with much the same result as gastric lavage. Salts of bismuth, magnesium oxide, and calcium carbonate may be employed as antacids and protectives to relieve irritation and vomiting. Vomiting caused by other conditions may be relieved by central nervous system depressants, antihistaminics, and tranquilizers. Chlorpromazine is regarded as an unusually potent antiemetic acting primarily to block the chemoreceptor trigger zone. Dimenhydrinate (Dramamine), meclizine (Bonine), and several others are employed effectively for motion sickness. These are discussed elsewhere (see Index).

■ Diagnostic aids
Agents used to determine gastric acidity
Histamine

Histamine is such a potent stimulant of the gastric glands that, when injected subcutaneously or intramuscularly in doses of approximately 0.3 to 0.5 mg., its failure to stimulate secretion of hydrochloric acid is considered proof of achlorhydria. The injection may produce side effects, such as a wheal at the site of injection, headache, vertigo, superficial vasodilatation, larger vessel vasoconstriction, and sometimes a drop in blood pressure.

Preparation, dosage, and administration. The following are available histamine preparations.

Histamine phosphate, **U.S.P., B.P.** This drug is also known as histamine diphosphate or histamine acid phosphate. When given during an augmented histamine test, it is accompanied by simultaneous administration of an antidote (usually epinephrine) so that all effects of histamine, except those on gastric secretions, are antagonized. It is given subcutaneously in doses of 0.04 mg. per kilogram of body weight, and the patient is to have had nothing by mouth since midnight.

Betazole hydrochloride, **U.S.P. (Histalog).** This preparation, an analog of histamine, is used more frequently than histamine phosphate because of its lower incidence of side effects. The routine administration of an antihistaminic compound is unnecessary, and augmentation of gastric secretion is equally effective. Betazole hydrochloride is to be used cautiously in patients with allergies. It is administered subcutaneously or intramuscularly in doses of 0.5 mg. per kilogram of body weight. Oral administration is under investigation.

Azuresin, N.F. (Diagnex Blue)

Azuresin is a preparation utilized to detect achlorhydria without intubation. As such, it has come to replace the older quinine carbacrylic resin for tubeless gastric analysis. The blue dye in the azuresin can be displaced by the hydrogen ions of hydrochloric acid, if acid is present. The test results do not furnish exact quantitative data, but the test is a convenient screening device.

Preparation, dosage, and administration. Since the patient is to have nothing by mouth after midnight in preparation, the test is usually performed in the early morning hours. Upon awakening, the patient is instructed to void, and this urine is discarded. Then 500 mg. of caffeine are administered in one glass of water in order to stimulate gastric secretions. Histamine phosphate may be substituted. One hour later, the patient is instructed to void and this urine is saved as a control specimen. Two grams of azuresin are then administered in one-fourth glass of water. Two hours after administration of the resin, the patient is again instructed to void. The concentration of dye in this last specimen is then determined by comparison of urine color to color standards. The patient should know that his urine will range from green to blue in color and that this condition may persist for several days.

Agents used for roentgenographic studies
Barium sulfate, U.S.P.

Barium sulfate is a fine, white, colorless, tasteless, and bulky powder free from grittiness. It is more impermeable to roentgen rays than are tissues and is therefore employed as an opaque contrast medium for radiologic examination of the gastrointestinal tract. Its property of insolubility renders it safe to use, for all soluble

barium salts are exceedingly poisonous. The patient is usually first examined by means of a fluoroscope, and flat plates are later taken to determine the rate of barium passage through the digestive tract and to locate sites of abnormality.

Preparation, dosage, and administration. For examination of the stomach, the patient is to have had nothing by mouth since midnight and is given barium orally in doses of 300 Gm. (usually in 400 ml. of water). Saccharin and vanillin may be used to improve the palatability of this mixture. If the large bowel is to be examined, the patient should have nothing by mouth after midnight in addition to cathartics and/or cleansing enemas. The barium is then given in enema form. The patient should be instructed to attempt to retain the barium during the radiologic examination, a feat that sometimes proves difficult. After the examination, either cleansing enemas or cathartics should be administered, so that the remaining barium does not contribute to bowel obstruction. In both cases the patient should be informed that his stool will be very light in color after the examination.

Meglumine diatrizoate injection, U.S.P. (Gastrografin)

Diatrizoate compounds, which are utilized in varied concentrations for specific radiographic examinations, are also sometimes used for gastrointestinal examinations. A 76% oral solution of meglumine diatrizoate injection is a water-soluble, iodinated contrast agent known as Gastrografin. Because of its hypertonicity and tendency to cause distention of the bowel, it is somewhat less satisfactory than barium.

Organic iodine compounds for cholecystography

A number of organic iodine compounds are used as diagnostic aids in examination of the liver, gallbladder, and bile ducts. These compounds are excreted by the liver into the bile and concentrated in the gallbladder. Since they cast a shadow on x-ray film, they are utilized to visualize the gallbladder outline and the presence of stones and to determine whether the organ fills and empties normally. If the gallbladder is not functioning, it does not absorb the dye and is not visualized on the film. An empty stomach and a clear intestinal tract are necessary for visualization of the gallbladder, so that patients are prepared with fat-free suppers and cathartics and may have nothing by mouth after midnight. Occasionally, after films are taken, the patient is given a fat-containing meal and additional films are taken to determine the ability of the organ to contract.

It is recommended that iodinated compounds be used cautiously, if at all, for patients with severe renal or hepatic disease. These compounds are contraindicated for patients sensitive to iodine, and their use will interfere with diagnostic radioactive isotope uptake studies.

Iodoalphionic acid (Priodax)

This compound produces fewer side effects than iodophthalein sodium. It is eventually excreted chiefly by the kidneys. Untoward effects include dysuria, nausea and vomiting, diarrhea, dryness of the mouth, and general weakness. The drug is available in 0.5-Gm. tablets for oral administration. The usual adult dose is 3 Gm. taken with several glasses of water.

Iopanoic acid, U.S.P., B.P. (Telepaque)

Iopanoic acid is a radiopaque medium used in cholecystography. It is claimed that undesirable side effects seldom occur and that it produces greater opacification of the gallbladder. When they do occur, they include nausea, diarrhea, and dysuria. The usual dose is 3 Gm. given orally 10 hours before the roentgenogram is to be made. The drug is available in 500-mg. tablets.

Drugs that affect the intestine

■ Cathartics

Cathartics are oral drugs administered to induce defecation. They may be administered for the following purposes:

1 In preparation of abdominal viscera prior to roentgen examination
2 To produce some degree of dehydration in cases of edema (cerebral or cardiac)
3 In cases of food and drug poisoning to promote the elimination of the offending substance from the gastrointestinal tract; saline cathartics are considered useful for this purpose
4 To keep the stool soft when it is essential to avoid the irritation or straining that accompanies the passage of a hardened stool (a rectal disorder, irritated polyps in the bowel, or cases in which straining should be avoided, as after the repair of a hernia or after a cerebral vascular accident)
5 To expel parasites and toxic anthelmintics; cathartics are routinely prescribed after certain anthelmintics for the purpose of expelling the parasites as well as the anthelmintic, which may be toxic
6 To secure a stool specimen to be examined for parasites; a saline cathartic is often preferred

The laity, however, frequently misuses cathartics, and misconceptions about the function of the bowel have long been harbored by mankind.

Almy and Steinberg state:

Drugs have been used since time immemorial for the purpose of promoting defecation. Such agents are widely self-administered by lay persons. Whatever the psychological basis, there is a durable attitude, spanning many centuries and many cultures, that associates excrement with evil and its elimination with the expiation of guilt. The practical result is that most people in our society still regard even transitory constipation as something to be directly and promptly treated with a cathartic. In the past the medical profession has abetted these tendencies by the empiric and nonspecific use of purgation in the treatment of systemic disease (even the common cold) and has been slow to disown the theory of intestinal autointoxication. As a consequence, more patients now consult the physician because of the untoward effects of chronic use of cathartics than for any condition that can be relieved by them.*

*From Almy, T. P., and Steinberg, H.: The choice of drugs for gastrointestinal disturbances. In Modell, W., editor: Drugs of choice 1962-1963, St. Louis, 1962, The C. V. Mosby Co., p. 339.

Constipation is a functional impairment of the bowel that prevents it from producing stool of normal consistency and frequency. Chronic constipation is sometimes caused by organic disease, such as benign or malignant tumors, which produces obstruction in the bowel, megacolon, hypothyroidism, anal and rectal disorders, and diseases of the liver and gallbladder. Patients who suffer from disorders of the gastrointestinal tract frequently complain of constipation. On the other hand, many persons complain of constipation when no organic disease or lesion can be found. A number of factors may operate to cause constipation in such persons.

1. Faulty diet and faulty eating habits (A diet that provides inadequate bulk and residue will contribute to the development of constipation. The gastrointestinal tract should function normally if fluids and residue are supplied in sufficient quantities to keep the stool formed but soft.)
2. Failure to respond to the normal defecation impulses and insufficient time to permit the bowel to produce an evacuation
3. Sedentary habits and insufficient exercise (Bedridden patients may be constipated because of inactivity or unnatural position for defecation.) Constipation, when not due to organic causes, is generally attributable to the above three factors.
4. The effect of drugs (The use of morphine, codeine, or ganglionic blocking agents often leads to constipation as a side effect.)
5. Febrile states, psychosomatic disorders, anemias, and sick headaches (Constipation can be a symptom of both functional and organic disorders.)
6. Atonic and hypertonic conditions of the musculature of the colon (These may result from habitual use of cathartics.)

Responsibilities of the nurse

As is true for all medications, the nurse must exercise caution in giving advice about cathartics. Persons who seek help because they are becoming increasingly dependent upon cathartics should be encouraged to seek the advice of a physician. Not infrequently, powerful, self-prescribed cathartics empty the whole colon, which then requires time to collect material. In the meantime, the patient may again be distressed because there has been no daily bowel movement and take another cathartic, thereby initiating a vicious cycle that may lead to dependency. Whatever the case, the patient should be helped to overcome his dependency.

The nurse should direct her efforts toward teaching the patient practices that promote normal bowel habits. In doing so, she must bear in mind that teaching in this area may be met with some resistance, so that she should attempt to achieve a nonthreatening atmosphere. The patient's bowel complaints should be listened to, and habits explored in order to determine the possible cause of the bowel disorder. Appropriate teaching can then be directed to the problem in relation to the patient's intellectual level, his socioeconomic background (which influences the type of food he eats), and his receptivity. Not infrequently, entire families have similar bowel habits and sometimes the mother is an excellent intermediary for change.

Elderly persons who have some degree of constipation cannot be treated in the same way as younger patients. They cannot be expected to change the habit patterns of a lifetime or to subject themselves to tiresome diets that disturb the peace required by the elderly person. It may be decidedly unwise to urge an elderly person to increase the roughage of his diet. He may not have the teeth or the type of bowel to make such an adjustment happily. After an examination the doctor frequently prescribes a laxative for more or less regular use, and if it produces satisfactory results (no griping or gaseous distention), there is probably little need to worry about the cathartic habit.

Conditions for which cathartics may be contraindicated

There are a number of conditions for which cathartics should be given with caution, if at all.

1. Inflammatory disorders of the alimentary tract, such as appendicitis, typhoid fever, and chronic ulcerative colitis
2. Cases of undiagnosed abdominal pain; should

the pain be caused by an inflamed appendix, a catharitic may bring about a rupture of the appendix by increasing intestinal peristalsis

3 After some operations such as repair of the perineum or rectum (for a time, at least)
4 Pregnancy and severe anemia; debilitated patients
5 Chronic constipation and spastic constipation
6 Bowel obstruction, hemorrhage, or intussusception

A number of ill effects may follow the use or overuse of irritant cathartics in particular; one of these is a disturbance of electrolyte balance. The small intestine contains an abundance of sodium, potassium, chloride, and bicarbonate ions that will be lost when the bowel is emptied vigorously. This can result in alkalosis or acidosis, dehydration, and potassium deficiency. Young and healthy adults may recover from the purgation without noticeable ill effect, but the same may not be true in the elderly or the debilitated patient or the patient with renal impairment.

Classification

Cathartics may be classified according to their source, site of action, degree of action, or method of action. The latter two classifications will be described.

Degree of action
1 Laxatives—stimulate few bowel movements, which are formed and usually unaccompanied by cramping
2 Purgatives—produce more frequent bowel movements, which are soft or liquid in nature and are frequently accompanied by cramping

Method of action
1 Irritant cathartics—increase peristalsis in the colon by irritating sensory nerve endings in the mucosa
2 Bulk cathartics—increase the volume of non-absorbable intestinal contents, thereby distending the bowel and initiating reflex bowel activity
3 Saline cathartics—retain and increase water content of feces by virtue of osmotic qualities; may also be considered as bulk cathartics
4 Intestinal lubricants—mechanically lubricate feces in order to facilitate defecation
5 Fecal softening agents—act as dispersing wetting agents, facilitating mixture of water and

fatty substances within the fecal mass; when a homogenous mixture is produced, the feces become soft

Nonchemical irritant cathartics— anthracene cathartics (Emodin cathartics)

The principal members of this group are botanical drugs obtained from the bark, seed pods, leaves, and roots of a number of plants. Cascara, senna, rhubarb, and aloe yield anthraquinones in the alkaline portion of the small intestine; these are absorbed and later secreted to produce irritation in the large intestine. These compounds are partially absorbed from the intestine and may cause discoloration of the urine. They have also been found to impart a purgative effect to the milk of nursing women. The anthracene cathartics act in 6 to 12 hours and exert their main action on the large intestine, which explains their tendency to produce cramping. Aloe and rhubarb are almost obsolete irritant cathartics.

Cascara sagrada

Cascara sagrada is obtained from the bark of the *Rhamnus purshiana,* a shrub or small tree, and is one of the most extensively used cathartics. Its action is mainly on the large bowel and, although its effects are comparatively mild, it does act by irritation. It is less likely to cause griping than some of the other cathartics belonging to this group of compounds. The active ingredients reach the large bowel by way of the bloodstream, after absorption in the small bowel, as well as by passage along the alimentary tract.

Preparation, dosage, and administration. The following are available preparations of cascara sagrada.

Aromatic cascara fluidextract, U.S.P.; *cascara elixir,* B.P. This compound is made more palatable than the plain fluidextract by extraction with boiling water and by the addition of magnesium oxide as well as a number of flavoring agents. The magnesium oxide is used to form insoluble anthraquinone derivatives that are then removed. This makes this preparation less harsh than the fluidextract. The dose is 5 to 15 ml., and it is given orally. The dose of cascara elixir is 2 to 4 ml. Bowel evacuation occurs in about 8 hours.

Cascara sagrada fluidextract, **N.F.;** *cascara liquid extract,* **B.P.** This preparation has a very bitter taste. The adult dose is 1 to 4 ml.

Cascara tablets, **N.F., B.P.** These forms are available in 120-, 200-, and 300-mg. tablets. The average dose is 300 mg. (gr. 5) for adults. The dose of cascara tablets, B.P., is 120 to 250 mg.

Senna

Senna is obtained from the dried leaves of the plant, *Cassia acutifolia,* a cathartic well known to the Arabians. The dried leaves have been used to make a homemade infusion of the drug, which is decidedly potent. It produces a thorough bowel evacuation in 4 to 6 hours and is likely to be accompanied by griping. It resembles cascara but is more powerful. It is found in the proprietary remedies Castoria and Syrup of Figs.

Senna tea is an infusion of senna leaves made from a teaspoonful of leaves to a cup of hot water.

Preparation, dosage, and administration. The following are preparations of senna.

Senna syrup, **N.F.** The usual dose is 8 ml. orally.

Senna fluidextract, **N.F.** The usual dose is 2 ml. orally.

A powdered concentrate of senna, obtained from the pod of the plant, is said to contain the desirable laxative components but to be free of the impurities that in previous preparations have been the cause of griping. This compound is sold under the name of Senokot (tablets and granules), and the usual adult dose is two tablets or 1 teaspoon of the granules.

Cathartics that act by chemical irritation
Castor oil, U.S.P., B.P. (Oleum Ricini)

Castor oil is obtained from the seeds of the castor bean, *Ricinus communis*, a plant that grows in India but that is also cultivated in a number of places where the climate is warm. Castor oil is a bland, colorless emollient that passes through the stomach unchanged, but, like other fatty substances, it retards the emptying of the stomach and for this reason is usually

given when the stomach is empty. In the intestine the oil is hydrolyzed to glycerol and a fatty acid, ricinoleic acid. This fatty acid is responsible for the irritation of the bowel, especially the small intestine. It rarely reaches the large intestine before causing irritation. Its irritating effect causes a rapid propulsion of contents from the small intestine, including any of the oil that may have escaped hydrolysis. A therapeutic dose will produce several copious semiliquid stools in 2 to 6 hours. Some persons have little or no griping or colic-like distress, whereas others may experience considerable abdominal cramping and exhaustion. Patients who have an irritable bowel or lesions in the bowel may be made very ill.

The fluid nature of the stool is caused by the rapid passage of the fecal content rather than by a diffusion of fluid into the bowel. Castor oil tends to empty the bowel completely; hence, no evacuation is likely to occur for a day or so after its administration. The drug is excreted into the milk of nursing mothers.

Uses. Castor oil is used much less often today than formerly. It continues to be used in the preparation of certain patients who are to have a roentgen examination of abdominal viscera. Because of its irritant action it is contraindicated for patients who have ulcerative lesions of the bowel, for pregnant women, or for nursing mothers.

Preparation, dosage, and administration. The usual adult dose of castor oil is 15 ml. and it is given orally. As much as 60 ml. may be ordered.

The natural oil may be unpleasant and nauseating. This may be overcome by the use of fruit juices or pharmaceutical mixtures to emulsify and disguise the oil.

Phenolphthalein tablets, N.F., B.P.

Phenolphthalein, a phenol derivative, is a synthetic substance, the cathartic action of which is similar to that of the anthracene group. It is a white powder insoluble in water but soluble in the juice of the intestine, where it exerts its relatively mild irritant action. Evacuation is produced in 6 to 8 hours, unaccompanied by griping. It acts upon both the small and large bowel, particularly the latter. When given orally, part of the drug is absorbed and resecreted into the bile and thus a prolonged cathartic action may be obtained.

Repeated doses may cause nausea, and in some susceptible individuals a skin rash may appear. In other cases a prolonged and excessive purgative effect may indicate individual idiosyncracy. The drug is odorless and tasteless and relatively pleasant to take; it is found in a number of proprietary preparations and is sold in a candy-like form and in a chewing gum. Children should not be allowed free access to these preparations, since they are likely to regard them as ordinary candy or gum and may get an overdose of the drug. Deaths have been reported from such accidents, although the dose causing toxicity is large.

Preparation, dosage, and administration. Phenolphthalein tablets are available in 60- and 120-mg. amounts. The usual dose is 60 mg. orally.

Phenolphthalein is found in some proprietary preparations with other cathartics such as agar, liquid petrolatum, as well as with other irritant cathartics.

Bisacodyl, N.F., B.P. (Dulcolax)

Bisacodyl is a relatively nontoxic laxative agent that reflexly stimulates peristalsis upon contact with the mucosa of the colon. Having grown into popular use, bisacodyl has been successful in the treatment of various types of constipation. In larger doses, it is also widely used for cleansing of the bowel prior to some surgeries and proctoscopic and radiographic examinations. Bisacodyl is insoluble in neutral or alkaline solution and should not be taken within 1 hour after antacids have been administered.

Preparation, dosage, and administration. Bisacodyl is available in tablets containing 5 mg. for oral administration and suppositories containing 10 mg. for rectal administration. The suppositories act within 15 to 60 minutes, while the tablets produce evacuation of the bowel in 6 to 12 hours.The suppositories may cause a burning sensation and proctitis. The tablets are enteric coated and should not be chewed (to avoid release of the drug in the stomach and the possibility of emesis).

Bulk-forming cathartics

Hydrophilic colloids stimulate peristalsis by increasing bulk and therefore modifying the consistency of the stool. This mechanism of cathartic action is a normal stimulus and is one of the least harmful. These drugs do not interfere with absorption of food, but they can cause fecal impaction and obstruction, so it is important to give them with adequate fluids. The effect of these cathartics may not be apparent for 12 to 24 hours, and their full effect may not be achieved until the second or third day after administration. Some physicians maintain that bran and dried fruits (such as prunes and figs) exert the same effect, and they prefer to advise these foods rather than the cathartics.

Agar, U.S.P.

Agar is a dried mucilaginous substance obtained from several varieties of algae, which is rich in indigestible cellulose. It may be obtained in the powdered, granular, or flaked form. The granular preparation is usually the one most desirable. When moistened, it swells, forming a mass of material that passes through the intestine without being affected by the digestive juices, and by its blandness and bulk it makes the stool large and soft so that it is easily moved along the colon and into the rectum.

The effect of agar is not noticed immediately. It may require a week or two to establish satisfactory evacuation, but as soon as results seem satisfactory, the dose should gradually be reduced to the smallest amount needed for a satisfactory bowel movement. Doses should then be omitted occasionally until its use is no longer necessary. This gradual reduction and cessation of dosage should constitute a principle underlying the use of all laxative cathartics to avoid undesirable reactions and habit formation.

Preparation, dosage, and administration. Agar is best taken twice daily in doses of 4 to 16 Gm. accompanied by plenty of fluid. Some find agar more palatable when it has been allowed to soak in hot water and is then added to such food as cereal, soup, or mashed potatoes or is merely taken in the soft semisolid form. When the dry agar is used, it likewise may be added to soup, cereal, potatoes, pudding, and so on. It also may be emulsified with liquid petrolatum (Petrogalar). Cascara, phenolphthalein, or milk of magnesia is sometimes added to the emulsified form.

The mineral oil and agar emulsions are widely advertised but are of little value because the agar content is so small (2% to 6%). The laxative effect of these emulsions is usually caused by the addition of some other cathartic.

Plantago seed, N.F. (psyllium seed)

Plantago seed is the dried ripe seed of the *Plantago psyllium, Plantago indica,* or *Plantago ovata.* The seeds are small, brown or blond seeds that contain a mucilaginous material that swells in the presence of moisture to form a jelly-like indigestible mass. The main disadvantage lies in the fact that, although the seeds swell, their ends remain sharp and may be the cause of irritation in the alimentary tract. At present, only the preparations of the extracted gums are available, and these have the advantage of causing less mechanical irritation.

Preparation, dosage, and administration. The following are preparations of plantago.

Psyllium hydrophilic mucilloid (Metamucil). This compound is a white to cream-colored powder containing about 50% powdered mucilaginous portion (outer epidermis) of blond psyllium seeds and about 50% dextrose. This mixture is used in the treatment of constipation because it promotes the formation of a soft, water-retaining gelatinous residue in the lower bowel. In addition, it has a demulcent effect on inflamed mucosa. The dose is 4 to 7 Gm. one to three times daily. It should be stirred into a glass of water or other fluid, drunk while in suspension, and followed by an additional glass of fluid.

Plantago ovata coating (Konsyl). This form is a cream- to brown-colored granular powder obtained from the *Plantago ovata* (blond psyllium,

mucilaginous portion). The dose is 5 to 10 Gm. three times daily before meals in a glass of water or milk. It should be swallowed before it thickens.

Methylcellulose, U.S.P. (Cellothyl, Hydrolose, Methocel, Syncelose)

Methylcellulose is a synthetic hydrophillic colloid. It is a grayish white, fibrous powder that, in the presence of water, swells and produces a viscous, colloidal solution in the upper part of the alimentary tract. In the colon this solution loses water and forms a gel that increases the bulk and softness of the stool.

Preparation, dosage, and administration. Methylcellulose is available in 500-mg. tablets or as a syrup (200 mg. per milliliter). It is administered orally two to four times daily in doses of 1 to 1.5 Gm. It should be accompanied by one or two glasses of water. The dosage is gradually reduced as normal defecation reflexes establish a normal pattern for the behavior of the bowel. Tablets should not be chewed to avoid risk of esophageal obstruction.

Sodium carboxymethylcellulose, U.S.P. (Carmethose, CMC Cellulose Gum, Thylose Sodium)

Sodium carboxymethylcellulose is a synthetic, hydrophilic, colloid gum. It is similar to methylcellulose in that it forms a soft bulk in the intestine after oral ingestion. It is insoluble in gastric juices, which is not true of methylcellulose.

Preparation, dosage, and administration. Sodium carboxymethylcellulose is available in 225- and 500-mg. tablets and in 5% solution for oral administration. The usual dose is 1.5 Gm. three times daily with one or two glasses of water. Tablets should not be chewed before swallowing.

Saline cathartics

The saline cathartics are soluble salts that are only slightly absorbed from the alimentary canal. Because of their osmotic effect these salts retain and increase the water content of feces. An isotonic saline solution will inhibit absorption of water from the bowel and will therefore increase the total fluid bulk. Peristalsis will be increased and several liquid or semiliquid stools will result. A hypertonic saline solution will cause diffusion of fluid from the blood in the wall of the bowel and into the lumen of the organ until the solution has been made isotonic. This type of fluid is especially effective in relieving edema, although the action may prove exhausting to the patient. Catharsis results in 1 to 4 hours.

The intestinal membrane is not entirely impermeable to the passage of saline cathartics. Some find their way into the general circulation only to be excreted by the kidney, in which case they act as saline diuretics. Hypertonic saline solutions in the bowel may result in so much loss of fluid that little or no diuretic effect will be possible. Some ions may have a toxic effect if they accumulate in the blood in sufficient quantity. This may occur with magnesium ions if a solution is retained in the intestine for a long time or if the patient suffers from renal impairment. It may also occur when large doses of the salt are given intravenously.

Uses. The saline cathartics are the cathartics of choice for the relief of edema (cerebral, cardiac) and for securing a stool specimen for examination as well as for use with certain anthelmintics and in some cases of food and drug poisoning.

When the object is merely to empty the intestine, magnesium citrate, magnesium sulfate, sodium phosphate, or milk of magnesia is effective. Milk of magnesia (magnesium hydroxide) is the mildest of the salines and is often the cathartic of choice for children. Heavy magnesium oxide is better for adults, as a rule. Magnesium sulfate is probably the best to relieve edema, although it has a disagreeable taste. Sodium sulfate is the most disagreeable and is seldom prescribed, except in veterinary practice. The effervescent preparations are the most agreeable to take.

Preparation, dosage, and administration. The following salts, when given for their cathartic effect, are usually given orally. Certain of them may be given rectally as an enema. The salts

tend to have a rapid action, especially if administered in the morning before breakfast. Patients sometimes complain of gaseous distention after taking saline cathartics. All preparations should be accompanied by a liberal intake of water, since the salts do not readily leave the stomach unless well diluted and may cause vomiting. On the other hand, if the saline is given to reduce edema, the patient's total daily intake of fluids will probably be restricted.

When a salt such as magnesium sulfate is administered to a patient, it should not only be dissolved in an adequate amount of water but it should also be disguised in fruit juice. Grape juice is excellent unless the patient is nauseated, in which case it is better to give it in plain water (chilled) or on chipped ice since the grape juice, if vomited, will stain bedclothing.

Sodium sulfate, B.P. (Glauber's Salt). This compound occurs as a white powder that is readily soluble in water. It has a strong, disagreeable saline taste that may be improved with lemon juice. It is one of the least expensive of saline cathartics and is the basis of many proprietary saline cathartics such as Sal Hepatica. The usual dose is 15 Gm.

Magnesium sulfate (Epsom Salt), **U.S.P., B.P.** This agent occurs as glassy, needle-like crystals or as a white powder and is readily soluble in water. It has a bitter saline taste. The usual dose for cathartic effect is 15 Gm. ($^1/_2$ ounce), although the range of dosage may be from 10 to 30 Gm.

Milk of magnesia, **U.S.P.;** ***magnesium hydroxide mixture,*** **B.P.** Milk of magnesia is also used as an antacid. In the stomach the magnesium hydroxide reacts with the hydrochloric acid to form magnesium chloride, which is responsible for the cathartic effect. The usual dose for adults is 15 ml. ($^1/_2$ fluidounce), although the range of dosage is 5 to 30 ml. *Magnesium hydroxide tablets,* N.F., contain 0.3 Gm. of the drug.

Magnesium oxide, **U.S.P.** This preparation depends on the conversion of the oxide into soluble salts of magnesium, which are themselves responsible for the cathartic effect. The usual laxative dose is 1 to 4 Gm.

Heavy magnesium carbonate, **B.P.**; *light magnesium carbonate,* **B.P.** This cathartic is a bulky white powder that is practically insoluble in water. It is used as an antacid as well as a cathartic. Cathartic effect is dependent upon the formation of a soluble salt of magnesium. The usual dose is 2 to 8 Gm.

Magnesium citrate solution, **N.F.** This preparation is not very soluble, hence the need for a relatively large dose. It is not unpleasant to take because it is carbonated and flavored. The usual dose is one-half to one bottle (6 to 12 ounces).

Sodium phosphate, **N.F., B.P.** This is a white crystalline substance readily soluble in water. Its taste is less disagreeable than that of either sodium sulfate or magnesium sulfate. The usual dose is 4 Gm.

Effervescent sodium phosphate, **N.F.** This preparation is made effervescent by the addition of sodium bicarbonate and citric and tartaric acids. The usual dose is 10 Gm.

A concentrated aqueous solution of sodium biphosphate and sodium phosphate is available under the name of Fleet Phospho-Soda. The usual dose as a cathartic is 4 to 15 ml. It is also marketed in a disposable enema unit.

Potassium sodium tartrate, **N.F. (Rochelle Salt).** The usual dose is 10 Gm. ($^{1}/_{3}$ ounce) orally. This preparation occurs as crystals or white powder, is very soluble, and has a not unpleasant taste.

Mineral waters. Mineral waters are usually artificially prepared solutions made in a factory and contain magnesium sulfate or sodium sulfate or both. Their use in the treatment of constipation is thought inadvisable.

Lubricant or emollient cathartics
Mineral oil, U.S.P.; liquid paraffin, B.P.

Mineral oil (liquid petrolatum) is a mixture of liquid hydrocarbons obtained from petroleum. The oil is not digested and absorption is minimal. It softens the fecal mass and prevents excessive absorption of water. It is especially useful when it is desirable to keep feces soft and when straining at stool must be reduced, as after rectal operations, repair of hernias, or cerebrovascular or spinal cord accidents. It may be useful for patients who have a chronic type of constipation because of prolonged inactivity. Such might be the case in patients with orthopedic conditions.

Some physicians object to the use of mineral oil on the basis that it dissolves certain of the fat-soluble vitamins and bile salts and inhibits their absorption. Others maintain that only the precursor to vitamin A (carotene) is so affected and that natural vitamin A is quantitatively absorbed from the intestine in the presence of mineral oil. Another objection to its use is that in large doses it tends to seep from the rectum, which may interfere with healing of postoperative wounds in the region of the anus and perineum. Although absorption of mineral oil is very limited, it is said to give rise to a chronic inflammatory reaction in tissues where it is found after absorption. Indiscriminate use by the aged and weak should not be encouraged. Mineral oil may also produce a lipid pneumonia if drops coating the pharynx gain access to the trachea.

Preparation, dosage, and administration. Mineral oil is administered in doses that range from 15 to 30 ml. (adults) and is best given between meals or at bedtime. It should not be given immediately after meals, since it may delay the passage of food from the stomach. Most patients may have a slice of orange or glass of orange juice to relieve the oily taste in the mouth. Mineral oil is also to be found as the major ingredient of some oil retention enemas.

Olive oil, U.S.P., B.P.; corn oil, U.S.P.; cottonseed oil, U.S.P.

Olive oil and cottonseed oil are digestible oils, but if given in sufficient quantity, they may act as emollient cathartics, since part of the oil will escape hydrolysis.

When administered in doses of 30 ml., these oils act as laxatives. They may be given orally or rectally.

Fecal moistening agents

With the introduction of fecal moistening agents and other less toxic synthetic drugs, there seems to be more restricted use of irritant cathartics. Fecal moistening agents are constantly being improved and have achieved a level of popular therapy.

Dioctyl sodium sulfosuccinate, N.F.

Dioctyl sodium sulfosuccinate acts in a manner similar to that of detergents and permits water and fatty substance to penetrate and to be well mixed with the fecal material. Thus, this agent promotes the formation of soft, formed stools and is a useful aid in the treatment of constipation.

It is said to have a wide margin of safety and negligible toxicity. There is some question about the advisability of giving it with mineral oil, since there is a possibility that it may promote absorption of the oil.

Uses. It is indicated for patients with rectal impaction, chronic constipation, and painful conditions of the rectum and anus and for those who should avoid straining at the time of defecation.

Preparation, dosage, and administration. The following are available preparations of dioctyl sodium sulfosuccinate.

Dioctyl sodium sulfosuccinate (**Colace, Doxinate**). This preparation is available in 50-, 60-, 100-, and 240-mg. capsules; in solution, 10 mg. per milliliter; and as a syrup, 4 mg. per milliliter. The usual adult dose is 50 to 100 mg. daily; 10 to 20 mg. for infants and children. Solutions of the drug are best given in fruit juice or milk.

Peri-Colace. Peri-Colace includes casantranol, which provides gentle peristaltic stimulation. Either dioctyl sodium sulfosuccinate or casantranol produces a bowel movement in 8 to 12 hours.

Dioctyl calcium sulfosuccinate, N.F. (**Surfak**). This drug is claimed to provide superior surfactant activity to the older chemical, dioctyl sodium. It is indicated in conditions in which cathartic therapy is undesirable but in which prevention of constipation is necessary. A wide margin of safety is claimed. The drug is administered in 240-mg. capsules; the usual dose is one capsule daily.

Dialose. Dialose is a combination of dioctyl sulfosuccinate and sodium carboxymethylcellulose. It combines the advantages of both drugs —fecal-moistening and bulk-producing agents. Dialose Plus also includes oxyphenisatin acetate, which is a peristaltic stimulant. Recommended dosages are one capsule two or three times a day, taken with a glass of water.

■ Antidiarrheics

Diarrhea is a symptom of a disorder of the bowel associated with rapid passage of intestinal content, frequent fluid stools, and griping. The remedies ordered to relieve diarrhea are selected on the basis of causation. The causes may be many and varied and include (1) the eating of contaminated or partially decomposed food, (2) bacterial or protozoan infection, (3) nervous disorders, (4) disturbances of gastric physiology, such as the absence of hydrochloric acid or the effects of resectional surgery of the stomach, (5) inflammatory processes of the intestine or adjacent viscera, and (6) the effects of certain drugs in the intestine (such as some of the broad-spectrum antibiotics).

The antidiarrheic drugs are less likely to be used without medical supervision than are the cathartics. Diarrhea may at times produce serious consequences in terms of dehydration, exhaustion, loss of electrolytes, vitamins, and food materials. In view of the numerous possible causes it is evident that effective treatment depends on discovering the cause and removing it if possible. In a few instances the administration of a cathartic that brings about the emptying of the entire bowel may be the best way to relieve diarrhea by elimination of contents irritating the bowel. Since diarrhea is looked upon as a defense mechanism on the part of the bowel against irritants or toxins, the diarrhea should not be checked until the cause has been determined.

The drugs used in the treatment of diarrhea include (1) demulcents and protectives, (2) adsorbents, (3) astringents, (4) carminatives, (5) antiseptics, and (6) sedatives and antispasmodics.

Demulcents and protectives

The demulcents are preparations that have a soothing effect on the irritated membrane of the gastrointestinal tract by coating membrane surface and thereby protecting underlying cells from irritating stimuli. The preparations used are salts of bismuth, calcium carbonate, and magnesium oxide. They are of limited efficacy and used only in mild disturbances.

Adsorbents

Preparations that adsorb gas or toxic substances from the stomach and bowel have been used extensively, but their value in the control of diarrhea has come to be questioned. If they are effective adsorbents, they adsorb not only undesirable substances but desirable ones such as enzymes and food nutrients as well. Hydrophilic substances such as psyllium hydrophilic mucilloid are sometimes combined with adsorbents for use as antidiarrheics. They contribute adhesiveness to the stool but do not necessarily stop the diarrhea. Adsorbents have an advantage of being inexpensive and nontoxic.

Preparation, dosage, and administration. The following are adsorbent preparations.

Activated charcoal, **U.S.P.** In a dry state this is one of the most efffective adsorbent substances. It was formerly used to relieve flatulence and diarrhea. It is now used chiefly as a general purpose antidote for certain types of poisoning.

Kaolin, **N.F.**; *light kaolin,* **B.P.** This is a naturally occurring aluminum silicate (clay) long used by the Chinese for the relief of diarrhea. It is given suspended in water in doses of 15 to 60 Gm. every 3 or 4 hours until relief is obtained.

Kaolin mixture with pectin, **N.F. (Kaopectate).** This mixture contains kaolin and pectin and acts as both an adsorbent and demulcent. Pectin is a coarse, yellowish powder that, when mixed with water, has a mucilaginous consistency. Ground raw apples constitute a good source of it and have been used in the treatment of diarrhea, especially diarrhea in children. Kaopectate is effective but must be given in relatively large doses, 15 to 30 ml. several times a day.

Astringents

Astringents are substances that shrink swollen and inflamed tissues such as the intestinal mucosa of the patient suffering from diarrhea. Astringents precipitate proteins and form an insoluble substance (a protein salt) over the mucous membrane and thus protect it from irritating substances. Astringents also inhibit secretions. Tannic acid has long been used as an astringent in the treatment of diarrhea, but there is some doubt concerning its effectiveness beyond the stomach because it may combine with food substances and be destroyed by hydrolysis.

Present-day therapy is directed at the cause of the diarrhea and at the maintenance of normal extracellular fluids. For this, better agents are available.

■ Carminatives

Carminatives are mild, irritant drugs that increase gastrointestinal motility and aid in expulsion of gas from the stomach and intestine. The active ingredients are, with few exceptions, aromatic substances such as volatile oils that possess an irritant action. Carminatives are more likely to be used in the home than in the hospital. Elderly patients may prefer them, partly because they may be accustomed to using them for the relief of mild symptoms. Whiskey or brandy in hot water or a few drops of peppermint (peppermint oil, U.S.P., or peppermint water, N.F.) in hot water are remedies commonly used in the home.

Mylicon is a drug utilized for the relief of flatulence. It is composed of simethicone (40 mg.) and relieves flatulence by its defoaming action. It acts in the stomach and intestines by changing the surface tension of gas bubbles, causing them to coalesce and enabling the patient to eliminate gas by erutating or passing flatus. The drug is available in tablet form to be chewed.

Phazyme is a phased tablet that releases pepsin, diastase, and simethicone in the stomach and pancreatin in the small intestine. It provides enzymes and gas-releasing agents to minimize gas formation and discomfort due to distention. It is administered in doses of one tablet with meals and at bedtime.

Antiseptics
Sulfonamides

Several of the sulfonamide compounds that are poorly absorbed from the intestine have been used in the treatment of certain cases of bacillary dysentery. These have included sulfa-guanidine and succinylsulfathiazole. However, sulfadiazine (which is absorbed from the bowel) has come to be the preparation of choice. It is also the preparation of choice for the treatment of cholera. The usual full doses of the drug are employed. The initial dose is usually 2 to 4 Gm. followed by 1 Gm. every 4 to 6 hours. Adequate fluid intake should be provided for the patient.

Salicylazosulfapyridine (Azulfidine) is employed in the treatment of secondary infections of patients who suffer from chronic ulcerative colitis. One gram is administered every 4 hours around the clock or, when the patient becomes ambulatory, 1 Gm. may be given after meals and at bedtime for a period of 1 or 2 weeks.

Antibiotics

Several of the antibiotics are bactericidal when administered orally (streptomycin, chloramphenicol, and the tetracyclines). Combinations of penicillin and streptomycin may also be given intramuscularly for certain infections of the bowel. Methicillin or vancomycin may be prescribed if *Staphylococcus aureus* is identified in the stool of patients suffering from diarrhea.

Neomycin sulfate, U.S.P., is an antibiotic that is also poorly absorbed from the gastrointestinal tract when given in oral form. It has been used as a bactericidal agent to sterilize the tract before surgery and in treatment of bacterial diarrheas. For sterilization of the intestinal tract, two tablets (0.5 Gm. each) are recommended hourly for 4 hours, then two tablets every 4 hours for four doses. The drug is contraindicated in the presence of intestinal obstruction because of the possibility of increased absorption from the diseased bowel. Caution is expressed regarding the possibility of superinfection. Chronic toxicity is manifest in renal damage and in damage to the eighth cranial nerve.

Kanamycin sulfate, U.S.P. (Kantrex), may also be used for similar purposes in 1- to 4-Gm. oral doses. Toxicity is low and affects the eighth cranial nerve.

Other drugs. A number of other drugs have been used for their antiseptic effect in the intestine. They include drugs such as methylene blue, gentian violet, and phenylsalicylate. Certain arsenicals, emetine, the iodohydroxyquinoline compounds, as well as certain antibiotics, are used in the treatment of amebic dysentery (see Chapter 30).

Sedatives and antispasmodics

The sedatives most often used to relieve diarrhea are preparations of opium, such as paregoric and laudanum. Codeine and morphine are sometimes used but should not be employed for chronic conditions because of the danger of producing drug dependence. Phenobarbital is used in conjection with anticholinergic drugs, a combination that is a common base for many antispasmodic drugs.

Belladonna and its alkaloids, either natural or synthetic, are frequently employed for their antispasmodic action on the intestine. These preparations are manufactured in varied proportions and under differing trade names. Some of the more commonly used include those described in the following paragraphs.

Chardonna is a drug consisting of phenobarbital, charcoal, and extract of belladonna. It depresses cholinergic stimulating effects. It is indicated for spastic conditions of the gastrointestinal tract in doses of one tablet three times daily, to be given before meals.

Donnagel combines kaolin, pectin, atropine, and belladonna for adsorbent, demulcent, anticholinergic, and spasmolytic effects. It is specifically indicated for antidiarrheal use in doses of 1 to 2 tablespoons every 3 hours.

Donnatal is a mixture of atropine, scopolamine, and phenobarbital. It also contains belladonna alkaloids for antispasmodic use.

Diphenozylate is used in combination with atropine (Lomotil) to control diarrhea in patients with irritable bowel syndrome and functional diarrhea. Dosage is variable. It is available in tablets and liquid form; each tablet or 5 ml. contains 2.5 mg. of diphenoxylate and 0.025 mg. of atropine. It is a very effective drug that acts by increasing intestinal tone and decreasing gastrointestinal motility. It is an opiate-like drug and may cause euphoria or slight sedation. It is an exempt narcotic.

Pamine (methscopolamine bromide) is a parasympatholytic drug that inhibits gastric secretion and also decreases gastrointestinal motility. The recommended dose is 2.5 mg. before meals and at bedtime.

Questions

for study and review

1 Differentiate between systemic and nonsystemic antacid characteristics.
2 Why is betazole hydrochloride (Histalog) preferred over histamine phosphate in diagnostic stimulation of hydrochloric acid secretion?
3 Define the mechanism of action of the Diagnex Blue test. In relation to this test, what would you consider important to tell the patient?
2 When using a salt solution for a gargle, why is it preferable to use a physiologic salt solution rather than a strong salt solution?
5 Mention some of the ways drugs may affect the stomach.
6 Name several simple emetics.
7 Name several preparations that are useful to check vomiting.
8 What are several popular misconceptions about constipation?
9 Name several conditions in which cathartics are contraindicated.
10 When a person walks into a drugstore and asks for a cathartic, why is a good druggist likely to inquire whether the person has any nausea or abdominal pain?
11 If a patient is scheduled to have a cholecystogram and a T_3 uptake on the same day, what nursing judgment would be exercised?
12 Identify and define the major modes of cathartic action, giving a drug example of each.
13 In case of food poisoning, why would castor oil be a more suitable cathartic than cascara?
14 What suggestions would you give to a person who asked you what could be done to overcome habitual constipation?
15 Evaluate the claims made for cathartics on present-day television and radio programs.
16 Identify two major objections to the use of mineral oil.

Multiple choice

Circle the answer of your choice.
17 For which of the following reasons is syrup sometimes used in medicines?
   a. as an antacid
   b. to increase caloric content
   c. as a flavoring agent
   d. as a digestant
18 Which of the following is a good example of a systemic antacid?
   a. calcium carbonate
   b. sodium bicarbonate
   c. lime water
   d. rhubarb and soda
19 Which of the following is a good example of a nonsystemic antacid?
   a. aluminum hydroxide   c. sodium bicarbonate
   b. calcium chloride   d. sodium carbonate
20 Which of the following represents the most outstanding precaution to observe when giving hydrochloric acid to a patient?
   a. dilute well with water
   b. give with meals
   c. give after meals
   d. follow administration with a drink of water
21 A potent stimulant of gastric secretions is:
   a. hydrochloric acid   c. histamine phosphate
   b. alcohol 7%   d. glutamic acid
22 All of the following preparations act both as an antacid and as a cartharic except:
   a. phenolphthalein
   b. magnesium hydroxide
   c. magnesium oxide
23 Kaopectate can be expected to relieve diarrhea by producing which of the following effects?
   a. cathartic and demulcent
   b. adsorbent and demulcent
   c. adsorbent and astringent
   d. carminative and sedative
24 In which of the following classifications might essence of peppermint belong?
   a. digestant   c. carminative
   b. antiemetic   d. antidiarrheic
25 Which of the following substances is responsible for the cathartic effect when milk of magnesia is administered?
   a. magnesium citrate
   b. magnesium chloride
   c. magnesium carbonate
   d. magnesium hydroxide
26 Methylcellulose is a cathartic that acts in which of the following ways?
   a. irritation of the intestine
   b. formation of bulk
   c. stimulation of bile flow
   d. detergent action
27 What is the chief present-day use for activated charcoal?
   a. as an emetic
   b. as a nonsystemic antacid
   c. as an antidote for poison
   d. as a purgative
28 Of the following cathartics which would you say is the one of choice for children?
   a. castor oil

b. senna syrup
c. milk of magnesia
d. sodium sulfate

29 The physiologically least harmful of the following cathartics is:
   a. cascara sagrada   c. Dulcolax
   b. milk of magnesia   d. Metamucil

30 If a young mother approached you for advice regarding her 7-year-old son, saying:"Johnny seems to be perfectly well, but he has not had a bowel movement for 2 days. What kind of a cathartic do you think I should give him?" Which of the following replies would you consider the safest and the most helpful?
   a. "You had better see your doctor; cathartics can be dangerous if used at the wrong time."
   b. "A dose of castor oil should take care of him nicely."
   c. "The use of a glycerin suppository will probably take care of his immediate needs and then see that he gets plenty of fruits and vegetables in his diet."
   d. "A teaspoonful of milk of magnesia is a mild cathartic and well suited to the needs of children."

31 Indicate whether each of the following antacids is constipating or diarrheal.
   a. aluminum hydroxide gel
   b. magnesium trisilicate
   c. calcium carbonate
   d. milk of magnesia

32 Bile acts to aid digestion by:
   a. activating pepsin
   b. hydrolyzing protein
   c. lowering surface tension of fats
   d. flushing bile ducts

33 A sulfonamide of choice for bacillary dysentery is:
   a. sulfadiazine   c. Azulfidine
   b. sulfathiazole   d. Sulfasuxidine

References

A. D. A. Council on Dental Therapeutics: Evaluation of Crest toothpaste, J.A.D.A. **61:**129, 1960.

American Dental Association: Accepted dental remedies, ed. 29, Chicago, 1965, Council on Dental Therapeutics, American Dental Association.

DiPalma, J. R., editor: Drill's pharmacology in medicine, New York, 1965, McGraw-Hill Book Company.

Diserena, R. V., Beman, F. M., and DeLor, C. J.: Medical management of gastric ulcer, Amer. J. Digest. Dis. **9:**191, 1964.

Editorial: Is there a therapeutic dentifrice? J.A.M.A. **155:**366, 1954.

Fordtran, J. S., and Collyns, J. A. H.: Antacid pharmacology in duodenal ulcer, New Eng. J. Med. **274:**921, 1966.

Frohman, I. P.: Constipation, Amer. J. Nurs. **55:**65, 1955.

Gambill, E. E.: Drugs in peptic ulcer, Minn. Med. **37:**787, 1954.

Ginsberg, M. K.: A study of oral hygiene nursing care, Amer. J. Nurs. **61:**67, 1961.

Ginsberg, M. K., and Yoder, A. E.: The effectiveness of some traditional methods in oral hygiene nursing care, J. Peridont. **35:**513, 1964.

Goodman, L., and Gilman, A., editors: The pharmacological basis of therapeutics, ed. 4, New York, 1970, The Macmillan Company.

Ingelfinger, F. J.: Anticholinergic therapy of gastrointestinal disorders, New Eng. J. Med. **268:**1454, 1963.

Kirsner, J. B.: Facts and fallacies of current medical therapy for uncomplicated duodenal ulcer, J.A.M.A. **187:**423, 1964.

Kirsner, J. B., Palmer, W. L., and Gutman, A. B., editors: Treatment of peptic ulcer, current concepts, Amer. J. Med. **29:**793, 1960.

Kirsner, J. B., and others: Problems in the evaluation of gastrointestinal drugs, Clin. Pharmacol. Therap. **3:**510, 1962.

Knutson, J. W.: Fluoridation, where are we today? Amer. J. Nurs. **60:**196, 1960.

Kutscher, A. H., editor: Pharmacotherapeutics of oral disease, New York, 1964, McGraw-Hill Book Company.

Markham, J.: Care of the mouth, Nurs. Times **58:**1384, 1962.

Modell, W., editor: Drugs of choice 1972-1973, St. Louis, 1972, The C. V. Mosby Co.

Morgan, J. W.: The harmful effects of mineral oil purgatives, J.A.M.A. **117:**1335, 1941.

Redman, B. K., and Redman, R. S.: Oral care of the critically ill patient. In Bergersen, B., editor: Current concepts in clinical nursing, vol. 1, St. Louis, 1967, The C. V. Mosby Co.

Tronquet, A. A.: Oral hygiene for hospital patients, J.A.D.A. **63:**215, 1961.

Ziter, F. M. H.: Cathartic colon, New York J. Med. **67:**546, 1967.

Minerals, vitamins, hormones

If the student stops to consider the place of certain drugs in the body economy, she will quickly recognize that in some instances substances given as medicaments are not foreign to the body but are provided as replacement therapy. They stand in contrast to a large number of drugs, the "foreign" compounds such as the anesthetics, antibiotics, and antihistaminics given to achieve a desirable pharmacologic effect. This "normal" group of drugs are natural constituents of the body or diet that are required in certain quantities to preserve healthy function. When absent, as in nutritional deficiency diseases, they must be replaced if the disease is to be cured. However, they may also be given when a deficiency is not present to obtain physiological actions available only at high blood levels.

■ Water

Dehydration resulting from vomiting, diarrhea, or excessive sweating may cause disturbance in electrolyte balance. Diseases such as diabetes and adrenal cortical insufficiency are associated with this type of imbalance and require expert medical management in selecting the proper parenteral fluids and electrolyte replacement. Simple dehydration involving water loss without electrolyte loss (as may be caused by insufficient water intake) can be remedied by restoration of water by mouth or parenterally by giving isotonic (5%) glucose solution.

The diuresis induced by administration of large amounts of water may lead to potassium depletion. Thus a potassium supplement is a frequent adjunct to prolonged intravenous fluid therapy or hydration therapy.

In the presence of any kind of intravenous fluid therapy, the nurse should be alert to fluid balance maintained by the patient. For this reason, intake and output records are vital. Quantities exceeding 3000 ml. per 24 hours for intra-

435

venous administration are rarely ordered because of the danger of circulatory overload. Geriatric patients, particularly, should have intravenous fluids administered at relatively slow rates of flow.

Excesses of water in relation to salt produce the symptoms known as water intoxication or miner's cramps, with muscular pains, spasmodic movements, and convulsions. It is a moot question whether this condition should be regarded as water excess or salt lack.

The most common form of water excess occurs after extensive losses of water and electrolytes by sweating, followed by drinking large amounts of plain water. Its prevention and treatment involve normalizing the tonicity of body water by increasing the intake of salt, often in the form of salt tablets, to balance the water ingested.

Minerals

Sodium and potassium

These cations (positive ions) are the principal ones in the extracellular and intracellular spaces, respectively. Normally, their concentration is automatically regulated by renal excretion, but a number of disease states can produce serious alterations in their levels. In addition, the possibility of administering concentrated solutions of the electrolytes parenterally makes it possible to produce sodium and potassium loading during efforts to correct deficiencies.

Sodium loss tends to occur in a number of pathologic states such as loss of gastric secretions, in metabolic disorders such as Addison's disease, and in prolonged diuresis with mercurial drugs. Loss of sodium decreases extracellular fluid and eventually leads to shock. Replacement can be made by parenteral means; hypertonic solutions of sodium chloride can be given intravenously if rapid restoration is necessary.

Sodium excess is typical of edema of congestine heart failure, advanced kidney disease, and cirrhosis of the liver. Withholding dietary sodium is frequently practiced in these conditions to promote gradual net loss of sodium through excretion.

Potassium loss is also a consequence of certain metabolic diseases, kidney diseases, loss of gastrointestinal secretions rich in this ion, diuretic therapy, or infusions of solutions not containing potassium. Potassium deficit affects the functions of both skeletal and cardiac muscle and may lead to paralysis of skeletal muscles or cardiac arrest. One hazard of the parenteral correction of potassium deficiency is the production of potassium poisoning, and the administration of potassium salts intravenously must be performed cautiously to avoid reaching a concentration that can cause asystole.

Preparation, dosage, and administration

Potassium chloride, **U.S.P., B.P.** This agent is available in 300- and 500-mg. as well as 1-Gm. tablets for oral administration and in 10-, 20-, 30-, and 40-mEq. solutions for parenteral administration. Whenever an intravenous solution containing a potassium salt is prescribed, the nurse should know how fast the solution is to be administered. Rapid infusion of potassium chloride frequently causes pain or burning at the infusion site or arrhythmias.

Potassium citrate, **N.F., B.P.** This form is administered orally.

Potassium Triplex. This is a nonofficial preparation of potassium acetate, potassium bicarbonate, and potassium citrate in aqueous solution. It contains 1 Gm. of each of these salts in each 10 ml. of solution, which provides 27 mEq. of potassium. It is administered orally, well diluted in fruit juice or water.

Kaon. Kaon is a nonofficial preparation of potassium gluconate used for replacement in hypokalemia. It is available in a sugar-coated tablet that is designed to dissolve in the stomach and as palatable elixir. The tablets are usually administered four times daily. The usual adult dose of Kaon elixir is 15 ml. Each milliliter supplies 20 mEq. of elemental potassium. Complaints of gastrointestinal disturbances during administration of the drug may be indication for discontinuing therapy.

K-Lyte. K-Lyte effervescent tablets, when

dissolved in water, supply potassium citrate, potassium bicarbonate, and potassium citrate, potassium bicarbonate, and potassium cyclamate. The tablets are individually foil wrapped and, when dissolved in 3 to 4 ounces of water, provide a lime-flavored drink.

Calcium

Calcium is necessary to the body for the growth of bone, for regulation of activities of nerves, muscles, and glands, for maintenance of cardiac and vascular tone, and for normal coagulation of blood. The intake of calcium in a balanced diet is sufficient for normal body needs, but in diseased conditions associated with calcium deficiency the drug is administered in the form of its soluble salts, chloride or lactate. When the calcium concentration of the blood is below normal continued administration of soluble calcium salts increases the calcium content to some extent, but it falls rapidly when the drug is discontinued.

Deficiency in calcium salts affects the peripheral neuromuscular mechanism, resulting in excessive irritability. A deficiency or excess of calcium salts alters cardiac function. The absence or deficiency of calcium salts results in undue heart relaxation and asystole. An excess of calcium salts produces a prolonged state of contraction known as "calcium rigor."

The absorption of calcium will depend upon how well it is kept in solution in the digestive tract. An acid medium favors calcium solubility; hence, calcium is absorbed mainly in the upper intestinal tract. Absorption is decreased by the presence of alkalies and large amounts of fatty acids with which the calcium forms insoluble soaps. Adequate intake of vitamin D appears to promote calcium absorption. A normal person excretes calcium in both the feces and the urine.

Daily requirements. The average adult needs approximately 0.8 Gm. of calcium daily, but pregnant or lactating women need 1.2 to 1.3 Gm. Children age 6 to 18 need from 0.9 to 1.4 Gm.

Patients who are bedridden tend to develop a negative calcium balance because the ion is lost from bones and is excreted. This effect is likely to be serious only when long immobilization of the patient is necessary.

Uses. Calcium salts are used as a nutritional supplement, particularly during pregnancy and lactation. They are specific in the treatment of hypocalcemic tetany. They have also been used for their antispasmodic effects in cases of abdominal pain, tenesmus, and colic resulting from disease of the gallbladder or painful contractions of the ureters. The basic salts of calcium are used as antacids.

Preparation, dosage, and administration

Calcium chloride, **U.S.P., B.P.** This is a salt of calcium irritating to tissues when given parenterally other than by intravenous injection. Care must be taken that the needle does not slip out of the vein and cause serious tissue irritation. Calcium chloride may be given orally but tends to cause gastric disturbance. When administered orally, it is best given in capsules. It is an acidifying salt and for that reason promotes the absorption of calcium. The average adult dose for oral administration is 1 Gm. (gr. 15) four times a day.

Calcium gluconate, **U.S.P., B.P.** This preparation is a white, crystalline or granular powder, which is odorless and tasteless. It has an advantage over calcium chloride since it is more palatable for oral administration and can be given parenterally. It should not be administered intramuscularly to children, however, since there is danger of abscess formation and tissue slough. For severe hypocalcemic tetany, calcium gluconate injection, N.F., B.P., is administered slowly in a 10% solution, intravenously (5 to 30 ml.). For mild hypocalcemic tetany, calcium gluconate may be given orally, 5 Gm. three times a day after meals. It is available in tablet form for oral administration. One part of calcium gluconate is soluble in 30 parts of cold water or in 5 parts of boiling water.

Calcium lactate, **N.F., B.P.** This compound is given orally. Its physical properties are similar to those of calcium gluconate. The usual adult dose is 5 Gm., which may be repeated three or four times a day. It is marketed in 300- and 600-mg. tablets. Calcium lactate is more soluble in hot water than in cold and should be dissolved

437

Table 21-1 Minerals and human nutrition

Mineral	Source	Daily requirements in adult male	Specific functions	Deficiency clinical state
Sodium	Common salt Citrate and tartrate in fruits	0.5 to 1.0 Gm.	Control of body water Electrophysiology of nerve, muscle, gland cells Regulation of pH, isotonicity	*Hyponatremia* Lassitude, hypotension, vomiting, cramps, hemoconcentration
Potassium	Present in all plant and animal food	2.0 Gm.	Necessary for electrophysiology of cell membranes Regulation of pH, isotonicity	*Hypopotassemia, hypokalemia* Mental changes, loquacity, hallucinations Limp, soft, weak muscles EKG: prolonged QT, depressed ST, inverted T
Calcium	Milk, cheese, flour	0.8 Gm.	Calcification of bones and teeth, blood clotting, excitation-coupling mechanisms, cofactor in enzyme reactions	Hypocalcemia Tetany Osteomalacia
Magnesium	Fruit, peas, beans, nuts, flour	0.4 Gm.	Electrophysiology, enzyme reactions	Neuromuscular disorders
Iron	Meat, liver, kidney, fruits, vegetables, cereals	12 mg.	Hemoglobin	Iron-deficiency anemia
Copper	Liver, oysters, salmon, fruits	1 to 2 mg.	Hemoglobin synthesis	Anemia

in hot water before giving it to the patient. Calcium lactate is not given parenterally. Some hospital pharmacies prepare a solution of calcium lactate for oral administration, such as calcium lactate solution (1-liter bottles containing 2 Gm. in 40 ml. of water).

Vitamins

Vitamins have great biochemical importance for they are essential for maintenance of normal metabolic function, growth, and health. The name *vitamin* means "vital for life." Originally

Treatment	Excess clinical state	Treatment

Ringer's solution
Sodium chloride 0.9%
  solution
	Hypernatremia
	  Edema, hypertonicity
		Dextrose and water intravenously

Potassium chloride tablets
  or injection
	Hyperpotassemia, hyperkalemia
	  Central nervous system stimulation
	    and paralysis
	  EKG: peaked T waves, prolonged
	    QRS, PR interval
	  Listlessness, weakness, numbness
		Intravenous glucose and insulin
		Extracorporeal dialysis
		Calcium gluconate

Intravenous calcium chloride
  or calcium gluconate
Oral calcium lactate or
  calcium gluconate
	Hypercalcemia
	Renal calculi
		EDTA

Magnesium ion replacement	Diminished excitability of muscle
	  fibers
	Hypotension
	Respiratory paralysis
		Intravenous injection of calcium
		  salts
		Artificial respiration

Ferrous sulfate and gluconate	Hemosiderosis	Chelating agent
—	—	—

the word was spelled with an "e" on the end (vitamine), since it was believed that these substances were amines; the "e" was dropped upon recognition that all vitamins were not amines.

Only a few vitamins are synthesized in the body; vitamin K is formed by bacteria in the gut and vitamin D is produced by exposure of the skin to sunlight. Thus most vitamins must be ingested in food or in their pure form as dietary supplements. Only small amounts of the vitamins are necessary for growth and health, and

439

an adequate and varied diet will provide all the vitamins needed except during pregnancy and infancy. Restricted diets as a result of cultural or idiosyncratic beliefs, alcoholism, poverty, ignorance, or disorders of the gastrointestinal tract that interfere with absorption will lead to vitamin deficiency. In these cases, vitamin preparations are therapeutic. In the United States and Canada, mild forms of avitaminosis are more common than the pronounced deficiency states of beriberi, pellagra, rickets, or scurvy.

Vitamins are classified as being *fat soluble* or *water soluble*. Fat-soluble vitamins are A,D,E, and K. They are stored in the liver and fatty tissue in large amounts, and a deficiency in these vitamins occurs only after long deprivation from an adequate supply or disorders preventing their absorption. Water-soluble vitamins include the B group and C. These vitamins are not stored in the body in large amounts, and short periods of inadequate intake can lead to a deficiency. Vitamins are important components of enzyme systems that catalyze the reactions for protein, fat, and carbohydrate metabolism.

The sale of vitamins in the United States constitutes a multimillion-dollar business. They are widely used, and often unjustifiably, primarily because of successful advertising that vitamins will improve even normal health. The indiscriminate use of vitamins is not likely to decline in the near future.

The potency of vitamins A and D, when described on a label, must be in U.S.P. units, but the vitamin content of ascorbic acid, thiamine, riboflavin, nicotinic acid, nicotinamide, pyridoxine, and menadione and other vitamin K preparations, when expressed, must be in terms of milligrams.

■ Fat-soluble vitamins

Vitamin A

Vitamin A, the fat-soluble, growth-promoting vitamin, is essential for growth in the young and for maintenance of health at all ages. The chemistry of this vitamin has been established and is related to the carotenoid pigments of plants,

especially carotene. In fact, the term *vitamin A* may be applied to vitamin A, alpha-carotene, beta-carotene, gamma-carotene, and cryptoxanthin. The last four bodies are formed in plants and are precursors of vitamin A in the body. Beta-carotene in the body is hydrolyzed to form two molecules of vitamin A.

Chemists have failed to discover vitamin A in any plant foodstuff. The carotene of plants, therefore, seems to supply the provitamin from which the body tissues prepare vitamin A. The amount of chlorophyll in the plant is a rough indication of the amount of carotene present. Animal fats, such as those found in butter, milk, eggs, and fish liver, are sources of the carotenoids; they were originally derived from plants and stored in animal tissue.

Vitamin A is essential in man to promote normal growth and development of bones and teeth and to maintain the health of epithelial tissues of the body. Its function in relation to normal vision and the prevention of night blindness has been carefully studied. Vitamin A actually makes up a portion of one of the major retinal pigments, rhodopsin, and is thus required for normal "rod vision" in the retina of man and many of the animals.

Vitamin A is also functional in conversion processes resulting in corticosterone and cholesterol.

Absorption, storage, and excretion. Vitamin A and carotene are readily absorbed from the normal gastrointestinal tract. Efficient absorption is dependent on fat absorption and, therefore, on the presence of adequate bile salts in the intestine. Certain conditions, such as obstructive jaundice, some infectious diseases, and the presence of mineral oil in the intestine, may result in vitamin A deficiency in spite of the fact that the amount ingested was normal.

Vitamin A is stored in the liver to a greater extent than elsewhere. The liver also functions in changing carotene to vitamin A; this function is inhibited in liver diseases and in diabetes. The amount of vitamin A stored depends upon the dietary intake. When intake is high or excessive, the stores formed in the liver may become sufficient to last a long time. Vitamin A is lost

Vitamin A

Beta-carotene (provitamin A)

chiefly by destruction. Little is lost through the ordinary channels of excretion.

Uses. Vitamin A is used to treat or relieve symptoms associated with a deficiency of vitamin A (avitaminosis), such as night blindness (nyctalopia), keratinization of epithelial cells, retarded growth, xerophthalmia, keratomalacia, weakness, and increased susceptibility of mucous membranes to infection.

The diet low in vitamin A should be corrected with foods rather than with drugs. It appears that large doses of vitamin A may be given with no apparent harm to the adult, although excessive doses have been known to produce toxic effects in rats and in young children.

There are times when vitamin A concentrates have a legitimate use as supplements to the diet. Increased need occurs during pregnancy and lactation, in infancy, and in conditions characterized by lack of normal absorption and storage of vitamin A.

Daily requirement. It has been conclusively established that the vitamin A daily requirement is a rather large one, if optimum conditions of nutrition are to be maintained. The minimum daily requirements for vitamin A are 1500 units for infants, 2000 to 3500 units for children, and 5000 units for adults. During pregnancy and lactation, requirements equal 6000 to 8000 units, respectively. Therapeutic dosages may be three times these amounts. Although larger doses have been used in experimental studies, there is no evidence that justifies the use of more than 25,000 units per day. It has not been shown that excess dosage over and above the daily requirement is of value in the prevention of colds, influenza, and so on. Dosages in excess of 200,000 units are injurious to infants.

When the vitamin A requirement is met in the form of carotene or the provitamin A, twice as many units of the carotene are required to produce the same effect.

Preparation, dosage, and administration. The following are preparations of vitamin A and combinations of vitamins A and D.

Vitamin A, U.S.P. This is either fish liver oil, fish liver oil diluted with vegetable oil, or a solution of vitamin A concentrate in fish liver oil or vegetable oil. Vitamin A Capsules are available, containing 1.5, 7.5, and 15 mg. of vitamin A (5000, 25,000, and 50,000 U.S.P. units). The usual therapeutic dose is 7.5 mg. (25,000 units) daily.

Oleovitamin A and D capsules, N.F. These contain 5000 units of vitamin A and 100 units of vitamin D.

441

Vitamin A ester concentrate, B.P. This contains not less than 485,000 units of vitamin A activity in each gram.

Cod liver oil, N.F., B.P. This is partially destearinated. The usual dosage is 4 ml. orally, which contains 3000 U.S.P. units of vitamin A and 300 U.S.P. units of vitamin D. Cod liver oil is one of the cheapest sources of vitamins A and D.

Nondestearinated cod liver oil, N.F. The dosage is 4 ml. orally. Each gram contains not less than 850 U.S.P. units of vitamin A and 85 U.S.P. units of vitamin D.

Halibut liver oil, B.P. Usual daily prophylactic dose for infants and adults is 0.1 ml. ($1\frac{1}{2}$ minim). Halibut liver oil contains in each gram not less than 60,000 units of vitamin A and not less than 600 units of vitamin D. In 0.1 ml. there are 5000 units of vitamin A.

Halibut-liver oil capsules, B.P. Each capsule contains 4500 units of vitamin A activity. The dose is one to three capsules daily.

A and D ointment. A and D ointment is a preparation containing both vitamins together with hexachloraphene. It is used in treatment of epithelial lesions, such as diaper rash, burns, and excoriations.

Vitamin D

Vitamin D₂ (calciferol)

Vitamin D is a term applied to two or more substances that affect the proper utilization of calcium and phosphorus in the body. Two forms of naturally occurring vitamin D have been isolated. One of these forms is obtained as one of the products of irradiated ergosterol and is known as D_2 or calciferol. Ergosterol has therefore been shown to be a precursor of vitamin D. Investigation has shown further that there are a number of precursors that can be changed by irradiation into compounds that have vitamin D activity. Irradiation of 7-dehydrocholesterol results in the formation of vitamin D_3 and is the form of vitamin found in irradiated milk and fish oils. It is formed also in skin exposed to sunlight. Irradiated ergosterol (calciferol) is the active constituent in various vitamin preparations such as viosterol and irradiated yeast.

Vitamin D_2 and vitamin D_3, as well as other products of irradiated ergosterol, are capable of antirachitic activity.

Although vitamin D is an essential vitamin, it is contained in only a few foods of the average American diet. Small amounts are present in herring, sardines, salmon, tuna fish, eggs, and butter. Vitamin D is found in high concentrations in a number of fish oils (cod, halibut).

At present, milk is the chief commercial food product enriched by the addition of vitamin D concentrate. By federal regulation, milk products are standardized at 400 International Units per quart, which represents a day's requirement of vitamin D.

Action and result. The exact mechanism by which vitamin D functions in the metabolism of calcium and phosphorus is not known. There is evidence that a complex relationship exists between vitamin D and parathyroid hormone, but this is not yet conclusive. The vitamin seems to be concerned directly with the absorption of calcium and phosphorus from the intestinal tract and their deposition in bone and teeth. In the absence of vitamin D the amount of these substances absorbed from the bowel is diminished to such an extent that even though the calcium and phosphate intake is adequate, rickets results in the child and osteomalacia in the adult.

An enzyme called alkaline phosphatase exists in the body and is closely related to phosphorus metabolism. It is distributed widely in the animal body and is particularly active in ossifying cartilage. When rickets is present the level of phosphatase in blood serum is high. This is thought to be caused by leakage from the diseased bone. Administration of vitamin D causes the enzyme to return to normal slowly.

Symptoms of deficiency. The chief indication of vitamin D deficiency is rickets, characterized by irritability, craniotabes, prominent frontal bones, delayed closing of the fontanels, soft bones, pigeon breast, rachitic rosary, flaring ribs, epiphyseal enlargement at wrists and elbows, muscular weakness, protruding abdomen, bowed legs, delayed eruption of teeth, abnormal ratio of calcium and phosphorus in the blood, and tetany.

Daily requirement. It is thought that either the human requirement of vitamin D is relatively low or else it is met by the action of sunlight on the skin. A daily intake of 400 units is considered adequate to meet the ordinary requirements of all age groups.

Older children and adults who live in a climate where they do not have access to abundant sunshine need to supplement their vitamin D intake. The amount supplied probably should be up to the minimum requirements for the infant. To prevent the development of rickets, it is important to start the administration of vitamin D early in the infant's life, and full dosage should be given by the second month.

Uses. The prevention of rickets in young children is one of the most justified uses of vitamin D. The initial dose should be about 200 units daily, with an increase in dosage up to 800 units by the second month. Premature infants or those who seem to be especially susceptible to the development of rickets need a larger intake (800 to 1200 units usually). When children already have rickets the dosage is also greater. The average daily dose usually is about 1200 to 1500 units, but in some instances it may be increased to as much as 60,000 or more units daily. Vitamin D–resistant rickets is a condition that does not respond to usual doses of vitamin D but requires unusually large doses. If nausea or anorexia appears, the vitamin should be discontinued temporarily.

In adults osteomalacia also calls for large doses of vitamin D, along with improved dietary and living conditions and more exposure to sunlight.

Patients suffering from bone fractures, especially elderly individuals, may benefit from the administration of vitamin D, thus promoting optimum conditions for bone healing.

Vitamin D may be administered in a number of conditions such as arthritis, psoriasis, diarrhea, and steatorrhea, if there is good evidence that a deficiency of this vitamin exists. Large doses of vitamin D are also of value in the treatment of lupus vulgaris.

Preparation, dosage, and administration

Ergocalciferol, **U.S.P.;** *calciferol,* **B.P. (vitamin D$_2$, Drisdol).** The preparation of this vitamin is available in capsules, each containing 50,000 U.S.P. units (1.25 mg.) and in solution, 0.25 mg. (10,000 U.S.P. units) per gram for oral administration. The average therapeutic dose for rickets is 1200 U.S.P. units (30 μg.). The normal daily intake for adults is 400 U.S.P. units (10 μg.). This preparation is especially suitable for severe or refractory rickets. Therapeutic dosage varies from 30 μg. to 5 mg.

Side effects and toxic effects. Certain pathologic changes have been noted in animals after the administration of excessive doses of vitamin D$_1$. This vitamin represents the exceptional case of a vitamin in which excessive dosage can cause disease. Initial symptoms of hypervitaminosis D are those associated with hypercalcemia. Doses greatly in excess of the usual therapeutic level can so increase the renal excretion of phosphate and calcium that these elements are withdrawn from bone, producing demineralization and calcium deposition in soft tissues. It is curious that both a lack and an excess of vitamin D may produce softening of the bones, although by different mechanisms. Elevation of serum calcium above 12 mg. per 100 ml. is considered a danger signal, and dosage should be reduced or temporarily discontinued.

Vitamin E, N.F.

Vitamin E was known as the antisterility vitamin until further studies revealed more widespread applications. It is a fat-soluble vitamin, the richest source of which is wheat germ oil, although it occurs in other vegetable oils such as cottonseed oil and peanut oil. It is also found in green leafy vegetables.

A number of compounds have been found

Alpha-tocopherol

that exhibit vitamin E activity. The most active of these are the tocopherols, of which three are naturally occurring compounds known as alpha-, beta-, and gamma-tocopherol. The most biologically potent of these compounds is alpha-tocopherol.

In laboratory animals a lack of vitamin E manifests itself by infertility or failure of the female to carry a pregnancy to term. Absence of vitamin E in the diet of rabbits and guinea pigs is followed by muscular dystrophy and paralysis of the hindquarters, and cardiac lesions have been noted in some species. In humans a deficiency of vitamin E results in hemolysis of erythrocytes.

Vitamin E in human physiology does not appear to be of value in the treatment of sterility or prevention of abortions.

Vitamin K

Vitamin K is also a fat-soluble vitamin that has been presented in Chapter 10.

■ Water-soluble vitamins
Vitamin B complex

The vitamin B complex refers to a group of vitamins that are often found together in food, although they are chemically dissimilar and have different metabolic functions. Grouping them together is based largely on the historical basis of their having been discovered in a sequential order. They have little in common other than their sources and the fact that they are water soluble. There is a sensible and increasingly popular trend to discard such names as B_1 and B_2 and to refer to these vitamins as thiamine and riboflavin. Vitamin B complex includes thiamine, riboflavin, nicotinic acid, pyridoxine, pantothenic acid, biotin, choline, inositol, and para-aminobenzoic acid.

Thiamine (vitamin B_1)

Thiamine is also known as the antineuritic or antiberiberi vitamin. It was first synthesized in 1937. It is found abundantly in yeast, in whole grain cereals, and in pork and liver.

Thiamine is believed to play an essential role in the intermediate steps of carbohydrate metabolism. Specifically, thiamine is a major portion of the coenzyme, cocarboxylase, necessary for the normal metabolism of pyruvic acid and other compounds as well. Thus it plays a part in the metabolism of all living cells.

Thiamine deficiency is recognized as being of fundamental importance in beriberi. This disease is still found in Asia but is seldom encountered in the United States and Europe except in persons whose dietary pattern is abnormal. The symptoms of thiamine deficiency are particularly related to changes in the nervous and cardiovascular systems and include the following: muscular weakness, disturbances of sensation, tenderness over nerve trunks, polyneuritis, loss of appetite, dyspnea, epigastric disorders, and irregularities of heart action. Milder symptoms may consist of muscular aches and pains, anorexia, tachycardia, irritability, and mental depression. Deficiency states in the United States are much less common since white flour has been enriched with thiamine.

Daily requirement. It has been estimated that adult females require 1 mg. of thiamine chloride daily. The recommended amount for males is from 1.2 to 1.4 mg. For the infant, 0.2 to 0.5

444

mg. is the optimum daily dose, increasing to 1.1 to 1.5 mg. between the ages of 10 and 18 years. Requirements are increased during pregnancy and lactation and when the metabolic rate is increased or the body is unable to absorb or utilize the vitamin. Treatment of thiamine deficiency states requires several times the amount ordinarily needed. Thiamine is found to some extent in all body tissues but, like all B vitamins, exists in high concentrations in the liver. It is absorbed from the gastrointestinal tract as well as from parenteral sites of administration.

Uses. The only therapeutic value of thiamine is in the treatment or prevention of thiamine deficiency. Since deficiency in one of the vitamin B factors may be accompanied by deficiency in others, some authorities prefer to give several components of the vitamin B complex. This is best accomplished by an adequate diet or preparations rich in the B factors, such as brewers' yeast. Thiamine is indicated for treatment of beriberi and polyneuritis and for the relief of symptoms that accompany milder forms of thiamine deficiency.

Thiamine replacement is necessary for patients receiving nourishment parenterally and only in the form of dextrose. Carbohydrate metabolism is increased and, therefore, requires additional amounts of thiamine.

Preparation, dosage, and administration

***Thiamine hydrochloride*, U.S.P.; *aneurine hydrochloride*, B.P.** This preparation is marketed in tablets for oral administration and in solution for injection. When injected, it is usually administered subcutaneously, or it may be added to intravenous fluids. The usual dosage of thiamine hydrochloride is 1 to 50 mg. daily. It is marketed under a number of trade names such as Berocca, Betalin, and Betaxin.

***Thiamine mononitrate*, U.S.P.** This form is available in 3-, 5-, 10-, and 25-mg. tablets.

***Dried yeast*, N.F.** Dried yeast must contain in each gram not less than 0.12 mg. of thiamine hydrochloride, 0.04 mg. of riboflavin, and 0.30 mg. of niacin. The usual dose is 10 Gm. four times a day. Dried yeast tablets, N.F., contain 500 mg. of dried yeast in each tablet.

Side effects and toxic effects. Large doses of thiamine when given intravenously have been known to cause anaphylactic shock, probably because of allergic responses to the preparation. However, the incidence of toxicity is so low as to be almost nonexistent.

Riboflavin (vitamin B₂)

Crystals of riboflavin are an orange-yellow color and are slightly soluble in water. Thiamine contains sulfur; riboflavin does not. Riboflavin was identified first in milk. Later it was identified in other substances and was called lactoflavin because of its intense yellow color. Its relationship to the vitamin B complex was not appreciated until it was observed that concentrates of vitamin B_2 had a yellow color, the intensity of which was related to the potency of the concentrate. At present, vitamin B_2 is synthesized and all doubt of its identity has been removed. It was named riboflavin because of the presence of ribose in its structure.

Metabolic function. Riboflavin seems to function in cellular respiration and is a constituent of all cells. It is slightly water soluble and heat stable. Many enzymes contain the riboflavin molecule as an essential portion of their molecule. These so-called flavo-enzymes include a number of oxidizing enzymes such as those that oxidize the common amino acids to ketoacids. In addition, flavo-enzymes form part of the chain of "electron transport" by which the energy obtained from oxidizing foodstuff is stored as chemical energy in the form of adenosinetriphosphate (ATP). The flavo-enzymes can carry out their function because the riboflavin molecule can be easily oxidized and reduced (loss and gain of electrons) so that it can act as a link in the bridge by which electrons are removed from organic compounds and transferred to oxygen.

The functions of flavo-enzymes are therefore **445**

Table 21-2 Vitamins and human nutrition

Vitamin	Source	Daily requirements in adult male	Specific functions	Deficiency	Therapeutic source
A	Dairy products, carrots, green vegetables, liver, kidneys, eggs	5000 I.U.*	Visual pigments Maintenance of epithelial tissue	Nightblindness Corneal softening Hyperkeratosis	Halibut liver oil Cod liver oil
C	Fruits, fresh green vegetables, potatoes, tomatoes, rose hips	70 mg.	Oxidation-reduction processes Maintenance of normal connective tissue Adrenal-cortical function	Scurvy Swelling, redness, and bleeding of gums Petechiae Capillary fragility Anemia	Ascorbic acid tablets and injection Decavitamins
D	Egg yolk, butter, milk, fish liver oils	400 I.U.	Absorption of calcium from intestine Deposition of mineral in bone	Rickets in children Osteomalacia in adults	Cod liver oil Halibut liver oil Calciferol tablets Sunlight
E	Wheat germ, egg yolk, liver, leafy vegetables	30 I.U.	Essential for normal hematopoiesis	Hemolytic anemia†	Multivitamins Tocopherol capsules and tablets
B complex Thiamine (B₁)	Cereal grains, yeast, meat, peas, beans	1 to 2 mg.	Carbohydrate metabolism	Central and autonomic nervous system disturbances Fatigue Neuritis Beriberi	Thiamine hydrochloride tablets or injection Multivitamins
Riboflavin (B₂)	Yeast, yeast extracts, dairy products	1.7 mg.	Coenzymes for metabolism of respiratory proteins	Glossitis Dermatitis Stomatitis	Riboflavin tablets and injection Decavitamins
Niacin (nicotinic acid)	Yeast, lean meat, liver	18 mg.	—	Pellagra	B complex vitamins
Pyridoxine (B₆)	Yeast, cereal grains, egg yolk, liver, beans, peas, potatoes, meat, fish	1 to 2 mg.	Formation of aminobutyric acid, an inhibitory transmitter substance Metabolism of amino acids, nucleic acids, protein	Convulsions Hyperirritability Neuritis Edema	Pyridocine tablets Decavitamins

*I.U., International Units, which are identical to U.S.P. units.
†Not well established.

Vitamin	Source	Daily requirements in adult male	Specific functions	Deficiency	Therapeutic source
B complex— cont'd Pantothenic acid	—	10 mg.	Component of coenzyme A	Neurologic disturbances Irritability Fatigue Muscle cramps Dry, scaly skin Adrenal hypofunction	Decavitamins
Biotin	Egg yolk, liver, tomatoes	—	Coenzyme for carbon dioxide fixation	Anorexia Malaise Dermatitis	Multivitamin preparations

so extensive and important that it becomes difficult to pinpoint single specific reactions that result from a riboflavin deficiency.

Symptoms of deficiency. Deficiency in human beings is associated with superficial fissures about the angles of the mouth (cheilosis) and nose at the junction between the mucous membrane and the skin, visual disturbances, glossitis, and a peculiar red color of the tongue. Actual tissue changes in the eye may occur. Riboflavin deficiency is likely to occur along with a deficiency of other members of the B complex.

Milk is one of the most important sources of riboflavin. Other sources include yeast, liver, kidney, eggs, lean meat, and leafy vegetables. The addition of riboflavin to white flour has helped to increase the intake of this vitamin for many persons.

Daily requirement. The requirement of riboflavin does not appear to be related to caloric intake or to muscular activity, but there does seem to be a relationship to body weight. The Food and Nutrition Board of the National Research Council in 1968 recommended 1.5 mg. for women and 1.7 mg. for men as a daily requirement for optimal nutrition. During preg-

nancy and lactation the recommended allowance should be increased by 0.3 to 0.5 mg. per day. For infants the recommended daily allowance is from 0.4 to 0.6 mg. and for children ages 1 to 18 the daily recommended allowance is from 0.6 to 1.5 mg.

Uses. Riboflavin is used to prevent and to treat deficiency states and is used along with niacin in the treatment of pellagra.

Preparation, dosage, and administration

Riboflavin, **U.S.P., B.P.*** (Lactoflavin). Riboflavin is usually administered orally because it is well absorbed from the gastrointestinal tract. Tablets of 5 and 10 mg. are available for oral administration. Riboflavin injection, U.S.P., 0.5 to 10 mg. per milliliter, can be given subcutaneously. The usual therapeutic daily dose is 5 mg., although 2 to 20 mg. daily may be needed, depending upon the degree of deficiency. Yeast preparations are also given for their riboflavin content.

Side effects and toxic effects. Riboflavin is completely nontoxic and reactions to it do not seem to occur. No side effects have been noted after relatively large doses.

*Spelled riboflavine in the B.P.

Niacin (nicotinic acid)

Niacin

Niacinamide

Niacin is related chemically to nicotine but possesses none of the latter's pharmacologic properties. Niacin is converted in the body to niacinamide, a dietary essential, the lack of which is responsible for the symptoms of pellagra. Pellagra is characterized by disturbances of the gastrointestinal tract, skin, and nervous system. In a milder degree of deficiency, patients are nervous or irritable and have indigestion, diarrhea or constipation, and abnormal skin pigmentation.

Pellagra occurs among persons of low economic means and has been noted especially among peoples who eat a good deal of corn (maize) but whose total diet is limited in protein. It is also seen as a result of dietary fads and disease of the gastrointestinal tract in which there is poor intestinal absorption.

Lean meats, poultry, and fish have been found to be a better source of niacin than vegetables and fruits. Milk and eggs are good sources of the precursor substance, tryptophan. The enrichment of white flour has made an appreciable contribution to the increase of niacin in the average diet in the United States.

Unlike some of the other water-soluble vitamins, man can synthesize niacin from the essential amino acid, tryptophan. Diets low in both niacin and tryptophan are the most likely to produce clinical deficiency.

Metabolic function. As in the case of riboflavin, a large group of enzymes depends for their function on coenzymes containing niacin. The vital oxidation-reduction coenzymes, di-

phosphopyridine nucleotide and triphosphopyridine nucleotide, are required for the early reactions of many metabolic pathways.

Ribose-phosphate-phosphate-adenine

Both contain the nicotinamide molecule as part of their structure. No biologic role of niacin is known except for its presence in coenzymes, but so many metabolic processes are dependent on the pyridine nucleotides that this is ample to explain the widespread symptoms caused by niacin lack.

Daily requirement. The National Research Council (U. S. A.), in its 1968 revision of Recommended Dietary Allowances, states the daily niacin requirements in terms of niacin equivalents, assuming that 60 mg. of tryptophan will supply 1 mg. of niacin. Requirements are estimated on the basis of body weight and caloric intake and then increased by 50% to provide for varying physiologic needs and dietary situations. The requirement for women is given as 13 mg. and is 14 to 18 mg. daily for men. For pregnancy and lactation an increase of from 2 to 7 mg. per day is recommended. For infants the daily recommended intake is 5 to 8 mg. equivalents. The recommended allowance for children ages 1 to 18 is 8 to 20 mg. equivalents daily.

Uses. Both nicotinic acid and nicotinamide are used in the treatment and prophylaxis of pellagra, but since pellagra is a disease associated with multiple vitamin deficiencies, riboflavin and thiamine are also indicated. Optimal treatment of the disease must include the administration of all members of the vitamin B complex as well as a diet adequate in animal protein. Results of therapy are frequently dramatic. Some positive results have been noted when niacin has been administered to patients with a variety of diagnoses, ranging from sprue to Meniere's syndrome. It has been used to reverse some characteristics of aging, in lowering cholesterol levels, and in psychiatric contexts to differentiate between psychoses of dietary and nondietary origin.

Preparation, dosage, and administration. The following are available preparations of niacin.

Niacin, N.F.; nicotinic acid, B.P. Nicotinic acid is available as a powder and in tablet form of 25, 50, and 100 mg. for oral administration.

Niacin injection, N.F. This form is available in 10-ml. ampules containing 100 mg. of the drug for parenteral use.

Niacinamide, U.S.P.; nicotinamide, B.P. Official preparations include tablets of 25, 50, and 100 mg. and ampules containing a solution for injection. The concentration of the solution is 50 or 200 mg. per milliliter.

These vitamins are usually given orally but they may also be given parenterally. The dose for the treatment of pellagra may be as much as 500 mg. daily by mouth in divided doses or 100 to 200 mg. by injection. The dose must be determined by the degree of deficiency being treated.

Side effects and toxic effects. The administration of large doses of nicotinic acid (especially when given intravenously) causes flushing of the face and neck, which may be associated with burning and pruritus. This does not occur after the administration of nicotinamide, which is therefore preferred for parenteral administration. In spite of this transient reaction, niacin is considered a nontoxic substance.

Pyridoxine hydrochloride, U.S.P. (vitamin B6)

Vitamin B_6 occurs as a group of chemically related compounds—pyridoxine, pyridoxal, and pyridoxamine. In the body tissues these compounds can be converted from one form to another. Pyridoxine is changed into pyridoxal, which seems to be especially active. Pyridoxal phosphate functions as a coenzyme and is involved in changing tryptophan to the nicotinamide portion of the pyridine coenzymes. It plays an important role in the metabolism of amino acids and fatty acids and is said to participate in energy transformation in the brain and nerve tissues.

Pork and glandular meats are said to be especially rich in the vitamin B_6 group of enzymes, although these substances are found in many different foods.

Although no specific deficiency disease has been recognized in man, convulsive disorders have been observed in infants who were fed a diet deficient in vitamin B_6 and adults who have received a vitamin B_6 antagonist have developed seborrheic dermatitis, lesions on mucous membranes, and peripheral neuritis. Patients with an unusual type of hypochromic anemia have responded well to the administration of vitamin B_6.

Daily requirement. The daily recommended allowance of vitamin B_6 is from 0.2 to 0.4 mg. for infants and from 0.5 to 1.4 mg. for children ages 1 through 12. The requirement ranges from 1.6 to 2 mg. for adolescents and is 2 mg. for adults. An increase of 0.5 mg. daily is recommended during pregnancy and lactation.

Uses. Pyridoxine hydrochloride is used as an adjunct in the treatment of nausea and vomiting of pregnancy and irradiation sickness.

Isoniazid, an antituberculosis drug, acts as an antagonist of vitamin B_6, and when used over a period of time it may produce a vitamin deficiency unless additional amounts of vitamin B_6 are administered.

Preparation, dosage, and administration. Official preparations are available in 5-, 10-, 25-, and 50-mg. tablets for oral administration and in solution (concentrations varying from 50 to 100 mg. per milliliter) for intramuscular or intravenous injection. The usual dosage is 5 mg. daily, although as much as 25 to 100 mg. has been administered.

Pantothenic acid

Pantothenic acid is widely distributed in nature. It is believed to be a constituent of coenzyme A, which plays an important role in the release of energy from carbohydrates, and in   **449** the synthesis and degradation of fatty acids, sterols, and steroid hormones. Pantothenic acid is believed to be essential for human beings, although what constitutes the daily requirement is uncertain. An average American diet is said to provide 8.7 mg. daily. It is known to prevent nutritional dermatosis in chicks and to promote normal growth in rats. Calcium pantothenate, U.S.P., is available in 10-mg. tablets. It is included in many multivitamin preparations. The usual dose is 10 mg.

Biotin

Biotin is a substance that plays a role in metabolism as a coenzyme with an important function in carbon dioxide fixation. Deficiency states have been reported in man only when fed a diet containing a large amount of raw egg white. Avidine, a protein found in egg white, binds the biotin and prevents its absorption from the intestine. This results in the development of anorexia, malaise, and dermatitis. Daily administration of 150 to 300 μg. will prevent the development of these symptoms in human beings. This amount is found in an average American diet.

Choline; inositol; para-aminobenzoic acid

These compounds have been included in the vitamin B complex, but their status is uncertain. Choline and inositol have been found to have a lipotropic (exhibiting an affinity for fat) effect. The lipotropic effect of choline was first noted in the liver, and this led to its use for the treatment of fatty infiltration of the liver and other disorders of fat metabolism. However, the evidence to support claims for clinical usefulness is questionable.

Vitamin B$_{12}$; folic acid

Vitamin B$_{12}$ and folic acid (pteroylglutamic acid) were discussed in Chapter 10.

Ascorbic acid (vitamin C)

Scurvy was formerly common among sailors deprived of fresh fruits and vegetables during long voyages. The well-known effects of lemon and orange juices in curing this disease led to attempts to concentrate the active principle by chemical means. Crystalline ascorbic acid in large amounts has been prepared from Hungarian red pepper. Biologic tests show that ascorbic acid is pure vitamin C, which is now synthesized on a commercial scale. Ascorbic acid is a powerful reducing agent and is therefore sensitive to oxidation. It is relatively stable in an acid medium but quickly oxidized in an alkaline medium. It is believed to be concerned in the oxidation-reduction reactions of living cells.

However, less is known about its function than is known about many of the other water-soluble vitamins already discussed. Ascorbic acid is concerned with the formation of collagen in all fibrous tissue, including bone, and with the development of teeth, blood vessels, and blood cells. It is also involved in carbohydrate metabolism. It is believed to stimulate the fibroblasts of connective tissue and thus promote tissue repair and the healing of wounds. It is said to help maintain the integrity of the intercellular substance in the walls of blood vessels, and the capillary fragility associated with scurvy is explained on this basis.

A deficiency in the intake of vitamin C results in scurvy, the chief symptoms of which are spongy, bleeding gums; loosened teeth; hemorrhagic tendencies in regions subjected to trauma or mechanical stress; sore, swollen joints; fatigue; pallor; and anemia. Vitamin C deficiency is thought to be a contributory factor in dental caries, pyorrhea, and certain oral infections.

Foods rich in vitamin C include citrus fruits (oranges, lemons, limes, and grapefruit) as well as tomato juice, raw cabbage, broccoli, and strawberries.

Daily requirement. Vitamin C is constantly being destroyed in the body, probably through the process of oxidation. If deficiency is to be avoided, daily requirements must be met. The optimum daily intake of ascorbic acid for an adult male is 60 mg.; for women, 55 mg.; for infants, 35 mg.; and 40 mg. for children. During pregnancy and lactation the requirement is 60 mg.

Uses. The specific use of vitamin C is in the

prevention and treatment of scurvy and for the subclinical manifestations of this disease. An optimum amount of ascorbic acid should be supplied for individuals of all ages to prevent the development of scurvy. In the absence of vitamin C changes occur in the collagen of fibrous tissues, in the matrix of tooth substance (dentin), in bone and cartilage, and in the endothelium of blood vessels. Since vitamin C is not stored to any appreciable extent, deficiency can develop easily. Patients who do not eat well or who do not receive a diet adequate for their needs or those who must be fed intravenously for a long time may develop a deficiency unless they are given ascorbic acid as a dietary supplement. Vitamin C deficiency may result in delay in wound healing, or it may actually cause a breakdown in the healing process. Its prophylactic use to prevent colds is highly controversial.

The administration of vitamin C is not considered specific treatment for pyorrhea, dental caries, and certain gum infections, unless these symptoms are associated with vitamin C deficiency. In fact, bleeding gums are a rather common finding among otherwise healthy individuals. Vitamin C deficiency to the extent necessary to cause capillary bleeding is quite rare. It is therefore most unreasonable to treat bleeding gums with an increased and supernormal intake of ascorbic acid.

Nurses who instruct young parents should stress the importance of not heating orange juice or adding vitamins to formula before it is heated, because heat destroys the vitamin C.

Preparation, dosage, and administration. The following are preparations available of ascorbic acid.

Ascorbic acid, **U.S.P., B.P.** Ascorbic acid is available in 25-, 50-, 100-, 250-, and 500-mg. tablets. A number of multiple-vitamin preparations also contain vitamin C.

Ascorbic acid injection, **U.S.P.** This is a preparation of ascorbic acid suited for parenteral administration.

Ascorbic acid may be given orally because it is well absorbed from the intestinal tract, or the injectable form may be given intramuscularly or added to intravenous fluids. The therapeutic dose for adults is 500 mg. daily.

Multiple-vitamin preparations

The daily intake of principal vitamins recommended by the Food and Nutrition Board of the National Research Council (1968 revision) is as follows for adults who are normally vigorous and living in a temperate climate: vitamin A, 5000 units; vitamin D, 400 units; thiamine (vitamin B_1), 1 to 1.4 mg.; riboflavin, 1.5 to 1.7 mg.; niacin, 13 to 18 mg.; ascorbic acid (vitamin C), 55 to 60 mg.

Many of the multiple-vitamin preparations that have come into extensive use in recent years contain amounts of the aforementioned vitamins that bear no relation to established therapeutic dosage or to normal daily requirements. In addition, many such preparations contain purified vitamins that are not yet known to be represented by any known deficiency diseases.

Certain multiple-vitamin preparations not only have excessive amounts of each vitamin but also contain vitamins whose importance in human nutrition is open to question. The cost of "overstuffed" vitamin preparations is unnecessarily high. Vitamin requirements may be abnormally high, for a time, in individuals who are acutely and severely ill, but that is another matter.

Decavitamin Capsules, **U.S.P.;** *Decavitamin Tablets,* **U.S.P.** These preparations contain in each capsule or tablet not less than 1.2 mg. (4000 U.S.P. units) of vitamin A, 10 μg. (400 U.S.P. units) of vitamin D, 70 mg. of ascorbic acid, 10 mg. of calcium pantothenate, 1 μg. of cyanocobalamin, 50 μg. of folic acid, 20 mg. of niacinamide, 2 mg. of pyridoxine hydrochloride, 2 mg. of riboflavin, and 2 mg. of thiamine hydrochloride. The usual daily dose is one capsule or one tablet. These preparations are the only official multiple-vitamin therapeutic drugs.

Hormones

The hormones are natural chemical substances that act after being secreted into the

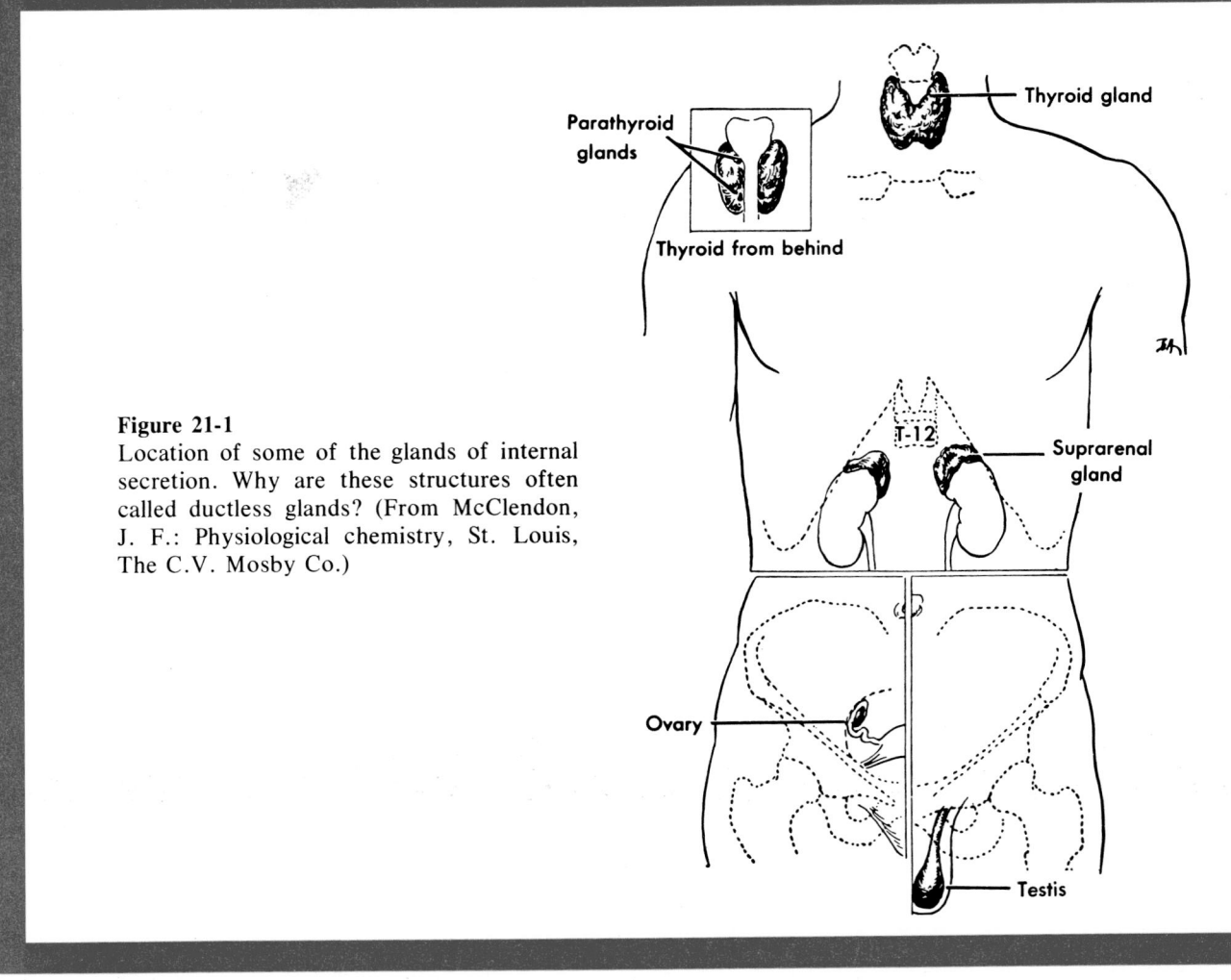

Figure 21-1
Location of some of the glands of internal secretion. Why are these structures often called ductless glands? (From McClendon, J. F.: Physiological chemistry, St. Louis, The C.V. Mosby Co.)

bloodstream from the ductless or endocrine glands.

Specific endocrine substances have a widespread effect, act on many other tissues and organs, and in a general way regulate the rates of certain metabolic processes, such as growth of the body, growth and development of the sex organs, or, as in the case of the pituitary hormones, growth and function of the ductless glands.

One of the major developments of this century in the fields of biology and medicine has been

the recognition and then the isolation, purification, and chemical understanding of most of the hormones we now know. In addition, once their chemical structure is known, it becomes hypothetically possible to duplicate them by chemical synthesis. This has been accomplished for some hormones, although not for all.

Exactly what should be called a hormone and what should not is not well defined. A broad definition could be any chemical substance released by one tissue, circulated by the blood, and having characteristic effects on other tissues. This would include many substances not ordinarily classed as hormones, such as carbon dioxide. In common usage, hormones are confined to those well-recognized and chemically specific products of the various endocrine glands that have specific well-defined physiologic effects on metabolism. The list of major hormones includes the products of the secretions of the anterior and posterior pituitary, the thyroid hormone, insulin and glucogen from the pancreas, epinephrine and norepinephrine from the adrenal medulla, several potent steroids from the adrenal cortex, and the gonadal hormones of both sexes.

In medicine these substances are generally used in two ways: (1) for replacement when a patient lacks sufficient endogenous hormone, exemplified by the use of insulin in diabetes or the use of adrenal steroids in Addison's disease, and (2) for pharmacologic effects beyond those of replacement, exemplified by the use of large doses of the adrenal steroids for their anti-inflammatory effects.

■ Pituitary hormones

Because the hormones of the pituitary gland exert an important effect in regulating the secretion of the other hormones, it is fitting that they be considered first.

The pituitary body is about the size of a pea and occupies a niche in the sella turcica of the sphenoid bone. It consists of an anterior lobe, a posterior lobe, and a smaller pars intermedia composed of secreting cells. The anterior part is particularly important in sustaining the life of the individual. The function of the pars intermedia is not well known. It should be noted that the oral administration of any part of the whole gland is without visible effect because it is destroyed by proteolytic enzymes and the pituitary hormones are protein or peptide in nature.

Anterior pituitary hormone

Present evidence indicates that a number of factors are concerned in the action of extracts of the anterior lobe of the pituitary gland. How many hormones are secreted by the gland is unknown, but at least six extracts have been prepared in a relatively pure state, and they have definite specific action.

1 A growth factor influences the development of the body. It promotes skeletal, visceral, and general growth of the body. Acromegaly, gigantism, and dwarfism are connected with pathology of the anterior lobe of the pituitary gland.

 The growth hormone or somatotropin has recently been obtained as a small crystalline protein, but thus far the growth hormone has found no established place in medicine, and its use in various clinical conditions is largely experimental. It tends to increase the blood sugar and antagonize insulin, and it may be the "diabetogenic" hormone postulated some years ago.

2 The follicle-stimulating hormone (FSH) stimulates the growth and maturation of the ovarian follicle, which in turn brings on the characteristic changes of estrus (menstruation in women). This hormone also stimulates spermatogenesis in the male. FSH appears to be a protein or is associated with a protein, but it has not yet been obtained in a highly purified form.

3 Luteinizing hormone (LH), also known as the interstitial cell–stimulating hormone (ICSH), together with FSH causes maturation of the graafian follicles, ovulation, and the secretion of estrogen in the female. It causes spermatogenesis, androgen formation, and growth of interstitial tissue in the male. The luteinizing hormone also promotes the formation of the corpora lutea in the female.

4 Thyrotropic hormone (TSH) is necessary for normal development and function of the thyroid gland and, if present in excess, is known to produce hyperthyroidism and an increased size of the gland in laboratory animals.

5 A lactogenic factor (luteotropic hormone) may play a part in proliferation and secretion of the mammary glands of mammals. This may be identical with the hormone responsible for the development of the corpus luteum. In its absence the corpus luteum fails to produce progesterone.

6 The adrenocorticotropic hormone (corticotropin or ACTH) stimulates the cortex of the adrenal gland.

Although the hormones produced by the an- **453**

terior lobe of the pituitary gland are important physiologically, a number of reasons explain their limited usefulness. Only in relatively recent times have purified preparations been available, at least for clinical study, and such preparations are both expensive and limited in supply. Increased application of their effects may be expected in the future, however, as chemically defined preparations become available.

The only anterior pituitary hormone that has been synthesized, the adrenocorticotropic hormone (corticotropin or ACTH), exerts its action primarily on the cells of the adrenal cortex and causes it to secrete its entire spectrum of hormones.

The ultimate effects in the body, therefore, are the effects of the various adrenocortical steroids and, in general, these effects are similar to those of cortisone. Corticotropin is effective only if a functioning adrenal gland is present. The present source of corticotropin is from the pituitary glands of hogs, cattle, and horses in the United States and from whales in the Scandinavian countries. The labor involved in the removal of the glands is such that this source is an expensive one.

During conditions of stress and strain the activity of the adrenal cortex is increased. This is thought to be the result of an increased secretion of corticotropin. One explanation for the regulation of corticotropic activity is that during stress the tissues of the body utilize more of the adrenal hormones than usual, which results in a decreased concentration of the adrenocortical hormones in the blood. This in turn brings about stimulation of cells in the anterior pituitary gland and the production of more corticotropin. On the other hand, when the situation of stress has subsided, the tissues use less of the adrenocortical hormones, their concentration in the blood increases, and this causes activity of the pituitary gland as well as the adrenal cortex to be decreased.

Absorption. Corticotropin is destroyed by enzymes in the gastrointestinal tract and therefore cannot be given orally. It is absorbed readily from sites of injection when given intramuscularly or intravenously. It is said to disappear from the blood rapidly after intravenous injection. Its effects rarely last longer than 6 hours. This necessitates frequent intramuscular injections, administration by slow intravenous drip, or the use of a preparation that is absorbed slowly. Its effectiveness depends upon the presence of normal adrenal glands capable of responding to the stimulant made by the pituitary gland.

Uses. Corticotropin is used for many of the same conditions for which cortisone and hydrocortisone are used, such as rheumatic diseases, skin diseases, ocular diseases, and allergic manifestations. It has the advantage of rapid absorption and rapid utilization, but it is more expensive than the cortical steroids.

Preparation, dosage, and administration. The following are preparations of corticotropin.

Corticotropin injection, U.S.P., B.P.* (Acthar). This preparation is marketed as a powder for injection in 10, 25, and 40 U.S.P. units and in solution of 10 to 40 U.S.P. units per milliliter. The average dose of corticotropin for adults is 20 U.S.P. units four times daily when given intramuscularly. When the drug is administered intravenously, 5 to 20 U.S.P. units are dissolved in 500 ml. of 5% glucose solution or isotonic saline (unless salt is restricted for the patient), and the solution is administered slowly over an 8-hour period.

Repository corticotropin injection, U.S.P. (Corticotropin Gel). This is a preparation of corticotropin dissolved in a gelatin solution, which results in slow absorption and more satisfactory clinical effect per unit of activity. Repository corticotropin is administered intramuscularly. A daily injection exerts a prolonged and continuous effect. The usual daily intramuscular dose is 40 U.S.P. units. The maintenance dose is 20 U.S.P. units two or three times a week.

Sterile corticotropin–zinc hydroxide suspension, U.S.P. This is a preparation of purified corticotropin adsorbed on zinc hydroxide. Absorption after parenteral administration is de-

---

*Spelled corticotrophin in the B.P.

layed, and thus its action is prolonged. It is administered intramuscularly and is available as a suspension containing 100 and 200 U.S.P. units in 5 ml. The usual initial dose is 40 U.S.P. units; the maintenance dose is 20 U.S.P. units two or three times a week.

Side effects and toxic effects. Effects are much the same as those noted after administration of cortisone or hydrocortisone (see pp. 464 and 465).

Pituitary gonadotropic hormone

The pituitary gonadotropic hormones are discussed in Chapter 26.

Posterior pituitary hormone

When solutions of extracts of the posterior lobes of the pituitary glands of animals (domestic) are administered parenterally, a number of effects have been observed: (1) stimulation of the uterine muscle (oxytocic effect), and (2) promotion of the absorption of water in the renal tubules (antidiuretic effect), and (3) stimulation of the muscle of the superficial blood vessels (pressor effect) and of the intestine.

A great advance in the pharmacology of the posterior lobe has been the recent identification and chemical analysis of two major hormones obtained from the gland in pure form. These compounds, oxytocin and vasopressin (antidiuretic hormone, ADH), are both peptides, each containing eight amino acids. After their isolation and determination it proved possible to synthesize them chemically. Availability of the oxytocic and vasopressor pituitary hormones in pure form has clarified a number of uncertainties about their action and has also encouraged their better-controlled therapeutic use. It is known, for example, that there is a certain overlap of pharmacologic action even in the pure preparation; pure oxytocin has some vasopressor activity, and vice versa. Vasopressin is also the antidiuretic hormone, its antidiuretic potency being much more marked than its pressor potency. Although the cruder preparations of oxytocic and vasopressor activity are still used, it may be expected that eventually the pure compounds will replace the older extracts.

Uses for vasopressin. Vasopressin is used chiefly in the treatment of diabetes insipidus, a condition in which the patient excretes a large amount of urine because sufficient antidiuretic hormone is not secreted. Since it stimulates gastrointestinal motility, it is also sometimes used for the relief of intestinal gaseous distention. It is rarely used to elevate the blood pressure, since more effective drugs are available for this purpose.

Preparation, dosage, and administration. The following are available preparations of vasopressin.

Posterior pituitary injection, **N.F.** It contains 10 U.S.P. posterior pituitary units in each milliliter of aqueous solution. The usual dose is 10 U.S.P. units subcutaneously. The preparation contains a mixture of hormones.

Vasopressin injection, **U.S.P., B.P. (Pitressin).** This is a purified preparation of antidiuretic and pressor hormone separated from the oxytocic hormone. The usual dose is 1 ml., and it is given subcutaneously or intramuscularly. It contains 20 pressor units per milliliter.

Vasopressin tannate **(Pitressin Tannate).** This compound is marketed in solution for intramuscular injection (5 pressor units per milliliter); 0.3 to 1 ml. (5 to 15 minims) is injected at intervals of 36 to 48 hours. Its effect is more prolonged than that of vasopressin. It cannot be given intravenously. Nurses who administer this drug are reminded that prolonged rotation of the ampule is necessary in order that all of the particles be included in the suspension. Failure to shake the ampule thoroughly can result in inaccurate dosage and inadequate therapeutic response.

Posterior pituitary powder. This powder is dried pituitary gland, which can be snuffed into the nose. Absorption from the nasal mucous membrane makes it possible to use it for the relief of symptoms of diabetes insipidus. It is less expensive than the injectable forms.

Side effects and toxic effects. Vasopressin can cause spasm of coronary arteries, and caution is recommended when it is administered to patients with inadequate coronary circulation. Water retention and occasionally water intoxication have been known to occur. The patient with diabetes insipidus will probably have to take the drug the remainder of his life. Large doses may cause intestinal and uterine cramps.

■ Parathyroid hormone

Lying just above the thyroid, or, in some animals, embodied in it, are a variable number of bean-shaped glands (two pairs in man) known as the parathyroids. The primary function of the parathyroids is the maintenance of adequate levels of calcium in the extracellular fluid. The most significant function of parathyroid hormone is mobilization of calcium from bone. It also reduces phosphate concentration, permitting more calcium to be mobilized. Hypoparathyroidism leads to manifestations of hypocalcemia and tetany, the symptoms of which include muscle spasms, convulsions, gradual paralysis with dyspnea, and death from exhaustion. Before death gastrointestinal hemorrhages and hematemesis frequently occur. At death the intestinal mucosa is congested and the calcium content of the heart, kidney, and other tissues is increased.

The symptoms of tetany are relieved by the injection of parathyroid extracts and by calcium salts. Because the action of parathyroid hormone is slow, it is usually necessary to administer calcium salts intravenously for rapid relief. Large doses of vitamin D are also useful to relieve tetany and to restore the normal level of calcium in the blood.

The patient is hospitalized because a frequent check on the blood calcium and phosphate levels is essential. Hypoparathyroidism is the specific indication for the use of hormonal therapy.

Preparation, dosage, and administration. The following is the available preparation of parathyroid hormone.

Parathyroid injection, **U.S.P.** Usual dose is 40 U.S.P. units intramuscularly every 12 hours. One milliliter of the parathyroid injection possesses a potency of not less than 100 U.S.P. parathyroid units, each unit representing one hundredth of the amount required to raise the calcium content of 100 ml. of the blood serum

of normal dogs 1 mg. within 16 to 18 hours after administration.

■ Thyroid hormones and drugs used in diseases of the thyroid gland

The thyroid gland stores an iodine-containing protein known as thyroglobulin, which is essential for the proper regulation of metabolism. Thyroxin is released from this protein into the bloodstream and, in the blood, is transported bound to one of the proteins in the plasma, also a globulin. Thyroxin was isolated by Kendall in 1915, who found that it contained 65% iodine. Thyroxin has been found to exhibit the same physiologic effects as the original protein.

Thyroxin has been known for many years and until recently was regarded as the thyroid hormone or at least the active portion of thyroglobulin.

Within the past few years a closely related compound, identical with thyroxin except that it contains one less iodine atom, liothyronine, has been found to be a natural component of thyroid tissue and is even more potent than thyroxin. Although thyroxin is more abundant in man than liothyronine, it is not certain which hormone is physiologically dominant. Both have essentially the same action.

Thyroxin (tetraiodothyronine)

Liothyronine (triiodothyronine)

Physiologic action. Although the exact mechanism of action of the thyroid hormones is not known, their primary effect is an acceleration of cellular metabolism. This is reflected in the way tissues grow and develop. Deficiency causes not only a slowing of growth in the young but also affects many reactions both in the young and in the adult; water and salt metabolism is affected, and muscular inefficiency, circulatory disturbances, and disturbance of the central nervous system may be noticed.

Thyroid and other endocrines

The thyroid gland is an important member of the endocrine group and is affected by other endocrine glands, especially by the thyrotropic factor from the anterior lobe of the pituitary. The thyroid also exerts an influence on other endocrines—the thymus, adrenals, and gonads. Hyperthyroidism results in increased calcium excretion and also hypertrophic changes in the parathyroid.

Iodine deficiency and its effect on the thyroid gland

The synthesis of the thyroid hormones and their maintenance in the blood in adequate amounts depend in large part upon an adequate intake of iodine. Iodine ingested by way of food or water is changed into iodide and is stored in the thyroid gland before reaching the circulation. Prolonged iodine deficiency in the diet results in an enlargement of the thyroid gland, known as a simple goiter. When thyroid hormones fail to be synthesized because of a lack of iodine, the anterior lobe of the pituitary is stimulated to increase the secretion of thyrotropic hormone, which in turn causes hypertrophy and hyperplasia of the gland. The enlarged thyroid then mobilizes to remove residual traces of iodine from the blood. This type of goiter (simple or nontoxic) can be prevented by providing an adequate supply of iodine for the young. Iodine is not abundant in most dietary items except fish and seafoods, and iodized salt is frequently the primary resource for iodine.

Hypothyroid states

Cretinism. Hypothyroidism in the young child is known as cretinism and is characterized by cessation of physical and mental development, which leads to dwarfism and idiocy. Patients with cretinism usually have thick, coarse skin, a thick tongue, gaping mouth, protruding abdomen, thick, short legs, poorly developed hands and feet, and weak musculature. This condition may result from faulty development or atrophy of the thyroid gland during fetal life. Failure of development of the gland may be caused by lack of iodine in the mother.

Myxedema (Gull's disease). Hypothyroidism in the adult is called myxedema. Its development is usually insidious and causes a gradual retardation of physical and mental functions. There is a gradual infiltration of the skin and loss of facial lines and facial expression. The formation of a subcutaneous connective tissue causes the hands and face to appear puffy and swollen. The basal metabolic rate becomes subnormal, the hair becomes scanty and coarse, movements become sluggish, and the patient becomes hypersensitive to cold.

Thyroid preparations

Thyroid is a yellowish powder obtained from the thyroid glands of domesticated animals used for food by man.

Thyroid or thyroxin is specific in the treatment of hypothyroid conditions. Patients with cretinism or myxedema will probably require therapy all of their lives. This dosage must be adjusted to the needs of the patient. For most patients an official preparation of thyroid in tablet form is the cheapest and most convenient form and at the same time is very effective. The object of treatment of the patient with myxedema is to rid him of symptoms, not necessarily to raise the metabolic rate to normal. In the treatment of the patient with cretinism, however, it may be necessary to raise the metabolic rate to normal or above in order to ensure adequate development. It is most important to start treatment of this patient very early in life, which means before the child is 6 months old if at all possible. Otherwise, both the physical retardation and mental retardation are likely to be permanent. In myxedema, mental and physical characteristics are restored and complete cure often results.

Thyroid preparations have been used extensively in the treatment of obesity. At best, the use of thyroid is a palliative measure and is not unaccompanied by the danger of inducing severe symptoms of toxicity. Thyroid hormone or thyroid extract should be regarded as a potent substance and should never be used indiscriminately. No one should take it who is not under direct medical supervision. If the obesity is primarily the result of hypothyroidism, its use may be indicated, but most authorities agree that obesity usually is caused by overeating and must be cured by reducing the caloric intake. Uncontrolled use of the drug has caused death.

Thyroid preparations have also been used in connection with low metabolic levels associated with rheumatoid arthritis, rickets, various skin diseases, and menstrual disturbances. Although thyroid is not considered specific for these conditions, good results have been reported in some cases. Sterility and habitual abortion are sometimes successfully treated with thyroid.

Side effects and toxic effects. The symptoms of overdosage are, in general, those of hyperthyroidism: palpitation, tachycardia, pain over the heart, dyspnea, nervousness, insomnia, tremor, hyperglycemia, sweating, and loss of weight.

It should be remembered that symptoms come on slowly and may last a long time. It is best, therefore, that a small dose be used at first and the patient be watched closely. One of the first symptoms of overdosage that the nurse may have occasion to note is an increase in the pulse rate. She should always count the pulse before giving the next dose of the drug. In some hospitals it is the rule to withhold the drug if the pulse rate has reached 100 beats per minute. For younger children the pulse rate may be higher, yet within the range of safety. The rate will vary with the age of the child. In mild cases withdrawal of the drug will result in return to the normal metabolic level. In severe cases it is important to allow the patient to rest in a comfortable position. A sedative also may be indicated.

Thyroid, U.S.P., B.P.

Thyroid is available in tablets containing 15, 30, 60, 125, 200, 250, and 300 mg. each for oral administration. The usual oral dose is 100 mg. daily, although the dose must be determined by the needs of the patient. Range of dosage for 1 day may be 15 to 180 mg. or more.

Thyroxine; thyroxine sodium, B.P.

Thyroxine is no longer an official drug in the United States. It is thought to have little or no advantage over crude preparations of thyroid, except that it can be administered parenterally. Since a latent period exists before the drug exhibits its peak effects, there is no advantage in giving the drug parenterally. It is more expensive than thyroid tablets.

Thyroxine sodium is available in tablet form. The dosage is 0.05 to 0.5 mg. daily. It should be protected from light.

Sodium levothyroxine, U.S.P. (Synthroid Sodium)

This is the sodium salt of the levo isomer of thyroxin. It is more effective than a mixture of D-thyroxine and L-thyroxine. It is given orally. Usual doses range from 100 to 600 μg. daily. Increase in dosage is made on the basis of patient's response. Official tablets are available containing 0.05, 0.1, 0.2, and 0.3 mg.

Sodium liothyronine, U.S.P. (Cytomel)

This is the active isomer of triiodothyronine. It exhibits a rapid onset of action, but after administration is stopped the duration of effect is correspondingly brief. From 5 to 200 μg. is given daily for adults being treated for hypothyroid states. Some patients will require higher dosage levels. It is available in 5- and 25-μg. tablets for oral administration.

Hyperthyroid states (thyrotoxicosis) and antithyroid drugs

Excessive formation of the thyroid hormones and their escape into the circulation result in a state of toxicity called thyrotoxicosis. This occurs in the condition known as exophthalmic goiter (Graves' disease) or in some forms of adenomatous goiters.

Hyperthyroidism leads to symptoms quite different from those seen in myxedema. The metabolic rate is increased, sometimes as much as a plus 60 or more. The body temperature frequently is above normal, the pulse rate is fast, and the patient complains of feeling too warm. Other symptoms include restlessness, anxiety, emotional instability, muscle tremor and weakness, sweating, and exophthalmos.

Prior to the advent of antithyroid drugs treatment was more or less limited to a subtotal resection of the hyperactive gland. Since these patients usually are poor operative risks, they may be hospitalized for a time and prepared for surgery by giving them as much mental and physical rest as possible, a diet particularly rich in carbohydrate and vitamins, and iodine. Thyroidectomy is indicated when the pulse has been slowed and the basal metabolic rate lowered to a somewhat stationary level. Antithyroid drugs provide less rapid control of hyperthyroidism than do surgical measures. Radioactive iodine is less rapid than surgical therapy, but it is one of the more effective antithyroid drugs.

An antithyroid drug is regarded as a chemical agent that lowers the basal metabolic rate by interfering with the formation, release, or action of the hormones made by the thyroid glands. Those that interfere with the synthesis of the thyroid hormones are known as goitrogens. A wide variety of compounds might be included in this category of antithyroid drugs, but only iodine (iodide ion), radioactive iodine, and certain derivatives of thiouracil will be included.

Iodine; iodide

Iodine that has pharmacologic or biochemical significance is either inorganic iodine (iodine ion) or iodine that is bound in an organic compound such as thyroxin. There is thought to be little in common between the physiologic effects of elemental iodine, the iodide ion, and organic compounds that contain iodine in their structure, as is true of thyroxin. Confusion seems to have arisen from the incorrect or loose usage of the word *iodine.*

When elemental iodine is administered locally, a certain proportion of it is converted to iodide and is absorbed. This brings about general systemic effects of iodide. Lugol's Solution contains elemental iodine, but it is changed into iodide before absorption. As a result, significant amounts of iodide reach the bloodstream and are effective in the treatment of toxic goiter.

Action and result. Iodide is the oldest of the antithyroid drugs. The response of the thyrotoxic patient frequently is remarkable. The metabolic rate falls at about the same rate as after surgical removal of the gland and many of the symptoms of hyperthyroidism are relieved. Maximum effects usually are attained after 10 to 15 days of continuous administration of iodide. Enlargement of the gland and hyperplasia are reduced, and the gland rapidly stores colloid, which contains highly potent thyroid hormone. The mechanism by which iodide accomplishes its beneficial effect is not fully understood. One explanation is that iodide temporarily promotes storage of hormone in the thyroid gland and at the same time lowers the amount delivered to the circulation. Another hypothesis is that iodide interferes in some way with the action of the thyrotropic hormone or that it diminishes the activity of the anterior lobe of the pituitary gland.

During the time when the metabolic rate is somewhere near the normal range, the surgeon may be able to operate upon a patient who is nearly normal instead of on a very sick individual. Unfortunately, the beneficial effects are not prolonged indefinitely. In a few weeks the symptoms are likely to reappear and may be intensified. The thyroid gland has been filled with active hormone that, when released, may plunge the patient into a critical state.

Uses. The chief use of iodide in the treatment of thyrotoxicosis is in preparation of the patient for thyroidectomy. Patients with severe hyperthyroidism are frequently prepared first with propylthiouracil or a related compound, and during the last part of the treatment iodide is given to prevent the development of a friable, highly vascular gland, which would increase the hazards of surgery. A certain number of patients, however, may be controlled and prepared for surgery with iodide alone.

Preparation, dosage, and administration. Con-   **459**

venient preparations are Lugol's solution and saturated solutions of sodium or potassium iodide; 0.3 ml. (0.1 to 1 ml.) of these preparations can be given orally three times a day. They should be well diluted in one-third to one-half glass of milk or another vehicle that may be preferred by the patient.

Strong iodine solution, **U.S.P. (Compound Iodine Solution, Lugol's Solution);** *aqueous iodine solution,* **B.P.** This preparation contains iodine and potassium iodide.

Sodium iodide, **U.S.P., B.P.** This drug may be given as an expectorant; dosage ranges from 300 mg. to 1 Gm. daily.

Potassium iodide solution, **N.F.;** *potassium iodide,* **B.P. (Saturated Potassium Iodide Solution).** Nurses may see this preparation ordered as SSKI, which means "Saturated Solution of Potassium Iodide." It is usually administered in 5- to 10-drop dosages diluted with fruit juice. Since the medication evaporates rapidly, it should not stand open to air for long periods before administration.

Radioactive iodine

Iodine 131 is a radioactive isotope of iodine that has given evidence of being useful in medicine. It has a half-life of 8.08 days, which means that at the end of about 8 days 50% of its atoms have undergone disintegration and in another 8 days 50% of the remaining amount has disappeared, and so on until an inappreciable amount remains. The radioactivity of this material is therefore dissipated in a relatively short time. The energy liberated during the period of radioactivity is in the form of beta particles and gamma rays. This radiation brings about the same tissue changes as are secured from radium emanations or from roentgen rays.

Radioiodine is absorbed rapidly from the stomach, and most of the dose is in the blood within the first hour. The cells of the thyroid gland have an unusual affinity for iodine and will concentrate the elements to a marked degree. Radioiodine is useful because it may be located, because of its radioactivity, even when present in extraordinarily small amounts. Radioiodine behaves exactly as does ordinary nonradioactive iodine; hence, an infinitesimal quantity of it can be used to trace or follow the behavior of any amount of ordinary iodine with which it is mixed. Such tiny doses, appropriately called "tracers," when given to a patient are used to tag all of the ordinary iodine in the patient's body and to permit the observers to trace the behavior of the radioiodine. It has become a useful tool with which to study problems of physiology and disease of the thyroid gland. It is also of value in diagnosing functional states of the thyroid gland, in treating selected cases of cancer of the thyroid gland, and in treating certain cases of hyperthyroidism. Some physicians believe that radioiodine is most effective as a therapeutic agent when used in treatment of patients more than 50 years of age, those who have severe complicating disease, those who have recurrent hyperthyroidism after previous resection of the thyroid, and those who have extremely small glands.

After the oral ingestion of a tracer dose of iodine 131, the following determinations are made: (1) the rate and amount of urinary excretion, (2) the rate and amount of uptake of the radioiodine by the gland, and (3) the rate and degree of incorporation of the radioiodine into the hormonal iodine of the blood. These determinations can be of value because they can be used to help differentiate the patient with a normally functioning thyroid gland from the one with hyperthyroidism or hypothyroidism.

Because radioiodine can be taken by mouth and is collected and concentrated by the thyroid tissue, a much greater degree of irradiation can be secured than is possible with radium or roentgen rays because of the danger of damaging normal tissue, particularly the skin, when large doses of the latter are used. The results of treatment of the patient with toxic goiter have been encouraging, although the theoretical danger of radiation injury has limited the treatment largely to older patients (beyond the child-bearing period) and to those who are considered poor surgical risks. For the latter type of patient this treatment is thought to be superior to the use of other antithyroid drugs, although it may never be used as widely as certain other antithyroid drugs because of the care and caution with which radioiodine must be handled. However, the chief disadvantage of use of radioiodine is that it may promote the formation of carcinoma. At present this is thought possible but unlikely.

When cancer is present in the thyroid gland, the tissue exhibits a variable degree of capacity to collect iodine, depending on the degree of function of the tissue in the tumor. Therefore, the possibility of treating cancer of the thyroid gland with radioiodine appears to be somewhat limited. Metastasis from a malignant tumor of the thyroid gland sometimes can be traced with the use of the Geiger-Müller counter and definite locations of metastatic lesions found. Prolonged treatment with radioiodine may in some cases arrest widespread involvement of this nature.

Preparation, dosage, and administration. The following are preparations available of radioiodine.

Sodium iodide I^{131} solution, **U.S.P., B.P.** This is a solution containing iodine 131 suitable for either oral or intravenous administration. Tracer doses range from 1 to 100 microcuries (μc.); therapeutic doses range from 1 to 100 millicuries (mc.). When diagnostic tracer tests are done for evaluation of thyroid function, 1 to 100 μc. of iodine 131 given along with 100 μg. of nonradioactive sodium iodide as a recommended dosage. This may be given in the morning before breakfast. The test will be invalidated, however, if the patient has been receiving thiouracil or iodine in any form during the preceding week or potassium thiocyanate during the preceding month. Therapeutic dosage is determined by the size of the gland, the severity of the condition being treated, and the results of the preliminary study of the excretion of tracer amounts or the percentage of the tracer dose observed in the thyroid gland.

Sodium iodide I^{131} capsules, **U.S.P.** These are gelatin capsules and contain a radioactive isotope of iodine.

Side effects and toxic effects. Although administration of this substance is in one sense very simple, since it can be added to water and given to the patient to swallow as he would a drink of water (for it has no color or taste), the radia-

tion from this substance is dangerous in the same way and to the same extent as are the effects from radium and roentgen rays. It follows that exposure to radioiodine, like exposure to radium or roentgen rays, should be avoided or minimized as much as possible. Special precautions must be observed, because it is frequently in a form that can be spilled on persons or property. The contamination that may result from spilling a dose of radioiodine or the spilling of urine or other excreta from patients who have received the radioactive substance means that surroundings must be checked and measured with special monitoring instruments, usually by small portable Geiger counters. It is particularly undesirable for nurses and technicians to contaminate their persons with radioiodine, and therefore rubber gloves should be worn whenever the radioiodine is given to patients and during the disposal of their excreta.

Propylthiouracil and related compounds

Propylthiouracil and related compounds interfere with the synthesis of the hormone produced by the thyroid gland. As a result the gland is depleted of hormone, less hormone reaches the tissues of the body, and the rate of metabolism is lowered. Because of the creation of a thyroid hormone deficiency, the thyrotropic hormone made by the anterior lobe of the pituitary gland is increased, and hyperplasia of the thyroid gland occurs. The inhibition of hormone synthesis is sufficiently effective to make these compounds useful in bringing about relief of symptoms of hyperthyroidism. The exact manner in which these drugs prevent synthesis of the thyroid hormone is not known. However, after administration of these compounds is stopped, the thyroid gland rapidly regains its ability to synthesize the hormone as well as to store colloid, which contains thyroxin. Propylthiouracil and related compounds are used chiefly to control the signs and symptoms of hyperthyroidism in Graves' disease and in toxic nodular goiter and to prepare the patient who must undergo surgery of the thyroid gland. It is true that the gland is made more friable and vascular with their use, but this is overcome with

461

the simultaneous administration of iodide 10 to 15 days prior to the operation.

Preparation, dosage, and administration. Propylthiouracil and related compounds are readily absorbed from the gastrointestinal tract and are administered by mouth only. Since all have the same mechanism of action, the choice depends on the incidence of side effects and on the duration of action. To ensure adequate and effective therapy these drugs should be administered at evenly spaced intervals during the day. Maintenance doses are determined in accordance with the metabolic rate.

Methylthiouracil, N.F., B.P. (Methiacil, Muracil, Thimecil). This drug is marketed in 50-mg. tablets. The usual daily dose is 200 mg. given in divided doses. It may prove useful for patients who are refractory to other antithyroid drugs.

Propylthiouracil, U.S.P., B.P. This preparation is similar to methylthiouracil and is marketed in 50-mg. tablets. The usual daily dose is 50 mg. every 8 hours. In severe hyperthyroidism, initial doses of 100 mg. every 8 hours may be required. In some instances much larger doses are given.

Iothiouracil sodium (Itrumil Sodium). This drug is said to exert the combined effects of a thiouracil derivative and an iodide. It is available in 50-mg. tablets. The usual daily dose is 150 to 200 mg. in divided doses.

Methimazole, U.S.P. (Tapazole). This is one of the most active of the thyroid-inhibiting drugs and its antithyroid activity is ten to twenty times stronger than that of propylthiouracil. It is marketed in 5- and 10-mg. tablets. Initial doses of 5 to 10 mg. every 8 hours are recommended.

Carbimazole, B.P. This compound is available in 5-mg. tablets. The maintenance dosage is 5 to 20 mg. daily given in divided doses. Claims have been made that this preparation causes less hyperplasia of the thyroid gland than certain of the other preparations of this group of drugs.

Side effects and toxic effects. Drugs of this group vary in their capacity to cause toxic reactions. Thiouracil is most likely to cause toxic effects and has been discarded in favor of propylthiouracil and other less toxic substitutes.

However, they are all capable of causing serious untoward effects, which may include leukopenia, skin rash, drug fever, enlargement of the salivary glands and lymph nodes in the neck, hepatitis, loss of the sense of taste, and edema of the lower extremities. The most grave complication is granulocytopenia. Many of the aforementioned reactions necessitate discontinuing administration of the drug and giving appropriate supportive treatment. Patients should be instructed that if they develop sore throat, a head cold, fever, or malaise they should report the symptoms immediately to their physician. The nurse should be alert to note warning symptoms as well. The incidence of untoward reactions is said to be between 3% and 5%. The incidence of agranulocytosis is said to approach 0.5%. The need for close medical supervision of patients receiving these drugs is obvious.

■ Hormones of the adrenal gland

The adrenal glands are located just above the kidneys and consist of two parts, the inner medulla and the outer cortex. Epinephrine, a secretion of the medullary portion, is discussed in Chapter 9. The secretion of the cells of the adrenal cortex is distinctly different from epinephrine. Adrenalectomized animals die within a few days unless they are given injections of adrenal cortex or adrenocortical hormones, whereas removal of the medullary portion of the gland does not necessarily result in death.

Adrenocorticosteroids

The three main groups of adrenocortical hormones are as follows.

Mineralocorticoids—aldosterone and desoxycorticosterone. Both of these compounds exhibit sodium-retaining and potassium-excreting properties. Aldosterone is the more potent compound.

Glucocorticoids. Hydrocortisone and cortisone have a specific effect upon carbohydrate metabolism (in that they promote the mobilization of glucose from glycogen reserves), maintain blood sugar by supporting gluconeogenesis, and promote the utilization of glucose to meet the needs of the body during an emergency.

They also affect protein and fat metabolism and produce antiinflammatory, antirheumatic, and antiallergic effects. They lower the number of eosinophils in the blood and suppress activity of the lymphatic system. Cortisone and hydrocortisone also help to regulate electrolyte exchange in the kidney but to a lesser degree than desoxycorticosterone.

Prednisone, prednisolone, methylprednisolone, triamcinolone, and dexamethasone are examples of synthetic glucocorticoids. Dexamethasone is the most potent antiinflammatory glucocorticoid available.

Hydrocortisone and related glucocorticoids produced by the adrenal gland are secreted in response to the influence of ACTH (adrenocorticotropic hormone) produced by the anterior lobe of the pituitary gland. When the adrenal gland secretes more cortical hormones than normal or when exogenous adrenocortical hormones are administered, secretion of ACTH by the pituitary gland is inhibited, and this in turn brings about decreased activity of the cells of the adrenal cortex.

Androgenic steroids. The chemical structure of the cortical steroids is similar to that of the sex hormones. Some of the adrenocortical steroids exhibit androgenic and some exhibit estrogenic properties. They are not of great consequence under normal conditions. Adrenal tumors, on the other hand, can cause increased formation of estrogen or androgen, which helps to explain abnormal feminization or masculinization in patients.

Although a rather large number of steroids have been isolated from the secretion of the cortical portion of the adrenal gland, only a few have been found to have a significant capacity to maintain life in an animal whose adrenal glands have been removed. Among these are desoxycorticosterone, cortisone, hydrocortisone, and a recently isolated steroid first called electrocortin and now known as aldosterone. Note the points of similarity and difference in the accompanying structural formulas.

These as well as a number of other chemically related hormones of the adrenal gland resemble the sex hormones.

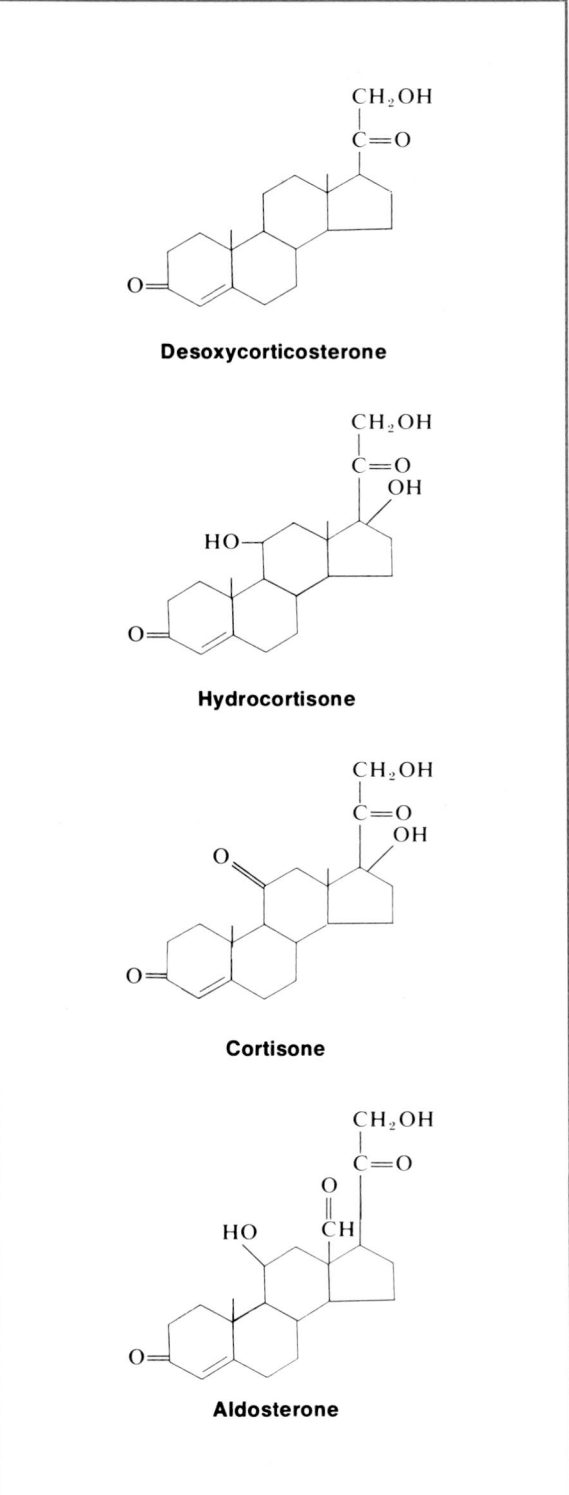

Desoxycorticosterone

Hydrocortisone

Cortisone

Aldosterone

Adrenal cortex injection

Adrenal cortex injection is a sterile solution of a mixture of natural adrenocortical hormones derived from the cortex of adrenal glands of healthy animals used for food by man. This preparation has been used in the prevention and treatment of acute adrenal insufficiency. It is usually administered intramuscularly or intravenously. It is of value in acute stress situations such as are encountered in patients with extensive burns or severe infections. Adrenal cortex injection is expensive, however, and as the availability of the pure adrenocortical steroids has increased, and particularly the availability of the different groups of steroids with their different effects, the use of the whole crude extract has diminished. It may be anticipated that, like liver extract and other crude preparations, it may soon be completely superseded.

Preparation, dosage, and administration. Adrenal cortex injection is available in 10- and 50-ml. vials. The range of dosage is 10 to 100 ml.

Desoxycorticosterone acetate (Doca Acetate)

Desoxycorticosterone acetate is a white, crystalline powder, insoluble in water and slightly soluble in vegetable oils. In small amounts it has been isolated from the adrenal cortex and is synthesized as the acetate.

The activity of desoxycorticosterone acetate appears to be limited to the metabolism of sodium, potassium, and water. It is particularly effective in correcting defects in the sodium-potassium balance. It promotes the retention of the sodium ions and water and the excretion of potassium. The site of action is seemingly the renal tubule of the kidney, where reabsorption is modified. It has no noticeable effect on carbohydrate and protein metabolism.

Patients with chronic adrenal insufficiency, such as patients with Addison's disease, may progress satisfactorily with the administration of desoxycorticosterone and sodium chloride. Some physicians prefer to use cortisone and hydrocortisone with sodium chloride along with maintenance doses of desoxycorticosterone. In acute adrenal insufficiency adrenocortical extract, cortisone, hydrocortisone, and desoxycorticosterone as well as other adrenal steroids may be used. Patients treated only with desoxycorticosterone are highly affected by states of stress or infections, and an addisonian crisis may be precipitated.

Since the advent of newer drugs, desoxycorticosterone acetate is not used as widely as in the past.

Preparation, dosage, and administration. The following are preparations available of desoxycorticosterone acetate.

***Desoxycorticosterone acetate,* U.S.P. (Doca Acetate, Percorten, Decortin, Decosterone); *deoxycortone acetate,* B.P.** This is available as a solution for injection (5 mg. per milliliter) and in 2- and 5-mg. buccal tablets. The tablets should be held in the buccal cavity or under the tongue. The solution is given by intramuscular injection.

***Sterile desoxycorticosterone pivalate suspension,* N.F.** This is a microcrystalline suspension of the drug. One injection lasts approximately 4 weeks for the patient with Addison's disease. It is administered intramuscularly. The usual dose is 50 mg.

The maintenance dose of desoxycorticosterone acetate varies from 1 to 7 mg. daily, depending on the response of the patient and the intake of sodium chloride (the higher the intake of salt, the lower the requirement of adrenal steroid). In the management of an acute crisis 10 to 15 mg. once or twice a day may be needed along with cortisone or other adrenal steroids.

Side effects and toxic effects. When large doses of desoxycorticosterone are given, patients may develop edema, pulmonary congestion, or congestive heart failure, and even death may result. A fair number of patients develop hypertension after several months or years of receiving this drug. The blood pressure should be taken periodically, and if hypertension develops, the dosage of the steroid and probably also the salt intake should be carefully adjusted. Excessive loss of potassium may account for electrocardiographic changes and sudden attacks of weakness.

Aldosterone

For some years desoxycorticosterone was the only potent steroid available that had selective action in favoring water and salt retention in the patient with Addison's disease. This hormone was lifesaving in the treatment of persons with low or absent adrenal cortical function. Desoxycorticosterone was originally obtained by chemical synthesis and has been found in adrenal glands in only trace levels. There have been reasons to doubt its role as a naturally occurring hormone of importance in regulating salt and water balance. Within the past few years a new steroid that seems much more likely to be the natural salt-retaining hormone of the adrenal cortex has been discovered in body fluids and in the adrenal gland. This is aldosterone, a compound much more potent in its electrolyte effects than desoxycorticosterone. Aldosterone has not yet established a therapeutic status comparable to that of desoxycorticosterone. Its use has been limited because of its cost and relative unavailability and because it must be administered intramuscularly. The amount of aldosterone secreted by the adrenal cortex is apparently affected by the concentration of sodium in body fluids rather than by the stimulation of the adrenal cortex by ACTH.

Cortisone; hydrocortisone

Cortisone and hydrocortisone are adrenal steroids that are particularly concerned with carbohydrate metabolism and are known as glucocorticoids. Cortisone was isolated from the adrenal gland in 1935 and for a time was known simply as Compound E. Hydrocortisone has been known also as Compound F. The activity of these two adrenal steroids is similar, although hydrocortisone is more potent in its physiologic and antirheumatic effects and is less irritating to synovial membranes when injected into joint cavities. However, it is less soluble in body fluids than cortisone; hence, it is less suited to intramuscular injection.

Sources. Cortisone is a white, crystalline substance that at the present time is made from an acid obtained from the bile of oxen and sheep. Desoxycholic acid was subjected to some thirty steps whereby changes were made to synthesize the substance now known as 17-hydroxy-11-dehydrocorticosterone. This name was shortened to cortisone. Total synthesis has since been accomplished. The partial chemical synthesis of hydrocortisone also was achieved soon after that of cortisone. Hydrocortisone, too, is a white, odorless, crystalline powder.

Action and result. Cortisone and hydrocortisone affect carbohydrate, protein, and fat metabolism. They promote glucogenesis, a rise in blood sugar, glycosuria, and a negative nitrogen balance. Large doses over a period of time produce an increased excretion of potassium and retention of sodium. The patient, therefore, must be watched closely to prevent imbalance of electrolytes. Administration of either hormone leads to an increased white cell count and a reduced eosinophil count. These hormones also inhibit activity of the lymphatic system, causing lymphopenia and reduction in size of enlarged lymph nodes. Therapeutic doses of cortisone and hydrocortisone depress the function of cells in the adrenal cortex as well as cells of the anterior lobe of the pituitary gland, which produce corticotropin. If administration is prolonged and large amounts of these hormones are given, atrophy of the adrenal cortex will develop. The gland usually recovers, but it must be kept in mind that permanent damage is always a possibility. Administration of the hormones should be withdrawn gradually rather than abruptly, for while termination of their use does not necessarily bring about symptoms of acute adrenal insufficiency, patients are known to experience muscular weakness, lethargy, and exhaustion after administration has been discontinued. Such symptoms are interpreted to mean that there is depression of cortical function.

It has also been noted that most patients respond to these medications with an elevated mood, which is a result of remission of symptoms or a direct result of central nervous system effects. However, neurosis and psychosis have been noted in patients with Cushing's syndrome.

Both cortisone and hydrocortisone are potent substances that exert widespread physiologic as well as pharmacologic effects in the human body.

There is evidence that some of the effects are therapeutically beneficial, others are of no apparent therapeutic significance, and still others are likely to be hazardous to the patient. Although the exact mode of action is unknown, Hench and his associates were of the opinion that in diseases influenced by cortisone and corticotropin, these hormones act as buffer substances against the known or unknown irritant to which the tissues of the body are reacting rather than remove the cause of the disease or repair damaged tissues.

In other words, cortisone and the closely related hydrocortisone permit the patient to have certain diseases without having the characteristic symptoms thereof or without being injured or destroyed by the disease, in some cases at least. In spite of the fact that they do not cure the disease, they bring about relief of symptoms in many patients, and in addition they have provided a remarkable new research tool for medical science.

Uses. Cortisone and hydrocortisone are indicated chiefly for replacement therapy in conditions of adrenal insufficiency, such as may be found after adrenalectomy, Addison's disease, and hypopituitarism. For these conditions these hormones are lifesaving.

These hormones and their synthetic derivatives may also be used therapeutically for a variety of nonendocrine conditions. It is believed that, by virtue of their antipyretic, antiinflammatory, and mood-elevating properties, they can do more good than harm.

In acute rheumatoid arthritis or arthritis, conditions unresponsive to other therapeutic measures, many experts advise glucocorticoid therapy. Intraarticular injection of cortisone has been practiced but with inconclusive results.

In patients with rheumatoid arthritis there is rapid and marked reduction in the symptoms and signs of the disease. Muscle and joint stiffness, muscle tenderness and weakness, and joint swelling and soreness are diminished. The patient getting the drug for the first time usually notices distinct improvement within a few days. Appetite and weight increase; fever, if present, disappears; and the patient feels more energetic.

Sedimentation rates usually are reduced or become normal and remain so as long as adequate doses of the hormone are given. Anemic patients usually have a rise in hemoglobin and in the number of red blood cells.

However, anatomic changes that have taken place prior to the administration of the hormones are unaffected, and joint deformities that have resulted from damage to bone and cartilage do not improve. After the withdrawal of the hormones symptoms generally reappear within a varying period of time, frequently within a short time.

Nephrotic syndrome has been effectively treated with glucocorticoids, as have cerebral edema and chronic ulcerative colitis. Glucocorticoids are also among the most useful therapeutic agents in the treatment of leukemias.

These hormones are used to relieve allergic manifestations such as may be seen in patients with serum sickness, severe hay fever, status asthmaticus, and exfoliative dermatitis. The tissue response to the allergic reaction is somehow modified by the hormones, but the precise mode of action is not understood.

Inflammatory conditions of the eye, such as uveitis, iritis, acute choroiditis, purulent conjunctivitis, allergic blepharitis, and keratitis, are also controlled. Prednisone or prednisolone is considered the steroid of choice in treatment of severe ocular inflammation requiring therapy.

Cortisone and hydrocortisone have been used extensively for the so-called collagen or mesenchymal diseases, such as lupus erythematosus, dermatomyositis, and periarteritis nodosa. In these diseases, particularly lupus erythematosus, a sensitivity seems to have been developed after some acute infection, and the brunt of the sensitivity is borne by the connective tissues of the body. Apparently, the response of connective tissues to mechanical or chemical injury as well as to states of hypersensitivity such as may be produced by disease or by drugs is somehow altered. The reactivity of the connective tissue is suppressed regardless of the cause. This effect of cortisone or hydrocortisone seems to explain their capacity to relieve symptoms in a variety of conditions.

In acute rheumatic fever the muscle tissue of the heart and the connective tissue of the heart valves respond a good deal like other muscle and connective tissues of the body of the patient with rheumatoid arthritis. These hormones suppress the signs and symptoms of the disease, but they neither shorten the natural duration of the disease process nor cure the disease. They do nothing to modify preexisting valvular damage or hypertrophy of the heart.

Glucocorticoids are also presently being used in shock, specifically shock with gram-negative bacteremia, but also shock of other etiologies. It has been postulated that the cortisones sometimes lead to "hemodynamic restoration" in circulatory shock when other measures have been futile, although the exact mechanism of action is not clear.

It must be remembered that in all of these conditions the administration of corticosteroids is primarily symptomatic, not curative, therapy.

Absorption. Cortisone acetate is absorbed effectively after both oral and intramuscular injection. The response after oral administration is often more rapid than after intramuscular injection, but the effect is less sustained. Since a constant level of the hormone in the tissues is highly desirable, several doses of intramuscular cortisone may be given during the first days of therapy, after which the size of the maintenance dose is determined. After oral administration the absorption of hydrocortisone is highly similar to that of cortisone. Absorption of hydrocortisone from an intramuscular site of injection, however, takes place much more slowly.

Preparation, dosage, and administration. The following are preparations available of cortisone and hydrocortisone.

Cortisone acetate, **U.S.P., B.P. (Cortone Acetate, Cortogen Acetate).** Official preparations are available in 5-, 10-, and 25-mg. tablets for oral administration and as a suspension for injection, 25 or 50 mg. per milliliter. There are also available an ophthalmic suspension (0.5% and 2.5%) and an ophthalmic ointment (1.5%). Cortisone acetate is administered parenterally, orally, or topically. Dosage varies greatly with the nature and severity of the disease being treated and with the responsiveness of the patient. In severe disorders as much as 300 mg. may be ordered the first day, 200 mg. the second day, and 100 mg. daily thereafter, reducing the dosage gradually to the minimum amount that will bring about the desired effects. Its use in the treatment of acute self-limiting conditions is usually discontinued as soon as feasible, and to avoid undesirable side effects dosage must be carefully regulated when used for chronic conditions. For rheumatoid arthritis tolerable doses are frequently less than was considered satisfactory at one time. The patient's age and sex greatly affect the dose. Women, and particularly postmenopausal women, are especially sensitive to adrenocortical steroids. The average maximal daily dose for long-term therapy is 25 to 30 mg. for women and 40 to 45 mg. for men.

Hydrocortisone, **U.S.P., B.P. (Cortef, Cortril, Hydrocortone).** Hydrocortisone is available in 5-, 10-, and 20-mg. tablets, as a suspension (2 mg. per milliliter) for oral administration, as a 1% lotion for topical application, and as a solution for injection (5 to 25 mg. per milliliter). Additional preparations include a cream (1% and 2.5%) and an ointment (1% and 2.5%) for topical application. Hydrocortisone is administered orally, intramuscularly, intravenously, and topically. The dosage of hydrocortisone is said to be about two thirds that of cortisone. Adjustments in dosage are made to meet changes in the needs of the patient. Withdrawal of therapy is sometimes necessary but is avoided when the patient is subjected to additional stress and strain. The usual oral dose is 20 mg. two or three times a day.

Hydrocortisone acetate, **U.S.P., B.P. (Cortef Acetate, Cortril Acetate, Hydrocortone Acetate).** This drug is available as a suspension for injection (25 to 50 mg. per milliliter); as an ophthalmic suspension (0.5% and 2.5%); as an ointment (0.5%, 1.5%, and 2.5%); and as an ointment for topical application. The dose for intraarticular injection varies greatly with the degree of inflammation, size of the joint, and response of the patient. Doses vary from 5 to 50 mg. Ophthalmic applications also vary but may be used freely since there is no systemic reaction.

467

***Hydrocortisone sodium succinate*, U.S.P., B.P. (Solu-Cortef).** This is a highly soluble salt of hydrocortisone, which lends itself to parenteral therapy in smaller volumes of diluent. It is recommended for short-term emergency therapy. Dosage is the same as for hydrocortisone. It is available in vials containing 100 mg. of the powder for injection.

When given especially for antirheumatic effects, the daily dose of the glucocorticoids should be given in approximately equal amounts throughout the 24-hour period. When a dose is due, it should be given promptly so intervals between doses are neither too long nor too short.

Side effects and toxic effects. Toxic effects resulting from the therapeutic use of corticosteroids fall into two categories: those resulting from withdrawal and those resulting from prolonged administration in large doses. Side effects do not often constitute a problem when cortisone or hydrocortisone is given for conditions that are benefited after a short period of administration. This is also true of corticotropin. When large doses or prolonged therapy is necessary, the altered reactions of tissue cells to infections, toxins, and mechanical or chemical injury may bring about serious untoward effects. Healing of wounds may be delayed because of interference with the formation of fibroblasts and their activity in forming ground substance and granulation tissue. Growth of blood vessels into new tissue is also impaired.

Since peptic ulcers may also result from therapy, corticosteroids should be administered with meals or milk. In patients who already have peptic ulcer and have been receiving cortisone, neither fever nor abdominal rigidity occurs when perforation of the ulcer and peritonitis develop. Perforation of the bowel has been reported in patients with chronic ulcerative colitis during treatment with cortisone or corticotropin. Because of the lack of symptoms the diagnosis may be missed, and healing may be impaired seriously because of the effect on new scar-forming tissue. This failure of tissue response also explains a breakdown and active manifestation of tuberculosis in persons in whom the infection has been quiescent.

Other side effects that have been noted include amenorrhea, which presumably is caused by inhibition of the anterior lobe of the pituitary gland; disorders of calcium metabolism, seen particularly after the menopause in women who have developed osteoporosis and spontaneous fractures; and increased incidence of thrombosis and embolic formations. Still other symptoms include those associated with Cushing's syndrome—a rounded contour of the face, hirsutism, purplish or reddish striae of the skin, transient retention of salt and water, cervicothoracic hump, and the appearance of edema. Psychic phenomena have also been observed in the form of restlessness, insomnia, euphoria, and even manic states. The psychic status of a patient is, therefore, considered before these hormones are administered.

Administration of the glucocorticoids may reduce the resistance of the patient to certain infectious processes and to some viral diseases. It is thought, therefore, that acute or subacute infections should be brought under control before starting the administration of these drugs when this is at all feasible. On the other hand, should an infection occur during the course of treatment with these hormones, it may be necessary to increase the dosage to help deal with the added stress occasioned by the infection.

It has become increasingly important to remember that any patient who has received a significant amount of cortisone or related glucocorticoids is likely to have a certain amount of atrophy of the adrenal cortex. The amount of hormone that will produce atrophy is not known, nor is it known how long the atrophy will persist, but acute adrenal insufficiency results from too rapid withdrawal of therapy. Withdrawal syndrome symptoms include weakness, lethargy, restlessness, anorexia, and nausea. Muscle tenderness is common. Withdrawal should be carried out slowly and under close supervision.

A patient who must undergo surgery and who has received treatment with cortisone should be prepared preoperatively with the administration of cortisone. Its administration should be continued postoperatively in decreasing doses for several days. The nurse should be alert to pick up this type of information; she should note whether or not a patient has received treatment with cortisone, and if so, such information should be reported to the physician. It is just possible that it might be overlooked. If patients go to surgery with atrophy of the adrenal gland, it is altogether possible that they will be unable to cope with the stress of such procedure and death may result.

Some physicians recommend that patients who receive cortisone, related adrenocortical steroids, or corticotropin be given cards similar to those carried by diabetic patients, so that the physician in charge of emergencies may be aware of this fact in the event of an accident.

Contraindications. Glucocorticoids are contraindicated for patients with psychoses, peptic ulcer, acute glomerulonephritis, vaccinia or varicella, herpes simplex of the eye, and infections uncontrolled by antibiotics. Myasthenic crisis may be induced if these drugs are administered to patients with myasthenia gravis. Pregnancy is an indication for cautious use, if at all, since adrenal insufficiency in both mother and child is a possibility at the time of delivery. Moreover, abnormalities in the fetus are possible. Cautious use is recommended in the presence of hypertension, congestive heart failure, diabetes mellitus, thrombophlebitis, convulsive disorders, renal insufficiency, osteoporosis, and diverticulitis.

Synthetic corticoids

There is evidence that the compounds already discussed are all natural components of the adrenal gland, although hydrocortisone is considered to be the main steroid found in the bloodstream with corticoid activity. In recent years chemical modifications of the basic steroid structure of the corticoids have been made, with the aim of producing more potent and more selectively acting compounds. If an additional double bond is inserted on ring A of cortisone or hydrocortisone, the compounds called prednisone or prednisolone result (see structural formulas—ring A is the one at lower left of formula).

Prednisone and prednisolone are considerably more active in their antiinflammatory effect but have less salt-retaining action as compared to the parent compounds on a weight basis. Hence, there is less risk of undesirable side actions related to the retention of salt, hypertension, and formation of edema when the newer compounds are used for their antirheumatic activity. The addition of a methyl group in the 6 position of ring B of prednisolone produces an even greater effect (see methylprednisolone).

Other modifications recently introduced involve adding a fluorine atom in one of the positions (9) of the steroid ring of cortisone and hydrocortisone. This leads to a great increase in both antiinflammatory and salt-retaining activity. Because the newer fluoro derivatives have such potent salt- and water-retaining action, they have been used less for systemic administration than for topical administration in skin disorders.

***Prednisone,* U.S.P., B.P. (Meticorten, Deltasone, Deltra).** Prednisone is available in 1-, 2.5-, and 5-mg. tablets for oral administration. Dosage varies with the severity of the disease and the response of the patient. A dose of 30 to 50 mg. may be required to suppress severe symptoms, although some physicians prefer to start therapy with a relatively small dose. After 2 to 7 days, dosage is gradually reduced and a maintenance dose established. A dose of 5 to 10 mg. (or less) daily may suffice for milder conditions. The daily allotment should be divided into installment doses and should be given on a regular 6- or 8-hour schedule. Not only the total daily dose but frequently individual doses in the course of the day must be adjusted to meet the needs of the patient. Patients vary in their need and tolerance to all antirheumatic steroids. The nurse should exert great care that the correct dose is given at the right time. When administration of the drug is to be discontinued, it is usually withdrawn gradually, and in the event of a medical or surgical emergency or period of unusual stress the drug is given again to prevent the possibility of acute adrenal insufficiency. This applies to all cortical steroids given for systemic effects.

***Prednisolone,* U.S.P., B.P. (Meticortelone, Delta-Cortef).** Prednisolone is available in 1-, 2.5-, and 5-mg. tablets for oral administration **469**

Prednisone (synthetic analogue of cortisone)

9-Alpha-fluorohydrocortisone (fludrocortisone)

Prednisolone (synthetic analogue of hydrocortisone)

Methylprednisolone

and as an ointment for topical administration. It has about the same potency as prednisone, and the dosage is approximately the same.

Prednisolone acetate, **U.S.P. (Sterane).** This is marketed as an aqueous suspension, 125 mg. in 5 ml., for intramuscular injection. Dosage is the same as for orally administered prednisolone. Prednisolone acetate, B.P., is available in 5-mg. tablets.

Prednisolone butylacetate **(Hydeltra-T.B.A.).** This compound is marketed as a suspension, 20 mg. per milliliter, for injection into joints, bursae, or synovial sheaths. Dosage varies from 4 to 30 mg. Relief of symptoms may not occur for a day or two because the drug is not very soluble.

Methylprednisolone, **N.F. (Medrol).** This drug is available in 2-, 4-, and 16-mg. tablets for oral administration. Dosage is individually determined, but in general, it is about two thirds that of either prednisone or prednisolone. Suppressive doses for severe conditions range from 20 to 60 mg. daily; for less severe conditions the initial daily dosage may be from 6 to 20 mg. The daily dose is divided into four parts and is given after meals and at bedtime with food. The daily maintenance dose is frequently about half the initial dose.

Prednisolone sodium phosphate, **U.S.P. (Hydeltrasol).** This preparation is more soluble than prednisolone or its acetate or butylacetate. After parenteral administration it has a rapid onset and short duration of action. It is administered parenterally and topically to the skin, eye, or external ear.

Dexamethasone, **U.S.P., B.P. (Decadron, Deronil, Gammacorten).** This preparation is a synthetic glucocorticoid structurally similar to hydrocortisone. It is a particularly potent antiinflammatory agent. In contrast to cortisone and hydrocortisone, it may exhibit diuretic effects in patients made edematous by the administration of other adrenocortical hormones. Dexamethasone lacks mineralocorticoid activity and hence is not suited to replacement therapy for adrenal insufficiency. It is used primarily for its antiinflammatory and antiallergic effects.

Dexamethasone is administered orally or

Table 21-3 Relative potency of corticoids in treatment of nonendocrine disease

Corticoid	Potency (relative to cortisone)	Trade name	Equivalent dose
Cortisone	1	Cortogen Acetate Cortone Acetate	25 mg.
Hydrocortisone	1.2	Cortril Cortef Hydrocortone	20 mg.
Prednisone	4 to 5	Meticorten Paracort Deltasone	5 mg.
Prednisolone	4 to 5	Delta-Cortef Hydeltra Meticortelone Paracortol Sterane	5 mg.
6-Methylprednisolone	5 to 6	Medrol	4 mg.
Triamcinolone	4 to 8	Aristocort Kenacort	4 mg.
Dexamethasone	16 to 30	Decadron Deronil Dexameth Gammacorten Hexadrol	0.75 mg.
Betamethasone	16 to 30	Celestone	0.6 mg.

topically. As is true for other adrenal steroids, the dosage varies considerably, depending upon the severity of the symptoms to be controlled and the response of the patient. Usual dose ranges form 0.5 to 6 mg. daily. For topical use the drug is applied as an aerosol spray. The drug is marketed in 0.5- and 0.75-mg. tablets, as an elixir, 0.1 mg. per milliliter, and as an aerosol.

Dexamethasone sodium phosphate, U.S.P. This drug is a derivative of dexamethasone, is more soluble than dexamethasone, and is suited for injection (intramuscular, intravenous, and intrasynovial).

Although dexamethasone is said to have little tendency to cause retention of salt and water, in other respects its side effects are similar to those produced by other glucocorticoids.

Betamethasone, N.F. (Celestone). Betamethasone is structurally similar to dexamethasone and has an approximately equal level of potency. It is administered orally and is available in 600-μg. tablets. A suspension containing betamethasone sodium phosphate and betamethasone acetate is available for intramuscular or local injection.

Triamcinolone, U.S.P. (Aristocort, Kenacort). This is a potent glucocorticoid that is said to produce effects comparable to prednisolone but with lower dosage. It apparently is less likely to produce retention of sodium and water than many of the related compounds and seemingly does not affect excretion of potassium except after large doses. Prolonged use and large doses, however, bring about negative protein and calcium balance and impaired carbohydrate metabolism as well as symptoms of hyperadrenalism. It is administered orally and is available in 1-, 2-, 4-, and 16-mg. tablets. The usual initial dose varies from 8 to 20 mg. daily, given in divided portions. Maintenance dosage is determined in relation to each patient.

Triamcinolone acetonide, U.S.P. (Aristocort, Acetonide, Kenalog). This is a derivative of triamcinolone and is suited for topical administration and treatment of acute and chronic dermatoses. It is available as a cream, a lotion, and an ointment (all in a 0.1% concentration).

Fludrocortisone acetate (Florinef Acetate, F-Cortef Acetate). This preparation is marketed as a lotion and as an ointment for topical application. Because of its intense sodium-retaining effect, it is not used systemically, except for Addison's disease. At present it is used primarily for the management of allergic dermatoses. A small quantity is applied to the area of involvement several times a day. Vigorous rubbing at the time of application should be avoided. The part being treated should be carefully cleansed before the application is made. This drug is a derivative of hydrocortisone acetate. It is also marketed as a tablet for oral administration.

Hydrocortamate hydrochloride (Magnacort). This drug is marketed as an ointment for topical application. It is a derivative of hydrocortisone and is used in treatment of dermatoses with an allergic or inflammatory basis. The ointment is applied to the infected areas two or three times a day.

Side effects and toxic effects. Although prednisone, prednisolone, and closely related compounds may achieve their effects with lower dosage, their capacity to produce many of the same side effects as cortisone and hydrocortisone continues to pose problems. A gain in weight, abnormal growth of hair on the face (hypertrichosis), the development of supraclavicular fat pads, increase in blood pressure, euphoria, emotional instability, undue fatigability, and menstrual irregularities are symptoms of a developing hypercortisonism that are more difficult to treat than to prevent. Postmenopausal women and young children are especially susceptible to the adrenal steroids and are more likely to develop hypercortisonism than younger women or men. Many physicians recommend that the patient be kept on doses that can be tolerated by the patient even though all the symptoms of rheumatoid arthritis may not be completely relieved and that the patient have the benefit of other therapy in the form of salicylates, physical therapy, and plenty of rest during both day and night.

All of the adrenal steroids used clinically have distinctive and individual qualities. Cortisone is still useful and in some cases is thought to be preferable to other steroids. It is the least costly to synthesize. Hydrocortisone is superior to cortisone, especially for local injection into joints. For prolonged systemic administration, when it is important to avoid disturbances produced by loss of potassium or retention of sodium and to minimize the amount of steroid used, some authorities consider prednisone or prednisolone the steroid of choice.

The production of new synthetic compounds has demonstrated that the steroid molecule can be altered to produce compounds with more selective effects and has paved the way for the synthesis of compounds with even greater selectivity of effects.

■ Hormones from the pancreas

Secretions from the pancreas that have an effect on blood sugar levels are glucagon and insulin. These hormones have an important role in the therapy of patients with diabetes mellitus.

Glucagon

Glucagon, like insulin, is a pancreatic extract and is thought to oppose the action of insulin. Glucagon is a product of the alpha cells of the islands of Langerhans; insulin is from the beta cells. Glucagon acts primarily by mobilizing hepatic glycogen, which produces an elevation of the concentration of glucose in the blood. Thus, it is primarily used in the treatment of hypoglycemic reactions in patients who are receiving insulin therapy for diabetes or psychiatric disorders. A patient in hypoglycemic coma will usually respond within 5 to 20 minutes after he has been given an injection of glucagon hydrochloride. However, in most patients, after the initial rise in the concentration of glucose in the blood, it will fall to normal or hypoglycemic levels within $1^{1}/_{2}$ hours. In order to prevent the patient from relapsing into coma after he has been aroused by glucagon, dextrose or another readily absorbable sugar is administered. Because patients who receive glucagon require close medical supervision, the drug is not recommended for home use or self-administration.

Preparation, dosage, and administration. Glucagon is available in vials containing powder suitable for injection. One milliliter of diluent is used for each milligram of glucagon. The usual dosage for the diabetic patient is 0.5 to 1 mg. If the patient does not respond in 20 minutes, additional doses may be given. The drug may be given by intravenous, intramuscular, or subcutaneous injection.

Side effects and toxic effects. Nausea and vomiting are the most frequent side effects observed in patients who have received glucagon, but these effects may be caused by hypoglycemia rather than the drug. Hypotensive reactions immediately after the administration of glucagon have also been reported. Because glucagon is an agent of protein derivation with unknown potential toxicity, nurses need to be alert to detect early signs of hypersensitivity. Glucagon has a positive inotropic effect on the heart.

Insulin

The discovery of insulin began with Johann Conrad Brunner (1653-1727), the discoverer of Brunner's glands in the duodenum. In 1683 he made incisions in the pancreas of a dog, after which the dog had extreme thirst and polyuria. Brunner suggested that there is a connection between the pancreas and diabetes. This seems to have been a pioneer experiment on the internal secretions of the pancreas.

In 1889 von Mering and Minkowski showed that removal of the pancreas from dogs produced symptoms identical with diabetes mellitus. In 1906 Minkowski showed that this experimental diabetes could be prevented by pancreatic grafts. This work practically proved that the pancreas produces an internal secretion or hormone that controls carbohydrate metabolism. Corroborative findings soon followed. Partial removal of the pancreas produced a mild diabetes in animals, and transfusion of normal blood ameliorated the symptoms. In autopsy of many diabetic patients, changes in the islets of Langerhans were found. This indicated that the hormone was produced in the islets.

Repeated attempts to isolate the hormone failed until Banting and Best, in 1921, isolated it in a sufficiently pure state to permit its use in diabetic patients. Extracts from fetal pancreata were found to cause a great reduction of blood sugar. Repeated daily injections permitted animals with the pancreas removed to live beyond the span of life usual under such conditions. Later, methods were developed for the extraction of insulin from an adult pancreas, and continuous improvement in the method of extraction has been made. Insulin is now prepared from mammalian pancreata (sheep, hogs, cattle).

Chemistry of insulin. Insulin is a protein that, upon hydrolysis, yields a number of amino acids. In its crystalline state it appears to be chemically linked with certain metals (zinc, nickel, cadmium, or cobalt). Normal pancreatic tissue is rich in zinc, a fact that may be of significance in the natural storage of the hormone. Insulin keeps rather well in a slightly acidified state but is unstable in dilute alkali. Slight changes in its chemical structure greatly change its behavior, and for this reason it cannot be given by mouth.

One of the major advances in the knowledge of insulin came within the last few years, when an English group headed by Frederick Sanger determined the complete amino acid sequence of insulin. Insulin, as a result of this work (for which Sanger received the Nobel prize), is known to consist of two polypeptide chains and to contain 48 amino acids, the exact sequence of which is known. There are slight differences in the order of amino acids in insulin from different species of animals.

Action and result. Since relatively small amounts of insulin are necessary in the body tissues, it is thought that insulin acts as a catalyst in cellular metabolism.

Carbohydrate metabolism is controlled by a finely balanced interaction of a number of endocrine factors (adrenal, anterior pituitary, thyroid, and insulin), but the particular phase of carbohydrate metabolism that is affected by insulin is not entirely known. When insulin is injected subcutaneously, however, it produces a rapid lowering of the blood sugar. This effect is produced in both diabetic and nondiabetic persons. Moderate amounts of insulin in the diabetic animal promote the storage of carbohydrate in the liver and also in the muscle cells, particularly after the feeding of carbohydrate. In the normal animal there is also an increase in the deposit of muscle glycogen but apparently no increase in the level of liver glycogen. In both diabetic and nondiabetic individuals the oxygen consumption increases and the respiratory quotient rises.

Diabetes mellitus. Diabetes mellitus is a disease of metabolism characterized particularly by an inability to utilize carbohydrate. The blood sugar becomes elevated, and when it exceeds a certain amount, the excess is secreted by the kidney (glycosuria). Symptoms include increased appetite, thirst, weight loss, increased urine output, weakness, and itching such as pruritus vulvae.

There are two types of diabetes mellitus—growth onset and maturity onset. Growth-onset diabetes seems to be the result of reduced or absent secretion of insulin and generally has its onset before age 20. This type of diabetes gen-

erally requires conscientious therapy, including administration of insulin. Maturity-onset diabetes, however, is the result of inability to utilize the insulin that is secreted. It generally occurs after the age of 30 and can frequently be controlled by oral hypoglycemic agents and/or diet.

In diabetes mellitus there is a failure to store glycogen in the liver, although the conversion of glycogen back to glucose or the formation of glucose from other substances (gluconeogenesis) is not necessarily impaired. As a result, the level of blood sugar rapidly rises. This derangement of carbohydrate metabolism results in an abnormally high metabolism of proteins and fats. The normal short-chain fatty acids, which result from oxidation of fatty acids, accumulate faster than the muscle cells can oxidize them, resulting in the development of ketosis and acidosis. The course of untreated diabetes mellitus is progressive. The symptoms of diabetic coma and acidosis are directly or indirectly the result of the accumulation of acetone, beta-hydroxybutyric acid, and diacetic acid. Respirations become rapid and deep, the breath has an odor of acetone, the blood sugar is elevated, the patient becomes dehydrated, and stupor and coma develop unless treatment is promptly started.

Therapeutic uses of insulin. Insulin is a specific in the treatment of diabetic coma and acidosis. The administration of glucose intravenously often accompanies the administration of the insulin, although not all physicians advocate that glucose be used early in the treatment of acidosis. Glucose and insulin promote the formation and retention of glycogen in the liver, and the oxidation of fat in the liver is arrested. Therefore, the rate of formation of acetone bodies is slowed and the acidosis is checked. Other supportive measures such as the restoration of the fluid and electrolyte balance of the body are exceedingly important.

Insulin has its principal use in the control of symptoms of diabetes mellitus when this disease cannot be satisfactorily controlled by a diet alone. Certain mild cases of the disease can be treated by diet alone, but many patients require insulin in order to live active and useful lives. The dosage must be determined for each individual patient and can best be done when the patient is under the direct observation of the physician for a period of time. A number of factors determine the amount of insulin needed by the patient, and a patient's needs are not always constant. Adjustments in dosage may be necessary if infection is present, if the patient has an anesthetic, if emotional strain and stress are prominent, or if his amount of activity is increased or decreased.

It is important that the symptoms of diabetes be adequately controlled. The more nearly the blood chemistry of the diabetic patient is restored to normal, the more normal his metabolism and nutrition will be and less degenerative damage will occur in organs such as the eye and the heart.

Insulin has been used also in some hospitals for the purpose of producing hypoglycemic shock for its effect on the patient with schizophrenia. It is a dangerous treatment with a relatively high mortality rate and should be used only by those who are well equipped, qualified, and familiar with the procedure. It has been replaced, to a great extent, by electroshock therapy and other drugs.

Preparation, dosage, and administration. A number of different types of insulin preparations are used in medicine. All preparations have the same fundamental pharmacologic action. Differences are those related to the time and duration of absorption of the injected insulin into the circulation, providing faster or slower, shorter or more prolonged effects.

All insulin preparations should be refrigerated. Vials of insoluble preparations (all except regular insulin) should be rotated between the hands and inverted end to end several times before a dose is withdrawn. A vial should not be shaken vigorously or the suspension made to foam.

Insulin is given subcutaneously into the loose connective tissues of the body, usually into the arms or thighs. It cannot be given by mouth because it is destroyed by digestive enzymes. Regular insulin is usually given about 20 minutes be-

fore meals. It is somewhat irritating, and since the tissues of the diabetic patient are likely to be less resistant to the invasion of pathogenic organisms than normal tissue, the technique used in administration of insulin should be flawless. The same site of injection should not be used repeatedly, but a plan of rotation should be followed so that the same site is not used more often than once a month.

There is no average dose of insulin for the diabetic; each patient's needs must be determined individually. These needs are frequently determined by testing for glycosuria and ketonuria. Unless complications are present, insulin is not used if the patient's glucose tolerance is sufficiently high to permit him to have a diet sufficient for light work.

Dosage of insulin is expressed in units rather than in milliliters or minims. Insulin injection is so standardized that each milliliter contains 20, 40, 80, or 100 U.S.P. units per milliliter. One insulin unit will, on the average, promote the metabolism of approximately 1.5 Gm. of dextrose. To estimate the necessary insulin dosage for the patient the physician must know how much dextrose will be obtained from the diet and what the patient's glucose tolerance is—how much insulin the patient is able to make for himself. Insulin must be regularly administered and must be accompanied by carefully estimated diets of known composition.

Insulin injection, U.S.P., B.P. This is an acidified aqueous solution of the active principle of the pancreas that affects the metabolism of glucose. This preparation is marketed in 10-ml. vials in strengths of 40, 80, 100, and 500 U.S.P. units per milliliter of the injection. The maximum degree of lowering of the blood sugar occurs in 2 or 3 hours. The onset of its activity is 1 hour, and the duration of activity is 6 to 8 hours.

Protamine zinc insulin suspension, U.S.P.; *protamine zinc insulin injection,* B.P. This is a preparation of insulin to which has been added an appropriate amount of protamine and a zinc salt, which has the effect of slowing absorption. The effects produced by protamine zinc insulin are the same as those of insulin, except that the

475

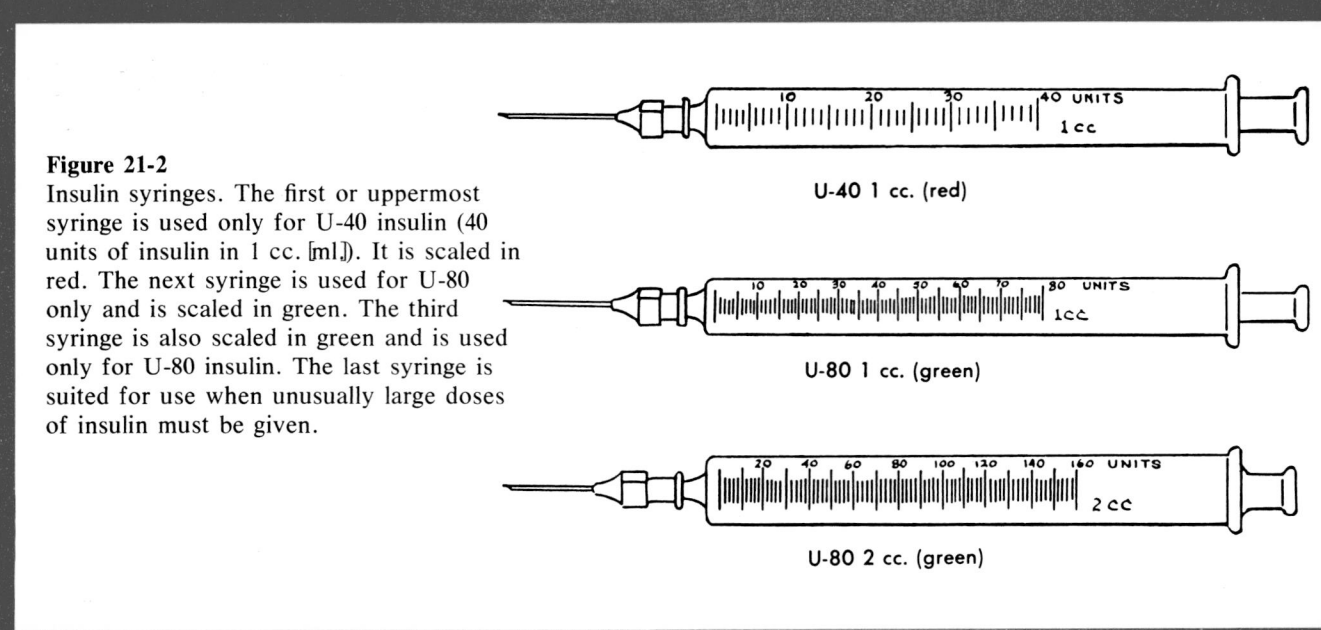

Figure 21-2
Insulin syringes. The first or uppermost syringe is used only for U-40 insulin (40 units of insulin in 1 cc. [ml]). It is scaled in red. The next syringe is used for U-80 only and is scaled in green. The third syringe is also scaled in green and is used only for U-80 insulin. The last syringe is suited for use when unusually large doses of insulin must be given.

U-40 1 cc. (red)

U-80 1 cc. (green)

U-80 2 cc. (green)

blood sugar–lowering action is much more prolonged. It may be used in place of unmodified insulin or in combination with it. The chief indications for its use are in those cases where the unmodified insulin does not provide control of symptoms unless it is given in several daily doses or in cases where lack of control is evidenced by frequent hypoglycemic reaction, ketosis, or pronounced fluctuations in levels of blood sugar. Usually protamine zinc insulin is administered either in the morning, 30 minutes to 1½ hours before breakfast, or in the evening, 1 hour before supper or before retiring. Its maximum blood sugar–lowering action is about 16 to 24 hours after administration. Its onset of action is 4 to 6 hours, and its duration of action is 24 to 36 hours or longer.

Hypoglycemic reactions from this drug are recognized less easily than those that occur with the regular insulin. Sometimes the main symptom is a feeling of pronounced fatigue out of proportion to the degree of activity. Treatment consists of giving a combination of a rapidly absorbed and a slowly absorbed carbohydrate, something like bread and honey. Many patients carry hard candy. Protamine insulin is of no value in emergencies such as diabetic coma. A combination of protamine insulin and rapid-acting insulin is frequently necessary if adequate control of symptoms is to be maintained. It is administered subcutaneously, never intravenously. It should be mixed well (but not made to foam) before withdrawal from container in order to obtain a uniform suspension. The vial is rotated, not shaken. It is available in concentrations of 40 or 80 U.S.P. units of insulin per milliliter of injection.

Globin zinc insulin injection, **U.S.P., B.P.** This is a preparation of insulin modified by the addition of globin and zinc chloride. The globin is obtained from globin hydrochloride prepared from beef blood. Each milliliter of the finished product contains 40 or 80 units of insulin. The action of this preparation is between that of regular insulin and protamine zinc insulin. The period of maximum effect extends from 8 to 16 hours after injection. It is beneficial for those patients who require more than a single injection of regular insulin, for those who are sensitive to protamine, and for those whose levels of blood sugar are not satisfactorily controlled by other forms of insulin. It is said to produce fewer local reactions than regular insulin. It is not given when rapid effects are desired, and it should never by given intravenously or intramuscularly. It should be administered only by deep subcutaneous injection. The dosage must be regulated according to the patient's needs. The initial dose may be two thirds to three fourths of the daily dose of regular insulin and then increased gradually as needed.

Isophane insulin suspension, **U.S.P. (NPH Insulin).** This preparation is a modified protamine zinc insulin. N indicates that it is a neutral solution; P stands for protamine zinc insulin; and H means that it originated in Hagedorn's laboratory. It is marketed in concentrations of 40 or 80 U.S.P. units per milliliter of suspension. Its action places it between globin insulin and protamine zinc insulin. Its onset of action is within 2 hours, while peak effect is reached in 10 to 20 hours, and the duration of its action is 28 to 30 hours. Isophane insulin may be mixed with regular insulin. It is an intermediate-acting insulin preparation and should not be used when a quick-acting insulin is needed. It is given only by subcutaneous injection.

Lente insulins

Lente insulins consist of insulin precipitated with zinc and resuspended in an acetate buffer rather than a phosphate buffer, which is usually used in insulin preparations. By varying the way the insulin is prepared it is possible to obtain suspensions that contain particles of different size and form. It has been found that the larger crystals produce a longer but less intense effect, and this preparation is known as ultralente insulin; its action resembles that of protamine zinc insulin. Semilente insulin contains smaller particles, and its action falls between that of NPH and crystalline insulin. Insulin zinc suspension, U.S.P., B.P. (Lente Insulin), contains a mixture of ultralente and semilente insulins. Lente insulins are available in quantities of 40 and 80 units per milliliter of suspension. The duration of lente insulin is much like that of NPH insulin, and the two can be used interchangeably. Its characteristics of action place it between regular insulin and protamine zinc insulin.

The principal advantage of the lente insulins is their lack of sensitizing substances such as protamine or globin. They are useful for the treatment of diabetic patients who are allergic to other types of insulin or for those whose disease is difficult to control.

The injection should be made deep into subcutaneous tissue but not into muscle, and it should never be given intravenously. The usual time of administration is in the morning before breakfast. The dosage must be individualized for each patient. It is not used in the treatment of acidosis or for conditions that demand a rapid-acting insulin.

Symptoms of overdosage. The symptoms of hypoglycemia develop in the patient who is given an overdose of insulin or in the patient with hyperinsulinism as a result of certain changes in the pancreas. When caused by an overdose of insulin, the fall in blood sugar is in proportion to the amount of insulin given. In man, toxic symptoms occur when the blood sugar falls below 79 mg. per 100 ml. The point at which the symptoms become noticeable varies greatly, however. For each person there is a level at which severe symptoms or the convulsive stage of hypoglycemia is reached. The symptoms of hypoglycemia depend on the speed with which it develops. Symptoms resulting from protamine zinc insulin are especially insidious.

Early symptoms include a feeling of weakness, sweating, nervousness and anxiety, pallor or flushing, and a vague feeling of apprehension. If the patient does not receive treatment, the symptoms may be intensified with the development of aphasia, convulsive seizures, coma, and even death. When the first mild symptoms are noted, the patient should receive treatment at once. Prolonged hypoglycemia is associated with diminished oxygen consumption and irreparable injury of the nervous system. Symptoms of hypoglycemia are quickly relieved by the administration of a soluble carbohydrate

Table 21-4 Tabulation of commercially available insulins*

Type of insulin	Time and route of administration	Time of onset (hours after administration)	Peak action (hours after administration)	Duration of action (hours)	Time when glycosuria most likely to occur	Time when hypoglycemia most likely to occur
Crystalline zinc† (pH 3-3.5; Zn. 0.02-0.04 mg./100 units) (regular)	Intravenously (emergency); 15 to 20 min. before meals; subcutaneously	Rapid—within 1 hr.	2 to 4	5 to 8	During night	10 a.m. to lunch
Semilente† (amorphous zinc) (pH 7.2; Zn. 0.2-0.25 mg./100 units)	30 to 45 min. before breakfast; deep subcutaneously; never intravenously	Rapid—within 1 hr.	6 to 10	12 to 16	During night	Before lunch
Globin zinc (pH 3.4-3.8; Zn. 0.25-0.35 mg./100 units)	30 min. to 1 hr. before breakfast; subcutaneously	Intermediate—rapidity of onset increases with dose—within 2 to 4 hr.	6 to 10	18 to 24; also increases with dose	Before breakfast and before lunch	3 p.m. to dinner
Lente† (combination of 30% semilente and 70% ultralente) (pH 7.1-7.4; Zn. 0.2-0.25 mg./100 units)	1 hr. before breakfast; deep subcutaneously; never intravenously	Intermediate—within 2 to 4 hr.	8 to 12	28 to 32	Before lunch	3 p.m. to dinner
NPH (neutral-protamine-Hagedorn) or Isophane (pH 7.1-7.4; Zn. 0.016-0.04 mg./100 units)	1 hr. before breakfast; subcutaneously	Intermediate—within 2 to 4 hr.	8 to 12	28 to 30	Before lunch	3 p.m. to dinner
Protamine zinc (ZPI) (pH 7.4; Zn. 0.2-0.25 mg./100 units)	1 hr. before breakfast; subcutaneously	Slow-acting—within 4 to 6 hr.	16 to 24	24 to 36+	Before lunch and at bedtime	2 a.m. to breakfast
Ultralente† (pH 4.8-5.7; Zn. 0.2-0.25 mg./100 units)	1 hr. before breakfast; deep subcutaneously; never intravenously	Very slow—8 hr.	16 to 24	36+		During night; early morning

*From a monograph on diabetes mellitus by the Upjohn Company, Kalamazoo, Mich., 1960, p. 65.
†Contains no modifying protein (protamine or globin).

in the form of orange juice or two or three lumps of sugar by mouth or a soluble carbohydrate intravenously if the patient is comatose.

Ambulatory patients learn to recognize sudden hunger, sweating, and nervousness as subjective signs of insulin overdosage and learn to carry a few lumps of sugar with them. A night nurse may find a diabetic patient asleep but in a pool of perspiration, a fact that would lead her to suspect he was having an insulin reaction and that he should be awakened and given a soluble carbohydrate.

Other untoward effects. Repeated injections of insulin at the same site may cause local reactions of the subcutaneous tissues. These can be avoided by changing the site of injection.

Some patients experience a disturbance of vision thought to result from a change in the crystalline lens of the eye. This disappears after a few weeks. Edema of the face and sometimes of the extremities is observed occasionally, especially in young women. This, too, tends to disappear, but if troublesome it may necessitate restriction of sodium chloride and the use of a mild diuretic.

A few patients exhibit allergic reactions in the form of urticaria, redness, and itching in the region where the insulin has been injected. These symptoms can usually be controlled by changing to a different brand of insulin.

An occasional diabetic patient fails to respond to an ordinary therapeutic dose of insulin. In these cases, there has developed what is known as insulin resistance. Enormous doses may be required to lower the blood-sugar level and to prevent acidosis. The cause of this condition is not entirely understood. In some instances it appears to be caused by the formation of antibodies, and in other cases it is thought to result from disturbance of the pituitary, adrenal, or thyroid glands. Most patients respond to large doses of insulin and the condition tends to be self-limiting.

Oral hypoglycemic agents

$$CH_3 - \langle\ \rangle - SO_2-NH-CO-NH-(CH_2)_3-CH_3$$

Tolbutamide (Orinase)

$$NH_2 - \langle\ \rangle - SO_2-NH-CO-NH-(CH_2)_3-CH_3$$

Carbutamide

$$Cl - \langle\ \rangle - SO_2-NH-CO-NH-(CH_2)_2-CH_3$$

Chlorpropamide (Diabinese)

In the early days of insulin therapy many attempts were made to obtain a preparation or modification of insulin active after oral administration. None was successful, and it is unlikely that any can be, since polypeptides and proteins are both susceptible to destruction in the gastrointestinal tract and are poorly absorbed in an intact state.

In recent years certain drugs have been found which do have blood sugar–lowering or "insulin-like" action when given by mouth. They are principally the group of sulfonylureas. These compounds were originally discovered after observing that some of the antibacterial sulfonamides had hypoglycemic effects. These drugs are sometimes called "oral insulins," although this definitely is incorrect, since, chemically, they are completely different from insulin. They also differ from insulin in origin and mode of action.

The sulfonylureas are thought to act by increasing the pancreas' own ability to secrete insulin. They are most efffective, therefore, in relatively mild diabetes when there is still some reserve islet capacity such as the adult patient in whom the diabetes is recognized after the age of 30 years and who can be controlled with less than 40 units of insulin per day. They are less effective or ineffective in severe diabetes or juvenile diabetes in which it is presumed that no functional islet tissue is left to respond. It has also been noted that long-continued high doses of the sulfonylureas administered to normal animals can produce diabetes, apparently by permanently exhausting the capacity of the islet cells to make insulin.

Although much interest and enthusiasm have greeted this new development and although these drugs have considerable scientific impor-

479

tance, they cannot be said to have fully replaced insulin in the treatment of diabetes. Nurses should recognize that the need for instruction that stresses dietary restrictions is even greater for patients receiving oral hypoglycemic agents than for those taking insulin, and it must be remembered that these patients, too, must be taught how and when to test for glycosuria and ketonuria, to maintain diet and personal hygiene, and to recognize dangerous symptoms. Since insulin is indispensable for management of complications, the patient must also be instructed in the use of insulin.

It must be noted that sulfonylurea drugs depress radioactive iodide uptake and may cause misleading results in diagnostic tests.

Preparation, dosage, and administration. The following are preparations of oral hypoglycemic drugs.

Tolbutamide, **U.S.P., B.P. (Orinase).** This drug, a sulfonylurea derivative, is marketed in 500-mg. tablets for oral administration. Therapeutic trial with this drug is initiated with 3 Gm. on the first day and 2 Gm. on the second day; then dosage is gradually reduced until the minimum dose for satisfactory control of blood sugar has been determined. Maintenance dosage may vary from 0.5 to 2 Gm. per day. The drug is preferably given in divided doses and after meals. Traces of the drug have been found in plasma 1 hour after administration and the drug has a half-life of about 4 to 6 hours. Diabetic patients require close medical supervision, especially when the drug is first tried.

When tolbutamide therapy is begun, it will frequently be effected with a concurrent, gradual reduction of insulin dosage. During this conversion period, the nurse must be alert to the occurrence of hypoglycemic reactions that might indicate a need for modification of the dosage schedules.

Carbutamide. This drug causes allergic reactions in human beings and has not been released for use in the United States.

Tolazamide, **U.S.P. (Tolinase).** Tolazamide is a sulfonylurea compound pharmacologically related to tolbutamide, but it is absorbed more slowly. The average half-life of tolazamide is 7 hours, with maximal effects persisting for about 10 hours. Tolazamide is administered orally in doses ranging from 100 mg. to 1 Gm. daily. Dosage in excess of 1 Gm. is not recommended. Side effects are similar to those of other sulfonylurea drugs.

Chlorpropamide, **U.S.P., B.P. (Diabinese).** Chlorpropamide belongs to the sulfonylurea group and has a biologic half-life of 30 to 36 hours. The drug is available in 100- and 250-mg. scored tablets for oral administration. A dosage in excess of 750 mg. daily is not recommended. Side effects are similar to those of other sulfonylurea drugs but may be more severe. The patient must be observed closely during the first 6 weeks of therapy. Hypersensitivity reactions may occur and are an indication for discontinuation of the drug. The drug may also prolong the action of sedatives and hypnotics. It is contraindicated in pregnancy, severe hepatic or renal dysfunction, other endocrine dysfunction, and Raynaud's disease.

Phenformin hydrochloride **(DBI).** Phenformin is not a sulfonylurea compound but a biguanide derivative. Its exact mode of action has not been clearly defined, but it seems to act by supplementing insulin effects in peripheral utilization of glucose. Its effectiveness requires the presence of some insulin, either exogenous or endogenous. It has been used in combination therapy with sulfonylureas when either drug alone does not produce maximal results. Side effects may include an unpleasant, metallic or bitter taste, anorexia, cramps, nausea, and sometimes vomiting and diarrhea. Phenformin should be withdrawn if vomiting occurs. Phenformin is available for oral administration in 25-mg. tablets and in 50-mg. extended-release tablets (DBI-TD). Maintenance doses range from 50 to 150 mg. daily.

Acetohexamide **(Dymelar).** This is a sulfonylurea compound closely related to tolbutamide but about twice as potent. It is available in 250- and 500-mg. scored tablets, and its usual dosage range is from 250 mg. to 1.5 Gm. Dosage in excess of 1.5 Gm. is not recommended. Side effects are similar to those of other sulfonylurea drugs.

Side effects and toxic effects. Side effects that have been reported include gastrointestinal upsets, weakness, paresthesia, headache, ringing in the ears, and intolerance to alcohol. A mild type of leukopenia has been reported. Oral hypoglycemic agents may interfere with some enzymatic reactions in the liver, and therefore their use for patients with hepatic damage is not recommended. The incidence of toxicity seems to be low. It is important that the diabetic patient observe dietary restrictions as carefully as when taking insulin. The drug does not cure the diabetes. Some patients develop allergic reactions that may require that administration of the drug be stopped and that therapy with insulin be resumed. Patients should be carefully instructed concerning the limitations of tolbutamide. Overdosage produces characteristic hypoglycemic reactions.

Questions

for study and review

1 Explain why some patients with diabetes mellitus require insulin injections while others are controlled with oral hypoglycemic agents.
2 What is the universal function of vitamins in the body?
3 What are the richest natural sources of B vitamins?
4 Prolonged intravenous infusions of 5% glucose in water with no dietary intake may have an undesirable effect on electrolyte balance and requirements for a specific vitamin. Identify these effects.
5 Why would administration of corticosteroids be contraindicated during pregnancy?

Multiple choice

6 Vitamin D helps to prevent rickets in which of the following ways?
  a. promoting the absorption of calcium from the bowel
  b. stimulating the bone cells to deposit calcium salts
  c. increasing activity of the parathyroid gland
  d. inhibiting activity of cells in the adrenal cortex
7 Preparations of posterior lobe pituitary can be expected to contain which of the following?
  a. growth hormone
  b. antidiuretic hormone
  c. thyrotropic hormone
  d. oxytocic principle
8 Which of the following preparations would you expect to see prescribed for a patient with myxedema?

  a. iodized salt
  b. Lugol's Solution
  c. radioactive iodine
  d. thyroid tablets
9 Effective therapy with ACTH is dependent upon a normal state of function of which of the following?
  a. thyroid gland
  b. adrenal gland
  c. islands of Langerhans
  d. anterior lobe of pituitary gland
10 Insulin must be administered parenterally for which of the following reasons?
  a. it acts more promptly when given parenterally
  b. oral administration of insulin is most likely to cause gastrointestinal irritation
  c. insulin is subject to destruction by proteolytic enzymes in the digestive tract
  d. insulin is not well absorbed from the gastrointestinal tract
11 Which of the following patients is likely to have a daily dose of ascorbic acid prescribed for him?
  a. a patient recovering from a stroke
  b. a patient recovering from a surgical operation
  c. a patient with acute coronary insufficiency
  d. a patient with pernicious anemia
12 A patient receiving insulin for diabetes mellitus is receiving a form of therapy that can be compared to which of the following?
  a. thyroid for cretinism
  b. streptomycin for tuberculosis
  c. cortisone for rheumatoid arthritis
  d. morphine for severe pain
13 Which of the following constitutes a significant side effect in a patient receiving cortisone?
  a. emotional instability
  b. polyuria
  c. increased appetite
  d. pigmentation of the skin
14 Prednisone differs from cortisone in which of the following respects? It is less likely to:
  a. cause retention of water and salt
  b. inhibit healing of tissues
  c. produce symptoms of hypercortisonism
  d. bring about depression of the adrenal cortex
15 One of your patients has rheumatoid arthritis for which her doctor has prescribed daily doses of aspirin. If she says to you: "I don't understand why my doctor only gives me aspirin; why can't I have a medicine like cortisone?" which of the following statements would you consider most appropriate and helpful?
  a. Cortisone is prescribed by many physicians, but your physician probably wants to take a conservative approach to your problem.
  b. Cortisone can be a dangerous drug and can produce many undesirable side effects.
  c. For the pain associated with rheumatism and arthritis, aspirin is considered one of the safest and best drugs on the market.

481

d. Cortisone is a relatively expensive drug whereas aspirin is inexpensive.

References

Amatruda, T. T., Jr., Hurst, M. M., and D'Esopo, N. D.: Certain endocrine and metabolic facets of the steroid withdrawal syndrome, J. Clin. Endocrin. **25:**1207, 1965.

Astwood, E. B., and Cassidy, C. E., editors: Clinical pharmacology II, New York, 1968, Grune & Stratton.

Astwood, E. B., Cassidy, C. E., and Aurbach, G. D.: Treatment of goiter and thyroid nodules with thyroid, J.A.M.A. **174:**459, 1960.

Aurbach, G. D., and Potts, J. T., Jr.: Parathyroid hormone, Amer. J. Med. **42:**1, 1967.

Bartter, F. C., editor: The clinical use of aldosterone antagonists, Springfield, Ill., 1960, Charles C Thomas, Publisher.

Beaser, S. B.: A survey of current therapy of diabetes mellitus, Diabetes **13:**472, 1964.

Bond, V. P., moderator: Symposium on insulin, Amer. J. Med. **40:**651, 1966.

Bush, I. E.: Chemical and biological factors in the activity of adrenocortical steroids, Pharmacol. Rev. **14:**317, 1962.

Chapman, E. M., and Maloof, F.: The use of radioactive iodine in diagnosis and treatment of hyperthyroidism: ten years' experience, Medicine **34:**261, 1955.

Clinical usefulness of aldosterone antagonists, Brit. Med. J. **2:**1005, 1961.

Cooley, D. G.: What is a vitamin? Today's Health **41:**20, 1963.

Cooper, L. F., and others: Nutrition in health and disease, Philadelphia, 1963, J. B. Lippincott Co.

Council on Foods and Nutrition—Youmans, J. B.: Deficiencies of the fat soluble vitamins, J.A.M.A. **144:**34, 1950.

DeGroot, L. J.: Current views on formation of thyroid hormones, New Eng. J. Med. **272:**243; 272:297; 272:355, 1965.

Editorial: Pharmacologic effects of adrenal corticosteroids, New Eng. J. Med. **273:**875, 1965.

Finch, C. A.: Iron balance in man, Nutr. Rev. **23:**129, 1965.

Fisher, A. M.: Insulin preparations, J. Canad. Med. Ass. **73:**1, 1955.

Gastineau, C. F., and Arnold, J. W.: Clinics on endocrine and metabolic diseases: 12. Thyroid disorder in Addison's disease: 1. Myxedema and goiter, Proc. Staff Meet. Mayo Clin. **38:**323, 1963.

Goodman, L., and Gilman, A.: The pharmacological basis of therapeutics, ed. 4, New York, 1970, The Macmillan Company.

Graber, A. L.: Natural history of pituitary-adrenal recovery following long-term suppression with corticosteroids, J. Clin. Endocrin. **25:**11, 1965.

Graham, G. G.: Johns Hopkins conjoint clinic on vitamins, J. Chron. Dis. **19:**1007, 1966.

Grodsky, G. M., and Forsham, P. H.: Insulin and the pancreas, Ann. Rev. Physiol. **28:**347, 1966.

Harris, L. J.: Vitamins in theory and practice, Cambridge, 1935, Harvard University Press.

Hench, P. S., and others: The effects of the adrenal cortical hormone 17-hydroxy-11-dehydrocorticosterone (Compound E) on the acute phase of rheumatic fever; preliminary report, Proc. Staff Meet. Mayo Clin. **24:**277, 1949.

Hench, P. S., and others: The effect of a hormone of the adrenal cortex (17-hydroxy-11-dehydrocorticosterone; Compound E) and of pituitary adrenocorticotropic hormone on rheumatoid arthritis; preliminary report, Proc. Staff Meet. Mayo Clin. **24:**181, 1950.

Hench, P. S., and others: Symposium on cortisone and ACTH in clinical medicine, Proc. Staff Meet. Mayo Clin. **25:**474, 1950.

Hench, P. S., and others: The antirheumatic effects of cortisone and pituitary ACTH, Trans. Stud. Coll. Physicians Philadelphia **18:**95, 1950.

Henderson, E. D., and Peterson, C. E.: Hydrocortisone and prednisolone; local injection in skeletal diseases, Orthopedics **1:**6, 1958.

Hilf, R.: Mechanism of action of ACTH, New Eng. J. Med. **273:**798, 1965.

Homwi, G., and Skillman, T.: The clinical usefulness of orally administered hypoglycemic agents, Postgrad. Med. **27:**687, 1960.

Jeffries, W. M.: Low dosage glucocorticoid therapy, Arch. Intern. Med. **119:**265, 1967.

Kendall, E. C.: The story of cortisone, Hosp. Management **70:**72, 1950.

Kendall E. C.: Cortisone, Quart. Phi Beta Pi **47:**187, 1951.

Levine, R.: Concerning the mechanism of insulin action, Diabetes **10:**421, 1961.

Liddle, G. W.: Clinical pharmacology of the antiinflammatory steroids, Clin. Pharmacol. Therap. **2:**615, 1961.

Lukens, F. D. W.: The rediscovery of regular insulin, New Eng. J. Med. **272:**130, 1965.

Lukens, F. D. W.: Insulin and protein metabolism, Diabetes **13:**451, 1964.

McKenzie, J. M.: Pathogenesis of Graves' disease: role of the long-acting thyroid stimulator, J. Clin. Endocrin. **25:**424, 1965.

National Research Council: Recommended dietary allowances, rev. 1968, ed. 7, Publ. 1694, Washington, D. C., 1968 U. S. Government Printing Office.

Orten, J. M., and Neuhaus, O. W.: Biochemistry, ed. 8, St. Louis, 1970, The C. V. Mosby Co.

Peterson, R. E., and Wyngarden, J. B.: The physiological disposition and metabolic fate of hydrocortisone in man, J. Clin. Invest. **34**:1779, 1955.

Polley, H. F.: Adrenocorticoid steroid therapy for rheumatic diseases, Arch. Phys. Med. **41**:497, 1960.

Rall, J. E.: The role of radioactive iodine in the diagnosis of thyroid disease, Amer. J. Med. **20**:719, 1956.

Rasmussen, H.: Parathyroid hormone—nature and mechanism of action, Amer. J. Med. **30**:112, 1960.

Rasmussen, H., and others: The relationship between vitamin D and parathyroid hormone, J. Clin. Invest. **42**:1940, 1963.

Reveno, W. S., and Rosenbaum, H.: Observations on use of antithyroid drugs, Ann. Intern Med. **60**:982, 1964.

Rieser, P.: Insulin, membranes and metabolism, Baltimore, 1967, The Williams & Wilkins Co.

Rivlin, R., and Asper, S. P.: Tyrosine and the thyroid hormones, Amer. J. Med. **40**:823, 1966.

Sharp, G. W. G., and Leaf, A.: Mechanism of action of aldosterone, Physiol. Rev. **46**:593, 1966.

Simoons, F. J., and others: Symposium on food prejudices and taboos, Food Technol. **10**:42, 1966.

Slocumb, C. H., and others: Hypercortisonism in patients with rheumatoid arthritis, Postgrad. Med. **25**:185, 1959.

Sodee, D. B.: Clinical usefulness of the I[131] triiodothyronine erythrocyte uptake test, J.A.M.A. **185**:100, 1963.

Sparberg, M., and Kirsuer, J. B.: Steroid therapy and infections, J.A.M.A. **188**:680, 1964.

Symposium on steroids: a decade of anti-inflammatory steroids, from cortisone to decamethasone, Ann. N.Y. Acad. Sci. **82**:799, 1959.

Symposium on thyroxine, Mayo Clin. Proc. **39**:546, 1964.

Thorm, G. W.: Clinical consideration in the use of corticosteroids, New Eng. J. Med. **274**:775, 1966.

Tucker, H. A.: Oral antidiabetic therapy; 1956-1965, Springfield, Ill., 1965, Charles C Thomas, Publisher.

Ward, E. E., and others: Prednisone in rheumatoid arthritis; metabolic and clinical effects, Ann. Rheum. Dis. **17**:145, 1958.

Ward, L. E., and others: Cortisone in the treatment of rheumatoid arthritis, J.A.M.A. **152**:119, 1953.

Wilkins, L.: The thyroid gland, Sci. Amer. **202**:119, 1960.

Williams, R. H., and Euswich, J. W.: Secretion, fates and actions of insulin and related products, Diabetes **15**:623, 1966.

Wollaeger, E. E.: Untoward effects of cortisone and corticotropin on the gastrointestinal tract, Minn. Med. **37**:626, 1954.

22 Enzymes

Enzymes as a group are among the newest agents used in therapy, but it may be anticipated that their application in medicine will increase greatly in future years. Enzymes are specific structures that act as catalysts of the many chemical reactions that go on in living systems. Catalysts are substances that accelerate chemical reactions (often stimulating a thousandfold or greater the speed of reaction) without themselves being used up in the reaction. The catalytic action of enzymes can be illustrated by catalase, an enzyme present in many living cells that speeds up a reaction in which hydrogen peroxide decomposes to form water and oxygen.

$$H_2O_2 \xrightarrow{\text{Catalase}} H_2O + \tfrac{1}{2}\,O_2$$

Catalase permits this reaction (moles of H_2O_2 decomposing per minute) to go on many thousand times the rate that could be observed without catalase; each molecule of catalase present in solution can stimulate the decomposition of millions of molecules of hydrogen peroxide.

The role of enzymes in living organisms is an important one, because these catalysts of living origin permit the chemical reaction to go on, and this makes life possible.

One feature of enzymes of great interest to possible pharmacologic application is their specificity. Each separate enzyme catalyzes a distinct chemical reaction or reaction type, and the thousands of chemical reactions characteristic of living cells* each require their corresponding enzyme.

Because the usefulness of drugs depends to a large measure on their specificity or selectivity, the high specificity of enzymes in catalyzing a given reaction and in influencing no other is a promising feature. However, their potential usefulness in medicine has been limited by certain other properties. The fact that they are proteins means that they need a high degree of purification before administration; and even pure proteins derived from other species may be antigenic and cause toxic reactions of an immunologic type. Also, as proteins, most enzymes would need to be given parenterally in order to

---

*Examples of large groups of reaction types are: hydrolysis of peptide bonds in proteins, oxidation of aldehydes to acids, and transfer of electrons.

short-circuit destruction by the protein-digesting enzymes of the gastrointestinal tract. In addition, proteins cannot yet be synthesized, and the preparation of purified enzymes from natural sources is often a laborious process, yielding small amounts of ultimate product. Finally, therapeutic agents that are proteins are limited in that they do not pass into cells readily, unlike the small molecules that constitute most of the drugs considered elsewhere in this book. A further limitation is that enzymes catalyze single specific chemical reactions, and symptoms of disease are not yet understood in such simple chemical terms.

Within these limitations, however, some enzymes have become useful for certain symptomatic purposes: protein-digesting enzymes such as trypsin have been used to remove dead tissue by enzymatic digestion (chemical debridement); enzymes that digest deoxyribonucleic acid have been used to digest thick purulent exudates whose viscosity depends on large amounts of this type of nucleic acid. A beginning has also been made in the use of enzymes that can destroy specific toxic or allergenic substances in the body; for example, the use of penicillinase to remove penicillin from the body fluids of a person suffering an allergic reaction to penicillin. The detoxicating action of enzymes has promise because of the specificity of enzymes that might be employed. It is possible that much wider use will be made of this specific way of removing unwanted drugs or other compounds from the body.

Hyaluronidase; hyaluronidase for injection, N.F. (Alidase, Diffusin, Hyazyme, Wydase)

Hyaluronic acid is a polysaccharide that constitutes an essential component of intercellular ground substance. It is present in the form of a gel in many parts of body tissues, where it serves as an intercellular cement and acts as a barrier to the diffusion of invading substances.

Hyaluronidase is a mucolytic enzyme prepared from mammalian testes. It is capable of hydrolyzing and depolymerizing hyaluronic acid. It acts as a spreading factor to facilitate absorption and distribution of infusions, local anesthetics, and drugs and to increase diffusion and absorption of local accumulations or transudates of blood.

It is especially useful to facilitate administration of fluids by hypodermoclysis. The resulting increased rate of dispersion and absorption of the injected fluid reduces tissue tension and pain. The rate of absorption, however, should not be greater than that of an intravenous infusion. Special care must be exercised when administering the drug to children—the speed and total volume administered must be controlled to avoid overhydration.

Preparation, dosage, and administration. Hyaluronidase is available in a stable dried form in vials containing 150 and 1500 N.F. units in a solution for injection, 150 N.F. units in 1 ml. or 1500 N.F. units in 10 ml. A dose of 150 N.F. units is dissolved in 1 ml. of isotonic sodium chloride solution and is then added to 1000 ml. of fluid for hypodermoclysis, or it is injected into the proposed site of the clysis.

Side effects and toxic effects. Hyaluronidase has a low level of toxicity, but caution is recommended when it is administered to patients with infections. It should not be injected into or around infected areas since it will produce spread of the infection by the same mechanism of action that causes spread of injected solutions. Patients occasionally exhibit hypersensitivity to this substance.

Streptodornase

Streptodornase is an enzyme produced by the growth of hemolytic streptococci. It promotes depolymerization of deoxyribonucleic acid and deoxyribonucleoprotein from degenerating white blood cells and injured tissue cells. Much of the stringy, slimy, viscous material in purulent exudates results from their presence. Streptodornase changes the thick purulent material to a thin, liquid material, sometimes in a very short time. Fortunately, streptodornase has no effect on nucleoprotein or the nuclei of living cells. The action of this enzyme requires the presence of the magnesium ion, but this is freely present in tissues. Activity of the enzyme is inhibited by citrate and heparin. It is most active at a pH between 7 and 8.5. Streptodornase is antigenic and may cause a sensitivity reaction.

Streptokinase

Streptokinase is an extracellular enzyme activator that is formed during the growth of various groups of hemolytic streptococci, prominent among which are the human strains of Lancefield's Group C. Streptokinase activates a factor present in human plasma known as plasminogen. Plasminogen is present in purulent, serous, and sanguineous exudates and, when activated by streptokinase, it forms an active enzyme, plasmin. Plasmin in turn promotes lysis of fibrin from a gel to a liquid and is accompanied by the formation of large polypeptides. This explains the dissolution of blood clots and fibrinous exudates. Streptokinase is therefore essentially a proteolytic enzyme active in the solution of fibrin. It exerts its maximal activity between a pH of 7.3 and 7.6.

Streptokinase-streptodornase (Varidase)

This preparation is a mixture of the two enzymes described previously. In addition to their proteolytic activity, they are capable of producing two additional reactions. One reaction is local and consists of an outpouring of white blood cells and fluid at the site of application. The second is a pyrogenic effect, especially when the enzymes are injected into a closed space with limited or delayed drainage. It is thought that the elevation of temperature is caused by the absorption of toxic products resulting from activity of the enzymes.

Uses. Streptokinase-streptodornase are used to liquefy coagulated blood, remove clots, and dissolve fibrinous material and purulent accumulations present after trauma or inflammation. The enzyme action helps the action of antiinfective forces, such as the action of antibiotics, and encourages the healing of tissues.

Preparation, dosage, and administration. Streptokinase-streptodornase is available in the form of buccal tablets (10,000 units of streptokinase and 2500 units of streptodornase); as a

powder for topical use (100,000 units of streptokinase and 25,000 units of streptodornase); as a powder for injection (20,000 units of streptokinase and 5000 units of streptodornase); and as a jelly (100,000 units of streptokinase and 25,000 units of streptodornase). The usefulness of this preparation after intramuscular or buccal administration is not fully established. It is applied topically in the form of wet dressings or as a jelly, or it is injected into cavities. Maximum effects usually occur in 12 to 24 hours. Solutions lose their potency when kept at room temperature but will keep for a week at a temperature 2° to 10° C.

Side effects and toxic effects. These enzymes are employed as supplements to, rather than as substitutes for, surgical debridement and drainage. They are not recommended for use in the presence of active hemorrhage or acute cellulitis, because they may interfere with the clotting of blood or promote the spread of a nonlocalized infection. In the absence of adequate drainage the patient may develop fever, urticaria, nausea, and vomiting when this preparation is injected into a closed cavity. The preparation should not be administered intravenously.

Trypsin, crystallized, N.F. (Tryptar, Parenzyme)

Crystallized trypsin is a purified preparation of the pancreatic enzyme obtained from mammalian pancreatic glands. It exerts a proteolytic action when brought into contact with clotted blood, exudate, and necrotic tissue. It is not harmful to living tissues because of the presence in serum of a specific trypsin inhibitor and other nonspecific inhibitory substances.

Crystallized trypsin is useful as an adjunct to surgical treatment of necrotic wounds, abscesses, empyema, sinuses, and fistulas. It is also used to liquefy hematomas and blood clots. It is sometimes employed in the treatment of bronchopulmonary conditions to reduce the viscosity of tenacious secretions that do not respond to expectorant drugs.

It is contraindicated in cases of severe hepatic disease, for use in actively bleeding cavities, and for debridement of ulcerated carcinomas. It should be used with caution in cases of tuberculous empyema.

Preparation, dosage, and administration. Crystallized trypsin is available in the form of buccal tablets (5 mg.), as a suspension for injection (5 mg. per milliliter), as a solution for injection (5 mg. per milliliter), and as a powder in vials containing 25 mg. Crystallized trypsin is applied to surface lesions either in a dry form by means of a blower or as a freshly prepared solution in the form of wet dressings. For less accessible lesions it may be instilled or used as an irrigant. Solutions or suspensions, when given by injection, are given by deep intragluteal injection. It should never be given intravenously. It is effective within a pH range of 5 to 8.

Side effects and toxic effects. Pain and induration may occur at the site of intramuscular injection. Hives and urticaria occur occasionally. A severe burning sensation may be experienced on surface lesions after topical application, and fever and an increased heart rate may result after injection. The latter reaction can be prevented by the administration of an antihistaminic. Toxic effects are considered negligible when the use of the enzyme is limited to local or topical administration.

Chymotrypsin, N.F. (Chymar, Enzeon)

Chymotrypsin is another protein-digesting enzyme that is being used to prevent and treat inflammatory reactions that cause pain, edema, and blood and lymphatic effusions associated with bruises, contusions, and fractures. It is marketed under the name of Chymar and is available for intramuscular injection. For systemic effects it is available in the form of buccal tablets.

Bromelains (Ananase)

Bromelains is a mixture of proteolytic enzymes obtained from the pineapple plant. It is claimed that this oral preparation is an adjunct to the treatment of inflammation resulting from trauma, operations, and skin infections. The effectiveness of proteolytic enzymes as antiinflammatory drugs is very difficult to appraise. There is no certainty about the usefulness of this drug in the management of inflammatory conditions.

Questions

for study and review

1 Explain what is meant by the term *chemical debridement*.
2 Discuss the use and differences between the following drugs.
   a. streptokinase-streptodornase
   b. hyaluronidase
   c. trypsin
   d. penicillinase
3 What precautions should be taken with the storage and use of enzymatic drugs?

References

A. M. A. Council on Drugs: Buccal and intramuscular use of streptokinase and streptodornase (Varidase), J.A.M.A. **172:**701, 1960.

A. M. A. Council on Drugs: New drugs, Chicago, 1967, American Medical Association.

Beckman, H.: Pharmacology; the nature, action, and use of drugs, Philadelphia, 1961, W. B. Saunders Co.

Goodman, L. S., and Gilman, A.: The pharmacological basis of therapeutics, New York, 1970, The Macmillan Company.

Hamilton, I., and Miller, J. M.: Effect of penicillinase on the activity of penicillins, Nature **201:**867, 1964.

Krantz, J. C., and Carr, C. J.: Pharmacologic principles of medical practice, Baltimore, 1965, The Williams & Wilkins Co.

Payton, W. D. M., and Payne, J. P.: Pharmacological principles and practices, Boston, 1968, Little, Brown and Company.

Topacek, M.: Basic chemistry of life, New York, 1968, Appleton-Century-Crofts.

23 Dermatologic agents

Preparations that soothe
Antiseptics and parasiticides
Stimulants and irritants
Keratolytics
Antipruritics
Protectives
Cleansers
Some cutaneous disorders

The skin is the largest organ of the body, but absorption from the skin is poor and uncertain. The flat cells of the outermost layer of the skin contain keratin, a substance that serves to waterproof the skin and to prevent absorption of water and other substances. Absorption is affected, however, by the presence of sweat pores and of sebaceous glands, which penetrate the epidermis from the deeper subcutaneous tissue and corium. Hair follicles, pigment cells, nerve endings, nerve networks, and blood vessels as well as collagenous and elastic fibers all contribute to the functions of the skin. Although the skin is not known for its powers of absorption, drugs that cannot penetrate the horny first layer are sometimes absorbed by way of the sebaceous glands. Absorption is increased if the skin is macerated either by water or perspiration. It is more likely to occur if the epidermis is thin, as it is in the axilla or in the skin of a child. Absorption will take place rapidly from raw or denuded surfaces.

Methyl salicylate rubbed on the skin can be found in the urine in 30 minutes. Alcohol and volatile solvents promote absorption. The nature of the vehicle affects absorption—drugs that are fat soluble can be absorbed more rapidly than water-soluble drugs, and natural fats make a better vehicle to carry the drug into the skin than do substances such as petrolatum.

Drugs excreted by way of the skin

Drugs may be excreted by the skin in small amounts. Silver, copper, arsenic, mercury, bromides, borates, phenol, salicylates, antipyrine, methylene blue, and phenolphthalein may be deposited in the skin and sweat glands, and this may explain the skin eruption sometimes noticed after their use. Many other drugs can be the cause of skin eruption.

Symptoms associated with cutaneous disorders

Reactions or disorders of the skin are manifested by symptoms such as itching, pain, or tingling and by signs such as swelling, redness, papules, pustules, blisters, and hives.

A reaction of the skin that makes the patient uncomfortable or unsightly may be attributable to or related to sensitivity to drugs, allergy, infection, emotional conflict, hormonal imbalance, or degenerative disease. Many times the cause of the skin disorder is unknown and the treatment may be empiric in the hope that the right remedy will be found.

■ Preparations that soothe
Emollients

Emollients are fatty or oily substances that may be used to soften or soothe irritated skin and mucous membrane. An emollient may also serve as a vehicle for application of other medicinal substances. Olive oil and liquid petrolatum are frequently used to cleanse dry areas that would be irritated by water.

Fixed oils. These are used as emollients and include olive oil, flaxseed oil, and cottonseed oil.

Benzoinated lard. This is made by incorporating 1% benzoin with lard and then straining the preparation. The addition of the benzoin hinders the development of rancidity. The preparation is used as an ingredient of ointments.

Glycerin, **U.S.P., B.P. (Glycerol).** In pure form this tends to have a drying effect, but when diluted with water or rose water it is useful for application to irritated lips and skin.

Lanolin, **U.S.P.;** *hydrous wool fat,* **B.P.** Lanolin is made by combining the purified fat of sheepswool with 25% to 30% water. It is used as an ointment base. It does not become rancid, and as much as twice its weight of water can be incorporated with it. It has a somewhat unpleasant odor. It requires dilution for use in ointments, and from 20% to 100% of petrolatum may be added for this purpose.

Hydrophilic ointment, **U.S.P.** This is an ointment in which the oil in it is dispersed in the continuous water phase. It is an oil-in-water emulsion, and when medicaments are incorporated, the wetting agent in the emulsion enables the drugs to come in more direct contact with the skin and sebaceous glands. It is less greasy and more easily washed off than other ointments. Inflamed or irritated skin is often intolerant of this kind of ointment.

Petrolatum, **N.F.;** *soft paraffin,* **B.P. (Petroleum Jelly).** This is a purified, semisolid mixture of hydrocarbons derived from petroleum and used as a vehicle for medicinal agents for local application. It is an important ointment base.

Rose water ointment, **N.F.** This is a pleasant-smelling water-in-oil emulsion of the cold cream type. It contains spermaceti and white wax as emulsifying agents in addition to expressed almond oil, sodium borate, rose water, oil of rose, and distilled water. Nonallergic cold creams do not contain perfume, to which some patients are intolerant.

Cold cream, **U.S.P.** This is like rose water ointment, N.F., except that mineral oil is substituted for almond oil or persic oil.

Theobroma oil, **U.S.P., B.P. (cacao or cocoa butter).** This preparation is a fixed oil that is expressed from the roasted seeds of *Theobromo cacao*. It is a yellowish white solid having a faint, agreeable odor and a bland taste resembling chocolate. It is used chiefly for making suppositories and, to some extent, as a lubricant for massage and for application to sore nipples.

White ointment. This is a mixture of white wax and white petrolatum. It is mostly petrolatum with a little white wax added to give it stiffness. It is used as an ointment base.

Yellow ointment, **N.F.** This contains yellow wax and petrolatum.

Zinc oxide ointment, **U.S.P.** This contains 20% zinc oxide in a base of liquid petrolatum and white ointment.

Zinc ointment, **B.P.** This contains 15% zinc oxide in a base of simple ointment.

Vitamin A and D ointment. This contains vitamin A and vitamin D in a lanolin-petrolatum base.

Solutions and lotions

Soothing preparations may also be liquids that carry an insoluble powder or suspension, or they may be mild acid or alkaline solutions, such as boric acid solution, limewater, or aluminum subacetate. The bismuth salts (the subcarbonate or the subnitrate) and starch are also commonly used for their soothing effect.

Aluminum acetate solution, **U.S.P. (Burow's Solution).** This contains 545 ml. of aluminum subacetate solution and 15 ml. of glacial acetic acid in 1000 ml. of aqueous medium. It is diluted with 10 to 40 parts of water before application.

Aluminum subacetate solution, **U.S.P.** This preparation contains 160 Gm. of aluminum sulfate, 160 ml. of acetic acid, and 70 Gm. of precipitated calcium carbonate in 1000 ml. of aqueous medium. It is applied topically after dilution with 20 to 40 parts of water as a wet dressing.

Calamine lotion, **U.S.P., B.P.** Prepared calamine, zinc oxide, bentonite magma, glycerin, and calcium hydroxide solution are included in this lotion. It is a soothing lotion used for the dermatitis caused by poison ivy, insect bites, prickly heat, and so on. It is patted on the involved skin area.

Zinc stearate, **U.S.P.** This is a compound of zinc and variable proportions of stearic and palmitic acids. It contains about 14% zinc oxide and is similar to zinc oxide. It is used as a dusting powder, but caution should be observed with its use, particularly around infants, to prevent inhalation of the powder.

■ Antiseptics and parasiticides

It is generally agreed that thorough washing of the skin with warm water and a mild soap should precede the application of antiseptics to the skin. It is impossible to sterilize the skin, but adequate soaping and washing will do much to remove bacteria and the outer, loose epithelium. Strong antiseptics may do more harm than good by producing an irritation that will decrease the natural resistance of the skin to bacterial invasion. Antiseptics that are used to lower bacterial content are presented in Chapter 27.

A number of skin conditions for which antiseptics are used are caused by staphylococci and streptococci. Invasion by these organisms is likely to occur, especially when the normal protective mechanisms of the skin are broken down.

Antibiotics

Although relatively costly, bacitracin and tyrothricin are very useful in the local treatment of infectious lesions. Bacitracin is most often used in an ointment, although it can be used to moisten wet dressings or as a dusting powder. It is odorless and nonstaining and its use seldom results in sensitization. Tyrothricin is said to be more effective in wet dressings than in a cream or an ointment. Tyrothricin does not cause local irritation and its use rarely is attended by sensitization. Neomycin has been used successfully in the treatment of a number of infections of skin and mucous membrane. It is applied topically but occasionally it irritates the skin. An ointment combining neomycin, bacitracin, and polymyxin B may be more efficacious in mixed infections than when these agents are used singly. Vioform and xeroform are helpful in skin infections; there is seldom any irritation, but temporary discoloration of the skin and linen occurs. A number of antibiotics can be given orally or parenterally for treatment of infections of the skin.

Ammoniated mercury ointment, **U.S.P., B.P.** The U.S.P. preparation contains 5 Gm. of ammoniated mercury in each 100 Gm. of finished preparation along with liquid petrolatum and white ointment. In this strength local irritation seldom occurs. The preparation has no odor and does not stain. It occasionally causes sensitization, particularly when combined with salicylic acid.

Nitrofurazone, **N.F. (Furacin).** This is a synthetic, bright yellow, antibacterial substance that is inhibitory to bacteria in concentrations of 1:100,000 to 1:200,000 and bactericidal in concentrations of 1:50,000 to 1:75,000. It is effective against a variety of both gram-positive and gram-negative organisms. It is least effective against *Pseudomonas aeruginosa* and *Diplococcus pneumoniae.*

Nitrofurazone is useful when applied topically in the treatment of superficial mixed infections associated with contaminated wounds, burns, ulcerations, and impetigo. It is also useful in the preparation of areas for skin grafting. Applications of nitrofurazone may produce a generalized allergic skin reaction in certain individuals. Its internal use is not recommended, although it appears to have a low level of toxicity. Any systemic untoward effects as a result of absorption from dressings seem unlikely.

Nitrofurazone is applied locally in a 0.2% ointment-like base or as a 0.02% to 0.2% solution. It is either applied directly to the area or applied to a dressing that is then applied to the infected area. Since the base is water soluble and softens at body temperature, special reinforcement of the dressing may be required to maintain an effective contact with the area or to limit absorption into the dressing.

Antifungal agents

Salicylanilide, **N.F. (Salinidol).** This antifungous preparation is used externally for the treatment of ringworm of the scalp. It is available as a 5% ointment and is applied alone or along with less irritating fungistatics. The ointment is rubbed into the affected areas once or twice a day for 6 days of the week over a period of about 8 weeks.

Gentian violet, **U.S.P.** This is available for external application in a solution containing 1% of the dye in an alcohol-water solvent. Its principal disadvantage is that it stains clothing.

Potassium permanganate solution, **U.S.P. (1:100 to 1:10,000).** This solution is sometimes prescribed for foot soaks for epidermophytosis of the feet (athlete's foot). It is inexpensive and odorless but leaves brown stains on fabrics, skin, and nails.

Sulfur ointment, **U.S.P.;** *sulphur ointment,* **B.P.** Sulfur ointment contains about 10% of the precipitated sulfur in a base of liquid petrolatum and white ointment and is used in the treatment of ringworm and seborrhea. An ointment containing precipitated sulfur, salicylic acid, and resorcin may be more helpful than sulfur alone in the treatment of seborrheic dermatitis and fungous infections.

Benzoic and salicylic acid ointment **(Whitfield's Ointment).** This ointment contains salicy-

lic ointment. It is used for epidermophytosis of the feet.

Nystatin, **U.S.P., B.P. (Mycostatin).** This drug is an antibiotic substance used to treat infections of the skin and mucous membranes caused by *Candida albicans.* Vaginal infections are treated with suppositories or tablets, each containing 100,000 units, once or twice daily. An ointment and cream are available (100,000 units per gram) for moniliasis of the skin and should be applied to the affected areas once to several times a day.

Griseofulvin, **U.S.P., B.P. (Fulvicin, Grifulvin).** This preparation is an important addition to the treatment of superficial fungous infections, particularly those caused by the trichophyton and microsporon organisms. It is given orally in a dosage of 1 Gm. per day (in children the dosage is decreased by half). It has a fungistatic action by combining with the keratin of skin, hair, and nails. Topical therapy should be continued while the griseofulvin is ingested. It is available in 250-mg. tablets for oral administration.

Tolnaftate, **U.S.P. (Tinactin).** A 1% cream and a 1% solution and powder have been recently introduced for the topical treatment of superficial fungous infections caused by trichophyton and related organisms. The drug is ineffective against *Candida albicans* and against gram-positive and gram-negative bacteria. Treatment twice a day for 2 to 3 weeks is usually adequate.

Pediculicides—scabicides

The following agents are used to kill lice or scabies caused by itch mite (7-year itch).

Gamma benzene hexachloride, **U.S.P., B.P. (Gexane, Kwell).** This white, crystalline powder acts both as a pediculicide and scabicide. It is toxic and its use should be supervised by a physician. One application is sufficient to remove the active parasites. The preparation does not dissolve nits and, after 1 week, a second application may be given if necessary. Repeated use should be avoided because the substance tends to cause skin irritation. It should be kept away from the eyes, since it is irritating to mucous membranes. It is applied topically as a 1% lotion or ointment. A small brush may be used to facilitate application to the scalp. All clothing and bed linen should be sterilized by boiling to prevent reinfection. Wool clothing should be dry cleaned. The patient should not bathe or wash the hair until 24 hours after the treatment. A 10% solution of acetic acid or vinegar will help to remove nits from hairy regions but should be followed by a cleansing bath.

Isobornyl thiocyanoacetate-technical (**Bornate**). This preparation is one of the thiocyanates that kill lice. It may be mildly irritating to the skin of certain persons, but it does not seem to act as a sensitizing agent. It should not be applied near the eyes or on mucous membranes.

An oil emulsion is used in amounts of 30 to 60 ml., depending on the amount of hair at the site of infestation. It is applied and worked into a lather, after which it is allowed to remain for 10 minutes. In a scalp treatment, the hair is then combed with a fine-tooth comb and washed with a bland soap and water. The preparation should not remain on the skin too long. More than two applications should be avoided.

Benzyl benzoate lotion, **N.F., B.P.** (**Benylate, Albacide**). Benzyl benzoate is applied in a 10% to 30% lotion or emulsion. Application is sometimes followed by a slight, transient, burning sensation. In patients with sensitive skin severe irritation sometimes develops. It should be kept away from the eyes.

The entire body should be bathed, and the lesions caused by the itch mite should be well scrubbed with soap and warm water. Then the entire body surface, except the face, should be covered with the drug in the form of the emulsion or lotion, the application being made with a swab or brush. Particular care should be given to the region of the nails. After the first application has dried, a second one should be made to the most involved areas. Sterilization of clothing and bed linen is essential. Twenty-four hours later, clean clothing is put on after a warm soaking bath. A second or third treatment should be given if the parasite has not been eradicated.

■ Stimulants and irritants

Stimulants are those substances that produce a mild irritation and in that way promote healing and the disappearance of inflammatory exudates. Most of the irritant drugs exert a stimulating effect when applied in low concentrations. Examples of preparations that may have a stimulating effect are the tars obtained from the destructive distillation of wood and coal.

Tars, when diluted, act as antiseptics as well as irritants. Official preparations include juniper tar, N.F., coal tar, U.S.P., and prepared coal tar, B.P. The tars are sometimes prescribed in the treatment of psoriasis and chronic eczematous dermatitis. The official tars are seldom employed full strength. Coal tar is the most antiseptic but also the most irritant, and it has the most disagreeable odor. Ichthammol, N.F., B.P., derived from destructive distillation of coal, is used in the form of an ointment for eczema and seborrheic conditions of the skin.

Vulneraries are a form of tissue stimulant that are used to hasten the granulation of wounds or stimulate the growth of cells over a denuded area.

Compound benzoin tincture, U.S.P., is useful as a stimulant and protective for ulcers, bedsores, cracked nipples, and fissures of the lips, anus, and the like.

Preparations made of red blood cells also have been used to stimulate healing of indolent wounds and ulcers.

■ Keratolytics

Keratolytics (keratin dissolvers) are drugs that soften scales and loosen the outer horny layer of the skin. Salicylic acid, U.S.P., B.P., and resorcinol, U.S.P, B.P., are drugs of choice. Their action makes possible the penetration of other medicinal substances by a cleaning of the lesions involved. Salicylic acid is particularly important for its keratolytic effect in local treatment of scalp conditions, warts, corns, fungous infections, and chronic types of dermatitis. It is used up to 20% in ointments, plasters, or collodion for this purpose.

■ Antipruritics

Antipruritics are drugs given to allay itching of skin and mucous membranes. There is less need for these preparations as the constitutional treatment of patients with skin disorders is better understood. Dilute solutions containing phenol as well as tars have been widely used. They may be applied as lotions, pastes, or ointments. Dressings wet with potassium permanganate 1:4000, aluminum subacetate 1:16, boric acid, or physiologic saline solution may cool and soothe and thus prevent itching. Lotions such as calamine or calamine with phenol (phenolated calamine, U.S.P.) and cornstarch or oatmeal baths may also be employed to relieve itching.

Local anesthetics such as dibucaine and benzocaine may decrease pruritus, but their use is not recommended because of their high sensitizing and irritating effects. The application of hydrocortisone in a lotion or ointment in a strength of 0.5% to 1% has proved to be one of the best methods of relieving pruritus and decreasing inflammation. It has the additional advantage of possessing a low sensitizing index. It may be necessary to administer sedatives that have a systemic effect. Some physicians prefer not to use barbiturates because they decrease cortical control of the scratch reflex. Tranquilizers such as meprobamate are usually effective and safe when given in small doses. Trimeprazine, one of the phenothiazine derivatives, is said to be effective for the relief of itching. Trimeprazine tartrate is administered orally. The usual dose for adults is 2.5 mg. four times a day.

In addition to the aforementioned measures to relieve itching, preparations of ergotamine are used to relieve the generalized itching associated with jaundice, cirrhosis of the liver, Hodgkin's disease, and so on. Ergotamine tartrate, U.S.P., is one of the preparations, and there are others, one of which is dihydroergotamine. This preparation is said to relieve itching in a way similar to ergotamine tartrate without producing the common undesirable side effects of that preparation (nausea, vomiting, and cardiovascular reactions).

Other preparations used to relieve itching related to allergic reactions are the antihistaminic drugs (see Index). Calamine and Benadryl, marketed under the name of Caladryl, are examples of combined drugs given to relieve itching.

■ Protectives

Protectives are soothing, cooling preparations that form a film on the skin. Protectives, to be useful, must not macerate the skin, must prevent drying of the tissues, and must keep out light, air, and dust. Nonabsorbable powders are usually listed as protectives, but they are not particularly useful because they stick to wet surfaces and have to be scraped off and do not stick to dry surfaces at all.

Collodion, **U.S.P.** Collodion is a 4% solution of pyroxylin, or guncotton, in a mixture of ether and alcohol. When collodion is applied to the skin, the ether and alcohol evaporate, leaving a transparent film that adheres to the skin and protects it.

Flexible collodion, **U.S.P., B.P.** This is a mixture of collodion with 2% camphor and 3% castor oil. The addition of the latter makes the resulting film elastic and more tenacious. Styptic collodion contains 20% of tannic acid and is, therefore, astringent as well as protective.

Adhesive tape. Adhesive tape is a tenacious preparation that is solid at ordinary temperature but pliable and adhesive at the temperature of the body. It consists of rubber, lead plaster, and petrolatum spread on linen or muslin. Besides its use as a general protective agent, adhesive tape is widely used to reinforce weak muscles, cover ulcers, limit effusions, and keep dressings in place.

Nonabsorbable powders. These include zinc stearate, zinc oxide, certain bismuth preparations, talcum powder, and aluminum silicate. The disadvantages associated with their use have been mentioned previously.

Although it is safe to say that no substances known at present can stimulate healing at a more rapid rate than is normal under optimal conditions, preparations that act as bland protectives may help by preventing crusting and trauma. In some instances they may reduce offensive odors.

***Water-soluble chlorophyll derivatives* (Chloresium).** A mixture of water-soluble derivatives of chlorophyll is employed topically to produce a bland, soothing effect, to deodorize, to promote tissue repair, and to relieve itching in ulcers, burns, or wounds. It is applied in solution or as an ointment. These derivatives of chlorophyll may aid in producing a clean, granulating wound base suitable for the normal repair of tissues, but they do not take the place of antiinfective agents for the treatment of infections.

Solutions containing 0.2% water-soluble chlorophyll derivatives are applied one or more times daily. A 0.5% ointment may be spread over affected areas and covered with a fine mesh gauze or dressing.

■ Cleansers
Baths

Baths may be employed to cleanse the skin, to medicate it, or to reduce temperature. The usual method of cleansing the skin is by the use of soap and water, but this may not be tolerated in skin diseases. In some cases even water is not tolerated and inert oils must be substituted. Persons with dry skin should bathe less frequently than those with oily skin. It is possible to keep the skin clean without a daily bath. Nurses are sometimes accused of overbathing hospital patients, causing the patient's skin to become dry and itchy. An oily lotion is preferable to alcohol for the dry skin.

To render baths soothing in irritative conditions, bran, starch, or gelatin may be added in the proportion of about 1 to 2 ounces to the gallon. Oils such as Alpha-Keri, Lubath, and oilated oatmeal in a proportion of 1 ounce to the tub of water decrease the drying effect of water and thus help to relieve the itching of a sensitive, xerotic skin.

Soaps

Ordinary soap is the sodium salt of palmitic, oleic, or stearic acids or mixtures of these. They are prepared by saponifying fats or oils with the alkalies. The fats or oils used vary considerably.

The oil used for castile soap is supposed to be olive oil. Some soaps are made with coconut oil to which the skin of some persons is sensitive. Soaps contain glycerin unless it has been removed from the preparation. The consistency of the soap depends upon the predominating acid and alkali used.

Although all soaps are alkaline, the presence of an excess of free alkali or acid will constitute a potential source of skin irritation. The best soaps are only slightly alkaline, and they are likely to be found among the inexpensive soaps rather than in the highly scented, highly colored, and expensive varieties.

Medicated soaps contain antiseptics and other added substances, such as cresol, thymol, and sulfur, but soaps per se are antiseptic only insofar as they favor the mechanical cleansing of the skin.

The belief that soap and water are bad for the complexion is erroneous for the most part. A clean skin helps to promote a healthy skin. The soap used in maintaining a clean skin should be mild and contain a minimum of irritating materials.

Soaps are irritating to mucous membranes, and they are used in enemas mainly because of this action. They are also used in the manufacture of pills, liniments, and tooth powders. If soaps contain much free alkali their use on the skin may cause eczema. One of the mildest soaps is shaving soap.

■ Some cutaneous disorders
Burns

It is said that approximately 6000 or more people die each year of burns in the United States alone. The chief cause of death is shock, a fact of considerable significance in any effective plan of treatment.

Consideration of what takes place in the damaged tissues clarifies many points of treatment. At first there is an altered capillary permeability in the local injured area. That is, the permeability is increased and a loss of plasma and weeping of the surface tissues result. If the burn is at all extensive, considerable amounts of plasma fluid may be lost in a relatively short time.

This depletes the blood volume and causes a decreased cardiac output and diminished blood flow. Unless the situation is rapidly brought under control, irreparable damage may result from the rapidly developing tissue anoxia. Lack of sufficient oxygen and the accumulation of waste products from inadequate oxidation result in loss of tone in the minute blood vessels, and the increased capillary permeability then extends to tissues remote from those suffering the initial injury. Thus, a generalized edema often develops and the vicious cycle once established tends to be self-perpetuating. One of the aims in the treatment of burns is, therefore, to stop the loss of plasma insofar as it is possible and replenish that which is lost as quickly as possible.

Partial- or full-thickness burns must be thought of as open wounds with the accompanying danger of infection. The infection must be prevented or treated. The treatment, however, must be such that it will not bring any further destruction of tissue or of the small islands of remaining epithelium from which growth and regeneration can take place.

First aid treatment of burns

An important first aid treatment for minor and major burns, regardless of cause (chemical, electric, thermal), is to immediately cool the wound to remove irritants, prevent afterglow, and constrict blood vessels; this reduces the permeability of the blood vessels and checks edema formation. Cold tap water can be used to thoroughly flush the wound and to cool hot clothing. The more quickly the wound is cooled, the less tissue damage there is likely to be, and the more rapid will be the recovery. No greasy ointments, lard, butter, or dressings should be applied, since these agents will inhibit loss of heat from the burn, which will increase both discomfort and tissue damage. The burn may be left exposed to the air or cold wet compresses may be applied until the patient can be transported to a place where he can receive medical attention.

Prevention and treatment of infection. Penicillin and streptomycin are frequently used for the early treatment of burned patients other than those with a minor partial-thickness burn and an intact skin. These agents are given parenterally during the first few days and are then discontinued until debridement has been performed or until there is evidence of infection. Some physicians feel that in the treatment of burns that are not grossly contaminated it may be better to wait until there is evidence of infection, obtain a culture, and follow with the antibiotic of choice.

A booster dose of tetanus toxoid is given to the patient who has been previously immunized, and active immunization is started for those not previously immunized.

Para-aminomethylbenzene sulfonamide acetate (Sulfamylon). One of the most important therapeutic agents developed to combat burn infection has been the discovery of Sulfamylon, which is also known as Linberg's butter. Sulfamylon is a water-soluble ointment that is applied topically to the burn wound with sterile gloves following wound cleansing and debridement. The exposure method of therapy is preferred, although occasionally dressings may be applied; however, this may result in tissue maceration.

The ointment forms a protective coating over the burn. It rapidly diffuses through partial- and full-thickness burns and has proved to be one of the most effective means for preventing and retarding bacterial invasion in burn wounds. It has decreased deaths resulting from septicemia and decreased extension of the wound from infection. It has decreased the number of burn cases requiring plastic surgery or skin grafting. However, eschar separation is delayed.

Sulfamylon is relatively nontoxic. It is rapidly broken down in the body and eliminated via the urinary tract. Since this drug is a strong carbonic anhydrase inhibitor, acidosis may occur. The patient should be carefully observed for any signs of respiratory embarrassment. If rapid or labored respirations occur, the ointment should be washed off the wound. Therapy can be interrupted for 2 to 3 days without impairing the bacterial control of the wound.

Sulfamylon may cause some discomfort when first applied—a burning sensation may

495

occur that lasts from a few minutes to as long as an hour.

This is a highly stable drug. It remains active for several years and does not need to be refrigerated except in tropical countries.

***Silver nitrate,* U.S.P.** An aqueous solution of silver nitrate, 0.5%, has been used extensively in some burn centers during the past few years. As a 0.5% solution it is a relatively safe antiseptic agent. Dressings soaked in silver nitrate, 0.5%, are applied to the burn; the dressings must be kept moist and must not be allowed to dry in order to prevent precipitation of silver salts into the wound, which would cause irritation. Concentrations of silver nitrate above 1% produce tissue necrosis; concentrations below 0.5% are not antiseptic. Silver nitrate stains anything with which it comes in contact. The brown or black tissue discoloration is usually not permanent. Silver nitrate solution, 0.5%, is a hypotonic solution, and when it is used on extensive burns or for extensive periods of time it may cause electrolyte imbalance. Blood electrolytes should be frequently determined and patients observed for symptoms of sodium or potassium depletion (change in behavior, confusion, and so on).

Silicone fluid (dimethyl polysiloxane). Silicone fluid has been used to treat hand burns. The hands are placed in plastic bags containing silicone fluid. This is a stable agent; it is inert, has a low specific gravity, and is not harmful to normal or burned skin. The buoyancy of the silicone fluid is a result of its low specific gravity. This permits the patient to move his fingers freely without great discomfort.

Sunburn

Sunburn is an acute erythema caused by too long an exposure to the rays of the sun. In some cases, especially if a large area is involved, it may be serious, and the skin surface should be treated as in any serious burn. Exposure to the sun should be done gradually, a few minutes each day, when a general tan is desired. As would be true for any minor partial-thickness burn, when the epithelium is intact and remains so, ordinary protective demulcents or emollients are sufficient to allay irritation.

Questions

for study and review

1 What are some of the nursing problems unique to the care of patients with disorders of the skin?
2 What are some of the points for or against giving a hospital patient a daily, complete bath with soap and water?
3 What information or help would you give a patient who complains of a dry, itchy, skin?
4 What constitutes a good soap? What can and cannot be expected from a soap?
5 Why is an extensive burn of the skin likely to be dangerous? What are some of the main points in treatment of burns? How are patients with burns treated in your hospital?
6 Discuss the therapeutic effectiveness and precautions to take when an extensively burned patient is treated with para-aminoethylbenzene sulfonamide acetate (Sulfamylon) and with silver nitrate solution.
7 Define each of the following and give an example of each:
   a. emollients
   b. keratolytics
   c. antipruritics
8 What preparations are used in your hospital for prevention or treatment of decubitus ulcers?
9 A 1:5000 solution of potassium permanganate has been ordered for treatment of a patient with epidermophytosis. To entirely cover the feet with the solution, 10,000 ml. are required; on hand are gr. $7\frac{1}{2}$ tablets (0.5 Gm.). How many tablets will be required to make a 1:5000 solution?

References

A. M. A. Council on Drugs: New drugs, Chicago, 1967, American Medical Association.

Baker, T. J.: Open technique in the management of burns, Amer. J. Nurs. **59:**1262, 1959.

Bettley, F. R.: Some effects of soap on the skin, Brit. Med. J. **1:**1675, 1960.

Blank, I. H.: Action of emollient creams and their additives, J.A.M.A. **164:**413, 1957.

Carney, R. G.: Topical use of antibiotics, J.A.M.A. **186:**646, 1963.

Council on Pharmacy and Chemistry: Pharmacologic and toxicologic aspects of DDT (Chlorophenothane, U.S.P.), J.A.M.A. **145:**728, 1951.

Criep, L. H.: Dermatologic allergy, Philadelphia, 1967, W. B. Saunders Co.

Epstein, E.: Allergy to dermatologic agents, J.A.M.A. **198:**517, 1966.

Fay, N., and Demes, L. C.: Care of severely burned patients. In Bergersen, B., editor: Current concepts in clinical nursing, vol. 1, St. Louis, 1967, The C. V. Mosby Co.

Gerou, F. J., and Weeder, R. S.: Fluid silicone continuous immersion in the treatment of burns, Bull. Gersinger Med. Cent. **16:**17, 1964.

Goodman, L., and Gilman, A.: The pharmacological basis of therapeutics, New York, 1970, The Macmillan Company.

Lentz, M., Seaton, R., and Macmillan, B.: Silver nitrate treatment of thermal burns, J. Trauma **6:**399, 1966.

Lindberg, R. B., and others: The successful control of burn wound sepsis, J. Trauma **5:**601, 1965.

McCarthy, J. T., and Nelson, C. T.: Common bacterial infections of the skin, Med. Clin. N. Amer. **3:**499, 1956.

Montcrief, J. A., and others: The use of a topical sulfonamide in the control of burn wound sepsis, J. Trauma **6:**407, 1966.

Moyer, C. A., and others: Treatment of large human burns with 0.5 percent nitrate solution, Arch. Surg. (Chicago) **90:**812, 1965.

Order, S. E.: The burn wound, Springfield, Ill., 1965, Charles C Thomas, Publisher.

Pillsbury, D. M., Shelly, W. B., and Klingman, A. M.: A manual of cutaneous medicine, Philadelphia, 1961, W. B. Saunders Co.

Rattner, H., and Norins, A.: Care of the aged skin, Postgrad. Med. **32:**82, 1962.

Report of S.M.A. Committee on Cosmetics: Ways and means to safe sunbathing, J.A.M.A. **161:**1480, 1956.

Russell, B.: Parasitic infestations of the skin, Practitioner **192:**621, 1964.

Sulzberger, M. B.: Symposium on disease of the skin, Med. Clin. N. Amer. **46:**633, 1959.

Antineoplastic drugs

Neoplastic diseases of blood-forming organs

Classification of drugs used in neoplastic diseases

Alkylating agents

Antimetabolites

Hormones

Radioactive isotopes

Miscellaneous agents

As malignant diseases have become significant causes of death and disability, chemical agents for the treatment of cancer and related disorders have become increasingly important in therapeutics. The drugs are grouped together in a single chapter because they are employed with the same aim: the pharmacologic eradication or control of malignant tumors. However, it should be pointed out that the various groups of drugs presented act in different ways and that individual types of tumors may represent basically different kinds of disorders. It also should be clearly stated that at present there is no known drug that cures malignant disease. True cures of malignant tumors are produced only by early surgery and irradiation and in varying percent-

ages. The use of drugs—*antimalignant, antineoplastic,* and *carcinostatic*—is therefore confined to malignant disease after it has become metastatic and is no longer curative by surgery or to diseases such as leukemia or lymphosarcoma, which start out as disseminated malignant processes.

Malignant tumors are those made up of cells that grow rapidly and without normal tissue controls and restraints. Such tumors are locally invasive, growing into surrounding tissues and destroying them by pressure or usurping their supply of nutrients and oxygen. Malignant tumors may also metastasize and send off daughter cells by way of the blood or lymphatic streams, or by the serous fluids in the body cavities, to form new colonies of tumor. Such tumors may arise from cells of virtually any tissue of the body, and, in general, they are always fatal if not totally eradicated by surgery or irradiation.

Since the basic process of origin of malignant cell growth is not understood, there can be no rationally based pharmacologic treatment. Instead, the types of chemical agents that have been useful have been obtained primarily by empirical screening of many different kinds of compounds. Furthermore, the compounds employed today are not highly selective; they are not able to destroy invaders without appreciably harming the host cells. Many effective antineoplastic agents are active because they are toxic to all rapidly proliferating cells. Since many normal cells are also rapidly proliferating they may be damaged by antineoplastic agents. This means that this group of agents is a comparatively toxic one, and many of the drugs used could not be considered safe enough for use if the type of disease being treated did not itself make the situation desperate.

Since depression of bone marrow is a common serious toxic effect of the antimalignant drugs, it should be emphasized that extraordinary precaution must be observed to prevent the development of infection in the patient who has leukopenia or depression of bone marrow. This patient needs protection from individuals who harbor microorganisms against which he is relatively defenseless. Everything that comes in contact with the patient should be scrupulously clean.

Antineoplastic drugs are also known as *cytotoxic* drugs. Since these drugs also damage normal cells, a favorable response is usually caused by cancer cells being more sensitive to the drug than normal cells. The normal cells most often affected are those that are rapidly produced, such as blood cells (3 million red blood cells are produced per second) and gastrointestinal epithelium (100 kg. of new gastrointestinal epithelium each year). Neoplasms as a rule do not produce cells at this rate. Thus, drugs designed to affect cell growth or reproduction will destroy more normal cells than tumor cells.

Although the expenditure of time, effort, and money for the development of drugs that would effectively destroy cancer cells without affecting vital cells or metabolic processes is of a magnitude that is awe-inspiring, such drugs are not yet available. Yet the search goes on in the hope that some day man will be able to overcome and eventually eradicate the disease that today ranks second as a major destroyer of human life.

■ Neoplastic diseases of blood-forming organs

A number of the drugs mentioned in this chapter are used in treatment of neoplastic conditions that affect the blood and blood-forming tissues. A brief description of several of these disorders follows.

Leukemia

Leukemia is a neoplastic disease characterized by excessive production of white blood cells. It affects the bone marrow, lymph nodes, and spleen. For reasons not understood, the blood-forming tissues produce white blood cells wildly and excessively and the bone marrow becomes infiltrated with abnormal cells. The production of erythrocytes and thrombocytes is reduced and the patient tends to become anemic and to exhibit hemorrhagic tendencies. The type of white cell that predominates in the blood determines the type of leukemia. Myelogenous leukemia means that the type of white cell found most often is a granulocyte or its precursor. Lymphatic leukemia is characterized by a large number of lymphocytes. Both types of leukemia may be acute or chronic. Immature white blood cells are found in the blood of the patient with acute leukemia, whereas more fully matured cells are seen in the case of chronic leukemia. Although the number of white blood cells may be excessive, they afford little protection against infection. Cells other than lymphocytes and granulocytes that are normally found in hematopoietic tissues may also become active in neoplastic proliferation. The cause of this disorder is not known.

Lymphoma

Lymphomas are tumors that involve the lymph nodes. Lymphosarcoma is a disease in which the lymphocytes multiply excessively and involve the lymph nodes, spleen, and lymphoid tissues of other organs. Almost any part of the body may become involved. Hodgkin's disease also involves lymph nodes as well as nonnodal tissues, but the reticulum cells rather than the lymphocytes are involved. These diseases are usually fatal within a few years. The lymph nodes, liver, and spleen become enlarged in lymphomas. Fever, itching, and hemorrhagic tendencies as well as anemia and thrombocytopenia present special clinical problems.

X-ray therapy is the treatment of choice, although the nitrogen mustards and related compounds are considered valuable as adjunctive forms of treatment.

Polycythemia vera

Polycythemia vera is a disease characterized by excessive formation of erythrocytes, the number per cubic millimeter sometimes being many times the normal number. Increased numbers of leukocytes and thrombocytes may be present.

Classification of drugs used in neoplastic diseases

The antineoplastic drugs can be divided into several large groups on the basis of their probable manner of actions.

Alkylating agents. These drugs are also referred to as *radiomimetic* drugs since they affect cells in much the same way as irradiation. Nitrogen mustards and related compounds are highly reactive chemically and act by transferring alkyl groups to receptor molecules. The precise mechanism by which alkylating agents cause cellular injury is not entirely clear, but DNA appears to be more vulnerable than other cell components. Alkylating agents inhibit cell division in the premitotic or resting phase and thus inhibit multiplication of malignant cells as well as certain normal cells. It is postulated that they act as anticancer agents by reacting with essential molecules in the cells of the tumor, such as nucleic acids. In general, rapidly reproducing cells are sensitive to the alkylating agents, so that many of these compounds are also toxic to the gastrointestinal tract and the bone marrow.

Common toxic effects of alkylating agents
  Nausea and vomiting
  Bone marrow depression—leukopenia; thrombocytopenia
  Bleeding—hemorrhage
  Marked lowering of resistance to infection

Attempts continue to be made to develop agents that will produce injury to specific types of neoplastic cells. The following outline gives examples of drugs.

Alkylating or radiomimetic drugs
  Nitrogen mustard (mechlorethamine)
  Triethylenemelamine (TEM)
  Chlorambucil (Leukeran)
  Busulfan (Myleran)
  Melphalan (Alkeran)
  Uracil mustard
  Thiotepa
  Cyclophosphamide (Cytoxan)
Antimetabolites
  Methotrexate (Amethopterin)
  Mercaptopurine (Purinethol)
  Thioguanine
  Fluorouracil

Hormones
  Adrenal steroids
  Sex hormones
Radioactive isotopes
  Phosphorus (^{32}P)
  Gold (^{198}Au)
  Iodine (^{131}I)
Miscellaneous
  Actinomycin D
  Urethan
  Azathioprine
  Vinblastine (Velban)
  Vincristine (Oncovin)

Antimetabolites. Antimetabolites are compounds whose chemical structures are close to but not identical with substances normally used by cells for growth and metabolism. Just as sulfanilamide acts as an antimetabolite for the normal bacterial metabolite para-aminobenzoic acid and is therefore toxic for certain bacteria, certain artificial relatives (analogs) of some of the vitamins or the components of nucleic acids can be toxic for rapidly growing human or other mammalian cells. Antifolic acid compounds resemble folic acid and act by competitively preventing the conversion of folic acid to a biologically more active derivative, thereby blocking biosynthesis. These drugs are metabolized in the liver and excreted by the kidneys. Thus good liver and renal function is important to avoid severe toxic effects in these organs.

Hormones. The hormones are believed to slow the growth of tumors by making environment less favorable. Certain tumors of secondary sexual tissue origin, such as prostatic cancer, are somewhat dependent for their growth on a supply of the male sex hormone. If this is removed (as by castration) and if estrogens are added to the environment, the growth of malignant cells of the prostate gland may be slowed. Comparably, some mammary cancers are slowed by the administration of androgenic hormone. A further example, although not so well understood, is the inhibiting effect that adrenocorticotropic hormone (ACTH) and adrenal steroids have on certain types of leukemia.

Radioisotopes. Radioisotopes act essentially as the roentgen ray does, by liberating cell-destroying ionizing radiation in the vicinity of the tumor. The chemical nature of the radioisotope, however, may take advantage of pharmacologic principles by guaranteeing delivery of the radioactivity to the proper target. Radioiodine is used to treat some diseases of the thyroid so that the damaging effects of the radiation are brought to the site desired. Other examples are radioactive phosphate ($^{32}PO_{4}^{\equiv}$) and colloidal radiogold (^{198}Au).

Miscellaneous agents. A final group not easily classified in any of the aforementioned groups includes urethane, actinomycin D, and azaserine. Azaserine has not proved to be of unique therapeutic value.

Some of the most important individual drugs will be discussed in more detail with reference to clinical indications, the method of administration, dosage, and toxicity. In cooperation with the National Cancer Institute, Public Health Service, a chemotherapy program is being carried out in which the resources of hospitals, research laboratories, industry, and government have been mobilized in an effort to find effective agents for cancer. Thousands of compounds are being tested annually on laboratory animals in a search for chemicals with anticancer properties. About forty substances are approved yearly for clinical trials on human patients.

▪ Alkylating agents
Nitrogen mustards and related compounds
Mechlorethamine hydrochloride (Mustargen Hydrochloride)

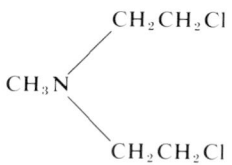

The nitrogen mustard that has been used most extensively is mechlorethamine, which is the prototype of the alkylating agents. It is an analog of sulfur mustard gas used in World War I. Nitrogen mustard was first used to treat patients in 1942 and 1943 but was not reported until 1946 because of wartime security restrictions of World War II. In certain respects it has an action on cells of the body similar to that of radiation. It exerts a selective cytotoxic effect on rapidly growing cells such as those found in blood-forming tissues and malignant tumors. Like other nitrogen mustards and the related compounds it inhibits mitosis by action at some premitotic phase of cell division. There is evidence that such compounds react selectively with certain groups of DNA and interfere with the reproduction of cells. As a result, cells may exhibit altered structure of their chromosomes. The normal tissues that react significantly after clinical use of the compounds are those of the bone marrow and the lymphoid organs.

Mechlorethamine is capable of producing severe tissue damage when it comes in direct contact with the skin, subcutaneous tissue, eyes, or respiratory tract.

Nitrogen mustard often provides dramatic relief of symptoms (relief of fever, improved appetite and strength, reduction of size of liver and spleen, relief from itching and pain). The duration of the remission may vary from a few weeks to several months.

Uses. Mechlorethamine is used in the treatment of Hodgkin's disease, lymphosarcoma, bronchogenic carcinoma, certain types of chronic leukemia, lymphoblastomas of the skin, and mycosis fungoides. This is a drug of choice for hospitalized patients when prompt treatment is indicated. It is considered most effective when the disease has become generalized or the patient is refractory to x-ray therapy, but is use in terminal stages of the disease is not thought to be justifiable.

Preparation, dosage, and administration. The following is the preparation available.

Mechlorethamine hydrochloride for injection, U.S.P. (Mustargen Hydrochloride); mustine injection, B.P. (nitrogen mustard). This drug is available in vials containing 10 mg. of the powder and 90 mg. of sodium chloride. Prior to **501**

injection the drug is dissolved in 10 ml. of distilled water. It is usually administered intravenously by injecting the solution into the tubing of an intravenous infusion. Dosage is calculated on the basis of body weight (0.1 mg. per kilogram on each of 4 successive days in most cases). The drug is preferably given in divided doses. Single doses of more than 8 to 10 mg. are not recommended.

After intravenous administration, nausea and vomiting usually occur within a few minutes to half an hour. Lymphopenia occurs within a few hours and persists for about 2 weeks. Bone marrow cell necrosis and disintegration appears within 12 hours and continues for 4 to 6 days; a return to normal cellularity takes 3 to 4 weeks. Blood samples will show a low white count (2500 to 3000 per cubic millimeter) on the fifth to sixth day after administration and persists until the tenth or twelfth day. Thereafter, blood samples will show an increase in the leukocyte count.

Because of the depressant effects on bone marrow, mechlorethamine injections are limited to intervals of 4 to 6 weeks.

Side effects and toxic effects. The margin of safety between the therapeutic dose of this drug and the toxic dose is very narrow, necessitating utmost caution in its administration. Thrombosis or thrombophlebitis may occur as a result of its effect on veins. Leakage of the solution around the needle may cause sloughing of adjacent tissues. Both the powder and the solution act as a vesicant and strong nasal irritant.

Systemic toxic effects include severe nausea and vomiting and decreased formation of blood cells. Granulocytopenia, lymphopenia, thrombocytopenia, and anemia may occur. Agranulocytosis has been known to develop. Gastrointestinal and gonadal injury also occurs. The toxic effects are directly proportional to the dosage; therefore, careful calculation of dosage usually will prevent severe reactions. Nausea and vomiting may be prevented by giving the drug late in the day and sedating the patient for the night. Sodium phenobarbital along with chlorpromazine, given intramuscularly, may prove effective.

Additional therapy with this drug is not undertaken until there is satisfactory recovery in the bone marrow. Subsequent courses of therapy do not, as a rule, produce responses as satisfactory as those of the preceding course.

Triethylenemelamine, N.F. (TEM)

Triethylenemelamine is related to the nitrogen mustards and exhibits actions and has uses similar to them (see mechlorethamine). It differs from mechlorethamine in that it can be given orally as well as parenterally, does not produce a blistering effect (vesicant action), and causes less nausea and vomiting; the onset and duration of its action are also more prolonged.

Uses. Although used for many of the same conditions for which mechlorethamine is used, best results probably have been obtained in patients with widely disseminated Hodgkin's disease. Remissions may last from 2 to 14 weeks. During this time the patient has some relief of itching, anorexia, and weakness, and the enlarged lymph nodes and tumor masses decrease in size.

Preparation, dosage, and administration. Triethylenemelamine is available in 5-mg. tablets for oral administration. The drug is inactivated by the presence of acid and food and therefore should be given an hour or more before breakfast along with 2 Gm. of sodium bicarbonate. The latter substance enhances both absorption and activity of the drug. During initial therapy, 2.5 mg. is given on two successive mornings. If anorexia does not develop a third dose of 2.5 mg. may be prescribed. Whether or not administration is continued depends upon the condition being treated and the response of the patient (condition of the appetite and the blood cell count). Maintenance therapy is sometimes carried out if periodic examinations of the blood can be made. Maintenance dose is 0.5 to 5 mg. weekly or every 2 to 5 days. This drug can also be administered intravenously (0.04 mg. per kilogram of body weight) daily for 3 days. Therapy should be discontinued if the white cell count falls rapidly or below accepted range of normal.

Side effects and toxic effects. The effects are the same as those for the nitrogen mustards, with the exception that this preparation produces less nausea and vomiting and no vesicant action. Slow onset of action and prolonged effects are its main disadvantages.

Chlorambucil, U.S.P., B.P. (Leukeran)

$$ClCH_2CH_2 \diagdown N \diagup (CH_2)_3—COOH$$
$$ClCH_2CH_2 \diagup$$

Chlorambucil is a derivative of nitrogen mustard, and its action and uses are similar to those of mechlorethamine hydrochloride and triethylenemelamine. Chlorambucil is useful in bringing about remissions in neoplastic diseases, especially when there is involvement of the hematopoietic tissues and when the patient has become refractory to radiation therapy. Patients with chronic lymphocytic leukemia may show marked improvement during clinical remissions; the white blood cell count may be rapidly lowered. Patients with Hodgkin's disease may experience relief of pain, reduction in the size of the liver and spleen, gain in weight, and a general increased sense of well-being.

Uses. Chlorambucil is used as a palliative treatment of chronic lymphocytic leukemia, lymphosarcoma, and Hodgkin's disease. Unfortunately, it does not seem to increase the survival time of persons ill with these diseases any better than the nitrogen mustards. Weekly blood examinations are recommended.

Preparation, dosage, and administration. Chlorambucil is available in 2-mg. tablets for oral administration. The initial dosage for patients with Hodgkin's disease is 0.2 mg. per kilogram of body weight, but it is reduced to a maintenance level after a response is obtained.

For patients with leukemia or lymphosarcoma, the dose is usually 0.1 mg. per kilogram of body weight daily for 4 to 6 weeks. It is usually well tolerated. It causes little nausea and vomiting.

Side effects and toxic effects. Excessive dosage or prolonged administration may cause severe depression of bone marrow. However, its absorption is said to be more predictable; it is easier to handle and produces fewer side effects than some of the other alkylating agents. Patients occasionally complain of gastric distress.

Busulfan, U.S.P., B.P. (Myleran)

$$CH_3—\overset{O_2}{\underset{\|}{S}}—O—(CH_2)_4—O—\overset{O_2}{\underset{\|}{S}}—CH_3$$

Busulfan is an active alkylating agent that pharmacologically resembles the nitrogen mustards and triethylenemelamine. Its cytotoxic action, however, is restricted chiefly to the cells of the bone marrow. In patients with chronic granulocytic leukemia remission of symptoms is characterized by improved sense of well-being, reduction in the size of the spleen, increase in the hemoglobin level, increase in the erythrocytes, and reduction in the number of circulating white blood cells. Following initial treatment with busulfan, 90% of the patients have remissions.

Uses. Busulfan is preferred to other antineoplastic drugs in the treatment of chronic myelogenous leukemia because of its depressant effect on the production of granulocytes.

Preparation, dosage, and administration. This drug is available in 2-mg. tablets for oral administration. The initial dose is usually 2 to 6 mg. daily until clinical improvement occurs. Some physicians prescribe appreciably larger doses but over a relatively short period of time.

Side effects and toxic effects. Busulfan offers the advantages of oral administration and a low incidence of side effects. It causes little nausea and vomiting. In addition it can be used in maintenance therapy of ambulatory patients. Overdosage or prolonged administration may produce irreversible damage to cells of the bone marrow. Weekly blood examinations are recommended. Bleeding tendencies may result from

503

reduced numbers of thrombocytes in the blood. Darkening of the skin, amenorrhea, and renal damage have been reported from the use of busulfan.

Melphalan, U.S.P. (Alkeran)

Melphalan is also known as phenylalanine nitrogen mustard. The drug is used in the treatment of multiple myeloma. Both objective and subjective improvement occurs with melphalan in 70% to 80% of patients. Improvement may last 6 months to 2 years; thus, melphalan prolongs life in these patients.

Preparation, dosage, and administration. Melphalan is available in 2-mg. tablets. Dosage is 6 mg. daily by mouth for 2 to 3 weeks. When the white count begins to rise, a maintenance dose of 2 mg. daily may be instituted. Other dosage regimens have been reported, including 4-day courses of treatment each month or every 6 to 8 weeks.

Toxic effects. Toxic effects are similar to those of other orally administered nitrogen mustards.

Uracil mustard

Uracil mustard is an alkylating agent similar to mechlorethamine and other alkylating agents. Its cytotoxic action is believed to result from its effect on DNA. Uracil mustard is well absorbed from the gastrointestinal tract. This drug appears to act slowly in some patients, and clinical response may not occur for 2 to 3 months after therapy is initiated.

Uses. Uracil mustard is used in the treatment of chronic lymphocytic leukemia, lymphomas, and Hodgkin's disease. Beneficial effects have been reported from its use in other malignant diseases such as ovarian cancer.

Preparation, dosage, and administration. Uracil mustard is available in 1-mg. capsules for oral administration. Two dosage schedules have been suggested for the gradual dosage schedule. From 1 to 2 mg. is given daily until clinical improvement or bone marrow depression occurs. When the patient's condition has deteriorated, 1 mg. daily is given for 3 out of every 4 weeks.

When the intensive dosage schedule is used, 3 to 5 mg. is given daily for the first 7 days, after which 1 mg. daily is given for 3 out of every 4 weeks.

Side effects and toxic effects. Nausea, vomiting, and diarrhea are the most common side effects. Skin reaction such as pruritus or dermatitis may occur. In addition, alopecia, nervousness, irritability, and depression have been reported. Tolerance to uracil mustard is reduced if patients have recently received other antineoplastics or irradiation therapy.

Thiotepa, U.S.P.

Thiotepa is one of the alkylating agents that produce effects similar to those produced by nitrogen mustard, triethylenemelamine, and chlorambucil.

Uses. It is used for many of the same conditions for which other drugs belonging to this group of preparations are used. Some authorities prefer not to use thiotepa for the initial treatment of malignant disease but advocate its use only after surgery and radiation therapy are not effective or are not feasible. It is ineffective for acute leukemia. It is particularly useful for therapy of cancer of the breast, ovaries, and urinary bladder.

Preparation, dosage, and administration. Thiotepa is available in vials containing 15 mg. of powdered drug. The maximum daily dose for initial therapy by intramuscular, intravenous, or intraarterial injection is 0.2 mg. per kilogram of body weight. It may also be injected into serous cavities and tumor masses. The dosage for maintenance therapy is determined by the clinical response of the patient and changes in the patient's blood. The powder should be refrigerated, and when solutions are prepared they should be used immediately or discarded. Because this preparation has no vesicant action and because solutions can be prepared at a pH that produces no irritation of tissues, it is suitable for all routes of parenteral administration.

Side effects and toxic effects. Thiotepa has a slow onset of action, and immediate side effects such as nausea and vomiting are minimal, although they do occur. It is capable of producing cumulative toxic effects in the blood-forming tissues and therefore caution in its use is recommended. Irreversible aplastic anemia has been known to develop.

Cyclophosphamide, U.S.P., B.P. (Cytoxan)

$$Cl-CH_2-CH_2 \quad\quad NH-CH_2$$
$$N-P \quad\quad CH_2 \cdot H_2O$$
$$Cl-CH_2-CH_2 \quad O \quad O-CH_2$$

Cyclophosphamide is one of the alkylating agents whose antineoplastic activity is similar to that of mechlorethamine hydrochloride. Although the uses and the precautions associated with the two drugs are similar, cyclophosphamide is not a vesicant or tissue irritant, a factor that affects administration of the drug. It is employed in the treatment of patients with lymphoma, lymphosarcoma, Hodgkin's disease, chronic lymphocytic leukemia, reticulum-cell sarcoma, and other malignancies.

Preparation, dosage, and administration. Cyclophosphamide is marketed in vials containing 100, 200, and 500 mg. of the drug for intravenous administration. The drug is dissolved in saline solution prior to administration. It is also marketed in 50-mg. tablets for oral use. The usual initial dose is 2 to 3 mg. per kilogram of body weight per day (intravenously) for 6 to 8 days. Maintenance dosage (oral or intravenous)

is determined in part by the white blood cell count of the patient. The drug is frequently given in doses of 100 to 200 mg. daily for 2 weeks or longer. It is also given intramuscularly and by intrapleural, intraperitoneal, and intratumor injection. The injectable form of the drug is unstable and must be used soon after it has been prepared.

Side effects and toxic effects. The incidence as well as the severity of side effects such as loss of appetite and nausea and vomiting are said to be less with this drug than with nitrogen mustard. It is capable of producing severe depression of the bone marrow. Leukopenia can be expected within a week or two after therapy has been started. Loss of hair from the scalp (partial or complete) has been reported in 50% or more of the patients treated. Regrowth usually occurs within a few months even though administration of the drug is continued.

Occasionally, patients develop a sore mouth with mucosal ulceration, dizziness, and disturbance of hepatic function.

Pipobroman, N.F. (Vercyte)

Pipobroman is an alkylating agent that is a derivative of piperazine. It is indicated primarily for the treatment of polycythemia vera, but it has also been shown to be clinically useful for treatment of chronic granulocytic leukemia, particularly when it has become resistant to treatment with busulfan.

Preparation, dosage, and administration. Pipobroman is available in 10- and 25-mg. tablets. When it is used for polycythemia vera an initial daily dose of 1 mg. per kilogram of body weight for about 30 days is recommended. The maintenance dose is 0.1 to 0.2 mg. per kilogram daily when the hematocrit level has been reduced to within normal limits.

For chronic granulocytic leukemia the initial daily dose recommended is 1.5 to 2.5 mg. per kilogram (about 5 to 175 mg.). This is continued until a desired clinical picture and leukocyte count are obtained.

Side effects and toxic effects. Since pipobroman, like other alkylating agents, is cytotoxic to bone marrow, a serious fall in platelets, leukocytes, and hemoglobin may occur. Blood transfusion may be necessary to overcome the anemia. Complete blood counts should be done once or twice a week during therapy, and leukocyte counts should be taken daily.

Other side effects that may occur include nausea and vomiting, abdominal distress, diarrhea, and skin rash.

Regional perfusion

In carefully selected patients, perfusion of certain parts of the body (for example, an extremity) with a high concentration of an alkylating agent has caused a regression of certain types of cancer, especially melanomas. The development of an adequate extracorporeal circulatory system similar to the kind used in cardiac surgery has made the perfusion technique possible. A tourniquet is used to isolate the area being treated, and a higher concentration of the alkylating agent can be used than would be possible with parenteral injection. Perfusion of parts other than the extremities is always more dangerous because of the possibility that the toxic agent will escape into the general circulation.

■ Antimetabolites

Antimetabolites include the folic acid antagonists (methotrexate), purine antagonists (mercaptopurine), and pyrimidine antagonists (fluorouracil). These agents also act as immunosuppressants.

Folic acid antagonists are used primarily in treating acute leukemias in children; they are less effective against leukemias in adults. They have been used to treat solid tumors, but with limited success.

Folic acid is a vitamin that acts as a catalytic agent in the synthesis of nucleic acid, an essential component of cellular protein. For this activity folic acid is converted to a biologically more active form known as folinic acid. Folic acid antagonists block the formation of folinic acid from folic acid. This brings about interference with the synthesis of DNA. Cells are not prevented from going into cell division, but normal mitotic progress is arrested. Cells proliferating rapidly, such as white blood cells in the

leukemic patient, are particularly affected. These drugs have a damaging effect on embryonic tissue and should not be given to pregnant women.

Remission is characterized by disappearance of fever, relief of pain in bones, improved appetite, and reduction in the size of enlarged organs such as the liver, spleen, and lymph nodes; in general the child seems to feel better and stronger. The blood picture may become comparatively normal.

The purine and pyrimidine antagonists also interfere with DNA synthesis. The first clinically useful folic acid antagonist was aminopterin; this drug is not currently available in the United States. It has been superceded by methotrexate.

Methotrexate, U.S.P. (amethopterin)

The official name methotrexate is preferred to amethopterin because of the similarity in spelling and pronunciation of amethopterin and aminopterin. Methotrexate is a folic acid antagonist.

Uses. Its principal use is in treating acute leukemia in children. It is occasionally used for adults who are refractory to other forms of therapy. In women, it is also used in the treatment of a rare type of cancer known as choriocarcinoma, a tumor composed of cells of fetal origin. Methotrexate is also used for continuous regional infusion. It may be accompanied by the administration of folinic acid (leucovorin), which acts as an antidote to lessen toxicity of the methotrexate.

Preparation, dosage, and administration. Methotrexate is available in 2.5-mg. tablets for oral administration. It is usually administered orally since it is readily absorbed from the gastrointestinal tract. A parenteral preparation is also available in vials containing 5 mg. of the drug. It can be given intramuscularly, intravenously, or intrathecally. Dosage for children varies from 1 to 2.5 mg. daily. The usual daily dose for adults is 5 mg. The drug may be given twice weekly to maintain a remission.

Side effects and toxic effects. Although claims have been made that methotrexate is less toxic than aminopterin, some investigators have found that when biologically equivalent doses

Mercaptopurine   Adenine   Hypoxanthine

are given, there is little or no difference in the toxicity and therapeutic effectiveness of the two drugs.

Mercaptopurine, U.S.P., B.P. (6-mercaptopurine, Purinethol)

Mercaptopurine acts as an antagonist to certain purines that are constituents of nucleic acids, thus interfering with the formation of nucleic acids. Chemically, mercaptopurine resembles constituents of nucleic acid—adenine and a purine base known as hypoxanthine (see accompanying formulas). Both compounds are needed for the synthesis of nucleic acid by cells; they are needed especially when cells are growing and multiplying rapidly. Mercaptopurine resembles adenine and hypoxanthine, but it cannot truly take their places, and therefore it interferes with normal cell processes.

The effects of mercaptopurine can be observed chiefly in the tissues in which there is rapid cellular growth and a high rate of metabolism of nucleic acid. As a result of its effects on the bone marrow, there is a reduction in the formation of leukocytes, thrombocytes, and reticulocytes. In the gastrointestinal tract injury of epithelium results in anorexia, nausea and vomiting, and diarrhea (in which the stools may become bloody), and large doses may bring about degenerative changes in the liver.

Uses. Mercaptopurine is used chiefly in treating acute leukemia in children. Careful use of the drug may bring about remission in the disease and prolongation of life in a fairly large number of patients. Remissions vary from a few weeks to several months. Leukemia in the adult may also respond to this drug, but the incidence of remissions is lower than for children. The administration of a folic acid antagonist and/or hormone therapy is often considered preferable as an initial form of treatment. When the patient no longer responds satisfactorily, mercaptopurine may be substituted. The reverse is also true; some physicians prefer to employ hormonal treatment as a last resort. Some patients with chronic myelogenous leukemia seem to respond favorably to mercaptopurine.

Preparation, dosage, and administration. Mercaptopurine is marketed in 50-mg. tablets for oral administration. Dosage is regulated in accordance with the amount of clinical improvement in the patient and the response made by his blood. The usual initial dose (both for children and adults) is 2.5 mg. per kilogram of body weight daily. From 3 to 6 weeks of therapy may be necessary before a remission is achieved.

Side effects and toxic effects. Resistance to mercaptopurine is said to develop fairly rapidly. Interruption of treatment brings about relapse rather quickly. The chief toxic effect is depression of the bone marrow, resulting in marked leukopenia, thrombocytopenia, and anemia. It is less toxic to the epithelium of the gastrointestinal tract than the folic acid antagonists, but it can cause nausea, vomiting, and diarrhea; large doses may result in ulcerations of the mucosa. Frequent examination of the patient's blood during therapy is indicated.

Thioguanine, N.F.
(2-amino-6-mercaptopurine)

Thioguanine is a chemical analog of the physiologic purines that have the same antineoplastic action as mercaptopurine. It is partially absorbed from the gastrointestinal tract. It is partially detoxified by the liver and excreted from the urinary and intestinal tracts.

Uses. It is used to treat acute leukemia and chronic myelocytic leukemia. Remissions in children are greater than those in adults. Thioguanine is recommended for use only after the patient has received treatment with busulfan or mercaptopurine and resistance or toxicity has developed.

Preparation, dosage, and administration. Thioguanine is available in 40-mg. tablets for oral administration. Initial and maintenance therapy is usually continued until resistance develops. Dosage is based on clinical and hematologic response and must be highly individualized.

Side effects and toxic effects. Thioguanine is a toxic drug, and its side and toxic effects are similar to those of mercaptopurine. Jaundice has also been reported, and thioguanine should be used cautiously in patients with impaired liver function.

Fluorouracil, U.S.P. (FU)

This drug is believed to affect specific steps in pyrimidine metabolism in such a way as to interfere with the synthesis of thymine, an essential part of deoxyribonucleic acid. It also inhibits the synthesis of ribonucleic acid (RNA) and is incorporated into the latter to form a fraudulent molecule of RNA. As a result, synthesis of proteins and proliferation of cancer cells are inhibited. Certain strains of cancer have been known to develop resistance to the drug. It is said to differ from the alkylating agents in that it does not lose its effectiveness after the first recurrence of the tumor.

Fluorouracil has been found to be particularly effective in bringing about remissions in patients with nonresectable carcinoma of the rectum, sigmoid, and colon. Patients with advanced cancer of the breast and ovaries have also been known to obtain temporary benefit. At least while the patients are receiving therapy they may have remarkable relief of pain, and they are often able to be up and about and function to some extent until the termination of life. Most patients who are given this opportunity for a temporary remission are happy to have it even when they understand that it may be brief and that they may experience distressing toxic effects. Remissions in patients with gastrointestinal cancer may last from 6 months to 4 years.

Preparation, dosage, and administration. Dosage is determined on the basis of the patient's weight. The initial dose is 15 mg. per kilogram of body weight for 4 or 5 days by intravenous injection. The dose is later reduced and given daily or every other day. The drug is available in 10-ml. vials (50 mg. per milliliter) for intravenous administration. A variety of dosage schedules is used.

Side effects and toxic effects. Early symptoms of developing toxicity include redness and dryness of the lips and soreness of the mouth, followed by ulceration of the lips and buccal mucosa. The patient may complain of oral discomfort before the ulcerated lesions are visible. The physician is likely to countermand the order for administration of this drug when these symptoms occur to avoid more serious toxic effects—severe diarrhea, extensive ulceration of the mouth, and marked leukopenia. Loss of hair from the scalp occurs fairly often, which is particularly distressing to women. Although the hair usually grows again within a few months, the patient should be prepared to face temporary alopecia. Some degree of anorexia and vomiting is seen in most patients receiving the drug. Some deaths have been reported that were believed to be the result of the toxic effects of this drug.

One of the nursing problems associated with the care of these patients who develop sore mouth is the maintenance of adequate nutrition. The physician may prescribe a topical anesthetic such as dyclonine hydrochloride (Dyclone). The patient can rinse the mouth with an aqueous solution of this drug, after which he is able to eat in greater comfort. Only limited relief is achieved, however. Care must be exercised so that the food provided for him is warm rather than hot to avoid thermal injury in a mouth that is already sore.

Related compounds. Other analogs of fluorouracil have been subjected to investigation. 5-Fluorodeoxyuridine (5-FUDR) is the one most widely used at present. Its toxicity is said to be increased when it is given in continuous intravenous infusion over a period of 4 to 5 days. The same is not thought to be true of fluorouracil. The recommended therapeutic dosage for 5-FUDR is 30 mg. per kilogram daily when given by rapid intravenous injection.

■ Hormones

The adrenotropic hormone (ACTH) and the cortical hormones made by the adrenal gland are known to inhibit the growth of cells, especially young actively growing and multiplying cells. The mechanism of their action is not known. Prednisone and prednisolone are most frequently used in the treatment of leukemia and lymphomas. Their action is highly similar to that of cortisone, but they cause somewhat less retention of fluid and salt. Prednisone is administered orally in doses of 50 to 100 mg. for adults and 50 mg. for children. This dosage is given daily in divided portions. Critically ill patients may be given ACTH by continuous intravenous infusion.

Temporary remissions are achieved with these hormones in an appreciable number of children who have acute leukemia. Less satisfactory results are obtained in adults. These hormones are also used to produce remissions in patients with Hodgkin's disease, lymphosarcoma, multiple myeloma, and chronic lymphatic leukemia. Some physicians reserve the use of hormones for the treatment of complications of lymphoma and chronic lymphatic leukemia, believing that true remissions are rarely achieved with hormones.

Side effects and toxic effects associated with overdosage are given in Chapter 21.

Hormones used in treating cancer of the breast include androgens such as testosterone propionate and fluoxymesterone. Estrogens such as diethylstilbestrol are sometimes administered, if the patient is well past menopause. Estrogens may increase the growth and metastasis of cancer in women who are still menstruating. Cancer of the prostate gland in the male is treated with an estrogen such as diethylstilbestrol or by a combination of an orchiectomy and administration of an estrogen.

A relatively high percentage of patients who have cancer of the breast or of the prostate show subjective improvement; they have less pain, their appetites improve, and, in general, they feel better. The malignant process may not have changed much, however, even though some patients receive benefit for a number of years. For side effects and dosage, see Chapter 26.

■ Radioactive isotopes

The radiations produced by radioactive isotopes are spoken of as alpha, beta, and gamma rays.* Alpha rays penetrate poorly into tissues, not more than a fraction of a millimeter. Beta rays penetrate tissues to the extent of a few millimeters, whereas gamma rays are highly penetrating. All radioactive isotopes represent a potential hazard to the patient and to all persons

*Radiation from radioactive materials is more correctly spoken of as alpha and beta particles and gamma rays.

who handle the preparations. The cytotoxic action of these preparations is the result of their ability to ionize molecules in a cell by injecting electrons. Tissues vary in sensitivity to ionizing radiations; cells with a short life and a high rate of reproduction are especially vulnerable. Cells of the body that are particularly affected therefore are the germinal cells of the ovaries and testes, bone marrow, lymphocytes, and the epithelial cells of the gastrointestinal tract. This helps to explain some of the symptoms of radiation sickness, such as nausea and vomiting, diarrhea, weakness, and reduction of cells in the circulating blood. Death may result from depression of the bone marrow, hemorrhage, or infection.

Among the radioactive isotopes used in medicine are sodium radiophosphate, radiogold colloid, and sodium radioiodide.

Sodium radiophosphate, U.S.P.

Sodium radiophosphate (^{32}P), when undergoing disintegration, emits only beta rays. The effects produced resemble those of radium or roentgen rays. It has a half-life of 14.3 days. Like ordinary phosphorus it is incorporated into the nucleoprotein of growing cells and reaches a high level in the rapidly proliferating and neoplastic cells. The cells of the bone marrow are thus subjected to considerable radiation, and large doses may result in severe depression.

Uses. This particular radioactive isotope has been used extensively in the treatment of polycythemia vera. The cells from which the red blood cells develop as well as other cellular elements of the bone marrow are depressed. It thus also helps to control excessive formation of white blood cells and thrombocytes and decreases the size of the enlarged liver or spleen. Remissions usually last for a period of months and occasionally for a year or more. They tend to be longer after the use of this preparation than after the use of x-ray therapy or other drugs.

Sodium radiophosphate (^{32}P) is also used to produce clinical remissions in chronic myelogenous and chronic lymphatic leukemia. Patients with acute leukemia are not benefited.

The drug is excreted in the urine, which necessitates careful disposal of this excretion.

Preparation, dosage, and administration. The following are the preparations available of sodium radiophosphate.

Sodium phosphate P^{32} solution, U.S.P. (^{32}P, Phosphotope). This radioisotope is administered intravenously or orally in aqueous solution. It is supplied in glass containers, but great care must be exercised in handling the material to prevent radiation burns from accidental contact with the skin. Its activity as indicated on the label is expressed in millicuries or microcuries.*

For polycythemia vera, the initial dose may vary from 2.5 to 5 mc. (millicuries). After 2 or 3 months an additional dose of 3 to 4 mc. may be indicated. For chronic myelogenous leukemia, the dosage is 1 to 2 mc. in a week. Dosage must be adjusted in accordance with the needs and response of the patient.

Sodium phosphate (^{32}P) injection, B.P., is suited for intravenous administration.

Side effects and toxic effects. The indications and contraindications for this form of therapy are much the same as those for x-ray irradiations. This preparation does not cause radiation sickness, but it can produce serious depression of the bone marrow. The chief untoward effects are leukopenia, anemia, and thrombocytopenia. Frequent blood examinations are indicated to detect developing states of toxicity. It is relatively inexpensive and usually produces fewer complications than a number of other effective agents.

Radiogold colloid

Gold Au^{198} injection, U.S.P. (Aurcoloid, Aureotope). This radioisotope emits both beta and gamma rays and has a half-life of 2.7 days. It is used to treat recurrent pleural effusion and ascites associated with metastatic malignancy. It does not cure the malignancy, but it contributes to the comfort of the patient by reducing the accumulation of fluid. It is administered by injection into the pleural or peritoneal cavity.

---

*One microcurie is the quantity of a radioactive material that is breaking down at the rate of approximately 2 million nuclear disintegrations per minute.

Mild radiation sickness may occur after 3 to 4 days, and a decrease in the number of white blood cells may take place.

This preparation offers a greater hazard to nursing personnel than ^{32}P because ^{198}Au emits the penetrating gamma rays whereas ^{32}P emits only beta rays.

Sodium radioiodide

Sodium iodide I^{131} solution, U.S.P. is presented in Chapter 21. It is used for palliative therapy of thyroid cancer.

■ Miscellaneous agents
Azathioprine (Imuran)

Azathioprine is related to mercaptopurine. The drug is used not so much in the treatment of leukemias as for prolonging the life of transplanted tissue. It is an immunosuppressive agent that tends to prevent or delay the rejection of transplanted organs by blocking cellular immunity and primary and secondary serum antibody responses. It is used primarily for maintaining renal homografts. It is presently being studied in relation to disorders caused by altered immunologic reactivity.

Azathioprine is well absorbed from the gastrointestinal tract. Oral doses vary from 2 to 5 mg. per kilogram of body weight daily. It may also be administered intravenously, 2 mg. per kilogram every 24 hours. Reduction of dosage is required to prevent dangerous cumulative effects. Allopurinol may be administered concomitantly since it interferes with enzymatic oxidation of azathioprine, thereby increasing the exposure of cells to azathioprine.

Side effects are usually mild. Toxic symptoms are those of bone marrow depression. Some patients have been treated with azathioprine for more than 2 years.

Vinblastine sulfate, U.S.P. (Velban)

The principal usefulness of vinblastine is as a supplemental or alternative drug in the treatment of Hodgkin's disease. It is also used for patients with choriocarcinoma who have become resistant to methotrexate and patients with breast cancer who have not responded to other forms of therapy. Thrombocytopenia is less severe with vinblastine than with alkylating agents.

Preparation, dosage, and administration. Vinblastine is prepared in 10-mg. vials for intravenous administration. It should not be given more often than once in 7 days. Initial dose is 0.1 mg. per kilogram of body weight; the dose is increased by increments of 0.05 mg. per kilogram until the white cell count falls to 3000 per cubic millimeter of blood, the tumor decreases in size, or a maximal dose of 0.5 mg. is reached. A maintenance dose of 10 mg. once or twice a month may be given. Weekly white cell counts should be done and the drug discontinued if the cell count falls below 3000.

Side effects and toxic effects. Nausea, vomiting, malaise, mental depression, paresthesia, headache, diarrhea, partial alopecia, anorexia, and stomatitis may occur. Excessive doses may permanently damage the central nervous system.

Vincristine sulfate, U.S.P. (Oncovin)

Although vincristine is chemically related to vinblastine, it exhibits different antitumor activity. It is used primarily in acute leukemias of children. Clinical studies report a 50% to 60% remission in children treated solely with vincristine; when vincristine is combined with corticosteroids, the remission rate rises to 85%. Vincristine is also used in treatment of other childhood neoplasms and in adults with Hodgkin's disease and lymphosarcoma.

Its neurotoxicity, which may cause permanent neural damage (loss of deep tendon reflexes and ataxia), limits its usefulness. In addition, duration of induced remissions is relatively short (4 to 16 weeks).

Preparation, dosage, and administration. Vincristine is supplied in powdered form in vials of 1 and 5 mg. to be diluted with 2 ml. distilled water for each milligram of vincristine. This drug is given intravenously, usually at weekly intervals. For children the usual dose is 2 mg. per square meter of body surface, or 0.05 mg. per kilogram of body weight initially with increments weekly to a maximum dose of 0.15 mg.

per kilogram of body weight. After remission, dosage is usually reduced. For adults the range of dosage is 0.025 to 0.075 mg. per kilogram of body weight weekly. The dose must be individually adjusted.

Dactinomycin, U.S.P. (actinomycin D, Cosmogen)

Dactinomycin is one of the actinomycins produced by a species of streptomyces that has been under reinvestigation for possible therapeutic uses. It has been found particularly useful for the control of metastases of Wilms' tumor (nephroblastoma). It is used alone or in combination with surgery or radiation. The precise mechanism of action of dactinomycin is unknown, but it evidently inhibits cellular activity and cell reproduction. Like other cytotoxic agents, it also inhibits the normal rapidly proliferating cells of the body.

The usual adult dose is 0.5 mg. intravenously for 5 days. This regimen may be repeated if toxicity does not develop; single doses of 2 mg. per week for 3 weeks have also been used. Drug dosages and regimens vary and depend on the individual patient and clinician.

The usual dose for children is 15 mg. per kilogram of body weight given intravenously for 5 days.

Side effects and toxic effects. Nausea and vomiting often occur during treatment. Toxic effects occur several days after treatment. Toxic effects include oral ulcerations, skin eruptions, diarrhea, and bone marrow depression with platelet depression. Extravasation produces severe local reactions.

Urethan, N.F. (ethyl carbamate); urethane, B.P.

Urethan was originally introduced into medicine as a hypnotic, but it is not considered useful for this purpose. In a manner that is not fully understood it interferes with cell division, possibly with the metabolism of nucleic acid. It depresses the bone marrow of patients with leukemia and inhibits cell division of neoplastic cells.

Uses. Urethan has been used in the treatment of leukemia; better results have been obtained in chronic myelogenous leukemia than in the lymphatic type. It is also used in the treatment of multiple myeloma. It is of no value in acute leukemia.

Preparation, dosage, and administration. Urethan is available for oral administration in 300-mg. tablets, enteric-coated, and as a 10% solution for intravenous administration. The usual daily dose is 3 Gm. It is administered after meals in three equal portions. The drug has a cumulative action.

Side effects and toxic effects. Side effects include nausea and vomiting, loss of appetite, and sometimes drowsiness and dizziness. The more toxic effects include severe leukopenia, anemia, hemorrhagic tendencies, and depression of the bone marrow. Disseminated, focal degeneration of the central nervous system and liver necrosis constitute serious complications from the use of urethan.

Nursing care measures for patients on antineoplastic therapy

Because of depression of antibody formation, red and white cell production, as well as anorexia, patients on antineoplastic therapy have lowered resistance and are prone to infections. Medical asepsis should be strictly enforced when caring for these patients.

These patients should be closely observed for bleeding tendencies—purpura or ecchymosis, bleeding gums, and so on. In addition, precautions should be taken to avoid physical trauma to the patient (bruising or undue pressure on body parts), since this may further enhance bleeding into body tissues.

Observation for neural involvement is also important; signs of paresthesia (numbness or tingling sensations), loss of reflexes, ataxia, and mental depression should be recorded and reported.

When the patient has stomatitis, he should be provided with foods that are highly nutritious, bland, and nonirritating. The patient should not be given foods that contain a high amount of acid (such as tomatoes or fresh fruit), are highly seasoned, or are mechanically or physically irritating (such as raw vegetables).

It is important that the nurse check frequently on the laboratory reports of the patient's blood examinations and liver tests and plan her nursing care accordingly.

Undoubtedly one of the most important nursing care aspects is that of providing emotional support to the patient with a destructive disease who is receiving drug therapy that is so physically distressing that it is also psychologically stressful. The patient needs to be assured that the symptoms arising from drug therapy will pass, the nausea and vomiting will subside, the hair will regrow after drug therapy is stopped, and so on. Patients receiving treatment with antineoplastic drugs should be prepared for the temporary symptoms that may occur. Such preparation tends to reduce the patient's emotional reaction to the distressing effects of this type of therapy. Necessary precautions should be taken when the patient is being treated with radioactive materials.

Questions

for study and review

1 Explain why antineoplastic drugs may destroy more normal cells than tumor cells.
2 Differentiate between an alkylating agent and an antimetabolite. Give an example of each.
3 Explain the important aspects of nursing care for patients on antineoplastic therapy.
4 What is the action for which radioactive isotopes are used? What aspects are important for the care of the patient receiving these drugs?
5 What is meant by emotional support? How can a nurse provide emotional support for an adult receiving antineoplastic therapy? For a child receiving antitumor or antileukemic therapy?

References

Alston, F., and others: Perfusion, Amer. J. Nurs. 60:1603, 1960.

A. M. A. Council on Drugs: New drugs, Chicago, 1967, American Medical Association.

American Cancer Society: Hormones and chemotherapy for cancer, Cancer 18:1517, 1965.

Ansfield, F. J.: Chemotherapy of disseminated solid tumors, Springfield, Ill., 1966, Charles C Thomas, Publisher.

Brockman, R. W.: Mechanisms of resistance to anticancer agents, Advances Cancer Res. 7:129, 1963.

Brodsky, I., Kohn, S. B., and Moyer, J. H.: Cancer chemotherapy, New York, 1967, Grune & Stratton, Inc.

Busch, H., and Lane, M.: Chemotherapy, Chicago, 1967, Year Book Medical Publishers, Inc.

Creech, O., Jr., and Krementz, E. T.: Cancer chemotherapy by perfusion, Advances Cancer Res. 6:111, 1961.

Crile, G., Jr.: Chemotherapy of cancer, Postgrad. Med. 28:242, 1960.

Dustin, P., Jr.: New aspects of the pharmacology of antimitotic agents, Pharmacol. Rev. 15:449, 1963.

Ellison, R. R.: Treating cancer with antimetabolites, Amer. J. Nurs. 62:79, 1962.

Golbey, R. B.: Chemotherapy of cancer, Amer. J. Nurs. 60:521, 1960.

Goth, A.: Medical pharmacology, ed. 6, St. Louis, 1972, The C. V. Mosby Co.

Greenwald, E. S.: Cancer chemotherapy, New York J. Med. 66:2532, 2670,1966.

Hiatt, H. H.: Cancer chemotherapy—present status and prospects, New Eng. J. Med. 276:157, 1967.

Hitchings, G., and Elion, G. B.: Chemical suppression of the immune response, Pharmacol. Rev. 15:365, 1963.

Johnson, I. S., and others: The vinca alkaloids: a new class of oncolytic agents, Cancer Res. 23:1390, 1963.

Karnofsky, D. A.: Triethylene melamine in treatment of lymphomas and leukemias, Med. Clin. N. Amer. 38:541, 1954.

Karnofsky, D. A.: Cancer chemotherapeutic agents, CA 11:58, 1961.

Knock, F. E.: Newer anticancer agents, Med. Clin. N. Amer. 48:501, 1965.

Modell, W., editor: Drugs of choice 1972-1973, St. Louis, 1972, The C. V. Mosby Co.

Moertel, C. G., and Reitemeir, R. J.: Experience with 5-fluorouracil in palliative management of advanced carcinoma of the gastrointestinal tract, Proc. Staff Meet. Mayo Clin. 37:520, 1962.

Neuss, N., and others: The vinca alkaloids, Advances Chemother. 1:133, 1964.

Oliverio, V. T., and Subrod, C. G.: Clinical pharmacology of the effective antitumor drugs, Ann. Rev. Pharmacol. 5:335, 1965.

Schwartz, S. A., and Perry, S.: Patient protection in cancer chemotherapy, J.A.M.A. 197:623, 1966.

Selawry, O. S., and Hananian, J.: Vincristine treatment of cancer in children, J.A.M.A. 183:741, 1963.

Sutou, W. W.: Chemotherapy in childhood cancer: an appraisal, Cancer 18:1585, 1965.

Venditti, J. M., and Goldin, A.: Drug synergism in antineoplastic chemotherapy, Advances Chemother. 1:397, 1964.

Wilson, H. E.: Leukemia, Amer. J. Nurs. 56:601, 1956.

25 Serums and vaccines

Agents containing antibodies: immune serums
Antigenic agents used to produce active immunity
Agents for cutaneous immunity tests
Allergens

Immunity is of two kinds, natural and acquired. If an individual is so constituted that the microbes causing a disease will not grow in his tissues or the toxins of those microbes are harmless to him, he is immune to that particular disease. Such immunity is called *natural immunity.*

When natural immunity is not effective and bacteria attack the tissues and live and grow at their expense, the body protects itself by preparing substances destructive to the particular organism making the attack. These substances are called antibodies. They are present in the blood and other body fluids and are carried to the point of infection by the blood and lymph. The antibodies gradually disappear from the blood, but the body cells have seemingly acquired the ability to continue to resist the same bacteria. Immunity resulting from these antibodies and the special ability to produce them is known as *acquired immunity.* Since the individual himself developed the antibodies, the immunity is known as *active immunity.* It is usually present after an attack of an infectious disease such as smallpox or typhoid fever and may be induced artificially by the injection of substances known as antigens. The antigen may be a suspension of living microorganisms, such as the vaccinia virus, or a suspension of dead microorganisms, such as typhoid vaccine. It may be an extract of the bodies of bacteria, as tuberculosis vaccine or a soluble toxin produced by bacteria, of which diphtheria toxin is an example.

Passive acquired immunity against certain diseases is secured by transferring to a person the blood serum of an animal that has been actively immunized by injections with the specific organisms or toxins of those diseases; it may also be secured by injection of the blood serum of an immune person. Immunity acquired in this way is called passive immunity because the body plays no part in the preparation of the antibodies. The body cells are not prepared to resist infection as they are in active immunity, and as the blood is renewed the antibodies are lost and the patient is in the same condition as if no antibodies had been administered.

514

Federal regulations control the manufacture and sale of these potent and, in some cases, dangerous products; firms are licensed under the supervision of the National Institutes of Health of the U. S. Public Health Service to import, export, or sell these biologic products in interstate commerce.

A number of these products may cause untoward reactions when they are administered as therapeutic or prophylactic agents. Individual sensitivities to animal products, especially horse serum and egg, are primarily responsible for adverse symptoms, and idiosyncrasies toward the products of bacterial metabolism are responsible for the others.

■ Agents containing antibodies: immune serums

An immune serum is the serum of a human being or an animal that has antibodies in the bloodstream.

Serum treatment consists of the transfer of the immune serum into the circulation of the patient. This immune serum contains specific antibodies that act upon disease germs.

There are two kinds of immune serums: the naturally produced and the antitoxic.

Naturally produced human serums

Naturally produced human serums are preparations obtained from normal blood, such as plasma, serum, or globulins or serum from patients who have recovered from a disease and retain the immune bodies in their blood serum.

Immune serum globulin, U.S.P.

This is a sterile solution of globulins that contains those antibodies normally present in adult human blood. Each lot of the preparation is derived from an original plasma or serum pool that represents at least 1000 individuals. It is thought to be as useful as convalescent serum and is more readily available. It is useful in the prevention of measles as well as in the treatment of that disease and for the prevention of infectious hepatitis.

The dosage varies with a number of factors. It is administered intramuscularly. The usual prophylactic dose of measles immune globulin, U.S.P., is 0.25 ml. per kilogram of body weight, and the usual dose for modification of measles is 0.02 to 0.05 ml. per kilogram.

Human gamma globulin

Human gamma globulin is available in a sterile solution for prevention or attenuation of measles and for the prevention of rubella, poliomyelitis, and infectious hepatitis.

Pertussis immune globulin, U.S.P.

This is the liquid or dried serum of blood obtained from donors who have recovered from pertussis (whooping cough) and who for the preceding 7 or more days have been without active clinical manifestations of the disease, or from donors immunized with pertussis vaccine. The usual intramuscular dose is 1.25 to 2.5 ml. repeated one or two times at 1-week intervals. Therapeutic dose is the same but injections are repeated at 1-day intervals.

Poliomyelitis immune globulin (human)

Poliomyelitis immune globulin is a sterile solution of globulins derived from pooled adult human blood. It is also obtained from placental blood.

It is used for the attenuation or prevention of poliomyelitis, measles, and infectious hepatitis. It is administered only by intramuscular injections, preferable in the buttock, using care to avoid accidental intravenous injection. The dosage varies considerably, depending on the purpose of the injection; for protection against paralytic poliomyelitis, the average dose to be injected is calculated on the basis of 0.31 ml. per kilogram of body weight.

Antitoxic serums of animal origin

Antitoxic serums are formed in the bodies of animals that have been actively immunized by a specific toxin. The animal is then bled and the serum separated from the blood. The serum is purified in most instances to remove inactive substances and to concentrate the antibodies. Antitoxins are given to neutralize the toxins produced in certain diseases.

515

Horses and rabbits are the animals most often utilized for artificial production of immune serums. One inoculation with the animal product may sensitize a patient to the blood components of that species, and subsequent inoculations of products from the same species may cause serum sickness or anaphylactoid shock. Tests for sensitivity to horse serum or other suspected antigens should be made on patients before injection of serums.

Diphtheria antitoxin, U.S.P., B.P.

Diphtheria antitoxin is a sterile solution of antitoxic substances obtained from the blood serum or plasma of a healthy animal immunized against diphtheria toxin. It contains not less than 500 antitoxic units per milliliter. It is used to confer passive immunity to the individual exposed to diphtheria or ill with the disease. The usual prophylactic dose is 1000 to 10,000 units and the therapeutic dose is 20,000 units, although it may range from 10,000 to 100,000 units. It is administered intramuscularly and intravenously.

Mixed gas gangrene antitoxin, B.P.

Mixed gas gangrene antitoxin is a sterile solution of antitoxic substances obtained from the blood of healthy animals that have been immunized against the toxins of *Clostridium perfringens, Clostridium septicum*, and *Clostridium oedematiens*. The usual initial therapeutic or prophylactic dose is the contents of one or more packages, given parenterally.

Tetanus antitoxin, U.S.P., B.P.

Tetanus antitoxin is prepared from the horse in much the same way as diphtheria antitoxin; the animal has been immunized against tetanus toxin or toxoid. The usual therapeutic dose is 10,000 to 100,000 units; the prophylactic dose range is 1500 to 10,000 units given subcutaneously or intravenously.

Tetanus and gas gangrene antitoxins, N.F.

This antitoxin is made by mixing the serums of horses individually immunized to the toxins of tetanus and gas gangrene. Each package of

the antitoxins contains not less than 1500 units of tetanus antitoxin and not less than 2000 units of each of the other component antitoxins *(Clostridium perfringens* and *Clostridium septicum)*. The usual dose is the contents of one or more packages, given parenterally, as a prophylactic measure.

Botulism antitoxin, U.S.P.

Botulism antitoxin is obtained from the serum of animals immunized with the toxin of *Clostridium botulinium,* type A, B, or E. It is available as pooled polyvalent antitoxin. Prompt injection of the antitoxin as soon as the diagnosis of botulism is made is essential to neutralize the toxins before they are *irreversibly bound* to receptor sites. Hypersensitivity tests should be made before injection. Usual dose is 20,000 to 43,000 units intravenously, which may be repeated at 2-to 4-hour intervals as necessary.

■ Antigenic agents used to produce active immunity
Vaccines

Vaccines are suspensions of either attenuated or killed microorganisms that are administered for the prevention or treatment of infectious diseases. The viruses for vaccines are commonly grown in living tissues, such as chick embryos; this type of vaccine is absolutely contraindicated in persons with a history of hypersensitivity to egg, chicken, or chicken feathers. Vaccines do not afford immediate protection. An interval of days or several weeks elapses between inoculation and the production of antibodies. Because of this, if there is danger of immediate infection and there is a serum available, a prophylactic dose of serum is first given to afford immediate protection, followed later by the vaccine injection to ensure a prolonged immunity.

Cholera vaccine, U.S.P., B.P.

Cholera vaccine is a sterile suspension of killed cholera vibrios *(Vibrio cholerae)* in isotonic sodium chloride solution or other suitable diluent. At the time of manufacture, cholera vaccine contains 8 billion cholera organisms in each milliliter of suspension. The usual subcutaneous dose is 0.5 ml., followed by another dose of 1 ml. 4 weeks later, making a total of two injections. If necessary, a 0.5-ml. dose may be repeated every 6 months.

Influenza virus vaccine, monovalent, type A (Asian strain)

This vaccine is a sterile suspension of formaldehyde-killed influenza virus, type A, grown in chick embryos. It is administered subcutaneously in doses of 1 ml. for adults and 0.5 ml. for children from 5 to 12 years of age. For children between 3 months and 5 years, the dose of 0.1 ml. given subcutaneously or intracutaneously is suggested. It is also suggested that these doses for infants and children be repeated within 1 or 2 weeks.

Influenza virus vaccine, U.S.P.; influenza vaccine, B.P.

This vaccine is a suspension of inactivated influenza virus cultivated in chick embryos. Influenza virus vaccine is used prophylactically to produce active immunization against influenza. The maximum amount of antibody formation occurs during the second week after vaccination, and the titer remains constant for about 1 month, after which there is a gradual decline. The vaccine should not be given to persons sensitive to material derived from chick or egg protein. Dosage for prophylactic active immunization is 0.5 to 1 ml. given subcutaneously, followed by 0.5 to 1 ml. in 2 months.

Mumps vaccine

Mumps vaccine is a sterile suspension of mumps virus grown in chick embryos, inactivated by ultraviolet light or formaldehyde. It is administered subcutaneously in two doses of 1 ml. each, given at an interval of 1 to 4 weeks.

Mumps virus vaccine, live, attenuated (Mumpsvax)

This is a preparation of live organisms of the Jeryl Lynn (B level) strain of mumps virus that has been grown in chick embryo tissue culture. It should be refrigerated at 2° to 8° C. and used within 8 hours after its reconstitution. Unused portions should be discarded. The vaccine should be protected from bright light and sunlight.

Duration of immunity has not been determined, but evidence indicates that good protection exists for 1 to 2 years after vaccination. It is not recommended for use in children under 1 year of age or in pregnant women.

Dosage is 0.5 ml. of vaccine given subcutaneously into the upper arm. Antibodies develop in about 28 days. Serious reactions are rare. Fever, redness, and soreness at the injection site may occur.

Pertussis vaccine, U.S.P., B.P. (whooping cough vaccine)

Pertussis vaccine is a sterile suspension of killed pertussis bacilli. Field studies show that this vaccine possesses sufficient antigenic value to afford considerable protection against whooping cough. It does not always prevent attacks of the disease, but it lowers the death rate from the disease. The usual dose is three injections of 0.5 to 1 ml. 4 to 6 weeks apart. Pertussis vaccine is given subcutaneously or intramuscularly.

Adsorbed pertussis vaccine, U.S.P.

Adsorbed pertussis vaccine is a sterile suspension of the killed pertussis bacilli of a strain or strains selected for high antigenic efficiency and adsorbed or precipitated by the addition of alum, aluminum phosphate, or aluminum hydroxide and resuspended. Because of the adsorption, there is a delay in absorption. The dose is the same as that for pertussis vaccine and is given intramuscularly.

Poliomyelitis vaccine, U.S.P.

Poliomyelitis vaccine is a sterile solution of inactivated poliomyelitis virus of types 1, 2, and 3, grown separately on cultures of renal tissue of monkeys. It is administered by subcutaneous or intramuscular injection. It is given in three doses of 1 ml. each; the second injection is given 4 to 6 weeks after the first, and the third injection, 7 months after the second dose.

517

Live oral poliovirus vaccine, U.S.P.; poliomyelitis vaccine (oral), B.P.

Attenuated live virus strains 1, 2, and 3 were introduced by Dr. Albert Sabin. This vaccine can be cultured in renal tissue cells of monkeys. Strains 1, 2, and 3 represent the three separate monovalent vaccines for the prevention of poliomyelitis caused by types 1, 2, or 3 of the poliovirus. This liquid vaccine is intended for oral administration only, not for injection. It is stored in the frozen state. When thawed for use, it is stored at refrigeration temperatures up to 50° F. and must be used within 7 days. The dosage varies with the potency of the pharmaceutical preparation used. Preparations of higher potency may be dropped on a lump of sugar before ingestion. Preparations of lower potency may be taken from a cup or teaspoon. For some infants it may be desirable to administer the drug by dropper. Each of the three types administered separately at intervals of 4 to 6 weeks and a fourth reinforcing dose 8 to 12 months later will ordinarily be expected to induce immunity. It is an active immunizing agent. Immunization should be done during the period of November to May when incidence of enterovirus infection is lowest, since this may result in failure of immunization.

Rabies vaccine, U.S.P., B.P.

This vaccine is a sterile freeze-dried suspension of killed rabies virus prepared from duck embryo or from brain tissue of rabbits infected with this virus. The virus obtained from the brain tissue is either attenuated or killed.

The administration of rabies vaccine may rarely result in paralysis of one or more extremities. Because paralysis is more likely to occur following undue exertion, it is suggested that activity be reduced during the vaccination period.

Rabies vaccine is injected subcutaneously for 14 to 21 days. When the killed virus vaccine is administered, 2 ml. of 5% suspension is given daily. When the attenuated virus vaccine is given, 1 ml. of the 5% suspension is administered.

Smallpox vaccine, U.S.P., B.P.

Smallpox vaccine was the first vaccine prepared. It consists of a glycerinated suspension of vaccinia viruses that have been grown in healthy vaccinated animals of the bovine family or in membranes of the chick embryo. It loses its potency if kept at a temperature above 8° C. Failure of vaccination is often caused by inactive virus and indicates that the vaccination should be repeated. The usual dose is the contents of one container, administered by multiple puncture of the skin. No bleeding or pain should occur with properly administered vaccine.

Typhoid and paratyphoid vaccine, U.S.P.; typhoid-paratyphoid A and B vaccine, B.P.

This vaccine is a suspension of killed typhoid and paratyphoid A and B bacilli in suspension in physiologic saline solution. The dose given subcutaneously is 0.5 ml., to be repeated three times; the interval between doses should be 7 to 28 days. With the use of the mixed vaccine, typhoid and paratyphoid infections may be entirely prevented. Within 12 hours a local reaction develops, and usually there is slight fever and a general lack of energy that lasts about a day. The patient should avoid activity as much as possible during that period. Immunity lasts for 2 to 4 years.

Typhoid vaccine, U.S.P.

Typhoid vaccine is a sterile suspension of killed typhoid bacilli in physiologic saline solution or other suitable diluent. The usual prophylactic subcutaneous dose is 0.5 ml., to be repeated two to three times at intervals of 28 days.

Typhus vaccine, U.S.P., B.P.

Typhus vaccine is a sterile suspension of the killed rickettsial organism of a strain or strains of epidemic typhus rickettsiae cultured in chick embryos. The usual dose, subcutaneously, for active immunization is 0.5 to 1 ml., to be repeated once 4 weeks later. The typhus vaccine listed in B.P. contains the killed murine typhus rickettsiae as well as the epidemic rickettsiae.

Tuberculosis vaccine, BCG vaccine, U.S.P.; bacillus Calmette-Guérin vaccine, B.P.

This is a freeze-dried preparation of the culture of an attenuated strain of the bovine tubercle bacillus.

The vaccine is used only in individuals who are negative in their reaction to the tuberculin test. Conversion of negative tuberculin-tested subjects to positive reactors after vaccination is usually considered presumptive evidence that immunity has developed similar to that which follows a naturally resisted or healed primary sensitizing infection. Physicians have a choice either of using the vaccine to reduce the risk of clinical disease or of not using the vaccine and having the tuberculin skin test for early diagnosis and as a guide to the need for further study and treatment.

Tuberculosis vaccine is usually administered by multiple puncture or by intradermal injection. The dose in drops varies, depending on the gauge of the needle or other openings from which the vaccine is deposited on the skin. For example, using the resuspended vaccine (50 mg. per milliliter) 4 drops from a 22-gauge needle would be used for the multiple-puncture method. For intradermal injection 0.1 ml. (equivalent to 0.2 mg.) is further diluted and injected as superficially as possible with a tuberculin syringe and a 26-gauge needle so that a wheal of 8 to 10 mm. is produced.

Yellow fever vaccine, U.S.P., B.P.

The U.S.P. preparation of yellow fever vaccine is the living virus of an attenuated strain of the yellow fever virus, prepared by culturing the microorganism in the chick embryo. It is dried from the frozen state; the powder is rehydrated immediately before use. It is administered subcutaneously, and the usual dose is 0.5 ml. A single dose provides protection for at least 6 years.

Live attenuated measles virus vaccine, U.S.P. (Lyovac Rubeovax)

Live, attenuated measles virus vaccine is prepared from measles virus grown in chick embryo tissue culture. It also contains streptomy-

cin, penicillin, and neomycin. The vaccine is lyophilized and must be reconstituted with the diluent before use.

Following a single dose, the vaccine induces an active form of immunity that lasts at least 4 years. Most children experience a febrile response following vaccination, which is generally mild but may be moderately severe.

This vaccine is available as an injectable suspension of 0.5 ml., which is administered subcutaneously in the upper arm. At the same time immune serum may be given intramuscularly in the other arm to reduce the severity of reaction to the live vaccine.

Adverse effects and contraindications. The live vaccine can reproduce most of the symptoms of measles, although it is a noncommunicable form of the disease. The simultaneous administration of immune globulin tends to reduce the incidence and severity of the reaction. The live vaccine should not be given to pregnant women or to those patients who suffer from severe or debilitating illnesses or whose resistance is lowered by steroids, irradiation, or toxic antineoplastic drugs. It is also contraindicated in patients who are allergic to some of the constituents of the vaccine preparation, such as egg proteins or the antibiotics that are present in the preparation.

Measles virus vaccine, inactivated (Vax-Measles-K)

Inactivated measles virus vaccine is obtained from monkey kidney tissue culture, and the virus is inactivated by formaldehyde. The suspension also contains neomycin sulfate, benzethonium chloride, and phenol red as indicator.

The vaccine may be given to infants as early as 3 to 4 months of age. It is recommended particularly for children who suffer from some debilitating disease such as cystic fibrosis, tuberculosis, asthma, or heart disease.

Measles virus vaccine, inactivated, should be administered by the intramuscular route. Dosage is 0.5 ml., with three doses given at monthly intervals. Most children are protected by this procedure for at least 6 months. Precautions are the same as those for other immunizing biologicals.

Toxoids

A toxoid is a toxin modified so that it is nontoxic but still antigenic. Formaldehyde is the agent generally used for the detoxification of toxins. Toxoids are supplied in the plain form and as precipitated and adsorbed preparations. Alum is used for the precipitated products, and aluminum hydroxide and aluminum phosphate are employed to provide an adsorption surface for toxoids. The precipitated and adsorbed products are absorbed more slowly by the circulating and tissue fluids of the body and excreted slowly; therefore, they provide higher immunizing titers than does plain toxoid.

Diphtheria toxoid, U.S.P.

Diphtheria toxoid is an aqueous solution of the products of the growth of *Corynebacterium diphtheriae*, so modified by formaldehyde that it has lost its toxic effects for guinea pigs but not its power to produce immunity. From 0.5 to 1 ml. is administered subcutaneously to produce active immunity in three doses with 4-week intervals between doses. A fourth reinforcing dose is given 6 to 12 months later. Since some general as well as local reactions are observed in adults and older children, a test dose should be given to determine sensitivity.

Adsorbed diphtheria toxoid, U.S.P.

Adsorbed diphtheria toxoid is a sterile suspension of diphtheria toxoid precipitated or adsorbed by the addition of aluminum hydroxide, aluminum phosphate, or alum. For active immunization it is given subcutaneously, 0.5 or 1 ml., two injections 4 weeks apart, and a third reinforcing dose 6 to 12 months later.

Diphtheria vaccine, B.P.

Diphtheria vaccine is prepared from diphtheria toxin and is indicated as alum-precipitated toxoid, purified toxoid aluminum phosphate, formol toxoid, and toxoid-antitoxin floccules. It is given subcutaneously or intramuscularly.

Tetanus toxoid, U.S.P.; tetanus vaccine, B.P.

Tetanus toxoid is a sterile solution of the products of growth of *Clostridium tetani*, so modified by formaldehyde that it has lost the ability to cause toxic effects in guinea pigs but retains the property of inducing active immunity. Usual subcutaneous dose is 0.5 or 1 ml. according to label specifications, repeated three times at intervals of 3 to 4 weeks.

Adsorbed tetanus toxoid, U.S.P.

This is tetanus toxoid precipitated or adsorbed by the addition of alum, aluminum hydroxide, or aluminum phosphate. Dosage for active immunization is two injections of 0.5 or 1 ml. at intervals of 4 to 6 weeks, given intramuscularly. This toxoid preparation is used as a booster for the actively immunized person who sustains superficial puncture wounds or lacerations that are potentially infected. For adequate protection the actively immunized person needs booster doses every 4 years.

Adsorbed diphtheria and tetanus toxoids and pertussis vaccine, U.S.P. (D.P.T.)

This preparation is a sterile mixture of diphtheria toxoid, tetanus toxoid, and pertussis vaccine adsorbed on aluminum hydroxide, aluminum phosphate, or alum. The antigens are combined in such proportion as to yield a mixture containing one immunizing dose of each in the total dosage prescribed on the label. The dosage is three injections of 0.5 or 1 ml., as specified on the label, 3 to 4 weeks apart, and a fourth reinforcing dose 12 months later. It is administered subcutaneously.

Adsorbed diphtheria and tetanus toxoids, U.S.P. (D.T.)

This preparation is a sterile suspension prepared by mixing suitable quantities of the adsorbed forms of diphtheria and tetanus toxoids. Two injections of 0.5 or 1 ml., as specified on the label, are given intramuscularly, 4 to 6 weeks apart, and a third reinforcing dose is given 6 to 12 months later. This combination is used for adults for whom the triple vaccine including pertussis is not recommended.

Diphtheria and tetanus toxoids; pertussis vaccine, U.S.P., B.P.

This preparation is administered subcutaneously or intramuscularly in doses of 0.5 or 1 ml. three times at intervals of 4 to 6 weeks, with a fourth reinforcing dose 12 months later.

Preparations of tetanus toxoid, diphtheria toxoid, and pertussis vaccine are available for separate administration. However, "triple toxoid" (a combination of the three) is preferred for childhood immunization.

Prior to the development of tetanus toxoid, passive immunization with tetanus antitoxin was the only effective method of tetanus prevention. Although there is an increasing number of actively immunized persons, the majority of our population still does not have this protection. Therefore, antitoxin is the most commonly used method of preventing tetanus in puncture wounds. Even for the patient who has been actively immunized, the physician may elect to use antitoxin for deep puncture wounds or for definitely contaminated compound fractures and extensive burns. Because tetanus antitoxin is obtained from horse serum, sensitivity tests are done prior to administration. Hospital policies may vary regarding who administers the serum. Nurses should administer horse serum under the supervision of a physician, and the patient should be observed closely for any untoward reaction.

■ Agents for cutaneous immunity tests
Diagnostic diphtheria toxin, U.S.P.; Schick test toxin, B.P.

Diagnostic diphtheria toxin is the toxin for the Schick test, which is done to determine the susceptibility of an individual to diphtheria. The toxin that is used is carefully standardized on human beings. The usual dose is 0.1 ml. This is injected intracutaneously, usually on the forearm. If the person is susceptible to diphtheria (if his blood does not contain a sufficient amount of antitoxin to protect him from the disease), a small area of redness, usually with

some infiltration, will occur at the point of injection in 24 to 28 hours. This is known as a positive reaction. It persists about 7 to 10 days and then fades slowly.

Old tuberculin, U.S.P., B.P. (Koch's tuberculin)

Old tuberculin is prepared by filtering a glycerin bouillon culture of the tubercle bacillus through a Berkefeld filter. It contains the toxins of the tubercle bacilli and is used largely in diagnosing tuberculosis. It is given by intracutaneous injection. If the patient has been infected with tuberculosis at some time, there is an area of redness, usually with a papule at the point of application of the tuberculin. The usual dose for diagnostic purposes is 0.1 ml. of a 1:1000 dilution. A reaction indicates that the patient has at some time been infected with tuberculosis but not necessarily that he has clinical tuberculosis.

Purified protein derivative of tuberculin, U.S.P., B.P.

This preparation is a sterile soluble purified product of the growth of the *Mycobacterium tuberculosis,* which is prepared in a special liquid medium free from protein. It is used chiefly as a diagnostic aid. Dosage is 0.01 to 5 μg. in 0.1 ml. of solution given intracutaneously.

■ Allergens

Allergy is a condition of hypersensitivity to certain antigens; these are usually proteins such as the pollens of plants, the proteins present in the hair or skin of animals or the feathers of fowl, and the proteins of food, serums, bacteria, and the like. The person who comes in contact with the proteins to which he is unusually sensitive develops such symptoms as sneezing, coryza, headache, fever, hives, and asthmatic attacks.

Allergens are extracts prepared from the proteins of various substances and are used to determine the susceptibility of the patient to proteins and to prevent and relieve the conditions caused by hypersensitivity.

The patient's susceptibility is tested by intradermal injection of the allergen. If the patient is sensitive to that particular protein, an urticarial wheal or elevated red spot results.

Prevention and treatment of allergy

When the identity of the particular protein causing the symptoms has been determined, the attacks of the disease may frequently be prevented by removing the causative factor—by omitting certain foods from the diet, by eliminating contact with cats and dogs, or by removing the hair mattress or the feather pillows, and so on, depending upon the cause of the allergy.

In hay fever the patient may have to be immunized against the specific pollens causing the attack. This process is called desensitization. It consists of a series of ten or more injections of dilute solutions of the specific pollens in graduated strengths given at intervals of about 5 days. The treatment should be begun sufficiently early so that the maximum dose is reached by the time of the first attack of the disease, and this dose is repeated once a week during the pollen season. Immunity lasts only about a year. In some cases of asthma and urticaria the patient may be desensitized to the specific proteins causing their symptoms. Antihistaminic drugs have become prominent in the treatment of allergic manifestations since it was recognized that histamine or a histamine-like substance is released in allergic reactions. For further discussion see Chapter 12. Cortisone, hydrocortisone, and related compounds have been found to provide symptomatic relief of allergy and allergic manifestations. They should not be used, however, for minor allergic conditions such as hay fever because of their serious side effects.

Questions

for study and review

1 Differentiate between an immune serum, a toxoid, and a vaccine. Give an example of each.
2 Differentiate between active and passive immunity.
3 Explain the difference between a toxoid and an antitoxin.
4 What precautions are necessary when immunization or vaccination is contemplated?

References

Advisory Committee on Immunization Practices of the U.S. Public Health Service: Immunization against typhoid, Ann. Intern. Med **65**:1300, 1966.

Advisory Committe on Immunization Practices of the U.S. Public Health Service: Smallpox vaccination, Ann. Intern. Med. **66**:358, 1967.

Anderson, G., Arnstein, M., and Lester, M.: Communicable disease control, New York, 1962, The Macmillan Company.

Anderson, R.: Smallpox immunization, Practitioner **195**:281, 1965.

Browne, C. M.: Pertussis immunization, Practitioner **195**:292, 1965.

Butler, N. R., and Benson, P. F.: Measles immunization, Practioner **195**:284, 1965.

Cahill, K. M.: Yellow fever, New York J. Med. **63**:2990, 1963.

Cannon, D. A.: Poliomyelitis immunization, Practitioner **195**:302, 1965.

Cole, L.: Tetanus immunization, Practitioner **195**:296, 1965.

Council on Drugs: Current status of measles immunization, J.A.M.A. **194**:1237, 1965.

Cox, C. A., Knowelden, J., and Sharrod, W. J.: Tetanus prophylaxis, Brit. Med. J. **2**:1360, 1963.

Davenport, F. M.: Factors of importance in the control of influenza, Med. Clin. N. Amer. **47**:1185, 1963.

Donaldson, A. W.: Current status of national immunization programs, Med. Clin. N. Amer. **51**:831, 1967.

Fox, J. P.: Immunization against epidemic typhus, Amer. J. Trop. Med. **5**:464, 1956.

International Conference on Tetanus: Prevention of tetanus, Ann. Intern. Med. **65**:1079, 1966.

Rubbo, S. D.: New approaches to tetanus prophylaxis, Lancet **2**:449, 1966.

Sabin, A. B.: Oral poliovirus vaccine: history of its development and prospects for eradication of poliomyelitis, J.A.M.A. **194**:872, 1965.

Von Magnus, H.: Measles vaccines present status, Med. Clin. N. Amer. **51**:599, 1967.

Sex hormones and other drugs that act on the reproductive system

26

Drugs that affect the myometrium
Drugs that increase uterine motility

Sex hormones that affect the ovaries
Pituitary gonadotropic hormones
Gonadotropic hormones of placental origin
Ovarian hormones

Male sex hormones

The reproductive system of the female consists of the ovaries, the uterine (fallopian) tubes, the uterus, and the vagina; in the male, it consists of the testes, the seminal vesicles, the prostate gland, the bulbourethral glands, and the penis. The reproductive organs of both the male and the female are largely under the control of the endocrine glands, especially the pituitary gland. The ovaries and testes are known as gonads and not only produce ova and sperm cells but also form endocrine secretions that initiate and maintain the secondary sexual characteristics in men and women. When gonadal function diminishes and finally ceases, the secondary sexual characteristics gradually change and reproductive function ceases. The period of change is marked in women by the cessation of menses and is known as the menopause. In men, diminution of output of the sex hormone also occurs in later life, but it is less clearly definable and is sometimes called the male climacteric.

Drugs that affect the myometrium

The uterus is a highly muscular organ that exhibits a number of characteristic properties and activities. The smooth muscle fibers extend longitudinally, circularly, and obliquely in the organ. The uterus has a rich blood supply, but when the uterine muscle contracts, blood flow is diminished. Profound changes occur in the uterus during pregnancy. The uterus of women increases in weight during pregnancy from about 50 Gm. to approximately 1000 Gm. Its capacity increases tenfold in length, and new muscle fibers may be formed. These changes are accompanied by changes in response to drugs. Since the uterine smooth muscle responds sensitively to many drugs, the uterus of virgin guinea pigs or rabbits is used in standardizing a number

523

of drugs that have a stimulating action on smooth muscle.

The uterus, both in situ and when excised, contracts rhythmically. Both pendular and peristaltic movements may be seen. In nongravid animals, peristaltic movements are relatively slight and, just as in the intestine, pauses occur between peristaltic contractions. These vary greatly with the condition of sexual activity. Movements are depressed early in pregnancy but increase later. Parturition is accomplished by powerful peristaltic waves, which cause labor pains.

Drugs that act upon the uterus include (1) those that increase the motility of the uterus and (2) those that decrease uterine motility.

■ Drugs that increase uterine motility
Oxytocics

In the human being, stimulation of either the sympathetic or the parasympathetic division of the autonomic nervous system may bring about increased uterine contractions. However, the response of the human uterus to cholinergic or adrenergic drugs is not dependable. There are drugs that exert a selective action on the smooth muscle of the uterus; these drugs are known as oxytocics. The ones used most are alkaloids of ergot and extracts from the secretion of the posterior pituitary gland, although there are many other drugs that may exhibit some effect on uterine motility.

Ergot

Ergot is the dried sclerotium (mycelium) of the parasitic fungus *Claviceps purpurea*, which grows on many species of grain but especially on rye, where it forms long black bodies on the ears of the rye. It is especially prevalent when the weather is moist and warm. It grows in the grain fields of North America and Europe. Ergot was known as an obstetric herb to midwives long before it was recognized by the medical profession.

Lysergic acid

Active constituents. Both levorotatory and dextrorotatory alkaloids have been isolated from ergot, but only the levorotatory compounds are pharmacologically significant. These are derivatives of a substance called lysergic acid. The basic structure of the diverse and complex group of alkaloids of ergot is that of the substance lysergic acid. The individual ergot alkaloids are all compounds in which substitutions have been made at the carboxyl group.

The entire large group of individual alkaloids derived from ergot can be further divided into three groups: the ergotamine group, the ergotoxine group, and the ergobasine group. Members of each group have certain common chemical features and certain common pharmacologic actions. The first two have a peptide chain substituted at the carboxyl group of lysergic acid, whereas alkaloids of the ergobasine group are chemically simpler and contain a relatively small side chain, that of an amino alcohol. In ergonovine, alaninol is linked to lysergic acid (see structural formula).

Ergonovine

Action and result. All three groups of the alkaloids of ergot increase the motor activity of the uterus. Some of them also have other pharmacologic actions, which are referred to elsewhere under appropriate headings (see Index for uses of ergotamine). For convenience the other effects will be classified here.

Ergotamine and ergotoxine groups. The major groups of alkaloids of ergot are contrasted and compared as follows.

Uterus. Ergotoxine* and ergotamine exert their most powerful effect on the uterus. The mechanism of action is a direct muscular stimulation since it occurs in the uterus after removal as well as when it is in the body. Small doses produce normal uterine contractions that may be spastic in nature. A gravid uterus is more sensitive to the alkaloids of ergot than a nongravid or immature uterus. Ordinary therapeutic doses of the alkaloids produce an effect in the gravid or parturient uterus that is unaccompanied by side actions. Very high doses can cause sustained contracture.

Circulatory system. The action on blood vessels, particularly the smaller vessels, is peripheral vasoconstriction. This effect is of value in reducing uterine hemorrhage after childbirth. When ergotamine and related alkaloids are administered in large doses, there follows a definite rise in blood pressure. The effect on blood pressure is less powerful than that of epinephrine, but it lasts longer.

Both ergotamine and ergotoxine are capable of damaging the capillary epithelium, which in turn may give rise to thrombosis and possible gangrene. Man is particularly sensitive to this toxic effect of the alkaloids of ergot.

Sympathetic nervous system. Ergotamine and ergotoxine act as autonomic blocking agents to paralyze the effector cells and make them nonreponsive to epinephrine. This action is not significant in man, provided the dosage remains within therapeutic limits.

Ergobasine group—ergonovine. Ergonovine resembles ergotamine and ergotoxine in its effect upon the uterus, although it appears to have a greater selective action on uterine muscle and produces its effects more rapidly. Ergotamine and ergotoxine are poorly and irregularly absorbed from the gastrointestinal tract, whereas oral doses of ergonovine are readily absorbed; it is therefore effective in smaller doses and weaker concentrations than the other alkaloids. Because small doses are effective and because the parturient uterus is especially sensitive to

*When the term *ergotoxine* is used, reference is being made to the alkaloids ergocristine, ergocornine, and ergokryptine.

ergonovine, side actions rarely accompany its use in obstetrics. Its duration of action is thought to be somewhat less than that of the other two alkaloids.

Ergonovine differs from ergotoxine and ergotamine in that it appears to stimulate the effector cells connected with adrenergic nerves rather than paralyze them. In therapeutic doses it produces little or no rise in blood pressure, and although it shares with the other alkaloids the ability to cause gangrene, it appears to be definitely less toxic than ergotamine and ergotoxine. Ergonovine is the preparation of ergot most used in obstetrics.

Uses. Preparations of ergot, especially ergonovine and methylergonovine, are used primarily to promote involution of the uterus and to prevent or control postpartum hemorrhage. Routine use of oxytocics during the first and second stages of labor is not recommended. The contractions that these drugs produce are such that the life of the mother and the fetus may be endangered by their use.

Ergotamine tartrate has been advocated for the relief of migraine headache and for relief of excessive itching associated with jaundiced conditions (see p. 493).

Preparation, dosage, and administration. The following are preparations used in obstetrics. Ergonovine is effective by oral, sublingual, rectal, intravenous, or intramuscular administration.

Ergonovine maleate, **U.S.P.** **(Ergotrate Maleate);** *ergometrine maleate,* **B.P.** This drug is available in 0.2-mg. tablets for oral administration and insolution for intramuscular or subcutaneous injection, 0.2 mg. per milliliter. The usual oral dose is 0.2 to 0.4 mg. repeated two or three times daily for a period of 2 to 3 days. Some physicians prescribe 0.2 mg. every 4 hours for six doses, starting immediately after delivery. The usual dose for parenteral administration is also 0.2 to 0.4 mg. Prolonged therapy should be avoided.

Methylergonovine maleate, **U.S.P.** **(Methergine Maleate);** *methylergometrine maleate,* **B.P.** This agent is a synthetic oxytocic and is available in 0.2-mg. tablets for oral administration and in solution for parenteral administration, 0.2 mg. per milliliter. The usual dose is 0.2 mg. This preparation is chemically related to ergonovine, but it is more potent and its action is said to be more prolonged. It has less tendency to cause an elevation of blood pressure and is preferred for patients who are threatened with eclampsia or in cases in which the condition is actually present. Although toxic effects are not ordinarily encountered, they can occur.

Side effects and toxic effects. Toxic effects of acute poisoning seen after the administration of ergonovine and similar alkaloids usually result from stimulation of the central nervous system and include nausea and vomiting, tremor, weakness, excitement, convulsive seizures, dilated pupils, and rapid pulse.

The ergotamine and ergotoxine alkaloids usually produce symptoms of circulatory disturbances before they produce effects in the nervous system. Such symptoms include tingling, itching, coldness of the skin, and rapid weak pulse. Other symptoms are thirst, headache, nausea, vomiting, dizziness, and diarrhea and abdominal cramps. They may develop after ingesting large doses in an attempt to induce abortion. It has been observed that increased sensitivity to alkaloids of ergot seems to accompany hepatic disease and febrile and septic states.

Chronic ergotism is now of rare occurrence where modern milling methods are used, but before the cause was known, it was frequent in wet seasons and times of poor harvest because of the ergot in the grain.

Chronic ergotism may occur in two forms: gangrenous and convulsive. Gangrene results from prolonged constriction of the blood vessels, which at the same time fill with a hyaline substance that blocks the circulation. Prolonged constriction of cerebral blood vessels results in degenerative changes in the brain, while constriction in retinal vessels may cause blindness. The most striking symptom of ergotism is the dry, painless gangrene of some part of the body such as fingers or toes. The part affected first becomes cold, numb, and dark in color and then shrivels up and drops off without pain or bleeding. These symptoms occur because the blood supply to the part is shut off by the constriction

of the vessels. The disease was once called "St. Anthony's fire" or "hell fire." The cure at that time was a pilgrimage to the shrine of St. Anthony, hence the name.

Treatment of ergot poisoning requires complete withdrawal of the medication, the use of symptomatic measures such as the use of vasodilator drugs and sedatives, and sometimes the injection of calcium gluconate to relieve muscular pain.

Posterior pituitary hormone

The pituitary gland is a small ductless gland situated in a small cup-shaped depression in the sphenoid bone at the base of the brain and consists of two lobes, the anterior and the posterior, and an intermediate portion called the pars intermedia. Extracts are obtained from the posterior lobe of the pituitary glands of cattle and sheep, and when injected they produce the following effects: (1) stimulation of uterine muscle (oxytocic effect), (2) promotion of water absorption in the tubules of the kidney (antidiuretic effect), and (3) constriction of peripheral blood vessels (pressor effect).

A great advance in the pharmacology of the posterior lobe has been the recent identification and chemical analysis of the two major hormones obtained from the gland in pure form. These compounds, oxytocin and vasopressin, are both peptides, each containing eight amino acids. After their isolation and determination it proved possible to synthesize them chemically. Availability of the only oxytocic and vasopressor pituitary hormones in pure form has clarified a number of uncertainties about their action and has also encouraged better-controlled therapeutic use. It is now known, for example, that there is a certain overlap of pharmacologic action in the pure preparations: pure oxytocin has some vasopressor activity and vice versa. Vasopressin is also the antidiuretic hormone, its antidiuretic potency being much more marked than its pressor potency. Although clinicians still use mainly the cruder preparations of oxytocic and vasopressor activity, it may be expected that eventually the pure compounds will replace the present extracts.

Action and result. Posterior pituitary injection

and particularly oxytocin stimulate the uterine muscle and produce rhythmic contractions. The action in the human being is modified by the pregnant or nonpregnant state as well as by the stage of pregnancy. Sensitivity to the extract increases as the pregnancy progresses. The effects of the pituitary preparation are produced rapidly as compared to ergot, which acts more slowly.

Posterior pituitary preparations stimulate certain contractile tissues in the mammary gland and promote the emptying of the milk into the larger ducts and reservoirs and contribute to milk ejection. They do not affect the total amount of milk formed over a period of time.

A transient fall in blood pressure is sometimes observed after the administration of oxytocin, which is thought to be the result of myocardial depression. Fortunately it does not last long.

Uses. Posterior pituitary injection and oxytocin injection are used to increase contractions of the uterus at the time of childbirth. Oxytocin may be used either to initiate contractions or to increase the force and rate of existing contractions. They may be used in a long labor when normal contractions do not bring about expulsion of the fetus or to constrict the uterus and decrease hemorrhage after delivery of the placenta. Oxytocics should be used with caution and avoided when the cervix is not thoroughly effaced and easily dilatable. They are usually contraindicated during the first stage of labor. If used when the cervix is undilated and rigid, severe laceration and excessive trauma are likely to result. Ill-advised use of oxytocics is thought to contribute to high maternal and infant mortality rates.

Preparation, dosage, and administration. The following are preparations available.

Posterior pituitary injection, **N.F.** This preparation is available in ampules containing 0.5 and 1 ml. of sterile aqueous solution prepared from the pituitary glands of domestic animals. The official preparation possesses in each milliliter the activity equivalent to 10 U.S.P. units and contains a mixture of hormones. The usual dose is 0.3 to 1 ml. This

preparation is sometimes known as obstetric Pituitrin. It is administered subcutaneously.

Oxytocin injection, **U.S.P., B.P. (Pitocin).** This solution is available in 0.5- and 1-ml. ampules. It is a sterile aqueous solution of the oxytocic principle, which is the preparation of choice when an oxytocic effect rather than a pressor effect is desired. Dosage depends upon the stage of labor. The usual intramuscular postpartum dose is 0.5 to 1 ml. Each milliliter of this preparation contains the equivalent of 10 U.S.P. units. When used to induce labor, 1 ml. in 1000 ml. of 5% dextrose in water may be given slowly by intravenous drip. This method of administration must be used cautiously.

Synthetic oxytocin **(Syntocinon).** This preparation is available in 0.5- and 1-ml. ampules. Dosage and administration are the same as those for oxytocin injection.

Preparations of vasopressin are presented on p. 455.

Side effects and toxic effects. In the human being the response of the myometrium to posterior pituitary extracts is variable and is influenced by many factors. Overdosage may produce uterine tetany followed by increasing clonic contractions. Uterine rupture and fetal death can result. These preparations are contraindicated or given with great caution to patients with cardiovascular disease, to those who have previously had a cesarean section, when there is a malpresentation of the fetus, or when rupture of the uterus threatens for any reason at all.

Patients receiving oxytocin or related drugs during labor should be under constant observation. This means the blood pressure should be taken frequently, careful and periodic check of the fetal heart tones should be made, and the strength and duration of the uterine contractions should be noted. Prolonged contractions of the uterus result in diminished blood flow and decreased oxygen for the fetus.

■ Drugs that decrease uterine motility

There are times when the inhibition of uterine contractions is indicated, as when a patient begins premature labor or when uterine tone is high and contractions are unusually frequent

527

and uncoordinated. Drugs that combat these conditions include certain depressants of the central nervous system and antispasmodics.

Analgesics and sedatives

Large doses of opiates, general anesthetics, and barbiturates tend to decrease uterine motility. Average doses of barbiturates probably have little or no effect. Morphine is effective because it not only relieves pain but also alters the patient's emotional reaction to pain, allaying fear and anxiety. Methadone is excellent to relieve pain, but it has no effect on fear and anxiety. Meperidine as compared to morphine has less effect on respiration, although this may not be so when equianalgesic doses of the two drugs are compared. Its analgesic potency is somewhere between that of morphine and codeine. Codeine, especially when combined with aspirin, is useful to relieve the discomfort associated with repair work on the perineum, but it has little use during the course of labor. Promethazine hydrochloride is utilized clinically for obstetric sedation. It relieves apprehension and potentiates the action of drugs such as morphine sulfate and meperidine hydrochloride, permitting a reduction in their dosage.

Antispasmodics

Antispasmodics reduce muscle spasm or relax muscles. They include drugs that exhibit various mechanisms of action and include a number of depressants of the nervous system that act by decreasing reflex hyperactivity. In addition, there are several other agents that are used.

Relaxin (Releasin)

Relaxin is a naturally occurring substance that, for commercial purposes, is extracted from the ovaries of pregnant sows. It exhibits an ability to inhibit uterine contractions. Its use as an agent to prevent the onset of premature labor has been recommended, but its value for this form of therapy has not been established. The results of a number of experiments on animals led to its clinical trial as a drug to soften and relax the cervix and thus shorten the course

of labor. Differences of opinion exist about its merits as such an agent. It has also been proposed for the relief of dysmenorrhea. Only time and careful research studies can determine the true worth of this preparation.

Preparation, dosage, and administration. Relaxin is available in solution, 20 mg. per milliliter, for intramuscular and intravenous injection. It is given in doses of 20 to 40 mg. When administered intravenously, it is given slowly by intravenous drip in 250 to 500 ml. of sterile diluent.

Side effects and toxic effects. Relaxin contains a pork protein and may induce hypersensitivity in patients; this may range in severity from chills to acute anaphylaxis after intravenous administration.

Lututrin (Lutrexin)

Lututrin is a protein-like substance that is extracted from the corpus luteum of the ovaries of the sow.

Action. This drug is related to relaxin and decreases muscular contractions of the human uterus.

Uses. Lututrin is used in the treatment of severe functional dysmenorrhea. Its value in the treatment of premature labor and threatened abortion is uncertain.

Preparation, dosage, and administration. Lututrin is available in tablets containing 2000 units each, the units being determined by the assay of the relaxing effect on the uterus of the guinea pig. For dysmenorrhea, initial doses of 4000 to 6000 units are given prior to the onset of symptoms and followed by 4000 to 6000 units every 3 to 4 hours as needed. As much as 50,000 units have been administered without observable untoward effects. Clearly defined dosage schedules for prevention of premature labor and abortion have not been agreed upon.

Magnesium sulfate, U.S.P., B.P.

Many students will think of magnesium sulfate as a saline cathartic only. The fact of the matter is that when this salt is administered parenterally it not only will depress the central nervous system but also depress all forms of muscular tissue (smooth, skeletal, and cardiac).

Uses. Magnesium sulfate is effective to counteract uterine tetany that may occur after large doses of oxytocin or when the myometrium is contracting abnormally. Because of its depressant effect on the central nervous system and skeletal muscle, it is employed in the treatment of eclampsia when patients are threatened with convulsive seizures.

Preparation, dosage, and administration. Magnesium sulfate is administered intramuscularly and sometimes intravenously. For rapid effect an intravenous dose of 20 ml. of a 20% solution may be given. Effects last approximately 30 minutes. It is poorly absorbed after oral administration.

Side effects and toxic effects. Parenteral administration of magnesium sulfate is not without attendant danger. Respiratory depression and failure can occur. Abrupt injection of large doses can cause cardiac arrest. The patient receiving magnesium sulfate parenterally should never be left alone. An injection of calcium gluconate (10% solution) is an effective antidote since it counteracts the effect of magnesium sulfate on muscle tissue. Artificial respiration may also be indicated.

Sex hormones that affect the ovaries

The hormones concerned with ovarian function include the *anterior pituitary hormones*, which are required for the normal development and function of the gonads; the *gonadotropic hormones* of placental origin; and the *ovarian hormones* themselves. The ovarian hormones include the naturally occurring steroids, the synthetic and partly synthetic steroids, and the nonsteroid compounds, such as stilbestrol, which have an ovarian hormone-like function.

A similar group of hormones plays corresponding roles in regulating gonadal growth and function in the male.

■ Pituitary gonadotropic hormones

The endocrine gland that exerts the chief gonadotropic influence in the body is the anterior lobe of the pituitary gland. How many hormones are made by this gland is uncertain, but three are believed to have an effect on the ovary. One stimulates the development of the graafian follicle and is known as the follicle-stimulating hormone (FSH). Another, the luteinizing hormone (LH) or interstitial cell-stimulating hormone (ICSH), promotes the growth of the interstitial cells in the follicle and the formation of the corpus luteum. A third hormone is known as the luteotropic hormone (LTH); it is probably identical with the lactogenic hormone. The follicle-stimulating hormone initiates the cycle of events in the ovary. Under the influence of both FSH and LH the graafian follicle grows, matures, secretes estrogen, ovulates, and forms the corpus luteum. The LTH promotes the secretory activity of the corpus luteum and the formation of progesterone. In the absence of LTH the corpus luteum undergoes regressive changes and fails to make progesterone.

In the male, FSH acts only on the seminiferous tubules and promotes the formation of sperm cells. ICSH stimulates the interstitial cells in the testes and promotes the formation of androgen.

The clinical use of the pituitary gonadotropic hormones has been handicapped by the lack of sufficiently refined preparations. Commercial preparations often contain other proteins and inert substances that make injections painful and make allergic reactions possible.

Some degree of success has accompanied the use of these gonadotropic extracts when used in the treatment of amenorrhea, Frohlich's syndrome, sterility, undescended testicle (cryptorchidism), and hypogenitalism. Lack of success in treatment can sometimes be attributed to the fact that when a deficiency of one of the pituitary hormones exists, it is more than likely that there is a deficiency in a number of others that may not be of a direct gonadotropic nature.

There are no official gonadotropic preparations from the anterior pituitary gland.

529

■ Gonadotropic hormones of placental origin

Gonadotropic substances are formed by the placenta during pregnancy in the human being and in certain animals. Human chorionic gonadotropic hormone differs from pituitary gonadotropins, both biologically and chemically. It produces little of the follicle-stimulating effect but affects principally the growth of the interstitial cells and the secretion of luteal hormone. In women, it is capable of prolonging the luteal phase of the menstrual cycle. Its normal role seems to be to enhance and to prolong the secretion of the corpus luteum during early pregnancy. It does not initiate the formation of corpus luteum, however.

In the male, it stimulates the interstitial cells of the testes, causing them to increase production of androgen, which in turn promotes the growth and development of accessory sex organs.

Chorionic gonadotropin has also been found in the blood of pregnant mares, but only the human chorionic gonadotropin is used therapeutically because, since it is of human origin, it does not induce the formation of antihormones in the patient. It is believed to be the substance that forms the basis of some pregnancy tests (Friedman and Aschheim-Zondek). This substance was originally thought to come from the anterior pituitary gland, but it is now recognized as coming from the placenta. The reason that the urine of pregnancy can be used to test for the gravid state is that the laboratory animal used for this test is usually a rodent, and in these animals the chorionic gonadotropic factor stimulates growth of the follicle as well as the corpus luteum.

Uses. Gonadotropic hormones are used in the treatment of cryptorchidism when there is no anatomic obstruction to prevent testicular descent. It is being used experimentally in the treatment of hypogonadism and functional uterine bleeding, but there is considerable difference of opinion about its value.

Preparation, dosage, and administration. The following is the preparation available of a gonadotropic hormone.

Chorionic gonadotropin, U.S.P., B.P. (Follutein, Entromone). Chorionic gonadotropin is a water-soluble gonadotropic substance obtained from the urine of pregnant women. It is a glycoprotein containing about 12% galactose. The dosage used in treating cryptorchidism is 500 to 1000 international units two times a week. Therapy should be discontinued if there are signs of precocious maturity.

■ Ovarian hormones

The ovaries are the female sex glands that are situated on either side of the uterus. They not only develop and periodically discharge the ripened ova but also secrete the ovarian hormones.

One of the ovarian hormones is made by the cells of the graafian follicle and is referred to as the follicular hormone. The other is the luteal hormone made by the cells of the corpus luteum. Normal development and activity of the reproductive organs are dependent in part on the right state of balance between these hormones. They are secreted in sequence under the influence of the gonadotropins of the anterior pituitary gland.

Estrogens

The follicular hormone is responsible for the development of the sex organs at puberty and for the secondary sex characteristics—the growth and distribution of hair, texture of skin, distribution of body fat, growth of the breasts, and character of the voice and the maintenance of these characteristics throughout adult life. The follicular hormone apparently exists not as an entity but as a number of related polymorphic forms that differ in their activity. These substances, which exhibit similar estrogenic activity, are called estrogens. The group includes both the natural estrogens and the synthetic substances that have similar effects in the body.

Chemistry. The naturally occurring estrogens are steroids in which ring "A" (ring at the lower left of the accompanying formula) is a benzene (aromatic ring) in place of the saturated ring of the other major steroids. (Compare formulas with those of the adrenal steroids in Chapter

21.) The primary natural estrogen believed to be secreted by the follicle is estradiol (estrin), so named for the two hydroxyl groups.

Estradiol

Estrone

Both estrone (Theelin) and estradiol are naturally occurring estrogens. In the body, estrone can be converted into estradiol and vice versa. There are a number of other naturally occurring estrogens.

The synthetic estrogens include both *steroid* and *nonsteroid* forms. The steroid forms include modifications of the naturally occurring steroid estrogens so as to increase potency (ethinyl estrogens). The more important group, however, consists of the nonsteroid synthetic estrogen compounds that do not closely resemble the natural estrogens chemically yet have remarkably similar pharmacologic action. A typical member of this group is diethylstilbestrol.

Diethylstilbestrol

Natural estrogenic substances are found in a variety of places in both plants and animals. They are found in the blood of both sexes, testicular fluid, feces, bile, and the urine of pregnant women and pregnant mares. Estrogens have also been found and isolated from the adrenal gland. These substances vary somewhat chemically in accordance with the source from which they are obtained.

Pharmacologic action and result. When estrogenic substances (natural or synthetic) are injected into immature animals such as rats, they are capable of hastening sexual maturity and producing estrus. In these animals the vaginal epithelium changes after the administration of estrogens and appears as it does in mature animals. This is the basis of bioassay and standardization of preparations of these substances.

When estrogens are administered in doses that compare favorably with the amount normally secreted by the ovaries, the effect is like that produced by the natural secretion of these glands. When estrogens are administered in larger amounts than these, however, other effects may be produced.

One effect is that of inhibiting hyperactivity of the pituitary gland. Increased activity of the pituitary gland is believed to occur at menopause or after surgical removal of the ovaries. This may cause symptoms such as flushing, sweating, and hot flashes. The administration of estrogen prevents hyperactivity of the pituitary gland at least temporarily or while the estrogen continues to be given.

When estrogens are administered, the same changes occur in the myometrium and endometrium as occur naturally; the myometrium and endometrium proliferate (cells reproduce rapidly). When the estrogen is withdrawn, uterine bleeding frequently occurs. It sometimes occurs even with continued administration of the estrogen.

Estrogens naturally stimulate the development of the breasts, that is, the development of the ducts in the gland and possibly both the ducts and the alveoli. Whether this occurs as a direct action on the mammary gland or because of indirect effect on the pituitary gland is not clear. Estrogens are known to inhibit the secretion of milk.

Estrogens exhibit effects in other parts of the body, such as the skeletal system. Large doses **531** *lg dose*

inhibit the development of the long bones by causing premature closure of the epiphyses and by preventing the formation of bone from cartilage (endochondral bone formation). On the other hand, some aspects of the bone formation are augmented by the presence of estrogens, and when these substances are lacking osteoporosis may develop, such as is seen in women after menopause.

Estrogens resemble the hormones made in the adrenal cortex in that large doses affect water and electrolyte balance and are prone to cause retention of sodium and development of edema. Their ability to do this is much less significant than that of the adrenal steroid hormones, however. It is known that the estrogen level in the blood is high just prior to menstruation, and at this time retention of water and electrolytes is recognized as a cause of gain in weight.

Some of the responses to estrogens in the body can be antagonized by the administration of androgens (male hormones), and the reverse is also true.

Uses. Estrogens are used for a variety of conditions in which there is a deficiency of these substances, such as to relieve certain symptoms associated with menopause. At the time of menopause the normal endocrine balance is disturbed by the gradual cessation of ovarian function. The pituitary gland apparently attempts to compensate for the lack of ovarian activity by temporary hyperfunction. Symptoms caused by this compensatory reaction respond well to estrogenic therapy because large doses of ovarian hormones depress the secretion of the gonadotropic hormones of the anterior pituitary. Vasomotor disturbances and headache can often be relieved. Symptoms that are of psychic origin do not respond to this type of therapy as a rule. The estrogenic substances may be administered orally, intravaginally, or parenterally. Both the dosage and the method of administration must be decided in relation to each individual patient. Postmenopausal osteoporosis has also been treated with estrogens with symptomatic but not roentgenographically visible benefit.

Senile vaginitis and kraurosis vulvae respond well to estrogen therapy. Some lower urinary tract infections that are part of postmenopausal atrophy have also been successfully treated with estrogens.

Functional uterine bleeding, failure of ovarian development, and acne have been known to exhibit positive responses to estrogen therapy.

Estrogens are also used to relieve engorgement of the breasts in a postpartum patient when lactation is to be suppressed. Administration of estrogens is believed to suppress the formation of the lactogenic hormone made by the pituitary gland.

Estrogenic material may serve as a substitute for castration for the relief of discomfort associated with prostatic carcinoma and its metastasis. Limited palliative effect has also been noted in postmenopausal women who have inoperable breast cancer with metastasis to the soft tissues.

Natural estrogens—preparation, dosage, and administration

natural

Estrone, **N.F. (Theelin).** Estrone is a crystalline estrogenic substance that is marketed in 1-ml. ampules or 10-ml. vials containing estrone in oil or aqueous suspension. The concentration varies from 0.2 to 1 mg. per milliliter for the preparation in oil and from 1 to 5 mg. per milliliter for the aqueous suspension. Estrone is also available in vaginal suppositories containing 0.2 mg. of the drug. For menopausal symptoms the drug is usually administered intramuscularly in doses of 0.2 to 1 mg. once or twice weekly.

Estradiol, **N.F. (Dimenformon, Progynon).** This drug is marketed as an aqueous suspension and in pellets, tablets, and suppositories. Preparations for injection contain 0.25 to 1 mg. per milliliter. It is administered topically, orally, or parenterally.

Estradiol benzoate, **N.F. (Diogyn B, Dimenformon Benzoate);** *oestradiol benzoate,* **B.P.** This form is less subject to destruction in the tissues than the parent substance and hence is suitable for parenteral administration (intramuscularly). Dosage varies from 0.1 to 5 mg., depending on the condition for which it is given and the severity of the symptoms.

Estradiol dipropionate, **N.F.** **(Ovocylin Dipropionate).** This preparation is absorbed more slowly and excreted more slowly than estradiol, but in other respects its effects are similar to other estradiol compounds. It is administered intramuscularly as a solution in oil and is available in 1-ml. ampules containing 1, 2.5, and 5 mg. of the drug or in 10-ml. ampules containing 10 to 50 mg. of the drug. Dosage ranges from 0.1 to 5 mg. given weekly or biweekly.

Estradiol cypionate, **N.F.** **(Depo-Estradiol Cypionate).** This preparation may produce more prolonged effects than the estradiol compounds mentioned previously and injection of 5 mg. may cause effects to persist for 3 to 4 weeks. It is available as an oil solution (10 mg. in 1 ml. or 25 mg. in 5 ml.). It is administered by intramuscular injection. For maintenance effects 1 to 5 mg. may be administered weekly for 2 to 3 weeks and then every 3 or 4 weeks.

Ethinyl estradiol, **U.S.P.** **(Estinyl).** This preparation is a potent estrogen made suitable for oral administration. It is available in tablets, 0.01, 0.02, 0.05, and 0.5 mg., and as an elixir, 0.006 to 0.03 mg. per milliliter. Dosage varies greatly with the condition treated. For control of menopausal symptoms 0.02 to 0.05 mg. is given one to three times a day.

Conjugated estrogens—preparation, dosage, and administration

Estrogenic substances, conjugated **(Premarin, Conestron, Amnestrogen).** This preparation contains water-soluble, conjugated forms of mixed estrogens from the urine of pregnant mares. The principal estrogen present is sodium estrone sulfate. These preparations are available in tablets and in solution for oral administration. They are also available in the form of topical creams and lotions as well as in powder for injection (intramuscular or intravenous). The action and uses of conjugated estrogens are similar to those of other estrogens. Dosage of 1.25 mg. daily is usually sufficient to control menopausal symptoms. Senile vaginitis and pruritus vulvae are usually relieved with doses of between 1.25 and 3.75 mg. For palliation of breast cancer a daily oral dose of 30 mg. is recommended.

Piperazine estrone sulfate **(Sulestrex Piperazine).** This preparation has the same actions and uses as the naturally occurring conjugated estrogens. It is administered orally. For the control of menopausal symptoms the dosage is usually 1.5 mg.; for the treatment of senile vaginitis and pruritus vulvae, 1.5 to 4.5 mg.; for breast engorgement, 4.5 mg. at intervals of 4 hours for five doses.

Synthetic estrogens—preparation, dosage, and administration

Diethylstilbestrol, **U.S.P.;** *stilboestrol,* **B.P.** This drug is a relatively inexpensive synthetic estrogenic substance that duplicates practically all known actions of the natural estrogens. It is relatively active when given by mouth as well as when given parenterally. It is not significantly more toxic than the natural estrogens. It is available in plain tablets, enteric-coated tablets, and capsules for oral administration, in solution for injection, and in the form of vaginal suppositories. These dosage forms are available in a wide range of concentrations. The average oral dose for treatment of menopausal symptoms is 0.5 to 1 mg. daily. The dosage is reduced if discomfort results. For the suppression of lactation, 5 mg. once or twice daily for 2 to 4 days is considered sufficient; for prostatic cancer, 3 mg. daily (intramuscularly) reduced to 1 mg. daily or 0.5 mg. three times a day (orally); and for the palliation of mammary cancer, 15 mg. is the daily oral dose recommended. Dosage of all preparations should be kept at the minimum necessary for the relief of symptoms.

Side effects are relatively common after oral administration and include nausea, vomiting, and headache.

Diethylstilbestrol dipropionate, **N.F.** This form is prescribed for the same conditions for which other estrogenic substances are used. It is given intramuscularly in oil and is said to have a rather prolonged effect; hence, reactions such as nausea, vomiting, headache, and dizziness occur less frequently than with free diethylstilbestrol. It is also administered orally as tablets. Dosage for the relief of menopausal symptoms is 0.5 to 2 mg. two or three times a week; larger doses are required for suppression of lactation and for the treatment of prostatic cancer.

Dienestrol, N.F., B.P. (Restrol, Synestrol). This is a nonsteroid estrogen that can be administered orally. It is said to cause fewer side effects than diethylstilbestrol and is less potent. Dosage for the relief of menopausal symptoms is 0.1 to 1.5 mg. daily. Larger doses may be ordered for the patient with mammary cancer. Dienestrol also can be given subcutaneously and intramuscularly. It is available in 0.1-, 0.5-, and 10-mg. tablets for oral administration; in a suspension for injection, 50 mg. in 10 ml.; and as a vaginal cream, 0.1 mg. per gram.

Chlorotrianisene, N.F. (Tace). This drug in general shares the actions and uses of other estrogenic substances, although it exhibits some points of difference. The compound is stored in body fat, from which it is slowly released. Therefore, its action extends beyond the time when administration of the drug has been discontinued. It is effective in the relief of mammary engorgement, but its use in large amounts is not recommended for cancer of the breast of patients beyond the age of menopause because it may induce uterine bleeding. Average oral dose for relief of menopausal symptoms is 12 to 24 mg. daily; in cases of prostatic cancer, 24 mg. daily; for relief of mammary engorgement, 48 mg. daily. The last-mentioned dosage is to be continued only for 1 week. It is available in 12- and 25-mg. capsules and in liquid form for oral administration.

Hexestrol. This is a compound that is less potent and less toxic than diethylstilbestrol. It is used for many of the same conditions for which the latter estrogen is used. It is available in 1- and 3-mg. tablets for oral administration. The dosage recommended for the control of menopausal symptoms is 2 to 3 mg., which is reduced as the symptoms are brought under control.

Methallenestril (Vallestril); benzetrol (Benzestrol); promethestrol dipropionate (Meprane Dipropionate). These are additional synthetic estrogens that produce effects similar to those produced by diethylstilbestrol.

The synthetic estrogens offer the advantage of ease of administration since they can be given orally, and they are also relatively inexpensive.

Side effects and toxic effects. Side effects seen in connection with estrogen therapy frequently include nausea and vomiting, diarrhea, and skin rash. The symptoms are usually mild and related to dosage, potency of the compound, and route of administration. Other symptoms include edema and an increased amount of calcium in the blood of patients who have been given prolonged therapy. Adjustment of dosage, substitutions of another estrogen, and perhaps parenteral rather than oral administration may relieve the gastrointestinal symptoms. Periodic tests of the blood and tests of renal function are recommended.

Tenderness of nipples and breast engorgement may occur in young women, and males may manifest gynecomastia.

Estrogens are carcinogenic when administered experimentally in animals that have inherited sensitivity to certain types of carcinoma. Many clinicians believe that estrogens are therefore contraindicated for women who have a personal or family history of malignancy of the reproductive system. Estrogens are used, however, for inoperable breast cancer.

Luteal hormone

The secretion of progesterone by the corpus luteum is under the influence of one of the pituitary hormones, luteotropin (LTH). The chemical structure of progesterone resembles that of the estrogens and also the androgens (see formula, p. 540).

The chemistry of progesterone and related compounds differs from the estrogens in that ring "A" (ring at the lower left of the accompanying structural formula) is not aromatic and there is also a two-carbon side chain at the 17 position (upper right). Chemically, this group is closely related to the adrenal steroids (see Chapter 21).

The luteal hormone functions in the preparation and maintenance of the lining of the uterus for the implantation and nourishment of the embryo. It supplements the action of the follicular hormone in the action on the uterus and also in the mammary glands. It suppresses ovulation during pregnancy and keeps the uterus in a quiescent state by decreasing the irritability of the uterine muscle. After the third month of pregnancy its production is taken over by the placenta.

Progesterone was formerly obtained from the corpus luteum, but it is now prepared synthetically because the naturally occurring hormone is inactivated or extremely weak in its effect when taken orally.

Uses. It was thought at one time that progesterone had therapeutic usefulness in the treatment of dysmenorrhea, menorrhagia, and habitual abortion, but positive evidence is insufficient to support this conclusion. It is of value in the treatment of functional uterine bleeding and endometriosis. After the endometrium is primed with estrogen, progesterone may be used in the treatment of amenorrhea. Some of the newer preparations are given to promote fertility when failure to conceive is the result of a luteal phase defect. Some have been reported to be helpful in cases of habitual abortion.

Some progestogens are components of oral contraceptives, which suppress ovulation. Norethindrone and norethynodrel are more effective in this respect than are other progestogens.

Preparation, dosage, and administration. The following are available preparations of luteal hormone.

Progesterone, **N.F., B.P. (Corlutone, Lipo-Lutin, Progestin, Proluton).** This preparation is available in an oil solution or aqueous suspension for injection. It is ineffective when given orally. The solution in oil is administered intramuscularly and the suspension may be administered subcutaneously. It is given in doses up to 25 mg. or more daily. Tablets of 10 and 25 mg. are available for sublingual administration up to four times a day.

Ethisterone, **N.F., B.P. (Anhydrohydroxy-progesterone, Lutocyclol, Pranone).** Ethisterone is a synthetic derivative of progesterone that can be given orally. It is available in 5-, 10-, and 25-mg. tablets. The usual dose is 25 mg. up to four times a day.

Norethindrone, **U.S.P. (Norlutin).** This is a semisynthetic compound chemically related to ethisterone and testosterone. It produces effects similar to those produced by progesterone and has some androgenic qualities. When administered at certain times during the menstrual cycle, the drug apparently inhibits ovulation, and continuous administration causes delay of menstruation for prolonged periods of time. Norethindrone has been used successfully in suppressing ovulation when given with estrogen. On the other hand, when given to women who are amenorrheic but who have received estrogen therapy, the drug will usually produce bleeding within 24 to 72 hours after administration has been stopped. It is being used chiefly for the treatment of patients who have amenorrhea, menstrual irregularity, and infertility. It is available in 5-mg. tablets and is administered orally in doses of 10 to 20 mg.

Norethynodrel, **U.S.P.** This is a synthetic progestogen similar to norethindrone but with fewer androgenic qualities. It is available for clinical use in combination with mestranol, an estrogen, and is marketed under the name of Enovid. In such, it is used to provide cyclic control, to prevent breakthrough bleeding, and to suppress ovulation. It is available in 2.5-, 5-, and 10-mg. tablets with varying amounts of mestranol.

As an oral test for pregnancy, 10 mg. may be administered daily for 5 days. Withdrawal bleeding occurs 2 to 7 days after the last dose if the patient is not pregnant.

This drug may also be administered in cases of threatened abortion and in treatment of habitual abortion.

Medroxyprogesterone acetate, **U.S.P. (Provera).** This synthetic substance differs from progesterone mainly in that it is active after oral administration. It can be used for all conditions for which progesterone is indicated and is more potent than ethisterone. It is available in 2.5- and 10-mg. tablets or as a suspension for injection.

Hydroxyprogesterone caproate, **U.S.P. (Delalutin).** A synthetic derivative of progesterone, it is a great deal like progesterone except that

535

it has a longer duration of action after parenteral administration. It is available in oil solution, 250 mg. in 2 ml., for intramuscular injection. The usual single dose is 125 to 250 mg., and one dose every 4 weeks may be sufficient in treatment of menstrual disorders and ovarian and uterine dysfunction.

Side effects and toxic effects. Preparations of luteal hormone or related compounds appear to have a low order of toxicity. Patients occasionally have gastrointestinal symptoms, headache, dizziness, and allergic manifestations. Cases have been reported in which masculinization of female infants occurred in connection with the administration of progesterone to the mothers during pregnancy.

Prolonged high dosages of progestogens may cause gastrointestinal disturbances, edema and weight gain, headache and vertigo, oligomenorrhea, and breast congestion.

Ovulatory suppressants

Contraception is as old as history and has been practiced in many forms, including the use of mechanical devices and ingestion of various herbs. Not until recently, however, has there been any consistent measure of reliability in these practices. The introduction of Enovid in 1960 dramatically demonstrated the unfailing suppression of ovulation by a combination of progesterones and estrogens. This event was preceded by a decade of research, the elucidation of which was largely the responsibility of Rock, Pincus, and Garcia. Evidence of the contraceptive effect of norethynodrel was published by this group in 1956 and followed by a number of controlled studies, most notably in Puerto Rico. By 1965 refined forms of this drug were multiplied, and over 5 million American women were using oral contraceptives.

Few drugs have been studied as ambitiously and intensively as have the oral contraceptives because of (1) the interest aroused concerning the effects these drugs might have on the human body when hormone levels and relationships are altered for the sole purpose of preventing conception, (2) the need for a simple method of population control in densely populated coun-

tries, and (3) the desire by many couples for planned parenthood.

Pharmacologic action and result. The development of the oral contraceptives was based on the knowledge that ovulation did not occur during pregnancy and that large amounts of estrogen and progesterone were produced by the extended function of the corpus luteum and by placental secretion.

In addition, a review of physiology of the menstrual cycle reveals that:

1 Ovulation is dependent upon the anterior pituitary gland to secrete two hormones:
  a. FSH—for maturation of the ovum
  b. LH—for release of the mature ovum from the ovary
2 The hypothalamus regulates the secretion of these hormones by the anterior pituitary by secreting hormones known as releasing factors.
3 Large amounts of estrogen (secreted by the maturing follicle and, following ovulation, by the corpus luteum) inhibit the hypothalamus releasing factors, which inhibits FSH and LH release and blocks ovulation.
4 Progesterone (secreted by the corpus luteum) inhibits the hypothalamic releasing factor for the luteinizing hormone, which also interferes with ovulation.
5 Estrogen and progesterone are responsible for endometrial buildup; decreased production of estrogen and progesterone results in endometrial sloughing and menstrual bleeding.

From this information, it can be readily understood why the administration of progesterone derivatives and estrogenic substances prevents ovulation without preventing menstruation and why these substances are the ingredients of oral contraceptives.

It is generally accepted that oral contraceptives act, at least in part, by inhibiting the secretion of gonadotropins from the pituitary gland. Other possible actions may include a direct inhibitory effect on the ovary, changes in tubal motility, or changes in the endometrium that would result in failure of implantation of fertilized ova.

The combination of drugs rapidly transforms the early secretory stage of the endometrium to one resembling secretory exhaustion. The drug is therefore judged effective because the estrogen encourages proliferative change that inhibits ovulation, while progesterone ensures that withdrawal bleeding will be physiologic, prompt, and brief.

Preparation, dosage, and administration. Although the use of exogenous estrogenic substances alone will inhibit ovulation, undesirable bleeding frequently occurs during the latter phase of the cycle. If estrogen levels are increased to prevent this, severe nausea and breast tenderness occur. It is for these reasons that estrogens are combined with progesterones in oral contraceptives.

Since naturally occurring progesterone is inactivated or extremely weak in its effect when taken orally and must be given by injection to be effective, steroidal compounds related to progesterone have been developed. These are termed progestogens. The majority of the oral contraceptives contain a synthetic progestogen, which is either norethynodrel or norethindrone.

Norethynodrel

Norethindrone

Norethynodrel is a basic progestin, while norethindrone is a more androgenic progestin. The latter is sometimes recommended for patients with excess side effects from estrogen, such as greater weight gain and amenorrhea. Norethynodrel, on the other hand, is good for patients with oily skin, acne, hirsutism, and breakthrough bleeding.

Two methods of oral contraception are used; one is termed "combination therapy," and the other is termed "sequential therapy." Combination therapy consists of taking tablets containing a progestogen and an estrogen. Sequential therapy consists of taking a tablet containing only estrogen for 15 days, then taking a tablet containing a mixture of estrogen and progestogen for 5 days (this is usually a differently colored tablet).

In both forms of therapy, 20 tablets are taken during each menstrual cycle. The first day of menstruation is day 1; on day 5 the first tablet is taken regardless of whether menstruation has ceased. One tablet is then taken each day for the next 20 days. Menstruation will occur within 2 to 7 days after the last tablet has been taken. The fifth day after the start of menstruation, the cycle begins again.

These two methods of therapy are equally effective. Most authorities claim them to be 100% effective; failures are the result of missed dosage. It is important that patients be instructed in the following:

1 The patient should take one tablet every day for the 20-day period without fail. Eliminating one tablet may lead to ovulation or breakthrough acyclic bleeding.

2 If breakthrough bleeding occurs, administration of the drug should be continued and the physician should be consulted. What may be required is a different balance of estrogen or a different progestogen. Breakthrough bleeding may occur only in the first cycles of treatment until the patient adjusts to the hormones. Spotting or slight brownish discharge is not breakthrough bleeding, and it eventually disappears. If bleeding is similar to that of menses, the patient is usually advised to stop taking the drug and begin the medication again 5 days later beginning a new cycle.

3 Even if menses does not occur following completion of a medication cycle, patients should be cautioned to begin another medication cycle on the seventh day and not to wait for menstruation to begin, since ovulation may occur within 9 or 10 days after stopping the medication. Ovulation can occur in the presence of a delayed or missed menstruation.

537

Table 26-1 Combination therapy oral contraceptives

Trade name	Tablet composition			
	Estrogen	Dose (mg.)	Progestogen	Dose (mg.)
Enovid	Mestranol	0.15	Norethynodrel	9.85
Enovid	Mestranol	0.075	Norethynodrel	5
Enovid-E	Mestranol	0.1	Norethynodrel	2.5
Ortho-Novum	Mestranol	0.06	Norethindrone	10
Ortho-Novum	Mestranol	0.075	Norethindrone	5
Norinyl, Novulen, Noralestrin	Mestranol	0.1	Norethindrone	2
Norlestrin, Prolestrin, Orlestrin, Etalontin	Ethynylestradiol	0.05	Norethindrone acetate	2.5
Ovulen, Metrulen-N	Mestranol	0.1	Ethyndiol diacetate	1
Provest, Proverstral, Provestrol	Ethynylestradiol	0.05	Medroxy progestrone acetate	10

Table 26-2 Sequential therapy oral contraceptives

Trade name	Estrogen component	Number of days	Estrogen and progestogen	Number of days
C-Quens	Mestranol, 0.08 mg.	15	Mestranol, 0.08 mg. and chloramadinone, 2 mg.	5
Oracon	Ethynylestradiol, 0.1 mg.	16	Ethynylestradiol, 0.1 mg. and dimethisterone, 2.5 mg.	5
Ortho-Novum SQ Tablets	Mestranol, 0.08 mg.	14	Mestranol 0.08 mg. and norethindrone, 2 mg.	6

4 Women who are early ovulators or have a shortened menstrual cycle (they menstruate every 21 days or less) should be cautioned to use another method of birth control during the first medication cycle. Under steroid therapy, these women will usually convert to a 28-day cycle.

5 The patient should be instructed to establish a definite pattern for taking the tablet at the same time each day; however, anytime within a 24-hour period is adequate.

6 The patient should be examined and reevaluated for oral contraceptive therapy at least once yearly and should report any untoward symptoms to her physician.

Side effects and toxic effects. Most common side effects are the result of either the estrogen-

Plate 8
Claviceps purpurea (rye ergot).

ic or progestogenic components of oral contraceptives. Nausea and vomiting, breast fullness, and mastalgia are largely caused by estrogen; headache, vertigo, depression, apathy, and fatigue result from progesterone derivatives. These symptoms generally subside with succeeding cycles. Fluid retention and weight gain may also occur but are usually self-limiting. Chloasma may be noted. There has been no evidence of production of carcinoma in women taking the drugs, and fertility is apparently unaffected. There is increasing evidence of thromboembolic phenomena and visual changes occuring in women taking these drugs, but this evidence is yet inconclusive. A general agreement exists that there has been too little time since the introduction of these drugs to make full assessment of all possible dangers.

Contraindications include a history of thromboembolic disease, hepatic disease, mammary or genital carcinoma, large uterine fibroids, migraine headache, asthma, epilepsy, and blood dyscrasias. Oral contraceptives should not be taken if pregnancy is suspected because of the danger of possible masculinization of the fetus.

Ovulatory stimulants

Anovulation is physiologic in patients who are pregnant, breast feeding, and postmenopausal. It becomes suspected pathology in situations characterized by abnormal bleeding or infertility. The incidence of anovulation is unknown and cannot be ascertained, but diagnostic tests may determine its presence.

Methods of ovulation induction include use of gonadotropins, thyroid preparations, cortisones, estrogens, and synthetic steroids.

Gonadotropins

The use of either human or equine gonadotropins has yielded inconsistent results in inducing ovulation. A combination of human pituitary gonadotropin for follicle maturation and human chorionic gonadotropin for ovulation and luteinization has been used with favorable results. Side effects of the latter include cystic ovaries, multiple births, and a marked febrile response.

Thyroid preparations

Thyroid preparations are used in hypothyroid or hyperthyroid conditions, which are often associated with anovulation.

Cortisone preparations

Cortisone preparations suppress adrenal activity, thereby decreasing androgen and estrogen secretions and encouraging release of human pituitary gonadotropins. This treatment is appropriate when adrenal gland dysfunction is etiologic in anovulation, as in adrenogenital syndrome.

Estrogens

These hormones act to induce ovulation in two ways: (1) by stimulating the release of pituitary gonadotropin and increasing secretion of FSH and LH and (2) by making the ovary more responsive to the influence of gonadotropin. Short-term therapy may be stimulating to the ovary, but long-term estrogen therapy depresses gonadotropin, which results in anovulation.

Ovulation-inducing agents

Several synthetic agents have recently become available. The mode of action of these drugs in inducing ovulation is not yet well established, but they may act either directly on the enzyme systems, suppressing estrogen production and secondary stimulation of gonadotropin, or directly on the hypothalamus, pituitary gland, or both, stimulating secretion of gonadotropin.

Side effects with any of these therapies are common, including gastrointestinal disturbances similar to those in pregnancy, breakthrough bleeding, abdominal pain, and weight gain.

Clomiphene citrate. This is a drug bearing a close structural relationship to the potent synthetic estrogen chlorotrianisene (Tace). It is generally suitable for patients with amenorrhea of pituitary origin, the Stein-Leventhal syndrome, and the Chiari-Frommel syndrome. Dosage is 50 to 100 mg. per day for 5 to 7 days. Short-term therapies have been found more effective than long-term ones. Side effects include hot flashes and the presence of ovarian enlargement with or without cyst formation. Incidence

539

of ovulation has been ascertained as 76% in one study, although further research is needed. Multiple pregnancies may occur in 10% of patients.

Human menopausal gonadotropin (HMG) is a powerful ovulation-inducing agent. It has caused multiple pregnancies in a high percentage of patients.

Male sex hormones

Androgens

Normal development and maintenance of male sex characteristics depend on adequate amounts of the male sex hormones, which are called androgens. All androgenic compounds have a steroid nucleus. In fact, natural estrogens, androgens, and some of the hormones of the adrenal cortex all exhibit an interesting similarity in their structural formulas.

There are about five steroidal hormones that manifest androgenic activity, and all are derivatives of androsterone. The most potent is testosterone, which is chemically similar to progesterone. Androgens chemically similar to testosterone are excreted in the urine and are usually referred to as 17-ketosteroids because there is a ketone group attached to carbon 17 of the steroid structure (see androsterone). It should be remembered, however, that the urinary 17-ketosteroids are also products of the adrenal cortex in both men and women. Androsterone is one of the 17-ketosteroids found in the urine. Testosterone is not excreted, as such, in the urine.

Testosterone
(male sex hormone)

Progesterone
(female sex hormone)

Androsterone
(one of 17-ketosteroids found
in urine of both sexes)

Action and result. The androgens function in the development and maintenance of normal states in the sex organs. Administration to immature males causes growth of the sex organs and the appearance of secondary sex characteristics. When administered for therapeutic purposes, they simply replace the missing hormone. When a high concentration of androgenic substances is maintained in the circulation, anterior pituitary secretion is inhibited and spermatogenesis is retarded.

In mammals, both sexes form male and female hormones, although they are antagonistic to each other. The administration of testosterone can suppress menstruation and cause atrophy of the endometrium.

Another effect produced by androgens is concerned with anabolism—the formation as well as the maintenance of muscular and skeletal protein. The administration of androgenic substances is associated with an increase in muscular development and weight. They bring about retention of nitrogen (essential to the formation of protein in the body) and also affect the storage of inorganic phosphorus, sulfate, sodium, and potassium.

The retention of nitrogen, prevention of atrophy in bones from disuse, and promotion of the healing of wounds are effects of testosterone and related compounds that have been reported. These effects are of particular significance in patients who are paraplegic after trauma to the spinal cord, because in these patients the maintenance of adequate nutrition, prevention of atrophy in muscles and bones, and prevention as well as treatment of decubitus ulcers constitute serious problems. Similar problems are encountered in the care of patients who are chronically ill or malnourished or who have a wasting disease such as carcinoma.

Uses. Androgens have been used in replacement therapy for patients with hypogonadism and eunuchoidism (castrates). They produce marked changes in sex organs, body contour, and voice, provided the deficiency state has not been present too long. Androgens have little effect on senile men and on patients with psychogenic impotence. They may increase libido in women.

Alone or with gonadotropic substances, androgens have been employed in the treatment of cryptorchidism.

Androgens have also been used in the treatment of dysmenorrhea and menopausal states and for the suppression of lactation and breast engorgement. Favorable results are sometimes obtained from their use to relieve subjective symptoms associated with the male climacteric, just as estrogens are of value in relieving symptoms of similar origin in women.

Androgens have been employed for palliative relief of advanced inoperable cancer of the breast. Their mechanism of action is not clear. Subjective improvement (improved appetite, gain in weight, and relief of pain) seems to be greater than objective improvement. Improvement is temporary and seldom exceeds a period of 1 year. Androgens are preferred for patients with this condition prior to or during menopause, since estrogens may promote the development of the cancer at this time.

Preparation, dosage, and administration. The following are preparations of androgens.

Testosterone, **N.F., B.P.** Testosterone produces effects similar to testosterone propionate. When given in aqueous suspension its duration of androgenic effects is slightly longer than those of testosterone propionate. It is available in 75-mg. pellets, as an aqueous injectable suspension of 25 mg. per milliliter, and as tablets for oral and sublingual administration. For dosage, see testosterone propionate.

Testosterone propionate, **U.S.P., B.P. (Oreton, Andronate).** This form is available in 5- and 10-mg. buccal tablets (these are held in the space between the teeth and cheek) and as a

solution for intramuscular injection. Dosage ranges from 10 to 60 mg. two to six times weekly, depending upon the response obtained and the effect desired. From 5 to 10 mg. daily may be sufficient as maintenance doses for therapy in men. For relief of symptoms of breast cancer, 150 to 300 mg. weekly (in several doses) may be administered. This preparation is synthesized from cholesterol or extracted from bull testes.

Testosterone enanthate, **U.S.P. (Delatestryl).** This preparation is administered as a solution in oil and provides a prolonged effect of 3 weeks or more. The usual intramuscular dose is 200 mg. every 2 to 4 weeks.

Deladumone. This is a preparation of testosterone enanthate and estradiol valerate dissolved in sesame oil. It is given to suppress lactation and prevent engorgement of the breasts. One intramuscular injection immediately after delivery is usually sufficient.

Methyltestosterone, **N.F., B.P. (Oreton M, Metandren).** This preparation is available in 5-, 10-, and 25-mg. tablets for oral administration, in 10-mg. buccal tablets, and in 5- and 10-mg. tablets for sublingual administration. Absorption from the buccal membranes is more effective than from the gastrointestinal tract. The indications and actions of this compound are essentially the same as those for testosterone propionate. The usual oral dose is 10 mg. three times a day. Doses for the suppression of lactation are larger. Dosage is adjusted according to the needs and response of the patient.

Testosterone cypionate, **U.S.P.** Although highly similar to testosterone propionate, this exhibits the advantage of more prolonged androgenic effects. It is available in solution, 100 mg. per 1 ml. and 500 mg. and 1 Gm. in 10 ml. It is administered intramuscularly in doses from 10 to 50 mg. at intervals of 1 or 2 weeks.

Stanolone **(Neodrol).** Stanolone is an androgen that has the same action and uses as testosterone and related compounds. It is used clinically for its anabolic effects and for its effects on inoperable or metastatic carcinoma of the breast. For cancer of the breast the average effective dose is 100 mg. daily, which is given

541

intramuscularly as long as the patient shows improvement or is able to tolerate the metabolic and masculinizing effects.

Norethandrolone, **N.F., B.P. (Nilevar).** This is a synthetic androgen that is chemically and pharmacologically related to testosterone. It is not used as an androgen because its androgenic properties are less significant than its ability to affect protein anabolism (see action of androgens). Its major effects include: (1) retention of nitrogen, phosphorus, and potassium in amounts required for protein anabolism, (2) retention and utilization of calcium, (3) sense of well-being, and (4) improved appetite. Patients receiving anabolic hormones should be on high-calorie, high-protein diets, if possible. It is administered orally and intramuscularly in amounts that range from 30 to 50 mg. daily in divided doses. It is available as a solution, 8.3 mg. per milliliter, and in 10-mg. tablets for oral administration. Large doses can produce androgenic effects like those encountered with the other androgens.

Fluoxymesterone, **U.S.P., B.P. (Halotestin, Ultandren).** This compound is a synthetic halogenated derivative of methyltestosterone. It is available in 2- and 5-mg. tablets for oral administration. It is several times more potent than methyltestosterone from the standpoint of both androgenic and anabolic activity. Dosage for anabolic effects ranges from 4 to 10 mg., and for palliation of breast cancer 6 to 20 mg. daily have been used. Dosage varies greatly with the condition being treated and the response of the patient. The daily dose is given at one time or divided into three or more portions.

Nandrolone phenpropionate, **N.F., B.P. (Durabolin).** This is a synthetic steroid hormone related to norethandrolone. Similarly, its anabolic effects are prominent while androgenicity is low. This drug is administered intramuscularly, and usual adult dosage ranges from 25 to 50 mg. once weekly.

Nandrolone decanoate, **N.F., B.P. (Deca-Durabolin).** Its duration of action is longer than nandrolone phenylpropionate and the usual dosage is 50 to 100 mg. once a month.

542   **Side effects and toxic effects.** Effects that are regarded as untoward in the female include deepening of the voice, hirsutism (excessive growth of hair), flushing, acne, regression of the breasts, enlargement of the clitoris, and general masculinization. Less prominent effects, but probably more serious, are the retention of sodium, potassium, water, and chloride, which can contribute to heart failure. Jaundice has occasionally been observed after the administration of methyltestosterone and norethandrolone and means that administration of the androgen will probably be discontinued. Nausea and gastrointestinal upsets occur occasionally. Patients receiving androgens should be observed carefully for hypercalcemia, acceleration of the disease being treated, and the appearance of edema. Edema is sometimes controlled with the use of diuretics and a diet low in salt.

Contraindications. Androgens are contraindicated for patients with prostatic cancer and serious cardiorenal dysfunction.

Questions

for study and review

1 Describe the objectives of androgen therapy.
2 Differentiate between combination therapy and sequential therapy oral contraceptives.
3 Identify some common side effects and some contraindications of oral contraceptive therapy.

Multiple choice

4 Diethylstilbestrol belongs to which of the following groups?
  a. gonadotropins
  b. androgens
  c. estrogens
5 A drug that is a male sex hormone is said to be an:
  a. estrogen
  b. androgen
  c. gonadotropin
6 Which of the following preparations is sometimes used to relieve symptoms associated with menopause?
  a. progesterone
  b. methyltestosterone
  c. diethylstilbestrol
  d. ergonovine maleate
7 Meperidine (Demerol) may be preferred to morphine for

the obstetric patient for which of the following reasons? It:

a. is a more potent analgesic
b. produces less respiratory depression
c. acts more quickly
d. does not affect the bowel

8 All central nervous system depressants tend to be used in small doses for the patient in labor to avoid:

a. prolongation of labor
b. excessive response by the mother
c. respiratory depression in the fetus

9 Which of the following reasons may explain why estrogens are sometimes used in treatment of mammary cancer (in patients past menopause) in preference to androgens?

a. They are less expensive.
b. They produce relief of symptoms more quickly.
c. They produce no side effects.
d. They can be administered orally.

10 Which of the following preparations might you expect to see ordered for the suppression of lactation?

a. chlorotrianisene (Tace)
b. oxytocin (Pitocin)
c. lututrin (Lutrexin)
d. methylergonovine maleate (Methergine Maleate)

11 Patients receiving oxytocin (Pitocin) to induce labor must be watched especially for:

a. tetanic contractions of the uterus
b. maternal exhaustion
c. drop in blood pressure
d. prolapse of the umbilical cord

12 What is the primary purpose of giving promethazine hydrochloride (Phenergan Hydrochloride) to a patient in labor?

a. to relieve pain
b. to reduce the amount of postpartum nausea
c. to reduce the amount of narcotic needed by the mother
d. to produce sleep

13 Which of the following preparations might you expect to see ordered for a patient who is inactive and whose muscular and osseous tissues seem to be wasting away?

a. diethylstilbestrol
b. chlorotrianisene (Tace)
c. lututrin (Luxtrexin)
d. norethandrolone (Nilevar)

14 Which of the following is a synthetic estrogen that is stored in body fat from which it is slowly released?

a. testosterone propionate
b. chlorotrianisene
c. estradiol benzoate
d. relaxin

15 Which of the following preparations might you expect to see used to produce central nervous system depression and relief of edema in an obstetric patient with toxemia?

a. morphine sulfate
b. phenobarbital
c. magnesium sulfate
d. promethazine hydrochloride

References

Arrata, W. S. M., and Arronet, G. H.: Norethynodrel with mestranol (Enovid) in infertility, Fertil. Steril. **16**:430, 1965.

Astwood, E. B., and Cassidy, C. E.: Clinical endocrinology. II. New York, 1968, Grune & Stratton, Inc.

Barger, G.: Ergot and ergotism, London, 1931, Gurney and Jackson.

Beckman, H.: Pharmacology; the nature, action, and use of drugs, Philadelphia, 1961, W. B. Saunders Co.

Berczeller, P. H., Young, I. S., and Kupperman, H. S.: The therapeutic use of progestational steroids, Clin. Pharmacol. Therap.**5**:216, 1964.

Borell, U.: Contraceptive methods—their safety, efficacy and acceptability, Acta Obstet. Gynec. Scand. **45** (supp.1):5, 1966.

Clegg, H.: Pituitary hormones for infertility, Brit. Med. J. **2**:316, 1965.

Clinical aspects of oral gestogens, WHO Technical Report Series, No. 326, 1966.

Davis, M. E., Strandjord, N. M., and Lanze, L. H.: Estrogens and the aging process, J.A.M.A. **196**:219, 1966.

Drill, V. A.: Oral contraceptives, New York, 1966, McGraw-Hill Book Company.

Evaluation of oral contraceptives, J.A.M.A. **199**:650, 1967.

Francis, W. G.: Long term estrogen and progestin Rx, Appl. Ther. **9**:833, 1967.

Franklin, R. R., and others: Induction of ovulation, Amer. J. Med. Sci. **254**:875, 1967.

Gemzell, C., and Roos, P.: Pregnancies following treatment with human gonadotropins, with special reference to the problem of multiple births, Amer. J. Obstet. Gynec. **94**:490, 1966.

Goodman, L., and Gilman, A.: The pharmacological basis of therapeutics, New York, 1970, The Macmillan Company.

Goth, A.: Medical pharmacology, ed. 6, St. Louis, 1972, The C. V. Mosby Co.

Greenblatt, R. B.: Estrogen therapy for postmenopausal females, New Eng. J. Med. **272**:305, 1965.

Lamb, E. J., and Guderian, M.: Clinical effects of clomiphene in anovulation, Obstet. Gynec. **28**:505, 1966.

Lammert, A.: The menopause; a physiologic process, Amer. J. Nurs. **62**:56, 1962.

Lipsett, M. B., and Kocenman, S. G.: Androgen metabolism, J.A.M.A. **190**:757, 1964.

Loraine, J. A., and Bell, E. T.: Fertility and contraception in the human female, Baltimore, 1968, The Williams & Wilkins Co.

McLennon, C. E.: Reflections on the physiology of menstruation, J.A.M.A. **156**:578, 1954.

Moir, J.C.: The history and present-day use of ergot, Canad. Med. Ass. J. **72**:727, 1955.

Morand, P., and others: The steroidal estrogens, Chem. Rev. **68**:85, 1968.

Mussey, E., and Malkasian, G. D.: Progestogen treatment of recurrent carcinoma of the endometrium, Amer. J. Obstet. Gynec. **94**:78, 1966.

Nathan, K.: Medical induction of ovulation in anovulatory infertility, Conn. Med. **31**:695, 1967.

Novak, E. R.: The menopause, J.A.M.A. **156**:575, 1954.

Pildes, R. B.: Induction of ovulation with clomiphene, Amer. J. Obstet. Gynec. **91**:466, 1965.

Rudel, H. W.: Mechanisms of action of hormonal antifertility agents, Pharmacol. Physicians **2**(2):1, 1968.

Rudel, H. W., and Kind, F. A.: The biology of anti-fertility steroids, Acta Endocrin. **51**(supp. 105):1, 1966.

Stevens, V. C., and others: Regulation of patient function by sex steroids, Abstr. Gynec. Survey **22**:781, 1967.

Taylor, E. S.: Problems associated with administration of estrogen, Arizona Med. **25**:42, 1968.

Taylor, E. S.: Changing concepts in infertility, Pacif. Med. Surg. **76**:1, 1968.

Tyler, E. T., and Olson, H. J.: Fertility promoting and inhibiting effects of new steroid hormonal substances, J.A.M.A. **169**:1843, 1959.

Vande Wiele, R. L., and Turksoy, R.: The use of human menopausal and chorionic gonadotropins in patients with infertility due to ovulatory failure, Amer. J. Obstet. Gynec. **93**:632, 1965.

Wilkins, L.: Masculinization of female fetus due to use of orally given progestins, J.A.M.A. **172**:1028, 1960.

Williams, R. H.: Textbook of endocrinology, Philadelphia, 1962, W. B. Saunders Co.

Yannene, M. E.: Use of hormones in the menopause, J. Iowa Med. Soc. **57**:1099, 1967.

Antiseptics and disinfectants

Early in the history of mankind it was found that certain gums, balsams, and resins had the power to prevent decay in the bodies of the dead, and today the Egyptian mummy is an evidence of the efficiency of the materials used. Some of these substances were also used for healing wounds, but it was not until the latter part of the nineteenth century, when Pasteur made his astounding discoveries regarding the germ theory and Lister, in consequence, began the systematic use of carbolic acid in his surgical work, that antiseptics came into general use.

Local antiinfectives now include a wide variety of agents used for many purposes. A number of the older agents continue to be used for such purposes as the preparation of the skin prior to surgical incision or parenteral administration of drugs, the disinfection of thermometers, and the treatment of contaminated clothing and infected human excreta. Local antiinfectives are used in the home for the treatment of minor wounds and abrasions, and in the community at large they play a role in the safe handling of sewage, in the purification of water supplies, and in the preservation of food supplies.

Definitions

There continues to be some misunderstanding about the terms used when speaking about groups of antiinfective agents. An *antiseptic* is a chemical agent that inhibits the growth and development of microorganisms but does not necessarily kill them. It is synonymous with the term *bacteriostatic*. It means against sepsis or, more literally, "against putrefaction or decay." This term was used long before bacteria were known to exist. It is now used especially to mean agents applied to living tissues, such as an antiseptic for the skin.

Disinfectants, germicides, or *bactericides* are agents that produce rapid death of harmful microorganisms, and the terms are used synonymously. There is a trend to use the word *disinfectant* to refer to germicides used on inanimate objects. Whether a given agent kills microorganisms or inhibits their growth may depend upon a number of factors, such as the mechanism of action, the length of time the organisms are subjected to the agent, the number of microorganisms present, the concentration of the chemical agent, the temperature, and the presence and amount of organic matter.

The older disinfectants were used for killing harmful microorganisms on dishes, instruments, or the surface of the skin, but they were generally found to be too poisonous to be used internally. The introduction of antibiotics, however, changed this concept of bactericidal agents, since antibiotics include many effective bactericidal agents that are quite nontoxic for man. Although in theory antibiotics could also be used topically like the older disinfectants, they are generally too costly to be used for instruments, and their topical use on the skin is often objectionable because of their capacity to induce allergic reactions in the individual. Exceptions are found in the use of bacitracin and neomycin, which exhibit a low incidence of hypersensitivity reactions when applied topically or when they act locally. Agents used to treat local fungal, viral, or parasitic infections may also be thought of as local antiinfectives.

■ Mechanisms of action

Antiinfectives may act in three ways. (1) They may bring about a change in the structure of the protein of the microbial cell (denaturation), which often proceeds to coagulation of protein with increased concentration of the chemical agent. (2) They may lower the surface tension of the aqueous medium of the parasitic cell. This increases the permeability of the plasma membrane, and the cellular constituents are destroyed by lysis. The cell is unable to maintain its equilibrium in its environment. (The surface-active agents are thought to act this way.) (3) They may interfere with some metabolic processes of the microbial cells in such ways as to interfere with the cell's ability to survive and multiply.

Concern about the effectiveness of disinfectants has been heightened by the problem of hospital-acquired infections caused by antibiotic-resistant staphylococci. On the other hand,

these microorganisms are apparently no more resistant to the usual chemical disinfectants than they ever were. A good antiinfective must be more effective against the parasitic cells than against the cells of the host. Many good antiinfectives are so toxic to all cells that they cannot be used except on inanimate objects, and they constitute a hazard around a home or anywhere human beings may be accidentally poisoned. Both physical and chemical agents are used in disinfection, but in this chapter emphasis is given to chemical agents. There is no ideal chemical agent suitable for all purposes for which these agents are needed.

■ Criteria for evaluating disinfectants

An ideal disinfectant may never be found. It should be able to destroy all forms of infectious agents without being toxic to the cells of human tissues, and it should not induce sensitization. In present-day practice, what constitutes a satisfactory germicide for a given article depends on whether only vegetative organisms must be destroyed or whether fungi, tubercle bacilli, viruses, and spores also must be killed, since the latter are generally more resistant to germicides. It is important to select the best antiinfective to accomplish the results desired. All germicides and disinfectants recommended for hospital use must be effective against gram-negative enteric organisms and gram-positive pyogenic organisms, when used as directed. The demands made of a good disinfectant have gradually become greater as better disinfectants have been developed. Some authorities now say that a solution of a disinfectant should be expected to kill within 10 minutes all vegetative bacteria and fungi, tubercle bacilli, animal parasites, and viruses with the possible exception of the viruses causing hepatitis. (The disinfectant cannot be expected to kill spores.) Not all disinfectants in present-day use will do this, at least not in a few minutes. Some may do so when several hours of exposure to the disinfectant are provided. The ideal disinfectant should not only kill all the organisms mentioned but should also act in the presence of organic material and be stable, noncorrosive, and inexpensive.

It should never be overlooked that heat, and particularly moist heat under pressure (autoclaving), is the method of choice for killing all forms of living organisms, but since not all things that require disinfection can be autoclaved, there continues to be a need for satisfactory chemical disinfectants.

Phenol and related compounds

Within the phenol group of compounds a relationship between chemical structure and antimicrobial activity has been noted. For this reason the chemical formulas have been included. This relationship has not been observed for all chemical agents.

Phenol, U.S.P., B.P. (carbolic acid)

OH

Phenol is a crystalline compound with a characteristic odor. The needle-shaped crystals may become pinkish upon standing. Phenol was introduced into medicine as an antiseptic by Sir Joseph Lister in 1867. Its use was so firmly established that it has been employed as a standard against which the antibacterial activity of other similar compounds (particularly other phenols) is measured. The relative power of a disinfectant as compared to phenol is known as the phenol coefficient (P/C). A disinfectant thirty times as efficient as phenol (producing the same killing effect at one thirtieth the concentration) is said to have a phenol coefficient of 30.

Solutions of phenol are antiseptic, germicidal, or escharotic (scarring to tissue), depending upon the concentration used. Antiseptic solutions are irritating or toxic to tissues, and concentrated solutions may produce death when taken internally or when applied topically to abraded surfaces of the skin. When applied locally, phenol penetrates the skin and exerts a local anesthetic effect on sensory nerve endings. This explains its presence in certain lotions or ointments used to relieve itching (antipruritic).

Phenol is believed to exert its germicidal action by altering the structure of the protein in the parasitic cells (denaturation). In high concentrations it precipitates cellular protein. It is not affected much by the presence of organic matter or by high concentrations of bacteria. The use of phenol has declined because better disinfectants have been found that are less irritating, less toxic to human tissues, and more efficient in killing microorganisms. Bacterial spores and viruses tend to be resistant to phenol. Phenol is occasionally used in full strength (89% aqueous solution) to cauterize small wounds such as snake bites, in 5% strength to disinfect sinks, toilets, and excreta, and in dilute solution (0.5% to 1%) to relieve itching.

Liquefied phenol, U.S.P., B.P. This is an 89% aqueous solution of phenol (80%, B.P.).

Phenolated calamine lotion, U.S.P. This is 1% phenol in calamine lotion.

Cresol, N.F., B.P.

Cresol is made available as a mixture of the ortho-, meta-, and para-methyl phenols and is derived from coal tar. Cresols are phenols in which one of the hydrogen atoms in the benzene ring has been replaced by a methyl group (CH_3).

OH CH_3 OH CH_3 OH CH_3

o-cresol   *m*-cresol   *p*-cresol

Cresol is a thick, heavy, straw-colored liquid with a phenol-like odor. It is two to five times as active as phenol but no more toxic. It is only slightly soluble in water but is soluble in liquid soap. Preparations of cresol are used for disinfecting excreta, sinks, bedpans, toilets, and the like. All are poisonous and should be used for external purposes only or as mentioned.

Saponated cresol solution, N.F. This is a 50% solution of cresol in vegetable oil (saponified). This is also known as Lysol.

Cresol and soap solution, B.P. This is essentially the same as the saponated cresol solution.

Lysol forms a milky emulsion in water, but it is more soluble than pure cresol. Its action is not hampered by the presence of organic material. It is used in 2% to 5% strength to disinfect excreta, sinks, toilets, bedpans, and similar utensils. It is like the other cresols and phenol in that it is poisonous.

Hexachlorophene, U.S.P. (Gamophen, pHisoHex, Surgi-Cen, Surofene); hexachlorophane, B.P.

Hexachlorophene is a chlorinated diphenol. It is a white to light tan powder, relatively insoluble in water but soluble in alcohol, fats, and soaps. It is incorporated into detergent creams, oils, soaps (Dial soap), and other media for topical application to reduce numbers of pathogenic bacteria on the skin and to reduce the incidence of pyogenic skin infections. It is much more effective against gram-positive than gram-negative bacteria. Optimum effects are secured only when regular and repeated applications are made. If other cleansing agents are substituted, a rapid increase of organisms normally found on the skin may be observed.

Hexachlorophene should not be looked upon as a substitute for mechanical cleansing of the skin, although products containing this substance are used for preoperative preparation of the skin. It is also used by food handlers and dentists. Its activity is reduced by the presence of organic material and blood serum. Alcohol and other organic solvents should be avoided when hexachlorophene is used. Hexachlorophene is an active ingredient in a number of deodorants.

***Hexachlorophene liquid soap*, U.S.P.** The soap contains between 225 and 260 mg. of hexachlorophene in each 100 ml. of 10% to 13% potassium soap base.

Resorcinol, U.S.P., B.P.

Resorcinol resembles phenol in effectiveness, but it is less toxic, irritating, and caustic. It is used chiefly as an antiseptic and keratolytic (softening or dissolving the keratin-containing epidermis) in the treatment of various diseases of the skin. It is used in strengths that vary from 2% to 20%. It acts by precipitating cell proteins.

This compound occurs as colorless needle-shaped crystals with a faint odor. It is applied topically as an ointment, lotion, or paste.

Compound resorcinol ointment, N.F., contains 6% resorcinol in a number of media to make a suitable ointment.

Hexylresorcinol, N.F., B.P.

Hexylresorcinol was first introduced as a urinary antiseptic. Much of its efficiency is the result of its low surface tension. This accounts for the name "ST 37" that is used for a 1:1000 solution of hexylresorcinol in glycerin and water.

Hexylresorcinol is stainless and odorless, but it may be irritating to tissues. Persons who become hypersensitive to it may exhibit allergic reactions. One of its more important uses is the treatment of patients with worm infestations. Its use as an anthelmintic will be discussed later.

Thymol, U.S.P., B.P.

Thymol is a colorless crystalline solid with an aromatic odor and taste. Chemically, it is related to one of the cresols and is more effective than phenol. It possesses fungicidal properties, and it is an effective anthelmintic for hookworm. Because of its pleasant odor and taste it is an ingredient of many gargles and mouthwashes.

O-syl and Amphyl

O-syl and Amphyl are both phenol derivatives.

A combination of *o*-phenyl phenol and potassium resinoleate furnishes the active ingredient of O-syl. A similar compound is marketed under the name of Amphyl. These compounds do not have the typical odor of phenolic compounds. When used in 3% concentrations they are said to be effective against vegetative forms of microorganisms, but they do not kill spores. They are moderately active against tubercle bacilli and viruses. They are suitable as germicidal solutions to be used for cleaning of walls, furniture, and floors.

■ Dyes

Certain dyes are used as antiseptics and antiprotozoal agents as well as to promote the healing of wounds. Because they are rapidly adsorbed on proteins, they exhibit limited ability to penetrate tissues, and their germicidal action tends to be slow.

Triphenylmethane dyes (rosaniline dyes)

Triphenylmethane dyes are a group of basic dyes that include crystal violet, gentian violet, methyl violet, brilliant green, and fuchsin. Solutions of these dyes are used in the form of antiseptic dressings on wounds, serous surfaces, and mucous membranes, or they are applied topically for the treatment of superficial fungous or gram-positive infections of the skin and mucous membranes. Gentian violet is also used in the treatment of certain types of worm infestation. Concentrations of 1:1000 to 1:5000 are used for direct application to tissues. For instillation into body cavities the concentration is decreased to 1:10,000.

Gentian violet, **U.S.P.**; *crystal violet*, **B.P.** This dye is available in bulk powder and in tablet form, 10, 15, and 30 mg.

Gentian violet solution, **U.S.P.** The solution consists mainly of gentian violet with some admixture of the other two violet compounds. It is a 1% solution of the dyes in 10% alcohol.

Carbol-fuchsin solution, **N.F. (Castellani's paint)**. This preparation contains fuchsin, phenol, resorcinol, and boric acid in an acetone-alcohol-water solution. It is used in the treatment of fungous infections. Fuchsin is para-rosaniline chloride and is a red dye.

Azo dyes

The azo dyes are more effective as agents that promote the healing of wounds than they are as antiseptics. They appear to stimulate the growth of epithelium and are sometimes used in the treatment of burns, chronic ulcers, and bedsores. Difference of opinion, however, exists regarding their effectiveness.

Scarlet red ointment. This preparation contains 5% scarlet red in olive oil, wool fat, and petrolatum.

Pyridium (phenyl-azo-diamino pyridine hydrochloride). Pyridium is used for its analgesic action on irritated mucous membrane of the urinary tract. It is for this reason that it is found in combination with urinary antiseptics, such as Azo Gantrisin.

Acridine dyes

Acridine dyes have been called "flavines" because of their yellow color. They are applied to open wounds in 0.1% to 1% solutions or ointments. In this strength they are relatively nonirritating and they do not retard the healing of wounds. They are bactericidal and bacteriostatic upon a variety of microorganisms, with greatest activity against gram-positive bacteria in an alkaline medium.

Acriflavine; proflavine hemisulfate, **B.P.** Both of these preparations are used in solution or ointment in the aforementioned strengths.

■ Heavy metals
Mercury compounds

Inorganic compounds. Inorganic compounds of mercury were among the earliest antiseptics to be used, and they long were regarded as potent germicides. Investigation has shown that their action, in many instances, is bacteriostatic rather than bactericidal, since their effects can be reversed under some conditions and microorganisms have been revived that were previously considered dead. Although the mercuric ion brings about the precipitation of cellular proteins, its bacteriostatic action is said to be the result of inhibition of specific enzymes of bacterial cells. Mercurial antiseptics may also exert toxic effects on the tissue cells of the host when taken internally. The mercurials fall far short of being ideal antiseptics or germicides. The inorganic compounds are irritating to tissues, penetrate poorly, are toxic systemically, are adversely affected by the presence of organic materials, have little or no action on spores, and are corrosive to metals. However, they are effective bacteriostatic agents for certain uses. Some of the organic compounds are more potent than the inorganic ones, especially if they are in alcoholic solution. Some authorities believe that certain organic mercurials are useful antiseptics if used appropriately in proper concentration.

Mercury bichloride; mercuric chloride, **B.P.** **(Corrosive Sublimate).** This is the oldest of the mercurial antiseptics. Tablets of mercury bichloride are coffin shaped and are stamped with a skull and crossbones and the word "Poison." They are colored blue to prevent their solutions from being mistaken for water. Mercuric chloride is available in 0.5- and 0.12-Gm. tablets. It is occasionally used in a 1:1000 concentration to disinfect objects that would be harmed by heat or to disinfect hands that have previously been scrubbed with soap and water.

Mercurial ointments. A number of compounds of mercury and metallic mercury are incorporated into ointments for use as antiseptics. The drug slowly dissolves in the tissues to release a low concentration of mercuric ions and thus exerts a prolonged effect. A number of such ointments are listed in *The National Formulary.* Two official ointments are included here.

Ammoniated mercury ointment, **U.S.P., B.P.** **(White Precipitate Ointment).** The U.S.P. preparation contains 5% ammoniated mercury; the B.P. preparation contains 2.5%. The U.S.P. preparation has a base of white ointment and liquid petrolatum. The B.P. preparation is made with simple ointment. Ammoniated mercury is also used in ointments of 2% to 10% concentrations as antiseptics and local stimulants in cases

of suppurating dermatitis, eczematous and parasitic skin diseases, and particularly impetigo.

Ammoniated mercury ophthalmic ointment. This contains 3% ammoniated mercury and is applied as an antiseptic to the eyelids.

Organic mercurial preparations. Organic mercurial compounds are less toxic and less irritating than the inorganic mercurial antiseptics.

Merbromin **(Mercurochrome).** Although widely used at one time, merbromin has been supplanted by more effective agents since it is primarily bacteriostatic. It was the first organic mercurial to be used.

Thimerosal, **N.F. (Merthiolate).** Thimerosal is a light cream-colored, crystalline powder. It contains about 50% mercury. It can be used safely as a skin antiseptic on abraded skin in concentrations of 1:1000, and aqueous solutions can be used on mucous membranes. Thimerosal solution, N.F., is an aqueous solution that has been colored red by a suitable coal-tar color. Thimerosal solutions are incompatible with acids, salts of other heavy metals, and iodine. Thimerosal tincture (an acetone-alcohol solution) and thimerosal ointment are also listed in the N.F.

Nitromersol, **N.F. (Metaphen);** *nitromersol tincture,* **N.F.** This is a 0.5% solution of nitromersol in acetone, alcohol, and water. It is used chiefly as a skin disinfectant. Nitromersol solution, N.F., is an aqueous solution sometimes used to disinfect instruments in concentrations of 1:1000 to 1:5000; to disinfect the skin it is used in a concentration of 1:1000 to 1:5000; and for irrigation of mucous membranes (eye and urethra) it is used in a concentration of 1:5000 to 1:10,000.

Acetomeroctol **(Merbak).** This is an organic mercurial applied topically as an antiseptic. Its activity and effectiveness are similar to those of other organic mercurials. A 1:1000 concentration contains 50% alcohol and 10% acetone, which contribute to its effectiveness.

Phenylmercuric compounds. Phenylmercuric compounds are active against a variety of pathogenic bacteria and exhibit a low level of toxicity in human tissue. Like other mercurial antiseptics, they cannot be depended upon to kill spores. These compounds occasionally cause irritation and poisoning in persons of undue sensitivity. Buffered solutions are odorless, colorless, and stainless and do not react with body proteins. They are noncorrosive to metals with the exception of aluminum, and they do not destroy rubber.

Phenylmercuric nitrate, **N.F., B.P. (Merphenyl Nitrate Basic).** This drug is applied topically in 1:1500 solutions for prophylactic disinfection of intact skin and minor injuries and in 1:1500 to 1:24,000 solutions for mucous membranes and wet dressings.

Silver compounds

Inorganic salts. Silver compounds are used in medicine for their antiseptic, caustic, and astringent effects, which are caused by the release of free silver ions. The soluble salts of silver ionize readily in solution, whereas the colloidal silver compounds dissociate only slightly. Silver ions will precipitate cellular protein; inorganic salts of silver are germicidal in solution but colloidal preparations are bacteriostatic. It is thought that silver, like mercury, is capable of interfering with important metabolic activities of microbial cells.

Silver nitrate, **U.S.P., B.P.** Silver nitrate occurs as flat, transparent crystals that become grayish black on exposure to light and in the presence of organic material. It is odorless and has a bitter strongly metallic taste. It is freely soluble in water, ionizes readily, and is germicidal. Silver nitrate reacts with soluble chloride, iodides, and bromides to form insoluble salts; therefore, the action of silver salts can be stopped by contact with a solution of sodium chloride. This chemical property also explains why solutions of silver salts penetrate tissues slowly as a result of the precipitation of silver ions in the tissues by chlorides or phosphates. A 1:1000 solution is antiseptic. Weak solutions are astringent on mucous membranes, and strong solutions are caustic when applied to mucous membranes or the skin. Silver salts stain tissues black because of the deposit of silver. This discoloration slowly disappears.

Silver nitrate is used on inflamed mucous membranes and ulcerated surfaces. For diseases of the conjunctiva, solutions varying in strength from 0.2% to 2% may be used. To prevent the development of gonorrheal conjunctivitis in the newborn infant, a drop or two of 1% solution is instilled into each eye as soon as possible after delivery. A stronger solution has been used, but it is dangerous, because strong solutions will kill tissue in a short time and may permit the gonococcus to enter and spread into deeper tissues. Blindness has been caused in this way. To stop the action if too much has been used, the eye should be washed with physiologic saline solution. Even a 1% silver nitrate solution produces a chemical conjunctivitis in a rather large number of cases. For this reason, some physicians have advocated the use of penicillin ointment. Solutions of silver nitrate that vary in concentration from 1:1000 to 1:10,000 are used for irrigation of the bladder and urethra. A 1:1000 solution is germicidal but irritating. Long-continued use of any silver preparation may produce permanent discoloration of the skin and mucous membranes, a condition known as argyria.

Toughened silver nitrate, **U.S.P., B.P. (Lunar Caustic).** This form is a white solid generally used in the form of pencils or cones. It is applied as a mild caustic to wounds, ulcers, and granulation tissue. It should be moistened before use and, to avoid blackening the fingers, should be held with forceps. It may be fused on a probe for application to parts with difficult access. The mucous membranes to which solutions of silver nitrate are applied should receive a preliminary cleansing to remove mucus, pus, and food that would interfere with drug action.

Colloidal silver preparations. Colloidal preparations do not ionize readily and do not act as corrosives, irritants, or astringents. They penetrate tissue more readily than do the solutions of simple salts of silver. They exert a bacteriostatic effect because of the concentration of silver ions that is gradually produced.

The terms *strong* and *mild* refer to the relative antiseptic values and not to the amount of silver they contain, for the strong contains about 8% silver and the weak contains about

20%. The antiseptic value depends on the extent of ionization in any given liquid. Mild silver protein preparations should be freshly made and dispensed in amber-colored bottles.

Strong silver protein (Protargol). This compound contains not less than 7.5% and not more than 8.5% of silver.

Mild silver protein, N.F. (Argyn, Silvol). The mild form contains from 19% to 23% silver. It is entirely nonirritating but it also has less antiseptic action than the strong silver protein. It is usually employed in concentrations of 5% to 25%. A concentration of 5% is commonly used for bladder irrigation, 10% to 15% in the nose, and 20% to 25% in the eye.

The colloidal preparations of silver are used as antiseptics, particularly on mucous membranes of the nose and throat, the urinary bladder, the urethra, and the conjunctiva. Gonococci are particularly susceptible to the action of silver compounds.

■ Halogens
Chlorine

Chlorine is a nonmetallic element that occurs in the form of a greenish-yellow gas. It has an intensely disagreeable odor. One part of chlorine in 10,000 parts of air causes irritation of the respiratory tract, and exposure to a 1:1000 concentration is fatal after 5 minutes. It causes spasm and pain of the muscles of the larynx and bronchial tubes, coughing, a burning sensation, fainting, unconsciousness, and death. Its extensive use for the purification of water, however, makes it one of the most widely used disinfectants. One part of chlorine in 1 million parts of water will destroy most bacteria in a few minutes. Acid-fast organisms such as *Mycobacterium tuberculosis* are unusually resistant to it. Chlorine is effective against amebas, viruses, organisms of the colon-typhoid group, and many of the spore-forming pathogens. The antibacterial action of chlorine is said to be caused by the formation of hypochlorous acid, which results when chlorine reacts with water. Hypochlorous acid is a rapidly acting bactericidal agent. Its effect is partly the result of its oxidizing action and partly of its effect on microbial enzymes that are concerned with the metabolism of glucose.

The activity of chlorine and chlorine-releasing compounds is influenced by a number of factors, such as the presence of organic material, the pH of the solution, and the temperature. Chlorine is more effective when there is a minimum of organic matter, when the medium is acid in reaction, and when the temperature is elevated. Chlorine is an efficient deodorant and a strong bleaching agent, and it corrodes many metals.

Gaseous chlorine has limited usefulness because it is difficult to handle. There are a number of compounds that yield hypochlorous acid and that are useful for certain kinds of disinfection.

Sodium hypochlorite solution, N.F. This is a 5% solution of sodium hypochlorite. This concentration is too great to be used on living tissues.

Diluted sodium hypochlorite solution, modified Dakin's solution, N.F. This preparation is a 0.5% aqueous solution of sodium hypochlorite. It was once used extensively in the treatment of suppurating wounds. Although it is useful in cleansing wounds, it also interferes with the formation of thrombin, delays clotting of blood, and is irritating to the skin. Dilute solutions have been used to prevent the development of athlete's foot (epidermophytosis). A 0.5% solution of sodium hypochlorite is also used to disinfect walls, furniture and especially floors. Preparations of sodium hypochlorite are unstable and need to be freshly prepared.

Chloramines. Several compounds are available in which chlorine is linked with nitrogen. The chloramines exert their effects by the release of chlorine to form hypochlorous acid and also by direct action of the parent compound. The chloramines are more stable, less irritating, and slower acting than the hypochlorites. Their action is more prolonged and they are less readily affected by the presence of organic material.

Chloramine-T; chloramine, B.P. This compound is used in 0.1% to 2% aqueous solutions for irrigations of wounds or for dressings.

Halazone, U.S.P. Halazone is available in

4-mg. tablets and is employed for the sterilization of drinking water. All pathogens usually found in water will be killed in 30 to 60 minutes by the addition of one to two tablets (4 to 8 mg.) per liter of water.

Iodine

Iodine is a heavy, bluish-black, crystalline solid that has a metallic luster and a characteristic odor. It is slightly soluble in water but is soluble in alcohol and in aqueous solutions of sodium and potassium iodide. Iodine is volatile, and its solutions should not be exposed to air except during use. The mechanism of disinfectant action is not entirely known. The concentration at which iodine acts as a disinfectant is similar for all bacteria. Iodine is thought to be one of the more efficient chemical disinfectants in present-day usage. Its activity does not vary greatly for vegetative pathogens; it is effective over a wide range of pH, and it is effective against spores, viruses, and fungi. It is not affected by the presence of organic material found in body fluids and exudates. In combination with alcohol, iodine in 0.5% to 1% solution will kill tubercle bacilli. However, iodine does not kill spores readily, and it has the disadvantage of staining skin and clothing. In rare instances, individuals exhibit hypersensitivity reactions to iodine when it is applied to the skin. Toxic effects on tissues are said to be low. Iodine is used chiefly for disinfection of small wounds and abraded surfaces and in the preoperative preparation of skin surfaces. A fact often overlooked is that aqueous solutions as well as alcoholic solutions of iodine are germicidal. Aqueous solutions are less irritating and are best used on abraded areas of the skin. Iodine penetrates the skin and slight amounts are absorbed.

Another use that may be made of iodine tincture is the emergency disinfection of water that is suspected of harboring pathogenic amebas. One drop of iodine tincture to a quart of water will kill amebas and bacteria in 15 minutes without making the water unpalatable.

Iodine stains the skin and linens a brown color. These stains can be removed from the skin with alcohol or ammonia and from fabrics with boiling water.

Iodine tincture, **U.S.P.** This preparation contains 2% iodine and 2.4% sodium iodide in 46% ethyl alcohol. It has to a great extent replaced the strong iodine tincture. Weak iodine solution, B.P., contains approximately the same amount of iodine along with potassium iodide and 90% ethyl alcohol.

Strong iodine tincture. This form is an alcoholic solution containing 7% iodine and 5% potassium iodide in 83% ethyl alcohol.

Strong iodine solution, **U.S.P. (Lugol's Solution).** Strong iodine solution is similar in preparation to strong iodine tincture. The aqueous solution contains 5% iodine and 10% potassium iodide. It is given orally for the treatment of goiter rather than for its antiseptic effect.

Iodine solution, **N.F.** This aqueous solution contains 2% iodine and 2.4% sodium iodide.

Iodophors. Iodophors are complex combinations of iodine and a carrier or agent that increases the water solubility of iodine. The word literally means "iodine carrier." The combination contains and slowly releases iodine as it is needed but does not stain as aqueous solutions of iodine do. As used today, it frequently means a combination of iodine and a detergent. Wescodyne is one that is said to kill tubercle bacilli as well as other organisms sensitive to iodine. Undecoylium chloride-iodine (Virac) is a combination of iodine and a cationic detergent that is said to make a useful surface-acting agent. Polyvinylpyrrolidone iodine, known as PVP iodine or povidone-iodine, is a stable, nonirritating compound that, when dissolved in water slowly, liberates iodine. It is claimed to be as effective and less irritating than aqueous solutions of free iodine. It is marketed as an antiseptic for external use under the name Betadine. It contains 1% available iodine.

■ Oxidizing agents

Certain oxidizing agents are destructive to pathogenic organisms but mild enough to be used on living tissues. Their activity is caused by the oxygen that they liberate. Oxygen combines readily with organic matter and, once combined, it is inert. Oxygen is especially harmful to anaerobic organisms. On the whole, microorganisms vary considerably in their sensitivity to oxygen.

Hydrogen peroxide solution, U.S.P., B.P.

The U.S.P. preparation of hydrogen peroxide solution is a 3% solution of hydrogen peroxide in water.* It is a colorless, odorless liquid that deteriorates upon standing. It should be kept in a cool, dark place and should be well stoppered. Hydrogen peroxide decomposes to water and oxygen. This reaction occurs rapidly when the solution is in contact with organic matter. It is an active germicide only while it is actively releasing oxygen. Solutions have a high surface tension and do not penetrate readily. The effervescence (caused by rapid formation of oxygen bubbles) that accompanies decomposition helps to clean suppurating wounds, but it should not be injected into closed body cavities or into abscesses from which the newly formed gas cannot easily escape. The official solution is usually diluted with 1 to 4 parts of water before it is used. It is used for the cleansing of wounds, for repair of cleft lip, and for the treatment of Vincent's infection (trench mouth). In the latter case it is employed full strength for a limited period of time. Nurses use it frequently to remove collections of mucus from the inner cannula of a tracheostomy tube.

Medicinal zinc peroxide

Medicinal zinc peroxide consists of zinc peroxide, zinc carbonate, and zinc hydroxide. Upon hydrolysis it yields hydrogen peroxide. It has some value in the disinfection and deodorization of wounds, especially those infected with anaerobic organisms. It leaves a residue of zinc oxide that is slightly astringent in effect.

Potassium permanganate, U.S.P., B.P.

Potassium permanganate occurs as dark purple crystals that are soluble in water (1:15). It decomposes on contact with organic matter and

*The preparation described in B.P. is approximately a 6% solution.

liberates oxygen, which combines with bacteria and inhibits their growth or destroys them. The bactericidal efficiency of solutions of potassium permanganate vary with the type of organism and the amount of organic material present. Solutions stronger than 1:5000 may be irritating to tissues. It used in vaginal douches in concentrations of 1:1000 to 1:5000 and is applied topically in concentrations of 1:500 to 1:10,000. After potassium permanganate solutions have lost oxygen they appear brown and are inert. Stains may be removed with dilute acids (lemon juice, oxalic acid, or dilute hydrochloric acid).

Potassium permanganate solutions produce irritant, astringent, deodorant, as well as germicidal effects. It is used much less now than formerly.

Sodium perborate. This is a white powder soluble in water. In solution it forms hydrogen peroxide. It is used as a dusting powder or in 2% solution as an oral antiseptic. Its chief use is in the treatment of Vincent's infection.

■ Surface-active agents

Surface-active agents are also known as wetting agents, emulsifiers, and detergents. In some respects, certain of these agents are considered superior to ordinary soap because they can be used in hard water, are stable in both acid and alkaline solutions, decrease surface tension more effectively, and are less irritating to the skin than ordinary soaps. They all lower surface tensions and aid in the mechanical removal of bacteria and soil. Many also exert a bactericidal action. Many are believed to depress metabolic activities of bacteria, but how they do it is not fully known. They have a weak antibacterial action against fungi, acid-fast organisms, spores, and viruses. Their activity is reduced greatly by the presence of organic matter. If the active portion of the surface-active agent (surfactant) carries a negative electric charge, it is known as an anionic compound; if the active portion carries a positive charge, it is known as a cationic surfactant or surface-active agent.

Cationic agents. The most effective cationic agents have been the quaternary ammonium compounds (sometimes referred to as "quats").

These compounds combine detergent and antiseptic action. In general, they are more effective antiseptics than the anionic group of compounds. They inhibit both gram-positive and gram-negative organisms. Soap inactivates cationic detergents and therefore it must be removed before the detergent is used. Hard water also inactivates these agents and causes precipitation. Although they are recommended in the final rinse of laundry materials, they are often ineffective because traces of soap or hard water remain. Cationic detergents cannot be relied upon to sterilize instruments and articles that cannot be subjected to heat, but they are sometimes used to preserve sterility of stored materials. They have also been used in aerosols to increase the penetrating power of antibiotics.

Benzalkonium chloride, **U.S.P., B.P. (Zephiran Chloride).** When employed in proper concentration, benzalkonium chloride is an effective, relatively noninjurious surface disinfectant. It is germicidal for a number of pathogenic nonspore-forming pathogens, including fungi after several minutes of exposure. However, it has no effect on tubercle bacilli. Its viricidal activity is said to be limited. Benzalkonium chloride solutions have a low surface tension and possess keratolytic, detergent, and emulsifying properties. Solutions of soap reduce its germicidal activity unless well rinsed from the area to be disinfected. Seventy percent alcohol serves to diminish the reaction of soap and the disinfectant and may well follow the use of soap and water preparation of the skin before the application of the disinfectant.

Solutions of benzalkonium chloride have a relatively low level of toxicity under the conditions of use for which they are recommended.

It is suitable for prophylactic disinfection of the intact skin and in the treatment of superficial injuries when used in 1:1000 concentration (tincture).

Solutions of 1:1000 are used for preservation of metallic instruments and rubber articles. For disinfection of operating room equipment, solutions of 1:5000 may be used.

Benzethonium chloride, **N.F. (Phemerol Chloride).** This is a detergent that exerts an inhibitory effect on the growth activities of commonly occurring bacteria and fungi. Tincture of phemerol chloride, 1:500, and benzethonium chloride solution, N.F., 1:1000, are used full strength as general germicides and antiseptics except for use in the nose and eye. For the latter, the aqueous solution is used and diluted with 4 parts of water.

Cetylpyridinium chloride, **N.F., B.P. (Ceepryn Chloride).** This agent is used for preoperative disinfection of intact skin, in the treatment of minor wounds, and for the therapeutic disinfection of mucous membranes. Its effectiveness is reduced by detergents, ordinary soap, and serums and tissue fluids, and it is ineffective against clostridial spores. Strengths used vary from 1:100 for skin preparations and 1:1000 for minor abrasions to 1:5000 and 1:10,000 for mucous membranes.

Methylbenzethonium chloride, **N.F. (Diaparene Chloride).** This preparation produces bacteriostasis of urea-splitting organisms. It is used for disinfecting babies' diapers; they should be free of soap, however, before being rinsed in this disinfectant. It is available in 0.09-Gm. tablets, and the solution is made by dissolving one tablet in 2000 ml. of warm water. This amount is sufficient for rinsing six diapers. They should remain immersed in disinfectant for 3 minutes.

Anionic surface agents. Anionic surface agents are the neutral or faintly alkaline salts of acids of high molecular weights. Common soaps and a number of other compounds belong to this group. They are incompatible with cationic compounds. They act best in an acid medium and are most effective against gram-positive organisms.

Tincture of green soap, **N.F.** This preparation is an alcoholic solution containing about 65% soft soap perfumed with oil of lavender. It is called green because it was first made from oils that contained chlorophyl-like coloring matter. Modern "green soap" may be colorless.

Green soap, **N.F.;** *soft soap,* **B.P.** This is a potassium soap made by the saponification of vegetable oils without the removal of glycerin. Soft soap has little antiseptic value but is used as a cleansing agent.

555

Hexachlorophene liquid soap, **U.S.P.** This is a potassium soap to which hexachlorophene has been added.

Sodium tetradecyl sulfate **(Sodium Sotradecol).** This is an anionic surface-acting agent that lowers surface tension of certain antiseptic solutions to which it may be added. It is also used as a sclerosing agent in the treatment of varicose veins and internal hemorrhoids.

Other anionic surface agents include pHisoderm, which is a synthetic compound sometimes used as a substitute for soap. It is available as a cream or creamy emulsion. It is sometimes used for certain dermatologic conditions when soap is contraindicated. pHisoHex is pHisoderm to which 3% hexachlorophene has been added. It exerts a prolonged antiseptic as well as emollient effect when used routinely. pHisoHex is used frequently for preoperative preparation of patient's skin.

■ Miscellaneous agents

Alcohol

Alcohol, ethanol, ethyl alcohol, **U.S.P., B.P.** Alcohol is one of the oldest and most widely used of the skin disinfectants. Both ethyl alcohol and isopropyl alcohol are used as disinfectants, and their germicidal power is said to be underrated. They are used extensively to prepare the skin prior to venipuncture, subcutaneous and intramuscular injection, and ear or finger pricks for samples of blood. Ethyl alcohol is reported to be most effective in concentrations of 50% to 70%. The growth of some organisms is said to be inhibited by a 1% solution, although the bactericidal action is unreliable when the concentration falls below 20% or is above 95%.

Isopropyl alcohol, **N.F.** This form is slightly more antiseptic than ethyl alcohol. It is employed full strength (99%) or as *isopropyl rubbing alcohol,* N.F., which is a 70% aqueous solution. It is also used extensively as a 75% aqueous solution for the disinfection and storage of oral thermometers. It can be combined with other disinfectants, such as formaldehyde solution, to make an effective germicide.

Formaldehyde solution, U.S.P., B.P.

Formaldehyde in a gaseous form is a powerful parasiticide because of its penetrating power, but it is active only in the presence of abundant moisture. It was used formerly for the fumigation of rooms.

Formaldehyde solution is a 37% solution of formaldehyde (by weight) known as formalin. It is a clear, colorless liquid that, on exposure to air, liberates a pungent, irritating gas. In proper concentration formaldehyde solution is germicidal against all forms of microorganisms. A 0.5% solution will kill all organisms, including spores, in 6 to 12 hours. Higher concentrations are effective in less time. It is not affected by organic matter, and it is effective against viruses. It acts as a precipitant of protein.

Formaldehyde solution hardens tissues, and for this reason it is used as a preservative for specimens and as an astringent. When it is combined with isopropyl alcohol or hexachlorophene, it is probably the most powerful germicidal solution available at the present time. Various modifications of the Bard-Parker germicidal solution are made with formaldehyde solution, isopropyl alcohol, and antirust agents for the disinfection of instruments and articles that cannot be subjected to heat. These solutions are sometimes called "cold sterilization solutions."

The chief disadvantage encountered in using solutions of formaldehyde is that it is irritating to tissues and mucous membranes and has an unpleasant odor.

Boric acid, N.F., B.P.

Boric acid is a mild antiseptic and astringent. Dilute solutions of boric acid are nonirritating and therefore suitable for use on delicate structures such as the eye. Boric acid is an ingredient of many antiseptic solutions used as washes and gargles. It is still widely used for conditions of the skin in the form of wet dressings, dusting powders, and ointments. It is also used in solution form for irrigations of mucous membranes such as the urinary bladder.

Although boric acid is not customarily considered a toxic substance since it is used externally, serious poisoning and deaths have resulted from its ingestion. Solutions of boric acid should be colored to help prevent accidents. Toxic reactions have occurred from topical application to large denuded areas because of the absorption that took place.

Boric acid solution is a 5% aqueous solution of boric acid.

Ethylene oxide

Ethylene oxide has come to be used for gaseous sterilization of materials that cannot be subjected to heat or pressure, such as certain plastic parts of machines and optical instruments.

Ethylene oxide is a colorless gas at ordinary temperatures; it has a rather pleasant ethereal odor, and its toxicity when inhaled is said to compare with ammonia gas. It is flammable and when confined is capable of explosive violence. This agent is therefore used in small cabinets or in a mixture of ethylene oxide with carbon dioxide so that the flammable point is not reached. A preparation of 10% ethylene oxide and 90% carbon dioxide is on the market under the name Carboxide.

Ethylene oxide is apparently effective against all types of microorganisms, including viruses and tubercle bacilli. It is also effective against spores. Its action is bactericidal rather than bacteriostatic. It is a more expensive form of sterilization than that achieved with heat or other chemical agents, but it has good penetrating power and can be used for many things that would be injured by heat.

Questions

for study and review

1 Explain how antiseptics and disinfectants exert their bacteriostatic or bactericidal action.
2 Make a list of the preparations of heavy metals used as antiseptics or disinfectants in the hospital in which you obtain your clinical experience. For what particular purposes are these substances used?
3 An antiseptic is a substance that:
   a. inhibits all microorganisms
   b. kills bacteria
   c. does not sterilize the surface being treated
   d. inhibits growth of infectious agents
4 Which of the following statements are correct?
   a. Increasing the concentration of an antiseptic at the site of action increases its effectiveness.
   b. Phenol antiseptics are not used to disinfect skin or tissue because they precipitate or coagulate proteins.
   c. Phenol antiseptics are effective against bacterial spores.
   d. The development of phenol-resistant organisms is not a problem.
5 The disinfectant activity of ethyl alcohol is:
   a. inferior to that of isopropyl alcohol 70%
   b. greatest at a concentration of 95%
   c. most effective at a concentration of 50% to 70%
   d. very limited
6 Select the *incorrect* answer.
   Anionic surface agents:
   a. are incompatible with cationic surface agents
   b. have a selective action against gram-negative bacteria
   c. act best in an acid medium
   d. have reduced effectiveness in the presence of organic matter (such as blood)
7 Iodine as a chemical disinfectant:
   a. is effective against spores, viruses, and fungi
   b. does not have reduced effectiveness in the presence of organic matter
   c. will kill tubercle bacilli when used in combination with alcohol as a 1% solution
   d. is nonirritating to human tissue

References

A. M. A. Council on Drugs: New drugs, Chicago, 1967, American Medical Association.

Caswell, H. T.: Staphylococcal infections among hospital personnel, Amer. J. Nurs. **58:**822, 1958.

DiPalma, J. R., editor: Drill's pharmacology in medicine, ed. 3, New York, 1965, McGraw-Hill Book Company.

Goodman, L., and Gilman, A.: The pharmacological basis of therapeutics, ed. 4, New York, 1970, The Macmillan Company.

Goth, A.: Medical pharmacology, ed. 6, St. Louis, 1972, The C. V. Mosby Co.

Hugo, W. B.: The mode of action of antiseptics, J. Pharm. Pharmacol. **9:**145, 1957.

Johnstone, F. R. C.: Skin antiseptics: an appraisal and attempted correlation with wound infection, J. Surg. Res. **4:**128, 1964.

Modell, W., editor: Drugs of choice 1972-1973, St. Louis, 1972, The C. V. Mosby Co.

Reddish, G. F., editor: Antiseptics, disinfectants, fungicides and chemical and physical sterilization, Philadelphia, 1957, Lea & Febiger.

Richards, R. C.: Some practical aspects of surgical skin preparation, Amer. J. Surg. **100:**575, 1963.

Spaulding, E. H., and Emmons, E. K.: Chemical disinfection, Amer. J. Nurs. **58:**1238, 1958.

Spaulding, E. H., Emmons, E. K., and Guzara, M. H.: Ethylene oxide sterilization, Amer. J. Nurs. **58:**1530, 1958.

Zintel, H. A., and Know, W. G.: A comparative environmental investigation of surgeon's skin germicides, Ann. Surg. Res. **4:**128, 1964.

Three distinct eras of chemotherapy can be identified. The first period is characterized by the use of natural plant products, extracts, and alkaloids to cure infections. The second period is the era of synthetic antimicrobial compounds. This marks the beginning of effective treatment of bacterial infections. It dates from the discovery of salvarsan by Ehrlich in 1909 to the discovery of the sulfonamides in 1935. Domagk actually discovered the antibacterial action of Prontosil in 1932 but did not publish his findings until 1935, when he had accumulated conclusive evidence concerning its antibacterial effectiveness. Domagk found that Prontosil protected mice against previously fatal doses of hemolytic streptococci. Later it was discovered that Prontosil is converted in the body to para-animo-benzene-sulfonamide, which was later named sulfanilamide. The third period can be characterized as the antibiotic era and a return to natural products, the molds and bacteria that form antibiotics. This era dates from 1940 when the first account of penicillin appeared to the present.

Chemotherapy is the use of agents producing a systemic antimicrobial action. An *antibiotic* is a substance produced by microorganisms that is antagonistic to the growth or life of other microorganisms. Not all antibiotics are clinically useful; many are too toxic to man. All effective antimicrobial drugs have the characteristic of *selective toxicity;* that is, they are more toxic for the parasite than for the host cell.

Sulfonamide compounds

Sulfonamides are widely used throughout the world as antimicrobial drugs, chiefly because of low cost and effectiveness in treating common bacterial infections. All sulfonamides are prepared synthetically.

Chemistry. All of the sulfonamides used therapeutically contain the para-amino-benzene-sulfonamide group ($H_2N—C_6H_4—SO_2NH—$), which gives them their common characteristics. To this group is attached hydrogen or another group that gives each compound its individually characteristic features.

Some 5000 sulfonamides have been made and tested since Domagk's discovery of the antibacterial action of Prontosil. Of these, twenty to thirty are clinically useful. Except under unusual circumstances, all of these are bacteriostatic (in clinically achieved concentrations) rather than bactericidal. All act basically in the same general way. The chemical differences among the various sulfonamides largely determine factors such as the quantitative aspect of antibacterial potency and the distribution, excretion, and toxicity of the drug in the tissues of the patient. Most of the sulfonamides are white, crystalline powders that are relatively insoluble in water and more soluble in an alkaline than an acid pH. Their sodium salts are readily soluble.

Sulfanilamide
Shows H attached to *p*-amino-benzene-sulfonamide group

Sulfadiazine
Shows pyrimidine ring attached to *p*-amino-benzene-sulfonamide group

Although sulfanilamide was not the first of these compounds to be synthesized, it is considered the parent substance of most other sulfonamides. All active members contain a free NH_2 group.

Action and result. Sulfonamides are primarily bacteriostatic agents that check bacterial growth, permitting normal phagocytic processes to eradicate the infection. Sulfonamides act as antimetabolites of para-aminobenzoic acid (PABA) and interfere with the synthesis of

coenzymes from PABA and with the incorporation of PABA into the folic acid molecule. Sulfonamide effectiveness is dependent on the fact that PABA is an essential nutrient for many bacteria. It is also believed that the sulfonamides act by competititive inhibition of PABA; the chemical similarity of these substances may account for the microorganisms taking in the sulfonamide. Bacteriostasis is achieved only in bacteria that must synthesize their own folic acid. Organisms that must utilize preformed folic acid (including man and other mammals) are not affected by sulfonamides.

The sulfonamide drugs

Para-aminobenzoic acid (PABA)

R = a variety of nitrogen-containing groups

Bactericidal effects of the sulfonamides are known to occur in the urine, where the drug becomes concentrated and the organisms are at a disadvantage, because urine is naturally a poor culture medium.

Absorption, diffusion, and excretion. Many of the commonly used sulfonamides (sulfadiazine, sulfamerazine, sulfamethazine, and sulfisoxazole) are well absorbed from the gastrointestinal tract and can therefore be administered orally. Some of the sulfonamides, such as succinylsulfathiazole and phthalylsulfathiazole, are poorly absorbed and are used therefore to reduce bacterial growth in the colon.

One of the outstanding features about the sulfonamides is the ease with which many of them diffuse into all body fluids. Readily absorbed sulfonamides are soon found in the cerebrospinal fluid and in the peritoneal and synovial fluids in concentrations that are therapeutically significant. Obviously, the amount of drug present at any one time depends on how rapidly it is absorbed and how rapidly it is excreted as well as on certain other factors, such as the degree to which it is bound by protein and the extent of acetylation.

Acetylation is the major process by which the sulfonamides are metabolically inactivated. This change is probably caused by the action of the liver. Acetylation is important to the physician when choosing a drug because the acetylated forms are believed to be nontherapeutic, but they may produce toxic symptoms. A sulfonamide with a low percentage of acetylation in the tissues could be given in smaller doses than one that undergoes greater acetylation, other factors being equal.

Excretion of the sulfonamides is chiefly by way of the kidney, where both the free and the acetylated forms of the drug are filtered through the glomerulus. Most sulfonamides are reabsorbed to some extent in the kidney. Some of the sulfonamides are relatively insoluble in neutral or acid media, and as the kidney concentrates the urine and it becomes acid in reaction, there is some danger that the sulfonamide will precipitate out of solution causing crystalluria, hematuria, and even renal shut down. The forcing of fluids to keep the urine dilute and the administration of an alkaline substance such as sodium bicarbonate help to keep a number of the sulfonamides in solution in the urine. However, this is no longer a clinical problem. Sulfonamides such as sulfisoxazole and sulfacetamide are now available and are quite soluble even in acid urine. The problem of solubility in the urine can also be dealt with by combinations of small doses of two or three different sulfonamides. The saturation point of each is not reached in this way and each drug remains in solution. Sulfonamides are also excreted by way of milk, bile, saliva, tears, sweat, and various other body fluids. Sulfamethazine and sulfamerazine are excreted more slowly than sulfadiazine. Some of the sulfonamides are excreted so slowly that one or two doses daily are suffi-

cient to maintain an effective blood level. Sulfamethoxypyridazine and sulfadimethoxine are examples of slowly excreted sulfonamides.

Uses. The choice of sulfonamide to be used depends upon the organism causing the infection, the clinical efficacy of the drug, and the variety, frequency, and severity of the toxic reactions that may be produced. They have the advantage of low cost and ease of administration. Many infections that were formerly treated with one of the sulfonamides are now treated with an antibiotic or with a sulfonamide and an antibiotic.

With the availability of many antibiotics the systemic sulfonamides are indicated only in the treatment of the following conditions (although they may be useful occasionally in others):

1. Chancroid
2. Trachoma
3. Inclusion conjunctivitis
4. Nocardiosis
5. Urinary infections caused by susceptible organisms such as *Escherichia coli, Klebsiella-Aerobacter, Staphylococcus aureus, Proteus mirabilis,* and less frequently *Proteus vulgaris.*
6. Toxoplasmosis—as adjunctive therapy with pyrimethamine
7. Malaria caused by chloroquine-resistant strains of *Plasmodium falciparum*
8. Meningococcal meningitis in which susceptible organisms have been demonstrated
9. *Haemophilus influenzae* meningitis—along with parenteral streptomycin
10. Prophylaxis of rheumatic fever—as an alternative to penicillin

Sulfonamides are of no value in the treatment of tuberculosis, leprosy, typhoid fever, tetanus, syphilis, most viral diseases such as measles and the common cold, and rickettsial diseases.

Resistance. It was early noted that a number of microorganisms were able to develop resistance to the effects of sulfonamides. Some organisms seem to develop an ability to circumvent the interference of the sulfonamide molecule in their enzyme systems. This type of resistance may develop rapidly, but seemingly it is also rapidly lost. Another type of resistance develops more slowly from the emergence of a

Table 28-1 Sulfonamides currently in clinical use

Official name	Trade names	Preparations available	Recommended dose	Remarks
Sulfacetamide, U.S.P., B.P.	Sulamyd	Ophthalmic ointment, 10% Ophthalmic solution, 10%, 30% Oral tablets, 500 mg.	2 to 3 Gm. per day	Rarely produces hypersensitivity of the eye—widely used Used for urinary tract infections
Sulfadiazine, U.S.P., B.P.	Pyramil	Oral tablets, 250, 300, and 500 mg. Injectable (intravenous) solution, 2.5 Gm. in 10 and 50 ml.	500 mg. to 4 Gm. per day 4 Gm. in 5% solution	Slowly absorbed and excreted May cause crystalluria Useful in meningitis Also available as ophthalmic ointment, cream, suppository
Sulfamerazine, U.S.P.		Oral tablets, 500 mg.		Excreted more slowly and bound to plasma proteins to a greater extent than sulfadiazine
Sulfamethazine, U.S.P.; sulphadimidine, B.P.	Diazil	Oral tablets, 500 mg.	Initial dose 2 to 3 Gm., then 1 Gm. every 6 hours	Highly soluble Low toxicity Slowly excreted
Sulfisoxazole, U.S.P.; sulphafurazole, B.P.	Gantrisin	Oral tablets, 500 mg.	Initial dose 3 to 4 Gm., then 4 to 8 Gm. per day	Rapidly excreted and useful for urinary infections Low toxicity Highly soluble
Acetylsulfisoxazole, N.F.	Gantrisin Acetyl	Oral tablets, 500 mg. Pediatric suspension, 0.5 Gm. in 5 ml. Syrup, 0.5 Gm. in 5 ml.	Initial dose 4 Gm., then 1 to 2 Gm. every 4 to 6 hours Adult dose 8 to 10 Gm. per day	Similar to sulfisoxazole
Sulfisoxazole diethanolamine	Gantrisin Diethanolamine	Injectable (intravenous, intramuscular, subcutaneous), 2 Gm. in 5 ml. Ophthalmic ointment and solution Nasal and ear solutions	2 to 4 Gm. every 8 to 12 hours	Caution when used for patients hypersensitive to sulfa drugs
Sulfamethoxazole, N.F.	Gantanol	Oral tablets, 500 mg.	Initial dose 1 to 2 Gm., then 0.5 to 1.0 Gm. every 12 hours	Long activity, slowly absorbed and excreted Used for minor infections of urinary and upper respiratory tracts and soft tissue High degree of acetylation; force fluids
Sulfamethoxypyridazine, B.P.	Kynex Midicel	Oral tablets, 500 mg.	Initial dose 1 Gm., then 0.5 Gm. per day	Readily absorbed but slowly excreted; diffuses rapidly into cerebrospinal fluid Drug reactions and headache common Fatalities have occurred from Stevens-Johnson syndrome Careful observation of patient required

Official name	Trade names	Preparations available	Recommended dose	Remarks
Sulfadimethoxine, N.F.	Madribon	Capsules and tablets, 500 mg.	Initial adult dose 1 to 2 Gm., then 0.5 to 1.0 Gm. per day	Long activity, slow renal excretion, prolonged blood levels
		Chewable tablets, 250 mg. Oral suspension, 250 mg. in 5 ml.	Children less than 80 pounds: 12.5 to 25 mg. per pound of body weight	May cause nausea, vomiting, Stevens-Johnson syndrome Observe patient closely, force fluids Effective against staphylococci
Sulfisomidine	Elkosin	Oral tablets, 500 mg. Syrup, 62.5 mg. per milliliter	Initial adult dose 3 Gm., then 1 to 1.5 Gm. every 6 hours	Useful general purpose drug Low toxicity, rapid excretion
Sulfamethizole, N.F., B.P.	Thiosulfil	Oral tablets, 250 mg. Oral suspension, 50 mg. per milliliter	0.25 to 0.5 Gm. every 4 to 6 hours	Rapidly excreted Useful for urinary infections
Succinylsulfathiazole, U.S.P., B.P.	Sulfasuxidine	Oral tablets, 500 mg.	5 to 10 Gm. per day	Used in intestinal disinfection and in pre- and postoperative bowel surgery Poorly absorbed
Phthalylsulfathiazole, N.F.	Sulfathalidine	Oral tablets, 500 mg.	10 to 20 Gm. per day	Similar to succinylsulfathiazole

few resistant organisms, which then increase in number. Although the latter type of resistance may disappear after a period of time, it tends to be permanent.

The problem of resistance necessitates the maintenance of adequate dosage at all times, since it is believed that inadequate dosage fosters development of resistant strains. It also emphasizes the hazards associated with indiscriminate and unnecessary use of these compounds.

Preparation, dosage, and administration. The sulfonamides are usually administered orally. These drugs should be stored in tight light-resistant containers to prevent decomposition. When, for some reason, a patient is unable to take the drug by mouth, sodium salts of a number of the sulfonamides are available for intravenous administration. Topical application fosters hypersensitivity and is therefore not recommended. Exceptions are ophthalmic ointments and sulfamylon for extensive burns. For the treatment of systemic infections the initial dose is frequently 0.1 Gm. per kilogram of body weight (usually about 4 Gm.) and then 1 Gm. every 4 hours (day and night) until the temperature has been normal for 72 hours. Patients with minor infections may be given correspondingly smaller doses. A concentration of 15 mg. of the drug in 100 ml. of blood is thought to be desirable when severe infection is present, and 5 to 10 mg. per 100 ml. is usually satisfactory for less severe infections. Peak action occurs 2 to 3 hours after oral administration. Experience seems to indicate that when a standard course of therapy is followed, it produces, in most in-

563

stances, an adequate concentration of the drug in the blood and tissue fluids.

Side effects and toxic effects. Some of the effects seen formerly when sulfanilamide, sulfathiazole, and sulfapyridine were extensively used are now seen much less often since these preparations are seldom used. With the preparations employed at the present time, the incidence of toxicity is relatively rare; however, when toxicity does occur it is likely to be the result of the development of hypersensitivity, renal disturbance, or personal idiosyncrasy on the part of the patient. Those that are poorly absorbed are naturally unlikely to cause symptoms of toxicity. When renal function is impaired, the incidence of toxicity is increased. Although the incidence of toxic effects is lower with the newer sulfonamides, they must be administered with the same precautions used with the older preparations. Some reactions are relatively mild and more of a nuisance than a real threat to the welfare of the patient. Toxic and side effects include the following:

1 Nausea and vomiting occur less often than formerly but still occur in as many as 5% of the patients. Stopping administration of the drug is not usually indicated.
2 Other undesirable reactions include dizziness, headache, mental depression, restlessness and irritability, drug fever, and dermatitis.
3 Among the more severe reactions are granulocytopenia, agranulocytosis, hemolytic anemia, and jaundice. The development of symptoms associated with these conditions means that administration of the drug probably must be discontinued. However, it is felt that the occasional severe toxic effect on the blood should not exclude the use of sulfonamides when they are clinically indicated.
4 Symptoms associated with renal damage include oliguria, crystalluria, and anuria. These may result from precipitation of the drug in the renal tubules. This happens when a sulfonamide that is not very soluble in urine is administered or when the fluid intake is inadequate.
5 Particularly with the long-acting sulfonamides, the skin eruptions of Stevens-Johnson syndrome may occur. This complication is fatal in 25% of the cases. The drug should be stopped at the first sign of a rash.

A number of toxic effects of the sulfonamides are more easily prevented than treated. It is important for the nurse to remember that damage to the kidneys can be minimized by making certain that the patient has an adequate fluid intake. Although this is not the problem that it was with the older compounds, it is still believed to be advisable to regulate fluid intake so that there will be an output of at least 1500 ml. daily. Preparations such as sulfadiazine are made more soluble in the urine if the urine is kept alkaline, and for that reason sodium bicarbonate is sometimes prescribed to be given with it. This precaution is not considered necessary when the more soluble (in urine) preparations are used.

Patients should be instructed that if at any time they develop a sore throat, fever, rash, or hematuria during treatment with these drugs, they should stop taking the drug immediately and contact their doctor.

The advantages of the sulfonamides may be listed as follows: (1) they are drugs of choice for treatment of some diseases, (2) they are easy to administer, (3) they are relatively inexpensive, and (4) it is thought they they rarely produce superinfection.

Sulfonamide mixtures

A number of preparations composed of two or more sulfonamides have been marketed. Their introduction was a major step in solving the problem of renal complications associated with therapy with the sulfonamides.

Triple mixtures have been found to reduce the incidence of renal complications more than dual mixtures. Other untoward effects, however, are not affected by combining the drugs.

It is believed that the incidence of sensitization is directly related to dosage; therefore, a decreased dose of each drug in the mixture is believed to reduce the danger of sensitization of the patient.

Trisulfapyrimidines oral suspension, U.S.P., and trisulfapyrimidines tablets, U.S.P., are official preparations of sulfadiazine, sulfamerazine, and sulfamethazine. Sulfonamide mixtures are now being replaced by the newer and more soluble sulfa drugs.

Questions

for study and review

1 Name a specific sulfa preparation used for:
   a. urinary tract infection
   b. preoperative bowel preparation
   c. meningitis
   d. bacillary dysentery

For the following statements indicate whether they are true or false, and explain the reason for your choice.

2 The sulfonamides are drugs of choice for the treatment of various urinary tract infections.

3 Sulfa preparations used to suppress the growth of bacteria in the large bowel prior to surgery are those that are poorly absorbed from the gastrointestinal tract.

4 To be effective in treating urinary tract infections, a sulfa drug must be highly soluble in urine.

5 Crystalluria becomes a hazard with the use of sulfa preparations that are insoluble in an acid medium.

6 Sulfonamides exert their major antibacterial action by interfering with the incorporation of PABA into the folic acid molecule.

7 Sulfonamides penetrate well into cerebrospinal fluid and the meninges and therefore are important drugs in the treatment of meningitis.

8 The development of sulfonamide-resistant organisms does not readily occur.

References

A. M. A. Council on Drugs: New drugs, Chicago, 1967, American Medical Association.

Bagdon, R. E.: Experimental pharmacology and toxicology of sulfonamides. In Schnitzer, R. J., and Hawking, R., editors: Experimental chemotherapy, vol. 2, New York, 1964, Academic Press, Inc.

Bass, A. D.: Chemotherapy of bacterial infections: II. Sulfonamides. In Di Palma, editor: Drill's pharmacology in medicine, ed. 3, New York, 1965, McGraw-Hill Book Company, p. 110.

Bauer, A. W.: The present status of bacterial resistance to sulfonamides, Chemotherapia (Basel) 9:88, 1964.

Bauer, A. W., and Sherris, J. C.: The determination of sulfonamide susceptibility of bacteria, Chemotherapia (Basel) 9:1, 1964.

Beckman, H.: Pharmacology; the nature, action, and use of drugs, Philadelphia, 1961, W. B. Saunders Co.

Carroll, G.: Neg Gram (nalidixic acid), a new antimicrobial chemotherapeutic agent, J. Urol. 90:476, 1963.

Draper, J. W.: Development of sulfonamides: historical account, Current Med. Digest. 32:855, 1965.

Goodman, L., and Gilman, A., editors: The pharmacological basis of therapeutics, ed. 4, New York, 1970, The Macmillan Company.

Holsinger, D. R., Hanlon, D. G., and Welch, J. S.: Fatal aplastic anemia following sulfamethoxypyridazine therapy, Proc. Staff Meet. Mayo Clin. 33:679, 1958.

Janovsky, R. C.: Fatal thrombocytopenic purpura after administration of sulfamethoxypyridazine, J.A.M.A. 172:155, 1960.

Leher, D.: Clinical toxicity of sulfonamides, Ann. N. Y. Acad. Sci. 69:417, 1957.

Ritz, N. D., and Fisher, M. J.: Agranulocytosis due to administration of salicylazosulfapyridine (azulfadine), J.A.M.A. 172:237, 1960.

Schwartz, M. J., and Norton, W. S., II: Thrombocytopenia and leukopenia associated with the use of sulfamethoxypyridazine, J.A.M.A. 167:457, 1958.

Today's drugs: sulphonamides, Brit. Med. J. 1:483, 1964.

Warning against prolonged-action sulfonamides, Med. Letter 8:13, 1966.

Weinstein, I., Madoff, M. A., and Samet, C. A.: The sulfonamides, New Eng. J. Med. 263:793, 1960.

29 Antimicrobial drugs — antibiotics

In 1928 Alexander Fleming observed that a mold contaminating a culture of *Staphylococcus aureus* inhibited bacterial growth. He extracted the substance produced by the mold (genus, *Penicillium*) and called it penicillin. Florey, Chain, and their group at Oxford became interested in the chemistry of penicillin and in 1940 isolated small amounts of impure penicillin. They used penicillin in man and achieved striking results, although these were only temporary because their supply soon became exhausted. In 1941, under the stimulus of wartime need, the manufacture of penicillin was started in the United States. The work in the United States was largely a search for improved methods of growing the mold, for strains of mold that would produce the highest yield of penicillin, and for methods of purifying penicillin.

Since the discovery of penicillin practically no other bactericidal antibiotics with low toxicity have been produced. Streptomycin, colistin, and bacitracin, three bactericidal drugs produced since the discovery of penicillin, have limited usefulness. Their toxicity is of such magnitude that administration in large doses over long periods of time is precluded. For this reason hope and enthusiasm are aroused whenever a new antibiotic is discovered. The use of antibiotics is widespread, and annual production is measured in millions of pounds. Penicillin remains the most widely used of all antibiotic agents and accounts for some 40% of all antibiotic production.

■ Antibiotic action

The ability of antibiotics to inhibit or kill microorganisms without seriously damaging human cells depends upon their interference with metabolic functions essential to the microorganism and not present in man. Bacteria possess rigid cell walls and thus cell wall synthesis for which there is no counterpart in mammalian cells. Bacteria without rigid cell walls cannot survive in most body fluids and tissues. Since penicillin prevents bacteria from forming new cell wall material, leading to their

Table 29-1 Bactericidal and bacteriostatic antibiotics

Group I (bactericidal)	Group II (bacteriostatic)
Penicillin	Chlortetracycline
Streptomycin	Chloramphenicol
Bacitracin	Oxytetracycline
Neomycin	Erythromycin
Polymyxin	Tetracycline
Kanamycin	Lincomycin

eventual destruction, penicillins are bactericidal antibiotics.

Antibiotics exert their antibacterial effects by: (1) inhibition of cell wall synthesis, (2) inhibition of protein synthesis, and (3) interference with the function of the cytoplasmic membrane.

Antibiotics that interfere with protein synthesis in bacteria include chloramphenicol, erythromycin, the tetracyclines, lincomycin, streptomycin, kanamycin, and neomycin. Some of these drugs are bacteriostatic while others are bactericidal. See Table 29-1.

The bacterial cytoplasmic membrane controls the internal composition of the cell. It functions as a selective permeable membrane that permits the bacteria to selectively concentrate certain low molecular substances as amino acids, nucleotides, and inorganic ions, resulting in high osmotic pressure within the cell. Damage to the cytoplasmic membrane releases the concentrated internal solutes and it can no longer function effectively. The cytoplasmic membrane is rich in enzymes and a site for synthesis of other cell components.

Antibiotics that alter the cytoplasmic membrane include: the polymyxins, amphotericin B, tyrocidin, nystatin, and novobiocin. The polymyxins are bactericidal, novobiocin is bacteriostatic.

Antibiotics are bacteriostatic or bactericidal. Whether an antibiotic is bacteriostatic or bactericidal is dependent upon the concentration and nature of the agent, the age of the organism, and the nature of the environment. Bacteria are most readily destroyed during immaturity and at the time of rapid multiplication of the organisms. When an antibiotic is used as a bacteriostatic agent, the normal body defenses, white blood cells and immune bodies, are depended upon to kill the inhibited microorganisms.

When the antibiotic blocks a metabolic reaction common to a large number of organisms, it is known as a broad-spectrum antibiotic because it has a large range of action. When an antibiotic blocks a reaction that can be bypassed by most but not all classes or organisms, it has a narrow range of activity and is known as a narrow-spectrum antibiotic.

Antibiotics may be additive, synergistic, or antagonistic to one another. On the basis of studies to determine these effects, antibiotics have been divided into two groups (see Table 29-1). Combinations of Group I drugs are considered synergistic, additive, occasionally indifferent, but never antagonistic. Group II combinations are never synergistic or antagonistic, but they are additive. Group I and Group II compounds may be used together. Group II compounds generally reduce the effectiveness of Group I compounds if the offending organism is sensitive to Group I drugs, but a synergistic action is obtained if the organism in question is resistant to Group I compounds.

■ **Aspects of antibacterial therapy**

The penicillins, streptomycin, the tetracyclines, and erythomycin are among the most effective and widely used antibiotics. Certain infections can be effectively treated with the use of only one antibiotic. In other infections any one of several agents may be effective. When a choice can be made, ease of administration, toxicity, and drug cost must be considered.

Initial and maintenance doses must be adequate to bring about recovery from illness as soon as possible and to discourage development of drug resistance by the microorganism. Excessive dosage, however, increases the likelihood of toxic reactions and adds to the patient's expense.

With the advent of widespread antibiotic therapy, hospital admissions and deaths from pneumococci and beta-hemolytic streptococci decreased sharply, while the number caused by gram-negative enteric bacteria increased markedly. Use of antistaphylococcal penicillins (such as methicillin) has resulted in a decline of hospital infections caused by *Staphylococcus aureus.*

Resistance. Bacteria develop resistance to penicillin by being *drug tolerant* and/or *drug destroying. Drug-tolerant* organisms have surfaces impermeable to the drug or have developed metabolic pathways not sensitive to drug action. Thus these organisms can survive and grow in antibiotic concentrations lethal for sensitive cells. *Drug-destroying* organisms produce enzymes that inactivate drugs. The most important of these enzymes is penicillinase.

Bacteria can also acquire antibiotic resistance by spontaneous mutation followed by selection of the resistant mutant in a drug environment. Some bacteria contain a resistant transfer factor (RTF) and one or more genes that confer resistance to one or more antibiotics. Direct cell-to-cell contact permits the transfer phenomenon. This probably accounts for antibiotic-resistant mixed infections. Staphylococci and gram-negative bacilli are known to be capable of transferring genetic material conferring antibiotic resistance. Thus pathogenic bacteria possess several effective means for coping with antibiotics, and the problem of bacterial resistance to antibiotics will undoubtedly continue to be of great importance.

The majority of disease-producing bacteria remain susceptible to antibiotics. *Proteus* and *Pseudomonas* are two of the few kinds of bacteria that tend to be resistant to most anti-microbial agents.

Microbial resistance to antimicrobial drugs is often effected in an environment containing a significant level of antimicrobial drugs. This applies not only to the internal environment of a single human being but also to an environment shared by many people (hospitals). Resistance occurs (1) when the drugs suppress the normal flora, creating a void that must be filled and thereby permitting entry and proliferation of resistant organisms, and (2) when the drugs suppress the drug-sensitive bacteria, permitting spontaneous resistant mutants to proliferate without restraint.

The problem of resistance may be somewhat overcome by reducing the abuse of antimicrobial agents. This means abolishing the indiscriminate use of antibiotics for trivial ailments, viral infections, or chemoprophylaxis in noninfectious disorders (such as cerebrovascular accidents). People are safer with their own flora and with building up their own resistance to infections. Therefore the nurse should check with the physician periodically to make certain that he wants administration of an antibiotic continued. Unreasonable confidence in antimicrobial drugs may result in deterioration of aseptic practices. It is important that nurses emphasize the need for asepsis, isolation, and cleanliness to reduce the spread of drug-resistant organisms.

Superinfections. Superinfections may occur when the normal flora of the body, which prevents other microorganisms from getting a foothold, is disturbed. Often this leads to nutritional imbalance and affects the integrity of the mucous membrane of the host, thereby giving entry to an organism that normally would be unable to penetrate healthy mucosa. Microorganisms not ordinarily pathogenic may then cause disease. For example, *Candida albicans* has caused monilial vaginitis when antibiotics killed the bacteria normally found in the vagina. Staphylococcal enteritis (pseudomembranous enterocolitis) has occurred when the normal pattern of intestinal flora has been disturbed. When superinfection develops, the use of the antibiotic is usually stopped or another antibiotic is employed to destroy the microorganisms causing the superinfection.

In considering antibiosis it should be remembered that in dealing with living organisms one deals with constant change. Man adapts to his environment, which includes the microorganisms with which he must live. The microorganisms, in turn, represent populations of billions of cells that can divide as often as every 20 minutes. Many random mutational changes may occur, permitting microorganisms to adapt to new conditions. Therefore, the status and usefulness of antibiotics change as man and microorganisms adapt to their changing environment.

Characteristics of a good antibiotic

An ideal antimicrobial drug for clinical use should be harmless to human tissues, especially those of the blood and the blood-forming organs, the liver, and the kidney. For an antibiotic to be effective it must remain in the body tissues for a relatively long period of time, and if the infection is a severe one, the dosage as well as the length of time during which it is administered may have to be increased; hence, low toxicity is a primary qualification. There are other characteristics of a good antibiotic:

1 It should be a stable substance, not destroyed by tissue enzymes, not inhibited by the presence of serum, pus, or blood, and not eliminated too rapidly by the kidney.
2 Infecting microorganisms should not be able to develop resistance to it, and it should be powerful in its action against some microorganisms.
3 It should be soluble in water and salt solutions.
4 It should diffuse readily through body tissues, and it should not sensitize the patient.
5 It should not alter the normal body flora, which may result in superinfections.
6 It should be well absorbed from the intestinal tract and be tolerated when given by other routes of administration.
7 It should not be antagonistic to other antibiotics.

No antibiotic, however, meets all of these requirements.

Systemic antibiotics generally used

Penicillins

General characteristics

Penicillin is an antibiotic derived from a number of strains of *Penicillium notatum* and *Penicillium chrysogenum*, common molds often seen on bread or fruit. Commercially, the mold is grown in corn-steep liquor, and to this medium may be added sugar, inorganic salts, and certain organic compounds that the mold incorporates into the penicillin molecule to form the type of penicillin desired. The various penicillins are known as penicillin F, G, K, O, V, and X. Penicillin G has been synthesized chemically, but the synthetic preparation is not practical because of the increased cost and difficulties encountered. The most commonly used penicillin is penicillin G; it is easy to manufacture and is widely used at present in the form of its sodium or potassium salt. Penicillin O and penicillin V are also used therapeutically. The other penicillins are not used therapeutically because of various disadvantages. The penicillins just mentioned differ from each other in that different side chains are attached to the basic nucleus of the molecule. The following is the basic formula

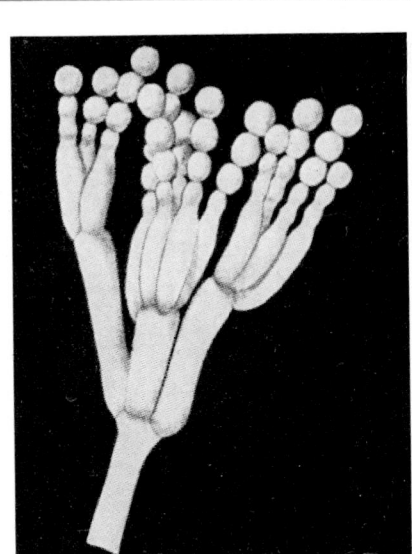

Figure 29-1
Typical penicillus of *Penicillium notatum;* Fleming's strain. (From Raper, K. B., and Alexander, D. F.: J. Elisha Mitchell Sc. Soc. **61**:74, 1945.)

for the penicillins. The *R* stands for the different side chains attached to the group common to all penicillins.

Basic formula for penicillins

Formula for penicillin G or benzyl penicillin

For two other commonly used penicillins the *R* in the formula is as follows:

Allylmercaptomethyl penicillin (O)

Phenoxymethyl penicillin (V)

The penicillins are organic acids, white or slightly yellow in color. The dry preparations are stable; however, in solution the penicillins are relatively unstable so that the expiration date should be noted when a nurse prepares the solution. Of the various penicillins, penicillin G is usually considered the most active. Penicillin G is the penicillin referred to in the following discussion unless specified otherwise.

Standardization. Penicillin is standardized by comparing the effect of the penicillin to be assayed on the growth of a test organism *(Staphylococcus, Streptococcus,* or *Bacillus subtilis)* with the effect of a standard penicillin

570

preparation. The U.S.P. unit is the antibiotic activity of 0.6 μg. of the U.S.P. penicillin G sodium reference standards, 1 mg. being equal to 1667 units.* Reference standard means a specific lot of penicillin G that serves as the standard of comparison in determining potency.

Penicillin dosage is still expressed in units, but the use of doses measured according to weight in milligrams is increasing.

The desired end result of the action of penicillin is eradication of infection with reduction of fever, improved appetite, and an increased sense of well-being; in other words, a return to a state of health.

Absorption, distribution, and excretion. Penicillin G and penicillin O are partially inactivated by gastric juice and by the enzyme penicillinase formed by bacteria in the intestine; therefore, their absorption from the intestine is uncertain unless they are buffered by an antacid such as calcium carbonate. The benzathine or aluminum salts of penicillin G are only slightly soluble and so can withstand the action of gastric juice. Penicillin V (phenoxymethyl penicillin) and phenethicillin are stable in gastric acid and so pass through the stomach unchanged, but they are not completely absorbed.

Penicillin diffuses readily into most body tissues, with the exception of the brain, spinal fluid, bone marrow, and fluids of the eye; in these, levels of penicillin are considerably lower than levels in the blood. Inflammation of limiting membranes, such as meninges, tends to make them more permeable to penicillin. Penicillin also passes easily from the maternal blood into the blood of the fetus.

Most of the penicillin absorbed is excreted quickly by the kidneys because, like certain other drugs, penicillin is not only filtered through the glomeruli but is also secreted directly across the epithelium of the kidney tubules. A small amount appears in the bile, saliva, and serous sacs. After an intramuscular injection of

---

*The U.S.P. states that 1 mg. of other kinds of penicillin contains different numbers of units. For example, 1 mg. of potassium phenoxymethyl penicillin represents 1530 U.S.P. units and 1 mg. of benzathine penicillin G represents 1211 U.S.P. penicillin units.

an aqueous solution of penicillin the drug appears in the urine in 10 minutes, and most of it is excreted within 2 hours. Because penicillin is absorbed so quickly from the muscles, ways have been devised to slow the passage from the muscle into the bloodstream. Relatively insoluble salts, such as procaine and benzathine penicillin, pass slowly into the bloodstream; placing penicillin in vehicles such as insoluble oils also slows its absorption.

To decrease the rate of excretion of penicillin, it is possible to give a drug that inhibits its excretion from the kidney. Probenecid (Benemid) is a drug that can be used for this purpose; however, penicillin is now relatively inexpensive, and it is usually simpler to give large doses to make up for urinary losses.

Uses. Penicillin should be used for any patient who is not allergic to it and who has an infection caused by a penicillin-sensitive organism. These include the following:

1 Gram-positive bacteria—all sensitive strains of staphylococci, *Streptococcus pyogenes, Streptococcus viridans, Diplococcus pneumoniae, Bacillus anthracis, Actinomyces bovis, Clostridium tetani,* the clostridia of gas gangrene, and *Corynebacterium diphtheriae*
2 Gram-negative bacteria—*Neisseria gonorrhoeae, Neisseria meningitidis,* and Vincent's organism
3 Others—*Treponema pallidum* and *Treponema pertenue*

Penicillin is not effective against infections caused by (1) protozoa, such as those causing malaria and amebiasis, (2) the gram-negative bacilli, such as the colon-typhoid dysentery group of organisms, (3) the tubercle bacillus, (4) the rickettsias, (5) the true viruses, and (6) the fungi. It is somewhat effective against the larger viruses of psittacosis and lymphogranuloma venereum.

Most of the organisms originally susceptible to the action of penicillin have remained susceptible. Penicillin has almost eradicated fatal hemolytic streptococcal infections. It is highly effective in pneumococcal pneumonia, syphilis, gonorrhea, bacterial endocarditis, and actinomycosis. However, the staphylococci have become increasingly resistant to penicillin, and resistant strains of gonococci are appearing. It will be remembered that penicillinase inactivates penicillin. Agreement does not exist as to whether penicillinase is produced through the use of too low a concentration of penicillin, whether it represents the emergence of mutants, or whether the strains originally were resistant because of their inherent ability to produce this penicillin antagonist. Probably all three factors play a part in the production of penicillinase.

In deciding on the use of penicillin against the organisms listed, the doctor's decision depends on a number of factors related to the microorganism, the patient, and the disease. The microorganism may prove to be resistant to penicillin; the patient may be known to be allergic to penicillin; past experience with the disease may indicate that penicillin should be combined with another agent (in diphtheria and clostridial infections penicillin is used with antitoxin, and in meningococcic infections sulfonamide may be given simultaneously).

Administration

Crystalline penicillin is very soluble in water and can be given by almost any method of administration. When it was first used, it was commonly given by intramuscular injection; because it was excreted quickly, it was administered every 3 hours. With further study it was found that maintenance of high blood levels was not essential in many patients, and this, added to the fact that frequent injections are inconvenient and uncomfortable, has led to the use of preparations of penicillin that are absorbed more slowly after intramuscular injection and to the use of oral preparations. Although these preparations do not lend themselves to the maintenance of high blood levels, in most cases they have been found to be therapeutically satisfactory.

Crystalline preparations may be dissolved in sterile distilled water, isotonic solution of sodium chloride, or 5% dextrose solutions. They diffuse quickly and are excreted rapidly. They are usually administered by the intramuscular route, although the intravenous method is also used. They are used for severe infections or infections in which the organism is only moderately susceptible to penicillin. They are also used when the organism is not very accessible, as in subacute bacterial endocarditis in which the infecting organism is protected by vegetative lesions. In these cases the dose may total many millions of units per day. When given intramuscularly they are given at frequent intervals. A continuous intravenous drip may be employed in treating of severe infections.

Noncrystalline preparations are used for prolonged action, since they are absorbed very slowly.

Parenteral. Parenteral administration includes intramuscular, intravenous, and subcutaneous injection.

Intramuscular administration is the most common parenteral method of administration. The slowly absorbed, insoluble depot preparations are those used most; procaine penicillin G and benzathine penicillin G are the most popular preparations at present.

For *intravenous* injection water-soluble salts of penicillin, such as penicillin G sodium and penicillin G potassium, are given when treatment of severe infections requires fast action and high blood levels. Continuous intravenous drip is employed for infections in which a large dose of penicillin is needed to conquer the infection.

Subcutaneous injection is seldom used because the blood levels attained tend to be unpredictable.

Preparation and dosage of crystalline penicillin. The following are the usual preparations and dosages of penicillin for parenteral use.

Potassium penicillin G for injection, **U.S.P.;** *benzylpenicillin injection.* This is potassium penicillin G or sodium penicillin G buffered with sodium citrate. The usual intramuscular dose is 400,000 U.S.P. units four times a day. The usual intravenous dose is 10 million units daily.

Potassium penicillin G (Benzyl Penicillin Potassium), **U.S.P.;** *benzylpenicillin,* **B.P.** The usual intramuscular dose is 400,000 U.S.P. units per day. The intravenous dose is usually 10 million units daily.

Sodium penicillin G (Benzyl Penicillin Sodium), **N.F.;** *benzylpenicillin,* **B.P.** The usual intramuscular dose is 400,000 U.S.P. units per day. The usual intravenous dose is 10 million U.S.P. units per day.

Sodium methicillin, **U.S.P.** (Staphcillin, Dimocillin-RT); *methicillin injection,* **B.P.** Sodium methicillin is a semisynthetic penicillin administered parenterally for treatment of staphylococcal infections that do not respond to other penicillins. Sodium dimethoxyphenyl penicillin (sodium methicillin) is available in vials for intramuscular and intravenous administration. The usual recommended dose is 1 to 2 Gm. every 4 to 6 hours. Patients may become allergic to it, and depression of bone marrow has been reported.

Preparation and dosage of noncrystalline penicillin. The following preparations are examples of relatively insoluble penicillin G preparations called "depot" preparations because they remain in the muscle a long time. Since they are slowly absorbed, their action lasts a longer time than the crystalline preparations and permits them to be given less often. They are administered intramuscularly only.

Benzathine penicillin G, **U.S.P., B.P.** (Bicillin). The usual intramuscular dose is 600,000 U.S.P. units, repeated as necessary. The usual range of dosage is 300,000 to 3 million units.

Sterile benzathine penicillin G suspension, **U.S.P.** The dose is the same as that for benzathine penicillin G. Benzathine penicillin G is very slowly absorbed. Depending on the size of the dose, a single intramuscular injection produces a demonstrable blood level for 1 to 4 weeks or longer. It may be used when prolonged action at low levels is desirable, for example, to prevent streptococcal infections in patients who have had rheumatic fever. For primary and secondary syphilis a single dose of 2,400,000 units is considered effective.

Procaine penicillin G, **U.S.P., B.P.** The usual intramuscular dose is 300,000 U.S.P. units once or twice a day. The usual dosage range is 300,000 to 1,200,000 units.

Sterile procaine penicillin G suspension, **U.S.P.;** *procaine penicillin injection,* **B.P.** The dose is the same as that for procaine penicillin G.

Sterile procaine penicillin G with aluminum stearate suspension, U.S.P. The intramuscular dose is 300,000 U.S.P. units on alternate days. The usual dosage range is 300,000 to 1,200,000 units.

Fortified procaine penicillin injection, B.P. This is a sterile suspension of procaine penicillin in water for injection containing benzylpenicillin in solution. The dose is determined by the physician in accordance with the needs of the patient.

Procaine penicillin is usually given once or twice a day, and the procaine penicillin in oil with aluminum monostearate needs to be given only every 24 to 48 hours. The amount of procaine in these preparations is small, but if a patient is allergic to procaine these preparations should not be used. Some preparations of procaine penicillin have crystalline penicillin G in them; this would provide both a rapid and a slow action in cases of severe infection.

Oral. Oral administration is highly desirable because it eliminates the need for injections and because anaphylactic reactions to orally administered penicillin are infrequent. It is not as effective as parenteral administration, for high blood levels are not easily attained and certain oral preparations tend to be excreted rapidly. However, oral administration is satisfactory for most infections except those that are very severe.

Preparation and dosage of penicillin for oral administration. The following are the usual preparations and dosages of penicillin for oral administration.

Phenoxymethyl penicillin, U.S.P. (Penicillin V), B.P. (Compocillin-V). Official preparations of phenoxymethyl penicillin include capsules, oral suspension, and tablets. The usual dose is 125 to 250 mg. (approximately 200,000 to 400,-000 U.S.P. units) four to six times a day. The usual dosage range is 500 mg. to 2 Gm. (approximately 800,000 to 3,200,000 units) daily.

Potassium phenoxymethyl penicillin (Penicillin V Potassium), U.S.P. (Compocillin-VK, Pen-Vee-K, V-Cillin-K). The dose is the same as that for phenoxymethyl penicillin. The official preparations include tablets and capsules.

Potassium phenethicillin, N.F. (Syncillin, Darcil, Chemipen, Maxipen). This is a semisynthetic penicillin that is water soluble and relatively resistant to the destructive action of acids. It is given orally in doses of 125 or 250 mg. three times daily. Larger doses may be used if indicated. It is available in the form of tablets and a solution for pediatric use.

Sodium oxacillin, U.S.P. (Prostaphlin, Resistopen). The preparation is a semisynthetic penicillin that has been found to be resistant to acid and penicillinase. It is available in 250- and 500-mg. capsules for oral administration, and parenteral preparations have been marketed for intramuscular and intravenous administration. The recommended dose for severe to moderately severe staphylococcal infections is 1 Gm. every 4 hours. When given orally, the drug should be given between meals, because the presence of food seems to delay absorption from the intestinal tract.

Sodium cloxacillin, U.S.P. (Tegopen). Sodium cloxacillin is very similar in all respects to sodium oxacillin. It is used primarily against staphylococci resistant to penicillin G. It is acid resistant and can be administered by mouth. Parenteral form is also available. The recommended dose is 0.5 to 1 Gm. every 4 to 6 hours by mouth.

Potassium penicillins G and O may be administered orally, but because they are, to a great extent, inactivated by gastric juice and intestinal bacteria, approximately three fourths of the dose is destroyed, leaving only one fourth to be absorbed and potentially effective. As a result, doses approximately five times greater than the parenteral doses must be given. The newer penicillins (penicillin V, phenethicillin, and oxacillin) are currently popular as oral preparations of penicillin. Their absorption may also be erratic, although not as much as when they are taken on an empty stomach. In any case, they should not be relied upon in the treatment of severe infection, in which case injectable preparations may be essential.

Aerosol. When penicillin is administered by

Table 29-2 The penicillins

Approved name	Other name	Resistant to gastric acid	Resistant to penicillinase	Antibacterial spectrum	Remarks
Benzylpenicillin (penicillin G)	Penicillin G	No	No	High activity against gram-positive bacteria Low activity against gram-negative bacteria	Only one-third oral dose absorbed, so oral dose must be three to five times that given parenterally For maximum absorption give oral dose 1 hour before or 2 to 3 hours after meal
Methicillin	Staphcillin	No	Yes	Like penicillin G but with lower activity; only $^1/_{150}$ as potent	Use only for penicillinase-producing staphylococci Intramuscular injections quite painful
Phenoxymethyl penicillin (penicillin V; Compocillin V)	Pen-Vee	Yes	No	Like penicillin G but less potent	Yields a serum peak level two to five times greater than penicillin G Can be given orally
Phenethicillin	Syncillin Chemipen Darcil	Yes	No	Like penicillin G but slightly less active against gram-positive cocci More active against penicillinase-producing *Staphylococcus aureus*	Give between meals since food delays absorption
Oxacillin	Prostaphlin Resistopen	Yes	Yes	Less active than penicillin G, more active than methicillin	Give between meals since food delays absorption
Cloxacillin	Tegopen	Yes	Yes	Effective against staphylococci resistant to penicillin G Like methicillin	Yields a serum peak level two times that of oxacillin Available only for oral use
Nafcillin	Unipen	—	Yes	Staphylococci, pneumococci, Group A beta-hemolytic streptococci More active than methicillin	Irregular absorption when given orally
Ampicillin	Polycillin Penbriten	Yes	No	Like penicillin G but more active against gram-negative bacteria	
Dicloxacillin	Dynapen Pathocil Veracillin	Yes	Yes	Like methicillin	Yields a serum peak level four times that of oxacillin
Carbenicillin		No	—	Like ampicillin High activity against some *Proteus* species Moderate activity against *Pseudomonas aeruginosa*	Not absorbed when given orally Under clinical investigation

inhalation as a fog or fine dust, the local concentration is high in the respiratory tract and absorption is such that satisfactory blood levels are reached. However, administration is cumbersome, sensitization is more likely to occur, and the effects on respiratory infections are satisfactory by other means of administration. Therefore, aerosol administration has limited usefulness.

Intrathecal. Penicillin administered orally or parenterally normally does not diffuse into the spinal fluid in large amounts. When the meninges are irritated, the diffusion is increased but high levels in the spinal fluid are not reached. Penicillin is toxic to the central nervous system, so that the amount and concentration of solutions of penicillin injected intrathecally must be carefully regulated. For this reason, intrathecal administration of penicillin has limited usefulness.

Topical. Topical administration of penicillin is associated with a higher incidence of allergic reactions than any other route of administration, and hence it is given this way infrequently. Other safer antimicrobial agents should be used.

Side effects and toxic effects

Penicillin is remarkably low in toxicity for man and other mammals. The only tissue injured by penicillin is that of the central nervous system when penicillin is placed in direct contact with it; headache, tenseness, muscular twitching, convulsions, and cyanosis may occur when it is applied to the brain during surgical operations.

Superinfections may occur as a result of the growth of insensitive or resistant organisms. These include staphylococcal enterocolitis and monilial infections. Blacktongue is the result of an overgrowth of fungi, usually *Candida*. Nausea, vomiting, diarrhea, and dehydration in patients receiving penicillin limit the excretion of the drug and raise the blood titer of the drug to toxic range.

Allergic reactions to penicillin are not uncommon. These constitute by far the most important type of untoward effects to penicillin and include contact dermatitis, urticaria, asthma, pruritus, local reaction at the site of injection, fever, erythema, polyarthritis, and exfoliative dermatitis. Anaphylactic shock is rare, but it is

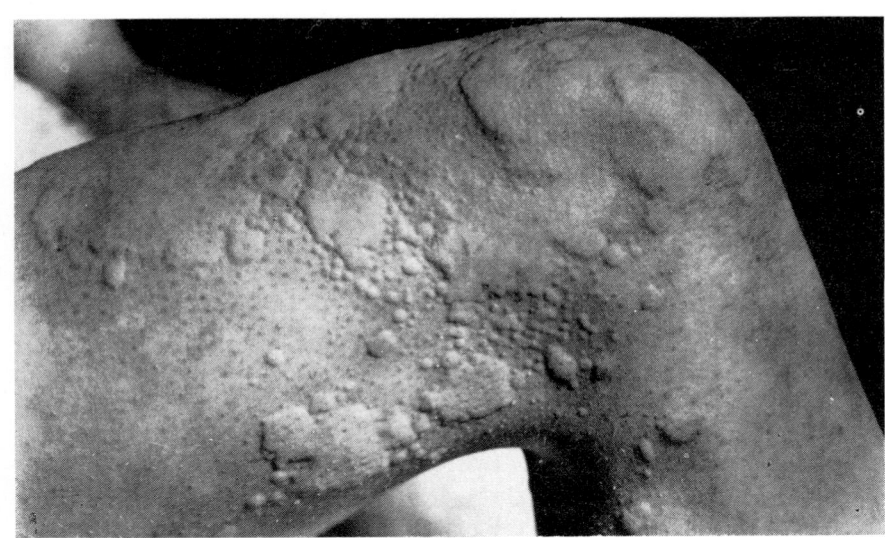

Figure 29-2
Urticaria such as may be seen in patients who are sensitive to penicillin.

increasing in frequency; death has followed in some instances. Patients known to have atopic allergy or a previous reaction to a drug need a skin or conjunctival test prior to the administration of penicillin. Furthermore, it is recommended that such patients remain close to medical facilities for at least 30 minutes after an injection.

Patients who are sensitive to penicillin G may be able to tolerate penicillin O; if this does not prove feasible another antibiotic is used. To treat minor allergic reactions one of the antihistaminic drugs such as diphenhydramine hydrochloride (Benadryl) or tripelennamine hydrochloride (Pyribenzamine) may be prescribed. For acute reactions, such as anaphylactic shock, epinephrine should be available. For severe reactions one of the adrenocorticosteroids may be helpful, although the presence of infection makes it somewhat hazardous to use them. It is of interest that some persons who are hypersensitive to penicillin may react to it even when they encounter it on a nontherapeutic basis, such as in poliomyelitis vaccine, in milk from penicillin-treated cows, or even from contact with penicillin prescribed for another patient.

Superinfections can sometimes be successfully treated with a different antibiotic; for example, nystatin may be used for moniliasis. In other cases of superinfection the use of penicillin must be stopped.

The amount of penicillin that can be safely administered to a human being is limited more by the cation of the salt than by the drug's toxicity. One million units of potassium penicillin contains about 0.2 Gm. potassium, and this can result in significant restriction of the use of penicillin in patients with renal insufficiency. Nevertheless, the most frequent untoward reactions to penicillin are attributed to hypersensitivity to the antibiotic.

Semisynthetic penicillins

Semisynthetic penicillins represent important additions to the drug therapy of infectious diseases. The purpose in the development of these new drugs was to overcome some of the disadvantages possessed by penicillin G, such as (1) destruction by staphylococcal penicillinase,

which makes staphylococci resistant to the antibiotics, (2) lack of acid stability, which prevents absorption from the gastrointestinal tract, (3) narrow antibacterial spectrum, which limits the usefulness of penicillin G to certain infections, and (4) allergic reactions to penicillin.

The semisynthetic penicillins include methicillin (p. 572), oxacillin (p. 573), cloxacillin (p. 573), phenethicillin, sodium nafcillin, and ampicillin. Methicillin, oxacillin, and cloxacillin appear to be highly effective in the treatment of severe staphylococcal infections, particularly those infections resistant to penicillin G. Phenethicillin, oxacillin, and cloxacillin have the advantage of being suited to oral administration. However, penicillin G is still believed to be the most effective penicillin if the infecting organisms are susceptible to it.

Sodium nafcillin and ampicillin are also effective against the staphylococci. Nafcillin, ampicillin, and oxacillin are stable in acid. A broader antibacterial spectrum than that of any of the other penicillins is characteristic of ampicillin. In the new penicillins the mold still produces the basic molecule, but chemists attach to it any one of a variety of R groups (see p. 570 for formula). The great advantage of this is that *R* groups have been found that make the penicillin molecule more stable and more resistant to destruction by the penicillinase of bacteria. The chemical addition of part of a molecule whose basic structure is obtained from natural sources (a plant or bacterial culture) is sometimes called semisynthesis.

Sodium nafcillin (Unipen). Sodium nafcillin is a readily soluble, semisynthetic penicillin that can be administered in both oral and parenteral dosage forms. It is resistant to staphylococcal penicillinase. Although primarily designed as an antistaphylococcal penicillin, it is effective also in the treatment of infections caused by pneumococci and Group A beta-hemolytic streptococci.

It is used in the treatment of lobar pneumonia, bronchopneumonia, tonsillitis, furunculosis, cellulitis, septicemia, osteomyelitis, and other infections produced by staphylococci or other microorganisms that are susceptible to the antibiotic.

Sodium nafcillin may be administered by several routes.

Oral route. For adults, a dose of 250 to 500 mg. (one to two capsules) every 4 to 6 hours is recommended for mild to moderate infections. In severe infections, four capsules every 4 to 6 hours may be necessary, or parenteral therapy may be advisable.

Intravenous route. Dosage of 500 mg. every 4 hours, or more often, is recommended in very severe infections. The required dose is dissolved in 15 to 30 ml. of sterile distilled water or sterile physiologic saline and injected over a 5- to 10-minute period through the tubing of an intravenous infusion. The drug may also be dissolved in 100 to 150 ml. and given by intravenous drip at a rate of 100 to 150 drops per minute.

Intramuscular route. For adults, 500 mg. every 6 hours, or more often, should be given. For infants and children, a dose of 25 mg. per kilogram, administered once or twice daily, is recommended.

Allergic reactions may occur in patients who are allergic to any of the penicillins or in those with a history of hay fever, asthma, or urticaria. Epinephrine should be available for allergic emergencies. Since thrombophlebitis may result from the intravenous injection, the intramuscular route is preferred if treatment must be continued for more than a day or two. Intramuscular injections may cause pain and tissue injury.

Ampicillin, **U.S.P. (Polycillin, Penebriten, Principen, Omnipen).** Ampicillin is often referred to as a broad-spectrum penicillin because it is effective not only against the organisms that are susceptible to penicillin G but also against some gram-negative organisms such as *Haemophilus influenzae, Escherichia coli, Klebsiella,* and a few others.

It is somewhat stable in the presence of acid and is absorbed moderately well from the gastrointestinal tract. Ampicillin is destroyed by staphylococcal penicillinase and is not an antistaphylococcal drug.

Uses. It is most useful in urinary infections and in systemic diseases in which the causative agents, often gram-negative bacteria, are sus-

ceptible to its action. Ampicillin dosages vary with the kind and severity of infection. The average oral dosage for moderate infections is 2 to 6 Gm. per day. In more severe infections parenteral dosage may range from 4 to 12 Gm. per day.

There is promise that other penicillins will be synthesized, and it is hoped that at least some of them will exhibit significant improvements over the ones now available. It is hoped that penicillins will be developed that will not induce hypersensitivity in the patient, that will not be too rapidly excreted, and that will be useful against other pathogenic organisms not affected by present-day antibiotics.

Penicillinase (Neutrapen)

Penicillinase is an enzyme produced by *Bacillus cereus, Escherichia coli,* and many strains of staphylococci. It hydrolyzes penicillin to penicilloic acid. Penicillinase has been recommended for the treatment of allergic reactions to penicillin.

Penicillin is virtually nontoxic to human beings except for hypersensitivity reactions to it; these are frequent and occasionally severe enough to constitute a considerable hazard in its use. The cortical steroids and the antihistaminics are both useful agents in the treatment of allergic responses to penicillin and to other allergens. A more direct attack is the use of the enzyme penicillinase. Penicillinase is an enzyme secreted by a number of bacteria, which hydrolyzes a portion of the penicillin molecule and produces a derivative that is inactive as an antibiotic and that is believed to have little or no antigenic or allergenic activity. Reports have suggested that penicillinase, particularly when used early in the course of a penicillin reaction, may be an effective way of relieving symptoms. Adjunctive use of more rapidly acting drugs such as epinephrine is recommended, however.

Preparation, dosage, and administration. Penicillinase is available as a lyophilized* stable powder and is marketed in single-dose vials con-

---

*Lyophilized means to be dehydrated from a frozen state by means of a vacuum.

taining 800,000 units* of the enzyme. It is administered by deep intramuscular injection. The content of the vial is dissolved in 2 ml. of sterile distilled prior to injection. A dose of 800,000 units may be repeated in 3 to 7 days, if necessary.

Side effects and toxic effects. Penicillinase is believed to have a low level of toxicity, but because it is an enzyme and therefore a protein, it is capable of producing allergic reactions, both mild and severe.

In case of anaphylactic shock it can be given intravenously, followed by an intramuscular injection. The injection should be made deep into the muscle to avoid pain and tenderness at the site of injection.

Tetracyclines

The tetracycline family consists of chlortetracycline, oxytetracycline, tetracycline, demethylchlortetracycline, rolitetracycline, and methacycline hydrochloride. Chlortetracycline, the first to be discovered, was isolated from *Streptomyces aureofaciens.* Oxytetracycline was isolated from *Streptomyces rimosus,* and tetracycline, which was obtained from another *Streptomyces,* has also been prepared chemically by removing chlorine from chlortetracycline. Demethylchlortetracycline is produced by a mutant strain of *Streptomyces aureofaciens.*

As can be noted from their formulas, the tetracyclines are chemically similar to each other. They form salts that are soluble in water. The dry salts are stable, but in aqueous solution there is progressive loss of antibacterial activity. The acid solutions are generally more stable and are used for parenteral administration.

The tetracycline compounds can be considered together because their action against bacteria is the same. Cross resistance between them is common. Tetracycline has largely supplanted the use of chlortetracycline and oxytetracycline. It is the most stable and the least likely to produce gastrointestinal symptoms, and it passes

more easily into the cerebrospinal fluid than do the older members of the family. Demethylchlortetracycline is said to be more stable at elevated temperatures and in acid and basic media than the older tetracyclines. Essentially, all have the same antibacterial propensities.

The tetracyclines are bacteriostatic when used in therapeutic doses against susceptible microorganisms by inhibiting synthesis of bacterial protein.

Absorption, distribution, and excretion. The tetracyclines are readily absorbed when administered orally. They are widely distributed through the body, except in the cerebrospinal fluid, where levels are much lower than in the blood plasma. The tetracyclines are excreted chiefly by the kidneys. Demethylchlortetracycline is excreted more slowly than the other tetracyclines. It is important to keep in mind that gastric antacids containing calcium and magnesium salts, aluminum gels, milk, and milk products interfere with the absorption of the tetracyclines.

Uses. The tetracyclines are "broad-spectrum" antibiotics, meaning that they are useful against a wide variety of microorganisms, gram-negative and gram-positive bacteria, including *Brucella,* the larger viruses of the psittacosis-lymphogranuloma group, the rickettsias (Rocky Mountain spotted fever and typhus fever), *Actinomycetes* (actinomycosis), and *Entamoeba histolytica* (amebiasis). They are particularly useful against infections caused by gram-negative bacilli, since penicillin and many of the other antibiotics do not have much action on this group. The tetracyclines are said to be effective in certain stages of syphilis, but they appear to be less effective than penicillin. They seem to be as effective as penicillin for yaws. A combination of tetracycline and streptomycin is recommended for treatment of certain severe infections, such as acute brucellosis and infections caused by bacteria of enteric origin.

Preparations. The following are the various preparations available of the tetracycline compounds.

***Chlortetracycline hydrochloride,* N.F., B.P. (Aureomycin Hydrochloride).** The B.P. lists

---

*One unit is the amount of penicillinase that will inactivate 1 unit of penicillin per minute or 60 units of penicillin per hour at a temperature of 25° C. and a pH of 7.

Chlortetracycline

Oxytetracycline

Tetracycline

Demeclocycline

Formulas for the tetracyclines

chlortetracycline capsules, whereas the N.F. lists that preparation and also chlortetracycline ophthalmic and chlortetracycline injection. Other preparations listed are topical ointment, ophthalmic ointment, powder for injection, nasal powder, ophthalmic powder, otic powder, tablets, and troches.

Oxytetracycline hydrochloride, **N.F., B.P. (Terramycin).** Preparations include capsules, oral suspensions, and solutions for injection.

Tetracycline hydrochloride, **N.F., B.P. (Achromycin).** Tetracycline hydrochloride is available in a number of dosage forms for oral, topical, and parenteral administration.

Tetracycline phosphate complex, **N.F. (Panmycin Phosphate, Sumycin, Tetrex).** Tetracycline phosphate complex has the same actions and uses as the parent antibiotic tetracycline or its hydrochloride. However, the phosphate complex is more rapidly and completely absorbed from the digestive tract and therefore produces higher blood levels of the drug. In other re-

spects it does not differ from other preparations of tetracycline. It is administered orally.

Demeclocycline hydrochloride, **N.F., B.P. (Declomycin).** This drug is available in 75- and 150-mg. capsules and as an oral suspension (75 mg. in 5 ml.).

Methacycline hydrochloride, **N.F. (Rondomycin).** Methacycline hydrochloride is a new broad-spectrum antibiotic synthetically derived from oxytetracycline. Its antibacterial activity, indications, and uses are similar to those of tetracycline. It is available as capsules containing 150 and 300 mg. methacycline hydrochloride and as a syrup containing 75 mg. of the drug per milliliter in a cherry-flavored suspension.

Dosage and administration of tetracyclines. The tetracyclines are usually given orally in doses of 250 to 500 mg. every 6 hours. Solutions buffered with a suitable agent may be given intravenously in emergencies or when patients cannot tolerate the drug by mouth. For intravenous administration 500 mg. is given every 6 to

12 hours. Phlebitis after intravenous administration is not uncommon. The drugs may be administered topically in suitable preparations. Intramuscular absorption is fairly satisfactory, except with chlortetracycline. The intramuscular doses range from 100 to 200 mg. every 6 to 8 hours. Demeclocycline and methacycline hydrochloride are given by mouth only, and the adult dose is lower than that for the older tetracyclines—600 mg. daily in divided doses.

Side effects and toxic effects. The tetracyclines are relatively nontoxic. When used in ordinary doses they do not injure the kidneys, the eighth cranial nerve, or the liver. However, high doses may cause some liver damage. The chief reactions occur in the gastrointestinal tract and include nausea, vomiting, and diarrhea. These occur more often with the tetracyclines than with any of the other commonly used antibiotics. Tetracycline is the least likely to cause these symptoms. Part of the gastrointestinal reaction is caused by local irritation. Irritation may also occur at the site of injection when tetracyclines are given intramuscularly or intravenously.

In addition to the local irritation, gastrointestinal symptoms may be caused by the suppression of the normal intestinal flora, which allows resistant or insensitive organisms to become established. Staphylococcal enterocolitis is one of the most serious of these superinfections and requires that administration of the drug be discontinued immediately. Other antibiotics may be employed against the staphylococci if the organisms are sensitive to them.

Demeclocycline is said to cause photosensitivity reactions more often than the other tetracyclines. This includes redness of the skin and sometimes edema when the skin has been exposed to sunlight. It may be followed by increased pigmentation.

Superinfections with fungi such as *Candida albicans* may also occur. Nystatin is sometimes used to treat monilial infections.

Symptoms of stomatitis, gastrointestinal irritation, or vaginitis, which indicate that superinfections have developed, should be promptly reported when a patient is receiving antibiotics. Anaphylaxis and blood dyscrasias are extremely rare.

The tetracyclines can cause yellow, gray, or brown discoloration of children's teeth with short or prolonged treatment. Pigmentation of the teeth has followed use of the drug either by the mother late in pregnancy or by the child during the period of tooth development. The affected teeth may have faulty enamel formation. The permanent teeth as well as the deciduous teeth may be affected, particularly when the pigmentation of the deciduous teeth is severe. The tetracyclines are deposited in teeth and bones by formation of a tetracycline-calcium-orthophosphate complex. There is some question whether deposition of the drugs in bones might inhibit their linear growth in premature infants. Discoloration of the nails has also been observed.

Antianabolic effects have resulted from the use of tetracyclines. Some of the symptoms associated with this are weight loss, negative nitrogen balance, and an increased urinary loss of nitrogen and sodium. The antianabolic action may reflect inhibition of amino acid and incorporation into protein. Caution is recommended in the use of these drugs in patients with renal insufficiency.

Outdated, unused, or degraded tetracycline should be discarded, since a degradation product of tetracycline (epianhydrotetracycline or anhydrotetracycline) is suspected as the etiologic factor in renal toxicity.

Nurses should check tetracycline for the manufacturer's expiration date and discard the drug accordingly. These drugs should be stored in airtight containers away from the heat, since heat and high humidity are factors capable of causing tetracycline degradation. A reversible Fanconi syndrome characterized by defective renal tubular reabsorption has been observed in patients who ingested outdated or degraded tetracycline.

Streptomycin; dihydrostreptomycin

Streptomycin is an antibiotic obtained from certain strains of *Streptomyces griseus*. Dihydrostreptomycin is produced by the hydrogenation of streptomycin. The dry powders of these drugs are stable; the solutions are stable for 7 to 10 days under refrigeration. These antibiotics inhibit the growth of and, in sufficient concentrations, destroy susceptible pathogens.

Absorption, distribution, and excretion. The streptomycins are poorly absorbed from the intestinal tract. When given parenterally they are distributed to all parts of the body, although they pass poorly into the cerebrospinal fluid. Excretion by the kidneys is slow. Its mode of action is to prevent synthesis of protein by bacteria; it also increases the permeability of the cytoplasmic membrane.

Uses. The main use of streptomycin is in the treatment of tuberculosis. It is also effective against a wide variety of gram-negative organisms, such as the gram-negative intestinal bacilli, and the *Pasteurella, Haemophilus,* and *Brucella* organisms. It is used occasionally against gram-positive organisms that are penicillin resistant. Infections of the urinary tract may respond well to therapy with streptomycin.

The streptomycins exert a marked suppressive action in tuberculosis. Because the treatment of tuberculosis is prolonged, resistance in the organisms may develop and toxicity may occur. To delay the appearance of resistance, PAS is given with the streptomycins. Some believe that it is best not to give streptomycin and isoniazid together except in extreme need, so that resistance to both drugs at the same time will not deprive the patient of the two most powerful antituberculosis drugs. To prevent toxicity during treatment of tuberculosis, the dosage of streptomycin is carefully regulated. In all types of tuberculosis, except the miliary and meningeal forms, 1-Gm. doses of streptomycin are recommended to be given intramuscularly two or three times a week along with PAS for 120 days. In tuberculous meningitis, intrathecal administration of 50 mg. of streptomycin every day or two may be given along with the streptomycin intramuscularly. In acute miliary tuberculosis, 2 Gm. or more of streptomycin is given daily.

Originally, a number of gram-negative and gram-positive bacteria were susceptible to the streptomycins. However, these drugs have a great tendency to induce resistance in bacteria. The majority of strains of certain gram-negative pathogens, such as *Proteus vulgaris, Pseudomonas aeruginosa,* and *Aerobacter aerogenes,* now being isolated in infections are resistant. In addition, many organisms, with the exception of the tubercle bacillus, that are sensitive to streptomycin are sensitive to the tetracyclines. The latter are safer to use, and organisms usually do not acquire resistance to the tetracyclines as rapidly as they do to streptomycin. Therefore, it is recommended by many authorities that streptomycin be limited to the treatment of tuberculosis and to infections in which the bacteria are resistant to other, safer antibiotics but susceptible to streptomycin.

Streptomycin is administered in combination with penicillin for certain infections, such as subacute endocarditis caused by *Streptococcus viridans,* and streptomycin-tetracycline therapy is advocated for brucellosis.

Preparation, dosage, and administration. The commercial preparations of streptomycin sulfate are powders for injection and solutions for injection containing 500 mg. in 1 ml., 1 Gm. in 2 ml., or 5 Gm. in 10 and 20 ml. The dose stated in the U.S.P. for these preparations of streptomycin is the equivalent of 1 Gm. of the base daily intramuscularly. The dose for dihydrostreptomycin is the equivalent of 500 mg. of the base every 6 hours intramuscularly. For systemic effects these antibiotics are usually given intramuscularly. Other methods of administration for streptomycin include intravenous drip, oral, intrathecal, topical, and nebulizer. When given orally, it is used as an intestinal antiseptic, but more effective medications are available for this purpose.

Side effects and toxic effects. Damage to the eighth cranial nerve, resulting in deafness and severe vertigo, is one of the most serious toxic effects of the streptomycins. Streptomycin causes more vertigo but less deafness then dihydrostreptomycin. The peculiar specificity of these toxic reactions is not understood. At one time it was believed that a half-and-half mixture of streptomycin and dihydrostreptomycin would result in less damage to the eighth cranial nerve. Later evidence revealed that loss of hearing occurred more often with the mixture than with streptomycin alone. Because the therapeutic results of the two drugs are similar and the toxicity of streptomycin is less distressing than the irreversible deafness that may result from dihydrostreptomycin, streptomycin is the drug of choice. Although dihydrostreptomycin may still have limited use in seriously ill patients who are sensitive to streptomycin, its use has greatly diminished because this serious complication of deafness may appear very late and after only a small amount of drug. It is no longer an official drug.

Streptomycin may produce toxic effects in the liver and kidney. Allergic reactions include erythema, rashes, urticaria, fall in blood pressure, headache, nausea, vomiting, and drug fever. Contact dermatitis may develop in persons who handle these drugs, so protective measures such as the use of rubber gloves are advised.

Erythromycin

Erythromcin is an antibiotic obtained from *Streptomyces erythreus.*

Absorption, distribution, and excretion. Erythromycin is readily absorbed from the gastrointestinal tract. Because it has a bitter taste and is destroyed by the gastric acid, it is administered in enteric-coated tablets or in the form of insoluble preparations that are slowly hydrolyzed. It diffuses through most of the body but is not found in appreciable amounts in the cerebrospinal fluid. It passes from the maternal blood to the fetus in amounts sufficient to be antibacterial. It is excreted by the kidneys and liver. It blocks intracellular protein metabolism in bacteria.

Uses. Erythromycin is similar to penicillin in its range of antibacterial activity. It is more effective against gram-positive than gram-negative bacteria. However, it does inhibit *Neisseria gonorrhoeae, Bordetella pertussis,* the rickettsias, the larger viruses, and to some extent the spirochetes. It is also useful for the treatment of

amebiasis. Penicillin is chosen in most cases in preference to erythromycin; however, the latter is used when organisms are penicillin-resistant or when the patient is allergic to penicillin. Unfortunately, the staphylococci develop resistance to erythromycin quite rapidly. In hospital infections caused by staphylococci, penicillin-resistant strains are often erythromycin-resistant.

Preparation, dosage, and administration. The following are the preparations available of erythromycin.

Erythromycin, **U.S.P., B.P. (Ilotycin, Erythrocin).** The official preparations of erythromycin include tablets, sterile solutions for injection, and an oral suspension. Orally, as the base or in the form of a suitable derivative, the dose is the equivalent of 250 mg. of erythromycin base every 6 hours. Intravenously, it is given in the form of a suitable derivative, in a dosage the equivalent of 250 mg. of erythromycin base, as a 0.1% solution every 6 hours. The usual dosage range is 1 to 2 Gm. daily.

Erythromycin estolate, **N.F., B.P. (Ilosone).** This is an oral preparation available in capsules, drops, or oral suspension. The usual adult dose is the same as that for erythromycin. There is a suggestion that erythromycin estolate is hepatotoxic.

Erythromycin ethylcarbonate, **U.S.P.** This is an oral preparation. The dose is the same as that for erythromycin.

Erythromycin ethylsuccinate, **N.F. (Pediamycin).** In addition to preparations for intramuscular use, an oral suspension is available. When administered parenterally, it should be given only by deep intramuscular injection and it is not recommended for small children without sufficient muscle mass.

Erythromycin gluceptate, **U.S.P.** This intravenous preparation has the same dose as erythromycin.

Erythromycin lactobionate, **U.S.P.** This water-soluble salt is suitable for intravenous and intramuscular injection and ophthalmic use in the form of an ophthalmic ointment, 1%.

Erythromycin stearate, **U.S.P.** This is prepared in a suspension and tablet form for oral administration. The dose is the same as that for erythromycin.

Side effects and toxic effects. Erythromycin is relatively nontoxic. Mild gastrointestinal symptoms may be produced. Large doses cause nausea, vomiting, diarrhea, and prostration. It rarely causes superinfection because of the suppression of the intestinal flora. It appears to have little tendency to produce hypersensitivity.

Lincomycin, U.S.P. (Lincocin)

Lincomycin, a new antibiotic unrelated structurally to other antimicrobial agents, appears to be effective against streptococci, staphylococci, and pneumococci. It may occupy a place similar to that of erythromycin in antibacterial chemotherapy. It is formed by the actinomycete *Streptomyces lincolnensis.*

Uses. It has been effective in the treatment of respiratory tract infections, skin and soft tissue infections, as well as infections of the urinary tract, bones and joints, meninges, and other areas in which the causative agents, usually streptococci, pneumococci, or staphylococci, are susceptible to the action of this antibiotic.

Preparation, dosage, and administration. Lincomycin as the hydrochloride monohydrate (Lincocin) is supplied in 250- and 500-mg. capsules, 2-ml. ampules, and 10-ml. vials. Each milliliter of sterile solution contains lincomycin hydrochloride monohydrate equivalent to 300 mg. of lincomycin base. It also contains water for injection and benzyl alcohol as a local anesthetic.

Oral route. Dosage is 500 mg. three times a day or more often in severe infections.

Intramuscular route. Dosage is 600 mg. every 12 hours or more often, depending on the severity of the infection.

Intravenous route. For adults, the dosage is 600 mg. dissolved in 250 ml. given by infusion every 8 to 12 hours. For children, 10 to 20 mg. per kilogram should be given by infusion in two or three doses at 8- to 12-hour intervals.

Adverse effects. Diarrhea and other gastrointestinal disturbances may occur, but no serious toxic reactions have been encountered. As in the case of all new drugs, however, it should be kept in mind that special precautions are needed in the newborn infant, in pregnant women, and in patients with preexisting kidney, liver, or metabolic diseases.

Chloramphenicol (Chloromycetin)

Chloramphenicol is an antibiotic originally derived from *Streptomyces venezuelae*, but it is now produced synthetically. Chloramphenicol is a bitter substance, whereas chloramphenicol palmitate is a tasteless but therapeutically effective derivative. Crystalline chloramphenicol is stable, as are the neutral and acid solutions.

Absorption, distribution, and excretion. Chloramphenicol is absorbed from the gastrointestinal tract and widely distributed throughout the body. It is excreted by the kidney and liver; that excreted in the bile is again absorbed, so that the kidney is the eventual place of excretion.

Uses. Chloramphenicol is a broad-spectrum antibiotic that is effective against a wide range of gram-positive and gram-negative bacteria, the rickettsiae, and certain of the large viruses (psittacosis and the lymphogranuloma group). It is the antibiotic of choice in typhoid fever and in the treatment of rickettsial infections. It should not be used indiscriminately because it depresses the bone marrow and may cause aplastic anemia. Because of the serious toxic effects of chloramphenicol its use should be reserved for treatment of typhoid fever, other salmonellas, and infections that do not respond to less potentially dangerous drugs.

Preparation, dosage, and administration. The following are the preparations of chloramphenicol.

Chloramphenicol, U.S.P., B.P. The U.S.P. lists the following as official preparations: Chloramphenicol capsules, chloramphenicol ophthalmic ointment, and chloramphenicol for ophthalmic solution. The usual dose is 50 mg. per kilogram of body weight daily, in divided doses, every 6 hours orally or every 8 to 12 hours intramuscularly. The usual dosage range is 50 to 100 mg. per kilogram of body weight daily, orally or intramuscularly. For external use, it is applied topically as a 0.5% to 1% ointment or solution.

Chloramphenicol palmitate, **U.S.P.** The U.S.P. lists chloramphenicol palmitate oral suspension as an official preparation. The usual dose is 86 mg. daily (the equivalent of 50 mg. of chloramphenicol per kilogram of body weight) in divided doses, four times a day. The usual dosage range is the equivalent of 50 to 100 mg. of chloramphenicol base, daily.

Side effects and toxic effects. Nausea, vomiting, and diarrhea may occur, although these occur less often with chloramphenicol than with other broad-spectrum antibiotics. The diarrhea is partly caused by irritation, but most often it is the result of a change in intestinal flora.

The most serious toxic effect is depression of the bone marrow, resulting in blood dyscrasias such as aplastic anemia and agranulocytosis. Although the incidence of this toxicity is low, it has limited the use of chloramphenicol. Careful selection of cases and frequent blood studies to detect early signs of toxicity should reduce the hazards of its use.

Gray cyanosis and respiratory insufficiency (gray syndrome) have been observed in newborn infants after administration of chloramphenicol; therefore, its use is contraindicated in these patients.

■ Systemic antibiotics occasionally used

The systemic antibiotics previously discussed are among the most effective and widely used or are ones that have a special use in certain diseases. Those that follow are used less often but are very valuable in certain cases (see Table 29-3). A number of them are used to treat staphylococcal infections in which either the infecting organism is resistant to penicillin G or the patient is unable to take one of the newer penicillins, such as methicillin. Other microorganisms also have developed mutants that are resistant to a number of the older and sometimes safe antibiotics. Such organisms included *Proteus, Pseudomonas,* and the coliform bacteria. The following antibiotics are listed alphabetically, not in the order of frequency of use.

Cephalothin (Keflin)

Cephalothin is a cephalosporin C derivative with some structural similarity to the penicillins. Cephalothin is a semisynthetic compound and a broad-spectrum antibiotic. It is active against gram-positive cocci, including staphylococci resistant to penicillin G, and gram-negative bacteria, including *Escherichia coli, Proteus mirabilis,* and *Klebsiella.* It is recommended for use in mixed infections and in patients allergic to penicillin. The drug, however, is not well absorbed from the gastrointestinal tract and should not be given by the oral route for systemic infections.

Uses. It has been used successfully in infections of the respiratory tract, urinary tract, soft tissues and skin, gastrointestinal system, and other areas in which the causative agent proved to be susceptible to cephalothin.

Preparation, dosage, and administration. Cephalothin is available as the sodium salt. For injection, each gram should be diluted with 4 ml. of sterile water. This solution will provide two 0.5-Gm. doses of 2.2 ml. each. Solutions should be stored in the refrigerator and should not be used after 48 hours. The adult dose is 0.5 to 1 Gm. given four to six times daily intramuscularly, but it may also be administered intravenously.

Adverse effects. Skin rashes have occurred following the use of cephalothin. It is believed, however, that most patients allergic to penicillin can tolerate cephalothin without significant reactions. Neutropenia and thrombophlebitis have occurred in an occasional patient following intravenous use of cephalothin.

Patients will experience pain following intramuscular injection of the 1-Gm. dose; this tends to increase with repeated injections. Induration, tenderness, and sterile abscesses may also occur. For these reasons it is necessary to emphasize the need for deep intramuscular injection into a large muscle mass.

Cycloserine, B.P. (Seromycin)

Cycloserine is an antibiotic obtained from strains of *Streptomyces orchidaceus, lavendulae,* or *garyphalus.* It exhibits a wide range of

Table 29-3 Antibiotics with limited
usefulness

Antibiotic	Uses
Amphotericin B	A systemic fungistatic agent used in treatment of deep-seated mycotic infections such as moniliasis, histoplasmosis, and North American blastomycosis.
Bacitracin	Limited usefulness when given parenterally because of possible toxic effects in kidney. Used locally for treatment of wounds and superficial infections of skin and to reduce flora in gastrointestinal tract. Has been found effective for amebiasis. Low incidence of bacterial resistance and patient hypersensitivity.
Cephalothin	Used for systemic infections caused by gram-positive or gram-negative organisms. It is administered intravenously or intramuscularly. It has low toxicity and is used for patients sensitive to or allergic to penicillin and for treatment of penicillin-resistant infections. Organisms do not readily acquire resistance to cephalothins. Superinfections may occur with its use.
Cycloserine	Used in treatment of streptomycin-resistant tuberculosis; usually combined with isonicotinic acid hydrazid (INH).
Gentamicin	Inhibits the growth of many strains of staphylococci and streptococci. It is particularly effective against *Pseudomonas aeruginosa.* It is both neurotoxic and nephrotoxic. It is administered intramuscularly. It is recommended for use in severe infections when less toxic drugs are not effective.
Griseofulvin	Fungistatic antibiotic given orally for ringworm of the scalp, body, and nails. Its use is not recommended for infections that respond to topical antifungal agents alone.
Kanamycin	Reserved for treatment of infections that do not respond to other antibiotics, for patients unable to take penicillin, and for treatment of infections of urinary tract. Possible toxic effects include deafness and renal damage.
Neomycin	Used to lower bacterial flora of intestinal tract and locally for superficial infections of skin. Occasionally used for systemic infections that do not respond to other antibiotics. May be toxic to kidney and to eighth cranial nerve when given parenterally.
Novobiocin	Occasionally used against staphylococcal infections that do not respond to other antibiotics and for infections caused by *Proteus vulgaris* and *Streptococcus faecalis.*
Nystatin	Effective against *Candida albicans,* a monilial organism. Given orally for intestinal moniliasis and topically for moniliasis of mouth, nails, skin, and vagina.
Oleandomycin	Has been used against staphylococcal infections. Its action and uses are similar to those of erythromycin.
Paromomycin	Has a similar antimicrobial spectrum to neomycin and is used in intestinal sterilization, amebiasis, shigellosis, and salmonellosis.
Polymyxin	This antibiotic is especially effective against *Pseudomonas aeruginosa.* Nephrotoxic and neurotoxic effects limit its usefulness for systemic infections.
Ristocetin	Active against gram-positive organisms, especially staphylococci and enterococci. It is administered intravenously. It is locally irritating and may cause hematologic complications.
Triacetyloleandomycin	This antibiotic has been promoted as a substitute for oleandomycin. It is said to be absorbed more readily than oleandomycin.
Vancomycin	This drug must be given intravenously, and its use is limited to the treatment of severe infections that do not respond to other antibiotics. It is an antistaphylococcal antibiotic of choice for patients who cannot take the new semisynthetic penicillins.
Viomycin	Tuberculostatic agent less active than streptomycin and more active than PAS. Potentially toxic to eighth cranial nerve.

antibacterial activity, inhibiting both gram-positive and gram-negative organisms. However, its antimicrobial activity is said to be less than that of many antibiotics in general use. It is being used along with other tuberculostatic drugs in the treatment of tuberculosis, although its effectiveness is not as pronounced as that of streptomycin, isoniazid, and probably para-aminosalicylic acid (PAS).

Absorption, distribution, and excretion. Cycloserine is rapidly absorbed from the gastrointestinal tract, and effective blood levels are reached 4 to 8 hours after administration, depending on the size of the dose. Significant concentrations in the cerebrospinal fluid are said to be reached after oral administration. It is excreted in the urine and feces.

Uses. It is indicated in the treatment of severe pulmonary tuberculosis in patients who do not respond to other tuberculostatic drugs or whose organisms have developed resistance to the older drugs named previously. It is not recommended as the initial form of chemotherapy for tuberculosis. It is also used in the treatment of stubborn urinary tract infections that do not respond to other forms of therapy because of bacterial resistance or hypersensitivity on the part of the patient. It is ineffective against *Proteus vulgaris*, *Pseudomonas*, and *Neisseria gonorrhoeae*. Bacterial resistance to cycloserine develops, although the rate of development is uncertain.

Preparation, dosage, and administration. Cycloserine is available in 250-mg. capsules for oral administration.

The patient receiving cycloserine should be hospitalized, where close observation can be provided and accurate blood-level determinations can be made. The usual daily dose is 250 to 500 mg.

Side effects and toxic effects. Cycloserine is more toxic than other drugs commonly used for the treatment of tuberculosis. Side effects include dizziness, lethargy, headache, psychotic reactions, and convulsive seizures.

Cycloserine should not be given to patients who have a history of mental disturbance or epilepsy. Renal insufficiency is also a reason for withholding the drug or for giving it with caution.

Gentamicin sulfate, U.S.P. (Garamycin)

This new antibiotic, derived from *Micromonospora purpurea*, has demonstrated antibacterial activity against gram-positive and gram-negative pathogens, including strains that have developed resistance to the commonly used antibiotics.

Uses. Topically, gentamicin proved effective in the treatment of pyogenic skin infections. Systemically, the antibiotic has been found useful in the treatment of urinary tract infection, burns, and pulmonary infections caused by gram-negative pathogens. For systemic use the drug is still experimental.

Preparation, dosage, and administration. Gentamicin sulfate is available as a 0.1% cream and 0.1% ointment. Although the drug has been used also by the intramuscular route, its systemic use is still in an investigational stage.

Side effects and toxic effects. When applied topically allergic skin reactions and photosensitivity reactions have been noted. Systemically the most serious effect of gentamicin has been irreversible vestibular damage.

Kanamycin sulfate, U.S.P. (Kantrex)

Kanamycin is an antibiotic derived from *Streptomyces kanamyceticus* that resembles neomycin and streptomycin. Its mode of action is not clear, but it may interfere with cytoplasmic membrane permeability and protein synthesis.

Uses. Kanamycin appears to be active against many strains of staphylococci, *Neisseria*, *Mycobacterium*, *Salmonella*, *Shigella*, *Klebsiella*, *Aerobacter*, *Escherichia coli*, and some strains of *Proteus*. Some patients with tuberculosis seem to respond favorably to kanamycin but it is not often used because of its neural and renal toxic effects when administered over a long period of time. It appears to be relatively inactive against the majority of strains of *Streptococcus*, *Pneumococcus*, *Clostridium*, *Pseudomonas*, *Brucella*, and some strains of *Proteus*. A number of microorganisms have been known to develop resistance to kanamycin.

Preparation, dosage, and administration. Kanamycin sulfate is usually given intramuscularly for systemic effect. The daily intramuscular dose for adults and children should not exceed 15 mg. per kilogram of body weight given in two or three divided doses. Intravenous administration is recommended only for very ill patients. For local effect the drug may be administered orally, intraperitoneally, by inhalation as an aerosol, or by instillation into cavities. The drug is only slightly absorbed when given orally. For preoperative preparation of the large intestine, it is given orally in doses of 1 Gm. every hour for 4 hours, then 1 Gm. every 6 hours for 36 to 72 hours before surgery. It has also been used orally for antibacterial effects within the intestine in infections caused by organisms susceptible to it.

Commercial preparations include 500-mg. capsules and solutions for injection containing 500 mg. in 2-ml. containers and 1 Gm. in 3-ml. containers.

Side effects and toxic effects. Toxic effects include impaired renal function, damage to the eighth cranial nerve, abnormal sensations (such as numbness and tingling), dermal reactions, and pain on injection. The drug should be given with caution to patients with renal damage; it is excreted by the kidneys, and if it is not excreted adequately, damage to the eighth cranial nerve is likely to occur. Patients require a high fluid intake and should be observed for symptoms such as tinnitus. Deafness can be partial or complete and, in most cases, has been irreversible.

Neomycin sulfate, U.S.P., B.P.

Neomycin is an antibiotic obtained from *Streptomyces fradiae.*

Uses. Neomycin is effective against a variety of gram-positive and gram-negative bacteria. Its antibacterial spectrum is broader than that of bacitracin, penicillin, or streptomycin. It is sometimes effective in the treatment of strains of *Pseudomonas* and *Proteus,* which are resistant to most antibiotics.

Unfortunately, it is toxic to the kidneys and to the eighth cranial nerve when given parenterally. Systemic administration is reserved for

infections that are sufficiently serious to warrant its use and in cases in which safer antibiotics are not successful.

Because it is not absorbed from the intestinal tract, it is useful as a preoperative intestinal antiseptic when given orally; it aids in achieving bactericidal concentrations in the intestine. Topically, it is effective and nonirritating and is often used for superficial infections of the eyes and skin. It appears to have a low but definite capability of sensitization.

Preparation, dosage, and administration. Neomycin sulfate is administered topically in the form of a 0.5% ointment or solution. Intramuscularly, the dose is 10 to 15 mg. per kilogram of body weight per day, not to exceed a total of 1 Gm. daily, and it is injected at 6-hour intervals. Orally, the dose is 1 Gm. every 4 hours for 24 to 72 hours prior to surgery.

Side effects and toxic effects. In addition to kidney damage and injury to the eighth cranial nerve, fever, tingling and numbness of the hands and feet, tinnitus, and dizziness occur. A mild laxative effect results when it is given orally. Superinfection by resistant organisms such as *Candida albicans* may occur.

Novobiocin

The calcium and sodium salts of the antibiotic novobiocin, derived from *Streptomyces niveus* or *Streptomyces spheroides*, are used mainly for the treatment of staphylococcal infections. The antibiotic has a moderate antimicrobial spectrum, the scope of which has not been completely determined. It inhibits the growth of many gram-positive organisms and a few gram-negative organisms. Novobiocin is indicated for the treatment of certain staphylococcal infections. Because of its side effects and the ease with which resistance may develop, it is best reserved for serious infections in which the patient is allergic to other drugs or for patients with penicillin-resistant staphylococcal infections. It has also been used for *Proteus* infections, especially urinary infections that are resistant to other drugs. There is no cross resistance with older antibiotics.

Absorption, distribution, and excretion. Novo-   **587**

biocin is rapidly absorbed from the intestinal tract. It is well distributed in the body but not into the cerebrospinal fluid. It is excreted in the feces and urine.

Preparation, dosage, and administration. The following are the dosages and preparations of novobiocin.

Sodium novobiocin, **N.F., B.P. (Albamycin Sodium, Cathomycin Sodium).** The commercial preparations are marketed as 250-mg. capsules and 500 mg. of powder for injection.

Novobiocin sodium is usually administered orally. The dosage commonly used is 250 mg. every 6 hours or 500 mg. every 12 hours. In more severe infections, 500 mg. every 6 to 8 hours may be necessary. It may be administered intravenously when oral administration is not advisable; the intravenous injection should be given slowly to avoid venous irritation. The drug can be given intramuscularly, if necessary, though this usually causes pain and irritation at the site of injection.

Calcium novobiocin, **N.F., B.P. (Albamycin Calcium, Cathomycin Calcium).** The novobiocin calcium preparation has the same actions and uses as the sodium salt but is more stable in aqueous suspension; thus, it is better suited for oral administration in liquid form.

Side effects and toxic effects. Novobiocin has relatively high index of sensitization. Skin rashes, urticaria, and fever have occurred. Leukopenia, thrombocytopenia, and agranulocytosis have been reported. Therefore, frequent examinations of the peripheral blood are likely to be requested. Yellowing of the sclerae as the result of a pigment produced in the metabolism of the drug is sometimes seen.

Oleandomycin phosphate, N.F. (Matromycin)

Oleandomycin is an antibiotic produced by *Streptomyces antibioticus.*

It is most active in vitro against gram-positive organisms such as staphylococci, streptococci, and pneumococci. It also inhibits a few gram-negative organisms, notably *Haemophilus influenzae* as well as gonococci and meningococci.

Uses. The main use of oleandomycin has been in the treatment of staphylococcal infections in which the organisms are resistant to penicillin, erythromycin, streptomycin, and the tetracyclines. Prolonged therapy with oleandomycin has produced resistant strains of staphylococci.

Preparation, dosage, and administration. Oleandomycin is available in capsules of 100 and 250 mg. and in 500 mg. of powder for injection; for adults the dose ranges from 250 to 500 mg. every 6 hours. The preferred route of administration is oral, but it may be given intravenously at a slow rate. Because oleandomycin is irritating, the intramuscular route is used when neither oral nor intravenous therapy is feasible. It is mixed with procaine and given by deep intragluteal injection.

Extreme care should be taken to avoid injection of the procaine-containing solution into a vein, into subcutaneous tissue, or into fatty tissue.

Side effects and toxic effects. Nausea, vomiting, diarrhea, and occasional skin rashes may occur.

Troleandomycin, N.F. (Cyclamycin, Tao)

Troleandomycin has the same actions and uses as oleandomycin phosphate, but it is more rapidly and completely absorbed from the gastrointestinal tract and less frequent doses are necessary. It is administered orally and the dose is the same as that for the phosphate. The preparations consist of capsules containing 125 and 250 mg.; a suspension containing 25 mg. per milliliter; and drops (oral), 100 mg. per milliliter. Troleandomycin has been found to produce hepatic toxicity.

Ristocetin (Spontin)

Ristocetin is an antibiotic produced by *Nocardia lurida*, a species of actinomycetes. The commercial product contains two components, ristocetin A and ristocetin B, the chemistries of which are not completely known.

Uses. Ristocetin is active in vitro against the following gram-positive organisms: streptococci, enterococci, pneumococci, and staphylococci.

It is not as active, as a rule, as other antibiotics, such as penicillin, and is not absorbed when given orally. For these reasons, penicillin and certain other antibiotics, such as the tetracyclines, are usually used as first choice for various infections. However, against staphylococci and enterococci, both of which tend to become resistant to other antibiotics, ristocetin may be the drug of choice. For pneumococci and beta-hemolytic streptococci, which rarely, if ever, develop resistance to other antibiotics, ristocetin is not usually indicated. Bacterial resistance to ristocetin has not developed to the same degree as with certain other antibiotics; this may change with increasing use of the drug.

Preparation, dosage, and administration. Ristocetin is available in vials containing 500 mg. of powder for injection.

It is administered intravenously only because it is inadequately absorbed after oral administration and is too irritating to the tissues to be given extravascularly. It irritates the veins and should not be given in too high a concentration. The drip technique is preferred, and the drug should be given slowly. For staphylococcal infections the usual total daily dose is 25 to 50 mg. per kilogram of body weight. In certain serious infections, doses as high as 75 mg. per kilogram may be used.

Side effects and toxic effects. Side effects of ristocetin include depression of white blood cells, with relative neutropenia, drug fever, skin rash, and diarrhea. Therefore, blood counts including a differential leukocyte count are done at frequent intervals. Occasional allergic reactions consisting of skin rashes, either at the site of the injection or all over the body, have occurred. To date, anaphylactic reactions have not been reported. Thrombocytopenia and toxic effects on the eighth cranial nerve have been reported. Because of its irritating effect, thrombophlebitis has occurred; extravasation of the drug into the tissues should be avoided.

Vancomycin hydrochloride, U.S.P., B.P. (Vancocin)

Vancomycin is an antibiotic derived from strains of *Streptomyces orientalis*. It is highly active against gram-positive cocci, including streptococci, pneumococci, and staphylococci.

Uses. Vancomycin should be reserved for critically ill patients with life-endangering infections caused by staphylococci and other microorganisms that are resistant to the commonly used antibiotics. The drug is not intended for routine use or for mild infections. Cross resistance to other antibiotics has not been observed.

Preparation, dosage, and administration. Vancomycin is supplied in 10-ml. ampules containing 500 mg. of powder for intravenous administration only. For adults the usual dose is 2 Gm. in 24 hours and is administered in amounts of 500 mg. every 6 hours by slow infusion over a period of 30 minutes; some investigators have used two infusions of 1 Gm. each at a 12-hour interval. Doses of 3 to 4 Gm. should be used only in desperately ill patients who have normal renal function. For children the daily dose is 20 mg. per kilogram of body weight. It is not well absorbed when given orally.

Side effects and toxic effects. Toxic symptoms include impairment of auditory acuity, thrombophlebitis because it is irritating, macular skin rashes, and febrile reactions. Toxicity is minimal for most short-term therapy. The drug should be used with caution in patients with renal damage because it may accumulate in the blood and the chance of ototoxicity is increased. If doses of more than 2 Gm. per day are used, periodic determinations of the blood urea nitrogen level are suggested.

Viomycin sulfate, B.P. (Vinactane Sulfate, Viocin Sulfate)

Viomycin sulfate is the salt of an antibiotic obtained from *Streptomyces puniceus* or *floridae*.

Uses. Because of its potential toxicity, its use should be restricted to the treatment of patients who are unable to tolerate other antituberculosis drugs or patients with tuberculosis caused by organisms resistant to these drugs. Apparently cross resistance does develop between viomycin and streptomycin or isoniazid.

Preparation, dosage, and administration. Viomycin sulfate should be administered by slow intramuscular injection; desirable levels in the blood are not achieved after oral administration.

Intravenous injection should be avoided because it results in greater danger of toxic reactions.

When administered intramuscularly in tuberculosis, the usual dose is 2 Gm., given in two doses of 1 Gm. each, 12 hours apart, every third day. It can be given alone or with aminosalicylic acid orally. This dosage can be continued at least 4 to 6 months. In special instances, dosage might be increased (for not more than 1 month), but the patient must be carefully watched for toxic symptoms.

Side effects and toxic effects. Viomycin sulfate is a potentially toxic drug. Toxic symptoms include allergic reactions, renal irritation, eosinophilia, edema, electrolyte disturbance, dizziness, and partial loss of hearing.

■ Antifungal antibiotics
Amphotericin B, U.S.P. (Fungizone)

Amphotericin B is an antibiotic agent that gives evidence of usefulness as an effective antifungal drug. It is derived from a species of *Streptomyces*. It is used in the treatment of disseminated mycotic infections, including coccidioidomycosis, cryptococcosis, disseminated moniliasis, histoplasmosis, and North American blastomycosis.

Preparation, dosage, and administration. Amphotericin B is available in vials containing 50 mg. of dry powder. The powder should be stored in the refrigerator and protected from light. Any unused material should be discarded after 24 hours.

Because only a minimal amount of absorption occurs on oral administration, it is administered parenterally for systemic infections. It is recommended that it be given by slow intravenous infusion over a period of approximately 6 hours. The recommended concentration is 0.1 mg. per milliliter of 5% dextrose in water for intravenous administration. Dosage varies with the tolerance of each patient. An initial daily dose of 0.25 mg. per kilogram of body weight is recommended. Total dosage may increase to 1 mg. per kilogram of body weight. Within this range the dosage should be maintained at the highest level not accompanied by toxic manifestations. Intrathecal injection of the drug dissolved in ster-

ile water may be given in coccidioidal meningitis.

Side effects and toxic effects. Side effects and toxic effects include phlebitis at the site of injection, chills, fever, vomiting, diarrhea, and headache. More serious effects such as anemia, hypokalemia, cardiac disturbances, and renal and liver damage can occur. These effects can be minimized by gradual increases in dosage and slow infusion. Tests of renal function need to be done periodically for patients receiving prolonged therapy.

Nystatin, U.S.P., B.P. (Mycostatin)

Nystatin is an antibiotic obtained from *Streptomyces noursei*.

Action and uses. Nystatin is primarily useful in treating infections caused by the monilial organism *Candida albicans* but is also effective against some other species.

Preparation, dosage, and administration. Nystatin is available in the following official preparations: oral suspension, ointment, tablets, and vaginal suppositories.

For gastrointestinal moniliasis, the proposed dose is 500,000 to 1,000,000 units, given orally three times a day. To prevent intestinal moniliasis, patients undergoing oral therapy with broad-spectrum antibiotics may be given nystatin concurrently. The oral route may be used concurrently with local application in resistant anal or vaginal moniliasis to decrease the possibility of reinfection from the intestine.

For monilial lesions of the mouth (thrush), suspensions of nystatin containing 100,000 units per milliliter may be dropped into the mouth or applied locally by applicator. Vaginal tablets or suppositories containing 100,000 units are inserted once or twice a day for vaginal moniliasis.

Side effects and toxic effects. Patients may complain of mild gastrointestinal discomfort after oral administration.

Griseofulvin, U.S.P., B.P. (Fulvicin, Grifulvin)

Griseofulvin is a fungistatic agent obtained from *Penicillium griseofulvum*. After absorption it is incorporated into the keratin of the nails, skin, and hair in therapeutic amounts. The infecting fungus is not killed, but its growth into new cells is prevented. As cells are shed or removed they are replaced by new ones that are free from the infection.

This antibiotic has been employed with particular success in the management of tinea capitis (ringworm of the scalp). Relief of itching is said to occur within a few days after treatment is started. Within 2 weeks other signs of improvement may be seen. These include decreased erythema, loosening of infected hairs, and scaling of the skin. Cure of this condition is ordinarily achieved in 4 to 6 weeks. The wearing of a protective cap, the use of keratolytic agents, and frequent shampoos are recommended as well as clipping of infected hairs after a few weeks of treatment.

Ringworm of the body, nails, and feet is also treated with this drug. Ringworm of the nails responds slowly, and sometimes complete cure is not achieved even when treatment is continued. Griseofulvin is more effective for chronic fungal infections of the feet than for acute conditions. It is not recommended for deep and systemic fungal infections or for infections caused by yeasts.

Preparation, dosage, and administration. Griseofulvin is available in both capsules and tablets for oral administration. The adult dose is 0.5 to 1 Gm. daily in divided portions. For mild infections 0.5 Gm. may be adequate; for severe infections 2 Gm. daily may be required. For children 10 mg. per pound of body weight per day as a single dose or in divided doses is recommended.

Side effects and toxic effects. Although serious reactions to this drug appear to be infrequent, it can produce a number of undesirable side effects, including headache, epigastric distress, nausea, diarrhea, skin eruption, and leukopenia. The latter explains why the physician is likely to order periodic examination of the blood when the patient is receiving this drug. In rare instances large doses have produced mental confusion and difficulty with routine activities such as driving an automobile. Care must be taken to prevent reinfection.

■ Other antibiotics
Bacitracin, U.S.P., B.P. (Baciguent)

Bacitracin is an antibiotic obtained from *Bacillus subtilis.*

Action and uses. Bacitracin is bactericidal. It is effective against a wide variety of gram-positive bacteria (streptococci, staphylococci, pneumococci, clostridia of the gas gangrene group, and corynebacteria) and the spirochete of syphilis. It has little effect against most gram-negative bacteria, except the neisseriae. It has been successfully used in the treatment of intestinal amebiasis.

Because it is toxic to the kidneys and its antibacterial spectrum is similar to penicillin and other antibiotics, the use of bacitracin has been limited to topical application. However, bacitracin may be used for infections in which the organisms are resistant to the more commonly used antibiotics but sensitive to bacitracin. Fortunately, patients rarely become hypersensitive to it and bacteria are slow in developing resistance to it.

Preparation, dosage, and administration. The commercial preparations of bacitracin are marketed as ophthalmic and topical ointments, as powder for injection and topical use (2000 and 10,000 units in 20-ml. vials; 50,000 units in a 50-ml. vial), and as soluble tablets containing 2500 units.

For systemic action bacitracin is administered intramuscularly in doses of 20,000 units every 8 hours. It can be administered by local injection into circumscribed areas of infections, such as abscesses. It is also used as an intrathecal or intraventricular injection, as an aerosol mist, and as a topical application. Because little is absorbed from the intestine when given orally, it is used as an intestinal antiseptic; it has been found useful against staphylococcal enterocolitis.

Side effects and toxic effects. Pain at the site of intramuscular injection may occur. Damage to the kidney may occur; albuminuria and an increase in the concentration of urea in the blood are indications that renal injury is occurring. The fluid intake should always be adequate (2500 ml. per day) for patients receiving bacitracin intramuscularly. If the urine output remains above 1000 ml. and there is no undue retention of urea, nephrotoxicity probably does not exist. Bacitracin is only rarely allergenic when applied topically.

Polymyxin; colistin

Polymyxin is a name used to designate several related antibiotics derived from different strains of *Bacillus polymyxa*. Polymyxin B is the least toxic of the polymyxins that have been studied.

Colistin is an antibiotic produced by the soil bacterium *Bacillus polymyxa* (var. *garyphalus*). It is closely related to polymyxin B. Two compounds of colistin are available: colistin sulfate (Coly-Mycin Pediatric Suspension) and sodium colistimethate (Coly-Mycin Injectable).

Uses. Polymyxin B is effective against many gram-negative organisms, including the coliform bacteria. Because of its toxicity, polymyxin B is usually reserved for the treatment of infections caused by organisms such as *Pseudomonas aeruginosa* that are resistant to most antibiotics.

Colistin sulfate is effective in the oral treatment of intestinal infections in infants and children when the infection is caused by certain gram-negative bacilli, particularly *Pseudomonas* and *Escherichia coli*.

Sodium colistimethate, a water-soluble derivative of colistin, is employed for the treatment of systemic infections caused by certain gram-negative bacilli, particularly in meningitis, bacteremia, peritonitis, and urinary tract infections caused by *Pseudomonas aeruginosa*. It is administered intramuscularly.

Preparation, dosage, and administration. The following are the usual preparations and dosages used for polymyxin and colistin.

Polymyxin B sulfate, **U.S.P., B.P. (Aerosporin Sulfate).** The commercial preparations are marketed in the form of an ophthalmic ointment, powder for injection, topical powder, otic solution, and tablets.

Polymyxin B sulfate is administered orally, topically, or parenterally. Intramuscularly, the usual daily dose is 10,000 to 20,000 units per kil-

ogram of body weight, given in divided portions every 6 hours. Because it is not absorbed from the intestinal tract, oral doses, when used, are given to combat intestinal infections. The usual oral dose is 750,000 units four times a day.

Colistin sulfate, **N.F. (Coly-Mycin Sulfate).** This is available as a powder (oral) in a 300-mg. bottle to be suspended in 37 ml. of distilled water prior to dispensing, providing 5 mg. colistin per milliliter. For infants and children 3 to 5 mg. of the base per kilogram of body weight is given daily in three divided doses.

Sodium colistimethate, **U.S.P. (Coly-Mycin Injectable).** This is available in vials containing 150 mg. of colistin base with dibucaine hydrochloride in the powder form. The dosage for intramuscular administration is 2.5 mg. of the base per kilogram of body weight daily; the maximal dose of 5 mg. per kilogram daily should not be exceeded.

Side effects and toxic effects. When given parenterally polymyxin B may produce nephrotoxic and neurotoxic effects, but the level of toxicity is low when it is administered within the range of recommended dosage. The neurotoxic effects are mild and subjective (dizziness, weakness, and paresthesias). Fever and pain at the site of injection also occur.

Sodium colistimethate, like polymyxin B sulfate, is capable of causing both renal and neural damage. In the case of colistin sulfate toxic effects are not as likely, because absorption from the gastrointestinal tract is limited.

Tyrothricin, N.F. (Soluthricin)

Tyrothricin is an antibacterial substance produced by *Bacillus brevis*. It consists of two substances called gramicidin and tyrocidine and is active against many gram-positive bacteria. However, it is rapidly inactivated in the body and causes so many toxic reactions that it cannot be used systemically.

Its usefulness is limited to topical applications in the form of lozenges, irrigating solutions, sprays, and ointments. With caution, it may be used in body cavities if there is no direct connection with the bloodstream.

Preparation, dosage, and administration. For

Table 29-4 Summary of some major allergic and toxic effects of antibiotics*

Anaphylaxis	Aplastic anemia	Nephrotoxicity	Injury to eighth cranial nerve	Staphylococcal ileocolitis
Penicillin Streptomycin Chloramphenicol Tetracyclines (rare)	Chloramphenicol (low incidence but high mortality)	Amphotericin B Bacitracin Colistin Kanamycin Neomycin Polymyxin B Streptomycin Gentamicin	Dihydrostreptomycin Neomycin Streptomycin Kanamycin Ristocetin Vancomycin Gentamicin	Tetracyclines

*Many of the toxic effects listed are not encountered unless the antibiotic is administered in a manner to produce systemic effects.

local application, a solution containing 500 μg. per milliliter is used. The N.F. lists tyrothricin spray and troches in addition to the solution.

Questions

for study and review

1 Which of the following has constituted the richest source of antibiotic substances?
a. molds
b. bacteria
c. *Streptomyces*
d. chemical synthesis

2 Antibiotics are:
a. bacteriostatic rather bactericidal
b. produced by microorganisms
c. frequently synergistic
d. antigrowth substances

3 A bacteriostatic agent:
a. kills bacteria on contact
b. does not inhibit normal intestinal flora
c. inhibits proliferation of bacteria
d. reduces the necessity for asepsis

4 Which of the following statements about the penicillins are correct?
a. They are very stable in aqueous solutions.

b. Staphylococci that develop penicillin resistance produce penicillinase.
c. Hypersensitivity reactions to penicillin occur most frequently with injected procaine penicillin G.
d. Penicillin is very effective against hospital strains of *Staphylococcus aureus.*

5 Select the *incorrect* answer from the following.
a. Administration of probenecid will slow the renal excretion of penicillin.
b. Activity of penicillin is decreased in the presence of blood or pus.
c. Penicillin G is susceptible to inactivation by penicillinases.
d. Penicillin kills bacteria by suppressing the formation of the cell wall.

6 A comparison between the action and effects of penicillin and tetracyclines indicates that:
a. tetracycline stains the teeth of children; penicillin does not
b. there is more effective penetration into cerebrospinal fluid by penicillin
c. superinfections are more likely to occur from the use of tetracyclines
d. tetracyclines have a wider range of antibacterial activity

7 Which of the following semisynthetic antibiotics is effective against many staphylococcal infections?
a. penicillin G   c. methicillin
b. phenethicillin   d. penicillin V

8 Serious side effects may result from the use of antibiotics. Of the following, which is an *incorrect* statement?

a. Chloramphenicol can cause severe bone marrow depression resulting in agranulocytosis and aplastic anemia.

b. Both streptomycin and kanamycin can cause damage to the eighth cranial nerve, resulting in deafness.

c. Skin eruptions are the most common type of allergic reactions ot the penicillins.

d. Antibiotics that can cause severe renal damage are polymyxin and vancomycin.

9 Which of the following constitutes the most distinct advantage of tetracycline over penicillin?

a. wider range of antibacterial activity

b. no side effects

c. satisfactory blood levels result from the usual oral dosage

d. less expensive

10 Which of the following pairs of antibiotics have been found effective in the treatment of certain viral and rickettsial infections?

a. streptomycin and neomycin

b. oxytetracycline and tetracyline

c. bacitracin and tyrothricin

d. penicillin and streptomycin

11 If a patient becomes hypersensitive to penicillin, which of the following statements best explains the situation?

a. The infecting organisms are more affected by penicillin than usual.

b. The patient will not react to penicillin one way or the other.

c. The patient will show allergic symptoms when given penicillin.

d. The infecting organisms will be able to grow in spite of the presence of penicillin.

12 When in the course of treatment with an antibiotic resistance is said to have developed, which of the following will have developed the resistance?

a. the antibiotic

b. the patient's body cells

c. the infecting organisms

d. immune bodies in the patient's blood

13 Which of the following reasons *best* explains why penicillin is not prescribed for an ordinary cold (no complications)?

a. The cold virus develops resistance easily.

b. The patient may be sensitized.

c. Penicillin has no effect on the virus causing a cold.

d. Penicillin is very expensive.

References

General references

Abraham, E. P.: The chemistry of new antibiotics, Amer. J. Med. **39**:692, 1965.

Burchall, J. J., Ferone, R., and Hitchings, G. H.: Antibacterial chemotherapy, Ann. Rev. Pharmacol. **5**:53, 1965.

Busch, H., and Lane, N.: Chemotherapy, Chicago, 1967, Year Book Medical Publishers, Inc.

Chain, E. B.: The development of bacterial chemotherapy, Antibiot. Chemother. **4**:215, 1954.

DiPalma, J. R., editor: Drill's pharmacology in medicine, ed. 4, New York, 1971, McGraw-Hill Book Company.

Dowling, H. F.: Present status of therapy with combinations of antibiotics, Amer. J. Med. **39**:796, 1965.

Dubos, R.: Mirage of health, New York, 1959, Harper & Row, Publishers.

Feingold, D. S.: Antimicrobial chemotherapeutic agents: the nature of their action and selective toxicity, New Eng. J. Med. **269**:900, 1963.

Flick, J. A.: Antibiotic resistance to staphylococci: problems and mechanisms of development, Clin. Pediat. **3**:215, 1964.

Gale, E. F.: Mechanisms of antibiotic action, Pharmacol. Rev. **15**:481, 1963.

Gill, A. F., and Hook, E. A.: Changing patterns of bacterial resistance to antimicrobial drugs, Amer. J. Med. **39**:780, 1965.

Griffith, R. S., and Black, H. R.: Cephalothin—a new antibiotic, J.A.M.A. **189**:823, 1964.

Hall, J.W.: Drug therapy in infectious diseases, Amer. J. Nurs. **61**:56, 1961.

Jager, B. V.: Untoward reactions to antibiotics, Amer. J. Nurs. **54**:966, 1954.

Kunin, C. M.: Effects of antibiotics on the gastrointestinal tract, Clin. Pharmacol. Therap. **8**:495, 1967.

Martin, W. J.: Antibacterial therapy; newer observations on the older agents, Minn. Med. **47**:839, 1964.

Modell, W., editor: Drugs of choice 1972-1973, St. Louis, 1972, The C. V. Mosby Co.

Petersdorf, R. G., and Plorde, J. J.: Colistin—a reappraisal, J.A.M.A. **183**:123, 1963.

Poth, E. J.: Intestinal antisepsis in surgery, J.A.M.A. **153**:156, 1953.

Riggs, B. L., Geraci, J. E., and Prickman, L. E.: Untoward reactions to antibiotics, Collect. Papers Mayo Clin. **52**:802, 1960.

Rollo, I. M.: Antibacterial chemotherapy, Ann. Rev. Pharmacol. **6**:209, 1966.

Sidell, S., and others: New antistaphylococcal antibiotics, Arch. Intern. Med. **112**:21, 1963.

VanArsdel, P. P., Jr.: Allergic reactions to penicillin, J.A.M.A. **191**:238, 1965.

Yaffe, S. J.: Antibiotic dosage in newborn and premature infants, J.A.M.A. **193**:818, 1965.

Tetracyclines

Koch-Weser, J., and Gilmore, E. B.: Benign intracranial hypertension is an adult after tetracycline therapy, J.A.M.A. **200**:345, 1967.

Kunin, C. M., and Finland, M.: Clinical pharmacology of the tetracycline antibiotics, Clin. Pharmacol. Therap. **2**:51, 1961.

Mull, M. M.: The tetracyclines: a critical reappraisal, Amer. J. Dis. Child. **112**:483, 1966.

Shils, M. E.: Some metabolic aspects of tetracyclines, Clin. Pharmacol. Therapy. **3**:321, 1962.

Shumacher, G. E.: A tetracycline tableau: chemistry, pharmacy, pharmacology, Amer. J. Hosp. Pharm. **20**:580, 1963.

Toxicity of tetracyclines, Lancet **2**:283, 1963.

Witkap, C. J., Jr., and Wolf, R. O.: Hypoplasia and intrinsic staining of enamel following tetracycline therapy, J.A.M.A. **185**:1008, 1963.

Wruble, L. D., Ladman, A. J., and Britt, L. G.: Hepatotoxicity produced by tetracycline, J.A.M.A. **192**:6, 1965.

Chloramphenicol

McCurdy, P. R.: Plasma concentration of chloramphenicol and bone marrow suppression, Blood **21**:363, 1963.

Smith, C. G.: Chloramphenicol, Progr. Indust. Microbiol. **4**:137, 1963.

Weiss, C. F., Glazko, A. J., and Weston, J. K.: Chloramphenicol in the newborn infant: a physiological explanation of its toxicity when given in excessive doses, New Eng. J. Med. **262**:787, 1960.

Erythromycin

Griffith, R. S., and Black, H.R.: Erythromycin, Pediat. Clin. N. Amer. **8**:1115, 1961.

Haight, T. H., and Finland, M.: The antibacterial action of erythromycin, Proc. Soc. Exp. Biol. Med. **81**:188, 1952.

Indications for erythromycin, Brit. Med. J. **1**:563, 1961.

Wolfe, A. D., and Hohn, F. E.: Erythromycin: mode of action, Science **143**:1445, 1964.

Penicillin

Dowling, H. F.: The newer penicillins, Clin. Pharmacol. Therap. **2**:572, 1961.

Fleming, A.: Penicillin; its practical application, London, 1950, Butterworth & Co. (Publishers) Ltd.

Friend, D. G.: Penicillin therapy—newer semisynthetic penicillins, Clin. Pharmacol. Therap. **7**:706, 1966.

Friend, D. G.: Pencillin G, Clin. Pharmacol. Therap. **7**:421, 1966.

Hamilton-Miller, J. M.: Effect of penicillinase on the activity of penicillins, Nature **201**:867, 1964.

Hyman, A. L.: Anaphylactic shock after therapy with penicillinase, J.A.M.A. **169**:593, 1959.

Kern, R. A.: Anaphylactic drug reactons, J.A.M.A. **179**:19, 1962.

Klein, J. O., and Finland, M.: The new penicillins, New Eng. J. Med. **269**:1019, 1963.

Martin, W. I.: Newer penicillins, Med. Clin. N. Amer. **51**:1107, 1967.

Park, J. T., and Strominger, J. L.: Mode of action of penicillin: biochemical basis for the mechanism of action of penicillin and for its toxicity, Science **125**:99, 1957.

Reisch, M.: Penicillinase therapy—clinical report of severe reactions, J.A.M.A. **169**:594, 1959.

Rose, A. H.: New penicillins, Sci. Amer. **204**:66, 1961.

Weinstein, L., Lerner, P. I., and Chew, W. H.: Clinical and bacteriological studies of the effect of "massive" doses of penicillin G on infections caused by gram-negative bacilli, New Eng. J. Med. **271**:525, 1964.

Weinstein, L., Samet, C. A., and Chew, W. H.: Studies of the effects of penicillin-sulfonamide combinations in man, Amer. J. Med. Sci. **248**:408, 1964.

Streptomycin and dihydrostreptomycin

Carr, D.T., and others: Neurotoxic reactions to dihydrostreptomycin, J.A.M.A. **143**:1223, 1950.

Ormerod, F. C.: Discussion on the toxic effects of streptomycin and dihydrostreptomycin on the acoustic and vestibular systems, Proc. Roy. Soc. Med. **45**:779, 1952.

Spotts, C. R., and Strainer, R. Y.: Mechanism of streptomycin action on bacteria: a unitary hypothesis, Nature **192**:633, 1961.

Waksman, S. A.: Tenth anniversary of the discovery of streptomycin, the first chemotherapeutic agent found to be effective against tuberculosis in humans, Amer. Rev. Tuberc. **70**:1, 1954.

Weinstein, L., and Ehrenkrauz, N. J.: Streptomycin and dihydrostreptomycin, Antibiotics Monographs, No. 10, New York, 1958, Medical Encyclopedia Inc.

Others

Abraham, E. P.: The cephalosporins, Pharmacol. Rev. **14**:473, 1962.

Andriole, V. T., and Kravetz, H. M.: The use of amphotericin B in man, J.A.M.A. **180**:269, 1962.

Butler, W. T.: Pharmacology, toxicity and therapeutic usefulness of amphotericin B, J.A.M.A. **195**:371, 1966.

Geraci, J. E., and Heilman, F. R.: Vancomycin in the treatment of staphylococcal endocarditis, Proc. Staff Meet. Mayo Clin. **35**:316, 1960.

Geraci, J. E., Nichols, D. R., and Wellman, W. E.: Vancomycin in serious staphylococcal infections, Arch. Intern. Med. **109**:507, 1962.

Jaco, R. L., and Jackson, G. G.: Gentamicin sulfate; a new antibiotic against gram-negative bacilli, J.A.M.A. **189**:817, 1964.

Nord, N. M., and Hoeprich, P. D.: Polymyxin B and colistin—a critical comparison, New Eng. J. Med. **270**:1030, 1964.

Petersdorf, R. G.: Colistin—a reappraisal, J.A.M.A. **183**:123, 1963

Weinstein, A., Kaplan, K., and Chang, T.: Treatment of infections in man with cephalothin, J.A.M.A. **189**:829, 1964.

30 | Specific chemotherapy

Tuberculostatic drugs
Drugs used in treatment of leprosy
Antiprotozoan agents
Antiviral chemotherapy
Anthelmintics
Amebiasis and amebicides

Chemotherapy of various parasitic diseases is of worldwide concern but in some cases is a primary concern of the tropics and subtropics. Tuberculosis and malaria continue to be responsible for millions of deaths each year throughout the world. Eradication or control of parasitic disease is highly important to international health work.

■ Tuberculostatic drugs

Tuberculosis continues to be an important disease, with 50,000 new cases occurring in the United States each year and 10,000 cases returning for retreatment. Efforts continue for improving therapeutic regimens and developing new, less toxic, and more effective drugs.

A rather large number of drugs exhibit tuberculostatic effects, but their usefulness is limited by the toxic effects they produce or by their lack of therapeutic potency. Drugs of greatest value in the treatment of tuberculosis are streptomycin, para-aminosalicylic acid (PAS), and the isonicotinic acid derivatives. Antituberculosis drugs act chiefly by preventing the tubercle bacilli from multiplying. The ultimate defeat of the organisms is caused by the immunity the human body develops against the infection. One of the greatest problems encountered in the chemotherapy of this disease is how to prevent emergence of resistant tubercle bacilli. The administration of two or more of these drugs at the same time has been reasonably successful in delaying development of resistance. Once chemotherapy has been started it should be continued without interruption until the physician decides to stop the treatment. Interruptions in drug therapy encourage the development of resistant organisms. An essential part of the nurse's role in caring for the patient with tuberculosis is helping him to understand the need for prolonged therapy.

Para-aminosalicylic acid (PAS)

$$NH_2-\text{⟨benzene ring⟩}-COOH \quad (OH)$$

Para-aminosalicylic acid is a synthetic, white, crystalline powder with a faint fruity odor. It is only slightly soluble in water, but its sodium salt is much more soluble.

Action and result. This drug inhibits the action of virulent tubercle bacilli, but it is less potent than streptomycin or isoniazid. It has little or no effect on other microorganisms. The precise mechanism of its action seems to be controversial. Some authorities contend that an antagonism exists between PAS and PABA (para-aminobenzoic acid) similar to the competition that exists between the sulfonamides and PABA.

PAS, as well as its salts, is well absorbed from the gastrointestinal tract after oral administration. The drug diffuses rapidly into pleural fluids and into various tissues, although its diffusion into cerebrospinal fluid is erratic and not dependable. It is excreted chiefly by way of the kidneys, although it is not effective for tuberculosis of the urinary tract since it is subject to change in the liver and the resulting metabolic products are therapeutically inactive. Since it is rapidly excreted, large doses, 8 to 20 Gm. daily, are required to maintain effective blood levels.

Resistance. The tubercle bacilli develop resistance to PAS slowly. Several months of treatment may elapse before the organisms are insensitive to the drug.

Uses. Aminosalicylic acid is not very effective when used alone, but when combined with streptomycin or isoniazid it delays the emergence of resistant tubercle bacilli and increases the effectiveness of these drugs. This sometimes makes it possible to reduce the dosage and decrease chances of toxic reactions.

Preparation, dosage, and administration. The following are the preparations and dosages of aminosalicylic acid. Discolored preparations are toxic and should be discarded.

Aminosalicylic acid, **U.S.P. (Para-Pas, Pamisyl, PAS).** This preparation is available in 300- and 500-mg. and 1-Gm. tablets for oral administration. The recommended daily dose is 8 to 16 Gm. Some physicians recommend dosage up to 20 Gm. daily. The drug may be given as a single dose or in four or more doses with or after meals. It is also available as a powder from which 2% to 5% solutions can be made for use in cavities and sinuses.

Calcium aminosalicylate, **N.F., B.P.** This form is available in 500-mg. tablets and capsules for oral administration. It has no advantages over the sodium salt except that it may be given to patients whose dietary intake of sodium is restricted. Dosage is similar to that for PAS.

Potassium aminosalicylate, **U.S.P. (Parasal Potassium, Paskalium).** This form is available in 500-mg. tablets and is given orally. The average adult dose is 12 Gm. daily. It may cause fewer symptoms of gastric irritation than the acid or the sodium salt.

Sodium aminosalicylate, **U.S.P., B.P. (sodium para-aminosalicylate).** This drug is marketed in 500-mg. capsules and in tablets containing 500 mg. and 1 Gm. of the drug. The sodium salt is said to produce less gastrointestinal irritation than the parent drug. Usual dose is 3 Gm. five times a day.

Side effects and toxic effects. Gastrointestinal symptoms are said to develop in approximately 10% to 15% of the patients. Such symptoms include nausea and vomiting, loss of appetite, and diarrhea. To help overcome this difficulty the drug should be given with meals. In addition, the physician may prescribe an antacid or adjust the dosage. Gastrointestinal symptoms are apparently caused entirely by local irritation. Allergic reactions often occur from the third to eighth week of therapy and include skin eruption, fever, painful joints, and a variety of neurologic symptoms. In addition, patients very occasionally develop hepatitis, renal failure, hemolytic anemia, and leukopenia. After therapy has continued for some time the clotting time of the blood is likely to be prolonged. This can be prevented by the administration of vitamin K. PAS has antithyroid activity, and patients on prolonged therapy should be checked for hypothyroidism. Other salicylates such as sodium salicylate and aspirin should be avoided, if possible, during therapy with PAS because of the possibility of severe salicylate poisoning.

Isoniazid, U.S.P., B.P. (INH, isonicotinic acid hydrazide)

$$N \underset{O}{\overset{\displaystyle}{\parallel}} \text{—C—NH—NH}_2$$

Isoniazid is a synthetic substance derived from isonicotinic acid. It is a white, crystalline, odorless compound. It is freely soluble in water.

Action and result. Isoniazid exerts a selective action against *Mycobacterium tuberculosis* and produces a bacteriostatic effect. Little is known about the mechanism of its action, but it probably acts as an antimetabolite by inhibiting essential enzyme systems of the tubercle bacilli. Of the three most effective agents against tuberculosis (PAS, streptomycin, and isoniazid), isoniazid is the most potent as long as the organisms remain sensitive to it.

Therapeutic effects are manifested by reduction of fever, improvement in the patient's appetite, and a gain in weight. The patient may feel so much better that his mental reactions at times may approach a state of euphoria. Coughing is diminished, and the number of acid-fast organisms in the sputum may diminish in number or disappear altogether.

The drug is speedily absorbed from the gastrointestinal tract and it diffuses readily into all body tissues and fluids, including cerbrospinal fluid. Peak serum levels occur 1 hour after administration. It is excreted chiefly by way of the kidney. It is inexpensive and relatively nontoxic when dosage is kept within the usual therapeutic range.

Uses. Isoniazid is used alone or concurrently with PAS or streptomycin or occasionally with both. Any regimen that includes isoniazid is considered superior to any drug or combination of drugs that does not contain it. Isoniazid-PAS and isoniazid-streptomycin are at present considered especially effective combinations. The isoniazid-PAS combination is the most convenient regimen, since both drugs can be given orally. Therapy for at least 1 year is considered advisable for minimal tuberculosis and for a longer period (2 to 3 years) when the disease is advanced or cavitation has occurred.

Preparation, dosage, and administration. Isoniazid is available in 50- and 100-mg. tablets and as a syrup, 10 mg. per milliliter for oral administration, also as a solution, 1 Gm. in 10 ml. for intramuscular injection.

The usual adult dose is 3 to 5 mg. per kilogram of body weight divided into two or three portions. A patient may receive as much as 300 mg. daily along with 8 to 16 Gm. of PAS. Higher dosage is sometimes employed. Rate of metabolism varies among individuals. Rapid metabolizers excrete more of the drug in acetylated form and have no drug in the serum 6 hours after administration. Slow metabolizers have one third of the peak level 6 hours after administration. Rapid metabolizers require higher dosage.

A dosage form is now available that contains isoniazid and streptomycin in combination. It is marketed under the trade name of Streptohydrazide. It is available as a vial of dry powder to which water for injection is added prior to intramuscular administration. The vial contains the equivalent of 1 Gm. of streptomycin and 236 mg. of isoniazid.

Side effects and toxic effects. Isoniazid resembles streptomycin in that tubercle bacilli readily become resistant to it. Undesirable side effects are more likely to occur when the dosage is elevated. The less serious effects include constipation, dryness of the mouth, headache, visual disturbances, insomnia, orthostatic hypotension, slight anemia, and occasionally albuminuria. With elevated doses, convulsive seizures and peripheral neuritis may develop. Symptoms of peripheral neuritis include pain, numbness and tingling, inability to grasp objects, and sometimes a tendency to drop things. The disturbance of the peripheral nerves can be prevented by the administration of pyridoxine (vitamin B_6), and the administration of 300 mg. daily reduces the incidence of neurotoxicity after large doses of isoniazid have been given. Isoniazid evidently causes a pyridoxine deficiency.

The drug is used with caution for patients with epilepsy or for those with a history of convulsive seizures.

Pyrazinamide; viomycin sulfate; cycloserine; ethionamide

Pyrazinamide

Since isoniazid, streptomycin, and PAS cannot always be prescribed for the treatment of tuberculosis for reasons such as (1) the organisms have become resistant, (2) the patient has become hypersensitive to the drug or drugs, (3) toxic effects have been produced, or (4) the drugs have failed to be effective, secondary drugs may be valuable as reserve agents to be used individually or in combination with one of the older drugs.

Pyrazinamide, U.S.P., B.P. (PZA, Aldinamide). This is a synthetic drug made from nicotinamide. It is considered an effective drug, especially when given with isoniazid for short-term therapy, such as that which precedes surgery of patients in whom the causative organism is resistant to other drugs. It is prone to cause liver damage, and the tubercle bacilli develop resistance to the drug relatively quickly. It is available in 500-mg. tablets for oral administration. A dose of 1.5 to 2 Gm. daily (after meals) in two or three equally divided portions is recommended. Jaundice is occasionally observed in patients; hence, it is used only when regular tests of liver function (the transaminase test) can be performed to detect a developing toxic reaction.

Viomycin sulfate, U.S.P., B.P. (Vinactane, Viocin). This is an antibiotic produced by *Streptomyces puniceus.* This preparation is said to possess definite although limited value as a tuberculostatic agent. It is given in doses of 2 Gm. twice weekly intramuscularly along with a more potent agent such as cycloserine or PAS. In large doses it may cause renal and auditory damage.

Cycloserine, U.S.P., B.P. (Seromycin). This agent exhibits some activity against the organisms causing human tuberculosis, especially when administered in combination with isoniazid. Its chief disadvantage is that it can be high-ly toxic to the nervous system and can cause convulsive disorders. Other toxic effects include headache, visual disturbances, skin lesions, and mental symptoms that may progress to psychosis. It is usually administered orally in doses of 0.5 Gm. daily. The initial dose is less, but subsequent doses are gradually increased.

Several other antibiotics have been undergoing study and investigation. These include streptovaracin, thiocarbanidin, and kanamycin. The first two drugs are thought to have minor value as drugs in the treatment of tuberculosis. Kanamycin has moderate antituberculosis activity, but it has been found to be toxic to the eighth cranial nerve, causing loss of hearing. Its use (as a last resort) is likely to be restricted to short periods of therapy.

Ethionamide, U.S.P., B.P. (Trecator). This drug is generally used only when the patient cannot tolerate the usual combination of drugs. It is not considered as effective and is more toxic. Anorexia, nausea and vomiting, postural hypotension, and impotence are commonly noted adverse effects. The usual dosage is 500 mg. to 1 Gm. daily in divided doses and with meals.

Ethambutol (Myambutol)

This is a new tuberculostatic drug. It is readily absorbed from the gastrointestinal tract and quite rapidly excreted in the urine. Resistance to the drug develops quite rapidly. It can be used with most other antituberculosis drugs and may be substituted for PAS in initial treatment.

Preparation, dosage, and administration. Ethambutol is available as 100- and 400-mg. tablets. Average daily dose is 25 mg. per kilogram of body weight (0.8 to 2 Gm. per day). The most serious toxic effects are visual: loss of green-red perception suggesting retrobulbar neuritis, retinal damage, and partial loss of vision.

Rifampin

Rifampin is a semisynthetic derivative of the antibiotic *rifamycin.* It is well absorbed from the gastrointestinal tract. It is said to be comparable to isoniazid as a single drug or in combination with other drugs. Oral dosage is usually 450 to

599

600 mg. per day. Rifampin appears to be well tolerated and adverse reactions have not yet been reported. It is an experimental drug under intensive study.

Capreomycin

Capreomycin is a peptide antibiotic obtained from *Streptomyces capreolus.* It is not active orally. It is administered intramuscularly in doses of 0.5 to 1.5 Gm. per day. After 60 days of treatment, 1.0 Gm. may be given every other day. Resistance to capreomycin develops slowly. Toxic reactions of renal damage and deafness have been reported. This drug may replace streptomycin in combined antituberculosis therapy. It is still undergoing intensive study.

■ Drugs used in treatment of leprosy

Leprosy is a chronic disease caused by the acid-fast bacillus *Mycobacterium leprae.* For many years chaulmoogra oil or one of its derivatives was used in the treatment of leprosy, but since it is no longer believed that either the oil or its derivatives have any therapeutic significance, they are no longer official preparations in the United States.

Sulfones

The sulfones in current use are synthetic compounds chemically related to the parent drug, diaminodiphenylsulfone. The latter substance was found to be an effective antibacterial agent, but because it was used in doses that produced toxic reactions it was soon replaced by less toxic sulfones. The members of this group of drugs that have been studied most extensively are sulfoxone sodium, glucosulone sodium, and thiazosulfone.

Action and results. To be effective, the more complicated derivatives apparently are changed into the parent compound prior to or after absorption. Although the sulfones have an antibacterial spectrum similar to that of the sulfonamides, their chief usefulness is in the treatment of leprosy. Their action is probably similar to the sulfonamides, that is, they interfere with the nutrition of bacteria. They exert a bacteriostatic effect on *Mycobacterium leprae,* evidenced by the slow disappearance of the organisms from leprous lesions. They bring about a suppression of the disease, prevent new lesions from appearing, promote the healing of many lesions, and allow the defense mechanisms of the body to keep the disease inactive. Their action is slow, and improvement may not be seen for several months. The most encouraging feature about their use is that they almost universally bring about sufficient improvement to permit many patients to become presentable members of society again. However, even though the disease apparently becomes inactive, maintenance doses should be continued indefinitely to prevent relapses.

The sulfones are excreted mainly by the kidneys. The body tissues retain considerable amounts of the drug and release it slowly for some time after administration is discontinued.

Preparation, dosage, and administration. The following are the preparations and dosages of sulfone.

Sulfoxone sodium, **U.S.P. (Diasone).** This compound is available in 330-mg. enteric-coated tablets for oral administration. The usual adult dose is 300 mg. daily, which is gradually increased to 900 mg. unless toxic symptoms occur. Periodic rest periods are advocated. At least 6 months of treatment are required to evaluate therapeutic effects.

Sodium glucosulfone injection, **U.S.P. (Promin).** This drug is available as a solution for intravenous injection (5 Gm. in 12.5 ml.). The intravenous dose is 2 to 5 Gm. given 6 days of each week. Periodic rest periods are recommended, but the treatment may continue over many months.

Dapsone, **U.S.P., B.P. (Avlosulfon, DDS).** The initial dosage is 25 to 50 mg. twice weekly, increasing by 50 to 100 mg. every month until 200 to 400 mg. are given twice weekly.

Side effects and toxic effects. The administration of the sulfones is not recommended unless there is adequate medical supervision and access to adequate laboratory facilities. Toxic effects include nausea and vomiting, anemia, dermatitis, hepatitis, glandular enlargement, and, occasionally, liver damage and psychosis.

Toxic reactions are associated with increased concentrations of the drug in the blood. If the sulfones are employed in minimum effective doses with rest periods interspersed between courses of therapy, serious reactions tend to be rare and the patient may be able to tolerate the medication for years.

■ Antiprotozoan agents
Antimalarial drugs

Malaria is one of the most prevalent of all diseases in spite of efforts to control the causative organisms and their insect vectors. The organisms that cause this disease are protozoa called *Plasmodium vivax* or tertian parasite, *Plasmodium malariae* or quartan parasite, and *Plasmodium falciparum* or estivoautumnal parasite. Each of these causes a different type of malaria. Each species is made up of several strains, each with idiosyncrasies that modify response to treatment.

Plasmodium falciparum is thought to be the most recently acquired malarial infection of man. It causes the highest mortality and has the simplest life cycle. Eradication of the blood forms of this species is relatively easy. *Plasmodium vivax* is better adapted to the tissues of the human host and is more difficult to eradicate. The malarial parasites undergo two phases of development: the sexual cycle, which takes place in the mosquito, and the asexual cycle, which occurs in the human body. The mosquito that bites an infected human being ingests the asexual forms, known as schizonts, and the sexual forms, known as gametocytes. In the mosquito the asexual forms are destroyed, but the female gametocytes are fertilized by the male gametocytes and development into asexual forms results. These are introduced into the blood of human beings by the bite of the anopheles mosquito.

The parasites, when injected into man by the mosquito bite, are known as sporozoites. Shortly after their introduction into the blood they disappear and enter fixed tissue cells (reticuloendothelial cells of liver) and possibly certain other organs where development and multiplication take place. For a period of time, which varies with the different plasmodia (6 to 14 days or longer), the patient exhibits no symptoms, no parasites are found in erythrocytes, and the blood is noninfective. This is known as the *prepatent* period or *tissue phase*. The parasites are called primary tissue schizonts or preerythrocytic forms. After the prepatent period the parasites burst from the tissue cells as merozoites, enter the bloodstream, penetrate erythrocytes, and begin the *erythrocytic phase* of their existence. In the case of *P. vivax* (but not *P. falciparum*) some of the merozoites invade other tissue cells to form secondary exoerythrocytic forms. The relapses in *P. vivax* malaria are believed to be caused by the successive formations of merozoites produced by various secondary exoerythrocytic forms of the parasite. Drugs that affect malarial parasites in the bloodstream do not necessarily destroy those in the exoerythrocytic or tissue stage.

The erythrocytic phase of development refers to the activity of the parasite within the red blood cell. The merozoites bore into the cell, undergo development and multiplication, and finally cause rupture of the red cell to set free many more merozoites. Some of the merozoites may be destroyed in the plasma of the blood by leukocytes and other agents, but many more enter other erythrocytes to repeat the cycle. The recurring chills, fever, and prostration that are prominent clinical symptoms of malaria occur when the red cells rupture and release the young parasites. This process takes place in malaria caused by *P. falciparum*, particularly in the capillaries of internal organs, and explains the pernicious nature of this kind of malaria, for example, comatose type in which the parasites accumulate in capillaries of the brain.

After a few cycles some of the asexual forms of the malarial parasites develop into sexual forms called gametocytes (the female form is called a macrogamete and the male is a microgamete). When the mosquito bites a person infected with malarial parasites and ingests the sexual forms, a rather complicated phase of sexual development takes place in the stomach of the mosquito. The female parasite is fertilized by the male, enters the wall of the stomach of the mosquito, where it becomes encysted, and forms many spindle-shaped forms known as sporozoites. After a time the cyst ruptures and the sporozoites find their way into the saliva of the mosquito and are thus transferred to the next victim of its bite.

Persons who harbor the sexual forms of the plasmodia are called carriers, since it is from carriers that mosquitos receive the forms of the parasite that perpetuate the disease. The asexual forms cause the clinical symptoms of malaria.

The life cycle of the *P. malariae* is similar to that of *P. vivax*.

Characteristics of a good antimalarial drug. The ideal antimalarial drug should be effective in the treatment of all forms of malaria, effective both as a prophylactic agent to destroy the exoerythrocytic forms and as a suppressive agent to prevent the development of clinical symptoms. It should also bring about a rapid curative action, and it should not create parasitic resistance. It should be excreted slowly so that the drug need not be given often. It should be palatable, inexpensive, and readily available. No drug is known that combines all these qualities, but research continues. Quinine is of historic importance and will be presented first, although it is now one of the least important drugs used for malaria. It is sometimes used for strains of *P. falciparum* that are resistant to newer drugs.

Quinine sulfate, N.F., B.P.

Cinchona bark is the source of quinine, the alkaloid that was long considered a specific in the treatment of malaria. The cinchona trees are indigenous to South America, but because of the great demand for quinine they were introduced into the East Indies, Jamaica, Java, and other countries.

The most important alkaloids belonging to the cinchona group are quinine and quinidine. The latter is discussed in Chapter 10, under heart depressants.

Action and result. Quinine acts as a selective parasiticide. In sufficient concentration it is fatal to all cells and has been called a "general proto-

plasmic poison." It affects protozoa more than it affects bacteria. In therapuetic doses it is effective against the plasmodia that cause malaria. Adequate doses promptly suppress the symptoms of the disease, killing the asexual forms of all types of malaria. It kills the sexual forms of both *P. vivax* and *P. malariae* but not of *P. falciparum*. It is not effective against the preerythrocytic forms of the parasite; hence, relapse is likely to occur when treatment is discontinued for infection caused by *P. vivax* or *P. malariae*.

Quinine has:

1 Analgesic and antipyretic action similar to salicylates
2 A distinct curare-like action. It decreases response of the motor end-plate to tetanic stimulation and to acetylcholine and is a competitive inhibitor of cholinesterase.
3 Cardiovascular effects identical to those of quinidine
4 A powerful local anesthetic effect when injected near a peripheral nerve
5 A slight oxytocic effect on the pregnant uterus during the third trimester of pregnancy
6 A peripheral vascular dilating effect

These numerous actions account for the wide diversity of side and toxic effects resulting from administration of quinine.

Uses. Quinine is used in some parts of the world when other antimalarials are not available or are too expensive. It has a number of disadvantages, among which are the following: the inconvenience of daily administration (doses should not be missed), bitter taste, and the likelihood of side effects associated with therapeutic dosage. However, it can be used to cure vivax malaria with a drug such as primaquine. Quinine has been used against strains of *P. falciparum* resistant to newer drugs.

It has been used alone or in combination with other drugs to lower fever. Occasionally, it is used as an analgesic for relief of headache and pain in muscles and joints.

Preparation, dosage, and administration. When used in the treatment of malaria, the oral route of administration is preferred. When oral administration is not feasible, quinine hydrochloride may be given intravenously, but this method is recommended only for emergencies, and the injection should be made slowly, for a dangerous lowering of blood pressure usually occurs. EKG monitoring is also important to detect cardiac arrhythmias.

Quinine sulfate, **U.S.P., B.P.** Usual oral dose is 1 Gm. daily for 2 days, then 600 mg. three times a day for 5 days. Quinine sulfate is available in tablets.

Side effects and toxic effects. When taken orally, large doses cause nausea, vomiting, and diarrhea. When injected intramuscularly, it is likely to cause abscesses. When injected intravenously, it causes irritation of the intima, which may result in thrombosis. Quinine has the disadvantage of a bitter taste. It must be taken daily when used for malaria. When the maximum therapeutic dosage is administered, symptoms of cinchonism are likely to occur. Such symptoms include ringing in the ears, headache, nausea, dizziness, and disturbance of vision. More severe poisoning may be indicated by the following: renal damage; acute hemolytic anemia; and involvement of the central nervous system, which includes stimulation of the respiratory center and eventual respiratory arrest.

Quinacrine hydrochloride, U.S.P. (Atabrine); mepacrine, B.P.

Quinacrine is a synthetic drug of the acridine dye series that is used in treatment of malaria. It is yellow in color. Although quinacrine was the drug of choice for malaria between 1940 and 1945, it has been replaced by chloroquine and amodiaquin. Quinacrine is also used as an anthelmintic (500 mg. with 500 mg. sodium bicarbonate).

Preparation, dosage, and administration. Quinacrine hydrochloride is available in 100-mg. tablets for oral administration. To suppress symptoms the dose for adults is 100 mg. daily for 6 days a week. For treatment of a clinical attack, 200 mg. of quinacrine with 1 Gm. of sodium bicarbonate is administered every 6 hours for five doses and then 100 mg. three times daily for 6 days. All doses of the drug should be accompanied by a full glass of water or sweetened fruit juice and taken after meals. Quinacrine hydrochloride can also be administered intramuscularly.

Side effects and toxic effects. The untoward effects are usually mild and consist of nausea, headache, vomiting, and diarrhea. Discoloration (yellow color) of the skin occurs, and the urine becomes yellow. This color change usually disappears a few weeks after the drug is discontinued. The drug is not toxic to the liver and kidneys. Toxic psychosis and aplastic anemia have been known to occur after long periods of suppressive therapy.

The treatment must suit the symptoms. Mild poisoning usually subsides when the medication is discontinued. In the more severe forms body temperature must be maintained and respirations supported.

Chloroquine; amodiaquine; primaquine; pyrimethamine; chloroguanide

More important than quinine or quinacrine is a series of synthetic drugs that are active antimalarials and that share certain chemical features with the naturally occurring cinchona alkaloids. These synthetic drugs include chloroquine, amodiaquine, primaquine, pyrimethamine, and chloroguanide. The structural similarities can be seen by studying the following formulas. It should be noted that many of these drugs contain the quinoline nucleus and also share certain general types of side chains.

Chloroquine, amodiaquine, pyrimethamine, and primaquine are among the drugs most often employed in programs for eradication of malaria. At the present time no drug is available that will act with equal effectiveness on all species and all developmental stages of the malarial parasites.

Chloroquine and amodiaquine are especially useful in the treatment of acute malaria. They are also effective for suppressive therapy for all kinds of human malaria. However, since they do not affect the primary or secondary tissue forms of the parasites, they do not prevent infection or relapse.

Pyrimethamine is said to be the most effective single suppressive agent. Single weekly

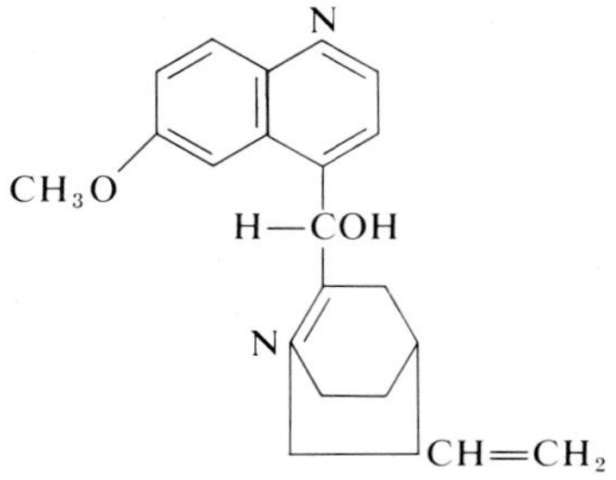

Quinine

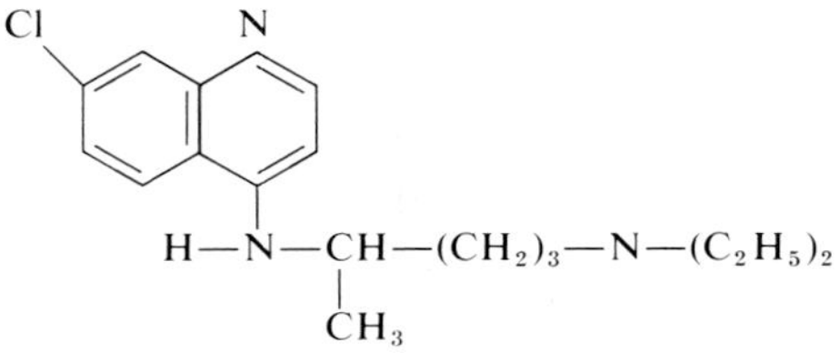

Chloroquine

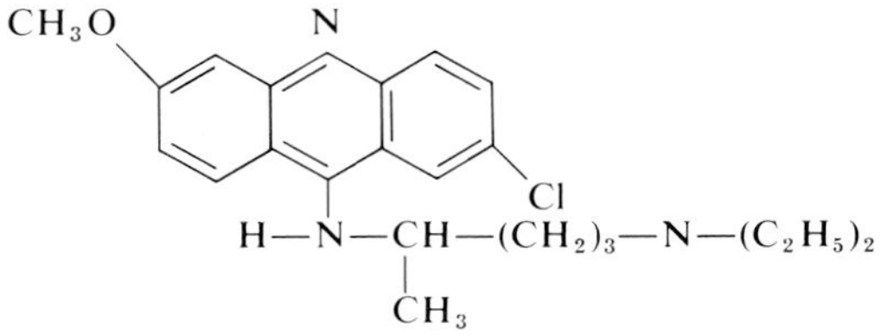

Quinacrine

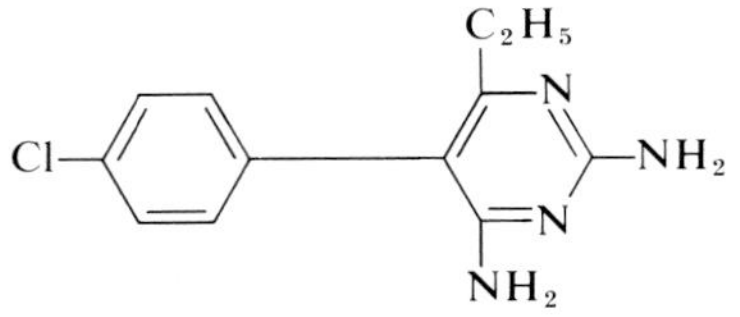

Pyrimethamine

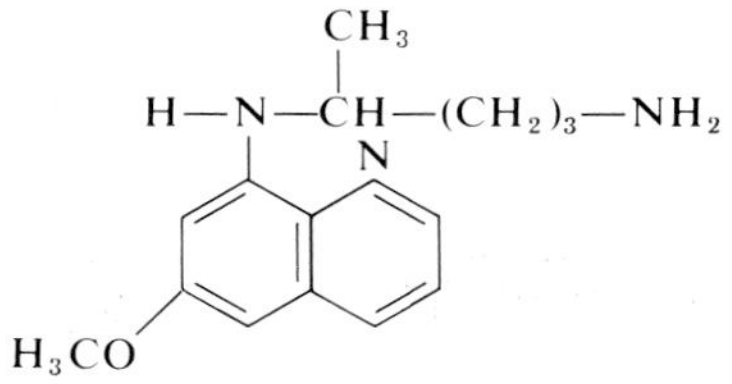

Primaquine

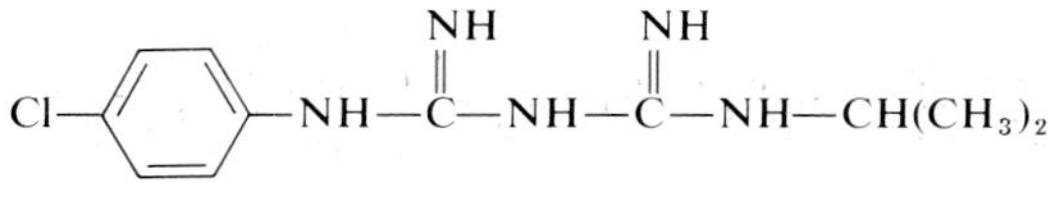

Chloroguanide

doses will prevent clinical attacks of malaria associated with all species of human malarial parasites so that the mosquito is unable to transmit the disease after feeding on persons taking this drug. Primaquine and related members of this group of drugs also have the advantage of destroying persistent exoerythrocytic parasites in the liver that are known to cause relapses of malarial infections.

In some parts of the world antimalarial drugs such as chloroquine are added to salt in much the same way that iodine is added to salt to prevent goiter. This would appear to be a useful way of dealing with malaria in places where difficulties are encountered in using other methods of eradication.

***Chloroquine phosphate*, U.S.P., B.P. (Aralen).** Chloroquine is a synthetic antimalarial drug. It was synthesized in Germany in 1934 and introduced in the U.S. for the treatment of malaria in 1944. It is the most effective and least toxic antimalarial drug. The mechanism of its action is to block the enzymatic synthesis of DNA and RNA. It is effective against the asexual forms of all plasmodia causing human malaria. It abolishes acute attacks of falciparum malaria and brings about complete cure of the infection (suppressive cure). However, it does not kill the sexual forms, and therefore patients continue to be infective to mosquitoes for a period of time. It does not cure malaria caused by *P. vivax*, but it is an effective suppressive agent, terminates attacks, and delays relapse. Chloroquine is not effective against the preerythrocytic forms of the plasmodia (tissue phase). Only falciparum infections, in which there are no persistent tissue forms, are radically cured by this drug. Some falciparum strains have become resistant to chloroquine. Chloroquine also possesses amebicidal properties.

Chloroquine is rapidly and almost completely absorbed from the gastrointestinal tract, with maximum plasma concentrations occurring 1 to 2 hours after administration. A portion of it is slowly eliminated in the urine.

Chloroquine phosphate is available in 125- and 250-mg. tablets for oral administration before or after meals. For acute attacks, an initial dose of 1 Gm. is followed by 500 mg. after 6 or 8 hours and by 500 mg. on each of 2 successive days. This dosage is sufficient to eradicate most infections caused by *P. falciparum* and to terminate an acute attack caused by *P. vivax*. Suppressive doses of 500 mg. every 7 days prevent clinical attacks of vivax malaria.

Chloroquine phosphate injection, B.P., is available for parenteral (intramuscular or intravenous) use. The B.P. also lists chloroquine sulfate and chloroquine sulfate injection for oral and parenteral administration, respectively.

When given in therapeutic doses the drug is well tolerated. However, mild headache, itching, gastrointestinal disorders, and visual disturbances are sometimes observed even with therapeutic doses. These symptoms disappear when administration is discontinued. When given intravenously, chloroquine may produce effects on the heart similar to quinidine.

Chloroquine can cause both corneal and retinal damage. For this reason frequent eye examinations are necessary when prolonged therapy with the drug is undertaken.

Chloroquine and amodiaquine have the advantage of low toxicity and rapid action, which makes possible a short course of treatment.

***Amodiaquine hydrochloride*, N.F., B.P. (Camoquin).** Amodiaquine is a synthetic antimalarial drug that greatly resembles chloroquine both in its effectiveness for treatment of malaria and in its level of toxicity. Like chloroquine, it is effective only in the erythrocytic stages of malaria. It is capable of producing a radical cure only when the infection is caused by *P. falciparum*. It does not effect a similar cure for other forms of malaria, but it is effective in the treatment of an acute attack, relieves symptoms, and delays relapse. It is therefore an effective suppressive agent in areas of the world where malaria is endemic.

Like chloroquine, amodiaquine is rapidly absorbed from the gastrointestinal tract and concentrated in the liver, spleen, kidney, and blood cells. It is said to be concentrated slightly less than chloroquine.

Amodiaquine hydrochloride is available in 200-mg. tablets for oral administration. The usual single dose for adults in an acute attack of the disease (in term of the base) is 400 to 600 mg. For suppression of endemic malaria the usual dose is 400 to 600 mg. administered once every 2 weeks. The dosage for children is reduced in accordance with the age of the child.

Side effects include nausea and vomiting, increased flow of saliva, and diarrhea. Large doses may produce spasticity, incoordination of movement, and convulsions, but these are seldom encountered. It does not discolor the skin. Prolonged usage in high doses may also result in corneal and retinal damage, blood dyscrasias, and hepatitis.

***Primaquine phosphate*, U.S.P., B.P.** Primaquine, pamaquine, and pentaquine are all synthetic antimalarial drugs that belong to the same chemical group of drug (8-aminoquinolines). The latter two members are more toxic and less potent than primaquine and hence will be omitted from this edition.

Primaquine exerts a distinctive action on all

605

gametocytes (sexual forms), especially those of *P. falciparum.* The gametocytes cause no clinical symptoms, but they are responsible for the transmission of malaria to the mosquito and thus keep the mosquito effective in the malarial cycle. The drug is ineffective or only slightly effective against asexual forms of the parasites *(P. falciparum);* hence, effective treatment of acute attacks of malaria is dependent on simultaneous administration of another antimalarial such as chloroquine. Its greatest value lies in its ability to destroy the late tissue forms (which can cause secondary erythrocytic parasites) and thus treat relapses of vivax malaria. If it is administered during the latent period (period between the time the person is bitten by an infected mosquito and the time that the parasites enter the red blood cells), radical cure of vivax malaria can be secured by this drug alone.

Primaquine phosphate, U.S.P., is available in tablets containing 26.3 mg. of the drug for oral administration. For the treatment of relapsing vivax infections, one tablet each day for 14 days is considered adequate to produce a radical cure. If the patient has symptoms of an attack or a relapse, primaquine phosphate is supplemented with chloroquine or amodiaquine.

When given in the dosage recommended, primaquine exhibits a low level of toxicity, but it can cause all the toxic effects associated with pamaquine (depression of the bone marrow, hemolytic anemia, and agranulocytosis). Epigastric distress, nausea and vomiting, and abdominal pains occur occasionally. Large doses result in hemolytic effects, particularly in persons belonging to the deeply pigmented races, and the drug should be stopped immediately on any sign of darkening of the urine or a sudden drop in hemoglobin concentration or leukocyte count. Its main disadvantages are its narrow margin of safety between therapeutic and toxic dose and ineffectiveness against asexual forms of *P. falciparum.*

Pyrimethamine, U.S.P., B.P. (Daraprim). Pyrimethamine is a potent antimalarial agent especially valuable as a suppressive agent. It therefore prevents the clinical attacks of all forms of malaria, and it interrupts the malarial cycle by preventing the formation of sporozoites in the mosquito. If suppressive therapy is continued long enough, suppressive cure of vivax infections may occur. Its use as a suppressive agent for falciparum infections results in a radical cure in most cases. This is because the gametocytes eventually disappear spontaneously after the asexual blood forms are eliminated by the suppressive drug. Pyrimethamine acts slowly and should not be used in the treatment of acute primary attacks.

Pyrimethamine is available in 25-mg. tablets for oral administration. The usual suppressive dose is 25 mg. per week. It is recommended that this dosage be continued indefinitely in areas where malaria is endemic. The dosage is 12.5 mg. for children under the age of 15 years. Therapeutic dosage (adults) is 25 mg. daily for 2 days.

Pyrimethamine has a wide margin of safety, and toxic effects are seldom encountered, although overdosage can result in anemia and leukopenia. Plasmodia that are resistant to chloroguanide may develop resistance to pyrimethamine. Therefore its use is not recommended in areas of the world where it is known that the plasmodia have developed resistance to chloroguanide.

Chloroguanide; proguanil, B.P. Chloroguanide has been used as an antimalarial agent, but it is no longer official in U.S.P. Its chief disadvantage is that it has resulted in the development of resistant strains of plasmodia.

Drugs of choice in treatment of malaria

According to current concepts the following are the drugs of choice for various forms of malaria:

1 Uncomplicated attacks by any plasmodia—chloroquine phosphate, amodiaquine hydrochloride, injections of chloroquine hydrochloride (if infection is severe)
2 Malaria caused by resistant strains of *P. falciparum*—quinine sulfate plus pyrimethamine and sulfadiazine
3 Prevention of disease in endemic area—chloroquine phosphate, 500 mg. once a week. The individual may develop the disease when discontinuing the medication upon leaving the area.

Other antiprotozoan agents
Trypanocidal drugs
Pentamidine (Lomidine)

Pentamidine, a trypanocidal drug, is the drug of choice for the prevention and treatment of *Trypanosoma gambiense* and *Trypanosoma rhodesiense* forms of trypanosomiasis (sleeping sickness). It is not effective for treating late stages of African sleeping sickness. It is also used for treatment of leishmaniasis. The basic mechanism of action of pentamidine is unknown but the organisms are known to accumulate high concentrations of the drug. *In vitro* experiments have shown that pentamidine inhibits no fewer than twenty enzyme systems. Pentamidine has both bactericidal and fungicidal action.

Pentamidine is poorly absorbed from the gastrointestinal tract and must be given intramuscularly or intravenously. After injection the drug is quickly taken up by the liver, kidney, and adrenal gland. Very little of the drug penetrates the central nervous system. Signs of a trypanocidal effect are evidenced by disappearance of organisms from the blood and lymph.

Side effects and toxic effects. The most common side effect is itching. Intravenous injection causes peripheral vasodilation and a sharp fall in blood pressure that is only partially blocked by atropine. This may be caused by release of tissue-bound histamine and peripheral adrenergic blockade.

Pentamidine may cause central nervous system depression, which may produce a rise of blood-urea-nitrogen and nonprotein nitrogen. Toxic effects are rare but tremor, convulsions, nystagmus, ataxia, vomiting, and death have been reported.

Preparation, dosage, and administration. Pentamidine is available as a dry powder in ampules of 200 mg. It is available in the United States only from the Parasitic Disease Drug Service, U. S. Public Health Service. Average dose is 4 mg. per kilogram of body weight intramuscularly daily or on alternate days. In the early stages of trypanosomiasis, pentamidine is given in dosages of 1.5 to 4 mg. intramuscularly every 1 to 2 days for 10 days. For chemoprophylaxis, 3 mg. per kilogram of body weight is given intramuscularly every 3 to 6 months.

Suramin, B.P.
(Antrypol, Germanin, Naphuride)

Suramin is a nonmetallic dye that is used both as a prophylactic and as a therapeutic agent for trypanosomiasis. This disease, which is caused by a parasitic protozoan organism that is spread by the bite of the tsetse fly, is also known as African sleeping sickness. There is more than one species of the parasite, and they are not equally virulent. Therapy in which suramin is given with an arsenical (tryparsamide) or alternated with it is particularly successful. This drug is excreted slowly and tends to persist in the tissues for some time after administration is discontinued.

Preparation, dosage, and administration. Suramin is not manufactured in the United States because it is used very little in this part of the world. The usual single dose is 1 Gm. given intravenously. A course of treatment consists of five to ten weekly injections.

Side effects and toxic effects. The drug is said to be somewhat toxic to the kidney, causing albumin, casts, and sometimes red blood cells to appear in the urine. It occasionally produces hemolytic reactions. Periodic urine and blood examinations are therefore recommended. In addition, the following symptoms may be seen: headache, chills, fever, itching, and dermatitis.

Trichomonicidal drugs
Metronidazole, U.S.P. (Flagyl)

Metronidazole is a highly effective drug for the treatment of *Trichomonas vaginalis*. It does not alter the normal vaginal flora. It is rapidly and almost completely absorbed from the gastrointestinal tract and suitable for both male and female patients. About 70% of the drug is excreted in the urine unchanged; it is also excreted in the saliva, milk, semen, and vaginal secretions. Maximum excretion is reached in 3 hours; the urine may be colored a deep red brown. About 90% of *T. vaginalis* infections can be cured with a single course of metronidazole therapy, and 90% of treatment failures will respond to retreatment. It has also been found to be effective in the treatment of disease caused by *Entamoeba histolytica,* acute ulcerative gingivitis, and some tropical diseases.

Preparation, dosage, and administration. Metronidazole is available in 250-mg. tablets and 500-mg. vaginal inserts. For *T. vaginalis* infections average dose is 250 mg. three times a day for 10 days for females and 250 mg. twice a day for 10 days for males. For treatment of severe intestinal amebiasis, the drug is given in a dosage of 750 mg. three times a day for 5 days.

Adverse reactions. Most commonly known noted side effects are a disagreeable metallic taste, gastric upset, and darkening of the urine. Headache, dizziness, glossitis, and stomatitis may occur. Symptoms of central nervous system irritation have not as yet been reported in man, but if they occur the drug should be stopped immediately. Alcohol should be avoided during treatment since metronidazole may inhibit several enzyme systems concerned with the metabolism of alcohol.

■ Antiviral chemotherapy

Until recently prevention or treatment of viral infections by synthetic chemicals was entirely nonexistent. Viruses consist essentially of nucleic acids having a protein coat. Their replication takes place inside the mammalian cell with the utilization of the host cell's enzyme systems. These facts make a chemotherapeutic attack on viral infections extremely difficult.

Despite these difficulties, at least one agent has become clinically useful by blocking the entry of certain viruses into the mammalian cell. This drug is amantadine hydrochloride (Symmetrel). Another agent, idoxuridine (Stoxil), is used topically in the eye in the treatment of keratitis caused by herpes or vaccinia viruses. It inhibits the synthesis of viral DNA but is too toxic for systemic use.

Amantadine hydrochloride, N.F. (Symmetrel)

Amantadine hydrochloride is the first synthetic chemical effective in the prophylaxis of some forms of influenza, a viral disease. It apparently acts by preventing penetration of the host cell by the virus. It is therefore a prophylactic agent.

Uses. Amantadine hydrochloride has been found effective in the prevention of Asian (A_2) influenza respiratory illness. It is recommended especially for the elderly and other high-risk patients in whom influenza could be dangerous.

Preparation, dosage, and administration. Amantadine hydrochloride is available as capsules containing 100 mg. of the drug. It is also available as a syrup containing 50 mg. of amantadine hydrochloride in each 5 ml.

The adult daily dosage is 200 mg. This may be given as a single dose or in two divided doses. Children under 9 years of age should receive a smaller dose. For details on doses the package insert should be consulted.

Side effects and toxic effects. Nervousness, insomnia, dizziness, ataxia, and psychic reactions have occurred following the use of amantadine hydrochloride. Blurred vision, dry mouth, gastrointestinal upset, tremors, and skin rashes have also occurred. The drug is quite new and much further experience is necessary in order to establish its ultimate safety. Nevertheless it is generally considered a breakthrough in the prevention of viral infections.

Idoxuridine, U.S.P. (Stoxil, Herplex, Dendrid)

Idoxuridine inhibits the replication of certain viruses, probably by blocking RNA synthesis in vaccinia-infected cells. It is useful by topical application in the treatment of keratitis caused by herpes and vaccinia viruses. It is available as a 0.1% solution. One or two drops should be instilled into the conjunctival sac every hour during the day and every 2 hours at night. Idoxuridine is too toxic for the treatment of viral infections by systemic administration.

■ Anthelmintics

Anthelmintics are drugs used to rid the body of worms (helminths). The use of anthelmintics (*anti,* against; Gr. *helmins,* worms) is among the most primitive types of chemotherapy. It has been estimated that over 800 million people, or one third the world's population, are infested with these parasites.

Helminths may be present in the gastrointestinal tract, but several types also penetrate the tissues and some undergo developmental changes, during which they wander extensively in the host. Diagnosis of helminthiasis is often made by finding the parasite, ova, or larva in the feces, fluids, or tissues of the host.

Undesirable effects that may result from helminthiasis. Parasitic infestations do not necessarily cause clinical manifestations, although they may be injurious for a number of reasons:

1 Worms may cause mechanical injury to the tissues and organs. Roundworms in large numbers may cause obstruction in the intestine; filariae may block lymphatic channels and cause massive edema; and hookworms often cause extensive damage to the wall of the intestine and considerable loss of blood.
2 Toxic substances made by the parasite may be absorbed by the host.
3 The tissues of the host may be traumatized by the presence of the parasite and made more susceptible to bacterial infections.
4 Heavy infestation with worms will rob the host of food. This is particularly significant in children.

Classification of helminths. Worms that are parasitic to man may be classified as cestodes, nematodes, and trematodes. The *cestodes* are the tapeworms, of which there are four varieties: (1) *Taenia saginata* (beef tapeworm), (2) *Taenia solium* (pork tapeworm), (3) *Diphyllobothrium latum* (fishworm), and (4) *Hymenolepis nana* (dwarf tapeworm). As indicated by the name of the worm, the parasite enters the intestine by way of improperly cooked beef, pork, or fish or from contaminated food, as in the case of the dwarf tapeworm.

The cestodes are segmented flatworms with a head and a number of segments or proglottids, which in some cases may extend for 20 or 30 feet in the bowel. The tapeworms, with the exception of the dwarf tapeworm, spend part of their life cycle in a host other than man—pigs, fish, or cattle. The dwarf tapeworm does not require an intermediate host.

The nematodes are round, unsegmented worms that vary in length from a fraction of an inch to a foot or more. They include *Ascaris lumbricoides* (roundworm), *Necator americanus* and *Ancylostoma duodenale* (two species of hookworms), *Trichuris trichiura* (whipworm), *Trinchinella spiralis* (which produces trichinosis and for which there is no effective anthelmintic), *Oxyuris (Enterobius) vermicularis* (pinworm), *Wuchereria bancrofti* (causing filariasis), and *Strongyloides stercoralis* (infestation with which is known as strongyloidiasis).

The trematodes are flukes, among which are several blood flukes—*Schistosoma mansoni, japonicum,* and *hematobium.* There are other flukes parasitic to man. Schistosomiasis is a disease caused by blood flukes. They penetrate the skin of persons who bathe in contaminated waters or in some other way come in contact with the infected water in which snails serve as the intermediate host. The adult blood flukes live in the veins of the mesentery and pelvis of man and accumulate in the portal tube. The liver and spleen are the organs mainly involved.

Properties of a good anthelmintic. Anthelmintics should be relatively safe and at the same time sufficiently potent to achieve their purpose. Many anthelmintics are toxic to man as well as to the parasite. A good anthelmintic has a minimal toxic effect on the host and a maximal toxic effect on the parasite. Other desirable properties include easy administration and low cost.

Effective treatment of the patient demands knowledge of the type of worm or worms, the best anthelmintic to use, and a method for determining success of treatment. Although the technique of treatment necessarily varies with the drug used, maximum effects are often related to how well the intestinal tract is emptied before the drug is administered and how well it is evacuated afterward. Some of the newer anthelmintics do not require that the patient be purged and starved to promote effectiveness of the drug.

Drugs used against cestodes and nematodes
Aspidium (male fern)

The male fern is one of the oldest of the anthelmintic agents. The official drug is obtained from *Dryopteris filix-mas*, a fern commonly found in England and Europe. The anthelmintic action is caused by the presence of several closely related substances (filicic acid, filmaron, and so on). This drug is no longer admitted to U.S.P. Because of its toxicity and limited usefulness, it has been supplanted by quinacrine hydrochloride.

Quinacrine hydrochloride, U.S.P. (Atabrine); mepacrine, B.P.

Quinacrine hydrochloride is usually effective against the beef tapeworm after a single dose. It is also effective against pork and fish tapeworm. A saline purgative is given the evening before the administration of the drug. The next morning no food is allowed, but quinacrine hydrochloride may be given orally in divided doses along with sodium bicarbonate, or it may be given in solution through a duodenal tube. The usual adult dose is 0.5 to 1 Gm. together with 1 Gm. of sodium bicarbonate. The latter agent helps to prevent gastric irritation and vomiting. A saline cathartic is again given 2 hours after administration of the drug.

Quinacrine hydrochloride is also an antimalarial agent and, as such, is discussed earlier in this chapter.

Piperazine salts

Piperazine compounds were introduced into medicine as agents for the treatment of gout. Although they proved to be ineffective for this condition, they have come to be considered drugs of choice for the treatment of roundworms and pinworms. They seem to induce a state of narcosis and paralysis in the worms, and they are then expelled by intestinal peristalsis in the patient. The drug appears to have a selective action on the myoneural junction of the worms. Since the worms may revive after expulsion from the body, general hygienic measures should be used.

It is more effective on the mature than on the immature forms of the worm; therefore, an interrupted treatment schedule is advisable. These drugs have the advantage of being low in toxicity. Furthermore, starvation and purgation need not accompany their administration.

Preparation, dosage, and administration

Piperazine citrate, **U.S.P. (Antepar).** This agent is available in 250- and 500-mg. tablets and as a syrup, 100 mg. per milliliter, for oral administration. The daily dose is calculated on a basis of 50 mg. per kilogram of body weight, but a daily dose of 2 Gm. should not be exceeded. For pinworms, a single course of treatment for 7 days is recommended. For roundworms (ascaris), the usual dose is 75 mg. per kilogram of body weight with a maximum dose of 5 Gm. daily. A single course of treatment of 5 to 7 days is usually satisfactory.

Piperazine tartrate **(Piperat).** This form is available in 250- and 500-mg. tablets and as an oral solution, 100 mg. per milliliter. Administration and dosage are the same as for piperazine citrate.

Piperazine calcium edetate **(Perin).** This form is available in 500-mg. wafers and as a syrup, 100 mg. per milliliter, for oral administration. For pinworms, the proposed dosage is 75 mg. per kilogram of body weight per day (children and adults), administered at one time or in two divided doses for a period of 15 days; for roundworms, 100 mg. per kilogram of body weight is administered.

Piperazine adipate and *piperazine phosphate.* These preparations are official in B.P.

Side effects and toxic effects. As mentioned previously, these drugs are among the least toxic of the anthelmintics. Excessively large doses may produce urticaria, muscular weakness, blurred vision, and vomiting. The symptoms disappear when the drug is discontinued.

Diethylcarbamazine citrate, U.S.P., B.P. (Hetrazan)

Diethylcarbamazine is a piperazine derivative that has been used for a number of years in the treatment of filariasis. More recently it has been found effective for the treatment of roundworms (ascariasis). Like the piperazine preparations, its use need not be accompanied by purgation and starvation. It appears to offer no advantage over salts of piperazine in the treatment of ascariasis.

Preparation, dosage, and administration. Diethylcarbamazine citrate is available in 50-mg. tablets and as a syrup, 30 mg. per milliliter, for oral administration. The usual dosage for ascariasis consists of 13 mg. per kilogram of body weight daily for 4 days. For the treatment of filariasis, the dose is 2 mg. per kilogram of body weight three times daily after meals for 7 to 21 days.

Side effects and toxic effects. Fever, leukocytosis, and swelling and tenderness of the lymphatic glands are frequently seen in patients treated for filariasis. Other symptoms include allergic manifestations, headache, nausea, and vomiting.

Hexylresorcinol, N.F., B.P.

Hexylresorcinol is an effective anthelmintic against roundworm, hookworm, pinworm, and the dwarf tapeworm. It exerts a paralyzing effect on the muscle of the parasite. It is less potent than some of the other anthelmintics, but it has the advantages of low toxicity and mildness that permit it to be used for children and debilitated individuals, for whom some of the other anthelmintics are contraindicated. It is useful when mixed infestations are present.

Preparation, dosage, and administration. Hexylresorcinol is available in pills containing 100 and 200 mg. of the drug. They are coated with a tough gelatin covering. A single oral dose of 1 Gm. for adults and 0.1 to 0.6 Gm. for preschool children may prove effective in a large number of infections. A saline purgative the evening before and also 2 to 4 hours after administration of the drug is recommended. Food is withheld during the treatment. The procedure may need to be repeated after 3 to 4 days.

When the capsules of hexylresorcinol are administered, it is important that they be swallowed intact. If broken in the mouth, extensive irritation may result.

Side effects and toxic effects. The main untoward effect of hexylresorcinol is that of local irritation. Therapeutic doses do not seem to cause systemic toxicity.

Tetrachloroethylene, U.S.P., B.P.

Tetrachloroethylene is a drug that has been used against hookworm. It is especially effective against *Necator americanus.* It is not particularly effective against other intestinal parasites. It has, to a great extent, replaced carbon tetrachloride as an anthelmintic because of the toxic effect of the latter on the liver. It is relatively insoluble in water, and in the absence of alcohol and fat in the intestine, very little drug is absorbed after oral administration. This probably explains its low level of toxicity.

Tetrachloroethylene should not be used for ascariasis because it irritates the worms, and in their attempt to escape the drug they may migrate into the bile ducts and liver or cause intestinal obstruction and perforation. In mixed infestations of both hookworm and ascaris (which often occurs), hexylresorcinol or piperazine should be administered first. Tetrachloroethylene has to some extent been supplanted by a new drug, bephenium hydroxynaphthoate.

Preparation, dosage, and administration. Gelatin capsules containing 0.2, 1, and 5 ml. of tetrachloroethylene are available for oral administration. The adult dose is 3 ml., and the dose for children is 0.2 ml. for each year up to the age of 15 years. The patient should remain at rest 2 to 4 hours after administration of the drug.

The drug should be stored in a cool place to avoid formation of the poisonous substance phosgene. The effectiveness of the drug is increased by a saline purge the evening before as well as after the administration of the drug. Food is withheld the morning of treatment, and fats, oils, and alcohol should be avoided throughout the treatment. Patients should be kept at bed rest and under observation for 4 hours after administration of the drug. One dose of the drug may prove sufficient unless ova are found in the stools after a period of 1 week.

Use of the drug is contraindicated in debilitated patients, small and seriously ill children, patients with liver disease, pregnant women, and alcoholism patients.

Side effects and toxic effects. Dizziness, drowsiness, giddiness, nausea, and vomiting occur occasionally.

Pyrvinium pamoate, U.S.P. (Povan)

Pyrvinium is a cyanine dye effective in the treatment of pinworm infections; both the worm and its ova are eliminated. About 90% or more of patients treated with pyrvinium are cured when a single adequate dose is given. Like dithiazaine, pyrvinium interferes with the respiratory enzyme of the parasite and inhibits its oxygen uptake and carbohydrate metabolism.

Preparation, dosage, and administration. Pyrvinium is available in 50-mg. tablets and as an oral suspension containing 50 mg. in 5 ml. The usual dose for children and adults is 5 mg. per kilogram of body weight. Periodic treatment at intervals of 2 or 3 weeks is recommended because of repeated recurrence of the parasite.

This dye colors the stools bright red. Clothing may become stained a bright red; vomitus may also stain clothing or furniture.

Side effects. Pyrvinium is essentially nontoxic. Nausea, vomiting, and cramping have occurred. A case of photosensitization has been reported.

Bephenium hydroxynaphthoate (Alcopar)

Bephenium hydroxynaphthoate is an effective drug for the treatment of human hookworm and ascaris infections. The recommended dose is 5 Gm. for adults given as a suspension on an empty stomach. Nausea, vomiting, and abdominal pain have been reported as side effects. However, it is a safe, well-tolerated drug with low toxicity.

The drug is available in 5-Gm. packets. The dose should be mixed with milk, orange juice, or carbonated beverages just prior to administration. Food should be withheld for 2 hours after ingestion of the drug. Children are usually given half the adult dose.

Thiabendazole, U.S.P. (Mintezole)

Thiabendazole is a new drug with a wide spectrum of anthelmintic activity. It is effective in the treatment of threadworms, cutaneous larva migrans, and pinworms. It is also used to treat other forms of worm infestations.

Preparation dosage, and administration. The drug is available as a suspension of 500 mg. per 5 ml. Average dose is 25 mg. per kilogram of body weight twice a day for 2 days; for pinworms the dosage is 25 mg. per kilogram of body weight twice a day for 1 day with dosage repeated in 1 week.

Side effects. Side effects are common but usually mild and transient. They occur 3 to 4 hours after ingestion of the drug and last 2 to 8 hours. Side effects are decreased if the drug is given after meals. Most common side effects are dizziness, anorexia, nausea and vomiting, abdominal cramping, diarrhea, headache, drowsiness, lethargy, and pruritus.

Drugs used in the treatment of schistosomiasis

Schistosomiasis is a disease caused by a parasite that burrows through the skin. The drugs used in treatment include antimony potassium tartrate, stibophen, and lucanthone hydrochloride. These preparations are not equally effective for all types of blood flukes that may cause this disease.

Antimony potassium tartrate, U.S.P., B.P. (Tartar Emetic)

Antimony potassium tartrate is administered intravenously as a 0.5% solution. The initial dose recommended is 30 mg. Dosage thereafter is gradually increased. The total dosage for a course of treatment is 1.5 to 2 Gm. Therapy with this drug has been known to result in changes in the heart and liver and sometimes in other organs. The drug may aggravate kidney disease. Patients should be hospitalized during treatment and remain recumbent for several hours after the drug is given. Numerous side effects are common.

Stibophen, U.S.P., B.P. (Fuadin)

Stibophen is a compound of antimony that is considered the drug of choice for treating schistosomiasis. It is administered intramuscularly. It is available in a solution (300 mg. in 5 ml.).

Small doses are given initially and gradually increased. Therapy is interspersed with rest periods. The initial dose is 100 mg., and this is increased to as much as 300 mg., up to a total dose of 6.3 Gm. This drug may cause nausea and vomiting, and occasionally muscle and joint pains may occur.

Lucanthone hydrochloride, U.S.P., B.P.

Lucanthone hydrochloride is a relatively new synthetic preparation. Its precise mode of action is unknown, but it interferes with the reproductive function of the parasite (egg production) and eventually causes its death. It can be administered orally in enteric-coated tablets. Dosage is calculated on the basis of 10 to 20 mg. per kilogram of body weight. It is given in divided doses daily for approximately 10 days. Nausea, vomiting, and gastric distress are sometimes experienced. The skin may turn yellow or orange with treatment, but this usually disappears in about 4 weeks. Insomnia, headache, convulsions, psychosis, and hepatic and renal damage have been reported. Toxic dosage is said to border closely on therapeutic dosage.

Therapeutic résumé

The drugs of choice for the treatment of helminthiasis include the following:

1 Against tapeworms—quinacrine, aspidium, and hexylresorcinol
2 Against roundworms—piperazine salts and diethylcarbamazine
3 Against whipworms—dithiazanine (although its potential danger should limit its use) and hexylresorcinol
4 Against pinworms—piperazine salts and hexylresorcinol. Pinworms do not cling to the intestinal wall and may also be expelled by the use of a cathartic or enema. The anal region must be kept clean, and scratching of the anal region must be avoided if reinfection is to be prevented. Underclothing, washcloths, and so on must be boiled to kill the eggs of the parasite. Reinfection is a major problem.
5 Against hookworms—tetrachloroethylene, hexylresorcinol, and bephenium
6 For strongyloidiasis—dithiazanine

7 For schistosomiasis—antimony compounds (antimony potassium tartrate and stibophen)
8 For filariasis—diethylcarbamazine, especially for the removal of the microfilariae, although the adult form of the worm is not much affected

■ Amebiasis and amebicides

Although a number of nonpathogenic amebas may be found in the human bowel, amebiasis or amebic dysentery is a disease caused by the *Entamoeba histolytica*. The disease is worldwide and not limited to tropical regions. The parasite occurs in two forms: the active motile form, known as a trophozoite, and the cystic form, which is inactive, resistant to drugs, and present in the intestinal excretions. In the lumen of the intestine, the ameba forms a cyst when living conditions, for some reason, become unfavorable. Outside the body the cyst becomes the source of infection to others when transmitted by flies or contaminated food and water. Only the cystic forms of the parasite can cause amebiasis because the motile forms are killed by gastric acid.

The initial infection of the bowel is known as intestinal amebiasis and is associated with diarrhea and the presence of motile parasite forms in the stools.

Secondary amebiasis means that the parasites have migrated to other parts of the body, such as the liver (where an amebic abscess may develop), spleen, and lungs. Only motile forms of the parasite invade the tissues. The amebas live at the expense of the host and always produce areas of tissue destruction in the bowel, although in certain individuals few symptoms of the disease may be noted. Apparently in these persons tissue repair keeps up with the tissue destruction.

Complete cure of the disease is difficult to attain because it is necessary to kill all of the parasites if relapse is to be avoided.

Drugs used in the treatment of amebiasis include those drugs used for extraintestinal amebic infection (emetine and chloroquine) and those used for intestinal amebiasis, which includes organic arsenicals, halogenated oxyquinolines, and antibiotics. Many physicians are

613

of the opinion that the disease is best treated by using a combination of several drugs.

Drugs used for extraintestinal amebiasis
Ipecac and emetine hydrochloride, U.S.P., B.P.

Ipecac is the dried root of the *Caphaëlis ipecacuanha*, a perennial shrub that grows in Brazil and other South American countries. It was long used by native people in the treatment of diarrhea. It contains two alkaloids, emetine and cephaeline, both of which are amebicidal, although emetine is the more potent agent. Emetine apparently has a direct lethal action on the *Entamoeba histolytica* when it is in a motile form, but it has little effect on amebic cysts. It is readily absorbed from parenteral sites of administration but is excreted rather slowly. It may therefore produce cumulative effects in the tissues.

Uses. The chief use of emetine is to control the symptoms of acute amebic dysentery or the symptoms that may suddenly develop during chronic phases of the disease. It has come to be regarded as second only to chloroquine for the treatment of amebic hepatitis and amebic abscess in the liver. It should not be used for the relief of mild symptoms or for the treatment of carriers. Preparations of ipecac are seldom used because of their tendency to cause gastrointestinal irritation.

Preparation, dosage, and administration. Emetine hydrochloride is available in 1-ml. ampules containing 30 or 60 mg. of the drug in solution. The usual daily adult dose is 1 mg. per kilogram of body weight. The dosage range for adults may be from 30 to 60 mg. For children, the dose is 10 to 20 mg., depending on their weight and age. The drug is given both by deep subcutaneous and deep intramuscular injection over a period of 5 to 10 days. Enteric-coated tablets have been given orally, but they are prone to cause irritation of the digestive tract.

Side effects and toxic effects. Emetine is a general protoplasmic poison and causes a variety of toxic reactions. Degenerative changes in the liver, heart, kidney, and muscles may occur. Cardiac changes may vary from disturbance in rhythm to acute myocarditis and heart failure. Other symptoms of poisoning include dizziness, nausea and vomiting, severe diarrhea, and albuminuria. Pain is often experienced at the site of injection. Emetine is contraindicated for patients with organic disease of the heart and kidneys. It is not used for pregnant, aged, or debilitated persons.

From 6 weeks to 2 months should intervene between courses of treatment.

Chloroquine phosphate, U.S.P., B.P. (Aralen)

Chloroquine is one of the antimalarial drugs that also exhibits amebicidal activity. Because it reaches many parts of the body and localizes in organs such as the liver, it is highly effective for the treatment of extraintestinal amebiasis, particularly amebic hepatitis and amebic abscess. It is not recommended for intestinal forms of amebiasis, partly because it is well absorbed from the small bowel and partly because the tissue in the wall of the bowel fails to concentrate the drug as well as does the liver. Since hepatic involvement may occur early in amebiasis with few if any clinical signs, some physicians recommend early use of chloroquine or emetine along with a drug that is effective against the intestinal forms of the disease, such as one of the arsenicals or one of the oxyquinoline drugs.

Preparation, dosage, and administration. Chloroquine phosphate is available in 125- and 250-mg. tablets. For extraintestinal amebiasis the usual oral dose for adults is 500 mg. two times daily for 2 days, followed by 250 mg. two times a day for 2 weeks or more. The course of treatment may be repeated or alternated with emetine therapy. To effect a cure it is necessary to administer this drug along with another drug known to be effective for intestinal amebiasis.

Side effects and toxic effects. Severe side effects or toxic effects are not associated with therapeutic doses of chloroquine phosphate. However, patients may complain of headache, itching, visual disturbances, and gastrointestinal upsets. These symptoms subside when the administration of the drug is stopped. However, retinal damage can be very serious.

Drugs used for intestinal amebiasis

Organic arsenicals

Pentavalent arsenic compounds such as acetarsone and carbarsone, as well as trivalent compounds such as thioarsenites, are amebicidal. Some arsenicals first used for syphilis have been found effective for amebic dysentery.

Carbarsone, N.F.

Carbarsone is one of the organic arsenicals and contains 28.5% arsenic. It is absorbed after oral or rectal administration and excreted rather slowly by the kidney.

It is especially effective for chronic intestinal amebiasis uncomplicated by hepatic involvement. It is not effective against amebas in abscesses of the liver or other organs. It is also used in treatment of trichomonal infections of the vagina.

Preparation, dosage, and administration. Carbarsone is available in 250-mg. tablets for oral administration and in suppositories containing 2 grains of the drug. The adult oral dose of amebiasis is 250 mg. two or three times daily for 7 to 10 days. For acute amebiasis, a retention enema (for adults) may be prepared by dissolving 2 Gm. of the drug in 200 ml. of a warm 2% sodium bicarbonate solution. The enema may be repeated every other night for five times. A cleansing enema should preferably precede the treatment. For trichomonal infections the dose is one suppository daily.

Side effects and toxic effects. Although carbarsone is considered one of the least toxic of the arsenicals, overdosage can produce damage to the liver and kidneys. Serious toxic effects rarely occur, however, although cutaneous rash, loss of weight, abdominal distress, and diarrhea have been noted. Exfoliative dermatitis, encephalitis, and damage of the optic nerve are almost unknown, but such effects must be kept in mind when an arsenical drug is being administered. Since excretion of the drug is rather slow there is a tendency to develop cumulative effects. BAL is effective in the treatment of arsenical poisoning.

Carbarsone is contraindicated for patients who have renal or hepatic pathology.

Glycobiarsol, N.F. (Milibis)

Glycobiarsol is a pentavalent arsenical combined with bismuth (15% arsenic and 42% bismuth). It is recommended for the treatment of intestinal amebiasis only. It exhibits low toxicity because it is not very soluble and is poorly absorbed. It needs to be supplemented with other therapy when amebic hepatitis or deep-seated infestation is present. This drug has also been used for monilial and trichomonal infections of the vagina.

Preparation, dosage, and administration. Glycobiarsol is available in 250- and 500-mg. tablets and in vaginal suppositories, 250 mg. The usual adult dose for amebiasis is 500 mg. three times daily for 1 week. Larger doses are sometimes necessary when diarrhea is severe. Additional course of treatment is indicated if pathogenic amebas continue to be found in the stool. This drug turns the stools black.

Side effects and toxic effects. This drug is not very toxic, but the presence of arsenic in the compound necessitates caution in its use.

Arsthinol (Balarsen)

Arsthinol is an organic thioarsenical compound that has been found effective for intestinal amebiasis and also for yaws.

Preparation, dosage, and administration. This compound is available in 100-mg. tablets for oral administration. The daily oral dose is 10 mg. per kilogram of body weight, not to exceed 500 mg. daily. It is given over a period of 5 days.

Side effects and toxic effects. The side effects are said to be minor, but the possibility of arsenic poisoning should not be overlooked. Rest periods between courses of treatment are recommended.

Iodohydroxyquinoline compounds

Included in this group of compounds are diiodohydroxyquin and iodochlorhydroxyquin. The following formulas indicate why these compounds are also called halogenated hydroxyquinolines.

Diiodohydroxyquin (Diodoquin)

**Iodochlorhydroxyquin
(Vioform)**

Diiodohydroxyquin, U.S.P. (Diodoquin); di-iodohydroxyquinoline, B.P.

Diiodohydroxyquin is an oxyquinoline derivative that contains about 64% iodine. It is directly amebicidal, although the mechanism of its action is not known. It is useful for intestinal amebiasis but not for amebic abscess or amebic hepatitis. Difference of opinion exists about its value as an amebicide. Some authorities consider it a valuable amebicide, especially when given with emetine.

It is also used in the treatment of trichomonas infections of the vagina.

Preparation, dosage, and administration. Diiodohydroxyquin is available as a bulky powder and in tablets, containing 210 and 650 mg. (300 mg., B.P.). It is administered orally as an amebicide and by insufflation for vaginitis. The adult dose is 650 mg. to 1 Gm. three times a day and is given preferably between meals.

Side effects and toxic effects. Diiodohydroxyquin exhibits a low level of toxicity, which is probably explained by the fact that it is not very soluble. Symptoms of iodism may develop (itching, dermatitis, abdominal discomfort, diarrhea, and headache). It is contraindicated for patients who have liver damage and for those who are hypersensitive to iodine.

Iodochlorhydroxyquin, N.F. (Vioform)

Iodochlorhydroxyquin has an iodine content of approximately 40%. It is poorly soluble, although some intestinal absorption does occur. Like the other drugs of this group of compounds, it is most effective for intestinal amebiasis and is ineffective for amebic abscesses or amebic hepatitis. It is expensive, and its administration does not require bed rest for the patient. It stains clothing and linens a yellow color. Some authorities consider this least effective of the iodohydroxyquinolines, but differences of opinion exist about their relative values. It is also employed in treatment of trichomonas infections of the vagina and for various types of dermatitis.

Preparation, dosage, and administration. Iodochlorhydroxyquin is available as a powder, as 250-mg. tablets, and as an ointment. The powder is suitably buffered for use as a vaginal insufflate. The usual adult dose is 250 mg. three times a day for 10 days. The drug may be used alternately with carbarsone—courses of treatment with one drug may follow the use of the other drug.

Side effects and toxic effects. Toxic reactions are seldom encountered. Mild symptoms of iodism may occur, and some patients may experience a severe gastritis.

Antibiotics for amebiasis

A number of antibiotics have been used in the treatment of amebiasis but only a few such as paromomycin have been found to be directly amebicidal. Other antibiotics, such as erythromycin and oxytetracycline, are effective indirectly by decreasing the number of intestinal bacteria on which the *Entamoeba histolytica* depends for some essential factor or factors.

Intestinal amebiasis appears to be controlled only as long as the associated bacteria are held in check. The tetracyclines and erythromycin are discussed elsewhere. One of the disadvantages of drugs such as oxytetracycline is that, while it may be effective for mild amebiasis, it may produce gastrointestinal symptoms (diarrhea) more troublesome than the mild amebiasis.

Since antibiotics are not effective for extraintestinal amebiasis, the concomitant administration of a drug such as chloroquine is advocated.

Paromomycin, N.F. (Humatin)

Paromomycin is an antibiotic obtained from *Streptomyces rimosus*. It is said to have a direct amebicadal action and also an antibacterial action on both normal and pathogenic microorganisms found in the bowel. Its range of antibacterial action is said to resemble that of neomycin. Little of the drug is absorbed into the systemic circulation.

Uses. Paromomycin appears to be effective for both acute and chronic forms of amebiasis, but it does not seem to be effective for extraintestinal forms of the disease.

Preparation, dosage, and administration. Paromomycin sulfate is available in capsules (250 mg. of the base) and as a syrup (125 mg. in 5 ml.) for oral administration. The dosage recommended is 35 to 60 mg. per kilogram of body weight daily. It is administered in divided doses at mealtime for 1 to 2 weeks.

Side effects. Paromomycin is nephrotoxic when administered parenterally but not when given orally. The chief side effect is diarrhea. Other side effects include nausea, vomiting, abdominal cramps, headache, pyrosis, and skin rash. Paromomycin is contraindicated for patients with intestinal obstruction.

Questions

for study and review

1 Suppressive treatment of malaria refers to:
   a. radical cure of the malarial infection
   b. eradication of malarial mosquitos
   c. prophylactic therapy
   d. prevention of clinical symptoms
2 Which of the following antimalarial drugs is capable of completely eradicating the infection when it is caused by *Plasmodium vivax?*
   a. quinine
   b. primaquine
   c. quinacrine
   d. chloroquine
3 Antituberculosis drugs:
   a. are primarily bactericidal
   b. effectively prevent development of resistant tubercle bacilli
   c. can only arrest, not cure, the disease
   d. are relatively nontoxic
4 Choose the *incorrect* statement about chemotherapy of tuberculosis.
   a. Para-aminosalicylic acid (PAS) is less potent than streptomycin or isoniazid.
   b. Isoniazid used alone or in combination with PAS or streptomycin is superior to any form of antituberculosis therapy not containing isoniazid.
   c. PAS increases the effectiveness of streptomycin and

delays emergence of resistant strains of tubercle bacilli.
   d. A combination of streptomycin and hydrocortisone is an extremely effective form of antituberculosis therapy.
5 Explain how the various anthelmintics exert their therapeutic effect.
6 What precautions must be taken when patients are treated with the following drugs?
   a. hexylresorcinol
   b. quinacrine
   c. tetrachloroethylene
   d. emetine
7 What instructions should patients receive to prevent reinfection or the spread of infection to others?

References

Antituberculosis drugs

Cohen, A. C.: The drug treatment of tuberculosis, Springfield, Ill., 1966, Charles C Thomas, Publisher.

Crofton, J.: The chemotherapy of tuberculosis with special reference to patients whose bacilli are resistant to the standard drugs, Brit. Med. Bull. **16:**55, 1960.

DesPrez, R. M., and Muschenheim, C.: The chemoprophylaxis of tuberculosis, J. Chronic Dis. **16:**599, 1962.

Frenay, Sister M. A. C.: Drugs in tuberculosis control, Amer. J. Nurs. **61:**82-85, 1961.

Grunberg, E., editor: Current status of tuberculosis, Ann. N. Y. Acad. Sci. **106:**1, 1963.

Hinshaw, H. C., and Garland, L. H.: Diseases of the chest, Philadelphia, 1963, W. B. Saunders Co.

Pfuetze, K. H., and Pyle, M. M.: Recent advances in treatment of organ tuberculosis, J.A.M.A. **187:**805, 1964.

Pfuetze, K. H., and Radner, D. B., editors: Clinical tuberculosis—essentials of diagnosis and treatment, Springfield, Ill., 1966, Charles C Thomas, Publisher.

Treatment of drug-resistant tuberculosis: a statement by the Committee on Therapy, Amer. Rev. Resp. Dis. **94:**125, 1966.

Weiss, M.: Chemotherapy and tuberculosis, Amer. J. Nurs. **59:**1711, 1959.

Leprosy

Canizares, P.: Diagnosis and treatment of leprosy in the United States, Med. Clin. N. Amer. **49:**801, 1965.

Fasal, P., Fasal, E., and Levy, L.: Leprosy prophylaxis, J.A.M.A. **199:**905, 1967.

Trantman, L. R.: The management of leprosy and its complications, New Eng. J. Med. **723:**756, 1965.

Antimalarial drugs

Alvarado, C. A., and Bruce-Chwatt, L. J.: Malaria, Sci. Amer. **206:**86, 1962.

Bartelloni, P. J.: Combined therapy for chloroquine-resistant plasmodium falciparum infection, J.A.M.A. **199:**173, 1967.

Bruce-Chwatt, L. J.: Changing tides of chemotherapy of malaria, Brit. Med. J. **1:**581, 1964.

Davey, D. G.: Chemotherapy of malaria. In Schmitzer, R. J., and Hawking, F., editors: Experimental chemotherapy, vol. 1, New York, 1963, Academic Press, Inc.

Elsager, E. F., and Thompson, P. E.: Parasite chemotherapy, Ann. Rev. Pharmacol. **2:**193, 1962.

Huff, C. G.: Man against malaria, Amer. J. Trop. Med. **14:**339, 1965.

Powell, R. D.: The chemotherapy of malaria, Clin. Pharmacol. Ther. **7:**48, 1966.

Tamber, E.: Ocular complications of chloroquine therapy, Calif. Med. **103:**30, 1965.

Thompson, P. E.: Parasite chemotherapy, Ann. Rev. Pharmacol. **7:**77, 1967.

Anthelmintics and amebicides

Brown, H. W.: The action and uses of anthelmintics, Clin. Pharmacol. Therap. **1:**87, 1960.

Bueding, E., and Swartzwelder, C.: Anthelmintics, Pharmacol. Rev. **9:**329, 1957.

Bumbalo, T. S.: Single dose regimen in treatment of pinworm infection, New York J. Med. **65:**248, 1965.

Busch, H., and Lave, M.: Chemotherapy, Chicago, 1967, Year Book Medical Publishers, Inc.

Davis, J. H.: Newer drugs in therapy of pinworm infestation, Med. Clin. N. Amer. **51:**1208, 1967.

Elsager, E. F., and Thompson, P. E.: Parasite chemotherapy, Ann. Rev. Pharmocol. **2:**193, 1962.

Goodman, L., and Gilman, A., editors: The pharmacological basis of therapeutics, ed. 4, New York, 1970, The Macmillan Company.

Kean, B. H., and Hoskins, D. W.: Drugs for intestinal parasitism. In Modell, W., editor: Drugs of choice 1972-1973, St. Louis, 1972, The C. V. Mosby Co.

Mansour, T. E.: The pharmacology and biochemistry of parasitic helminths, New York, 1964, Academic Press, Inc.

Most, H.: Treatment of the more common worm infections, J.A.M.A. **185:**874, 1963.

Royer, A., and Berdnikoff, K.: Pinworm infestation in children: the problem and its treatment, Canad. Med. Ass. J. **86:**60, 1962.

Saz, H. J., and Bueding, E.: Relationships between anthelmintic effects and biochemical and physiological mechanisms, Pharmacol. Rev. **18:**871, 1966.

Woolfe, G.: Chemotherapy of amebiasis. In Schnetzer, R. J., and Hawking, F., editors: Experimental chemotherapy, vol. 1, New York, 1963, Academic Press, Inc.

Antiviral drugs

Council on Drugs: The amantidine controversy, J.A.M.A. **201:**372, 1967.

Eggers, H. J., and Tanim, I.: Antiviral chemotherapy, Ann. Rev. Pharmacol. **6:**231, 1966.

Isaacs, A., and Lindenmann, J.: Virus interference: I. Interferon, Proc. Roy. Soc. London (Biol.) **147:**258, 1957.

■ Calculation of drug dosages

The responsibility of drug administration to patients on pediatric services requires of nurses a specific knowledge and technique. Physicians prescribe the dosage of medication, but it is the nurse's responsiblility to know the safe dosage range of any medication she administers to children. A standard dosage of medication is nonexistent in pediatrics; medications are ordered according to the weight or body surface area of the child. Pharmaceutical companies continue to supply most medications in a standard adult dosage strength, and the nurse must calculate the correct dosage before administering the medication.

Since many pharmacology textbooks or drug reference books are geared to standard adult dosages, the nurse must have other resources for estimating safe dosages for children. The methods used to calculate a safe dosage for an individual child are based on the weight or body surface area of the child. Following are some formulas for calculating estimated safe dosages. The formula based on weight is preferred whenever possible since it is considered most accurate.

$$1 \quad \frac{\text{Average adult dose} \times \text{Weight of child in pounds}}{150} = \text{Estimated safe dose}$$

Example: How much aspirin should a 1-year-old child weighing 21 pounds receive if the average adult dose is 10 grains?

$$\frac{\overset{10}{\text{(grains)}} \times \overset{21}{\text{(weight in pounds)}}}{150} = \text{gr. } 1\frac{2}{5}$$

$$*2 \quad \frac{\text{Average adult dose} \times \text{Age of child in years}}{\text{Age} + 12} = \text{Estimated safe dose}$$

Example: How much atropine sulfate should an 8-year-old child receive if the adult dose is gr. $\frac{1}{150}$?

*Age alone does not provide a good basis for calculating estimated safe doses. A 1-month-old infant could weigh 3 pounds, 7 pounds, or 16 pounds.

$$\frac{8}{8+12} \times \text{gr. } \frac{1}{150} = \text{gr. } \frac{1}{375} = \frac{\text{Estimated}}{\text{safe dose}}$$

$$*3 \quad \frac{\overset{\text{Average}}{\text{adult dose}} \times \overset{\text{Age in}}{\text{months}}}{150} = \text{Estimated safe dose}$$

> Example: The adult dose of atropine is 0.6 mg. How much should a 2-month-old infant receive?

$$\frac{0.6 \times 2}{150} = \frac{1.2}{150} = .008 \text{ mg.}$$

A nurse preparing calculated dosages of digitalis, insulin, barbiturates, and narcotics should have the calculations as well as the prepared medication dosage checked by another nurse before she administers the drug. Pediatric dosages are often minute, and a slight mistake in calculating the amount of medication to be administered results in greater proportional error.

Body surface area as a basis

More than 100 years ago, Hufeland suggested that drug doses should be calculated on size or a proportional amount of body surface area to weight. Many physicians continue to use weight as the basis for calculating drug doses and body surface area for calculating fluid requirements. Most clinicians advocate using body surface area for determining drug dosage for adults as well as children. Physicians usually carry a simple slide rule or nomogram such as the West nomogram (Figure 31-1) to make rapid conversions from weight alone.

Although the previously stated rules have been devised for relating adult doses to infants and children, it must be emphasized that there are *no* rules or charts that are adequate to guarantee safety of dosage at any age, particularly in the neonate. None of these methods takes into account all variables, particularly individual tolerance differences. Astute, accurate nursing observations of the reactions of individual children to drugs can be of great assistance to the

---

*Age alone does not provide a good basis for calculating estimated safe doses. A 1-month-old infant could weigh 3 pounds, 7 pounds, or 16 pounds.

physician as he chooses drugs and regulates the dosage of drugs for his patients.

■ Some variables affecting drug responses in neonates, infants, and children

The pharmacologic effects of a drug are determined by the drug's action and the individual receiving the drug. Since the biochemical make-up of individuals may be markedly different, the wide variety of responses to drugs is not surprising, even among adults. The introduction of other variables such as maturation processes and maturity accentuate physiologic and biochemical differences in infants and children. Many articles have appeared on the subject of iatrogenic damage caused by drugs in the fetus, premature infant, and full-term newborn infant. The precautions and dangers of giving drugs to an immature organism can be readily summed up by saying that *most* drugs can be harmful to the immature neonate and *very few* drugs are indicated in his care.

Other variables that add to the problems of drug responses in children are absorption, distribution, biotransformation, excretion, developmental effects, difficulty in evaluating drug response, and actual administration of drug. Add to these variables the influence of disease on an easily disturbed acid-base equilibrium, and there exists a situation that frequently calls for constant observation of a child by physicians and nurses.

Immaturity and maturation process

Pharmaceutical researchers have done few studies on the reactions of drugs in very young animals. Thus there is little basis for knowledge of drug action and toxicity in children except as they may have been delineated in mature animal studies. Immaturity may alter drug actions and toxicities because of inability to excrete medications as rapidly as necessary for the prescribed dosage. Hopefully, future research will give a sounder basis for choice of drugs in immature organisms. The need for this type of research as well as the need for pediatric pharmacologists is evident.

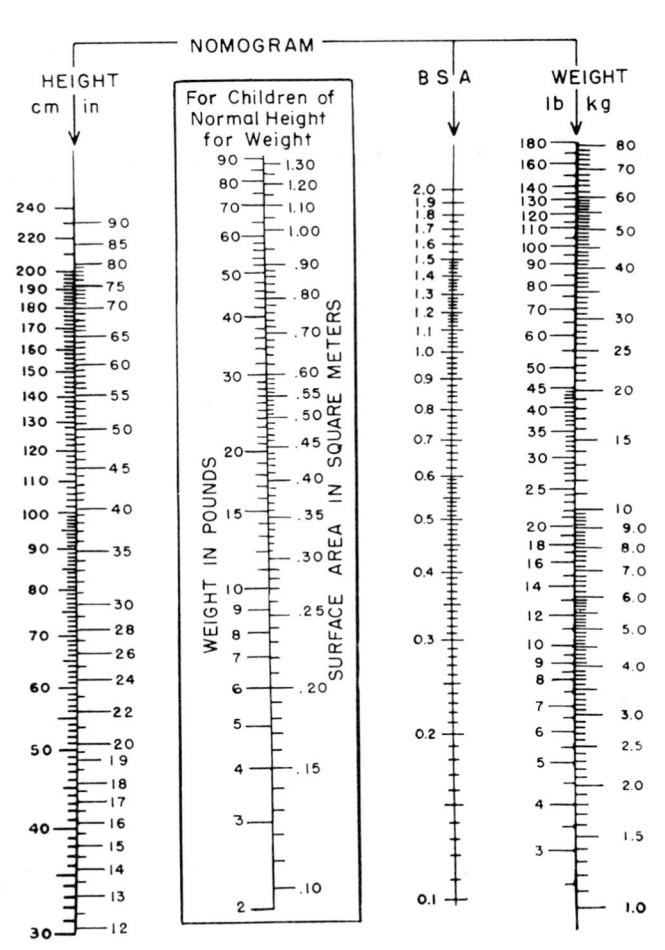

NOMOGRAM

Figure 31-1
BSA is indicated where straight line that connects height and weight levels intersects BSA column or, if patient is about average size, from weight alone (enclosed area). (Modified from data of E. Boyd by C. D. West. From Shirkey and Barba.)

During the neonatal period, there is rapid physical growth and daily changes in organ functions produced by biochemical fluctuations within the cells. If enzyme systems responsible for metabolizing drugs are not fully developed, drugs may have profound effects on the developmental processes occurring in the child. Histologic and laboratory studies have demonstrated that in early infancy normal kidney function is significantly different from that of an adult. The newborn infant has fewer glomeruli than the adult, and there is diminished or immature reserve capacity. This is of critical importance when administering drugs excreted via the renal system.

Drug administration routes

Even assuming that the nurse has some knowledge of medications and some experience and skill in giving medications to adult patients, she will find the administration of medications to infants and children challenging, as well as frustrating at times. The ability to give injections skillfully will enhance her security and help her to successfully gain a child's cooperation when giving injections. A sound knowledge of growth and development will also provide the nurse with information as to how a child at a certain age might be approached, whether trying to reason with him will help or hinder the process, and also whether she will need assistance to hold the child securely. Many of the principles of safe administration of medications apply to all age groups, but children are different from adults, and the nurse has certain added responsibilities.

Ideally, a nurse who has established a positive relationship with a child will find it easier to secure his cooperation when administering medications. If the child associates the nurse with daily hygiene, feeding, holding, play, and happy times, he may also find it easier to accept from her the discomforts associated with injections and some oral medications. Along with this, the nurse herself experiences fewer feelings of guilt and finds it less uncomfortable to inflict pain when she realizes that the child sees her as someone who brings him pleasure and comfort most of the time, as well as some discomfort necessary to his getting well.

Regardless of what kinds of external stimuli produce fear or anxiety in a child, his natural response will be to strike out at the frustration or avoid it. If the nurse accepts this and is convinced that this behavior is a natural response to some type of frustration or discomfort, she will then be able to tell him that she knows that the medication doesn't taste good or bothers him and that other children respond the same way. She will also be honest about the "hurt" associated with injections. She will tell the child: "Yes, it will hurt. I know you are afraid. It is all right to cry if it helps. You hold very still, and I'll help hold you still so that it will go very fast."

Many children are courageous, or like to be considered so, and appealing to their courage is sometimes effective. A child 4 years old or over may choose to hold his own medicine cup, to drink unassisted, and to take his pills from the container without any assistance from the nurse. Because of the sense of achievement that

follows, he may want to save the medicine cups to show his mother and father.

Honest explanations to children are essential, and the timing and type of explanation should be geared to his ability to perceive and understand. Each child has a right to some explanation of any procedure that concerns him. For the child 2 years of age or younger very simple explanations such as "I have some medicine for you to drink" or "I have an injection to give you, and it will hurt a little" will be sufficient. Long explanations to children up through 5 years of age do little more than delay his anticipated pain and increase his anxiety or his fear. Telling a child of 4 to stop (when he has responded to being told that he is to receive a medication with kicking, hitting, or other avoidance behavior) only conveys to the child that he is not understood and that he will receive little or no help with his feelings of frustration.

Oral medications. Success in administering oral medications usually requires a kind but firm approach with a positive attitude. There should be no evidence of doubt in the nurse's choice of words or in her tone of voice that the child will take his medicines. She might say: "Jimmy, it's time to take your yellow medicine." This is an indication that she expects him to cooperate and to do it willingly. An unwise approach that reveals doubt on the part of the nurse might be: "I have your yellow pill, Jimmy. Will you take it for me, please?"

Nurses should by all means be aware of the taste of medicines they are giving to anyone, adult or child, so that they can answer such questions as: "Does it taste bad? Will it burn my mouth?" If the nurse knows what a medication tastes like she might then reply: "It tastes like cherry to me. Tell me what it tastes like to you." Often the child will accept the suggestion to taste and find out. However, if the medication is bad tasting, attempting deceit or lying to the child is pointless.

Disagreeable tasting medications should be disguised if at all possible. Small amounts of honey, syrup, jam, fruit, and some fruit juices are suitable sweet substances that might provide a vehicle for less palatable drugs. Pills can be crushed and suspended in small amounts of any of these. Many liquid medications are more readily swallowed by infants and children if they are mixed with any of the suggested sweet substances or diluted with a small amount of water. If large amounts of water or other substances are used and the child refuses to take all of the mixture, it is difficult to estimate the amount of medication the child received. Fortunately, many drugs are available in the form of syrups or suspensions that are palatable and well suited for administration to infants and children. The following suggestions may be helpful:

1 Parents are frequently good sources of information about sucessful methods or vehicles for giving medications to their children.

2 Try to avoid the use of essential foods such as milk, cereal, or orange juice, since the child may become conditioned against future acceptance of that food in his diet.

3 Never underestimate the reaction of a child. He may not require that the taste of his medication be disguised.

4 A sip of fruit juice, a popsicle, or a mint-flavored substance before and after the administration of an unpalatable medicine may effectively dull its taste.

5 Sugarless vehicles such as those sweetened by saccharin should be used to disguise the taste of medications given to diabetic children or those on a ketogenic diet.

6 Honey and syrup are ideal for suspending drugs that do not dissolve easily in water.

7 Since fruit syrups are usually acid in reaction, they should not be used for medicines that react in an acid medium (for example, sodium bicarbonate, soluble barbiturates, and salicylates).

8 Elixirs have an alcohol base that, when undiluted, may cause the child to cough and choke. Small amounts of water added to elixirs of phenobarbital, chloral hydrate, and the like will make them easier to swallow.

9 Much nursing time will be saved if the child's care plan is utilized to communicate the most successful method of administering medications.

It is relatively easy to give oral medications to neonates and young infants, but caution must be exercised to prevent aspiration. It is important to give the medications slowly and in small amounts to avoid causing the infant to choke. Liquid medications may be administered via nipple, plastic medicine cup, plastic dropper, or a plastic syringe without the needle. Glass cups, droppers or syringes should be avoided at all costs because of the obvious danger of breakage in the child's mouth. A dropper or syringe is best suited for placing a liquid medication along one side of the infant's tongue. Older infants and toddlers seem to prefer to take their medications from a plastic medicine cup. If the child is held or placed in a sitting position, he will be less likely to aspirate the medication than if he is lying on his back. When administering a medication with a dropper or syringe, the nurse may purse the infant's lips with one hand to keep the medicine from running out of his mouth.

If the child is still refusing to cooperate after explanations and encouragement by the nurse, she may have to ask the child whether he is going to take the medication himself or whether he would like her to give it to him. Physical coercion is seldom necessary, but if and when it is, it should be a mild form used with dispatch and firmness, since there is danger of aspiration. It is important, however, not to combine force with anger, nor should force be resorted to because one nurse has been unable to administer the medication. Careful consideration should be given to such factors as: Why does the child resist? Does he disapprove only of this one nurse? Have his past experiences with medications given at home or in the hospital frightened him? Will forcing a medication cause a struggle that will counteract the effects of the drug if the medication is intended to sedate the child? The use of mild force, when necessary, should be explained to the child in such a way that he gets the idea that this form of treatment is necessary to his well-being. The cooperation of the child cannot be gained if he feels that force was used as a punishment for his inability to cooperate, and often his confidence in all personnel will be lost.

Intramuscular injections. The principles and techniques of the administration of injections are the same for children as they are for adults. There has been considerable concern, however, about the advisability of using the buttocks as a site for intramuscular injections for infants and children. Many authorities believe that the risk of sciatic nerve injury is too great to warrant the use of this site of administration. The sciatic nerve is the largest nerve in the body, and its normal pathway is the hollow midway between the ischial tuberosity and the greater trochanter, covered by the gluteus maximus muscle. This, however, varies a great deal from individual to individual. In addition, the small size of the gluteal mass in the infant or neonate and the potential neurotoxicity of many drugs enhance the possibility of iatrogenic trauma secondary to intramuscular injections. According to Chutorian, iatrogenic trauma of this kind is the leading cause of sciatic neuropathy in infancy. A lesion at this height of the sciatic nerve is usually tragically associated with marked permanent disability. The gluteal musculature develops more fully after the child begins to walk, so it is inadvisable to use this site for injection until he has at least reached the toddler stage.

The quadriceps muscle of the midanterolateral aspect of the thigh is the site of choice for injections in infants, children, and adults. Injection sites should be rotated frequently, and if multiple injections over a long period of time necessitate the use of the buttocks in older children, the nurse must be extremely cautious. A method that is relatively safe and adaptable for older children is to establish landmarks by placing the thumb on the trochanter and the middle finger on the iliac crest. The index finger is placed midway between the thumb and middle finger and above them to form a triangle. The index finger indicates the safe area for the injection site. Anatomic landmarks must always be felt, not arrived at by looking at the child, because of individual differences in body construction. Other sites that can be utilized are the deltoid area and the soft flesh inferior to the crest of the ilium.

As stated previously, injections should be given as rapidly as possible to avoid prolonging a fear-provoking experience. The child must be adequately restrained before attempting to give an injection. Children will often tell the nurse that they will "hold still" for an injection, but a wise pediatric nurse will be sure to have another person there to hold the patient so that she can safely administer the injection. Stabilizing a child over 4 years of age in order to give an injection in the thigh may require more than two persons.

Rectal administration. When oral administration is difficult or contraindicated, the rectal route is often advised. A number of drugs are available in suppository form, for example, sedatives, aspirin, and antiemetics. Suppositories made with a cocoa butter base will melt rapidly at normal body temperature, releasing the drug for absorption. After a suppository is inserted in an infant, the buttocks should be held or taped together for 5 to 10 minutes to relieve pressure on the anal sphincter and thereby help to ensure retention and absorption of the medication. Infants and children with diarrhea, however, may easily expel suppositories with their explosive stools. Likewise, a suppository inserted into a child with a constipation problem or a rectum full of stool will be surrounded with stool with little chance for absorption of its contents.

Pharmacists and nurses often have to cut suppositories to obtain correct doses. This is a dangerous practice, since all of the medication might be contained in one area of the suppository. If divided doses must be administered, the pharmacist should be the one to divide the suppository; they should be cut lengthwise and weighed in order to ensure as accurate a dosage as possible.

Nose drops, ear drops, and eye drops. Aqueous preparations of nose drops are the only safe preparations to use, if it is deemed necessary to use them at all, because of the danger of aspiration. Many nose drop preparations act as vasoconstrictors and prolonged or excessive use may be harmful. Infants are nose breathers, and nasal congestion will inhibit their sucking. For this reason, nose drops should be instilled 20 minutes to 1 half hour before feedings.

To instill nose drops:

1 Hold the infant in your arm, allowing his head to fall back over the edge of your arm, or place a small pillow under the shoulders and allow his head to fall back over the edge of the pillow.
2 Place your free arm so that the forearm is around the far side of the child's head, stabilizing his head between your forearm and your body. Use your hand to stabilize his arms and hands.
3 With your free hand you can then instill the prescribed drops with minimum struggle and maximum accuracy.

The instillation of ear drops requires a knowledge of anatomic structure, since the shape of the auditory canal of a young child is different from that of an adult. In children 3 years of age or younger the nurse must gently pull the pinna of the ear slightly down and straight back to properly instill ear drops. In older children and adults, the pinna should be held up and back. Gentle massage of the area immediately anterior to the ear will facilitate the entry of the drops into the ear canal.

Eye drop instillation is done in the same way on children as with adults. The lower lid of the eye is gently pulled down and out so that it has a cup effect into which the correct number of drops is instilled. Many eyedrops cause a burning sensation in the eye for a few seconds, so if both eyes are to be medicated it is wise to do the second instillation quickly before the patient begins to blink and tear as a reaction to the burning sensation occurring in the first eye medicated.

Aqueous preparations of nose, ear, and eye drops may support the growth of bacteria and fungi. For this reason small volumes of such medications are ordered and should be used for only *one* individual (not shared by family members). Examination of these types of drops for clearness of fluid (hold the dropper up to the light) is a good method of checking for contamination. Contaminated fluid will appear cloudy when held up to the light.

Eye and ear drops are more comfortably tolerated if they are warmed before instillation.

This can be achieved by running warm water over the side of the bottle without the label or immersing the bottle in some warm water in a medicine cup. Even carrying the bottle in your pocket for half an hour or so will take the chill off of the drops.

Intravenous medications. The use of intravenous drug therapy is widespread on most pediatric services for several reasons. In children with vomiting and diarrhea, medications given by mouth may be vomited so that precious time is lost in drug management of disease processes. These same children may have poor absorption of drugs and fluids as a result of dehydration or peripheral vascular collapse, so that drugs administered via the intramuscular route may be ineffective. Prior to the now widespread use of the midanterolateral thigh muscle for intramuscular injections, there was a great danger of sciatic neuropathy and other neurologic sequelae associated with injections in the gluteal area. For these reasons, as well as the advantages associated with administering long-term drug therapy more accurately via a relatively simple vehicle, the use of intravenous therapy has increased greatly. Considering the dangers and contraindications of intravenous drug therapy, however, its use must be justifiable.

The pediatric nurse responsible for the *administration* of intravenous drugs may find the following suggestions helpful.

1 Intravenous drug therapy should only be utilized when other channels of drug administration have failed. Pediatric nurses skilled in the administration of medications to children via other routes may greatly influence the physician's decisions regarding channels of drug administraton.
2 Too rapid intravenous injection causes "speed shock": rapid fall in blood pressure, respiratory irregularity, incoagulability of the blood, and even death.
3 Once a drug is injected intravenously, it is impossible to exert further control except by specific antidote.
4 Drugs must be properly diluted. Too much emphasis cannot be placed on the caution: give the smallest possible dose at the slowest possible rate.

625

Most older children may be given fluids or drugs intravenously following the same principles and techniques utilized for adults. The younger and smaller the child, the greater the difficulty of administration and the greater the dangers associated with it.

Neonates, infants, and children must be adequately restrained so as not to dislodge or pull out an infusion needle once it is in place. Some of the following may be helpful hints to the nurse *caring* for a patient receiving intravenous therapy.

1   The needle should be fixed with plastic tape.
2   When a loop of tubing directly above the needle is secured to the tape, it relieves some of the pressure on the needle.
3   Since most children move about or are restless, it will be necessary to support the limb and immobilize the site of intravenous therapy.
4   Support should extend to the joints above and below the site (with arm boards or intravenous boards).
5   Tape backed with gauze can be used to secure the limb to the support.
6   If the infusion bottle is too high, it will increase the pressure in the vein and cause fluid seepage into the surrounding tissues.

Other conditions influencing the dosage of drugs in infants and children

Laboratory studies have shown that the same individual under almost identical situations at different time intervals will exhibit variations in measured drug responses. Frequent altering of drug dosage in relation to insulin administration, digitalis administration, and oral enzyme therapy are but a few examples.

Some of the variables influencing drug dosage were mentioned briefly at the beginning of this chapter (for example, age, size, weight, immaturity, and routes and time of administration). A few other variables will be considered here with some specific examples.

Tolerance to drugs exists in infants and children just as it does in adults, and the same principles are followed to handle such a problem. Either a larger dose of the drug is administered or a different drug is selected, preferably one without cross tolerance.

As previously discussed, the dosage of most agents is roughly proportional to the age, weight, and size of the child. According to Barnett, opiates, for example, can be given in dosages proportional to body weight, 0.15 to 0.2 mg. of morphine sulfate per kilogram of body weight being a safe level. On the other hand, infants are more sensitive than adults to a few drugs, so that smaller dosages than those proportional to weight and size are recommended. Atropine sulfate is one of these drugs. For many years atropine was used in the medical treatment of pyloric stenosis as an antispasmodic to relax the pylorospasm. The reason for sensitivity to atropine in infants is not well known, but it may be contingent on the immaturity of the central nervous system. Products less toxic than atropine itself (atropine methylnitrate or Eumydrin) are being utilized with much greater success in the treatment of pylorospasm.

Among the drugs to which older infants and children are more tolerant are epinephrine, barbiturates, and many of the other biologic preparations. Pentobarbital (Nembutal) is such an example. Roughly half of an adult dose will be easily tolerated by a child 2 to 4 years of age and one fourth of the adult dose by an infant of 6 months. Long-term experience with adult doses of pentobarbital given to children ages 3 to 6 in preparation for heart catheterizations has greatly influenced clinical opinions of its tolerance levels in children.

Nadas and co-workers showed that infants and children are more resistant to the effects of digitalis preparations than are adults. At any age, however, digitalis preparations should be administered based on individual tolerance, and suggested safe dosages should be used only as a guide.

Presence of disease

The presence of disease or any basic abnormality in a child may alter his response to drugs. For example, in children with any of the metabolic diseases such as diabetes mellitus, melituria, galactosemia, or phenylketonuria, one can expect altered drug responses. Since the liver, kidneys, intestines, and lungs are the chief channels of drug elimination, the presence of disease in any one of these organs will require that medications be administered with much knowledge and deliberation. It remains the nurse's responsibility in pediatrics to administer medications, to recognize and interpret the child's response to drug therapy, and to teach parents about the drugs their children are receiving. All ethical opportunities for learning about the pharmacodynamics of drugs should be maximally exploited by physicians and nurses alike so that children can benefit sooner from advances in medicine.

■ Summary

Pediatric nurses have a legal, moral, and ethical responsibility associated with drug administration to children. In addition to that, the responsibility of teaching children and parents about the drugs they are receiving, using sound knowledge of pharmacodynamics, has further expanded the nurse's role in relation to drug therapy. These factors, along with a knowledge of principles and techniques of drug administration to children and the application of knowledge of growth and development, will greatly enhance the pediatric nurse's ability to be the decision maker in rapidly changing health care delivery systems.

Questions

for study and review

1 Briefly explain the relationship of weight and drug dosage in children.
2 Explain why the variable of age alone is not a good basis for calculating safe drug doses for children or adults.
3 Identify and describe four conditions or variables that influence or alter drug dosage in children.
4 Identify and describe four factors that might influence a nurse's ability to administer oral medications to a 4-year-old child.
5 Using the formula based on the weight of the child in pounds, calculate the estimated safe dose of Benadryl for a 1-year-old child weighing 21 pounds if the average adult dose is 50 mg.
6 Identify and explain five factors that will enable a nurse to give an injection most effectively.
7 Identify and explain the responsibilities of a nurse administering drug therapy.

References

Barnett, H. L.: Pediatrics, ed. 14, New York, 1968, Appleton-Century-Crofts.

DiPalma, J. R.: Drill's pharmacology in medicine, ed. 4, New York, 1971, McGraw-Hill Book Company.

Goodman, L. S., and Gilman, A.: The pharmacological basis of therapeutics, ed. 4, New York, 1970, The Macmillan Company.

Modell, W.: Drugs of choice 1972-1973, St. Louis, 1972, The C. V. Mosby Co.

Shirkey, H. C., editor: Pediatric therapy, ed. 4, St. Louis, 1971, The C. V. Mosby Co.

32 Toxicology

Toxicology is the study of poisons, their action and effects, methods for their detection, and diagnosis and treatment of poisoning. A poison can be defined as any substance that in relatively small amounts can cause death or serious bodily harm by chemical action. All drugs are potential poisons when used improperly or in excess dosage. Poisoning may be *acute* or *chronic*. In acute poisoning the effects are immediate. In chronic poisoning the effects are insidious as a result of cumulative effects of small amounts of poison absorbed over a prolonged period of time. Chronic poisoning causes chronic illness that may or may not be reversible.

■ General symptoms of poisoning

When poisoning is suspected, the nurse should send for the physician. In the meantime, since time is such a precious factor, particularly in cases of acute poisoning, she should learn as much about the patient as possible and apply suitable first-aid measures.

There is reason to suspect that a poison has been taken when sudden, violent symptoms occur, such as severe nausea, vomiting, diarrhea, collapse, or convulsions. It is important to find out (if possible) what poison has been taken and how much. Additional information that might prove helpful to the physician in making a diagnosis includes answers to questions or reports of observed phenomena, as follows:

1 Did the symptoms appear suddenly in an otherwise healthy individual? Did a number of persons become ill about the same time (as might happen in food poisoning)?
2 Is there anything unusual about the person, his clothing, or his surroundings? Is there evidence of burns about the lips and mouth? Are the gums discolored? Are there needle (hypodermic) pricks, pustules, or scars on the exposed and accessible surfaces of the body? (These may be seen in examination of drug addicts.) Is there any skin rash or discoloration?
3 The odor of the breath, the rate of respiration, any difficulty in respiration, and cyanosis should be noted.

4 The quality and rate of the pulse should be noted.

5 If vomitus is seen, what is its appearance and its odor? Is or was vomiting accompanied by diarrhea or abdominal pain?

6 Any abnormalities of stool and urine should be noted; change in color or the presence of blood may be significant.

7 For signs of involvement of the nervous system, the presence of excitement, muscular twitching, delirium, difficulty in speech, stupor, coma, constriction or dilatation of the pupils, and elevated or subnormal temperature should be looked for.

The nurse should save all specimens of vomitus, urine, or stool in case the physician wishes to examine them and perhaps turn them over to the proper authority for analysis. This is of particular importance not only in making or confirming a diagnosis but also in the event that the case has medicolegal significance.

■ Source and incidence of poisoning

Poisoning is common in the United States, with about 1 million cases occurring each year.

Most poisonings are *accidental* and caused by drug intoxication. Some poisonings are *suicide* attempts. *Criminal* poisonings are rare, since modern scientific methods permit highly accurate detection of poisons and most large cities maintain toxicologic laboratories in conjunction with law enforcement agencies. *Industrial* poisonings are increasing, since modern technology exposes man to numerous toxic agents in exhaust gases, radioactive substances, insecticides, and the like.

In the adult, five common drugs account for most poisonings from medicinals—barbiturates, salicylates, glutethemide, meprobamate, and phenothiazines. Scopolamine, bromides, and ethylene glycol also rank high as poisoning agents. Carbon monoxide is a chief cause of both accidental and suicidal death.

While most poisonings occur in the adult, one third of the accidental poisonings occur in children under age 5. Children are normally curious and will taste or ingest that which is easily accessible within their environment. Most of these poisonings are from medicines found within the

Table 32-1 Common poisoning agents and the symptoms and treatment of poisoning

Drug	Estimated fatal oral dose	Symptoms	Treatment
Barbiturates		Respiratory depression, hypotension, hypothermia, renal failure, coma	Respiratory assistance, renal dialysis, diuresis
Short acting	3 Gm.		
Long acting	5 Gm.		
Glutethimide	10 Gm.	Hypotension, apnea, mydriasis, flaccid paralysis	Gastric lavage, respiratory assistance, renal dialysis, diuresis
Salicylates	10 to 20 Gm.	Hyperpnea, respiratory alkalosis, metabolic acidosis occurring later, hypoprothrombinemia	Alkaline diuresis, renal dialysis, vitamin K
Phenothiazines	50 mg. per kilogram of body weight	Miosis, irritability	Supportive measures, control of convulsions
Meprobamate	12 Gm.	Respiratory depression, hypotension, coma	Respiratory assistance, renal dialysis

home—aspirin, laxative tablets, barbiturates, iron pills, and tranquilizers. Other frequent causes of poisoning in children are cleaning agents, pesticides, bleaches, paint thinners, and lye. Lead and arsenic poisoning is encountered in fruit-growing areas where unwashed fruit-bearing residues of insecticidal sprays are available to children and in ghetto areas where children often eat old peeling paint and plaster containing lead and arsenic. In the emergency department of a large midwestern hospital the chief cause of poisoning among children was found to be aspirin. In most cases the children had apparently mistaken the sweetened gr. 1 tablets for candy.

■ Poison control centers

Physicians have long been concerned about the incidence of poisoning especially among young children, and as a result of such concern the first poison control center was started in Chicago in 1953 as a cooperative and integrated community activity. This idea spread to other cities in many states, and similar programs have been started, the administration of which may be the function of the local medical society, a medical school, the health department, a hospital, or a combination of these groups. Their main purpose is to serve as centers from which information about poisons can be obtained. There are now over 200 of these centers in the United States. With thousands of products on the market known only by their trade names, one of the major problems in treating the victim of a supposed poison is the proper identification of the ingredients of the product so that adequate treatment may be given or the victim and his family can be assured that the product was harmless. The collection of data that help to identify a poison is an important contribution of the center, although it has other functions. Data on all cases of poisoning are collected and centrally reported and followup visits to homes are often made to help prevent further cases of poisoning. The National Clearinghouse of Poison Centers is maintained by the National Institutes of Health for compilation of data and dissemination of information on poisons.

■ Classification of poisons

The classification of poisons is as broad as the classification of drugs, since any drug is a potential poison in the tissues of the right person or when used in excess.

Poisons might be classified in various ways. They might be grouped according to chemical classifications as organic and inorganic poisons; as alkaloids, glycosides, and resins; or as acids, alkalies, heavy metals, oxidizing agents, halogenated hydrocarbons, and so on.

Another way in which they might be grouped is by locale of exposure—poisons found in the home, poisons encountered in industry, poisons encountered while camping, and so on.

Still another way in which poisons may be classified is according to the organ or tissue of the body in which the most damaging effects are produced. Some poisons injure all cells with which they have contact. Such chemical substances are sometimes called protoplasmic poisons or cytotoxins. Others have more effect on the kidney (nephrotoxins), the liver (hepatotoxins), or on the blood or blood-forming organs.

Poisons that affect chiefly the nervous system are called neurotoxins or neurotropic poisons. They must be studied separately, because different symptoms characterize each one. Symptoms of toxicity have been mentioned in connection with each of these drugs as they were presented in previous chapters. Although symptoms of this group of poisons are to some extent specific, it is also true that certain symptoms are encountered repeatedly and are associated with a large number of poisons. Drowsiness, dizziness, headache, delirium, coma, and convulsive seizures always indicate central nervous system involvement. On the other hand, one learns to associate dry mouth, dilated pupils, and difficult swallowing with overdosage of atropine or one of the atropine-like drugs; ringing in the ears, excessive perspiration, and gastric upset are associated with overdosage with salicylates.

■ Mechanisms of toxic actions of poisons

Poisons produce injurious effects in a number of ways. Many times the precise mechanism of action is not known; death may be caused by respiratory failure but exactly what happens to cause depression of the respiratory center may not be known.

It is apparent that the human body is dependent upon a constant supply of oxygen if various physiologic functions are to proceed satisfactorily. Anything that interferes with the use of oxygen by the cells or with the transportation of oxygen will produce damaging effects in cells and in some cells faster than in others.

Carbon monoxide from automobile engines and unvented gas heaters is one of the most widely distributed toxic agents. It poisons by producing hypoxia and finally asphyxia. Carbon monoxide has a great affinity for hemoglobin and forms carboxyhemoglobin. Thus the production of oxyhemoglobin and the free transport of oxygen is interfered with, and oxygen deficiency soon develops in the cells. Unless exposure to the carbon monoxide is terminated quickly and before 40% of hemoglobin has been changed to carboxyhemoglobin, the anoxia may produce serious brain damage; death occurs when 60% of the hemoglobin has been changed to carboxyhemoglobin.

The cyanides act somewhat similarly in that they bring about cellular anoxia, but they do so in a different manner. They inactivate certain tissue enzymes so that cells are unable to utilize oxygen. Death may occur very rapidly.

Curare and the curariform drugs in toxic amounts bring about paralysis of the diaphragm, and again the victim dies from lack of oxygen.

Certain drugs have a direct effect on muscle tissue of the body such as that of the myocardium or the smooth muscle of the blood vessels. Death results from the failure of circulation or cardiac arrest. The nitrites, potassium salts, and digitalis drugs may exert toxic effects of this type.

Arsenic is an example of a protoplasmic poison or cytotoxin. Compounds of arsenic inhibit many enzyme systems of cells, especially those that depend on the activity of their free sulfhydryl groups. The arsenic combines with these SH groups and makes them ineffective. Hence, extensive tissue damage in the body occurs.

Methyl alcohol owes its toxic effect to an intermediate product of metabolism—formic acid. This produces a severe acidosis, lowered pH of the blood, reduced cerebral blood flow, and decreased consumption of oxygen by the brain. There is also a selective action on the retinal cells of the eye, but the exact cause of this injury is unknown.

Benzene is an example of a poison that acts by inhibiting the formation of all types of blood cells. In some instances the precursor of one type of blood cell is injured more than another. Depression of the formation of any of the blood cells can cause death.

The strong acids and alkalies denature and destroy cellular proteins. Examples of corrosive acids are hydrochloric, nitric, and sulfuric acids. Sodium, potassium, and ammonium hydroxides are examples of strong or caustic alkalies. Locally, these substances cause destruction of tissue, and death may result from hemorrhage, perforation, or shock. Corrosive poisons may also cause death by altering the pH of the blood or other body fluids, or they may produce marked degenerative changes in vital organs such as the liver or the kidney.

Many of the central nervous system depressants cause death by producing excessive depression of respiration and respiratory failure. The general anesthetics, barbiturates, chloral hydrate, and paraldehyde are examples of such drugs.

Central nervous system stimulants such as pentylenetetrazol, strychnine, and others in toxic amounts cause convulsive seizures, exhaustion, and depression of vital centers.

■ First-aid measures for poisoning

As mentioned previously, the duty of the nurse is to send for a physician and, pending his arrival, to ascertain if possible the cause of the symptoms and to apply suitable first-aid measures. The treatment of acute poisoning is always an emergency. Recommendations on first-aid measures for poisoning were made by the Committee on Toxicology of the American Medical Association and are presented on pp. 633 and 634.

631

Treatment of poisoning

Treatment of poisoning includes a number of general principles of action. Under many circumstances good first aid may save the patient's life and make the physician's task easier. To some extent, first aid and the later treatment may overlap. There are many things that may be done for the patient that can be done only under the direction and supervision of a physician, but the more the nurse knows about the poison and what to expect and what to have ready for use, the more help she is to all concerned. Occasionally, a nurse must deal with an emergency alone or at best under the direction of a physician she is able to contact by telephone.

When living in or near a city it is faster and more satisfactory to bring a patient to a hospital, clinic, or physician's office than it is to wait for the physician to call at home. Professional ambulance service, the police, or the fire department will frequently provide transportation, but a family car or that of a neighbor may be a faster way of solving the problem. Treatment of poisoning frequently involves (1) removal of the poison, (2) administration of a suitable antidote, (3) promotion of elimination, and (4) supportive treatment of the patient.

The order of these measures may need to be reversed, depending on the poison taken and the general condition of the patient. Sometimes the prompt removal of the poison is all the treatment that is needed.

◼ Removal of poison

When poisons are on the external surface of the body, in the nasal or oral cavities, or in the eye, attempts to remove them should be made by irrigating with copious amounts of plain water; this will prevent additional trauma resulting from the use of a weak base or acid. Toxic oils should be removed with organic solvents or warm, soapy water. If the poison has been swallowed recently, it is advisable to remove it from the stomach as soon as possible to decrease chances of absorption. The simplest way, provided the patient is conscious and cooperative,

is to persuade him to drink an excess of tepid water and induce vomiting. Other emetics can be used, but some of them must be used with caution. Tepid water with mustard (1 teaspoon to a glass), weak salt water, starch water, or weak soap solution can do little harm, although the mustard may accentuate the discomfort of the raw mucous membranes. Copper sulfate is sometimes added to water and used as an emetic, especially for arsenic poisoning, but it has been known to kill infants when the excess cupric ion was not removed. Apomorphine, gr. $^{1}/_{10}$, can be given hypodermically. It acts promptly but tends to be depressing and hence is not widely used. The best emetic is probably the mildest and the one most readily available.

Use of the stomach tube to remove poisons can be hazardous. This is especially true if there is (1) danger of perforating a corroded esophagus or stomach, (2) danger of aspirating the poison, or (3) danger of precipitating a convulsive seizure such as might occur in strychnine poisoning.

Use of the stomach tube is probably preferable to the use of emetics in many cases, because the tube has greater efficiency in emptying the stomach and because less prostration is likely to follow its use than when the patient is made to vomit.

◼ Administration of suitable antidote

After the stomach has been emptied, it is necessary to administer the proper antidote. An *antidote* is any agent used to counteract the action of a poison. There are three kinds of antidotes: (1) physical or mechanical, (2) chemical, and (3) physiologic.

A *physical antidote* is one that envelops or mixes with the poison and prevents its absorption, soothes and protects the tissues, and may aid in removal of the poison.

Demulcents, emollients, emetics, cathartics, and the stomach tube are used as physical antidotes.

Milk, white of egg, boiled starch or porridge, gruels, barley water, mashed potato, and mucilage of acacia are suitable demulcents. Fixed oils such as olive, cottonseed, cod liver, or liq-

First-aid measures for poisoning*

The following recommendations on first-aid measures for poisoning have been adopted by the Committee on Toxicology. These recommendations are made in response to numerous requests to the American Medical Association for general instructions for poisoning emergencies. They are intended for use in educating the public in what to do when poisoning occurs.

Emergency telephone numbers:
PHYSICIAN .... FIRE DEPT ....
HOSPITAL ...... (resuscitator) ....
PHARMACIST .... POLICE ....
RESCUE SQUADS ....

The aim of first-aid measures is to help prevent absorption of the poison. SPEED is essential. First-aid measures must be started at once. If possible, one person should begin treatment while another calls a physician. When this is not possible, the nature of the poison will determine whether to call a physician first or begin first-aid measures and then notify a physician. Save the poison container and material itself if any remains. If the poison is not known, save a sample of the vomitus.

Measures to be taken before arrival of physician

I. Swallowed poisons

Many products used in and around the home, although not labeled "Poison," may be dangerous if taken internally. For example, some medications which are beneficial when used correctly may endanger life if used improperly or in excessive amounts.

In all cases, *except those indicated below,* REMOVE POISON FROM PATIENT'S STOMACH IMMEDIATELY by inducing vomiting. This cannot be overemphasized, for it is the essence of the treatment and is often a life-saving procedure. Prevent chilling by wrapping patient in blankets if necessary. Do not give alcohol in any form.

A. Do not induce vomiting if:
  1. Patient is in coma or unconscious.
  2. Patient is in convulsions.
  3. Patient has swallowed petroleum products (kerosene, gasoline, lighter fluid).
  4. Patient has swallowed a corrosive poison (symptoms: severe pain, burning sensation in mouth and throat, vomiting). CALL PHYSICIAN IMMEDIATELY.
    (a) Acid and acid-like corrosives: sodium acid sulfate (toilet bowl cleaners), acetic acid (glacial), sulfuric acid, nitric acid, oxalic acid, hydrofluoric acid (rust removers), iodine, silver nitrate (styptic pencil).
    (b) Alkali corrosives: sodium hydroxide-lye (drain cleaners), sodium carbonate (washing soda), ammonia water, sodium hypochlorite (household bleach).

If the patient can swallow after ingesting a *corrosive poison*, the following substances (and amounts) may be given:
  For acids: milk, water, or milk of magnesia (1 tablespoon to 1 cup of water).
  For alkalies: milk, water, any fruit juice, or vinegar.
  For patient 1-5 years old – 1 to 2 cups.
  For patient 5 years and older – up to 1 quart.

B. Induce vomiting when non-corrosive substances have been swallowed:
  1. Give milk or water (for patient 1-5 years old – 1 to 2 cups; for patient over 5 years – up to 1 quart).
  2. Induce vomiting by placing the blunt end of a spoon or your finger at the back of the patient's throat, or by use of this emetic – 2 tablespoons of salt in a glass of warm water.

When retching and vomiting begin, place patient face down with head lower than hips. This prevents vomitus from entering the lungs and causing further damage.

II. Inhaled poisons

  1. Carry patient (do not let him walk) to fresh air immediately.
  2. Open all doors and windows.
  3. Loosen all tight clothing.
  4. Apply artificial respiration if breathing has stopped or is irregular.
  5. Prevent chilling (wrap patient in blankets).
  6. Keep patient as quiet as possible.
  7. If patient is convulsing, keep him in bed in a semi-dark room; avoid jarring or noise.
  8. Do not give alcohol in any form.

Continued.

III. Skin contamination

1. Drench skin with water (shower, hose, faucet).
2. Apply stream of water on skin while removing clothing.
3. Cleanse skin thoroughly with water; rapidity in washing is most important in reducing extent of injury.

IV. Eye contamination

1. Hold eyelids open, wash eyes with gentle stream of running water *immediately*. Delay of few seconds greatly increases extent of injury.
2. Continue washing until physician arrives.
3. *Do not use chemicals;* they may increase extent of injury.

V. Injected poisons (scorpion and snake bites)

1. Make patient lie down as soon as possible.
2. Do not give alcohol in any form.
3. Apply tourniquet above injection site (e.g., between arm or leg and heart). The pulse in vessels below the tourniquet should not disappear, nor should the tourniquet produce a throbbing sensation. Tourniquet should be loosened for 1 minute every 15 minutes.
4. Apply ice-pack to the site of the bite.
5. Carry patient to physician or hospital; DO NOT LET HIM WALK.

VI. Chemical burns

1. Wash with large quantities of running water except those burns caused by phosphorus).
2. Immediately cover with loosely applied clean cloth.
3. Avoid use of ointments, greases, powders, and other drugs in first-aid treatment of burns.
4. Treat shock by keeping patient flat, keeping him warm, and reassuring him until arrival of physician.

Measures to prevent poisoning accidents

A. Keep all drugs, poisonous substances, and household chemicals out of the reach of children.
B. Do not store nonedible products on shelves used for storing food.
C. Keep all poisonous substances in their original containers; do not transfer to unlabeled containers or to food containers such as soft drink bottles.
D. When medicines are discarded, destroy them. Do not throw them where they might be reached by children or pets.
E. When giving flavored and/or brightly colored medicine to children, *always* refer to it as medicine — *never* as candy.
F. Do not take or give medicine in the dark.
G. READ LABELS before using chemical products.

uid petrolatum may be used, but in cases where the poison is soluble in the oil, like cantharides or phosphorus, the stomach should be emptied after giving the oil.

A *chemical antidote* is one that reacts with the poison and neutralizes it. Common salt (sodium chloride) is an excellent antidote for silver nitrate. The products formed, silver chloride and sodium nitrate, are both harmless. Magnesium oxide, milk of magnesia, or baking soda are chemical antidotes for acids. In general, it is to be remembered that alkalies counteract acids and vice versa. Care should be used when sodium bicarbonate is given, because if too much gas results from the reaction, the pressure may rupture the corroded stomach. For this reason,

milk of magnesia or calcium carbonate may be preferable. Lemon juice, grapefruit juice, and vinegar are suitable weak acids to neutralize strong bases. Poisoning with irritant metallic salts is best treated with albumin in the form of egg white, since an insoluble albuminate is formed. The antidote for the vegetable alkaloids such as morphine, atropine, or strychnine is tannic acid or potassium permanganate. Both the tannic acid and the potassium permanganate (1:2000) may be used to wash out the patient's stomach. Tannic acid can be obtained from strong green tea; it brings about precipitation of alkaloids while potassium permanganate causes oxidation of alkaloids.

Chemical antidotes act only on such portions

Table 32-2 Some specific poisons, symptoms, and emergency treatment

Poison	Symptoms	Treatment
Acids (such as hydrochloric or nitric)	Parts in contact with acid are first white, later colored (brown or yellow) Pain in throat, esophagus, and stomach; dysphagia, diarrhea, shock, circulatory collapse Death may result from asphyxia from edema of glottis	Avoid stomach tube, emesis, and solutions of carbonate, such as sodium bicarbonate Give milk of magnesia, aluminum hydroxide, mild soap solution, plenty of milk or water with egg white Copious amounts of water Keep patient warm and quiet Corticosteroids to reduce fibrosis and possibility of esophageal stricture
Arsenic (found in weed killers, insecticides, sheepdip rodenticides, and so on)	Rapidity of onset of symptoms related to whether or not poison is taken with food Odor of garlic on breath and stools Faintness, nausea, difficulty in swallowing, extreme thirst, severe vomiting, gastric pain, "rice water" stools, oliguria, albuminuria, cold, clammy skin Collapse and death	Universal antidote, 5 to 6 teaspoonfuls, followed by repeated lavage with warm or weak sodium bicarbonate solution or by an emetic (warm water, salt water, or mustard water) repeated until vomiting occurs Intravenous fluids Sedation, analgesics Dimercaprol (BAL) is the antidote of choice (see p. 639) Keep patient warm
Bromides	*Acute poisoning* 　Deep stupor 　Ataxia 　Extreme muscular weakness 　Collapse *Chronic poisoning* (bromism) 　Bromide acne is seen on face, chest, and back 　Salty taste in mouth 　Foul breath 　Gastrointestinal disturbance 　Mental depression 　Faulty memory 　Pronounced apathy 　Ataxia—slurred speech 　Muscular weakness 　Malnutrition 　Anemia	Stop the drug Large doses of physiologic salt solutions are given to hasten excretion of drug As a rule, symptoms of bromism rapidly abate if drug is withdrawn Diuretics are given to hasten excretion of the drug
Carbon monoxide (present in coal gas, illuminating gas, exhaust gas from motor cars, and so on)	Symptoms vary with concentration of carbon monoxide in blood Headache, dizziness, impaired hearing and vision, drowsiness, confusion, loss of consciousness Slow respiration, rapid pulse Coma, cherry-red lips and nails	Remove patient to fresh air; artificial respiration; high concentration of oxygen preferably under positive pressure Bed rest for 48 hours Keep patient warm

Continued.

Table 32-2 Some specific poisons, symptoms, and emergency treatment—cont'd

Poison	Symptoms	Treatment
Carbon tetrachloride (found in some dry-cleaning fluids and in some home fire extinguishers)	*When inhaled:* headache, nausea, vomiting, diarrhea, jaundice, oliguria, albuminuria, dark-colored urine *When swallowed:* headache, nausea, vomiting, sometimes blood in vomitus, abdominal pain, disturbance of hearing and vision, jaundice, profuse diarrhea, albuminuria, anuria	Remove patient from poisoned atmosphere; administer oxygen or oxygen with carbon dioxide Simple emetics to produce repeated vomiting if lavage not available; if possible, lavage followed by saline cathartic High-protein, high-carbohydrate, high-calcium diet General supportive measures
Chlorophenothane (dichlorodiphenyl-trichloroethane, or D.D.T.)	Headache, nausea, vomiting, diarrhea, paresthesias of lips and tongue, numbness of extremities, malaise, sore throat Coarse tremor, convulsions, respiratory failure	Induce vomiting or use gastric lavage if convulsions do not threaten Give saline cathartic, force fluids, give strong tea or coffee Avoid fats, fat solvents, and epinephrine Wash contaminated skin areas with soap and water
Cyanides	An odor of oil of bitter almonds on breath; headache, rapid breathing, dyspnea, palpitation of heart, feeling of tightness in chest, cyanosis, convulsions Death may come within few minutes	Prompt treatment sometimes successful Amyl nitrite (several pearls broken into gauze and given by inhalation), followed by 1% sodium nitrite intravenously slowly, in 10-ml. doses, to a total of 50 ml. in an hour, and this followed by slow intravenous administration of sodium thiosulfate (50 ml. of a 25% solution) Oxygen, artificial respiration, and blood transfusion may be indicated
Fluoride (found in insecticides)	Nausea, vomiting, abdominal pain, diarrhea, muscle weakness, difficult swallowing, facial paralysis, inability to speak, convulsions at times, respiratory failure and circulatory collapse	Give emetic containing soluble calcium salts (calcium lactate or gluconate) or use plenty of warm water and follow with plenty of milk Preferable to lavage promptly with 1% calcium chloride to inactivate fluoride General supportive measures
Hydrocarbons (present in kerosene, gasoline, naphtha, cleaning fluids, insecticides)	Symptoms of intoxication similar to those of of alcohol; burning sensation in mouth, esophagus, and stomach Vomiting, dizziness, tremor, muscle cramps, confusion, fever Cold, clammy skin, weak pulse, thirst, unconsciousness, coma Death from respiratory failure	Emetics and lavage usually avoided unless large amounts swallowed; saline cathartics after small amounts taken Some authorities recommend large doses of mineral oil for severe poisoning, followed by lavage with 1% or 2% sodium bicarbonate solution General supportive measures

Poison	Symptoms	Treatment
Iodine	Brown-stained lips, tongue, and mouth, which are painful Odor of iodine in vomitus Intense thirst, fainting attacks, giddiness, vomiting, burning, abdominal pain, diarrhea, shock	Give plenty of water promptly, with starch or flour or mashed potatoes Gastric lavage if possible with thin, cooked suspension of starch or 5% sodium thiosulfite solution Give drinks of milk or white of egg, with water
Lye (a severe caustic)	Severe burning pain in mouth, throat, and stomach Strong soapy taste in mouth Early violent vomiting with mucus and blood in vomitus Mucous membranes become white and swollen; lips and tongue swell; throat may become constricted Respirations difficult Skin cold and clammy Pulse rapid Violent purging Great anxiety	Emetics and lavage frequently not recommended Give large amounts of water containing weak acids, lemon, vinegar, lime juice, and so on; later give demulcents, white of egg, gruel, olive oil or salad oil Analgesics, parenteral fluids Corticosteroids
Mercury and its compounds	Burning sensation of throat Nausea and vomiting (vomitus blue if antiseptic tablets of bichloride used) Sense of constriction in throat and esophagus Ashen-gray color of mucous membranes that have been in contact with poison Bloody, profuse diarrhea, with shreds of mucous membrane in stool and vomitus Shock, albuminuria, and hematuria During acute phase, pain and prostration; late, progressive uremia	Give 5 to 6 heaping teaspoonfuls of universal antidote and then lavage with 5% sodium formaldehyde sulfoxylate solution followed by sodium bicarbonate solution If not feasible, give emetic of mustard water or salt water until vomiting has occurred repeatedly Give milk and egg white in water Dimercaprol indicated as specific antidote (see p. 639) Parenteral fluids Keep patient warm Recovery depends on dose taken, amount of absorption, and amount of kidney damage
Nicotine (Black Leaf 40 contains about 40% nicotine sulfate)	Burning sensation in mouth and throat, increased flow of saliva, abdominal pain, vomiting, diarrhea, headache, sweating, confusion, weakness, dilatation of pupils, faintness, death from respiratory paralysis	Universal antidote, 6 to 8 teaspoonfuls; lavage with 0.5% tannic acid or 1:5000 potassium permanganate Artificial respirations Wash contaminated skin with cold water

Continued.

Table 32-2 Some specific poisons,
symptoms, and emergency
treatment—cont'd

Poison	Symptoms	Treatment
Paris green (copper arsenite and copper acetate)	Vomiting of green material followed by gastric and abdominal pain; diarrhea with dark and sometimes bloody stools; metallic taste; neuromuscular weakness Thirst, oliguria, anuria Cold, clammy skin Coma, convulsions, death	Potassium ferrocyanide, gr. 10 in water as soon as possible (forms an insoluble salt of copper), followed by lavage with sodium bicarbonate solution or a mustard-water emetic until stomach cleansed Demulcents (milk, egg white in water, gelatin) Supportive measures
Phenolic compounds (carbolic acid, cresol, Lysol, creosote)	Corrosion of mucous membranes that have come in contact with poison Severe pain, vomiting, bloody diarrhea, headache, dizziness Cold, clammy skin Oliguria, hematuria, unconsciousness, slow respiration, respiratory failure Urine dark and turns very dark on exposure to air	Of utmost importance to remove poison before absorption, prompt lavage with olive oil (a good solvent); leave some oil in stomach after lavage; give egg white and milk for demulcent effect Parenteral fluids, oxygen, carbon dioxide, analgesics Other supportive measures Phenol on skin can be removed with 50% solution of alcohol, followed by thorough rinsing with water, or wash external burns with olive oil or castor oil
Strychnine (symptoms occur within 15 or 20 min. after drug has been taken)	Feeling of stiffness in muscles of face and neck Twitching of face and limbs Violent convulsions of whole body, at intervals varying from a few minutes to an hour Death may result from asphyxia caused by spasm of respiratory muscles or during period of relaxation from respiratory paralysis	Administer anesthetic agents or barbiturates to control convulsive seizures (sodium salt of amobarbital or pentobarbital intravenously) If barbiturates are not available, chloroform, paraldehyde, or tribromethanol are recommended Gastric lavage may be done with solutions of potassium permanganate 1:1000 or 2% tannic acid After convulsions have been checked, chloral hydrate or phenobarbital may be needed to prevent convulsions from returning During treatment patient should be in cool, quiet room and protected from sudden noise, jarring, or change of any kind that might precipitate another seizure
Quaternary ammonium compounds (such as Zephiran)	Burning pain in the mouth and throat, nausea and vomiting, apprehension and restlessness; muscle weakness, collapse, coma, sometimes convulsions	Induce vomiting or use gastric lavage if it can be done promptly; mild soap solution will serve as antidote for unabsorbed portions Give cathartic

of the poison as have not been absorbed, and they must be given promptly. They are frequently added to the lavage solution.

A *physiologic antidote* is one that produces the opposite systemic effects from that of the poison. If a person has taken or been given too much pilocarpine, the sweating is readily counteracted by the hypodermic use of atropine (gr. $^1/_{60}$ to $^1/_{30}$). Caffeine is a physiologic antidote for morphine and sedatives like pentobarbital, and an anesthetic is an antidote for strychnine poisoning. If there are spasms, ether should be used first, a sedative later.

Antidote kit

The following materials have been suggested to cope with poison emergencies. Others may be added (see Table 32-2). A nurse is often responsible for keeping up the supplies and for seeing that clear legible labels are maintained. However, the pharmacist should relabel all medications.

Alcohol
Amyl nitrite
Apomorphine tablets, 2 mg.
Aromatic spirit of ammonia
Atropine tablets, 1 mg.
Bicarbonate of sodium
Caffeine-sodium benzoate
Calcium gluconate, 10%, ampules
Charcoal, activated
Chloroform
Cupric sulfate, powdered
Dextrose, 50%, ampules
Dimercaprol
Epinephrine tablets, 1 mg.
Ephedrine hydrochloride, 16-mg. tablets
Limewater
Magnesia, calcined
Methylene blue, 50 ml., 1% in 1.8% sodium sulfate
Metrazol, 10%, 1-ml. ampules
Morphine sulfate tablets, 10 mg.
Nalorphine, 10 mg. in two ampules
Nitrite of sodium, 2%, 10-ml. ampules
Olive oil
Pentobarbital sodium, 0.5-Gm. ampules
Picrotoxin, 3%, 20 ml.
Potassium permanganate, 1% solution, to be diluted twenty times
Thiosulfate of sodium, 30%, 10-ml. ampules

Tincture of iodine
Whiskey

A hypodermic syringe and a stomach tube with a funnel should be available. The following usually can be secured at the home of the patient: boiled water, hot strong black coffee, eggs, milk, mustard, salt, starch, tea, and vinegar.

Universal antidote

This old and previously widely used antidote consists of 1 part of tannic acid, 1 part of magnesium oxide, and 2 parts of activated medicinal charcoal. The magnesium oxide neutralizes acid without forming gas, the tannic acid brings about the formation of insoluble salts (of alkaloids and metals), while the charcoal is an excellent adsorbent of a variety of substances. The recommended dosage is $^1/_2$ ounce or 4 to 5 heaping teaspoonfuls. The preparation is light and fluffy and must be stirred into a glass of water to form a thin paste before it is swallowed. It can be swallowed quickly after the ingestion of certain poisons but should be removed by emesis or lavage before the stomach content has time to pass into the intestine. This antidote is now seldom used since the effectiveness of the charcoal is probably decreased by the other two ingredients.

Heavy metal antagonists

Dimercaprol, U.S.P., B.P. (BAL)

Dimercaprol was developed during World War II as an antidote for the arsenic-containing blister gas, Lewisite; hence, the name "BAL" for "British Anti-Lewisite." It was used to decontaminate the skin and eyes of persons who had been in contact with the gas, but later it was found to be of value in treatment of various forms of arsenic poisoning.

Dimercaprol is a colorless liquid with a rather offensive odor. It is dispensed in 10% solution in peanut oil for intramuscular injection. One milliliter contains 100 mg.

Arsenic compounds produce their toxic effects by combining with the sulfhydryl groups of enzymes, which are necessary for normal metabolism. As a result, the processes of oxidation and reduction in the tissues are seriously hindered. BAL interferes with this combination, forms a stable combination with the arsenic, neutralizes its toxic effects, and hastens its excretion from the body.

BAL is also indicated in the treatment of gold and mercury poisoning. Treatment should begin as soon as possible after poisoning has occurred.

Results in the treatment of poisoning from other heavy metals are disappointing or inconclusive. Although the toxicity of BAL is less among patients suffering from arsenic, gold, or mercury poisoning than among persons in normal condition, doses of 300 mg. may cause the following symptoms: nausea and vomiting, headache, a burning sensation of the mouth, throat, and eyes, a constricting sensation in the chest, muscular aching, and tingling in the extremities. This drug can also cause blood pressure elevation, capillary damage, and a condition resembling diabetic acidosis. Hypersensitivity reactions are common. BAL is a potentially dangerous drug.

In the treatment of arsenic or gold poisoning, the dose is 2.5 to 5 mg. of dimercaprol per kilogram of body weight, given intramuscularly every 4 hours the first 2 days, reduced to two injections on the third day, and then daily for the next 5 days. In mild cases the dose may be reduced. In mercury poisoning the dosage is sometimes increased.

Other heavy metal antagonists

While dimercaprol is a highly effective antidote to arsenic, gold, or mercury poisoning, other new antidotes are very useful for the treatment of some other intoxications caused by heavy metals. Most important are calcium disodium edetate and penicillamine.

Calcium disodium edetate, U.S.P. (Calcium Disodium Versenate)

Calcium disodium edetate is most useful in the treatment of lead poisoning. It combines with the heavy metal in the body and favors its renal excretion.

Calcium disodium edetate is available as a 20% solution for injection and in tablets containing 500 mg.

For the treatment of lead poisoning the drug is administered by slow intravenous infusion. One gram is added to 250 or 500 ml. of 5% dextrose in water or to isotonic saline. Infusions may be given twice a day for 3 to 5 days. Dosage for children should be kept below 1 Gm. per 30 pounds of body weight. The drug is given in 5-day courses with a 2-day rest period between courses. Daily urinalysis should be done and dosage reduced if there is indication of renal impairment.

The drug may also be injected intramuscularly, but a local anesthetic may have to be added to the solution in order to decrease pain at the site of injection. In mild cases calcium disodium edetate may be administered orally; the usual dose for adults is 4 Gm. a day.

It is important not to confuse this drug with the trisodium salt of ethylenediamine tetraacetic acid, the administration of which would be extremely dangerous.

Adverse effects. If more than the recommended dosage is used, renal damage may occur, particularly in children. Symptoms of acute lead poisoning, particularly cerebral symptoms, may be aggravated at the beginning of therapy. If this happens, dosage should be reduced.

Penicillamine, U.S.P., B.P. (Cuprimine)

$$H_3C - \underset{\underset{\underset{H}{|}}{\underset{S}{|}}}{\overset{\overset{CH_3}{|}}{C}} - \underset{\underset{NH_2}{|}}{CH} - \overset{\overset{O}{||}}{C} - OH$$

Penicillamine is used to treat poisoning caused by copper and for removing copper from the body in hepatolenticular degeneration (Wilson's disease). It may also be used as a chelator of lead and mercury.

The recommended dose of penicillamine is 250 mg. four times a day by mouth.

Adverse effects. Rashes, blood dyscrasias, and possibly renal damage may occur following the use of penicillamine. The drug is relatively safe, however, and adverse effects do not occur frequently.

Desferrioxamine (Desferal)

Desferrioxamine binds iron and promotes its excretion. As a consequence, it may be useful in the treatment of iron poisoning and in diseases such as hemochromatosis in which there is a chronic accumulation of iron in the body.

Desferrioxamine is administered intravenously, 400 to 600 mg., once or twice a day. In cases of acute iron poisoning several grams may be given by stomach tube and followed by intravenous medication.

Organophosphorus insecticide antidotes

Many organophosphorus insecticides, as well as some therapeutic agents, are highly toxic because they inactivate cholinesterase in the body. Atropine is an important antidote for poisoning caused by anticholinesterase drugs. Another antidote, pralidoxime (PAM), has been developed that actually reactivates the cholinesterase enzymes in the body when they are inhibited by the organophosphorus compounds, thereby removing the block at the myoneural junction. Since many widely used insecticides owe their toxicity to the fact that they combine with cholinesterase drugs, knowledge of antidotes for such poisonings is of very great importance.

Along with atropine, pralidoxime is useful for the treatment of poisoning by anticholinesterase drugs and chemical warfare agents of the organophosphorus type. Since such anticholinesterase drugs are also used in ophthalmology, pralidoxime also may find some application in that specialty.

Pralidoxime methiodide should be administered by intravenous infusion in a dosage of 50 mg. per kilogram dissolved in 1000 ml. of saline.

Promotion of elimination

Promotion of elimination may be accomplished by the use of certain cathartics, such as saline cathartics or castor oil, or by rectal irrigation. After gastric lavage 1 ounce of 50% magnesium sulfate may be left in the stomach, followed by administration of copious amounts of water. Magnesium sulfate helps to cleanse the lower part of the bowel. In case of anuria, the artificial kidney may be life saving.

Supportive care of the patient

In an effort to find the right antidote for a poison, the most important aspect of care of the patient may be overlooked. Sometimes the greatest need of the patient is met by giving artificial respiration. Shock is an important factor to be considered. Intravenous administration of physiologic saline or glucose solution is important for the maintenance of adequate circulation and for replacement of fluid that may be lost by diarrhea from gastrointestinal irritation. Attention to fluid needs may also help to conserve kidney and liver function, particularly in the presence of certain poisons. At times depressant drugs are indicated, at other times stimulants. Often attention must be given to keeping the patient warm and, if stuporous or comatose, to see that his position is changed periodically to prevent hypostatic pneumonia.

Moral support of the patient and his significant others is always an important aspect of nursing care.

Poisonous foods

Many foods, because of their content of inherently poisonous chemicals (mushrooms and other fungi) or the presence of bacterial exotoxins, produce symptoms of poisoning when eaten. The symptoms are diverse, but intense gastrointestinal irritation is common to all of them, and they may therefore by appropriately classed as irritants. Mushroom poisoning arises through mistaking various fungi, such as poisonous mushrooms, toadstools, and truffles, for edible varieties. The toxin of many of these plants is muscarine, a deadly alkaloidal poison that causes violent vomiting, colic, thirst, dyspnea, paralysis, and death. Many of the cases of food poisoning seen especially in the warm season of the year are caused by soluble exotoxins that result from bacterial contamination of food. Foods that seem prone to cause symptoms of poisoning are corned beef, sausage, pickled or decaying fish, shellfish, ham, home-canned vegetables, salads, whipped cream, and custards. Poisoning is more likely to occur, especially from salads, whipped cream, and custards, when large amounts are made at one time and are improperly prepared and refrigerated. The treatment of food poisoning, from whatever cause, is prompt evacuation of the stomach, preferably by stomach tube. In the process of this evacuation plenty of water is used and tannic acid or strong tea is administered; a large dose of magnesium sulfate or castor oil is given to empty the bowel and prevent absorption therefrom. Morphine may be given for abdominal pain, and stimulants may be indicated if there is prostration.

Questions

for study and review

Circle the answer of your choice.

1 Which of the following conditions would lead you to suspect acute poisoning?
   a. gradual loss of weight
   b. anorexia, undue lassitude
   c. onset of sudden violent symptoms
   d. weakness, anemia, headache

2 Which of the following factors is likely to be the crucial one in the successful treatment of early and acute poisoning?
   a. amount of supportive treatment
   b. immediate removal of poison from the body
   c. control of shock
   d. administration of the right antidote

3 Which of the following kinds of antidotes are represented when sodium chloride solution is used in the treatment of silver nitrate poisoning?
   a. chemical   c. universal
   b. physical   d. physiologic

4 If you were working in the chemistry laboratory of the school of nursing and splashed some hydrochloric acid in your eye, what is the first thing you would do?
   a. rush to the emergency room
   b. search for a weak base and instill some in your eye
   c. neutralize the acid with solution of sodium hydroxide
   d. wash eye with copious amounts of plain water

5 BAL (British Anti-Lewisite) is a recommended antidote for poisoning from:
   a. hydrocarbons
   b. strong acids
   c. phenolic compounds
   d. certain heavy metals

6 Death from carbon monoxide is likely to be caused by:
   a. changes in bone marrow
   b. damage to liver and kidney
   c. depression of heart
   d. anoxia

7 Death from a poison like methyl alcohol is likely to result from:
   a. destruction in the kidney
   b. perforation, hemorrhage, or both
   c. acidosis
   d. depression of the respiratory center

8 Which of the following kinds of foods are least likely to be a source of bacterial contamination and food poisoning?
   a. lobster salad
   b. boiled dinner of cabbage, meat, and potatoes
   c. chicken salad, Boston cream pie
   d. ham sandwiches, iced tea

9 Which of the following statements best explains why children are often poisoned by medicines left around the house?
   a. children are naturally curious about things
   b. children mistake sweet-tasting tablets or pills for candy
   c. children like to explore new things with their mouths
   d. children like to imitate other members of the household

10 Which of the following would you do if present at the scene of a poisoning and the patient had been vomiting?
   a. note odor and color of the vomitus before flushing down the toilet
   b. save a specimen of vomitus and add a preservative if possible
   c. save a specimen of vomitus (an early one if possible) for the doctor
   d. discard emesis as fast as possible to avoid offense to the patient

References

Adams, E.: Poisons, Sci. Amer. **201:**76, 1959.

Adams, W. C.: Poison control centers: their purpose and operation, Clin. Pharmacol. Therap. **4:**293, 1963.

Castell, D. O., and Morrison, C. C.: Management of common adult intoxications, G.P. **33:**105, 1966.

Done, A. K.: Pharmacologic principles in the treatment of poisoning, Pharmacol. Physicians **3:**1, 1969.

Dreisback, R. H.: Handbook of poisoning: diagnosis and treatment, Los Altos, Calif., 1966, Lange Medical Publications.

Frazer, A. C.: Pesticides, Ann. Rev. Pharmacol. **7:**319, 1967.

Gleason, M. N., Gosselin, R. E., and Hodge, H. C.: Clinical toxicology of commercial products, Baltimore, 1963, The Williams & Wilkins Co.

Gosselin, R. E., and Smith, R. P.: Trends in the therapy of acute poisonings, Clin. Pharmacol. Therap. **7:**279, 1966.

Goth, A.: Medical pharmacology, ed. 6, St. Louis, 1972, The C. V. Mosby Co.

Henderson, I. W., and Merrill, J. P.: Treatment of barbiturate intoxication, Ann. Intern. Med. **64:**876, 1966.

Hollister, L. E.: Overdose of psychotherapeutic drugs, Clin. Pharmacol. Therap. **7:**142, 1966.

Keehn, R. J.: Home accidents resulting from gas, Amer. J. Nurs. **55:**720, 1955.

Medved, L. I., and Kagan, J. S.: Toxicology, Ann. Rev. Pharmacol. **6:**293, 1966.

Press, E.: Poison control centers, Nurs. Outlook **5:**29, 1957.

Price, E. C.: A remote village, a neighborhood nurse, and an antidotes chart, Amer. J. Nurs. **59:**688, 1959.

Tonyan, A.: The nurse's part in poison control, Amer. J. Nurs. **58:**96, 1958.

Upholt, W. M., and Kearney, P. C.: Pesticides, New Eng. J. Med. **275:**1419, 1967.

West, I.: Pesticide-induced illness—public health aspects of diagnosis and treatment, Calif. Med. **105:**257, 1966.

INDEX

Index

Index

Index

681

Metric doses and apothecary equivalents

Reprinted from U.S.P. XVIII

Liquid measure

Metric		Approximate apothecary equivalents	
1000	ml.	1	quart
750	ml.	1½	pints
500	ml.	1	pint
250	ml.	8	fluid ounces
200	ml.	7	fluid ounces
100	ml.	3½	fluid ounces
50	ml.	1¾	fluid ounces
30	ml.	1	fluid ounce
15	ml.	4	fluid drams
10	ml.	2½	fluid drams
8	ml.	2	fluid drams
5	ml.	1¼	fluid drams
4	ml.	1	fluid dram
3	ml.	45	minims
2	ml.	30	minims
1	ml.	15	minims
0.75	ml.	12	minims
0.6	ml.	10	minims
0.5	ml.	8	minims
0.3	ml.	5	minims
0.25	ml.	4	minims
0.2	ml.	3	minims
0.1	ml.	1½	minims
0.06	ml.	1	minim
0.05	ml.	¾	minim
0.03	ml.	½	minim